Johannine Grammar

Ancient Language Resources
K. C. Hanson, Series Editor

Arno Poebel
*Fundamentals of Sumerian Grammar/
Grundzüge der sumerischen Grammatik*

A. H. Sayce
Assyrian Grammar

Samuel A. B. Mercer
Introduction to Assyrian Grammar

The Student's Concise Hebrew-English Lexicon of the Bible

Heinrich Ewald
Syntax of the Hebrew Language of the Old Testament

S. R. Driver
A Treatise on the Use of the Tenses in Hebrew

William R. Harper
Hebrew Vocabularies

M. H. Segal
A Grammar of Mishnaic Hebrew

William B. Stevenson
Grammar of Palestinian Jewish Aramaic

Carl Brockelmann
Lexicon Syriacum

J. Payne Smith
Compendious Syriac Dictionary

William Jennings
Lexicon to the Syriac New Testament

Eberhard Nestle
Syriac Grammar

Theodor Nöldeke
Compendius Syriac Grammar

Theodor Nöldeke
*Mandaean Grammar /
Mandäische Grammatik*

August Dillmann and Carl Bezold
Ethiopic Grammar

William W. Goodwin
A Greek Grammar

William W. Goodwin
Syntax of the Moods and Tenses of the Greek Verb

Ernest D. Burton
Syntax of the Moods and Tenses in New Testament Greek

J. B. Smith
Greek-English Concordance to the New Testament

Edwin A. Abbott
Johannine Grammar

W. E. Crum
A Coptic Dictionary

Thomas O. Lambdin
Introduction to the Gothic Language

Johannine Grammar

Edwin A. Abbott

New Foreword and Bibliography
by K. C. Hanson

Wipf & Stock Publishers
Eugene, Oregon

JOHANNINE GRAMMAR
Ancient Language Resources

Copyright © 2006 Wipf & Stock Publishers. All rights reserved. Except for brief quotations in critical publications or reviews, no part of this book may be reproduced in any manner without prior written permission from the publisher. Write: Permissions, Wipf & Stock, 199 W. 8th Ave., Suite 3, Eugene, OR 97401.

Originally published London: A. & C. Black, 1906.

ISBN: 1-59752-546-4

Cataloging-in-Publication data:

Abbott, Edwin A. (1838–1926)
    Johannine grammar / by Edwin A. Abbott. New foreword and bibliography by K. C. Hanson.

    ISBN: 1-59752-546-4

    Ancient Language Resources

    xxix, 687 p.; 23 cm.
    1. Bible. N.T. John—Criticism, interpretation, etc. 2. Greek language, Biblical—Grammar. I. Hanson, K. C. (Kenneth C.). II. Title. III. Series.

    BS2555 A3 pt 6 2006

Manufactured in the U.S.A.

Series Foreword

The study of languages forms the foundation of any study of ancient societies. While we are dependent upon archaeology to unearth pottery, tools, buildings, and graves, it is through reading the documentary evidence that we learn the nuances of each culture—from receipts and letters to myths and legends. And the access to those documents comes only through the basic work of deciphering scripts, mastering vocabu-lary, conjugating verbs, and untangling syntax.

Ancient Language Resources (ALR) brings together some of the most significant reference works for the study of ancient languages, including grammars, dictionaries, and related materials. While most of the volumes will be reprints of classic works, we also intend to include new publications. The linguistic circle is widely drawn, encompassing Egyptian, Sumerian, Akkadian, Ugaritic, Phoenician, Hattic, Hittite (Nesite), Hurrian, Hebrew, Aramaic, Syriac, Ethiopic, Arabic, Greek, Coptic, Latin, Mandaean, Armenian, and Gothic. It is the hope of the publishers that this will continue to encourage study of the ancient languages and keep the work of groundbreaking scholars accessible.

—K. C. Hanson
Series Editor

Foreword

Edwin Abbott Abbott (1838–1926) is not a well-known figure in the history of biblical studies, but this is perhaps more the result of his career path than his abilities. He was educated at St. John's College, Cambridge, where he took highest honors in classics, mathematics, and theology. He was then made a fellow of St. John's and ordained to the priesthood a year after his graduation. He taught at King Edward's School and then Clifton College before becoming headmaster at the City of London School in 1865. In 1876 he was invited to give the prestigious Hulsean Lectures at Cambridge. He is probably most famous for his novel, *Flatland: A Romance of Many Dimensions*, which combined clever social satire with multidimensional geometry.

Retiring from the City of London School in 1889 at the age of fifty, he devoted himself to scholarly pursuits. His literary output was prodigious, but several of his works he published under pseudonyms. He wrote *Shakespearian Grammar* in 1870, which remains a major contribution to English philology. This was followed by *Philochristus* (1878), *Onesimus* (1882), *Bacon and Essex* (1885), *The Kernel and the Husk* (1886), *Philomythus* (1891), *The Anglican Career of Cardinal Newman* (1892), *St. Thomas of Canterbury* (1898), and *Sitanus* (1906).

Eventually he turned his attention to the New Testament, with particular emphasis on the gospels. He produced the numerous volumes of a series he called Diatessarica: *Clue: A Guide through Greek to Hebrew Scripture* (1900), *The Corrections of Mark Adopted by Matthew and Luke* (1901), *From Letter to Spirit* (1903), *Paradosis* (1904), *Johannine Vocabulary* (1905),

Johannine Grammar (1906), *Notes on New Testament Criticism* (1907), *The Son of Man* (1910), *Light on the Gospel from an Ancient Poet* (1912), *The Fourfold Gospel* (5 vols. 1913–17), and *Indices to the Diatessarica, with a Specimen of Research* (1907). These are all lengthy volumes of detailed grammatical, literary, and theological analyses.

TO

MY DAUGHTER

BY WHOM THE JOHANNINE MATERIALS FOR THIS WORK
WERE GATHERED AND ARRANGED
AND THE RESULTS CORRECTED AND REVISED
"JOHANNINE GRAMMAR" IS DEDICATED

PREFACE

IT was said in the first half of this work, *Johannine Vocabulary* (**1879**), "There are more ambiguities in the Fourth Gospel than in all the Three taken together, and it is easy to put one's finger on the cause of many of them." One object of *Johannine Grammar* is to classify, with the view of ultimately explaining, these ambiguous passages[1]. For example, what Browning calls *Hoti* on my title-page may mean "*that*" or "*because.*" Browning extols his Grammarian —alas! an ideal—who "settled *Hoti's* business." This work tries to help to "settle" it—unquestionably it has not yet been "settled"—for passages in the Fourth Gospel, in some of which our translators halt between "*that*" and "*because.*"

Again, Johannine commentators of repute disagree as to who is speaking in certain portions of the Gospel. Take, for example, i. 16—18 "For he was before me. *For of his fulness we all received......the only begotten Son, which is in the bosom of the Father, he hath declared* [*him*]." Origen attributed the italicised passage to the Baptist. So did Irenaeus. Heracleon, and many critics in Origen's time, maintained that it proceeded partly from the Baptist, partly from the evangelist. Alford and Westcott assert that the whole of it proceeds from the evangelist.

Next take iii. 15—21 "...that whosoever believeth may in him have eternal life. *For God so loved the world, that he*

---

[1] See Index, "Ambiguity," pp. 666—7.

PREFACE

gave his only begotten Son that whosoever believeth in him should not perish, but have eternal life. For God sent not the Son...that they have been wrought in God." Concerning the italicised passage Westcott says "It contains the reflections of the evangelist and is not a continuation of the words of the Lord." Alford says that this view—although held by many commentators—is "as inconceivable as the idea of St Matthew having combined into one the insulated sayings of his Master." Westcott maintains that his own conclusion is consistent with the tenor of the passage and "appears to be firmly established from details of expression." Some of these details—such as "only begotten Son," "believe in the name of," "do truth," which are characteristic of the evangelist—belong to vocabulary rather than grammar. But in favour of Westcott's view there is a small point of grammar to which attention might have been called, as will be seen from the two passages to be next quoted.

One of these, according to Westcott, follows—or, according to Alford, is part of—the last words of the Baptist, thus: iii. 30—36 "He must increase, but I must decrease. *He that cometh from above is above all...For he whom God hath sent speaketh the words of God; for he giveth not the Spirit by measure...the wrath of God abideth on him.*" Concerning the whole of these six verses ("He that cometh...abideth on him") Westcott says that the section "contains reflections of the evangelist"; and he calls attention to the use of the title "Son" absolutely, and to other details, as well as to the tenor of the passage, as justifying his conclusion. Alford calls this view (which is not peculiar to Westcott) an "arbitrary proceeding"; but he himself abstains from any argument based on grammatical or verbal detail.

The next instance occurs in the Dialogue between our Lord and the Samaritan woman, iv. 9 (R.V.) "How is it that thou, being a Jew, askest drink of me, which am a Samaritan woman? (*For Jews have no dealings with Samaritans*)."

PREFACE

Chrysostom takes the italicised words as uttered by the woman. The meaning would then be, "Jews as a rule do not condescend to have dealings with Samaritans: yet thou askest a favour from me!" But some authorities omit the italicised words. Alford and Westcott (the latter, with the *caveat* "if genuine") say that they are an explanatory note of the evangelist.

In favour of this last conclusion (that "Jews…Samaritans" is an evangelistic explanation) is the following grammatical argument. There are two words, ὅτι and γάρ, used by John[1] to express the conjunction "for." For the most part, in Christ's words, he uses the former; in his own comments, the latter (**2066**). The latter occurs not only in the Samaritan Dialogue but also in the two previously quoted passages. It is a matter of minute detail; but, so far as it goes, it confirms Westcott's view—favoured also by other grammatical considerations—that all three are evangelistic comments (**1936**).

The labour has been much greater, and the book longer, than I anticipated or desired. But the more fully I studied the Gospel and its most ancient MSS, versions, and commentators, the more necessary it seemed to give the evidence, if at all, at full length. Conclusions stated confidently, and with abundance of references, frequently assume an entirely different complexion when the references are verified and quoted accurately with their complete contexts.

As to the lines on which the book is constructed, they are the same as those of my Shakespearian Grammar—published nearly forty years ago but presumably still found useful as it is still in demand. Besides many points of

---

[1] By "John" is meant, throughout the whole of this volume, the writer of the Fourth Gospel, of which the originator may have been (as the Gospel suggests) John the son of Zebedee, but of which the writer, the exact nature of the origination, and the exact extent to which the writer paraphrased, commented, and blended allegory with fact are (in my opinion) at present unknown.

PREFACE

similarity in detail, the two works have two broad assumptions in common.

The Shakespearian Grammar assumed that Shakespeare wrote, with a style of his own, in English that he read and spoke. Hence North's Plutarch, Florio's Montaigne, the Elizabethan dramatists—and especially his own works compared with one another—were treated as safer guides to his meaning than Milton, Dryden, and Pope. A similar assumption is made in the Johannine Grammar. The Johannine language in general has been carefully classified with a view to the elucidation of particular passages; and the LXX, the Synoptists, the New Testament as a whole, Epictetus, and the Papyri of 50—150 A.D. have been recognised as safer guides than writers of the third century and far safer than those of the fourth. This assumption is even truer about John than about Shakespeare, to whom was given, in some measure, the very rare privilege of anticipating, or shaping, the language of posterity.

My Shakespearian Grammar also assumed that Shakespeare was a great poet. About John, I have tried to subordinate strictly to grammatical inferences my conviction that he, too, is a master of style and phrase, as well as an inspired prophet; but I have felt bound to assume that he did not at all events misuse words like the author of "the Second Epistle of St Peter," or "use one word for another" like a modern journalist describing a cricket-match or a boat-race. For example, where John is represented by our Revised Version as saying that Jesus "bowed his head" upon the cross, I argued, in "Johannine Vocabulary," that it must be rendered "laid his head to rest," and that, if so, the expression mystically implied "rest on the bosom of the Father." This rendering was based entirely on dry hard grammatical evidence shewing that *the phrase had no other meaning in the Greek language.* I have subsequently

PREFACE

discovered that Origen thrice assumes this to be the meaning ("*inclinasse caput super gremium Patris*").

Besides these two assumptions, the Johannine Grammar recognises one strong probability—namely, that the author was an honest man (a fact that some commentators hardly seem to recognise), writing indeed some seventy years or more after the Crucifixion, but still with some knowledge of what he wrote about, and with some sense of responsibility to those for whom he wrote. His Christian readers (I assume) had read earlier Gospels, which, if authoritative, an honest writer of a new Gospel was bound to take into account. For example, the Synoptists express themselves differently and somewhat obscurely as to the "authority" possessed by Christ and imparted by Him to the disciples. The meaning of true "authority" is of great moral importance, and much discussed by Epictetus. It is assumed as probable that John's teaching on this point was intended to elucidate that of the Synoptists.

I venture to think that the Index to N.T passages will supply something like a continuous commentary on the Fourth Gospel, and that the Index to Greek words will help the reader to compare Johannine, Synoptic, literary, and vernacular Greek. The English Index contains copious references to Origen, Nonnus, Chrysostom, Philo, and Epictetus, indicating lines of thought illustrative of the circumstances amid which the Gospel issued from its originator, was committed to writing by its author, and was interpreted by the earliest extant commentaries.

Many of the grammatical details must of course be abstruse and unsuitable for any but Greek scholars. But an attempt has been made—by translating literally many of the quotations, by comparing the Authorised with the Revised Version, and by illustrating Greek from English idiom—to make several interesting peculiarities of Johannine

PREFACE

style intelligible to readers unacquainted with Greek literature except through translations. In order to give easy access to all such oases in the classical desert, and a bird's-eye view of some of them, the English Index has been made very copious. It contains, for example, two columns on "Ambiguity." The reader will also find references to "Allusiveness," "Emphasis," "Mysticism," "Narrowing Down," "Parenthesis," "Quotation," "Repetition," and "Self-correction." Many of these subjects will—I sincerely believe—be better understood by a student with little or no knowledge of Greek but much knowledge of literature, than by one case-hardened against intellectual interests by a long course of "the classical languages" unintelligently and unwillingly studied.

For my "Notes on preceding Paragraphs" (**2664--799**) I am under great obligations to Professor Blass's Grammar of New Testament Greek, even where I have been led to differ from its conclusions[1]. To Dr Joseph B Mayor, in whose works on the Epistle of St James and on Clement of Alexandria I have found rich stores of Greek learning, and to Dr W Rhys Roberts, Professor of Greek at the University of Leeds, whose editions of Longinus, Dionysius, and Demetrius, are full of interesting and stimulative information on Greek style, I am indebted for correction of my proofs and for very useful criticisms and suggestions; nor must I omit brief but hearty thanks to the Cambridge University Press.

EDWIN A. ABBOTT.

Wellside
  Hampstead
    20 *Dec.* 1905

---

[1] See note on p xxvii.

CONTENTS

	PAGE
REFERENCES AND ABBREVIATIONS	xxv—xxvii

INTRODUCTION .   .   .   .

§ 1 The scope of the proposed work (**1886—7**)
§ 2 The arrangement and proportions of the work (**1888—93**)

BOOK I

FORMS AND COMBINATIONS OF WORDS

General warning as to use of Index (**1894***)

ADJECTIVES

  (i) Used predicatively (**1894**)
  (ii) Special
    (a) Μόνος (**1895, 2664**)
    (β) Πρῶτος (**1896—1901, 2665—7**)

ADVERBS

  (i) Intensive (**1902**)
  (ii) Special
    (a) Ἄνωθεν (**1903—8**)
    (β) Ἄρτι, see νῦν (**1915** (i))
    (γ) Ἐγγύς (**1909**)
    (δ) Εὐθέως and εὐθύς (**1910—15**)
    (ε) Νῦν and ἄρτι (**1915** (i)—(vi))
    (ζ) Οὕτως (**1916—7**)
    (η) Παρρησία (**1917** (i)—(vi))
    (θ) Τάχειον (**1918**)

CONTENTS

ANACOLUTHON
- (i) Generally (**1919**)
- (ii) The Subject suspended (**1920—2**)
- (iii) Digression (**1923—4**)
- (iv) Impressionism (**1925—7**)

AORIST, see Index

APODOSIS, see Index

APPOSITION
- (i) With proper names (**1928**)
- (ii) In subdivisions (**1929—30**)
- (iii) Explaining, or defining (not with Participle) (**1931—6**)
- (iv) With Participle (**1937—45**)
- (v) Noun repeated in Apposition (**1946**)
- (vi) Of Pronoun with preceding Subject (**1947**)

ARTICLE (see also **2669—74**)
- (i) Before Nouns in general (**1948**)
- (ii) Inserted, or omitted, before special Nouns
  - (a) Fathers (**1949—50**)
  - (β) Feast (**1951**)
  - (γ) Heaven (**1952—8**)
  - (δ) Man (**1959—61**)
  - (ε) Mountain (**1962—3**)
  - (ζ) Only begotten (**1964**)
  - (η) Prophet (**1965**)
  - (θ) "Teacher [of Israel]" (**1966**)
- (iii) Before Names (**1967—70**)
- (iv) With Participle and "is" or "are" (**1971—81**)
- (v) With Non-Possessive Adjectives (**1982—6**)
- (vi) With Possessive Adjectives (**1987—9**)
- (vii) Omitted, or misplaced (**1990—4**)
- (viii) With Infinitive (**1995**)

ASYNDETON
- (i) Johannine use of (**1996—9**)
- (ii) Classification of references (**2000—8**)

CONTENTS

CASES

I ACCUSATIVE
- (i) Adverbial (2009—11)
- (ii) Absolute, or suspensive (2012)
- (iii) Denoting time, but not duration (2013)
- (iv) Cognate (2014)
- (v) With special verbs
  - (a) Ἀκούω (2015)
  - (β) Γεύομαι (2016—8)
  - (γ) Προσκυνέω (2019)

II DATIVE
- (i) Of instrument (2020)
- (ii) Of time (completion) (2021—4)
- (iii) Of point of time (2025—6)
- (iv) With παρά (2027)

III GENITIVE
- (i) Absolute (2028—31)
- (ii) Objective or subjective (2032—40)
- (iii) Partitive (2041—2)
- (iv) Before Nouns (2043)
- (v) Special passages
  - (a) With πρῶτος and πρῶτον (2044)
  - (β) Τιβεριάδος (2045)
  - (γ) Ἡ διασπορὰ τῶν Ἑλλήνων (2046)
  - (δ) Τὰ βαία τῶν φοινίκων (2047)
  - (ε) Παρασκευὴ τοῦ πάσχα (2048)

IV NOMINATIVE
- (i) Special passage
  - (a) Ὁ κύριός μου (2049—51)

V VOCATIVE (see also 2679—82)
- (i) Special passages
  - (a) Πατήρ (2052—3)

CONJUNCTIONS (1894*) for ἄν, ἐάν, ὅταν, ὅτε, see Index
- (i) Johannine use of (2054)
- (ii) Ἀλλά
  - (a) Ἀλλά = contrariety, "not this but that, or, something more" (2055—7)

xv   b 2

CONTENTS

  (β) 'Αλλά = difference, "nevertheless" (**2058—9**)
  (γ) Special passages (**2060—2**)
  (δ) 'Αλλ' ἵνα (**2063—4**)

(iii) **Γάρ**

  (a) Synoptic and Johannine use (**2065—6**)
  (β) Special passages (**2067—8**)

(iv) **Δέ**

  (a) Consecutive or adversative (**2069—73**)
  (β) Third word, or later, in its clause (**2074—6**)
  (γ) Μέν...δέ (**2077**)

(v) **Εἰ**

  (a) Εἰ, corresponding to ἄν, in Words of the Lord (**2078—9**)
  (β) Εἰ δὲ μή (**2080—6**)

(vi) **'Επεί**

  (a) 'Επεὶ παρασκευὴ ἦν (**2087—8**)

(vii) **"Εως**

  (a) Not confused with ὡς (**2089**)

(viii) **"Η and ἤπερ**

  (a) "Η (**2090—1**)
  (β) "Ηπερ (**2092**)

(ix) **"Ινα** (see also **2686—90**)

  (a) In John, expresses, or implies, purpose (**2093**)
  (β) In John, never merely appositional (**2094—6**)
  (γ) Special passages (**2097—2103**)
  (δ) "Ινα and Subjunctive, compared with Infinitive (**2104**)
  (ε) Omission of principal verb before ἵνα (**2105—12**)
  (ζ) Dependent on verb implied in question (**2113**)
  (η) With Indicative (**2114**)
  (θ) Connexion of (**2115**)
  (ι) "Ινα...ἵνα (**2116—21**)

(x) **Καθώς**

  (a) Suspensive (**2122**)
  (β) Followed by καί or κἀγώ in Apodosis (**2123—7**)
  (γ) Supplementary (**2128—32**)

(xi) **Καί**

  (a) Καί in narrative (Hebraic) (**2133—4**)
  (β) Καί connecting affirmation and negation (**2135**)
  (γ) Καί = "and yet" (**2136—40**)

CONTENTS

- (δ) Special instances of καί = "and yet" (2141—5)
- (ε) Καί introducing an exclamation (2146)
- (ζ) Καί meaning "also" (2147)
- (η) Καί in Apodosis, after ἄ, εἰ, καθώς etc. in Protasis (2148)
- (θ) Καὶ ὑμεῖς (2149)
- (ι) Καί in Crasis (2150)
- (κ) Κἀκεῖνος (2151)
- (λ) Καί "also," connexion of (2152—3)
- (μ) Καί "also" in viii. 25 (2154—6)
- (ν) Καί meaning "[indeed] and" (2157)
- (ξ) Καὶ ἐάν (2158—9)
- (ο) Κἄν (2160)
- (π) Καί καί, "both...and" (2161—6)
- (ρ) Καὶ γάρ (2167)
- (σ) Καί omitted between two adjectives (2168)

(xii) Μέν, μέντοι (2169—70)

(xiii) Ὅπου (2171—2)

(xiv) Ὅπως (2173)

(xv) Ὅτι (see also 2694—5)
- (α) Ὅτι (1) suspensive, (2) explanatory (2174—7)
- (β) Ὅτι introducing (1) cause of action, (2) ground of statement (2178—80)
- (γ) Ὅτι (?) "that" or "because" (2181—6)
- (δ) Ὅτι μή (2187)
- (ε) Οὐχ ὅτι (2188)
- (ζ) Ὅτι recitativum (2189—90)

(xvi) Οὖν
- (α) In Christ's words (2191—7)
- (β) Applied to Christ's acts (2198—2200)

(xvii) Ὡς
- (α) Ὡς (?) for ἕως (2201)
- (β) Ὡς "as it were" (2202)

(xviii) Ὥστε (2203, 2697)

ELLIPSIS

(i) Of two kinds (2204)

(ii) Contextual (2205—9)
- (α) Ἐὰν οὖν θεωρῆτε (2210—2)

CONTENTS

(iii) Idiomatic
  (α) Ellipsis of " some " (2213—5)
  (β) Ellipsis (?) of " gate " (2216)
  (γ) Ellipsis of " daughter " (or " wife "?) (2217)
  (δ) Ἀλλ' ἵνα, see 2063—4 and 2105—12
  (ε) Οὐχ ὅτι (2218—9)
  (ζ) Ellipsis after " I am " (2220—8)
  (η) Ellipsis of ἐστί (2229—30)

IMPERATIVE, see Index

INFINITIVE, see Index

INTERROGATIVE SENTENCES
  (i) Interrogative particles (2231)
    (α) Οὐ μή (2232)
    (β) Οὐκοῦν (2233—4)
    (γ) Μή (2235)
  (ii) Interrogative tone (2236—47)
  (iii) Questions without interrogative particle (2248)
  (iv) Indirect interrogative (2249—51)

MOOD
  (i) Imperative, Indicative, Infinitive, and Subjunctive, see Index
  (ii) Optative (2252)

NEGATIVE PARTICLES
  (i) Μή (2253—4)
  (ii) Οὐ μή with Future and Subjunctive (2255)
  (iii) Εἰ οὐ (2256)
  (iv) Οὐ...οὐδείς (2257)
  (v) Οὔτε...καί (2258—9)
  (vi) Οὐ (or μή) combined with πᾶς (2260—3)
  (vii) Οὐ v.r. οὔπω (2264—5)
  (viii) Οὐχί (2265 (i))

NUMBER
  (i) Plural referring to preceding Singular (2266)
  (ii) Plural Neuter with Plural Verb (2267)
  (iii) Special words
    (α) Αἵματα (2268—9)
    (β) Ἱμάτια (2270)

CONTENTS

PARTICIPLE (1894*)

  (i) Causal (2271—3)

  (ii) Tenses of (see also Tense 2499—2510)

    (α) Τυφλὸς ὤν (2274)
    (β) Ὁ ὢν ἐν τῷ οὐρανῷ (2275)
    (γ) Ἡ ἐκμάξασα (2276)

  (iii) Present with ἦν (2277)

  (iv) Agreement of (2278)

  (v) Prefatory use of (2279)

PREPOSITIONS (for σύν see 2799 (ii))

Introductory Note (2280)

  (i) Ἀνά (2281—3)

  (ii) Ἀντί (2284—7)

  (iii) Ἀπό

    (α) Ἀπό and ἐκ meaning "[some] of," see 2213—5
    (β) Ἀπό, transposition of (2288)
    (γ) Ἀπό and ἐκ describing domicile or birthplace (2289—93)
    (δ) Ἀπό, ἐκ, and παρά, with ἐξέρχομαι, see 2326—8

  (iv) Διά (see also 2705, 2715)

    (1) Διά with Accusative of Person (2294—2300)
    (2) Διά with Genitive of Person (2301—4)

  (v) Εἰς (see also 2706 foll.)

    (α) For πιστεύειν εἰς, see **1480** foll.
    (β) Εἰς without verb of motion (2305—9)
    (γ) Εἰς, "to" or "into" (2310—11)
    (δ) Εἰς ζωὴν αἰώνιον (2312—6)
    (ε) Ὄψονται εἰς (2317—8)
    (ζ) Εἰς τέλος (2319—23)

  (vi) Ἐκ

    (α) Ἐκ meaning "some of," see 2213—5
    (β) Ἐκ meaning "native of," as distinguished from ἀπό "coming from," or "resident in," see 2289—93
    (γ) Ἐκ μέτρου (2324)
    (δ) Ἐκ with σώζω and τηρέω (2325)
    (ε) Ἐκ, ἀπό, and παρά, with ἐξέρχομαι (2326—8)
    (ζ) Ἐκ with πληρόω and γεμίζω (2329)

  (vii) Ἔμπροσθεν (2330)

CONTENTS

(viii) **Ἐν**
  (a) Ἐν used metaphorically, *e.g.* "abide in," see **1881**
  (β) Ἐν used temporally (2331)
  (γ) Ἐν quasi-instrumental (2332)
  (δ) Ἐν used locally, ἐν τῷ γαζοφυλακίῳ (2333—4)

(ix) **Ἐνώπιον** (2335)

(x) **Ἐπί**
  (1) Ἐπί with Accusative (2336)
  (2) Ἐπί with Dative (2337—9)
  (3) Ἐπί with Genitive
    (a) Ἐπὶ τῆς θαλάσσης (2340—6)
    (β) Ἐπὶ τοῦ σταυροῦ (2347)

(xi) **Κατά** (2348)

(xii) **Μετά**
  (a) Μετὰ Ἰουδαίου (2349—50)
  (β) Οἱ μετ' αὐτοῦ ὄντες (2351)
  (γ) Μετά compared with παρά (2352—3)

(xiii) **Παρά**
  (1) Παρά with Accusative (2354)
  (2) Παρά with Dative
    (a) Παρά with Dative and μετά with Genitive, see **2352—3**
    (β) Synoptic and Johannine use (2355)
  (3) Παρά with Genitive (2356)
  (4) Παρά with Genitive and with Dative interchanged (2357—9)

(xiv) **Περί** (2360)

(xv) **Πρό**
  (a) Πρὸ ἐμοῦ (2361—2)
  (β) Πρό transposed, see **2288**

(xvi) **Πρός**
  (1) Πρός with Accusative, with verb of rest (2363—6)
  (2) Πρός repeated after verb of motion (2367)
  (3) Πρός with Dative (2368)

(xvii) **Ὑπέρ** (2369—71, see also 2718—22)

(xviii) **Ὑπό** and ὑποκάτω (2372)
  (1) Ὑπό with Accusative (2372)
  (2) Ὑπό with Genitive (2373)

CONTENTS

PRONOUNS

I DEMONSTRATIVE

(i) Αὐτός (2374—80, see also 2723—7)

(ii) Ἐκεῖνος (2381—5, see also 2729—32)

(iii) Οὗτος (2386)

   (α) Διὰ τοῦτο (2387—91)

   (β) Ἐν τούτῳ (2392—3)

   (γ) Μετὰ τοῦτο or ταῦτα (2394)

   (δ) Αὐτοῦ omitted and ταῦτα repeated (2395—7)

(iv) Τοιοῦτος (2398)

II PERSONAL

(i) Insertion for emphasis (2399—2400)

(ii) Ἐγώ (2401)

(iii) Σύ (2402—4)

III RELATIVE

(i) Ὅς

   (α) Attraction of the Relative (2405—7)

   (β) Ἐν τῷ ὀνόματί σου ᾧ δέδωκάς μοι (2408—11)

   (γ) Ἐντολὴν καινὴν…ὅ (2412)

(ii) Ὅστις (2413)

   (α) Ὅστις ἄν, or ἐάν (2414—6)

SUBJECT

(i) Collective or noun group (2417—8)

(ii) Neuter plural (2419—20)

(iii) Suspended (2421)

   (α) Πᾶν ὃ δέδωκας (2422, 2740—4)

(iv) Omitted in partitive clauses (2423)

(v) "They" non-pronominal (2424—6)

(vi) "We" non-pronominal (2427—8)

   (α) "We know (οἴδαμεν)" (2429—35)

TENSE

Tense-rules and word-rules (2436)

I IN THE IMPERATIVE MOOD

Aorist (first) and Present (2437—9 (v))

CONTENTS

II IN THE INDICATIVE MOOD
  (i) Aorist (see also **2747—55** and **2785—90**)
    (1) Aorist compared with Perfect (**2440—9**)
    (2) Aorist of special verbs
      (α) Ἀκούω (**2450—2**)
      (β) Ἀποστέλλω (**2453**)
      (γ) Δίδωμι (**2454—5**)
      (δ) Εἶπον (**2456**)
      (ε) Ἔρχομαι and ἐξέρχομαι (**2457**)
      (ζ) Μένω (**2458**)
    (3) Aorist for English Pluperfect (**2459—62**)
  (ii) Future, see **2484** foll. and **2255**
  (iii) Imperfect
    (1) The Imperfect in general (**2463—6** (i))
      (α) Ἔλεγον (**2467—70**)
      (β) Ἤθελον (**2471—2**)
  (iv) Perfect
    (1) As the result of Johannine style (**2473—5**)
    (2) As the result of Johannine thought (**2476—7**)
    (3) Second Perfects (**2478—9**)
  (v) Pluperfect (**2480—1**)
  (vi) Present (see also **2760—6** (i))
    (1) Historic Present (**2482—3**)
    (2) Present of Prophecy and Present of Law (**2484—94**)

III IN THE INFINITIVE MOOD
  (i) Infinitive compared with ἵνα and Subjunctive (**2495**)
  (ii) Aorist and Present (**2496—8, 2767**)

IV IN PARTICIPLES
  (i) Aorist (**2499—2505**)
  (ii) Perfect (**2506**)
  (iii) Present (**2507—10**)

V IN THE SUBJUNCTIVE MOOD
  (i) Aorist and Present (**2511**)
    (α) In Deliberative Subjunctive (**2512**)
    (β) With ἐάν (or ἄν) "if" (**2513—5** (i))
    (γ) With ἄν and Relative (**2516**)

CONTENTS

 (δ) Ἄν τινων κρατῆτε (2517—20)
 (ε) With ἐὰν μή (2521—3)
 (ζ) With ἵνα (2524—9)
 (η) Ἵνα μὴ ἀποθνήσκῃ (vi. 50, in Codex B) (2530)
 (θ) With ὅταν (2531—5)

VOICE

 (i) Middle
  (a) Αἰτοῦμαι (2536)
  (β) Ἀποκρίνασθαι (2537)
 (ii) Passive
  (a) Ἐκρύβη (2538—43)

BOOK II

ARRANGEMENT, VARIATION, AND REPETITION OF WORDS

CHAPTER I

ARRANGEMENT AND VARIATION

§ 1 Variation in repetition or quotation (2544—53)
§ 2 Chiasmus (2554—7)
§ 3 The Possessive Genitive (2558—69, see also 2776—84)
§ 4 Miscellaneous (2570—86)

CHAPTER II

REPETITION

§ 1 The nature of Johannine repetition (2587)
§ 2 Jewish canons of repetition (2588—90)
§ 3 Repetition through negation (2591)
§ 4 Repetition in the Synoptists (2592—3)
§ 5 The Johannine Prologue (2594—7)
§ 6 Johannine repetition through negation (2598—2600)
§ 7 Twofold repetition in the Baptist's teaching (2601—2)

CONTENTS

§ 8 Twofold repetition in Christ's words (2603—6)
§ 9 Twofold repetition in narrative (2607)
§ 10 Twofold or threefold repetition (2608—11)
§ 11 Threefold repetition (2612—23)
§ 12 Sevenfold repetition (2624—7)

CHAPTER III

CONNEXION OF SENTENCES

§ 1 Self-corrections (2628—30)
§ 2 Parentheses (2631—5 (ii))
§ 3 Instances of doubtful connexion (2636—40)

APPENDIX I

TWOFOLD MEANINGS AND EVENTS

§ 1 Our Lord's Sayings (2641—2), § 2 The Sayings of the Disciples and of the Evangelist (2643—4), § 3 The Sayings of others (2645), § 4 Events (2646—9)

APPENDIX II

READINGS OF CODEX VATICANUS NOT ADOPTED BY WESTCOTT AND HORT

§ 1—2 Introductory Remarks; Tischendorf and the Photograph (2650—3), § 3 List of Readings (2654—62), Pause-spaces (2663)

NOTES ON PRECEDING PARAGRAPHS (2664—2799)

For summary of Contents, see pp. 506—7

INDICES

To Johannine Vocabulary, (i) N.T. Passages, (ii) English, (iii) Greek, pp. 625—51

To Johannine Grammar, (i) N.T. Passages, (ii) English, (iii) Greek, pp. 652—87

REFERENCES AND ABBREVIATIONS

REFERENCES

(i) *Black Arabic numbers* refer to paragraphs in this volume (1886—2799) or in preceding volumes of Diatessarica —

    1— 272 = *Clue*
    273 - 552 = *Corrections*
    553—1149 = *From Letter to Spirit*
    1150- -1435 = *Paradosis*
    1436—1885 = *Johannine Vocabulary*.

(ii) The Books of Scripture are referred to by the ordinary abbreviations, except where specified below. But when it is said that Samuel, Isaiah, Matthew, or any other writer, wrote this or that, it is to be understood as meaning *the writer, whoever he may be, of the words in question*, and not as meaning that the actual writer was Samuel, Isaiah, or Matthew.

(iii) The principal Greek MSS are denoted by ℵ, A, B, etc., the Latin versions by *a*, *b*, etc., as usual. The Syriac version discovered by Mrs Lewis on Mount Sinai is referred to as SS, i.e. "Sinaitic Syrian." It is always quoted from Mr Burkitt's translation. I regret that in the first three vols of Diatessarica Mrs Lewis's name was omitted in connexion with this version.

(iv) The text of the Greek Old Testament adopted is that of B, edited by Professor Swete[1], of the New, that of Westcott and Hort.

(v) Modern works are referred to by the name of the work, or author, vol., and page, e.g. Levy iii 343 *a*, i.e. vol iii p 343, col 1

ABBREVIATIONS

Aq. = Aquila's version of O. T.
Apol = Justin Martyr's First Apology
Blass, see Addendum on p xxvii
Buhl = Buhl's edition of Gesenius, Leipzig, 1899
Burk. = Mr F. C. Burkitt's *Evangelion Da-mepharreshe*, Cambridge University Press, 1904.

---

[1] Codex B, though more ancient than Codex A, is often less close to the Hebrew than the latter (*Clue* 33)

REFERENCES AND ABBREVIATIONS

C. before numbers = circa, "about" (*e.g.* c. 10).
Canon. LXX = *the canonical books* of LXX.
Chr. = *Chronicles.*
Chri. = *the words of Christ*, as distinct from narrative, see **1672***.
Clem. Alex. 42 = Clement of Alexandria in Potter's page 42.
Dalman, *Words* = *Words of Jesus*, Eng. Transl. 1902; *Aram. G.* = *Grammatik Aramäisch*, 1894.
Demosth. 433 = Teubner's marginal page 433 of Demosthenes; but Demosth. (Preuss) xxvii. 3 = p. 3 of Orat. xxvii. in Teubner, as in Preuss's Concordance.
Diatess. = the Arabic Diatessaron, sometimes called Tatian's, translated by Rev. H. W. Hogg, B.D., in the Ante-Nicene Christian Library.
Ency. = *Encyclopaedia Biblica.*
Ephrem = Ephraemus Syrus, ed. Moesinger.
Epistle, the = the First Epistle of St John.
Euseb. = the Ecclesiastical History of Eusebius.
Field = Origenis Hexaplorum quae supersunt, Oxford, 1875, also Otium Norvicense, 1881.
Gesen. = the Oxford edition of Gesenius.
Heb. LXX = that part of LXX of which the Hebrew is extant.
Hor. Heb. = *Horae Hebraicae*, by John Lightfoot, 1658—74, ed. Gandell, Oxf. 1859.
Iren. = the treatise of Irenaeus against Heresies.
Jer. Targ. (or Jer.) I and II = severally the Targum of "Jonathan Ben Uzziel" and the fragments of the Jerusalem Targum on the Pentateuch.
K. = *Kings.*
Levy = Levy's *Neuhebräisches und Chaldäisches Wörterbuch*, 4 vols., Leipzig, 1889; Levy Ch. = *Chaldäisches Wörterbuch*, 2 vols., 1881.
L.S. = Liddell and Scott's Greek Lexicon.
Narr. = *in narrative*, as distinct from (*a*) speech of Christ, (*b*) speech generally (**1672***).
Origen, Huet, or Lomm., ii. 340 = vol. ii. p. 340 of Huet or Lommatzsch severally. The reader is also sometimes guided by reference to the text, *e.g.* Numb. xiv. 23 in O.'s commentary on Numbers.
Oxf. Conc. = *The Oxford Concordance to the Septuagint.*
Papyri are indicated by *Pap.* [from the] *Berlin* [Museum]; and *Pap.* [of the] *Egypt* [Exploration Society], vols. i—vi, viz. *Oxy*[rynchus] i—iv, *Fayûm* v, *Tebt*[unis] vi.
Pec., affixed to Mt., Lk., etc., means peculiar to Matthew, Luke, etc.
Philo is referred to by Mangey's volume and page, *e.g.* Philo ii. 234, or, as to the Latin treatises, by Aucher's pages (P. A.) (see **1608**).
Resch = Resch's *Paralleltexte* (4 vols.).
S. = *Samuel*; s. = "see."
Schöttg. = Schöttgen's *Horae Hebraicae*, Dresden and Leipzig, 1733.

REFERENCES AND ABBREVIATIONS

Sir = the work of Ben Sira, *i.e.* the son of Sira. It is commonly called Ecclesiasticus (see **20***a*). The original Hebrew has been edited, in part, by Cowley and Neubauer, Oxf. 1897; in part, by Schechter and Taylor, Camb. 1899.

   SS, see (iii) above
   Steph. or Steph. Thes. = Stephani Thesaurus (Didot)
   Sym = Symmachus's version of O.T.
   Theod = Theodotion's version of O.T.
   Tromm. = Trommius' *Concordance to the Septuagint*
   Tryph = the Dialogue between Justin Martyr and Trypho the Jew.
   Wetst. = Wetstein's *Comm. on the New Testament*, Amsterdam, 1751
   W H = Westcott and Hort's New Testament

(*a*) A bracketed Arabic number, following Mk, Mt, etc., indicates the number of instances in which a word occurs in Mark, Matthew, etc., *e.g.* ἀγάπη Mk (0), Mt (1), Lk. (1), Jn (7).

(*b*) Where verses in Hebrew, Greek, and Revised Version, are numbered differently, the number of R.V. is given alone.

ADDENDUM

Blass = Second English Edition of Professor Blass's Grammar of New Testament Greek, Macmillan and Co., 1905. It did not come into my hands till this volume was in the press. But I have made copious use of it in foot-notes, and still more in the "Notes on Preceding Paragraphs" (2664—799). Dr Blass regards as interpolations some passages that I should treat as evangelistic comment; and he appears to me to attach too much importance to the testimony of Chrysostom (concerning whom Field, Chrys *Comm. Matth.* vol. III. p. 153 uses the weighty words, "Chrysostomo, Scriptori in libris citandis incuriosissimo," of which the reader will find ample proof in the following pages) and too little to that of Origen. But even where, as is frequently the case, my conclusions differ from his, I gladly acknowledge my obligation for his succinct statement of the evidence favouring his views, and for calling attention to points that had escaped my notice.

INTRODUCTION[1]

§ 1. *The scope of the proposed work*

[1886] Obscurity of style in an inflected language is caused by ambiguity (1) in words[2], (2) in inflexions of words[3], (3) in combinations of words[4] The First Part of this work, *Johannine Vocabulary*, dealt with characteristic, or characteristically used, Johannine words, such as "believe," and "authority," with the principal Johannine synonyms, and with the relation between the Johannine and the Synoptic Vocabularies But the words were almost exclusively verbs, nouns, adjectives, and adverbs. The article could not be represented statistically in the Vocabularies, nor could many of the pronouns and conjunctions; and only a general view could be given of the difference between the Johannine and the Synoptic use of prepositions. These words must therefore now be added to the two subjects above mentioned as remaining to be discussed—namely, inflexions, and combinations of words.

---

[1] See references on pp. xxv foll. This is the sixth part of the series entitled *Diatessarica*. The fifth part of the series ("*Johannine Vocabulary*") terminated with subsection **1885**

[2] *E g* "apprehend" (**1443**, **1735** *e—g*) may mean "understand" or "take prisoner"

[3] "Inflexions" include those of all parts of speech

[4] "Combinations" include those in phrases, in clauses, in sentences, and in paragraphs (or sections)

[1887] INTRODUCTION

[1887] In *Johannine Grammar* it is proposed to treat of these matters with a view to two objects. The first object is to ascertain the evangelist's meaning; the second is to compare or contrast his Gospel with those of the Synoptists. A great deal will be omitted that would be inserted in a Grammar of New Testament Greek, or in a Grammar that proposed to examine the differences between Johannine and, for example, Pauline style. On the other hand, a great deal will be inserted that would not find place in a treatise attempting simply to elucidate the obscurities of the Fourth Gospel. As in *Johannine Vocabulary*, so in *Johannine Grammar*, many remarks that may seem superfluous for explaining the special passage under discussion may be found to be justified hereafter by the use made of them in a commentary on parallel passages in the Four Gospels[1].

§ 2. *The arrangement and proportions of the work*

[1888] Logical arrangement, symmetry, and completeness, will be subordinated to the object of illuminating the Fourth Gospel as a whole, and passages of recognised difficulty in particular, by ready reference to groups of similar Johannine idioms. For this purpose, English alphabetical order will be adopted as regards subjects, *e.g.* Adjectives, Adverbs, Anacoluthon, Asyndeton etc., and Greek order, for the most part, as regards Greek words discussed separately under these several headings. Under "Adjectives"—in accordance with the promise to omit all that did not bear on Johannine style—very little will be said except as to John's use of two or three special words. For the rest, the reader will be referred to "Article"—since the repetition of the article with an adjective makes the latter emphatic. The same rule will apply to Adverbs. On the other hand, under "Anacoluthon" (*i.e.* want

---

[1] See *Johannine Vocabulary*, Pref. p. ix.

of grammatical sequence) space will be given to the discussion of several difficult passages; and "Asyndeton"—*i e* the omission of connecting particles between clauses and sentences—will receive a space proportioned to the number of instances in which it causes ambiguity.

[1889] Under "Mood," the reader will find hardly anything except a reference to other headings and especially to "Tense." The reason is that many Johannine distinctions of mood—occasionally (**2511** foll) so important as almost to amount to a distinction of word—arise from the evangelist's distinction between the present and the aorist in the same mood and may be most conveniently discussed as Presents and Aorists rather than as Imperatives, Subjunctives etc. Concerning the ambiguous πιστεύετε in xiv. 1 rendered by R.V. "*Ye believe* in God, believe also in me," with a marginal alternative "*Believe* in God," it was remarked three centuries and a half ago, "It may be read in four ways[1]." There are several other passages of a similar character about which much the same thing is likely to be said till doomsday unless some conclusion can be arrived at by a grouping of similar Johannine ambiguities. The best heading for these appeared to be, not "Indicative" or "Imperative," but "Interrogative."

[1890] Under "Prepositions" will be given ἀνά, although it occurs in only one Johannine passage, ii. 6 "two or three firkins *apiece*," and ἀντί, although that, too, occurs only in i. 16 "grace *for* grace" In the latter, not much doubt as to the meaning exists; in the former, none at all. But some space has been given to both, because it happens that expressions similar to these occur in the Book of the Revelation of St John and in the works of Philo, and, if questions should arise hereafter, in dealing with the Fourfold Gospel, as to allusiveness or latent mystical meanings in either passage, these external quotations may be of use. Similarly, under

---

[1] So Suicer (ii 721) quotes Erasmus, "Quadrifariam legi potest."

[1891] "Pronouns," in treating the Johannine "I am," an attempt will be made to ascertain, by reference to Hebrew and LXX usage (as well as to Johannine passages) when John uses it (if he ever does) to mean simply "I am the person you speak of," and when he uses it to mean (or to suggest) the divine I AM.

[1891] In those parts of the work which relate to the order and arrangement of words, something will need to be said about Philonian and Rabbinical canons of sacred expression, and about the repetitions so frequent in Hebrew poetry and in Jewish liturgy. For these may explain some curious twofold and threefold repetitions of the same statement, and some (logically speaking) superfluous combinations of affirmation and negation. But even when the most is made of these, much in the Johannine style will remain inexplicable, perhaps, except by particular influences and circumstances. The book seems to combine the occasional diffuseness of an old man with the general and pervasive subtlety of a master of words in the prime of intellect. It has curious sevenfold arrangements of events and sayings that strike a modern reader as highly artificial, and likely to have required much forethought and elaboration. Yet sometimes it halts, adds after-thoughts, breaks into parentheses, seems to make inexact statements and to correct them, and it certainly mixes words of the Lord and of other speakers with remarks of the evangelist in such a way that the most careful commentators are tasked to disentangle them.

[1892] Some of the phenomena above mentioned resemble phenomena that we find in the Apocalypse. Others indicate a subtle use of Greek grammatical forms quite unlike anything in that book. Yet the Gospel has not two styles. Indeed, as has been pointed out in the Preface, it has such a sameness of style that the words of the Baptist or of Christ—although distinguishable on close examination—appear to have been confused by some able critics with words of the evangelist. There may, however, have been one originator who did not write, and one writer, who did not originate. In other words, there may have been, in effect, two authors, of whom the second and later—while impressing his own character on the style of the whole—may have preserved here and there with special fidelity (sometimes at the cost of clearness, **1927** *c*) the traditions of the first, in whose name he wrote nominally as an amanuensis but actually as an expounder and interpreter. These considerations will come before us (**2427—35**) in discussing the remarkable textual variations in the passage about "the disciple that beareth witness of these things," but they ought to be always so far present that our minds may be kept open to all evidence bearing on the question of authorship.

[**1893**] The Fourth Gospel is admitted by all Greek scholars to be, in parts, extraordinarily obscure. No honest writer of history is obscure, as a rule, except through carelessness or ignorance—ignorance, it may be, of the art of writing, or of the subject he is writing about, or of the persons he is addressing, or of the words he is using, but, in any case, ignorance of something. But an honest writer of poetry or prophecy may be consciously obscure because a message, so to speak, has come into his mind in a certain form, and he feels this likely to prove the best form—ultimately, when his readers have thought about it. Instances will come before us, for example, where ὅτι may mean "that" or "because," and where καθώς may look back to what precedes or forward to what follows: and as to these we may say that the writer may have preferred to let the reader think out the meaning or the connexion for himself. But what are we to say to x. 38 "that ye *may come to know definitely* (γνῶτε) and that ye *may continue in the ever growing knowledge* (γινώσκητε) that the Father is in me"? Here the difference between the aorist and the present subjunctive is so great as to amount almost to the difference between two distinct words:

but is it like a poet or a prophet to write after this fashion? We must frankly admit that such language—of which there are many instances (**2524**)—would appear highly artificial in any Greek writer unless there were special reasons for it, as, for example, a desire to protest tacitly against some popular and erroneous notions about "knowing" and "knowledge." A Grammar is not the place to discuss the question whether such notions existed and whether the evangelist would be likely to protest against them; but it may be of use here to prepare the reader for a multitude of such minute grammatical distinctions. In an ordinary book, we should stigmatize them as pedantry; in the Fourth Gospel, they must be explained (we may feel sure) by very different reasons. The business of the Grammar will be to collect and classify these and other peculiarities so as to lead the way to an explanation that lies beyond the limits of a grammarian.

BOOK I
FORMS AND COMBINATIONS OF WORDS

BOOK I

FORMS AND COMBINATIONS OF WORDS

General warning as to use of Index

[1894*] N B For all matter affecting Adjectives, Adverbs, Anacoluthon etc., and not occurring under these several headings, the reader is referred to the Index For example, under the heading "Adjectives" in the following paragraphs nothing will be found about their frequent use with the reduplicated article for emphasis, nor about their occasional use with the ellipsis of a noun But these deficiencies will be supplied under the heading "Adjectives" in the Index at the end of the book, where the reader will find references to "Article," to "Ellipsis," and to passages dealing with emphasis. Also, as regards some special adjectives, discussed at considerable length, but not here (*e.g* ἴδιος, πολύς, προβατική), the reader will be referred to the paragraphs dealing with them by the two Indices of Greek words, where they will be found in their alphabetical order The Index to the "Vocabulary" will give the statistics of the words; the Index to the "Grammar," their grammatical use.

Adjectives

(i) **Used predicatively**

[1894] The adjective is used predicatively in iv 18 τοῦτο ἀληθὲς εἴρηκας, which is quite different from τοῦτο ἀληθῶς εἴρηκας. The latter might have meant (1) "*Truly*, i e *in truth*, thou hast said this," or (2) "Thou hast said this *truly*, i e *with truth*" But the former means "*This, at all events*, among all that thou hast said, is true"—implying that hitherto the woman has talked in a reckless and trifling way[1].

(ii) **Special**

(*a*) Μόνοc

[1895] Μόνος occurs as follows in v. 44 (W.H.) "How can ye believe, receiving glory from one another:—and the glory that comes from *the only* [*God*] (τὴν δόξαν τὴν παρὰ τοῦ μόνου [θεοῦ]) ye seek not!" Θεοῦ is here omitted not only by B but also by *a* ("gloriam *ab unico* non quaeritis") and *b* ("honorem *ejus qui est solus*")[2]. If the omission occurred in B alone, it might be explained as an omission—sometimes occurring in that excellent MS.—in a group of similar letters[3]. But it occurs also in Origen[4], which demonstrates that the reading was much earlier than the draughting of B. Moreover, the omission, being unusual, would suggest a lacuna, which scribes would be tempted to fill up, conforming the passage to "the *only* true *God*" later on, and to general usage[5]. The Greek "only" is used (as in Shakespeare, "the *only* man of Italy[6]") to mean "unique"—more than merely "first." In N.T. "only" is connected with ascriptions of glory[7]. Horace speaks of Jupiter as having "no like or second" although Pallas occupies "the place next in honour[8]." Aristotle says that the heaven is "one and *alone* and perfect[9]." But

---

[1] [1894*a*] R.V. ("this hast thou said truly") is ambiguous, and might agree with ℵ *b*, *f*, ἀληθῶς "thou hast *indeed* (or, *in truth*) said." Comp. Demosth. (Teubn. p. 87) τοῦτό γε ἀληθές (but better MSS. ἀληθῆ) λέγουσιν. Such a predicative use is prob. without another parall. in N.T.

[1894*b*] In xiii. 34 ἐντολὴν καινὴν δίδωμι ὑμῖν ἵνα ἀγαπᾶτε ἀλλήλους—καθὼς ἠγάπησα ὑμᾶς, ἵνα καὶ ὑμεῖς ἀγαπᾶτε ἀλλήλους, the adj. "new" is not predicative. The meaning is, "I give you a *new* commandment": and it is "new" because it enjoins a new kind of "love," not revealed through the Prophets, but for the first time through the Son and through His love of men. Comp. 1 Jn ii. 7—8 "*Not a new commandment do I write to you*......on the other hand (πάλιν) *a new commandment do I write to you*—which [paradox] (ὅ) is true in him and in you," *i.e.* it is "old" yet made "new" in Christ and in His newborn disciples.

[2] [1895*a*] The Lat. *f* has "quae a Deo solo," *ff* "quae ab illo solo est Deo" (where "Deo" looks like an interpolation out of place). Neither of these retains the Gk order as in *d* ("gloriam ab unico deo") and *e* ("gloriam a solo dō").

[3] [1895*b*] See **2650**: ΘΥ might be omitted coming between the ΟΥ of μόνου and that of Οὐ.

[4] Orig. Huet i. 392, and see **2664**. [5] Jn xvii. 3, Rom. xvi. 27, 1 Tim. i. 17.

[6] [1895*c*] *Much Ado* iii. 1. 92. See also Lucian (ii. 386, *Demon.* 29) where a man boasts that he is μόνος καὶ πρῶτος τῶν διαλεκτικῶν, and is rebuked for being illogical. [7] Rom. xvi. 27, 1 Tim. i. 17, Jude 25, Rev. xv. 4.

[8] *Odes*, I. xii. 19—20. [9] *De Cael.* i. 9. 8.

ADJECTIVES [1897]

no passage is alleged in the Thesaurus where Greeks call God ὁ μόνος: and such a use, if it existed, must have been rare among the Jews¹. More to the point is the saying of Philo that the words "It is not good for man to be *alone*" are uttered because "It is good that *the Alone* should be alone²," meaning the Only God. On the whole, it seems fairly probable that, when speaking about "glory" and its source, the evangelist used ὁ Μόνος—with allusion to the connexion of the word with "glory" both in Hebrew and Greek—to mean briefly "He that is *alone* glorious" *i.e.* "He from whom *alone* all glory comes."

(β) Πρῶτος

[1896] Πρῶτος is followed by a genitive, and is said by some to mean "first in regard of," in (*a*) i. 15 (R.V.) "He that cometh after me is become before me (ἔμπροσθέν μου); for he was *before me* (ὅτι πρῶτός μου ἦν)" and i. 30 (R.V.) "After me cometh a man which is become before me; for he was *before me*" (R.V. marg. in both verses "*first in regard of me*"). It is rendered by the conjunction "before," supplying a verb, in (*b*) xv. 18 (R.V.) "If the world hateth you, ye know that it hath hated me *before* [*it hated*] you (πρῶτον ὑμῶν)."

[1897] To deal first with (*a*). Stephen's Thesaurus quotes from Aelian³ "those who have investigated these things *before me* (οἱ πρῶτοί μου ταῦτα ἀνιχνεύσαντες)." But πρῶτός τινος ἐποίησά τι is different from πρῶτός τινος ἦν. More to the point is πρῶτος ὤν in the Scholiast's Preface to the *Phoenissae* of Euripides quoted in the Thesaurus thus: "Eteocles, *as though he were first* [*in regard*] *of his brother* (ἅτε πρῶτος ὤν τοῦ ἀδελφοῦ)," given by Dindorf (presumably correcting the text) as τῶν ἀδελφῶν. Another Scholiast explains (*Hecuba* 458) "*firstborn* palm (πρωτόγονός τε φοῖνιξ)" by saying "created *first* [*in regard*] *of* the bay-tree (πρῶτον γεννηθέντα τῆς δάφνης)." Origen seems to take πρῶτός μου as parallel to, and

---

¹ [1895 *d*] Levy ii. 234 *b* quotes *Genes. Rab.*, on Gen. iii. 22 "one of us," explained as "like the Only One of the universe," and Levy *Chald.* i. 331 *b* quotes a Targ. on Job xiv. 4 "not one," explained as "shall not *the Only One*?" (so Vulg. "nonne tu qui solus es?").

² Philo i. 66 Διὰ τί τὸν ἄνθρωπον, ὦ προφῆτα, οὐκ ἔστι καλὸν εἶναι μόνον; Ὅτι, φησί, καλόν ἐστι τὸν μόνον εἶναι μόνον. Μόνος δέ, καὶ καθ' αὑτόν, εἷς ὤν, ὁ θεός, οὐδὲν δὲ ὅμοιον θεῷ.

³ [1897 *a*] Ael. *N. A.* viii. 12. Steph. also quotes Plut. *Vit. Cat. Min.* § 18 οὔτε πρῶτός τις ἀνέβη...Κάτωνος οὔτε ὕστερος ἀπῆλθε: but he thinks πρότερος should be restored here, and he expresses doubt about the quotation from Aelian.

[1898] ADJECTIVES

included in, πρωτότοκος πάσης κτίσεως¹, *i.e.* "firstborn [brother] of all creation," so that πρῶτός μου would mean "firstborn [brother] of me," *i.e.* "my eldest brother." His words are: "The Baptist teaches [us] how Jesus 'is become before him [by] being first [in regard] of him (ὧν πρῶτος αὐτοῦ)' since He was *the firstborn* (πρωτότοκος) of every creature²"; and the same view is suggested by παρά (implying the metaphor of a household) in the following words, "I understand that He was first[born in respect] of me and more honourable *in the house of the Father* (παρὰ τῷ Πατρί)." Chrysostom, without using the word "firstborn," argues that the words must refer to precedence *in point of time*³—not *in point of rank*, rank having already been expressed (as he says) by the words "become before me."

[1898] According to Luke, the Baptist was born before Jesus. If that was recognised as a historical fact by the earliest readers of the Fourth Gospel, "first in regard of me" could not appear to them to mean "born before me [on earth]." But some have supposed it to mean "begotten before me in the beginning." If so, why did the Baptist omit "in the beginning," which is essential, and insert "before me," which, had "in the beginning" been inserted, would not have been essential? Many will feel great difficulty in believing that John the Baptist, at this stage in his testimony to Jesus (if indeed in any stage) proclaimed to the Jews (1) the pre-existence of Jesus, as being the Messiah—and proclaimed Him, too, as pre-existent, not "from eternity" nor "from the beginning," but (2) relatively to himself. The former doctrine, the eternal pre-

---

¹ [1897 *b*] Col. i. 15 πρωτότοκος πάσης κτίσεως, comp. the genitive in Rev. i. 5 πρωτότοκος τῶν νεκρῶν, and see Col. i. 18 ἡ ἀρχή, πρωτότοκος ἐκ τῶν νεκρῶν, Gen. xlix. 3 πρωτότοκός μου, σὺ ἰσχύς μου καὶ ἀρχὴ τέκνων μου, Rom. viii. 29 εἰς τὸ εἶναι αὐτὸν πρωτότοκον ἐν πολλοῖς ἀδελφοῖς, Col. i. 18 ἵνα γένηται ἐν πᾶσιν αὐτὸς πρωτεύων, and 2 S. xix. 43 πρωτότοκος ἐγὼ ἢ σύ (LXX error). These passages shew that πρωτότοκος, suggesting supremacy among brethren, might be replaced by πρωτεύων, or πρῶτος, if one wished to say "my firstborn [brother]," because "my firstborn" would naturally be taken to mean "my firstborn [*son*]." The phrase "my elder [brother]," πρεσβύτερός μου, would convey none of the old associations of the blessing and supremacy belonging to the Firstborn.

² Orig. Huet ii. 99.

³ [1897 *c*] "It is not to be supposed, says [the Baptist], that, whereas I was first, He, by outstripping me (so to speak) in the race, cast me behind [Him] and 'has become before' [*i.e.* superior]. On the contrary 'He was first [in regard] of me [in point of time],' for all that He is coming last into [view]," Οὐδὲ γὰρ ἔκ τινος, φησί, προκοπῆς πρῶτόν με ὄντα ὀπίσω ῥίψας ἔμπροσθεν γέγονεν, ἀλλὰ Πρῶτός μου ἦν, εἰ καὶ ὕστερος παραγίνεται. He explains ἔμπροσθεν as λαμπρότερος, ἐντιμότερος. On σοῦ πρῶτός εἰμι in the Leyden Papyri, see 2667.

12

existence of the Messiah, may possibly have been entertained by some Jews in the Baptist's time: but, even if it was, it is difficult to believe that the Baptist gave it such prominence and in such a shape.

[1899] The Synoptists[1], instead of "*first in regard of me*," have "*mightier than I*." This suggests that some word capable of meaning "firstborn" might also be interpreted as "superior to," "stronger than[2]." The Hebrew *Rab*, the root of "Rabbi," "Teacher," is capable of the two meanings (**1897** *b*). The Baptist may have said, in effect, "Jesus of Nazareth numbers Himself among my disciples, but He was from the first my Teacher, or *Rab*." Now whenever a Jewish Teacher spoke about the divinely ordained relations between the elder and the younger, so prominent in Hebrew history, he might use the word *Rab* (**420**) to mean "firstborn," alluding to the supremacy of Jacob preordained in the words "the *elder* shall serve the younger[3]." But *Rab* is also used for "mighty" in Messianic passages such as "*mighty* to save" and "a portion with the *mighty*[4]." John may have taken the word in the former sense, the Synoptists in the latter.

[1900] Apart from the question—which cannot be answered with certainty—as to the original word used by the Baptist, we may be sure that this rare expression πρῶτός μου means something more than μείζων μου. Probably the writer had in view the Johannine traditions "I am *the First* and the Last[5]." As one can speak of "*my God*," "*my Rock*," "*my Light*," so one might speak of "*my First*," having in view the Firstborn of God, the Beginning. The evangelist, without supposing that the Baptist consciously intended hereby to set forth to the world the eternal pre-existence of Christ as the Logos, might very well represent him as unconsciously including in his language (after the manner of all the Prophets and the Psalmists) more than he included in his thought. According to this view, the Baptist *meant* "He was from the cradle *my superior*, *my elder brother*"; but he *said* words that might be interpreted as meaning

---

[1] Mk i. 7, Mt. iii. 11, Lk. iii. 16.

[2] [1899 *a*] In 2 S. xix. 43, the LXX, confusing "in David" with "firstborn," uses the latter as a comparative adjective, "I am firstborn than thou," πρωτότοκος ἐγὼ ἢ σύ. But the Hebrew word there erroneously read by the LXX never means "strong."

[3] Gen. xxv. 23.   [4] Is. lxiii. 1, liii. 12.

[5] Rev. i. 17, xxii. 13.

"He was, from the beginning, my *First*," i.e. the Firstborn of God, the object of my worship.

[1901] We come now to the use of πρῶτον with the genitive in (*b*), xv. 18 "If the world hateth you, ye know that it hath hated me (R.V.) *before* [*it hated*] *you*." No precedent is alleged from Greek literature for such a rendering of the italicised words. But πρῶτον rendered as above will make sense here: "It hath hated me, *your First*, i.e. *your Chief*." Something like this ("priorem vobis") is the rendering of the Vulgate and of one of the oldest Latin MSS.; and others, though they omit "you," take πρῶτον as an adjective ("priorem[1]")." Thus rendered—if "first" be taken as suggesting "firstborn brother"—the words prepare the disciples for the new sphere of life and thought that was to follow the Resurrection, wherein Christ was to become "the firstborn of the dead, the ruler of the kings of the earth[2]." He was not to be alone. He was to be "the firstborn among many brethren[3]." The whole Church was to be "the Church of the firstborn[4]," and He Himself was to be the First of the firstborn, the "first-fruits of them that had fallen asleep[5]." The Johannine context leads the disciples to regard themselves as branches in the Vine, "friends" (no longer "slaves") of the Son— "friends" that must henceforth partake in His life and in His secret counsels[6]. Being now destined to become younger brothers of the Firstborn, they must expect to share the Elder Brother's sufferings: "If the world now hateth you, adopted brethren of the Family of God, remember that it hath hated *me—the First*[*born*] *of you* [*all*][7]." Possibly the evangelist wishes not so much to say this as to

---

[1] [1901 *a*] "You" is om. by *a* ("me prius odiit") and *e* ("me primo odiit") and also by D (*d* has "me primum odiuit"); *b* and *ff* have "me priorem odio habuit," *f* and Vulg. "me priorem vobis odio habuit." See **2665** foll.

[2] Rev. i. 5, quoting Ps. lxxxix. 27, where David is declared "firstborn."

[3] Rom. viii. 29.   [4] Heb. xii. 23.

[5] 1 Cor. xv. 20.   [6] Jn xv. 15.

[7] [1901 *b*] In i. 41 εὑρίσκει οὗτος πρῶτον τὸν ἀδελφὸν τὸν ἴδιον Σίμωνα, several authorities have πρῶτος: *b* and *e* have "mane," apparently having read πρωί. The Syriac (Burk.) has "And he, Andrew, saw Simon Kepha and saith to him...," SS "And he, Andrew, saw Simon his brother on that day." It is generally supposed (**1720** *i*) that the meaning is, "Andrew first found his own brother [before Andrew's companion John the son of Zebedee found *his own* brother James the son of Zebedee]." But there may be also some allusion to ancient traditions in which πρῶτον Σίμωνα, or (as in Mt. x. 2) πρῶτος Σίμων, occurred at the head of a list of the Apostles. If πρῶτος were read above, it would lay rather more stress on the fact that Andrew was the first Christian disciple that made a convert.

suggest this, by expressing the phrase "before you" in a manner that would convey more than one meaning. See also 2665—7.

Adverbs

(i) Intensive

[1902] The adverbs λίαν, περισσῶς etc. are rarely used by John, who differs greatly in this respect from Mark and Matthew, and slightly from Luke[1]. When John wishes to emphasize an adverb or adverbial phrase he gives it an unusual place, *e.g.* at the beginning of the sentence, xvi. 31 Ἄρτι πιστεύετε, xii. 27 Νῦν ἡ ψυχή μου τετάρακται, xvi. 30 ἐν τούτῳ πιστεύομεν, vii. 14 ἤδη δὲ τῆς ἑ. μεσούσης, vii. 37 ἐν δὲ τῇ ἐσχάτῃ ἡμέρᾳ..., xiii. 1 πρὸ δὲ τῆς ἑορτῆς τ. πάσχα, xvi. 22 πάλιν δὲ ὄψομαι ὑμᾶς[2]. See 2636 c and 2668. On ἀμὴν ἀμήν see 2611 a.

(ii) Special

(a) Ἄνωθεν

[1903] The most important adverb in the Fourth Gospel is ἄνωθεν, as used in iii. 3—7 (R.V. marg.) "Except a man be born *from above* (ἄνωθεν) he cannot see the kingdom of God....Marvel not that I said unto thee, Ye must be born *from above*." Nicodemus takes this as meaning "born a second time"; and he replies, "Can a man enter *a second time* into his mother's womb and be *born*?" Chrysostom says that our Lord here speaks obscurely in order to lead Nicodemus on to further question; and he adds, "Ἄνωθεν here means, some say '*from the heaven*,' others '*from the beginning*[3].'" The following facts indicate that our Lord is intended by the evangelist to mean "*from*

---

[1] [1902 a] Λίαν occurs Mk (4), Mt. (4), Lk. (1), Jn (0): σφόδρα, Mk (1), Mt. (7), Lk. (1), Jn (0): περισσῶς, Mk (2), Mt. (1), Lk. (0), Jn (0). Mk has adverbial forms of πολύς more freq. than Mt. Lk. Jn taken together.

[2] [1902 b] But see 1914 as to the position of εὐθύς, and comp. xi. 29 ἠγέρθη ταχύ with xi. 31 ταχέως ἀνέστη, where ταχέως (2554 b) before its verb appears to be more emphatic than ταχύ on which the voice does not rest. An adverb may also be emphasized by coming at the end of a sentence.

[3] [1903 a] Chrys. himself, in a very long comment, gives the impression that he takes ἄνωθεν to mean "from heaven" and that Nicodemus materialises it: "Why draggest thou," he says, apostrophizing Nicodemus, "the meaning (λόγον) down to earth? This kind of birth is *above* such birth-pangs (ἀνώτερός ἐστι τῶν τοιούτων ὠδίνων οὗτος ὁ τόκος)." Origen's comment *ad loc.* is lost, but elsewhere he contrasts γεννᾶται ἄνωθεν with ἐκ τῶν κάτω γίνεται in such a way as to demonstrate that he took the former to mean "born *from above*." See 2573.

heaven," and that Nicodemus is intended to be regarded as misunderstanding Him, or affecting to misunderstand Him, as though He meant "a second time."

[1904] Ἄνωθεν occurs in N.T. thirteen times. Apart from the passage under consideration, it never means "from the beginning" except thrice, and then it is joined to "again" or "knowing," or "ascertaining[1]." The Thesaurus shews that (1) it often means "from the beginning" in connexion with the tracing of a genealogy, describing one's ancestry or early life, or a friendship of long date, relating ancient history, or speaking of ancient times, or repeating a story over again from the beginning; and Suicer shews that ἄνωθεν is thus used in connexion with πάλιν, and with ἐξ ἀρχῆς. On the other hand (2) it means "from above" in a spiritual sense in Jn iii. 31 "he that cometh *from above*," xix. 11 "given to thee *from above*." In the Epistle of St James, it refers once to "every perfect gift" as being "*from above*, coming down from the Father of lights...By his will (βουληθείς) he brought us forth (ἀπεκύησεν) by the word of truth" —thus connecting "*from above*" with spiritual generation: in two other passages St James connects it with "the wisdom that is from above[2]." In the LXX, it always has a local meaning, except once (where it is joined with πάλιν) in the Wisdom of Solomon[3].

[1905] Apart from LXX and N.T. usage, the rendering "from above" in the Dialogue with Nicodemus is also favoured by the probability that the intention is to fix the attention not on being born "*over again*"—which might be a change for the worse—but upon being born into a higher life. This latter thought is approximated to by Philo, in various phrases including ἄνωθεν, when he speaks of "him that is inspired *from above*" (in connexion with those who avoid the life of the flesh and live to God) and of those who "philosophize, so to speak, *from above*[4]." Commenting, also, on the *calling up* of Moses to Mount Sinai, he describes it as "a second

---

[1] Lk. i. 3, Acts xxvi. 5, Gal. iv. 9.

[2] [1904 a] Jas i. 17—18, iii. 15, 17. In Jn xix. 23 ἐκ τῶν ἄνωθεν ὑφαντός, its meaning is "from above."

[3] [1904 b] Wisd. xix. 6. In Is. xlv. 8 "Let the heaven drop *from above*," Ibn Ezra says, "This is a commandment to the angels that they shall drop righteousness."

[4] [1905 a] Philo i. 482 ὁ καταπνευσθεὶς ἄνωθεν, i. 264 οἱ ἄνωθέν πως φιλοσοφήσαντες, comp. ii. 442 τοῦ θείου πνεύματος ὅπερ ἄνωθεν καταπνευσθὲν εἰσῳκήσατο τῇ ψυχῇ, i. 498 ἀπ' οὐρανοῦ καταπνευσθεὶς ἄνωθεν.

birth better than the first," where there is "no mother, but only a father, the Father of all¹."

[1906] The use of "*from above*" to describe a heavenly ideal is common in Jewish literature. St Paul speaks of "Jerusalem that is *above*" as being free, in contrast with "the present Jerusalem," which is in bondage². The Apocalypse speaks of "the *new* Jerusalem," but adds "*coming down from heaven*³." Somewhat similarly St Paul says that the first man is of the earth, earthy, "the *second* man is *from heaven*⁴." In the one case "*new*," and in the other "*second*," might be used to paraphrase the expression "*from heaven*"; and similarly "generate *anew*" might be a substituted paraphrase for "generate *from heaven*." But to say that a man on earth must be "born *from above*" implies that he must also be "born *anew*," so that the former has the advantage of being ampler. The former is also more in accordance with Johannine doctrine, as well as with Johannine use of ἄνωθεν. Again, all the Synoptists say that Jesus asked the Jews whether "the baptism of John" was "*from heaven* or from men⁵"; and "*from heaven*" in such a context might naturally be expressed by the Aramaic "*from above*." Moreover, the very beginning of the Bible describes, shortly after the motion of the Spirit on the waters, a separation between "the waters and the waters," or, as the Jerusalem Targum has it, "*the waters above* and the waters below."

[1907] Thus, from several points of view, if a Rabbi came to consult Jesus about baptism, and if our Lord wished to insist on the need of a spiritual, and not a mere external, regeneration, we might expect that the phrase "*from above*" would occur in His mention of the operation of the Spirit. If Christ had said "*new*" or "*anew*," this could not have been misunderstood; for the Aramaic "new," like the Greek καινός, cannot be confused with "above." Moreover if the evangelist had desired to represent in Greek the mere thought of "regeneration" he might have used ἀναγεννᾶν. But "regenerate"—unless qualified as it is in St Peter's

---

¹ [1905 *b*] Philo (on Ex. xxiv. 16) P. A. 502 "Sursum autem vocatio prophetae secunda est nativitas (sive regeneratio) priore melior...cuius non est mater; sed pater solus, qui etiam universorum."
² Gal. iv. 25—6.
³ Rev. xxi. 2.   ⁴ 1 Cor. xv. 47.
⁵ Mk xi. 30, Mt. xxi. 25, Lk. xx. 4.

Epistle[1]—does not necessarily convey the notion of a birth unto righteousness. Nicodemus was familiar with the doctrine of "new birth" applied to baptized proselytes, and he knew that very often it did not mean much[2]. But this doctrine of Jesus about "birth *from above*," he dimly felt, meant a great deal more, some fundamental change—what he would call a "miraculous" change. He therefore asks what the miracle is to be: "It cannot be that a man is to be literally born a second time[2]?"

[1908] In deciding this question we have to consider, not only what our Lord may have said, but also how the author of the Fourth Gospel,—in view of the misunderstandings of what He had said as

---

[1] [1907 a] 1 Pet. i. 3 "*the God and Father of our Lord Jesus Christ*, who regenerated us *into a living hope*...," i. 23 "having been regenerated, *not from corruptible seed, but from incorruptible, through the word of God, living and abiding.*" Comp. Jas i. 18 "he brought us forth *by the word of truth*."

[2] [1907 b] On our Lord's opinion of some proselytes, see Mt. xxiii. 15 "twofold a child of hell."

[3] [1907 c] There are naturally some cases where ἄνωθεν is ambiguous, *e.g.* Clem. *Anc. Hom.* ch. 14 τὴν ἐκκλησίαν οὐ νῦν εἶναι ἀλλὰ ἄνωθεν. This (as in the above quoted Gal. iv. 25—6 τῇ νῦν......ἡ δὲ ἄνω) might conceivably mean, "that the Church is not *of this present age* ([τοῦ] νῦν [αἰῶνος]), but *from heaven.*" But such an ellipsis is unlikely; and the contrast is more probably between οὐ νῦν [πρῶτον], "not now [for the first time]" (οὐ νῦν πρῶτον being freq. in Greek) and "but *from the beginning.*" Epict. i. 13. 3 "Wilt thou not bear with thy brother, who hath Zeus for his ancestor, [and who] (ὥσπερ, ? ὃς ὥσπερ) as a son, is born from the same seed and from the same *celestial* sowing (τῆς αὐτῆς ἄνωθεν καταβολῆς)" might be, but less probably, "*initial* sowing." Philo ii. 141 ἠρχαιολόγησεν ἄνωθεν ἀρξάμενος τῆς τοῦ παντὸς γενέσεως probably means "beginning *from the beginning* [*i.e.* the First Cause]"—having in mind the ancient Greek saying "Let us *begin from Zeus*," and "*In the beginning* God created." He proceeds to say that the first object was to set forth "the Father and Maker of the world," and then man obeying the Maker's laws.

[1907 d] Justin Martyr *Tryph.* 63 ἄνωθεν καὶ διὰ γαστρὸς ἀνθρωπείας (describing the birth of Christ) appears to mean [" by the action of the Spirit] *from above* and through a mortal womb" (although the Psalm (cx. 3) from which Justin has quoted refers to birth (LXX) "before the morning star"). Comp. Epiphanius (*Haer.* li. ch. 6, vol. i. 428) about Mark as "nowhere saying [that] the birth [was] *from above* (οὐδαμοῦ ἄνωθεν λέγων τὴν γέννησιν)" and (*ib.*) τῆς ἄνωθεν καταγωγῆς θεοῦ λόγου. So Simon Magus (Hippol., ed. Duncker, vi. 18) speaks of the generating principle as "*from above.*" In Artemid. *Oneirocr.* i. 13, γεννᾶσθαι ἄνωθεν undoubtedly means "to be born *again,*" but there the meaning is prepared for in a peculiar way by the context: "If a man *dreams that he is being born*......this indicates that he will have a *son in every respect like himself: for thus he might seem to be born over again* (οὕτω γὰρ [ἂν] ἄνωθεν αὐτὸς δόξειε γεννᾶσθαι)." And there it should be noted that the meaning is *not* "*to be born into a better life,*" but "*to be born over again in every respect like what one was before.*"

it had been recorded by the Synoptists—might think it right to recast the saying. Christ's doctrine, "Become ye as one of these little ones," might be in danger of being misunderstood literally (somewhat after the manner of Nicodemus) as encouraging childishness rather than childlikeness (1 Cor. xiv. 20). It is in accordance with the Johannine method that John should illustrate this danger by exhibiting a great Rabbi as actually misunderstanding the doctrine at its first utterance. It is also in accordance with his method of "narrowing down" (**2290**) that he should first introduce a general term "from above" including as St James says "every perfect gift" that comes from heaven—and then define it as a spiritual influence. The saying of Christ, that a proselyte,—who was compared by the Jews to a new-born child,—might be made a "*child of hell*," is of itself sufficient to explain why it might be necessary to emphasize the truth that regeneration must be "*from above.*" See **2573**.

(β) Ἄρτι see νῦν (**1915** (i) foll.)

(γ) Ἐγγύς

[**1909**] This adverb is used (**1718**) more frequently by John than by the Synoptists all together. In Jn it never describes the nearness of a person except in vi. 19, "they behold Jesus walking on [the edge of?] the sea and *becoming near* the boat (ἐγγὺς τοῦ πλοίου γινόμενον)." Ἐγγίζω, "draw near," is frequent in O.T. and N.T., and the Synoptists sometimes (Luke most frequently) apply it to Christ, but John never uses it. Under "Prepositions" (**2340—6**) reasons will be given for thinking that John regards the Lord as "*on the sea shore*," and not as advancing over the sea to the boat. If so, he may use γινόμενον ἐγγύς as we speak of the coast "*coming into view*" when we ourselves "*come*" within sight of it. The words and their context are susceptible of a spiritual interpretation. At first the disciples, in terror and unbelief, beheld (**1598**) Jesus "*becoming near.*" Then (vi. 21) "they willed to receive him"; and "straightway the boat was on the land." That is to say, like the Ephesians, "they that had been far off were made to be near[1]."

(δ) Εὐθέως and εὐθύς

[**1910**] Mark (**1693**) never uses εὐθέως, but he uses εὐθύς abundantly. Matthew uses both pretty often. Luke uses εὐθέως and παραχρῆμα pretty often, but εὐθύς only once. John uses εὐθέως

---

[1] Eph. ii. 13 ὑμεῖς οἵ ποτε ὄντες μακρὰν ἐγενήθητε ἐγγύς.

thrice, and εὐθύς thrice. *Whenever Matthew uses εὐθύς (7), it is found in the parallel Mark.* The question arises whether John distinguishes between the two words, or whether he uses now one, now another, as Matthew appears to do, because he uses now one, and now another, source of evangelic tradition.

[1911] As to εὐθύς "straightway," Phrynichus blames "many" who used εὐθύ ("straight away") instead of it. Hesychius says about it simply Εὐθύς, ἀντίον, which indicates that he took it to mean "straight opposite [to]," "coming face to face with." He also says, Εὐθύ, ὀρθόν, ἁπλοῦν, ἐγγύς, παραχρῆμα, εἰς εὐθεῖαν. Bonitz's Index shews that Aristotle uses εὐθύς of place, before ὑπό, πρός, μετά to mean "*immediately* under," etc. and also to mean "to take the first instance that presents itself," *i.e.* "for example," which it also means in Epictet. i. 19. 2 (where Schweigh. refers to many other passages)[1]. In LXX, as a rendering of Hebrew, εὐθύς occurs only in Gen. xv. 4 καὶ εὐθὺς φωνὴ Κυρίου ἐγένετο πρὸς αὐτόν, xxiv. 45 εὐθὺς Ῥεβέκκα ἐξεπορεύετο, xxxviii. 29 καὶ εὐθὺς ἐξῆλθεν ὁ ἀδελφὸς αὐτοῦ, where the Hebrew has "behold!" Similarly, parallel to Mk xiv. 43 "and *straightway*...there cometh up," Matthew and Luke have "*behold!*" A Scholiast on Thucydides, who describes the Plataeans as "killing their prisoners *straightway*," says that here εὐθύς does not mean immediately but offhand and without reflection[2], which is probably implied. Very likely Mark's εὐθύς may be a loose rendering of an original Semitic "behold[3]." But even without any such hypothesis the above-mentioned variety of meanings suffices to explain why Luke almost always avoids the word.

[1912] Mark's non-use of εὐθέως does not require explanation in view of the fact that it is never used by Aeschylus and (though thrice by Sophocles[4]) only once by Euripides in a fragment[5], whereas both writers use εὐθύς frequently. In the Indices of Epictetus and Lucian, εὐθύς is found, but not εὐθέως, and Bonitz's Index to Aristotle shews a very great preponderance of the former. The LXX Concordance

---

[1] Εὐθέως in Polyb. xii. 5. 6 is perh. similarly used.
[2] [1911 *a*] Steph. on Thuc. ii. 5 οἱ δὲ Πλαταιῆς......ἀπέκτειναν τοὺς ἄνδρας εὐθύς, "Hic enim schol. ait εὐθύς non esse παραχρῆμα, sed ἐξευθείας et ἀσκόπως."
[3] [1911 *b*] It has been shewn (352—3) that "behold" in Mt.-Lk. freq. corresponds to some verb of "coming to" in Mk. This may be illustrated by Hesych. εὐθύς, ἀντίον i.e. "coming to meet."
[4] Sophocles also uses εὐθύς 7 times.
[5] *Fragm.* 31. The Egypt. Pap. Indices have εὐθέως (11), εὐθύς (2).

gives εὐθέως as only once representing a Hebrew word. It occurs almost exclusively in Maccabees (especially book II). The insertion of such a word (whether in Hebrew or in Greek) might depend on the author's taste. The Jerusalem Targum has (Gen. i. 3) "And *immediately* there was light," and in Susannah (29) LXX and Theodotion severally insert εὐθέως and omit it. Aquila uses the word (Micah ii. 7) to mean "straightforwardly," "righteously."

[1913] In N.T., apart from the Gospels, εὐθέως is used frequently in the Acts, and occasionally elsewhere[1]. Εὐθύς occurs nowhere except in Acts x. 16 "Now this was done thrice and *straightway* (εὐθύς) the vessel was taken up to the heaven." This occurs in a Petrine passage describing the vision that resulted in the conversion of Cornelius. But when Luke rewrites this in Peter's speech, he alters the expression (Acts xi. 10) "Now this was done thrice and everything was *caught up again* to the heaven[2]." This indicates (1) that εὐθύς might be expected in a Petrine Gospel such as Mark's is generally believed to be, (2) that Luke, although occasionally retaining it as part of an old document, might be expected to alter it in re-editing or re-writing.

[1914] Coming to Johannine usage we find (*a*) εὐθέως in the Cure at the Pool of Bethsaida, the Walking on the Water, and the Denial of Peter[3]. Only as to the last of these ("immediately the cock crew") does the word occur in the parallel Synoptic narrative— where Mark has εὐθύς but many authorities omit it, Matthew has εὐθύς but many authorities read εὐθέως, Luke has παραχρῆμα[4]. (*b*) Εὐθύς occurs in Jn xiii. 30—2, "Having taken the sop, therefore, he [Judas] went out *straightway* (ἐξῆλθεν εὐθύς). Now it was night. When, therefore, he went out, Jesus saith, (lit.) Now was the Son of man glorified and God was glorified in him. And God will glorify him in himself and will *straightway* glorify (εὐθὺς δοξάσει) him," xix. 34 "One of the soldiers pierced his side with a spear and there

---

[1] Acts ix. 18, 20, 34, xii. 10, xvi. 10, xvii. 10, 14, xxi. 30, xxii. 29, Gal. i. 16, Jas i. 24, 3 Jn 14, Rev. iv. 2.

[2] [1913*a*] Acts x. 16 εὐθὺς ἀνελήμφθη τὸ σκεῦος, xi. 10 ἀνεσπάσθη πάλιν ἅπαντα. Also the Hebraic use of "all...not" is altered from x. 14 οὐδέποτε ἔφαγον πᾶν κοινόν into xi. 8 κοινὸν......οὐδέποτε εἰσῆλθεν εἰς τὸ στόμα μου.

[3] Jn v. 9, vi. 21, xviii. 27.

[4] [1914*a*] Mk xiv. 72, Mt. xxvi. 74, Lk. xxii. 60 παραχρῆμα ἔτι λαλοῦντος αὐτοῦ. In the Walking on the Water, Mk vi. 50 ὁ δὲ εὐθὺς ἐλάλησεν, Mt. xiv. 27 εὐθὺς δὲ ἐλάλησεν are not quite parallel to Jn vi. 21 εὐθέως ἐγένετο τὸ πλοῖον...

came out *straightway* (ἐξῆλθεν εὐθύς) blood and water." Comparing (*a*) and (*b*) we must bear in mind that the Cure at the Pool has many points of resemblance with the Cure of the Paralytic where Mark and Luke describe the act as immediate, and that the Walking on the Water is recorded by Mark and Matthew—so that we may say generally that the instances in (*a*) have some connexion with Synoptic narrative while those in (*b*) have not. In xiii. 30 the emphasis rests on εὐθύς, which comes at the end of the sentence ("rushed forth *straightway*"). In xix. 34 the voice passes on from εὐθύς to αἷμα καὶ ὕδωρ, but the adverb indicates that the "fountain" against "sin and uncleanness" (Zech. xiii. 1) was foreordained and ready to gush forth. Having regard to the rarity of the adverb we seem justified in thinking that, in xiii. 30—2, John deliberately uses it twice in one and the same passage concerning the "immediate" departure of Judas and the "immediate" advent of "glory," the former being subordinate to the latter.

[1915] The conclusion is, that εὐθύς and εὐθέως are used in N.T., not indiscriminately but with reference to meaning, or because they occur in documents of this or that style. The only instance of εὐθύς in Luke is in the passage about the house without foundation (vi. 49) "against which the river burst and *straightway* it fell in a heap (εὐθὺς συνέπεσε)," where Matthew (vii. 27) differs. It is quite intelligible that Luke might be willing to apply to the fall of a house an adverb that he might think unfit to apply to the actions of Christ.

(ε). Νῦν and ἄρτι

[1915 (i)] In **1719**, νῦν was shewn to mean "at the present time" (as distinct from ἄρτι "at this moment") and to imply, in Jn, a contrast for the most part between the present and the past. This is its general use in the Epistles, especially in contrasting the past darkness with the present light ("ye were once darkness but *now* are ye light in the Lord[1]"). But the interpretation of καὶ νῦν in xi. 22 (**1719**) is complicated by the use of the phrase in LXX, where "*and now*" is often connected with the thought "*And now* in this crisis, or, at this stage, or, in these difficulties, or, in conclusion, what is

---

[1] [1915 (i) *a*] Eph. v. 8 ἦτε γάρ ποτε σκότος νῦν δὲ φῶς ἐν Κυρίῳ. Of course in special phrases such as ὁ νῦν αἰών, ἡ νῦν Ἰερουσαλήμ etc. the contrast is with the future as in 2 Pet. iii. 7, 18 (the only instances of νῦν in that Epistle). But in 1 Pet. i. 12, ii. 10 (*bis*), ii. 25, and iii. 21, the contrast is with the past.

to be done?" e.g. "*And now*, Israel, what doth the Lord thy God require from thee?" "*And now*, Lord, what wait I for? My hope is in thee[1]?" So Peter, after reproaching the Jews for crucifying Christ, says, "*And now*, brethren, I know that in ignorance ye did it," where the underlying thought appears to be, "*And now*, what is to be done? Acknowledge your past ignorance[2]."

[1915 (ii)] In 2 Thess. ii. 5—6, the words "Remember ye not that while I was still with you I used to say these things to you," come after a prediction about "the man of lawlessness" and before the words "*And now* ye know that which hindereth (καὶ νῦν τὸ κατέχον οἴδατε)," where Lightfoot doubtfully inclines to the logical meaning ("*Well, then*, ye know") and says "this usage is particularly noticeable with οἶδα following." But he suggests alternatively "and *as to the present time* ye know what it is that restraineth"—a transposition like that in Jn iv. 18 "for thou hast had five husbands, *and he whom thou now hast* (καὶ νῦν ὃν ἔχεις) *is not thy husband*[3]."

[1915 (iii)] These facts indicate that καὶ νῦν, especially in an author like John, prone to transposition and asyndeton, will

---

[1] [1915 (i) *b*] Deut. x. 12, Ps. xxxix. 7, see Gesen. 774 *a* quoting Gen. iii. 22 and many other instances. The LXX regularly represents the phrase by καὶ νῦν, and it is extremely frequent, *e.g.* 2 S. vii. 28 (sim. 1 Chr. xvii. 26) "*And now*, O Lord God, thou art God, and thy words are truth......now therefore, let it please thee," where it might almost be translated "And in conclusion." It suggests (1) the conclusion of a prayer, (2) a logical or inferential conclusion.

[2] [1915 (i) *c*] Acts iii. 17. In Acts this is often καὶ τὰ νῦν, *e.g.* Acts iv. 29 "*And now* (κ. τὰ νῦν), Lord, look on their threats," v. 38 "*and now* (κ. [τὰ] νῦν) I say unto you, desist from these men." In Acts xx. 22—32 καὶ νῦν ἰδού, "and now behold," is used first temporally ("and at the present time...I go bound"), then with a suggestion of logical meaning ("and now behold I know") and lastly καὶ τὰ νῦν ("*and now* [*in conclusion*] I commend you to the Lord").

[3] [1915 (ii) *a*] Theoretically, the italicised words might begin a new sentence in asyndeton, "*The one that thou hast even now* is not thy husband." But, even in an author so prone to asyndeton as Jn, this is hardly possible. Col. i. 24 Νῦν χαίρω ἐν τοῖς παθήμασιν, coming at the beginning of a paragraph and after a description of the wealth of God's mercy, is explained by Lightfoot "*Now*, when I see the full extent of God's mercy...," no doubt correctly. But he adds "compare also 2 Cor. vii. 9 νῦν χαίρω, οὐχ ὅτι κ.τ.λ., where again there is no connecting particle." This, however, instead of coming at the beginning of a paragraph, is printed by W.H. thus, 2 Cor. vii. 7—9, "...ὥστε με μᾶλλον χαρῆναι. ὅτι εἰ καὶ ἐλύπησα ὑμᾶς ἐν τῇ ἐπιστολῇ, οὐ μεταμέλομαι· εἰ καὶ μετεμελόμην, (⸢βλέπω⸣ ὅτι ἡ ἐπιστολὴ ἐκείνη εἰ καὶ πρὸς ὥραν ἐλύπησεν ὑμᾶς,) νῦν χαίρω....." It might be printed otherwise. But, however printed, the context indicates that νῦν may be temporal. According to W.H., the meaning would naturally be, "I may perhaps have repented once, I rejoice *now*."

depend, for its meaning, on its context. As in 2 Thess. ii. 5, there is a reference to past teaching in 1 Jn ii. 18, παιδία, ἐσχάτη ὥρα ἐστίν, καὶ καθὼς ἠκούσατε ὅτι Ἀντίχριστος ἔρχεται, καὶ νῦν ἀντίχριστοι πολλοὶ γεγόνασιν, the meaning is "even as ye heard the prediction in past time, *even so* (καί) *at the present time* (νῦν) it is fulfilled[1]." There is also some reference to past time in 1 Jn ii. 27—8, but the passage comes at the end of a section enjoining "[steadfast] abiding," and καὶ νῦν appears to be logically or rhetorically (not temporally) used, "But as (ὡς) his anointing teacheth you...and even as (καὶ καθώς) it taught you, abide in it. *And now* [*in conclusion, I repeat*] abide in it[2]."

[1915 (iv)] There is again a reference to past teaching in 1 Jn iv. 3, "and this is the [spirit] of antichrist, [as to] which ye have heard that 'it cometh,' *and now* (καὶ νῦν) in the world it is *already* (ἤδη)[3]." Without any addition, καὶ νῦν might have meant "and [accordingly] at the present time [in accordance with past prediction]": but by adding ἤδη, the writer shews that he intends the meaning to be "before expectation." In 2 Jn 5 there is reference to past teaching, "I have found some of thy children walking in the truth, even as we received commandment from the Father, *and now* (καὶ νῦν) I ask thee...that we love one another," where the temporal and the logical meaning seem combined, but the latter predominates. These are all the instances of καὶ νῦν in the Johannine Epistles. Νῦν, apart from καί, occurs in them only once, 1 Jn iii. 2 "beloved, *now* are we children of God." This follows the mention of what the Father's love *has* done for us, and precedes the mention of what we shall become; and νῦν suggests the thought of the isthmus between the past and the future.

---

[1] [1915 (iii) *a*] But probably there is a double force in καί so that it also suggests "*even now* is antichrist here."

[2] [1915 (iii) *b*] 1 Jn ii. 27—8 ...καὶ καθὼς ἐδίδαξεν ὑμᾶς μένετε ἐν αὐτῷ. Καὶ νῦν, τεκνία, μένετε. Theoretically the first μένετε might be indicative; but this would be against Jn's general use of the word, and does not seem necessitated by τὸ χρίσμα μένει ἐν ὑμῖν in the context: for the meaning may be "the Spirit of Christ abides in you...take care to abide in Him." Μένει ἐν ὑμῖν is an instance of the rule *laudando praecipere*: the Spirit abideth in you—if ye are Christ's. The repetition of "abide" imperatively is like Phil. iv. 4, "Rejoice in the Lord alway, *again I will say Rejoice.*"

[3] [1915 (iv) *a*] As above, καὶ νῦν might theoretically mean "even now" and is perhaps intended to suggest "even now," which, however, is made clearer by adding ἤδη.

[1915 (v)] Returning to xi. 22 καὶ νῦν οἶδα ὅτι ὅσα ἂν αἰτήσῃ... we find that many MSS. and versions insert ἀλλά before καί so as to make the meaning (A.V.) "*But...even now...*" R.V. has "*And even now,*" apparently taking καὶ νῦν as "even now" and supplying "and" for the sake of English connexion. This indicates a tendency to take the phrase according to classical Greek idiom. But, having regard to the fact that καὶ νῦν or καὶ νῦν ἰδού, with οἶδα, occurs in N.T. elsewhere Hebraically (1915 (i) *c*) or with a suggestion of Hebraic meaning, and that καὶ νῦν in the Johannine Epistles is frequent and sometimes Hebraic, we are justified in preferring a Hebraic meaning here, like that of the Psalmist ("*And now* Lord, for what do I wait?"). In that case the meaning will be: "Lord, if thou hadst been here, my brother had not died. [But it pleased thee to be absent although we sent unto thee.] *And now* [Lord, what am I to say? *My hope is still in thee.*] I know that whatsoever thou shalt ask God, God will give it to thee." This is confirmed by two other passages where καὶ νῦν seems to introduce a last word, before the speaker passes from one subject to another: xiv. 29—30 "*And now* I have said [it] to you before it come to pass...No longer shall I speak much with you," xvii. 4—5 "I have glorified thee on the earth having perfected the work...*and now* glorify thou me."

[1915 (vi)] Ἄρτι is distinguished from νῦν as "this moment" is distinguished from "this present time[1]." Ἄρτι is practically (485 *b*) not a LXX word, and ἀπ' ἄρτι does not occur in LXX at all. "The present [dispensation]," τὸ νῦν, might be said to date "*from the moment* (ἀπ' ἄρτι)" when the revelation of the Father had been consummated through the Son[2], and Jesus says to the disciples, "From this moment ye know him (the Father)." Ἕως ἄρτι is used in v. 17 ("My Father worketh (A.V.) *hitherto*") of that which has been going on "*up to the present moment*" *and is still continuing*, as also in 1 Jn ii. 9 ("is in the darkness *up to this very*

---

[1] [1915 (vi) *a*] Comp. Mt. xxvi. 64 ἀπ' ἄρτι ὄψεσθε "ye shall see *from this moment* the Son of man seated," with Lk. xxii. 69 ἀπὸ τοῦ νῦν δὲ ἔσται, which presents much less difficulty than Mt. because ἀπὸ τοῦ νῦν might mean "from the [beginning of the all but] present [age]." Lk. xii. 52 again uses ἀπὸ τοῦ νῦν, which Jn never uses (except in viii. 11 interpol.).

[2] xiv. 7 ἀπ' ἄρτι γινώσκετε αὐτόν. Ἀπ' ἄρτι also occurs in xiii. 19. "*From this moment* I tell you before it come to pass." On ἀπ' ἄρτι, or ἀπαρτί, "exactly," see 485 *c*.

moment[1]"). In the following, a distinction (though a slight one) is drawn between ἄρτι and νῦν, xiii. 33—7, "And as I said to the Jews 'Where I go ye cannot come,' *to you also I say* [*it*]—*for the moment* (καὶ ὑμῖν λέγω ἄρτι)." Then, in answer to Peter's question, "Whither goest thou?" Jesus replies "Where I go, thou canst not follow me *at the present time* (νῦν), but shalt follow later (ὕστερον)." The saying is only "for the moment," but He gradually reveals to the disciples that the absence will be more than momentary extending through "the present time." Peter, in his second question, is not content with the promise that he shall follow "later," nor even "*at the present time* (νῦν)." "Why," he asks, "can I not follow thee *at this moment* (ἄρτι)?[2]"

(ζ) Οὕτως

[1916] "Thus" in iv. 6 (R.V.) "Jesus...being wearied (κεκοπιακώς)...sat *thus* (οὕτως) by the well," is scarcely intelligible. But R.V. marg. says "or, *as he was*." In classical Greek, οὕτως is often used of something that happens *before circumstances have time to alter*, e.g. of a speaker "departing *thus*," i.e. without another word, of an assailant "departing *thus*," i.e. without suffering in return. Similar to these is "I cannot answer *thus*," i.e. offhand. So here the meaning is, "he sat down *just as he was*, being thoroughly tired out." Probably Chrysostom is right in suggesting that the adverb calls attention to the "sitting" as being in some sense casual, although it was divinely foreordained to bring about the conversion of the Samaritans. It also suggests, as he says, the indifference of the true King to the external symbols of royalty[3]. Almost all the

---

[1] [1915 (vi) *b*] R.V., in both, "*even until now*," but in xvi. 24 R.V. and A.V. have "*Hitherto* have ye asked nothing in my name." Comp. 1 Cor. iv. 13, viii. 7, xv. 6. In v. 17 the meaning appears to be, "My Father worketh [*on the sabbath from the beginning*] *until this moment*, and I accordingly work [such acts as my Father prescribes on the sabbath]."

[2] [1915 (vi) *c*] Comp. 1 Cor. xiii. 12 "For we see *for the moment* (ἄρτι) through a mirror." When Jn uses νῦν thus, he adds μέν in xvi. 22 "and ye *now indeed* (νῦν μέν) have sorrow...but I will see you again and your joy none shall take from you."

[1915 (vi) *d*] Νῦν, in Mk xiii. 19, Mt. xxiv. 21 ἕως τοῦ νῦν, Mk xv. 32, Mt. xxvii. 42, καταβάτω νῦν ἀπὸ τ. σταυροῦ, and also in Mt. xxvi. 65, xxvii. 43 has almost the meaning of ἄρτι, "at this moment." But in Mk x. 30 νῦν ἐν τ. καιρῷ τούτῳ it means "at the present time." These are all the instances in Mk-Mt. In Lk. (1719) it is much more frequent.

[3] [1916*a*] Chrys. *ad loc.*: Διὰ τὸν κόπον (Cramer τόπον) ἡ καθέδρα γέγονε, διὰ

Latin MSS. omit the adverb, and SS has "sat [so] that he might rest himself," perhaps confusing κοπιάω and κοπάζω.

[1917] This passage prepares us for the true reading, and rendering, in xiii. 25 (R.V.) "He [the beloved disciple] leaning back, *as he was* (οὕτως), on Jesus' breast, saith unto him, 'Lord, who is it?'" where many authorities omit οὕτως. The meaning probably is, that the beloved disciple, instead of turning round to speak to Jesus (which would have attracted attention) merely "leaned back a little, *keeping the same attitude.*" But further, if any reader asked, "How could any of the disciples venture to ask such a question?" this adverb suggested an answer, "He did it, at Peter's suggestion, and being so close to the Lord, '*just as he was*,' i.e. *unpremeditatedly*[1]."

(η) Παρρηcίᾳ

[1917 (i)] Παρρησία, "speaking all [one's mind]," "freedom of speech," when applied to language, may be opposed—as Lightfoot (on Col. ii. 15) says—"either (1) to 'fear,' as John vii. 13, Acts iv. 29, or (2) to 'ambiguity, reserve,' Joh. xi. 14, xvi. 25, 29; but 'misgiving, apprehension' in some form or other seems to be always the correlative idea. Hence when it is transferred from words to actions, it appears always to retain the idea of 'confidence, boldness'....The idea of publicity may sometimes be connected with the word as a secondary notion, *e.g.* in Joh. vii. 4, where ἐν παρρησίᾳ εἶναι 'to assume a bold attitude' is opposed to ἐν κρυπτῷ ποιεῖν (comp. xviii. 20); but it does not displace the primary sense." Hence, in Col. ii. 15 (R.V.) "he made a shew of them *openly* (ἐν παρρησίᾳ) triumphing over them in it [*i.e.* in the cross]," Lightf. substitutes "*boldly*," and (earlier) paraphrases thus, "As a mighty

---

τὸ καῦμα, διὰ τὸ περιμεῖναι τοὺς μαθητάς· ᾔδει μὲν γὰρ συμβησόμενον τὸ κατὰ τοὺς Σαμαρείτας, οὐκ ἐπὶ τοῦτο δὲ ἦλθε προηγουμένως...Τί δέ ἐστιν, Οὕτως; Οὐκ ἐπὶ θρόνου, φησίν, οὐκ ἐπὶ προσκεφαλαίου, ἀλλ' ἁπλῶς καὶ ὡς ἔτυχεν ἐπ' ἐδάφους.

[1] [1917 a] Οὕτως in the Gospels almost always looks *backward*, "thus *as has been said above.*" It seldom means "thus, namely, *as follows*" (*e.g.* Mt. i. 18, vi. 9, Jn xxi. 1). Mk iv. 26 Οὕτως ἐστιν ἡ β. τ. θεοῦ ὡς..., "the kingdom of heaven is *even so as* [if] a man were to cast seed...," is exceptional in the Gospels and also non-classical. Οὕτως ὥστε occurs in Jn iii. 16, Acts xiv. 1, but, in Jn with indic., in Acts with infin.: Jn's construction, unique in N.T. (**2203**), is frequent in classical Greek and is one of many proofs that the passage was not regarded by the evangelist as a saying of the Lord, but was written as an evangelistic comment in a somewhat less Hebraic style (see Preface, p. viii).

conqueror He displayed these His fallen enemies to an astonished world, leading them in triumph on His cross."

[1917 (ii)] This view of the adverbial παρρησίᾳ, namely, that it "appears always to retain the idea of 'confidence, boldness,'" is confirmed by its use as a noun in the rest of N.T. where R.V. regularly renders it to that effect[1]. Moreover in the Johannine Epistle it occurs four times, and always to express the "boldness," or "confidence" of Christ's followers, confidence "toward God," or confidence as to future judgment[2]. Even in xi. 14 "then therefore Jesus said to them *without more reserve* (παρρησίᾳ) 'Lazarus is dead,'" the meaning may be, that Jesus, having prepared His disciples for the disclosure, revealed the truth without (as Lightfoot says above) "misgiving or apprehension" lest their faith should fail: for a teacher will not use παρρησία unless he is "confident" as regards his pupils, that they are ready to receive the teaching. This, too, may explain xvi. 25 "I will announce to you *without reserve* concerning the Father"; and xvi. 29 "Behold, now speakest thou *without reserve*," i.e. frankly, and fully, and clearly.

[1917 (iii)] There remain two questions as to παρρησία in the Gospels. (1) Why do Matthew and Luke omit it in the single passage where Mark employs it (viii. 32) "and he [*i.e.* Christ] was *boldly* (R.V. *openly*) speaking the word"? (2) What is the reason for the abundant use of the word in the Johannine Gospel and Epistle where it occurs thirteen times, as often as in all the rest of N.T. together (setting aside the Acts, where it occurs five times)? Out of these may arise a third question. (3) Is there any reason for thinking that this is one of the many passages where John intervenes to explain something in Mark that is omitted by Matthew and Luke?

[1917 (iv)] In order to understand Mark's use of "boldly" (Mk viii. 32 "*boldly* speaking the word") we must bear in mind that Christ's prediction of His own crucifixion was the prediction of a Gospel that proved "to the Jews a stumbling block and to the

---

[1] [**1917** (ii) *a*] See Acts iv. 13, 29, 31, xxviii. 31, 2 Cor. iii. 12 (where A.V. has "plainness of speech," but R.V. "boldness of speech"), vii. 4 etc. Sim. Acts ii. 29 (R.V.) "I may say unto you *freely*," (A.V.) "let me *freely* speak unto you."

[2] 1 Jn ii. 28, iii. 21, iv. 17, v. 14.

Gentiles foolishness[1]." The shock caused by "the word" to the disciples, and especially to Peter, shews that their Master had need of "boldness" (not for Himself in facing death, but for them in predicting it—boldness in believing that He would ultimately carry them with Him and that they would not abandon Him irrevocably). But still, to readers that did not realise the circumstances of the moment, Mark's brief phrase might seem obscure. Some might take παρρησίᾳ as "*openly*," i.e. *to all the world*. These might say that the phrase was misplaced, since Christ was addressing the disciples alone. Others might take the view of the Sinaitic Syrian, the Arabic Diatessaron, and the Codex Bobbiensis, which agree (1252) in making the words *part of a prediction of Christ, that, after death, He would rise again and speak the word "openly" or "with confidence" to the disciples*. Matthew and Luke—perhaps for one of these two reasons—omit the phrase. Clearly this tradition called for explanation on the part of any writer of a fourth authoritative Gospel.

[1917 (v)] Moreover, at the close of the first century, there were special reasons why attention should be called—among Christians, among non-Christian Jews, and among Greeks—to παρρησία as the mark of a great Teacher of divine truth. It was a time of religious impostures. Many people made money out of them. St Paul lays great stress on his own "sincerity," "confidence," and "boldness" (or "frankness"). He is not one (he says) of those who "water down" the Gospel for gain[2]. Speaking from another point of view, there was a "veil," he adds, on the face of Moses proclaiming the Law (which was unto death) but not on the face of Christian teachers: "Having such a hope [as I have above described] we use great *boldness*—and not as Moses used to put the veil on his face[3]."

---

[1] [1917 (iv) *a*] Comp. Rom. i. 16 "For I am *not ashamed of the Gospel, for it is the power of God*...to the Jew first and also to the Greek" with 1 Cor. i. 23—4 "*We preach Christ crucified*—unto Jews a stumbling block and unto Gentiles foolishness, but, unto them that are called, both Jews and Greeks, *Christ the power of God* and [Christ] the wisdom of God."

[2] 2 Cor. ii. 17 "watering down" or "making merchandise" καπηλεύοντες, "of sincerity" ἐξ εἰλικρινείας, iii. 4 "confidence," πεποίθησιν.

[3] [1917 (v) *a*] 2 Cor. iii. 12 ἔχοντες οὖν τοιαύτην ἐλπίδα πολλῇ παρρησίᾳ χρώμεθα.... Comp. 2 Cor. vii. 4, Eph. iii. 12, vi. 19, Phil. i. 20, Col. ii. 15, 1 Tim. iii. 13, Philem. 8, Heb. iii. 6, iv. 16, x. 19, 35; also Acts xx. 20 οὐδὲν ὑπεστειλάμην, at first limited by τῶν συμφερόντων, but repeated xx. 27 οὐ γὰρ ὑπεστειλάμην τοῦ μὴ ἀναγγεῖλαι πᾶσαν τὴν βουλὴν τ. θεοῦ ὑμῖν, where "*all the counsel of God*" implies the fore-ordained sacrifice on the cross, which was, to some, "foolishness" or "a stumbling block."

Philo, describing the freedom of speech used by Abraham toward God, classes παρρησία among "admirable virtues," the sign of a "good conscience," and quotes with approval the saying of a comic poet that a slave may be a storehouse of knowledge and yet "a rascal" unless you "give him a spice of παρρησία[1]." Arrian, too, publishing the sayings of Epictetus, just as he had heard them, describes them as intended to be "notes to remind himself of the teacher's understanding and παρρησία[2]." Epictetus had been a slave; but his teaching is permeated with a twofold παρρησία. He is free from all misgivings as to the truth of his teaching; he is also absolutely free from personal fear as to the consequences of uttering what he thinks right to utter.

[1917 (vi)] These facts may well explain the prominence given by John to Christ's παρρησία, and the different circumstances in which he mentions it—so as to suggest that traditions might vary about it and yet might be reconciled. For example, Christ's brethren urge Him, indirectly, to "*take a bold attitude*[3]." He refuses, at the moment, because His "hour was not yet come." Soon afterwards, the multitude is represented as "not speaking *boldly* through fear of the Jews," and this timid multitude testifies to Christ, "Behold, he speaketh *boldly*[4]." Later on, it is said that Jesus would no longer walk and teach "*boldly*" among the Jews; but this is almost immediately followed by His final journey to Jerusalem and to death[5]. To the Jews, who say "If thou art the Christ, tell us *boldly*," He replies in a dark saying; yet to the High Priest He protests "I have spoken *boldly* to the world[6]." The impression left by these

---

[1] [**1917** (v) *b*] Philo i. 473 ὡς καὶ τὸ κωμικὸν ἀψευδῶς μᾶλλον ἢ κωμικῶς εἰρῆσθαι δοκεῖν—

"Ἂν πάνθ' ὁ δοῦλος ἡσυχάζων μανθάνῃ
Πονηρὸς ἔσται· μεταδίδου παρρησίας.

[2] [**1917** (v) *c*] Letter of Arrian to Gellius, introducing the *Dissertations*: Οὔτε συνέγραψα ἐγὼ τοὺς Ἐπικτήτου λόγους οὕτως ὅπως ἄν τις συγγράψειε τὰ τοιαῦτα· οὔτε ἐξήνεγκα εἰς ἀνθρώπους αὐτός ὅς γε οὐδὲ συγγράψαι φημί. ὅσα δὲ ἤκουον αὐτοῦ λέγοντος, ταῦτα αὐτὰ ἐπειράθην, αὐτοῖς ὀνόμασιν ὡς οἷόν τε ἦν γραψάμενος, ὑπομνήματα εἰς ὕστερον ἐμαυτῷ διαφυλάξαι τῆς ἐκείνου διανοίας καὶ παρρησίας. Aristotle *Eth. Nic.* iv. 3. 28 says that the μεγαλόψυχος must be παρρησιαστικός. Plutarch ii. 68—9 (*De Adulatore* 27—9) has a long discussion on the good and bad παρρησία rather inclining against παρρησίαν κυνικὴν κ. λόγους τραχεῖς.

[3] See **1917** (i), where Lightf. is quoted as rendering Jn vii. 4 "assume a bold attitude."

[4] vii. 13, 26.   [5] xi. 54, xii. 1.   [6] x. 24, xviii. 20.

superficial inconsistencies is that our Lord always spoke "boldly," but not always "clearly,"—at least not clearly to the disciples because the disciples were "not able to bear[1]" the clear and full doctrine as yet. They also suggest a probability that John may have had in view misunderstandings arising from the doctrine of Mark, that "Jesus taught the word boldly." Perhaps, too, he may have had before him a version of Mark like that of SS, namely, that Christ would "*rise from the dead and speak the word boldly*": for this is very much like the Johannine tradition, "The hour cometh when I shall no longer speak to you in proverbs, but shall announce to you *without reserve* concerning the Father[2]."

(θ) Τάχειον

[1918] Τάχειον (or τάχιον) occurs in xiii. 27 and xx. 4 "the other disciple ran on before *more quickly* than Peter." In N.T., it occurs also in Hebrews xiii. 19 (R.V.) "that I may be *the sooner* restored to you," and xiii. 23 "if he come (R.V.) *shortly*," but the meaning is doubtful (2554 *d*)[3]. John also uses both ταχέως and ταχύ[4]. We pass to the important passage xiii. 27 ὃ ποιεῖς ποίησον τάχειον. R.V. renders this "do *quickly*." But it seems reasonable to suppose that John does not use the form τάχειον exactly like ταχέως and ταχύ. And it makes excellent sense to suppose that Judas, *who had not been originally purposing to commit the act of treachery on that night, was*

---

[1] xvi. 12.

[2] [1917 (vi) *a*] xvi. 25. It is interesting to note that the disciples, in spite of this warning as to the need of waiting for the παρρησία, persist in affirming that Christ *already speaks* (xvi. 29) ἐν παρρησίᾳ. It should be added that παρρησία occurs (5 or 6) in Canon. LXX, but only once (cf. Oxf. Conc. Lev. xxvi. 13 "upright," *i.e.* "with head erect as freemen") with correct Heb. equiv. Levy iv. 103—4 says that the Hebraized word may mean (1) "publicly," (2) "mit lauter Stimme."

[3] [1918 *a*] The Thesaurus indicates that θᾶσσον is frequently used (perhaps meaning θᾶττον λόγου, "quicker than one can tell it") for "at once," as it is also in the second book of Maccabees iv. 31, v. 21, xiv. 11 (A.V. "in all haste," "no sooner but"), and τάχιον is also thus used, though not nearly so many instances are given. Τάχιον occurs thus in Diod. Sic. and in Plut. *Moral.* 240 D "Unless you turn the stranger (ξενύλλιον) out of doors *at once*, he will corrupt you." It belongs to vernacular Greek and is condemned by Phrynichus.

[4] [1918 *b*] xi. 29 ταχύ, xi. 31 ταχέως. In Wisd. xiii. 9, τάχιον means "sooner." In 1 Macc. ii. 40 ἐὰν...μὴ πολεμήσωμεν...νῦν τάχιον ἡμᾶς ὀλεθρεύσουσιν, the context allows the meaning to be (1) "quickly" or (2) "all the more quickly," "sooner." In view of general usage, (2) is probable. In N.T., ταχέως, ἐν τάχει, and ταχύ, are all in use, so that there was no lack of words to express "quickly" regularly and accurately. On the variation in xi. 29—31, see 2554 *b*.

driven to quicker action by the words of Jesus. In other words, Judas had in his mind some thought similar to that expressed by the chief priests in Mark and Matthew[1], "Not on the feast day lest there be an uproar of the people": but he was forced to do the deed "*more quickly.*" And so it was brought about that the crucifixion took place on the Day of the Passover. Luke omits all mention of this original intention to delay the arrest of Christ. If John's τάχειον refers to it, it is one of the many instances where Luke omits and John intervenes.

ANACOLUTHON

(i) **Generally**

[1919] Anacoluthon[2] (lit. "*not following*") is the name given to a grammatical irregularity wherein, though the meaning may be clear, what is expected to follow *does not follow*, e.g. xv. 6 (R.V.) "If a man (τις) abide not in me, he is cast forth as a branch and is withered; and they gather *them* (αὐτά) [*i.e.* the branches] and cast them into the fire." Here "as a branch" is simile, but "he is withered" is metaphor: and strictly "*them*" ought to be "*it.*" Moreover, the following words tell only what becomes of the branches, not what becomes of the man. But the sentence is clear in meaning and calls for little comment.

(ii) **The Subject suspended**

[1920] Several instances may be illustrated by the Hebrew custom of putting the subject at the beginning of a sentence, and then repeating it as a pronoun, e.g. "*The Lord*, he is God." So in Revelation (iii. 12, 21) "*He* that conquereth (ὁ νικῶν)" is followed by "I will make *him* a pillar," "I will give *to him.*" Somewhat more correct Greek is given earlier (Rev. ii. 7, 17) "To him that conquereth I will give to him." Compare Josh. ix. 12 οὗτοι οἱ ἄρτοι... ἐφωδιάσθημεν αὐτούς, Ps. ciii. 15 ἄνθρωπος, ὡσεὶ χόρτος αἱ ἡμέραι αὐτοῦ etc. The following passages may be thus explained.

---

[1] Mk xiv. 2, Mt. xxvi. 5.
[2] The Johannine passages quoted under this head are i. 15, v. 44, vi. 39, vii. 38, 49, viii. 53, x. 35—6, xii. 35, xiii. 29, xv. 2—6, xvii. 2, xx. 18, xxi. 12: also 1 Jn ii. 24—7.

[1921] vi. 39 "...In order that *all* (πᾶν) that he hath given me I may lose none of it"; vii. 38 "*He that believeth* (ὁ πιστεύων)... rivers...shall flow from his belly"; x. 35—6 "*Whom* (ὅν) the Father sanctified...do ye say [to him] 'Thou blasphemest,'" best explained as [ἐκεῖνος] ὅν (in the light of the preceding passages); xv. 2—5 "Every *branch* (κλῆμα) in me that beareth not fruit he taketh it away...and every [one] (πᾶν) that beareth fruit he purifieth it...*he that abideth* (ὁ μένων) in me and I in him, *he* (οὗτος) beareth much fruit"; xvii. 2 "In order that *all* (πᾶν) that thou hast given to him [*i.e.* to the Son] he [*i.e.* the Son] should give to them eternal life." Here, grammatically, the meaning would be that the Son should *give all that He has received from the Father, namely, eternal life*. But the meaning is that He should *give eternal life to the whole Church* (comp. vi. 39 above). See **2422**.

[1922] 1 Jn ii. 24—7 "*Ye* (emph.) (ὑμεῖς), that which ye heard from the beginning—let it abide in you. If in you there abide that which ye heard from the beginning, ye also shall abide in the Son and [in] the Father...And *ye* (emph.) (ὑμεῖς), the chrism that ye received from him abideth in you, and ye have no need that any man should be teaching you." Here the writer emphasizes those that confess Christ ("ye") as opposed to those previously mentioned, who deny Him; and he may perhaps have begun by intending to say, "*Ye*, abide *ye* (imperat.) in the Son." But he deviates into saying, "let the chrism of the Son abide in you and then ye will abide in the Son."

Having regard to the instances in which the initial word ("*he* that conquereth," "*he* that believeth," "*ye*") is clearly nominative, it is probable that it is nominative in other cases, where the ambiguous neuter (πᾶν, κλῆμα) would allow the accusative.

(iii) **Digression**

[1923] In the last section, anacoluthon sprang from the desire to insist and repeat. More often it digresses, *e.g.* in v. 44 "How can ye (*emph.*) believe, receiving glory from one another and—the glory that [is] from the only God *ye seek not*?" The writer perhaps began with the intention of saying "receiving from one another...and *not seeking* from God," and then strayed away into the definite statement "ye seek not." In viii. 53 "Art thou greater than our father Abraham, who (ὅστις) is dead? *and the prophets are dead*; whom makest thou thyself?," as in the preceding example, the writer deviates from the logical continuation of the interrogative ("and greater than the prophets who are dead?") into a more brief and trenchant affirmation. This deviation is favoured by ὅστις ἀπέθανεν, which may imply an affirmation, "*Now he* (or, *for he*) is dead," so as to prepare the way for a second affirmation. In xii. 35 "Walk as (ὡς) (2201) ye have the light, lest (ἵνα μή) the darkness overtake you and [then]—he that walketh in the darkness knoweth not where he goeth," the speaker digresses from a particular consequence ("and lest ye walk in darkness and know not") into a general one ("and then—what is the consequence? A man that walketh in darkness, knoweth not whither he goeth").

[1924] It was pointed out above (1919) that after mentioning "branch" John speaks of "*them*" instead of "*it.*" So he has vii. 49 "This multitude that understandeth not the Law—[they] are [all] accursed (ἐπάρατοί εἰσιν)," which is more emphatic than the singular. Also xxi. 12 "No one (οὐδείς) of the disciples was bold enough to question him, 'Who art thou?' *knowing* [*all of them*] (εἰδότες) that it was the Lord," though ungrammatical, is brief and clear[1].

(iv) **Impressionism**

[1925] Anacoluthon in John often proceeds from his desire to let readers receive impressions of things in his pages as they receive them in nature, that is to say, first seeing the most striking of a group of things at a glance, and then gradually taking in the rest. In order to effect this, he may even deliberately let pass a statement that he afterwards corrects, as where he says that Jesus was baptizing and then adds that He Himself did not baptize, but His disciples did (iii. 22, iv. 1—2). Take, for example, the way in which he introduces (*a*) the Baptist's testimony concerning the coming of Christ, (*b*) Mary Magdalene's testimony concerning the Resurrection: (*a*) i. 15 (W.H. marg.) Ἰωάνης μαρτυρεῖ περὶ αὐτοῦ καὶ κέκραγεν λέγων, Οὗτος ἦν ὃν εἶπον· ὁ ὀπίσω (or,...ὃν εἶπον Ὁ ὀπίσω) μου

---

[1] [1924*a*] Clear so far as concerns the pl. But the participle, in such a context, suggests two interpretations, (1) "They did not dare to question *though* they knew it was he," (2) "They did not dare to question *because* they knew it was he." The Latin has the pl. part., SS has "*because* they were believing that it was he," (Walton) "*since* they knew that it was our Lord." See **2273**.

ANACOLUTHON [1927]

ἐρχόμενος...(W.H. txt λέγων—οὗτος ἦν ὁ εἰπών—'Ο ὀπίσω...)[1], (b) xx. 18 ἔρχεται Μαριὰμ ἡ Μαγδαληνὴ ἀγγέλλουσα τοῖς μαθηταῖς ὅτι Ἑώρακα τὸν κύριον καὶ ταῦτα εἶπεν αὐτῇ.

[1926] In the latter (b), W.H. give no various reading: but A.V. follows a text (similar to that of D and some Latin versions) that creates regularity by turning both clauses into reported speech, "M. M. came and told the disciples that *she had seen* the Lord and [that] he had spoken these things unto her[2]." The true text, however, gives prominence to the all-important words—all-important, at least, for the speaker—"I have seen the Lord." Then there is a drop into reported speech ("and he said these things to her," where "these things" refers to the message just recorded by the evangelist and therefore not repeated). Some might have expected ὅτι to be omitted before the direct speech, and to be inserted before the reported speech. But the writer reverses this, apparently using ὅτι (2189—90) to mean "these were her words," as the sign of quotation, (lit.) "There cometh M. M. bringing tidings to the disciples that"—*i.e.* these were her words—"'*I have seen the Lord*'—and [that] he said these things to her[3]."

[1927] In the earlier passage (a) above quoted (1925), we should expect οὗτος ἦν ὅν (or, περὶ οὗ) εἶπον ὅτι—if the meaning had been "This was he [concerning] whom I said *that* he that cometh after me is become before me[4]." Consequently we are led to another

---

[1] [1925 a] The best MSS. give ο ειπων: but (1) SS (Burk.) supports W.H. marg., (2) the scribal difference turns on a point on which the evidence of B is comparatively weak, (3) the sequence of similar syllables, ΟΕΙΠΟΟΟΠΙϹⲰ, may have been a special cause of confusion (1961, 2650—2).

[2] [1926 a] SS has "and the things which he revealed to her she said to them," D και α ειπεν αυτη εμηνυσεν (d adnuntiauit) αυτοις, a "et haec dixit illi," b "et haec dixit," f "et omnia quae dixit ei," e "et quae dixit ei manifestauit." Confusion may have arisen from reading ΤΑΥΤΑΕΙΠΕΝ as ΤΑΥΤΑΔΕΙΠΕΝ and from supplying what then seemed needful to complete the sentence.

[3] [1926 b] Jn xiii. 29 "For some thought...that Jesus was saying (λέγει) to him [*i.e.* to Judas Iscariot] Buy (ἀγόρασον) the things we have need of for the feast, or, that he should give something to the poor (ἢ τοῖς πτωχοῖς ἵνα τι δῷ)" is perhaps hardly to be called anacoluthon, but rather variation, the sentence passing from a direct to an indirect imperative. The change seems to be one from definiteness to vagueness, from the authoritative "buy" to "instructions about giving"—as to which Judas, the (Jn xii. 6) "thief," might be supposed to need a stimulus ("do (1918) more quickly").

[4] [1927 a] For the construction of the relative, comp. Jn viii. 54 ὃν ὑμεῖς λέγετε ὅτι...

rendering, "This was he that I *said*," i.e. "meant, or contemplated, [in all my utterances]"; and the following words ("He that cometh") may be a new statement of the Baptist's. Later on, the Baptist uses a preposition, thus "This is [*he*] *in behalf of whom* (or, *about whom*) I said, 'After me cometh a man...[1].'" It is reasonable to infer that in the first passage the Baptist must not be supposed to mean "*in behalf of whom* (or, *about whom*)," for else the evangelist would not have varied the phrase[2]. On the whole we may believe that, at some cost of immediate clearness of detail, the evangelist wishes to put briefly before his readers the essence of the Baptist's testimony as being, from the beginning, twofold:—in the first place one of prediction, or anticipation, in the next place one of subordination. Then he can fill in the details afterwards. The first point is that when Jesus first appeared, the Baptist at once testified "This was *he that I said*," the second, "*After me yet before me*." Later on, he connects the two. At first he places them side by side without connexion[3].

Aorist, see Index

Apodosis, see Index

Apposition

(i) **With proper names**

[1928] Apposition is a method of expressing the phrase "that is to say" without writing it, by "apposing" a second word with a case-ending to a first word with the same case-ending, as in xi. 16 "Thomas, [*that is to say*] he that is called Didymus," xx. 24 "Thomas, [*that is to say*] one of the Twelve, [*that is to say*] *he that is called* Didymus," vi. 71 "This man (*i.e.* Judas Iscariot) was

---

[1] Jn i. 30 οὗτός ἐστιν ὑπὲρ οὗ ἐγὼ εἶπον, Ὀπίσω μου ἔρχεται ἀνήρ....

[2] [1927 *b*] See **2360, 2369—70.** Supposing ὑπέρ to be used for περί "concerning," as it is used by many authors, the argument will still hold good, that John would not have used ὑπὲρ οὗ to denote exactly the same thing as ὅν.

[3] [1927 *c*] After all attempts at explanation it remains difficult to understand how any writer—and particularly one that shews himself so subtle and careful occasionally in distinguishing various shades of meaning—could here express himself with such extraordinary irregularity, abruptness, and obscurity. Possibly we have here **(1892)** some clause of ancient tradition inserted with the result of dislocating the context. The expression "This was he that I said"—if it means longing expectation—is similar to that in *The Gospel of the Hebrews* **(1042)** "Fili mi, in omnibus Prophetis exspectabam te."

destined to deliver him up [(?) *that is to say*] *one* of the Twelve," xii. 4 "Judas Iscariot, [*that is to say*] *one* of his disciples, *he that was destined* to deliver him up." This construction conduces to brevity and force, but sometimes to obscurity as is seen in the above queried vi. 71 οὗτος γὰρ ἔμελλεν παραδιδόναι αὐτόν—εἷς ἐκ τῶν δώδεκα. This may be mere apposition, but it may be an abbreviation of εἷς ὤν, "being one," understood to mean "*though* he was one[1]." There is also serious ambiguity in xix. 25 "His mother and the sister of his mother Mary the [daughter] of Clopas and Mary Magdalene." Here it is impossible to tell, from the text apart from other evidence, whether "the sister of his mother" is "Mary the [daughter] of Clopas," or whether they are two persons.

(ii) **In subdivisions**

[1929] Apposition is used after a broad statement to define its parts. But the first of the instances given below is not a certain one. John is referring to a previous statement that Jesus "found in the Temple *those that were selling oxen and sheep and doves.*" What follows may mean that Jesus (ii. 15) "drove all [of them] out of the Temple, *both sheep and oxen* (πάντας ἐξέβαλεν ἐκ τοῦ ἱεροῦ, τά τε πρόβατα καὶ τοὺς βόας)*," *i.e.* the men and what they sold, indicating that "all [of them]" included their belongings, "sheep sellers and ox sellers, sheep and oxen." And this may be his meaning in using τε—which occurs nowhere else in this Gospel without introducing a verb[2]. If so, the instance is appositional. Whatever the con-

---

[1] [1928 *a*] Comp. Mk xiv. 10 Ἰσκ. ὁ εἷς τῶν δώδεκα, Mt. xxvi. 14 εἷς τ. δώδ. ὁ λεγόμενος Ἰ. Ἰ., Lk. xxii. 3 Ἰούδαν τὸν καλούμενον Ἰσκ., ὄντα ἐκ τοῦ ἀριθμοῦ τ. δώδ., where Mk's ὁ is very curious. Later on, W.H. read Mk xiv. 43 [ὁ] Ἰ., εἷς τ. δ., parall. to Mt. xxvi. 47 Ἰ. εἷς τ. δ., Lk. xxii. 47 ὁ λεγόμενος Ἰ. εἷς τ. δ. In illiterate Gk MSS. of the 1st cent., ο and ω being interchanged, the participle ὤν might be written ὄ and confused with the article.

[1928 *b*] It is worth noting that, in John, these appositional constructions have to do with (*a*) Thomas, who was called by some (*Enc. Bib.* 5058) "Judas Thomas," with (*b*) Judas Iscariot, and (xiv. 22) with (*c*) "Judas not Iscariot"—all of whom might need to be distinguished. But in other cases also, when the Gospels came to be read publicly in sections, there would be found great use and clearness in appositional clauses defining personality at the beginning of a section, even though such a clause had been already inserted on the introduction of the character in an earlier section.

[2] [1929 *a*] Τε occurs only thrice in this Gospel. The other two instances are iv. 42 τῇ τε γυναικὶ ἔλεγον, vi. 18 ἥ τε θάλασσα...διεγείρετο. In ii. 15, A.V. has "drove *them all* out...*and* the sheep," R.V. "cast *all* out of the temple, *both* the

struction may be, the context implies that Jesus dealt in one way with the sellers of cattle and in another with the sellers of doves.

[1930] R.V., in v. 3 "A multitude of them that were sick (ἀσθενούντων), blind, halt," apparently takes the participle as *parallel* to the adjectives; but A.V. takes the participle as *including* them, "a multitude of impotent folk," *i.e.* "of blind, halt...." In that case, the construction is appositional. If the former had been intended, we should have expected ἀσθενής the adjective, or some more special word, such as "paralysed." Other instances of subdivisional apposition in v. 29, ix. 2, xx. 12, are perfectly clear, and call for no comment.

(iii) Explaining, or defining (not with Participle)

[1931] In most of the following instances the writer places at or near the end of a sentence some word or clause introduced without any preparatory or connecting word. Often, but not always, the clause is of such a nature that we may suppose it to have taken the hearer by surprise, when first uttered. They may be conveniently grouped here together and discussed severally in **1932**—6.

i. 45 "[Him of] whom Moses...wrote...we have found—*Jesus, son of Joseph, the [Jesus] of Nazareth*"; iii. 13 "He that came down from heaven—*the Son of man*"; vi. 4 "Now there was at hand the passover, *the feast of the Jews*" (W.H. enclose "at...passover" in half brackets. Contrast vii. 2); vi. 27 "For him did the Father seal —*God*"; vi. 71 "For this [man] was destined to deliver him up— *one of the* Twelve," *i.e.* probably "*though* he was one of the Twelve"; vii. 2 "Now there was at hand the [great] feast of the Jews—*the feast of tabernacles*"; viii. 40 "Ye seek to kill me—(lit.) *a man, [me] who have spoken to you* the truth" (As to this difficult passage, see **1934**—5); viii. 41 "We have one Father—*God*"; viii. 44 "Ye are of [your] father—*the devil*"; ix. 13, 18 "They bring him (αὐτόν) to the Pharisees—(lit.) *the once blind [man]* (τόν ποτε τυφλόν)"..."they called his parents—[*the parents of*] *him that had recovered sight*[1]";

---

sheep and the oxen." The former is hardly in accordance with Gk idiom. But in a writer so fond of parenthesis as Jn the meaning might be, "He cast them all out of the temple—both the sheep and the oxen [did he cast out]—and he poured forth the money...."

[1] [1931 a] Τοὺς γονεῖς αὐτοῦ τοῦ ἀναβλέψαντος (which, strictly, belongs to apposition with participle, **1937**), would mean, in ordinary Greek, "the parents of *the very man that had recovered sight*." But this, besides making poor sense,

xii. 46 "I (emph.), *light*, have come into the world"; xiii. 14 "If I (emph.), then, have washed your feet—*the lord and the teacher*..." (perhaps generally interpreted as meaning "*though* I am the lord and the teacher," but possibly meaning "*because* I am the lord and the teacher," if Christ assumed that it was *the attribute of the lord to serve*); xiv. 16, 26 "And another Paraclete shall he give to you...*the Spirit of truth*," "But the Paraclete, *the Holy Spirit*...*he* shall teach you"; xv. 26 "But when the Paraclete shall have come—*the Spirit of truth*"; xvii. 3 "That they may grow in the knowledge of thee, *the only true God*, and of him whom thou sentest—*Jesus Christ*"; xviii. 16 "The other disciple—*the friend* (ὁ γνωστός) of the high priest...."

[1932] Some of the above quoted instances require little comment, being simply short and sudden ways of implying "*that is to say*," or "*and it is*," e.g. (viii. 41, 44) "We have one Father [*and it is*] God," "Ye are of [your] father [*and it is*] *the devil*." Similarly xviii. 16, "the other disciple, the friend..." means "*now he was, as I said before*, a friend of the high priest, and hence he was able to introduce Peter into the house." In i. 45, "son of Joseph" and "of Nazareth" are mentioned abruptly by Philip as attributes of the Messiah, whom he accepts. In i. 46 and vi. 42 the same phrases are mentioned as reasons for rejection[1]. The abruptness with which Philip obtrudes them (so to speak) on the learned Nathanael (who is shocked by "Nazareth") may be intended to illustrate Philip's character and faith. In iii. 13 the words "coming *down from heaven*" followed, not by "the Son of *God*," but by "the Son of *man*[2]," stimulate the reader to think of what was

---

would be a rare Johannine usage. In the only Johannine instance of αὐτὸς ὁ applied to persons (xvi. 27) "The Father *himself* (αὐτὸς γὰρ ὁ πατήρ)," it means, "*of himself*" (**2374**)—that is, unsolicited by me. These clauses ("the once blind" etc.) are not needed for clearness. They suggest the reason for the "bringing" and the "calling." More amply it might be expressed by "'Here,' said they, 'is *the man that was once blind*,'" or "full of astonishment at the cure of *the man that was once blind*."

[1] [**1932** *a*] Also in vii. 42, "Nazareth" is (in effect) tacitly indicated as an objection, by the mention of "Bethlehem" as the foreordained birthplace of the Messiah.

[2] [**1932** *b*] R.V. adds "which is in heaven": but this clause is not even placed in the marg. by W.H., being absent from the best MSS. and from ancient quotations, which stop short, omitting these words (W.H. *ad loc.*). Probably a feeling of abruptness and paradox originated the interpolation (if it is one).

meant by "heaven," and "coming down." In xiv. 16, 26, xv. 26, emphasis is laid on the Paraclete, or Advocate, as not being one of the ordinary kind—the kind that takes up a client's cause, good or bad, and makes the best of it—but as being *"holy,"* and—which is twice repeated—"a Spirit *of truth."*

[1933] In the above quoted xii. 46 "I, *light* (ἐγὼ φῶς), have come into the world," the appositional clause comes exceptionally near the beginning of the sentence. It is not parallel to iii. 2 "From God thou hast come *a teacher*[1]," because the emphasis in the former lies on "*I, light,*" but in the latter on *"from God"* (and the pronoun "thou" is not expressed). It may mean, either, "I, *though* I am and have been Light from the beginning, have come into this world of darkness," or, "I, *because* I am Light, and *because* it is the mission of Light to enlighten, have come into the world." The reader is probably *intended to think of both these meanings and to prefer the latter*, as being in harmony with the saying in the Prologue, "There was the Light, the true Light, enlightening every human being— coming [*as it does continually*] into the world."

[1934] In viii. 40, there is a very great difficulty fully appreciated by Origen and Chrysostom, and by the translators of some Latin versions. Our Lord is proving to the Jews that they are not true children of Abraham: "If ye are children of Abraham, the deeds of Abraham ye are doing (2078—9). But as it is ye are seeking to kill me, (lit.) *a human being* (or *man,* ἄνθρωπον), *who have told you the truth*, which I heard from God[2]." On this Origen has frequent comments, trying (2412 *a*) to explain the insertion of *"human being"* on the ground that it refers to Christ's human nature, which alone can be killed etc.[3] It is difficult to accept these explanations, and Chrysostom dispenses with the need of them by dropping "*human being*" thus: "Ye seek to kill me *because* (ὅτι) I have told you the truth." Also two Latin versions (*ff* and *e*) have "hominem qui locutus est" ("a man that *has*," not "a man, me who have"). Doubtless either Origen is right in thinking that "human being" has some definite and emphatic meaning, or Chrysostom is right in thinking that the text must be altered.

[1935] But the text may be retained and may receive a very natural and beautiful meaning if we suppose that our Lord assumed

---

[1] Ἀπὸ θεοῦ ἐλήλυθας διδάσκαλος.
[2] Νῦν δὲ ζητεῖτέ με ἀποκτεῖναι, ἄνθρωπον ὃς τὴν ἀλήθειαν ὑμῖν λελάληκα....
[3] Orig. Huet ii. 262 A, 298 B, 413 B, and comp. 297 A B, 363 B.

a connexion, in the minds of those whom He was addressing, between "Abraham" and "man" (in the sense of "mankind" or "human being"), and also between "Abraham" and "truth," so that Jesus might be understood to say "You say you are Abraham's children; but you do not act like him. *He loved men and loved God's truth. I am a man, and I am telling you God's truth, and you are seeking to kill me.*" Philo (ii. 30) speaks of Abraham's "*love of man* (φιλανθρωπία)[1]" as being the natural accompaniment of his piety. Abraham also is the first of Biblical characters to use the words "brethren" and "men" together in a passage in which he sets a precedent for peace-making. His words and his deeds all suggest "humanity," φιλανθρωπία. Again, the first mention of the word "*truth*" in the Bible is connected with God's manifestation of His "kindness and *truth*" to Abraham[2]. Moreover the statement (made a little later on) that the Patriarch "*saw the day*" of the Messiah "and rejoiced[3]," implies—if at least the Messiah is the ideal of humanity—that Abraham was the friend of man as well as the friend of God. These considerations indicate the meaning of part of this obscure passage to be, "Ye profess to be the children of Abraham the friend of man, and yet ye desire to kill a *man*."

[1936] On xvii. 3, "And this is life eternal, that they should know thee, the only true God, and [him] whom thou sentest— *Jesus Christ*," Westcott (*ad loc.*) says, "(1) The use of the name 'Jesus Christ' by the Lord Himself at this time is in the highest degree unlikely...(2)...'the only true God'...recalls 'the true God' (1 Jn v. 20) and is not like any other phrase used by the Lord, (3) the clauses, while perfectly natural as explanations, are most strange if they are taken as substantial parts of the actual prayer." These arguments demonstrate that this is one of the many[4] passages where evangelistic explanation of a Logion or utterance of the Lord has made its way into the Logion itself. But what distinguishes this from other cases is, that the saying not only retains the second person, but is also addressed to God. The Epistle says (1 Jn v. 20) "...that we should know the true [One] and be in the true [One] in

---

[1] [**1935** *a*] Gen. xiii. 8 (Heb. and LXX) "Let there be no strife, I pray thee, between me and thee...(lit.) *for men brethren* [*are*] *we*," ὅτι ἄνθρωποι ἀδελφοὶ ἡμεῖς ἐσμέν. See Origen on Ps. lxii. 3 "*a man*" (**2412** *a*).

[2] Gen. xxiv. 27.   [3] Jn viii. 56.   [4] See Index, "Speech."

his Son Jesus Christ. This is the true God and eternal life." The evangelist, or some editor, seems to have applied this definition of "eternal life" to the explanation of words in the Prayer (xvii. 2) "that all that thou hast given him—he may give to them eternal life"; and, in order to continue in the language of prayer, he perhaps changed the "*we*" of the Epistle into "*they*," and "*the true One*" into "*thee, the only true God.*"

(iv) **With Participle**

[1937] Apposition between a noun and a participle with the article may be ambiguous. For example, ὁ χριστὸς ὁ ἐρχόμενος might mean either (1) "the Christ that is to come" (like Tennyson's "the Christ that is to be"), or (2) "the Christ, He that is to come." The former would not be true apposition but definition. Possibly the first of the following instances may be of the nature of apposition, although the participle has no article: i. 6 "There came into being (ἐγένετο) a man (ἄνθρωπος)—[one] *sent* from God (ἀπεσταλμένος παρὰ θεοῦ)." Here (*a*) ἐγένετο seems to be contrasted with the previous ἦν in i. 1 ("In the beginning *was* (ἦν) the Word"), (*b*) ἄνθρωπος, "a man," with ὁ Λόγος, "the Word," and (possibly) (*c*) ἀπεσταλμένος παρά "sent from the house of," with ἦν πρός "was with" ("the Word was with God").

[1938] i. 18 "Only begotten, *God, HE THAT IS in the bosom of the Father*—he (emph.) declared him (Μονογενής, Θεός, ο ωΝ εἰς τὸν κόλπον τοῦ πατρός—ἐκεῖνος ἐξηγήσατο)." The passage is one of great difficulty: but it seems best to punctuate (differently from W.H.) as though the Logos here receives three distinct titles. Ἐκεῖνος, *i.e.* "He, and he alone," would be called an instance of apposition in a classical author; but, in John, it is the imitation of Hebrew idiom for the purpose of emphasis (**1920**). In i. 29 "The lamb of God—(?) he that taketh away the sin of the world (ὁ ἀμνὸς τοῦ θεοῦ—ὁ αἴρων τὴν ἁμαρτίαν τοῦ κόσμου)," theoretically the construction might be non-appositional, "the lamb that," *i.e.* "among lambs offered in sacrifice this is the one that taketh away sin." But practically the evangelist's fondness for apposition almost decides that the construction is appositional here, "the Lamb of God, He that taketh away the sin of the world."

[1939] ii. 9 "But the attendants knew—*those that had drawn*

APPOSITION [1941]

the water (οἱ δὲ διάκονοι ᾔδεισαν, οἱ ἠντληκότες τὸ ὕδωρ)," probably apposition, "—[that is to say, not exactly the attendants, but only] *the men that had drawn the water.*" Non-appositionally it would mean (as W.H. punctuate) "the *attendants that* had drawn," *i.e.* such of the attendants as had drawn. The meaning is the same in both cases, but the way of putting things is different. If there is apposition, it defines, or rather corrects, the larger and incorrect statement; and this corrective manner is a Johannine characteristic (**1925**). Moreover, if the participle had been non-appositional it would probably not have been separated from its noun by the intervention of the verb. In iii. 29 "But the friend of the bridegroom, [*that is to say*] *he that standeth and hearkeneth unto him* (ὁ δὲ φίλος τοῦ νυμφίου, ὁ ἑστηκὼς καὶ ἀκούων αὐτοῦ)," the construction is certainly appositional and W.H. punctuate it so. It does not mean "That one of the bridegroom's friends whose task it is to stand and hearken." "The 'friend' of the bridegroom" might be expressed in modern English, "The bridegroom's 'best man.'" In iv. 25, "I know that Messias cometh—he that is called Christ (Μ. ἔρχεται, ὁ λεγόμενος Χριστός)," the appositional clause is clearly an evangelistic addition. On iv. 23 "seeketh such—namely, those that worship him [in such wise]," see **2398**.

[**1940**] In iv. 26 "I am [Messiah] (**2205**)—*he that talketh to thee* (ἐγώ εἰμι, ὁ λαλῶν σοι)" the appositional clause is added as a repetition of a statement so startling that the Samaritan woman might hardly believe that she heard it rightly: "When I say 'I,' I mean 'he that talketh to thee.'" In vi. 14 "This is of a truth the prophet (?) [*he*] *that is to come into the world* (ὁ προφήτης (?) ὁ ἐρχόμενος)," W.H. place no comma after προφήτης. But John has, previously (i. 21), "Art thou *the prophet?*" as though that were a title by itself, familiar to the people; and Matthew and Luke both represent the Baptist as sending to say to Jesus (Mt. xi. 3, Lk. vii. 19) "Art thou *he that is to come* (ὁ ἐρχόμενος)?" On the whole, the evidence of Johannine usage (**1635**—9) favours apposition, "the prophet, he that is to come." This applies also to xi. 27 "The Christ, the Son of God, he that is to come into the world."

[**1941**] In xi. 45 "Many therefore of (ἐκ) the Jews,—*those that had come to Mary and beheld* (πολλοὶ οὖν ἐκ τῶν Ἰουδαίων, οἱ ἐλθόντες πρὸς τὴν Μαριὰμ καὶ θεασάμενοι)...," A.V. has "the Jews which came." R.V. inserts a comma, "the Jews, which came." Perhaps neither version would be generally understood to mean what the

Greek means, namely, "Many therefore of the citizens of Jerusalem[1] —[by 'many,' I mean] those that had come to Mary[2]."

[1942] The passage presents great difficulty. That John should here use "Jews" not in his usual hostile sense but apparently to mean citizens of Jerusalem (as also seemingly in xi. 18, 19, 31 and xii. 9) need not surprise us much: but the sense seems to demand, after "Jews," the genitive τῶν ἐλθόντων, " Many therefore of the Jews [I mean many] *of those [Jews] that had come* to Mary...believed, but *some of them* [i.e. *of those Jews that had come to Mary*] gave information to the Pharisees." This is actually the reading of D[3]. But Origen, in a very long comment in which he mentions the phrase "those that had come unto Mary" some seven or eight times, gives express reasons why τῶν ἐλθόντων should not be read[4]. Chrysostom does not commit himself to anything definite in his brief statement, "Some marvelled; but others went and carried word to the Pharisees[5]."

---

[1] [**1941** *a*] Jn uses Ἰουδαῖοι to mean citizens of Jerusalem in xi. 18, 19, where he says that, as Bethany was close to Jerusalem, " many of *the Jews* (apparently meaning citizens) had come out to Martha and Mary to comfort them ": so, too, in xi. 31 and in xii. 9, " the common people therefore of *the Jews*." Elsewhere (**1702**), the word "Jews," in Jn, is often almost synonymous with " Pharisees."

[2] [**1941** *b*] " Many " is a relative term. It would probably mean a very much larger number in (1) "*Many* of the citizens died of the plague," than in (2) "*Many* of the citizens used to come out to see us as our village was only a couple of miles off." In xi. 45, there was need to define " many." It needed no definition in xi. 18—19 where the context defined it.

[**1941** *c*] The difficult question remains, Why does Jn repeat a phrase ("many of the Jews ") that meant one thing above (xi. 18—19), and would mean quite a different thing here—unless he hastened to explain it? The explanation may be, that the original text presupposed some distinction between (xi. 19) those Jews that "came to Martha and Mary," and those that came to (? SS "because of ") Mary at the tomb of Lazarus. Some may have remained in the house when Mary went out of it. In that case, (1) "the Jews" in xi. 45 mean the Jews above mentioned, who "came to Martha and Mary." (2) "Many of these [Jews]" had " come to Mary " at the tomb of Lazarus and "believed." (3) "But some of these [Jews]" did not come to Mary at the tomb, and these did not believe but gave information to the Pharisees.

[3] [**1942** *a*] SS, quite altering the sentence, has " Many Jews that *came unto Jesus because of Mary* from that hour believed in Jesus."

[4] Orig. Huet ii. 353.

[5] [**1942** *b*] Cramer *ad loc.*, in an extract closely resembling Chrysostom's context, has γενομένου δὲ τοῦ θαύματος, οἱ μὲν ἐπίστευσαν τῶν θεασαμένων, οἱ δὲ ἀπήγγειλαν τοῖς Φαρισαίοις—which commits itself to the view that the informers had beheld the miracle.

[1943] The impression left by Origen's long commentary is that he distinguishes the Jews that followed Mary to the tomb from other Jews that remained in the house. All had come to comfort the two sisters; but only those that followed Mary, in the belief that she was going to weep at the tomb, *were by her means drawn out of the house so that they unexpectedly met Jesus and witnessed the miracle.* Concerning these one might say, in the words of SS, that "they came *unto Jesus because of Mary.*" Origen speaks of them as the persons for whose sake the miracle was mainly wrought[1]. Perhaps he regards them as a type of the Church or of the Jewish section of it.

[1944] Justin Martyr and Irenaeus[2] regarded Rachel as the type of the Church. Origen, according to an extract from Cramer, connects Rachel with persons weeping for their children and not yet instructed by the Resurrection of Christ, and says that she is a type of the Church[3]. Whether Origen connected Rachel weeping for her children with Mary weeping for Lazarus we do not know, as his comment on the weeping is lost: but he compares the stone rolled away by Jacob (for Rachel) with the stone rolled away from the grave of Lazarus[4]. Origen censures Martha's want of faith. Justin says that Leah, because she had weak eyes, was a type of the Synagogue, and Irenaeus says that Rachel was a type of the Church because she "had good eyes." By this is meant that Rachel could discern the truth, which Leah could not. The Johannine narrative does not justify anyone in drawing this marked distinction between Martha and Mary; but it certainly leaves on us the impression that Mary was in some way superior to Martha, and that in very ancient times, "those that came to Mary" were regarded as typical of those Jews "who came to Jesus because of Mary," and that this coming was associated with the message of Resurrection[5].

---

[1] [1943 a] Orig. Huet ii. 352 D. In what follows, he says that Jesus raised Lazarus "that *the majority of the Jews* (οἱ πολλοί, not πολλοί), *having come* to Mary (ἐλθόντες πρὸς Μ., not οἱ ἐλθόντες)...might believe in him." Then he adds, "The language is somewhat ambiguous."

[2] Iren. iv. 21. 3, Just. Mart. *Tryph.* 134.

[3] Cramer on Mt. ii. 18.   [4] Orig. Huet ii. 343 B.

[5] [1944 a] This phrase ("those that came to Jesus because of Mary") might come into use in connexion with the part played by Mary Magdalene as the first announcer of Christ's Resurrection. A great deal remains to be explained about the different Maries, about the sisters Mary and Martha, and the household of

[1945] xii. 4 "Judas Iscariot, one of his disciples—*he that was destined to deliver him up* (εἰς τῶν μαθητῶν αὐτοῦ, ὁ μέλλων αὐτὸν παραδιδόναι)." Judas Iscariot has been previously mentioned in the same connexion, vi. 71 "for *he was destined* (ἔμελλεν) *to deliver him up*—one of the twelve": and now, reversing the clauses, John repeats the statement, when explaining that the words xii. 5 "Why was not this ointment sold?" were uttered, not (as Matthew says) by "*the disciples*," or (as Mark says) by "*certain persons*," but by "*one of his disciples*," namely, Judas Iscariot. It happens that Luke omits, in his description of the Last Supper, the words of the Lord reported by Mark and Matthew, "*One of you shall deliver me up*[1]." To these Mark alone adds "*One of the twelve*[2]." John follows Mark and Matthew in the former statement, "*One of you shall deliver me up*[3]"; and it is perhaps in view of this pathetic utterance of Jesus—"*one of you*," or "*one of the twelve*"—that he prepared his readers for it at the very first mention of Judas Iscariot, and now repeats it.

(v) **Noun repeated in Apposition**

[1946] A noun is repeated in apposition in i. 14 "And we beheld his glory—*glory* as of [an] only begotten." This is perhaps intended to suggest that the "glory" cannot be defined by such words as "light," "splendour," "brightness," or by anything except repetition, with some qualifying phrase to denote unique personality.

(vi) **Of Pronoun with preceding subject**

[1947] On the apposition, or quasi apposition, of a pronoun with a preceding subject, as in i. 33 ὁ πέμψας....ἐκεῖνος, see **1920** and **2386**. Bruder (Moulton) p. 678 gives this construction (of ὁ with participle etc. followed by demonstrative pronoun) as occurring Mk (3), Mt. (6) (including Mt. iv. 16 where it is a transl. of the Heb. idiom in Is. ix. 1), Lk. (1), Jn (17). On κἀκεῖνος thus used, see **2151**.

Bethany. Besides many other variations, SS has the following in Jn xi. 5—45 "Now Jesus *was loving to these three, the brother* [*and sisters*] *Mary, Martha, Lazar* (R.V. loved Martha, and her sister, and Lazarus)......(19) *that they might comfort Martha and Mary* (R.V. to M. and M. to console them concerning their brother)...(45) *And many Jews that came unto Jesus because of Mary from that hour believed in Jesus* (R.V. Many therefore of the Jews, which came to Mary and beheld that which he did, believed on him)."

[1] Mk xiv. 18, Mt. xxvi. 21.

[2] [**1945***a*] Mk xiv. 20 "One of the twelve, he that dippeth with me in the dish," Mt. xxvi. 23 "he that has dipped his hand with me in the dish," omitting "one of the twelve."

[3] Jn xiii. 21.

ARTICLE

(i) **Before Nouns in general**

[1948] The Fourth Gospel, more than the Three, represents Jesus as using the Article to denote (1) ideals such as the Good Shepherd, the Way, the Truth, the Door, the Life, and (2) types, such as "the wolf," "the porter," "the bridegroom," "the woman [of the house]," *i.e.* the wife[1], "the grain." In the last instance, R.V. has xii. 24 "Except *a grain of wheat* (ὁ κόκκος τοῦ σίτου) fall into the earth," perhaps from a sense that in English, though we can say "*the* seed," we could not say "the wheat-grain." But we lose in this translation the recognition of the fact that "*the* grain" (no less than "*the* sower," and "*the* earth"), was present before our Lord as one of the familiar instruments, so to speak, in His Father's hand. Somewhat similarly Mark alone speaks of "*the* candle," where Matthew and Luke have dropped the article[2].

(ii) **Inserted, or omitted, before special Nouns**

(1) "Fathers"

[1949] vi. 58 "Not as *the fathers* ate and died," vii. 22 "Not that it [*i.e.* circumcision] is from Moses but from *the fathers*." In vi. 58, "the fathers" must mean "the generation that received the law and died in the wilderness." But, in the New Testament generally, "the fathers" means "the patriarchs" (and especially Abraham) regarded as the original receivers of the Promises of God[3]; and the language of the Epistle to the Hebrews, "God, who...spake to *the fathers* in the prophets[4]," is quite exceptional (2553 *e*). Hence, in the Acts, when the people of Israel (and not the Patriarchs) is denoted, "our" (or "your") is perhaps invariably inserted[5]: and we should expect a Jew to speak and write "*our*

---

[1] [**1948** *a*] xvi. 21 ἡ γυνὴ ὅταν τίκτῃ, *i.e.* the married woman, not "*a* woman." The meaning is "*the* woman [*of the home*]," or "housewife." Comp. Ruth iv. 11 "Like Rachel and like Leah, which two did *build the house* of Israel." Perh. there is allusion to this thought in the description of Jehovah as, so to speak, *building* the *builder*, Gen. ii. 22 "he *built* the rib into a woman." See **1019**.

[2] [**1948** *b*] Mk iv. 21 ὁ λύχνος, Mt. v. 15, Lk. viii. 16 λύχνον. A.V. has even rendered ὁ σπείρων "*a* sower" (but R.V. "the") in Mk iv. 3, Mt. xiii. 3, Lk. viii. 5.   [3] Rom. ix. 5, xi. 28, xv. 8, Acts xiii. 32 (comp. 2 Pet. iii. 4).

[4] Heb. i. 1.

[5] [**1949** *a*] Acts iii. 13, iii. 25 (ὑμῶν, marg. ἡμῶν), v. 30, vii. (Stephen's speech) 11, 12, 15, 38, 39, 44, 45 (*bis*), 51 (ὑμῶν), 52 (ὑμῶν), xiii. 17, xv. 10, xxii. 14, xxvi. 6, xxviii. 25. Note that, amidst frequent repetitions of "*our* fathers" in the course

fathers" when mentioning his own people. The preceding words are, "This is the bread that came down *from heaven*," whereas, in this Gospel, Jesus is always (**1952**—**8**) represented as saying "from *the* heaven." These facts suggest that vi. 58 may be an evangelistic summary of the Doctrine of the Bread from Heaven.

[**1950**] In vii. 22 "For this cause Moses gave you circumcision—not that it is from Moses but from *the fathers*—and on the sabbath ye circumcise a man (**1961**)," the exact historic truth would require, not "from the fathers," but "from *Abraham*." But "the fathers," meaning "the patriarchs," might be loosely used to express the fact that circumcision, beginning with the first of the Patriarchs, was continued by the rest of them, and was thus passed on to Moses, who, though he "gave," did not originate it. If John wrote vi. 58 in his own person, but vii. 22 in the person of Christ, it is comparatively easy to explain how "the fathers" might mean "Israel in the Wilderness" in the former, and "the Patriarchs" in the latter[1]. It is more in accordance with the Johannine method of expression that our Lord should speak of Abraham, Isaac, and Jacob as "the fathers" than that He should give this name to the generation that wandered forty years in the wilderness.

(2) "Feast"

[**1951**] vii. 2 "Now there was at hand *the* [*principal*] *feast* of the Jews, the feast of tabernacles (ἡ ἑορτὴ τῶν Ἰ. ἡ σκηνοπηγία)." Josephus calls this (*Ant.* viii. 4. 1) "by far the most holy and important feast among the Hebrews," and (*ib.* xv. 3. 3) "most of all observed among us." John's reason for calling attention to this is given in the context. The brethren of Jesus urge Him to shew Himself in

---

of Stephen's speech, "*the* fathers" (according to W.H., following אBD) occurs exceptionally thus, Acts vii. 19 "the same dealt subtilly with our race, and evil entreated *the fathers, that they should cast out their babes*." Is this to be explained from the special context, as meaning "*the fathers of newly born children*"? Stephen calls the sons of Jacob "*the patriarchs* (οἱ πατριάρχαι) when they sell Joseph, and "*our fathers*" when they are sent to buy corn, and subsequently (Acts vii. 9, 12, 15). In Acts iii. 22 (A.V.) the words "unto the fathers" are an interpolation. The title (in Sir. xliv.) "[The] Song of [the] Fathers," LXX ὕμνος πατέρων, is, in Heb., "Praise of the Fathers of the World."

[1] [**1950** *a*] Note that Jesus, in replying to the Jews (vi. 31 "*our fathers* ate the manna") has said vi. 49 "*your fathers* ate the manna...and died" (comp. Mt. xxiii. 30—2 "*Our fathers...your fathers*"). An evangelist, commenting on this in a Gospel for Greeks and Jews, not being able to say "*your* fathers," might substitute "*the* fathers."

public, "Manifest thyself to the world," and this particular feast was the best occasion for obtaining publicity[1].

(3) "Heaven"

[1952] The article is always used by John (16 times) with "heaven" except in i. 32 "I have beheld (τεθέαμαι) the Spirit descending as a dove *from heaven* (ἐξ οὐρανοῦ)"; vi. 58 "This is the bread that descended *from heaven* (ὁ ἐξ οὐρανοῦ καταβάς)—not as the fathers ate and died—he that eateth this bread shall live for ever." Of the sixteen instances of "heaven" with the article, thirteen occur in the phrase "*from the* heaven[2]." This makes the two exceptions all the more remarkable.

[1953] As a rule, "*the heaven*" means heaven regarded as a place distinct from "the earth," whereas "*heaven*" means what is heavenly or divine as distinct from what is mortal or human. In the Synoptic Tradition, "The doctrine of John, was it *from heaven* (ἐξ ὀ.) or from men[3]?," "*from heaven*" means divinely inspired, but "*from the heaven*" would have implied a suggestion of an angelic message, or vision (Acts xi. 5) "*sent down from the heaven.*" Different writers might take different views of the Lord "hearing from heaven." Solomon in the book of Kings uses the article, Nehemiah does not[4]. But the same author may reasonably be expected to take the same view, and not to use the phrase with and without the article indiscriminately.

[1954] John habitually represents Jesus as asserting that He has come down "from *the heaven*," using the noun metaphorically in a spiritual sense like "the *bosom* of the Father," "the *light* of the world," "the *bread* of life" etc. If he had used the phrase "*from heaven*," it would have predicated about our Lord what might also have been predicated—as we have seen above—concerning the doctrine of John the Baptist. Therefore in the Fourth Gospel both Christ and Christ's doctrine, the Bread of Life, are said as a rule to

---

[1] [1951 a] In v. 1, Μετὰ ταῦτα ἦν ἑορτὴ τῶν Ἰουδαίων, Tisch. reads ἡ ἑορτή. But W.H. reject the article without alternative. SS has "a feast of the Jews."

[2] [1952 a] All have ἐκ, except vi. 38 ἀπό.

[3] [1953 a] Mk xi. 30, Mt. xxi. 25, Lk. xx. 4. 1 Cor. xv. 47 ὁ δεύτερος ἄνθρωπος ἐξ οὐρανοῦ, and 2 Cor. v. 2 τὸ ἐξ οὐρανοῦ imply "spiritual" as opposed to "earthly," "fleshly."

[4] [1953 b] 1 K. viii. 32, 34, 36, 39, 43, 45, 49 εἰσακούσῃ ἐκ τοῦ ὀ., Nehem. ix. 13 ἐλάλησας πρὸς αὐτοὺς ἐξ ὀ., ix. 15 ἄρτον ἐξ ὀ. ἔδωκας αὐτοῖς, ix. 27 ἐξ ὀ. σου ἤκουσας, ix. 28 ἐξ ὀ. εἰσήκουσας. Contrast also Ps. liii. 2 ὁ θεὸς ἐκ τ. ὀ. διέκυψεν with Ps. cii. 19 κύριος ἐξ ὀ. ἐπὶ τὴν γῆν ἐπέβλεψε.

have descended "from *the heaven.*" Thus John reverses the usual custom of speech. Most writers would speak of "the birds of *the heaven,*" and would describe a bird as coming down "from *the heaven,*" meaning "the sky," whereas they would say that a prophet's message comes "from *heaven*, not from earth." But John prefers to take "the heaven" as a materialistic term used by him always in a metaphorical sense to imply that the Lord Jesus Christ, the Bread of Life, was not merely of a heavenly origin but came down in a unique manner from the abiding-place of the Eternal God.

[1955] What bearing has this on the first of the two above-mentioned exceptions, i. 32 "I have beheld the Spirit descending as a dove *from heaven* (ἐξ ὁ.)"? The answer is complicated by several facts. (1) The Baptist is speaking, not our Lord, nor the evangelist in his own person. (2) It is not clear whether "from heaven" should be taken with "as a dove" or with "descending." (3) Mark and Matthew in their parallel description of the descent of the Spirit, mention "*the heavens*" and "*from the heavens*": but Luke has "*the heaven*" and "*from heaven.*" If John had written "from the heaven," it might have been taken literally in connexion with "dove," so as to mean "like a dove from the sky"; or it might have been taken metaphorically, "from the very habitation of God." Perhaps neither of these meanings is contemplated in the Fourth Gospel. More probably John regarded the Baptist as speaking of a vision that came "*from heaven*" and as using the ordinary phrase about it. This phrase he places exceptionally in the Baptist's mouth in order to distinguish it, on the one hand, from any bodily dove visible to all, and, on the other hand, from those unique spiritual descents concerning which Jesus spoke, which were from "the heaven of heavens." See **685—724.**

[1956] The other instance, vi. 58 "This is the bread that came down *from heaven*" (οὗτός ἐστιν ὁ ἄρτος ὁ ἐξ οὐρανοῦ καταβάς), follows, in the same chapter, no less than eight instances of "bread *from the heaven*" or "come down *from the heaven,*" and, in particular, vi. 50—1 "This is the bread that is [continually] coming down *from the heaven*...I am the living bread that came down *from the heaven.*" The two challenge, as it were, comparison or contrast. So do their several contexts: (*a*) vi. 58 "This is the bread that came down from heaven—*not as the fathers ate and died*; he that feedeth on (τρώγων) this bread shall live for ever," (*b*) vi. 49—51 "*Your fathers ate in the wilderness the manna and died.* This is the bread that is continually coming down from the heaven *that anyone may eat thereof and not die* (ἀποθάνῃ) (or, *be liable to death*, ἀποθνήσκῃ). I am the living bread that came down from the heaven. *If anyone eat of this bread he shall live for ever.*"

[1957] The first point to be noted is that in (*a*) the passage under discussion, the eaters of the manna are called "*the* fathers," but in (*b*) "*your* fathers." This, as has been shewn above (1949), may indicate that (*b*) is a saying of the Lord, while (*a*) is evangelistic comment. The next point is that the anacoluthon, or breaking off, implied in "not as (οὐ καθώς)," is paralleled by Westcott here to 1 Jn iii. 12 "—not as Cain was of the evil one"; and neither here nor in the Epistle does Westcott refer to any other N.T. instance of such a construction[1]. These two peculiarities of John himself, as distinct from the words of Christ recorded by John, when combined with "*from heaven*"—instead of the phrase regularly assigned to Christ ("*from the heaven*") both here and elsewhere—indicate that the evangelist is here speaking in his own person and summing up the whole of the Eucharistic discourse. According to this view, the teaching of the Lord in the Synagogue at Capernaum concluded with the words (vi. 57) "He that feedeth on me, he also shall live for my sake." Then John himself thus sums up the doctrine and the circumstances in which it is delivered: "This is[2] the bread that came down *from heaven* [*not from men*]—*not as the fathers* [*of Israel*] ate in

---

[1] [1957 *a*] According to Bruder, οὐ καθώς—apart from 2 Cor. viii. 5 καὶ οὐ καθὼς ἠλπίσαμεν—is purely Johannine, occurring in Jn vi. 58, xiv. 27, 1 Jn iii. 12: in xiv. 27 (where it is in Christ's words) the construction is quite regular.

[2] [1957 *b*] "This is" both in (*a*) and (*b*) is ambiguous. It may mean, "*This* [*bread*] is the bread that came down," or "*This* [*man*] is the bread that came down (1974)." In Jn, Christ is never represented as saying οὗτός ἐστιν except here, and in His lips it probably means "This [*bread*] is." But it is quite characteristic of Jn that he should repeat the words of the Lord giving them their inner sense "This [*man*] is." The phrase occurs several times in testimony to Christ, i. 30 (from the Baptist) "*This is* he about whom I said," i. 33 "*This is* he that baptizeth," i. 34 "*This is* the Son (or, Chosen One) of God," iv. 42 (from the Samaritans) "*This is* in truth the Saviour of the world," comp. vi. 14, vii. 40 "*This is* in truth the prophet," vii. 41 "*This is* the Christ." In some of these passages, *e.g.* i. 34, iv. 42, it comes at the close of a narrative. In xxi. 24 it comes near the close of the Gospel, "*This is* the disciple that testifieth these things." In the Epistle it occurs thrice: ii. 22 "*This is* the antichrist," v. 6 "*This is* he that came through water and blood," v. 20 "*This is* the true God and eternal life." The phrase comes appropriately in Jn vi. 58 as part of an evangelistic utterance testifying to the truth of Christ's Eucharistic doctrine. Comp. 2621—2.

the wilderness and died. He that feedeth on this bread shall live for ever. These things he said in synagogue teaching in Capernaum."

[1958] In i. 51, "Ye shall see *the heaven* opened (perf.)," the meaning is probably something quite different from a vision of a "rending" in the sky such as might be inferred from Mark's use of the word "rend" in the description of Christ's baptism. Taken in conjunction with John's context about "angels ascending and descending," the words (**642**) "promise a continuous revelation and a permanent avenue opened up between heaven"—the *spiritual heaven*—"and earth." The evangelistic use of the word with the article in xii. 28 "There came therefore a voice from *the heaven*," and in xvii. 1 "Having lifted up his eyes to *the heaven*," perhaps denotes in both passages an outer and an inner meaning; for non-believers, that lower heaven which men call "the sky"; for believers, "the heaven of heavens[1]."

(4) "Man"

[1959] In the following passages, "*the* man" is used (like "*the* dog," "*the* vine" etc.) to mean "man in general," "mankind," or "human nature"; Jn ii. 24—5 "But Jesus himself (**2374**) would not trust himself to them because he understood all [men] (πάντας) and because he had no need that any one should testify about *human nature* (lit. *the man*) because he himself (**2374**) could understand what was in *human nature* (lit. *the man*)." Mark alone has (ii. 27) "the sabbath was made for *the man* and not *the man* for the sabbath." But Mk vii. 15 "There is nothing outside *the man* (i.e. *man in general*) that, going into him, is able to defile him" is imitated by Mt. xv. 11. In Genesis, vi. 5 "God saw that the wickedness of *the man*, i.e. *mankind*, was great," viii. 21 "the imagination of the heart of *the man*, i.e. *mankind*," LXX has 1st "*the men*," 2nd "*the man*." Comp. Eccles. iii. 11 "so that *the man* cannot find out," where LXX has "*the man*," but Aquila "*man*," and iii. 19 "*the man* hath no preeminence above the beasts," where LXX and Theod. have "*the man*," but Sym. "*man*." So 1 Cor. ii. 11 "Who among men knows the things of *the man*?" i.e. the facts of human nature. The Hebrew phrase is identical with "*the Adam*," so that the Pauline phrases "*the old man*," and "*the new man*," are equivalent severally

---

[1] For "judgment-seat" with and without the article, see **1745**.

to (1) "*the old Adam*," or "*first Adam*," and (2) "*the last Adam*," or "*second man*," who is said to be "from heaven."

[1960] In vii. 51, "*the man*" may very well refer to previous context, which describes an attempt on the part of the Sanhedrin to arrest Jesus. Nicodemus, a member of the Sanhedrin, pleads that Jesus ought at all events to be heard: "Will (or, doth[1]) our Law judge *the man* except it first hear from him...?" i.e. *the man you have been trying to arrest*. The term is perhaps slightly contemptuous, and exhibits Nicodemus as affecting to speak from a detached and superior position—in spite of the fact that he has visited Jesus by night. Somewhat similarly, in Matthew, Peter detaches himself under pressure of fear, and, when he is questioned about his Master, says, "I do not know *the man*[2]." In classical Greek, ὁ ἄνθρωπος often means "the poor man," "the poor creature," and there is probably a tinge of this mixture of pity and contempt in Pilate's saying (xix. 5) "Behold the man," i.e. "Behold *the poor creature—* whom you are persecuting, and who is surely beneath your hostility!" But Pilate, like Caiaphas (xi. 50), may also be regarded as speaking "not from himself," so that he unconsciously uses an expression that may mean "Behold *the* man!" i.e. the Man according to God's Image, the ideal Man[3].

---

[1] [1960 a] The scribe that accented B gives κρινεῖ fut., which favours the view taken above; κρίνει would favour the rendering "the man [from time to time brought before the Law]." Comp. Lk. xix. 22 κρινῶ—where W.H. (with most Lat. vss.) have κρίνω but R.V. κρινῶ.

[2] [1960 b] Mt. xxvi. 72, 74 τὸν ἄνθρωπον, Mk xiv. 71 τὸν ἀ. τοῦτον ὃν λέγετε. Lk. xxii. 58, 60 has ἄνθρωπε. Mk softens the harshness, Lk. gets rid of it.

[3] [1960 c] Epictetus' use of the term is worth considering here. He uses it to mean "the ideal man," what Philo would call "the man according to the image [of God]," St Paul "the new man," and some "the Son of man." It may be briefly expressed by "The Man" in the following extracts: (ii. 9 title) "How that, being unable to fulfil the promise implied in '*The Man*' (τὴν τοῦ Ἀνθρώπου ἐπαγγελίαν πληρῶσαι) we take in addition to [it] (προσλαμβάνομεν) that of 'The Philosopher,'" (ii. 9. 1 foll.) "Beware, then, lest thou do aught as a wild beast! Else, thou hast lost *The Man* (ἀπώλεσας τὸν ἄνθρωπον), thou hast not fulfilled the promise. Beware, lest [thou do aught] as a sheep! Else, thus also *The Man* is destroyed (ἀπώλετο ὁ ἄνθρωπος)." And again (Epict. ii. 10. 14) "But if, from being a man, a creature mild and sociable, you have become a wild beast, noxious, cunning at mischief, given to biting, have you lost (ἀπολώλεκας) nothing? What! Must you wait to lose the trash in your purse before you will confess to having suffered damage (ἀλλὰ δεῖ σε κέρμα ἀπολέσαι ἵνα ζημιωθῇς)? Is there no other loss that damages *The Man* (ἄλλου δ' οὐδενὸς ἀπώλεια ζημιοῖ τὸν ἄνθρωπον)?"

[1961] In vii. 23 "If *a man* (ἄνθρωπος) receiveth circumcision on the sabbath," W.H. have [ὁ] ἄνθρωπος, and B inserts ὁ. But the high authority of B is weakened as regards the article by the fact that it makes frequent mistakes (2650—2) about o and the similar letter c, *e.g.* v. 7 προcεμοy for προεμοy, vi. 19 ωcταδιογc for ωccταδιογc, vii. 38 ειεμε for ειcεμε, and even vii. 43 cχιμα for cχιcμα (where, as in vii. 23, the error of insertion or omission could not arise from the juxtaposition of similar letters). Possibly in vii. 23 the scribe of B may have referred to the previous words ("and on the sabbath ye circumcise a man") and he may have supposed the text to proceed, "if *the man [just mentioned]*...," In any case "man" is as emphatic here as it is in Mark's statement "*The man* is not made for the sabbath"; and the emphasis is illustrated by vii. 22 "On the sabbath ye circumcise *a man*." "A man" might have been omitted if emphasis had not required it. But the argument is: "You do not hesitate to break the sabbath by circumcising *a human being*. If *human beings* on the sabbath are allowed to receive this partial purification, are ye angry with me for having made a *whole human being* (ὅλον ἄνθρωπον) sound on the sabbath?" The plea is, in behalf of *humanity*, for a *humane* judgment ("judge righteous judgment"). And the whole passage illustrates the use of ἄνθρωπος alleged above (1934—5) to mean "*human being*" in connexion with Abraham whose "love of men" is eulogized by Philo.

(5) "Mountain"

[1962] In Genesis (xix. 17) (LXX) "Look not behind thee nor stand in any of the surrounding country (τῇ περιχώρῳ), escape into *the mountain*," the context defines "the mountain" as the mountainous country near Sodom. So in Mark, before the Choosing of the Twelve, (iii. 13) "he goeth up into *the mountain*," is defined by the previous mention of (iii. 7) "the sea"—presumably the sea of Galilee—as being the mountainous country near the sea of Galilee[1]: but the parallel Luke (vi. 12) "he went forth into *the* mountain to pray" is not defined by anything—unless we suppose it to follow closely on Christ's teaching in (vi. 6) "*the* synagogue," and assume this to mean the synagogue of Capernaum, so that "the mountain" means "the mountainous country" near that city. In Mark and Matthew

---

[1] Τὸ ὄρος means "*the* mountain," or "*the* mountainous country," defined by something implied or expressed, like "*the* Highlands," "*the* Lakes."

Christ's going "into *the mountain* to pray," after the Feeding of the Five Thousand, follows a previous mention of going in "a boat," presumably on the sea of Galilee[1]. In the story of the Gerasene demoniac, "the mountain" is also defined (in Mark and Luke) by a previous mention of "the sea," or "sailing," as well as by "Gerasa[2]." When the Transfiguration is described, Mark and Matthew speak of "*a* high mountain[3]" (as also does Matthew in the Temptation[4]) but Luke has "He went up into *the mountain* to pray[5]."

[1963] A review of the contexts of the passages in which Mark mentions "*the mountain*" makes it probable that he uses the phrase to mean *the mountainous country in view of Capernaum*—not that which was actually nearest to the city on the west of the Lake, but that which lay on the east of the Lake. The former, though near, could not be seen by the citizens of Capernaum who lived under it, so to speak: the latter, being constantly visible to them, might naturally be called "*the mountain.*" This is not always clear in the Synoptists. But John defines the position thus in the only passages in which "*the mountain*" is used by him absolutely, vi. 1—15 "Jesus went away *on the other side of the sea of Galilee*....Now Jesus came up into *the mountain*....he withdrew again into *the mountain.*" Luke makes no mention of "the mountain" in connexion with the Feeding of the Five Thousand, Mark and Matthew mention it once, John mentions it twice. It is a case where Luke omits and John intervenes.

(6) "Only begotten"

[1964] i. 18 "No man hath seen God at any time. *Only begotten* (Μονογενής), God, HE THAT IS in the bosom of the Father,— he hath declared him." Under the head of Apposition (**1938**) reasons have been given for punctuating as above, and for regarding "Only begotten," "God," and "HE THAT IS" (ὁ ὤν qualified by "in the bosom of the Father") as three titles of the Logos. The Greeks, and Philo (the Jewish interpreter of Greek philosophy) called God "that which is," τὸ ὄν, neuter. John adopts the Apocalyptic phrase "He that is," ὁ ὤν[6], so as to make God a Person, not a thing. He then adds "in the bosom of the Father" to indicate

---

[1] Mk vi. 46 "went away to pray," Mt. xiv. 23 "went up to pray," following Mk vi. 32, Mt. xiv. 13.
[2] Mk v. 11, Lk. viii. 32, following Mk v. 1, Lk. viii. 26.
[3] Mk ix. 2, Mt. xvii. 1.   [4] Mt. iv. 8.   [5] Lk. ix. 28.
[6] Rev. i. 4, 8 etc.

a Person, in whom the defining characteristic is not strength or wisdom but filial union with a Father. Thus an expression implying both paternal and filial love closes the list of titles and descriptions of the Logos enumerated in the Prologue. In the last three of these titles, the first place is given to "Only begotten," which, both in Greek and Hebrew—owing to the connexion between an only Son and a beloved son (803)—implied "beloved Son." It is not likely that John meant us to render the word "*an* only begotten," any more than to render θεός, "*a* God." As a Christian would not render Χριστός "*an* Anointed," but "*the* Anointed," or "Christ," so John intends us to render Μονογενής, "*the* only begotten," or else, as a proper name, Monogenes, *i.e.* "Only begotten." The alterations of this text are numerous and natural as John has strained to the utmost the elastic Greek language to express briefly the intensity of his conviction that the Father is known only through the Son.

(7) "Prophet"

[1965] In i. 21 "Art thou *the prophet?*" A.V. has "*that* prophet," apparently (unless "*that*" is "ille" as in 1 K. xviii. 7 (A.V.)) regarding it as a repetition of the previous question "Art thou Elijah?" Origen, with more probability, supposes it to refer to the "prophet" mentioned in Deuteronomy xviii. 15, 18, whom the Jews (825) seem not to have identified with the Messiah, although the prophet is thus identified in Acts iii. 22.

(8) "Teacher [of Israel]"

[1966] iii. 10 "Thou art *the teacher* of Israel (ὁ δ. τοῦ 'Ι.) and knowest not these things!" is probably ironical, meaning "*the [well-known] teacher.*" That John would not indiscriminately insert and omit the article in such phrases, may be inferred from his general carefulness and subtlety in linguistic discrimination and, in particular, from i. 49 "thou art *the Son* of God, thou art *King* of Israel," the utterance of Nathanael, as compared with xii. 13 "*the king* of Israel," the utterance of the crowd, in the Entry into Jerusalem. "The Son of God" *reigns over, or is "king of," all the nations of the earth including Israel.* David, or Hezekiah, or a merely Jewish Messiah, might naturally be called "*the king of Israel*," i.e. the king for the time being. Nathanael is made to utter a confession much more inclusive than that of "the great multitude[1]."

---

[1] [1966 *a*] In classical Gk a distinction is drawn between βασιλεύς, *i.e.* "King"

(iii) **Before Names**

[1967] The article before a name may mean (1) "the [above-mentioned]," (2) "the [well-known]." This leaves room for great variety of usage in different writers, and even in the same writer (when writing in different moods). Mark is singularly consistent in his use of the article with the nominative, "Jesus." He omits it in the first mention of the name (i. 9) but never again, except in the phrase (x. 47) "Jesus the Nazarene"—where custom requires its omission as the name is defined by "the Nazarene." Matthew and Luke omit the article at first, but omit it also (with the non-predicative nominative) in about five and eight instances, severally, later on (besides the parallel to Mk x. 47).

[1968] In John—excluding such instances as "Jesus the Nazarene" and others where we might expect omission—we find the article omitted about sixty-five times[1]. With λέγει, John, more often than not, has ὁ Ἰησ., but he has ἀπεκρίθη Ἰησ. about twenty-two times and ἀπεκρίθη ὁ Ἰησ. only once for certain[2]. In phrases with ἀπεκρίθη and names, the LXX regularly omits the article. John may have been influenced, in using this word, by LXX usage, while, in the use of λέγει, he follows Greek usage. With indeclinable names, case-inflexions are sometimes indicated by the article for the apparent purpose of clearness; and perhaps it is sometimes inserted in accordance with an unconscious sense of rhythm so as to avoid monotony in the long dialogues that characterize the Fourth Gospel.

[1969] John's general rule is to *introduce* a personal name uniquely, the name given to the sovereign of the East, and ὁ βασιλεύς, "*the* king" of this or that barbarous tribe. There is perhaps an inner evangelistic meaning in the protest of the priests, xix. 21 "Write not, '*the king* of the Jews,' but that 'He said, *I am king* of the Jews (β. τῶν Ἰ. εἰμί),'" besides some allusiveness to the Synoptic differences concerning the inscription. See **2669**.

[1] [1968 a] The statistics are doubtful owing to the similarity of o to c and the weakness of codex B on this point (**1961** and **2650—2**). But 65 is probably the minimum.

[2] [1968 b] vi. 29. In iii. 5, xviii. 37, W.H. have [ὁ]. On the other hand where αὐτοῖς is inserted after ἀπεκρίθη we often find ὁ or [ὁ] before Ἰησοῦς. Perhaps where αὐτοῖς or αὐτῷ is inserted, *referring back* to the person spoken to, a corresponding ὁ is more often inserted to *refer back* to Jesus.

[1968 c] Johannine variations may be illustrated by the use of "John (the Baptist)" which occurs with article (13), without (5), doubtful (1). Contrast i. 28 ἐν Β....ὅπου ἦν ὁ Ἰ. βαπτίζων (where there has been much said about John in context) with x. 40 εἰς τὸν τόπον ὅπου ἦν Ἰ. τὸ πρῶτον βαπτίζων.

without the article[1], and there appear only three or four exceptions to this. One is "Pilate" in xviii. 29 "There went out therefore *the [governor] Pilate*," and this may be paralleled by Luke's first mention of him in the Passion, "they led him to *the [governor] Pilate*," where Mark has no article ("they delivered him up to *Pilate*") and Matthew "they delivered him up to *Pilate the governor*[2]."

[1970] The other exceptions are indeclinable nouns: i. 43—5 "He findeth Philip...now *the [aforesaid]* Philip was from Bethsaida... Philip findeth (lit.) *the Nathanael* (τὸν Ναθαναήλ)." Here "Philip" is introduced, according to rule, without the article; "Nathanael," against the rule, with the article: i. 45 "We have found Jesus, (lit.) a son of *the Joseph* ('Ι. υἱὸν τοῦ Ἰωσήφ)." Contrast this with vi. 42 "Is not this Jesus, the [well-known] son of Joseph ('Ι. ὁ υἱὸς Ἰωσήφ)?" In iv. 5 "the well that Jacob gave to *[the] Joseph* his son," the reading is doubtful, and W.H. bracket τῷ. Ἰωσήφ is shewn to be dative by υἱῷ αὐτοῦ, but the article conduces to immediate clearness. If "Nathanael" were not indeclinable, we might suppose the article to imply distinction such as is implied in the words of the Lord ("Behold an Israelite indeed"), but can this be the meaning of the article just afterwards ("a son of *the* Joseph"), and does it seem likely that John would speak of anyone as distinguished ("*the [great]* Nathanael") when describing his first approach to Jesus[3]?

---

[1] [1969 a] "Solomon" (x. 23 ἐν τῇ στοᾷ τοῦ Σ.) could hardly be said to need "introducing." In xviii. 40 "Not this man but *the [great]* Barabbas," it is the crowd, not the evangelist, that speaks; and the same applies to xix. 12 "*the [great]* Caesar."

[2] [1969 b] Jn xviii. 29, Lk. xxiii. 1, Mk xv. 1, Mt. xxvii. 2. Mk subsequently has ὁ Π. invariably, Mt. has it except in xxvii. 62 (pec.), Lk. has it exc. in xxiii. 6, 13, 24. Jn has ὁ Π. 19 times, and once, according to W.H., (xviii. 31) simply Π. Probably W.H. are wrong in following B here, especially as ο may have been omitted after the preceding c in ΑΥΤΟΙC (**1961, 2650**—2).

[3] [1970 a] Possibly i. 45 υἱὸν τοῦ Ἰωσήφ may shew traces of some tradition about "the carpenter Joseph," and the evangelist may intend a contrast between the beginning of the Gospel (when Jesus was described as υ. τοῦ Ἰωσήφ) and the development of the Gospel (after which Jesus was described as ὁ υ. Ἰωσήφ).

[1970 b] The article *before names of persons introduced for the first time* is rare in LXX; but it occurs in 2 K. xxii. 3 to represent *eth*, the sign of the objective case, before "Shaphan...the scribe." The parall. 2 Chr. xxxiv. 8 has *eth*, but LXX omits τόν. For the article with *names of places*, see **2670** foll.

(iv) **With Participle and "is" or "are"**

[1971] In the Synoptists, this construction is comparatively rare, e.g. "Who is *it that smote* thee (τίς ἐστιν ὁ παίσας σε)[1]?", "These are *they that were sown*[2]," "These are *the things that defile* (ταῦτά ἐστιν τὰ κοινοῦντα) the man[3]," "Who is *it [really] that gave* (τίς ἐστιν ὁ δούς) thee this authority[4]?" In the last instance, the parallel Mark and Matthew have "Who *gave* thee?" The construction with the article assumes the existence of some person or thing defined as doing something. Isaiah writes, "There is at hand *one-justifying-me*," LXX renders this, "There is at hand *he that justified* me (ὁ δικαιώσας με)." Isaiah proceeds, "Who will contend against me?" varying the construction. But LXX does not vary it, "Who is *he that contendeth* with me (τίς ὁ κρινόμενός μοι)?" The Epistle to the Romans loosely follows LXX "God [is] *he that justifieth*: who is *he that shall condemn*[5]?". In classical Greek it is necessary to insert the article in representing the Hebrew "one justifying me." If ὁ were omitted above before δικαιώσας, the meaning of the Greek would be "he is at hand, having justified me[6]."

[1972] Whereas Luke scarcely ever uses this construction in the Words of the Lord[7], John uses it frequently as follows (1) v. 31—2 "If I be testifying about myself my witness is not true. Another *is [really] he that testifieth* (ἄλλος ἐστὶν ὁ μαρτυρῶν) concerning

---

[1] Mt. xxvi. 68, Lk. xxii. 64, not in Mk (**490—1**).

[2] [1971 *a*] Mk iv. 16—20, Mt. xiii. 19—23, comp. Lk. viii. 12, 14, the explanation of the Sower.

[3] [1971 *b*] Mt. xv. 20 (? Mk vii. 15), not in Lk. Mt. also has this construction in iii. 3 οὗτός ἐστιν ὁ ῥηθείς.

[4] Lk. xx. 2 parall. Mk xi. 28, Mt. xxi. 23 τίς σοι ἔδωκεν;

[5] Rom. viii. 34 (quoting Is. l. 8) θεὸς ὁ δικαιῶν, τίς ὁ κατακρινῶν;

[6] [1971 *c*] In Proverbs xi. 24 (lit.) "there *exists* one scattering and yet increasing," the LXX paraphrases, "there are those who (εἰσὶν οἵ), [while] scattering, make things more," but Aq. and Sym. ἔστι σκορπίζων, comp. Prov. xii. 18, xiii. 7.

[1971 *d*] In classical Greek prose it would probably be hard to find an instance of ἐστί and a participle, without ὁ, meaning e.g. "is scattering"—unless the meaning were "*is really* scattering." The instances given by Jelf § 376. 4 are mostly from poetry and not in the present. Plat. *Legg.* 860 E (and Demosth. p. 853. 29) ταῦτα οὕτως ἔχοντά ἐστιν means "these things *are really so*."

[7] [1972 *a*] Lk. xx. 17 τί οὖν ἐστιν τὸ γεγραμμένον is (apart from the Parable of the Sower (**1971** *a*)) the only exception, if it can be called one. Outside the words of Christ, the constr. occurs (in Lk.) only in xxii. 64, xxiv. 21 ὅτι αὐτός ἐστιν ὁ μέλλων λυτροῦσθαι τὸν Ἰσραήλ.

me...," and then Jesus goes on to say that this "Testifier" is not the Baptist, nor even the works that He Himself does, but the Father, invisible to those whom He is addressing. Ἄλλος ὁ μαρτυρῶν would have sufficed (like St Paul's θεὸς ὁ δικαιῶν) if the meaning of "is" were not intended to be emphatic. The meaning really is twofold (1) "Another and distinct from myself is he that testifieth," (2) "Another [*really*] exists [*whose existence ye perceive not*], namely, he that testifieth." The first is expressed, the second is suggested. Ἄλλος means "another [of the same kind]" (2675—7).

[1973] (2) v. 45 "Do not imagine that I (*emph.*) (ἐγώ) will accuse you to the Father. *There is* [*indeed*] (ἔστιν) *he that accuseth* you, [namely] Moses...," *i.e.* "The very person to whom you look for testimony in your behalf (because you claim to be observing his law) is all the while testifying against you[1]."

[1974] (3) vi. 33 "For the bread of God *is* [not a thing of the past but of the present] *the* [*one*] *that is ever descending* from heaven and offering life to the world[2]." Here comes into play the ambiguity (comp. 1957 *b*) sometimes inherent in ὁ with the participle, since it may refer to the masculine noun last mentioned, namely "bread," or "loaf," ἄρτος "the loaf of God is *the* [*loaf*] *that* is descending." And this the Jews take to be the meaning, for they proceed to ask "Give us evermore this bread." But Jesus replies "I am the bread of life." Ἐστίν is not here so emphatic as in the last instance: but the context indicates that stress is being laid on the difference between the manna—a detail of the historic past—and the ever present, ever descending, bread of life. It is probable that John intends "the [one] that is ever descending" to mean the Man, quite as much as the Bread, or, primarily, the Man, and secondarily, the Man regarded as the Bread.

[1975] (4) vi. 63 "The spirit is that which giveth life (τὸ πνεῦμά ἐστιν τὸ ζωοποιοῦν), the flesh doth not profit at all[3]." The words

---

[1] [1973 *a*] Comp. viii. 50 ἔστιν ὁ ζητῶν καὶ κρίνων, "*There* [*really*] *exists he that seeketh*...." This and other passages, and the Johannine love of apposition, are against the rendering "He that accuseth you is Moses," or "Moses is he that accuseth you."

[2] [1974 *a*] A.V. "the bread of God is *he which*," R.V. "*that which*," ὁ γὰρ ἄρτος τοῦ θεοῦ ἐστιν ὁ καταβαίνων.

[3] [1975 *a*] Here ℵ omits "the," before "spirit," so as to mean "That which giveth life is of a spiritual nature." SS (Burk. marg.) has "He is the Spirit that giveth life to the body, but ye say 'The body nothing profiteth.'"

might mean: "The Spirit (*i.e.* the Holy Spirit) is [distinguished from all other spirits by being] the [spirit] that giveth life," repeating πνεῦμα after ζωοποιοῦν: and it may be fairly argued that similarly R.V. (against A.V.) has repeated ἄρτος in the passage last quoted ("the loaf is *the* [*loaf*] *that* descends"). But in that instance there was perhaps a deliberate ambiguity, and possibly the primary meaning did not require the repetition. Here there is no question of any distinction between one spirit and another, but only between "the spirit" and "the flesh."

[1976] The words are of very great difficulty owing to the different meanings that may be attached, not only to them (taken by themselves) but also to their context (**2210** foll.). One meaning may be "It is the spiritual part of man that must give vitality to all doctrine by receiving it spiritually," as St Paul says[1], and this suits the antithesis of "the flesh." But we have to bear in mind that (1) the phrase "life-giving spirit" is rare, (2) it occurs here in connexion with a preceding mention of "the Son of man ascending" and it is followed by a mention of "words" that are "life," (3) in N.T. elsewhere it occurs twice: "The letter killeth, *the spirit giveth life*[2]," "The last Adam [became] *a life-giving spirit*[3]," (4) the verb occurs twice in John elsewhere concerning the Father, who "*giveth life*" and the Son who "*giveth life*[4]." In the light of these facts does it seem likely that John would use the phrase "give life" concerning the Spirit of *man*? Would he not more probably use it of the Spirit of Christ, "the last Adam," the Son of Man in heaven? If so, the meaning here would seem to be, "*the Spirit* [*of the Son*] is that which giveth life[5]."

---

[1] 1 Cor. ii. 13—14.   [2] 2 Cor. iii. 6.
[3] 1 Cor. xv. 45.   [4] Jn v. 21 (*bis*).
[5] [1976 *a*] Perhaps there is a play on the word "spirit" as meaning also "breath" in Hebrew and Greek, that cannot well be reproduced in English. As there is a spirit that gives life beneath the *letter* that killeth, so there is a spirit that gives life beneath *words* that (taken literally) may "kill." The disciples of Jesus have to go back beyond the sound of His uttered *words* to the breath, spirit, or personality, that uttered them. Compared with the inner meaning, breath, or "spirit," of a word, the outward meaning or sound may be called its "flesh." "The words that I have spoken to you," says our Lord, "they are *spirit* and they are *life*, because they have not been mere 'flesh words,' or external sounds, but have passed, breathing life, into your spirits." And accordingly Peter says (vi. 68) "Thou hast words of eternal life."

[1977] Some such thought appears to have been in the mind of the originator of the version in SS, "*He* [i.e. the Son of Man] *is the Spirit that giveth life to the body.*" He arrives at this by repeating "Son of Man" as the subject of "is," by taking τὸ π. τὸ ζ. as "the Spirit that giveth life," and by altering the subsequent words. The version may be of value as testifying to a very early interpretation connecting "giving life" to the dead with "giving life" to words, and both of these with the Son of man.

[1978] (5) viii. 50—1 "I honour my Father and ye dishonour me. But I seek not my own glory; *there is* [*indeed*] *he that seeketh and judgeth* (ἔστιν ὁ ζητῶν καὶ κρίνων)," i.e. as explained above (1971—3) "there is, all the while, though ye know it not." And the "judging" is regarded as going on (iii. 18) "already." Later on it is said (xii. 48) "He that is rejecting me and not receiving my words (ῥήματά μου) *hath him that judgeth him* (ἔχει τὸν κρίνοντα αὐτόν)," where a clause in the future follows: "The word (λόγος) that I spake—that (ἐκεῖνος) shall judge him in the last day." The Logos is judging *now*, and the judgment will be summed up hereafter.

[1979] (6) viii. 54 "If I (*emph.*) should glorify myself, my glory is nothing. *It is* [*indeed*] my Father *that is glorifying* me, of whom *ye* (emph.) say that he is your God, and [yet] ye have not recognised him; but I know him[1]." Here the context indicates that the emphatic "is," expressed by ἔστιν at the beginning of a sentence, describes an action going on in the presence of men ignorant both of the action and of the agent. The "glorifying" is manifested by the works that the Son receives from the Father to do in the presence of men.

[1980] (7) xiv. 21 "He that hath my commandments and keepeth them, he *it* [*really*] *is that loveth me* (ἐκεῖνός ἐστιν ὁ ἀγαπῶν με)." This follows xiv. 15 "If ye be loving me ye will keep my commandments," and it adds, in effect, "If ye keep them, *then, and*

---

[1] [1979 *a*] Ἐὰν ἐγὼ δοξάσω ἐμαυτόν, ἡ δόξα μου οὐδέν ἐστιν. ἔστιν ὁ πατήρ μου ὁ δοξάζων με ὃν ὑμεῖς λέγετε ὅτι θεὸς ὑμῶν (marg. ἡμῶν) ἐστίν, καὶ οὐκ ἐγνώκατε αὐτόν, ἐγὼ δὲ οἶδα αὐτόν. The ἔστιν at the end of the first sentence is quite unemphatic and almost superfluous. But, if it were omitted, the following ἔστιν might be taken to be final instead of initial. Moreover, the juxtaposition of the two lays unusual emphasis on the second. "*It really is* my Father."

only then, will ye be really loving me," or, in the third person, "He that keeps them, *he and he alone*, is really loving me[1]."

[1981] Besides occurring in the Words of Jesus, this construction is found in the words of the Baptist and other speakers. Thus, whereas the Synoptists represent the Baptist as saying concerning the future Messiah "*He shall baptize* you," John gives the words as "*He it is that is baptizing* you[2]": and the Jews and others also speak thus[3]. But the phrase appears to have commended itself to the evangelist as especially suited to the Logos, who Himself sees everything, and describes it to others, as it really is, going on visibly before His eyes, though not before theirs.

(v) **With Non=Possessive Adjectives**[4]

[1982] The reduplication of the article changing a noun-adjective phrase, *e.g.* (1) "the third day" to (2) "the day *the* third," adds weight and emphasis to the adjective. In Christ's predictions of the Resurrection Matthew always gives the former: Luke, in the parallel to one of these, gives the latter. The latter is also used in the formal and traditional enumeration of the appearances of Christ after death in the First Epistle to the Corinthians[5]. The Revelation has the former in speaking of "the third living creature," or "the third angel"; but in more solemn phrases we find "he opened the seal *the* third," "the woe *the* third cometh quickly[6]."

[1983] In the Synoptists, the reduplication—apart from words of Christ and the Voice from Heaven ("My Son my beloved")—

---

[1] [1980 *a*] Other instances of ὁ with the participle and ἐστί are iv. 10 "If thou hadst known who *it* [*really*] *is that saith* unto thee (τίς ἐστιν ὁ λέγων σοι)...," iv. 37 ἄλλος ἐστὶν ὁ σπείρων καὶ ἄλλος ὁ θερίζων where ὁ σπείρων and ὁ θερίζων are, in effect, nouns. In ix. 37 καὶ ἑώρακας αὐτὸν καὶ ὁ λαλῶν μετὰ σοῦ ἐκεῖνός ἐστιν, the subject is ὁ λαλῶν, and ἐκεῖνος is not (as mostly) repetitive but means "that very Son of Man about whom you ask 'Who is he?' as though he were far off."

[2] Jn i. 33, Mk i. 8, Mt. iii. 11, Lk. iii. 16.

[3] Jn v. 12 "Who is *the man that said*...?" v. 15 "...that Jesus was (lit. is) *he that had made* him whole," xxi. 20 "Who is *he that is to deliver thee up*?"

[4] [1982 *a*] This excludes noun-participle phrases, *e.g.* "the people that [was] sitting (ὁ λαὸς ὁ καθήμενος)," "the miracles *that* [*were*] *wrought* (αἱ δυνάμεις αἱ γενόμεναι)" etc. For phrases with possessive adjectives see **1987—9**.

[5] [1982 *b*] Mt. xvi. 21, xvii. 23, xx. 19. The parall. Mk has μετὰ τρεῖς ἡμέρας, Lk. ix. 22 has τῇ τ. ἡμ. in a prediction of Christ, and also in his account of what the Saviour said (xxiv. 46) after the Resurrection. But Lk. xviii. 33 (parall. to Mt. xx. 19) has τῇ ἡμ. τῇ τρ., the form used in 1 Cor. xv. 4.

[6] [1982 *c*] Rev. iv. 7, vi. 5, viii. 10, contrasted with Rev. vi. 5, xi. 14.

is very rarely used, except in a few special phrases. Lk. ii. 7 has "her Son her firstborn"; Mark has often, and Luke twice (viii. 29, ix. 42) "the spirit the unclean"; Luke has (i. 26) "the month the sixth" (ii. 26, iii. 22, also Mk iii. 29, xiii. 11, Mt. xii. 32) "the Spirit the Holy[1]."

[1984] John, as a rule, reduplicates the article only in utterances of the Lord or in weighty sayings about Him, as in the Prologue, "This was the light, the true [light][2]." In the less weighty clauses of the Lord's utterances he does not reduplicate it, as in "the true worshippers[3]," contrasted with "I am the Vine the true [vine][4]."

[1985] One or two perplexing instances of reduplication in John may be perhaps explained by a desire to suggest to the reader some latent thought, as when he says that Andrew "findeth first *his brother his own* [brother] Simon[5]." Here the evangelist is supposed to mean that Andrew's unnamed companion *also* found *his* brother, James the son of Zebedee, but not till Andrew had "first" found Simon. Antithesis is certainly expressed elsewhere in "his name his own [name][6]," "his glory his own [glory][7]." In "the day the third [day]" at Cana—if the text is correct—there is perhaps a mystical meaning[8]. In "the five loaves the barley [loaves][9]" and "the ear the right [ear]" of Malchus[10], symbolism may be latent, apart from the fact that (comp. **1983** *a*) John is adding details not mentioned by Mark and Matthew[11].

---

[1] [**1983** *a*] Mk v. 7, [Lk. viii. 28] assign to the demoniac the words, "Son of the God the Highest"; Lk. vi. 6, xxii. 50—*when adding facts unmentioned by* Mk-Mt., namely, that the "hand," and the "ear," severally, were "the right one"—reduplicates the article.

[2] i. 9.

[3] [**1984** *a*] iv. 23 "The hour cometh......when *the true worshippers* shall worship the Father in spirit and truth." The italicised words do not predicate anything about the Logos, and they are subordinate in emphasis to what follows.

[4] xv. 1.   [5] i. 41.   [6] v. 43.
[7] vii. 18.   [8] ii. 1.   [9] vi. 13.

[10] [**1985** *a*] xviii. 10. Luke may not have intended symbolism. The two evangelists must be judged in the light of their several Gospels, taken as wholes.

[11] [**1985** *b*] In xviii. 17, the person previously described as (xviii. 16) "*She that kept the door*," is now called "*the 'maid,' she that kept the door*." This is probably not emphasis but afterthought; the evangelist wishes to retain the old Synoptic tradition that the Apostle was confused and abashed by a mere "maid," whom he had previously described as "she that kept the door." The meaning, then, is, "*The maid, she* [*whom I described above as the one*] *that kept the door*."

[1986] The following are the instances in Greek :

(α) i. 9 Ἦν τὸ φῶς τὸ ἀληθινόν. Comp. vi. 32 τὸν ἄρτον ἐκ τοῦ οὐρανοῦ τὸν ἀληθινόν, xv. 1 ἡ ἄμπελος ἡ ἀληθινή. Contrast iv. 23 οἱ ἀληθινοὶ προσκυνηταί. See above (1984).

(β) i. 41 εὑρίσκει οὗτος πρῶτον τὸν ἀδελφὸν τὸν ἴδιον Σίμωνα (1985). Comp. v. 43 ἐν τῷ ὀνόματι τῷ ἰδίῳ, vii. 18 τὴν δόξαν τὴν ἰδίαν. In all these there is antithesis. Contrast iv. 44 ἐν τῇ ἰδίᾳ πατρίδι, x. 3 τὰ ἴδια πρόβατα, where there is no expressed antithesis. In the latter, there is no antithesis till x. 12.

(γ) ii. 1 τῇ ἡμέρᾳ τῇ τρίτῃ γάμος ἐγένετο, but marg. τῇ τρίτῃ ἡμέρᾳ (1982 b).

(δ) In iii. 16, τὸν υἱὸν τὸν μονογενῆ, "He gave *his only begotten son,*" the adj. is more emphatic than in iii. 18 τὸ ὄνομα τοῦ μονογενοῦς υἱοῦ τοῦ θεοῦ, "because he hath not believed in the name of *the only begotten Son* of God," where "God" attracts much of the emphasis.

(ε) iv. 9 ἡ γυνὴ ἡ Σαμαρεῖτις (the context lays stress on her Samaritan origin, "from me being a woman that is a Samaritan").

(ζ) vi. 13 ἐκ τῶν πέντε ἄρτων τῶν κριθίνων, "from the five loaves— that were, as I have said, of barley." This detail is not given by the Synoptists (1985).

(η) x. 11, 14 ὁ ποιμὴν ὁ καλός (3 times). Contrast ii. 10 (*bis*) τὸν καλὸν οἶνον.

(θ) xviii. 10 τὸ ὠτάριον τὸ δεξιόν (1985).

(ι) xviii. 16 ὁ μαθητὴς ὁ ἄλλος ὁ γνωστὸς τοῦ ἀρχ. (? distinguished from Peter, who was *not* "an acquaintance of the High Priest"). Contrast xx. 2, 3, 4, 8 ὁ ἄλλος μ., xx. 25, xxi. 8 οἱ ἄλλοι μ.

(κ) xviii. 17 ἡ παιδίσκη ἡ θυρωρός (called previously (xviii. 16) "the door-keeper" (fem.), and now, "the maid that [as I said] was doorkeeper").

(vi) **With Possessive Adjectives**

[1987] The adjective is frequently possessive, and, in that case, is almost always accompanied by a reduplicated article. Instances are given below in Greek. The student will find in almost every case that the phrase with the reduplicated article, *e.g.* x. 26—7 "the sheep *that are my own* (τὰ π. τὰ ἐμά) hearken to my voice," lays more stress on the owner than is laid in the phrase with the possessive genitive xxi. 16—17 "feed my sheep (τὰ π. μου)." The "love" of Christ is to be regarded as unique, and the command to "*love one another*" *with that kind of love* is a "new commandment," which our Lord might call *His own* special commandment. Hence He says, xiv. 15, " If ye love me, ye will keep *my own* [*special*] commandments (τὰς ἐ. τὰς ἐμάς)." But this is followed by an unemphatic repetition of the clause because the emphasis is to be thrown on something else, xiv. 21 " He that hath my commandments (τὰς ἐ. μου) and keepeth them—*he it is that really loveth me*." So the emphatic is followed by the unemphatic in xv. 9—10 " Abide in *my* [*special*] *love* (ἐν τῇ ἀ. τῇ ἐμῇ)...If ye keep my commandments ye will abide in my love (ἐν τῇ ἀ. μου)," where the last words amount to little more than, " Ye will do this." On the other hand, the unemphatic is followed by the emphatic in xv. 10—12, " If ye keep my commandments (τὰς ἐ. μου)...this is *my* [*special*] *commandment* (ἡ ἐ. ἡ ἐμή) that ye love one another even as I have loved you." Here, as often elsewhere, an if-clause, being less emphatic than a predicate, expresses ownership in the unemphatic form.

[1988] The following are the instances in Greek:

(α) iii. 29 αὕτη οὖν ἡ χαρὰ ἡ ἐμὴ πεπλήρωται. There is harmony, not antithesis, between " *my* [*own*] joy " and "*your* joy " in xv. 11 ἵνα ἡ χαρὰ ἡ ἐμὴ ἐν ὑμῖν ᾖ καὶ ἡ χαρὰ ὑμῶν πληρωθῇ. Ὑμέτερος (1774) is very rare. Comp. xvi. 22, 24, τὴν χαρὰν ὑμῶν and xvii. 13 ἵνα ἔχωσιν τὴν χαρὰν τὴν ἐμὴν πεπληρωμένην ἐν ἑαυτοῖς.

(β) v. 30, viii. 16, ἡ κρίσις ἡ ἐμὴ δικαία (ἀληθινή) ἐστιν.

(γ) v. 30, vi. 38, τὸ θέλημα τὸ ἐμόν (antithesis in context).

(δ) vii. 6 ὁ καιρὸς ὁ ἐμός...ὁ δὲ καιρὸς ὁ ὑμέτερος (antithesis). On repetition the writer (1987) adopts the less emphatic form vii. 8 ὁ ἐμὸς καιρός.

(ε) viii. 17 καὶ ἐν τῷ νόμῳ δὲ τῷ ὑμετέρῳ, "yea, and even in your very own law." There is no antithesis but very strong emphasis. Contrast vii. 51, x. 34, xviii. 31, ὁ νόμος ὑμῶν (ἡμῶν).

(ζ) viii. 31 ἐὰν ὑμεῖς μείνητε ἐν τῷ λόγῳ τῷ ἐμῷ, 37 ὁ λόγος ὁ ἐμὸς οὐ χωρεῖ ἐν ὑμῖν, 43 τὸν λόγον τὸν ἐμόν, xvii. 17 ὁ λόγος ὁ σός. Contrast v. 24 τὸν λόγον μου, viii. 51 τὸν ἐμὸν λόγον, 52 τὸν λόγον μου, xiv. 23 τὸν λόγον μου, 24 τοὺς λόγους μου, xvii. 6 τὸν λόγον σου, 14 τὸν λόγον σου.

(η) viii. 43 τὴν λαλιὰν τὴν ἐμήν. Contrast iv. 42 τὴν σὴν λαλιάν (marg. τὴν λαλιάν σου).

(θ) viii. 56 τὴν ἡμέραν τὴν ἐμήν, emphatic in a Messianic sense.

(ι) x. 26, 27 τὰ πρόβατα τὰ ἐμά emph. Contrast xxi. 16, 17 τὰ προβάτιά μου.

(κ) xii. 26 ὁ διάκονος ὁ ἐμός, " my own [true] minister."

(λ) xiv. 15 τὰς ἐντολὰς τὰς ἐμάς, xv. 12 ἡ ἐντολὴ ἡ ἐμή. See **1987** and contrast xiv. 21, xv. 10 τὰς ἐντολάς μου.

(μ) xv. 9 μείνατε ἐν τῇ ἀγάπῃ τῇ ἐμῇ, (*ib.* 10) μενεῖτε ἐν τῇ ἀγάπῃ μου (see **1987**).

(ν) xvii. 24 τὴν δόξαν τὴν ἐμήν. Contrast viii. 50, 54 ἡ δόξα μου.

(ξ) xviii. 35 τὸ ἔθνος τὸ σόν (contemptuously emphatic on the part of Pilate).

(ο) xviii. 36 ἡ βασιλεία ἡ ἐμή (*bis*)...οἱ ὑπηρέται οἱ ἐμοί. There is antithesis implied between "my own kingdom" and kingdoms derived "from this world," and the same applies to "my own officers (**1388** *a*)."

[**1989**] The non-reduplicated article before a possessive adjective is rare, but occurs as follows: iv. 42 οὐ διὰ τὴν σὴν λαλιάν (marg. τὴν λαλιάν σου) fairly emphatic, being antithetic to an implied "because of our own hearing," v. 47 τοῖς ἐμοῖς ῥήμασιν, antithetic to τοῖς ἐκείνου γράμμασιν. In vii. 8 ὁ ἐμὸς καιρός occurs after an emphatic (vii. 6) ὁ καιρὸς ὁ ἐμός. The non-reduplicated form (though more emphatic than ὁ καιρός μου would have been) is probably not so emphatic as the reduplicated. In vii. 16 ἡ ἐμὴ διδαχὴ οὐκ ἔστιν ἐμή, "that which is [in one sense] my teaching is [in another sense] not [really] mine," the first ἐμή is moderately emphatic. In viii. 51 τὸν ἐμὸν λόγον, "if anyone keep my word," the emphasis is moderate. This construction seems to indicate an emphasis greater than that of the possessive pronoun but less than that of the possessive adjective with the reduplicated article. As regards xiv. 27 εἰρήνην τὴν ἐμήν, which must be taken with its context, see **1993**.

(vii) Omitted, or misplaced

[**1990**] In xi. 19 "Now many of the Jews had come to Martha and Mary (πρὸς τὴν Μάρθαν καὶ Μαριάμ) to comfort them (αὐτάς) concerning their brother (περὶ τοῦ ἀδελφοῦ)," we should have expected τήν either to be omitted before Μάρθαν, or, if not, to be repeated before Μαριάμ. D omits it before Μάρθαν: A has "*to the household* (πρὸς τὰς περί) of M. and M.," and so too has C³ (περη): SS (Burk.) has "went forth to *Beth Ania* that they might comfort Martha and Mary," omitting "concerning their brother." The facts indicate that "the *Martha-and-Mary*" was felt by some scribes to be a combination intended to mean "*the household*" of the two sisters, and hence they (perhaps influenced also by the proximity of [αὐ]τὰς περὶ τοῦ ἀδελφοῦ [?taken as an error for "*the household* of the deceased brother, τ. π. τὸν ἀδελφόν]) substituted τὰς περί for τήν. The reading of SS suggests that the translator took [αὐ]τὰς περὶ τοῦ ἀδελφοῦ to mean "Martha and Mary," as being "the household of the brother (Lazarus)." "To Beth Ania" may have been supplied by SS for sense or may be a further error arising out of "household," confused by SS with "house," *Beth.*

[1991] The best Greek MSS. have probably preserved the correct text, the intention of the writer being to represent, by the unusual omission of the article, that Martha and Mary now made up one household, of which Martha was the leader. Comp. 1 Thess. i. 7—8 ἐν τῇ Μακ. καὶ ἐν τῇ Ἀχ....ἐν τῇ Μ. καὶ Ἀχ. (R.V.) "an ensample to all that believe *in M. and in A.*...not only in *M. and A.* but in every place" (A.V. (*bis*) "in M. and A.")—where the article is omitted in the second clause, partly because one abbreviates in repetition, but more because there is, in the second clause, an antithesis between "M. and A." (as being *one place*)[1], and "*every* [*other*] *place.*"

[1992] xii. 9—12 (W.H.) ἔγνω οὖν ὁ ὄχλος πολὺς ἐκ τῶν Ἰουδαίων.... Τῇ ἐπαύριον ὁ ὄχλος πολὺς ὁ ἐλθὼν εἰς τὴν ἑορτήν is uncertain owing to the variation of MSS. But it has been suggested above (1739—40) that it is written with allusion to Mk xii. 37 ὁ πολὺς ὄχλος, and that John took advantage of some irregular expression in ancient tradition, in order to shew that he regards the phrase as meaning, not "the illiterate rabble," but "the multitude in full force."

[1993] In xiv. 27 εἰρήνην ἀφίημι ὑμῖν, εἰρήνην τὴν ἐμὴν δίδωμι ὑμῖν, if Jn had written, in the second clause, τὴν ἐ. τ. ἐμήν, the article would have suggested, for the moment, a reference to the ἐ. in the first clause ("the peace just mentioned"). Instead of that, the writer breaks off to indicate that it is something more than the common kind of peace: "Peace I leave unto you. *Peace* [*do I say? nay, a new kind of peace*] *the* [*peace*] *that is mine* I give you." In this special context the phrase with the single article conveys even more emphasis than the phrase with the article doubled.

[1994] In iv. 34 ἐμὸν βρῶμά ἐστιν ἵνα ποιήσω... we ought not to say that the article is omitted but rather that the predicate is placed

---

[1] [1991*a*] When "the chief priests" are mentioned before "Pharisees," the article is omitted before "Pharisees" where the two classes are regarded as forming one council in vii. 45 "came to *the chief priests and Pharisees.*" But the article is repeated before "Pharisees" where they are regarded as two distinct classes combining in hostility against Jesus (vii. 32 ἀπέστειλαν, xi. 47 συνήγαγον, xi. 57 δεδώκεισαν ἐντολάς).

before the subject¹. The words might have run otherwise, "To do the will of the Father—that is food for me (or, my food)." But the disciples were saying to themselves, in effect, "What is his food?" ("Hath any man brought him aught to eat?"). And Jesus answers their implied question by putting it foremost in His reply, because it is foremost in their thoughts: "*My food*, you ask: What is *my food*? it is to do the Father's will." The subject of the sentence is the subject of Christ's thought, namely, doing the Father's will².

(viii) **With Infinitive**

[1995] The Article with the Infinitive is almost non-occurrent in John. Its rarity deserves notice as being in striking contrast with its frequency in Luke, in whom alone there are more instances than in the other three Gospels together³.

ASYNDETON

(i) **Johannine use of**

[1996] A sentence in Greek is mostly connected with the preceding one by some conjunction. This has the disadvantage of sometimes defining rather narrowly the relation between one thought and another: and a foreigner, writing Greek without a native knowledge of its conjunctions, might define the relation wrongly. But it has great advantages, especially for readers of an ancient Greek MS.—written before punctuation had been introduced. For it often helps us to discern the beginning of a sentence. From the want of such a conjunction springs the ambiguity noted by R.V. marg. in the words "Without him was not made *anything*. That which (ὅ)

---

¹ [**1994 a**] In i. 1 θεὸς ἦν ὁ λόγος, iv. 24 πνεῦμα ὁ θεός, the predicate comes first for emphasis, and the subject, distinguished by the article, is placed last. It is very rare to have a noun predicate thus before a noun subject. An adj. in such a position is more freq., as vi. 60 σκληρός ἐστιν ὁ λόγος οὗτος, "hard [indeed] is this saying," and πιστός and εὐλογητός are often thus placed (though not in Jn).

² [**1994 b**] In Jn iv. 43 (R.V.) "after *the* two days," A.V. has omitted "the." It refers to iv. 40 "they besought him to abide with them and he abode there two days," and it means that He abode there *those two days and no more*. In Jn xviii. 3 (R.V.) "*the* band (marg. cohort)," A.V. ("*a* band") has missed the reference to "*the* band" that regularly kept guard in the fortress called Antonia.

³ [**1995 a**] Bruder (1880) gives τό with inf., Mk c. 15, Mt. c. 24, Lk. c. 70, Jn only 4, namely i. 48 πρὸ τοῦ σε Φ. φωνῆσαι, xiii. 19 πρὸ τοῦ γενέσθαι, xvii. 5 πρὸ τοῦ τὸν κόσμον εἶναι, ii. 24 διὰ τὸ αὐτὸν γινώσκειν.

hath been made," where many have taken the meaning to be (as R.V. text) "*anything that hath* been made[1]."

[1997] The omission of the conjoining words commonly called conjunctions is called "Asyndeton," *i.e.* "not fastened together." John abounds in instances of asyndeton of the most varied and unexpected kind, too numerous to quote, especially with an initial verb ("[There] cometh Mary," "[There] findeth Philip Nathanael" etc.); with any form of the pronoun "*this*"; with the conjunctions "*if*" and "*even as*"; with an adverbial phrase ("*in him* was light"); with a participle with the article ("he that believeth (ὁ πιστεύων)," or sometimes "everyone that (πᾶς ὁ) believeth"). Sentences frequently begin abruptly with "*now*" or "*already*," or with the emphatic "I" or "ye," expressed by Greek pronouns, which would not be inserted if emphasis were not intended. There is hardly any part of speech, or word, that might not come at the beginning of a Johannine sentence without a conjunction, *e.g.* "*Because* I live ye shall live also," "*Excommunicated* shall they make you[2]."

[1998] The contrast in the use of asyndeton between the Fourth Gospel and the Three is well illustrated by what the evangelists place severally after the statement of the Baptist that *he* baptizes with water:

Mk i. 8	Mt. iii. 11	Lk. iii. 16	Jn i. 26
"I baptized you with water, *but* he shall baptize (δέ)...."	"I *on the one hand* (μέν) baptize you in water to repentance, *but* he that (ὁ δέ)..."	"I *on the one hand* (μέν) baptize you with water, *but* there cometh (δέ)..."	"I baptize in water: midst of you standeth (μέσος ὑμῶν στήκει) one..."

[1999] Under the head of "Conjunctions, καθώς," instances will be found where the absence of a γάρ, δέ, or καί, makes it difficult to tell whether καθώς is to be taken as beginning a new sentence or continuing a preceding one. Moreover, in the same sentence, the absence of conjunctions makes it sometimes difficult to determine which is the most prominent of two or three clauses in it, or whether each clause is to be regarded as a separate sentence, *e.g.* "There

---

[1] [1996 a] Jn i. 3—4. The meaning "That which..." would have been clearly conveyed by ὃ δέ, or (if the writer disliked ὃ δέ as confusable with ὅδε) by ὅσα δέ.
[2] xiv. 19, xvi. 2.

came into being (ἐγένετο) [as distinct from ἦν applied to the Logos] a man (ἄνθρωπος) [as distinct from θεός applied to the Logos] sent from God. His name was John. This [man] came for witness[1]...." The presence of asyndeton is most remarkable in the Prologue of the Gospel (i. 1—18) and in the Prayer to the Father (xvii. 1—26). The absence of asyndeton is very remarkable in xvi. 2—11 (which includes, as initial conjunctions, ἀλλά, καί, ἀλλά, δέ, δέ, ἀλλ', ἀλλ', γάρ, δέ, καί, μέν, δέ, δέ). Ἀλλά, "nay," "but indeed," "but on the contrary," often occurs in emotional utterances in Greek literature generally. Both the presence and the absence of asyndeton appear appropriate to the tenor of these two passages.

(ii) **Classification of references**

The following attempt at classification of instances of asyndeton —according to the part of speech in connexion with which the conjunction is omitted—may be of use to students investigating the connexion between sentences in the Fourth Gospel.

[2000] (1) With Adverbs, or Adverbial Phrases:

(α) ἕως ἄρτι, ἀπ' ἄρτι, νῦν, οὐκέτι, ἤδη, iv. 36, xii. 27, 31 (*bis*), xiii. 19, xiv. 7, 30, xv. 3, 15, xvi. 24, 30, xvii. 7; ἔτι, xvi. 12; μικρὸν καί, xvi. 16.

(β) ἔπειτα, εἶτα, xi. 7, xiii. 5, xx. 27; οὕτως, iii. 8.

(γ) τῇ ἐπαύριον, i. 29, 35, 43, vi. 22, xii. 12.

(δ) ἐν ἐκείνῃ τῇ ἡμέρᾳ, xiv. 20, xvi. 26.

See also 2006 for διὰ τοῦτο, μετὰ ταῦτα etc.

[2001] (2) With Conjunctions:

(α) ἐάν, ἄν, εἰ, iii. 12, v. 31, 43, vi. 51, vii. 4, 17, 23, viii. 19, 46, ix. 33, x. 24, 35, 37, xi. 9, 48, xii. 26, xiii. 17, xiv. 7, 14, 15, 28, xv. 6, 7, 10, 18, 19, 20 (*bis*), 22, 24, xviii. 36, xx. 23 (*bis*).

(β) καθώς, and οὐ καθώς, v. 30, vi. 57, x. 15, xiv. 27, xv. 4, 9, xvii. 18, xx. 21.

(γ) ὅτι, xiv. 19 ὅτι ἐγὼ ζῶ καὶ ὑμεῖς ζήσετε.

(δ) ὅταν, iv. 25, viii. 44, ix. 5, x. 4, xv. 26.

[2002] (3) With Imperatives:

ii. 16, iii. 7, v. 8, 28, v. 39 (?) ἐραυνᾶτε τὰς γραφάς (but see 2439 (i)), v. 45, vi. 20, 27, vii. 24, 52, xii. 35, xiv. 1, 11, 27, 31, xv. 4.

(4) With Interrogatives:

v. 44 πῶς, vi. 42 πῶς, vii. 19 οὐ Μωυσῆς, vii. 42 οὐχ ἡ γραφή.

---

[1] i. 6.

(5) With Negatives:

i. 8, v. 30, v. 37 οὔτε, vi. 44 οὐδείς, vii. 7, viii. 27, 29, xiii. 18, xiv. 6 οὐδείς, xiv. 18, xv. 16, xvii. 9, 15, xxi. 12 οὐδείς.

[2003] (6) With the Object:

(α) Object followed by Verb, vi. 68, viii. 26, 41, ix. 21, 25, x. 18, xiii. 34, xiv. 27 (*bis*).

(β) Object followed by Verb with Adverb or Clause intervening, v. 41, xiii. 37.

(γ) Object qualified by Relative or Participial Clause, xiv. 10, xv. 2; or with Adj., xvi. 2 ἀποσυναγώγους ποιήσουσιν ὑμᾶς, xv. 13 μείζονα ταύτης ἀγάπην οὐδεὶς ἔχει.

[2004] (7) With Participles:

(α) Participle without Article, i. 42 ἐμβλέψας αὐτῷ, xiii. 25 ἀναπεσὼν ἐκεῖνος οὕτως, xx. 16 στραφεῖσα ἐκείνη λέγει αὐτῷ, xxi. 20 ἐπιστραφεὶς ὁ Πέτρος.

(β) Participle preceded by Article (with or without intervening Adverb or Adverbial Phrase), iii. 6, 18 (*bis*), 29, 31 (*bis*), 33, 36, v. 23, vi. 35, 54, 58, vii. 18, 38, viii. 12, 47, xi. 26, xii. 25, 48, xiv. 9, 21, 24, xv. 5, 23.

(γ) Participle preceded by Article and πᾶς, vi. 45, xviii. 37, xix. 12.

(8) With Prepositions:

(α) Preposition and Noun, i. 1, 10, 11, iv. 31, ix. 32, xiv. 2, xvi. 33, xvii. 16.

(β) Preposition and Pronoun, v. 3, x. 9. See also 2006.

[2005] (9) With Pronouns:

(α) ἐγώ (apart from ἐγώ εἰμι) iv. 38, v. 43, vii. 8, 29, viii. 15, 23, x. 10, 30, xii. 46, xiii. 18, xvi. 33, xvii. 4, 9, 14, xviii. 20, 37.

(β) ἐγώ εἰμι vi. 48, 51, viii. 18, x. 9, 11, 14, xv. 1, 5.

(γ) ἡμεῖς ix. 4 (accus.), ix. 24, 29; at beginning of speech viii. 41, xii. 34, xix. 7; at beginning of clause iv. 22.

(δ) σύ xxi. 17 (πάντα σὺ οἶδας, σὺ γινώσκεις).

(ε) ὑμεῖς iv. 22, v. 33, vii. 8, viii. 15, 23, 41, 44, xiii. 13, xiv. 17, xv. 14, xvi. 20.

(ζ) ἄλλο(ι) iv. 38, v. 32, vii. 41, ix. 9 (*bis*), x. 21, xii. 29.

(η) αὐτός ix. 21, iii. 28 αὐτοὶ ὑμεῖς

(θ) ἐκεῖνος iii. 30, v. 35, viii. 44, ix. 9, xvi. 14, xx. 15.

(ι) οὗτος (apart from ταῦτα) i. 2, 7, 30, iii. 2, iv. 18, 47, v. 6, vi. 50, 58, viii. 40, x. 3, xxi. 14, 24.

(κ) ταῦτα i. 28, vi. 59, viii. 30, ix. 6, 22, xi. 11, xii. 16, 36,

ASYNDETON [2008]

xii. 41, xiii. 21, xiv. 25, xv. 11, 17, xvi. 1, 25, 33, xvii. 1, xviii. 1, xx. 14 (for μετὰ ταῦτα, see 2006).

(λ) οὗτος, ταύτην, ταῦτα etc. in agreement, ii. 11, viii. 20, x. 18, x. 6, xv. 12 αὕτη ἐστὶν ἡ ἐντολὴ ἡ ἐμή.

[2006] Forms of οὗτος with Prepositions:
(α) διὰ τοῦτο vii. 22, viii. 47, ix. 23, x. 17, xii. 39, xiii. 11, xvi. 15, xix. 11.

(β) ἐκ τούτου vi. 66, xix. 12.

(γ) ἐν τούτῳ xiii. 35, xv. 8, xvi. 30.

(δ) μετὰ τοῦτο ii. 12, xix. 28.

(ε) μετὰ ταῦτα iii. 22, v. 1, 14, vi. 1, xxi. 1.

[2007] (10) With Relative clauses introduced by ὅ, ὅπου, ὡς, ὅτε: i. 4, iii. 32, viii. 21, xii. 36, xvii. 12.

(11) With the Subject:

(α) Subject followed immediately (or with intervening Adverb or Adverbial Clause) by Verb[1], i. 15, iii. 8, 35, iv. 20, vi. 49, 63, viii. 13, 35, 52, 56, ix. 41, x. 10, 11, xviii. 35, xix. 29. (In xvii. 17 the verb is ἀλήθειά ἐστιν.)

(β) Subject qualified by Relative Clause or by Participle, i. 18, vi. 37, 63, x. 8, 12, 25, xii. 48[2].

[2008] (12) With the Verb (not including ἀπεκρίθη, εἶπε, or λέγει)[3]:

(α) Verb absolute, or followed by Adverbial Phrase, iv. 30, xiv. 1, xvi. 28 (*bis*, the second time preceded by πάλιν), xxi. 3.

(β) Verb followed immediately by Subject or Predicate, i. 6, 9, 40, 41, 45, 47, ii. 17, iv. 7, 50, v. 15, vii. 32, viii. 50, 54, ix. 4, 35, xi. 35, 44, xii. 22, xiii. 23, xvi. 25, xviii. 25, xx. 18, 26, xxi. 13.

(γ) Verb followed thus, but with Adverb or Adverbial Phrase intervening, x. 22, xiii. 22 ἔβλεπον εἰς ἀλλήλους οἱ μ., xxi. 2.

(δ) Verb followed immediately by Object (with or without intervening Adverb or Possessive Genitive), i. 42, vii. 34, ix. 13, x. 30, xiii. 33, xvii. 6.

(ε) Verb followed by ὅτι, viii. 37, ix. 31, οἶδα and οἴδαμεν, xiv. 28 ἠκούσατε.

(ζ) To these add vi. 45 ἔστιν γεγραμμένον, ix. 40 ἤκουσαν ἐκ τῶν Φαρισαίων ταῦτα, where ἐκ τῶν Φ. is the Subject.

---

[1] In xvi. 21 ἡ γυνὴ ὅταν τίκτῃ, a conjunction intervenes.
[2] Asyndeton is also found in i. 39, iv. 7, xix. 14 ὥρα ἦν, and x. 22 χειμὼν ἦν.
[3] Asyndeton with these initial verbs is too frequent to permit or need a collection of all the references.

CASES

I Accusative

(i) **Adverbial**

[2009] This occurs in Jn vi. 10 τὸν ἀριθμόν, viii. 25 τὴν ἀρχήν, on which see **2154—6**, xv. 25 δωρεάν (from Ps. lxix. 4) which needs no comment. The present section will deal only with vi. 10 (R.V.) "Make the people (τοὺς ἀνθρώπους) sit down...So the men (οἱ ἄνδρες) sat down *in number* about five thousand (τὸν ἀριθμὸν ὡς πεντακισχίλιοι)." A distinction is probably intended by R.V. between "*the people*," i.e. the whole number, including women and children, and the "*men*," who are described by Matthew as (xiv. 21) "about five thousand *men* (ἄνδρες) *beside women and children*." But, if this distinction were insisted on in the R.V. of John, the meaning would be that although the Lord commanded that *all the "people"* should be made to sit down, including the women and children, yet, for some reason or other, only "*the men*" sat down. We can however retain a distinction between ἄνθρωποι and ἄνδρες by dropping οἱ with W.H. marg. "they sat down therefore, [*being*] *men* [exclusive of women] to the number of five thousand[1]."

[2010] "In number" is not inserted by the Three Synoptists in the Five Thousand narrative, nor by the Two in the Four Thousand. Cramer quotes a Greek commentator, "He numbers *the men alone*, following the customs of the Law[2]"; and it is probable that John means this. John may have considered that Matthew was right in *inferring, from some ancient phrase about the "numbering," that "women and children" were not included*: but if the old Tradition did not mention "women and children," and Mark and Luke did not mention them, John may have preferred to return to the exact words, while suggesting the truth of Matthew's interpretation by the contrast between "men" and "people."

[2011] The noun "number," apart from Lk. xxii. 3 "Judas... being of the number of the twelve," and Rom. ix. 27 (Hos. i. 10) is

---

[1] [2009 a] (W.H.) ἀνέπεσαν ⌜οὖν οἱ ἄνδρες⌝ τὸν ἀριθμὸν ὡς πεντακισχίλιοι (marg. οὖν, ἄνδρες). Less probably, οὖν, οἱ ἄνδρες might be read, "they sat down therefore —the men [*were*, or, *being*] five thousand."

[2] [2010 a] Cramer ii. 242 Παρουσῶν δὲ γυναικῶν σὺν τέκνοις μόνους τοὺς ἄνδρας ἀριθμεῖ ταῖς κατὰ τὸν νόμον συνηθείαις ἀκολουθῶν.

used only in Acts and Revelation. In the former, it is always (with one exception) used to describe the growth of the Church[1]; and it is appropriate here in a narrative that is typical of that growth. In the Pentateuch, it is frequently used in connexion with numbering prescribed by the Law, and κατ' ἀριθμόν is frequent. But the adverbial τὸν ἀριθμόν rarely or never occurs in canon. LXX[2].

(ii) **Absolute, or suspensive**

[2012] On vi. 39 ἵνα πᾶν...μὴ ἀπολέσω ἐξ αὐτοῦ (where π. may possibly, but not probably, be accus., see 1921—2), and on xv. 2 πᾶν κλῆμα...αἴρει αὐτό...πᾶν τὸ καρπὸν φέρον καθαίρει αὐτό, see 1920—2.

(iii) **Denoting time, but not duration**

[2013] iv. 52—3 "'Yesterday, [about] the seventh hour (ὥραν ἑβδόμην) the fever left him.' The father, therefore, recognised that [it had left him] at that same hour (ἐκείνῃ τῇ ὥρᾳ)[3]." The accus. is freq. in LXX in the phrase τὴν ὥραν ταύτην αὔριον, which was apparently intended by the translators to mean "about this time to-morrow" (but see Gesen. 453) representing the Hebrew "as the time" or "at the like of the time": and it occurs in Rev. iii. 3 "thou shalt not know *what hour* (ποίαν ὥραν) I will come against thee[4]." It is perhaps vernacular, like our "*what time* did it happen?" If so, the servants speak in the vernacular, as well as loosely, not knowing that their master wanted to know the time exactly. Subsequently the dative is used to denote *the exact point of time*. The father, hearing the words "about the seventh hour," recognised the coincidence between "*seventh*" and the exact hour when Jesus pronounced the words "Thy son liveth."

---

[1] Acts iv. 4, vi. 7, xi. 21, xvi. 5. The exception is v. 36.

[2] [2011 a] It occurs in 2 Macc. viii. 16 ὄντας τὸν (A om.) ἀ. ἑξακισχιλίους, 3 Macc. v. 2 τοὺς ἐλέφαντας ποτίσαι ὄντας τὸν ἀ. πεντακοσίους, also in Susan. 30 of the kinsfolk and attendants ὄντες τὸν ἀριθμὸν πεντακόσιοι παρεγένοντο (Theod. om.). In classical Gk it is freq. *e.g.* Aristoph. *Av.* 1251.

[3] [2013 a] Strictly, the sense demands "The father, therefore, inquired further and ascertained that it was not only *about*, but *precisely at*, the time when....' But the text is according to nature. The father—fastening on the word "seventh" apart from its context—says "That was precisely the number." See 2025—6.

[4] [2013 b] See Ex. ix. 18, 1 K. xix. 2, xx. 6. In Acts x. 3 ὡσεὶ περὶ ὥραν ἐνάτην τ. ἡμέρας, D is wanting, and W.H. follow the best MSS. in inserting περί. The accus. of duration in Jn is too frequent and regular to need comment. Mk xiii. 35 μεσονύκτιον is prob. an adverb (2678).

(iv) Cognate

[2014] Such a cognate accusative as vii. 24 τὴν δικαίαν κρίσιν κρίνετε requires no comment. But it is very unusual that this construction should accompany an accusative of the person as in xvii. 26 ἡ ἀγάπη ἣν ἠγάπησάς με, and it is surprising that (according to Alford) no Greek uncial except D has substituted ᾗ for ἥν. It is probably more than a mere coincidence that the only other such combination of personal and cognate accusative is a similar phrase, Ephesians ii. 4 διὰ τὴν πολλὴν ἀγάπην αὐτοῦ ἣν ἠγάπησεν ἡμᾶς. But there the relative may have been attracted to the case of the antecedent. Here no such explanation is possible, and the dative might have been used as in iii. 29 χαρᾷ χαίρει, "rejoiceth *with joy*." Possibly the evangelist, in these last and most solemn words of the Son's Last Prayer, shrank from representing the love of God as instrumental ("wherewith"). God, he says elsewhere, "*is* love," and the love "wherewith" men would describe Him as loving, is really a part of Himself, emanating from Himself. Therefore a cognate accusative is preferred even though combined—uniquely in N.T.— with an accusative of the personal object[1].

(v) With special verbs

(α) Ἀκούω

[2015] Ἀκούω with accusative is sometimes to be distinguished from ἀ. with genitive, the former meaning "perceive by hearing," "catch the *sound* of," while the latter means "understand by hearing," "catch the *meaning* of." See **1614**.

(β) Γεύομαι

[2016] Γεύομαι with accusative occurs in ii. 9 (R.V.) "And when the ruler of the feast *tasted the water now become wine* (ὡς δὲ ἐγεύσατο ὁ ἀ. τὸ ὕδωρ οἶνον γεγενημένον) and knew not whence it was (but the servants which had drawn the water knew) the ruler of the feast calleth the bridegroom...." A.V. has "the water *that* was made wine," which would require τό to be repeated after ὕδωρ. R.V. marg. has "tasted the water *that it had become wine*." This would explain the construction here as parallel with that of γεύομαι meaning

---

[1] [2014 a] I have not found in classical Gk an instance of ἀγαπᾶν τινα with ἀγάπην. But comp. *Odyss.* xv. 245 ὅν...φίλει (*i.e.* ἐφίλει) παντοίην φιλότητα, and Soph. *Electra* 1034 τοσοῦτον ἔχθος ἐχθαίρω σ' ἐγώ.

"taste and see that," in Hebrews "Having *tasted* [*and seen that*] the word of God [is] good¹." But that construction is very rare. The writer is there quoting from the Psalms, and perhaps erroneously, as he differs both from the Greek and from the Hebrew.

[2017] In Jn viii. 52 "he shall not taste of death," the genitive is used, and the question in ii. 9 is, whether the accusative is used like the genitive to mean "taste of" or to mean "taste and perceive that." Outside LXX γεύομαι is rarely used with accusative: but in LXX the accusative is fairly frequent². In N.T., γεύομαι is never used with the accusative except in Hebrews as above mentioned and here³. On the whole the grammatical evidence favours the view (of R.V. marg.) that John would not have used the accusative if he had not meant something different from "tasted *of* the water." But there is great difficulty in harmonizing with the context the marginal reading of R.V. "tasted the water that it had become wine." For this is the first indication in the narrative that the water has become wine, and we should expect—if the taster knew that the liquid had recently been water—"tasted the water and found to his astonishment that it had become wine." Besides, if John meant "taste and see that," why did he use the accusative and not ὅτι as in Proverbs (2016 *a*)? The context indicates that the taster knew nothing of the conversion of the water to wine but simply pronounced the wine unusually good.

---

¹ [2016 *a*] Heb. vi. 5 καλὸν γευσαμένους θεοῦ ῥῆμα (the nearest approach to which is Herod. vii. 46 γλυκὺν γεύσας τὸν αἰῶνα "having made us *taste*, i.e. *perceive, life to be sweet*") is a free quotation from Ps. xxxiv. 8 "*taste and see that* (γεύσασθε καὶ ἴδετε ὅτι) the Lord is good." In the context (Heb. vi. 4) γεύομαι occurs with the ordinary genitive ("having tasted of the heavenly gift"). Γεύομαι means "taste [and see] that (ὅτι)" "*i.e.* perceive that" in Prov. xxxi. 18. It also means "discriminate the taste of" and governs accus. in Job xii. 11 σῖτα (parall. to διακρίνει), xxxiv. 3 βρῶσιν (parall. to δοκιμάζει), comp. Sir. xxxvi. 19 "As the palate *discriminates* (γεύεται) the flesh of beasts of the chase (βρώματα θήρας) so doth the understanding heart [*discriminate*] false words."

² [2017 *a*] Steph. quotes only Antig. Caryst., Leonid., and the dictum of Suidas, γεύομαι, αἰτιατικῇ. In LXX (besides the instances above mentioned) γεύομαι is found with (1 S. xiv. 29—43) βραχὺ τ. μέλιτος τούτου...βραχὺ μέλι, (Tob. vii. 11) οὐδέν, (Jon. iii. 7) μηδέν: but always with ἄρτου (1 S. xiv. 24, 2 S. iii. 35, 1 Esdr. ix. 2). In LXX, the accus. with γεύομαι is always neuter, except where it is parall. (Job xxxiv. 3) to δοκιμάζει. See 2016 *a*.

³ [2017 *b*] The instances with genit. are Mk ix. 1, Mt. xvi. 28, Lk. ix. 27 θανάτου, Lk. xiv. 24 γ. μου τ. δείπνου, Jn viii. 52 θανάτου, Acts xxiii. 14 μηδενός, Heb. ii. 9 θανάτου, vi. 4 δωρεᾶς.

[2018] These facts are almost conclusive against R.V. margin. The difficulty of R.V. text may be diminished by punctuating some of the words as part of a parenthesis and by rendering γεύομαι with the accusative (as in Proverbs) "tasted" in the sense of "tested." The writer speaks of "the water—[now] become wine," somewhat as he speaks of the blind man of Siloam, when healed, in different phrases—"the formerly blind," "the blind," "the man that had recovered sight[1]." So here, the wine might be called "the formerly water" or "the now wine." The attendants brought it as "water," the master of the feast tested it as "wine." The evangelist combines the facts thus: "Now when the master of the feast tasted the water—[*now*] *become wine* (and[2] (καί) he knew not whence it was, but the attendants knew, they that had drawn the water)—the master of the feast called the bridegroom and said...." This is almost equivalent to "Now when he tasted the water—[*I say water, but*] *it had become wine*...[3]." This brief and parenthetic statement of the first of Christ's miracles—in which the reader is let into the secret in two words ("become wine") while the master of the feast talks, outside the secret, in twenty ("Every man—until now") is highly characteristic of the Fourth Gospel.

(γ) Προσκγνέω

[2019] Προσκυνέω in the following passage is used, first, with dative, then with doubtful case, then again with dative, and then with accusative: iv. 21—3 "Ye shall *worship the Father* (dat.) Ye *worship* [*that*] *which* (?) ye know not, we *worship* [*that*] *which* (?) we know[4]... shall *worship the Father* (dat.)...the Father seeketh...those *worshipping him* (accus.). God is Spirit, and they that *worship him* (accus.) must worship in spirit and truth." See **1640—51**, where it is shewn that (1) the dative is the regular form in LXX, but the accusative in classical Greek; (2) the dative emphasizes the notion of "prostrating oneself *to* a person, idol, or God," while the accusative means "adore" without this emphasis. Here, as between the Jews and the Samaritans, Jesus uses the Hebrew construction "Neither in this

---

[1] ix. 13, 17, 18.

[2] Possibly καί means "and yet," or "but," see **2136—45**.

[3] [**2018** *a*] Codex *a* actually reads "aqua," but probably through scribal error: "cum autem gustasset architriclinus aqua vinum factum......."

[4] [**2019** *a*] In iv. 22 π. ὃ οὐκ οἴδατε......ὃ οἴδαμεν, the antecedent may be dat. or accus. Heracleon (Orig. *Comm.* Huet ii. 213 B ᾔδεσαν τίνι προσκυνοῦσι) took it to be dative.

mountain nor in Jerusalem shall ye bow yourselves down to the Father"; and this is repeated: "They shall bow down to the Father [not in any *place* but] in spirit and truth." But when the doctrine proceeds to base this prediction on the general statement that God is Spirit, and seeks such worshippers, the Greek phrase is used, "those *worshipping him* (accus.).''

II DATIVE†

(i) **Of instrument**

[2020] xxi. 8 "But the other disciples came *by the little boat* (τῷ πλοιαρίῳ ἦλθον)," appears to mean something different from coming "*in* (ἐν) the boat," the phrase used by Mark[1]. In Mk vi. 32, Tischendorf follows the authorities that omit ἐν[2], and there the meaning may be that Jesus avoided the multitude by departing "*by boat*," as distinct from "*on foot*" which is mentioned by Mark in the context. Chrysostom here contrasts "*coming by the boat*" with "swimming[3]."

(ii) **Of time (completion)**

[2021] ii. 20 (R.V.) "Forty and six years was this temple in building," τεσσεράκοντα καὶ ἓξ ἔτεσιν ᾠκοδομήθη ὁ ναὸς οὗτος, is generally taken by modern commentators as referring to the Herodian Temple, which, it is supposed, was still being built at the time when the Jews uttered these words, so that they would mean, in effect, "Forty-six years is it since the building of this Temple began [and it is not yet finished]." This would practically give a "dative of duration of time." Such a dative is found in late Gk, *e.g.* Joseph. *Ant.* i. 3. 5 τὸ ὕδωρ ἡμέραις τεσσαράκοντα ὅλαις κατεφέρετο, Euseb. v. 1 πολλοῖς ἔτεσιν...διατρίψας, but always in passages where there is no possibility of confusing the dative of duration with *the dative of*

---

† For the dative with special verbs, *e.g.* πιστεύω, προσκυνέω, see the special verbs in Index.

[1] Mk v. 21, vi. 32, with διαπεράσαντος and ἀπῆλθον. Mt. xiv. 13 also has ἐν πλοίῳ (but without the article) with ἀνεχώρησεν.

[2] [2020 *a*] In Mk vi. 32 ἀπῆλθον. ἐν τῷ πλοίῳ W.H. ins. ἐν without alternative: the text there varies greatly.

[3] [2020 *b*] 'Αλλ' οὐδὲ οὕτως ἐκαρτέρησε τῷ πλοίῳ πρὸς αὐτὸν ἐλθεῖν ἀλλὰ νηχόμενος παρεγένετο.

completion, which is the natural construction here, "was built [*and completed*] *in* forty-six years¹."

[2022] Heracleon referred the words to Solomon's temple. Origen points out that Solomon's temple was built in seven years, and adds that there are no means of clearly connecting "forty-six years" with Ezra's temple². He takes it for granted that ᾠκοδομήθη means "was built" in past times, but appears to give up the problem. The Herodian theory he does not so much as mention. The details given by Josephus (*Ant.* xv. 11. 1 foll. and elsewhere) make it clear that a Jew would say about Herod's temple, "This work took from eight to ten years to finish, and the completion was celebrated with great splendour in Herod's lifetime." It is true that, after the great fire in the reign of Archelaus and some sinking of the foundations, the Temple constantly needed repairs: but, even if we could suppose with probability that the Jews were referring to these repairs as "building," the number of years would not suit the supposition. For according to Lightfoot (*B.E.* p. 31) the Jews, at the time of the Passover, might have said *forty-seven* years, and, according to Westcott (*ad loc.*), *forty-nine*. It is against nature to suppose that they would have definitely understated this as "*forty-six.*" Much more probably they would have said "*some fifty* years."

---

¹ [2021 *a*] *E.g.* there is no possibility of confusing Ezr. v. 16 ἀπὸ τότε ἕως τοῦ νῦν ᾠκοδομήθη καὶ οὐκ ἐτελέσθη, parall. 1 Esdr. vi. 19 ἀπ' ἐκείνου μέχρι τοῦ νῦν οἰκοδομούμενος οὐκ ἔλαβε συντέλειαν.

² [2022 *a*] Westcott does not mention Origen's and Heracleon's views, and the former is represented in Clark's transl. as saying "Someone else will say that the temple...was...the temple built at the time of Ezra, *with regard to which the forty-six years can be shewn to be quite accurate.*" But Huet gives, *for the words I have italicised* (ii. 188 E) περὶ οὗ οὐκ ἔχομεν τρανῶς τὸν τῶν τεσσαράκοντα καὶ ἐξ ἐτῶν ἀποδεῖξαι ἀληθευόμενον λόγον, i.e. "with regard to which *we are not able clearly to demonstrate that the statement of forty-six years is truly stated*"—implying that Origen knew that there were arguments for it, but not such as were clearly demonstrative. Clark proceeds, "But in this Maccabean period things were very unsettled with regard to the people and the temple, and I do not know if the temple was really built in that number of years." But the words are, ἔοικε δὲ καὶ κατὰ τὰ μακκαβαϊκὰ πολλή τις ἀκαταστασία γεγονέναι περὶ τὸν λαὸν καὶ τὸν ναὸν καὶ οὐκ οἶδα εἴ ποτε ᾠκοδομήθη τοσούτοις ἔτεσιν ὁ ναός. Steph. gives μακκαβαϊκά as meaning "the books of the Maccabees" and ποτε appears to mean "ever" or "at any rate"—"I do not know whether the temple was *ever* built in this number of years." The Latin has "tunc" (reading τότε). Origen introduces all this with the words (Huet ii. 187 E) "How the Jews [can] say they built the temple in forty-six years we are not able to say if we are to follow the history exactly," πῶς τ. κ. ἐξ ἔτεσιν ᾠκοδομῆσαι (*sic*) φασι τὸν ναὸν οἱ Ἰουδαῖοι λέγονται (marg. λέγειν) οὐκ ἔχομεν εἰ τῇ ἱστορίᾳ κατακολουθήσομεν.

[2023] But the definite *"forty-six* years" can be explained as follows in accordance with Jewish feeling, with the views of Heracleon, with the chronology of Eusebius, with the text of LXX, and with the language of Josephus. It was an error relating to the second temple, the temple of Ezra, which the Jews, among themselves, would regard as merely repaired by Herod, not as rebuilt. The edict for rebuilding was issued (Ezr. v. 13) "in the first year of Cyrus *king of Babylon*" i.e. 538 B.C. But LXX omits "of Babylon" having "Cyrus *the king*." And the Hebrew itself has gone further in Ezra i. 1 "In the first year of Cyrus *king of Persia*." But this is 559 B.C. Josephus (*Ant.* xi. 1. 1) says that the edict was issued "in the first year of the reign of *Cyrus*," which is ambiguous: he also says that the temple was completed in the ninth year of Darius, *i.e.* B.C. 513. Now from 559 B.C. to 513 B.C. gives "*forty-six* years," as is stated in the chronology of Eusebius extracted from Syncellius (vol. ii. p. 81) "Now from the second year of Darius until the sixth it [the temple] was fully completed... within *forty-six entire years* from the first year of Cyrus[1]."

[2024] When the Herodian temple was destroyed it was not unnatural that Talmudic traditions should dwell upon its splendour: but it is very unlikely that Jews born in the reign of Herod the Idumaean would recognise him as a Builder like Solomon or Ezra. Possibly when it fell into disrepair they would console themselves—as with the proverb "Rome was not built in a day"—by reflecting that the building of the Temple in former times lingered through two reigns, and by repeating to one another that "In the days of Cyrus and Darius *this temple took forty-six whole years to build*." Josephus, though his chronology may have led to this error, did not himself commit the error: and possibly our evangelist did not. He may have taken it as the mere chatter of the "Jews" whose ignorant talk he elsewhere holds up to ridicule. But, in any case, no reliance can be placed on "forty-six" as determining the date at which the Jews were speaking, or as evidence of the evangelist's presence as an ear-witness. He may have obtained this detail from books.

(iii) **Of point of time**

[2025] iv. 53 "The father therefore recognised *that* [*it was*] *at that same hour* (ὅτι ἐκείνῃ τῇ ὥρᾳ) *in the course of which* (ἐν ᾗ)...."

---

[1] Ἀπὸ δὲ δευτέρου ἔτους Δαρείου ἕως ἔκτου ἀνεπληρώθη...ἐν μϛ´ ἔτεσιν ὅλοις ἀπὸ τοῦ πρώτου ἔτους Κύρου.

The majority of MSS. (Alford) insert ἐν before ἐκείνῃ. Its omission by the best MSS. gives us "the dative of the point of time": and this exactness is more suitable to the contrast, indicated above (2013), with the accusative in iv. 52 "*about* the seventh hour," which the father interprets as "precisely at the seventh hour."

[2026] The phrase "in (ἐν) that same hour" occurs in Matthew's account of the healing of the centurion's son or servant, where the parallel Luke merely says that the messengers *returned and found the servant healed.* So where Matthew says that the Syrophoenician's daughter "was healed *from* (ἀπό) *that same hour*," Mark merely says that she *returned and found her healed.* These are the only two instances of healing at a distance in the Synoptists. Evidential proof needed an instance that should combine (1) "*returning and finding*" with (2) "*at that same hour.*" John's single tradition of healing at a distance—which has many points in common with Matthew's and Luke's narrative—contains this combination. It should be added that "at that same hour" is peculiar to this passage of John[1].

(iv) **With** παρά

[2027] The Synoptic παρὰ θεῷ—in the phrases "possible *with* God[2]," "favour *with* God[3]," "ye have no reward *with* your Father which is in heaven" (A.V. (txt) "of your Father[4]")—rather gives the impression of meaning "*in the sight of* God." But the exact meaning of the preposition is "by the side of"; and this may be interpreted (in accordance with a frequent use of παρά in Greek literature) as meaning "*in the house of*." John brings out this, which one may call "the domestic meaning," much more clearly, viii. 38 "That which I have seen *in the house of* the Father," xvii. 5 "And now glorify thou me, O Father, *in thine own house* (παρὰ σεαυτῷ) with the glory that I had *in thy house* [παρὰ σοί] before the world was." The latter may be compared with the saying of Wisdom about herself and the Creator, "Before his works of old...or ever the earth was...I was *by him* (ἤμην παρ' αὐτῷ)[5]." Both here and

---

[1] [2026 a] Luke has "in (ἐν) that same hour" once, vii. 21 "in that same hour he healed many of diseases." But he prefers ii. 38, xxiv. 33 αὐτῇ τῇ ὥρᾳ "at that very hour," x. 21, xii. 12, xiii. 31, xx. 19 ἐν αὐτῇ τ. ὥ., "in that very hour."

[2] Mk x. 27, Mt. xix. 26, Lk. xviii. 27.   [3] Lk. i. 30, ii. 52.
[4] Mt. vi. 1.   [5] Prov. viii. 22—30.

in John, we might render παρά "by the side of" or "in the bosom of." On the distinction between παρὰ τῷ πατρί and παρὰ τοῦ πατρός in Jn viii. 38, see 2355—7.

III Genitive

(i) Absolute

[2028] Mark uses this construction somewhat monotonously for the most part to introduce the circumstances of a new narrative in such phrases as "when it was late," "when he was going forth," "while he was yet speaking" etc. In four of these instances the parallel Matthew and Luke employ the same construction[1]. Mark never uses it in Christ's words, except once in the Parable of the Sower[2].

[2029] Matthew, in the Triple Tradition, uses it freely, like Mark, in the temporal clauses of narrative (often however with δέ where Mark has καί). He introduces it thrice in Christ's words, all in the Parable of the Sower and its explanation; and one of the three agrees with Mark[3]. As in Mark, the implied conjunction is "when" or "while," with perhaps one exception[4].

[2030] In the Triple Tradition, Luke introduces it twice into Christ's Discourse on the Last Days in insertions peculiar to himself[5], once in Christ's instructions for the preparation of the Passover[6], and once in the words of our Lord at His arrest[7]. Luke appears to use it causally in xxiii. 44—5 "There came a darkness...the sun failing, or, being eclipsed," and quasi-causally in xxii. 55 "Now as they had lighted (περιαψάντων δέ) a fire...," xxiv. 5 "Now as they were terrified (ἐμφόβων δὲ γενομένων)." Except in these three

---

[1] [2028 a] Mk i. 32, ix. 9, xi. 27, xiv. 43, and parall. Mt.-Lk. The vb. is not the same in all these cases. I have not noticed more than these four agreements of Mt.-Lk. with Mk in about 30 instances of the genit. abs. in Mk. In Mk the clause is almost always preceded by καί.

[2] [2028 b] Mk iv. 17 εἶτα γενομένης θλίψεως, Mt. xiii. 21 γενομένης δὲ θλίψεως, Lk. viii. 13 καὶ ἐν καιρῷ πειρασμοῦ.

[3] Mt. xiii. 6, 19, 21.

[4] [2029 a] Mt. xxvi. 60 καὶ οὐχ εὗρον πολλῶν προσελθόντων ψευδομαρτύρων.

[5] Lk. xxi. 26 ἀποψυχόντων ἀνθρώπων, xxi. 28 ἀρχομένων δὲ τούτων γίνεσθαι.

[6] Lk. xxii. 10 Ἰδοὺ εἰσελθόντων ὑμῶν εἰς τὴν πόλιν (Mk xiv. 13, Mt. xxvi. 18 Ὑπάγετε εἰς τὴν πόλιν).

[7] Lk. xxii. 53 καθ' ἡμέραν ὄντος μου (Mk xiv. 49 ἤμην, Mt. xxvi. 55 ἐκαθεζόμην).

passages, Luke appears, like Matthew and Mark, to imply "when" or "while."

[2031] *In no case does John use the genitive absolute in recording Christ's words.* Elsewhere he employs it with more elasticity of meaning than is found in the Triple Tradition. A causal meaning ("*as*" or "*because*") is implied, probably or certainly, in ii. 3, v. 13, vi. 17. "*Though*" is certainly implied in xii. 37, xxi. 11, and perhaps in xx. 19 "There cometh Jesus, the doors being shut, *i.e.* (?) *though* the doors were shut¹."

(ii) **Objective or subjective**

[2032] In Greek, as in English, such a phrase as "the love *of God*" may imply one of two propositions:—(1) "God (*subject*) loves man," (2) "Man loves God (*object*)." "*Of God*," if it implies the former, is called a *subjective* genitive; if the latter, an *objective* genitive. "The love of God" occurs frequently in the Johannine Epistle but only once in the Gospel, v. 42 "But I know you, that ye have not *the love of God* in you," ἀλλὰ ἔγνωκα ὑμᾶς ὅτι τὴν ἀγάπην τοῦ θεοῦ οὐκ ἔχετε ἐν ἑαυτοῖς, where the question arises whether the genitive is subjective or objective. The following considerations make it probable that in the Gospel, as in the Epistle, it is subjective, "the love that God gives to man."

[2033] In the first place, ἀγάπη in N.T. is very rarely used with objective genitive, perhaps only once or twice². It is never thus

---

¹ [2031 *a*] The meaning "though" is necessitated by the context in xii. 37 "*He having wrought* so many signs *they did not believe*," that is, "*though he had wrought.*" This suggests that in Lk. xxii. 53 ὄντος may be intended to mean, "*though I was* [in the temple by day, ye did not lay hands on me]."

² [2033 *a*] Westcott, on 1 Jn ii. 5, says that the genit. with ἀγ. "once marks the object of love, 2 Thess. ii. 10 ἡ ἀγ. τῆς ἀληθείας." He omits Lk. xi. 42 παρέρχεσθε τὴν κρίσιν καὶ τὴν ἀγάπην τοῦ θεοῦ. There it is possible that the words mean "ye neglect *God's judgment and God's love*," i.e. the way in which God judges and loves : " Ye neglect the things that God condemns and God loves, and condemn the things He loves, and love the things He condemns." But Cyril (Cramer) assumes the meaning to be ἀγάπη ἡ εἰς θεόν (Winer and Alford are silent) and most people would probably take the meaning to be "[just] judgment and *love toward God.*"

[2033 *b*] In 2 Thess. iii. 5 " And [may] the Lord guide your heart safe (κατευθύναι ὑμῶν τ. καρδίαν) into *the love of God*," the regular Pauline usage would of itself suffice to make it almost certain that it means "*the love of God* [toward men]" (like "the peace of God") sometimes regarded (Rom. v. 5) as a gift of God shed forth in man's heart, but here regarded as a goal or haven. This is confirmed

used by St Paul, who always regards "the love of God," and "the love of Christ," as, so to speak, divine inmates in man's heart, sent from God. As "the peace of God" constrains a man to be peaceful, and "the [social] fellowship of the Holy Spirit" constrains him to be social, so "the love of God" constrains him to be loving, both to God his Father and to men the children of the Father. Thus "*the love of God" for man* causes "*the love of God" in man*, i.e. causes man to love God. But this consequent love of man for God or for Christ is not what St Paul primarily means when he says, "the love of Christ constraineth us." He means Christ's love as a divine fire in the heart, driving out the fires of "this world." This is invariably the meaning of the phrase in the Pauline Epistles.

[2034] And this, almost (if not quite) always, holds good in the very numerous instances in which the Johannine Epistle mentions "the love of God." The writer thinks of it as a gift, spirit, or germ, that comes from God not from ourselves ("Not that we loved God but that He loved us"). It enables us to love, as the light of the sun enables us to see; but, as the latter remains "the light of the sun," so the former remains "the love of God." "The love of God" in our heart, like any other vital germ, needs to be (1 Jn ii. 5) "perfected" by responsive human action, and it cannot grow and expand without pushing out the love of the world[1].

[2035] Greek scholars, familiar with ἡ ἀγάπη meaning "the [feeling of] love," may sometimes think that John uses the article thus. But apparently he never does. The context always indicates that he uses "*the love*" (as Jews used "*the* Name" and "*the* Will") to mean "*the* love of God revealed to men in Christ," or "the real love as distinct from love so called by the world," or "the love wherewith the Son loved us and bade us love one another." This seems to be the meaning in 1 Jn iii. 16 "Herein know we *the love*

---

by the use of κατευθύνω in Lk i. 79 "guide safely *into the way of peace*" and by general Greek usage (Steph.), especially by that of Clem. Alex. 654 (Steph., but ? ref.) "*guide* the ship *safe*," and by Ps. cxli. 2 (LXX) "Let my prayer *go straight [to heaven]* as incense before thee (κατευθυνθήτω)" quoted by Clem. Alex. 857. In the Pauline Epistles, both "the love of God" and "the love of Christ" always mean the love of God, or of Christ, *for us*.

[1] [2034 a] But the writer does not speak of "the love of the world" as an entity in the same way in which he speaks of "the love of God." He prefers the verb, thus (1 Jn ii. 15) "if any man *love the world* the love of the Father is not in him." It is the Epistle of St James that speaks of (iv. 4) "the friendship of the world."

[*revealed by the Son of God*] because he laid down his life for us," and in 1 Jn iii. 23—iv. 10 "Let us love one another as he gave commandment to us....Let us love one another, because *the love* [wherewith he commanded us to love one another] is from God...... Herein *the love of God* was manifested in us because he hath sent his only begotten Son......herein is *the love* [of God], not because we have loved God, but because he loved us." Unloving conduct on the part of a Christian is a proof that this divine entity is not in his soul, 1 Jn iii. 17 "Whoso shutteth up his heart...how abideth *the love of God* in him?"

[2036] These statements about "*the* [*real*] love" or "*the* love [*of God*]" as an entity given to men and abiding in men, reach a climax in the doctrine that God Himself is "love," and that "the love of God" has the power of expelling fear if only it is allowed scope so as to be perfected. The writer begins by saying "And as for us, our whole knowledge, yea, our whole faith, consists in *the love* that God hath in us[1]." That is to say, as we are in the sunlight even

---

[1] [2036 *a*] 1 Jn iv. 16 καὶ ἡμεῖς ἐγνώκαμεν καὶ πεπιστεύκαμεν τὴν ἀγάπην ἣν ἔχει ὁ θεὸς ἐν ἡμῖν. The writer seems to have begun with the intention of saying "We have a full knowledge of the love." Then it occurs to him that not only our knowledge, but our faith is wrapped up in this "love." To have used the dative "we fully trust to the love of God" would not have expressed the meaning, which is that, as we may be said to "love [with] love" (cogn. accus. ἀγαπᾶν ἀγάπην (2014)), so we may be said to "trust [with] trust" (πιστεῦσαι πίστιν), or rather to trust with something more than trust—to "trust [with] love (πιστεῦσαι ἀγάπην)." Love is the atmosphere breathed by faith as well as the object of knowledge.

[2036 *b*] As to 1 Jn iv. 16 τὴν ἀγάπην ἣν ἔχει ὁ θεὸς ἐν ἡμῖν, Westcott gives several instances of ἀγ. ἔχειν but none of ἀγ. ἔχειν ἔν τινι except Jn xiii. 35 ἐὰν ἀγ. ἔχητε ἐν ἀλλήλοις, where ἐν ἀλλήλοις—a phrase capable of being applied to intercourse hostile as well as friendly (Aesch. *Prom.* 200 στάσις τ' ἐν ἀλλήλοισιν: but mostly friendly, Mk ix. 50 εἰρηνεύετε ἐν ἀ., Rom. xv. 5 τὸ αὐτὸ φρονεῖν ἐν ἀ.)— appears to be disconnected from ἔχειν and to mean "in your dealings with one another." Perhaps "keep love" is intended to come as a climax: xiii. 34—5 "*Love* one another......as I *loved* you, *love* one another......thus shall men know you to be my disciples if ye *keep love* among one another." In Phil. ii. 1—2, "Comfort in Christ...consolation of love...fellowship of the Spirit...*having the same love*," the meaning seems to be that the Philippians are to "*keep*" in their hearts one and "the same" quickening, consoling and comforting "love [of Christ]" as also the same "Spirit [of Christ]." In 1 Pet. iv. 8 τὴν εἰς ἑαυτοὺς ἀγ. ἐκτενῆ ἔχοντες the meaning is, "*keeping constantly* in the full tension of exercise and practice, not letting it become slack." By analogy—until there can be found some instances where ἀγ. ἔχω ἐν σοί means "I have love for thee"—we must take 1 Jn iv. 16 "the love that God *hath in us*" to mean "the spark, or spirit, or vitalising power, of love, which God keeps in our hearts as His representative and as our comforter."

while the sunlight is in us, so it is with love. Then he proceeds, "God is love, and he that abideth in *the love [of God]* abideth in God, and God [abideth] in him. Herein hath *the love [of God]* been perfected [working in our souls] along with us...Fear hath no existence in *the love [of God]*, but *the perfected love [of God]*[1] casteth out fear......We (emph.) are loving [now, simply] because he first loved us[2]."

[2037] In the following passage, however, the objective genitive seems at first sight intended, 1 Jn v. 2—3 "Herein know we that we are loving the children of God when we are loving God and doing his commandments. For this is *the love of God* (lit.) in order that (ἵνα) we should be keeping his commandments...." Here some might suggest the following paraphrase: "Hereby we know that we are loving God's children, not selfishly as our playthings or amusements, but genuinely as our brethren, when we are loving God Himself and doing His will: for '*Our love of God can only be shewn in the effort to fulfil His will*[3].'" But the "effort," or purpose, may, in this passage, be divine, not human. For (1) it will be shewn (2093 foll.) that, when our Lord says "This is my commandment *in order that* ye may love one another," an "*effort*," or "*object*," *is implied on the part of the Son for the good of men*, and (2) *the Johannine phrase* αὕτη ἐστιν ἡ *regularly introduces the definition of something that comes not from man, but from God* (2396—7). Hence we may with more probability paraphrase 1 Jn v. 2—3 as follows: "Hereby know we that we are loving the children of God [with the real love] when we are loving God in our hearts and doing His will with our hands:—*for this is the meaning and purpose of the love of God* [*His gift in our hearts*, namely] *that we should be keeping His commandments*...." This agrees with what is said elsewhere, "If a man does not *do* God's will, how dwelleth *the love of God* in him?" So here, "What is the object of *the love of God* in you except that you should do His will?"

---

[1] 1 Jn iv. 16—18 ἡ τελεία ἀγάπη, *i.e.* perfected, or fullgrown, in us, corresponding to (iv. 17) τετελειωμένη.

[2] [2036 *c*] 1 Jn iv. 19 ἡμεῖς ἀγαπῶμεν, ὅτι αὐτὸς πρῶτος ἠγάπησεν ἡμᾶς. I have quoted 1 Jn ii. 5—iv. 19 fully, because Lightfoot (2 Thess. iii. 5) refers to these passages as indicating that "it is very seldom possible...to separate" the meaning "love of God for us" from the meaning "our love for God"—a conclusion different from the one maintained above.

[3] The words italicised are Westcott's paraphrase of αὕτη γάρ ἐστιν ἡ ἀγάπη τοῦ θεοῦ ἵνα τὰς ἐντολὰς αὐτοῦ τηρῶμεν.

[2038] We return to the single mention of "the love of God" in the Gospel. It follows the Healing on the Sabbath. Jesus charges the Jews with rejecting Him on account of this act of kindness and with refusing the testimony of His works: v. 37—42 "The Father that sent me, he hath borne witness to me...*ye have not his word* (λόγον) *abiding in you* (ἐν ὑμῖν μένοντα), [I say this] because him whom he sent ye believe not......ye desire not to come to me that ye may have life......I know you that *ye have not the love of God in yourselves* (τὴν ἀγ. τ. θεοῦ οὐκ ἔχετε ἐν ἑαυτοῖς)." Theoretically, and taken by themselves apart from N.T. and Johannine usage, these last italicised words might mean, "Ye have no love *for* God," but that this is not the case is probable for the two following reasons.

[2039] (1) Whenever this writer describes a believer as "*having*" or "*to have*" something "*in himself*," he always means "*having in his heart some vitalising germ placed there by God.*" Unstable believers are described by Mark as "having no root *in themselves*," and Matthew follows Mark. Luke omits "in themselves[1]." Perhaps Luke thought that "the root" of a Christian life is in God. There is a difficulty in defining how far the divine seed in the heart of man is still God's, and how far it is now man's, when it takes root there. But John, though he rarely uses the metaphor of a seed, habitually regards the life-giving entity as a gift from God: iv. 14 "the water that I shall give him will become *in him* a fountain of water," v. 26 "as the Father *hath life in himself* so also to the Son gave he to *have life in himself*," vi. 53 "Except ye eat the flesh of the Son of man and drink his blood ye have not *life in yourselves*." So in the Epistle (iii. 15) "no murderer hath *eternal life abiding in him* (marg. *in himself*)." In one passage, the fountain of life is described not as "in" the believer but as gushing forth *from* him (vii. 37—8) in "rivers." But in every case the evangelist, while insisting that each believer must have this vitalising source "in his very self"—for that is the meaning of ἐν ἑαυτῷ—always regards it as the gift of God, not as the thought of man.

[2040] (2) The second reason is the parallelism between "Ye have not in yourselves *the love of God*" and the preceding "Ye have

---

[1] [2039 a] In the explanation of the Parable of the Sower, Mk iv. 17 οὐκ ἔχουσιν ῥίζαν ἐν ἑαυτοῖς, Mt. xiii. 21 οὐκ ἔχει δὲ ῥίζαν ἐν ἑαυτῷ, Lk. viii. 13 simply ῥίζαν οὐκ ἔχουσιν. [So Mark alone has (ix. 50) "Have salt *in yourselves* (ἐν ἑαυτοῖς) and be at peace with one another (ἐν ἀλλήλοις).")

not abiding in you *his Logos*," i.e. "*the Logos that proceeds from God.*" The writer assumes here (as in the Prologue) that even before the Logos came to "his own," bringing Light into the world, all men had some affinity to the Logos and some glimmerings of the Light, But some stifled the sound of the Logos and shut out the Light, so that when the crisis came—the moment for accepting or rejecting the incarnate Logos—they had not a trace of the Logos in them, nor a trace of the Love of God, that might have helped their hearts to go forth responsively to meet the Love incarnate. In accordance with this parallelism, "the love of God" would mean "the love *that proceeds from God*": and this rendering agrees with the Johannine usage elsewhere and also with the contextual phrase "*have in yourselves.*"

(iii) **Partitive**

[2041] In partitive phrases with πολύς, John never uses Matthew's and Luke's expression πολλοὶ τῶν..., "many of the...[1]." But he sometimes uses a modified form of it, interposing a verb or participle, *e.g.* "Many therefore *having heard it* [*many I mean*] of his disciples, said...." In such cases, the genitive is sometimes preceded by the Hebraic ἐκ[2]: iv. 39 ἐκ δὲ τῆς πόλεως ἐκείνης πολλοὶ ἐπίστευσαν εἰς αὐτὸν τῶν Σ., vi. 60 πολλοὶ οὖν ἀκούσαντες ἐκ τῶν μαθητῶν αὐτοῦ εἶπαν, xii. 11 πολλοὶ δι' αὐτὸν ὑπῆγον τῶν Ἰουδαίων, xix. 20 τοῦτον οὖν τὸν τίτλον πολλοὶ ἀνέγνωσαν τῶν Ἰουδαίων. Comp. vii. 44 τινὲς δὲ ἤθελον ἐξ αὐτῶν πιάσαι αὐτόν.

[2042] A construction almost if not quite peculiar to John is the partitive genitive, with or without ἐκ, (*a*) *before the governing word,* or (*b*) *with no governing word.* In (*b*), ἐκ τῶν Φαρισαίων means "from the Pharisees [some]." Obviously, with a verb of motion in the context this may create ambiguity, because the meaning may be (1) "*Some of* the Pharisees came, were sent etc.," (2) "They came, were sent etc. *from* the Pharisees." This ambiguity (on which see Ellipsis, 2213—5) occurs in the first of the instances quoted below :—

---

[1] [2041 *a*] Πολλοὶ τῶν does not occur at all in Mk (Bruder) but is in Mt. iii. 7, Lk. i. 16, Acts iv. 4, viii. 7, xiii. 43 etc., also in Rev. viii. 11.

[2] [2041 *b*] The Hebraic "many *from* (ἐκ)," "some *from* (ἐκ)," which is also used by the Synoptists (though very rarely by Mark) is fairly frequent in Jn, especially in the Raising of Lazarus, *e.g.* xi. 19, 37, 45, 46. It is quite distinct from the selective ἐκ in classical Gk, *e.g.* ἄριστοι ἐκ.

i. 24 (?) καὶ ἀπεσταλμένοι ἦσαν ἐκ τῶν Φαρισαίων, i. 35 ἱστήκει 'Ι. καὶ ἐκ τῶν μαθητῶν αὐτοῦ δύο, vi. 11 (?) ὁμοίως καὶ ἐκ τῶν ὀψαρίων ὅσον ἤθελον, vi. 64 ἀλλὰ εἰσὶν ἐξ ὑμῶν τινὲς οἵ, vi. 70 καὶ ἐξ ὑμῶν εἷς διάβολός ἐστιν, vii. 31 ἐκ τοῦ ὄχλου δὲ πολλοὶ ἐπίστευσαν εἰς αὐτόν, vii. 40 ἐκ τοῦ ὄχλου οὖν ἀκούσαντες τῶν λόγων τούτων ἔλεγον, ix. 16 ἔλεγον οὖν ἐκ τῶν Φαρισαίων τινές,' ix. 40 ἤκουσαν ἐκ τῶν Φαρισαίων ταῦτα οἱ μετ' αὐτοῦ ὄντες, xii. 42 ὅμως μέντοι καὶ ἐκ τῶν ἀρχόντων πολλοὶ ἐπίστευσαν εἰς αὐτόν, xvi. 17 εἶπαν οὖν ἐκ τῶν μαθητῶν αὐτοῦ πρὸς ἀλλήλους, xviii. 9 οὐκ ἀπώλεσα ἐξ αὐτῶν οὐδένα.

(iv) **Before Nouns**

[2043] The Synoptists place the possessive αὐτοῦ mostly after its noun, *e.g.* τὸν ἱμάντα αὐτοῦ. John frequently places it before *the article and its noun, e.g.* αὐτοῦ τὸν ἱμάντα[1]—somewhat like the Latin dative "loose for him the shoe-latchet": this throws the emphasis from the pronoun on the noun. See 2558 foll.

(v) **Special passages**

(α) With πρῶτος and πρῶτον

[2044] i. 15, 30 πρῶτός μου ἦν, xv. 18 ἐμὲ πρῶτον ὑμῶν μεμίσηκεν, see **1896—1901** and **2665—7**, where it is maintained that the latter means "me *your chief*," and that ὑμῶν is a possessive genitive.

(β) Τιβεριάδος

[2045] In vi. 1 "Beyond the sea of Galilee [*i.e.* the sea] *of Tiberias*," the apparently superfluous genitive (Τιβεριάδος) has been thought by some to be corrupt. But it is probably to be explained as one of the many instances of Johannine intervention coincident with, or consequent on, Luke's deviation from the Synoptists. Mark and Matthew always have "the sea of Galilee," Luke calls it "the lake [of] Gennesaret," and afterwards "the Lake[2]." But Mark and Matthew speak of Gennesaret as a place at which the disciples disembark[3]. John mediates, as it were, between the two names, but inclines towards the ancient tradition "sea of Galilee," only explaining it by a name more familiar to his readers. Perhaps variations in the application of the term Galilee induced Luke

---

[1] Mk i. 7, Lk. iii. 16, Jn i. 27. Τὸν αὐτοῦ ἱμάντα would emphasize αὐτοῦ.
[2] Lk. v. 1, 2, viii. 22, 23, 33.   [3] Mk vi. 53, Mt. xiv. 34.

GENITIVE [2046]

to substitute Gennesaret[1]. But "Gennesaret" was supplanted by "Tiberias" in Talmudic Tradition and the latter (which was also used by Pliny) was preferred by John, who, later on, makes (xxi. 1) "the sea of Tiberias" the scene of Christ's last manifestation to His disciples. Τιβεριάδος in vi. 1 is a genitive of possession ("belonging to")[2] governed by "sea" which must be understood as appositionally repeated.

(γ) Ἡ Διασπορὰ τῶν Ἑλλήνων

[2046] This phrase occurs in vii. 35 "Will he go to *the Dispersion of the Greeks* (τὴν διασπορὰν τῶν Ἑλλήνων) and teach the Greeks?" In LXX, we find "*the Dispersion of Israel*," and "*the Dispersions of Israel*[3]," as one might speak of "the church, or churches, of the Christians." But this phrase might be followed by another genitive describing the city or country to which the Dispersion belonged: "the Dispersion of Israel of, *i.e.* belonging to, Egypt, Pontus, Cappadocia etc." Then "of Israel" might be assumed, and dropped for brevity, and so we might get (1 Pet. i. 1) "to the elect sojourners of *the Dispersion of Pontus, Galatia* etc.," and here "*the Dispersion of the Greeks*," meaning, "the Dispersion belonging to the Greek-speaking countries." It may be asked why the sentence does not proceed thus, "and teach the Dispersion of the Greeks"? One answer may be, "For brevity." But another answer, and a more satisfactory one, is that the words are intended to represent the Jews as unconsciously predicting the manner in which the Spirit of the risen Saviour, travelling abroad in His disciples, would teach, first, the Dispersion among the Greeks, and then the Greeks themselves (2645)[4].

---

[1] [2045 a] "Gennesar," or "Gennesaris," is used mostly by Josephus, and is also recognised as the popular name for the Lake by Pliny (v. 15) "Plures Genesaram vocant."

[2] [2045 b] Wetstein (Jn vi. 1) quotes *Erachin* 32 a "Tiberiadi mare murus est." *Hor. Heb.* i. 142 says that the lake called in O.T. "the sea of Chinnereth" is called "in the Targumists 'the sea of *Genesar, Genesor, Ginosar*,' it is the same also in the Talmudists, but most frequently 'the sea of *Tiberiah*.'"

[3] [2046 a] Is. xlix. 6 τὴν δ. τοῦ Ἰσραήλ, Ps. cxlvii. 2 τὰς δ. (Aq. and Sym. τοὺς ἐξωσμένους) τοῦ Ἰσραήλ. Westst. *ad loc.* quotes *Paralipom. Jeremiae* MS. ὁ δὲ Βαροὺχ ἀπέστειλεν εἰς τὴν διασπορὰν τῶν ἐθνῶν.

[4] [2046 b] In xii. 20, "Greeks" means Greek proselytes to the Jewish faith. The congregations of the Dispersion would contain a large admixture of these: and so the name "Greeks" might be given contemptuously to congregations of Jews in Alexandria, Antioch etc.

[2047] CASES

(δ) Τὰ βαῖα τῶν φοινίκων

[2047] The difficulty about this phrase xii. 13 τὰ βαῖα τῶν φοινίκων is that both βαῖα and φοίνικες, separately, may mean "palm-branches" (though the latter may also mean "palm-trees")[1], so that the phrase might mean "palm-branches of palm-branches." One word (it would seem) might have sufficed. The LXX, with various readings and accents, has βαιων, βαιν, βαεων etc., and sometimes φοῖνιξ, but never βαῖα φοινίκων, except as an anonymous rendering in Lev. xxiii. 40 "branches of palm-trees." Possibly βαῖα may have been loosely used for "bunches of twigs" of any sort used in festal processions. The parallel Synoptists mention no palm-branches taken in the hands, but Mark xi. 8 mentions στιβάδας "bed-litter." Matthew has the common word κλάδους for "branches," and these (like Mark's "bed-litter") are supposed to be strewn in the road. Luke omits all mention of "branches." In Mark, A, C, and Origen, have στοιβαδας, where SS omits the clause, D has εστιβαδας[2], and some inferior authorities στειβαδας and στυβαδας. John's rare word βαῖα has different forms, βαινας, βαιας, βαεις, and possibly one of these has been corrupted by Mark into στιβάδας. If so, it is a case where Mark errs, Luke omits, and John intervenes. This hypothesis would also explain why John took special pains to define the βαῖα as belonging to φοίνικες.

(ε) Παρασκευὴ τοῦ πάσχα

[2048] xix. 14 ἦν δὲ παρασκευὴ τοῦ πάσχα does not present any grammatical difficulty. If the phrase were used consciously as meaning "preparing the Passover" it would be objective genitive. More probably it is possessive—the word "Preparation" having come to mean "the eve [of]," and being applied to any feast but most frequently to the sabbath, so that it is used in the second century absolutely to mean (*Didach.* viii. 1 and *Mart. Polyc.* vii. 1) "Friday." But what makes the phrase interesting is that John's insertion of τοῦ πάσχα differentiates his use of παρασκευή from that of the Synoptists, two of whom connect it with the sabbath, and

---

[1] See Wetstein *ad loc.* and 1 Macc. xiii. 51, 2 Macc. x. 7, xiv. 4 (comp. 1 Macc. xiii. 37).

[2] [2047 a] If an early Greek Gospel used (Jelf § 817) ἔστι δ' οἵ for ἄλλοι δέ, "and others [carried] palms," εστιδοιβαιας, it might explain the readings of Origen and D. Βαῖα φ. may be illustrated by L. S. on λύγος and μόσχοισι λύγοισι.

NOMINATIVE [2049]

none with (2087—8) the passover. Mark xv. 42 is most definite, ἦν παρασκευὴ ὅ ἐστιν προσάββατον. If that "sabbath" happened also to be the first day of Unleavened Bread, Mark's statement, though true, might be misleading. Hence John might intervene in three ways, (*a*) by defining the Preparation here, (*b*) by stating (xviii. 28) that the paschal lamb had not yet been "eaten," and also (*c*) by saying (xix. 31) that the approaching "sabbath" was "a great day." Thus the genitive in xix. 14 may illustrate—not grammatically but as a specimen of Johannine methods of dealing with Synoptic tradition—the genitive just discussed (xii. 13 τὰ βαΐα τῶν φοινίκων)[1].

IV Nominative

(i) **Special passage**

(*a*) Ὁ κύριός μου

[2049] On the Nominative used suspensively see **1920** foll. Only one passage needs separate discussion, xx. 27—8 "'...and be not unbelieving but believing.' Thomas answered and said to him, '*My Lord and* (?) *my God*' (ὁ κύριός μου καὶ ὁ θεός μου)." Here the nominatives are said to be vocatives by Wetstein, who alleges (1) the LXX use of ὁ to represent the vocative, (2) classical Greek usage of nominative for vocative. But (1) Wetstein alleges no LXX instance (except one, explicable by special context) of ὁ κύριος thus used, although there are many LXX instances of ὁ θεός, and also of κύριε ὁ θεὸς ἡμῶν (which is the regular rendering of "O Lord our God[2]"). (2) In classical Greek, the instances of quasi-vocative with ὁ are (*a*) accompanied by οὗτος, or σύ, or they are like our "Mr" in vernacular speech ("you, Mr cricketer, Mr Yorkshireman etc."); (3) or else, as in ὦ φίλος, they are found (Steph. "metri causa") only in poetry. (4) The one instance of the combined quasi-vocatives quoted by Wetstein is Epict. ii. 16. 13 κύριε ὁ θεός which tells against him, shewing that, although Epictetus could use ὁ θεός

---

[1] For the genit. gov. by ἀκούω, see **1614**, gov. by γεύομαι, see **2017**.

[2] [2049 *a*] 2 K. xix. 19, 1 Chr. xxix. 16, 2 Chr. xiv. 11, Ps. xcix. 8 etc. The exception is Ps. xxxv. 23 "My God and my Lord (Adonai)," LXX ὁ θεός μου καὶ ὁ κύριός μου. In the preceding verse, "my Lord (Adonai)" is rendered Κύριε as it is regularly in LXX when applied to God (see Gesen. 11 *a* ref. to Gen. xx. 4, Ex. xv. 17 etc.). But here, as it *follows* the nominatival form of the vocative, ὁ θεός μου, it is rendered for conformity ὁ κύριός μου. In Jn, ὁ κύριος *precedes* ὁ θεός. Steph. 876 c gives many instances of voc. φίλος but all from poetry.

vocatively, he could not use ὁ κύριος thus. The Egyptian Papyri use κύριε freely, but never, so far as alleged, ὁ κύριος vocatively. Thus, a great mass of evidence from all extant Greek shews that, had the vocative been intended, κύριε would have been employed. This is confirmed by the Latin versions, which have "dominus."

[2050] What then is the meaning? "Lord" certainly cannot mean "Jehovah." "My Jehovah" would be an unheard of monstrosity. But "my Lord" might mean "my dear Lord," or "my dear Master" as the term is used by Mary Magdalene[1]. And it would be appropriate that this almost unique appellation should be used by Thomas, as by Mary, in connexion with a manifestation of the risen Saviour[2]. If it is so used here, is "my Master" subject or predicate? If it were predicate we should have to supply "*Thou art*," or "*It is*," which is inserted in xxi. 7 "it is the Lord (ὁ κύριός ἐστιν)." But could ἐστιν have been omitted there? In any case it could hardly be omitted here, since the meaning required would be "*it is indeed* my Lord," so that it would be emphatic[3]. But if we take "My [dear] Lord" as subject, we may readily imagine a pause after it, while the speaker, overwhelmed with amazement and joy, is attempting to express his feeling about the Lord. He might have added "has indeed risen from the dead" or "has been indeed restored to me," but he means a great deal more than that. When he has uttered "my Lord," he feels that "there is none in heaven" whom he could "desire in comparison" with this "Lord[4]." In effect, his Lord has become to him one with his God, so that he may say "My Lord is also my God."

[2051] This accords well with the frequency of the emphatic καί in John. As for the omission of ἐστι, it undoubtedly causes some obscurity; but might not this seem to the evangelist to have the merit of forcing his readers to think out the full meaning of this confession —which is, as it were, wrung from the Apostle in a moment of

---

[1] Jn xx. 13, comp. Phil. iii. 8.

[2] [2050 a] "My Lord" occurs in O.T., like the French "monsieur," with the third person, in respectful address, Josh. v. 14 "What saith *my Lord* (but not LXX) unto his servant," Dan. x. 19 "Let *my Lord* speak." But perhaps here affection is predominant over respect, and Thomas speaks *about* his Master in the act of replying *to* his Master.

[3] [2050 b] See Jn i. 49 σὺ εἶ...σὺ...εἶ, "*thou art* the Son of God, *thou art* King of Israel."

[4] Ps. lxxiii. 25.

inspired conviction[1]? Thomas, logically speaking, had no more right to say to the risen Saviour that He was "his God" than a Jew would have to say the same thing to Enoch or Elijah, in the event of their being manifested to men on earth. But Thomas, spiritually speaking, might feel (justified is not the right word but) necessitated to say what he said. His Master—he suddenly found—was, at all events, "*his* God," the equal of whom did not exist for him in heaven or earth as claiming his worship. We are not, then, to suppose that Thomas argued, like St Paul, that Jesus was "defined to be Son of God by the resurrection from the dead[2]." There may have been no arguing in the matter. According to the view taken above, Thomas, regaining Jesus of Nazareth from the dead, was instantaneously possessed with the conviction that his Lord was also his God, and the conviction forced its way out in utterance[3].

---

[1] [**2051** *a*] In N.T. the rule is that ὁ κύριος means "the Lord [Jesus]," and the article before κύριος differentiates this confession from Hos. ii. 23 "Thou [art] my God," κύριος ὁ θεὸς μου εἶ σύ, Zech. xiii. 9 "the Lord [is] my God," κύριος ὁ θεὸς μου, where some copies (Field) insert "thou art" (κύριος εἶ). At the same time it was hardly possible for John to write down the Greek words "my Lord and my God" without considering their association in LXX to express "Jehovah our God": and he probably desired to convey to his readers an impression of the providential way in which the most unbelieving of the Twelve was led on by the intensity of affection for his regained Master to utter words that suggested the highest Biblical expression of belief in His divine nature. Both in Hosea and in Zechariah, the confession comes from penitents, who had gone astray.

[2] [**2051** *b*] Rom. i. 4 "defined as the Son of God with power, according to the spirit of holiness by the resurrection of the dead." The mention of "holiness," however, distinguishes the "defining" from any merely miraculous revivification.

[**2051** *c*] Among many instances of κύριε and ὁ θεός in Boeckh *Inscr.* 9110 foll. with ἀνάπαυσον, ὑπόμνησον etc., there is 9124 ("lapis in marginibus valde corrosus") μ]η[νὶ] Παειν[ὶ] ι̅α̅. Ὁ κ(υρι)ος ἀνά[π]αυσον. But the usual abbreviation for κυριος is not κοc but κ̅c̅. Moreover, after the month, and before ἀνάπαυσον, it is usual (though not invariable) to insert ινΔ *i.e.* ινδ(ικτιῶνος) with a number. Possibly this has been corrupted into οκοc, and ἀνάπαυσον is used here (as it often is) without κύριε or ὁ θεός. The corroded condition of the stone and the exceptional form οκοc make it probable that some error underlies οκοc. It might be simply an error for the very frequent ο θ̅c̅, *i.e.* ὁ θεός.

[3] [**2051** *d*] But this is not quite satisfactory. For xiii. 13 φωνεῖτέ με ὁ διδάσκαλος καὶ ὁ κύριος, and Rev. iv. 11 ἄξιος εἶ, ὁ κύριος καὶ ὁ θεὸς ἡμῶν, ought to have been mentioned above. For these, and for further remarks on the vocative use of ὁ, indicating that Jn may have used it here exceptionally, see **2679** foll.

V Vocative[1]

(i) Special passages

(a) Πατήρ

[2052] According to W.H.[2], the word πατήρ is used vocatively by our Lord (a) in the regular form πάτερ, in the Raising of Lazarus, xi. 41 "*Father*, I thank thee," (b) after the Voice from Heaven, and xii. 27—8 "What (2512 b—c) should I say? '*Father*, save me from this hour'? ...*Father*, glorify thy name," and (c) thrice in the Last Prayer, xvii. 1—11 "*Father*, the hour hath come—glorify thou me, *Father*,...*holy Father* (πάτερ ἅγιε), keep them in thy name." In all these cases πάτερ is used. But, towards the conclusion of the Last Prayer, when the Son prays for the unity of the Church that is to be, He thrice uses the form πατήρ: xvii. 21—5 "that all [of them] may be one even as thou, *Father*, in me...*Father*, that which thou hast given me I will that where I am they also may be...*Righteous Father* (πατὴρ δίκαιε)...." The final instance is a remarkable contrast with πάτερ ἅγιε (if πάτερ is the correct reading), the form and place of the adjective being the same in both, but the form of the noun different.

[2053] It will be found that the Johannine Last Prayer, in its earlier portion, down to the words (xvii. 15) "Keep them from the evil [one]," follows the lines of the Lord's Prayer in which the form πάτερ is used by Matthew and Luke. Possibly John desired to draw a distinction between that part of the Prayer, which was merely for the present Disciples, and the latter part which was for the whole Church[3].

---

[1] In xx. 28, ὁ κύριός μου is probably not vocatively used, see **2049—51**.

[2] See **2053** c, where attention is called to the readings of B, which have, in one instance, been incorrectly given by Tischendorf.

[3] [**2053** a] Ὁ πατήρ occurs in Mk xiv. 36, Mt. xi. 26, Lk. x. 21, and is the regular Hebraic vocative; but Alford and Steph. give no instance that I can find of πατήρ thus used, without the article.

[**2053** b] In xvii. 21, καθὼς σύ, πατήρ, ἐν ἐμοί, might mean "even as thou [being] Father, art in me [as being Son]." And xvii. 24 πατήρ, ὃ δέδωκάς μοι may be compared with x. 29 ὁ πατήρ μου ὃ δέδωκέν μοι. If x. 29 is to be rendered "that which the Father hath given me," may not xvii. 24 mean "that which thou, being Father, hast given me"? Theoretically, it would be possible to take the last two instances as appositional, at the end of the sentence xvii. 23 καθὼς ἐμὲ ἠγάπησας—πατήρ, xvii. 24 ὅτι ἠγάπησάς με πρὸ καταβολῆς κόσμου—πατήρ. But though John is extremely fond both of apposition and of abruptness, these instances would perhaps go beyond his limits. All we can say is that he has *some* definite and distinctive

Conjunctions (1894*)

(i) Johannine use of

[2054] The most remarkable characteristic of John, in his use of certain conjunctions that take the subjunctive mood, is, that he makes very subtle distinctions between the tenses with which they are used. This is especially the case with ἐάν and ὅταν which will therefore be discussed under "Tense" and not under "Conjunction." For the Johannine omission of conjunctions see 1996—2008. For his use of the participle in their place, see 2271—3, and 2031.

(ii) 'Αλλά

(*a*) 'Αλλά = contrariety, "not this but that, or, something more"

[2055] 'Αλλά is used by John more frequently than by Matthew and Luke taken together (1708). One reason for this, is that it is the appropriate conjunction for such phrases as "*not* this *but* that," or "this *but not* that," and John (2598) is fond of stating a truth in its negative and positive aspects. Theoretically, ἀλλά implies *difference*, or *contrariety*, not the mere negation of presence or absence. Nevertheless, in most instances, a negative is expressed or implied in the context of a Johannine ἀλλά.

[2056] In vi. 9, the negative ("this is true *but not* that") is implied by a question, "There is a lad here with five barley loaves... *but*[1] what are they...?" i.e. *but* they are *not* anything to the purpose. In vi. 34—6, the Jews say "give us this bread," and Jesus replies, "I am the bread...he that cometh to me shall not hunger...*But* I said unto you that ye have seen me, yet believe not." Here the meaning seems to be, "Ye have the bread visibly before you, *but* (as

---

meaning in the threefold use of πατήρ, following the threefold use of πάτερ, in the Lord's last prayer.

[2053 *c*] The question is complicated by the readings of B in the Voice from Heaven as well as the Last Prayer. In xii. 27—28 (W.H.) τί εἴπω; πάτερ, σῶσόν με...ταύτην. πάτερ, δόξασόν σου τὸ ὄνομα, the photograph of B has, most distinctly, first πατερ in the rejected prayer, and then πατηρ in the accepted prayer. [Tisch.'s txt of B neither reproduces πατηρ (2653)—though it reproduces B's reading μου τo ονομα for σου τ. ο.—nor comments on it as an error. Alford does not mention πατήρ. W.H. do not give it as an alternative.] This confirms the view that the scribe of B in both passages is recognising some distinction that goes beyond the province of grammar. Perhaps both he and the evangelist reserved the nominative form as best suited to the most exalted utterance (2679 foll.). Codex D, in xvii. 1—25, has πατερ throughout, except where συ precedes the noun, xvii. 5, 21.

[1] [2056 *a*] Here and elsewhere in this section, "*but*" = ἀλλά.

I said) ye do *not* accept it because ye do not believe." But, as the writer proceeds, the thought "as I said" becomes more and more prominent, and passes from an implied parenthesis into an expressed adversative statement[1].

[2057] In vii. 26 "*Can it possibly be that* (μή ποτε) it was recognised by (ἔγνωσαν) the rulers that this [man] is the Christ? *Nay, but* [as for] this man ('Ἀλλὰ τοῦτον) we know his origin...": here ἀλλά implies something quite different from that which has been suggested by the preceding context, and might be rendered by our exclamatory "*Why!*" which often means "Why ask such a question?" In vii. 48 "*Can it be said that a single one* (μή τις) of the rulers has believed in him, or a single one of the Pharisees? *But* (ἀλλά) this rabble...are accursed," there is a reference to an implied negation: "*Not* a single Pharisee has believed in him : *but* the rabble are ready to believe anything." The next instance resembles the last two, though the question is not asked by μή, ("Could I possibly say (μὴ εἴπω)?") but by τί ("What should I say (τί εἴπω)?") (for the various renderings of this see 2512 *b—c*) xii. 27 "What should I say (τί εἴπω)? 'Father, save me from this hour'? *Nay, but* (ἀλλά) for this cause came I, to [meet] this hour." 'Ἀλλά implies the negation, or opposite, of a prayer that is merely put forward as an impossible one for the Saviour to utter.

(β) 'Ἀλλά = difference, "nevertheless"

[2058] Passing over other instances (far too numerous to quote) where ἀλλά is used with an expressed or implied negative in the sense (1) "[not this] *but* [the opposite]" or (2) ["not this] *but* [something more]," we come to those where, without a negative in the context, it introduces something different from the past, something for which the past has not prepared us, but which *nevertheless* will take place, *e.g.* xi. 42 "I knew that thou hearest me always, *but* [*nevertheless*] for the sake of the multitude I said it," xvi. 20 "Ye shall sorrow, *but* [*nevertheless*] your sorrow shall become joy," xvi. 33 "In the world ye have tribulation, *but* [*nevertheless*] be of good cheer."

[2059] It is sometimes difficult to decide whether ἀλλά means "nevertheless" or "on the contrary," *e.g.* xv. 20—1 "If they persecuted me, they will also persecute you. If they kept my word, they

---

[1] [2056 *b*] Comp. vi. 63—4 "The words...are life. *But* there are some of you that believe not," where there is a contrast between the offering of a precious gift and the non-acceptance of it.

will keep yours also. *But all these things will they do unto you because of my name* because they know not him that sent me." Does this mean "If they kept my word they would keep yours: *but on the contrary*, instead of doing this, they will persecute you"? Or do the italicised words point back to the earlier part of the section (xv. 18 foll.) so that the ἀλλά does not refer to what immediately precedes, but to the tenor of the section, which is, to prepare the disciples for persecution? In that case, the meaning is "*Nevertheless [take courage from the thought that] they will do all this to you for my sake* and because they know not God." In view of the above quoted instances (xvi. 20, 33) where ἀλλά means "*nevertheless*" in Christ's utterances of consolation, this meaning becomes all the more probable here.

(γ) Special passages

[2060] Ἀλλά means, at first, "not this but more" in xvi. 1—7 "These [warnings about persecution] I have spoken unto you that ye may not be caused to stumble. Out of the synagogues will they cast you, *nay, more* (ἀλλά), there cometh a time when everyone that killeth you will think he is offering service [thereby] to God." But in the following verses, ἀλλά (1) first means "but, though it cannot be avoided," "but nevertheless," or "but at all events"; (2) then it means "but," as usual, after a negative; (3) then, again, it means "but nevertheless" (or "but still") :—xvi. 3—7 "And these things will they do because they have not known the Father nor me. *But at all events* [though actions arising from such ignorance cannot be hindered] I have spoken these things to you that when their time shall come ye may remember that I said [these things] to you...And (δέ) now I go to him that sent me: and *none* of you asketh me, Whither departest thou? *but* (ἀλλ'), because I have spoken these things to you, the grief thereof hath filled your heart. *But still* (ἀλλ') I tell you the truth, it is profitable for you that I should depart." In the last sentence, it is not clear whether the writer means "I cannot expect you to believe me, *but still* I tell you the truth," or whether the *real* contrast is between "grief" and "profitable," so that the meaning is, "Sorrow hath filled your heart, *but still* it is for your profit (as I have truly told you) that I should depart."

[2061] The use of ἀλλά in the following passage seems inexplicable as it stands, iv. 21—3, "Believe me, woman, that there is coming a time when neither in this mountain nor in Jerusalem shall ye worship the Father. [*Ye worship that which ye know not, we worship that which we know, because salvation is from the Jews.*] But there cometh a time and now is, when the true worshippers shall worship the Father in spirit and truth[1]."

It has been shewn elsewhere (1702, 1713 *m*) that "Jews" in the Fourth Gospel is almost always used in a bad sense, and that for this and other reasons (1649—51), the italicised and bracketed words should perhaps be transposed and *assigned to the Samaritan woman as her account of what the Rabbis say.* Then our Lord's words would be to this effect: "Not in Jerusalem or in Gerizim, *but* in spirit and truth shall the Father be worshipped."

[2062] It is hard to find a satisfactory explanation of viii. 26 "I have many things concerning you to say and to judge. *But* he that sent me is true, and [as for me] the things that I have heard from him these do I speak unto the world." Perhaps the meaning is, "*But*, though there is much to judge, the judgment must wait till the time appointed by the Father. He is the Truth. His word, which I utter (xii. 48), will be the judge[2]."

(δ) Ἀλλ' ἵνα

[2063] Where ἀλλ' ἵνα is preceded by another parallel ἵνα (expressed or implied) the verb in the first ἵνα clause may sometimes be regarded as repeated in the second ἵνα clause, as in i. 7—8 "he came *in order that* (ἵνα) he might bear witness concerning the

---

[1] [2061 a] Westcott explains "*But*" thus: "The old differences of more and less perfect knowledge were to be done away." He apparently means that the preceding sentence describes "more and less perfect knowledge" and that "but" introduces the perfect knowledge. But do the preceding words describe "more and less perfect knowledge"? Concerning the Samaritans it is said "*ye know not*"; concerning the Jews, "*we know.*" Is not this rather the "difference" between *knowledge* and *ignorance*? On 1 Jn ii. 19 ἐξ ἡμῶν ἐξῆλθαν, ἀλλ' οὐκ ἦσαν ἐξ ἡμῶν, where the meaning of ἀλλά may be affected by the meaning of ἐξῆλθαν, see 2110.

[2] [2062 a] Westcott explains "but" by a paraphrase differently thus: "The utterance of these judgments will widen the chasm between us. *But* they must be spoken at all cost; they are part of my divine charge; *he that sent me is true....*"

[2062 b] Chrys. says "I have many things both to say and to judge, yea, and not only to convict but also to punish, *but* He that sent me, *i.e.* the Father, doth not desire this (ἀλλ' ὁ πέμψας με, τουτέστιν, ὁ Πατήρ, οὐ βούλεται τοῦτο)." Theod. of Heraclea (Cramer) says "Even if ye do not take into your minds at present the day of judgment, *yet* He that sent me is true, and He hath decreed the day of requital (κἂν εἰς νοῦν μὴ λαμβάνητε τὸν τῆς κρίσεως καιρόν, ἀλλ' ὁ πέμψας με, φησίν, ἀληθής ἐστιν, ὃς ὥρισε τὸν τῆς ἀποδόσεως καιρόν)." This is the view taken above.

CONJUNCTIONS [2065]

light...: he was not the light, *but* [? came] *in order that* (ἀλλ' ἵνα) he might bear witness concerning the light." This, then, is perhaps a case of ellipsis supplied from context, called below (**2204—5**) "contextual" ellipsis as distinct from "idiomatic" (**2213**). Even where there is no preceding parallel ἵνα, a preceding verb may sometimes perhaps be supplied as, possibly, in ix. 3 "Neither this man sinned nor his parents; but [he was born blind] in order that the works of God might be manifested in him"—where "he was born blind" is regarded by some as repeated from the question of the disciples "Who sinned, that he was born blind?" But there (ix. 3) it is perhaps better to take ἀλλ' ἵνα as meaning "but [it was ordained] in order that." And even in i. 7—8 ἀλλ' ἵνα might have that meaning.

[**2064**] The ellipsis is certainly sometimes not contextual but idiomatic[1]. Instances must be considered separately, but generally it may be said that ἀλλ' ἵνα, even where it is a contextual ellipsis, conveys a notion of divine ordinance. In i. 31, the best rendering is, "And I knew him not, *but* [all things concerning him—whether I knew them or not—were ordained] *in order that* he should be manifested to Israel. For this cause came I baptizing in water." This has the advantage of keeping "for this cause" at the beginning of the sentence, where in John, it is almost invariably placed (see **2006** and **2387**).

(iii) Γάρ

(*a*) Synoptic and Johannine use

[**2065**] In Matthew and Luke (when both are independent of Mark) γάρ is hardly ever used in strict narrative[2], but almost always in the words of Christ and other speakers. Out of Matthew's twelve instances in strict narrative, *nine* ("*for* they were fishers," "*for* he was teaching them," "*for* she said...If I touch...," "*for* Herod having seized John," "*for* John repeatedly said to him," "*for* the wind was contrary," "*for* he was one that had great possessions," "*for* their eyes were weighed down," "*for* he knew that through envy they had delivered him up") *agree verbatim, or nearly so, with*

---

[1] *E.g.* xiii. 18 ἐγὼ οἶδα...ἀλλ' ἵνα ἡ γραφὴ πληρωθῇ, xv. 24—5 νῦν δὲ καὶ ἑωράκασιν καὶ μεμισήκασιν...ἀλλ' ἵνα πληρωθῇ ὁ λόγος.... See **2105—12**.

[2] [**2065** *a*] "Strict narrative" *excludes* the words of the Baptist, the disciples, the Pharisees etc., which are *included* generally in the term "narr.," as distinct from "Chri." (**1672***).

*Mark*¹. Γάρ is used by Luke altogether about a hundred times, and by Matthew still more frequently, but almost always in Christ's words (and in the words of other speakers). In strict narrative Luke uses it only eleven times; and *in three of the eleven he agrees substantially with Mark*². Mark uses γάρ *altogether about seventy times, and, of these, as many as thirty or more are in strict narrative. The use of γάρ, therefore, in strict narrative, is characteristic of Mark (as distinct from Matthew and Luke)*, and the fact that Matthew and Luke agree with Mark in so large a proportion of the few instances in which they use "strict narrative" γάρ indicates that they have copied these clauses from Mark.

[2066] John uses γάρ about twenty-seven times in Christ's words—exclusive of its use (about nine times) in the words of other speakers—and about twenty-seven times in strict narrative, so that he agrees (roughly) with Mark's usage. But there is this difference, that John's "strict narrative" includes what would commonly be called evangelistic comment, *e.g.* iii. 15 foll. "...that whosoever believeth may in him have eternal life. *For* God so loved the world that he gave...*For* God sent not the Son...and men loved the darkness rather than the light, *for* their works were evil. *For* every one that doeth ill hateth the light...." This use creates ambiguity. Many commentators have taken iii. 16—21 as Christ's words. Similarly Chrysostom³ appears to assign to the Samaritan woman the words, iv. 9 "*For* Jews have no dealings with Samaritans,"

---

¹ [2065 *b*] Mt. iv. 18, vii. 29, ix. 21, xiv. 3, 4, 24, xix. 22, xxvi. 43, xxvii. 18. The exceptional instances are Mt. xxviii. 2 ἄγγελος γὰρ κυρίου, which finds no apparent parallel in Mk xvi. 4 ἦν γὰρ μέγας σφόδρα, and Mt. ii. 5 οὕτως γὰρ γέγραπται..., iii. 3 οὗτος γάρ ἐστιν ὁ ῥηθείς....

² [2065 *c*] Lk. viii. 29, xviii. 23, xx. 19. Lk. uses γάρ twice in the short account, peculiar to his Gospel, of the mocking of Christ by Herod Antipas (Lk. xxiii. 8, 12) and once in the Miraculous Draught (Lk. v. 9).

³ [2066 *a*] Chrys. *ad loc.* Τί οὖν ἡ γυνή...λέγει, Πῶς σὺ Ἰ. ὤν......Σαμαρείταις... Καὶ πόθεν...ἐνόμιζεν...Οὐ γὰρ εἶπεν ὅτι Σ. τοῖς Ἰ. οὐ συγχρῶνται ἀλλ' Ἰουδαῖοι Σαμαρείτας οὐ προσίενται, *i.e.* "For she did not say that Samaritans have no dealings with the Jews but Jews repudiate Samaritans." Apparently Chrysostom thinks that οὐ συγχρῶνται means what his hearers would render οὐ προσίενται, which is a little stronger (see Steph.).

[2066 *b*] In other passages, the abundance of γάρ ought not to be ignored as a possible indication of evangelistic origin, *e.g.* v. 21, 22, 26. Here ὥσπερ γάρ twice occurs. ὥσπερ is not elsewhere found in John, and it would be possible to regard v. 21—3, and v. 26—7 as comment on the clauses addressed to the Jews in the second person.

which are regarded by many modern commentators as a comment of the evangelist, if not an interpolation.

(β) Special passages

[2067] Different interpretations have been given to iv. 43—4 "But after the two days he went forth thence to Galilee: *for* (γάρ) Jesus himself testified that a prophet in his own country hath no honour." Some have interpreted this (1), "He went to Galilee from His own country, *Judæa*, because He had not been honoured in the latter." A second interpretation might be (2), "After having acquired honour in Judæa, which was not His own country, He went to Galilee His own country, because He did not desire to gain honour at the expense of the Baptist, and He had testified that a prophet in his own country does not gain honour." The decision rests on several considerations that need separate discussion in a comparison of the Four Gospels: but the differences illustrate the vagueness of the inferences deducible from the mere statement of a motive with "for."

[2068] In vii. 41—2 "Others said, 'This is the Christ'; but others again said, '*For* can it be that (μὴ γάρ) the Christ is to come from Galilee?'" we must supply "No" before "for." Or, more accurately, the rule in such cases is that the preceding words should be mentally repeated in some phrase (expressing astonishment) equivalent to a statement, after which "for" follows, introducing the reason for this implied statement. ["This the Christ! Impossible!] *for*...." The same explanation applies to ix. 29—30—after the Pharisees have said concerning Jesus "But as for this [man] we know not whence he is"—where the man cured of blindness by Jesus replies "*For* herein is the wonder of wonders (ἐν τούτῳ γὰρ τὸ θαυμαστόν) because ye (*emph.*) know not whence he is and [yet] he opened my eyes." The man repeats the words of the Pharisees "[Ye 'know not whence he is'! A wonderful confession!] *for* herein is the wonder...¹." But the text is doubtful. See **2393, 2683**.

---

¹ [2068 a] So in Mk xv. 14, Mt. xxvii. 23, Lk. xxiii. 21 Pilate's reply "*For* what evil has he done?" coming as a reply to the demand "Crucify him!" may be explained "[An amazing request!] For what evil has he done?" Comp. Demosth. 43 λέγεταί τι καινόν; [An amazing question!] γένοιτο γὰρ ἄν τι καινότερον; Soph. *Ajax* 1125—6 σὺν δίκῃ... [An amazing statement!] δίκαια γάρ...; where καινόν and δίκη are, practically, repeated. So πῶς γάρ (or, γὰρ οὐ); means "[A surprising question!] For how could it be so [or, otherwise]?"

(iv) Δέ

(a) Consecutive or adversative

[2069] In classical Greek, δέ, calling attention to the second of two things, may mean (1) "*in the next place,*" (2) "*on the other hand,*" somewhat as our English word "other" may mean "*another [of the same kind]*" or "*other [in kind]*," i.e. different, opposite. The former may be called "narrative δέ" because it is frequently used to describe the sequence of events in a story. But in this sense John, as compared with Matthew and Luke, very rarely uses it except in the phrase "so when (ὡς δέ)[1]." He uses it much more frequently in the latter sense, though not nearly so often as Matthew and Luke.

[2070] But there is also another sense in which John uses δέ, to introduce that which comes second *not in point of time but in point of thought*, as being the next point to note, thus: "His mother saith unto the servants, Whatsoever he saith unto you, do it. *Now [the next point to note is that] there were* (ἦσαν δέ) six waterpots...Jesus saith unto them, Fill the waterpots[2]." Similarly in the Feeding of the Five Thousand, after recording the command, "Make the men lie down," John adds, "*Now [the next point to note is that]* there was much grass in the place[3]." And this quiet particle may occasionally introduce something of the nature of an epigram, *e.g.* "They cried out...'Not this man, but Barabbas.' *Now [the next point to note is that]* this Barabbas was a robber[4]"—thus briefly implying the condemnation (amplified in the Acts[5]) of the preference of a "robber" to the Prince of Life. This parenthetic or supplementary use of δέ to introduce to the reader the "next point" for him to notice is hardly found in the Synoptists.

[2071] It is sometimes difficult to decide whether δέ in John is adversative or consecutive, *e.g.* "They took his garments and made four portions, for each soldier a portion, and the tunic. *Now* the tunic was (ἦν δὲ ὁ χιτών) without a seam[6]," where the meaning

---

[1] [2069 a] ii. 9 "*So when* (ὡς δέ) he had tasted," ii. 23 "*So when* he was in Jerusalem." Comp. vi. 12, 16 etc. Bruder (1888) gives to the instances of δέ in Mt. and Lk. severally about 9 and 9¼ columns, in Mk 3¾ (less in W.H.), in Jn 4 (less in W.H. especially when the interpolation in viii. 1—11 is removed). The statistics, though rough, suffice to establish an enormous predominance of δέ in Mt. and Lk., as compared with Mk and Jn.
[2] ii. 6.
[3] vi. 10.   [4] xviii. 40.   [5] Acts iii. 14, 15.   [6] xix. 23.

may be either "*But* the tunic *on the other hand* [*as opposed to the cloak*]," or "Now [*the point to be here noted is that*] the tunic was seamless." In any case it would be an error to suppose that the events introduced with this particle are of secondary importance. For ἦν δέ is used to introduce Nicodemus ("Now there was a man of the Pharisees"), the man cured at Bethesda (or Bethsaida), Lazarus, and perhaps the "nobleman" whose son is cured near Cana[1]. On ὁ δέ in John, see 2684.

[2072] The uses of δέ, adversative and consecutive, may be illustrated by the only two instances in which it occurs in the body of Luke's Gospel after Ἰησοῦς without the article. The first introduces "Jesus" as representing a new character entering on the stage of public life[2]; the second represents contrast between Judas and Jesus[3]. The first of John's only two instances appears to be adversative, "They therefore took up stones to cast at him. *But* Jesus (Ἰ. δέ) was hidden from them and went forth from the Temple[4]." The second introduces Christ's last public words, and follows an evangelistic comment on the national rejection of the Light. W.H. place a space between the two, "...for they loved the glory of men rather than the glory of God. ‖ *But* Jesus (Ἰ. δέ) cried and said...[5]" It is not clear whether this merely introduces a new subject, and marks an interval (perhaps of time) or whether, as in the previous case, it implies a contrast between the rejection of the Light and Christ's protest against the rejection.

[2073] When δέ is used, without the article, after other proper names, there is a somewhat similar doubt. Probably however contrast is intended—Mary being distinguished from the two disciples, who had entered the tomb of the Saviour and had returned to their homes, one at least believing—in the words "*But* Mary (M. δέ) stood near the tomb outside weeping[6]." Similarly the words, "*But* Thomas (Θ. δέ)[7]," contrast Thomas, who had not seen the Lord,

---

[1] [2071 a] iii. 1, v. 5, xi. 1, and iv. 46 (marg.). In some of these cases Jn specifies time ("after these things," "after the two days" etc.) and place, and then introduces persons and circumstances. In ix. 14 "Now it was (ἦν δέ) the sabbath" introduces a point essential to the comprehension of what follows.

[2] [2072 a] Lk. iv. 1 Ἰ. δὲ πλήρης πνεύματος ἁγίου ὑπέστρεψεν....This follows the genealogy (iii. 24—38) which is preceded by iii. 23 καὶ αὐτὸς ἦν Ἰ. ἀρχόμενος.... The nom. (as subject) has previously occurred without the article in Lk. ii. 43 ὑπέμεινεν Ἰ. ὁ παῖς, ii. 52 καὶ Ἰ. προέκοπτεν..., iii. 23 καὶ αὐτὸς ἦν Ἰ. ἀρχόμενος....

[3] Lk. xxii. 48 Ἰησοῦς δὲ εἶπεν αὐτῷ, Ἰούδα....

[4] viii. 59. [5] xii. 44. [6] xx. 11. [7] xx. 24.

with the rest of the disciples, who had seen Him. In both cases, the particle introduces a new event and one of the deepest interest. And this, as a rule, is characteristic of John's use of δέ: it *draws attention*, sometimes to the beginning of a manifestly great event, sometimes to a detail, not manifestly, but really, important—either in itself or because of some latent symbolism.

(β) Δέ, third word, or later, in its clause

[2074] The instances are as follows, vi. 51 καὶ ὁ ἄρτος δὲ ὃν ἐγὼ δώσω ἡ σάρξ μου ἐστίν..., vii. 31 ἐκ τοῦ ὄχλου δὲ πολλοὶ ἐπίστευσαν εἰς αὐτόν, viii. 16 καὶ ἐὰν κρίνω δὲ ἐγώ, viii. 17 καὶ ἐν τῷ νόμῳ δὲ τῷ ὑμετέρῳ γέγραπται (comp. 1 Jn i. 3 καὶ ἡ κοινωνία δὲ ἡ ἡμετέρα), xv. 27 ἐκεῖνος μαρτυρήσει περὶ ἐμοῦ· καὶ ὑμεῖς δὲ μαρτυρεῖτε, xvi. 9—10 περὶ ἁμαρτίας μέν...περὶ δικαιοσύνης δέ, xvii. 20 οὐ περὶ τούτων δὲ ἐρωτῶ μόνον, xxi. 23 οὐκ εἶπεν δὲ αὐτῷ ὁ Ἰησοῦς... These may be classified according as δέ (1) is not, or (2) is, preceded by καί.

[2075] (1) In vii. 31, ἐκ δὲ τοῦ ὄχλου was perhaps avoided as it would lay too much stress on the preposition, which here means (in effect) "some of" and is so closely connected with τοῦ ὄχλου that ἐκ τοῦ ὄχλου might be regarded as almost a compound noun. In xvi. 9—10, μέν and δέ are placed third after preposition and noun as is frequently the case. In xvii. 20 οὐ δέ would have been against the rules of Greek. Compare 1 Jn ii. 2 περὶ τῶν ἁμαρτιῶν ἡμῶν, οὐ περὶ τῶν ἡμετέρων δὲ μόνον, ἀλλὰ καί.... But, in both, the unusual position of δέ probably calls rather more attention to the context as worthy to be noted. In xxi. 23, A, D, and *a, b, e, f* etc. read καὶ οὐκ εἶπεν for οὐκ εἶπεν δέ. The weight of ℵBC 33 and Origen is so great that we must accept δέ, as representing the earliest Greek text. But, on the other hand, καί—where we should naturally expect ἀλλά or μέντοι—is so difficult that it can hardly be a mere correction for regularity's sake. So far as regards difficulty, it would be more likely that the difficult καί would be corrected by a marginal δέ. When scribes began to transfer this to the text as a substitute for καί they could not place δέ after οὐκ, so they would place it after οὐκ εἶπεν. Possibly this very ancient tradition about the oldest of the Apostles may have been current in the Galilaean Church in a form in which the Hebraic "and" was used for "and yet." As it stands, οὐκ εἶπεν δέ is perhaps without parallel in Johannine Greek[1].

---

[1] [2075 *a*] Δέ is irregularly used in x. 41 Ἰωάνης μὲν σημεῖον ἐποίησεν οὐδέν, πάντα δὲ ὅσα εἶπεν Ἰ. περὶ τούτου ἀληθῆ ἦν. But there the irregularity arises from

[2076] (2) In the combination of καί and δέ, since καί would have sufficed to express mere addition, δέ seems to be devoted to the expression of emphasis, so that καὶ...δέ probably means "and...what is *more*," in the sense "and...what is *to be specially noted.*" Winer-Moulton (§ 53 p. 553) indicates two opinions as to καὶ δέ:—(1) that καί = "also," (2) that καί = "and." If καί meant "*also*," emphasizing the following word, Mt. xvi. 18 κἀγὼ δέ σοι λέγω would mean "I *also*," or "*Even* I"; and, in Jn vi. 51 καὶ ὁ ἄρτος would mean "*even* the bread" or "the bread *also*"—not likely interpretations. There are cases where initial καί is shewn by some special preceding context to be, not "and," but "also" or "even." But, as a rule, καί standing first in a sentence is to be assumed to mean "and." Καί in viii. 16, καὶ ἐὰν κρίνω δέ might possibly be emphatic (not connective) "*Even* if"; but, if so, the best course would be to treat both καί and δέ as contributing to emphasis, "*Yea, even* if I should judge."

(γ) Μέν...Δέ

[2077] In Johannine Words of the Lord, μέν occurs only twice, and there δέ follows. Both instances occur in the chapter containing Christ's last words to the disciples: (1) xvi. 9—11 περὶ ἁμαρτίας μέν ...περὶ δικαιοσύνης δέ...περὶ δὲ κρίσεως, (2) xvi. 22 καὶ ὑμεῖς οὖν νῦν μὲν λύπην ἔχετε· πάλιν δὲ ὄψομαι ὑμᾶς. In xvi. 11, περὶ κρίσεως δέ would have corresponded so exactly with the two previous περί clauses as to produce an artificial effect: and perhaps the writer wishes to call special attention to the clause "about judgment" and effects this by a slight variation of order. Μέν...δέ nowhere occurs in the Epistle.

(v) Εἰ

(a) Εἰ, corresponding to ἄν, in Words of the Lord

[2078] Mark (followed by Matthew) only once attributes to our Lord a saying about what "*would have happened*[1]," and such sayings are rare in Matthew and Luke[2]. But in John they

---

the position of μέν. Πάντα δέ would have corresponded to σημεῖον μέν. Or we might have expected ἀλλά or μέντοι following 'Ι. without μέν.

[1] [2078 a] Mk xiii. 20 (Mt. xxiv. 22) "If the Lord had not shortened those days no flesh would have been saved."

[2] [2078 b] Mt. xi. 21—3, Lk. x. 13 "If in Tyre...," also Mt. xii. 7 (pec.) "If ye had known...ye would not have condemned," Mt. xxiii. 30 (pec.) "Ye say, If we had been in the days of our fathers," Mt. xxiv. 43, Lk. xii. 39, "If the master

occur more often than in all the Synoptists together[1]. The only passage that requires comment is one in which W.H. omit ἄν, viii. 39 "If ye are children of Abraham, then ye are doing (ποιεῖτε) the deeds of Abraham. But as it is (νῦν δέ) ye are seeking to kill me[2]."

[2079] Here B alone has ποιεῖτε, and a scribe (possibly the first hand) has added ε in smaller characters, so as to make εποιειτε (without ἄν). L reads εποιειτε αν, D εποιειτε, ℵ εποιειται, corr. adds αν. The inferior MSS. have "If ye were (ἦτε)...ye would be doing (ἐποιεῖτε ἄν)." SS renders ποιεῖτε imperatively, "If ye are...do ye the deeds of Abraham": but no instance occurs in John of an imperative preceding νῦν δέ, "but as it is," which requires before it either "ye would be doing" or something equivalent to it[3]. We therefore have probably to choose between ποιεῖτε indicative and ἐποιεῖτε. The former would be a vivid and almost ironical way of saying "in that case you are doing," or "of course you are doing," the works of Abraham. The latter would be for ἐποιεῖτε ἄν. Omissions of ἄν are found in John elsewhere[4]: but *they are always with a negative.* Ποιεῖτε is therefore to be preferred here. In a similarly irregular passage, Lk. xvii. 6 εἰ ἔχετε πίστιν...ἐλέγετε ἄν, many MSS. alter the present ἔχετε into the imperfect; and the tendency to do the same here would naturally be strong. If Codex B had been lost and only a fair copy of it preserved, writing ᵉποιειτε as εποιειτε, not a single Greek uncial MS. would now preserve what appears to be the correct reading[5].

---

of the house had known..." Lk. xvii. 6 has εἰ ἔχετε πίστιν...ἐλέγετε ἄν, where Mk xi. 23 (? parall.) has ἔχετε πίστιν, Mt. xxi. 21 ἐὰν ἔχητε πίστιν, followed by future. In Lk. xix. 42 "If thou hadst known," the apodosis is dropped.

[1] [2078c] iv. 10, v. 46, viii. 19, ?viii. 39, ix. 41, xiv. 7, 28, xv. 19, xviii. 36; also with εἰ μή in xv. 22, 24, xix. 11. In these last three instances ἄν is omitted.

[2] Εἰ τέκνα τοῦ Ἀ. ἐστε, τὰ ἔργα τοῦ Ἀ. ποιεῖτε (marg. ἐποιεῖτε). νῦν δὲ ζητεῖτέ με ἀποκτεῖναι.

[3] [2079a] ix. 41, xv. 22, 24, xviii. 36. In all these cases, the sense is, "If so-and-so had happened things would have been different......*but as it is* (νῦν δέ)...." In xvi. 5, xvii. 13, the meaning is, "Things were different once......*but as it is* (νῦν δέ)...."

[4] [2079b] ix. 33, xv. 22, 24, xix. 11 εἰ μή in every case, ix. 33 is not a saying of Christ's. On ἄν omitted with indic. see **2213 a** and **2698**.

[5] [2079c] Origen's present text, when he is not expressly commenting on the passage, uses (Huet i. 72, ii. 96) the reading of the inferior MSS. But in his comment on the passage he agrees about six times (Huet ii. 286, 294—6) with W.H. txt, twice (*ib.* ii. 290, 293) with W.H. marg., comp. **2659 e**.

(β) Εἰ δὲ μή

[2080] Εἰ δὲ μή, without a verb, in LXX, almost always follows an expressed or implied imperative[1]. Apart from John, in N.T. (sometimes as εἰ δὲ μήγε) it follows (1) description of what ought to be done, (2) precept, (3) an if-clause[2]. In John, where it occurs twice, it follows an imperative in xiv. 11 "Believe me (μοι) that I [am] in the Father and the Father in me. *But if not* (εἰ δὲ μή), because of the mere works believe," *i.e.* if ye cannot believe *me* on the ground of my personality and the words that I utter, then believe because of the signs that I perform." This is according to rule. But the other instance, which comes earlier in the same chapter, is not according to rule—not, at least, as translated in the text of R.V., thus xiv. 1—3 "Let not your heart be troubled: ye believe in God, believe also in me. In my Father's house are many mansions; *if it were not so* (εἰ δὲ μή) I would have told you; for (ὅτι) I go (πορεύομαι) to prepare a place for you. And if I go (πορευθῶ) and prepare a place for you, I come again, and will receive you unto myself; that, where I am, [there] ye may be also. And whither I go (ὑπάγω) ye know the way."

[2081] (1) The first point to be noted about this difficult passage is that εἰ δὲ μή in this second instance—as in the first, though here at a somewhat longer interval—follows an imperative, and the imperative of the same verb as above ("believe"). According to the analogy of the first instance, and of all Biblical usage, endeavouring to connect εἰ δὲ μή with the imperative "believe," we must suppose the clause about "mansions" to be parenthetical; and the meaning will be, "Ye believe (or, Believe) in God. Believe [similarly] in me...*but, if [you can] not [rise to this]*—then,...."

[2082] (2) The next point to be noted is that R.V. has failed to represent a distinction drawn by our Lord here between "going on a journey" (πορεύομαι) and "going back, or home" (ὑπάγω) (1652—64). Earlier in the Gospel, the Jews themselves are dramatically described by John as failing in much the same way when Jesus says (vii. 33) "I go back (ὑπάγω) to him that sent me," and they say (vii. 35) "Where doth he purpose to *go* (πορεύεσθαι) *i.e.* journey?,"

---

[1] [2080 a] The exceptions are Gen. xviii. 21, Job xxiv. 25, xxxii. 22. In Sir. xxix. 6 εἰ δὲ μή follows ἐὰν ἰσχύσῃ. In 2 S. xvii. 6 ποιήσομεν...εἰ δὲ μή, the verb may be intended to imply an imperative, "let us do."

[2] Mk ii. 21, 22, Mt. ix. 17, Lk. v. 36, 37; Mt. vi. 1, Lk. x. 6, xiii. 9, xiv. 32, 2 Cor. xi. 16, Rev. ii. 5, 16.

adding "Doth he purpose to *go* to the Dispersion of the Greeks?" It is also noteworthy that, up to this point (xiv. 1) in the Gospel, Jesus has repeatedly described Himself as "going *home*, or *back* (ὑπάγω)" to the Father, but never, spiritually, as "going [on a journey (πορεύομαι)." In the preceding context He has just said to the disciples twice (xiii. 33, 36) "Where I *go home* (ὑπάγω) ye cannot come," and they have been perplexed and troubled, not being able to realise the Lord's "*going home*" and treating it simply as a separation. At this point Jesus Himself begins to speak of Himself as "*going* (πορεύομαι)," and the context suggests that He does this in order to adapt His language to the understanding of the disciples[1].

[2083] (3) A third point is, that εἶπον ἂν ὑμῖν ὅτι πορεύομαι, according to Greek usage in general as well as Johannine usage in particular, would naturally mean—unless some very clear prefixed context prevented the meaning—"I should have said to you *that* I am going." SS takes it thus. Chrysostom and many other authorities do the same, but omit ὅτι ("I should have said to you, 'I am going'"). On this point, see **2185—6**.

[2084] (4) Another consideration is that "If it were not so [as I have said]" would imply a supposition that Christ had stated an error; and this—even in the form of a supposition at once dismissed as impossible—is hardly in accordance with Johannine thought. There results a considerable negative probability, that εἰ δὲ μή does not mean εἰ δὲ μὴ οὕτως ἦν ("but if it were not so"). There is also a positive probability, if the text is not corrupt, that it relates to the imperative "believe" and means "otherwise," *i.e.* "if ye cannot do this."

[2085] According to this view, the disciples have been unable to realise all that was implied in the Son's "going *home*" to the Father. It meant that He could take His friends thither, and that the Father would find room for them all. It was not a strange place, or an inn, to which it was necessary that the Son should go first, to make preparations for the disciples. Nevertheless, if the disciples could not understand the unity of the Son with the Father and could not trust unreservedly in the Son's power without detailed assurances, He was willing to lower His language to their

---

[1] On ὑπάγω (not in Pap. Index, but colloquial, so that it has passed into modern Greek) and πορεύομαι, see **1652—64**. Jn carefully distinguishes them.

level and to ask them to trust in a special assurance. We may perhaps suppose Him to repeat, in thought, the precept "believe me" somewhat to this effect; "Ye believe (or Believe) in God? Believe also [similarly] in me—in my Father's house are many abiding places—: *but if not* [i.e. if ye cannot believe in me to this full extent, then believe me at least to this extent.]—I could have said to you [instead of speaking about 'going home'] that I was going on a journey to prepare a place for you."

[2086] This is not wholly satisfactory. For, strictly speaking, εἶπον ἄν means "I *should* have said," not "I *could* have said." But the whole passage is surcharged with emotion, and Christ may be represented as having two thoughts in His mind, (1) "If I had known your weakness I *should* have spoken differently," (2) "If you are so weak, believe me, I *could* have put things for you differently." From the objective point of view, the Son does not "go to prepare a place for the disciples" because the places are already (Mk x. 40) "prepared" (Mt. xx. 23) "by my Father." But, adapting His language to the weakness of their faith, Christ proceeds to say, "And if—to use the language suited to you—even if I should '*go and prepare a place for you*,' yet I come again...." Literally, the Lord can hardly be said to "go to prepare a place," like a courier engaging rooms in an inn; and Jesus seems to have implied this by His previous mention of "many abiding-places," as if He had said, "We shall be in my home—your home, large enough to hold all."

(vi) Ἐπεί

(*a*) Ἐπεὶ παρασκευή ἦν

[2087] This conjunction did not appear in *Johannine Vocabulary* because it occurs, though rarely, in each of the Gospels[1], and there is nothing grammatically remarkable in the two Johannine instances of it. But historically it is remarkable that Mark's only use of it is in connexion with the Preparation for the Passover, and that one of John's two instances is similarly connected. The Gospels all mention the Preparation, but differently:—(1) Mk xv. 42 "*since* (ἐπεί) it was *the Preparation,* which is 'eve of the sabbath,' there came Joseph of Arimathaea," (2) Mt. xxvii. 62 "But on the morrow,

---

[1] [2087 *a*] Mk only once (xv. 42 ἐπεὶ ἦν παρασκευή, ὅ ἐστιν προσάββατον), Mt. (3), Lk. (1+1 marg.), Jn xiii. 29 ἐπεὶ τὸ γλωσσ. εἶχεν Ἰ., xix. 31 ἐπεὶ παρασκευὴ ἦν.

which is [the day] after *the Preparation*, there were gathered together the chief priests and the Pharisees to Pilate," to ask him to guard the tomb, (3) Lk. xxiii. 53—4 "he placed him in the tomb...where no man had yet lain: and it was the day of *the Preparation* and the sabbath was dawning."

[2088] Ἐπεί means "*when*," as well as "*since*," and is interchanged with ἐπειδή, "*when*," in Daniel, Luke, and Acts[1]. Matthew and Luke, who omit ἐπεί above, may have supposed that here it meant simply "*when*," not perceiving that it stated the *cause* for the coming of Joseph. John intervenes, at great length. Whereas Mark and Luke, in different ways, connect the day with "the Sabbath," John, in the first mention of it, says (xix. 14) "it was the Preparation *of the Passover.*" He adds that the Jews desired the bodies of the crucified to be taken away (xix. 31) "*since* it was the Preparation," and that Joseph of Arimathea came hereupon and took the body of Jesus, and also that the body was buried as it was (apparently meaning buried in haste) "*because of* the Preparation." Thus he repeatedly brings out the causal meaning of Mark's ἐπεί, which is not represented in Matthew and Luke.

(vii) Ἕως

(*a*) Not confused with ὡc

[2089] Ἕως, with the present indicative, occurs perhaps once in Mark[2], but nowhere else in N.T. except 1 Tim. iv. 13 ἕως ἔρχομαι "*while I am* [*still*] *coming* [and not yet present]," and thrice in John, ix. 4 "we must work...*while* (ἕως, marg. ὡς) (SS "*while yet*") *it is day*," and xxi. 22—3 (bis) "*while I am* [*still*] *coming*." The Thesaurus gives many such phrases as "*While* (ἕως) there is [still] opportunity," "*While* he [still] has breath and power[3]," and—with "still (ἔτι)" inserted and verb omitted—"*While* the sea [is] still navigable," "*while* [there is] still hope" etc.[4] SS therefore expresses the sense in adding "*yet*." The importance of these facts consists in their indication that, when John uses ὡς later on in xii. 35 ὡς τὸ φῶς ἔχετε, he means something different from "*while*" (2201).

---

[1] [2088 *a*] Dan. iii. 22, Lk. vii. 1 (v. r.), Acts xiii. 46 (v. r.). 1 Esdr. vi. 14 ἐπεί is parall. to Ezr. v. 12 ἀφ' ὅτε, R.V. "after that," marg. "because that."

[2] [2089 *a*] In Mk vi. 45 (W.H. ἀπολύει) ℵBL have ἕως αὐτὸς (L αὐτοὺς) ἀπολύει, where D has αὐτὸς δὲ ἀπολύει and the other MSS. απολυσει or -ση: the parall. Mt. xiv. 22 has ἕως οὗ ἀπολύσῃ.

[3] [2089 *b*] Dem. 15. 5, Synes. *Epist*. 44. Ἐστί is om. in Plat. *Legg*. 789 E τὸ γενόμενον δὲ πλάττειν ἕως ὑγρόν.

[4] Thuc. vii. 47, viii. 40, also Xen. *Cyrop*. vii. 1. 18 ἕως ἔτι σοι σχολή.

(viii) Ἤ and ἤπερ

(a) Ἤ

[2090] In the Synoptists, ἤ, "or," is frequently used in Christ's words for rhetorical fulness or impressiveness ("tribulation *or* persecution," "under the bushel *or* under the bed" etc.)[1]. In John, where it seldom occurs, it is mostly outside Christ's words. In Christ's words it occurs only thrice[2]. Once it introduces a direct question as follows:—xviii. 34 "Sayest thou this from thyself, *or* (ἤ) did others say [it] to thee concerning me?"

[2091] This is our Lord's answer to Pilate's words, "Thou art [it seems] the king of the Jews!" which are probably (2234, 2236 foll.) to be read as a contemptuous exclamation expressed in an interrogative tone. It is clear that, as Chrysostom says, our Lord's reply is not a request for information. Pilate obviously did *not* say this from himself. Others *had* said it to him. In Greek questions, an absurdity is often put before the reality, thus: "When horses are injured do they become *better, or* worse?" "In states, are rulers *without error, or* liable to error?" "Do you *permit* [*a bad ruler*] *to rule, or* do you appoint another[3]?" There is nothing in the literal English rendering of our Lord's reply to indicate the meaning conveyed by this Greek usage. But the meaning might be fairly paraphrased as "Will you venture to assert that you say this from yourself, or will you admit, as you must be conscious, that you were prompted by others?"

(β) Ἤπερ

[2092] Ἤπερ occurs only once in N.T., namely in Jn xii. 43 "They loved the glory of men rather *than* (ἤπερ) (marg. ὑπέρ) the glory of God." Chrysostom, in his comment, quotes (v. 44) "How can ye believe...since *ye seek not* the glory that is from the only God?" And perhaps this is almost the meaning here:—"the glory of men *and not* the glory of God." Compare 2 Macc. xiv. 42

---

[1] [2090 *a*] In the Sermon on the Mount alone, it occurs about ten times.

[2] [2090 *b*] Two of these contain indirect questions, vii. 17 "He shall know... whether it is from God *or* I speak from myself," viii. 14 "Ye know not whence I come *or* where I return."

[3] [2091 *a*] Steph. quoting Plato 335 B, 339 B, Xen. *Cyrop.* iii. 1. 12 (to which add *ib.* "Do you let him [*i.e.* the bad ruler] *retain his wealth, or* do you reduce him to poverty?").

"desiring [rather] to die nobly than [i.e. *and not*]...to be subjected (θέλων ἀποθανεῖν ἤπερ...ὑποχείριος γενέσθαι)," and the variously interpreted *Iliad* i. 117 βούλομ' ἐγὼ λαὸν σόον ἔμμεναι ἢ ἀπολέσθαι, where ἤ (Eustathius says) was explained as being "for ἤπερ," so as to mean emphatically "than," not "or." According to this distinction, whereas (1) μᾶλλον ἤ might have meant that they loved the glory of God *somewhat* but the glory of men *more*, (2) μᾶλλον ἤπερ suggests that they loved the glory of men, and the glory of God they loved *not at all*. Compare the only other passage where John uses μᾶλλον ἤ, iii. 19 "The light hath come into the world and men loved *rather the darkness than the light* (μᾶλλον τὸ σκότος ἢ τὸ φῶς)." The likeness, and the unlikeness, are remarkable. The evangelist appears to condemn both "the world" and "the rulers," but the latter more severely. The "world" had perhaps *some* love for the light: the "rulers" had no love at all for the glory of God[1]. See **2685**.

(ix) Ἵνα

(*a*) Ἵνα, in John, expresses, or implies, purpose

[2093] The frequency of ἵνα in John (**2686**) illustrates in part his preference for colloquial as distinct from literary Greek, but in part also the tendency of his Gospel to lay stress on *purpose*, e.g. on the purpose of the Baptist's birth and mission[2], on the purpose of the Son's mission[3], on the purpose of His actions and words[4], and on the Father's purpose in appointing for Him these actions[5], which purpose may also be described as the Father's will[6]. John's view is that actions are appointed for men *in order that*, in doing them, they may do the will of their Father; and *the essence of the action consists in the motive*, namely, to do that will. In English, "*to* do" often means "doing," having quite lost its old notion of "*to* doing," i.e. "*toward* doing," i.e. *purpose*: but in John—whatever may be the case in other writers—ἵνα seems always to retain some notion, or suggestion, of purpose, or motive, as being the essence of action[7].

---

[1] [2092 *a*] Ἥπερ ("than") differs from ἤ ("or" or "than") in being non-ambiguous and emphatic. Ὑπέρ, v.r. for ἤπερ, substitutes a common for an uncommon word and weakens the sense.

[2] i. 7, 8 ἵνα μαρτυρήσῃ, comp. i. 31 ἵνα φανερωθῇ.

[3] iii. 17 etc.   [4] v. 34.   [5] v. 23, 36.

[6] vi. 40 τοῦτο γάρ ἐστιν τὸ θέλημα τ. πατρός μου ἵνα....

[7] [2093 *a*] Jn does not use the infinitive of purpose with τοῦ, or πρὸς τό, so that *a priori* we might expect him to use ἵνα as a substitute. Bruder gives the article

(β) ἽΝΑ, in John, never merely appositional

[2094] If ἵνα were merely appositional like our English "to," N.T. writers would be able to employ ἵνα, like "to"—irrespective of good or evil, of positive or negative—in such sentences as "It is good, or evil, for thee *to* do this," "I *command*, or *forbid*, thee *to* do this." But ἵνα can only be used with "good" and "command," not with "evil" and "forbid." The reason is that "goodness" and "command" suggest *a positive object to be attained or a positive object in commanding; and object suggests purpose*[1]. "Evil" and "forbid" do not—or at least not to the same extent. In xiii. 34, R.V. marg. has "A new commandment I give unto you, *that ye love* (ἵνα ἀγαπᾶτε) one another; even as I loved you, *that ye also may love* (ἵνα καὶ ὑ. ἀγαπᾶτε) one another," apparently taking the first ἵνα as introducing the *substance* of the command ("that ye *love*"), and the second as introducing its *purpose* "that ye *may* love." It seems better to give the same rendering in both cases, the second being an emphatic and much more definite repetition of the first. The meaning is, in both cases, "*My command is, and my purpose is, that ye love one another.*" But in the second clause the kind of love is defined ("Even as I loved you").

[2095] Similarly in xv. 13 "Greater love hath no man than this (μείζονα ταύτης ἀγάπην οὐδεὶς ἔχει)—that a man lay down his life (ἵνα τις τὴν ψυχὴν αὐτοῦ θῇ) for his friends," the ἵνα clause (in view of the frequency of Johannine apposition) is best taken as being in

---

and the inf. as occurring Mk (15), Mt. (24), Lk. (c. 70), Jn (4) (thrice πρὸ τοῦ, once διὰ τό). Ἵνα occurs in Jn almost as often (**1726**) as in all the Synoptists together.

[2093 b] In xii. 40 "*in order that* (ἵνα) they may not see with their eyes" represents the divine purpose of "blinding" those who do not wish to see: and this phrase, derived loosely from Isaiah (vi. 10), is quoted by Mark (iv. 12) and Luke (viii. 10), but not in the parallel Matthew who avoids it (xiii. 13 ὅτι...οὐ βλέπουσι, supplemented by xiii. 14 οὐ μὴ ἴδητε). When once the stupendous admission is made that evil in some sense may be decreed by God, there ceases to be any difficulty in xvi. 2, "The hour cometh [*decreed*] *in order that* whosoever killeth you shall *think* (δόξῃ) *he doeth God service*." If persecution is "decreed," it must be decreed that some shall persecute; and the evil is not always made worse by the fact that a man persecutes, thinking that "he doeth God service."

In v. 7, ἵνα depends on ἕτοιμον implied in ἔχω "I have no one [ready]."

[1] [2094 a] In the following, there is a notion of some standard of excellence to be attained, something desired or needed, some customary privilege that is prized and asked for, i. 27 "I am not worthy *that* I should loose the shoe latchet," ii. 25 "He had no need *that* anyone should testify," xviii. 39 "There is a custom [established] for you *that* I should release...." See **2104 a**.

apposition to ταύτης [τῆς ἀ.], but ἵνα τις θῇ is not the same as τοῦ θεῖναι. For the love is, *not "the laying down of life," but the spirit that prompts the laying down or stimulates one man that he may lay down his life for another.* And this suggestion of motive or effort is latent in ἵνα. So, too, iv. 34 "My meat is *in order that* I may do (ἵνα ποιήσω) the will of him that sent me" implies that the "meat" consists in the will to do His will. Comp. xvii. 3 "This is eternal life, *in order that* they may know thee," which perhaps combines (1) "*the effort to* know thee," (2) "*given to men that* they may know thee."

[2096] In answer to the question of the Jews, "What are we to do in order that we may work the works of God?" Jesus replies (vi. 29) "This is the work of God [namely] *in order that* ye may believe," which appears to mean that the "works" are not of the nature assumed by the questioners (*e.g.* sabbath-keeping, alms-giving etc.) but of the nature of *motive* or *purpose*: and if they are to do the works it will be because they take into their hearts God's purpose and will, which is an *effort* to make them believe, literally, an effort "*in order that* ye may believe." Similarly vi. 40 "For this is the will of my Father [and His purpose and effort] *in order that* everyone that beholdeth the Son...may have life eternal," and xv. 12 (comp. xiii. 34) "This is my commandment [and purpose] *in order that* ye may love one another." The following passages shew that John, differing from Epictetus and others, never uses ἵνα exactly for ὅτι or ὥστε (2697).

(γ) Special passages

[2097] In viii. 56 "Abraham, your father, rejoiced *that he might see* my day," the meaning is that Abraham, receiving the promise of the son in whom all the nations of the world were to be blessed, (Gen. xvii. 17) "*laughed*" *for joy*, being strengthened by God with hopeful faith, *in order that*, under God's providence, he might thus fulfil the overruling will of God working for the salvation of "the nations." Philo (i. 602—3) compares the "laughing" of Abraham to the "laughing" of the day in anticipation of the early dawn: and, playing on the meaning of the name of Isaac (*i.e.* "laughter") who was not yet born, he declares that "Abraham, so to speak, laughed before laughter existed, as the soul, through hope, rejoices before joy and delights before delight." The meaning is, that Abraham, being helped by God, performed a "work of God," namely, "believing" and "rejoicing," *in order that* he might fulfil a purpose of God, namely, might see the day of the Messiah[1]. See also 2688—9.

[2098] ix. 2 "Rabbi, who sinned, this [man] or his parents, *in order that* he might be born blind?" is answered by Jesus in language that does not deny *purpose* but calls attention to an *ulterior purpose*: "Neither did this [man] sin, nor his parents, but [it came to pass] *in order that* the works of God might be manifested in him."

[2099] In xi. 14—15 "Lazarus is dead, and I am glad, on account of you, that ye may believe, because I was not there[2]," the first question is, What is the verb, expressed or implied, on which there depends the clause "that ye may believe"?

(1) The only verb expressed is χαίρω: and, taken by themselves, the words "Lazarus is dead and I rejoice in order that ye may believe" might mean "I force myself to rejoice over it and to express my joy in order that ye may believe"—as a general, after the death of a brother in battle, might say to his soldiers, "I rejoice over it in order that you may be encouraged to follow his example." According to this view, the Son "rejoices" over His friend's death—foreseeing the triumph over death—being filled by the Father with joy in order that He may accomplish a work for the strengthening of the faith of the disciples.

[2100] (2) But we have not here χαίρω and ἵνα consecutively, (as above (2097) ἠγαλλιάσατο ἵνα). "For your sakes" intervenes. Now "for your sakes" implies that the speaker *desires* something *for the sake* of those spoken to. And, in answer to the question, "desiring what?" τί θέλων; the reply would be θέλων ἵνα πιστεύσητε, "desiring that ye may believe." Hence ἵνα may depend upon θέλω implied in δι' ὑμᾶς: "I rejoice for your sakes desiring that ye may believe."

[2101] (3) The next clause to consider is "because (ὅτι) I was not there." (a) This may depend upon "believe." Then it would mean, "that ye may believe in me because your faith has not been shaken at the spectacle of Lazarus dying in my presence when I, you might think, could have healed him." In this spirit, Martha and Mary say to Jesus, "If thou hadst been here, my brother had not died," and Martha may be supposed to add, "Yet even now [though

---

[1] [2097 a] Ἀγαλλιάομαι is never used in the Bible with ἵνα to mean "rejoice (to do)." Once, when meaning "rejoice to do," it is used with infin. (Ps. xix. 5) "rejoiceth *to run* (δραμεῖν) his course." For Origen's comment, see 2689.

[2] Λάζαρος ἀπέθανεν, καὶ χαίρω, δι' ὑμᾶς, ἵνα πιστεύσητε, ὅτι οὐκ ἤμην ἐκεῖ. I have added a comma after χαίρω.

the faith of some might have been shaken] I believe that whatsoever thou shalt ask from God, God will give thee." But is it likely that Christ would rejoice in the prospect of a belief so *negative* and frail that it depends upon His *absence*? More probably, if this were the grammatical construction, there would be a latent *positive* meaning, "That ye may believe *because* I was not there to save him from death and *because I shall consequently go thither to raise him from death*," *i.e.* that ye may believe because I shall raise him from death as a consequence of my absence. (*b*) Again, the words "because I was not there" may depend upon "rejoice," the meaning being, "I rejoice—on your account, desiring that ye may believe—because I was not there," *i.e.* "I rejoice that I was not there, not for my own sake, not to avoid the spectacle of his death, but for your sakes desiring that ye may believe."

[2102] (4) On the whole—having regard to John's frequent use of ἵνα to introduce divine preordinance and to the stress laid on Christ's knowledge of all that was happening to Lazarus, combined with His determination to remain at a distance till His "friend" was dead—we shall probably come closest to the meaning, if we take the words as signifying that the Son rejoiced over all the circumstances of the death of Lazarus, as He was ready to rejoice over His own death, and for the same reason—namely that, in both cases, the death would tend to the glory of God by strengthening men's faith in God. We are intended to listen to Jesus as the words dropped slowly from His lips, clause by clause. The same shock that the disciples would have felt we also are intended to feel, when we hear Jesus say, "Lazarus is dead, and I rejoice." Then we are to be in part comforted by His affection and in part bewildered by "for your sakes." Then some reassurance follows when we hear "in order that ye may believe." Then we are plunged into bewilderment again by the words "because I was not there." This is what we are to realise as the confused feeling of the hearers at the time. But realising it as readers, in the light of subsequent events, we are to interpret the oracular words as meaning that the Son *rejoiced in all that the Father revealed to Him*, in the death, and in His absence from His friend's death-bed, for the sake of His disciples, and that the death, the absence, and the rejoicing, were all ordained for the fulfilment of the divine purpose[1].

---

[1] [2102 *a*] Chrysostom's comment is "*Died and I rejoice on your account.* Why, pray, *on your account*? Because I foretold [it], not being there, and

[2103] In xii. 7 Ἄφες αὐτὴν ἵνα εἰς τὴν ἡμέραν τοῦ ἐνταφιασμοῦ μου τηρήσῃ αὐτό, obscurity arises, not from the construction of ἵνα τηρήσῃ "in order that she may keep," but from the doubtful meaning of the context (which will, I hope, be discussed in a future treatise) and from the possibility of some corruption[1].

(δ) Ἵνα and Subjunctive, compared with Infinitive

[2104] In xi. 50 "It is profitable for you (lit.) *in order that* one man should die for the people," and in xvi. 7 "It is profitable for you (lit.) *in order that* I may depart," ἵνα follows a word that suggests a profitable object to be pursued (as explained above 2094). But owing to the context, in each case, there is probably a notion of preordinance. For this reason, perhaps, ἵνα and the subjunctive are put into the mouth of the High Priest when he utters the words under higher influence than his own ("not of himself") as being a divine decree: but afterwards the evangelist, when referring to these very words, uses the infinitive, xviii. 14 "Now Caiaphas was he that gave counsel to the Jews that it was expedient that one man should die (ὅτι συμφέρει ἕνα ἄνθρωπον ἀποθανεῖν) for the people[2]."

(ε) Omission of principal verb before Ἵνα

[2105] As the *Iliad* declares its subject to be the wrath of Achilles but adds that the "purpose that was being accomplished" was that of Zeus, so, though in reverse order, the Fourth Gospel begins with the Logos and God and Light; and then, coming to "a man," indicates that the *purpose* of the man's "coming" is to bear witness about the Light. To express this purpose the evangelist

---

because, when I shall have raised [him] up [from the dead], there will be no suspicion (οὐδεμία ἔσται ὑποψία)." Theodorus (Cramer *ad loc.*) says "I rejoice, He says, for your sakes (ὑμῶν ἕνεκεν). For the fact that I was not there will contribute to your faith (τὸ γὰρ μὴ εἶναί με ἐκεῖ συντελέσει πρὸς τὴν πίστιν τὴν ὑμετέραν) since, if (εἰ μέν) I had been present, I should have healed him while still ailing (ἀρρωστοῦντα ἐθεράπευον), but such a wonder as that would have been slight for the manifestation of power."

[1] On xv. 8 ἐν τούτῳ ἐδοξάσθη ὁ πατήρ μου ἵνα καρπὸν πολὺν φέρητε, see 2393.

[2] [2104 a] Jn's preference of ἵνα to the infinitive is illustrated by (a) i. 27 "I am not worthy *that* (ἵνα)," contr. with "worthy *to*" in Lk. xv. 19, 21, Rev. v. 2, 4, 9, 12, and by (b) ii. 25, xvi. 30, 1 Jn ii. 27 χρείαν ἔχειν ἵνα, contr. with χ. ἔχειν and infinitive in Mt. iii. 14, xiv. 16, 1 Thess. i. 8 (comp. Heb. v. 12 τοῦ διδάσκειν). On the infinitive with τοῦ see 2093 a.

uses ἵνα for the first time[1]. As the man is described as "sent from God," the purpose of the "coming" may be supposed to be that of God, not of the man except so far as the man makes it his own as well. The Gospel then proceeds to subordinate the "man" to the "light" by saying, i. 8 "He was not the light, *but* [   ] *in order that* (ἀλλ' ἵνα) he might bear witness concerning the light."

[2106] How are we to fill the bracketed gap? R.V. supplies "came," and perhaps correctly: but the passage should be considered with others like it, ix. 3 "Neither did this man sin nor his parents, *but* [   ] *in order that*[2] the works of God should be manifested in him," xiii. 18 "I speak not concerning you all: I know whom (τίνας) I chose, *but* [   ] *in order that* the Scripture might be fulfilled...," xiv. 30—1 "And he [*i.e.* the prince of the world] hath nothing in me; *but* [   ] *in order that* the world may know that I love the Father and as the Father gave me commandment, even so I do. Arise, let us go hence," xv. 24—5 "If I had not done...they had not had sin; but now (νῦν δέ) have they both seen and hated me and my Father; *but* [   ] *in order that* the word that is written in their law might be fulfilled, They hated me without a cause." Similarly 1 Jn ii. 19 "They came forth [*i.e.* originated] from us, but (ἀλλ') they were not of us: for if they had been of us, they would have continued with us, *but* [   ] *in order that* they might be made manifest how that they all are not of us."

[2107] Attempting to supply these ellipses we may first take those passages in which ἀλλά is preceded by a negative. In these, where we can supply a verb by repeating it from the preceding context, it will be reasonable to do so: i. 8 "He was not the light *but on the contrary* [*was*, or *was sent*, or *came*] *in order that* he might bear witness concerning the light," repeating ἐγένετο, or ἀπεσταλμένος [ἦν], or ἦλθεν, from i. 6—7 (but see 2112)[3]: similarly ix. 3 "*Neither* did this man sin *nor* his parents *but on the contrary* [*he was born blind*] in order that the works of God should be manifested,"

---

[1] [2105 a] i. 6—7 ἐγένετο ἄνθρωπος ἀπεσταλμένος παρὰ θεοῦ...οὗτος ἦλθεν εἰς μαρτυρίαν, ἵνα μαρτυρήσῃ... Comp. Is. lv. 4 "I [*i.e.* Jehovah] have given him *for a witness* to the peoples."

[2] "But [   ] in order that," in the whole of this paragraph = ἀλλ' ἵνα.

[3] [2107 a] The view that ἀλλά means "*but on the contrary* [subordinated to the light]" and not, "*but still* [in some way connected with the light]" is favoured by Jn iii. 28 οὐκ...ἀλλ', "not...*but on the contrary*," uttered by the Baptist himself about his relation to Christ.

referring to the question of the disciples "Who did sin...that *he was born blind?*" (but see **2112**).

[**2108**] In xiv. 30—31 above quoted, the negative clause "hath nothing in me," means "he finds no sin in me." The opposite of this would be "he finds righteousness in me." But instead of supplying this or any clause, the best plan perhaps is to connect together "*But on the contrary*...even so I do (οὕτως ποιῶ)," so that the meaning is, "Satan does not find sin in me [and constrain me to die because of my sin], *but on the contrary—*[*unconstrained by any law of sin or Satan*] *in order that* the world may know..., and even as the Father gave me commandment—*so I do*," i.e. I act sinlessly and voluntarily for His glory. In that case, the principal verb is not omitted but is placed at the end of the sentence.

[**2109**] In the following instances, where there is no negative clause immediately preceding ἀλλά, the context suggests the ellipsis of some exclamation of sorrow for sin as being "[evil indeed], *but yet* [ordained] *in order that*" some divine purpose, or saying of Scripture, may be fulfilled : xiii. 18 "I know that you will not all be saved; I know whom I have chosen : [evil indeed] *but yet* [*it has so come to pass*] *in order that* the Scripture may be fulfilled." Similarly in xv. 24—5 ἀλλά means "but still," and the speaker falls back, in trust, upon the fulfilment of "the word that is written in their law" as being the only consolation: "They have both seen and hated me and my Father; *but still* [it has been so ordained] in order that...." The evil is regarded as evil, but as evil resulting in the fulfilment of the Law.

[**2110**] In 1 Jn ii. 19, where a negative precedes, but at some interval, ἀλλά appears to mean "*but still*," and to suggest, in the thought of a mysterious and divine justice, some compensation for the defection of disciples : "They went out from us, *i.e.* they originated from us, but they never really belonged to us. Had they belonged to us, they would have continued with us—[*evil, indeed*] *but* [*at all events an evil working for good*] *in order that* they might be manifested....[1]."

---

[1] [**2110** *a*] R.V. supplies "they went out" from what precedes, and takes it as "they *revolted*" or "*deserted*." Ἐξῆλθον might, in suitable context, apply to "coming forth" either (*a*) as sons from a home, soldiers from a camp etc., or (*b*) as runaways, deserters, rebels. Here, the following words, ἀλλ' οὐκ ἦσαν ἐξ ἡμῶν, rather suggest antithesis, "They [at first] came out from us [as children from our home, or soldiers from our camp] *but they were not really* [*in heart*] *belonging to us*...." For ἐξέρχομαι ἐκ, παρά, ἀπό, meaning "originate from" or "come from," see Jn viii. 42, xiii. 3, xvi. 28, 30, xvii. 8.

[**2110** *b*] Origen, however (Huet ii. 410 D), commenting on the going out of Judas

[2111] There is but one instance of ellipsis with ἀλλ' ἵνα in the Synoptic Tradition. It occurs in Mark alone, and the parallel Matthew and Luke are of interest as shewing how such a missing clause might be variously supplied. The Three Synoptists, after substantially agreeing that Jesus said "I was with you '[day] by day' in the Temple and ye did not seize me," give His following words thus:

Mk xiv. 49	Mt. xxvi. 56	Lk. xxii. 53
"*but in order that* (ἀλλ' ἵνα) the Scriptures might be fulfilled."	"*but* (δέ) *all this is come to pass* (γέγονεν) *in order that* the Scriptures of the Prophets might be fulfilled."	"*but* (ἀλλ') this is your hour and the power of darkness."

Here it would be an extremely weak interpretation, in Mark, to repeat the preceding verb, "seize" (so as to make the sense "but [ye have seized me] in order that"). A better course is to explain it as above, as being an exclamation of mingled sorrow and self-consolation at the temporary triumph of evil: "[evil and strange] *but yet, [ordained] in order that* the Scriptures might be fulfilled." Matthew takes it so, and expressly asserts that "all this" (τοῦτο ὅλον) came to pass according to divine decree. Luke, on the other hand, seems to emphasize the fact that the arrest took place by *night*: "Ye did not seize me by day; *but [now ye seize me by night]*, this is your [appointed] hour, fit for a deed of darkness."

[2112] In the light of this passage we must perhaps be prepared to say that in one at least of the Johannine instances (i. 8, ix. 3) explained above (**2107**) by a repetition of a preceding verb, John may have intended to supply, as Matthew does here, "now all this came to pass," so that the meaning of Christ's reply about the blind man (ix. 3) would be, "No particular sin of the parents or of the child in any pre-existing condition explains the facts: *the whole was ordained* for the glory of God." Possibly the same explanation applies also to the saying about the Baptist (i. 8). It is characteristic of John's style that he so often uses a phrase—

---

after receiving the sop from Jesus (xii. 30) says τέλεον ἐξῆλθεν ἀπὸ τοῦ Ἰησοῦ ἀνάλογον τῷ Ἐξῆλθον ἐξ ἡμῶν, apparently illustrating the "going out" in the Gospel by the "going out" in the Epistle, and taking the latter as revolt, or secession. According to that view, the rendering would be "They went out as rebels from us. [An evil, indeed,] *but still* they were never in heart belonging to us," *i.e.* but still the evil would have been greater if they had really belonged to us and had yet fallen away.

perhaps borrowed from the early Greek vernacular Gospel and retained in one instance by Mark alone of the Synoptists—that leaves the reader *in some doubt as to what is alleged to have happened, but insists that it happened for a certain purpose.*

(ζ) Ἵνα dependent on verb implied in question

[2113] i. 22 "They said therefore to him, Who art thou (τίς εἶ;)? *that* we may give an answer to them that sent us."

ix. 36 "He answered [and said], And who is he, Lord, *that* I may believe on him?"

"'Tell us," and (2157) "thou wilt surely tell me," may be severally supplied before "that."

(η) Ἵνα with indicative (2690)

[2114] Ἵνα with future indicative occurs in vii. 3 "*in order that* thy disciples also *shall behold* (θεωρήσουσι)," xvii. 2 "*in order that* all that thou hast given to him *he shall give* (δώσει) to them eternal life." This (comp. 1 Cor. ix. 18 ἵνα θήσω) is fairly frequent in N.T. But 1 Jn v. 20 "he hath given to us a mind that we may be recognising (ἵνα γινώσκομεν)" stands on a different footing, being probably a mere misspelling arising from the confusion of ο and ω (966 *a*). Compare Gal. vi. 9—12 θερίσομεν (אCFG etc. -ωμεν)...ὡς καιρὸν ἔχωμεν (so W.H. with אB*, but Lightf. (2696) ἔχομεν)...ἐργαζώμεθα (AB* -όμεθα)... διώκωνται (ACFG etc. -ονται). In the context, the writer says "See with what large (πηλίκοις, but B* ἡλίκοις) letters I have written to you *with my own hand.*" It is possible that the Apostle, like some writers in the Egyptian papyri, habitually interchanged ο and ω; and early reverence for the autograph may have preserved some traces of the interchange in the best Greek MSS. (2691). This however will not explain Jn xvii. 3 (ADL etc.) ἵνα γινώσκουσιν (*d* cognoscant) where possibly some scribes took the meaning to be "*so that* they know." In the difficult passage (1673 *c*) v. 20 ἵνα ὑμεῖς θαυμάζητε (SS "*and* do not wonder") אL have θαυμάζετε. In xii. 40 ἵνα μὴ ἴδωσιν...καὶ ἰάσομαι αὐτούς, John follows Is. vi. 10 (LXX, but Sym. ἰαθῇ), and so does Mt. xiii. 15. Compare Eph. vi. 3 ἵνα εὖ σοι γένηται καὶ ἔσῃ (which deviates from LXX both of Ex. xx. 12 and of Deut. v. 16). This resembles W.H. marg. in Jn xv. 8 ἵνα καρπὸν...φέρητε καὶ γενήσεσθε ἐμοὶ μαθηταί—a natural transition, but BDL have γένησθε.

(θ) Ἵνα, connexion of

[2115] A ἵνα clause generally follows the principal verb, but see 2108 and comp. xix. 31 (where ἵνα occurs with a negative) οἱ οὖν

Ἰουδαῖοι, ἐπεὶ π. ἦν, ἵνα μὴ μείνῃ...ἦν γάρ...ἠρώτησαν τὸν Π. ἵνα...[1]. The connexion is doubtful in xix. 28 μετὰ τοῦτο εἰδὼς ὁ Ἰησοῦς ὅτι ἤδη πάντα τετέλεσται ἵνα τελειωθῇ ἡ γραφὴ λέγει, Διψῶ. Chrysostom paraphrases thus, εἰδὼς οὖν πάντα πεπληρωμένα, λέγει, Διψῶ, πάλιν ἐνταῦθα προφητείαν πληρῶν, apparently connecting the ἵνα clause with λέγει, and the rhythm of the sentence being like that of xix. 31 somewhat favours this view. If that were correct, the best interpretation would be that the Son *felt the thirst and uttered the expression of it* in order that the Scripture might receive its fulfilment (not that He deliberately uttered the word in order that a particular passage of Scripture might be fulfilled (1722)). But, on the other side, Johannine usage decidedly favours the rendering "knowing that *all things were now accomplished in order that the Scripture might be perfectly fulfilled*"—provided that we read what follows in the light of these words. Then "He saith, 'I thirst'" will mean, "[Knowing, I say, that the time had come for the supreme perfection of the Father's will as expressed in Scripture] he saith, 'I thirst.'" The writer indicates (1) that all things were accomplished that the Scripture might be fulfilled, (2) that Jesus knew this when He uttered the words "I thirst." He leads us to infer that Jesus uttered the words as the crown of that accomplishment and with a view to that fulfilment. Our conclusion is, then, that according to Johannine *grammar* the ἵνα clause depends on τετέλεσται; but, according to Johannine *suggestion and intention*, the ἵνα clause is to be repeated so as to depend on λέγει.

(ι) Ἵνα...ἵνα

[2116] Such a sentence as "*In order that x may come to pass in order that y may come to pass*" would naturally mean that an immediate object *x* is to be attained with a view to the attainment of an ultimate object *y*—so that the second ἵνα clause would be grammatically (though not mentally) *subordinate* to the first. But the second clause may be reiterative—*y* being another form of expressing *x*—"in order that [I say] *y* may take place," so that

---

[1] [2115 a] In this sentence ἵνα μή could not depend on ἠρώτησαν, the principal verb, without changing the meaning into "asked Pilate that the bodies might not remain." But they "asked" for something rather different—"that their legs might be broken and they might be taken away." The sentence does not give grounds for supposing that in ordinary cases (where ἵνα is used without a negative and where no ἐρωτᾶν ἵνα follows) John would place a ἵνα clause before the principal verb.

the second clause is *coordinate* with the first. In xiii. 34 "A new commandment give I unto you, *that* (ἵνα) ye love one another—even as (καθώς) I loved you, *that* (ἵνα) ye (ὑμεῖς) also love one another," the second clause is reiterative (though amplified by the definition, "even as").

[2117] This sequence of ἵνα...καθώς...ἵνα ("In order that ye should love—[How love?] Even as I loved, that ye should love") suggests that we should arrange in the same way (as being an answer to the question "How glorify the Father?") xvii. 2 "Glorify thy Son *that* the Son may glorify thee—*even as* thou gavest unto him authority over all flesh, *that* all that thou hast given to him, he may give unto them life eternal." According to this view, we may briefly paraphrase the latter part of the sentence thus, "[How say I 'that the Son may glorify thee'? I mean] that the Son may glorify thee by giving to others even as thou hast given to him." It is implied that the Father is the Supreme Giver and that the supreme authority consists in "giving." Moreover the highest glorifying of the Father consists in giving. Whosoever gives to others, as from the Father, gives what he has received from the Father, and glorifies the Father in the hearts of those who "see his good works and glorify his Father who is in heaven[1]." Nearly the same sense might be obtained (but not in such accordance with Johannine style) by making the second ἵνα, not parallel with the first, but dependent on ἔδωκας, and by taking καθώς as, in effect, καὶ γάρ, "for indeed": "Glorify thy Son, that the Son may glorify thee: *for indeed* thou hast given all authority to him *in order that* he may give life to others [and that he may thus glorify thee]." A third arrangement, to take the second ἵνα clause as grammatically subordinate to the first ("that he may glorify thee... that he may give unto them eternal life") would be quite contrary to all Johannine thought as well as to the interpretation of the sequence in xiii. 34.

[2118] A similar sequence of ἵνα, καθώς, and ἵνα, but followed by a third ἵνα, is in xvii. 20—1 "But not about these alone do I pray but also about them that are to believe through their word in me, *that* all may be one—*even as* (καθώς) thou, Father, in me, and I in thee, *that* [*I say*] they also may be in us[2], *that* the world may

---

[1] Mt. v. 16.
[2] [2118 a] xvii. 21 (R.V.) "That they also may be *in us*," A.V. has "That they also may be *one in us*," reading ἵνα καὶ αὐτοὶ ἐν ἡμῖν ἓν ὦσιν, with ℵAC²L.

believe that thou didst send me," where the second ἵνα clause appears to be reiterative, and coordinate with the first, while the third ἵνα clause is subordinate. The same sequence, but perhaps not the same connexion, occurs in xvii. 22—3, which, if arranged like xvii. 20—1, would run thus, "And I too have given to them the glory thou hast given to me *that* they may be one—*even as* (καθώς) we (ἡμεῖς) [are] one, I in them, and thou in me, *that* they may be perfected into one, *that* the world may recognise that thou didst send me and didst love them even as thou didst love me." The sense, however, demanded in the latter passage seems to require "I in *thee*" [not "*them*"] "and thou in me"—if the words are to be arranged thus. If the words are not corrupt, it seems necessary to punctuate xvii. 22—3 as W.H., with no pause before καθώς: "*that* they may be one *even as* we [are] one, I in them and thou in me, *that* [I say] they may be perfected into one." But, even taken thus, the words seem to shew a want of parallelism. We seem to need either (1) "that they may be one...[namely] I in them and *they* in me," or (2) "even as we are one, [namely] I in *thee* and thou in me." The present text seems to confuse (1) and (2)[1]. If

---

SS has a blank in the MS. "may be [   ] that the world may believe." Burk. suggests "a possible restoration" meaning "united." On κἀγώ see **2127 b**.

[1] **[2118 b]** The passage may have been confused at an early date owing to (1) its various possibilities of connexion, (2) the juxtaposition of ⲉⲛ meaning "in" and ⲉⲛ meaning "one," (3) doctrinal controversies as indicated by Epiphanius (*Haer*. lxix. 19 and 69, 743 A and 793 B). Clem. Alex. quoting xvii. 21—23 as "gospel" and as "the Lord's utterance," says (140) "Ἕνα μὲν αὐτὸν [*i.e.* τὸν Θεόν] λέγει, "ἵνα πάντες ἓν ὦσι καθὼς σύ, πάτερ, ἐν ἐμοί, κἀγὼ ἐν σοί· ἵνα καὶ αὐτοὶ ἐν ἡμῖν ἓν ὦσι......ἵνα ὦσιν ἕν, καθὼς ἡμεῖς ἕν, ἐγὼ ἐν αὐτοῖς καὶ σὺ ἐν ἐμοί, ἵνα ὦσι τετελειωμένοι εἰς ἕν." But in the whole of this quotation there is nothing that contains a statement that "God is one," unless in σύ, πάτερ, ἐν and σὺ ἐν, Clement read ἕν for ἐν. ἐν ἐμοί might perhaps be taken to mean "one with me," as εἷς is used with a dat. by Plutarch (*Mor*. 1089 A) "having drunk from one and the same cup with [that of] Epicurus (ἐκ μιᾶς οἰνοχόης Ἐπικούρῳ πεπωκότες)." Origen uses ἓν ἅμα in connexion with the passage, (*Exhort. ad Mart.* 39) "Become worthy *of becoming one with* (τοῦ ἓν γενέσθαι ἅμα) Son and Father and Holy Spirit, according to the Prayer of the Saviour saying '*As I and thou are one* (Ὡς ἐγὼ καὶ σὺ ἕν ἐσμεν) *that they may be* (?) *one with us* (ἵνα καὶ αὐτοὶ ἐν ἡμῖν ἓν ὦσι, where "deest ἕν in edd. Wetst. et Ruaei").'" Here the last words may mean "in us" or "one in us," or—if ἕν takes a dat., like τὸ αὐτό—"one and the same with us." So Origen speaks of (*Cels*. viii. 12) τὸ Ἐγὼ καὶ ὁ πατὴρ ἕν ἐσμεν, καὶ τὸ ἐν εὐχῇ εἰρημένον ὑπὸ τοῦ υἱοῦ τοῦ θεοῦ ἐν τῷ, Ὡς ἐγὼ καὶ σὺ ἕν ἐσμεν.

[2118 c] Although the text of Clement, in the extract given above, now quotes Jn xvii. 21—3 as in A.V., it is not at all certain that he did so in the original text

the text is correct, the best plan will be to take "I in them and thou in me" as an appositional clause explaining the meaning of "*one*" in "that they may be *one*."

[2119] The underlying thought is, perhaps, as Clement says, that "one" means "God," and that the indwelling of God is the sole cause of unity. But how can God the Father dwell "in" men? Only if the Son dwells "in" men. If the Son dwells "in" men, and the Father dwells "in" the Son, it follows (spiritually as well as logically) that God the Father dwells in men, which means also that unity dwells in them, so that they are one. Probably this is the meaning: but the precise text and the precise grammatical explanation of it, must, at present, be given up as unascertainable.

[2120] The following instance has been placed last, out of order, owing to its special character, xv. 16 "Ye chose not me, but I chose you, and set you [in the vineyard] *that* (ἵνα) ye might go [the] way [that I go] (1659—60) and [that ye] might bear fruit and [that] your fruit might abide—*that* (ἵνα) whatsoever ye ask the Father in my name he may give you." "Fruit," as always in John[1], means the vintage or harvest of souls, which elsewhere the Apostles are said to

---

of his work. A long extract would naturally be conformed by scribes to the canonical text. They would take more pains about it than about a short quotation or allusion. Origen (*De Princip.* i. 6) quotes xvii. 22, 23 correctly, but, later on, he mixes up xvii. 24, 21, 22, giving, as part of the quotation (*ib.* ii. 3. 5) " and that, *as I and thou are one*, these also may be *one in us* (? one with us)," and, later still, (*ib.* iii. 6. 1) "and that *as thou and I are one*, they also may be one in (?) us," where Jerome confirms Rufinus in his translation of this quotation of Origen's (Clark transl. vol. ii. p. 264). Epiphanius, too, quotes as a saying of Jesus (*Haer.* 743 A) "and the saying, '*The two of us are one, that they also may be one*' (καὶ ὅτι, Οἱ δύο ἓν ἐσμεν ἵνα καὶ αὐτοὶ ἓν ὦσιν)" and (*ib.* 793 A) "Make them that they may be in me (? one with me) as *I also and thou are one* (ποίησον αὐτοὺς ἵνα ὦσιν ἐν ἐμοὶ ὡς κἀγὼ καὶ σὺ ἓν ἐσμεν)" and (*ib.* B) "the two of us are one (οἱ δύο ἓν ἐσμεν)."

[2118 *d*] xvii. 22—3 is thus given by W.H....ἵνα ὦσιν ἓν καθὼς ἡμεῖς ἕν, ἐγὼ ἐν αὐτοῖς καὶ σὺ ἐν ἐμοί, but by R.V. "that they may be one, even as we [are] one; I in them and thou in me," SS begins a new sentence at xvii. 23 thus: "...that they may be one even as we are one. *I shall be with them and thou with me*," introducing the new sentence with "I." Similarly Migne prints both *a* (which has "Et ego in illis") and *b* and *f* ("Ego in eis"). Many Gk and Lat. authorities ins. ἐσμεν before ἐγώ. All these facts indicate early differences of connexion. It may be worth noting that *a*, *b*, and *f*, have (at the end of xvii. 22) "sicut *et* nos," *e* "quomodo *et* nos"—facts that suggest confusion between καθως, και ως, and ως και.

[1] [2120 *a*] iv. 36, xii. 24, xv. 2—16. Comp. Rom. i. 13. To an Apostle, it was "gain" to die and be with Christ, but it was (Phil. i. 22) "fruit" to live and gain souls for Him.

"reap," but here they are said to "bear" it as a vine-branch bears its clusters[1].

[2121] The question is, Why does not the sentence end with "that your fruit might abide," *i.e.* that the Church of Christ might be spread? Is not that worthy to be the ultimate object? Is it not bathos to say to Apostles "*in order that* (ἵνα) the Church of Christ may be spread—*in order that* (ἵνα) your prayers may be answered"? It certainly would be bathos if we did not assume the last words to mean "in order that your prayers for more fruit and for more gaining of souls may continually be answered." Thus taken, the clause is not bathos. It reminds the Apostles that the more they succeed, the more they must remember that their success depends on God's answer to their prayers, and—since divine answer to human prayer depends on human unity with divine will—on the oneness of their will with His. According to this view, the meaning is, "*That* ye may save souls—*that* [*I say*] your prayers for the souls of men may ever be heard[2]."

(x) **Καθώς**

(a) Suspensive

[2122] Καθώς, when suspensive, keeps the reader's attention in suspense till he reaches the principal verb later on, *e.g.* "*even as* I... so do ye"; when supplementary or explanatory, it follows the verb ("Do ye...*even as* I"). Καθώς is never used suspensively in Matthew. Luke uses it thus thrice in the Double Tradition, where the parallel Matthew has ὥσπερ etc.[3] John has suspensive καθώς

---

[1] [2120 b] It is hardly possible that φέρητε can mean "carry home as vintagers." Apart from other reasons, the freq. καρπὸν φέρει in the context applied to (xii. 24) the grain of wheat, (xv. 2, 4, 5) vine-branches, precludes this.

[2] [2121 a] Comp. 1 Jn v. 15—16 "If we know that he heareth us whatsoever we ask, we know that we have the petitions that we have asked of him. If any man see his brother sinning a sin not unto death, he shall ask...." In xv. 16, if the 2nd ἵνα is subordinate to the 1st, the meaning is "*in order that* by saving souls, ye may acquire apostolic strength *in order that* your prayers for souls may be still more completely heard." This would be in accordance with the law, "He that hath, to him shall be added." So, he that gains "talents" for his Master, may be said to gain them "in order that" he may gain more. But the coordinate interpretation is more in accordance with Johannine usage.

[3] [2122 a] Lk. vi. 31 καθὼς (Mt. vii. 12 πάντα οὖν ὅσα ἐὰν) θέλετε......ποιεῖτε αὐτοῖς ὁμοίως, xi. 30, xvii. 26 καθὼς ἐγένετο......(Mt. xii. 40, xxiv. 37 ὥσπερ). Mk i. 2—3 may possibly be suspensive. Lk. xvii. 28 has ὁμοίως καθὼς.......

about a dozen times, always in Christ's words, and mostly indicating a *correspondence* between the Father and the Son, or between the Son and those whom the Son sends¹.

(β) Followed by καί or κἀγώ in apodosis

[2123] "*Even as*" in protasis naturally prepares the way for "*precisely so*," "*altogether so*," "*al(l)so*" in apodosis ("*even as* you do, he *also* will do"). In the Johannine Gospel, exhibiting the correspondence between the Father and the Son, as proclaimed by the latter, and between the Son and the children of the Father, cases of this idiom are necessarily frequent, and, in particular, "*Even as* he [the Father] does...*I also* (κἀγώ) do." In English, there is no ambiguity except that we may not feel quite sure whether "also" is intended to suggest "besides" or "in precisely the same way." But in Greek, where "also" is represented by καί, which regularly means "and," the words will be manifestly liable to ambiguity, if the sense admits of the rendering "*Even as* he does...*and* [*even as*] I do." Καθώς followed by κἀγώ occurs in the following five instances:—

[2124] (1) vi. 57 "Even as the living Father sent me *and I* (κἀγώ) live on account of (διά) the Father, *he also* (R.V. *so he*) that eateth me (καὶ ὁ τρώγων με)—he also [I say] (κἀκεῖνος) shall live on account of me." Here R.V. agrees with A.V. in rendering κἀγώ "*and I*," but Chrysostom and Severus of Antioch both render it "*so I*," and this makes good sense: "Even as the living Father sent me, *so I* live on account of the Father" [i.e. *so I*, *corresponding to His will, live* (2297 foll.) *merely to do His will, or on His account*], "*and* he that eateth me shall [in the same way] live on account of me²."

---

¹ [2122 *b*] Καθώς in i. 23, vi. 31, vii. 38 (? 2129), xii. 14 introduces (or follows) Scripture, and is supplementary, but is suspensive in iii. 14, v. 30, vi. 57 (Chrysost. agst. R.V.), viii. 28, x. 15 (2125—6), xii. 50, xiii. 15, 33, 34, xiv. 27, 31, xv. 4, 9, xvii. 18, xx. 21. In vi. 58, "*Not as* the fathers died [shall ye die]," the verb should probably be supplied *after* οὐ καθώς (as in xiv. 27 οὐ καθὼς ὁ κόσμος δίδωσιν ἐγὼ δίδωμι), and in that case καθώς would be suspensive. In v. 23 it does not introduce Scripture, and it is supplementary; but it may possibly be evangelistic comment, not words of the Lord (2066 *b*).

² [2124 *a*] See Cramer and Chrysost. *ad loc.* ζῶ ἐγὼ οὕτως ὡς ὁ Πατήρ. The words might, in theory, be connected with what precedes: vi. 56—7 ὁ τρώγων μου τὴν σάρκα καὶ πίνων μου τὸ αἷμα ἐν ἐμοὶ μένει κἀγὼ ἐν αὐτῷ, καθὼς ἀπέστειλέν με ὁ ζῶν πατὴρ κἀγὼ ζῶ διὰ τὸν πατέρα. But it would be against the suspensive usage of καθώς, and is in other respects improbable. In the next instance, however, R.V. treats καθώς as non-suspensive.

[2125] (2) Καθώς is taken as explanatory (not suspensive) by R.V. in x. 14—15 "I am the good shepherd; and I know mine own, and mine own know me, *even as* the Father knoweth me, *and I* know the Father; and I lay down my life for the sheep[1]." But the generally suspensive use of καθώς in Christ's words, up to and beyond this point in the Gospel[2], would suggest that it is to be taken as in A.V., "*As* the Father knoweth me, *even so* know I the Father, and I lay down my life for the sheep." It is true that there is an attractive symmetry and equality in a kind of double proportion between four terms in R.V. "*I* know *mine own* and *mine own* know *me*, even as the *Father* knoweth *me* and *I* know the *Father*." Moreover A.V. may have been somewhat influenced by inferior MSS., which alter "mine own know me" into "I am known by mine." But still there is something to be said for the view of Chrysostom, who says that "the knowledge is *not equal*" between the shepherd and the sheep but that it *is* "equal" between the Father and the Son[3].

[2126] According to this view, there would be (one might suppose) a distinct pause after the words "mine own know me," while Jesus is preparing to teach His disciples for the first time what is implied by *personal knowledge*. This has not yet been mentioned by Him, though He has spoken of knowing "concerning the teaching whether it be of God," of knowing "the truth," and even of knowing "that I AM[4]." According to the Greek doctrine, summarised in the epigram at Delphi "Know thyself," the knowledge of one's own nature was the highest knowledge. According to the Synoptic doctrine of Christ, some knowledge of one's own defects (the beam in one's own eye) was but a rudimentary preparation for "seeing clearly" to help one's neighbour. According to the Johannine doctrine, the highest knowledge of all was that knowledge,

---

[1] Ἐγώ εἰμι ὁ ποιμὴν ὁ καλός, καὶ γινώσκω τὰ ἐμὰ καὶ γινώσκουσί με τὰ ἐμά, καθὼς γινώσκει με ὁ πατὴρ κἀγὼ γινώσκω τὸν πατέρα, καὶ τὴν ψυχήν μου τίθημι ὑπὲρ τῶν προβάτων.

[2] [2125 a] Καθώς supplementary—apart from quotations of Scripture (2122 b)—is almost confined to the Last Discourse (2128—32).

[3] Chrys. (Migne) (reading as A.V.) Ἄκουσον τί ἐπήγαγε· Καὶ γινώσκω τὰ ἐμά, καὶ γινώσκομαι ὑπὸ τῶν ἐμῶν......Εἶτα, ἵνα μὴ τῆς γνώσεως ἴσον τὸ μέτρον νομίσῃς, ἄκουσον πῶς διορθοῦται αὐτὸ τῇ ἐπαγωγῇ· Γινώσκω τὰ ἐμά, φησί, καὶ γινώσκομαι ὑπὸ τῶν ἐμῶν. Ἀλλ' οὐκ ἴση ἡ γνῶσις· ἀλλὰ ποῦ ἴση; Ἐπὶ τοῦ Πατρὸς καὶ ἐμοῦ. Ἐκεῖ γάρ, Καθὼς γινώσκει με ὁ Πατήρ, κἀγὼ γινώσκω τὸν Πατέρα.

[4] vii. 17, viii. 28, 32.

or understanding, between the Father and the Son which, in some mysterious way, implied self-sacrifice : " I know mine own and mine own know me. [But what is this 'knowing'? It is a mystery to be perceived through experience, and to be felt and acted on, not to be expressed or comprehended in mere words]—Even as the Father knoweth me *so* I too know the Father and [this knowledge is the reason why] I lay down my life for the sheep."

[2127] (3) In xv. 9 (R.V.) "*Even as* the Father hath loved me, *I also* (κἀγώ) have loved you : abide ye in my love¹," (A.V.) "*As* the Father hath loved me *so* have I loved you," W.H. txt places only a comma before "abide," so that the meaning would be "Even as the Father loved me *and I* loved you, abide in (μείνατε ἐν) my love." But, if that were the meaning, might not John have marked the apodosis by inserting "ye also" (μείνατε καὶ ὑμεῖς)²? And is not R.V. (and A.V.) more consonant with the general meaning of κἀγώ in these sentences, and with the fact that John says "abide in *my* love" (not "in *our* love")? (4) In xvii. 18 "*Even as* thou didst send me into the world, *I also* (κἀγώ) sent them into the world," R.V. and A.V. agree in "*As* thou...*even so*...*I*." In (5) xx. 21 "*Even as* the Father hath sent me, *I also* (κἀγώ) send you," R.V. and A.V. have "*As*...*even so send I you*." A comparison of the five instances confirms the view that A.V. is right in (2) and that in each of the five κἀγώ should be rendered "I *also*," or, more idiomatically, "*even so*³ I."

(γ) Supplementary⁴

[2128] Outside Christ's words, supplementary καθώς occurs early in the Gospel in the phrases "even as Isaiah said" and "even as it is written," and, later on, "even as it is written" and "even as is the custom⁵." *But, in Christ's words,* the earlier portion of the

---

¹ Καθὼς ἠγάπησέν με ὁ πατήρ, κἀγὼ ὑμᾶς ἠγάπησα, (marg. ἠγάπησα·) μείνατε ἐν τῇ ἀγάπῃ τῇ ἐμῇ.

² [2127 *a*] Comp. xiii. 15 "For I have given an example to you that, *even as* I have done to you, *ye also* (καὶ ὑμεῖς) may do," xiii. 33 "And *even as* I said to the Jews I say *to you also* (κ. ὑμῖν)" (comp. xiii. 34).

³ [2127 *b*] In xvii. 21 "in order that all may be one—even as thou, Father, in me, (?) I also in thee—in order that they also may be......," the connexion is doubtful (**2132** *a*). It may be an exception. But it is quite consistent with John's style that the words "even as thou [art] in me, so [am] I in thee," may be a parenthetic explanation of the divine unity implied in "One."

⁴ This section includes doubtful cases.

⁵ i. 23, vi. 31, xii. 14, xix. 40.

Gospel affords hardly any instances. The first is v. 23 "that all may honour the Son *even as* they honour the Father." There are some indications (2066 *b*) that this may be evangelistic comment.

[2129] (?) vii. 37—8 "If any man thirst let him come unto me and drink: he that believeth on me—*even as* the Scripture said—rivers from his belly shall flow, of living water[1]." Here it is impossible to tell what passage or passages of Scripture the writer has in view (1722 *k*), and whether "even as" refers to what precedes or follows. Perhaps the most probable "Scripture" is Isaiah's invitation "Ho every one that thirsteth come ye to the waters," with the context describing the fertilising of the wilderness as the result of the Word of God[2]. "He that believeth on me (*i.e.* in the Word)" appears to be parallel to "If any man thirst [*i.e.* for the Word]"; and "the Scripture" may refer to what precedes (*i.e.* the "thirsting" or "believing") as well as to what follows (*i.e.* the "flowing" or diffusion). We cannot confidently say that καθώς here is suspensive or supplementary.

[2130] In xiii. 34 "A new commandment give I unto you that (ἵνα) ye love one another—*even as* I have loved you, that (ἵνα) ye also love one another[3]," R.V. txt and A.V. agree in making καθώς suspensive. If the second "that" had been omitted, καθώς would be manifestly suspensive ("Even as I...so ye"). As it is, after giving the simple precept "that ye love," the writer seems to repeat it emphatically in order to define the nature of the love of the brethren for one another and to shew its correspondence to the love of the Son for them: "that ye love one another—[*I mean*] *even as I* have loved you, that ye also love one another." It would be very weak to take καθώς supplementarily and the last clause as a mere repetition, "that ye love one another as I have loved you—that ye also [I say, likewise] love one another."

[2131] The last quotation, shewing an emphasis laid upon the nature of the New Commandment of Christ, prepares us to find

---

[1] Ἐάν τις διψᾷ ἐρχέσθω πρός με καὶ πινέτω. ὁ πιστεύων εἰς ἐμέ, καθὼς εἶπεν ἡ γραφή, ποταμοὶ ἐκ τῆς κοιλίας αὐτοῦ ῥεύσουσιν ὕδατος ζῶντος.

[2] Is. lv. 1—13.

[3] [2130 *a*] Ἐντολὴν καινὴν δίδωμι ὑμῖν ἵνα ἀγαπᾶτε ἀλλήλους καθὼς ἠγάπησα ὑμᾶς ἵνα καὶ ὑμεῖς ἀγαπᾶτε ἀλλήλους. W.H. have a comma after ἀλλήλους. R.V. marg. gives the last clause as "that ye also may love one another," apparently meaning "*in order that* ye may love" (2094). But that does not interfere with the suspensive nature of καθώς.

Him defining the future love that the brethren are to have for one another by reference to the past love that He has had for them: "love one another *even as I* have loved you." And, as a fact, in the Last Discourse, the hitherto almost invariably suspensive construction is occasionally exchanged for a supplementary one, *e.g.* xv. 10 "If ye keep my commandments ye will abide in my love *even as* I have kept the commandments of the Father and abide in his love," xv. 12 "This is my commandment that ye love one another *even as* I have loved you." Of the same character are the next four instances of καθώς in xvii. 2, 11, 14, 16.

[2132] This is not unnatural. As long as Christ is looking *forward* to His work on earth, He impresses on His disciples the truth that, "*even as*" this or that is in heaven, *so* He *will* do, or *is doing*, this or that on earth. But when His work on earth is on the verge of completion, He refers to it (after the manner of Jewish references to Scripture, "*even as* it is written") mentioning it as an accomplished fact, a new Law for His disciples, "obey *even as* I have obeyed," "love *even as* I have loved." And this view prevails in the Last Discourse except when He is looking forward to the future on earth, not now for Himself, but *for His disciples* (xvii. 18 and xx. 21), "Even as the Father hath sent me *I also* send you"—which is the last instance of all[1].

(xi) **Καί**

(*a*) Καί in narrative (Hebraic)

[2133] The opening words of the Bible exhibit a frequent Hebraic use of "and," *e.g.* "*And* the earth was...*and* darkness was...*and* the

---

[1] [2132 *a*] The occasional difficulty of distinguishing suspensive from supplementary καθώς may be illustrated by xvii. 21—2, punctuated by W.H. thus, ἵνα πάντες ἓν ὦσιν, καθὼς σύ, πατήρ, ἐν ἐμοὶ κἀγὼ ἐν σοί, ἵνα καὶ αὐτοὶ ἐν ἡμῖν ὦσιν, ἵνα ὁ κόσμος πιστεύῃ...κἀγὼ τὴν δόξαν ἣν δέδωκάς μοι δέδωκα αὐτοῖς, ἵνα ὦσιν ἓν καθὼς ἡμεῖς ἕν, ἐγὼ ἐν αὐτοῖς καὶ σὺ ἐν ἐμοί, ἵνα ὦσιν τετελειωμένοι εἰς ἕν, ἵνα γινώσκῃ ὁ κόσμος.... Here W.H. differentiate their punctuation, making the former clause apparently suspensive but the latter supplementary. Some reasons for this migh be alleged, based upon rhythm and possibly on the use of κἀγώ in the first sentence: but the difference is extremely subtle.

[2132 *b*] In the Epistle, καθώς (total 9) is sometimes suspensive, *e.g.* ii. 27 "And *even as* he taught you, abide" (**1915** iii *b*); sometimes supplementary, *e.g.* iii. 23 "That we may love one another *even as* he gave commandment." Its most noticeable use is in the phrase "*even as he*," where *He* means Christ, always expressed by ἐκεῖνος (**2382**), in passages bidding Christians do, and be, "*even as*" their Lord (ii. 6, iii. 3, 7, iv. 17).

spirit of God moved...*and* God said...*and* there was light...*and* God saw the light...*and* God divided the light...*and* God called...*and* the darkness he called...*and* there was evening *and* there was morning." Bruder, referring to this use of καί as "in oratione historica ex simplici Hebraeorum narrandi modo[1]," shews, by his tabulations, that John uses it very rarely as compared with any of the Synoptists. The short Gospel of Mark has it more than 400 times[2], John less than 100 times. It may be said that John does not deal much with narrative, but mainly with discourse. That holds good also of Matthew, and in some degree of Luke, so that it does not explain John's abstinence.

[2134] Besides, if we take the first and the last chapters of John, both of which consist almost wholly of narrative, how are we to explain that in the last chapter, consisting of twenty-five verses, Bruder gives the Hebraic καί as occurring only once[3], whereas in the first twenty-five verses of the first chapter we have about eighteen instances? For example, the Prologue begins "...*and* the Word was with God *and* the Word was God...*and* without him was not anything...*and* the life was the light...*and* the light shineth...*and* the darkness apprehended it not." The usage continues even when the writer brings us down from the Word to the testimony of John, "*And* this is the testimony... *and* he confessed *and* he denied not...*and* they asked him...*and* he saith...*and* he answered" etc. The explanation is probably this. In the opening of the Gospel John follows the style of the opening of Genesis, not in affectation, but with a symbolism natural to him, sympathetically describing what was "in the beginning" of spiritual Being, as Genesis describes what went on in the beginning of material creation. But after the Resurrection, when the Apostles are receiving their morning meal before going forth to convert the whole world, Greeks as well as Jews, "all things are become new," and the old-world Hebraic style is thrown aside. The Johannine use of καί in narrative, meaning "and" (as distinct from "also,"

---

[1] [2133 a] He inserts by error καί (for ὅτι) in i. 16 and omits καί in i. 4 καὶ ἡ ζωὴ ἦν. His list refers the reader elsewhere for the special phrases καὶ ἐγένετο, καὶ ἔσται, καὶ ἰδού. But these are not Johannine phrases. If they were included, John's abstinence from καί would appear still more clearly. Some of Bruder's instances might be otherwise classified; but his statistics suffice as a rough test.

[2] [2133 b] Of course, this is in part explained by the predominance of narrative in Mk. Mt. has it about 250, Lk. about 380 times.

[3] xxi. 19 καὶ τοῦτο εἰπὼν λέγει.

"even" etc.) seldom if ever causes ambiguity and calls for no detailed comment. The following sections, which will deal with καί in speech as well as in narrative, will confine themselves almost entirely to cases where the meaning is ambiguous or obscure, or where the precise emphasis is doubtful.

(β) Καί connecting affirmation and negation

[2135] In Hebrew, "*and*" is frequently used where English would use "*and yet*" or "*but.*" John adopts this usage in many cases, especially where one of the clauses connected by "and" has a negative, or a word implying a negative :—i. 10—11 "The world was made through him *and* [*yet*] the world knew him *not*. He came unto his own [house] *and* [*yet*] his own [household] received him *not*," iii. 11—12 "That which we have seen do we witness *and* [*yet*] our witness ye receive *not*....I told you *and* [*yet*] ye believe *not*," iii. 32 "What he hath seen and heard, this he witnesseth, *and* [*yet*] his witness *no one* receiveth," vii. 19 "Hath not Moses given you the law, *and* [*yet*] *none* of you doeth the law?" vii. 30 "They sought therefore to seize him, *and* [*yet*] *no one* laid his hand on him because his hour had not yet come," viii. 49 "I honour my Father *and* [*yet*] ye *dis*honour (ἀτιμάζετε) me" (where ἀ. has a negative force), viii. 54—5 "Of whom ye say that he is your God, *and* [*yet*] ye know him *not*," viii. 57 "Thou art *not* yet fifty years old *and* [*yet*] thou hast seen Abraham?" ix. 30 "Ye know *not* whence he is *and* [*yet*] he hath opened mine eyes," xiv. 9 "Have I been with you so long, *and* [*yet*] knowest thou me *not*, Philip?" xiv. 24 "He that loveth me not keepeth *not* my words *and* [*yet*] the word that ye hear is not mine but the Father's who sent me," xvi. 32 "There cometh a time....and ye shall leave me alone; *and* [*yet*] I am *not* alone, because the Father is with me," xx. 29 "Blessed are they that have *not* seen *and* [*yet*] have believed."

(γ) Καί = "and yet"

[2136] Καί is thus used in some cases where both the connected clauses are affirmative, or affirmatively interrogative ("is it not?"), but the sense implies contrariety: iii. 19 "The light hath come.... *and* [*yet*] men loved the darkness," iv. 20 "Our fathers worshipped in this mountain, *and* [*yet*] ye say that in Jerusalem is the place....," vi. 49 "Your fathers did eat the manna...*and* [*yet*] they died," i.e. *and yet* it did not save them from death, vi. 70 "Did not I choose you the twelve, *and* [*yet*] one of you is a devil?" ix. 34 "Thou wast altogether born in sins *and* [*yet*] thou teachest us!" x. 39 "They [therefore] sought again to seize him, *and* [*yet*] he came forth from their hand," xi. 8 "The Jews but now were seeking to stone thee *and* [*yet*] thou goest thither again!"

[2137] Contrast the Hebraic "*and*," used in the manifestation of the risen Saviour to Mary Magdalene, with the Hellenic "*however*" used in the manifestation to the Seven Disciples:—(1) xx. 14 "And she beholdeth Jesus standing *and* [*yet*] knew not that it was Jesus," (2) xxi. 4 "Jesus stood on the shore; the disciples did not *however* (οὐ μέντοι) know that it was Jesus."

[2138] Perhaps the construction with "*and*" is sometimes preferred by John because he wishes to emphasize the mystery of the ways of Providence. At all events, on two occasions, after saying that people wished to seize Jesus, or that He was teaching in the Temple, (vii. 30, viii. 20) "*and* no man" arrested Him, he adds "*because his hour had not yet come*." But elsewhere, when there is no such reference to the "hour," he does not use the Hebraic construction: vii. 44 "Now some wished to seize him, *but* [*in spite of that*] (ἀλλ᾽) no man laid hands on him."

[2139] Whatever his motive may be, the statistical fact is undeniable that the phrase "*and no one*" (καὶ οὐδείς) (unbroken by intervening words) is not often (perhaps only thrice) used by John in what we should call its natural sense, *i.e.* additively or consecutively, *e.g.* "My Father...is greater than I, *and no one* is able to snatch them out of my Father's hand[1]." More frequently (about six times) it may mean "*and yet* no one."

[2140] The same rule does not apply so frequently to the Johannine use of "*and not*," which is used in varied contexts, *e.g.* "A little while *and* ye behold me *not*," "They have taken the body of the Lord *and* we know *not* where they have laid him,"

---

[1] [2139 *a*] Jn x. 29. The text and the translation are doubtful (see **2496** *b*). The preceding context has the words (x. 28) "they shall assuredly not be lost... *and no one* (καὶ οὐ...τις) shall snatch them out of my hand." The other instances are viii. 33, xvii. 12. On iii. 13 see **2141**. [In xvi. 22 "*and* your joy *no one* taketh," the phrase is broken by the intervening words.] In xvi. 5 the meaning may well be "You are full of sorrow at the thought of my departure *and yet not one of you* (καὶ οὐδεὶς ἐξ ὑμῶν) asks me whither I am departing." "*And nothing*" occurs thus in vii. 26 "Is not this he that they seek to kill? And yet (καί) see! he speaketh openly *and nothing* (καὶ οὐδέν) do they say to him." It might be fairly maintained that the "yet" implied in the preceding καί runs on to the second καί.

"Thou knowest all things *and* hast *not* need," "Ye have neither seen him *and* ye have *not* his word abiding in you." Still, the instances in which "*and not*" is, or may be, adversative, slightly exceed the non-adversative¹. Nor is it fanciful to say that this curious Johannine characteristic reflects the writer's view of the world —its double nature of light and darkness, its disappointments, incongruities, and pathetic paradoxes, which he feels to be often expressible better by an "*and*" than by a coarse, commonplace, obtrusive "*but*": "He was in the world *and*—the world knew him not," "He came unto his own, *and*—his own received him not."

(δ) Special instances of καί = "and yet"

[2141] This general preponderance of adversative meaning must weigh in the interpretation of particular passages of which the meaning is disputed, *e.g.* i. 5 "The light shineth in the darkness *and* [*yet*] —the darkness apprehended it not" (1443, 1735 *e* foll.) [instead of "*and* the darkness overcame it not"]. In iii. 13 "If I told you earthly things and ye believe not, how shall ye believe [*i.e.* ye will assuredly *not* believe] if I tell you heavenly things? *And* [*yet*] *no man* hath ascended into heaven except him that descended out of heaven...," the meaning appears to be, "Ye will *not* believe *and yet* the truth is told you by him who alone knows the truth." In v. 39—40 ("*Ye search* the Scriptures, because ye think to have in them eternal life, and they are they that bear witness concerning me, *and* [*yet*] ye have *no* desire (καὶ οὐ θέλετε) to come unto me that ye

---

¹ [2140 *a*] This conclusion is reached by reference to οὐ in Bruder (1888) and by examining instances of καὶ οὐ. An examination of the same phenomena, under the same heading, in Luke, reveals very different results. In the first place, John uses οὐ more frequently than Luke does in the proportion of about 4½ to 2⅜— a testimony to John's predilection for contrasts and opposites. In the next place, whereas John exhibits this predilection even more in his Prologue than in the rest of his Gospel, Luke does not use καὶ οὐ adversatively till the end of his sixth chapter in the words of Christ, "Why call ye me Lord, Lord, *and* [*yet*] do not the things that I say?" Subsequently he uses it fairly often, mostly in words of Christ, or in parables, or in passages where he follows the Synoptic Tradition, especially in such antitheses as "They desired to see *and* [*yet*] they saw not," "He came seeking *and* [*yet*] he found not," "They shall seek *and* [*yet*] they shall not be able to find" etc.

[2140 *b*] In his first six chapters Luke freely uses the additive "*and* not," i. 7 "*and* they had *no* child," ii. 43 "*and* his parents knew *not*," ii. 50 "*and* they understood *not*," iv. 2 "*and* he ate *nothing*." Later on, in Luke's adversative instances, there is probably not one that presents any ambiguity.

may have life ") "ye search...and" is more probably correct than "*Search...and*" (**2439** (i)).

[**2142**] In vii. 27—8, the Jews first declare that they know the origin of Jesus, implying that consequently He cannot be the Messiah, "But [as for] this [man] we know whence he is, whereas (δέ) the Messiah—when he comes, no man is to know whence he is." Jesus replies, apparently *repeating their assertion of knowledge* as an exclamation of His own, and shewing its falsity: "(lit.) Both me ye 'know' and ye 'know' whence I am! *And* [*yet*] I have not come from myself, but he that sent me is true, whom ye know not," *i.e.* "Ye say ye know my origin, *and yet* I come from Him who is Truth whom ye know not[1]."

[**2143**] In x. 35 "If he [David] called them gods...and [if] the Scripture cannot be broken," the meaning might be "and [if nevertheless, in spite of so difficult a meaning] the Scripture[2] cannot be annulled." But οὐ, before δύναται, may be regarded as ἀ in ἀδύνατος, and καὶ οὐ δύναται may be regarded as differing little from a parenthetic ἀδύνατον δέ. And this perhaps is the best view: "If the Psalmist called *them* gods—and [all know that] the Scripture cannot be annulled—how can ye accuse me?"

[**2144**] In some cases the choice between "*and*" and "*yet*" may be called a mere matter of taste, as in the following:—

Mt. vi. 26 (A.V.)	Lk. xii. 24 (A.V.)
"...they sow not neither do they reap...*yet* (καί) [R.V. *and*] your heavenly Father feedeth them."	"...they neither sow nor reap... *and* (καί) [R.V. *and*] God feedeth them."

Isaiah vi. 9

R.V.	LXX and Mt. xiii. 14 (R.V.)
"Hear ye indeed *but* (Heb. *vaw*, "*and*") understand not."	"By hearing ye shall hear *and* (comp. Acts xxviii. 26 "*and*") shall in no wise understand."

---

[1] [**2142** *a*] Ἀλλὰ τοῦτον οἴδαμεν πόθεν ἐστίν· ὁ δὲ χριστὸς ὅταν ἔρχηται οὐδεὶς γινώσκει πόθεν ἐστίν. Ἔκραξεν οὖν...λέγων Κἀμὲ οἴδατε καὶ οἴδατε πόθεν εἰμί· καὶ ἀπ' ἐμαυτοῦ οὐκ ἐλήλυθα, ἀλλ' ἔστιν ἀληθινὸς ὁ πέμψας με, ὃν ὑμεῖς οὐκ οἴδατε. "Both me do ye know" is intended to reproduce the ambiguity of the original which may be either exclamatory or interrogative. Οἴδατε repeats οἴδαμεν ironically. Comp. ix. 29—30 "'*We know not*....' '*Ye know not*...!'"

[2] On ἡ γραφή, see **1722** *k*.

[2145] Apart from all questions of taste it is certain that our Lord, speaking in Aramaic, used the ambiguous *vaw*, capable of meaning "and" or "and yet," and certain also that any Greek translators of Aramaic Christian traditions or of Hebrew Gospels would have the alternative of rendering *vaw*, when used in the latter sense, either literally by καί or freely by words meaning "but," "however" etc. There results a reasonable probability that John, writing many years after the circulation of the Synoptic Tradition, which seldom uses the Hebraic καί in the sense "and yet," deliberately resorted to it as one of many means of forcing his readers to reflect on the many-sidedness of the Lord's doctrine and on the occasional inadequacy of the letter of the earliest Gospels to reproduce the living word. Whatever may have been his motive, or motives, the fact remains that he uses—with a frequency and boldness unparalleled in the Synoptists—the Greek additive conjunction in a non-Greek adversative fashion to introduce adversative clauses with a suddenness that heightens the sense of paradox, thus: v. 43 "I have come in the name of my Father *and*—ye do not receive me," v. 44 "How can ye believe, receiving glory from one another *and*—the glory that comes from the only God ye do not seek?" vi. 36 "Ye have both (καί) seen me *and*—ye do not believe," vii. 36 "Ye shall seek me *and*—ye shall not find."

(ε) Καί introducing an exclamation

[2146] Καί occasionally introduces an exclamation that may be treated as a question, implying incongruity with a previous statement: ii. 20 "This temple was built in forty-six years: *and* [*yet*] thou (emph.) (καὶ σύ) in three days wilt raise it up!" viii. 57 "Thou art not yet fifty years old, *and* [*yet*] thou (unemph.) hast seen Abraham (emph.) (καὶ 'Α. ἑώρακας; marg. καὶ 'Α. ἑώρακέν σε)!" xi. 8 "The Jews but now were seeking to stone thee, *and* [*yet*] again thou (unemph.) goest thither[1]!"

---

[1] [2146 a] In i. 16 "From his fulness did we all receive, *and* grace for (ἀντί) grace," the καί does not mean "namely," or "that is to say," but "and, what is more," "and indeed," or "yea" (see ἀντί, **2284—7**). There is probably no instance in Jn where καί means "namely." "Receive" is used absolutely (comp. **1315** and *Aboth* i. 3, 4, 7 etc.), and καί introduces a new statement about the nature of the reception.

(ζ) Καί meaning "also"

[2147] Καί *before* a noun or pronoun, corresponding to our "also" *after* a noun or pronoun, is sometimes used by John to predicate again, what has been predicated before, about a different person or thing[1]. Where "not only" precedes[2], attention is called to "*also*," and there is no ambiguity or obscurity. But the meaning is liable to be missed in passages where the previous predication is implied (not expressed) or expressed at a considerable interval, *e.g.* vii. 3 "Depart to Judaea that thy disciples *also* (ἵνα καὶ οἱ μ. σου) may behold thy works," *i.e.* "Here in Galilee, among thy countrymen and kinsfolk, thou hast no disciples worth mentioning: go to Judaea, where thou hast disciples, that they *also* may behold thy works[3]." In xii. 10 "But the chief priests took counsel that they might kill Lazarus *also*," the reference is to xi. 53, the meaning being, in effect, "I have said above (xi. 53) 'From that day forth therefore they took counsel that they might kill him [Jesus]': now I say that they included Lazarus *also* in their plans[4]."

(η) Καί in Apodosis after ἅ, εἰ, καθώc etc. in Protasis.

[2148] This construction is frequent in John because he dwells on the principle of *correspondence* between the visible and the invisible, between the incarnate Son below and the Father above: v. 19—26 "For what things soever he [*i.e.* the Father] doeth, these *the Son also* (καὶ ὁ υἱός) likewise (ὁμοίως) doeth.... For as the Father... raiseth up, so (οὕτως) *the Son also* (καὶ ὁ υἱός) quickeneth.... For as the Father hath life in himself so (οὕτως) to the *Son also* (καὶ τῷ υἱῷ) gave he to have life in himself," viii. 19 (comp. xiv. 7) "If ye knew

---

[1] [2147 *a*] This construction is most freq. in Lk. In Jn it is about as freq. as in Mt.

[2] [2147 *b*] "Not only," οὐ, or μή, μόνον (adv.), Jn v. 18 before verb, οὐ μόνον ἔλυε, elsewhere before noun, xi. 52 οὐχ ὑπὲρ τοῦ ἔθνους μόνον, comp. xii. 9, xiii. 9, xvii. 20. This precise constr. (Bruder) does not occur in the Synoptists exc. Mt. xxi. 21. When Mt. iv. 4, Lk. iv. 4 quote Deut. viii. 3 "Not by bread alone," they have οὐκ ἐπ' ἄρτῳ μόνῳ (adj.) (as LXX). In Jn xi. 52—xvii. 20, οὐ and μόνον (adv.) are always separated, "*not* for the nation *alone*," "*not* because of Jesus *alone*" etc.

[3] [2147 *c*] Comp. Rom. i. 13 "that I might have some fruit in *you also* (καὶ ἐν ὑμῖν)—as also (καθὼς καί) in the rest of the nations," where "in you also" would not have been quite clear unless the writer had added the subsequent words to make it clear.

[4] [2147 *d*] Καί, meaning "also," is preceded by δέ in ii. 2, iii. 23, xviii. 2, 5, 18, xix. 19, 39, xxi. 25 [But in ii. 2 δὲ καί may mean "now both..."].

me, ye would know *my Father also* (κ. τὸν π. μου)," xii. 26 " Where I am there shall be *my servant also* (κ. ὁ διάκονος ὁ ἐμός)[1]."

(θ) Καὶ ὑμεῖc

[2149] Καὶ ὑμεῖς, ὑμᾶς etc., meaning "ye also," "you also" etc., is so frequent in John[2], that the frequency almost suffices of itself to determine the sense in xiv. 19 "...but ye behold me : because (ὅτι) I (emph.) (ἐγώ) live, *ye also* (καὶ ὑμεῖς) shall live." Here R.V. marg. gives "*and* ye shall live." But this,—whether rendered "ye behold me...*and* ye shall live," or "because I live *and* [*because*] ye shall live" —makes very weak sense. R.V. txt makes perfect sense and accords with Johannine usage. In xvi. 21—22 "the woman hath sorrow...*and ye* (R.V.) therefore (οὖν) have sorrow," might, and probably should, be rendered "*ye also* therefore have sorrow," since καί implies correspondence, and not mere addition.

(ι) Καί in Crasis

[2150] Καί is always combined by crasis with ἐγώ (freq.), with ἐμοί (once, xvii. 6), and with ἐμέ (twice, vii. 28, xvi. 32) except in antithesis xv. 24 καὶ ἐμὲ καὶ τὸν πατέρα μου. It is combined with ἐκεῖ in xi. 54, but not in ii. 12, iii. 22, vi. 3. With the masculine ἐκεῖνος it is always combined, except in xix. 35 on which see **2383**. For κἄν, see **2160**.

(κ) Κἀκεῖνοc[3]

[2151] After a subject expressed by a participle, ἐκεῖνος is sometimes used appositionally for emphasis, "*he and no other*," and where καί is prefixed to it, the meaning is "*he also*," or "*he in the same way*," or "*he on his side*" etc. :—vi. 57 "He that eateth me, *he also* (κἀκεῖνος) shall live on account of me," *i.e.* just as I live on account of the Father (see context); xiv. 12 "He that believeth on me, the works that I do shall *he also* (κἀκεῖνος) do," *i.e.* as well as I myself. In vii. 29 "I am from him (παρ' αὐτοῦ) *and he* (emph.) sent me (κἀκεῖνός με ἀπέστειλεν)" the καί is probably additive, and the meaning is that Jesus comes not only from the presence of the Father

---

[1] [2148 a] On the possibility of ambiguity when καί, after a clause with καθώς, may mean "also" or "and," see **2123**, and on καθώς followed by κἀγώ in particular, see **2124—7**.

[2] vii. 47, ix. 27, xiii. 14, 15, 33, 34, xiv. 3, xv. 20. On viii. 38 καὶ ὑμεῖς οὖν... ποιεῖτε, see **2193—4** and **2359**.

[3] [2151 a] Καὶ ἐκεῖνος never occurs exc. in xix. 35, where ℵA read κἀκεῖνος (**2383**). In xvii. 6, ℵA καὶ ἐμοί—here with CD—again differ from W.H. κἀμοί.

but also by His express sending, "and *he, and no other*, sent me¹."
In x. 16 "And other sheep I have, which are not of this fold : *them also* (κἀκεῖνα) must I bring...," the meaning might be (theoretically) "*and them* must I bring," but John's predilection for asyndeton, and the appropriateness of the meaning "also" here, indicate that καί is emphatic, not additive. The only other instance is xvii. 24 "that where I (*emph.*) am *they also* (κἀκεῖνοι) may be together with me (μετ' ἐμοῦ)," *i.e.* "that they, as well as I, may be there"; the phrase μετ' ἐμοῦ suggests that they are to be not only in the same place but "together" in mind and spirit.

(λ) Καί, "also," connexion of

[2152] Καί, "also," before nouns and pronouns, has been discussed above. But καί, "also," before a verb, is sometimes liable to be confused with καί before the subject of the verb. Thus, διὰ τοῦτο καὶ ὑπήντησεν αὐτῷ ὁ ὄχλος might be confused with διὰ τοῦτο ὑπήντησεν αὐτῷ καὶ ὁ ὄχλος. Yet the former means (1) "For this cause the multitude went *also* to meet him," *i.e.* besides doing, or having done, something else, it did this additional act. The latter would mean (2) "But there went to meet him the multitude *also*," *i.e.* the multitude, as well as Christ's disciples, or companions.

[2153] This distinction is ignored by A.V. in xii. 18 διὰ τοῦτο καὶ ὑπήντησεν αὐτῷ ὁ ὄχλος, where A.V. has "for this cause the people *also*." R.V. has "for this cause *also* the multitude," which would naturally mean "for this cause *as well as for other causes*." But the words ought to mean that the multitude, *besides doing other things* (*e.g.* noising abroad the raising of Lazarus) *also*, or *actually*, took the extreme course of organizing a procession in Christ's honour, *i.e.* "went also to meet him," or "actually went to meet him²."

(μ) Καί "also" in viii. 25

[2154] There is great difficulty in viii. 25 "They therefore said unto him, Who art thou? Jesus said unto them, [In] the beginning

---

¹ [2151 *b*] Asyndeton ("He also") is less probable here. If that were the construction, the sentence and its context would mean "I (*emph.*) know him because I (*unemph.*) am from his presence: *he, on his side*, sent me."

² [2153 *a*] Possibly A.V. may have considered that καί represented a distinction between two multitudes, (1) xii. 12 ὁ ὄχλος πολύς, which came *out of* Jerusalem, (2) xii. 17 ὁ ὄχλος ὁ ὢν μετ' αὐτοῦ ὅτε τὸν Λ. ἐφώνησεν...which accompanied Jesus *into* Jerusalem, and which is said to have (*ib.*) "testified." John does distinguish between these two multitudes. But καί here has nothing to do with emphasizing the distinction.

whatever I also speak unto you (τὴν ἀρχὴν ὅτι καὶ λαλῶ ὑμῖν, punctuated by W.H. txt interrog., marg. affirm.)." Chrysostom's explanation is as follows, "Now what he means is to this effect, *Even at all to hear* the words that fall from me ye are unworthy, much more are ye unworthy to understand also who I am[1]." Cramer quotes Cyril thus, "I am justly punished, says [He], because I made *a beginning even of [receiving]* word[s] from you, because I have addressed to [you] aught of the things that know [? ειδοτωΝ ? εοικοτωΝ "that seem likely"] to profit [you] and took counsel [how] to deliver [you], I have been counted thus cheap in your estimation[2]." It will be observed that the two do not agree. Chrysostom apparently takes τὴν ἀρχήν as ὅλως, "at all," but Cyril takes it as "beginning." Chrysostom's interpretation would require οὐ, or τί καί, or some negative context, which is found with τὴν ἀρχήν when it means "at all" ("*never at all,*" "*not at all*" etc.)[3].

[2155] As regards ὅτι, Chrysostom apparently takes it as the neuter pronoun ("that which I even speak," paraphrased by him as "the words that fall from my lips," τῶν λόγων τῶν παρ' ἐμοῦ): Cyril takes it as "because" ("*because* I made a beginning"). Neither of them takes ὅτι interrogatively. Of the instances alleged by Westcott here for interrogative ὅτι, one is probably corrupt, and two are not parallel to the instance in question[4]. Even if the interrogative use in Mark could be proved, it would be alien from Johannine usage (2231 c—e).

---

[1] [2154 a] Ὁ δὲ λέγει τοιοῦτόν ἐστι· Τοῦ ὅλως ἀκούειν τῶν λόγων τῶν παρ' ἐμοῦ ἀνάξιοί ἐστε, μήτι γε καὶ μαθεῖν ὅστις ἐγώ εἰμι.

[2] [2154 b] Cramer *ad loc.* Δίκαια πάσχω, φησὶν, ὅτι καὶ λόγου παρ' ὑμῶν ἐποιησάμην ἀρχήν, ὅτι προσπεφώνηκά τι τῶν εἰδότων (?) ὠφελεῖν, καὶ διασώζειν ἐβουλευσάμην, εὐτελὴς οὕτω λελόγισμαι παρ' ὑμῖν. Perhaps there should be a full stop after ἀρχήν. Cramer also has a comment (resembling Chrysostom's) quoting the text as "τὴν ἀρχὴν ὅ τι καὶ λαλῶ ὑμῖν, πολλὰ ἔχω παρ' ὑμῶν λαλεῖν καὶ κρίνειν."

[3] [2154 c] It is very doubtful whether such a negative could be implied here from the tone of the answer ("[You ask me who I am. I give you no reply. I tell you not] *at all even* that which I say [much less that which I am]").

[2154 d] No negative v.r. is given by Alford. SS (Burk.) has "The chief [is] that I (*emph.*) should speak [myself] with you," *a* "initium quod loquor vobis," *b* "inprimis quia loquor vobis; cum...," *d* "initium quoniam et loquor vobis," *f* "principium quod et loquor vobis," *gat.* and *mm.* "principium, quod loquor," *e* and Vulg. "principium qui et loquor vobis."

[4] [2155 a] In Mk ix. 11, 28, ὅτι is preceded by ἐπηρώτων, and the best translation would probably be an affirmative—ὅτι or λέγοντες ὅτι being simply used to introduce the statement—"They questioned him saying, 'The scribes say Elijah must first come. [How is that?']," "They questioned him saying 'We could not

[2156] If ὅτι is a relative pronoun the meaning would seem to be that Jesus identifies Himself with that which He speaks, *i.e.* with the words which, as He says (xii. 48), "shall judge" those who reject Him. Then, perhaps, the καί may be explained with reference to what precedes—where He has said to the Jews, "If ye believe not that *I am*"—so that the meaning is, "[*I am*] that which I also *speak*." From an ordinary person, this would mean "I am as good as my word." From a prophet, it might mean "I am the messenger of God, nay, the message of God." But coming from the Logos—who is both the Word and the Act of God, the Messenger of righteousness and justice and also the Righteous Judge Himself—it implies a unique and mysterious identity between the Personality and the Word. As John the Baptist says (i. 23) "*I* [am not to be accepted as the son of Zachariah the priest, or on any other personal grounds, but as being] *a voice* (ἐγὼ φωνή)," so Jesus says "I am [not to be accepted as the Son of David, born at Nazareth, or Bethlehem, but as being] that which also I speak from the first," *i.e.* the Logos, as He had spoken it from the first, consistently[1].

(ν) Καί meaning "[indeed], and...?"

[2157] In ix. 36 "*And* who is he, Lord, that (2113) I may believe in him?" the question (uttered by the blind man whom Jesus had healed) follows the words, "Thou believest [dost thou not] in the Son of man?" The man is startled by the unusual

---

cast it out. [How was that?].'" In both cases, the question is implied in the tone, *and in the verb "questioned,"* which makes all the difference. In Mk ii. 7 διαλογιζόμενοι ἐν ταῖς καρδίαις αὐτῶν, Τί οὗτος οὕτως λαλεῖ; W.H. print ὅτι only in marg., and Swete gives, as the authority for it, only B (whose authority is weak on insertion and omission (**2650**) of O) and one cursive. See **2231** *d—e*.

The adv. ἀρχήν (and τὴν ἀρχήν) when meaning "at all" appears always (Steph.) to have a negative context expressed or implied. It is implied in *Clem. Hom.* vi. 11 τί καὶ τὴν ἀρχὴν διαλέγομαι; *i.e.* οὐ δεῖ διαλέγεσθαι. Comp. *ib.* xix. 6. Without a negative, it means "*at the first*," as in Gen. xli. 21, xliii. 18, 20, and Just. Mart. *Apol.* § 10 (*bis*).

[1] [**2156** *a*] So Nonnus, Τίς σὺ πέλεις; καὶ Χριστὸς ἀνίαχεν, ὅττι περ ὑμῖν Ἐξ ἀρχῆς ὀάριζον, ἔχων νήριθμα δικάζειν. This, though probably not an actual utterance of Jesus, may be a Johannine and mystical paraphrase of something expressed differently by the Synoptists, according to whom, Jesus expressed His desire to go back to the "beginning" of things, before the Law of Moses was given "because of the hardness of men's hearts." He also said that His "words" would "never pass away." He claimed for "the Son of man" that He was "Lord also of the Sabbath." Combining these statements we shall arrive at a claim on the part of the Son of man to identify Himself with the Father's Law or Word.

phrase ("believe in the Son of man"), and he craves additional explanation "[Thou sayest this] *and* [thou wilt surely tell me] who is he?" Somewhat similarly in answer to Christ's startling statement about the spiritual disability attendant on riches, the disciples reply, "[Thou sayest this] *and*—who [then] can be saved¹?" Probably, later on, John finds a parallel and a contrast between this question asked by a believer and the question asked by the unbelieving Jews, (xii. 34) "Who is this Son of man?" and the surprise of the former, together with his readiness to believe in what surprises him, brings out clearly the nature of the man's faith. He is ready to believe in anyone that Jesus bids him believe in. In effect—before Jesus had spoken—he already believed, heart and soul, in Jesus as a divine incarnation of kindness and power.

(ξ) Καὶ ἐάν (See also 2513—5 (i))

[2158] In Isaiah x. 22 "For *though* thy people Israel be as the sand...only a remnant shall return," LXX has καὶ ἐὰν γένηται. St Paul, for κ. ἐ. γένηται, has (Rom. ix. 27) ἐὰν ᾖ (A.V. "*though*," R.V. "*if*"). Probably St Paul used ἐάν with the consciousness that the apodosis gave it the meaning "even if," and LXX intended καί to mean "even." In an author like John, much given to asyndeton, there is an antecedent probability (in doubtful cases) that καὶ ἐάν would mean, not "and if," but "*even if.*"

[2159] Καὶ ἐάν occurs as follows: viii. 16 "I judge no man, (R.V.) yea, *and if* I judge (καὶ ἐὰν κρίνω δὲ ἐγώ), my judgment is true" (A.V. "*and yet if* I judge"). Perhaps, "yea, *even if* I judge"; xii. 46—7 (R.V.) "I am come...that whosoever believeth on me may not abide in the darkness. *And if* (καὶ ἐάν) any man hear my sayings and keep them not, I judge him not," better, perhaps, "*Even if* any man hear and disobey, I judge him not"; xiv. 3 (R.V.) "*And if* (καὶ ἐάν) I go and prepare a place for you, I come again, and will receive you...," better, perhaps, "*Even if* (or, *And even if*) I go...[yet] again do I come." There is great

---

¹ [2157 a] Mk x. 26, Lk. xviii. 26 (Mt. xix. 25 τίς ἄρα). So Xen. *Cyrop.* v. 4. 13 "'You are passing over a still greater marvel.' '[*Indeed*] *and* what might that be (καὶ τί δὴ τοῦτ' ἐστίν;)?'" And, in reply to Cyrus's orders as to the drawing up of soldiers for an attack, an officer replies (*ib.* vi. 3. 22) "[*Indeed*] *and* do you think we shall be strong enough (Καὶ δοκοῦμέν σοι, ἔφη, ὦ Κῦρε, ἱκανῶς ἕξειν)...?" Similarly, in English we might have "'Give him what he asks.' '*And* where am I to get it?'" So καὶ πῶς; freq. (Steph. 2305 B).

difficulty about the whole of this passage, but it seems to mean "I should not myself call it going on a journey (πορεύομαι) but going back to the Father (ὑπάγω): however, to use your word, *even if* I do 'go,' yet I will return" (2080—6). In the Epistle, καὶ ἐάν occurs twice. It is used with indic. in 1 Jn v. 15 καὶ ἐὰν οἴδαμεν "and if we know" (see 2515 (i)). R.V. "and if" does not seem adequate to the meaning in 1 Jn ii. 1—2, "I write...that ye sin not. *Grant however that one sin* (καὶ ἐάν τις ἁμάρτῃ) *we have a Paraclete.*" It is not meant that we have no Paraclete if we do not sin. The meaning is, "Even if we do sin [*let us remember that*] we have a Paraclete."

(*o*) Κἄν

[2160] Κἄν occurs four times in John and means "even if" certainly in viii. 14, x. 38, xi. 25, and possibly in viii. 55, (R.V.) "But I know him [*i.e.* the Father]; *and if* I should say (κἂν εἴπω) I know him not, I shall be like unto you, a liar." It is true that κἄν means "*and if*" in Luke, and in the Mark-Appendix[1]; and three Johannine instances are hardly enough to establish the necessity of a similar meaning in the fourth. Yet, having regard to the instances, so far as they go, and to the frequency of asyndeton in John, and to the extraordinary force and abruptness of the thought, the balance of probability inclines slightly toward the latter rendering: "I know him. *Even if* I say I know him not—[what then?] I shall be a liar."

(*π*) Καί...καί, "both...and"

[2161] In vi. 36 "But I said unto you that ye (*unemph.*) have *both* seen [me] and [yet] do not believe," ἀλλ᾽ εἶπον ὑμῖν ὅτι καὶ ἑωράκατέ [με] καὶ οὐ πιστεύετε, A.V. has "ye also," which would require καὶ ὑμεῖς. R.V. omits "*both.*" The word "*both*" increases the abruptness of the paradox, as in xv. 24 (where R.V. inserts it) "they have *both* seen and hated both me and my Father[2]." Possibly

---

[1] [2160 *a*] Κἄν, in Mk v. 28, vi. 56 means "though it were but," *i.e.* "merely," in Mt. xxi. 21, xxvi. 35, "even if." But in Lk. xii. 38, xiii. 9, Mk-App. [xvi. 18], Jas v. 15 (on which see Mayor), it means "and if." This evidence, so far as it goes, favours the view that John would always use the word in one sense as is the case in Mk, Mt., and Lk.

[2] [2161 *a*] In vi. 36, με is om. by almost all authorities exc. BD, prob. because the scribes did not understand that the reference was to vi. 26 "not because ye *saw* signs" combined with vi. 29 "this is the work of God that ye *believe*."

CONJUNCTIONS

R.V. omits it here because it is contrary to English idiom, and because the paradox is expressed by rendering the second καί "*and* [*yet*]." This however does not give the suspensive force of the first καί, which might be freely rendered "*though*" ("*though* ye have seen me *yet* ye do not believe").

[2162] This usage is almost peculiar to John in N.T. Other books use καί...καί to represent (1) the same verb applied to two nouns, *e.g.* "healing *both* the *blind* and the *lame*[1]," or (2) the same noun or pronoun applied to two verbs, *e.g.* "he began *both to do and to teach.*" But these and other instances ("both hungering and thirsting," and even "both to be filled and to be hungry[2]") are unlike the Johannine coupling (with "and [yet]"). Sometimes also John couples, not opposites, but correlatives, or correspondent statements like that of St Paul, "God *both* raised up the Lord *and* will raise up us[3]," where the text suggests that Redemption is one great foreordained plan including past and present. Thus the Voice from Heaven says xii. 28 "I have *both* glorified *and* will again glorify," *i.e.* as it was, so it shall be.

[2163] ix. 37 "Thou hast *both* seen him *and* he that is speaking with thee is he[4]," is the reply of our Lord to the man born blind, asking who "the Son of man" is, in whom he is to believe. Jesus does not at once say, as to the Samaritan woman, "*I that speak unto thee* am he." The words "Thou hast seen him" coming to the blind man from Jesus, who had just made him "see," and whose voice he would recognise, could hardly fail to be clear. The blind man could hardly think of asking, "But of all those whom I have seen since I received sight a few hours ago, which is he?" Perhaps,

---

The former implies that the Jews *had "seen" the Messiah manifested by "signs"*; the latter, that, in spite of this "seeing," they still *did not "believe" and needed to be commanded to "believe."*

[1] [2162 a] Comp. Mk iv. 41 "(?) *both* (R.V. *even*) the wind and the sea," sim. Mt. viii. 27. Luke in the parall. (viii. 25) by a difference of order (καὶ τοῖς ἀνέμοις ἐπιτάσσει καὶ τῷ ὕδατι, not καὶ τ. ἀνέμοις κ. τ. ὕδατι) perh. indicates that he takes καί...καί as "even...and."

[2] [2162 b] Phil. iv. 12 οἶδα καὶ ταπεινοῦσθαι, οἶδα καὶ περισσεύειν is interesting as shewing the Apostle in the act of writing καὶ ταπ. καὶ περισσ. and then changing his mind, inserting οἶδα : as Lightf. says, καὶ ταπεινοῦσθαι was "shaped in anticipation of the καὶ περισσεύειν which follows."

[3] [2162 c] 1 Cor. vi. 14 ὁ δὲ θεὸς καὶ τὸν κύριον ἤγειρεν καὶ ἡμᾶς ἐξεγερεῖ (B ἐξήγειρεν). B's reading would mean that "God *both* raised up the Lord *and* (ipso facto) raised up us," as part of one plan.

[4] Καὶ ἑώρακας αὐτὸν καὶ ὁ λαλῶν μετὰ σοῦ ἐκεῖνός ἐστιν.

therefore, Chrysostom has not chosen the right epithet in calling the clause "obscure[1]." But it is purposely preparatory and incomplete—as though beginning from the physical and passing to the spiritual. As, after the feeding of the Five Thousand, the Saviour says (vi. 63), "The flesh profiteth nothing, the words that *I have spoken to you are spirit and are life*," so, after the healing of the blind man, Jesus does not say, "I that healed thee am he," but describes the Son of man as "He that is *speaking with thee*." He thereby suggests another aspect of the Messiah. He is not only the Healer, but also the Speaker of the words of God[2].

[2164] Καί is not immediately before the verb in xvii. 25 (lit.) "O righteous Father, *both* (καί) the world did not recognise thee—but I (ἐγὼ δέ) recognised thee—and these (καὶ οὗτοι) recognised that thou didst send me." Here the first καί is intended to keep the reader in suspense, aware that the meaning is incomplete[3], and perhaps the sentence starts with the simple antithesis, "*Whereas* (καί) the world did *not...on the other hand* (καί) these *did*." But the sentence is broken by a parenthesis ("but I recognised") and this perhaps suggests the reason why "these did [recognise]," namely, because the Son imparted to the disciples His power of recognition—so that a new connexion is introduced, "but I did *and consequently* these did[4]."

[2165] These words (xvii. 25) resemble—spiritually, though not verbally—the saying in the Double Tradition, "I confess unto thee, O Father...because thou hast hidden these things from the wise... and revealed them unto babes. Yea, Father, for so it hath seemed

---

[1] Chrys. Οὐκ εἶπεν, Ἐγώ εἰμι· ἀλλὰ μέσος ἔτι καὶ ὑπεσταλμένος. Καὶ ἑώρακας αὐτόν. Τοῦτο ἔτι ἄδηλον ἦν· διὸ τὸ σαφέστερον ἐπήγαγεν· Ὁ λαλῶν μετὰ σοῦ, ἐκεῖνός ἐστι. By μέσος he seems to mean "going half way."

[2] Comp. vi. 68 "Thou hast the words of eternal life," which implies "Thou art the Saviour."

[3] [2164 a] As a rule, καὶ ὁ κόσμος, in such a position as this, would mean "*Even* the world," and in some contexts it would make good sense to render it thus, "*Even* the world, even God's own creation, did not know Him"; but this would not be appropriate in a context where "the world" is clearly regarded as an enemy.

[4] [2164 b] See 2162 b on Phil. iv. 12. In Jn xvii. 26, the words καὶ ἐγνώρισα... καὶ γνωρίσω might begin a new sentence (like xii. 28 καὶ ἐδόξασα...καὶ πάλιν δοξάσω) "I have *both* made known...and will make known," and this hypothesis of asyndeton is more in accordance with Johannine style than the hypothesis of καί "*and*" repeated thrice after καί "*both*."

good in thy sight[1]." There, too, the context says that no man knoweth the Father save the Son and he to whom the Son reveals Him. So, we might paraphrase the Johannine "*righteous* Father" as meaning substantially "I confess the righteousness of that which hath seemed good in thy sight." The Johannine antithesis between "the world" and "these" corresponds to the antithesis between "the wise" and "babes." Also the parenthesis "But I knew thee" followed by "and these knew that thou didst send me," suggests—what Matthew and Luke express—that the knowledge of the Father is peculiar to the Son and to those who receive the gift from the Son. The καί in the Fourth Gospel supplies the connexion between "hiding" from the "wise" (*i.e.* "the world" meaning "the worldly") and the revealing unto "babes" (*i.e.* the little ones of Christ, whom the Fourth Gospel calls "these"). The two are parts of one plan. In John, "hiding" and "revealing" are expressed by "not knowing" and "knowing." The thought is the same as in Matthew and Luke.

[2166] In xxi. 24, οὗτός ἐστιν ὁ μαθητὴς ὁ καὶ μαρτυρῶν περὶ τούτων καὶ ὁ γράψας ταῦτα is the reading of B. On the context, see 2169 and 2429—35. It would be against Greek usage to suppose that this means, "he that both testifieth and wrote," ὁ καὶ μαρτυρῶν καὶ γράψας. In B, therefore, we must take the first καί as "also": "This [*i.e.* the beloved disciple above described] is the disciple that *also* [besides seeing the Saviour in the way described above] testifieth concerning these things," *i.e.* he not only saw the Saviour but testifies to what he saw[2]. After these words the evangelist continues, "and the one that wrote these things," making a pause after τούτων and deliberately separating the two statements. As a rule, an apostle would "testify" and his amanuensis or interpreter would write (as in the case of St Paul's Epistles): but in this case the "beloved disciple" did both[3].

---

[1] Mt. xi. 25—7, Lk. x. 21—2.

[2] [2166 *a*] "These things" may perhaps not refer to the whole of the contents of the Gospel, but to the events just described, like ταῦτα in xii. 16 (2621—2): Codex *a* has "de Jesu" and *e* "de ihm," but these are perhaps confusions of "de his," read as "de ihs."

[3] [2166 *b*] Καί would naturally be omitted by scribes before μαρτυρῶν because it would seem to them, if genuine, intended to mean "both": and this it could not mean. If we omit it, the rendering will still be as above, only omitting the emphatic "also."

[2166 *c*] If we adopt the two marginal readings of W.H. and assume [ὁ], in the

[2167]   CONJUNCTIONS

(ρ) Καὶ γάρ

[2167] Καὶ γάρ occurs in John twice. Once αὐτοί intervenes (iv. 45 καὶ αὐτοὶ γὰρ ἦλθον, "for they *also* went") perhaps receiving special emphasis from its intervention (2692). The other instance is iv. 23, "For the Father *also* (καὶ γὰρ ὁ πατήρ) seeketh such for his worshippers (τοιούτους ζητεῖ τοὺς προσκυνοῦντας αὐτόν)," R.V. txt "*for* such doth the Father seek to be h. w.," marg. "*for* such the Father *also* seeketh." This rendering ("for...also") is more probable, here, than "for indeed." Καὶ γάρ may mean "for indeed"—emphasizing the cogency and truth of a causal proposition—*when there is no noun or pronoun that comes close afterwards.* But where there is such a noun or pronoun the force of καί is to emphasize it, as in "*For I also* am under authority*[1]*." Taken thus, the words are appropriate as a reply to the Samaritan woman, whose tone suggests that she may have thought it a mark of weakness in man, much more in God, to "seek," since "seeking" implied want and need[2]. Mark records a saying of the Son about Himself, "*For the Son of man also* (καὶ γὰρ ὁ υ. τ. ἀ.) came to be a minister[3]." John here records a similar saying of the Son about the Father, and with the same conjunction, "*For the Father also* (καὶ γὰρ ὁ π.) seeketh[4]."

On καὶ...δέ see 2076, and on οὔτε...καί see 2258—9.

(σ) Καί omitted between two adjectives

[2168] Such collections of adjectives as we find in the Pastoral Epistles (2 Tim. iii. 2 foll.) "Self-loving, money-loving, boastful, haughty etc." are not to be found in John, where two contiguous

---

second, to be part of the text, the translation will then be "This is the disciple that also testifieth concerning these things, the [disciple] that also wrote...." But the possibilities of combining various readings are so numerous that it is not worth while to enter into further detail.

[1] [2167 a] Mt. viii. 9, Lk. vii. 8. Comp. Mt. xxvi. 73 "for thy speech *also*," i.e. besides other suspicious circumstances, Mk x. 45 "for the Son of man *also*," i.e. He as well as others, not exempting Himself from the duty of common men, Lk. vi. 32 "for sinners *also*," i.e. as well as the righteous, etc.

[2] [2167 b] Christ had said to her "*Give me* to drink" and had then perplexed her by saying that He could *give her* to drink. The evangelist here represents the Son as saying "Give," just as a father might say to his children "Give me your hearts," and just as God is represented in O.T. as saying to Israel "Seek ye my face"—thus "seeking" them—in the hope that they may reply "Thy face, O Lord, will I seek."

[3] Mk x. 45.   [4] Jn iv. 23.

adjectives may always be explained by special circumstances. In xii. 3, νάρδου πιστικῆς (**1736** *d*) (perhaps intended to suggest an inward symbolical meaning) may be taken as a compound noun followed by πολυτίμου. In xvii. 3, σὲ τὸν μόνον ἀληθινὸν θεόν may be illustrated by Rom. xvi. 27 μόνῳ σοφῷ θεῷ, where μόνος perhaps implies (**1895, 2664** *a*) an adjective ("One") and an adverb ("uniquely"). It is characteristic of John that, instead of saying "the last and greatest day of the feast," he should say (vii. 37) "Now on the last day—the great one [too]—of the feast (ἐν δὲ τῇ ἐσχάτῃ ἡμέρᾳ—τῇ μεγάλῃ—τῆς ἑορτῆς)," adding "the great one" as a parenthetical remark[1].

(xii) Μέν, μέντοι

[2169] The Johannine use of μέν is interesting mainly in its bearing on the question whether οἴδαμεν in xxi. 24 may have been taken by Chrysostom as οἶδα μέν, on which point see **2429—35**. Apart from vii. 12 οἱ μὲν ἔλεγον...ἄλλοι [δέ], and xi. 6 τότε μὲν ἔμεινεν ...ἔπειτα μετὰ τοῦτο, it is generally followed by δέ, as in xix. 24 οἱ μὲν οὖν στρατιῶται...ἱστήκεισαν δέ, xix. 32 τοῦ μὲν πρώτου...ἐπὶ δὲ τὸν Ἰ., xx. 30 πολλὰ μὲν οὖν κ. ἄλλα...ταῦτα δέ. In x. 41 Ἰωάνης μὲν σημεῖον ἐποίησεν οὐδέν, πάντα δὲ ὅσα εἶπεν Ἰωάνης περὶ τούτου ἀληθῆ ἦν, the antithesis suggested by the beginning of the sentence is "John on the one hand did no sign, but this man, who was predicted by John, has fulfilled all John's predictions"—but the subject is changed in order to emphasize πάντα. The two remaining instances of μέν are in words of the Lord, xvi. 9 περὶ ἁμαρτίας μέν...περὶ δικαιοσύνης δέ...περὶ (**2077**) δὲ κρίσεως, and xvi. 22 κ. ὑμεῖς οὖν νῦν μὲν λύπην ἔχετε· πάλιν δὲ ὄψομαι ὑμᾶς, where, in strict regularity, the second verb should have continued in the second person ("but hereafter ye shall rejoice"), but the writer passes off to the cause of the future joy.

[2170] Μέντοι occurs nowhere in the Synoptists, but five times in John. In iv. 27 "No one, *however*, said, What seekest thou?" and in xx. 5 "He did not, *however*, enter in," a feeling of reverence is suggested: in vii. 13 "No one, *however*, spake freely about him," the reason is added—"owing to the fear of the Jews." In xii. 42—after having said "they did not believe"—the evangelist says "yet

---

[1] [2168 *a*] Some Latin translators have been perplexed by the Gk article and by taking ἑορτή as feast-day; *a* has "in novissima autem magna die festi Judaeorum," but *b* "in novissimo autem die magno ac solenne," *e* "in die autem novissimo magno die festo," *d* and *ff* "in novissimo autem die (*ff*+ illo) magno diei festi," SS "and on the great day of the feast."

however (ὅμως μέντοι) even of the rulers many believed in him, but owing to [fear of] the Pharisees they did not confess him." In xxi. 4 "Jesus stood on the beach. The disciples, *however*, did not know that it was Jesus" is the only remaining instance[1]. Reviewing the whole, we may say that μέντοι is never used except where the context indicates prevention of some action by fear, or reverence or some mysterious restraint. As bearing on the last instance comp. Lk. xxiv. 16 "But their eyes were holden that they should not know him."

(xiii) "Οπου

[2171] In classical Greek, ὅπου is not used after a definite mention of place, as it is in John, *e.g.* i. 28, "Bethany, beyond Jordan, *where* (ὅπου) John was...," xii. 1 "Bethany, *where* Lazarus was" etc. Compare especially xix. 17—18 "...to the place of a skull called in Hebrew Golgotha, *where* (ὅπου) they crucified him," *i.e.* almost equivalent to, "*and there* they crucified him." This Johannine use is not borrowed from the LXX, where ὅπου is so rare that it is non-occurrent in the Pentateuch, Joshua and Kings. Nor does the Thesaurus give instances of it. But Mark uses it thus four or five times, and Matthew—probably sometimes borrowing from Mark—uses it about thrice[2]. In connexion with the Resurrection, it

---

[1] [2170 a] Out of Jn, it occurs only 2 Tim. ii. 19 ὁ μ. στερεὸς θεμέλιος, Jas ii. 8 εἰ μ. νόμον τελεῖτε βασιλικόν, Jude 8 ὁμοίως μ. καὶ οὗτοι.

[2] [2171 a] Mk ii. 4 τὴν στέγην ὅπου ἦν...τὸν κράβαττον ὅπου ὁ παραλυτικὸς κατέκειτο, (?) iv. 15 οἱ παρὰ τὴν ὁδὸν ὅπου σπείρεται ὁ λόγος, ix. 48 γέενναν ὅπου ὁ σκώληξ αὐτῶν οὐ τελευτᾷ, xvi. 6 see below (2171 e): Mt. xiii. 5 (definite) τὰ πετρώδη ὅπου οὐκ εἶχεν γῆν πολλήν, but Mk iv. 5 (indefinite if καί is inserted) τὸ πετρῶδες [καὶ] ὅπου οὐκ εἶχεν γῆν πολλήν. In Mt. xxvi. 57, ὅπου follows Καιάφαν which implies "the palace of Caiaphas." Mt. xxviii. 6, see below (2171 e).

[2171 b] Mt. vi. 19—20 (Lk. xii. 33) is of a somewhat indefinite nature, and ὅπου in Mk xiv. 14 (Lk. xxii. 11) (Mt. om.) ποῦ ἐστὶν τὸ κατάλυμά μου ὅπου... φάγω, is interrogative, and, so far, indefinite.

[2171 c] "Οπου occurs, in the Acts, only in xvii. 1 Θεσσαλονίκην, ὅπου..., xx. 6 (v. r.) τὴν Τρῳάδα...ὅπου (W.H. οὗ). Lk. uses ὅπου five times, but never as above, unless an exception is to be recognised in Lk. xii. 33 (where Lk. follows Mt. vi. 20) ὅπου κλέπτης οὐκ ἐγγίζει.

[2171 d] The Johannine combinations of ὅπου with εἰμί above, as well as the non-use of εἶμι "go" in N.T., and almost complete absence of εἶμι in O.T., shew that ὅπου εἰμί (not εἶμι) must be read in vii. 34, "where I am" (rep. by the Jews in vii. 36) although the Jews refer to it in vii. 35 as πορεύεσθαι. If the meaning had been where I "go," ὑπάγω or πορεύομαι would almost certainly have been employed (as Jesus frequently uses both). A strong incompatibility is suggested by "where I *am*, there ye cannot come."

occurs in Mark and Matthew in an angelic utterance ("see the place"), but in John in a description of two angels in the tomb[1]. Here Matthew approaches a dependent interrogative, but Mark and John do not.

[2172] John frequently uses ὅπου, with or without a preceding τόπος, to denote that the place now mentioned had already been the scene of some notable action: iv. 46 "Cana...*where* (ὅπου) he had made the water wine," vi. 23 "near the place *where* (ὅπου) they ate the bread," vii. 42 "Bethlehem the village *where* David [once] was," x. 40 "the place *where* John [once] was, at the first, baptizing," xii. 1 "He came to Bethany *where* was Lazarus," *i.e.* "where (as I said above, xi. 1), Lazarus lived, whom Jesus raised from the dead." Had it not been for the other passages quoted above, this last might have been supposed to mean "where Lazarus was" at the time when Jesus "came." In i. 28, a comma should perhaps (2277 a) be inserted after ἦν, thus: "These things came to pass in Bethany beyond Jordan—(lit.) *where John was* (ἦν), baptizing (βαπτίζων)," and ἦν may mean "was and had been for some time" (2648). Under ordinary circumstances we should translate ὅπου ἔκειτο in xx. 12, "*where lay* the body of Jesus," but it is shewn by the context to mean "*where it had lain*[2]."

(xiv) Ὅπως

[2173] This (1695) occurs frequently in Matthew and Luke, but only once in Mark (iii. 6 "that they might destroy (ἀπολέσωσιν) him") and once in John (xi. 57 "that they might take (πιάσωσιν) him"). Matthew's parallel to Mark iii. 6 agrees with Mark verbatim, but Luke's differs[3]. Elsewhere, Matthew uses ὅπως (but Luke never)

---

[1] [2171e] Mk xvi. 6 ἴδε, ὁ τόπος ὅπου ἔθηκαν αὐτόν, Mt. xxviii. 6 ἴδετε τὸν τόπον ὅπου ἔκειτο, Jn xx. 12 θεωρεῖ δύο ἀγγέλους...ὅπου ἔκειτο τὸ σῶμα τοῦ Ἰησοῦ.

[2] [2172 a] A "where-clause," *e.g.* "Etam where (ἔνθα) Samson lived," is common in the *Onomasticon* of Eusebius, and such clauses are natural in works about sites of interesting scenes. But in John something more than this is apparent in the emphasis laid by him on the fact that the public work of Christ begins, and almost ends, in two places of the same name, Bethany. There is, perhaps, a feeling that history repeats itself and that things appear to move in a circle even when they are really going on, as when the Son (vi. 62) "goeth up *where he was before*." Comp. i. 28 ὅπου ἦν ὁ Ἰ. βαπτίζων and x. 40 ὅπου ἦν Ἰ. τὸ πρῶτον βαπτίζων.

[3] [2173 a] Mt. xii. 14. Lk. vi. 11 has διελάλουν πρὸς ἀλλήλους τί ἂν ποιήσαιεν τῷ Ἰησοῦ. On πιάζω see **1723** c and *Ox. Pap.* 812 (B.C. 5) πεπίασται Λοκρίων.

in similar contexts[1]. These facts suggest that ὅπως was current in Mark-Matthew traditions about the plots of the Jews "*in order to* destroy, or ensnare, Jesus," and that Luke avoided, while John adopted, this method of expression. See **2693**.

(xv) ″Οτι[2]

(*a*) ″Οτι (1) suspensive, (2) explanatory

[**2174**] ″Οτι is used by John much more frequently than by Luke, and somewhat more frequently than by Mark and Matthew taken together. One reason is, that John deals largely with causes, and uses ὅτι very frequently in the sense "because." In theory, ambiguity might arise from the fact that λέγω, πιστεύω, θεωρέω etc., followed by ὅτι, might mean "I say, believe, behold, *that*," or, "I say, believe, behold, *because*." In practice, however, such ambiguity, though not infrequent, is not very serious, except perhaps in one important passage to be considered later on—because John adheres to regular Greek usage, which would not sanction the conjunction after such verbs, except to mean "*that*," introducing the object of the verb.

[**2175**] A more serious cause of ambiguity is that ὅτι—like καθώς (**2122—32**)—may be used (1) suspensively ("*because* I live ye shall live") as well as (2) explanatorily ("ye shall live" [why?] "*because* I live"). The former construction is comparatively rare. Where it occurs, "because" ought to be, so to speak, protected from the preceding sentence by a δέ or other conjunction as in Gal. iv. 6 "*But because* (ὅτι δέ) ye are sons, God hath sent forth his Spirit." Else, "because ye are sons" might be connected with the last words of the preceding sentence. In the following passage the first ὅτι is *certainly* suspensive after οὕτως: the second ὅτι is probably suspensive—but *not certainly* (owing to the absence of a conjunction) Rev. iii. 16—17 " Thus (οὕτως), *because* (ὅτι) thou art lukewarm…I am about to spew thee out of my mouth. *Because* (ὅτι) thou sayest 'I am rich…' and knowest not…, I counsel thee to buy…." Here the construction might be "*Because* thou art lukewarm I purpose to spew thee out, *because* [*I say*] thou sayest…," and "I counsel"

---

[1] [**2173** *b*] Mt. xxii. 15 ὅπως αὐτὸν παγιδεύσωσιν ἐν λόγῳ, xxvi. 59 ὅπως αὐτὸν θανατώσωσιν. Blass (p. 211) on Jn xi. 57 says "for the sake of variety"; but the repetitions of ἵνα in **2116—20** are against this view.

[2] ″Οταν is discussed under Tense, Aorist and Present Subjunctive (**2531—5**).

might begin a new sentence; and the English Hexapla prints the words thus in all versions after that of 1380 A.D.[1].

[2176] The suspensive use of ὅτι in the Greek Testament is first found in Genesis iii. 14 "And the Lord God said unto the serpent, *Because* (ὅτι) thou hast done this, cursed art thou," and iii. 17 "Unto Adam he said, *Because* (ὅτι) thou hast hearkened...cursed is the ground." In the second case, it would be quite possible to take ὅτι as introducing the words of the speaker, "Unto Adam he said [that] 'Thou hast hearkened...Cursed is the ground.'" It is perhaps for this reason that in Deuteronomy (i. 27 "and said, '*Because* the Lord hated'") where the Hebrew is the same, the LXX has διὰ τό which Luke also has (xviii. 5 "Yet *because* this widow troubleth me"). In N. T., suspensive ὅτι is almost confined to the Johannine writings and the Apocalypse, and it is one of a few very interesting similarities of style suggesting that the author of the Gospel may have been a disciple, or younger coadjutor, of the author of the Apocalypse[2].

[2177] In John, the ambiguity of suspensive ὅτι is greatly increased by his excessive use of asyndeton, *e.g.* xiv. 19 "But ye behold me. *Because* (ὅτι) I live, ye also shall live." Here it is possible, theoretically, to connect "because" with what precedes, and R.V. marg. assumes this connexion, so as to give either (1) "But ye behold me because I live; and ye shall live," or (2) "But ye behold me, because I live and [because] ye shall live." If the words occurred in a Synoptic Gospel, one of these marginal renderings would be probable. But in John, regard being had to his suspensive use of ὅτι else-

---

[1] [2175 a] The suspensive construction is preferable (as in R.V.). It might also be adopted in Rev. xviii. 7 "How much soever she glorified herself...so much give her of torment and mourning. *Because* she saith in her heart, 'I sit a queen and am no widow and shall in no wise see mourning,' therefore (διὰ τοῦτο) in one day shall her plagues come...." Here, however, all the English versions have "*for* she saith in her heart" and begin a new sentence with "Therefore." Ὅτι is also suspensive in Rev. iii. 10 "...that they may know that I loved thee. *Because* (ὅτι) thou didst keep the word of my endurance I also (κἀγώ) will keep thee...," where it would be quite possible to render the words "that they may know that I loved thee *because* thou didst keep...*and* I......." That is to say, it would be theoretically possible. But no one familiar with the style of the author would so render it.

[2] [2176 a] Besides Gal. iv. 6 (above quoted) ὅτι suspensive occurs in 1 Cor. xii. 15—16 (*bis*) "If the foot shall say, '*Because* I am not the hand, I am not of the body' it is not therefore not of the body," and Rom. ix. 7 "Neither, *because* they are Abraham's seed, are they all children."

where[1], and to his habitual use of (2149) καὶ ὑμεῖς to mean "Ye also," the rendering given above, which is in the main that of R.V. text, may be pronounced the only possible interpretation.

(β) Ὅτι introducing (1) cause of action, (2) ground of statement

[2178] A doubt may sometimes exist whether ὅτι, "because," introduces (1) the ground or motive of an action ("he does this *because* he likes it") or the proof of the truth of an assertion ("You did this, [I know] *because* you were caught in the act"), where (in English) we should mostly use "for." Such a sentence as x. 5 "They will flee...*because* they know not," introducing a cause inherent in the persons spoken of, presents no difficulty. And in this way "because" would generally be used where it connects two verbs in the same person ("you (or, they) do this *because* you (or, they) do that"). But the meaning is not so clear in v. 38 "Ye have not his word abiding in you *because* (ὅτι) whom he sent him ye believe not." Does this mean (1) that, *because* they rejected Christ and refused to believe in Him, the Jews darkened their minds and made it impossible for the word of God to "abide" in them? In that case, ὅτι introduces *the reason why the "word" did not "abide."* Or does it mean (2) "Ye have not his word abiding in you: [I know this] *because* whom he sent him ye believe not"? In that case ὅτι introduces *the cause of the speaker's knowledge*, the proof of his assertion. The use of ὅτι to mean "[I say this] because," "[And this is true] because," is so frequent in John that the latter (2) is the more probable explanation. If John had meant the former (1) he would have probably written "*For this cause* (διὰ τοῦτο) ye have not his word abiding in you *because*"— a very common formula with him[2].

---

[1] [2177 a] Comp. i. 50 ὅτι εἶπόν σοι, xx. 29 ὅτι ἑώρακάς με, where ὅτι is suspensive and initial. Suspensive ὅτι is also initial with δέ in xv. 19, and ἀλλ' ὅτι is initial and suspensive in xvi. 6. In viii. 45 ἐγὼ δὲ ὅτι τὴν ἀλήθειαν λέγω, οὐ πιστεύετέ μοι, the δέ introduces an antithesis to the previous sentence: "Ye *on the one hand* are the children of the Father of lies and move in falsehood as your atmosphere: but I *on the other hand*—just because I say the truth, ye do not believe me."

[2] [2178 a] R.V. and A.V. "for." Westcott says (*ad loc.*) "*For* (because)...." This is not alleged as the ground but as the sign of what has been said. Comp. Luke vii. 47; 1 John iii. 14." The former passage ("her sins...are forgiven *because* she loved much") states the cause of being forgiven, in accordance with the Law of Forgiveness: the latter ("we *know* that we have passed from death... *because* we love the brethren") states the ground of "knowing," which may be

[2179] In ii. 18 "What sign shewest thou *because* thou doest these things?" the meaning of ὅτι seems to be "[We ask thee this question] because¹," and similarly in vii. 35 "Where doth this man purpose to go, [*we ask this*] *because* [according to what he says] we shall not find him?" In xii. 48—9, "The word that I spake, the same shall judge him in the last day, *because* I spake not from myself; but the Father...," the meaning may be explained by turning "because I spake" into "because it is spoken." "The word" will have the right to judge you, and will judge you, *because* it comes ultimately, not "from myself," but from the Father, the righteous Judge. In x. 12—13 "But the hireling...fleeth, and the wolf snatcheth and scattereth them *because* he is a hireling," some authorities insert "the hireling fleeth" before "because," and R.V. supplies these words in italics; but the sense may very well be that "the wolf scatters the flock—[*Why?*] *because* the shepherd is a hireling." Similarly the laziness of a sentinel is a contributory *cause* to disaster, and an enemy may be said to surprise a camp "*because* the sentinel was asleep." The passage illustrates John's varied use of ὅτι.

[2180] In i. 14—18, a complicated passage in which connexions of thought are broken by interventions of parentheses, ὅτι occurs thrice, and in each case seems to base a new statement on some preceding similar one, with a curious mannerism frequent in the Fourth Gospel but particularly noticeable here. Ὅτι seems to mean in each case "[I say *this*] because of *that*," where "this" and "that" are similar or identical words (like "*full*" and "*fulness*," "*first*" and "*before*," "*grace*" and "*grace*") thus: (*a*) "He is become *before* me, [*I say 'before'*] *because* he was *first* in regard to me"; (*b*) "the Logos tabernacled among us...*full* of...² [*I say 'full'*] *because* from his *fulness* did we all receive"; (*c*) "...and *grace* for *grace*, [*I say 'grace'*] *because*, whereas the Law [of God] was given [as a preparatory grace

---

also called the *cause* of knowledge. The analogy of both of these would seem to point to (1) rather than (2): but Westcott seems to favour (2), if "the sign of" means "the sign of the truth of."

¹ [2179 *a*] Somewhat less probable would be "*In consequence of* your taking upon yourself to do these authoritative works you must be certainly intending to prove your authority to us by working a sign—what is that sign?" See **2183** *a*.

² [2180 *a*] The intervening verse (i. 15 "John beareth witness......before me") is probably to be regarded as a parenthesis. It is so printed by W.H., but not by R.V.

or preparation for grace] through Moses, the [real] *grace* [of God] and the truth [of God] came into being through Jesus Christ."

(γ) Ὅτι (?) "that" or "because"

[2181] Ὅτι is interpreted "*because*" by Chrysostom, but "*that*" by R.V., in iii. 19 "And this is the judgment, *that* (αὕτη δέ ἐστιν ἡ κρίσις ὅτι) the light hath come into the world and men loved the darkness rather than the light." Here Chrysostom—taking "judgment" as condemnation bringing punishment with it—paraphrases thus, "What he means is to this effect, *For this cause* (διὰ τοῦτο) *they are punished because* they did not desire to leave the darkness and run to the light." But the use of a similar phrase in 1 Jn i. 5 and v. 14 "*And this is* the boldness that we have...[*namely*] *that*..." confirms the view that ὅτι here means "that." The very fact that men love darkness is their condemnation. Similarly (2187) iii. 18 ὁ μὴ πιστεύων ἤδη κέκριται ὅτι μὴ πεπίστευκεν is more accurately rendered "*found guilty of not having believed*," than "*found guilty because he has not believed*": and Ammonius (paraphrasing "found guilty" as "punished") suggests this view of ὅτι in his comment: "Disbelief is of itself a punishment[1]."

[2182] Ὅτι probably means "I say this because" in xvi. 8—11 "He will convict the world about sin and about righteousness and about judgment; in the first place (μέν) about sin, [*I say this*] *because* they believe not on me; in the next place (δέ) about righteousness, [*I say this*] *because* I go unto the Father and ye no longer behold me; in the next place (δέ) about judgment, [*I say this*] *because* the prince of this world hath been judged." The absence of the defining clause αὕτη δέ ἐστιν differentiates this passage from iii. 19, and the statement "I will judge the world about these three things" suggests to the reader "Why about these three in particular?" so as to prepare the way for a threefold "because."—"I say about sin, *because* it will be shewn that they are unbelieving and unbelief is at the bottom of sin; I say about righteousness, *because* it will be shewn that they drive me out of the world, and to be driven out of the unjust or unrighteous world"—as Aristides the just was driven out of unjust Athens—"is a proof of justice or righteousness[2]; I say about judgment, *because* the prince of this world, who—by means

---

[1] Cramer *ad loc.* αὐτὸ τὸ ἀπιστεῖν κόλασίς ἐστι.
[2] Comp. Heb. xi. 37 "Evil entreated, of whom *the world was not worthy*, wandering in deserts...."

of his agents, Pilate and the priests—will have judged and sentenced me to the death of a criminal, will himself have been judged and cast into hell, so that the judgment of this world will have been judged and condemned[1]."

[2183] R.V. and A.V. differ in ix. 17 "What dost thou (σύ) say about him, (R.V.) *in that* he opened thine eyes?" (A.V. "*that* he hath opened thine eyes?"). The object of "sayest" has preceded ("*What* sayest thou?") and the blind man has already said (ix. 15) in effect, "he hath opened mine eyes." Consequently, we may naturally expect ὅτι to introduce, not the object of "sayest," but a reason for the saying: "In consequence of this cure—what do *you* say about him?" At all events the blind man takes it in this way, for he replies "[I say] he is a prophet,"—and not, as the A.V. rendering would require, "Yes, I say that he *did* open my eyes." But, if R.V. is right, it would be better not to insert a comma (as R.V. does) before "in that" but to run the words on thus, in effect, "What sayest *thou* (emph.) about him *for having* [*as thou sayest*] opened thine eyes?" The comma of R.V. before ὅτι might lead the reader to give ὅτι the force of "we ask this because" or "for indeed"—as though the questioners acknowledged the miracle: but the next verse shews that they did not acknowledge it[2].

[2184] In the following, ὅτι certainly means "that"; but the instance may be conveniently placed here, because, as in the instances last discussed, ὅτι follows τί and a question. R.V. punctuates the sentence as two questions, A.V. as one. It represents what the Jews "kept saying" to one another while they "kept looking for" Jesus[3], asking one another whether He would come to the Feast, in view of the attempts, mentioned in the context, to kill or capture

---

[1] [2182 a] The "judgment" (or "condemnation") of "the prince of this world," would be regarded by Christians as demonstrated primarily by the Resurrection of Christ and its triumph over death. But external signs of it would also be looked for in all that subsequently befel Pilate, Herod Antipas, and the rulers of the Jews, who would be regarded as the agents of "the prince of this world."

[2] [2183 a] According to this view, this passage differs slightly from ii. 18, where a comma precedes ὅτι: "What sign art thou about to shew unto us—[*we ask this*] *because* thou doest these things (**2179**)?" Here the position of the authoritative ἡμῖν, in τί σημεῖον δεικνύεις ἡμῖν, indicates that the sign must be shewn "unto *us*," and that "*we*" have a right to ask for it.

[3] xi. 56 imperf. ἐζήτουν...ἔλεγον.

Him: xi. 56 "What think ye? *That* he will assuredly not come to the feast?" Τί δοκεῖ ὑμῖν; ὅτι οὐ μὴ ἔλθῃ εἰς τὴν ἑορτήν; The intention certainly is to give prominence to Christ's courage in the face of dangers recognised by everybody, and the meaning of the text appears to be: "What do *you* (emph.) think? [*Do you think, as we do,*] *that he will never dream of venturing to come* to the feast?" But the text is not quite certain[1]. The passage, however, comes usefully here as shewing how complex may be the considerations on which the meaning of ὅτι may depend, and how even the Greek commentators may be puzzled by John's use of it.

[2185] Other instances in the Fourth Gospel where A.V. and R.V. differ in this respect are unimportant *e.g.* iv. 35, (R.V.) "Lift up your eyes and look on the fields, *that* (ὅτι) they are white already unto harvest[2]." Here A.V. has "*for* they are white"; and, in favour of A.V., it might be fairly argued that if John meant "behold *that*...," he might have written "behold *that* the fields are white," as elsewhere (vi. 5) "beholding *that* (ὅτι) a great multitude cometh[3]."

---

[1] [2184 a] D reads Τί δοκεῖτε, *a, b, e,* Δοκεῖτε, "Do ye suppose?" (instead of Τί δοκεῖ ὑμῖν;). SS has "Do ye suppose that *perchance* he cometh not to the feast?" Origen *ad loc.* has at first τί ὑμῖν δοκεῖ οὐ μὴ ἔλθῃ... ("What do you think? He will never surely come [will he]...?") though quoting correctly afterwards. Chrysostom (Migne) *ad loc.* has δοκεῖτε, and "in the course of (ἐν) the Feast." He adds τουτέστιν, Ἐνταῦθα αὐτὸν ἐμπεσεῖν δεῖ, τοῦ καιροῦ καλοῦντος αὐτόν. Cramer has τί ὑμῖν δοκεῖ, ὅτι οὐ μὴ ἔλθῃ εἰς τὴν ἑορτήν, adding ὁ δὲ λέγει τοιοῦτόν ἐστιν, ἐνταῦθα αὐτὸν ἐμπεσεῖν δεῖ τοῦ καιροῦ καλοῦντος αὐτόν. Steph. iii. 882 gives ἐμπίπτω absol. "temere iruere." Chrysostom uses ἐμπεσεῖν again (on Jn vii. 10) about coming to a feast in the midst of excitement.

[2] [2185 a] In iii. 21 (A.V.) "that his deeds may be made manifest, *that* they are wrought in God," R.V. has txt "*that,*" marg. "*because.*" In vii. 52 (A.V.) "Search and see, *for*," R.V. has txt "*that,*" marg. "*for.*" In viii. 22 (A.V.) "Will he kill himself? *because* he saith..." i.e. "[*We ask this*] *because,*" R.V. has "*that*" he saith (presumably attempting to correct not the sense but the English). On xiv. 2 see **2186** foll. Cases of "not that" meaning "not because" are not included in this list.

[2185 b] In xviii. 37 (R.V. txt) "Thou sayest *that* I am a king," R.V. marg. has, "Thou sayest [it] *because* I am a king," on which Westcott justly says, "The translation '*Thou sayest* (*i.e.* rightly), *because I am*' seems to be both unnatural as a rendering of the original phrase, and alien from the context." In xxi. 23 οὐκ εἶπεν δὲ αὐτῷ ὁ Ἰησοῦς ὅτι οὐκ ἀποθνῄσκει, SS has "for that" *i.e.* because, "But Jesus, not *for that* he was not to die said he [it]." In such cases, the Latin *quod,* or *quia,* would often reproduce the ambiguity of the Greek.

[3] [2185 c] Θεᾶσθαί τι ὅτι foll. by indic. (like v. 42 ἔγνωκα ὑμᾶς ὅτι οὐκ ἔχετε) does not appear to exist elsewhere in N.T. Westc. says "For, rather *that,*" but gives no reasons; Thayer recognises τι as the ordinary accus., apparently favouring A.V.; Alford has no remark about the construction.

But perhaps R.V. is right in judging that John (even when an accusative intervened) would not use ὅτι (2174) after any verb of perception in any sense but "that," because to use it in any other sense would, as a rule, involve obvious and immediate misunderstanding[1].

[2186] In all the passages bearing on ὅτι, up to this point, no instance has been found of λέγω closely followed by ὅτι meaning "I say ...because." This makes it all the more remarkable that in one passage, according to R.V., John has used εἰπεῖν ὅτι to mean, "say [it] *because*," on which is based the following rendering (xiv. 1—2), "Let not your heart be troubled: ye believe (or, believe) in God, believe also in me. In my Father's house are many mansions; if it were not so, *I would have told you; for I go* (εἰ δὲ μή, εἶπον ἂν ὑμῖν ὅτι πορεύομαι) to prepare a place for you." It has been shewn, under the head of εἰ δὲ μή (2080—6), that there is no authority for the rendering "*if it were not so.*" Even if it were allowable to supply the sense in that way (εἰ δὲ μὴ [οὕτως ἦν]), it is doubtful whether such an ellipsis could be repeated as a second ellipsis, so as to make the sense "I should have said to you [that it was not so]" εἶπον ἂν ὑμῖν [ὅτι οὐχ οὕτως ἐστίν]. No authority has been alleged for this[2]. But, apart from all these facts, the regular Greek and Johannine use of λέγειν or εἰπεῖν ὅτι, "say *that*," should oblige translators to assume, in the first instance, that, if the text is not corrupt, the meaning here is, "I should have said to you *that I am going*[3]."

For ὅτι equivalent to ὥστε, in xiv. 22, see 2694.

---

[1] [2185 *d*] In Jn xx. 13 R.V. and A.V. have "*Because* they have taken away my Lord," but W.H. txt has λέγει αὐτοῖς ὅτι Ἦραν (marg. Ὅτι ἦραν), which—being more impassioned and more like xx. 18 ὅτι Ἑώρακα—is prob. correct, in spite of the fact that the words are an answer to the question "Why weepest thou?"

[2] [2186 *a*] The instances, Mt. xxviii. 7 "Behold I have said [it] to you," Mt. xxiv. 25 "I have said [it] to you before," Jn x. 25 "I said [it] to you and ye believe not" all refer to *something preceding, and more or less definitely expressed*. For example, Jn x. 25 "I said [it] (εἶπον) to you" refers to the preceding words. "If thou art the Christ *say* [*so*] (εἰπόν) *to us*." In xiv. 29. "I have said [it] (εἴρηκα) to you" (better than "I have told you") probably refers to xiv. 28 "I said (εἶπον) to you, I depart."

[3] [2186 *b*] For the new meaning that would be given to the whole passage by this interpretation the reader is referred to εἰ δὲ μή (2080—6). Here it may be added that several authorities (including *a* and *e*) omit ὅτι, and that the Syriac (including SS) has "I should have said *that* I go." In LXX, ὅτι "recitativum" is omitted after "I said" in Ps. xxx. 6 "I said I shall never be removed," xxxi.

CONJUNCTIONS

(δ) Ὅτι μή

[2187] In one instance, ὅτι μή in the Gospel curiously contrasts with ὅτι οὐ in the Epistle: Jn iii. 18 "He that believeth not (ὁ μὴ πιστεύων) hath been judged already *because he hath not believed* (ὅτι μὴ πεπίστευκεν) in the name of the only begotten Son of God," 1 Jn v. 10 "He that believeth not God (ὁ μὴ πιστεύων τῷ θεῷ) hath made him a liar; [I say this] *because he hath not believed* in the testimony that God testified (ὅτι οὐ πεπίστευκεν εἰς τὴν μαρτυρίαν)...." In the latter, ὅτι οὐ states the fact *objectively*; in the former, ὅτι μή states it *subjectively*, as the judgment pronounced by the Judge, "This man is guilty *in that he hath not believed*," so that the meaning is almost "hath been pronounced guilty *of not believing*." See 2695.

(ε) Οὐχ ὅτι

[2188] In classical Greek, οὐχ ὅτι often means "*not only*" and may be explained as "not [only do I say] that," so as to prepare the way for ἀλλὰ καί "but [I] also [say this]." But in N.T. it never has that meaning. When it comes immediately after a statement that is in danger of being misunderstood, οὐχ ὅτι might be explained as (1) "[*I say this*], *not because*...," (2) "[*I do*] *not* [*mean to say*] *that*...." The latter is generally the more probable. See Ellipsis, 2218—9.

(ζ) Ὅτι "recitativum"

[2189] Ὅτι "recitativum" is a Greek way of expressing our inverted commas, or the Hebrew "saying," as in i. 20 "he confessed that (ὅτι) *I am not the Christ*," i.e. "*saying* 'I am not the Christ.'" This is very frequent in Mark, frequent in John, somewhat less so in Luke, and comparatively rare in Matthew[1]. The use of ὅτι Ἐγώ in the case of the Baptist above and of the blind man in ix. 9 ἔλεγεν ὅτι Ἐγώ εἰμι, may be contrasted with the omission of ὅτι when "I am" is uttered by Jesus in xviii. 5 λέγει αὐτοῖς Ἐγώ εἰμι...ὡς οὖν εἶπεν αὐτοῖς Ἐγώ εἰμι. Neither here nor elsewhere—except in two or three instances where sayings of Christ are repeated for the second

---

22 "I said...I am cut off," xxxii. 5 "I said I will confess" etc. This may have influenced the scribes that omitted it here. If it did, the fact would indicate that the scribes regarded ὅτι as meaning "*that*," not "*because*."

[1] [2189 a] The mss. vary, and editors print the same text differently (*e.g.* ὅτι ἐγώ and ὅτι Ἐγώ) so that it is difficult to obtain exact statistics. W.H. print Mt. x. 7 κηρύσσετε λέγοντες ὅτι Ἤγγικεν, but Lk. vii. 4 λέγοντες ὅτι ἄξιός ἐστιν ᾧ παρέξῃ τοῦτο, ἀγαπᾷ γὰρ τὸ ἔθνος ἡμῶν....

CONJUNCTIONS   [2190]

time (2190)—does John use ὅτι before *direct* speech of the Lord after
"*he said*": consequently when we find "*I said*" a little later on,
xviii. 8 εἶπον ὑμῖν ὅτι ἐγώ εἰμι, there is some reason for thinking that
this is *reported* speech, "I said to you *that* I am¹." There are many
instances of this phrase ("I said that") because John (differing from
the Synoptists) frequently represents Christ as referring to what He
Himself has previously said, *e.g.* i. 50 "Because *I said unto thee that*
(ὅτι) I saw thee under the fig-tree," vi. 36 "But *I said to you that* ye
have seen me," viii. 24 "*I said...to you that* ye shall die in your
sins," xi. 40 "Did I not say to thee *that*, if thou wilt believe, thou
shalt see the glory of God?," xvi. 15 "For this cause I said to you
that he taketh from that which is mine and [that he] will declare
it unto you." In all these passages there is nothing to shew whether
ὅτι introduces (1) direct or (2) reported speech; but W.H. print the
text as the latter, and their view agrees with the general absence
of ὅτι recitativum elsewhere after "he said" introducing words of
Christ.

[2190] The text varies somewhat in xiii. 33 "Even as I said to
the Jews *that* 'Where I go, ye are not able to come,' [so] to you also
I say—for the moment"; but if the text is correct² and if the
reference is to viii. 21, then ὅτι recitativum is here used in exact
quotation of a saying of the Lord. The quotation is not exact in
xviii. 9 ἵνα πληρωθῇ ὁ λόγος ὃν εἶπεν ὅτι Οὓς δέδωκάς μοι οὐκ ἀπώλεσα

---

¹ [2189 b] For the omission of ὅτι elsewhere before ἐγώ εἰμι, in words of the
Lord, see vi. 20 λέγει αὐτοῖς Ἐγώ εἰμι, and vi. 35 εἶπεν αὐτοῖς ὁ Ἰησοῦς Ἐγώ εἰμι ὁ
ἄρτος τῆν ζωῆς.

[2189 c] In the Baptist's words, W.H. print iii. 28 εἶπον [ἐγώ] Οὐκ εἰμὶ ἐγώ ὁ
χριστός, ἀλλ' ὅτι Ἀπεσταλμένος εἰμὶ ἔμπροσθεν ἐκείνου. However printed, the text
seems to blend (1) "I said '*I am not the Christ but am one sent*,'" (2) "I did not
say '*I am the Christ*,' but I said, '*I am one sent*.'"

² [2190 a] Ὅτι is om. by אD b, e. SS has "that, where I go *they* cannot
come." Christ had said in vii. 34 "Where I *am*, ye are not able to come," and
(perhaps for this reason) a and e read "sum" in xiii. 33; b reads "eo" which may
be intended for ειμι accented εἶμι "I go" (in vii. 34, a renders εἰμι "I am" by
"vado" and sim. SS "go"). Another instance where ὅτι is omitted by Bruder
(following אA) but ins. by W.H. is xiii. 11 διὰ τοῦτο εἶπεν ὅτι Οὐχὶ πάντες καθαροί
ἐστε. What Jesus had actually said, was Ὑμεῖς καθαροί ἐστε ἀλλ' οὐχὶ πάντες, so
that this quotation is not exact. In view of a future consideration of Johannine
quotations it is worth while noting that (a) vii. 34 ὅπου εἰμὶ ἐγώ ὑμεῖς οὐ δύνασθε
ἐλθεῖν is exactly repeated by the Jews in vii. 36, that (b) viii. 21 ὅπου ἐγώ ὑπάγω
ὑμεῖς οὐ δύνασθε ἐλθεῖν is exactly repeated by the Jews in viii. 22, and that (c) the
second of these sayings is exactly repeated by Christ, with ὅτι in xiii. 33 ὅτι Ὅπου
ἐγώ...ἐλθεῖν.

ἐξ αὐτῶν οὐδένα, which is a certain instance of ὅτι recitativum before words of the Lord. It is assumed by Westcott and Alford that the reference is to xvii. 12 ἐτήρουν αὐτοὺς ἐν τῷ ὀνόματί σου ᾧ δέδωκάς μοι ...καὶ οὐδεὶς ἐξ αὐτῶν ἀπώλετο. But there is a great difference between "Those whom thou hast given me I lost not one of them" and "I kept them in thy name which thou hast given me...and not one of them was lost." Why does not the evangelist give the words exactly? This question must be considered under "Variation" (2544 foll.). It does not come under the present heading except so far as it suggests a possibility that the writer may sometimes use ὅτι to mean "[*to this effect*] *that*"—when he does not propose to give the exact words in a quotation[1].

(xvi) Οὖν

(*a*) In Christ's words

[2191] Οὖν, in Matthew and Luke, when used by our Lord, introduces a precept, or inference, as being based on something that precedes (often a parable or statement of considerable length) of a very cogent nature: "Be not ye *therefore* anxious," "Look to it *therefore* whether the light within thee be darkness," "If *therefore* ye,

---

[1] [2190 *b*] Thus our Lord says to the Jews ix. 41 λέγετε ὅτι Βλέπομεν, and x. 36 λέγετε ὅτι Βλασφημεῖς, meaning "Ye say in effect." In reality (1) they had not said, "We see," but "Are we blind also?" and (2) they had not said "Thou blasphemest," but "We stone thee for blasphemy and because thou, being a man, makest thyself God."

[2190 *c*] It will be found that almost all Jn's quotations and repetitions, with or without ὅτι, are given with variations (2544 foll.). But ὅτι introduces an exact quotation (soon after the passage last quoted) in x. 34 Οὐκ ἔστιν γεγραμμένον ἐν τῷ νόμῳ ὑμῶν ὅτι Ἐγὼ εἶπα Θεοί ἐστε, where a short saying is quoted exactly to illustrate the pervading thought in *the whole of what Jesus calls "your own Law,"* that those to whom the word of God comes are in some sense "gods." In xx. 18 ἀγγέλλουσα τοῖς μαθηταῖς ὅτι Ἑώρακα τὸν κύριον καὶ ταῦτα εἶπεν αὐτῇ, the tidings of Christ's Resurrection are first summed up in one phrase of direct speech "I have seen," and then the fact that He said certain things is expressed in reported speech.

[2190 *d*] In xvi. 17 τί ἐστιν τοῦτο ὃ λέγει ἡμῖν Μικρὸν καὶ οὐ...καὶ "Ὅτι ὑπάγω πρὸς τὸν πατέρα, ὅτι is probably "because." Jn would hardly omit ὅτι recit. before Μικρόν and insert it before Ὑπάγω—if both were the first words of quotations. "Because" may be the first word of "*Because* I go to the Father" repeated from xvi. 10 "*because I go to the Father* and ye no longer behold me." Several authorities interpolate the italicised words in xvi. 16, and it is clear that these took ὅτι as "*because*."

CONJUNCTIONS [2192]

being evil, know how to give good gifts to your children, how much more...?" "If *therefore* in the unrighteous mammon ye were not faithful, who shall entrust to you...¹?" John (**1883**) uses οὖν very frequently in his Gospel, about 195 times in all, but in Christ's words very rarely, only 8 times. It occurs most frequently when He is arguing with unbelievers or doubters; but He uses it twice in the Discourse with the disciples before the Passion, and, for the last time, to the soldiers arresting Him. He has twice asked them "Whom seek ye?" And they have twice replied, "Jesus of Nazareth." Now He replies (xviii. 8) "I told you that I am he. *Therefore*, if it is I that ye seek, let these depart." "Therefore," in R.V., has the advantage of uniformity, but "then" would sometimes be preferable.

[**2192**] The other instances in Christ's words are as follows: vi. 62 "Doth this cause you to stumble? (lit.) *If therefore ye should be beholding* (ἐὰν οὖν θεωρῆτε) the Son of man ascending where he

---

¹ [**2191 a**] Mt. vi. 31, Lk. xi. 35, Mt. vii. 11, Lk. xvi. 11. Luke often inserts it as follows—mostly in Christ's words—where the parall. Mk omits it:—

Mk	Mt.	Lk.
iv. 24 βλέπετε τί...	om.	viii. 18 βλέπετε οὖν πῶς]
iv. 30 καὶ ἔλεγεν, Πῶς	xiii. 31 ἄλλην παραβολὴν π.α. λέγων Ὁμοία	xiii. 18 ἔλεγεν οὖν, Τίνι
ix. 50 καλὸν τὸ ἅλας	v. 13 ὑμεῖς ἐστὲ τὸ ἅλας	xiv. 34 καλὸν οὖν τὸ ἅλας
xii. 9 τί ποιήσει	xxi. 40 ὅταν οὖν ἔλθῃ...τί ποιήσει	xx. 15 τί οὖν ποιήσει αὐτοῖς
xii. 10 οὐδὲ τὴν γραφὴν ταύτην ἀνέγνωτε	xxi. 42 λέγει αὐτοῖς ὁ Ἰησ. Οὐδέποτε ἀνέγνωτε	xx. 17 τί οὖν ἐστιν τὸ γεγραμμένον
xii. 20 ἑπτὰ ἀ. ἦσαν	xxii. 25 ἦσαν δὲ παρ' ἡμῖν ἑπτὰ ἀ.	xx. 29 ἑπτὰ οὖν ἀ. ἦσαν
xii. 23 ἐν τ. ἀ. τίνος αὐτῶν ἔσται γυνή	xxii. 28 ἐν τῇ ἀ. οὖν τίνος τῶν ἑπτὰ ἔσται γυνή	xx. 33 ἡ γυνὴ οὖν ἐν τ. ἀ. τίνος αὐτῶν γίνεται γυνή
xii. 37 Αὐτὸς Δ. λέγει αὐτὸν Κύριον	xxii. 45 εἰ οὖν Δ. καλεῖ αὐτὸν κύριον	xx. 44 Δ. οὖν αὐτὸν κύριον καλεῖ
xiii. 4 εἰπὸν ἡμῖν πότε ταῦτα ἔσται	xxiv. 3 as Mk	xxi. 7 πότε οὖν ταῦτα ἔσται
xiv. 61 Σὺ εἶ ὁ χριστὸς ὁ υἱὸς τοῦ εὐλογητοῦ	xxvi. 63 εἰ σὺ εἶ ὁ χριστὸς ὁ υἱὸς τ. θεοῦ	xxii. 70 (perh. parall.) σὺ οὖν εἶ ὁ υἱὸς τ. θεοῦ (see context).
xv. 9 θέλετε ἀπολύσω ὑμῖν	xxvii. 17 συνηγμένων οὖν αὐτῶν εἶπεν...τίνα θέλετε ἀπολύσω	xxiii. 16, 22 παιδεύσας οὖν αὐτὸν ἀπολύσω

In the last five passages of Lk., only Lk. xx. 44 is in Christ's words. The result indicates a general preference of οὖν in Lk.

was before—". Here there is an ellipsis of the apodosis—"What will ye do?" or "What is to happen?" The passage is extremely obscure (2210—12): but the meaning appears to be that, if they stumble already at the truth, they will, *as an inevitable consequence*, stumble again when a higher truth is set before them. In viii. 24 "I said *therefore* to you 'Ye shall die in your sins,'" after "Ye are of this world," Jesus assumes that "this world" (1 Jn v. 19) "lieth wholly in the evil [one]," *i.e.* in the hands of sin and death, so that those who "are of this world" will "*therefore* die" in their sins; in viii. 36 "The Son abideth [in the house] for ever. If *therefore* the Son shall free you, ye shall be free indeed," it is assumed that what the Son of the house does will be ratified by the Father, and "therefore" will be permanent and "real."

[2193] In the following difficult passage, οὖν may help to decide between the alternative renderings given by R.V., (viii. 37—8) (lit.) "Ye seek to kill me...The things that I (emph.) have seen in the house of the (παρὰ τῷ) Father I speak : *ye also therefore* (καὶ ὑμεῖς οὖν)—the things that ye heard from the (παρὰ τοῦ) father, ye do (ἃ ἠκούσατε παρὰ τοῦ πατρὸς ποιεῖτε)." Here R.V. txt has "*and ye also do*" (apparently rendering καί by "and," οὖν by "also"), but R.V. marg. "*do ye also therefore* the things which ye heard from the Father." In R.V. txt, it is *affirmed* that the Jews do the works suggested from the devil, who is to them "the father"; in R.V. margin, the Jews are *exhorted* to do the works suggested by the Father, God.

[2194] In favour of the former rendering ("ye do") there is the precedent of καὶ ὑμεῖς οὖν quoted from xvi. 22 above (2149, comp. 2196—7) with the indicative, where it meant "ye also *in a corresponding way.*" So here, the meaning seems to be that there is a *correspondence* between the conduct of Christ and that of His persecutors. They are as consistent in evil as He in good : "The things that I have seen in the house of Light I speak : ye, *by the law of your nature as I by the law of mine*—I do not say ye 'speak,' but, more than that—the things that ye have heard from the house of darkness, ye *do*[1]."

---

[1] [2194 *a*] It is implied that they "see" nothing, being children of darkness; but they execute the whispered suggestions of evil that come to them from "the father" of the house of darkness (somewhat as the mutterings of Satan are represented by Milton as coming to Eve in her sleep). There is a paradoxical antithesis : "What I *see*, I *speak*; what ye *hear*, ye *do*."

[2194 *b*] For "the father" used to mean "Satan," comp. viii. 44 "Ye are of

[2195] In xii. 49—50 "The Father that sent me—he hath given me commandment what I should say and what I should speak. And I know that his commandment is eternal life. The things *therefore* that I (emph.) speak—even as the father hath said [them] to me, so speak I," Chrysostom has excellently expressed the force of οὖν by the paraphrase "*It is not natural* (οὐκ ἔχει φύσιν τὸ πρᾶγμα) that the Father should say one thing and I utter another." The meaning is, "I not only know what I am commanded to say, but also know that it is my Life, Life Eternal, to fulfil the commandment, *it follows therefore* that I must speak the Father's words." There is an argument *a fortiori* in xiii. 13—14 "Ye address me [with the titles] 'the Teacher' and 'the Master (κύριος),' and ye say well, for such I am. If *therefore* I washed your feet—'the Teacher' and 'the Master'— ye also are bound to wash each other's feet." In Matthew and Luke this cogent "therefore" would perhaps have been accompanied by "*How much more!*" and SS has something like it here "And if I, your Rabbi...*how much* doth it behove you...!"

[2196] In xvi. 21—2 "The woman [or, wife] when she is in travail (ὅταν τίκτῃ) hath sorrow because her hour hath come: but when she hath given birth to (γεννήσῃ) the child she remembereth no more the anguish because of the joy that a man is born into the world. Ye also *therefore* (καὶ ὑμεῖς οὖν) now indeed (νῦν μέν) have sorrow: but I will see you again and your heart shall rejoice and your joy no man shall take from you," we may explain "therefore" in a broad and general way by saying that the argument takes child-

---

the father the devil." As in French "*the* head" means "*my, your, his* head" according to the context, so may "*the* father" in Greek; and the writer deliberately uses the ambiguous expression "*the* father" in order to prepare for the defining climax in viii. 44, (1) "the father," (2) "the devil," (3) "your father."

[2194 c] The view that ποιεῖτε is indicative is supported not only by the analogy of xvi. 22, but also by the fact it is in Jn's manner to repeat a statement twice or thrice with variations, and we find the indicative again in viii. 41 "*ye do* the deeds of your father," viii. 44 "*ye are fain to do* the lusts of your father." Moreover the imperative rendering, "Do ye also the things that ye heard from the Father," *i.e.* God, would imply that the Jews *had* heard the Father's voice, which (though theoretically arguable as referring to the Law of Sinai) is somewhat inconsistent with v. 37 and viii. 43. The statement in viii. 37 "ye seek to *kill* me" implies, "ye are doing the work of *your father* Satan," as appears from viii. 44 ("he was a *murderer* from the beginning") and from 1 Jn iii. 10—12 "in this the children of God are manifest and the *children of the devil*...Cain was of the evil one and slew his brother."

birth as a type of a fundamental law in human nature that all deep and lasting joy must be reached through pain and sorrow. But probably there is a more definite reference in the evangelist's mind. For Micah combines the prophecy about the Messiah from Bethlehem with a mention of affliction and temporary abandonment of Israel. "He will give them up *until the time that she which travaileth hath brought forth*[1]," and the phrase "birth-pangs of the Messiah" is associated with this prophecy in the Talmud, where it occurs several times[2].

[2197] Mark and Matthew represent our Lord as saying, just before His prediction of persecution for the disciples, "These things are the beginning of *travail-pangs* (ὠδίνων)[3]." Besides the "travail-pangs" of the Church collectively, it was necessary that there should be "travail-pangs" in the soul of each believer before it could give birth to the idea of the spiritual Christ[4]: and both these doctrines may have been in the mind of this evangelist, who is the only one that records, in exact words, the doctrine that a man cannot enter into the kingdom of Heaven unless he is "born from above." Thus a number of considerations, not present to modern readers, may have suggested the thought of inevitable consequence in the words "Ye also, *therefore*, now indeed have sorrow."

(β)   ΟὖΝ applied to Christ's acts

[2198] Setting aside instances where οὖν introduces words of the Lord, we find that it either introduces an act of special solemnity, or else—as is most frequently the case—it is applied to His various journeys. The writer perhaps had in view the objections of con-

---

[1] [2196 a] Mic. v. 2—4 "But thou Bethlehem Ephrathah...out of thee shall come unto me he that is to be ruler in Israel; whose goings forth are from of old, from everlasting. *Therefore will he give them up until the time that she which travaileth hath brought forth.* Then the residue of his brethren shall return unto the children of Israel, and he shall stand and feed his flock in the strength of the Lord."

[2] [2196 b] *Sanhedr.* 98 b. Levy ii. 5 a refers also to *Schabb.* 118 a, *Pes.* 118 a.

[3] [2197 a] Mk xiii. 8, Mt. xxiv. 8. The parall. Lk. omits this, but inserts (xxi. 12) "*Before all these things*," perh. intending this as a paraphrase of the metaphor.

[4] [2197 b] That appears to be the metaphor here, the "soul" being regarded as the mother in travail. From one point of view, the "new birth" is that of the soul itself: from another, it is that of the idea of Christ *within* the soul, which transforms the soul into His image.

troversialists, some of whom, like Celsus, might regard Jesus as a vagrant exorcist, or as a fugitive escaping from arrest. The first instance of all (iv. 1 "when *therefore* the Lord knew") represents Him as departing not from pursuit but from too much popularity. The next two (iv. 5, 6) represent His coming to Sychar and sitting at the well—actions providentially arranged with a view to the conversion of Samaria. The words (iv. 46) "He came *therefore* to Cana," introduce the healing of the nobleman's son. In vi. 11 occurs the first instance that does not apply to journeying, "Jesus *therefore* took the loaves," of which the symbolical importance needs no comment. In vi. 15, the multitude sought to make Jesus a king by force; "*therefore*" He retired. In the Raising of Lazarus, οὖν is four times used, first, paradoxically, "When *therefore* Jesus knew" of the sickness of Lazarus, "he abode" at a distance three days; "*therefore*," when He arrived, He "found that Lazarus had been four days in the tomb"; seeing Mary weeping Jesus "*therefore*... troubled himself"; some of the Jews ask, in effect, why Jesus did not save Lazarus, "Jesus *therefore*...cometh to the tomb[1]." The fourfold conjunction sounds strange in English. But the intention of the narrative as a whole is to represent the Raising of Lazarus as foreordained; and this repetition of "therefore" may be intended, in particular, to shew how the Son, step by step, moved forward in a regular and predetermined sequence to do the Father's will in performing the last and greatest of His "signs."

[2199] The next two instances refer to Christ, as first avoiding peril, and then confronting it, when the Jews took counsel to kill Him: xi. 54 "Jesus *therefore* no longer walked openly among the Jews," xii. 1 "Jesus *therefore* came to Bethany"—following immediately on the statement that the chief priests had taken steps to seize him! It is not surprising that Chrysostom alters this second οὖν to δέ. But the meaning, perhaps, is, that both in avoiding peril and in meeting it Jesus followed the Father's will, not the ways of ordinary men.

[2200] After the instance in the sacramental Washing of Feet (xiii. 6 "He cometh *therefore* to Simon Peter"), the next is in the narrative of Gethsemane, where, upon the arrival of Judas and the soldiers (xviii. 4) "Jesus, *therefore*, knowing all that was coming upon him, went forth and said to them, Whom seek ye?" There

---

[1] xi. 6, 17, 33, 38.

remain but two more instances. One ("Jesus *therefore* went out") introduces the exclamation of Pilate "Behold the man[1]!" The other introduces the first manifestation of the risen Saviour, "When *therefore* it was evening...came Jesus and stood in the midst[2]." The facts as a whole indicate that, although "therefore" is an exaggerated rendering of οὖν, yet the particle, when used in connexion with the acts of Christ, is often intended to suggest a sequence of cause and effect[3].

(xvii) Ὡς[4]

(*a*) Ὡc (?) for ἕωc

[2201] Ὡς is translated "while" by R.V. in xii. 35—6 "Walk *while* ye have the light...*while* ye have the light, believe in the light." Several MSS. and authorities read ἕως for ὡς, but the difficulty of the latter, and its double occurrence, demonstrate it to be the true reading. But that ὡς does not mean "while" is made highly probable by ix. 4 "I must work the works of my Father *while* (ἕως) (marg. ὡς) it is day." It is scarcely credible that a writer like John should use ὡς twice in precisely the same sense in which he has used ἕως. Ὡς in Gal. vi. 10 ὡς καιρὸν ἔχωμεν is doubtful. Lk. xii. 58 ὡς γὰρ ὑπάγεις is not quite parallel[5]. Taking the text as it stands,

---

[1] xix. 5. See **1960** and **2645**.   [2] xx. 19.

[3] [**2200** *a*] These instances are taken from Bruder (1888) with whom, in each case quoted above, W.H. agrees. There may be other instances in W.H. not included in Bruder. The list given above does not include vi. 5 ἐπάρας οὖν, xiii. 12 Ὅτε οὖν ἔνιψεν τοὺς πόδας αὐτῶν, xix. 26 Ἰ. οὖν ἰδὼν τὴν μητέρα, xix. 30 ὅτε οὖν ἔλαβε τὸ ὄξος, xxi. 15 ὅτε οὖν ἠρίστησαν, because the principal verb that follows is, in each case, "said" (not a verb of action). Perhaps, however, there might have been included (on the ground that "cry aloud" is a kind of action distinct from mere saying) vii. 28 ἔκραξεν οὖν ἐν τῷ ἱερῷ. This occurs as follows vii. 25—8 "Is not this he whom they seek to kill? And, lo, he speaketh openly ...no man knoweth whence he is. He cried aloud *therefore* in the temple...." See the context. It is uncertain whether the "therefore" means "in consequence of the words '*no man knoweth*,'" or "Accordingly, '*speaking openly*' in spite of the attempts to kill him." On οὖν used after parentheses, or resumptively, see **2631—5**. Of course it must be remembered that οὖν, being used by Jn freely (1) to introduce action of *any kind*, would naturally be used by him (2) to introduce actions of Christ without any intention to express providential sequence. Still, if the actions of Christ introduced by οὖν are compared with the actions of Christ introduced by δέ or by asyndeton, I think it will be found that the first class are specially important.

[4] On ὡς, "when," see **1775** *d—e*.

[5] See **2696**.

we may make fair sense of xii. 35—6 by rendering ὡς "as." Compare 1 Jn ii. 27 "*As* (ὡς) his anointing teacheth you [in the present]...and even as (καθώς) it taught you [in the past], abide[1] in it." This harmonizes with St Paul's precepts, "Walk by the Spirit," and "Live up to the standard you have reached [hoping for a higher one][2]." So here the meaning—or, at all events, the meaning of the best text—is "Walk according to your light as far as it goes." This rendering of ὡς enables us to take περιπατεῖν with an implied οὕτως, "Walk [*thus*, namely] as ye have light [to walk]," and delivers us from the necessity of taking it absolutely, "Walk [in the paths of righteousness]."

(β) Ὡc "as it were"

[2202] In vii. 10 "He went up [to the feast] not openly but *as it were in secret* (ὡς ἐν κρυπτῷ)," the meaning is "like one going up in secret," *i.e.* not actually in secret but in a manner resembling secrecy. Compare St Paul's words to Philemon (14) "in order that thy good deed may not be *as it were* compulsory (ὡς κατὰ[3] ἀνάγκην)." The particle may be a short way of saying "people might call it so," and it is perhaps inserted with a view to the vindication of the Johannine view of the publicity of Christ's life, as in xviii. 20, "In secret spake I nothing"; and in this very feast Christ is described as (vii. 26) "speaking openly (παρρησίᾳ)," and (vii. 28) "he cried aloud in the temple teaching." According to this view, "*as it were* in secret" means that Christ refused to take the advice of His brethren and to go up with them to the feast accompanied by such a multitude as attended Him when He "went up" finally. This going up was "*comparatively in secret*." But, in case any opponent of the Christians might refer to the saying of Christ's brethren (vii. 4) "No man doeth aught *in secret* and himself seeketh to be in publicity," the evangelist wishes to shew that there was nothing "*in secret*" *in the exact sense of the term*. For this purpose he inserts ὡς here and παρρησίᾳ later on.

---

[1] [2201 a] "Abide," imperative. The writer has admitted that it does (*ib.* 27) "abide" in them, and that they "have no need that anyone should teach" them. But still he *does* teach them as St Paul does after similar admissions (1 Thess. iv. 10 and elsewhere). See **2437—9**.

[2] Gal. v. 16, Phil. iii. 16 εἰς ὃ ἐφθάσαμεν τῷ αὐτῷ στοιχεῖν.

[3] [2202 a] Comp. 2 Cor. xi. 17 ὡς ἐν ἀφροσύνῃ, xiii. 7 ὡς ἀδόκιμοι. In Rom. ix. 32 οὐκ ἐκ πίστεως ἀλλ' ὡς ἐξ ἔργων, the meaning is "on a false basis of works," or "as though it could be attained from works."

(xviii) Ὥστε

[2203] This conjunction, which is found frequently in Mark and Matthew, and four times in Luke, occurs in John only once, and then with a unique construction, thus, iii. 16 οὕτως γὰρ ἠγάπησεν ὁ θεὸς τὸν κόσμον ὥστε τὸν υἱὸν τὸν μονογενῆ ἔδωκεν. In the rest of N.T., ὥστε occurs either (1) *at the beginning of a clause* ("so that" meaning "and so") with an emphatic *indicative* or *imperative* (Mk ii. 28 "*And so* the Son of man is lord of the sabbath," 1 Thess. iv. 18 "*And so* (or, *Therefore*) comfort one another") or else (2) *post-initially* with an *infinitive* (Mk i. 27 "*so that* they questioned together")[1]. Both these constructions are frequent. But ὥστε never occurs *post-initially with an indicative* except in John iii. 16[2]. This unique use of οὕτως and ὥστε with indicative is common in the best classical authors[3], but it is unlike the style of any evangelistic tradition in N.T. It is one of many proofs that the passage under consideration was not regarded by the writer as a saying of the Lord, but as an evangelistic explanation (see 2066 and 2697).

ELLIPSIS[4]

(i) **Of two kinds**

[2204] (1) Ellipsis, "leaving out," or "deficiency," may exist when something is *left out* that can be supplied from the preceding context, *e.g.* "I said, Go. But he would not [go]," "You have taken my book and left your own [book]." This ellipsis may be

---

[1] [2203 *a*] W.H. and R.V. in some cases punctuate differently from Bruder, and the classification is to some extent a matter of taste except where ὥστε is preceded by οὕτως, ὧδε, εἰς τοσοῦτον etc., so that the ὥστε cannot possibly be called initial. Bruder 1888 prints ὥστε "in principio periodi" separately, and always with indic. or imperat.: but he prints Gal. ii. 13 συνυπεκρίθησαν...ὥστε καὶ Β. συναπήχθη, under the same heading as Jn iii. 16 οὕτω γὰρ ἠγάπησεν...ὥστε...ἔδωκεν, and marks these as the only two passages (in the group) where the indic. is used. I should take Gal. ii. 13 quite differently, "*And the consequence was* that even Barnabas was carried away."

[2] [2203 *b*] Acts xiv. 1 ἐγένετο...λαλῆσαι οὕτως ὥστε πιστεῦσαι..., is the only other passage in N.T. where ὥστε is preceded by οὕτως. Heb. xiii. 6 ὥστε θαρροῦντας ἡμᾶς λέγειν rather suggests what we *may* say than states what we *do* say.

[3] See Steph. viii. 2128—9, and, in particular, the first definition of "log-rolling" in Plato 257 E οὕτως ἀγαπῶσι τοὺς ἐπαινέτας ὥστε προσπαραγράφουσι πρώτους οἳ ἂν ἑκασταχοῦ ἐπαινῶσιν αὐτούς.

[4] Steph. (quoting Athen. 14, p. 644 A σησαμοῦς κατ᾽ ἔλλειψιν τοῦ ἄρτος) calls it "Praetermissio, Omissio," adding "Potest vero et Defectus reddi."

called "*contextual.*" (2) Ellipsis may consist in the customary omission of words (apart from contextual influence) in certain condensed phrases, *e.g.* "Away!" for "[Go] away!" or "the first of the month" for "the first [day] of the month." This[1] may be called "*idiomatic.*"

(ii) **Contextual**

[2205] iv. 25—6 "'Messiah cometh...'I am [Messiah].'" This must be distinguished from (*a*) vi. 20 "I am," rendered by R.V. "It is I"—like our idiom in English, "It [that you see, or, hear] is I"— and also from (*b*) any special use of I AM with Hebraic associations. The present instance may be illustrated by xviii. 5, 6, 8 "I am [Jesus of Nazareth]"—which refers to the preceding mention of the name in xviii. 5 "'Whom seek ye?' 'Jesus of Nazareth'"—and also by ix. 9 "I am [(ix. 8) 'the man that used to sit and beg']." Here the Samaritan woman—who is described as saying aloud "Messiah cometh"—is to be regarded (comp. Lk. iii. 15 "reasoning in their hearts...whether he might be the Christ") as saying in her heart "Can it be that *this is* Messiah?" and Jesus answers her silent question, "I am [Messiah]."

[2206] iv. 52—3 "They said...[that] 'Yesterday, [about the] seventh hour (ὅτι Ἐχθὲς ὥραν[2] ἑβδόμην) the fever left him.' The father therefore recognised *that* [*it had left him*] at that [same] hour (ὅτι ἐκείνῃ τῇ ὥρᾳ)...." Phrase mentally repeated. In v. 11—12 "'He that made me whole, he [it was that] said to me, Take up thy bed (κράβαττον) and walk.' They asked him, 'Who is the man that said to thee, Take [it] up and walk?,'" the omission of the object of the verb[3] is somewhat harsh, and many MSS. and versions insert "bed."

[2207] viii. 16 "Yea, and even if I should judge, my judgment is true, because I am not alone but [am to be regarded as] I and the

---

[1] On this, see **2220**. Contextual ellipsis is sometimes called "brachylogy."

[2] [**2206** *a*] On the change of case, see **2013**, **2025**—**6**. In v. 6—7, after Christ's question, "Dost thou desire to be made whole?" we might expect the sick man to reply "Yes." But the man takes the question as an implied reproach on his sluggishness, and replies, "I have no man to put me in the pool." It is not a case of ellipsis but of an answer made to the spirit, rather than to the letter, of a question.

[3] [**2206** *b*] No other instance in this group omits the object thus. Κράβαττος, the word here used by the sick man and previously by our Lord, is (**1736** *a*) avoided by Luke and condemned by Grammarians as vulgar.

Father that sent me," ὅτι μόνος οὐκ εἰμί, ἀλλ' ἐγὼ καὶ ὁ πέμψας με [πατήρ]. Chrysostom says, "Hereby he hinted (ἠνίξατο) that it was not He Himself alone that was to condemn them (ὅτι οὐκ αὐτὸς μόνος αὐτοὺς καταδικάζει) but also the Father": and Cramer quotes Ammonius to the same effect. In that case we should have to supply the sense as follows: "I and the Father that sent me [are together as Judges]." But the simple repetition of εἰμί, so as to mean "But [I am] *I and the Father*[1]," seems more in accordance with Johannine ellipsis and with Johannine theology. This latter view, taking the words to declare the eternal unity of the Father and the Son, would also include their unity in the act of judging.

[2208] xiii. 8—9 "'Thou shalt assuredly not wash my feet.'... 'Except I wash thee, thou hast no part with me'....'Lord, do not (μή) [wash] my feet (πόδας) alone but also my hands and my head!'" Verb repeated. Here, μή implies an imperative, and the accusative shews that the construction cannot be "let not my feet (nom.) be washed alone," so that the grammar combines with the context to make the elliptic construction clearer than even in English. In xv. 4 "Abide in me, and I (or, I also) [abide] in you[2]," the verb is to be repeated, and the meaning may be paraphrased "Your abiding in me shall be mine in you," or "Cause yourselves to abide in me and [thereby] me also to abide in you." The two "abidings" are regarded as inseparable[3].

[2209] In xviii. 39—40 "'Desire ye therefore that I release unto you the king of the Jews?'....Do not (μή) [release] this man (τοῦτον)...," as in xiii. 8—9, the μή implies that the verb is to be repeated imperatively, but instead of repeating the object (μὴ τὸν βασιλέα τ. Ἰ.) a pronoun (τοῦτον) is substituted so that the Jews

---

[1] Or we might supply ἐστί, "But [it is more correct to say] 'I and the Father that sent me.'"

[2] [2208 a] There follows an ellipsis of δύνασθε καρπὸν φέρειν ἀφ' ἑαυτῶν, which has to be mentally supplied after οὐδὲ ὑμεῖς from the preceding δύναται κ. φ. ἀφ' ἑαυτοῦ.

[3] [2208 b] In xvii. 21 "that they may be all one: even as (καθώς) thou, Father [art] in me and I [am] in thee, that they also may be in us," if the punctuation were "that they may be all one even as thou, Father, [art] in me," it might be contended that "art" is supplied from what precedes. But, if a fresh sentence begins at "even as," "art" is omitted in accordance with Greek idiom and must be supplied in accordance with it—without any reference to what precedes. So it would not fall under this group of ellipses. See 2127 b, 2132 a.

ELLIPSIS [2211]

avoid calling Jesus "king." In xxi. 19—21 "'Follow me'......
[My] Lord, but *this man, what?*'" the δέ denotes antithesis and
implies a preceding μέν-clause, "My Lord, [I on the one hand am to
do this that thou sayest] but this man on the other hand—what [is
he to do?]" The preceding context describes Peter as first
receiving the command, "Follow," and then (while apparently in
the act of following) as "turning" and seeing the unnamed disciple
also "following." Hence the meaning might possibly be "I am
following thee as thou commandest, *but this man, what* [*is he doing,
following without command*]?" But the subsequent context ("If
I will that he tarry till I come...") points to the *future* as the object
of Peter's question: and both Origen and Chrysostom take it thus[1].

(*a*) Ἐὰν οὖν θεωρῆτε (vi. 62)

[2210] Perhaps the following extremely difficult passage is a case
of contextual ellipsis, vi. 62 "This [it seems] causes you to
stumble! If (ἐάν) therefore (οὖν) ye should be beholding (θεωρῆτε)
the Son of man ascending where he was before—[2]." The interpretation turns on (1) the connexion implied by "therefore," (2) the
meaning of "behold," whether literal or spiritual, and in good sense
or bad, (3) the nature of the "ascending," whether literal or spiritual,
(4) the words omitted in ellipsis.

[2211] (1) "Therefore," following an implied statement "ye
stumble at this," would naturally introduce an argument *a fortiori*,
"Much more, therefore, will ye stumble" (see οὖν, 2192) or something equivalent to it. (2) "Behold" θεωρῆτε (for which Chrysostom
reads ἴδητε) has been shewn (1598) to include vacant, unintelligent,
and unspiritual "beholding." (3) "Ascending to heaven," when
previously predicated concerning the Son of Man in this Gospel
(iii. 13 "No man hath ascended into heaven but only he that
descended from heaven, the Son of man") is connected with the
"lifting up of the serpent" in the wilderness, and apparently with
sacrifice for sin. If that is the meaning here, "ascending where he

---

[1] [2209 *a*] Ἀκολούθει μοι...Οὗτος δὲ τί; On this Origen says (Huet ii. 405 D) βουλόμενος μαθεῖν καὶ τὸ κατὰ τὸν Ἰωάννην τέλος, and Chrys. *ad loc.* οὐ τὴν αὐτὴν ἡμῖν ὁδὸν ἥξει; For an altern. ellipsis of γενήσεται see **2386** *c*.

[2] [2210 *a*] Τοῦτο ὑμᾶς σκανδαλίζει; ἐὰν οὖν θεωρῆτε τὸν υἱὸν τοῦ ἀνθρώπου ἀνα-
βαίνοντα ὅπου ἦν τὸ πρότερον; SS has "but if," *a* has "quod si," *b* and *e* "quid
si," *f* "si autem," *ff* "quid ergo cum." Though D has ἐὰν οὖν, *d* has "quid si."
ℵ om. οὖν.

was before" means "offering up in the flesh that supreme sacrifice which raises the incarnate Son to the place that He had in the bosom of the Father as the pre-incarnate Word." But the offering up of this sacrifice in the flesh is described by Jesus, in the passage under consideration, as giving His "flesh and blood" to be the food of men; and it is the announcement of this that has caused them to "stumble[1]."

---

[1] [2211 a] The explanation of the Johannine use of the words "ascend" and "exalt" and of their relation to Jewish thought does not strictly belong to Johannine Grammar: but some remarks on these points are necessary here. The Jews were familiar with the thought of the Deliverer "sitting on the right hand" of God, and with the image of one like unto a Son of man "coming with the clouds of heaven," as also with the Psalmist's apostrophe to the everlasting gates to open and admit "the king of glory." Jesus appears from the Fourth Gospel to have given a spiritual interpretation to these metaphors. To Him "the everlasting gates" were the gates of self-sacrifice. The "glory" was service. To sacrifice Himself for men was, relatively to men, giving Himself up entirely, to them and for them. But, relatively to God, it might be called the "ascending" of the Son to the place "where he was before."

[2211 b] The whole of Christ's life might be accurately described as a sacrifice, or a "glorifying" of God, or as a process of "ascending" to the Father: but the term "glorifying" is more particularly used for the Crucifixion and the Resurrection as summing up the essence of the life. The punishment of Crucifixion (as we know from Artemidorus' Manual of Dreams and from Jewish sources) was frequently referred to as a "lifting up"; and similar allusions are found in the Fourth Gospel, never in the Synoptists. Hence, when the Jews stood round the Cross of Christ "staring and gaping" upon Him, as the Psalmist says, they were really "beholding Him going up to the place where He was before." And some thought of this kind—some notion of unintelligent "staring and gaping"—may have been in John's mind when he described the soldier piercing Christ's side, as fulfilling the prophecy "they shall look on him whom they pierced."

[2211 c] On the late Jewish use of "lifted up" for "crucified," or "hanged," see Levy i. 549 b (quoted in 1003 c). Artemidorus, too, writing in the second century, connects dreams about "*lifting up*" and "stretching out of hands" with crucifixion, thus, i. 76 εἰ δέ τις ὑψηλὸς ἐπί τινος ὀρχοῖτο, εἰς φόβον καὶ δέος πεσεῖται· κακοῦργος δὲ ὢν σταυρωθήσεται διὰ τὸ ὕψος καὶ τὴν τῶν χειρῶν ἔκτασιν, and again in his special section on dreams "about the Cross" (ii. 53) ἀγαθὸν δὲ καὶ πένητι· καὶ γὰρ ὑψηλὸς ὁ σταυρωθεὶς καὶ πολλοὺς τρέφει, i.e. "Such a dream betokens good for a poor man also; for the crucified is '*lifted up*' and he '*feeds many*.'" "To feed many" means to be a rich man with plenty of slaves. But it also contains a grim allusion to the fact that the crucified "*fed the crows*" ("non pasces in cruce corvos"), which he refers to in the context, τὰς σάρκας ἀπολλύουσιν οἱ σταυρωθέντες, "the crucified *lose their flesh*." For a bachelor, he adds, the cross betokens a marriage, "but not at all a profitable one," by reason of the "*binding*." The cross also prevents a man from going forward (ἐπιβαίνειν) on the land and from staying where he would like to stay. To be crucified in a city (*ib.*) "signifies

[2212] According to this view, θεωρέω is used here, as in some other passages of the Fourth Gospel (1598) for unintelligent "beholding," seeing with the eyes of the flesh: and the meaning of the passage is, "Doth this cause you to stumble, [the mere setting forth, in word, of the doctrine of a self-sacrificing Messiah]? [*What*] *therefore* [*will ye do, and how much more grievously will ye stumble*] if ye behold[1] [the fulfilment, in act, of my doctrine, not your doctrine, of the Messianic glory; if, instead of gazing at the King of glory going up in visible splendour on the clouds of heaven, ye 'stand staring and gaping' at] the [crucified] Son of man, [going down as ye suppose to Sheol, but in fact] going up where He was before[2]?"

some office corresponding to the place wherein the cross is erected (ἀρχὴν τοιαύτην σημαίνει οἷος ἂν ᾖ ὁ τόπος ἐν ᾧ ὁ σταυρὸς ἔστηκεν)." In a later section about "carrying (βαστάζειν) and being carried (βαστάζεσθαι)" (ii. 56) he again refers to the cross. Some of these details are curiously similar to xxi. 18 "thou shalt (1) *stretch out thy hands*, and another shall (2) *gird* (i.e. bind) thee, and shall (3) *bear thee where thou dost not desire*," to which is added, "this he said signifying by what death he [*i.e.* Peter] should glorify God." See **2642** *b*.

[1] [2212 *a*] The present subjunctive may, perhaps, be regarded as prophetic present, or it may denote continuance, "what if ye find yourselves beholding...."

[2] [2212 *b*] Chrysostom, reading ἂν οὖν ἴδητε, likens this mention of "ascending" to Christ's promise to Nathanael ("thou shalt see greater things than these... [angels of God ascending]") and to Christ's argument with Nicodemus ("No man hath ascended to heaven except the Son of man..."). He seems to reject the interpretation given above, saying "Doth He knit perplexities with perplexities? No. God forbid! But by the grandeur of His doctrines, and by their abundance, He desires to attract them (τῷ μεγέθει τῶν δογμάτων καὶ τῷ πλήθει αὐτοὺς ἐπαγαγέσθαι βούλεται)."

[**2212** *c*] This feeling (namely, that Christ is looking forward to a time when the disciples will *not* "stumble") has probably caused the alterations in the text mentioned above (**2210** *a*). For, if δέ be read for οὖν, then contrast replaces inference, and the whole meaning is changed to something of this kind: "*This* (emph.) causeth you to stumble: *but* [*wait a little, what will ye say*] if ye should be [soon] beholding the Son of man visibly ascending [in triumph] where He was before? [Then ye will cease to stumble]." There is much against this. It involves an alteration of a difficult text to a less difficult one. Moreover, though all Christians (like the martyr Stephen) might be represented as seeing Christ *at* the right hand of God, only an exceptional few (Acts i. 2—13) could be represented as seeing Him *in the act of ascending* to God. It seems to take θεωρῆτε as being a fleshly "beholding" and yet as one that will remove a stumbling-block. It does not tell us who will thus "behold"—or when, and how, they will be delivered from "stumbling" by the "beholding." The Acts, which relates the Ascension, implies that a small number witnessed it. But those whom Christ was now addressing were apparently a large number, for He says to them (vi. 64) "There are some of you that believe not," and then it is added "Many of his disciples went back."

(iii) Idiomatic

(a) Ellipsis of "some"

[2213] The most important elliptical expression in John is the Graeco-Hebraic use of "I am" (without any predicate expressed or implied in the context) for which see **2220** foll. There are two or three omissions of ἄν with the indicative, which need little comment[1]. But the omission of "some" in the phrase "some of" requires notice. For the most part it is free from ambiguity, as in vi. 39 "that...I may not lose [*any*] of it (ἵνα...μὴ ἀπολέσω ἐξ αὐτοῦ)," where, strictly speaking, μηδέν would be supplied, not τι, vii. 40 "[*Some*] of the crowd, therefore (ἐκ τοῦ ὄχλου οὖν), having heard these words, said...," xvi. 17 "There said therefore [*some*] of (εἶπαν οὖν ἐκ) the disciples...," xxi. 10 "Bring [*some*] of (ἀπό) the fish."

[2214] The following is ambiguous, i. 24 Καὶ ἀπεσταλμένοι ἦσαν ἐκ τῶν Φαρισαίων, R.V. txt "And they had been sent from the Pharisees," R.V. marg. "and [certain] had been sent from among the Pharisees." In favour of R.V. marg. are the following facts. (1) The partitive use of ἐκ is very frequent in John[2]. (2) John has already told us who sent the deputation (i. 19 "The Jews sent to him"). (3) "Some of the Pharisees" makes excellent sense. "Priests and Levites" alone have been as yet mentioned: and they (we may suppose) have asked their questions, and have been silenced. They are on the point of going back to those who sent them, carrying a merely negative answer ("I am not the Christ" etc.). But now it is added that there were "Pharisees" on the deputation, men learned in the Law and the Traditions, given to ask "By what authority?" and not so easily silenced: these therefore intervene with the question, "Why baptizest thou then?" These arguments are not conclusive, but they make it probable that there is an ellipsis of "some[3]."

[2215] ix. 40 "[*Some*] *of the Pharisees* heard these things (ἤκουσαν ἐκ τῶν Φ. ταῦτα)—those that were with him (οἱ μετ' αὐτοῦ ὄντες)—and

---

[1] [2213 a] xv. 22, 24 ἁμαρτίαν οὐκ εἴχοσαν, xix. 11 οὐκ εἶχες ἐξουσίαν. In viii. 39, we ought probably to read, with W.H. txt, ποιεῖτε (not, with W.H. marg. ἐποιεῖτε), see **2078—9**. Ἄν is said to be (Winer p. 382) regularly omitted in modern Greek in such instances, and the omission is freq. in later classical Greek. It might also be a Latinism. Perhaps in N.T. it adds force, "they would assuredly have had no sin." See also **2698**.

[2] It is about as freq. in Jn as in Mk, Mt. Lk. together.

[3] [2214 a] Chrysostom and many scribes of various MSS. read οἱ before ἀπεσταλμένοι, as A.V. "they which were sent," so as to leave no ellipsis.

said, Are we also blind?" A.V. "And [*some*] *of the P.* which were with him," R.V. "*Those of the Pharisees* which were with him." John's frequent use of apposition (1928—47) combines here with his frequent use of partitive ἐκ, to make an ellipsis of τινες almost certain. Chrysostom in his comment ("There say unto Him [some] of those that were following Him¹") apparently takes it thus, and he suggests that the evangelist added the clause οἱ μετ' αὐτοῦ to shew that they were the same that had previously revolted and afterwards tried to stone Him². This construction ("[some] from," *i.e.* "[some] of") is frequent in Hebrew and fairly frequent in LXX. In both, it gives rise to ambiguities, *e.g.* Lev. xxv. 33 (R.V.) "If one *of* the Levites redeem," marg. "redeem *from* the Levites," where LXX (παρά) takes the latter view, but Aquila and Symmachus (ἐκ) the former³.

(β) Ellipsis (?) of "gate" (v. 2)

[2216] v. 2 (R.V.) "Now there is in Jerusalem *by the sheep* [*gate*] (ἐπὶ τῇ προβατικῇ) a pool...," A.V. "*by the sheep* [*market*] (marg. *gate*)." The text is probably corrupt. But in any case no solid grounds have been alleged for the hypothesis of an ellipsis of "gate." (1) Eusebius, Jerome, Chrysostom, and the ancient Latin and Syriac versions make no mention of "gate" in connexion with this passage. (2) Nehemiah mentions all the gates of Jerusalem, the "*sheep-gate*" among them, where the context would make his meaning quite clear without "*gate*"; yet the noun "gate" is never omitted by his narrative in Hebrew or Greek⁴. (3) No instance of such an ellipsis has ever been quoted from Greek literature (although it would probably have been frequently used if it existed in that language, as in German). (4) Wetstein has shewn that a Jewish

---

¹ Λέγουσιν αὐτῷ ἐκ τῶν ἀκολουθούντων αὐτῷ, Μὴ καὶ ἡμεῖς τυφλοί ἐσμεν;

² [2215 a] Οὐχ ἁπλῶς δὲ ὁ εὐαγγελιστὴς ἐμνημόνευσεν, ὅτι ἤκουσαν ἐκ τῶν Φαρισαίων ταῦτα οἱ μετ' αὐτοῦ ὄντες, καὶ εἶπαν· Μὴ καὶ ἡμεῖς τυφλοί ἐσμεν; ἀλλ' ἵνα σε ἀναμνήσῃ ὅτι οὗτοι ἐκεῖνοι ἦσαν οἱ πρότερον ἀποστάντες, εἶτα λιθάσαντες, καὶ ῥᾳδίως εἰς τοὐναντίον μεταβαλλόμενοι.

³ [2215 b] In Dan. i. 6 Theod. ἐκ "*of the number of*"=LXX ἐκ τοῦ γένους "*descended from.*" In 1 Esdr. v. 45 οἱ ἐκ alters the sense of the Heb. of Ezr. ii. 70 "*some of*," LXX ἀπὸ τοῦ. In 1 Esdr. i. 8, ἐκ τῶν βασιλικῶν "from the king's [treasures] (? king's officers)"=2 Chr. xxxv. 7—8 "from the king's substance. And his princes...."

⁴ [2216 a] Neh. ii. 13, 14, iii. 1, 3, 13, 14 etc. In Neh. xii. 31 "the dung-gate," LXX omits the whole; ℵ has τῆς κοπρίας, with τῆς πύλης superscr.

word similar to προβατική (and perhaps transliterated from it) was in use to mean "bathing place." (5) This might be interpreted in Greek as "pool (κολυμβήθρα)," besides being transliterated in the text as προβατική, "bathing place." (6) On the three occasions where προβατική occurs in LXX it happens to be joined to πύλη (Neh. iii. 1, 32, xii. 39) so that the adjective might naturally suggest the interpolation of "*gate*" to any persons perplexed by the apparent use of προβατική as a noun. (7) Thus the two words might be combined so as to give the sense of a "pool" near a "sheep-gate."

There may not be quite enough evidence to support this explanation; but, in any case, so far as we are acquainted at present with the Greek language, there is no evidence at all for the ellipsis of "*gate*[1]."

(γ) Ellipsis of "daughter" (or "wife"?)

[2217] xix. 25 (R.V.) "Mary *the* [*wife*] (ἡ) of Clopas." The almost universal practice in Greek writers is to use ἡ τοῦ 'A. to mean "the [daughter] of A." In a few special cases, where the relationship was historically known, ἡ τοῦ 'A. might mean "the mother, *or* sister, *or* wife, of A.," but these are not to the point here. In Latin, "Verania Pisonis" is used for "Piso's [wife] Verania," and such a use of the genitive is current in some parts of England: but obviously it would lead to confusion if "Clopas's Mary" could mean indiscriminately either "mother, daughter, or wife, of Clopas." The reasons for believing that ἡ τοῦ must here have been intended to mean "daughter" must be deferred to another work.

(δ) Ἀλλ' ἵνα, see 2063—4 and 2105—12.

(ε) Οὐχ ὅτι

[2218] Some verb or phrase is omitted in connexion with οὐχ ὅτι as follows: (1) vi. 45—6 (R.V.) "Every one that hath heard from the Father, and hath learned, cometh unto me. *Not that* (οὐχ ὅτι) any man hath seen the Father, save he which is from God, he

---

[1] [2216 *b*] As regards the possible ellipsis in v. 44 τὴν δόξαν τὴν παρὰ τοῦ μόνου [θεοῦ], and the question whether "the Alone" is here used for God, see **1895**. For the ellipsis of ἱματίοις in xx. 12 ἐν λευκοῖς, comp. Rev. iii. 4 περιπατήσουσιν...ἐν λευκοῖς, and Artemid. ii. 3 ἐν λευκοῖς ἐκφέρεσθαι, also Mt. xi. 8, Lk. vii. 25 ἐν μαλακοῖς. Wetst. on Jn v. 44 supplies more instances, Latin as well as Greek.

hath seen the Father[1]," (2) vii. 22 (R.V.) "For this cause hath Moses given you circumcision (*not that* it is of Moses but of the fathers); and on the sabbath ye circumcise a man" (A.V. "*not because* it is of Moses")[2]. Compare 1 Jn iv. 9—10 (R.V.) "Herein was the love of God manifested in us, *that* (ὅτι) (A.V. *because that*) God hath sent his only begotten son...Herein is love, *not that* (οὐχ ὅτι) we loved God but that (ἀλλ' ὅτι) he loved us and sent...[3]." In the Epistle ἐν τούτῳ...ὅτι appears to mean "Herein...[*I mean in the fact*] *that*," and ἐν τούτῳ...οὐχ ὅτι "Herein...[*I do*] *not* [*mean in the fact*] *that*."

[2219] As regards the two passages in the Gospel, it is not possible to demonstrate that ὅτι means "that" (and not "because")— just as, in English, it is not possible sometimes to decide whether the expression "*not that* I wish" means "[*I say this*] *not because* I wish" or "[*I do*] *not* [*mean to say*] *that* I wish." But, having regard to the classical[4] and the Pauline[5] uses of οὐχ ὅτι, and to the contexts of the two Johannine passages, we may conclude that "*I say*" (whether in the sense of "I mean" or otherwise) is to be supplied in both of them. That being the case, it will be more in accordance with

---

[1] [**2218 a**] Πᾶς ὁ ἀκούσας παρὰ τοῦ πατρὸς καὶ μαθὼν ἔρχεται πρὸς ἐμέ. οὐχ ὅτι τὸν πατέρα ἑώρακέν τις εἰ μὴ ὁ ὢν παρὰ [τοῦ] θεοῦ, οὗτος ἑώρακεν τὸν πατέρα. Origen (Huet ii. 293 A) ὁ ὢν παρὰ τῷ πατρί, and so SS "he that is with God," Chrys. 1st, ὁ ὢν παρὰ τοῦ θεοῦ, 2nd, ὁ ὢν ἐκ τοῦ θεοῦ.

[2] [**2218 b**] Διὰ τοῦτο Μωυσῆς δέδωκεν ὑμῖν τὴν περιτομήν,—οὐχ ὅτι ἐκ τοῦ Μωυσέως ἐστὶν ἀλλ' ἐκ τῶν πατέρων,—καὶ [ἐν] σαββάτῳ περιτέμνετε ἄνθρωπον. SS "not because...but because," *b, e*, and *f* "not because," *a* om. "because."

[3] [**2218 c**] Ἐν τούτῳ ἐφανερώθη ἡ ἀγάπη τοῦ θεοῦ ἐν ἡμῖν, ὅτι τὸν υἱὸν αὐτοῦ τὸν μονογενῆ ἀπέσταλκεν ὁ θεὸς...ἐν τούτῳ ἐστὶν ἡ ἀγάπη, οὐχ ὅτι ἡμεῖς ἠγαπήκαμεν τὸν θεόν, ἀλλ' ὅτι αὐτὸς ἠγάπησεν ἡμᾶς καὶ ἀπέστειλεν.... But Jn ix. 30 ἐν τούτῳ γὰρ τὸ θαυμαστόν ἐστιν ὅτι is to be explained differently, since "in this" means "in your not knowing" (comp. "we know not") and ὅτι means "because." See **2393**.

[4] [**2219 a**] In classical Greek οὐχ ὅτι means (1) "[I do] *not* [say only] *that*," i.e. "not only"; (2) "[I do] *not* [mention the fact] *that*," i.e. "I pass over the fact," *e.g.* Plat. *Protag.* 336 D "Socrates will not forget—*I take no account of the fact that* (οὐχ ὅτι) he jokes and says he is forgetful," *i.e.* "although he jokes," comp. *Gorg.* 450 E. Similarly, but with ἵνα μὴ λέγω σοι ὅτι, Philem. 19, "*not to say that* you owe me also yourself."

[5] [**2219 b**] In 2 Cor. vii. 9 "Now I rejoice, *not because*," the meaning is clear, and there is no ellipsis, and prob. in 2 Cor. iii. 4—5 "This great confidence we have...*not because*...," and 2 Thess. iii. 7—9: but in 2 Cor. i. 23—4 "I gave up my plan...from a desire to spare you," the best meaning of the following οὐχ ὅτι is attained by some insertion of "say" as "[*I say this*] *not because*," or "[*I do*] *not* [*mean to say*] *that*," and so in Phil. iii. 10—12, iv. 10—11, 17.

general Greek usage if we supply λέγω not before οὐχ ὅτι, but before ὅτι, giving λέγω the sense "I mean to say," which it repeatedly has in N.T., and in Greek generally, so that οὐχ ὅτι is equivalent to "[*I do*] *not* [*mean to say*] *that*." Then, in both passages, it will correct a possible misapprehension. In the former, vi. 45—6, the words "from the Father"—naturally meaning "from the home of" (2356) or "from the side of," the Father—might suggest a person seeing the Father face to face. This is disclaimed by the words "[*I do*] *not* [*mean*] *that* any one hath seen the Father." In vii. 22, there is a similar disclaimer, "Moses hath given you circumcision—[*I do*] *not* [*mean to say*] *that* he originated it, but it was from the fathers."

(ζ) Ellipsis after "I am"

[2220] In the Walking on the Waters it is usual to assume that vi. 20 ἐγώ εἰμι means "*I am* [*indeed that which I appear to be*]," "*I am* [*my very self*]," or, according to our English idiom, "*It is I*[1]." This would accord with what is stated in the parallel Mark-Matthew, namely, that the disciples "thought they saw a phantasm[2]." In opposition to this, Christ might naturally be supposed to say " *I am* [*not a phantasm but*] *I* [*myself*]." But there is no proof that the Greek words can mean this. And there is proof that, in the Discourse on the Last Days, Mark uses ἐγώ εἰμι to mean "*I am* [*the Saviour, Deliverer, or Christ*]." Moreover in that Discourse Luke (who omits the Walking on the Waters) agrees with Mark in the use of ἐγώ εἰμι, and Matthew shews that he understood the phrase thus by supplying the ellipsis, "*I am the Christ*[3]." Lastly, Luke indicates that he would not have agreed in rendering ἐγώ εἰμι "I am my very self" by the fact that elsewhere, when he actually attributes a meaning of this kind to our Lord, he adds αὐτός[4].

[2221] The N.T. use of "*I am*" to mean "*I am the Saviour*" is in accordance with passages in Deuteronomy and Isaiah, where

---

[1] The same interpretation is usually given to Mk vi. 50, Mt. xiv. 27 θαρσεῖτε, ἐγώ εἰμι, μὴ φοβεῖσθε. Jn vi. 20 om. θαρσεῖτε.

[2] Mk vi. 49 ἔδοξαν ὅτι φάντασμά ἐστιν, Mt. xiv. 26 ἐταράχθησαν λέγοντες ὅτι Φάντασμά ἐστιν.

[3] [2220 a] Mk xiii. 6, Mt. xxiv. 5, Lk. xxi. 8 all have πολλοί (Mt.-Lk.+γάρ) ἐλεύσονται ἐπὶ τῷ ὀνόματί μου λεγόντες (Mk+ὅτι) Ἐγώ εἰμι (Mt.+ὁ Χριστός). In Mk xiv. 62, ἐγώ εἰμι is not used absolutely but answers the question "Art thou the Christ?" where the parall. Mt. xxvi. 64 has σὺ εἶπας and the parall. Lk. xxii. 67—70 has, 1st, ἐὰν ὑμῖν εἴπω... and, 2nd, ὑμεῖς λέγετε ὅτι ἐγώ εἰμι.

[4] Lk. xxiv. 39 ἐγώ εἰμι αὐτός.

ἐγώ εἰμι corresponds to the Hebrew "*I* [*am*] *he* [*to whom all must look*]," and is applied to God. The LXX uses the same phrase to render the boast of Nineveh in Zephaniah, "*I* [*am*], and there is none else beside me[1]." Nor is there (as at present alleged) any solid evidence to shew that ἐγώ εἰμι could bear, at least in the first century, anything else but this meaning—derived through LXX from Hebraic sources—"*I am the Saviour*, or *Deliverer.*" The Thesaurus gives no instance of the meaning "I am my very self." Wetstein (on Mt. xiv. 27) quotes authority for phrases in the context, but none for "*I am*" in this sense. Westcott and Swete quote none to the point[2].

[2222] If therefore we are to be guided by evidence, we must suppose the meaning to be, not "I am myself, Jesus of Nazareth," but "I am your Saviour[3]." It is to be interpreted as a vestige of the poetic and Hebrew element underlying the story of the Stilling of the Storm, in which the disciples saw the form of Jesus, and heard Him saying, "I AM [HE]," meaning "I am He that helpeth." It is, then, a genuine case of ellipsis, for the meaning is not "*I am*" in the sense of "*I live*" or "*I exist-eternally*[4]." There is an ellipsis of HE meaning, in Jewish tradition, "Deliverer," but also implying more than this, as will appear in the next Johannine instance of "I am."

---

[1] Deut. xxxii. 39, Is. xliii. 10, Zeph. ii. 15. The Heb. has "*I he*" in the first two, and simply "*I*" in the third.

[2] [2221 *a*] Swete (on Mk vi. 50) says "ἐγώ εἰμι = 'It is I,' cf. Lc. xxiv. 39, ἐγώ εἰμι αὐτός, and the use of אני, LXX ἐγώ in the O.T. (B.D.B., p. 59)." But Lk.'s insertion of αὐτός separates his usage from that of Mk, and Gesen. p. 59 merely says that Heb. אני (LXX ἐγώ) is used "*alone in response to a question*," *e.g.* Gen. xxvii. 24 "Art thou my son Esau? And he said I [am]" ὁ δὲ εἶπεν, Ἐγώ. None of these instances are to the point.

[2221 *b*] Westcott (on Jn vi. 20) says, "It is I. Comp. iv. 26, viii. 24, 28, 58, (ix. 9), xiii. 19, xviii. 5, 6, 8; Mark xiii. 6, Luke xxi. 8." But (2205) these are either cases of contextual ellipsis or else of special and technical meaning, I AM: and indeed Westcott himself (on viii. 24) distinguishes the technical usage from "cases where the predicate is directly suggested by the context."

[3] [2222 *a*] Comp. Orig. on Mt. xiv. 27 (Huet i. 242 A—B) ταραχθησόμεθα πρὶν τρανῶς καταλαβεῖν ὅτι ὁ σωτὴρ ἡμῖν ἐπιδεδήμηκεν, which suggests how "Saviour" and "Jesus" might be interchanged, especially in translating from a language in which "Jesus" meant "Saviour."

[4] [2222 *b*] The Syr. of ἐγώ εἰμι is a reduplication of "I," which pronoun (Thes. Syr.) also represents the copula, so that "I I" may mean "I am."

[2223] viii. 24—5 "'For except ye believe that I AM, ye shall die in your sins.' They therefore said to him, 'Who art thou?' Jesus said to them, '[From] the beginning that which I also speak to you¹.'" The words "believe me and understand that I AM HE" occur in Isaiah, as follows, "Ye are my witnesses, saith the Lord, and my servant whom I have chosen, that ye may know and believe me, and understand that I [AM] HE...Yea, since the day was, I [AM] HE²." In the Psalms, this use of HE occurs with an ellipsis of "art" in addressing Jehovah, "Thou [art] HE and thy years shall not fail³." The Song in Deuteronomy says "See now that I, I, [AM] HE," where LXX has "See, see that I AM⁴." Here Philo paraphrases I AM as "that there is from the beginning a Cause of the Universe⁵." Ibn Ezra (on Isaiah xliii. 10—13) says, "This is the sublimest expression of the unity of God; for every other being is different from its real form"—apparently meaning that, whereas all other things deviate from their ideal, God alone is true to the Ideal. Hence God is Truth and also Perfection. Apparently he takes I [AM] HE to mean "I am he that is," *i.e.* is really, eternally, and unchangeably.

[2224] In LXX, the Hebrew I HE is regularly rendered ἐγώ εἰμι. Aquila certainly rendered it so once and presumably always⁶. In Hebrew, the personal pronoun "he" is so frequently used as a substitute for the verb "to be" that Greeks might well translate "he" by εἰμί in this phrase. In Aramaic also (Levy) "he" is "used for the copula" as well as for the personal pronoun⁷. Hence any Semitic Logia of Jesus using this idiom would probably be rendered in Greek for the most part by ἐγώ εἰμι. In the Psalms, HE in "Thou [art] HE" is once rendered ὁ αὐτός, "the same⁸." The Semitic I HE is perhaps latent under ἐγώ εἰμι αὐτός, assigned to Christ by Luke alone⁹. But the text is doubtful (2699 foll.).

---

¹ [2223 a] Ἐὰν γὰρ μὴ πιστεύσητε ὅτι ἐγώ εἰμι ἀποθανεῖσθε ἐν ταῖς ἁμαρτίαις ὑμῶν. As to "the beginning" and "that which I also speak," see **2154—6** and **2225**.

² Is. xliii. 10—13, comp. xlvi. 4, xlviii. 12 (**2224** a).

³ Ps. cii. 27 (lit. Heb.) R.V. "Thou art the same." ⁴ Deut. xxxii. 39.

⁵ [2223 b] Philo i. 258 ὅτι ἔστι τι καὶ ὑπάρχει τὸ τῶν ὅλων αἴτιον, and he paraphrases ὅτι Ἐγώ εἰμι ἴδετε as Τὴν ἐμὴν ὕπαρξιν θεάσασθε.

⁶ [2224 a] In Is. xlviii. 12, where LXX om. the phrase, Aq. Sym. and Theod. render I HE by ἐγώ εἰμι, and Aq. is so consistent in his general renderings that he may be presumed to have been consistent in this particular one.

⁷ Levy *Ch.* i. 195 b. ⁸ Ps. cii. 27. ⁹ Lk. xxiv. 39.

[2225] That John, when writing "believe that I AM," did not mean exactly "believe that I am the eternal God," may be inferred from several facts. (1) Christ's hearers (until they heard the words "before Abraham[1]") did not take I AM in that sense. Else they would have stoned Jesus at once. (2) The words are put by the Synoptists into the mouth of any false Messiah that might say, in effect, "I am the Deliverer." (3) John always represents the Son as claiming to reveal the Father and to be one with the Father, but never as claiming to be the One God. It is not so easy—probably it is impossible—to define exactly John's positive meaning: but some light may be thrown on it by the first of the passages in which Isaiah uses the phrase. It runs thus in Hebrew "Ye are my witnesses, saith Jehovah, and my servant whom I have chosen, in order that ye may know and believe in (lit. to) me, and may understand that I [AM] HE[2]." The Targum has (after "Jehovah") "my servant Christ whom I have chosen that ye may know and believe before me and may understand that I [AM] HE *that is from the beginning*." Thus, if we, as it were, interrogate the speaker in Isaiah as to the meaning of I HE and ask "What art thou?" the Targum answers "HE *that is from the beginning*." But this is curiously like the question and answer in John after Jesus had insisted on the necessity of believing "that I AM." The Jews had asked "Who art thou?" and the first word of Christ's reply is "[In] the beginning (τὴν ἀρχήν)[3]."

[2226] There are several interesting resemblances between the Hebrew doctrine of the I HE (or the Greek doctrine of the I AM) in Isaiah and the Johannine doctrine about the unity of the Father and the Son. For example, "My Father worketh from the beginning

---

[1] viii. 58.   [2] Is. xliii. 10.

[3] [2225 a] The Targ. paraphrases I HE elsewhere as follows, Deut. xxxii. 39 (Heb. "I, I, HE") (Jer. 1) "I [*am*] *He who Am and Was, and Will be*," (Jer. 11) "I *in my word* [*am*] *He*"; Ps. cii. 27 "Thou [art] *He that created us*"; in Is. xliii. 13 Heb. "From the day I HE" is (Targ.) "From eternity I HE"; in Is. xlvi. 4 "Even to old age I HE"=Targ. "Even to eternity I HE." Perh. the Targumist regarded "from eternity" and "to eternity" as attributes, and therefore did not in these last two passages insert such predicates as "that created us" or "that is from the beginning" etc. Comp. Is. lii. 6 "Therefore my people shall know my name, therefore [I say, they shall know] in that day that I [AM] HE that speaketh, behold me" (Ibn Ezra "when I shall proclaim, Behold it is I"). Swete punctuates the LXX ὅτι ἐγώ εἰμι αὐτὸς ὁ λαλῶν· πάρειμι, but there are many ways of combining the words. The Targ. is (Walton) "scietis, quoniam ego sum qui loquebar et Verbum meum permanet."

[2227]   ELLIPSIS

and I work," "I—and yet not I, but I and the Father that sent me," combined with the present passage ("I AM....From the beginning that which I speak unto you") appear to represent the Son as "from the beginning" at one with the Father in "working" the work of supporting and redeeming man. So in Isaiah, we find, in one and the same context, "I AM," together with *from the beginning* (in Hebrew, Aramaic and Greek[1]), and "I will *work*[2], who shall hinder it?" Another passage introduces "speaking," "I [AM] HE that speaketh[3]."

[2227] One of the most spiritually minded of the early Rabbis, Abba Saul, who flourished about 130 A.D., extracting the words I AND HE out of a passage of Scripture where they have no existence, paraphrases them thus, "I will be like Him [*i.e.* God]: as He is merciful and kind, so will I too be merciful and kind[4]." Commenting on the Isaiah passage (Is. xlvi. 3) that describes Jehovah as carrying His people, Ibn Ezra says "The idols of Babylon are carried by their worshippers but I, the God of Israel, carry the Israelites." This conception of man as being *in* "the *arms*" of God, his Father—and not as crouching *under* "the *arm*" of God, his Chastiser, pervades the whole of the Fourth Gospel. It may be taken as certain that the evangelist attaches some meaning of this kind to the Greek words I AM in virtue of their association with the thought of God carrying man in His bosom. It would be bathos to suppose that Jesus, after saying "I am the bread of life" and "I am the light of the world," now comes down to the bare "I am" implying nothing more than mere existence, conceivably bad as well as good.

---

[1] [2226 *a*] The Heb. is (Is. xliii. 13) "from the day" (R.V. txt "since the day was"), which is rendered by LXX "from the beginning." The Aramaic has here "from eternity," and inserts in xliii. 10 "he that is from the beginning."

[2] [2226 *b*] The Heb. of Is. xliii. 13 "work" is regularly rendered ἐργάζομαι (though LXX renders it "make (ποιῶ)" here) which is the word in Jn v. 17 "My Father worketh and I work."

[2226 *c*] The curious juxtaposition of "*know*" and "*believe*" in connexion with I AM in Is. xliii. 10, and the phrase (Is. lii. 6) "[they shall know] in that day that I [am] he that *speaketh*," may be compared with the Johannine form of Peter's confession (Jn vi. 68—9) "Thou hast *words* of eternal life, and *we know and believe* that thou art the holy one of God."

[3] Is. lii. 6.

[4] See **1022**. Bacher (*Die Agada*, ii. 367) shews that some versions have "Be thou like," but prefers the above.

[2228] Much more probably we may suppose I AM to come here, absolutely,—as a climax after the previous declarations about the "bread" and the "light"—conveying a great mass of meaning that would not be fully intelligible to any readers that had not pondered on the meaning of the divine I AM, and perhaps on the meaning of "I[1]." On the one hand I AM means more than "I am the Deliverer"; on the other, it means less than "I am the eternal God." Taken by itself, "Believe that I AM" might mean, as it means in Deuteronomy, "Believe in the unity of the Supreme God, the Deliverer of Israel": but, taken here, along with other declarations about what Jesus IS, it seems to call upon the Pharisees to believe that the Son of man is not only the Deliverer but also one with the Father in the unity of the Godhead. Many may be unable to believe that our Lord actually uttered these precise words in this sense and may yet find it quite possible to believe that they represent the essence of His doctrine, namely, that the Father is revealed to men in the ideal of humanity (with which He is at one) and not in a written law. Others may go further, and may believe that Jesus felt Himself to be thus absolutely at one with the Father.

---

[1] [2228 a] The doctrine of Epictetus (ii. 22. 15—20) concerning the "I" is worth noting in this connexion. Wherever the "I" and the "Mine" are, there, he says, will be every creature's inclination (compare "Where your treasure is there will be your heart also"): Every creature loves its own "profit ($\sigma \nu \mu \phi \acute{\epsilon} \rho o \nu$)" above all things, "This, *i.e.* profit, is father and brother and kindred and country and God." If therefore a man "identifies 'profit' with piety and honour and country and parents and friends, these are saved, all of them"; if not, they are outweighed by "profit." *This identification of the "profit" of the "I" with Goodness*, is what a Jew might express mystically by saying "*I am He.*" Epictetus adds (*ib.*) that we must needs desire to destroy anyone—brother, father, child—that comes between us and "profit" ("Unless a man hate his own father...he cannot be my disciple") but that if the "I" is identified with virtuous purpose, he will become a perfect friend, son, and father (Mk x. 30 "he shall receive a hundredfold...mothers...").

[2228 b] The Synoptic form of these doctrines may have influenced Epictetus and may have led him to think that virtuous philosophers might find their Son of man in themselves, each man in his own heart: "I will *not* 'lose my soul that I may find it.' I will *worship* my own soul, my own higher purpose, my spirit contending against the flesh." John may have written with some regard to such conclusions, putting the Synoptic doctrine in a new aspect, or developing it in an old aspect neglected by the Synoptists, in order to shew that the regeneration of man, if it was to be based on "I," must be based on a different one from the philosophic "Ego."

(η) Ellipsis of ἐcτί

[2229] In ii. 4 τί ἐμοὶ καὶ σοί, and in xxi. 22 τί πρὸς σέ; there is an ellipsis of ἐστί. Τί πρὸς σέ (of which Wetst. *ad loc.* alleges comparatively few instances) presents no difficulty, as meaning "What [is it] in relation to thee?" *i.e.* What does it concern thee? Wetst. quotes Glycas, *Annal.* iv. p. 255, *Anthol.* MSS. i. 1, and Epictet. (but without reference) μὴ προσέλθῃς· οὐδέν ἐστι πρός σε (*sic*), and τί πρὸς ἐμέ;

[2230] Τί ἐμοὶ καὶ σοί might, theoretically, be rendered "What does this concern me and thee?" for τί μοι, *by itself*, might mean "what does it concern me?" as in Epictet. iii. 22. 66 (foll. by infin.). But, as a fact, both in Hebrew and Greek (Wetst. on Mt. viii. 29) "What [is there] *to me and thee?*" always implies "*to me and thee in common*," so that the meaning is, "What have we to do with one another?" [Wetst. compares Josh. xxii. 24, 2 S. xvi. 10, 1 K. xvii. 18, 2 K. xvi. 10, 2 Chr. xxxv. 21, Joel iii. 4. But in Josh. xxii. 24, LXX omits καί, 2 K. xvi. 10 is a repetition (by error) of 2 S. xvi. 10, and in Joel iii. 4 LXX has (as Heb.) τί ὑμεῖς ἐμοί;] It occurs in Aristoph., Demosth., Epictet., Achill. Tat., Anacreon etc., and none of Wetstein's numerous quotations adds an explanatory phrase except Synesius, δήμῳ γὰρ δὴ καὶ φιλοσοφίᾳ τί πρὸς ἀλλήλους; The phrase was so common that no contemporary (2642 *a*) Greeks could doubt that πρὸς ἀλλήλους had to be supplied[1].

[2230 (i)] The ellipsis of ἐστί in the phrase ἔτι μικρόν is found in no Gospel but the Fourth, xiv. 19 "*Yet a little* (ἔτι μικρόν) and the world no longer beholdeth me: ye (emph.) behold me." The Epistle to the Hebrews, quoting from prophecy, says, "Ye have need of patience, that having done the will of God ye may gather

---

[1] [2230 *a*] In v. 36 "The witness that I have is greater than [that of] John," ἐγὼ δὲ ἔχω τὴν μαρτυρίαν μείζω τοῦ Ἰ., there is, perhaps, no ellipsis of τῆς μαρτυρίας before τοῦ Ἰ. Somewhat similarly we sometimes substitute the person for his work in vernacular English (as well as in Latin and Greek) especially when speaking about a picture or poem, "This is rather *like* Gainsborough," "*better than* Linnell," "almost *equal to* Tennyson," "*He* was *better than* his word," "How very *like him* to say that!" etc. Winer explains in the same way (Mt. v. 20) "Except your righteousness (lit.) *abound more than the scribes*," and gives frequent instances in Greek and Latin. Probably the meaning here is all the stronger for the omission of τῆς μ.: "The witness that I have is *above the level of John*."

in (κομίσησθε)¹ the promise, For *yet a little, just a little,* [and] he that cometh will come². " This illustrates the regular use of the phrase in O.T. in predictions announcing the approaching doom of the enemies of Jehovah and the deliverance of His people, who are exhorted to wait "yet a little³." The ellipsis of ἐστί after ἔτι is not mentioned in the Thesaurus and appears to spring from Hebrew sources.

[2230 (ii)] Similar ellipses of "are," with mention of time, occur in O.T. in connexion with the judgment of Jehovah that will surely come to pass in "yet seven days," "yet forty days," "yet a year" etc.⁴ Compare the *thought* in iv. 35 "Say ye not, '*Yet are four months and the harvest cometh*'? Behold, I say unto you, lift up your eyes and contemplate the lands how that they are white for reaping. *Already doth the reaper receive hire* and gather fruit for life eternal." As the Gospel connects this numbering of "*months*" with a subsequent mention of "*hire*," so does Isaiah, "Within *yet a year as the year of a hireling,*" and elsewhere he says, "Within *three years, as the years of a hireling,* and the glory of Moab shall be brought into contempt⁵," meaning apparently that Israel counted the days "like the days of an hireling, as a servant that earnestly desireth the shadow, and as an hireling that looketh for his wages⁶."

[2230 (iii)] As regards the period of "four months," it appears⁷ that the Jews divided the agricultural year into six periods of two months, the first four being "*seed-time*," "*winter*," "*winter-solstice*," "*harvest.*" It might therefore be common for farmers and labourers

---

¹ [2230 (i) *a*] Not quite the same as "receive," see L.S. quoting Dem. 304. 26 τοὺς καρποὺς κεκόμισθε " ye have *reaped* the fruits," and Herod. ii. 14 καρπὸν κ. "*gather in* corn."

² Heb. x. 37 ἔτι γὰρ μικρὸν ὅσον ὅσον, ὁ ἐρχόμενος ἥξει quoting from Is. xxvi. 20 ἀποκρύβηθι μικρὸν ὅσον ὅσον and from Hab. ii. 3 foll. (LXX).

³ [2230 (i) *b*] Comp. Rev. vi. 11 "that they should rest *yet a little time,*" and see Is. x. 25, xxix. 17, Jer. li. 33, Hos. i. 4.

⁴ [2230 (ii) *a*] Gen. vii. 4 (R.V.) "For yet seven days and I will..." ἔτι γὰρ ἡμερῶν ἑπτὰ ἐγώ (Heb. lit. "to days" and om. "and"), Is. xxi. 16 "Within yet a year as the year of a hireling and all the glory of Kedar shall fail," ἔτι ἐνιαυτὸς ὡς ἐ. μισθωτοῦ, ἐκλείψει ἡ δόξα τ. υἱῶν K., Jon. iii. 4 "Yet forty days and Nineveh shall be overthrown," LXX (by error) ἔτι τρεῖς ἡμέραι καὶ N. καταστραφήσεται.

⁵ Is. xvi. 14.

⁶ [2230 (ii) *b*] Job vii. 1—2. So Ibn Ezra (Is. xvi. 14) "*As the years of a hireling,* who daily counts when the end will come; so the prophet is satisfied, when he sees that the time of the calamity of Moab approaches."

⁷ *Hor. Heb.* on Jn iv. 35, quoting *Baba Mezia* 106 *b*.

at the conclusion of "*seed-time*," to say "*Yet four months* [i.e. *winter and winter-solstice*] and the *harvest* cometh," and from agriculturists the saying might pass into a proverb inculcating patient expectation. It is to be noted that Jn iv. 35 foll. is the only place in this Gospel where "*hire*" is mentioned. The meaning may be paraphrased thus: "Do not the farmers say, *Four months precisely, as the days of a hireling*—and then cometh the harvest? But I say to you, Lift up your eyes, and see the harvest already white, and *the hire of the reapers* already present[1]."

IMPERATIVE, see Index

INFINITIVE, see Index

INTERROGATIVE SENTENCES

(i) **Interrogative particles**

[2231] John's use of the interrogative οὐ[2], οὐχί, πῶς, πόθεν, and τί[3] seldom causes ambiguity and requires little comment. But his uses of οὐ μή and οὐκοῦν are unique in N.T. as follows:

---

[1] [2230 (iii) *a*] Comp. Jas v. 7 "Be therefore *long-suffering...the husbandman waiteth....*" In Jn iv. 35 τετράμηνός ἐστι, there is no ellipsis; but the *thought* is similar to that of the above quoted passages from O.T.

[2] [2231 *a*] In xix. 10 ἐμοὶ οὐ λαλεῖς; "To me thou speakest not!" οὐ has the force of *alpha* privative, "Thou refusest to speak to me!" As regards οὐχί—which (**1861**) is never used by Mk and is more freq. in Lk. than in Mt. and Jn taken together—there are abundant instances in N.T. of its use interrogatively as in Jn xi. 9. In vi. 42, W.H. has ⌜οὐχὶ⌝ (marg. οὐχ) οὗτός ἐστιν Ἰησοῦς ὁ υἱὸς Ἰωσήφ...; Comp. Mk vi. 3 οὐχ οὗτός ἐστιν ὁ τέκτων...; καὶ οὐκ...; Mt. xiii. 55 οὐχ οὗτός ἐστιν...; καὶ...οὐχί...; Lk. iv. 22 οὐχὶ υἱός ἐστιν Ἰωσὴφ οὗτος; In Mt. v. 46, 47, vi. 25, xii. 11, the parall. Lk. rejects οὐχί. But Lk. freq. has οὐχί interrog. elsewhere, in traditions peculiar to himself, and also in the parall. to Mt. x. 29. On οὐχί negative, see **2265** (i).

[3] [2231 *b*] On xii. 27 τί εἴπω, see **2512** *b—c*, which (the view taken in **933** being retracted) accepts the ordinary rendering "*What* should I say...?" In iv. 27 τί λαλεῖς, A.V. and R.V. give "*Why*," without alternative, and Westcott makes no comment. SS however has "*What* wast thou saying?" The Latin MSS. also have "*quid* loqueris" (following "*quid* quaeris") clearly meaning "*what*" (but Chrys. has οὐκ ἠρώτησαν τὴν αἰτίαν).

[2231 *c*] As to the interrogative use of τί generally, it has been noted (**939** *b*) that Jn never uses ἵνα τί. Διὰ τί he never uses without a negative. Τί, "*why?*" he uses frequently. Ὅτι, interrogatively used sometimes in LXX, Jn never uses thus.

INTERROGATIVE SENTENCES [2232]

(a) Οὐ μή

[2232] xviii. 11 "The cup that my Father hath given me *shall I not assuredly drink it* (οὐ μὴ πίω αὐτό)!" See 933—6, 1007, where it is maintained that this rare interrogative is rather an exclamation than an interrogation, and that it means literally "I am of course not to drink it [according to your desire]!" This view is confirmed by many details in this section shewing John's proneness to the exclamatory interrogative; and it also helps to explain (1508) one aspect of the meaning of iv. 48 "Except ye see signs and wonders ye will assuredly not believe (οὐ μὴ πιστεύσητε)!" addressed to the nobleman from Capernaum. Chrysostom suggests that "ye" may mean "ye citizens of Capernaum," and that our Lord is chiding and stimulating his faith as being weak like that of his fellow-citizens. But the words

---

[2231 *d*] As regards ὅτι, the LXX uses it to express a great number of Hebrew particles, and it often represents Heb. "Why?" "For what?" "Is not?" etc. But there is often v.r. τί ὅτι; and, where ὅτι introduces a speech, confusion may arise from the use of ὅτι *recitativum*, e.g. Gen. xviii. 13 εἶπεν K. πρὸς 'A. "Ὅτι ἐγέλασεν Σ. (D τί ὅτι) "*Wherefore* did S. laugh?" Comp. Judg. ii. 2 v.r. ὅτε, Judg. iv. 14 v.r. οὐχ ἰδού (where Swete marks no interrog. and ὅτι may mean "for indeed"), 2 S. vii. 7 v.r. τί and τί ὅτι, xii. 9 v.r. τί, 2 K. viii. 14 (Swete ὅ τι, called by Blass "v.l. (in AB) for τί," but Swete gives no v.l.), Job xxvii. 12 v.r. διὰ τί δέ etc. The instances are extremely numerous.

[2231 *e*] These special circumstances differentiate LXX Greek (and Greek influenced by LXX) from all other Greek, as to the use of ὅτι in particular and interrogative and relative particles in general. Blass says (p. 176) "the employment of ὅστις or even of ὅς in a direct question is quite incredible, except that ὅ, τι appears to be used as an abbreviation for τί ὅ, τι 'why.'" Blass (p. 331) mentions, as quoted against him, (1) Plut. *De Sera Vind.* 14 p. 558 E: but this is best punctuated τό γε σαφές...οὐδ'...ἀσφαλῶς εἰπεῖν ἔχομεν, οἷον, διὰ τί..., ἢ πάλιν δι' ἣν αἰτίαν.... (2) 2 K. viii. 14 (see 2231 *d*) which should not be mixed with non-LXX Gk, (3) [Justin] *Cohort. ad Graec.* 5 ad fin., where the txt is doubtful, but there is high authority for paraphrasing thus, "*For the same reason for which* (δι' ἣν αἰτίαν) you say Homer speaks the truth when he is on your side don't you think he speaks the truth when *we* prove (ἀποφηναμένων for ἀποφηνάμενος) from Homer a view opposite to yours?" (4) Euseb. *P.E.* vi. 7. 12 (Giff. p. 257 *d*) Ὧν δὲ ἕνεκα ταῦτα προσεισήνεγκα τῷ λόγῳ—ὅτι σε ἐκπέφευγεν..., rendered by G. "But do you ask the reasons for which...": but I should prefer: "And now to come to the reason for which I have introduced these matters—[it is] because...." To these may be added Euseb. *P.E.* vi. 7. p. 256 C, ἐκεῖνό μοι λέγε...ἆρά γέ τί ἐσμεν ἐγώ τε καὶ σύ; —φαίης ἄν—τοῦτο δὲ ὁπόθεν ἴσμεν; where I should suggest a repetition of λέγε. "Tell me this...Do we exist, you and I—yes, you say of course—but [tell me] whence we know this." Gifford renders, in note, "But do you ask whence do we know this?" The facts confirm Blass's conclusion.

apply to men of the world generally, "Ye that are rich and great will not believe without signs and wonders! [Is it to be so with thee[1]?]"

(β) Οὐκοῦν

[2233] xviii. 37 (R.V.) "Pilate therefore said unto him, Art thou a king then (οὐκοῦν βασιλεὺς εἶ σύ;)?" Οὔκουν, unaccented, may mean (1) "Not therefore," (2) "It is not, then?" (3) "Then it is so [is it not?]" In this last sense, in which it is commonly accented οὐκοῦν, it drops the negative and interrogative force, so that it can be used, in the sense "well then," even with an imperative, as in Kings (Heb.) "Be content, take two," where Symmachus has "*Well then*, take," οὐκοῦν (A οικουν, *sic*) λάβε[2]. In such cases it means, "You'll do it, then, won't you?" It may be paraphrased as "come" when Persephone coaxes her husband to make Protesilaus young again, "*Come*, husband, prithee do thou cure this ill, also[3]."

[2234] In xviii. 37, the force of οὐκοῦν cannot be understood without reference to context (and perhaps to the Synoptists). All the four evangelists agree exactly in words and order as to the question addressed by Pilate to Jesus, "Thou art [it seems] the king of the Jews[4]!" But as to our Lord's answer, "*Thou sayest* [*this*][5]," the Synoptists assert that it followed at once, whereas John says that Jesus answered at once, "*Sayest thou this* from thyself......?" Moreover, according to John, this answer provoked a contemptuous reply from Pilate, which led to Christ's explanation: "My kingdom

---

[1] [2232a] Comp. 1 Cor. i. 26, which says that "not many mighty, not many noble," are chosen, after stating that (i. 22) "Jews seek *signs* and Greeks wisdom."

[2] [2233a] 2 K. v. 23. Other copies have ἐπιεικῶς λάβε, "kindly take."

[3] [2233b] Lucian, *De Mort.* xxiii. 3 (i. p. 428) οὐκοῦν, ὦ ἄνερ, σὺ καὶ τοῦτ' ἴασαι.... Steph. quotes also *De Mort.* x. 4, xxiii. 2 with imperatives.

[4] [2234a] Mk xv. 2, Mt. xxvii. 11, Lk. xxiii. 3, Jn xviii. 33 Σὺ εἶ ὁ β. τ. Ἰουδαίων;

[5] [2234b] Σὺ λέγεις, but Jn has ἀπὸ σεαυτοῦ σὺ τοῦτο λέγεις at once, and afterwards (xviii. 37)—in answer to the question, οὐκοῦν βασιλεὺς εἶ σύ—σὺ λέγεις ὅτι β. εἰμι. On σὺ λέγεις, as a formula of assent, see Wetst. on Mt. xxvi. 25. His instances of "vos dixistis" are from Talmudic sources. They express assent to bad news ("'Num mortuus est Rabbi?' Respondit ille, 'Vos dixistis'") which a messenger shrinks from repeating to a questioner. So in Eurip. *Hippol.* 352 σοῦ τάδ' οὐκ ἐμοῦ κλύεις and fr. 379 (not in Dind.) σὺ δὲ λέγεις ταῦτ', οὐκ ἐγώ. His only instance from Gk prose is Xen. *Mem.* iii. 10. 15 αὐτός, ἔφη, τοῦτο λέγεις, where there is no bad news in the context. The use in the Gospels is prob. from Jewish sources.

is not from this world." Then, when Christ had thus admitted that He had, *in some sense*, a "kingdom," Pilate replies—dropping "*Jews*" and "*the*"—"*Well then* (οὐκοῦν) [we will not dispute about details, such as "*the* king" and "*the Jews*"] thou art *a king*." To this, and only to this—according to John—does Jesus assent by replying "*Thou sayest* that I am a king."

(γ) Μή

[2235] Μή ("it is not so, is it?" "can it be that?") is used interrogatively in the Fourth Gospel[1] more frequently than in all the Three Gospels taken together: but whereas the Three (Mark only using it once) restrict it to the words of Jesus, John almost restricts it to the words of others. There are but two instances of it in Christ's words, one being vi. 67, "*Can it be that* (μή) ye also (καὶ ὑμεῖς) desire to go away*?"

---

[1] [2235 *a*] It occurs about 17 times in Jn. Mk uses it only in ii. 19 (Mk xii. 15 being (**933** *h*) not to the point). In Jn v. 45 μὴ δοκεῖτε, imperative, SS takes μή as interrogative, "Can ye suppose?"

[2] [2235 *b*] The other is xxi. 5 Παιδία, μή τι προσφάγιον ἔχετε; Field says (*ad loc.*) "ἔχεις τι; is the usual question...answering to our 'Have you had any sport?'" By adding μή to the usual phrase, the negative expectation is emphasized, "You have caught no fish, have you?" But ought we not to read μήτι (**2702**)?

[**2235** *c*] On ἔχετε, Wetst. *ad loc.* quotes conclusively Schol. on Aristoph. *Nub.* 731, and Field adds, from Nonnus, ἦ 'ρ' ἔχομέν τι; where Schol. has ἆρα ἐθηράσαμέν τι; but the statement quoted by some from Euthymius that παιδία is a term freq. applied to labourers (ἔθος γὰρ τοὺς ἐργατικοὺς οὕτως ὀνομάζειν) is not proved (so as to be applicable to xxi. 5) by Aristoph. *Ran.* 37, *Nub.* 132 παιδίον, "boy!" rightly explained by Steph. as "servulus." A Greek could say παιδίον to the "boy [at the door]" of the house he was visiting, but not παιδία to strangers fishing. Chrys. and *a* omit παιδία. *Acts of John* § 2 represents Christ Himself as appearing on the bank to James as a παιδίον. See **2701**.

[2235 *d*] On προσφάγιον, Field, quoting A.V. "any meat," and R.V. "aught to eat," says "Rather, 'Have ye taken any fish?'" Steph. shews that προσφάγιον was a vernacular word for προσόψημα, ὀψάριον (or ὄψον, which Clem. Alex. 104 substitutes (**2307** *a*) when quoting this passage): and these words, though meaning literally "[relish] to food," were frequently used for "fish," in places where the habitual relish was "fish." In *Oxyr. Pap.* 736, προσφάγιον is rendered "relish" —after "beer, leeks,...asparagus, a cabbage"—"*a relish* half an obol," and again "*relishes* for the women on two days two and a half obols." Similarly 739 "*a relish* for the builder" thrice, 498 "each of us shall receive one loaf and a *relish* per diem." In 736, the editors also give "sauce (ὀψαρίου) one obol...sauce (ὄψου) one obol, sauce (ὀψαρίου) one obol." These entries are on three consecutive days, and—vegetables being excluded here by the mention of them in the context—it would seem probable that ὄψον means nearly the same thing as ὀψάριον and as προσφάγιον, namely "fish" in some form. Comp. *Fayum Pap.* cxix. 31 "for G.'s

(ii) Interrogative tone

[2236] There is frequent ambiguity in sentences where the interrogation, if it exists, is expressed not by a particle, but by tone[1]. In the first two of the following instances there is a protasis with a suspensive ὅτι, in the third there is not: i. 50 (R.V. and A.V.) "Because (ὅτι) I said unto thee I saw thee underneath (A.V. under) the fig-tree *believest thou*? thou shalt see greater things than these"; xx. 29 (R.V. txt and A.V.) "Because (ὅτι) thou hast seen me *thou hast believed*: blessed [are] they that have not seen and [yet] have believed" (R.V. marg. "*hast thou believed?*"); xiv. 1 (R.V.) "*Ye believe* (marg. *Believe*) (πιστεύετε) in God: believe (πιστεύετε) also in me[2]."

[2237] The following facts bear on the last (xiv. 1) of these ambiguous instances. The meaning of the ambiguous form of the 2 pers. pl. in -ετε, when it may be (theoretically) either interrogative or affirmative or imperative, is largely determined by special custom. Θέλετε, βούλεσθε, δοκεῖτε, would naturally be interrogative, "Do ye desire?" "Think ye?" Ἀκούετε and βλέπετε would naturally be imperative, "Hear ye," "See ye." Apart from such special custom, the ordinary meaning of -ετε would be—where the context does not decide otherwise—affirmative in classical Greek, because *the interrogative force, if intended, might have been expressed by an interrogative particle*, and because the imperative might (in many cases) be expressed by the unambiguous aorist, *e.g.* πιστεύσατε[3].

---

birthday feast send (?) fish (ὀψάρια) (*sic*) (edd. delicacies)...and an artaba of wheaten bread"; and *Oxyr.* 531 τοῖς ὀψαρίοις ἐξήλλαξας ἡμᾶς (?) "you won me over by the *fish* (edd. dainties)." The editors add that certain "cloaks" mentioned in the context may have been "in exchange for the ὀψάρια." Either interpretation would be compatible with the rendering "fish." Possibly, as "pickles" with us means "pickled (*vegetables*)," so the three Greek words above mentioned came to mean in certain localities, "[*fish*] for eating [with bread]," but different terms may have been applied to different kinds of fish, fresh, salt etc. *Oxyr. Pap.* 736 perhaps resembles Jn xxi. 5—9 in using 1st προσφάγιον and 2nd ὀψάριον to mean nearly the same thing. But in Jn the word may have a symbolic meaning (**2703**).

[1] [2236 *a*] This is much more frequent in Jn than in the Synoptists, *e.g.* xiii. 6 σύ μου νίπτεις τοὺς πόδας; "*Thou* dost wash my feet!"

[2] [2236 *b*] i. 50 Ὅτι εἶπόν σοι ὅτι εἶδόν σε ὑποκάτω τῆς συκῆς πιστεύεις; μείζω τούτων ὄψῃ, xx. 29 Ὅτι ἑώρακάς με πεπίστευκας; μακάριοι οἱ μὴ ἰδόντες καὶ πιστεύσαντες, xiv. 1 πιστεύετε εἰς τὸν θεόν, καὶ εἰς ἐμὲ πιστεύετε, marg. πιστεύετε, εἰς τὸν θεὸν καὶ εἰς ἐμὲ πιστεύετε.

[3] [2237 *a*] The unambiguous aorist imperative, though theoretically somewhat different in meaning, differs sometimes little (in practice) from the present

[2238] Πιστεύετε is certainly imperative twice in Mark[1] and thrice in John[2] (apart from the instance (xiv. 1) under discussion). St Paul's exhortation to the jailor in the Acts, "*Believe* in the Lord Jesus[3]" is in the singular besides being in the unambiguous aorist. But it reminds us how frequent would be the plural imperative use of the verb among evangelists during the period of numerous conversions in the early Church.

[2239] On the other hand, πιστεύετε occurs in Matthew's version of Christ's words previous to His healing two blind men—theoretically capable of meaning "*Believe,*" or "*Believe ye?*" or "*Ye believe [I suppose]*"—before the words "that I am able to do this[4]." Here it might have been plausibly argued that Jesus used the imperative to stimulate their faith, as He stimulates that of Jairus ("Be of good cheer, *only believe*[5]"): but this would be incompatible with the answer of the blind men, "*Yea*, Lord," which necessitates in πιστεύετε a meaning either directly interrogative ("Do ye believe?") or indirectly ("Ye believe [I assume before going further]?"). The latter is frequently used in English (*e.g.* "You will come with me?" "You will come with me, then?" for "You will come with me [will you not?]").

[2240] This last disconcerting instance from Matthew shews the difficulty and the danger of laying down a rule including all books of N.T. Each writer may have his own usage. But the usage of John (and of Mark, with whom John curiously agrees in some idioms) makes it probable that in the third Johannine instance above quoted (xiv. 1) πιστεύετε is imperative, "*Believe* in God,...[6]"

---

imperative. Comp. Mk v. 36 πίστευε = Lk. viii. 50 πίστευσον, and Sir. ii. 6 πίστευσον αὐτῷ, ii. 8 πιστεύσατε αὐτῷ, xi. 21 πίστευε τῷ κυρίῳ, with little apparent difference of meaning. Some writers may be more strict than others in discriminating between the two. Moreover, in particular verbs, *e.g.* ἔρχομαι, the use of the present and of the aorist imperative may vary according to special circumstances (**2438** *b*).

[1] Mk i. 15, xi. 24. [2] Jn xii. 36, xiv. 11 (*bis*).
[3] Acts xvi. 31 πίστευσον. [4] Mt. ix. 28.
[5] Mk v. 36, Lk. viii. 50. Comp. Mk xi. 24 "whatsoever ye pray...*believe* (πιστεύετε) that ye have received them."
[6] [**2240** *a*] Chrys. *ad loc.* says, "Πιστεύετε...καὶ εἰς ἐμὲ πιστεύετε." τουτέστι, πάντα παρελεύσεται τὰ δεινά (Cramer, πάντα φησὶ παρελθεῖν δεῖται(?) τὰ δεινά). Ἡ γὰρ εἰς ἐμὲ πίστις καὶ τὸν γεγεννηκότα δυνατωτέρα τῶν ἐπιόντων ἐστί (Cramer τυγχάνει) καὶ οὐδὲν ἐάσει κρατῆσαι τῶν δυσχερῶν. On this Erasmus says that it favours the rendering "*Creditis in Deum et in me creditis.* Atque ita legisse

[2241] The other two instances (i. 50, xx. 29) differ from the third, and agree together, in being preceded by a protasis with suspensive ὅτι ("Because I said unto thee...," "Because thou hast seen..."): and this leads us to ask what is John's usage after other Johannine instances of suspensive ὅτι. We shall find that there are four, and that the verb in the apodosis is always affirmative[1]. This turns the scale in favour of an affirmative in i. 50 and xx. 29 "Because I said unto thee, I saw thee under the fig-tree, *thou believest*!" "Because thou hast seen me, *thou hast believed*[2]!"

[2242] Similarly in the Acts, Paul says to Agrippa "Thou believest (πιστεύεις) the prophets [is it not so?]," and goes on to add the answer to this suggested question, "I know that thou believest[3]," and the Epistle of St James addresses a controversialist ironically thus, "*Thou* (emph.) (σύ) [*of course*] believest that there is one God[4]?"—assuming, before the writer goes further, that this must be so, but putting the assumption as an affirmation with an interrogative tone. In the Fourth Gospel, πιστεύεις is used by Jesus to Martha, "thou believest this [is it not so?][5]," and, with

---

videtur ex interpretatione sua Chrysostomus, quasi *fides quam habebant*...illis abunde præsidio esset." But might it not be consistent with an imperative rendering: "*Be not troubled.* Continue to believe....That is to say, Your terrors will all pass away. For the belief in me and in the Father is stronger than your enemies"? Erasmus says that Cyril interprets both verbs imperatively. SS and *a* have "credite...et creditis," *i.e.* "believe in God and then *ipso facto* ye will believe in me"; but if this had been the meaning, would not Jn have written "the Father" (instead of "God")? The Vulgate and *f* have "creditis...credite"; Diatess., Syr. (Walton), *b*, *d*, and *e* have "credite...credite." Erasmus enumerates four possible interpretations (1) "creditis...creditis," (2) "credite...credite," (3) "creditis ...credite," (4) "credite...creditis." To this may be added (5) (W.H. marg.), "credite, in Deum et in me credite" taking the 1st πιστεύετε absolutely; and possibly (6) "creditis in Deum? Et in me credite," "Do ye believe in God? Then believe also in me." The passage is one of the most conspicuous instances of Johannine ambiguity.

[1] Jn viii. 45, xiv. 19, xv. 19, xvi. 6, comp. Gal. iv. 6.

[2] [2241 *a*] But the *tone* in i. 50, xx. 29 is quite different from that of ordinary affirmation, *e.g.* xiv. 19 "Because (ὅτι) I live, ye also *shall live*," where the sentence ends and the reader rests on "shall live" as a natural consequence. In the two instances above mentioned, the sentence goes on to a contrast, and there is an implied exclamation: "Thou believest [but on how slight a ground]!" "Thou hast believed [it is true, but not with the highest belief]!"

[3] Acts xxvi. 27.

[4] [2242 *a*] Jas ii. 19. W.H. punctuate interrogatively, Mayor prefers an affirmation. The emph. σύ seems to mean, ironically, "thou, the orthodox disputant."

[5] xi. 26 "...he shall never die. Thou believest this?"

a different shade of meaning, σὺ πιστεύεις to the blind man: "He [Jesus] said, *Thou* (emph.) *believest* in the Son of man[1]." This apparently refers to the preceding facts—to the blind man's defence of Christ against the Pharisees, to his avowed belief in well-doing, and to his confidence that "God heareth" those who do His righteous will. If so, the meaning is, "*Thou [I am sure] believest* in the Son of man[2]," and there is little or nothing of the interrogative tone.

[2243] In xiii. 12—although R.V. and A.V. agree in the interrogative—"He said unto them, (R.V.) *Know ye* (γινώσκετε) what I have done to you?" the imperative is somewhat more probable, in view of xv. 18, "If the world hateth you, (R.V. marg.) *know ye* (γινώσκετε) that it hath hated me..." (1901, 2665—7), i.e. "*understand, recognise,* that the world hated me." The LXX usage rather favours the imperative[3]. In any case, we could not explain γινώσκετε in xiii. 12

---

[1] ix. 35.
[2] [2242 *b*] It may be said that Jesus could not have meant this, as the next words of the blind man are "And who is he, Lord?" But it may be replied that the blind man virtually believed in the ideal Son of man already, and that the Logos was supposed by the evangelist to discern this belief even before the blind man expressed it in the words (ix. 38) "I believe."
[3] [2243 *a*] Γινώσκετε does not mean "know" but "begin to know," "come to know," "recognise." It is therefore quite different from ἐγνώκατε (which is probably never imperatively used). Γινώσκετε is imperatively used in the LXX, after ἐὰν γὰρ ἀποστραφῆτε, in Josh. xxiii. 13. It is also imperative in Dan. iii. 15, 3 Macc. vii. 9 (and the sing. imperat. γίνωσκε occurs in LXX 4 times); the only indicative instances are either with ὑμεῖς inserted (Gen. xliv. 27) or in the phrase "Do ye know so-and-so?" (Gen. xxix. 5, Tob. vii. 4). In the Synoptists, the imperative and the indicative are about equally balanced. In 1 Jn ii. 29, γινώσκετε is taken by Westc. as prob. imperative, but by Lightf. (on Gal. iii. 7) apparently as indicative. In 1 Jn iv. 2, the mood is doubtful, but taken by Westc. as indicative. In Jn xiii. 12 it is generally taken interrogatively; it certainly cannot be affirmative. In xiv. 7 and xiv. 17 it is preceded severally by ἀπ' ἄρτι and ὑμεῖς and is indicative. In Heb. xiii. 23 "*know ye* that our brother Timothy hath been set at liberty," γινώσκετε is almost certainly imperative, and the only two Pauline initial uses of the verb (2 Cor. viii. 9 γ. γάρ, Gal. iii. 7 γ. ἄρα) indicate that γ. would seldom be placed at the beginning of a clause indicatively without some word such as γάρ, ἄρα, ὑμεῖς etc. to denote that the word is used affirmatively or argumentatively, or to emphasize fact. Indeed, in one of these two passages (Gal. iii. 7), R.V. txt and A.V. have the imperative. In Phil. ii. 22 τὴν δὲ δοκιμὴν αὐτοῦ γινώσκετε, the verb is non-initial, and the meaning appears to be "*Ye are alive to* his tried worth" (not quite the same as ἐγνώκατε): Chrys. paraphrases it as ὑμεῖς αὐτοὶ (v.r. αὐτόν) ἐπίστασθε. But even there it is not certain that the Apostle is not bespeaking respect for the somewhat retiring Timothy, whose quiet unselfish labours might fail to obtain due recognition even from those who (like the Philippians) were familiar with them: "For all seek their own interests, not

like πιστεύετε above, as "*Ye know [do ye not?]*." And the rendering, "*Understand* the meaning of what I have done to you," makes excellent sense. Origen (*ad loc.*) allows both renderings.

[2244] In two instances, a conditional clause ("if...as you cannot deny") prepares the way for something incongruous with that condition, which incongruity is expressed by an interrogative or exclamation of amazement: vii. 23 "If circumcision is received on the sabbath—[in the face of that fact] *are ye angry with me* (ἐμοὶ χολᾶτε) for healing on the sabbath?" x. 35—6 "If he called them gods...and the Scripture cannot be broken—[in the face of that fact] *do ye* (emph.) (ὑμεῖς) *say* (λέγετε), Thou blasphemest?" Here the emphatic "*ye*" means "ye guardians and interpreters of Scripture." Only under special circumstances could ὑμεῖς λέγετε, "*ye* (emph.) say," at the beginning of a clause, be used interrogatively.

[2245] An interrogative or exclamatory tone may be suggested by initial words that imply incongruity or the need of explanation, "*From Nazareth* can any good thing come[1]!" "*Thus* answerest thou the High Priest[2]!" "*Your king* am I to crucify[3]!" "*Our fathers worshipped in this mountain*, and [yet] (2136) ye say (ὑμεῖς λέγετε) that in Jerusalem is the place[4]!" Thus, an initial σὺ λέγεις, where there is no incongruity between the person and the utterance, would naturally mean "*thou* (emph.) sayest"; but an incongruity would make all the difference, *e.g.* "Dost *thou* [the General] say, 'Flee'?" "Dost *thou* [the Priest] say, 'Murder'?" Also such a sentence as "*From thyself* sayest thou this *or did others* say it to thee?" may be

---

those of Jesus Christ. But as for his tried worth, *I would have you recognise it*, because, like child with father, he did laborious service with me for the Gospel." It must be borne in mind that the pres. imper. γινώσκετε "be recognising," "try to recognise," would naturally be distinguished from γνῶτε "recognise [once for all]," by a careful writer (**2437—9**).

[**2243 b**] In Euripides, γίνωσκε freq. means "recognise [the facts of life etc.]," *Inus* fr. xxi. 1 γ. τἀνθρώπεια (comp. *Hec.* 227, *Alc.* 418, *Hel.* 1257) whereas γ. in 2nd pers. indic. does not occur except interrog. *Her.* 639. Also, in Xenophon and Lucian, the imperat. γίνωσκε (Steph.) is freq., especially in the phrase οὕτω γίνωσκε "make up your mind to this," which Lucian has in 2nd pers. pl. (i. 337, *Pluto* § 2) "*Make up your mind to this* that I shall not stop for a moment (οὕτω γινώσκετε ὡς οὐδὲ παυσομένου μου)." Clem. Alex. 759 quotes the Preaching of Peter thus, Πέτρος ἐν τῷ κηρύγματι λέγει, Γινώσκετε οὖν ὅτι εἷς θεός ἐστιν..., which can hardly be otherwise than imperative.

[1] i. 46. [2] xviii. 22. [3] xix. 15. [4] iv. 20.

interrogative, a question being suggested by the words "from thyself" followed by the alternative "or from others[1]?"

[2246] In xvi. 32, a contrast is implied between ἄρτι, "at the present moment" and the "hour" that "is coming and hath come" (1915 (i) foll.). Ἰδού here, as in the only other Johannine instance where our Lord uses it, is almost equivalent to the Greek δέ, "but[2]." As in the First Epistle to the Corinthians ("*For the moment* (ἄρτι) we see through a mirror darkly but *then* face to face[3]") so here, the antithesis, having an affirmative in the second clause, requires us to suppose an affirmative in the first clause also, thus, "*For the moment* (ἄρτι) [*indeed*] *ye believe*, [but] behold the hour cometh…when ye shall be scattered every man to his own." This rendering agrees with xvi. 27 "Ye *have believed*" and xvii. 8 "They [*have*] *believed*." Our Lord recognises that the disciples did really and truly "believe." They had said, however, too confidently (xvi. 30) "*Now (at last)* (νῦν) we know…herein *we believe*"; to which Jesus replies, in effect, "Do not say *Now at last*, say rather, *For the moment*. *Ye believe for the moment*, but the impending hour of trial will dissipate your belief."

---

[1] [2245 a] xviii. 34 Ἀπὸ σεαυτοῦ σὺ τοῦτο λέγεις, ἢ ἄλλοι εἶπόν σοι περὶ ἐμοῦ; This is clearly interrogative. But in xviii. 37—in answer to Pilate's second question, "Well then, thou art [it seems] *a king*?"—when Jesus replies Σὺ λέγεις ὅτι βασιλεύς εἰμι, there is no reason to suppose that this is interrogative (as it is punctuated in W.H. marg.). A distinction is clearly drawn between "*the king of the Jews*" and "*a king*." The former our Lord puts aside with contempt as a question dictated by "others," *i.e.* the chief priests. The latter was of a different kind. Everyone knew, even the boys in the streets of Rome, that the wise and virtuous philosopher claimed to be in some sense "*a king*," and the Book of Revelation (Rev. v. 10) claims that the followers of Christ are to be "kings and priests." To the latter, then, Christ assents in the words "thou sayest that I am a king." Comp. Lk. xxii. 70 "Ye say that I am [a king]." Mt. xxvi. 64 "Thou saidst [it]," σὺ εἶπας is parall. to Mk xiv. 62 ἐγώ εἰμι. At the same time it must be admitted that (2234 b) the use of σὺ λέγεις, outside N.T. (so far as Wetstein's evidence goes) generally implies bad tidings. It is a phrase that might be explained (as a saying of Christ) by various contexts. In the bringing of bad news, it means (1) "Thou sayest this [*not I*]"; but where there is no bad news, it might mean (2) "Thou [of thyself] sayest this, unprompted by others." Jn combines (1) with (2) taken interrogatively.

[2] [2246 a] Jn iv. 35 "Do not ye say…? *Behold*, I say unto you," *i.e.* "Ye are in the habit of saying, 'The harvest is coming.' *But* I tell you it is come." There, the first clause is, in effect, not a question, but the Hebraic interrogative (comp. "Is it not written?" etc.), which is a Greek affirmative.

[3] [2246 b] 1 Cor. xiii. 12. Ἄρτι is contrasted (Jn xiii. 7) with μετὰ ταῦτα, (xiii. 37) with a preceding ὕστερον, and (xvi. 12) with a preceding ἔτι.

[2247] In almost all the instances of affirmative, or exclamatory interrogation, it would be better for an English translator to imitate the Greek by leaving the sentence affirmative so far as concerns the words, trusting to context and punctuation to suggest the interrogative tone: "*Thou* (emph.) washest *my* feet!" If this were done, many sentences would be left less definite than in our R.V., but they would be closer to the meaning of the original.

(iii) **Questions without interrogative particle**[1]

[2248] The list of interrogative sentences in the footnote appended to this section will be limited to those that have no interrogative particle. Some have been discussed under καί meaning "and yet" (2136—45). In iii. 10, οὐ is in such a context that it might possibly be called an interrogative particle, "Thou art the teacher of Israel; and [yet] dost thou not know this?" But on the other hand the whole of the sentence may be regarded as exclamatory, and οὐ as merely equivalent to *alpha* privative ("The teacher of Israel...and ignorant of this!"). Hence the instance is included below[2]. The dozen or more of interrogatives with οὐ are excluded as they do not throw light on ambiguity[3].

---

[1] [2248 *a*] These are punctuated as in W.H. But in the preceding remarks, reasons have been given for punctuating many of them differently. Greek has no note of exclamation. That being the case, an editor of N.T. has to choose between two defective representations, a note of interrogation or a full stop.

[2] [2248 *b*] In vii. 19, (R.V.) "Did not M. give you the law, and [yet] none of you doeth the law?" is prob. preferable to W.H.'s text, which ends the question at "give you the law," and makes the following words a statement. In vii. 35, R.V. ("Whither will this man go *that* (ὅτι) we shall not find him?") gives the impression of meaning "*so that* we shall not find him." But that is not the meaning of the Greek. Jesus had previously said (vii. 34) "*Ye...shall not find me.*" The Jews now say in consequence "Where is he going? For [*according to his account*] (ὅτι) we shall not find him." The initial ὅτι means "[*We say this*] *because*" or "*for*," and introduces the reason for asking "Where is he going?" (2179).

[3] [2248 *c*] i. 21 ἠρώτησαν αὐτὸν Τί οὖν; [σύ] 'Η. εἶ; (marg. Τί οὖν σύ; 'Η. εἶ;)... Ὁ προφήτης εἶ σύ; i. 46 εἶπεν αὐτῷ Ν., Ἐκ Ν. δύναταί τι ἀγαθὸν εἶναι; i. 50 εἶπεν αὐτῷ Ὅτι εἶπόν σοι ὅτι εἶδόν σε ὑποκάτω τῆς συκῆς πιστεύεις; ii. 20 εἶπαν...Τεσσεράκοντα καὶ ἓξ ἔτεσιν οἰκοδομήθη ὁ ναὸς οὗτος, καὶ σὺ ἐν τρισὶν ἡμέραις ἐγερεῖς αὐτόν; iii. 10 εἶπεν αὐτῷ Σὺ εἶ ὁ διδάσκαλος τοῦ Ἰ. καὶ ταῦτα οὐ γινώσκεις; v. 6 λέγει...Θέλεις ὑγιὴς γενέσθαι; vi. 61 εἶπεν...Τοῦτο ὑμᾶς σκανδαλίζει; ἐὰν οὖν θεωρῆτε...; vii. 23 εἰ περιτομὴν λαμβάνει...ἵνα μὴ λυθῇ ὁ νόμος Μωυσέως, ἐμοὶ χολᾶτε ὅτι ὅλον ἄνθρωπον ὑγιῆ ἐποίησα ἐν σαββάτῳ; viii. 57 εἶπαν...πεντήκοντα ἔτη οὔπω ἔχεις καὶ Ἀ. ἑώρακας; ix. 19 ἠρώτησαν αὐτοὺς λέγοντες Οὗτός ἐστιν ὁ υἱὸς ὑμῶν, ὃν ὑμεῖς λέγετε

INTERROGATIVE SENTENCES [2250]

(iv) **Indirect interrogative**

[2249] This is rare in John. He prefers the direct interrogative even where it involves such a repetition as (xiii. 24) "Simon Peter beckoneth to him and saith to him, 'Say *Who is it?* about whom he saith [this],'" where many MSS. have (A.V.) "beckoned to him *that he should ask who it should be* (πυθέσθαι τίς ἂν εἴη)," an alteration made (no doubt) for style. But he uses the indirect form in two passages as follows.

[2250] (1) vii. 16—17 "My teaching is not mine but [is the teaching] of him that sent me. If any man have a will to do his will, he shall know concerning the teaching, *whether* (πότερον) *it is from God, or* [*whether*] *I am speaking from myself.*" Πότερον is not found elsewhere in N.T.[1] But it is here used deliberately to prepare the way for the weighty statement of an alternative that might at first sight seem superfluous—"*speaking from oneself.*" Why is not John content to say "He shall know *if* [i.e. *whether*] it is from God[2]," and there to stop? The answer is, that John desires to emphasize "*speaking from oneself,*" as being a crime. Some might urge that, according to the Synoptists, Christ taught "with authority," and that, in the Sermon on the Mount ("Ye have heard that it hath been said to them of old...but *I say*") He "spake from

---

ὅτι τυφλὸς ἐγεννήθη; ix. 34 εἶπαν...Ἐν ἁμαρτίαις σὺ ἐγεννήθης ὅλος, καὶ σὺ διδάσκεις ἡμᾶς; ix. 35 εἶπεν Σὺ πιστεύεις εἰς τὸν υἱὸν τοῦ ἀνθρώπου; x. 35—6 εἰ ἐκείνους εἶπεν θεούς,...ὃν ὁ πατὴρ ἡγίασεν...ὑμεῖς λέγετε ὅτι Βλασφημεῖς ὅτι εἶπον υἱὸς τοῦ θεοῦ εἰμι; xi. 8 λέγουσιν...Ῥαββεί, νῦν ἐζήτουν σε λιθάσαι οἱ Ἰουδαῖοι, καὶ πάλιν ὑπάγεις ἐκεῖ; xi. 26 οὐ μὴ ἀποθάνῃ εἰς τὸν αἰῶνα· πιστεύεις τοῦτο; xiii. 6 λέγει...Κύριε, σύ μου νίπτεις τοὺς πόδας; xiii. 12 εἶπεν...Γινώσκετε (**2243**) τί πεποίηκα ὑμῖν; xiii. 37—8 τὴν ψυχήν μου ὑπὲρ σοῦ θήσω. ἀποκρίνεται Ἰησοῦς Τὴν ψυχήν σου ὑπὲρ ἐμοῦ θήσεις; xiv. 9 λέγει...Τοσοῦτον χρόνον μεθ᾽ ὑμῶν εἰμὶ καὶ οὐκ ἔγνωκάς με, Φίλιππε; xvi. 19 εἶπεν...Περὶ τούτου ζητεῖτε μετ᾽ ἀλλήλων ὅτι εἶπον...; xvi. 30—1 πιστεύομεν ὅτι ἀπὸ θ. ἐξῆλθες. ἀπεκρίθη αὐτοῖς Ἰ. Ἄρτι πιστεύετε; xviii. 22 εἰπών Οὕτως ἀποκρίνῃ τῷ ἀρχιερεῖ; xviii. 33 εἶπεν...Σὺ εἶ ὁ βασιλεὺς τῶν Ἰουδαίων; xviii. 34 ἀπεκρίθη...Ἀπὸ σεαυτοῦ σὺ τοῦτο λέγεις ἢ ἄλλοι εἶπόν σοι περὶ ἐμοῦ; xviii. 37 ἀπεκρίθη...Σὺ λέγεις ὅτι βασιλεύς εἰμι; (so marg. but text, affirmative). xviii. 39 βούλεσθε οὖν ἀπολύσω ὑμῖν τὸν β. τῶν Ἰ.; xix. 15 λέγει...Τὸν βασιλέα ὑμῶν σταυρώσω; xx. 29 λέγει..."Ὅτι ἑώρακάς με πεπίστευκας; xxi. 15 λέγει...Σίμων Ἰωάνου, ἀγαπᾷς με πλέον τούτων; xxi. 16 λέγει...Σίμων Ἰωάνου, ἀγαπᾷς με; xxi. 17 λέγει...Σίμων Ἰωάνου, φιλεῖς με;

[1] [**2250** *a*] In LXX, it occurs only in Job, and there always (12 times) in direct interrogation.

[2] Comp. Jn ix. 25 "*If* (i.e. *whether*) (εἰ) he is a sinner I know not," also 1 Cor. vii. 16 etc.

himself." John represents Christ as affirming, some seven or eight times[1], that He is *not* sent "from himself," and that He neither says nor does anything "from himself." Not even the Holy Spirit speaks "from itself[2]." The spontaneous or originating power of the Son, and of the Spirit, springs from the Father, or from the Son in union with the Father. To do anything "from oneself" in this Johannine sense—that is, apart from the fountain head of life, order, and harmony—is always evil[3].

[2251] (2) x. 6 "This parable spake Jesus unto them: but they understood not what things they were that he spake unto them (ἐκεῖνοι δὲ οὐκ ἔγνωσαν τίνα ἦν ἃ ἐλάλει αὐτοῖς)." The apparently superfluous words in "what things they were that" (instead of "what things" or "the things that") are intended to emphasize the absolute ignorance of the persons addressed[4]. Jesus had been "talking (λαλέω)" about a shepherd that rules the flock with his voice and not by coercion. Those whom He was addressing had no conception of ruling except by Law and punishment. The evangelist might have expressed this by the phrase used in the First Epistle to Timothy[5], "did not understand *about what things* (περὶ τίνων)" Christ was teaching. But John wishes to say more, namely, *that the very language was foreign to them.* It might as well have been Iberian or Gallic. The thought must be compared with that in viii. 43 "Why do ye not understand my speech (λαλιάν)? Because ye are not able to hear my Word (ἀκούειν τὸν λόγον τὸν ἐμόν)," *i.e.* ye have not the spiritual sympathy that would give you a key to my language[6].

---

[1] v. 30, vii. 17, 18, 28, viii. 28, 42, xii. 49, xiv. 10.

[2] xvi. 13.

[3] [**2250 *b***] It is worth noting how indignantly Pilate—a mere puppet in the hands of the chief priests, whose charge against Jesus he at first assumes to be true (xviii. 33), instead of first attempting to ascertain whether it is true—disowns the notion suggested to him by Jesus that he is *not* speaking "from himself" (xviii. 34 "sayest thou this *from thyself*?").

[4] [**2251 *a***] In vi. 64 ᾔδει γὰρ ἐξ ἀρχῆς ὁ Ἰησοῦς τίνες εἰσὶν οἱ μὴ πιστεύοντες καὶ τίς ἐστιν ὁ παραδώσων αὐτόν, the meaning is that Jesus could distinguish from the crowd of apparent believers the real non-believers and even the future traitor—not that He knew all about them. "From the beginning" may mean "from the time when the Gospel of the Cross began to be preached publicly in Capernaum, when schism and desertion first appeared among the disciples" (see **2254**).

[5] 1 Tim. i. 7.

[6] [**2251 *b***] Λαλιά occurs, elsewhere in N.T., only in Mt. xxvi. 73 "thy [Galilaean] dialect," Jn iv. 42 "thy talk," *i.e.* the talk of the Samaritan woman. In classical

Mood

(i) **Imperative, Indicative, Infinitive and Subjunctive,** see Index, also **Tense** (in Contents) p. xxi.

(ii) **Optative**

[2252] The optative mood is practically non-existent in the Gospels except in Luke. For example, the optative of γίνεσθαι occurs in Lk. (2), and that of εἶναι in Lk. (7), but neither of these occurs in Mk, Mt., Jn. In Jn xiii. 24 the v.r. πυθέσθαι τίς ἂν εἴη (not in W.H.) is a corruption. In Mark, the forms iv. 29 παραδοῖ, v. 43 and ix. 30 γνοῖ, viii. 37 δοῖ are subjunctive: but xi. 14 καρπὸν φάγοι has a true optative corresponding to Mt. xxi. 19 καρπὸς γένηται. Compare 2 S. i. 21 μὴ καταβῇ δρόσος, B καταβοῖ, A καταβήτω, and Deut. xxxiii. 24 "let him be," LXX ἔσται; also *Oxyr. Pap.* 742 ἵνα πάλιν φ[ί]λος ἡμεῖν παραδοῖ.

Negative Particles

(i) **Μή**

[2253] In later Greek, μή encroached on οὐ, especially in connexion with participles[1]. In John, μή for οὐ is not so frequent

---

Gk λαλέω means "talk freely," as at table, or in one's family, or in gossip abroad. In N.T., it means "talk freely," sometimes in bad sense, 1 Tim. v. 13, Jude 15, 16 or with suggestion of bad sense; but much more often of the free and public proclaiming of the truth of the Christian Gospel, as freq. in the Acts and the Pauline Epistles, and also of spiritual song and prophecy. Hence John—who deprecates the view that Christ taught secretly or privately—uses this word more freq. than Mk and Lk. taken together, and *assigns it to Christ 33 times in the first person, whereas it is never thus used by any Synoptist (exc. Lk. xxiv. 44, after the Resurrection).* Comp. Jn xviii. 20 "I have *spoken* freely to the world and in secret *spake* I never (lit. nothing)." The word is used in Mk xiii. 11, Mt. x. 19, to represent the *unpremeditated* speech that was to flow from the disciples (when put on their defence before kings and rulers) under the influence of the Holy Spirit, when they would not speak "from themselves" but the Spirit would speak for them. That exactly represents the Johannine use of λαλέω when used by Jesus concerning His own teaching.

[1] [2253 a] Winer, p. 606 n. "In modern Greek the participle invariably takes μή." A striking instance of μή for οὐ is Mt. xi. 18 (Lk. vii. 33) ἦλθεν γὰρ 'Ι. μήτε (Lk. μή) ἐσθίων μήτε πίνων, and Mt. xxii. 12 πῶς εἰσῆλθες ὧδε μὴ ἔχων ἔνδυμα γάμου; Lucian (iii. 104 *Indoct.* §5) καὶ ὁ κυβερνᾶν οὐκ εἰδὼς καὶ ἱππεύειν μὴ μεμελετηκώς is an excellent instance of the context that might in a few rare cases cause ὁ οὐ to be used, namely where οὐ=*alpha* privative, "*absolutely ignorant* of steering and not having given much pains to riding."

as in the Synoptists. But it is probable that vii. 15 "How doth this man know letters *not having learned* (μὴ μεμαθηκώς)?" does not imply doubt as to the negation ("if as we are given to understand he has not learned") but means "being, as he is, one that has not learned," "one of the illiterate class[1]." In vii. 49 ὁ ὄχλος οὗτος ὁ μὴ γινώσκων, John could not have used οὐ without limiting the assertion to a particular crowd pointed out, whereas the meaning is "This multitude [these and their like, this rabble] that knoweth not the law are accursed." In iii. 18 "He that believeth not is already condemned because he hath not believed (ὅτι μὴ πεπίστευκεν)," the unbelief, though implied as a fact, is stated, *not* as a fact, but as the ground for condemnation, and the meaning "condemned for not having believed" (2187) approximates to "pronounced guilty of not believing." See 2695.

[2254] The words of Christ, vi. 64 "There are among you some that do not believe (εἰσὶν ἐξ ὑμῶν τινὲς οἳ οὐ πιστεύουσιν)" are followed by the comment "For Jesus knew from the beginning (lit.) who are those that are not believing (τίνες εἰσὶν οἱ μὴ πιστεύοντες) and who is he that shall betray him (καὶ τίς ἐστιν ὁ παραδώσων αὐτόν)." It had been previously stated, before any mention of Christ's preaching, that many in Jerusalem, being impressed by His "signs," "believed" in Christ after a fashion, in whom Christ Himself (ii. 24) did not believe—presumably knowing that they did not *really* believe. From the first, then, Christ had this power of distinguishing unreal from real belief, so that He could answer with an affirmative the question "Knowest thou who are they that do not really believe?" But, since that time, the Twelve had been appointed and the Gospel of the Bread of Life had been preached in Capernaum. And, from the beginning of this Gospel, Judas (it would appear) had shewn signs of his future treason. Here it is added that Jesus noted these signs and knew to what they pointed. (See 2251 *a*.) We are not to suppose, with some ancient Greek commentators, that "from the beginning" means "from the foundation of the world[2]." As to the

---

[1] [2253 *b*] This utterance however takes place at Jerusalem, among strangers, not in Nazareth or Galilee: and therefore it is not quite certain that the other meaning is wrong. Winer (p. 607) quotes Philostr. *Apoll.* iii. 22 ὃς καὶ γράφει μὴ μαθὼν γράμματα.

[2] [2254 *a*] Chrys. ἄνωθεν, Cramer πρὸ καταβολῆς κόσμου. Ἐξ ἀρχῆς, "from the beginning," is similarly used in xvi. 4, and ἀπ' ἀρχῆς in 1 Jn ii. 7, 24 etc.

change from οὐ πιστεύουσιν to μὴ πιστεύοντες, it is what might have been expected in consequence of the change from the indicative to the participle. On x. 12 ὁ...οὐκ ὢν ποιμήν, see **2704**.

(ii) **Οὐ μή with Future and Subjunctive**

[2255] Οὐ μή is comparatively rarely used with the future in N.T. In John it occurs fourteen times with subjunctive[1] and thrice with future, as follows: iv. 14 οὐ μὴ διψήσει εἰς τ. αἰῶνα, vi. 35 ὁ ἐρχόμενος πρὸς ἐμὲ οὐ μὴ πεινάσῃ κ. ὁ πιστεύων εἰς ἐμὲ οὐ μὴ διψήσει πώποτε, x. 5 ἀλλοτρίῳ δὲ οὐ μὴ ἀκολουθήσουσιν ἀλλὰ φεύξονται. The second instance (vi. 35) invites inquiry, in view of the parallel πεινάσῃ and διψήσει. But a review of N.T. usage indicates no settled or general distinction of meaning. Compare Heb. viii. 12 οὐ μὴ μνησθῶ, quoting Jer. xxxi. 34 correctly, with Heb. x. 17 οὐ μὴ μνησθήσομαι quoting the same incorrectly: also Mt. xxiv. 35 οὐ μὴ παρέλθωσιν with parall. Mk xiii. 31 (W.H. marg.) οὐ μὴ παρελεύσονται (W.H. txt om. μή) and parall. Lk. xxi. 33 οὐ μὴ παρελεύσονται. In John's three instances there occur severally (1) εἰς τὸν αἰῶνα, (2) πώποτε, (3) a following future (φεύξονται). These facts suggest that he had in his mind an emphasis laid rather on futurity, than on certainty (which would have been indicated by the subjunctive).

(iii) **Εἰ οὐ**

[2256] Εἰ οὐ never occurs in John, as an undivided phrase, except in antithesis (twice) v. 47, "If ye *fail to believe* (οὐ πιστεύετε) his writings how can ye [*succeed in*] believing my words," x. 37 "If I *fail to do* (οὐ ποιῶ) the works of my Father...but if I [*succeed in*] *doing* them...." In both cases οὐ has the force of *alpha* privative, or may be treated as part of a compound verb, the hypothesis being positive but the compound verb negative. It is not the same as a negative hypothesis ("*except* ye believe," "*except* I do"). In iii. 12 οὐ πιστεύετε is divided from εἰ, "If I have told you earthly things and ye *disbelieve* (οὐ πιστεύετε)."

---

[1] [2255 a] This includes xx. 25 οὐ μὴ πιστεύσω, which, so far as the form is concerned, might be future. On xi. 56 τί δοκεῖ ὑμῖν ὅτι οὐ μὴ ἔλθῃ... see **2184**. On xviii. 11 οὐ μὴ πίω see **2232**. In the Pauline Epistles οὐ μή occurs only six times: two of these instances are from LXX: one of the two (Gal. iv. 30) is in the future.

[2257]   NEGATIVE PARTICLES

(iv) Οὐ...οὐδείς¹

[2257] This particular phrase with the double negative, which Mark frequently uses in narrative but only once (Matthew and Luke never) in Christ's words², John uses, never in narrative, but frequently in Christ's words³. It is never ambiguous.

(v) Οὔτε...καί

[2258] This construction is of the nature of a Latinism in 3 Jn 10 "*he neither himself* (οὔτε αὐτός) receiveth the brethren *and* those that desire [to come] he hindereth*," where the sentence is long and periodic. It is quite different in Jn iv. 11 "Neither (οὔτε) a bucket hast thou—and the well is deep," where it is strange that more Greek MSS. have not adopted the obvious alteration introduced by D, οὐδέ, "not even a bucket" (so too SS). But οὔτε...καί is highly characteristic of the style of the woman's talk, which is somewhat flighty, passing from "*neither* bucket hast thou [*nor rope to let down the bucket*]"—which she had at first in her mind—to the thought of the "depth" of "the well." The construction is not alleged to occur in N.T. outside these two passages (Winer p. 619, Westc. on 3 Jn 10).

[2259] In v. 37—8, R.V. punctuates "Ye have neither (οὔτε) heard his voice at any time, nor (οὔτε) seen his form. And (καί) ye have not his word abiding in you," but W.H. better "Ye have neither at any time heard his voice nor seen his form, *and* [*as a consequence*, or, *besides*] ye have not his word abiding in you: [I say this] because...ye believe not." Perhaps R.V. was influenced by the supposition that "*because ye believe not*" introduced the cause why the Word was "not abiding in them," but see **2178**. "And," introducing the consequence, or accompaniment, of two negations, is perfectly regular; "nor" (in the place of "and not") would not have expressed the meaning.

---

¹ [**2257** *a*] This does not include οὐ...οὐκέτι, which does not occur in Jn but occurs 6 times in Mk (in Mt. and Lk. once, parall. to Mk xii. 34) nor οὐδέν...οὐ μή, which is in Lk. x. 19. On οὐ...τις see **2586** *d*—*e*.

² Mk iii. 27 οὐ δύναται οὐδεὶς εἰς τὴν οἰκίαν...ἰσχυροῦ εἰσελθὼν...διαρπάσαι.

³ [**2257** *b*] Jn v. 19 οὐ δύναται ὁ υἱὸς ποιεῖν ἀφ' ἑαυτοῦ οὐδέν, v. 22 οὐδὲ γὰρ ὁ πατὴρ κρίνει οὐδένα, v. 30 οὐ δύναμαι ἐγὼ ποιεῖν ἀπ' ἐμαυτοῦ οὐδέν, vi. 63 ἡ σὰρξ οὐκ ὠφελεῖ οὐδέν, viii. 15 ἐγὼ οὐ κρίνω οὐδένα etc. (about 12 times). It is also used in the words of others, iii. 27, vi. 33 etc. Jn has once οὐδέπω οὐδείς in xix. 41 μνημεῖον καινὸν ἐν ᾧ οὐδέπω οὐδεὶς ἦν τεθειμένος, which resembles Lk. xxiii. 53 μνήματι λαξευτῷ οὗ οὐκ ἦν οὐδεὶς οὔπω κείμενος.

(vi) Οὐ (or, μή) combined with πᾶς

[2260] A distinction must be drawn between (1) οὐ...πᾶς, (2) πᾶς ...οὐ, and (3) οὐ πᾶς. The first two belong mostly to Hebraic, the third—in which πᾶς follows οὐ without any intervening word except perhaps the verb "to be"—belongs mostly to Greek idiom. In (1) and (2) the meaning of πᾶς is generally to be expressed by "any," in (3) by "every." But in John a literal translation is sometimes preferable as will be seen below.

[2261] In Hebrew, when "not" and "all" occur (as mentioned above) in the same sentence, the "not" goes with the verb in a manner unusual in Greek and English, (Gen. ii. 5) *"all* plants of the field *were not as yet,"* i.e. no plants yet existed; (Gen. iv. 15) "for the *not-smiting* him of *all* finding him," *i.e.* that none finding him should smite him; (Ex. xii. 16) *"all* work shall *not be done"*[1] etc. The last sentence might well be understood to mean *"all kinds of work* must not be done, but only the following": and, generally, the Hebrew idiom might produce ambiguity, which we escape in English and Greek by saying *"not any* (or, *no*) work"—and in Greek sometimes by repeating the negative (*"no* work shall *not* be done"). In the Synoptists, we have but few instances of either (1) οὐ...πᾶς or (2) πᾶς...οὐ[2].

[2262] In John's Gospel, and perhaps in the Epistle, there are no instances of οὐ...πᾶς meaning "not any," but πᾶς followed by οὐ (or, μή) is very frequent in both. It is partly explained by the writer's love of universal propositions, especially in connexion with the Church ("all that thou hast given me," "every branch in me," "everyone that believeth[3]"). These are connected mostly with affirmatives, but (*a*) sometimes with negatives followed by affirmatives thus: iii. 16 "in order that *everyone* (πᾶς) that believeth should *not* (μή) perish but should have eternal life," vi. 39 "in order that

---

[1] [2261 *a*] Gesen. 482 *a*. Ex. xii. 16 Πᾶν ἔργον λατρευτὸν οὐ ποιήσετε ἐν αὐταῖς, πλὴν ὅσα... Comp. Ex. xx. 10 οὐ ποιήσεις ἐν αὐτῇ πᾶν ἔργον.

[2] [2261 *b*] See (1) οὐ...πᾶς in Mk xiii. 20, Mt. xxiv. 22 "not...*any* flesh," Lk. i. 37 "not...*any* word," (2) πᾶς...οὐ in Mk vii. 18 πᾶν...οὐ δύναται, Mt. xii. 25 πᾶσα...οἰκία μερισθεῖσα...οὐ σταθήσεται (parall. Mk iii. 25 ἐὰν οἰκία...μερισθῇ, οὐ δυνήσεται στῆναι), Lk. iv. 33 (pec.).

[3] [2262 *a*] In Is. xxviii. 16 "he that believeth," Heb. and LXX om. "all," but Rom. x. 11 inserts it, thus, Πᾶς ὁ πιστεύων ἐπ' αὐτῷ. Parallel passages in Kings and Chronicles freq. differ in inserting or omitting Heb. "all": and LXX freq. differs similarly from Hebrew.

everything that he hath given to me I should *not* (μή) lose [aught] from it but should raise it up": (*b*) sometimes with negatives implying a negation of death or darkness, xi. 26 "*everyone* that liveth and believeth in me shall *surely not* (οὐ μή) die," xii. 46 "in order that *everyone* that believeth in me may *not* (μή) abide in darkness[1]."

[2263] On the other hand, the Greek usage of οὐ πᾶς, "*not everyone*," is frequent in traditions that say, in different forms, what the Lord says in the Sermon on the Mount, "*Not everyone* (οὐ πᾶς) that saith unto me Lord, Lord, shall enter into the kingdom of heaven[2]." So in the Epistle to the Romans, "*Not all* that are *from* Israel" are really Israel, "*nor yet* (οὐδέ), because they are the seed of Abraham, are they *all* children"; the Gospel was preached to them "but *not all* hearkened[3]"; so to the Corinthians, "*Not in all* [men] is knowledge," "*Not with the most of them* (οὐκ ἐν τοῖς πλείοσιν αὐτῶν, Clem. Alex. πᾶσιν αὐτοῖς) was God well pleased." And in the Fourth Gospel Jesus says to the disciples (xiii. 10, 11, 18) "Ye are clean but *not all*," "*Not all* of you are clean," "*Not* about you *all* do I speak." Some uses of the phrase "*not all*" may be derived from Attic and colloquial Greek, as in the famous saying, familiar to us through Horace, but Greek in origin, "The voyage to Corinth is *not every man's*[4]." How naturally it might occur to evangelists

---

[1] [2262 *b*] In the Epistle, the negation is sometimes a negation of truth, life, light etc., ii. 21 "*every* lie is *not* of the truth," ii. 23 "*everyone* that denieth the Son hath also *not* the Father (οὐδὲ τὸν πατέρα ἔχει)," iii. 6 "*Everyone* that sinneth hath *not* seen him" (antithetical to iii. 6 "*Everyone* that abideth in him sinneth *not*"), iii. 10 "*Everyone* that doeth not righteousness is *not* of God," iii. 15 (lit.) "*Every* murderer hath *not* eternal life" (a sentence hardly English, and certainly not Greek, in form), iv. 3 "*Every* spirit that confesseth not Jesus is *not* of God." Πᾶς is followed, as in the Gospel, by negation of death, darkness etc. in 1 Jn iii. 6, 9, v. 18. In 1 Jn ii. 16 "everything that is in the world" is separated from "is not from the Father" by an intervening appositional clause—"the desire of the flesh and the desire of the eyes and the vain glory of life." To the negations of good may be added 2 Jn 9 "Everyone that...abideth *not* in the teaching of Christ hath *not* God."

[2] Mt. vii. 21.

[3] [2263 *a*] Rom. ix. 6—7, x. 16, 1 Cor. viii. 7, x. 5. It is also used in Mt. xix. 11 "*Not all* are capable of receiving this saying," 1 Cor. vi. 12 "*not all things* are profitable," x. 23 "*not all things* are profitable...*not all things* edify." In the two passages last quoted there is an antithesis to a previous "all," in "*all things* are lawful." And such an antithesis is generally implied in the Greek idiom "[*All may do that, but*] *not all* can do this."

[4] [2263 *b*] Lewis and Short quote Aul. Gell. i. 8. 4 οὐ παντὸς ἀνδρὸς εἰς Κόρινθόν ἐσθ' ὁ πλοῦς, and see Steph. vi. 567 on παντός ἐστι.

failing to make converts, or finding converts relapse into unbelief and hostility, is shewn by St Paul's prayer "that we may be delivered from unreasonable and evil men; for the faith [of Christ] *is not the portion of all* (οὐ γὰρ πάντων ἡ πίστις)¹."

---

¹ [2263 c] 2 Thess. iii. 2. This traditional use of οὐ πάντες to describe the falling away of Israel after the flesh, and the defection of converts, and the practical failure of mere professors, may have a bearing on the difficult and doubtful Johannine utterance about "antichrists" in 1 Jn ii. 19 "They went out [at first (but see **2110** *a*—*b*) as our soldiers] belonging to our camp (lit. from us, ἐξ ἡμῶν): but they were not [really] belonging to our camp; for, if they had been [really] belonging to our camp they would have remained on our side (μεμενήκεισαν ἂν μεθ᾽ ἡμῶν): but [their not remaining was foreordained] in order that they might be manifested [shewing] that *not all are* (or, *they are not all*) belonging to us (ἀλλ᾽ ἵνα φανερωθῶσιν ὅτι οὐκ εἰσὶν πάντες ἐξ ἡμῶν)."

[2263 *d*] Westcott paraphrases this, "that they may be made manifest that they are *not, no not in any case, however fair their pretensions may be*, of us." The words I have italicised indicate that he takes the negation as universal, "*not any of them*." He gives, as a reason, that "when the πᾶς is separated by the verb from the οὐ, the negation according to the usage of the New Testament is always universal." This is true; but does it apply when the verb is εἶναι, and in such a writer as John, who nowhere else uses the Hebraic οὐ...πᾶς? If, for example, John had written in xiii. 11 οὐκ ἐστὲ πάντες καθαροί (instead of οὐχὶ π. κ. ἐστε) should we have translated this, "Ye are not *any of* you clean"? I am disposed to think that 1 Jn ii. 19 does not afford a unique instance of the Hebraic οὐ...πᾶς, and that the words refer to the departure of "Israel after the flesh," and of other temporary converts, very much as the Epistle to the Romans mentions it. If so, there is a confusion between (1) φανερωθῶσιν ὅτι οὐκ εἰσὶν ἐξ ἡμῶν, and (2) φανερωθῇ ὅτι οὐ πάντες [οἱ δοκοῦντες] εἰσὶν ἐξ ἡμῶν. One thought is "*they were not really ours*"; another, "*not all* that seem to be ours are really ours." Origen illustrates the "going out" of Judas by the "going out" in the Epistle. Now concerning Judas it is said in the Gospel "*not all* of you are clean," and "*not all*" is repeated in this connexion. This seems to confirm the view that "*not all*" in the Epistle is similarly used as meaning that "many are called but *not all* chosen."

[2263 *e*] In viii. 35 "the slave doth not abide in the house for ever (ὁ δὲ δοῦλος οὐ μένει ἐν τῇ οἰκίᾳ εἰς τὸν αἰῶνα)," if we are to adopt here the meaning of οὐ (or μή, μηκέτι etc.)...εἰς τὸν αἰῶνα everywhere else in N.T. (Mk iii. 29, xi. 14, Mt. xxi. 19, Jn iv. 14, viii. 51, 52, x. 28, xi. 26, xiii. 8, 1 Cor. viii. 13) it should mean "*never*." Then the sentence would mean "The slave, *e.g.* Ishmael, shall *never [be allowed to] abide permanently in the house*," with allusion to the tradition quoted by St Paul (Gal. iv. 30, "*cast out the handmaiden and her son*"). The preceding words are "everyone that doeth sin is a slave [of sin]," but SS, D, *b*, and Clem. Alex. omit "of sin," which may be a gloss added to explain "slave." With this omission, the whole may be paraphrased, "Whosoever doeth sin is not a son but a slave. Now the slave, who is not under grace but under law and constraint, *has no abiding-place, and never shall have, in the family of the Father*."

[2263 *f*] The following words, "But the Son abideth for ever [in the house of the Father], if therefore the Son shall free you, ye shall be really free," may

[2264] NEGATIVE PARTICLES

(vii) Οὐ, v. r. οὔπω

[2264] In vii. 8 (R.V. txt and W.H. txt) "I go *not* up *yet* to this feast," the reading, "I go *not* up to this feast" is very strongly supported. W.H. and R.V. place it in their margin, and it is now confirmed by SS. Porphyry[1] attacked Christ for the change of purpose implied (by "go *not* up") in this passage, when contrasted with vii. 10—14 "then he also himself *went up*...now about the middle of the feast Jesus *went up* to the temple and began to teach." Chrysostom and Ammonius the Elder (Cramer) write apologetically on it without any apparent knowledge of such a reading as οὔπω[2]. It is almost incredible that οὔπω, if genuine—a reading that supplied so obvious an answer to all objections—should have been unknown to these commentators, and should have been supplanted in so many versions and MSS. by the difficult reading οὐ.

[2265] The explanation of "I go *not* up to this feast," and its reconciliation with what follows, must be sought perhaps in the

---

be paraphrased, "But the son and heir, like Isaac the child of promise and grace, abides for ever in the house : if therefore ye shall receive into your hearts the Son of God and the Spirit of Sonship, then shall ye be really free, being freed from all fear of being 'cast out,' and knowing that ye are the heirs and inheritors of the House." If the positive "*abideth for ever*" had preceded the negative "*abideth not for ever*," it might have been argued (though not cogently) that in this particular place "not...for ever" must be taken in an unusual sense because of antithesis. As it is, there is no basis for any rendering except "*never*" for οὐ...εἰς τὸν αἰῶνα.

[2263 g] Cyril (Cramer *ad loc.*) explains οὐ μένει εἰς τ. αἰῶνα by adding "for he will hurry into the outer darkness (δραμεῖται γὰρ εἰς τὸ ἐξώτερον σκότος)." Ammonius says, ὁ μὴ μένων εἰς τὸν αἰῶνα καὶ ὡσαύτως ἔχων ἀεὶ δοῦλός ἐστι τῇ φύσει...πάντα γὰρ δοῦλα τοῦ κτίσαντος, μένει δὲ εἰς τὸν αἰῶνα ὡσαύτως ἔχων ὁ Υἱὸς ὡς φύσει θεός, where the punctuation is doubtful but the phrase "all things are slaves of the Creator" suggests that he did *not* read "slave *of sin*." Chrysostom (Migne) thrice drops εἰς τὸν αἰῶνα after οὐ μένει and interprets the words "the slave doth not abide for ever," as implying a "gentle casting down (ἠρέμα καταβάλλει)" of the things of the Law and the sacrifices prescribed by Moses (comp. Heb. iii. 5—6). Perhaps he took the words to mean, "The slave [even though he be faithful, as one of the prophets, or as Moses himself, is still below the son and heir, and] *does not abide [as the son abides] in the house*."

[1] *Dict. Christ. Biogr.* "Porphyrius," p. 442 a, referring to Jerome, *Dial. c. Pelag.* ii. 17.

[2] [2264 a] Migne prints a quotation from Chrys. οὐκ ἀναβαίνω ἄρτι, and then (punctuating thus) Πῶς οὖν, φησὶν, ἀνέβη, εἰπών, Οὐκ ἀναβαίνω; Οὐκ εἶπεν καθάπαξ, Οὐκ ἀναβαίνω· ἀλλὰ, Νῦν, εἶπεν, τουτέστι, μεθ' ὑμῶν, where apparently the writer does not mean that Jesus *said* νῦν, but that He *meant* νῦν. In Cramer, this appears, with οὔπω, thus, Αὐτὸς δὲ πῶς ἀνέβη, φησὶν, εἰπών, "ἐγὼ οὔπω ἀναβαίνω...." It is clear that neither οὔπω nor νῦν nor ἄρτι was a part of the text thus commented on.

Johannine view of Christ's "going up" to Jerusalem as a whole. Two acts of this kind have been mentioned (ii. 13, v. 1), the first of which excites jealousy, the second hostility, and (v. 18) a desire to kill Him, in "the Jews." In view of this hostility, Jesus is regarded as now contemplating a time when He will "go up" to a feast and die, but this has not yet come: "I go not up to *this* feast, because my time is not yet fulfilled." Accordingly, though He goes up later, He does not *"go up" to keep the feast as a whole*, and does not enter the temple till the middle of the week. Ammonius the Elder says, fairly enough, "He has not contradicted His words by His actions, for *He did not go up to keep the feast*[1]..." But something more is probably intended to be implied: "When my hour has arrived, then and not till then shall I really go up to the feast": and we are also probably intended to think of Christ's habitual language about "going up," meaning, to heaven, or to the Father.

(viii) Οὐχί

[2265 (i)] Οὐχί presents nothing remarkable in ix. 9 ἄλλοι ἔλεγον Οὐχί, ἀλλὰ ὅμοιος αὐτῷ ἐστίν: for its use *before a pause*, and especially

---

[1] [2265 *a*] Ammonius also adds that He went up "not with joy as is customary with feast-goers." Joy was particularly characteristic of this feast, the feast of Tabernacles. Some authorities have inserted "this" in Christ's words to His brethren "Go ye up to *this* feast," and have substituted "the" later on, "I go not up to *the* feast," or have inserted "this" in both clauses. The difference, though subtle, is important: "Go ye up to *the* feast, as usual; I shall not go up to *this* feast, but to *another, before long, when the time will have arrived for what some call death, but what I call going up to the Father*." On Christ's uses of ἀναβαίνω elsewhere, see i. 51, iii. 13, vi. 62, xx. 17 where it is used of "going up to heaven."

[2265 *b*] The remaining instance of ἀναβαίνω in Christ's words is x. 1 "He that entereth not through the door into the fold of the sheep but *goeth up* from some other quarter (ἀναβαίνων ἀλλαχόθεν)—that [man] is a thief and a robber." Beside the literal meaning we are intended to think of the two kinds of "going up" mentioned in the Bible. Rezin and Pekah (Is. vii. 1) "*go up* to Jerusalem" as enemies. When our Lord said (Mk x. 33, Mt. xx. 18, Lk. xviii. 31) "Behold, we *go up* to Jerusalem," He added, in effect, that He was to "go up" as a sacrifice. John is probably alluding to these two kinds of "going up." Jews would contrast Hezekiah, who (Is. xxxvii. 14) "*went up* unto the house of the Lord" to supplicate as a mediator, with the Roman Emperors, who exalted themselves and sat in the temple of God, setting themselves forth as God (comp. 2 Thess. ii. 4) and who said (Is. xiv. 13) "I will *go up* into heaven."

[2265 *c*] The "door" is probably the door of service (not, as Chrys., the door of the Scriptures). The Shepherd goes in by the same door as that "of the sheep," making himself one with them not as a mere act of "voluntary humility,' but to guide them and protect them; the "robber" prefers to "go up" by the path of what men call "glory," to make himself "a mighty hunter" of men.

before a pause followed by ἀλλά, is frequent in Greek and in N.T. But neither N.T. nor the Thesaurus affords a parallel to the following, xiii. 10—11, "ye (emph.) are clean *but not all* (ἀλλ' οὐχὶ πάντες)... for this cause said he (lit.) *that 'Ye are not all clean,'* ὅτι, Οὐχὶ πάντες καθαροί ἐστε¹." Οὐχί is so frequently interrogative that, if the last tradition were found as a detached Logion of the Lord, we should certainly render it (as in Heb. i. 14 οὐχὶ πάντες εἰσὶν λειτουργικὰ πνεύματα) "Are ye not all clean?" But in Numbers ("I shall see him *but not* now") LXX has καὶ οὐχί², as John has in xiv. 22 ἡμῖν... καὶ οὐχὶ τῷ κόσμῳ. Greek writers seem to have differed among themselves—and John seems to have differed from most—in the use of οὐχί and its equivalents³.

Number

(i) Plural referring to preceding Singular

[2266] This occurs when the speaker passes from considering a multitude as a whole to considering them as units, vii. 49 "This multitude that knoweth not the Law—[they] *are* accursed," xv. 6 "If anyone abide not in me he is at once cast out as the branch [from the vine] (τὸ κλῆμα)...and they gather *them* (*i.e.* such branches, αὐτά)," xvii. 2 "In order that all (sing.) that thou hast given to him—*to* [*all of*] *them* (αὐτοῖς) he may give eternal life" (see **1919** foll. and **2417—20**).

(ii) Plural Neuter with Plural Verb

[2267] This construction, which is rare in classical Greek, is also rare in John. Ἐπερίσσευσαν is supported by BD against אAL (-σεν) in vi. 13 "[the fragments] that (ἅ) superabounded," where the previous mention of "twelve baskets," and the desire to emphasize

---

¹ [**2265** (i) *a*] In 1 Cor. x. 29 συνείδησιν δὲ λέγω οὐχὶ τὴν ἑαυτοῦ..., ἀλλά *follows*, as also in Lk. i. 60 οὐχί, ἀλλὰ κληθήσεται, xii. 51 οὐχί, λέγω ὑμῖν, ἀλλ' ἢ διαμερισμόν, Rom. iii. 27 οὐχί, ἀλλὰ διὰ νόμου πίστεως. The anomaly here is that ἀλλά *precedes*. Lk. xvii. 7—8 τίς...ἐρεῖ...ἀλλ' οὐχὶ ἐρεῖ...is interrogative.

² [**2265** (i) *b*] Numb. xxiv. 17, LXX δείξω αὐτῷ καὶ οὐχὶ νῦν, representing the Heb. *vaw* by καί. I have not found οὐχί in the Egypt. Pap. Indices.

³ [**2265** (i) *c*] Steph. (v. 2351) shews that Xenophon regularly says Οὐκ, ἀλλά whereas Epictetus says Οὐ, ἀλλά. It has been shewn above (**2231** *a*) that where Mt. has οὐχί interrog. the parall. Lk. sometimes differs. On the other hand where Lk. xii. 51 has the negative οὐχί, λέγω ὑμῖν, ἀλλ' ἢ διαμερισμόν, the parall. Mt. x. 34 has οὐκ...ἀλλά. Mt. never uses οὐχί otherwise than interrogatively. Mk does not use it at all. Steph. quotes Porphyr. for a freq. and peculiar use of οὐχὶ δέ.

plurality may explain the plural (if genuine). In xix. 31, ἵνα μὴ μείνῃ ἐπὶ τοῦ σταυροῦ τὰ σώματα...ἵνα κατεαγῶσιν αὐτῶν τὰ σκέλη καὶ ἀρθῶσιν, is, if genuine, an extremely remarkable variation of singular and plural verbs with neuter plural subjects—and that too in similar construction and order (ἵνα μὴ μείνῃ...ἵνα κατεαγῶσιν). But (in spite of the genitive αὐτῶν, 2419 *b*) σκέλη may be accusative: "that *they might have their legs broken* and be taken away." In the parable of the Good Shepherd, πρόβατα is at first regarded as the flock that (x. 3—4) "hears" and "follows" the shepherd. Then the reason is given (x. 4) "*they know* (οἴδασιν) his voice," and, having thus dropped into the plural, the writer continues to describe them individually: x. 5—8, "*they* will not follow," "*they* will flee," "*they* know not," "the sheep *heard* (pl.) them not (οὐκ ἤκουσαν αὐτῶν τὰ πρόβατα)." Finally the writer returns to the singular with οὐκ ἔστιν— an emphatic phrase frequent in classical Greek—describing the "hireling" as one (x. 12) "whose own the flock *is not* (οὗ οὐκ ἔστιν τὰ πρόβατα ἴδια)."

(iii) **Special words**

(*a*) Αἵματα (i. 13)

[2268] Concerning those who (i. 12) "received" the Logos it is said that "he gave them authority to become children of God," and that these (lit.) "not from *bloods* (αἱμάτων), nor yet from will of flesh, nor yet from will of man (ἀνδρός), but from God were begotten." The plural of "blood," both in classical Greek and in Hebrew, almost always means "bloodshed[1]." But *Horæ Hebraicæ* (*ad loc.*) calls attention to a passage of *Shemoth Rabba* (referring to Ezekiel), where Jerusalem is described as a babe born in uncleanness, but purified by Jehovah; and in Ezekiel the Hebrew four times uses the plural "*bloods*[2]" in such a way as to indicate that it might mean

---

[1] [2268 *a*] Gesen. 196 *b*, and Steph. αἷμα: but Steph. does not quote Eurip. *Ion* 693 (Chorus) ἄλλων τραφεὶς ἀφ' αἱμάτων where the context indicates that the meaning may be "born from another *mother*." Macarius (§ 27, p. 117) speaking of Peter, to whom "flesh and blood" did not reveal the Messiahship of Jesus, has οὐκ ἐξ αἱμάτων οὐδὲ σαρκῶν...παιδευθείς..., ἀλλ' ἐξ ἁγίου πνεύματος μαθών....

[2] [2268 *b*] Ezek. xvi. 6 (lit.) "in thy *bloods*" (thrice) LXX ἐν τῷ αἵματι...ἐκ τοῦ αἵματός σου (and om.) (Field, ὁ Ἑβραῖος ἐν τῇ ὑγρασίᾳ σου) rep. xvi. 22 LXX ἐν τῷ αἵματί σου.

there, as Chrysostom says it means here, "the fleshly pangs of childbirth[1]."

[2269] An objection that may be raised against this view is that it represents the evangelist as describing at great length (saying in effect "begotten of no mortal mother, nor of any fleshly union, nor of any mortal begetter," ἀνδρός as distinct from γυνή) what might have been expressed more briefly in one or other of the shapes in which the best Greek MS. and the earliest Fathers quote it[2]. Possibly one

---

[1] [2268c] Chrys. τῶν σαρκικῶν ὠδίνων, and similarly Cramer. Hesych. refers to αἵματος and γενεῆς in the *Iliad* vi. 211, as if the former meant birth from the mother, the latter from the father—no doubt erroneously as to Homer's meaning, but perhaps instructively as to the various meanings conveyed by αἷμα to Greeks in later times.

[2268d] In LXX, no attempt is made to render literally the Heb. pl. "bloods" in the Pentateuch, but αἵματα, "bloodshed," is freq. after Judges. "His *bloods* be upon him" is ἔνοχος ἔσται in Lev. xx. 9 etc., but Ἄλλος has αἷμα there and αἵματα in Lev. xx. 11. In the obscure passage about (Ex. iv. 25, 26) "a husband of *bloods*," connected with circumcision, LXX has αἷμα, but the rest of the translators have αἱμάτων in one or both of the verses.

[2] [2269a] Codex B omits (but ins. in marg.) οὐδὲ ἐκ θελήματος ἀνδρός, which is also perhaps omitted in a paraphrase by Clem. Alex. 460 τὸν οὐκ ἐξ αἱμάτων οὐδὲ ἐκ θελήματος σαρκός, ἐν πνεύματι δὲ ἀναγεννώμενον. Irenaeus (iii. 16. 2 and iii. 19. 2) twice omits ἐξ αἱμάτων, and has once "from *the will of* God." Tertullian (*De Carne Chr.* 19, and comp. 24) quotes the text several times, but scribes have conformed some of his quotations to the received text. The most trustworthy is perhaps "Quid utique tam exaggeranter inculcavit, non ex sanguine, nec ex carnis voluntate, aut viri, natum?" Origen (on Josh. i. 2) has "neque ex voluntate viri" before "neque ex v. carnis." Hippolytus (vi. 9, Dunck. i. p. 236) has ἐξ αἱμάτων καὶ ἐπιθυμίας σαρκικῆς. Irenaeus and Tertullian must have read, with *b*, ἐγεννήθη (natus est) for ἐγεννήθησαν: for both of them take the passage as describing the birth of Christ, and Tertullian accuses the Valentinians of altering the text so as to apply it to the above-mentioned "credentes" instead of Christ. SS has "in blood."

[2269b] Justin Martyr has several passages that indicate an ancient tradition, "Not of man's seed but of God," referring to Christ, and some of these mention "*blood.*" In the following extracts, γενηθῆναι is rendered "generated," to distinguish it from γεννηθῆναι, "begotten": *Apol.* 21 "That the Logos, which is the first *begotten offspring* (γέννημα) of God, has been *generated* (γεγενῆσθαι) without *sexual union* (ἐπιμιξίας), Jesus Christ our teacher..."; *Apol.* 22 "But even if [or But if also, referring to previous εἰ καὶ κοινῶς] we say that uniquely, contrary to common birth (γένεσιν), He has been generated (γεγενῆσθαι) from God [as] God's Logos, as we said above, let this be in common with you (κοινὸν τοῦτο ἔστω ὑμῖν) who say that Hermes is the Logos that brings messages from God"; *Apol.* 32 "For the phrase (Gen. xlix. 11) 'blood of the grape' was significant of the fact that He that was to appear would indeed have *blood*, but not from human seed but from divine power...: for as not man, but God, hath made (πεποίηκεν) the

of the two clauses θελήματος σαρκός and θελήματος ἀνδρός may be an interpolation; but ἐξ αἱμάτων is too original a phrase to be thus explained. It points to some allusive meaning such as that in Ezekiel above mentioned, which was interpreted Rabbinically as referring not only to the blood attendant on childbirth, but also to what may be called the Jewish sacraments of Circumcision and Passover, by which the Israelites were "brought into covenant[1]." If that allusion is included here, the meaning of "not from bloods" is twofold, 1st, "not from mortal generation," 2nd, "not from such sacramental regeneration as Jews could offer to Gentiles through the Law."

---

blood of the vine, so this *blood* also was hereby indicated as to be generated (ἐμηνύετο...γενήσεσθαι) not from human seed but from [the] power of God."

[2269 c] Justin's Dialogue has similar passages: *Tryph.* 54 "Christ hath indeed *blood*, but not from seed of man (ἀνθρώπου) but from the power of God (τοῦ θεοῦ). For as not man, but God (lit.) begot (ἐγέννησεν) *the blood of the vine*, so [the prophet] indicated beforehand that the *blood* of Christ also would be not from human birth (γένους) but from [the] power of God. Now this prophecy... demonstrates that Christ is not man from men begotten (γεννηθείς) in the common way of men (κατὰ τὸ κοινὸν τῶν ἀνθρώπων)"; *Tryph.* 61 "[The Logos] may be called by all [these] names from the fact that He ministers to the Father's desire and purpose and from the fact that He has been generated *by the Father by will* (καὶ ἐκ τοῦ ἀπὸ τοῦ πατρὸς θελήσει γεγενῆσθαι)"; *Tryph.* 63 "since *His blood* (lit.) has not been begotten from human seed (ὡς τοῦ αἵματος αὐτοῦ οὐκ ἐξ ἀνθρωπείου σπέρματος γεγεννημένου) but from [the] will of God (ἀλλ' ἐκ θελήματος θεοῦ)"; *Tryph.* 76 "For the phrase (Dan. vii. 13) '*like* a son of man' makes it clear that He was to appear and to have been brought into being (φαινόμενον καὶ γενόμενον) a man, but not from human seed...He was indeed to have *blood*, but not from men; even as not man, but God, begot *the blood of the vine*."

[2269 d] These passages indicate the existence of early discussions about "*blood*," in connexion with the birth and nature of Christ. [The mention of (Lk. xxiv. 39) "flesh and bones" (without "*blood*") suggests that there were other discussions about the nature of His body after the Resurrection.] Justin appears to have laid great stress on these; and they seem to have influenced Irenaeus, Tertullian, and others, to such an extent that they have modified John's text, perhaps taking αἱμάτων to mean, "*not from ordinary blood*," or "*not from mortal blood*." But, in fact, the Johannine tradition teaches that the truth applies to *all* the children of God, so that "*blood*," in any sense, may be excluded from a consideration of the nature of the birth.

[1] [2269 e] *Hor. Heb.* on Jn i. 13 says, "The Israelites were brought into covenant by three things; by circumcision, by washing, and by offering of sacrifices," and quotes *Shemoth Rab.*, sect. 19, and Gloss. in *Vajikra Rab.* fol. 191 as to "the blood of the passover mingled with the blood of the circumcised."

(β) Ἱμάτια

[2270] Ἱμάτια (pl.) occurs in John as follows, xiii. 4 "he layeth aside his garments," xiii. 12 "he took his garments," xix. 23 "the soldiers therefore...took his garments," xix. 24 (quoting Ps. xxii. 19) "they parted my garments among them." In the last passage, the writer distinguishes ἱμάτια from the χιτών (*i.e.* undergarment), and describes the former as being divided into four pieces. Although the word is in the plural—meaning "the upper clothes," all except the tunic—yet the plural might apparently denote "cloak" when, as would be the case with the poor, the "upper clothes" consisted of *a cloak alone,* and not of a cloak and doublet. Hence "garment" is parallel to "garments" in the Synoptists, and Matthew in one passage interchanges singular and plural[1]. All the Synoptists use the plural to describe the parting of Christ's "garments" among the soldiers. John does the same, but he indicates that the plural means a single cloak in seams capable of being divided equally among four soldiers. John adds a negative detail about "not rending the tunic[2]," but casting lots for it; and he quotes the Psalmist's prophecy "They parted my *clothes* (ἱμάτια) among them, and on my clothing (ἱματισμόν) they cast [the] lot." This prophecy may have afforded John an additional reason for preferring the plural ἱμάτια, even though our Lord wore nothing but the cloak over the tunic[3].

---

[1] [2270 a] Mk v. 28 ἱματίων = Mt. ix. 21 ἱματίου: Mk v. 27 has ἱματίου (but ib. 30 ἱματίων). Mk v. 27—30 has pl. in speech, sing. in narrative.

[2] [2270 b] The only Synoptic mention of "tunic" in the Passion is in Mk xiv. 63 "he rent his tunics," where the parall. Mt. xxvi. 65 has "garments." But this applies to the Highpriest. Luke omits it. In Acts xvi. 22 περιρήξαντες αὐτῶν τὰ ἱμάτια, two or three scribes have ἑαυτῶν, supposing that the praetors rent *their own* garments (2563 c); but the meaning is that they caused the garments to be rent off from the Apostles. "Rend (garments)" in Mk-Mt. is διαρήσσω, but in Jn σχίζω.

[3] [2270 c] In iii. 33 ὕδατα πολλά, the pl. of ὕδωρ, being freq. (Steph.) in non-hebraic Greek as well as in LXX, calls for little comment except as to the combination "many waters," which occurs in N.T. only here and Rev. i. 15, xiv. 2, xvii. 1, xix. 6. In Rev. xvii. 1 (Jer. li. 13, LXX pl.), it is used of turbulent forces (as in Is. viii. 7, LXX sing.). The first use of Heb. "many waters" (Gesen. 913 a) refers to the waters of Meribah (Numb. xx. 11, LXX sing.). In the Psalms xxix. 3, xxxii. 6, lxxvii. 19, xciii. 4, cvii. 23, cxliv. 7, ὕδατα πολλά denotes stormy violence, over which Jehovah rules, or from which He delivers the Psalmist. In Ezek. xvii. 5, 8, xxxi. 5, "many waters" (LXX ὕδωρ πολύ sing.) denotes fertilising streams, but in Ezek. xxvi. 19 (LXX sing.) it denotes destroying inundation.

Participle (1894*)

(i) Causal

[2271] This is more frequent in John than in the Synoptists. The Johannine phrase "answered *and* said," as distinct from the Synoptic "answering (ἀποκριθείς) said," shews that John avoids the participle as a substitute for "and." But he frequently—or at all events more frequently than the Synoptists—uses it for "because."

[2272] In iv. 6 "Jesus, therefore, *because he was wearied* (κεκοπιακώς) by the journey, was sitting, just as he was (οὕτως) by the well," κεκοπιακώς must be interpreted in the light of the fact that the word occurs in John only here and in the context (iv. 38) "I have sent you to reap that over which *ye have not wearied yourselves*: others have been *weary*." The "weariness" is that of the labourers in the harvest of God. And the "weariness" of the Messiah, thirsting, and preaching the Gospel in "the heat of the day[1]," prepared the way for the work of the Apostles in later times, as described in the Acts (viii. 25). The phrase "just as he was" indicates (from the human point of view) fortuitousness, or at all events (1916—7) absence of premeditation. But the narrative suggests that what might be called "casual" in all these details was really foreordained. On another occasion, when our Lord was apparently even more exhausted so that He fell asleep, Mark—and Mark alone[2]—says that the disciples conveyed Him "*as he was* (ὡς ἦν)" in the boat; and then He arises out of sleep to manifest Himself as Lord of the winds and waves. So here, the weariness is represented as the instrumental cause of an apparently casual consequence. It would have been somewhat too logical, and perhaps almost stilted, to say "*because* (ὅτι) he was wearied"; but the participle suffices to suggest it. And the story as a whole makes us feel that the journey itself, the intense weariness, and the sudden sitting down to rest just before the coming of the Samaritan woman, were all foreordained to divine ends.

---

[1] [2272 a] Mt. xx. 12, comp. Jn iv. 6 "it was about *the sixth hour*," i.e. noon. The "weariness" was not accidental but providential, like the journey itself (iv. 4 "*there was need* (ἔδει) that he should go through Samaria"). In Jn (as in Rev.) δεῖ always refers to *spiritual* decree or *spiritual* necessity, iii. 7, 14, 30, iv. 20, 24, ix. 4, x. 16, xii. 34, xx. 9.

[2] Mk iv. 36.

[2273] In the same narrative (iv. 9) "How is it that thou, *being* a Jew, askest drink from me, *being* a Samaritan?" the participles might be most obviously explained as "*though* thou art," and "*though* I am." But an explanation more in accordance with Johannine usage would be to render the participles by "*since*," having regard to the negative implied in the question: "Thou hast no right, *since* thou art a Jew, to ask drink from me; *since* I am a Samaritan." So, in English, we should say, "You, being under age—what right have you to vote?" or "how is it that you vote?" In iv. 39, "because of the word of the woman *testifying* (τῆς γ. μαρτυρούσης...)" means "testifying as she did," suggesting "*because* she repeatedly testified[1]": and in iv. 45, "having seen" means "*because* they had seen." It would be impossible to find such a group of causal participles in the Synoptists. In xxi. 12 εἰδότες probably means "*because* they knew," not "*though* they knew" (1924 *a*).

(ii) **Tenses of (see also Tense, 2499—510)**

(*a*) Τυφλὸc ὤn (ix. 25)

[2274] In ix. 25, "One thing I know, that [*though*] being [*once*] blind, now I see (τυφλὸς ὢν ἄρτι βλέπω)," the present participle is perhaps used for brevity and ποτέ is omitted because it has already been used (ix. 13 τόν ποτε τυφλόν). Compare ix. 17 "they say to *the blind* man" for "to *the once blind* man." But the writer may possibly intend to suggest that the blindness had been so recently cured that it was almost present, "being [up to this moment] blind."

---

[1] [2273 *a*] iv. 39 (A.V.) "the woman, which," (R.V.) "the woman, who." Possibly R.V. took it as τῆς γ. τῆς μαρτ., which Shakespeare would have rendered "the woman *that*," but which A.V. (according to its custom) renders "the woman *which*." R.V., which generally follows A.V. in this use of "which," deviates here, and adopts "who," presumably meaning "and she" or "for she." According to a convenient usage generally adopted in the English of Shakespeare and Addison, and one that would conduce to clearness in modern English, "*who*" should introduce a non-essential statement about the antecedent ("I heard it from the policeman, *who* heard it from the postman"). "*That*" should introduce a statement that is essential to the complete meaning of the antecedent ("I heard it from the boy *that* cleans the boots"). See the author's *How to Write Clearly*, Seeley and Co., and comp. **1493** *a*, **1564** *b*.

(β) Ὁ ὢν ἐν τῷ οὐρανῷ (iii. 13, R.V.)

[2275] In iii. 13 "No man hath ascended to heaven save he that descended from heaven, [even] the Son of man," R.V. text adds "who is in heaven," ὁ ὢν ἐν τῷ οὐρανῷ. W.H. reject the addition (without marginal alternative), pointing out that it is omitted in many early quotations in which the insertion of the words—had they been recognised by the quoters as genuine—might be described as "morally certain[1]." Without this addition the words appear to mean that the real and spiritual ascension to heaven has always been the result of a descent from heaven. The descending influence was referred to earlier in reverse order, (i. 51) "the angels of God *ascending* and *descending* on the Son of man," where it seems to mean the prayers of the Logos going up to heaven and returning to earth. Here the meaning seems to be that the Logos has always been descending on man to lift man up to God. This Logos, the express Image of God, is here identified with the incarnate Image of God, the "Son of man."

---

[1] [2275 a] W.H. point out that Origen's alleged quotations of the clause are only from the Latin of Rufinus, and elsewhere Origen omits it. They think the interpolation "perhaps suggested" by i. 18 ὁ ὢν εἰς τὸν κόλπον τ. πατρός. Possibly "the Son of man" seemed a weak ending, unless it was defined in some way as meaning the Divine Ideal of Man, the Man in Heaven. Some Greek conflation of ΟΥΣ ΤΟΥ ΑΝΟΥ (*i.e.* "the Son of man") and ΟωΝΕΝΟΥΝω (*i.e.* "who is in heaven") may have favoured the interpolation. A* omits ωΝ.

[2275 b] In v. 35 ἐκεῖνος ἦν ὁ λύχνος ὁ καιόμενος καὶ φαίνων there are perhaps two allusions. The first is to Christ's doctrine about lighting the candle (λύχνος) and putting it where all may see (Mk iv. 21, ἔρχεται, but Mt. v. 15 has καίουσιν and Lk. viii. 16 ἅψας), and prob. to a proverbial distinction between the candle that has to be thus daily "lighted" (ὁ καιόμενος) or "continually burns," and the sun, which needs no such lighting (comp. Philo i. 485 "for the one [the eye of the soul] is like *the sun* but these [the bodily eyes] are like *candlebearers* (λυχνούχοις))." The second may be to Sir. xlviii. 1 "his word [*i.e.* the word of Elijah] *burned continually* like a torch (ὡς λαμπὰς ἐκαίετο)"; but there the Hebrew ("His words were like a burning furnace"), and the Greek context, indicate that καίω has a different meaning from that in Mt. Does καιόμενος here mean "continually burning" or "lighted day by day"? In view of καιόμενος "steadily burning" in Lk. xii. 35 λύχνοι καιόμενοι, Rev. iv. 5 λαμπάδες πυρὸς καιόμεναι ἐνώπιον τ. θρόνου, xxi. 8 τῇ λίμνῃ τῇ καιομένῃ (comp. Rev. viii. 8, xix. 20) and ἐκαίετο in Sir. xlviii. 1, we are justified in concluding that the present participle means continuousness ("*steadily burning*") : but the verb itself ("*burn*") and the context, suggest that the continuousness is only for its appointed hour, and that the "candle" not only "*burns*" but also "*burns away.*"

(γ) Ἡ ἐκμάξαca (xi. 2)

[2276] In xi. 2 "Now Mary was the [Mary, or, woman] *that anointed*...," it is correct, but not enlightening, to say that the Anointing "presented itself to the writer as a past event[1]," and thus to explain the aorist participle used concerning an act that the evangelist records later on. Every event in the Fourth Gospel "presented itself to the writer as a past event." But, as to this particular event, the Anointing of Christ by a Woman—probably well-known, in some form, to all Christians at the end of the first century, but connected by Luke alone with a "sinner"—the Fourth Evangelist takes this opportunity (afforded by the necessity of mentioning Mary in connexion with Lazarus) to say, before he comes to the Anointing, that this same Mary was the Mary (or, woman) whose story was in everyone's mouth. It would have been tedious to say "the woman that will presently be described by me as anointing...."

(iii) **Present with** ἦν

[2277] The Hebraic use of ἦν διδάσκων, κηρύσσων etc. for the imperfect, "he was teaching, preaching etc." is quite distinct from such phrases as ἦν ἐκεῖ καθήμενος "there happened to be on the spot sitting" (where ἦν is separated from the participle) and also from ἦν with the perfect passive participle. In N.T., when ἦν is separated from the present participle, it is often better to supply some predicate from the context and to take the participle as in classical Greek, especially in those Gospels where the Hebraic participle is rare. In John, it is very rare. But there are approximations to the Hebraic participle in xiii. 23 ἦν ἀνακείμενος (which however resembles both in meaning and in sound the passive pluperfect) and in xviii. 30 εἰ μὴ ἦν οὗτος κακὸν ποιῶν, where perhaps the intention is, not to represent Hebraically the imperfect ἐκακοποίει ("if he had not been doing mischief") but to suggest "if he had not been a man continually doing mischief," *i.e.* an habitual mischief-worker (SS, *b*, and *f*, "if he had not been an *evildoer*[2]"). John's general separation

---

[1] Winer, p. 431.

[2] [2277 a] In Jn iii. 22—3 "Jesus and his disciples came into the land of Judaea and there (ἐκεῖ) he tarried with them and was baptizing (ἐβάπτιζεν). Now there was also John (ἦν δὲ καὶ [ὁ] Ἰ.) baptizing (βαπτίζων) in Aenon," the context suggests the meaning "*John, also, was in that neighbourhood*, namely, in Aenon," so that it is not quite like the ἦν κηρύσσων or διδάσκων of Mark and Luke.

of participles from ἐγένετο and ἦν favours their separation in i. 6 "There came [into being] (ἐγένετο) a man (ἄνθρωπος), sent from God (ἀπεσταλμένος παρὰ θεοῦ)," where (1937) ἐγένετο is contrasted with ἦν above, ἄνθρωπος with Λόγος above, and ἀπ. π. θεοῦ with ἦν πρὸς τὸν θεόν above. The same applies to i. 9 "There was [from the beginning] the light, the true [light], which lighteneth every man, coming as it does (ἐρχόμενον) [continually] into the world." On this, see 2508.

(iv) **Agreement of**

[2278] A singular noun, when plural in meaning, is often the subject of a plural verb, but is not so often followed by a plural participle, as in xii. 12 ὁ ὄχλος πολὺς ὁ ἐλθών...ἀκούσαντες...ἔλαβον. In ἔλαβον alone there would have been nothing remarkable, nor in ἀκούσαντες if it had followed ἔλαβον: but, coming before the plural verb, the unusual plural participle suggests a desire to emphasize the plurality of the crowd,—a desire also apparent in the extraordinary phrase ὁ ὄχλος πολύς (1739—40). In i. 48 πρὸ τοῦ σε Φίλιππον φωνῆσαι ὄντα ὑπὸ τὴν συκῆν εἶδόν σε the participle may agree with the first or second σε, see 2372 b.

(v) **Prefatory use of**

[2279] John uses prefatory participial clauses, to an extent unequalled in the Synoptists, to prepare the reader for some especially solemn utterance or act of Christ's. A combination of this use with the genitive absolute is particularly noticeable in the preface to the Washing of Feet: xiii. 1—4 "Now before the feast... Jesus *knowing* that his hour had come...*having loved* his own...he loved them to the end. And, *while supper was going on* (δείπνου γινομένου), *the devil having now put it* into the heart...*knowing* that the Father had given him all things into his hands, and that..., he riseth from supper." Similar phrases introduce some of the most important events in Christ's life[1].

---

[1] [2279 a] The conversion of the two disciples that constitute the firstfruits of the Church is preceded by i. 38 στραφεὶς δὲ ὁ Ἰ. καὶ θεασάμενος, the cure of the impotent man by v. 6 τοῦτον ἰδὼν ὁ Ἰ....καὶ γνοὺς ὅτι..., the feeding of the five thousand by vi. 5 ἐπάρας οὖν τοὺς ὀφθ. ὁ Ἰ. καὶ θεασάμενος ὅτι..., the spiritual explanation of the doctrine of the flesh and blood by vi. 61 εἰδὼς δὲ ὁ Ἰ. ἐν ἑαυτῷ ὅτι...(referring to the "murmuring" of some of the disciples), and Christ's last two utterances on the Cross by xix. 28—30 μετὰ ταῦτα εἰδὼς ὁ Ἰ. ὅτι ἤδη......ὅτε οὖν ἔλαβεν τὸ ὄξος ὁ Ἰ., where we have the subject preceded first by a participle and then by the equivalent of one.

Prepositions

[2280] For a brief comparison of the Johannine with the Synoptic use of prepositions in general and statistics bearing on the comparison, see **1881—5**. The following remarks will deal with particular prepositions in alphabetical order, including some passages that may be of interest (apart from grammatical usage) because of their bearing on Johannine thought and purpose as distinct from mere style.

(i) Ἀνά

[2281] Ἀνά occurs only once in John, as follows: ii. 6 "Now there were *six* waterpots of stone set there after the Jews' manner of purifying, containing *two or three* firkins *apiece* (χωροῦσαι ἀνὰ μετρητὰς δύο ἢ τρεῖς)." Ἀνά, with numbers, occurs elsewhere in N.T., though very rarely[1]. In the Apocalypse, it occurs in connexion with the "*six*" wings of the seraphs, whom Isaiah describes as with *two* covering the face, with *two* the feet, and with *two* flying[2]. Philo (2283 b) speaks mystically of the number "*six*" as "composed of *twice three*, having the odd as the male and the even as the female" and as generating the things that are "perfected by the *seven*." No one disputes that purifying vessels of the Jews may have held "*two or three firkins apiece*" and that ἀνὰ μετρητὰς δύο ἢ τρεῖς means this: but if the phrase is also symbolically intended[3], the symbolism may affect the grammatical interpretation of other parts of the narrative. According to a literal interpretation—which must be presumed to be part of the meaning even though the spiritual interpretation may be the chief part—the stone vessels were first filled to the brim by the attendants, and then they "drew" either (1) from them or (2) from the well[4], and "carried" to the Ruler of the Feast, who said that "the

---

[1] Mt. xx. 9, 10 "[one] denarius *apiece*," Lk. ix. 14 "*by* fifties," x. 1 "*by* twos," Rev. iv. 8 "six wings *apiece*," xxi. 21 "*each* one (ἀνὰ εἷς) of the several gates." In LXX, Oxf. Conc. mentions ἀνά (in any sense) as occurring—apart from ἀνὰ μέσον—only nine times.

[2] Rev. iv. 8, alluding to Is. vi. 2 (where ἀνά is not used).

[3] See *Enc.* 1796—7 ("Gospels" § 47) on the apparent symbolism of Johannine numbers generally and, in particular, the (xxi. 11) "one hundred and fifty three" fish.

[4] [2281 a] Field (*ad loc.*) "Οἱ ἠντληκότες τὸ ὕδωρ. This is generally understood of *drawing the water from the well*, as in Ch. iv. 7. So St Chrysostom: εἰ γὰρ ἔμελλόν τινες ἀναισχυντεῖν, ἠδύναντο πρὸς αὐτοὺς λέγειν οἱ διακονησάμενοι·

good wine" had been "kept to the last." (1) If the "drawing" was from the vessels, of which the contents were all changed into wine, then we have to suppose that 130 gallons of water were thus converted[1]. (2) If, as Westcott explains it, the "drawing" was from the well—which would be the usual sense of ἀντλέω—then we have to suppose the filling of the vessels to be a preliminary and independent act, as though Jesus had said, "Before the water from the well can be turned into the wine of the Gospel, it must first be used to fill the vessels of purification of the Law."

[2282] The former interpretation ("drawing from the vessels")—besides the difficulty of the supply of wine being very far in excess of the need—describes the wine as being in the "stone vessels" of which the interpreters of the Talmud said, "If anyone have water fit to drink, and *that water by chance contract any uncleanness, let him fill the stone vessel with it[2]*." Westcott's interpretation avoids these

---

ἡμεῖς τὸ ὕδωρ ἠντλήσαμεν· ἡμεῖς τὰς ὑδρίας ἐνεπλήσαμεν...." But Migne omits ἡμεῖς τ. ὑ. ἐνεπλήσαμεν and gives no v. r. The omission would leave the reader free to suppose that the attendants, according to Chrysostom, could say "We *drew the water [out of the vessels]*"—which accords with the view taken by Field. He apparently thinks that other attendants (or perhaps women) would have previously drawn water from the well for all the needs of the household, and that "the attendants" merely filled the vessels to the brim with this water and then "drew out" the water from the vessels. This is certainly more probable than that the attendants were sent away from the house to draw water from the well. Chrysostom clearly believes that the wine came out of the vessels—and not direct from the well (as Westcott suggests)—for he meets the objection of sceptics that perhaps these vessels had been used for vintage purposes and retained a savour of wine.

[1] A "firkin," μετρητής, Heb. "bath," was nearly 9 gallons, so that the 6 vessels would contain $6 \times 2\frac{1}{2} \times 9$ gallons.

[2] [2282 a] *Hor. Heb.* ad loc. quoting Gloss. (apparently) on *Kelim* cap. 1, hal. 1. The phrase "*the* stone vessel" suggests that *one* vessel sufficed most households. And it seems reasonable to believe that this would often be the case if the vessel held 22 gallons. As for the μετρητής, Steph. says that the Attic measure differed from the Roman or Italian, and also quotes Aristotle as mentioning a μετρητὴς Μακεδονικός. The grammarian Thomas said, ἀμφορεὺς λέγε, μὴ στάμνος μηδὲ μετρητής, εἰ καί τινες. It is applied, however, by Polybius ii. 15. 1 to wine in Gaul (τοῦ δ' οἴνου τὸν μετρητήν) as though it needed no explanation. In the Indices to Egypt. Pap. it does not appear except in the Fayum vol., where it is used as a measure for oil, 95, 96 etc. Steph. describes it as "vas magnae cujusdam capacitatis nulla certa definitum mensura." It is made the subject of witticism when a man gives another a μετρητής of wine on condition that it shall keep its name because of μετριότης, *i.e.* he is to drink moderately. On the other hand, Xenarchus the Rhodian was called μετρητής because of his vast drinking.

two difficulties—but at the cost of converting the "filling of the vessels" into a mere symbol, while still taking the rest of the story literally. Nor is the symbol quite clear. The water of the Gospel, the water that becomes wine, comes independently from the well or spring. The preliminary water goes into the vessels of the Law and stays there. It does nothing.

[2283] On the whole it seems more in accordance both with the literal and with the spiritual interpretation that the water of the Word should be supposed to be placed *first* in *the vessels of the Law*. Thence, having been transmuted, it is "drawn forth *now* (emph., νῦν)," at Christ's command, as the wine of the Gospel. To the objection that such water was "unclean" for purposes of drinking, might not the evangelist reply (like the voice that replies to Peter's objection in the Acts[1]) that what God hath "cleansed" is not to be called "common or unclean"? According to this view, Christ, in this symbolic story, transmutes the outwardly purifying element of the Law into the inwardly purifying element of the Spirit. If some such symbolism is really latent here, we should expect (according to the principle of Philonian interpretation) to find traces of it in the mention of the numbers "*two*," "*three*," and "*six*," here mentioned by John. In a history, describing the sinking of so many triremes or the destruction of so many soldiers, numbers would be simply numbers. But in a symbolic story unfolding the future transmutation of Law into Gospel, numbers (not necessary for the narrative) would rarely be inserted unless they lent themselves to symbolism. From the allegorizing point of view, the numbers "two," "three," and "six" are easily capable of an appropriate meaning[2].

---

[1] [2283 *a*] Acts x. 14. Comp. Ephrem p. 56 "Denique hoc miraculum fecit ut *res viles* in delicatas permutando doceret eas non esse natura malas"—where perhaps "viles" means "common," "cheap."

[2] [2283 *b*] Philo says (ii. 281) "The number *Six* is even and odd, composed of *twice three*, having the odd as the male and the even as the female, from which [numbers] are the origins [of things] according to the unalterable laws of nature," and "What things the *Six* generates these things the Seven exhibits when perfected." In Isaiah's above quoted description of the seraphim (each of which had "*six*" wings) giving glory to the Lord in the Temple, "six" might be taken as symbolizing the created world giving glory to the Creator, and Isaiah's mention of the uses of each of the three pairs of wings would favour Philo's allegorizing interpretation of the "*two*" and the "*three*" as making up the "*six*." A work like the Fourth Gospel, which appears, even when narrating facts, to set them forth with symbolism and allusion, might naturally illustrate this sign, apparently

(ii) 'Αντί

[2284] 'Αντί occurs only once in John as follows: i. 14—17 "And the Word became flesh and tabernacled in [the midst of] us...full of grace and truth...because from his fulness we all received and grace *in the place of* (ἀντί) grace: because [whereas] the Law through Moses was given [by God,] the grace [of God] and the truth [of God] through Jesus Christ came into being."

[2285] In classical Greek, ἀντί is used in phrases describing the *lex talionis* of "like *for*, i.e. *in the place of*, like." The Thesaurus quotes "man *for* man," "woman *for* woman," "insult *for* insult,"

---

performed on the sabbath, by a numerical detail suggesting "*two*" and "*three*" as part of the preparation for what Philo calls "*the Seven when perfected*."

[2283 c] Origen (*Philocal.* i. 12) explains ἀνὰ μετρητὰς δύο ἢ τρεῖς as referring to three different aspects of the Scriptures, and he adds ἓξ δὲ ὑδρίαι εὐλόγως εἰσὶ τοῖς ἐν τῷ κόσμῳ καθαριζομένοις γενομένῳ (Robinson γεγενημένῳ) ἐν ἓξ ἡμέραις ἀριθμῷ τελείῳ. By "perfect number" (Plato 546 B, and see Steph.) he means a number that is "perfected," or "completed," by adding the terms of an Arithmetical Progression. Thus 3, 6, and 10 are called perfect numbers, because $3 = 1 + 2$; $6 = 1 + 2 + 3$; $10 = 1 + 2 + 3 + 4$. Philo (ii. 183) and Clement of Alexandria (782) call 10 "the *all-perfect* or *all-perfecting* decad" (δεκάδι τῇ παντελείᾳ, ἡ δεκὰς δὲ ὁμολογεῖται παντέλειος εἶναι (the fem. in -εία should be recognised in L. and S.)), but six is also a "perfect" number and one that would commend itself to a Jew as symbolical of creation. Since six derives its "perfection" from the addition of "two" and "three" to unity, it is all the more intelligible that Jn should here introduce the "two" and "three" as well as the "six." It may be added that Augustine interpreted the "one hundred and fifty three" in xxi. 11 as being a "perfect number," the sum of $1 + 2 + 3$... up to 17, where 10 and 7 represent severally the "ten commandments" of the Law and "the seven spirits of God."

[2283 d] A number may be allegorized variously by different interpreters, and the variation may be alleged as proof that no allegory or inner meaning was ever intended. As an instance, however, to the contrary, see Gen. xiv. 14 "three hundred and eighteen," allegorized by Barn. ix. 8 and Clem. Alex. 782 as referring to the cross of Christ, but Hershon says: "Our sages say: 'He went in pursuit with *Eliezer alone*, whose *name* has the numerical value of three hundred and eighteen.'" The application of "numerical value" to names may be illustrated by the "number of the beast" in the Apocalypse, 666, a sort of parody, thrice repeated, of the "all-perfect number."

[2283 e] In renderings of O.T., μετρητής represents the Hebrew *bath*, a measure of liquid, as follows: Ezek. xlv. 14 "the *bath* of oil...tenth part of a *bath* out of the cor which is ten *baths*, even an homer; for ten *baths* are an homer," LXX thrice κοτύλη, Aq. (twice) μετρητής, Theod. twice βάτος: 2 Chr. iv. 5 "three thousand *baths*," LXX μετρητάς (Field) Ἄλλος· κεράμια (comp. Is. v. 10 "bath," κεράμιον, Οἱ λοιποί· βάτον), parall. 1 K. vii. 26 "two thousand *baths*," LXX om., A δισχιλίους χοεῖς: 1 Esdr. viii. 20 "an hundred *measures* (μετρητῶν) of wine," corresponding to Ezr. vii. 22 "an hundred *baths* of wine," ἀποθηκῶν, A βάδων. In Dan. Bel 3 LXX has ἐλαίου (Theod. οἴνου) μετρηταὶ ἕξ.

"blow *for* blow" etc., and the Sermon on the Mount has "eye *for* an eye," "tooth *for* a tooth¹." But, apart from contexts suggesting endless *vendetta*, ἀντί might mean "[coming constantly] in the place of," so as to denote "one thing [*following*] *upon* another"; and Origen actually paraphrases it so here, "a second grace *upon* (ἐπί) a former grace," though both in the preceding and in the following context he quotes the clause with ἀντί². Ἀντί is used by Philo³ similarly, but somewhat differently, to describe the succession of the graces of God, who *takes away the old*, and dispenses to us constantly "new *in the place of* old." Elsewhere He is said to pour them on us in an unceasing and continuous succession or orbit⁴.

[2286] There is probably in John, as in Philo, an intention to suggest the notion of *"exchange"* rather than that of mere succession. Both Origen and Chrysostom appear to discern, in this passage, a taking away of the old grace, or gift of the Law ("the Law was *given*"), in order to *substitute* the new gift of the grace and truth that are in Christ. The *Law* was given to Israel through Moses because (Deut. vii. 7) the Lord "loved" them and "chose" them, that is to say, God gave it as a gift, or grace; but His full grace and truth, latent under that Law, did not come into being till the Word became flesh as Jesus Christ in order to *"take away"* the first grace, *i.e.* the Law of Moses, so as to establish the second grace, *i.e.* the grace of freedom, or sonship,—the grace of the Father as manifested in the grace of the Son⁵.

[2287] "We all" is perhaps intended to mean more than the "we" that is so common in the First Epistle ("*we* know," "*we* are the sons of God" etc.). "We" means "we Christians." But "we all"—like "every man" at the beginning of the Prologue—may mean "every human being from the creation of man." All have

---

¹ [2285 *a*] "De rebus adversis dicitur," says Steph. Comp. Theogn. 342—3 εἰ μή τι κακῶν ἄμπαυμα μεριμνέων εὑροίμην, δοίην δ' ἀντ' ἀνιῶν ἀνίας. Alf. quotes Chrys. *de Sacerdot*. 6. 13 vol. i. p. 435 ἑτέραν ἀνθ' ἑτέρας φροντίδα.

² Orig. Huet ii. 95.

³ [2285 *b*] Philo i. 254 τὰς πρώτας ἀεὶ χάριτας, πρὶν κορεσθέντας ἐξυβρίσαι (so Wetst., Mang., by error, -εσθὲν -ίσε) τοὺς λαχόντας, ἐπισχών, καὶ ταμιευσάμενος, εἰσαῦθις ἑτέρας ἀντὶ ἐκείνων, καὶ τρίτας ἀντὶ τῶν δευτέρων καὶ ἀεὶ νέας ἀντὶ παλαιοτέρων, τοτὲ μὲν διαφερούσας, τοτὲ δ' αὖ καὶ τὰς αὐτὰς ἐπιδίδωσι.

⁴ [2285 *c*] Philo i. 342 ὁ τὴν τῶν δωρεῶν ἐπάλληλον φορὰν ἀπαύστως συνείρων, ὁ τὰς χάριτας ἐχομένας ἀλλήλων ἀνακυκλῶν.

⁵ Comp. Heb. x. 9 "He *taketh away* the first that he may establish the second."

received, in various degrees and kinds, gifts from the Pleroma, the Fulness of Him that filleth all in all[1].

(iii) Ἀπό

(α) Ἀπό and ἐκ meaning "[some] of," see 2213—5

(β) Ἀπο, transposition of

[2288] Ἀπό, meaning "off," is placed before πηχῶν in xxi. 8 "about two hundred cubits off (ἀπὸ πηχῶν διακοσίων)." It is a natural transposition arising from the desire to give prominence to the notion "distant," as in our "*distant* two hundred cubits," and then, illogically, allowing the preposition that signifies distance to govern "cubits." Similarly πρό is transposed in xii. 1 (lit.) "*before six days* the Passover (πρὸ ἓξ ἡμερῶν τοῦ πάσχα)," for "*six days before* the Passover," like the Latin "*before the fifth day* the Kalends" for "*the fifth day before* the Kalends." Abundant instances will be found in the Thesaurus, and there is nothing in the Johannine passages that needs comment, except that the former transposition may be largely the result of Latin influence, and that it is found in Revelation (xiv. 20) "*at a distance of*…furlongs (ἀπὸ σταδίων…)."

(γ) Ἀπό and ἐκ describing domicile or birth-place

[2289] Ἀπό and ἐκ occur in i. 44 "Now Philip was *from* (ἀπό) Bethsaida[2], *from out* (ἐκ) the city of Andrew and Peter[3]," and

---

[1] [2287 a] "Grace for grace" may be a different aspect of the saying "He that hath, to him shall be added," and of the Synoptic doctrine concerning "reward." A "talent" given by the Master of the House may be called a "grace" given by the Father. In the Parable of the Talents the Master gives the talents. The servant returns the talents doubled. Lastly, the servant receives, in return, the joy of his Lord. By calling the talent "a grace," a writer would indicate that the transaction is one of free gift, on both sides, with no thought of bargain. The child that returns to the Giver the grace or talent of childhood with interest, receives the grace or talent of youth, and the youth, again, the grace or talent of manhood, and, finally, that of old age. God, in each case, may be said either to "take away," or receive back, the first grace, that He may "establish" the second.

[2287 b] Perhaps, also, John wishes, at the outset of his Gospel, to indicate to his readers why he will very rarely use the Synoptic word, μισθός, i.e. "hire," "wages," or "reward." It expresses a truth: but, if used too often and without care, it might lead some to suppose that God bargains. The Fourth Gospel uses the word only once, when Jesus says (iv. 36) "*Already* is he that is reaping receiving *wages*," i.e. "The very act of reaping God's harvest is your 'wages,' just as the very act of doing God's will is my 'meat.'"

[2] Comp. xii. 21 προσῆλθαν (i.e. Ἕλληνες) Φιλίππῳ τῷ ἀπὸ B. τῆς Γαλιλαίας.

[3] [2289 a] A.V. "of B., the city," R.V. "from B., of the city." The Latin MSS. render ἀπό by "a," ἐκ by "de," "ex" (or om.).

i. 45—6 "We have found...Jesus son of Joseph,—him [that is] *from* Nazareth ('Ι. υἱὸν τοῦ Ἰωσὴφ τὸν ἀπὸ Ναζαρέτ)...*From out* (ἐκ) Nazareth can any good thing be[1]?" These two passages, so far as they go, suggest that (in both) ἀπό signifies domicile and ἐκ extraction. In the former, ἐκ may be used to imply that Philip, though resident in Bethsaida, had sprung "from" Capernaum, the city of Andrew and Peter; in the latter, to imply that the Messiah could not spring "from" Nazareth (instead of Bethlehem). But this rule seems broken in vii. 41—2 "But others said, Can it be that the Christ is to come *from out* (ἐκ) Galilee? Did not the Scripture say that *from out* (ἐκ) the seed of David, and *from* (ἀπό) Bethlehem, the village where David was (ὅπου ἦν Δ.), the Christ is to come[2]?" Here, where we might expect "*from out* Bethlehem," to denote that the Messiah was to be *born there*, the weaker preposition is substituted, perhaps because the stronger has been already used to denote *extraction* from the family of David.

[2290] Concerning xi. 1 (lit.) "Now there was one [lying] sick (ἦν δέ τις ἀσθενῶν) Lazarus *from* Bethany (Δ. ἀπὸ Βηθανίας) *from out* (ἐκ) the village of Mary and Martha her sister" Chrysostom says, "Not at haphazard does the evangelist tell us *whence Lazarus was* (πόθεν ἦν ὁ Λ.), but for a certain cause, which he will subsequently mention." By the "cause" Chrysostom (doubtless) means Christ's special affection for the whole family at Bethany. For this reason, we ought perhaps to connect "from Bethany," not with "Lazarus" adjectivally, but with "was" predicatively, thus: "Now a certain man, lying sick [at the time], Lazarus [by name], *was from* Bethany[3]," which agrees with the construction in (2289) "Now Philip *was from* Bethsaida." The writer proceeds on the principle of

---

[1] [2289 *b*] The Latin versions here translate both ἀπό and ἐκ by "a": and "Joseph a Nazaret(h) (or, Nazara)" in *a*, *b*, *e*, and *f*, might mean "Joseph of Nazareth"; *ff* has "Joseph qui est a Nazareth," which perhaps increases the ambiguity.

[2] [2289 *c*] Codex *a*, "de...de...a"; *b*, "ex...ex...(om.)"; *f*, "a...ex...de"; *e*, "de Galilaea...de semine David a Bethlehem de castello David venit." Mic. v. 2 has ἐκ, not ἀπό, in the prophecy about "Bethlehem" here alluded to.

[3] [2290 *a*] Comp. iii. 1 ἦν δὲ ἄνθρωπος, ἐκ τῶν Φ., Ν. ὄνομα αὐτῷ, ἄρχων τῶν Ἰ. οὗτος ἦλθε, where ἄρχων is certainly the emphatic, if not the predicative part, of the sentence. In xi. 1, *a*, *b*, *f* have "infirmus Lazarus nomine (*or*, nomine Lazarus) a Bethania," *i.e.* "a sick man, Lazarus by name, from Bethany"; *e* has "erat autem quidam Lazarus a Bethania qui tenebatur infirmitate magna"; all render ἀπό by "a," ἐκ by "de." But *d* has "de" for both.

"narrowing down." As Lazarus has not been mentioned before, he does not speak of "Lazarus from Bethany," but thus: (1) "one," (2) "lying sick," (3) "Lazarus," (4) "domiciled at Bethany," (5) "a native of the village of Mary and Martha." Then follow (6) "Mary was the woman that anointed the Saviour's feet," (7) "Lazarus her brother was sick," (8) "he whom thou lovest is sick[1]." It is not certain, he seems to say, that Lazarus was *born* in Bethany; but it is certain that he was born in the same village as his sisters, and that he was living now at Bethany. The passage suggests that the evangelist is writing cautiously, in view of differences of opinion; but it favours the conclusion that he uses ἀπό to mean domicile and ἐκ to mean extraction.

[2291] xix. 38 "But after these things Joseph *from* (ἀπό) Arimathaea asked Pilate...[2]." All the evangelists use ἀπό here. But the parallel Mark and Matthew have "came" in the context of "from Arimathaea" in such a way as to suggest that Joseph *came from that town* for the purpose of presenting his petition to Pilate. Luke and John make it clear that "from Arimathaea" indicates Joseph's domicile, and does not mean that he came on that day from that village[3].

[2292] From the Johannine combinations of ἀπό and ἐκ above we may conclude with certainty that John makes a distinction between them. Light on his motive may be thrown by the following facts. (1) Mark's only use of the phrase "Jesus *from* Nazareth" is connected with "come," so that it is ambiguous, "There *came* Jesus *from* (ἀπό) Nazareth of Galilee[4]," where the parallel Matthew omits "Nazareth" and has merely "from Galilee." (2) Matthew elsewhere says that Jesus left "the [city] *Nazara*" (in which Joseph of Bethlehem had settled on his return from Egypt[5]) and settled in Capernaum[6], but that the multitude called Him (not "Jesus *from* Capernaum" but) "the prophet, Jesus, the [man, *or*, prophet] *from*

---

[1] [2290 b] The process of "narrowing down," probably used unconsciously by many, was recognised by the Jews (*Sanhedr.* 89 b) in God's command to Abraham, (Gen. xxii. 2) "Take now thy son" (Abr. "But I have two"); "thine only son" (Abr. "but each is the only son of his mother"); "whom thou lovest" (Abr. "but I love them both"); "Isaac" (to which there is no reply except in act).

[2] The Latin codices mostly render ἀπό by "ab," but *e* by "qui ab" perh. reading ὁ ἀπ' 'A. with ℵ.

[3] Mk xv. 43, Mt. xxvii. 57, Lk. xxiii. 51.   [4] Mk i. 9.

[5] Mt. ii. 23 Ναζαρέτ.   [6] Mt. iv. 13 τὴν Ναζαρά.

Nazareth of Galilee¹." Luke never uses the phrase "Jesus *from* (or, the [man] *from*) Nazareth"; but, in his Introduction, he describes Nazareth as the home of Mary and Joseph from the beginning (although Jesus was born at Bethlehem), and, in the body of his Gospel, on the only occasion on which he mentions Nazareth, he says, "And he came to *Nazara* where he had been brought up²." The only mention of Nazareth in N.T. apart from the Gospels is in the speech of Peter to Cornelius "Jesus the [man] *from* Nazareth³."

[2293] This, then, is one of the very many instances where John uses a phrase used by Mark and Matthew and disused by Luke— probably because Luke thought it likely to make people suppose that Jesus was *born* at Nazareth instead of Bethlehem. John takes up the phrase ἀπὸ N. and puts it before the reader, at the outset of his Gospel, along with ἐκ N., leading us to infer that Jesus might be *domiciled* at Nazareth without having been *born* there. At the same time he makes us applaud the faith of Philip, who could accept as the Messiah "Jesus a son of Joseph," domiciled at Nazareth, on the strength of His personality alone⁴.

---

¹ Mt. xxi. 11 ὁ προφήτης Ἰησοῦς ὁ ἀπὸ N. τῆς Γαλιλαίας.

² Lk. iv. 16 ἦλθεν εἰς Ναζαρά, οὗ ἦν τεθραμμένος.

³ [2292 a] Acts x. 36—8, an inextricably confused sentence, or rather group of clauses, in which—without any certain grammatical construction—τὸν λόγον, and τὸ γενόμενον ῥῆμα, and "beginning *from* (ἀπό) Galilee" occur in connexion with "Jesus *from* (ἀπό) Nazareth." Possibly there was some early confusion between "Jesus beginning" and "the Word beginning," and between the "word" in two senses. W.H. have a long marginal alternative.

⁴ [2293 a] Ἀπό, of domicile, is not quoted in Steph. from secular authors, though there are abundant instances of it as denoting a school or sect, "*those from* (οἱ ἀπό) the Porch" (also "*those from* Aristarchus, Pythagoras etc."). Swete (on Mk xv. 43) quotes Joseph. *Ant.* xvi. 10. 1 (301) Εὐρυκλῆς ἀπὸ Λακεδαίμονος. But the quotation, after a parenthesis about the man's character, has ἐπιδημήσας ὡς τὸν Ἡρώδην, which suggests that ἀπὸ Λ. ἐ. may mean "*having come from* Lacedaemon *on a visit* to Herod." Even if that were not the exact meaning there, ἀπό would probably be *influenced* by the impending verb (like Soph. *Electr.* 135 τόν γ' ἐξ Ἀΐδα...λίμνας...ἀναστάσεις, quoted by Jelf §647). Thayer quotes no instances from secular authors. In LXX, between "Jephthah the Gileadite" and "Elon the Zebulonite," we have Judg. xii. 8 "Ibzan *from Bethlehem*," ἀπό (but A ἐκ), and sim. in 2 S. xxiii. 20 ἀπό (parall. to 1 Chr. xi. 22 ὑπέρ by error, al. ex. ἀπό). Comp. also the predicative use in Judg. xiii. 2 καὶ ἦν ἀνὴρ εἶς ἀπὸ (A ἐκ) Σαραὰλ ἀπὸ (A ἐκ) δήμου συγγενείας τοῦ Δανεὶ καὶ ὄνομα αὐτῷ Μανῶε, Judg. xvii. 1 καὶ ἐγένετο ἀνὴρ ἀπὸ (A ἐξ) ὄρους Ἐφραίμ, καὶ ὄνομα αὐτῷ Μειχαίας. The variations of A are useful as indicating that different writers might distinguish differently between ἀπό and ἐκ in phrases of domicile or extraction.

[2293 b] The difference between ἀπό and ἐκ may also be illustrated by the

(δ) Ἀπό, ἐκ, and παρά, with ἐξέρχομαι, see ἐκ, 2326—8

(iv) Διά

(1) Διά with Accusative of Person

[2294] An action may be done διά τινα when it is done "*because of* a person" in various aspects of causation: (1) (motive) "*because of* the doer's love of, or fear of, or, desire to please, the person," (2) (action) "*because* the person helped, prompted, or constrained, the doer." In the former aspect appear "The Sabbath was made *because of* [God's love of] man[1]," and similarly "*because of* the elect" and "*because of* Herodias[2]." The latter, if it occurs at all in N.T., may be exemplified by the phrase "*because of the multitude*," which in various contexts may suggest (1) because of some one's desire not to jostle, or press through, the multitude, or (2) because the multitude hindered, constrained etc. But in xi. 42 it means "for the sake of helping the multitude[3]." The Epistle to the Hebrews contains the only passage in N.T. that combines the personal accusative and the personal genitive thus: "It became him, *i.e.* the Father, *because of whom are all things and through whom are all things* (δι' ὃν τὰ πάντα καὶ δι' οὗ τὰ πάντα), in bringing many sons unto glory, to make the captain of their salvation perfect through sufferings[4]." It is also concerning the Father that the Epistle to the Romans says, "From him and *through him, and to him,* are all things[5]." But the Epistle to the Colossians says concerning the Son, "All things *through him and to him* have been created[6]."

[2295] These quotations, by themselves, would suffice to make it probable that, by the end of the first century, Greek Christians would be weighing and discussing the exact phrases by which they ought to express the mediatory action of the Son in the regeneration of the world. Philo actually exhibits such a discussion concerning

---

unique phrase (Jn xii. 49) ἐξ ἐμαυτοῦ οὐκ ἐλάλησα as compared with the usual οὐκ ἀπ' ἐμαυτοῦ λαλῶ. The former goes back more definitely to the fountain-head. It is also more emphatic and comes appropriately in the solemn protest that concludes Christ's public preaching.

[1] Mk ii. 27.   [2] Mk xiii. 20, Mt. xxiv. 22, and Mt. xiv. 3.
[3] [2294 a] Mk ii. 4, iii. 9, Lk. v. 19, viii. 19, διὰ τὸν ὄχλον. Comp. Mt. xxvii. 19 δι' αὐτόν = (1) "because of my thoughts about him," or (2) "because he terrified me in a vision." On xii. 11 "*for the sake of* [*seeing*] *him* [i.e. Lazarus] δι' αὐτόν)" (less probably "*by reason of* [*their having seen*] *him*") see 1652 *b*.
[4] Heb. ii. 10.
[5] Rom. xi. 36 ἐξ αὐτοῦ καὶ δι' αὐτοῦ καὶ εἰς αὐτὸν τὰ πάντα.   [6] Col. i. 16.

the mediatory action of the Logos. He finds fault with Eve and with Joseph for using the phrase "*through God* (διὰ τοῦ θεοῦ)[1]"—for which he would certainly have rebuked the author of the Epistle to the Hebrews, as implying that God was an instrument. Towards the creation of anything there must be, he says, a combination of several things. To make a house, for example, there must be (1) builder, (2) materials, (3) instruments. In the abstract, he adds a fourth term as follows: (1) the ὑφ' οὗ, "by what," τὸ αἴτιον, "the causal," (2) the ἐξ οὗ, "from what," ἡ ὕλη, "the material," (3) the δι' οὗ, "through what," τὸ ἐργαλεῖον[2], "the instrumental," (4) the δι' ὅ, "because of what," ἡ αἰτία, "the cause (*or*, reason)." Applied to the House of the Universe, the Causal is God, the Material is the four elements, the Instrument is the Word of God[3].

[2296] Philo lays great stress on this distinction between the Instrument and the Cause or the Causal. "It characterizes," he says, "those who love truth, and who desire true and wholesome knowledge: but those who say they have 'obtained a thing *through God*,' [wrongly] suppose the Causal, the Builder, to be a [mere] instrument, and [suppose] the instrument, the human mind, to be the Causal." The passage concludes with the assertion that salvation is not "*through* God," but "[*a gift*] *from* Him (παρ' αὐτοῦ) as being the Causal[4]."

---

[1] Gen. iv. 1, xl. 8.

[2] [2295 a] Philo i. 161—2. Instead of τὸ ἐργαλεῖον, he regularly uses τὸ ὄργανον, or τὰ ὄργανα, in the context. Aristotle defined a slave as "a living *organon*" and Philo says expressly here ὄργανα γὰρ ἡμεῖς, so that the term includes "living instruments."

[3] [2295 b] So far, so good; but as regards the Cause, the δι' ὅ or αἰτία, the parallel between the earthly house and the House of the Universe is not maintained. For, in dealing with the former, instead of asking the question "*Because of* what?" (Διὰ τί;) he asks "*On account of what?*" (Τίνος ἕνεκα;)— "*On account of what* [is the house built] except for *shelter and safety*...," Τίνος δὲ ἕνεκα πλὴν σκέπης καὶ ἀσφαλείας δι' ὅ τοῦτό ἐστιν; The sense seems to require τὸ δὲ δι' ὅ τοῦτό ἐστιν, "and this constitutes the δι' ὅ or Why." In his description of the necessary conditions for a material house, he enumerates only three, (1) architect, (2) stone and wood, (3) tools. He omits the cause or motive. Also, in speaking of the House of the Universe, he says that "*the cause* (αἰτία) *of its creation is the goodness of the Architect.*" Apparently he makes the *object* of the human architect, which he calls "shelter and security," parallel to the *motive* of the divine Architect, which he calls His "Goodness."

[4] [2296 a] Οὐ διὰ τοῦ θεοῦ, ἀλλὰ παρ' αὐτοῦ, ὡς αἰτίου, τὸ σώζεσθαι, where παρά implies proceeding from a *person*, whereas ἐκ might mean "from a *source*." The whole of the passage indicates a controversial attitude towards loose thinkers,

[2297] What, then, is the meaning of "because of the Father" and "because of me" in vi. 56—7 "He that eateth my flesh and drinketh my blood abideth in me and I in him. Even as the living Father sent me and I *live because of the Father* (διὰ τὸν πατέρα) so he that eateth me, he also shall *live because of me* (ζήσει δι' ἐμέ)[1]"? Starting from the second clause we begin by assuming that this is different from the corresponding phrase with the genitive in the Epistle, 1 Jn iv. 9 "In this was manifested the love of God in us because God hath sent his only begotten Son into the world that *we may live through him* (ζήσωμεν δι' αὐτοῦ)." The phrase ζῶ διὰ σέ may mean "I live *because of thee*" in two senses: (1) "I live because of thy action in the past [whether that of parents in giving life, or that of friends in saving it]," (2) "I live because I desire to serve thee, must serve thee, for the sake of serving thee [in the future][2]."

who confused these distinctions. Taken all together, these extracts from Philo strengthen the probability that John deliberately reserved the instrumental phrase, δι' αὐτοῦ, for the action of the Logos, or Son, both in the Gospel and in the Epistle, so that he would not apply it to the action of the Baptist (2302—4). But they also suggest that John would take pains to distinguish his doctrine of the instrumental action of the incarnate Logos from that of Philo which contemplated no incarnation and perhaps no personality in the Logos. In any case the facts make it absolutely certain—at least for those who regard the evangelist as a careful writer (not to speak of his being more than usually careful) writing after, and in the midst of, such discussions as these—that John would not use the δι' ὅν for the δι' οὗ or vice versa.

[1] [2297 a] A.V. "I live *by* the Father...he shall live *by* me." A.V. mostly uses "by" to translate διά with personal genitive when it refers to the action of the Logos. Apparently A.V. took διά with accusative here as meaning the same thing as διά with genitive.

[2] [2297 b] For (1) comp. Plut. *Vit. Alex.* § 8 (p. 668 d—e) concerning Alexander, who said he owed life to his father, but good life to Aristotle, δι' ἐκεῖνον μὲν ζῶν διὰ τοῦτον δὲ καλῶς ζῶν, Dion. Hal. 1579 διὰ τοὺς θεούς (478 δι' οὕς) μέγας ἐγενόμην (Sylb. "frequentius genetivum"), (?) Aristoph. *Plut.* 470, Plutus says δι' ἐμέ τε ζῶντας ὑμᾶς (ambig., perh. "to gain me"). In Hesiod *Works* 3—4, ὅν τε διὰ βροτοὶ ἄνδρες...Διὸς μεγάλοιο ἕκητι may mean "because of his action in the past...and thanks to whom (or, at whose mercy) in the future." Timaeus (quoted in Longinus iv. 3) says that Athens was punished as a whole, for the mutilation of the Hermae, more especially δι' ἕνα ἄνδρα, "because of one man," (Roberts) "the infliction of punishment was chiefly due to Hermocrates the son of Hermon, who was descended...from the outraged god."

[2297 c] For (2), Wetstein (on Jn vi. 57) quotes Xiphilinus in Caracalla p. 328 "I would fain *live because of you* alone (δι' ὑμᾶς μόνους ζῆν ἐθέλω) that I may be continually heaping favours on you [all]," and Eustathius, who (on *Iliad* v. 875 σοὶ πάντες μαχόμεσθα) says ἤγουν διὰ σέ, ὅμοιον τῷ Σοὶ ζῶ, ἤτοι διὰ σέ. This is important as indicating that ζῶ διὰ σέ was a familiar phrase meaning "I live for thy sake," *i.e.* to do thee service. Comp. Epictet. iv. 1. 150 (given by Wetst. as

But in later Greek the second of these interpretations predominates, especially with the word "live," and where the future is contemplated. Moreover the first interpretation ("I live because of thy action in the past") is scarcely to be distinguished from the genitival form "I live through thy action in the past." Hence we infer that in the present passage the phrase means—or perhaps it will be safer to say, includes as its first meaning—"he also shall live *to do me service*, or, *to do my will.*"

[2298] Going back to the parallel and preceding clause, "I live *because of* the Father," are we to infer that this means "I live *to do the will of* the Father"? This is certainly one aspect of the truth, and it agrees with the tenor of the whole Gospel, and particularly with the words "I am come down from heaven, not to do mine own will, but the will of him that sent me[1]." But Jesus also says "My *meat* is to do the will of him that sent me[2]," and this implies that the Father gives the Son "meat," that is, supports and strengthens, and *causes* the Son's life. Thus we have here the two aspects of causation mentioned above. The first is (motive) "I live *because I desire to serve the Father*"; the second is (action) "I live *because the Father gives me life.*"

[2299] It is quite in John's manner to avail himself of this twofold meaning in order to suggest to his readers something of the manysided mystery of the relation between the Father and the Son. Epictetus (2297 *e*) had implicitly denied that it was right for anyone

---

iii. 26) "For my part I had as soon not live, if one were bound to live *for the sake of* Felicion (διὰ Φιληκίωνα) [*i.e.* to do F. service] putting up with his frowns and fits of slave-like fury (δουλικοῦ φρυάγματος, *i.e.* such as one might expect from a slave promoted to office)." Also Winer (p. 498) quotes Long. *Pastor.* 2 p. 62 (Schaef.) διὰ τὰς νύμφας ἔζησε. So the philosopher in Epictetus says to God "I abide on earth merely *for thy sake* (διὰ σέ)" (**2705**).

[2297 *d*] Comparing the two groups, we see that later Greek takes διά τινα in the second sense, "to do anyone service," and especially in the phrase ζῶ διά. Where the future is in view, ζῶ διά would naturally have the second meaning.

[2297 *e*] Δι' ἄλλον, (δι' οὐδένα etc.) without ζῆν, occur in Epictetus in connexion with his doctrine that we ought not to regard ourselves as unfortunate or in evil case "because of another person," *e.g.* i. 9. 34 ἄλλος δι' ἄλλον οὐ δυστυχεῖ, and *Ench.* xxiv. 1 οὐ δύνασαι ἐν κακῷ εἶναι δι' ἄλλον. According to Epictetus, δυστυχῶ δι' ἄλλον means "I am made unfortunate *because of* [*my thoughts about*] another." And this, he says, we ought never to say. This may include both meanings "we are not to be unhappy *because of* what anyone has done in the past," or "*because of* what anyone may experience in the future."

[1] vi. 38. [2] iv. 34.

to live "*because of another.*" But here John speaks of the disciples as "living *because of the Son*" and of the Son as "living *because of the Father*" in a manner that suggests that this is the highest kind of life, hinting even at a reciprocal action, as though the Father also, from the beginning, might have "lived *because of the Son*"—as we may surely say that the Son "lived *because of the Church.*"

[2300] This passage, also, partially answers the question, Why does John altogether omit the Synoptic doctrine that the disciples are to do this and that "*for the sake of* (ἕνεκα)" *Christ*? The doctrine is here. It is implied that those who receive Christ's flesh and blood are so impregnated with the common life of the Church that henceforth they "live *because of* (διά)" *Christ*. They do not serve Him in this or that single act, by a separate effort on each occasion, but spontaneously as the branch develops in the vine according to the law of the vine—a metaphor not yet mentioned by John but prepared for in the preceding words "He that eateth my flesh and drinketh my blood abideth in me and I in him[1]."

(2) Διά with Genitive of Person

[2301] Strictly described, the author of an action (mentioned passively) is distinguished from his agent or instrument by two distinct prepositions, as in Matthew, "that which was spoken *by* (ὑπό) the Lord *through* (διά) the prophet[2]." But Luke only once uses this instrumental διά in connexion with "prophets" ("written (lit.) *through* (διά) the prophets"); and once he has "*through* (διά) *the mouth of* his holy prophets" (avoiding personal instrumentality)[3]. Where Matthew describes the Baptist as sending "*through* (διά) his disciples," Luke has "*two* (δύο τινάς) of his disciples[4]." In the Triple Tradition, this personal genitive with διά occurs only in the passages pronouncing woe on him "*through* whom (δι' οὗ) the Son

---

[1] [2300 a] Chrysostom comments thus: Καὶ ἵνα μὴ ἀγέννητον νομίσῃς προσέθηκεν εὐθὺς τὸ, Διὰ τὸν Πατέρα, οὐ τοῦτο δεικνὺς ὅτι ἐνεργείας τινὸς χρείαν ἔχει πρὸς τὸ ζῆν...Τί οὖν ἐστιν, Διὰ τὸν Πατέρα; Τὴν αἰτίαν ἐνταῦθα αἰνίττεται μόνον. Ὁ δὲ λέγει τοιοῦτόν ἐστι, Καθώς ἐστι ζῶν ὁ Πατὴρ οὕτω κἀγὼ ζῶ. He seems to take διά as "*because of* [the divine begetting]" (in sense (1) given above (2297)), and to interpret the clause as meaning "*because of* the life similar to His own transmitted to me permanently by the Father."

[2] Mt. i. 22. Comp. ii. 5, 15, 17, 23, iii. 3, iv. 14, viii. 17, xii. 17, xiii. 35, xxi. 4, xxiv. 15, xxvii. 9.

[3] Lk. xviii. 31, i. 70.   [4] Mt. xi. 2, Lk. vii. 19.

of man is to be delivered up[1]." In John, διά with genitive of person is repeatedly used to denote the agency of the Logos or of Christ, "All things came into being *through* him (δι' αὐτοῦ)," "The world came into being *through* him," "The grace [of God] and the truth [of God] came into being *through* Jesus Christ," "God sent not the Son into the world to judge the world but that the world should be saved *through* him[2]" etc.

[2302] There is ambiguity in i. 7 "This [man] came for witness that he might bear witness concerning the light (φωτός), in order that all might believe *through him* (or; *through it*, δι' αὐτοῦ). *He* (ἐκεῖνος) was not the light, but...." Is it meant (*a*) that all might believe *through John the Baptist*, or (*b*) that all might believe *through the Light*, or *through the Logos* in whom is "the Life" that is "the Light of men"?

In favour of (*a*) are these considerations. (1) John frequently speaks elsewhere of believing the Son, and on, or in, the Son, and of believing in the Light[3]; but (2) there is no other Johannine instance of "believe *through* the Son, or *through* Him, or *through* the Light." (3) The change from an unemphatic pronoun ("through him (αὐτοῦ)") to an emphatic "he (ἐκεῖνος)" may be illustrated by other instances in N.T.[4], so that there is no difficulty in supposing both pronouns to mean "the Baptist." (4) In view of i. 17 "the Law was given *through* Moses," where subordinate agency is clearly attributed to Moses, why may it not be attributed to John the Baptist?

[2303] In favour of (*b*) are the following arguments. (1) This is the first passage in which the word "believe" is mentioned. Now belief, in itself, may be either good or bad, belief in the true God or belief in false gods. Is it likely that the new "belief" should be introduced by the evangelist, as being "*belief* through" a "man"? (2) When first introducing a term, it is in accordance with the evangelist's style to use it in a broad sense, which he afterwards "narrows down"; and all that he may mean here is that the belief is to be "*through the Light*" (not, like superstitious beliefs, "through the darkness"). (3) "That *all* might *believe*

---

[1] Mk xiv. 21, Mt. xxvi. 24, Lk. xxii. 22. Comp. Mt. xviii. 7, Lk. xvii. 1.

[2] [2301 *a*] Jn i. 3, 10, 17, iii. 17 etc. In xiv. 6 "No man cometh to the Father save *through* me," the context ("I am the way") may justify the supposition that the phrase is metaphorical, and that the genitive is local, δι' ὁδοῦ.

[3] xii. 36 π. εἰς τὸ φῶς.

[4] See Field, *Otium* (on 2 Tim. ii.26).

through John the Baptist"—even if we admit that this was the will of God in sending the Baptist—is not so natural, in any Christian writer, as "that *all* might believe through *the Christ*, or through *the Son*," or "that *Israel* should believe through *the Baptist*."

[2304] (4) In the Fourth Gospel, which consistently subordinates the Baptist to the Messiah, and in which the former is called by the latter a mere lamp (v. 35), is it likely that the evangelist should say that this "lamp" was sent to bear witness concerning the Light "in order that all men should believe—through the 'lamp'"? (5) The agency attributed to Moses is merely the transmission (from God to man) of the written Law, which the context contrasts with "Grace and truth"; but the agency that would produce Belief is of a much higher and more subtle kind. (6) The work to be accomplished through the agency of the Baptist would be better described in his own language (*"in order that there may be manifested to Israel"*) as the manifestation of the Son, through whom "all" were to believe in the Father. (7) In xvii. 20 ("those who believe through their logos or word," *i.e.* through the word of the disciples) the evangelist avoids saying "believe *through them*" (although St Paul uses that phrase[1]) and this, too, although the disciples were destined to receive the Spirit: much more does it seem likely that John would avoid saying that "*all men*" were intended (in the divine Providence) to "believe *through the Baptist*[2]." (8) The pronoun αὐτός—with the exception of the unemphatic and parenthetic "his name was John" (ὄνομα αὐτῷ Ἰ.), rendered in Latin as well as in English "*whose*"—is used always in this Prologue for the Word, the Light etc.; and the words or phrases "through him," "without him," "in him," "it," "him" etc. occur so frequently that the interpretation of a particular "through him" as referring to John the Baptist carries with it a sense of incongruity. It may be added that the only instance of δι' αὐτοῦ in the Epistle refers to the Son ("that we may

---

[1] 1 Cor. iii. 5.
[2] [2304 a] The Epistles teem with phrases indicating that "through him (αὐτοῦ)," *i.e.* through Jesus, would be used in connexion with every gift of God to man, and, although πιστεύω is not thus used, the adjective πιστός in the First Epistle of St Peter (i. 20—1) describes the Messiah "foreknown before the foundation of the world but manifested at the last of the times for your sakes who *through him are made firm in trust to God* (τοὺς δι' αὐτοῦ πιστοὺς εἰς θεόν)."

live *through him*¹"). There appears a preponderance of probability in favour of the interpretation "that he might bear witness concerning the Light that all might believe *through that* [*Light*]²."

(v) **Εἰς** (see also **2706** foll.)

(α) For πιϲτεγω εἰc, see **1480** foll.

(β) Εἰc without verb of motion

[2305] This construction is used in the words of Christ, ix. 7 "Go wash *to* the pool of Siloam," repeated by the blind man thus, ix. 11 "He said to me, Go *to* Siloam and wash³." Motion is also implied in xx. 7 "the napkin...apart, rolled up [*and put*] *into* one place," which perhaps implies more deliberateness ("first rolled up and then carried into a place apart") than would have been implied by ἐν.

[2306] Far more important than these, are passages, in connexion with some spiritual doctrine of unity, where John uses εἰς with a verb that does not imply motion, such as xvii. 23 "that they may be *completely perfected into one* (τετελειωμένοι εἰς ἕν)." This is perhaps little more than a brief way of saying "that they may be completely perfected and brought into unity." But it is not so easy to explain 1 Jn v. 8 "Three are they that bear witness, the spirit and the water and the blood, and the three are *into* the one (οἱ τρεῖς εἰς τὸ ἕν εἰσιν)." Εἰσιν appears to be emphatic ("are essentially"), and the writer seems to suggest (1) the reality of three witnesses *tending* "*to*" *one truth*, and (2) the reality of three essences *harmonizing themselves* "*into*" *one nature*, namely, that of the crucified Son who first

---

¹ 1 Jn iv. 9 ἵνα ζήσωμεν δι' αὐτοῦ.

² [2304 *b*] Origen, after an exposition of the words "he came for witness to bear witness of the light," says (Huet ii. 85 D) "we must next consider what is to be thought about the words 'That all might believe through him.'" Unfortunately what should follow has been lost. Cramer, however, prints, as from Origen, "That is to say, so far as He was concerned (ὅσον ἐφ' ἑαυτῷ)—even though 'all' did *not* 'believe.' For [similarly], if all men should not receive the light that comes from the sun, one would not say, as a consequence, that the sun did not rise for the purpose of universal enlightenment; for the purpose of Him that sent him was that all should believe (ἡ γὰρ πρόθεσις τοῦ πέμψαντος αὐτὸν ἦν πιστεῦσαι πάντας)." This rather suggests that Origen took δι' αὐτοῦ to mean "through the Light—so far as the Light is concerned."

³ [2305 *a*] For λούειν εἰς, see Epict. iii. 22. 71 ἵν' αὐτὸ λούσῃ εἰς σκάφην (lit.) "to bathe the child *into* the tub." Νίπτω εἰς is not given by Steph. On εἰς for ἐν in the Synoptists and later Greek, see **2706** foll.

delivered up His Spirit to God and then poured forth from His side "water and blood" for the sake of men.

[2307] As regards the phrase twice[1] used to describe Christ's visitations after the Resurrection (xx. 19, 26) "and he stood (lit.) *to the midst of the disciples*," it is preceded in the former case by "Jesus came" and in the latter by "Jesus cometh," so as to preclude the explanation that it is a condensed form of "came to, and stood among, the disciples." And it is the more remarkable because, concerning a similar visitation, Luke has (xxiv. 36) "And while they were speaking these things he himself stood *in* the midst of them"; and the tradition about Jesus "*in* the midst" of the disciples is found in the Epistle to the Hebrews[2]. The writer of that Epistle regards Jesus as "singing the praises of God *in the midst of the disciples*." Justin Martyr takes the same view. He mentions the "singing" immediately after mentioning the Resurrection; he says that Jesus "stood in the midst of the disciples," and he appeals for confirmation to "the Memoirs of the Apostles." His language indicates that he has in view the manifestation to the Eleven described by Luke[3]. John—on the supposition that he knew this traditional phrase to have been connected with Christ's resurrection by Luke—may be presumed to have had some good reason for departing from Luke's

---

[1] [2307 a] In Jn xxi. 4 W.H. ἔστη Ἰησοῦς εἰς (marg. ἐπί) τὸν αἰγιαλόν, all the MSS. (Alford) exc. BC have ἐπί. The Latin versions have "in," exc. *d* which has "ad" corresponding to D ἐπί. In BC the juxtaposition of the two similar syllables ΙϹΕΙϹ suggests that ΙϹ may have been repeated as εἰς (comp. **2661** *c*) and may have supplanted ἐπί. There would also be a temptation to alter ἔστη ἐπί to ἔστη εἰς in order to assimilate the phrase to the two instances of ἔστη εἰς applied by Jn to manifestations after the Resurrection. Clem. Alex. 104 quotes freely as follows: ἐν γοῦν τῷ εὐαγγελίῳ, σταθείς, φησίν, ὁ Κύριος ἐπὶ τῷ αἰγιαλῷ πρὸς τοὺς μαθητάς—ἁλιεύοντες δὲ ἔτυχον—ἐνεφώνησέν (?) τε, Παιδία, μή τι (?) ὄψον ἔχετε;

[2] [2307 b] Heb. ii. 12 "He is not ashamed to call them *brethren*, saying, 'I will announce thy name to my brethren; *in the midst* of the assembly (ἐκκλησίας) I will sing of (ὑμνήσω) thee'" (Ps. xxii. 22). So Just. Martyr *Tryph*. 106 καὶ ὅτι ἐν μέσῳ τῶν ἀδελφῶν αὐτοῦ ἔστη, τῶν ἀποστόλων...καὶ μετ' αὐτῶν διάγων ὕμνησε τὸν θεόν, ὡς καὶ ἐν τοῖς ἀπομνημονεύμασι τῶν ἀποστόλων δηλοῦται γεγενημένον, τὰ λείποντα τοῦ ψαλμοῦ ἐδήλωσεν. Ἔστι δὲ ταῦτα. Διηγήσομαι τὸ ὄνομά σου τοῖς ἀδελφοῖς μου, ἐν μέσῳ ἐκκλησίας ὑμνήσω σε. The words "not ashamed to call them *brethren*" are illustrated by Jn xx. 17 "Go unto my *brethren*, and say to them, I ascend to my Father and your Father." This and Mt. xxviii. 10 are the only passages in the Gospels where Jesus uses the term thus definitely (**1749**).

[3] [2307 c] Mk xiv. 26 and Mt. xxvi. 30 place the "singing [of a hymn]" on the night before the Crucifixion. Lk. xxii. 39 omits it there.

language. Perhaps he wished to describe the Saviour, not as singing praises to God, but as bringing strength to men; and on that account he first mentions the "coming" (**1633** foll.) so as to suggest the Helper, and then he mentions Him as "standing *into* the midst of the disciples," so as to combine mystically the ancient notion of the firm, erect, and immoveable Deliverer with that of the Spirit passing "*into* the midst" of the Church, and "*into* the midst" of each of the disciples[1]. This view is somewhat confirmed by the next instance to be discussed.

[**2308**] i. 18 μονογενὴς θεὸς ὁ ὢν εἰς τὸν κόλπον τοῦ πατρός is the only passage where the Fourth Gospel uses εἰς with a form of εἶναι. SS has "an only [one] a Son from the bosom of his Father," and codex *a* "nisi unicus filius solus (? εἷς) sinum patris ipse enarravit." But there can be no doubt that εἰς τ. κόλπον is the true reading and that it is intended to mean something different from (xiii. 23) ἐν τῷ κόλπῳ[2]. In i. 1, ὁ λόγος ἦν πρὸς τὸν θεόν, καὶ θεὸς ἦν ὁ λόγος, the preposition πρός is used to describe "God, the Logos" as from the

---

[1] [**2307** *d*] The passage may be compared with 1 S. iii. 10 "And the Lord *came, and stood*, and called as at other times, Samuel, Samuel" (LXX κατέστη, but "Another" (Field) ἐστηλώθη). The Lord had been previously thrice described (1 S. iii. 4—8) as simply "calling" Samuel; but the latter did not recognise Him. Now at last, it is said, the Lord "came and *stood*, or *took up his stand* (Gesen. 426)"—and now Samuel recognises and replies, "Speak, for thy servant heareth." The Targum, understanding the meaning of the Lord's "coming" to be, *not that He really "came," but that He revealed Himself as present*, has "And Jehovah *was revealed* and *stood ready* (Levy Ch. ii. 250 *a*) and called." Both in Heb. and Aram. the word for "*stand*" here means "*stand fast*, or *ready*." There is little doubt that the Targum attached a spiritual meaning to the "*standing*" as well as to the "coming." A whole treatise might be compiled about Philo's views of God as "*standing* (ἑστῶτα)" and unchangeable, and of the Logos as "*standing* and health-giving" (i. 94 "None but the true God *standeth*," i. 93 "the *standing*, wholesome, and right Logos," comp. i. 269, 276, 425, 586, 591, 687, 688). Simon Magus (Clem. Alex. 456) claimed to be "*the standing One*." Origen (Huet ii. 82 (comp. ii. 129)) says that this "*standing*" denotes Christ's προηγουμένην ὑπόστασιν διήκουσαν ἐπὶ πάντα τὸν κόσμον κατὰ τὰς ψυχὰς τὰς λογικάς. Comp. *Log. Oxyrhynch.* "I *stood* (ἔστην) *in the midst* of the world (κόσμου) and in the flesh appeared to them." It is quite characteristic of John that he should introduce at the beginning and at the end of his Gospel similar yet varied traditions about the Logos, "standing in the midst" (**2646**—9).

[2] [**2308** *a*] Chrys., however, reprinted by Migne, after quoting the text ὁ ὢν εἰς at the head of his discourse, quotes it (*p.* 99) thus, εἰπών, ὅτι Ὁ ὢν ἐν τῷ κόλπῳ τ. πατρός, and henceforth has, consistently, ἐν (once (*p.* 100) ὡς ἐν τοῖς κόλποις ὄντος τοῖς πατρικοῖς).

beginning "[*looking*] *toward* (πρός) God." In xvii. 21 and elsewhere He is described as being "*in*" the Father and the Father "*in*" Him. But the present passage describes Him as Only begotten, incarnate, on earth, declaring the invisible mysteries of God to man. As He is "Only begotten," the word "bosom" is introduced to suggest the love of the Father for the Son; and as He is Mediator and Interpreter penetrating from earth *into* (εἰς) the deepest secrets of God in heaven,—where He IS, in Spirit, even when His body is on earth—He is described as "He that IS *into* the bosom of the Father."

[2309] As a whole, the evangelist's use of εἰς without verbs of motion leads to the conclusion that when he uses it of divine mysteries, he wishes to combine the notions of motion and rest as belonging to God and to the manifestations of God. From God, the Logos is ever coming *to* men and is also abiding *in* them. From Man the Logos is ever going up *to* God and is also abiding *in* Him. Hence concerning the Son incarnate on earth, but ever going up in thought and word and act *to* the Father, the evangelist says that "He IS *to the bosom of the Father.*" Again, concerning the Son, when He has ascended to heaven, but is ever coming down *to* the hearts of men, it is said that He "came, or cometh, and stood *to the midst of the disciples.*"

(γ) Εἰς, "to" or "into"

[2310] Εἰς is sometimes ambiguous, since it may mean "to" or "into." In iv. 5 "He cometh therefore *to a city* (εἰς πόλιν)," εἰς has not the same meaning as in iv. 8, 28 "had gone away, or, went away, *into the city* (εἰς τὴν π.)": for the context indicates that in the former passage εἰς means only "to the neighbourhood of." The ambiguity might have been avoided by writing "He draweth near to a city[1]," but John prefers to give the meaning vaguely first and to "narrow down" afterwards (2290). It follows that, in the account of the Resurrection, (xx. 1) "she *cometh to* (ἔρχεται εἰς) the tomb" may be John's way of expressing what Mark and Luke express by the preposition ἐπί, "*up to,*" or "*towards,*" where Matthew has "they came *to behold* the tomb[2]." John perhaps hardly ever uses ἐπί

---

[1] [2310 *a*] Comp. Mt. xxi. 1 ἤγγισαν εἰς 'Ι. καὶ ἦλθον εἰς B., Mk xi. 1 ἐγγίζουσιν εἰς 'Ι. εἰς B. Lk. xix. 29 has καὶ ἐγένετο ὡς ἤγγισεν εἰς B. preceded by xix. 28 καὶ εἰπὼν ταῦτα ἐπορεύετο ἔμπροσθεν ἀναβαίνων εἰς 'Ι.

[2] Mk xvi. 2, Lk. xxiv. 1, Mt. xxviii. 1.

of motion "up to" or "towards" a place (2336). After making this general statement about Mary Magdalene, he leads us to suppose that she did not go right up to the tomb but ran back—as soon as she perceived that the stone had been rolled away—to tell the story to Peter and his companion.

[2311] Mark and Luke describe the women as subsequently "entering (εἰσελθοῦσαι)." Matthew omits this. John has an account of the two disciples and Mary, in which the details—how the two "began to come to (ἤρχοντο εἰς)" (R.V. "went toward") the tomb, and the other disciple "came first," yet "entered not in," and how Peter "cometh" and "entered," and then the other disciple "entered" (he that "came first") and how Mary "stood outside"—are fully described in such a way as to suggest that the Fourth Evangelist desired to clear up obscurities in early tradition, and to shew how it came to pass that Mary Magdalene—although she did not actually "enter the tomb"—was the first to see the risen Saviour; and the unnamed disciple, though not the first to enter the tomb nor the first to see the Saviour, was the first to "believe."

(δ) Εἰς ζωὴν αἰώνιον

[2312] In vi. 27 "work not for *the food that perisheth*, but for the food *that abideth unto eternal life* (τὴν μένουσαν εἰς ζ. αἰώνιον)" if John had meant merely "abideth for ever," would he not have written, as elsewhere (viii. 35, xii. 34), "*abideth for ever* (μένει εἰς τὸν αἰῶνα)," and consequently does he not mean here "*abideth with a view to eternal life*" i.e. in order to produce eternal life? That meaning is probably included. But as the "bread" is itself called (vi. 51) "living," and the "water" also (iv. 10, 11) "living," the full meaning probably is "abideth *for* life eternal" in the double sense of our English "*for*," namely, (1) "*lasting for*," (2) "*for the sake of*," or "*for the purpose of producing*."

[2313] Another interpretation would make a pause after "abideth" (as in xv. 16 "That your fruit may *abide*)[1]," so that the meaning would be, "Work not for the transitory but for the abiding food—with a view to life eternal." The same doubt attends iv. 36, "Already doth he that reapeth receive wages and gather fruit—*with*

---

[1] [2313 a] Comp. 1 Pet. i. 23 "Having been begotten again, not from corruptible seed but from incorruptible, through the Word of God living and *abiding* (διὰ λόγου ζῶντος θεοῦ καὶ μένοντος)" and 1 Cor. xiii. 13 "And now *abideth* faith, hope, love."

a view to life eternal[1]," where the "view" is probably not man's view but God's. That is to say, the reaper is not described as working with *his* eyes fixed on life eternal, but the fruit is regarded as stored up, *in the eyes of God* (or according to the will of God), for eternal life.

[2314] In iv. 14 "The water that I will give him shall become in him a fountain of water leaping (ἁλλομένου)—*unto* (εἰς) *life eternal*," some have taken the meaning to be "*leaping into life eternal.*" This would imply that the water was, at first, in the human being, stagnant as in a cistern, and now became transmuted to a bubbling fountain. But all the Biblical traditions about the divine "Water," and especially those in John, suggest that the water from heaven is "living" from the first. Moreover, though "*leap into life*" is good English, the metaphor is not alleged to occur in Greek. Nor is ἅλλομαι alleged in the Thesaurus to be elsewhere applied to water. The Greeks have an abundant vocabulary to express a bubbling fountain[2]—but (so far as is known) they never use ἅλλομαι thus.

[2315] But a clue to the Johannine expression may be found in the fact that the evangelist always connects the "water" of heaven with the Spirit, directly or indirectly, and that he does this expressly in the words (vii. 38) "He that believeth on me...rivers from his belly shall flow—*of living water*," where he explains that this was "said about *the Spirit*," which was to be transmitted from Christ to the disciples and through them to the world in a continuous stream. Now ἅλλομαι, or ἐφάλλομαι, in LXX, is applied to the action of a "*spirit of God*," "forcing its way" or "falling violently" on Samson, Saul, and David[3].

[2316] These passages suggest that "leaping" is used in the Gospel with some special reference to the action of the Spirit. As the Spirit, when likened to wind, may be said to "blow" or "breathe" where it listeth, so, when likened to water from heaven—which leaps

---

[1] [2313 *b*] Ἤδη ὁ θερίζων μισθὸν λαμβάνει καὶ συνάγει καρπὸν εἰς ζωὴν αἰώνιον. In xii. 25 εἰς ζωὴν αἰώνιον φυλάξει, the nature and the position of the verb make the meaning certain.

[2] [2314 *a*] *E.g.* in Prov. xviii. 4 "the wellspring of wisdom is [as] a *flowing brook*" LXX ἀναπηδύει (al. ἀναπηδῶν), Aq. Sym. ἀναβλύζων, Theod. ἀνομβρῶν. Steph. quotes no passage except this to illustrate the use of ἅλλομαι "de aqua scaturiente."

[3] [2315 *a*] Ἅλλομαι in Judg. xiv. 6, 19, xv. 14, 1 S. x. 10, ἐφάλλομαι in 1 S. x. 6, xi. 6. In 1 S. xvi. 13 "The Spirit of the Lord *leapt on* David from that day forth," LXX has ἐφήλατο, Aq. has ἐνηυλίσθη, Sym. ὥρμησεν, Theod. ἐπέφανεν.

down upon the earth and fertilises it—the Spirit may be said to "leap" with a mighty rush; and indeed this notion of rushing down mightily is connected by Luke with the Pentecostal descent of the Spirit manifested in tongues of flame[1]. It is possible that there may be a double meaning in the word here. Superficially, and literally, it is intended to convey to the Samaritan Woman (or to readers in her position) the notion of a fountain "leaping *up*" (as in Numbers xxi. 17, "Spring *up*, O well") in opposition to a deep well. But mystically it appears to mean water "*leaping down*" to convey life, or else "*pulsing*" with life, the water of regeneration[2].

---

[1] Acts ii. 2.

[2] [**2316 a**] The noun ἅλμα (Steph.) is used for the pulsation of the heart and also for the first "leaping" of the unborn babe in the womb, corresponding to the verb σκιρτάω in Lk. i. 41 ἐσκίρτησεν τὸ βρέφος ἐν τῇ κοιλίᾳ αὐτῆς καὶ ἐπλήσθη πνεύματος ἁγίου ἡ Ἐλεισάβετ. It is, perhaps, a general belief that, in the Dialogue with Nicodemus, the words (Jn iii. 5) "unless a man be *begotten from Water and Spirit*" mean "unless a man's body be baptized in material water and his soul be regenerate from the Spirit." But the meaning appears to be "*begotten from spiritual water,*" *the water of inward generation.*

[**2316 b**] Origen often quotes iv. 14, sometimes blending it with vii. 38 "rivers of water," and seeming to interpret ἁλλομένου in different ways, occasionally altering εἰς to ἐπί to suit his interpretation. A passage in his Comm. *ad loc.* has ὥστε πηγήν...ἀναβλυσθάνειν ἐν αὐτῷ ἄνω πηδώντων ὑδάτων...ἄλλεσθαι καὶ πηδᾶν ἐπὶ τὸ ἀνώτερον, ἐπὶ τὴν αἰώνιον ζωήν. But he proceeds to quote Cant. ii. 8 "*leaping upon* the mountains, *skipping upon* the hills," πηδῶν ἐπὶ τὰ ὄρη διαλλόμενος ἐπὶ τοὺς βουνούς, which he explains of the Bridegroom—presumably the Holy Spirit, or the Word—"leaping" now upon the more exalted, now on inferior, souls; "Similarly here the fountain created in him that hath drunk of the water that Jesus giveth leapeth to eternal life." Then he adds "But perhaps also it will *leap after* (πηδήσει μετά) *the eternal life,* [namely] to (εἰς) the Father [who is] beyond the eternal life. For Christ is the life. But He that is greater than Christ is greater than life." Later on, he looks favourably on Heracleon's explanation of "leaping." Οὐκ ἀπιθάνως δὲ τὸ ἀλλομένου διηγήσατο, καὶ τοὺς μεταλαμβάνοντας τοῦ ἄνωθεν ἐπιχορηγουμένου πλουσίως καὶ αὐτοὺς ἐκβλύσαι εἰς τὴν ἑτέρων αἰώνιον ζωὴν τὰ ἐπικεχορηγημένα αὐτοῖς. Heracleon's rendering of εἰς ἀ. ζ., "*with a view to produce eternal life*" *in others,* agrees with the doctrine in vii. 38; but it will be observed that he does not paraphrase ἁλλομένου by ἀναβλύσαι but by ἐκβλύσαι. In Saul of Tarsus, for example, the water of life became a fountain—not merely "leaping [up]" to *his own* eternal life, but—"*leaping* [*out*]" to the eternal life of the Gentile world.

[**2316 c**] Comp. *Aboth* ii. 10—11 (ed. Taylor), where Rabban Jochanan, praising his five best pupils, calls Eliezer son of Hyrcanus "a plastered cistern, which loseth not a drop," and Eleazar son of Arak "a welling spring." He gave the palm to Eliezer, but the spiritually minded Abba Saul (**1022**) said, "If all the wise of Israel were in one scale of the balance, and Eliezer son of Hyrcanus with them, and Eleazar son of Arak in the other scale, he would outweigh them all."

(ε) Ὄψονται εἰς (xix. 37)

[2317] Εἰς τινα is used with ἰδεῖν, ὁρᾶν and βλέπειν to mean "looking *to*" a person for help or encouragement, or in regard and deference[1]. Εἰς is also used thus in LXX, sometimes without a verb ("our eyes [are] to the Lord") but sometimes with one, about "looking to" Jehovah, to Abraham etc.[2] Hence in xix. 37 "And another scripture saith, They shall *look to* (ὄψονται εἰς) him whom they pierced" we must be prepared to find the "looking" of a reverential kind. The "scripture" is from Zechariah's prophecy about "looking" and "mourning," where LXX and the other translators differ greatly[3], and quotations from Revelation, Barnabas, and Justin indicate early Christian divergences as to traditions about "looking to" or "looking at" Jesus, and "mourning[4]."

---

[1] [2317 a] Steph. (ὁράω, 2137, 2139, and εἰς 292) quotes abundant instances.

[2] [2317 b] With ἐμβλέπω in Is. xvii. 7, xxii. 11, li. 1, 2. The Heb. prep. "to" corresponding to εἰς (Gesen. 40 a) is used with verbs that imply looking to anyone in love, hope, expectation, or longing.

[3] [2317 c] Zech. xii. 10 "they shall look unto me (marg. him) whom they pierced and they shall mourn for him." LXX καὶ ἐπιβλέψονται πρὸς μὲ ἀνθ᾽ ὧν κατωρχήσαντο καὶ κόψονται ἐπ᾽ αὐτόν (al. exempl. ἐφ᾽ ἑαυτούς), Aq. σὺν ᾧ ἐξεκέντησαν καὶ κόψονται αὐτόν, Sym. ἔμπροσθεν ἐπεξεκέντησαν καὶ κόψονται αὐτόν, Theod. καὶ ἐπιβλέψονται πρὸς μὲ εἰς ὃν ἐξεκέντησαν καὶ κόψονται αὐτόν. The Targum renders "They shall look unto me" (Walton) "Rogabunt a facie mea," implying "they shall stand looking in expectation and in supplication before my face." The variant ἐφ᾽ ἑαυτούς should be noted. It *converts the "mourning" for the "pierced" into "mourning" for the piercers themselves, and quite transmutes the passage.*

[4] [2317 d] There was an early twofold application of Zech. xii. 10. Those who "looked" might be (1) Gentiles, (2) Jews; Gentiles, or "nations," might be taken to include (3) the whole world, when referring to the Last Judgment. Zech. xii. 12 "And the *land* shall mourn, every *family* apart," clearly refers to the "*land*" *of Judaea*, and the "families" are immediately mentioned as those of David, Nathan, Levi, and Simeon. But the LXX καὶ κόψεται ἡ γῆ κατὰ φυλὰς φυλάς, might be rendered "the earth...tribe by tribe," and this might be taken to mean "the tribes, or nations, of the earth." Moreover, in Zech. xii. 10, א has ὄψονται for κόψονται, and this indicates that ὄψονται αὐτόν, "shall see him," might be substituted for (Aq. Sym. Theod.) κόψονται αὐτόν, "shall mourn for him," by Greek corruption.

[2317 e] Rev. i. 7 has ὄψεται αὐτὸν πᾶς ὀφθαλμὸς καὶ οἵτινες αὐτὸν ἐξεκέντησαν, καὶ κόψονται ἐπ᾽ αὐτὸν πᾶσαι αἱ φυλαὶ τῆς γῆς, which applies the prophecy to the whole world under the term "tribes of the earth." But it drops the preposition after the verb of seeing, thus giving, "Every eye shall *see him*," instead of "Every eye shall *look to him*." However, it retains "for him" in "they shall mourn *for him*."

[2317 f] Mt. xxiv. 30 has καὶ τότε [φανήσεται τὸ σημεῖον τοῦ υἱοῦ τοῦ ἀνθρώπου ἐν οὐρανῷ καὶ τότε κόψονται πᾶσαι αἱ φυλαὶ τῆς γῆς καὶ] ὄψονται τ. υ. τ. ἀ. ἐρχόμενον

[2318] All the Synoptists mention a "*beholding* (θεωρεῖν)" of some kind immediately after the death of Jesus. But Mark and Matthew connect it simply with the women "standing afar off[1]" and do not mention any "mourning." Luke, besides mentioning the women, describes "all the multitudes that had come together to behold this," as "beholding the things that had come to pass, and

---

ἐπὶ τ. νεφελῶν. Here the three Synoptists agree in the words "And then shall they see the Son of man coming...," but the bracketed words, which are in Matthew alone, represent a version of the tradition of Revelation "they shall mourn *for him*," from which "*for him*" has been dropped, so as to represent the "*tribes of the earth*" as "*mourning*" *for their own sakes*—an entirely new departure.

[2317 g] Barnabas applies the prophecy to those who crucified the Lord, vii. 9 "Since *they shall see Him* (ὄψονται αὐτόν) then in the [last] day (Zech. xii. 10 "in that day") wearing the scarlet robe...and they shall say, 'Is not this He whom we crucified, having set Him at naught and pierced and spit upon Him?'" And he, too, drops the preposition that is essential to the meaning ("look *to*") and omits all mention of "mourning."

[2317 h] Justin expressly applies Zech. xii. 10 to the Jews, after mentioning a repentance that comes too late to prevent the tortures of hell, 1 *Apol.* 52 "And what the peoples (λαοί) of the Jews will say and do...was prophesied thus by Zechariah the prophet...They shall mourn (κόψονται) tribe to (πρός) tribe, and then they shall look to (?) Him whom they pierced (τότε ὄψονται εἰς ὃν ἐξεκέντησαν)"— a curious disarrangement, where perhaps Justin misunderstands "look to" (see below). *The preposition "to" is retained, though "look" is dropped*, when Justin, mentioning Hosea (!) and Daniel, says to Trypho (*Tryph.* 14) "Your people will see and understand *to* whom they have pierced (ὄψεται ὁ λαὸς ὑμῶν καὶ γνωριεῖ εἰς ὃν ἐξεκέντησαν)," and again (32) "one [Advent] in which He was pierced by you, but a second when ye shall recognise *to* whom ye pierced (ἐπιγνώσεσθε εἰς ὃν ἐξεκεντήσατε) and your tribes shall mourn (κόψονται) tribe to (πρός) tribe...," (64) "whom they that pierced Him are destined to see and mourn (ὃν ὁρᾶν μέλλουσι καὶ κόπτεσθαι οἱ ἐκκεντήσαντες αὐτόν)," (126) "who shall come again also and then your twelve tribes shall mourn (κόψονται)." In all these passages Justin drops the prophetic "*for him*," and makes the Jews "*mourn*" *for fear of punishment*. In two of them he alters "look" into "know" or "recognise" in such a way as to suggest that he takes ὄψονται εἰς ὃν ἐξεκ. to mean, "they shall see and recognise Him *against whom* they have raised their hands to pierce Him."

[2317 i] The Gospel of Peter says that after the crucifixion (§ 7) "the Jews and the elders and the priests...began to *mourn* (κόπτεσθαι) and to say, Alas for our sins," and also that (§ 8) "the scribes and Pharisees and elders...heard that the whole people (λαός) murmured and [mourned] beating their breasts (κόπτεται τὰ στήθη)." This resembles Lk. xxiii. 48 τύπτοντες τὰ στήθη (where SS and other authorities add a clause like that of the Gospel of Peter).

[1] [2318 a] Mk xv. 40, Mt. xxvii. 55 ἦσαν δὲ καὶ (Mt. ἐκεῖ) γυναῖκες ἀπὸ μακρόθεν θεωροῦσαι. Lk. xxiii. 49 mentions the women later καὶ γυναῖκες...ὁρῶσαι ταῦτα.

beating their breasts¹"—apparently indicating the dissent of the multitude of pilgrims from the act of the rulers of the Jews. John applies the prophecy of Zechariah (concerning the "looking" of the house of Judah "*to*" Him whom "they pierced"), not to the Jews but to the four soldiers used by the Jews as their instruments with the intention—so to speak—of "breaking the bones" of the Paschal Lamb. This intention is frustrated. Instead of "breaking the bones," one of the soldiers pierces the side of the Saviour, thereby drawing forth "blood and water." Then the four soldiers—representing the four quarters of the world—are supposed to stand "looking *to* him whom they pierced," and the reader is left to interpret this in a twofold sense, present and future. They look to Him now in amazement; they will look to Him for forgiveness and salvation².

(ζ) Εἰc τέλοc

[2319] Εἰς τέλος occurs in John once, in the only passage where he mentions τέλος, xiii. 1 (R.V.) "Jesus, knowing that his hour was come that he should depart out of this world unto the Father, having loved his own which were in the world, he loved them *unto the end* (marg. *to the uttermost*) (εἰς τέλος)." It will be shewn that the ambiguity of this phrase has influenced other passages in N.T. and that John probably desires to suggest to his readers *both* the meanings given by R.V.

[2320] In LXX, εἰς τέλος means "*to the end*" in the sense of "*to the [bitter] end*," i.e. utter destruction, or "*to the [good] end*," i.e. perfect deliverance or salvation. Hence it sometimes represents the Hebrew verb reduplicated for emphasis (Gen. xlvi. 4) "I will also *surely bring thee up again*," LXX "I will bring thee up *to the uttermost*, or, *in the end* (εἰς τέλος)." On the other hand, in Job, LXX has "let him not cut me off *to the [bitter] end* (εἰς τέλος)," where the Hebrew and Aquila have "*let loose the hand [for destruction]*³."

---

¹ Lk. xxiii. 48 καὶ πάντες οἱ συνπαραγενόμενοι ὄχλοι ἐπὶ τὴν θεωρίαν ταύτην, θεωρήσαντες τὰ γενόμενα, τύπτοντες τὰ στήθη ὑπέστρεφον.

² [2318 *b*] Any prophecy about Israel might be transferred by Christian evangelists (following St Paul) to the Gentile Churches as being "Israel after the Spirit." But this particular prophecy about the "tribes of the *land*" might lend itself in a special way to such a transference by being supposed to refer to the "tribes of the *earth*." Concerning the soldiers and their superiority to the Jews as regards expectation of forgiveness, see the early tradition in Lk. xxiii. 34.

³ Job vi. 9 Aq. Sym. ἐπιβαλὼν τὴν χεῖρα.

Elsewhere εἰς τέλος means "to consummation," or "*for ever*," in such phrases as "the poor will not be forgotten *for ever*," "Arise and cast us not away *for ever*," "Wherefore hast thou, O God, cast us away *for ever*[1]?" Somewhat different is its use in Ps. xvi. 11 "In thy right hand are pleasures [for] *evermore*" and (xlix. 9) "that he should still live *alway*[2]."

[2321] In Greek literature of all periods ἐς τέλος is almost always used of that which lasts "*to the end*," or "*turns out to be the fact when one comes to the end*[3]." Exceptionally, in Polybius (where it is very frequent indeed), it means "*perfectly*"; but the Thesaurus quotes no instance of this meaning from any other ancient author. Lucian perhaps uses it once to mean "*perfectly*[4]," but he certainly uses it once to mean "*persistently*[5]," and the former passage may mean "even though you have not yet come to the end of your experience of me." In any case the meaning "*to the end*" is unquestionably predominant.

[2322] In N.T. the usage of εἰς τέλος is as follows. In 1 Thess. ii. 16 ἔφθασεν δὲ ἐπ' αὐτοὺς ἡ ὀργὴ εἰς τέλος "the wrath [of God] hath come upon them *to [the bitter] end*," the meaning follows the LXX.

---

[1] [2320 a] Ps. ix. 18, xliv. 23, lxxiv. 1. Comp. Ps. ix. 6 etc. In the Psalms, these questions, or negations, may sometimes be said to imply the ultimate triumph of good because evil will "*not*" last "*for ever*." But in Hab. i. 4 (R.V.) "judgment doth *never* (marg. *not to victory*) go forth," this hopeful view is not taken. In Job xiv. 20 "thou prevailest *for ever* against him," xx. 7 "he shall perish *for ever*," it describes the destruction of man, but not in xxiii. 7 "So shall I be delivered *for ever*." The word rendered τέλος means illustriousness, eminence, enduringness, and is applied to God, in 1 S. xv. 29 (R.V.) "the *Strength* (marg. *Victory*, or *Glory*) of Israel" (LXX in error). Wisdom xvi. 5, xix. 1 uses μέχρι τέλους thus, "Not *to the end* did thy anger abide," "on the impious there pressed unpitying anger *to the end*."

[2320 b] Εἰς τὸ τέλος, Ps. iv. (title) R.V. "For the chief musician" (Aq. τῷ νικοποιῷ, Theod. εἰς τὸ νῖκος, Sym. ἐπινίκιος) represents a different form of the same Hebrew root that is rendered εἰς τέλος above. It is consistently given by LXX in the titles of the Psalms where R.V. has "For the chief Musician."

[2] [2320 c] Ps. xvi. 11 Aq. νῖκος, xlix. 9 Aq. εἰς νῖκος, Sym. εἰς αἰῶνα.

[3] [2321 a] Steph. (τέλος 1996—7) qu. Solon ap. Stob. Fl. 9, 25, 28 : Αἰεὶ δ' οὔτι λέληθε διαμπερὲς ὅστις ἀλιτρὸν θυμὸν ἔχει, πάντως δ' ἐς τέλος ἐξεφάνη. Eur. *Iph. A.* 161 θνητῶν δ' ὄλβιος ἐς τέλος οὐδείς. Steph. quotes no authors but Polybius and Theodor. Prodr. for the meaning "perfectly."

[4] [2321 b] Lucian *Somn.* 9 (i. 12) "I am Education, my child, a familiar acquaintance of yours for some time, even though you have never yet had a *perfect* experience of me (εἰ καὶ μηδέπω εἰς τέλος μου πεπείρασαι)."

[5] Lucian *Navig.* 28 (iii. 266) "you *keep on* jeering at my vow (ἐς τέλος... ἐπηρεάζων)," referring to (*ib.* 25) a previous mockery.

PREPOSITIONS [2322]

In Lk. xviii. 5 μὴ εἰς τέλος ἐρχομένη ὑπωπιάζῃ με, R.V. has "lest she wear me out by her *continual* coming," and this is probably correct, as the present subjunctive denotes a continuous "wearing out." Mark and Matthew assign to our Lord the saying, "He that endureth *to the end* he shall be saved," and this is (no doubt correctly) punctuated as meaning "He that endureth to the end—he shall be saved[1]." But even in Greek, apart from Hebrew originals, εἰς τέλος is liable to create confusion by being connected with what precedes instead of with what follows[2]. Much more, in Hebraic Greek, might a doubt arise, whether "to the end" ought not to be connected with "saved" ("he that endureth—*to the end* shall he be saved") as meaning "saved *to the utmost*," "saved *in body, soul, and spirit*." The parallel Luke omits "*to the end*," but has two clauses, "(1) A hair of your head shall surely not perish, (2) in your endurance ye shall win your souls[3]." This ("a hair of your head") resembles the saying to the Thessalonians "May the God of peace himself sanctify you *wholly*, and may your *spirit and soul and body be preserved entire* without blame at the coming of our Lord Jesus Christ[4]"; whereas the Epistle to the Corinthians rather resembles Matthew and Mark, "Waiting patiently for the revealing of our Lord Jesus Christ who also shall confirm you *to the end* (ἕως τέλους) unreproveable in the day of our Lord Jesus Christ[5]."

---

[1] Mk xiii. 13, Mt. x. 22, xxiv. 13.

[2] [2322 a] See Steph. τέλος 1996 D "Polyb. 8, 2, 2 : Τὸ μὲν γὰρ μηδενὶ πιστεύειν εἰς τέλος ἄπρακτον· ubi Schweigh. non recte disjungere εἰς τέλος ab seq. ἄπρακτον ostendit."

[3] [2322 b] Lk. xxi. 18—19. Comp. Jas v. 11 "We call blessed *them that endure*. Ye have heard of the endurance of Job and have seen the *end* of the Lord," where "end" seems to mean "final salvation," and "endure" is taken absolutely as in 2 Tim. ii. 12 "if we *endure*." It is also absolute in 1 Pet. ii. 20, Rom. xii. 12, and should almost certainly be taken so in Heb. xii. 7 "It is for [your] training that *ye endure*," i.e. God chastens you, not to give you pain, but to train you.

[4] 1 Thess. v. 23.

[5] [2322 c] 1 Cor. i. 7—8. Comp. Heb. vii. 25 σώζειν εἰς τὸ παντελὲς δύναται "to save *to the utmost*," which, however, Chrys. explains as meaning "to all time," ἀεί, and ἐκεῖ ἐν τῇ μελλούσῃ ζωῇ. Comp. 2 Clem. 19 ἵνα εἰς τέλος σωθῶμεν "be saved *unto the end*," i.e. "retain salvation to the end," differing little from "be saved in the end," Barn. iv. 6 "*utterly* (or, *for ever*) lost," εἰς τ. ἀπώλεσαν, x. 5 "*utterly* (or, *irrevocably*) impious and already adjudged to death," xix. 11 "*Utterly* (or, *for ever*) shalt thou hate the evil [one]." In Hermas *Vis*. III. x. 4—5 ἱλαρὰ δὲ εἰς τέλος follows, as a climax, on ἱλαρωτέρα, and means "joyful *to the uttermost*."

[2323] Returning to xiii. 1 εἰς τέλος ἠγάπησεν αὐτούς, we have to bear in mind that John must certainly have known (1) that εἰς τέλος was used in the first century to mean "*to the uttermost*" and "*to the end*," (2) that it was associated with traditions about final salvation after trial or temptation. Further, if we believe that he was acquainted with the first three Gospels, we must suppose him also to have known (3) that two of the three evangelists reported Christ's saying about the "saving" of those who should "endure *to the end*," and that the third had a parallel tradition (in effect) about being "*perfectly* saved" if men "endured." It may be also assumed (4) that John does not mean to say merely—a platitude beneath the level of this Gospel—that the Son of God continued steadfastly loving His disciples to the end. (5) It has been shewn (**1744** (iv) foll.) that in the Pauline Epistles and elsewhere the aorist ἠγάπησεν is applied to love expressed in action, and especially to the love of God for man expressed in the act of redemption. We may therefore infer that here, as in many other cases, John uses a phrase of ancient Christian tradition in *more than one meaning*—not excluding the interpretation of Aquila (**2320** *c*) suggesting victory as well as consummation—and that he means something to this effect: "Having loved them before, he now loved them *to the last, in a last and crowning act of victorious love*[1]."

(vi) Ἐκ

(α) Ἐκ meaning "some of," see **2213—5**

(β) Ἐκ meaning "native of," as distinguished from ἀπό "coming from," or "resident in," see **2289—93**

---

[1] [**2323** *a*] Chrys. appears to give two interpretations, taking εἰς τέλος ἀγ., 1st, as σφόδρα ἀγ., 2nd, as ἀγαπῶν διηνεκῶς:—(1) Εἶδες πῶς μέλλων ἐγκαταλιμπάνειν αὐτοὺς σφοδροτέραν τὴν ἀγάπην ἐπιδείκνυται; Τὸ γάρ, Ἀγαπήσας, εἰς τέλος ἠγάπησεν αὐτούς, τοῦτο δηλοῖ· Οὐδὲν ἐνέλιπεν ὧν τὸν σφόδρα ἀγαπῶντα εἰκὸς ἦν ποιῆσαι. Τί δήποτε δὲ οὐκ ἐξ ἀρχῆς τοῦτο ἐποίησε; Τὰ μείζονα ὕστερον ἐργάζεται..., (2) Τί δέ ἐστιν, Εἰς τέλος ἠγάπησεν αὐτούς; Ἀντὶ τοῦ, ἔμενεν ἀγαπῶν διηνεκῶς, καὶ τεκμήριον τῆς πολλῆς ἀγάπης τοῦτο λέγει.

[**2323** *b*] There is a similar expression with ὑπεραγαπᾶν and πέρας in Barnabas v. 8 πέρας γέ τοι διδάσκων τὸν Ἰσραὴλ κ. τηλικαῦτα τέρατα κ. σημεῖα ποιῶν ἐκήρυσσεν, κ. ὑπερηγάπησεν αὐτόν, where πέρας means "as a climax" (or "finally"), ὑπέρ means "to the utmost," and the aorist means that love was expressed in definite action.

PREPOSITIONS [2325]

(γ) Ἐκ μέτρογ

[2324] This phrase occurs in iii. 34 "For he whom God sent speaketh the words of God: for not (lit.) *from measure* doth he give the spirit. The Father loveth...." It is non-occurrent in LXX and the Thesaurus. Ἐν μέτρῳ means "in *small measure*" in Judith vii. 21, Ezek. iv. 11, 16, but "in *large measure*" in Ps. lxxx. 5 (where Aq. has τρισσόν, and Sym. μέτρῳ without ἐν[1]). The Thesaurus gives μέτρῳ for "in due measure," or "by measure," usually in a good sense, and ἐν μέτρῳ for "in metre." The text is uncertain[2]. If "he" could be taken as the Son, the meaning might be "[the Son] doth not give *from measure*," i.e. *from a limited store*, it being implied that the store is unlimited from what follows, namely, "He hath given all things into his hand." The objection remains that ἐκ μέτρου is not found in Greek literature[3]. See 2714.

(δ) Ἐκ with ςώzω and τηρέω

[2325] It has been shewn elsewhere (940) that in LXX, and in John, ἐκ, with σώζω and τηρέω, does not always imply "take me *out of* evils in which *I am*." It may be used in the prayer "Keep me *altogether*

---

[1] [2324 a] So, too, Apollinarius here (Cramer *ad loc.*) ἡμεῖς μὲν οὖν, φησί, μέτρῳ τὴν ἐνέργειαν τοῦ Πνεύματος ἐλάβομεν, αὐτὸς δὲ οὐχ οὕτως.

[2] [2324 b] B omits "the spirit" (but B² adds it in margin): Syr. Burk. "for not *by measure* did the Father give [the Spirit] to his Son, but he loveth...." SS is partly illegible, but reads "For not *by measure* gave God the Father, but to his Son [he was loving] and...." Cramer prints a comment of Ammonius, ὅλον ἔχει τὸ Πνεῦμα ὁ Υἱὸς οὐσιωδῶς, οὐ μὴν ἐκ μέρους ὡς κτίσμα: and Wetstein mentions ἐκ μέρους as a substitute for ἐκ μέτρου in three cursives. Many MSS. and versions insert ὁ θεός after δίδωσιν.

[3] [2324 c] Perhaps οὐκ ἐκ μέτρου is used with allusion to the LXX οὐκ ἐκμετρηθήσεται (Hos. i. 10, Jer. xxxiii. 22 (Theod.)) and to the LXX use of μέτρον for a "measure" of corn, oil etc. Origen on Ps. xvi. 5—6—after saying that "the knowledge of God is Christ's allotted portion (κληρονομία)" and that the Lord is this "lot (μερίς)"—comments on "lines (σχοινία)" as follows, Εἰ τὸ σχοινίον μέτρον ἐστί, πῶς γέγραπται ἐν τ. κ. Ἰ. εὐαγγ. (iii. 34); and he suggests that the term μέτρον is used οὐ πρὸς αὐτὴν τὴν γνῶσιν ἀλλὰ παρὰ τὸν ὑποδεχόμενον τῷ μὴ εἶναι αὐτὸν μείζονος δεκτικόν, "for," he adds, "the rain, though itself immeasurable, is measured in the vessels that receive it: ἐκληροδοτήθη δέ μοι, φησίν, ὥσπερ ἐκ μέτρου γῆ, ᾗ καὶ ἀρκοῦμαι. Apparently he takes ἐκ μέτρου as meaning, for the Psalmist, "*proportionate [to my wants]*" and οὐκ ἐκ μέτρου for Christ as "*immeasurable.*"

[2324 d] Ἐκ μέτρου might conceivably be a way of expressing ἔκμετρος i.e. "*outside measure*" so as to mean that the fulness of the gift of the Spirit to the incarnate Son was *not* "*beyond the measure* of His stature" (comp. Eph. iv. 13). But this adj., though freq. in non-Hebraic Greek, does not occur in LXX; and ἐκ μέτρου, in such a sense, is still more improbable. See 2714.

out of evil" and is probably thus used in xii. 27 "save me *from* (ἐκ) this hour" and xvii. 15 "keep them *from* (ἐκ) the evil [one] (τοῦ πονηροῦ)."

(ε) Ἐκ, ἀπό, and παρά, with ἐξέρχομαι

[2326] These three prepositions are used as follows to describe the coming forth of the Son from the Father:—

(1) (ἐκ) viii. 42 "For I came forth *from* (ἐκ) the Father and am come (ἥκω)," where the first clause expresses origin rather than coming, and the origin of the Son is contrasted with the origin of the Jews, who are said to be (viii. 44) "from their father the devil (ἐκ τοῦ πατρὸς τοῦ διαβόλου)": xvi. 28 "I came forth *from* (ἐκ) the Father and have come (ἐλήλυθα) into (εἰς) the world," where the preceding verse says παρὰ τ. πατρὸς ἐξῆλθον, i.e. "*from the side, bosom,* or *home,* of the Father," but this states merely origin, "*out of*" contrasted with "into," without the suggestion of domesticity or affection.

[2327] (2) (ἀπό) The words of the evangelist, xiii. 3 "Knowing that...*from* (ἀπό) God he came forth and unto (πρός) God he goeth back," are to be compared with those of the disciples, xvi. 30 "Herein we believe that *from* (ἀπό) God thou camest forth," where the disciples alter the words of their Master in repeating them, for Christ had said (xvi. 27) "I came forth *from the side of* (παρά) the Father," and (xvi. 28) "I came forth (lit.) *out of* (ἐκ) the Father." The disciples repeat neither of these prepositions. Possibly the same feeling that induces them to alter "Father" to "God" induces also the change from παρά and ἐκ to ἀπό. It is not for them to lay stress on the domesticity of the relation between the Father and the Son. The same feeling may have influenced the evangelist.

[2328] (3) (παρά) xvi. 27 "For the Father of himself taketh you as friends (φιλεῖ ὑμᾶς) because ye have taken me as friend (ἐμὲ πεφιλήκατε) and have believed that I came forth *from the side of* (παρά) the Father." Here the personal preposition is used because personal feeling predominates—the notion of a household bound together by affection. The same explanation applies to xvii. 8 "They [*i.e.* the disciples] recognised (ἔγνωσαν) in truth (ἀληθῶς) that I came forth *from thy side* (παρὰ σοῦ) and believed that thou didst send me." This is the last statement of the Son about His coming forth, and it seems appropriate that it should use the personal preposition. On φιλεῖ, see **1728** *p* and **2584** *c*.

(ζ) Ἐκ with πληρόω and γεμίζω

[2329] In xii. 3 "but the house was filled full (ἐπληρώθη) from (ἐκ) the odour of the ointment," B reads ἐπλήσθη (for ἐπληρώθη) and this is the word used in 2 Chr. vii. 1 "the glory of the Lord *filled* (ἔπλησε) the house," as also by ℵA in Is. vi. 4 "the house *was filled* (LXX ἐνεπλήσθη) with smoke." But perhaps John uses πληρόω to suggest spiritual filling, such as makes the Church really the Church, the full-filling, or Pleroma, of divine graces and powers. And some symbolism of this kind may also explain ἐκ, which is very rarely indeed used with verbs of filling in LXX and N.T.[1] It might be originally merely a Hebraistic form, such as may be found in the Apocalypse, in which ἐκ expressed the Hebrew preposition used with "fill." But John might give it a spiritual application by taking the house as the House of God, *i.e.* the Church, which is "fulfilled," *i.e.* brought into the fulness of the glory of Christ, *as a result of* (ἐκ) this sacrifice of sweet savour. Origen takes some such view of the "house," which he calls "omnem hujus mundi domum ac totius ecclesiae domum[2]."

[2329 (i)] In vi. 13 ἐγέμισαν δώδεκα κοφίνους κλασμάτων ἐκ τῶν πέντε ἄρτων τῶν κριθίνων ἃ ἐπερίσσευσαν τοῖς βεβρωκόσιν, is the connexion "filled [full] of fragments" or "baskets of fragments"? Our English versions adopt the former. A.V. has "filled twelve baskets *with the fragments* of the five barley loaves," R.V. "*with broken pieces* from the five barley loaves." Westcott does not dissent. His comment on A.V. is "fragments *i.e.* the pieces broken for distribution (Ezek. xiii. 19)." But John has not mentioned any "breaking" for distribution. Chrysostom *ad loc.* calls the fragments λείψανα, a word denoting "*fallen fragments.*" Origen speaks of "the barley loaves *from which* (ἀφ' ὧν) there superabounded the twelve baskets[3]." The Latin and Syriac versions indicate that κόφινοι

---

[1] [2329 *a*] See Winer xxx. 8 (*b*) p. 251 quoting Rev. viii. 5 γεμίζειν ἐκ, xix. 21 χορτάζειν ἐκ, xvii. 2, 6 μεθύειν, or μεθύσκεσθαι, ἐκ. Comparing Mt. xxiii. 25 ἔσωθεν γέμουσιν ἐξ ἁρπαγῆς with Lk. xi. 39 τὸ ἔσωθεν ὑμῶν γέμει ἁρπαγῆς, he thinks the former means that the contents of the vessels are *derived from* robbery.

[2] [2329 *b*] *Hom.* on *Cant.* i. 12. He takes the fragrance however to be that of the "odor doctrinae qui procedit de Christo et sancti Spiritus fragrantia."

[3] Origen *Comm. Matth.* about "the seven loaves."

κλασμάτων should be connected—as probably in Luke[1] (though Luke may mean "pieces broken for distribution")—and that the meaning may be, as in the Syriac, "filled twelve *baskets-of-fragments* from the five barley loaves[2]," taking γεμίζω and ἐκ together.

(vii) Ἔμπροσθεν

[2330] Ἔμπροσθέν σου occurs in Matthew and Luke (*"prepare... before thee"*) quoting Malachi about the messenger that was to "prepare the way," and applying the prophecy to John the Baptist as being the messenger. In Malachi, both the Hebrew and the LXX have "*before my face*," πρὸ προσώπου μου, instead of "*before thee*." Mark omits the clause with "prepare," but has "send my messenger *before thy face* (πρὸ προσώπου σου)," and attributes the prophecy to "Isaiah." These facts shew that there were early Greek variations as to ἔμπροσθεν applied to the Baptist as being the forerunner of Christ. Like the English "before" (in "placed *before*," "stands *before*," "ranked *before*") so ἔμπροσθεν, in certain contexts, might mean "superior to," "above [in esteem]." This word, belonging to the Matthew-Luke tradition, is put by John thrice into the mouth of the Baptist himself testifying twice, (i. 15, 30) "He is become *before me*," i.e. "*ranked before me*," and, in the third instance, (iii. 28) "I have been sent *before him*," i.e. as His herald or harbinger[3].

---

[1] [2329 (i) *a*] Lk. ix. 17 ἤρθη τὸ περισσεῦσαν αὐτοῖς κλασμάτων κόφινοι δώδεκα. This prob. means "*baskets of*," not "*superabundance of*." Comp. Lk. xiii. 8, where D and the Latin MSS. have "a basket of dung," and see Steph. for κόφινος meaning "a measure," and for the curious phrase οἴνου κόφινος.

[2] [2329 (i) *b*] The Syr. (Burk.) has "they gathered and filled twelve *baskets of fragments* from the five pieces of barley-bread—those which remained over from them that ate" (SS "they gathered them, the fragments that remained over of them and filled twelve baskets, the superabundance of those five loaves of barley and of those two fishes. Now the men that had eaten of that bread had been five thousand"). The Latin versions also have "fragmentorum" which prob. depends on "cophinos."

[3] [2330 *a*] See **830—5**, where this Johannine use of ἔμπροσθεν should have been noted. In Heb., Gesen. 817 *b* mentions only two instances of Malachi's word as denoting superiority, Gen. xlviii. 20 "set Ephraim *before* Manasseh (ἔθηκεν...ἔμπροσθεν)," Job xxxiv. 19 (LXX confused). Ἔμπροσθεν does not mean "superior" elsewhere in N.T., for Jn x. 4 "[the shepherd] goeth *before* them" is not an instance. No instance quoted by Steph. means "superior" except Plato 631 D ταῦτα δὲ πάντα ἐκείνων ἔμπροσθεν τέτακται φύσει, "these have a natural *superiority* to those," but comp. Plato 744 A σωφροσύνης ἔμπροσθεν ὑγίειαν...ποιῶν τιμίαν, and 805 D ἔμπροσθεν...θεῖμεν ἄν.

PREPOSITIONS [2331]

(viii) Ἐν

(α) Ἐν used metaphorically, *e.g.* "abide in," see **1881**

(β) Ἐν used temporally

[**2331**] ii. 19—20 "Destroy this temple and [*with*]*in* (ἐν) three days I will raise it up...thou *within* (ἐν)[1] three days wilt raise it up[2]!" The corresponding utterance in Mark and Matthew (omitted by Luke) has "*after an interval of* (διά) three days," and the context leaves the impression that no such words proceeded from Jesus but only from false witnesses. In the predictions of the Resurrection, whereas Mark has "*after* (μετά[3]) *three days*" (**1297, 1301**—2) Matthew and Luke have "*the third day*," and as these early variations cannot well be regarded as accidental, we are led to infer that something may be intended by John's variations here ("in" and "within"). B's reading represents Jesus as saying "*in* three days" and the Jews as quoting Him not quite correctly, "*within* three days." If the evangelist wrote this, his meaning may be that the Jews, while slightly exaggerating what Jesus had actually said[4], nevertheless (by a sort of irony of Providence) more exactly predicted that which actually came to pass: Christ *did* raise up the Temple of His body "*within* three days[5]." See **2715**.

---

[1] [**2331** *a*] Comp. Xen. *Mem.* iii. 13. 5 "*within* five or six days," Plato 240 B "*within* three days," Steph. (Vol. iii. 962) "Quod Hippocrates dixit Ἐν ἑπτὰ ἡμέρησιν ἀποθνήσκουσιν, interpr. Celsus, *Intra* septimum diem," also Xen. *Cyropaed.* v. 3. 28 "To come (lit.) less than within (μεῖον ἢ ἐν) six or seven days."

[2] [**2331** *b*] The first ἐν is om. by B but ins. by א, the second ἐν is om. by א, *a* has "in triduo...tribus diebus," *b* "in triduo...in triduo," *e* "in trib (*sic*) diebus ...in triduo."

[3] Mk xiv. 58, Mt. xxvi. 61.

[4] There are many other instances in which Jesus is not quoted exactly; but the whole subject of quotations and repetitions in Jn is attended with great difficulty: they are so frequently inaccurate (**2544—53**).

[5] [**2331** *c*] It would be wrong to translate Mk xiv. 58, Mt. xxvi. 61 διὰ τριῶν ἡμερῶν, "*within* three days," or anything but "*after an interval of* three days" (comp. Mk ii. 1 δι' ἡμερῶν), just as Mk viii. 31 μετὰ τ. ἡ. must be rendered "*after* three days." And these two expressions must be reconciled with τῇ τρίτῃ ἡμέρᾳ partly (see Field on Mt. xvi. 21) by Greek looseness of expression, and partly by Biblical influence. As regards Acts i. 3 δι' ἡμερῶν τεσσεράκοντα, Cramer publishes, as from Chrys., "he said not *for forty days* but (?) *at intervals during forty days*, for He was [during that time, now] approaching nigh and [now] removing again," οὐ γὰρ εἶπε τεσσαράκοντα ἡμέρας ἀλλὰ δι' ἡμερῶν τεσσαράκοντα· ἐφίστατο γὰρ καὶ ἀφίστατο πάλιν. If that is the writer's meaning, he gives to διά with ἡμερῶν an unprecedented rendering, which completely changes the sense. No authority

(γ) 'Εν *quasi-instrumental*

[2332] John does not use the Hebraic ἐν for "with" in such phrases as "slay *with* the sword[1]": but Hebraic influence may in part account for his use of ἐν τούτῳ where many would use διὰ τούτου "hereby": xiii. 35 "*By this* shall all men know that ye are my disciples, if ye have love one to another." In part it may arise from his proneness to see things as though they were going on in spiritual regions (*e.g.* light, darkness, love), "*In this region* shall men

---

for it is alleged by Blass (p. 313) except Mk xiv. 58, Mt. xxvi. 61, which, as stated above, must be rendered "*after an interval of.*" D omits διά in Acts but places it above the line between τεσσ. and ἡμ., *d* has "post dies quadraginta." This makes excellent sense, "*After an interval of forty days*, giving them a vision of himself (ὀπτανόμενος αὐτοῖς) and speaking of the things concerning the kingdom of God, and (?) uniting himself with [them] (συναλιζόμενος), he exhorted them not to separate from Jerusalem." This would vividly represent what the Lord said and did in His last manifestation. The words attributed to Chrys. are not quite incompatible with the meaning in D, "*After forty days* [from the Resurrection] appearing [for the last time]." Chrys. may mean, "Luke said '*after*,' not '*during*,'" for [during all those days] He came and went [not appearing continuously]."

[2331 *d*] Jn xx. 26 "after eight days," indicates that Christ had not appeared to the disciples since the appearance last (xx. 19) recorded, and favours the view that the manifestations after the Resurrection were not continuous. It also shews how divergent traditions about the intervals might arise; for the Hebraic phrase δι' ἡμερῶν "after [some] days," being as strange in classical Gk as in English, might be supposed to have accidentally omitted the number. Hence H̄, "eight," or M̄, "forty," might naturally be inserted, being supposed to have dropped out before H in HΜΕΡѠΝ. Even if Chrys. interpreted διά as meaning "at intervals during," it is impossible to accept his interpretation without a great deal of evidence for such a use of διά with a plural ("days," "years" etc.). See **2715**.

[2331 *e*] In Lk. ix. 37 τῇ ἑξῆς ἡμέρᾳ, D has διὰ τῆς ἡμέρας, *d* "per diem," Syr. "on that day again (SS om. again)." The Gk of D, if it is another way of saying τῇ ἑξῆς ἡ., must mean "after the interval of the day," but seems to have been taken by the Latin translator as meaning "in the course of the day."

[1] [2332 *a*] Rev. vi. 8 ἀποκτεῖναι ἐν ῥομφαίᾳ. Comp. Lk. xxii. 49 ἐν μαχαίρῃ. A Tebtunis Papyrus 16 (B.C. 114) has ἐν μαχαίρῃ—and others (*ib.* 41, 45, 46, 47) have the same phrase (in pl.)—to express "[armed] with a sword." Comp. *ib.* 48 Λύκος σὺν ἄλλοις ἐν ὅπλοις, foll. by καὶ σπασαμένων τὰς μαχαίρας. As ἐν ὅπλοις practically means ὁπλοφόρος, "bearing arms," so ἐν μαχαίρῃ by analogy might come to mean μαχαιροφόρος, "bearing a sword." None of these papyrus passages have a verb like ἀποκτείνω or πατάσσω, as in Rev., Lk., and LXX (2 K. xix. 37, Jer. xxvi. 23 etc., where ἐν represents Heb. "in"). So, too, 1 Cor. iv. 21 ἐν ῥάβδῳ ἐλθεῖν—until instances are alleged from non-Hebraic Gk of ἔρχομαι ἐν—must be regarded as akin to 1 S. xvii. 43 ἔρχῃ...ἐν ῥάβδῳ καὶ λίθοις, *ib.* 45 ἔρχῃ...ἐν ῥομφαίᾳ, 2 S. xxiii. 21 κατέβη...(Field) ἐν ῥάβδῳ, parall. 1 Chr. xi. 23 κατέβη...ἐν ῥάβδῳ. The Targum follows the Heb. in using "in," and Deissmann (p. 120) gives no reason for rejecting the obvious explanation that the Pauline phrase had a Semitic origin.

discern that...," namely, in Christian fellowship. So xvii. 10 "I have been glorified *in them*" does not, perhaps, mean merely "in their hearts" (still less merely "by them") but "in the Church" as represented by the small band of disciples: and xvi. 30 "*In this* we believe that thou camest forth from God" may be intended to suggest the thought that, after wandering in the dark, the disciples, finding that Jesus miraculously knows their thoughts, seem to themselves to have emerged into light: "*In* [*the light of*] *this* [*thy saying*], we believe...."

(δ) Ἐν used locally, ἐν τῷ γαζοφυλακίῳ (viii. 20)

[2333] viii. 20 "These words he spake *in* (ἐν) the Treasury teaching in the Temple." As no authority has been alleged for the supposition that the Treasury (γαζοφυλάκιον) was open to the public[1], it has been suggested that ἐν must here mean "near." But no authority for this hypothesis is alleged from N.T. Either therefore we must suppose that (1) a special part of the Women's Court, opposite the Treasury, was familiarly known as "the Treasury," or else that (2) John has used the expression loosely for some other reason. In support of (1), no instance has been alleged.

[2334] It is true that, according to the LXX of Nehemiah, the people were to bring their gifts "*to* the Treasury[2]," and this might suggest that the public had access to the Treasury. But according to Mark, Jesus stood "*opposite* the Treasury" when He taught the disciples to judge the widow's gift not as man sees it, but as God sees

---

[1] [2333 *a*] It would have been correct to say (1) "in the women's court," on which the Treasury abutted, or (2) "opposite the Treasure-chests" (called "Trumpets") into which offerings were put by people in the women's court, or (3) "opposite the Treasury" (Mk xii. 41) *i.e.* in that part of the women's court where one could see people "casting their gifts into the Treasury" (Lk. xxi. 1). Josephus says (*Wars* v. 5. 2) that a portico ran "in front of (πρό) the treasure-boxes (τῶν γαζοφυλακίων)," and (*Ant*. xix. 6. 1) that Herod Agrippa suspended a golden chain "up above the Treasury (ὑπὲρ τὸ γαζοφυλάκιον)" *i.e.* presumably on the wall of the Treasury abutting on the Court, where it would be visible to those in the Court. But none of these facts suggest that people had access to the Treasury, and the access is antecedently most improbable. *Hor. Heb.* i. 226 says, "When John saith, 'Jesus spake these words in the treasury,' it is all one as if he had said, 'He spake these words in the court of the women'..."—*i.e.* in the place where the "Trumpets" abutted on the women's court.

[2] [2334 *a*] Nehem. x. 37 "to the chambers of the house of our God," εἰς γαζοφυλάκιον οἴκου τοῦ θεοῦ. This might give the impression that the people came into the Treasury.

it; why then did not John adhere to Mark's tradition (supposing him to have known it) and say, "These things spake Jesus teaching *opposite* the Treasury"? May not the reason be that, from the symbolical point of view, the old phrasing was not quite appropriate? John perhaps accepted from the Synoptists the tradition that the Treasury was the scene of Christ's doctrine about judgment concerning gifts, as judged by man and as judged by God. But he may have also adopted a further tradition that His doctrine on that occasion included judgment in general (viii. 15 "ye judge after the flesh"), since the whole life of man may be regarded as a "gift" or "offering" to God[1]. From his point of view, then, the Treasury has

---

[1] [2334 b] Mt. xxiii. 23 and Lk. xi. 42 protest against the tithing of mint, when accompanied by the neglect of "judgment." Mt. xii. 7 says, "If ye had known what that means, 'I will have mercy and not sacrifice,' ye would not have condemned the guiltless." Compare the tradition of Micah (vi. 7—8) that "to do justly" is better than offerings of "thousands of rams," and "rivers of oil." The Treasury, the receptacle of God's offerings, might well seem an appropriate place for doctrine about "doing justly" or "judging righteous judgment."

Note also the following uses of ἐν :—

[2334 c] Ἐν χειρί in iii. 35 πάντα δέδωκεν ἐν τῇ χειρὶ αὐτοῦ is Hebraic as compared with xiii. 3 πάντα ἔδωκεν αὐτῷ εἰς τὰς χεῖρας. The second is the more emphatic—"gave him all things [giving them absolutely] into his hands." But indiscriminative writers or translators might use the two indifferently as in Josh. x. 30, 32 (*bis*) "*delivered into the hand* of Israel," Heb. "gave, or placed, *in* the hand," LXX εἰς χεῖρας...εἰς τὰς χεῖρας, but A ἐν χειρί...εἰς τὰς χεῖρας. Comp. Dan. i. 2 Theod. ἔδωκεν ἐν χειρὶ αὐτοῦ, LXX παρέδωκεν...εἰς χεῖρας αὐτοῦ.

[2334 d] The interpolation in v. 4 κατέβαινεν ἐν τῇ κολυμβήθρᾳ is probably from a Semitic source. Comp. Judg. vii. 9 κατάβηθι ἐν (A εἰς) τῇ παρεμβολῇ and 1 S. xiv. 21 "*into*" (marg. *in*) the camp," Josh. viii. 13 etc. Blass (p. 130) quotes Herm. *Sim.* i. 6 ἀπέλθῃς ἐν τῇ πόλει σου, and refers to *Clem. Hom.* i. 7, xiv. 6, and (p. 313) quotes Epict. i. 11. 32 ἀνέρχῃ ἐν Ῥώμῃ. But in *Clem. Hom.* i. 7 ἐν πυρὶ ἀσβέστῳ ῥιφθείσας τὸν αἰῶνα κολασθήσεσθαι, the meaning may be "punished *in* fire unquenchable." In *Clem. Hom.* xiv. 6 ἐν ἀλλοδαπῇ ὁρμήσασα is immediately described as ἐν ἀλλοδαπῇ γενομένη. The context lays stress on a voyage by sea, and suggests that the meaning may be, not "having set out *in* (for *to*)," but "*having found anchorage in* (ὁρμέω) a foreign coast." In Epictet., Schweig. says that ἀνέρχῃ covers an erasure, which, he says, may be ἀπέρχῃ. Comp. *ib.* ii. 20. 33 ἀπελθεῖν ἐν βαλανείῳ. This would reduce the two instances in Epict. to agreement with Herm. *Sim.* i. 6, and comp. Steph. 1289 D quoting Mustoxydis Anecd. ἀπελθόντος ἐν τῇ πατρίδι, and "alia non minus barbara schol. φοιτητὴς ὁ συνεχῶς παρὰ τῷ διδασκάλῳ ἀπερχόμενος." The facts indicate that in vernacular Gk, independent of Semitic influence, the use of ἐν was freq. with ἀπέρχεσθαι but not with other verbs of motion. Epictet. elsewhere uses ἀνέρχομαι with εἰς, and also absolutely (but not with ἐν), of "going up [to Rome]." Ἀπέρχομαι ἐν seems to have meant "I go and stay in [a place]." But the Fayûm Pap. 116, 138 give ἀπελθεῖν εἰς πόλιν (not ἐν, though the writers are illiterate).

a typical meaning. It belongs to the Father, and the Son comes to visit it in order to inspect the offerings made to His Father. In this light—the Son being regarded as Lord of the Treasury—it is more appropriate to think of Him as standing "*in*" it than "*opposite to*" it, or "*looking up*" to it[1].

(ix) Ἐνώπιον

[2335] Ἐνώπιον occurs only once, xx. 30 (lit.) "Many and other signs therefore on the one hand (πολλὰ μὲν οὖν καὶ ἄλλα[2] σημεῖα) did Jesus *in the sight of* (ἐνώπιον) the disciples," and once in the Epistle, 1 Jn iii. 22 "we do the things that are well pleasing *in his sight* (ἐ. αὐτοῦ)." Mark and Matthew never use it. Luke uses it twenty-two times, the last instance being (xxiv. 43) "he ate *in their sight*," i.e. "*in the sight of*" *the disciples*. This refers to the period after Christ's resurrection: and it is noteworthy that the only Johannine instance of the word refers apparently to the same period, and to events of the same kind *i.e.* to signs wrought by Jesus "*in the sight of*" *the disciples alone, and not in the sight of the world at large*. If the "signs" had not been restricted *to the* "*sight*" *of* "*the disciples*," the phrase (it seems probable) would not have been inserted.

(x) Ἐπί

(1) Ἐπί with Accusative

[2336] Ἐπί with accusative, which is frequently found in the Synoptists to express "coming up to" or "against" a person, thing, or place, is never used thus of literal motion by John except in xix. 33 ἐπὶ δὲ τὸν Ἰησοῦν ἐλθόντες. John uses it however of the Spirit (i. 33, 51) "coming down *on*" a person, and in vi. 16 "came down

---

[1] Lk. xxi. 1 ἀναβλέψας.

[2] [2335 a] This use of "and" after "many," though (Steph.) regular in classical prose, is not found elsewhere in N.T. except in Luke iii. 18 πολλὰ μὲν οὖν καὶ ἕτερα, and Acts xxv. 7. Jn xxi. 25 ἔστιν δὲ καὶ ἄλλα πολλά omits "and." Both in the use of ἐνώπιον, and in the insertion of καί, this passage resembles the style of Luke. Also μὲν οὖν, which occurs in Jn only here and xix. 24, is extremely frequent in the Acts. Ἐνώπιον, in Lk., in connexion with "eating," occurs in Lk. xiii. 26, "we did eat and drink *in thy presence*...," where Mt. vii. 22 has "we prophesied in thy name...." Justin Mart. *Apol.* 16, *Tryph.* 76 has "we did eat and drink *in thy name*." So has Origen repeatedly (Huet ii. 389—90, 393, *Cels.* ii. 49). Acts x. 41 has (Peter's speech) συνεφάγομεν κ. συνεπίομεν αὐτῷ, Ign. *Smyrn.* 3 συνέφαγεν [*i.e.* the Lord] αὐτοῖς καὶ συνέπιεν ὡς σαρκικός.... The narrative of Jn xxi. 13 describes the disciples as eating in Christ's presence and from His hand, but makes no mention of His eating.

[2337] PREPOSITIONS

on (R.V. *unto*) the sea." On the reading in xxi. 4 ἔστη ἐπί, where no verb of motion is expressed, see **2307** *a*.

(2) Ἐπί with Dative

[2337] Ἐπί, "close on," "at," "by," in iv. 6 ἐπὶ τῇ πηγῇ, and in v. 2 ἐπὶ τῇ προβατικῇ, calls for no comment. In the latter, ἐπί—since it might be thus used whether the meaning were "by a *gate*" or "by a *pool*"—throws no light on the disputed ellipsis (**2216**).

[2338] In iv. 27 "And *upon this* (ἐπὶ τούτῳ) came his disciples and were amazed that he was speaking with a woman," it has been shewn (**1673** *a*) that "amazed" probably conveys a notion of being "shocked" or "scandalized." "*Upon this*," literally "on the top of this," is frequent in classical Greek, where ἐπί occurs not only in such phrases as "evil *on* evil," "one *on* another," but also in the ordinary meaning of sequence, "on this," "hereon," "hereupon." But in N.T. this use of ἐπὶ τούτῳ—apart from some verb preparing the way for ἐπί—is unique[1]. Origen has ἐπὶ τοῦτο: SS has "while they [were] speaking"; the Latin versions, "meanwhile," "forthwith" etc.; Dא*, ἐν. Chrysostom says, "'*Upon this came His disciples*': they came most seasonably when the teaching of the Lord had been completed[2]"—perhaps meaning "Jesus had *just* time to utter the words, *I am He*," whereas the writer of SS ("while they were speaking [as above described]") perhaps means "The woman had *not* time to add a word of question." Both interpretations appear to recognise the exceptional meaning of "*upon this*" by an attempt to paraphrase it. The context supposes that the disciples did not hear Christ's words; else they would have been "amazed" at what He said, not at the mere fact that He "*spake with a woman*": but they came up just in time to prevent the woman from saying anything more.

[2339] In xii. 16 ταῦτα ἦν ἐπ' αὐτῷ γεγραμμένα, D reads περί (comp. v. 46 περὶ γὰρ ἐμοῦ ἐκεῖνος ἔγραψεν) which would be the usual preposition if the meaning were simply "concerning": but ἐπί "on the basis of" (not εἰς, "with a view to"), means that the Scripture was,

---

[1] The references given by Alford (*ad loc.*) are not to the point, as they have verbs ("rejoice," "console" etc.) in the context and mean "rejoice *at*," "console *over*" etc. Eph. iv. 26 μὴ ἐπιδυέτω ἐπί reproduces a phrase from Deut. xxiv. 15.

[2] [2338 *a*] Σφόδρα εἰς καιρὸν ἀπήντησαν τῆς διδασκαλίας ἀπαρτισθείσης. On Origen (*ad loc.*) ἐπὶ τοῦτο, note confusion of ο and ω. Nonnus is strangely confused, Χριστὸς ἐγὼ γενόμην· οὐ δεύτερος ἄλλος ἱκάνει· Οὐδέ μιν ἤρετο Πέτρος ἄτε θρασύς....

by foreknowledge, "based on," and "adapted to," the act of Christ that fulfilled it. The context is quite different in Lk. xxiii. 38 ἐπιγραφὴ ἐπ' αὐτῷ: but probably ἐπί, there too, means "suited to the case of," and hence "concerning"—not "over his head" (506 (i) *b*).

(3) Ἐπί with Genitive

(*a*) Ἐπὶ τῆς θαλάσσης (vi. 19, xxi. 1)

[2340] John seldom uses ἐπί with genitive, for it does not (1882) lend itself to metaphor. The only instance of ἐπί with the genitive in Christ's words is in xvii. 4 "I have glorified thee on the earth." But the following passages claim attention:—vi. 19—21 "They behold Jesus walking *on* (? *near*) *the sea* (περιπατοῦντα ἐπὶ τῆς θαλάσσης)...and straightway the boat (lit.) became *on* (? *near*) the land (εὐθέως ἐγένετο τὸ πλοῖον ἐπὶ τῆς γῆς) to which they were returning (εἰς ἣν ὑπῆγον)," xxi. 1 "After these things Jesus manifested himself again to the disciples *on* (? *near*) *the sea* (ἐπὶ τῆς θαλάσσης) of Tiberias."

[2341] In the latter, there is no intention to represent Jesus as *walking on the sea*, for it is expressly said that "Jesus *stood on the beach*[1]." Why, then, does not John use the customary[2] phrase "*by* (παρά) *the sea*"? Turning to the Synoptic account of the Walking on the Sea[3], we find that Matthew curiously differs from Mark and John. Matthew has the phrase first with the accusative, "He came toward them walking *on* (? *over*) the sea (ἐπὶ τὴν θ.)"; then with the genitive, "seeing him *on* the sea (ἐπὶ τῆς θ.) walking." This change of case may be explained as follows, from a desire to clear up an early obscurity attaching to the phrase "*on* the sea," and to the word "walk."

[2342] "*On* the sea" is ambiguous—capable of meaning "*near* the sea," as when we say that a city "lies *on* the sea"—and more ambiguous in Greek than in English. We could not say, of a person, "*he* stood *on* the sea," for "*on the edge* of the sea." But Greek and Hebrew can say this. Moreover περιπατεῖν means as a rule "walk about" and not "walk" in the sense of progression.

---

[1] [2341 *a*] xxi. 4 ἔστη εἰς (marg. ἐπί) τὸν αἰγιαλόν. For the reasons for preferring ἐπί, see **2307 *a***.

[2] [2341 *b*] "Customary," even where there is no verb of motion, both in LXX and in Mk-Mt. Comp. Mk iv. 1 διδάσκειν π. τὴν θ., v. 21 ἦν π. τὴν θ., Mt. xiii. 1 ἐκάθητο π. τὴν. θ.

[3] Mk vi. 48—9, Mt. xiv. 25—6, not in Lk.

[2342] PREPOSITIONS

In LXX it is used of "walking to and fro," on a roof, or palace wall[1], and in classical Greek it was so frequently used about the "walking up and down" of the philosophic teacher that it gave the name to the Peripatetic philosophy. Plutarch says that people use the term "walk about" concerning those who "move up and down in the porches," not about those who "walk (βαδίζοντας) into the country or to see a friend[2]." Hence περιπατεῖν could not well mean "walk forward" except in some special context, as where Herodian says "He used *to travel with them, mostly walking* (περιπατῶν), rarely in carriage or on horseback[3]." If therefore Matthew desired to use the verb in the sense of "advance," some change in the context might be usefully introduced to suggest this[4]. Now from the time of

---

[1] [2342 a] 2 S. xi. 2 π. ἐπὶ τοῦ δώματος, Dan. iv. 26 ἐπὶ τῶν τειχῶν (Theod. ἐπὶ τῷ ναῷ). Job ix. 8, Ps. civ. 3, describing Jehovah as "*walking about* (περιπατῶν)" on the waters, or on the wings of the wind, are prob. to be expl. in the light of Job xli. 23 (24) (LXX) "he reckoneth the abyss as *a portico* (εἰς περίπατον)," i.e. *as a place for walking up and down in*. Prov. vi. 28 "*walk about* on coals" conveys no notion of progressing. The accus. occurs in an erroneous rendering of Is. viii. 7 "go over all his banks," περιπατήσει ἐπὶ πᾶν τεῖχος ὑμῶν.

[2] [2342 b] Plut. *Mor.* p. 796 D τοὺς ἐν ταῖς στοαῖς ἀνακάμπτοντας περιπατεῖν φασίν...οὐκέτι δὲ τοὺς εἰς ἀγρὸν ἢ πρὸς φίλον βαδίζοντας.

[3] [2342 c] Steph. quotes Herodian, iv. 7. 11 τὰ πλεῖστά τε αὐτοῖς συνώδευε περιπατῶν, σπανίως ἅρματος ἢ ἵππου ἐπιβαίνων.

[4] [2342 d] It may be urged that Mark himself distinctly mentions advancing in the words "*cometh* (ἔρχεται) towards them." This is true, but the context indicates varieties of tradition. For (1) Mark adds "he *wished to* (lit.) *come past them* (ἤθελεν παρελθεῖν αὐτούς)." (2) Matthew omits this, but has ἦλθεν instead of ἔρχεται. (3) John also omits this ("wished to pass by") but has ἤθελον in quite a different context ("*they wished* to receive him"). (4) Παρελθεῖν, instead of "*pass by*," might mean "*come to* [*them*]" in classical Greek, and might be taken by some as having that meaning here. (5) The three words ΗΘΕΛΟΝ, ΗΘΕΛΕΝ, and ΗΛΘΕΝ might be easily confused. (6) The tradition that Jesus "wished to pass by the disciples"—and presumably gave up His wish—is fraught with great difficulty. (7) Matthew alone introduces a story about Peter here, asking Jesus to bid him "come" to Him "*over the waters* (ἐπὶ τὰ ὕδατα)," and then Peter "*walked over the waters* (περιεπάτησεν ἐπὶ τὰ ὕδατα)" and "came to Jesus." Taking all these facts into consideration we appear to be justified in inferring that Matthew's reason for deviating from Mark's use of the genitive (which is also the usage of the LXX) in the first instance in which he speaks about the "walking," was, that he desired to emphasize the meaning "walking *onward*," as distinct from "walking about."

[2342 e] Περιπατέω in N.T. means (1) "walk about," (2) "walk in love, faith, light etc." Applied to the lame, or paralysed, it may mean "recover the power of walking." When applied to Jesus, it probably means in most cases, as in classical Greek, "*walk about while teaching.*" Where Mark describes Jesus as (xi. 27) "*walking about* in the Temple," Matthew has (xxi. 23) "*came into* the

Homer and Hesiod, ἐπί with *the accusative of* θάλασσαν, πόντον etc. was extremely common in the sense of sailing, advancing etc. *over the sea or ocean*[1]. Consequently, by the slight change of the genitive

Temple," and Luke (xx. 1) "*teaching* the people in the Temple and *preaching the Gospel*"; and this is probably the real meaning of Mark's tradition. For several authors use the word thus (Steph.) Philostr. p. 21 "*lecturing* to one's audience (περιπατοῦντος ἐς τοὺς ἀκροωμένους)," *ib.* 302 "*lecturing* to people that are in a state of depression (π. ἐς ἀνθρώπους ἀθύμως ἔχοντας)," Diog. Laert. vii. 109 "Ask and answer and *lecture* (τὸ ἐρωτᾶν καὶ ἀποκρίνεσθαι καὶ περιπατεῖν)." As Jewish teachers "sat" while teaching, περιπατέω would not probably be applied to Jesus in this sense, except either as a Greek paraphrase, or as referring to His "going from place to place" while preaching the Gospel.

[2342 *f*] Mt. iv. 18 περιπατῶν (Mk i. 16 παράγων) δὲ παρὰ τὴν θάλασσαν τῆς Γ. occurs before the call of Peter. The corresponding narrative in Lk. v. 1 has ἐγένετο ἐν τῷ τὸν ὄχλον ἐπικεῖσθαι αὐτῷ καὶ ἀκούειν τὸν λόγον τοῦ θεοῦ καὶ αὐτὸς ἦν ἑστὼς παρὰ τὴν λίμνην Γεννησαρέτ. If this detail in Lk. is parallel to the detail in Mk-Mt., Lk. would seem, as above, to have taken π. as "teach." In Lk.'s sequel, Jesus goes into a boat and (v. 3) "sitting down, from (ἐκ) the vessel he taught the multitudes." This resembles an incident, omitted by Luke, but recorded by Mark and Matthew before the Parable of the Sower, where the three Synoptists relate the gathering of a crowd. Mark and Matthew add:—

Mk iv. 1	Mt. xiii. 2
"...so that he himself went into a boat and sat *in* (ἐν) *the sea*, and all the multitude were toward the sea on (or, on the edge of, ἐπί) the land (ἐπὶ τῆς γῆς)."	"...so that he himself went into a boat and *sat*, and all the multitude had taken up its stand on the beach (ἐπὶ τὸν αἰγιαλὸν ἑστήκει)."

[2342 *g*] The facts indicate that there were many traditions about Jesus teaching the disciples "*in* the sea" or "*by* the sea." It is not at all likely that περιεπάτησεν ἐπὶ τῆς θαλάσσης εἰς τοὺς μαθητάς originally meant (according to the idiom of Philostratus) "He *discoursed*, on the edge of the sea, *to the disciples*"—for the idiom was probably confined to educated writers. But, reversely, it is possible that the original and poetical tradition about Jesus walking on the sea to the disciples may have been explained by some as meaning that He "stood on the edge of the sea and *discoursed to* them," or else "He, in the sea, *i.e.* in a boat on the sea, *discoursed to* the disciples."

[2342 *h*] In Jn xii. 35 "*Walk about* (περιπατεῖτε) (R.V.) while (ὡς) ye have the light," the Syr. (Burk. txt) has "*walk in the light*"; and a little later (xii. 36) instead of "believe in (εἰς) the light," Chrysostom has "*walk* [having regard] to (εἰς) the light." If ὡς meant "while," we should have to interpret the former passage "*Be active*," "*be doing*," assuming that the "walking about" is in the paths of righteousness; but more probably (**2201**) ὡς means "as" and the sense is "Walk *according as* ye have the light."

[1] [2342 *i*] Steph. quotes abundant instances from Homer and Hesiod of ἐπί with accus. in this sense ("*over* the sea"), but none (nor do L. S. and Jelf) from later authors. Matthew, however, uses it twice in the story of Peter walking on the waters, as well as once in the Synoptic Tradition. And comp. Eurip. *Hec.* 446 ἐπ' οἶδμα, also *Hel.* 400, *Iph. T.* 395, 409. It seems a poetic idiom.

to the accusative, Matthew suggests that the meaning of the old tradition was not "*walking about on the edge of* the sea," but "*walking over* the sea [toward the disciples]." In the light of this, his readers would naturally interpret the next clause as "having beheld him, *on* the sea, walking [towards them]."

[2343] Mark's narrative suffers from ambiguity. He has the same two phrases as Matthew, but with the ambiguous genitive in both clauses. John has only one clause, and that contains the ambiguous genitive, "They behold Jesus walking on the sea (ἐπὶ τῆς θ.)¹."

[2344] The variations may be illustrated by the description (LXX) of Israel "encamped *by* the [Red] Sea." The Hebrew preposition means literally "upon." In the first instance, LXX renders this literally by ἐπί with the genitive, but a few verses afterwards by παρά with the accusative², which is the regular rendering all through the Bible, παρὰ θάλασσαν being very frequent whereas ἐπὶ θαλάσσης is extremely rare. When the latter occurs in the Psalms (R.V.) "terrible things *by* (Heb. *on*) the Red Sea," the Hebrew writer and the Greek translator (who uses ἐπί with the genitive) may be alluding to the passage in Exodus where the meaning is "*on the edge of* the sea³."

[2345] It appears, then, that the phrase used twice by Mark, "*on* the sea," is, both in Hebrew and in Greek, ambiguous. Matthew alters it in one case so as to make the meaning clear, "walking *over* the sea." John retains "walking *on* the sea." In view of Matthew's alteration, and of Luke's omission of the whole story, it is reasonable to conclude that there were early divergences of opinion as to the meaning of "on the sea" and to regard it as probable that John

---

¹ [**2343***a*] Mk vi. 48—9, Mt. xiv. 25—6, Jn vi. 19. Some of the Latin MSS. distinguish between the two clauses. In Mt., *a* has "ambulans supra mari...supra mare ambulantem" (*b* om. 2nd clause), *e* has "ambulans super mare...in mari ambulantem," *f* has "ambulans super mare...supra mare ambulantem," SS has "on the water...on the waves of the sea." In Mk, SS has "walking on the water...on the water [and] walking." In Mk, *a* has "ambulans Jesus super marem (*sic*)...ambulantem super mare." In Mk, D has π. ἐπὶ τῆς θαλάσσης twice. In Mt., D has two genitives; L has genitive first, accusative second.

² [**2344***a*] Ex. xiv. 2 ἐπὶ τῆς θ., xiv. 9 παρὰ τὴν θ. Ἐπὶ τὴν θ. occurs in Ex. xiv. 16, 21 etc. of Moses "stretching out his hand *over* the sea."

³ [**2344***b*] In Ps. cvi. 22, the Syr. and Vulg. have "*in* the Red Sea": Walton renders the Targ. "in," but the Heb. "super," but the preposition, in both, is the same as in Ex. xiv. 2 (Heb.).

intended "walking *on* the sea" to mean something different from Matthew's "walking *over* the sea"—something more in accordance with the usage of Polybius—who describes the Roman soldiers as "standing *on* (i.e. on the edge of) the sea[1]," and not venturing into it in order to attack the Carthaginians—and also in accordance with the LXX version of the Deliverance on the Red Sea and the allusion to it in the Psalms. And this hypothesis is made all the more probable because we thereby interpret the Johannine "*on* the sea" precisely as we are to interpret the Johannine "*on* the land" in the same story, and also as we interpret the Johannine "*on* the sea" in the narrative of the manifestation after the Resurrection. In each of these three cases "*on*" means "*close to*," "*on the edge of*."

[2346] It has been shewn elsewhere that John's use of the rare (1735 *b c*) word ΗΘΕΛΟΝ in the context indicates that he was writing with allusion to Mark's ΗΘΕΛΕΝ. Mark had said that Jesus "*willed*" to pass by the disciples. John says that the disciples "*willed*" to receive Jesus: and then there was a miracle. The boat was "immediately *on the edge of* the shore"! But the difference between the Synoptic and the Johannine miracle is this, that in the former the Lord comes to the disciples, in the latter He draws the disciples to Himself[2]. See also 2716—7.

---

[1] Polyb. *Bell. Pun.* i. 44 ἐπὶ δὲ τῆς θαλάσσης ἔστησαν [οἱ Ῥωμαῖοι] καταπεπληγμένοι τὴν τῶν πολεμίων τόλμαν.

[2] [2346 *a*] John, like Origen, may have regarded the story as typical of the Storm of Temptation. The narrative has some points of similarity to that of Adam and Eve, when they, after yielding to temptation, heard the voice of "the Lord God *walking* (περιπατοῦντος)," and they were afraid. Before they had tasted of evil, says Philo (on Gen. iii. 8), they were at rest themselves and believed God to be at rest: now, being themselves in commotion, they impute motion to Him. This is not the place to discuss the relation between the two Johannine descriptions of Jesus "*on the edge of the sea* (ἐπὶ τῆς θαλάσσης)" of Tiberias—one before, one after, the Resurrection. But, as regards the former, the facts indicate that John found this ambiguous phrase in the Original Greek Tradition. Instead of omitting it, or altering it, he desired to set forth what appeared to him true and spiritual traditions containing it. In other words, whereas Luke omits, John intervenes and explains.

[2346 *b*] The *Acts of John* says § 2 (ed. James) "When He had chosen Peter and Andrew, who were brethren, He cometh to me and to my brother James, saying, 'I have need of you: come unto Me.' And my brother <hearing> that, said 'John, what would this child have that called to us upon the shore?' (καὶ ὁ ἀ. μου τοῦτο εἶπεν, Ἰ. τὸ παιδίον τοῦτο <τὸ> ἐπὶ τοῦ αἰγιαλοῦ καλέσαν ἡμᾶς τί βούλεται;)."

[2346 *c*] The narrative goes on to say that, when they had "brought the ship to

(β) Ἐπὶ τοῦ ϲταυροῦ (xix. 19)

[2347] Jn xix. 19 ἐπὶ τοῦ σταυροῦ—which is parallel to Lk. xxiii. 38 ἐπ' αὐτῷ, R.V. "over him," but better, perhaps, "concerning him" (506 (i) *b*)—requires in itself no grammatical comment, but perhaps points to mistranslation of Semitic tradition by one or more of the evangelists.

(xi) **Κατά**

[2348] Κατά, in the Synoptists, is occasionally used of locality, both with genitive and with accusative. In John it is never thus used. In Mark, it occurs no less than seven times in the phrase κατ' ἰδίαν, "privately." John never represents Jesus as doing anything "privately" (comp. xviii. 20). This is one explanation of the rarity of κατά in John as compared with Mark. It is interesting to note that one out of two instances with the genitive, and one out of eight instances with the accusative, occur in interpolations (viii. 6, v. 4). The phrase εἷς καθ' εἷς is also part of an interpolation (viii. 9).

(xii) **Μετά**

(*a*) Μετὰ Ἰουδαίου (iii. 25)

[2349] Μετά with the accusative requires no comment, meaning almost always "after," of time, as in the Synoptists[1].

Μετά with the genitive of the person in N.T. regularly means "in company with," and frequently "associated with (as a friend)," "on the side of." Except in Revelation, it is not used in N.T. with verbs

---

land," the brothers presently saw Jesus "helping along with us to *settle* the ship (τὸ πλοῖον ἑδράσωμεν)." For this remarkable expression comp. (Steph.) Callixenus Athen. 15, p. 204 D ἑδρασθῆναι τὸ πλοῖον ἀσφαλῶς ἐπὶ τῶν φαλάγγων (*i.e.*, Steph. viii. 603, on the (1) "stocks" or (2) "rollers"), and Constantin. Basil. Mac. c. 34, p. 90 ἐπί τινος ἀσφαλοῦς ἐλπίδος ἑδρασθῆναι (metaph.). In N.T. also we have "hope" connected with steadfastness in two metaphors, (1) Col. i. 23 τεθεμελιωμένοι καὶ ἑδραῖοι καὶ μὴ μετακινούμενοι ἀπὸ τῆς ἐλπίδος..., (2) Heb. vi. 18—19 ἐλπίδος, ἣν ὡς ἄγκυραν ἔχομεν. This "settling the ship" is perhaps originally derived from some poetic metaphor.

[1] [2349 *a*] Μετά with accusative occurs (12) in the phrase μ. ταῦτα (or, τοῦτο) (**2394**), also in iv. 43 μετὰ δὲ τὰς δύο ἡμέρας, xx. 26 μεθ' ἡμέρας ὀκτώ. It is foll. by other nouns in [v. 4] μετὰ τὴν ταραχήν (interpol.), xiii. 27 μετὰ τὸ ψωμίον.

In the historical books of LXX, μετὰ ταῦτα is very common (much more so than μετὰ τοῦτο). It occurs (5) in 1 Mac., but not in 2 Mac., 3 Mac., 4 Mac. It occurs (3) in 1 Esdr. but never in Ezr., which has μετὰ τοῦτο twice. Μετὰ ταῦτα is non-occurrent in Mk and Mt., but it occurs Mk-App. xvi. 12, and in Lk. (both speech and narr.). It is very freq. in Rev. (i. 19, iv. 1, 2, vii. 9 etc.).

of contention *e.g.* "fight *with* (i.e. *against*)[1]," a use apparently confined to Hebraic Greek. In John, when it is used of people "talking," or "murmuring," or "questioning with one another (μετ' ἀλλήλων)[2]," the speakers *are all on one side*—either the Jews against Jesus, or the disciples wishing to question Jesus (not some for, others against, Him). And συνζητεῖν, ζήτησις etc. elsewhere are found with πρός or σύν or dative, but not with μετά[3]. These facts bear on the interpretation of iii. 25 (lit.) "There arose therefore a questioning *from* (? 2350) (ἐκ) the disciples of John *along with* (μετά) a Jew about purifying, and they came to John and said to him, Rabbi,...."

[2350] The whole of the context—which turns on the possibility of rivalry between the Baptist and Christ, who had come into the Baptist's neighbourhood—suggests that the Jews and some of the Baptist's disciples wished to incite the Baptist to jealousy. If we take ζήτησις to mean (as it does in the Acts and Pastoral Epistles) a quarrel[4], and a quarrel about some matter that seems to the writer unimportant, we can give μετά its usual Johannine signification by supposing (1) a parenthesis after "quarrel[5]," (2) an ellipsis of τινες, "some," after ἐκ (2213—5), (3) μετά meaning "allied with": "There arose therefore a quarrel—[some] of the disciples of John [*siding*] *with* a Jew [or, Jews] about purifying; and they came to John and said, Rabbi,..." *i.e.* they tried to rouse him to jealousy of Jesus[6]. Nonnus has ἔρις...Ἰωάνναο μαθηταῖς Ἑβραίου μετὰ φωτός.

---

[1] Rev. ii. 16, xi. 7, xii. 7, xiii. 4 etc. But comp. 1 Cor. vi. 6—7 ἀδελφὸς μετὰ ἀδελφοῦ κρίνεται...κρίματα ἔχετε μεθ' ἑαυτῶν. Steph. gives no instance.

[2] Jn xi. 56 ἔλεγον, vi. 43 γογγύζετε, xvi. 19 ζητεῖτε, all foll. by μ. ἀλλήλων.

[3] Mk viii. 11 dat., ix. 14, 16 πρός, Lk. xxii. 23 πρός, Acts xv. 2 πρός (v. r. σύν), Acts xxv. 19 πρός: Acts vi. 9 dat., ix. 29 πρός.

[4] [2350 *a*] Ζήτησις is not in LXX. In N.T. it occurs elsewhere 6 times. It implies strife in Acts xv. 2, 7, foolish discussion and pedantical wrangling in 1 Tim. vi. 4, 2 Tim. ii. 23, Tit. iii. 9, and prob. in Acts xxv. 20. Ζήτημα is also used in an unfavourable sense in Acts xv. 2, xviii. 15, xxiii. 29 etc.

[5] [2350 *b*] Comp. Rev. xii. 7 "And there was war in heaven—Michael and his angels making war with the dragon—and the dragon made war and his angels...."

[6] [2350 *c*] The Latin versions have "Jews" instead of "Jew" and render ἐκ as follows :—*a* and *f* "inter," *b* "ex," *e* "de," *d* "a." They render μετά thus :— *a* "et" (but *a* has "inter Judaeos et discipulos Johannis"), *b* and *e* "cum," *f* "et," *d* "ad." Syr. Burk. has (txt) "among the disciples of John with the Jews," but his marg. gives "of one of the disciples of John with a Jew (*or*, 'the Jews') *S*," and the Arabic Diatessaron has "between *one* of John's disciples and

[2351]   PREPOSITIONS

(β)   Οἱ μετ' ἀυτοῦ ὄντες (ix. 40)

[2351] In ix. 40 (lit.) "There heard [some] of the Pharisees these things—*those that were with him* (ἤκουσαν ἐκ τῶν Φ. ταῦτα οἱ μετ' αὐτοῦ ὄντες)," SS has "the Pharisees which were *near* him." This rendering, if allowable, would remove a great difficulty; for the context represents Christ as severely condemning them, so that "*on his side*," or "*his companions*"—the rendering demanded by usage[1]—seems out of place here. But (1) μετά is hardly ever used of mere proximity, (2) the article would surely have been omitted, since the sense would require "some, being casually with him." Chrysostom paraphrases it as "following him superficially (ἐπιπολαίως)": but how can the supposition of such an ellipsis be justified? It would be more allowable to suppose that, as in ix. 25 τυφλὸς ὤν means "being once blind," so here οἱ ὄντες means "those who once were." But there the context continues "now I see (ἄρτι βλέπω)," so that the antithesis and the context together make the meaning clear: "Being [known to everyone as] blind," or "being [up to this moment] blind," now I see. Here there is no such context, and no satisfactory explanation presents itself[2].

(γ)   Μετά compared with παρά

[2352] John only once says μένειν μετά[3], the reason being perhaps

---

one of the Jews." These last two renderings necessitate that the *two* must be described as going *together* to John and saying "Rabbi" etc.

[2350 *d*] Chrysostom supposes that the "Jew" was one of Christ's followers, one whom the disciples of John tried ineffectually to persuade. But this view, besides not explaining μετά, fails to explain why the evangelist here alone uses the word "Jew" instead of "a disciple of Christ," the term he elsewhere applies (xix. 38) to Joseph of Arimathæa.

[1] [2351 *a*] Even where Peter is represented as (xviii. 18) "*along with*" the High Priest's servants (as Judas is "*along with*" the soldiers that arrest Jesus) μετά probably suggests blame, "*making himself their companion*." And, with the article, the notion of *companionship* is strengthened.

[2] [2351 *b*] Ποτέ, "once," occurs in this narrative, a little earlier (ix. 13) "him that was *once* blind (τὸν ποτε τυφλόν)." And the context implies that, whereas "the *once* blind" had been caused to see, so, "those who had *once* seen"—*i.e.* those who, being Pharisees, had *once* been disciples of the Lord—had been made blind. It would therefore make good sense to read οἱ ποτε μετ' αὐτοῦ ὄντες, and ποτε might have been dropped owing to its similarity with ὄτες of which it seemed a repetition. But there is no variation in the MSS. except that A places ὄντες before μετ' αὐτοῦ.

[3] [2352 *a*] Jn xi. 54 "and there he abode *with* (μετά) *the disciples*" is shewn by the following words ("Now the passover of the Jews was nigh") to denote a brief period.

that μετά mostly implies companionship, friendly conversation, aid etc., for a special occasion, unless the contrary is implied by adding "for ever" etc.[1] When the Paraclete (*i.e.* Friend and Helper) is first mentioned, it is with μετά, but qualified by "for ever," then with παρά, "at home with," then with ἐν, as follows, xiv. 16—17 "another Paraclete will he give to you that he may be *in companionship with* you (μεθ᾽ ὑμῶν) for ever, even the Spirit of truth, which the world is not able to receive, because [the world] doth not behold it or understand it. Ye understand it because it abides, *as in a home, with* you (παρ᾽ ὑμῖν μένει) and *in* you it [really] is (καὶ ἐν ὑμῖν ἔστιν, v.r. ἔσται, W.H. txt ἐστίν)."

[2353] Here are three stages of revelation. The first is, that the new Friend—instead of being the companion of the disciples for a few months (like the Lord in the flesh) (μετά)—would be their companion, guide, and prompter, "for ever (εἰς τὸν αἰῶνα)." The second is, that since the companion was the Spirit of Truth and the disciples had a spiritual affinity with Truth, they were already in sympathy with the Spirit, and it was already (in the eyes of the Lord who saw things as they were) *at home with* them (παρά). The third statement is, that the Spirit was indeed *essentially* "*in* them," *i.e.* in their inmost being (ἐν)[2]. The MSS., except BD, read (xiv. 17) ἔσται "*shall be in you.*" But "ye understand it because *it shall be in you*" makes very poor sense. Our Lord has previously used the present tense to the disciples ("Ye are") telling them that they are (xv. 3) "pure" by reason of "the Word" that He has, as it were, spoken into the hearts of all but Judas. This "word" is regarded as being the beginning of the Spirit, which, therefore, He now says, "in you [essentially] is."

(xiii) Παρά

(1) Παρά with Accusative

[2354] This construction is never used by John. Whereas Mark and Matthew have "*by* the sea (παρὰ τὴν θάλασσαν)" with verbs of

---

[1] [2352 *b*] In xii. 7 "The poor ye have always *with you* (μεθ᾽ ὑμῶν)" is omitted (**1688** *b*) by SS and D. If it were genuine it would be Jn's only mention of πτωχοί in Christ's words.

[2] [2353 *a*] In some contexts, ἐν ὑμῖν might mean "*among* you all" and not "*in* you individually." But the whole passage indicates that the three prepositions describe three stages of spiritual help for each one of the disciples individually, the Spirit being (1) "by his side," (2) "at home with him," (3) "in his heart." Moreover, the Johannine ἐν almost always means "in," not "among."

rest or motion, and Luke twice has "*standing by* the lake (ἑστώς, or ἑστῶτα, παρὰ τὴν λίμνην)[1]," John, though he at least once describes Jesus as standing by the sea, never uses παρά thus. It has been shewn (2340—6) that once at least (and probably twice) he uses ἐπί with the genitive to mean "on the edge of the sea."

(2) Παρά with Dative

(*a*) Παρά with Dative and μετά with Genitive, see 2352—3

(β) Synoptic and Johannine use

[2355] In the Synoptists, παρὰ τῷ θεῷ, or τῷ πατρί, "with God," or "with the Father," mostly suggests "in the sight of God," "in the estimation of the Father," not "in His, [so to speak, literal] presence." But in John the sense is local and metaphorical, as in viii. 38 "that which I have seen *with* (παρά) the Father," that is "in the home of my Father," or "by the side of my Father." It means the spiritual region that we call "heaven." Compare xvii. 5 "glorify me...*by thy side* (παρὰ σεαυτῷ)...with the glory that I had *by thy side* (παρὰ σοί)." In xix. 25 "Now there stood (ἱστήκεισαν δέ) *by the cross* (παρὰ τῷ σταυρῷ) of Jesus his mother...," there occurs the only instance in N.T. where παρά is used with an impersonal dative. It is quoted by Chrysostom with παρεστηκέναι and the dative. Is it possible that "the cross" had already acquired a shade of suggestion of a "sign" or military "standard," so that when Christ's disciples had abandoned Him in the conflict, the women are described as still "standing by the cross," as soldiers "stand by the colours"?

(3) Παρά with Genitive

[2356] On παρά and ἐκ, with ἐξέρχομαι, see 2326—8. Παρὰ Κυρίου occurs in Mark and Matthew as a quotation in connexion with the Corner Stone ("This [thing] is from the Lord") and in Luke, in connexion with the Incarnation, just before the Magnificat[2]. In John, παρά with genitive almost always means "from [the bosom, or home, or hand, or immediate presence, of]" God[3].

---

[1] Lk. v. 1—2.
[2] [2356 *a*] Mk xii. 11, Mt. xxi. 42 (Ps. cxviii. 23). Lk. i. 45 ἔσται τελείωσις... παρὰ Κυρίου, and also i. 37 οὐκ ἀδυνατήσει παρὰ τοῦ θεοῦ πᾶν ῥῆμα (alluding to Gen. xviii. 14 "too hard *for the Lord*," παρὰ τῷ θεῷ ῥῆμα) refer to the Incarnation.
[3] In this sense it occurs about 18 times, in other senses about 7 times.

PREPOSITIONS [2359]

(4) Παρά with Genitive and with Dative interchanged

[2357] In the following, the dative construction is followed by the genitive construction (but D, and most Latin and Syriac versions, have assimilated the latter to the former) viii. 38 ἃ ἐγὼ ἑώρακα παρὰ τῷ πατρὶ λαλῶ· καὶ ὑμεῖς οὖν ἃ ἠκούσατε παρὰ τοῦ πατρὸς ποιεῖτε. Commenting on this, Origen adduces vi. 45—6 πᾶς ὁ ἀκούσας παρὰ τοῦ πατρὸς καὶ μαθὼν ἔρχεται πρὸς ἐμέ. οὐχ ὅτι τὸν πατέρα ἑώρακέν τις εἰ μὴ ὁ ὢν παρὰ [τοῦ] θεοῦ, οὗτος ἑώρακεν τὸν πατέρα. But in the latter Origen reads ὁ ὢν παρὰ τῷ πατρί instead of ὁ ὢν παρὰ [τοῦ] θεοῦ[1], and Chrysostom reads ὁ ἐκ τοῦ θεοῦ at least once[2].

[2358] Retaining the text in vi. 45—6, we may explain ὁ ὢν παρὰ [τοῦ] θεοῦ, like ὁ ὢν εἰς τὸν κόλπον τοῦ πατρός above (2308—9), as a combination of rest and motion, suggesting the divine nature of the Son on earth, not "*sent* from the side, or home, of God" like John the Baptist (i. 6 ἀπεσταλμένος παρά) but "BEING from the side of God," *i.e.* eternally existing and proceeding from God. There is a distinction between the believer—who (through the Law of Moses and of Nature) "hath heard" voices issuing from the Father's House and "hath understood" their humanising and loving tendency—and the Son, in the Father's House, who "hath seen the Father."

[2359] In viii. 38, the interpretation of the whole largely depends on the interpretation of ποιεῖτε as indicative or imperative, on which see 2193 foll. On this, too, rests in part the application of τοῦ πατρός to God, or to Satan (who is shortly afterwards described as the "father" of those whom Jesus is addressing). But in any case there is the same contrast as in vi. 45—6 between the distinctness with which the Son "sees" the things *in* the House of the Father and the

---

[1] [2357 *a*] Huet ii. 293 A ἕτερος συγχρώμενος καὶ τῷ, Πᾶς ὁ ἀκούσας παρὰ τοῦ πατρὸς καὶ μαθὼν ἔρχεται πρός με, οὐχ ὅτι τὸν πατέρα ἑώρακέ τις, εἰ μὴ ὁ ὢν παρὰ τῷ πατρὶ οὗτος ἑώρακε τὸν πατέρα, ἐρεῖ ὅτι εἰσί τινες τῶν ἐνσωματουμένων ψυχῶν πρὶν εἰς γένεσιν ἐλθεῖν, μεμαθητευμέναι παρὰ τῷ πατρί, καὶ ἀκούσασαι αὐτοῦ, αἴ τινες καὶ ἔρχονται πρὸς τὸν σωτῆρα....

[2] [2357 *b*] Chrys. Εἶτα ἐπάγει· Οὐχ ὅτι τὸν Πατέρα τις ἑώρακεν εἰ μὴ ὁ ὢν ἐκ τοῦ Θεοῦ· οὐ κατὰ τὸν τῆς αἰτίας λόγον ἐνταῦθα τοῦτο λέγων ἀλλὰ κατὰ τὸν τρόπον τῆς οὐσίας. Ἐπεὶ εἰ τοῦτο ἔλεγε, πάντες παρὰ τοῦ θεοῦ ἐσμέν· ποῦ οὖν τὸ ἐξαίρετον τοῦ Υἱοῦ καὶ κεχωρισμένον; That is to say, παρά would apply to "all men," ἐκ to the Eternal Son alone. One may infer from this that ὁ ὢν παρά, in Chrys., a few lines above, when the text is first introduced, is (as often in such cases) a corrupt conformation to the received text. Cramer reads ἐκ repeatedly, but has a strangely different text, with πάντες γὰρ ἐκ τοῦ θεοῦ ἐσμεν.

indistinctness with which men receive promptings *from* the invisible, whether for good or for evil. About the promptings for good Jesus said, "everyone that hath heard *and understood*." He does not here say, "the things that ye have heard *and understood*." Perhaps the evangelist wishes to suggest that the muttered instigations to evil need no such effort to "understand" them as is required by the promptings to good.

(xiv) Περί

[2360] Περί with accusative does not occur in John. On the v.r. in xi. 19 τὰς περὶ Μάρθαν, see **1990**. With the genitive, περί occurs in John almost as often as in all the Synoptists together, because of the frequency of the Johannine phrases "testify concerning," "speak concerning" etc. This makes it almost certain that περί, the reading of A etc. in i. 30 ὑπὲρ οὗ ἐγὼ εἶπον, is incorrect; for there would have been no temptation to alter it. It also demonstrates that ὑπὲρ οὗ, in that passage, cannot mean precisely "concerning whom," for, had that been the meaning, John would have written περί. See **2369—71**. The frequency of περί, and the existence of γράφειν περί in v. 46, shew that xii. 16 ἦν ἐπ' αὐτῷ γεγραμμένα does not mean quite the same as περὶ αὐτοῦ. See **2339**.

(xv) Πρό

(a) Πρὸ ἐμοῦ (x. 8)

[2361] In x. 8 "As many as came *before me* (πρὸ ἐμοῦ) are all thieves and robbers," the difficulty of "before me" has caused its omission in several versions and quotations, because the phrase might be used against the Prophets and Saints of Israel. Πρό, in some contexts, might mean "*in preference to*"—as in "Thou shalt have none other gods *before me*[1]," if rendered into classical Greek. But πρό, with ἐλθεῖν, could hardly mean anything except "in front of" or "previously to."

[2362] In the second of these two senses, however, the phrase will harmonize with the context, if "*before me*," referring to what has

---

[1] [2361 a] Ex. xx. 3, LXX πλὴν ἐμοῦ, Deut. v. 7, comp. Deut. xxi. 16. In Deut. v. 7, LXX has πρὸ προσώπου μου, but AF πλὴν ἐμοῦ. The LXX, so far as can be judged from the instances given by Trommius under seven Hebrew headings, never uses πρό to mean "preferred to."

just been said ("I am the Good Shepherd") can mean "*before the coming of the Good Shepherd in the dawn* to open the door of the fold and to bring out the flock for pasture." In contrast with Him, the evil shepherds, or hirelings, may be supposed to come prematurely, while it is dark, trying to force their way into the fold in order to steal and kill. Possibly πρὸ ἐμοῦ may be also intended to suggest a notion of "preferring himself to me," but the fundamental meaning is that of time. Only, we are not to suppose that "before me" means "before I became incarnate" or that it is limited (as Chrysostom seems to suggest) to leaders like Judas and Theudas[1]. It appears to be uttered by Christ in the character of the Good Shepherd—whether called the Shepherd of Israel, or the Shepherd of the world—and to mean "As many as have come to the flock, from the beginning, not waiting for the Good Shepherd's time, nor associating themselves with Him, but pressing forwards to rule mankind by the short methods of constraint."

(β) Πρό transposed

For xii. 1 πρὸ ἐξ ἡμερῶν τοῦ πάσχα, see **2288**.

(xvi) **Πρός**

(1) Πρός with Accusative, with verb of rest

[2363] The only Johannine passage that needs comment is i. 1 "In the beginning was the Word and the Word was *with* (πρός) God (τὸν θεόν)," where the question is, What is precisely meant by πρός? An evangelist might have used σύν "together with," or μετά "in companionship with," or παρά (with dat.) "by the side of," "in the household of"—as, in Proverbs, Wisdom personified, describing her close connexion with God, says, "Then [*i.e.* during the Creation] I was *by His side* (παρ' αὐτῷ)[2]." But John uses a preposition that is (so far as present evidence goes) not used in this connexion by any

---

[1] [2362 a] Origen says (Huet ii. 41 D) πρὸ γὰρ τῆς τελειώσεως τοῦ λόγου πάντα ψεκτὰ τὰ ἐν ἀνθρώποις ἄτε ἐνδεῆ καὶ ἐλλιπῆ. In his context he mentions the "*white horse*" in the Apocalypse (xix. 11) with Ps. xxxiii. 17 "A *horse* is deceitful for safety" and Ps. xx. 7 "Some trust in chariots and some in *horses*." The passages suggest a contrast between the true Deliverer, or Captain of Salvation, and the false Deliverer, between the Warrior and the Brigand.

[2] Prov. viii. 30.

Greek classical author, nor in LXX.¹ And this is all the more remarkable because παρά with dative is used by John to describe "abiding *with*," spiritually, as well as literally, and this is also used in classical Greek, and in the Synoptists, to mean "in the house of," "at home with."

[2364] In N.T. πρός τινα is frequently employed, to mean, not exactly "at home with," but "in familiar intercourse with," "close contact with," sometimes hostile, but in any case close, communication². In the Second Epistle to the Corinthians the Apostle says that he desires "to be at home *in converse with* the Lord (ἐνδημεῖν πρὸς τὸν Κ.)" and in any case to be "well pleasing" to Him; and he uses this preposition to describe his "staying *in converse with*" Peter, and to express his hope that the youthful Timothy may "be free from intimidation in his *intercourse with*" the Corinthians³.

[2365] According to the analogy of Mark's usage, ὁ λόγος ἦν πρὸς τὸν θεόν would mean "the word was *in converse with* God": and John, in writing the words, might possibly have in mind the two passages (2364 *a*) in Mark's Gospel where Christ speaks of Himself as "*having converse with*" men, and where, in each case, either Matthew or Luke has omitted or altered the preposition. As the Logos on earth ἦν πρὸς ἀνθρώπους, so from the beginning He was

---

¹ [2363 *a*] Steph. and Thayer give no instance of εἶναι πρός τινα from classical Greek. Wahl's classical instances bear on γράφεσθαι, or ἀπογράφεσθαι, πρός etc., and contain no example with εἶναι or with a verb of simple rest. Swete (Mk xiv. 49) says "see W. M., p. 504, and cf. ix. 19, note"; but ix. 19 note says simply "πρὸς ὑμᾶς=μεθ' ὑμῶν (Mt.), cf. vi. 3"; and vi. 3, commenting on πρὸς ἡμᾶς, simply says, "They were settled at Nazareth (ὧδε πρὸς ἡμῖν)"—presumably a misprint for ἡμᾶς. W. M. p. 504 gives no classical instance exc. Demosth. *Apat.* 579 *a* (Teubner 892) τοῖς μὲν ἐ...εἶναι τὰς δίκας πρὸς τοὺς θεσμοθέτας, *i.e.* "bring their suits *to*"—which is not to the point.

[2363 *b*] In 2 Chr. xxviii. 15 "they brought them to Jericho...unto their brethren," κατέστησαν αὐτοὺς εἰς Ἰ...πρὸς τοὺς ἀδελφοὺς αὐτῶν, motion is implied. No instance has been hitherto alleged of εἶναι πρός τινα in LXX.

² [2364 *a*] Mk vi. 3, Mt. xiii. 56 (Lk. diff.) "they are all *in familiar intercourse with us* (πᾶσαι πρὸς ἡμᾶς εἰσίν)," Mk ix. 19, Lk. ix. 41 (Mt. xvii. 17 μεθ' ὑμῶν) "How long shall I *hold converse with you* (πρὸς ὑμᾶς)!" Mk xiv. 49 (Mt. xxvi. 55 om., Lk. xxii. 53 μεθ' ὑμῶν) "I was daily *in converse with you* (πρὸς ὑμᾶς) in the Temple teaching and ye did not seize me." Comp. Mt. xxvi. 18 (Mk·Lk. diff.) πρὸς σὲ ποιῶ τὸ Πάσχα "I keep the Passover *in thy house.*" The context suggests a sign, and a secret arrangement, and confidential communication.

³ [2364 *b*] 2 Cor. v. 8, Gal. i. 18, 1 Cor. xvi. 10 ἀφόβως γένηται πρὸς ὑμᾶς. Comp. Gal. ii. 5 "that the truth of the Gospel might *abide in converse with you* (διαμείνῃ πρὸς ὑμᾶς)."

πρὸς τὸν θεόν, and the twofold application of the phrase "in converse with" prepares the way for the thought of a Mediator. Moreover, this preposition, being regularly used with many verbs of speaking[1], might seem appropriate to the definition of the Word.

[2366] But would an educated Greek at once understand ἦν πρὸς τὸν θεόν in this sense? In Mark, the context shews the meaning of εἶναι πρός, but it is not shewn thus at the beginning of the Fourth Gospel: and πρός with the accusative, in classical Greek, means "having regard to," as in πρὸς ταῦτα "having regard to these things," one of the commonest phrases in the language. Hence πρὸς τὸν θεόν might be taken by Greek readers to mean "having regard to God." And this would agree with abundant instances of ζῆν πρός τινα, in classical Greek, meaning "*to live in absolute devotion to anyone*," as where Demosthenes describes patriots as "living *with constant regard to* (πρός) their country[2]." This sense, too, suits the whole of the Fourth Gospel, which describes the Son as doing nothing except that which He sees the Father doing, so that the Logos is regarded as always, so to speak, ["looking] *toward*," or "*having regard to*," God. Probably John combines this spiritual meaning ("devoted to") with the more local meaning ("in converse with") and, in his own mind, the former is predominant[3].

---

[1] [2365 a] Not however so freq. in Jn as in Lk. Λέγειν and εἰπεῖν πρός in Jn occur only thrice of Christ's words, but more freq. as to the words of others.

[2] [2366 a] Aristot. *Rhet.* i. 9. 4 ἐλευθέρου γὰρ τὸ μὴ πρὸς ἄλλον ζῆν, Plut. *Mor.* 471 B ἐπεὶ πρὸς ἑτέρους ἢ πρὸς αὑτοὺς εἰθίσμεθα ζῆν, Demosth. 411. 33 τοῖς δὲ πρὸς ὑμᾶς ζῶσιν (comp. *ib.* 361. 4 πρὸς τοῦτον πάντ' ἐσκόπουν), Lucian iii. 312 πρὸς μόνον σε ζῶ. It is frequent in Aristotle.

[3] [2366 b] Πρός τινα with verbs of speaking—which is prob. non-existent in Mk-Mt. except in πρὸς ἀλλήλους or ἑαυτούς—is fairly frequent in Jn, but not nearly so frequent as in Lk. Jn seldom has it of words addressed by Jesus to others (iv. 48 "Except ye see signs...," vi. 5 "Whence are we to buy loaves?" viii. 31 "If ye abide in my word...," addressed to those who are soon afterwards called the children of the devil), but more frequently of words addressed to Jesus (ii. 3, iii. 4, iv. 15, 49 etc.). In Lk. it is so freq. as to occur six times in the first chapter. In LXX, πρός τινα in 1 Kings xii. 5, 7, 10, xxii. 18 etc. corresponds to τινί in 2 Chr. x. 5, 7, 10, xviii. 17 etc.

[2366 c] In Mk xii. 12, πρὸς αὐτοὺς εἶπεν means "*with reference* to (or, *against*) them." In Mk x. 26, W.H. read λέγοντες πρὸς αὐτόν without altern. following BCℵ, and this would mean "to Jesus." But the text varies greatly. SS omits "saying" and has "in themselves," and AD and the Latin vss. have πρὸς ἑαυτούς. There does not appear any reason why πρὸς αὐτόν, had it been in Mk, should have been altered to πρὸς ἑαυτούς. But if the ε in ἑαυτούς were dropped in some MSS. after the C in πρός, or if ἑαυτούς were spelt αὐτούς, it would be

(2) Πρός repeated after verb of motion

[2367] In xx. 2 "She runneth therefore and cometh *unto* (πρός) Simon Peter and *unto* (πρός) the other disciple whom Jesus loved and saith to them..." why is πρός repeated? The repetition would certainly indicate a desire to distinguish in a marked manner between the two, if πρός had been repeated in a brief phrase like πρὸς Σ. καὶ πρὸς Ἰωάνην. Perhaps here it means simply that the two were not living in the same house, and Mary is to be supposed as being accompanied by Peter to the house of the other disciple. No other instance quite like this is given by Winer-Moulton (p. 522, Part iii. sect. l. 7. a). Elsewhere prepositions are repeated to give distinctness and weight to separated clauses as in Jn xvi. 8 (and, without καί, in Eph. vi. 12).

(3) Πρός with Dative

[2368] This occurs four times in John (Mk (1), Mt. (0), Lk. (1)[1]) always meaning "at," "close to," xviii. 16 "Peter was standing *at* the door," xx. 11 "Mary was standing *at* the tomb outside," xx. 12 "two angels sitting one *at* the head and one *at* the feet." Πρός, "near," with dative of person, occurs in Sophocles (*Ant.* 1189, *Oed. Col.* 1268) (comp. Aesch. *Suppl.* 242) and might conceivably have been used (πρὸς τῷ θεῷ) in i. 1 if John had meant merely "near[2]."

(xvii) Ὑπέρ (see also 2718—22)

[2369] Ὑπέρ with accusative occurs as v.r. for (xii. 43) ἤπερ, see 2092. Ὑπέρ with genitive occurs 13 times in John, more than twice the number of instances in all the Synoptists. In almost all the Johannine instances it refers to the death of one for the many[3]. But in the

---

comparatively intelligible that αὐτούς (read as αὑτούς) should be changed to αὐτόν: and αὐτόν might be thought by the scribe of B to agree better with Mt.-Lk. and with the context, which describes Jesus as answering what is said by the disciples. W.H. reject B's reading of ἑαυτ. for αὐτ. in Mk viii. 37 and xi. 8, and place it in the margin in xi. 7. On the whole, in Mk x. 26, ἑαυτούς seems more probable than αὐτόν.

[1] Mk v. 11 ἦν δὲ ἐκεῖ πρὸς τῷ ὄρει, Lk. xix. 37 ἐγγίζοντος δὲ αὐτοῦ ἤδη πρὸς τῇ καταβάσει τ. ὄρους τῶν Ἐλαιῶν.

[2] [2368 a] Πλησίον, "near," deserves mention as a preposition peculiar to Jn in iv. 5 πλησίον τοῦ χωρίου, R.V. "*near to* the parcel of ground." Πλησίον, "near," occurs nowhere else in N.T., nor does Steph. quote it freq. except with genitive of person (but see Aesch. *Prom.* 364). Jn may have been influenced by LXX where it occurs (Tromm.) 10 times, once (Josh. viii. 33) in connexion with Gerizim, called in John (iv. 20—21) "this mountain."

[3] Jn xvii. 19 ὑπὲρ αὐτῶν ἁγιάζω ἐμαυτόν refers also to mediation.

following it is rendered by R.V. (as well as A.V.) "of": i. 30 "This is he *of* whom (ὑπὲρ οὗ) I said, After me cometh a man which is become (A.V. "is preferred") before me...."

[2370] Against this rendering is the fact that (2360) περί is the regular Johannine preposition in the phrase "speak *of*" meaning "speak about." Ὑπέρ, it is true, is used by some authors in a sense closely resembling that of περί, as we might use "on" ("*on* this subject the writer urges etc." often with a notion of advocacy): but in such cases the context—referring generally to a thing, not to a person—ought to be such as to make the meaning clear[1]. Here the context suggests "in behalf of." For the Baptist is speaking as a messenger or ambassador of the Messiah, and he might have used the words of St Paul "We are ambassadors *in behalf of* Christ[2]."

[2371] Ammonius[3], among other explanations, suggests that ἀνήρ is here applied to Christ by John the Baptist in the sense of νυμφίος, "bridegroom," and it is an undoubted fact that in the Fourth Gospel the singular of ἀνήρ is always capable of this sense[4]: and the Baptist is introduced later on in this Gospel as calling Christ the "bridegroom" and himself the "bridegroom's friend[5]." This suggests a new way in which we may interpret ὑπέρ in accordance with its legitimate meaning: "This is he *in behalf of whom* [*coming as the bridegroom's friend in behalf of the bridegroom*] I said, After me cometh a man...." It would be too much to substitute "husband" for "man": but a play upon the word, *suggesting* the former, may very well be intended. In the first statement of the Baptist's evidence the word "man" did not occur (i. 15) "This was he (lit.) that (1927) I said (οὗτος ἦν ὃν εἶπον), He that cometh after me...." The insertion of the word ἀνήρ is therefore all the more remarkable here: and so is the insertion of ὑπέρ. We may suppose that in the first moment of discovery the Baptist simply announces a superior. After an interval he is able to define the superiority: "He is the

---

[1] [2370 a] *E.g.* in Xen. *Cyrop.* vii. 15. 17 Abradates has been, in effect, pleading in behalf of the flanks of the army that they will be exposed while he himself will be so safe that he is almost ashamed to take the position assigned to him. Cyrus replies, "Well, if your part [of the army] is right, be not alarmed *for* them (εἰ τὰ παρὰ σοὶ καλῶς ἔχει θάρρει ὑπὲρ ἐκείνων)." See **2719** a.

[2] 2 Cor. v. 20.   [3] Cramer *ad loc.*

[4] [2371 a] In iv. 16, 17, 18 the context shews that it *must* mean "husband." In i. 13 οὐδὲ ἐκ θελήματος ἀνδρός, the use of ἀνήρ instead of ἄνθρωπος *may* indicate "husband," the meaning being "not by mortal begetting." See **2722** c.

[5] Jn iii. 29.

ἀνήρ, the lord, the husband of Israel. I came and spoke *in his behalf, preparing the way for him as the bridegroom*[1]." See 2718—22.

(xviii) Ὑπό **and** ὑποκάτω

(1) Ὑπό with Accusative

[2372] Ὑπό with accusative occurs only in i. 48 "Before Philip called thee being *under the fig-tree* I saw thee (πρὸ τοῦ σε Φίλιππον φωνῆσαι ὄντα ὑπὸ τὴν συκῆν εἶδόν σε)." This should be compared with the following, which contains the only instance of ὑποκάτω in John, i. 50 "Because I said to thee that I saw thee *underneath the fig-tree* (ὅτι εἶδόν σε ὑποκάτω τῆς συκῆς) thou believest!" Here a phrase with ὑπό and accusative is quoted with ὑποκάτω and genitive. Perhaps the more emphatic form ὑποκάτω, "under cover of," emphasizes the notion of secrecy: "Because I said to thee that I saw thee *under cover of a fig-tree* [as if that were, in thine eyes, so very marvellous]." The same substitution is found in Luke's, as compared with Mark's, description of the suppressed light. Mark has "*under* the bed," but Luke "*under cover of* a bed," or "*thrust down under* a bed[2]."

---

[1] [2371 *b*] For ὑπέρ with personal object and verb of speaking, comp. Xen. *Cyrop.* iii. 3. 14 ἐπεὶ οὖν σὺ σιωπᾷς ἐγὼ λέξω καὶ ὑπὲρ σοῦ καὶ ὑπὲρ ἡμῶν, Polyb. xxi. 14. 9 ταῦτα...ἀπεφήνατο ὑπὲρ παντὸς τοῦ συνεδρίου, xxviii. 16. 4 ὑπὲρ ἧς [πρεσβείας] ἐποιεῖτο τὸν χρηματισμὸν καὶ τοὺς λόγους.

[2] [2372 *a*] Mk iv. 21 ὑπὸ τὴν κλίνην, Lk. viii. 16 ὑποκάτω κλίνης. In LXX, (1) "under the tree, oak, pomegranate etc." is regularly ὑπό *with accusative*, but (2) "under every green tree," referring to idolatry, is regularly ὑποκάτω (in Is. lvii. 5, where LXX has ὑπό, Aq. and the rest have ὑποκάτω) with genitive. By so allusive a writer as Jn this distinction might be utilised here if the intention was to indicate in the second phrase (ὑποκάτω) that Nathanael was passing through some spiritual crisis and perhaps wrestling with the solicitations of evil thoughts just before Philip called him.

[2372 *b*] There is ambiguity in the first words, πρὸ τοῦ...συκῆν. The caller might be Nathanael or Philip, and either Philip or Nathanael might be under the fig-tree. We have to infer the meaning from the context. And, even when εἶδόν σε is added, there is still ambiguity. Ὄντα may agree with (1) the preceding or (2) the following σε: and the meaning may be (1) "[Long, or just] before Philip called thee at the moment when thou wast under the fig-tree—I saw thee," (2) "[Just] before Philip called thee—I saw thee in that moment when thou wast under the fig-tree."

[2372 *c*] Chrysostom has a long and not very clear commentary, in the course of which he seems to assert that Christ had seen Nathanael not only "*just before* (πρὶν ἢ φωνῆσαι)" the calling but also "*before this* (πρὸ τούτου)": only the time had not come to say this. And yet Chrysostom previously says "But Jesus

(2) Ὑπό with Genitive

[2373] Ὑπό with the genitive is avoided by John (1885) as he prefers to speak of an agent performing an action rather than of an act performed by (ὑπό) an agent. It occurs only in xiv. 21 ὁ ἔχων τὰς ἐντολάς μου κ. τηρῶν αὐτὰς ἐκεῖνός ἐστιν ὁ ἀγαπῶν με· ὁ δὲ ἀγαπῶν με ἀγαπηθήσεται ὑπὸ τ. πατρός μου, where perhaps the writer desires to repeat precisely the words ὁ ἀγαπῶν με so that they may constitute the two middle terms of the sentence (2544 a). Perhaps the frequency of the nominatives ὁ ἀγαπῶν and ὁ μὴ ἀγαπῶν in the Epistle (1 Jn ii. 10, iii. 10, 14, iv. 7 etc.) may partly explain the shape of the sentence here. Had the verb been τιμάω we should have expected ἐάν τις ἐμὲ τιμᾷ τιμήσει αὐτὸν ὁ πατήρ similarly to xii. 26.

PRONOUNS

I. DEMONSTATIVE

(i) Αὐτός (see also 2723—7)

[2374] Αὐτός (nom. sing.), in Luke[1], sometimes means "he" (unemphatic); but John uses it always to mean "himself," sometimes in a context mentioning other persons ("*himself* (αὐτός) and his mother," "*himself* and his household[2]") but more often without such context to mean "of his own knowledge, or motion," "unaided," "unprompted," *e.g.* ii. 24—5 "But Jesus [*of*] *himself* (ἀ. δὲ Ἰ.) would not trust himself to them because he understood [*of*] *himself* (διὰ τὸ αὐτὸν γινώσκειν) all men...for he knew [*of*] *himself* (αὐτὸς γὰρ ἐγίνω-

---

answered as God. For indeed He said I have known thee from the beginning...and 'But now (*i.e.* just now) did I see thee in the fig-tree (Καὶ γὰρ εἶπεν, ὅτι Ἀνωθέν σε οἶδα...καὶ, Νῦν εἶδόν σε ἐν τῇ συκῇ...).'" Probably καὶ γὰρ εἶπεν means "For indeed He *said* [*in effect*]" i.e. He meant. And Chrysostom perhaps implies that the words of Jesus *contained both* of the meanings above mentioned, though the time had not yet come when the former ("long before") could be clearly expressed. It will be noted that he paraphrases "*under* the fig-tree" as "*in* [*the covert of*] the fig-tree."

[1] [2374a] Comp. Lk. xix. 2 καὶ ἰδοὺ ἀνὴρ ὀνόματι Ζακ. καὶ αὐτὸς ἦν ἀρχιτελώνης with Judg. xvii. 7 καὶ ἐγενήθη νεανίας...καὶ αὐτὸς Λευείτης, a literal rendering of the Heb. "and he [was] a Levite," and see Lk. iv. 14—15, viii. 1 etc. In Lk., this use is probably Hebraic.

[2] [2374b] Jn ii. 12, iv. 2, 12, 53, xviii. 1 (R.V.) "*he* entered *himself* (ἀ.) and his disciples," (A.V.) "*he* entered and his disciples."

σκεν) what was in man¹," vi. 6 "*For he himself* (ἀ. γὰρ) knew [*i.e.* he knew of himself, although he asked a question]...."

[2375] So in vi. 15 "Jesus withdrew again into the mountain *himself alone*," αὐτὸς μόνος is in contrast with the multitude that wished to seize Him, and perhaps it does not merely mean "by himself alone." Several authorities omit αὐτός. Perhaps it has a mystical emphasis (2724—6). The same phrase, αὐτὸς μόνος, is applied to the grain of seed that will not die, xii. 24, A.V. "It abideth alone," but R.V. "it abideth *by itself* alone." It would be well to use the emphatic pronoun elsewhere, *e.g.* vii. 10 "Then he *himself* also went up [following his brethren]." In v. 20 "The Father loveth the Son and sheweth him all things that *he himself* doeth," R.V. has "*himself*," but does not have it in xii. 49 "The Father that sent me hath *himself* given me commandment (ὁ πέμψας με πατὴρ αὐτός μοι ἐντολὴν δέδωκεν)." In the latter, αὐτός is not quite the same as ἐκεῖνος, "He and no other"; it is rather, "He in His own person," or "He in His own character of Father²."

[2376] Αὐτούς (accus. pl. masc.) occurs very frequently in the Synoptic narrative, to denote disciples, multitudes, Pharisees etc., in relation to Jesus, describing how Jesus "taught *them*," "healed *them*," "called *them*," "sent *them*," "questioned *them*" etc. In John it occurs *thus* only four times³ (excluding one instance in an interpolated passage⁴). On the other hand it occurs nine times in Christ's Last Prayer referring to the disciples, when He is praying to the Father concerning "them⁵."

---

¹ [2374c] A.V. omits "self" in each of the three cases, R.V. in every case but the third. The threefold repetition of αὐτός is remarkable. In reality it does not mean "Jesus, by himself"—for Jesus repeatedly declared that He does nothing "from, or by, himself"—but Jesus being one with the Father or with the Spirit. Comp. the threefold repetition of ταῦτα in 2396—7.

² [2375a] In xii. 49 R.V. has "The Father which sent me, he hath given me...." In vii. 4 οὐδεὶς γάρ τι ἐν κρυπτῷ ποιεῖ καὶ ζητεῖ ⌜αὐτὸς⌝ ἐν παρρησίᾳ εἶναι, the txt, if correct, means "himself in opposition to his work." W.H. marg. has αὐτό, with BD *d*; but (1) c might be dropped before ε, (2) although Syr. Cur. omits αὐτός, SS inserts it, (3) ζητῶ with accus. and inf. is not found in N.T. See 2727.

³ Disciples in i. 38, vi. 17, xiii. 1, soldiers in xviii. 7.

⁴ viii. 2.

⁵ [2376a] xvii. 6—23. The nom. pl. αὐτοί is used (perh. in a more personal and emotional sense than ἐκεῖνοι) in Christ's Prayer for the disciples, xvii. 19 "that they may be also *themselves* hallowed," xvii. 21 "that they may be also *themselves* in us." In xvii. 8 καὶ αὐτοὶ ἔλαβον, there is perh. a notion of spon-

DEMONSTRATIVE [2378]

[2377] In xviii. 11 τὸ ποτήριον...οὐ μὴ πίω αὐτό, there is probably a combination of two constructions (1) "that very cup (αὐτὸ τ. π.)," *i.e.* the cup just as the Father presents it, and (2) the repetition of αὐτό (more usually ἐκεῖνο) to emphasize the object[1]. In xx. 2—15, after Mary has said "They have taken the Lord out of the tomb," the two disciples run thither, and one of them happens to be indicated by a pronoun (xx. 6 "Simon Peter following *him*"): but the narrative proceeds to describe how Peter (xx. 7) "entered into the tomb, and beholdeth...the napkin, which had [before] been upon *his* head," where "his," of course, means "the Lord's"—very naturally and dramatically since "the Lord" is in the mind of the evangelist and is assumed by him to be in the minds of sympathetic readers: and similarly Mary addressing, for the first time (as she supposes), the "gardener," says "Sir, if thou hast conveyed *him* away," although the "gardener" has merely said, "Whom seekest thou[2]?"

[2378] The meaning of αὐτοῦ is disputed in the following, viii. 44 " He (ἐκεῖνος) was a murderer from the beginning and stood (ἔστηκεν) not in the truth because there is no truth in him. Whenever he is speaking *that which is false* (τὸ ψεῦδος) he speaketh out of his own (ἐκ τῶν ἰδίων) (2728); because he is a false speaker (ψεύστης) and the father *of it* (αὐτοῦ).ʺ Here "*of it*" probably means "of that which is false." Falsehood is regarded as being slanderous, *i.e.* diabolic, or Satanic. Whenever Satan utters that which is false he speaks "out of the abundance of his heart," "out of his inmost nature"; but it is also suggested (by "your father" in the context) that, when the Slanderer causes men to slander, *he speaks out of them as "his family"*—ἰδίων being either masculine or neuter. For Origen's and Chrysostom's views see **2728**. R.V. has "speaketh *of* his own"—which, if "of" is meant for "from" (as in "give *of*," "take *of*"), is probably not English (**2728** *b*), or only the English of scholars.

---

taneousness, "and they *of themselves* received the words I gave them." (In xvii. 11 αὐτοί (v. r. οὗτοι), if genuine, is antithetical to the following ἐγώ.)

[1] [2377 *a*] Winer-Moulton p. 184, after quoting Jn xviii. 11, says "The pronoun is used for emphasis: so also in Mt. vi. 4, 1 Pet. v. 10 (Acts ii. 23), Rev. xxi. 6." But W.H. reject αὐτός in Mt. vi. 4, Rev. xxi. 6, not even giving it in the margin. In 1 Pet. v. 10 αὐτὸς καταρτίσει probably implies the willingness of the Father to strengthen those who resist temptation (not "*He* [as distinct from others]"). In such a solemn utterance as xviii. 11, it is hardly possible that αὐτό should be "pleonastic."

[2] On αὐτοῦ, as distinct from ἑαυτοῦ or ἴδιος, used possessively, see **1720** *a—i*.

[2379] Some have suggested that αὐτοῦ above (viii. 44) refers to τις "anyone," implied as the subject of λαλῇ, "Whenever anyone speaks...he is a liar, and *so is his father*," i.e. so is the devil. But (1) the alleged instances of the omitted τις are quite different from the context here[1]. (2) Such an end to a sentence as καὶ ὁ πατὴρ αὐτοῦ, leaving the reader to supply "is the same," or "likewise a liar," is quite unparalleled in this Gospel. (3) Where the subject is omitted, it would not be permissible (except in very special cases, such as Mt. xix. 3 ἔξεστιν [τινί], "a man may") to use a pronoun referring back to the non-existent subject.

[2380] In xi. 45—6 "Many therefore of the Jews, [by 'many' I mean] those that had come (οἱ ἐλθόντες) to Mary...believed in him: but some of *them* (τινὲς δὲ ἐξ αὐτῶν) went away to the Pharisees and told them...," the pronoun "*them*" may mean either "the Jews" or that section of the Jews which "had come to Mary." For a discussion of this see **1941** foll. It is not likely that those who "told the Pharisees" told them from good will to Jesus, desiring to glorify the latter: for, had that been the meaning, the writer would probably have used "and," or "therefore," instead of "but" ("*but* some of them went[2]").

---

[1] [2379 a] Of the instances alleged by Winer-Moulton p. 736 n. 3, Job xxviii. 3 has "man" supplied in R.V. but "He" (*i.e.* God) in A.V.; both R.V. and A.V. agree in supplying "God" in the context (xxvii. 22), and its poetic character makes it of little use as a parallel to Jn. In 2 S. xvi. 23, ὃν τρόπον ἐπερωτήσῃ is a literal rendering of Hebrew, "as though [one] were to take counsel," and has little bearing on independent Greek. In Mt. xix. 3, τινι may be easily supplied after ἔξεστιν, "[one] is permitted," and the parall. Mk x. 2 has ἀνδρί. In 1 Thess. iv. 9, the substantival infinitive in οὐ χρείαν ἔχετε γράφειν ὑμῖν is very doubtful, having regard to (1) εἴχομεν in B, ἔχομεν in other good authorities, γράφεσθαι in some authorities, and to (2) the likelihood of conformity to 1 Thess. v. 1 οὐ χρείαν ἔχετε ὑμῖν γράφεσθαι. In any case it supplies no parallel to λαλῇ in Jn viii. 44.

[2379 b] Winer himself does not recognise the omission of the indefinite τις in any instance except where the subject can be supplied by the reader from his own knowledge or reading, or where it means "God," "Scripture," "the sacred writer" etc.: and, though it is frequent in LXX (as literal transl. of Hebrew, *e.g.* Ezr. iv. 15 "that [one] may search" ἐπισκέψηται, but 1 Esdr. ii. 18 ἐπισκεφθῇ) it requires more support than is alleged by Winer-Moulton before it can be recognised in any book of N.T., and especially in John, who had other ways of expressing himself (ἐάν τις λαλῇ, ὁ λαλῶν etc.), so that antecedently he would not be likely to use such an ellipsis even if the other evangelists used it.

[2] [2380 a] It may be said that the impotent man cured by Jesus gave information similarly (v. 15) to the Jews. But we are not told that he "believed in Jesus"; and it is quite possible that the evangelist regarded him as ungrateful and unbelieving—a contrast to the blind man, of whom it is expressly said that (ix. 36—8) he "worshipped," after expressing "belief."

DEMONSTRATIVE [2382]

It is difficult to explain how some of those who "believed in" Jesus could (apparently) act against Him. Possibly, it is one of the instances of John's manner of stating a fact, first, loosely and (strictly speaking) even inaccurately, and then correcting the statement (1925). If so, the meaning may be "those that had come to Mary [as a whole or, almost without exception]...believed...but some [few] of them [did not believe, but] went away to the Pharisees..." For ὅς = αὐτός or ἐκεῖνος, see below[1].

(ii) Ἐκεῖνος (see also 2729—32)

[2381] This pronoun is used frequently by all the evangelists as an adjective, especially in temporal phrases such as "in those days," "from that hour" etc., and all the Synoptists have it in the phrase "woe unto that man (τῷ ἀνθρώπῳ ἐκείνῳ)[2]." But the singular, as a personal pronoun, is almost confined to John[3]. He uses it sometimes, without much apparent emphasis, in narrating a dialogue ("*he* answered," "*he* saith") to mean "*he, on his side*, replied, said, denied etc.[4]"

[2382] Outside dialogue, when John uses ἐκεῖνος in his own words, or in the words of others reported in the first person, it generally has considerable emphasis as in i. 8 "*He* was not the Light" (*i.e.* do not suppose that *he*, the Baptist, was the Light), i. 18 "The only begotten...*he* [*and no other*] hath declared," i. 33 "He that sent me...*he* [*and no other*] said to me," ii. 21 "[The Jews took the words literally] but *he* was speaking about...[5]." It is often used by the Son concerning the Father, v. 19 "Whatsoever things *he* doeth" and similarly in v. 38, vi. 29, viii. 42. The Samaritan woman also uses it about the Messiah, iv. 25 "when *he* (emph.) (ἐ.)

---

[1] [2380 *b*] In v. 11 ὃς δὲ ἀπεκρίθη αὐτοῖς, AB alone retain ὃς δέ, which is omitted or changed to ὁ δέ by other authorities. Ὃς δέ is prob. more emphatic than ὁ δέ and less emphatic than αὐτὸς δέ (which, in Jn, would mean "he [of] himself said"). Ὅς, in this sense, occurs in N.T. elsewhere only in Mk xv. 23 ὃς δὲ οὐκ ἔλαβεν (where אB and 33 almost alone preserve ὅς). It is one of several curious characteristics common to Mk and Jn. Steph. gives abundant instances of καὶ ὅς in Plato and Xen., but none of ὃς δέ. But comp. Job xxii. 18 ὃς δὲ ἐνέπλησεν, where ὅς represents the Heb. pron. "he" and is emphatic, Aq. and Theod. have καὶ αὐτός (A ὅτε γε), Tob. v. 13 ὃς δὲ εἶπεν, Ἐγὼ Ἀζαρίας (א καὶ εἶπεν αὐτῷ). Ὃς μέν...ὃς δέ does not occur in Jn. [2] Mk xiv. 21, Mt. xxvi. 24, Lk. xxii. 22.

[3] Lk. xviii. 14 has παρ᾽ ἐκεῖνον, Mk-App. xvi. 10 has ἐκείνη.

[4] Jn ix. 11, 25, 36 (?), xviii. 17, 21.

[5] Comp. the pl. in x. 6 "But *they* (ἐ. δὲ) did not know," xi. 13 "But *they* thought...."

cometh, he (unemph.) will tell us all things." In the Epistle, it is the pronoun used to denote Christ, as being the Person always before the writer's mind as his example. Ἐκεῖνος is used thus six times there, and in no other sense[1].

[2383] In John, ἐκεῖνος[2], when preceded by καί, is generally combined with it in the form κἀκεῖνος. The following is exceptional, xix. 35 "And he that hath seen hath borne witness, and his witness is true (ἀλ. αὐτοῦ ἐστὶν ἡ μαρτυρία) *and he* (καὶ ἐκεῖνος[3]) knoweth that he (unemph.) saith true (οἶδεν ὅτι ἀληθῆ λέγει), in order that ye also may believe." Here ἐκεῖνος might theoretically be a mere emphatic substitute for the preceding αὐτός. Then the meaning would be simply, "he that hath seen is quite certain that he himself is speaking the truth." But this does not make very impressive sense, whereas the occasion demands something not only impressive but uniquely impressive. Moreover it seems to demand *a combination of more witnesses than one*, as in the Gospel, where (viii. 17) "the testimony of two men" is mentioned, or in the Epistle, where (1 Jn v. 8) "three" witnesses are mentioned in connexion with "the water," "the blood," and "the spirit."

[2384] The passage may perhaps in some respects be illustrated by v. 32 "*Another is he that witnesseth* concerning me and I know that the witness..is true," where, though Chrysostom supposes Jesus to mean the Baptist, He probably means (2730) the Father, who "witnesseth" to the Son by the works that He (v. 36) "hath given" to the Son to accomplish. St Paul appeals sometimes to the testimony, as it were, or presence, of God or Christ[4]; and, on one occasion, not long after the words "the God and Father of the Lord Jesus Christ...knoweth that I lie not," he passes to "visions and revelations of the Lord[5]." So here, we appear to have a solemn appeal on the part of the evangelist touching the truth of a statement that he obviously regards as symbolical of a profound mystery not apparent to the soldiers at the crucifixion but revealed to him. To whom should he appeal except to the Lord Himself from whose side

---

[1] 1 Jn ii. 6 (see Westc.), iii. 3, 5, 7, 16, iv. 17. The fem. occurs in v. 16, the neut. never. Comp. 2 Pet. i. 16 ἐπόπται...τῆς ἐκείνου μεγαλειότητος.

[2] [2383 a] Perhaps the only exception in Jn, besides the one above discussed, is v. 39 "Ye search the Scriptures, and they are they (καὶ ἐκεῖναί εἰσιν) that testify concerning me."

[3] Alford reads κἀκεῖνος with ℵ.

[4] Rom. ix. 1, Gal. i. 20, 2 Cor. xi. 10—11.   [5] 2 Cor. xi. 31 *foll.*

(as he declares) there flowed forth "blood and water"? But, if so, we have seen from the Epistle (**2382**) that the evangelist might naturally speak of the Lord as ἐκεῖνος, when recording His testimony to the truth of a tradition revealed to "him that had seen it," whether in a vision or otherwise, "And he that hath seen hath borne witness, and his witness is true, and *He knoweth* that he saith true, that ye also may believe[1]." For a parallel from Barnabas, see **2731**.

[**2385**] Chrysostom has the following comment on vii. 11 ποῦ ἐστὶν ἐκεῖνος; "By reason of their great hatred and rancour they would not even call Him by His name[2]." The same pronoun that might mean, in the mouths of admirers, "*that [great] man*," might mean, in the mouths of enemies, "*that [notorious] man.*" In vii. 45 "There came therefore the officers to the chief priests and Pharisees and *they* (ἐκεῖνοι) said to them, Why did ye not bring him?"—we must bear in mind that John has previously described (vii. 32) "the chief priests and the Pharisees" as sending officers to arrest Jesus. Meantime, he has told us about the talk of "the multitude," of whom "some" say this, "others" that, some for, some against, Jesus: now, in contrast with the "division" in the multitude, he describes the fixed and virulent determination of the Pharisees by emphasising the pronoun in "*they* said[3]." See also **2732**.

---

[1] [**2384** *a*] If the evangelist is distinct from "him that hath seen," then this sentence implies three witnesses. It should be noted that this evangelist alone records that the Saviour, after the Resurrection, shewed the disciples His wounded side (xx. 20, 27). Nonnus (ἴδμεν) prob. read οἴδαμεν.

[**2384** *b*] On xix. 35 Blass (p. 172) says, "There is doubt about the whole verse, which is wanting in *e*, and Cod. Fuldensis of the Vulgate, about this particular clause [*i.e.* the ἐκεῖνος clause], about the text of this clause, as Nonnus read ἐκεῖνον οἴδαμεν, etc." But *e*, besides omitting the verse, alters the order of the preceding words "sanguis et aqua" to "aqua et sanguis"; and it is possible that the omission may be from homoeotel., in passing from -is in sanguis to the -is in " credatis" ("ut et vos credat*is*"). So difficult a verse might naturally be amended into ἐκεῖνον οἴδαμεν; but the emendation is manifestly based on xxi. 24 οἴδαμεν ὅτι ἀληθὴς αὐτοῦ ἡ μαρτυρία ἐστίν. But there is great force in Blass's warning against basing " theories as to the origin of the fourth Gospel on this verse," and in his objection to "the meaning ordinarily attached to it."

[2] So, too, Cramer, τίνος ἕνεκεν...; ὑπὸ πολλοῦ μίσους καὶ τῆς ἀπεχθείας συνεχόμενοι.

[3] [**2385** *a*] The antithesis is much more obvious in Acts iii. 13 ὃν ὑμεῖς μὲν παρεδώκατε...κατὰ πρόσωπον Πειλάτου κρίναντος ἐκείνου ἀπολύειν, "*Ye on your side* delivered up...when *he on his side* had decided to acquit." In the context of Jn there is no μέν and there is a considerable interval between ἐκεῖνος and the earlier member of the antithesis. Still, antithesis is the explanation.

[2386]　　　　　　　　PRONOUNS

(iii) Οὗτος

[2386] Οὗτος nom. sing. masc. is about as frequent in John as in Mark and Luke taken together. This arises partly from the frequency of testimonies to Christ from the Baptist and others ("this is he that...")[1], but partly also from the evangelist's habit of using οὗτος after a previous description to sum up, or repeat, i. 1—2 "In the beginning was the Word...*this* [*same*] was in the beginning with God." So, too, at the close of his Gospel, after the many hints and suggestions as to "the disciple that Jesus loved" etc., xxi. 24 "*This* [*same*] is the disciple that testifieth concerning these things...." Οὗτος is also used, in apposition, to sum up a collective participle, vi. 46 ὁ ὢν παρὰ [τοῦ] θεοῦ, οὗτος..., vii. 18 ὁ δὲ ζητῶν...οὗτος, xv. 5 ὁ μένων...οὗτος (where the meaning would be quite different if οὗτος were after a participle without a pause, *e.g.* ὁ μένων οὗτος, "this man that remains"). In all these cases, the meaning is that *if* a man does a certain antecedent act, then "this [same] man (οὗτος)" also does a consequent act[2].

---

[1] [2386 a] i. 15 (reading ὃν εἶπον), i. 30, 34, iv. 42, vi. 14, vii. 40. In i. 34 (W. H.) οὗτός ἐστιν ὁ υἱὸς τ. θεοῦ, the reading ἐκλεκτός for υἱός, supported by SS and ℵ (815), appears to have been in the txt of a papyrus of the 3rd century, *Oxyr. Pap.* vol. ii. p. 7, where the editors have shewn that a lacuna is prob. to be filled thus.

[2] [2386 b] In the Epistle, οὗτος nóm. sing. masc. occurs only thrice, ii. 22 ὁ. ἐστιν ὁ ἀντίχριστος, v. 6 ὁ. ἐστιν ὁ ἐλθὼν δι᾽ ὕδατος κ. αἵματος, v. 20 ὁ. ἐστιν ὁ ἀληθινὸς θεός. On the difference between οὗτος ὁ ἀ. and ὁ ἀ. οὗτος, see **2553** c. The following is exceptional, ix. 16 οὐκ ἔστιν οὗτος παρὰ θεοῦ—ὁ ἄνθρωπος (altered by many authorities, but probably meaning "This [man] is not from God—this fellow!" contemptuously, and at the same time perhaps intended by the evangelist to suggest an inner meaning—a radical sense of antagonism between "God" and "man," resulting in a rejection of the doctrine of the Incarnation). In xii. 18 ἤκουσαν τοῦτο αὐτὸν πεποιηκέναι—τὸ σημεῖον, the meaning seems to be "They heard that he had done this—[this great] sign."

[2386 c] On xxi. 21 οὗτος δὲ τί; Blass (p. 177) compares Acts xii. 18 τί ἄρα ὁ Πέτρος ἐγένετο, Lk. i. 66 τί ἄρα τὸ παιδίον ἔσται; Joseph. *Vit.* § 296 οἱ εἴκοσι χρυσοῖ τί γεγόνασιν; Xen. *Hell.* ii. 3. 17 τί ἔσοιτο ἡ πολιτεία, and gives the rendering "what will become of him?" This is possible. But in all these instances there is no ellipsis. And the context in xxi. 21 points (**2209**) to some *action*, something more than mere passive "becoming." Comp. Luc. *Dial. Mort.* vii. 2 (i. 357) ὁ γέρων δὲ τί πρὸς ταῦτα; "and the old man—*what* [*did*] he in consequence?" Plat. *Gorg.* 502 A τί δὲ ὁ πατὴρ αὐτοῦ Μέλης; *ib. Rep.* 332 E τίς δὲ πλέοντας [δυνατώτατός ἐστιν εὖ ποιεῖν] πρὸς τὸν τῆς θαλάττης κίνδυνον; Κυβερνήτης. Τί δὲ ὁ δίκαιος; All these imply contrast, "so-and-so did thus: *what shall this man do?*"—so that they are parallel to xxi. 21. Nonnus supplies τελέσσει.

DEMONSTRATIVE [2386 (i)]

[2386 (i)] Οὗτος, if connected with a noun and not used predicatively, requires an intervening article as in classical Greek[1]. In ii. 11 ταύτην ἐποίησεν ἀρχὴν τῶν σημείων, R.V. has "*this beginning of his signs*," following ℵ and Chrys., who read τὴν ἀρχήν[2]—an interpolation so natural that its non-prevalence in the MSS. is surprising. Basilides, after speaking of the ineffable spiritual life, likens it to the water at Cana and says, "This is the great and genuine 'beginning of the signs,' [that beginning] which Jesus wrought in Cana of Galilee[3]." Origen comments on the fact that the Synoptists did not give the title "beginning of the signs" to the first "wonders" or "mighty works" wrought at Capernaum. He takes "beginning" as appositional or predicative and as meaning "chief of signs (προηγούμενον σημείων)," and he justifies this by saying that the creation of the draughts of sober joy is greater than acts of healing[4]. A similar predicative use of ἀρχή occurs in O.T. once, and perhaps only once, Prov. viii. 22 κύριος ἔκτισέ με ἀρχὴν ὁδῶν αὐτοῦ, about the creation of Wisdom[5]. The Hebrew word there rendered κτίζω is *cana*—Targum *bara* "create"—and means κτάομαι as well as κτίζω: and Aquila and the rest substitute ἐκτήσατο. Κτῆσις, or κτῆμα, is accepted by Origen as representing the meaning of Cana[6]. In the first verse of Genesis, where LXX has ποιέω for the Hebrew *bara* "create," Aquila has κτίζω. Philo (i. 361), inveighing against drunkenness, quotes the passage from Proverbs thus, ὁ θεὸς ἐκτήσατό με πρωτίστην τῶν ἑαυτοῦ ἔργων[7]. These facts shew that ποιέω, κτίζω, and κτάομαι might be interchanged. Origen's direct comment on "Cana"

---

[1] [2386 (i) *a*] Ezr. x. 9 οὗτος μὴν ὁ ἔνατος is a literal rendering of Heb. and means "this [is] month the ninth," parall. to 1 Esdr. ix. 5 οὗτος ὁ μὴν ἔνατος—perhaps intended to mean, "this month [is] ninth in the year." Comp. 1 Chr. xi. 4 αὕτη Ἰεβούς "this [is] Jebus."

[2] [2386 (i) *b*] Alf. omits Chrys., but mentions "Eus₁ [-mss.]." As he does not mention Clem. Alex., he presumably refers to Eus. iii. 24. 11, quoting Clem. Alex. ταύτην ἀρχὴν ἐποίησε τῶν παραδόξων ὁ Ἰησοῦς. But Heinichen and Schwegler mention τήν only as an inferior reading (ταύτην τὴν ἀρχήν).

[3] [2386 (i) *c*] Hipp. v. 8 (pp. 107—9) αὕτη, φησίν, ἐστὶν ἡ μεγάλη καὶ ἀληθινὴ ἀρχὴ τῶν σημείων, ἣν ἐποίησεν ὁ Ἰησοῦς ἐν Κ. τῆς Γ. Nonnus has Πρωτοφανὲς τόδε θαῦμα...ἐτέλεσσεν.

[4] Lomm. vol. i. 295—6.

[5] [2386 (i) *d*] Comp. Sir. xxiv. 9 (A) πρὸ τοῦ αἰῶνος ἀπαρχὴν ἔκτισέ με.

[6] Lomm. ii. 117 βεβαιῶν ἑαυτῷ κτῆσιν τῶν ἀπὸ ταύτης τῆς γῆς πιστευόντων εἰς τὸν πατέρα δι' αὐτοῦ, *ib*. 128 παρὰ τὸ κτῆμα αὐτοῦ...Κανᾶ ὠνομάσθη.

[7] Philo proceeds (i. 362) to describe the infinite flow of the graces of God as a fountain (ἐπιρρεούσης τῆς τοῦ θεοῦ χαρίτων πηγῆς).

is lost; but he refers to what he had written as indicating that it denoted the "creation" or "acquiring" of the Church by Christ; and the Hebrew *cana* is used in O.T. of God (Gesen. 888—9) (1) "creating" heaven or Israel, and (2) "acquiring" or "redeeming" His people. The latter is symbolized in O.T. by wedlock. Using the same metaphor, Origen warns men to "abstain from the harlot Matter (ὕλη) and to be made one with the Logos that was in the beginning with God, and with His Wisdom, whom *He created as the beginning of His ways*[1]." The facts indicate that ii. 11 ταύτην ἐποίησεν ἀρχήν means τοῦτο ἐποίησεν ὡς (or ὥστε εἶναι) ἀρχήν, that it is intended to sum up a typical description of the marriage feast of the Logos or Wisdom of God, that it was based on the above-quoted passage in Proverbs, and that Origen has rightly interpreted its inner meaning.

(*a*) Διὰ τοῦτο

[2387] Διὰ τοῦτο, "for this cause," "consequently," is almost always placed by John at the beginning of the sentence. An exception is xv. 19 "If ye were of the world the world would love its own. But because ye are not of the world but I chose you out of the world—*for this cause* (διὰ τοῦτο) the world hateth you." The initial "for this cause" is so frequent elsewhere that we may infer that here, too, John writes with the *feeling* that he is introducing a new sentence, as though the last terminated with the statement "I chose you out of the world," as a consequence of which, "the world hateth" them[2]. Another exception, according to R.V., is i. 31 "And I knew him not; but that (ἀλλ' ἵνα) he should be made manifest to Israel *for this cause* came I baptizing with water." Here, however, there is probably (**2064**) an ellipsis, as in other cases, before

---

[1] [**2386** (i) *e*] Lomm. ii. 233. Origen perh. has in his mind the context in Proverbs which contrasts Wisdom, who cries to men "Drink of the wine that I have mingled" with Folly, or "the Foolish Woman," who cries "Stolen waters are sweet" (Prov. ix. 5—17). Epiphan. p. 443 A has τοῦτο πρῶτον σημεῖον ἐποίησεν, and Chrys. quoting with τὴν ἀρχήν, says εἴτε δὲ τοῦτο εἴτε ἕτερον πρῶτον σημεῖον ἐγένετο τῶν μετὰ τὸ βάπτισμα γενομένων οὐ σφόδρα διισχυρίζεσθαι ἀναγκαῖον εἶναί μοι δοκεῖ. Their words indicate that any Greek writer would naturally have used πρῶτον if he had meant merely "first," but that John meant something more.

[2] [**2387** *a*] The three instances in which N.T. (Bruder) quotes from O.T. clauses with διὰ τοῦτο, all have it at the beginning, Acts ii. 26, Rom. xv. 9, Heb. i. 9.

ἵνα, and the rendering should be "But [it came to pass] in order that he should be made manifest to Israel. *For this cause* came I etc."

[2388] In vii. 21—2, "...I did one work [on the sabbath] and ye all marvel. *For this cause* hath Moses given you circumcision... and on the sabbath ye circumcise a man," R.V. marg. gives "and ye all marvel *because of this*." But the text is to be preferred (in consequence of the regular Johannine usage) in spite of its difficulty, the meaning of *"for this cause"* being, perhaps, "in order to typify the subordination of the sabbath to man." The words point back to the cure just effected on the sabbath, at which the Jews, instead of welcoming it, "marvel," *i.e.* are amazed with a foolish and faithless amazement (1673 *a—e*). Rebuking them, Jesus says, *"For this cause,"* i.e., for the cause of kindness, to reveal love and not law as the key to the mysteries of the Father, there has been ordained the rite of circumcision, always on the eighth day after birth, so that ye are forced sometimes to circumcise on the sabbath.

[2389] Διὰ τοῦτο, with an interval, frequently precedes ὅτι, *"because,"* e.g. viii. 47 "He that is from God heareth the words of God. *For this cause* (διὰ τοῦτο) ye hear not, *because* (ὅτι) ye are not from God." Here, *"for this cause"* looks back to the general cause ("he that is...") and then forward to the particular cause ("ye are not..."). Some such restatement of a cause (*"because of this*, which I have just mentioned,...*because, in other words*, so and so happened") is very frequent in John. The phrase is almost always in asyndeton; but it is preceded by "and" and followed by "therefore" in one of the very few passages where it occurs in narrative, v. 15—18 "The man...told the Jews that it was Jesus that had made him whole. *And* (καί) *for this cause* did the Jews persecute Jesus; *because* [*in other words*] (ὅτι) he did these things on the sabbath. But he answered them, My Father worketh...and I work. *For this cause therefore* (οὖν) the Jews sought rather (2733 *a*) to kill him, *because* [*in other words, or, from their point of view*] he not only brake the sabbath but also called God his own Father...[1]."

[2390] It is sometimes difficult to define exactly the noun

---

[1] [2389 *a*] Διὰ τοῦτο follows ἀλλά and precedes εἰς in xii. 27 (see 2512 *b—c*), "And what should I say? 'Father, save me from this hour'? *Nay* (ἀλλά), *for this cause* (διὰ τοῦτο) came I, to [meet] (εἰς) this hour." Here "for this cause" looks back to "this hour," and forward to a phrase in which "hour" is repeated for emphasis ("to [meet] this hour").

represented by τοῦτο, *e.g.* in xii. 37—40 "But...they did not believe, in order that the word of Isaiah might be fulfilled, 'Lord, who [hath] believed...?' *For this cause* they were not able to believe, *because* again Isaiah said, 'He hath blinded their eyes....'" Apparently, however, "*this*" means the Law of fulfilment of Prophecy as being the Will of the righteous God. Isaiah's question ("Who hath believed?") amounted to a predictive statement, "None believed." John, having expressed the fulfilment of this statement in the form "they *were not able* to believe," goes on to explain this by another prophecy referring to retributive blindness[1].

[2391] An apparent, but only apparent, exception (to διὰ τοῦτο looking back) occurs in x. 17 "*For this cause* doth my Father love me *because* I lay down my life." No doubt, the immediately preceding sentence (about "other sheep") contains nothing to which the phrase could well point. But we must go back further and take the passage as a whole: "Even as the Father knoweth me....*I lay down my life for the sheep*—and other sheep I have...and they shall become one flock, one shepherd. *For this cause* doth my Father love me *because* I lay down my life that I may take it again." It will then appear that "*for this cause*" looks back, past the intervening parenthesis, to the words "*lay down my life for the sheep*," which are repeated, with modification, after "because." Similarly in 1 Jn iii. 1 "...and we are [the children of God]. *For this cause* the world knoweth not us because it knew not him," the reference of "*this cause*" is to the preceding words, "*and we are* [the children of God]"; and the meaning is, "*Because we are His children* the world knows us not—naturally, because it knows not the Father."

(β) Ἐν τούτῳ

[2392] Ἐν τούτῳ, (neut.) "in this," "herein," "hereby[2]," occurs five times in the Gospel and twelve times in the Epistle. The uses are not quite similar. In the Epistle, when followed by ὅτι or ἐάν, it

---

[1] [2390 a] For διὰ τοῦτο (1) looking back to a previous statement and at the same time (2) preceding a sentence with initial ὅτι, see Ps. xvi. 8—10 (Acts ii. 26—7) διὰ τοῦτο ηὐφράνθη ἡ καρδία μου...καὶ ἡ σάρξ μου κατασκηνώσει ἐπ' ἐλπίδι. ὅτι οὐκ ἐνκαταλείψεις.... Here διὰ τοῦτο merely looks backward. Ὅτι begins a new sentence and introduces a restatement of the cause for joy ("*for indeed* thou wilt not leave my soul to Sheol") stated previously in the words "Because he is at my right hand I shall not be moved."

[2] Not in the Synoptists exc. Lk. x. 20 "*In this* rejoice not."

seems sometimes to look forward, as in 1 Jn ii. 3 "And *hereby* know we that we know him—*if* we keep his commandments," *i.e.* by the following test. There is nothing in the preceding context to which "hereby" can well point. In the Gospel it always looks back. But (like διὰ τοῦτο) it may also look forward to something supplementary. This, however, is not the case in iv. 36—7, "He that reapeth receiveth wages and gathereth fruit unto life eternal; in order that he that soweth and he that reapeth may rejoice together. For *herein* is the saying true that 'One soweth and another reapeth.'" Here the meaning is, that in the joy of the sowers and the reapers of the heavenly harvest there is fulfilled in the real and spiritual sense— namely, in the sense that the sower rejoices to sow for others—the proverb current among men of this transient world in the unreal saying that "fools sow and clever men reap." The ὅτι clause has nothing to do with ἐν τούτῳ but defines ὁ λόγος.

[2393] But ἐν τούτῳ is explained by a following ὅτι clause in ix. 30, where, the Pharisees having said "We know not," the blind man just healed says "*Herein* [*i.e.* in your not knowing] is the marvel [namely] *because* (ὅτι) ye know not whence he is, and [yet] he opened mine eyes." In xiii. 35 "...even as I have loved you that ye also love one another. *Herein* shall all know that ye are my disciples, if ye have love one to another," the cause is first stated before "herein" and then repeated with slight modification—"if [I say] ye have love among one another"—as though the "love" were a book in which "all" could read the truth of their discipleship. In xv. 8 "*Herein* [i.e. *in your abiding in me*] my Father was glorified in order that ye might bear (ἵνα...φέρητε) much fruit and might become my disciples," the reference is to previous statements (xv. 5—7) that, if the disciples "abide" in Christ (as the branches abide in the vine) they will "bear fruit," and that this "abiding" will procure the accomplishment of all their prayers. Here, as a climax, it is said that in this abiding the Father "was glorified," in the fulfilment of His will and effort (2093—6) "in order that (ἵνα)" the disciples "may bear much fruit." Thus the ἵνα clause does not define "herein" (as though it meant "in the fact that ye bear") but explains the *object* of the "abiding."

(γ) Μετὰ τοῦτο, or ταῦτα

[2394] Μετὰ τοῦτο is rarer in John than μετὰ ταῦτα. The former occurs only as follows, mostly implying a short interval, ii. 12 "*After this* [i.e. after the sign at Cana] he went down...," xi. 7 "*after this* [i.e. after abiding two days] he saith," xi. 11 "These things he said, and *after this* [i.e. after saying these things] he saith to them," xix. 28 "*After this* [i.e. after giving His mother to the beloved disciple]...he saith 'I thirst.'" In all these instances there follows some word or deed of Jesus. This is not the case after μετὰ ταῦτα in xix. 38 "*after these things* Joseph asked Pilate"; but in v. 1 "*after these things* there was a feast of the Jews, and Jesus went up," an action of Christ practically follows as elsewhere[1]. In ii. 12 and xix. 28, μετὰ τοῦτο might refer to the completion of a definite period or act (like the Hebrew in Gen. xxiii. 19 "*After this* he buried Sarah[2]") as distinct from μετὰ ταῦτα referring to a collection of actions. But in xi. 7—11, the story of Lazarus, it is difficult to understand the twice-used phrase unless the intention is to describe the miracle as not being merely wrought at the grave but also prepared for, stage by stage, during the period of anticipation prescribed by the Father to the Son.

(δ) Αὐτοῦ omitted and ταῦτα repeated

[2395] For the most part, John avoids pronouns where classical Greek would use them, and prefers nouns, as in the Prologue and elsewhere ("In the beginning was the Word, and the Word was with God, and the Word was God," "not to judge the world but to save the world" etc.[3]). In the following, the MSS. vary (ii. 12) "He went down to Capernaum, himself, and his mother and [his?] brethren and his disciples." The Synoptists similarly vary when they describe Christ's family as seeking to speak to Him; Mark has "his" twice, "his mother (αὐτοῦ) and his brethren (αὐτοῦ)," but Matthew and Luke have "his mother and brethren (ἡ μ. καὶ οἱ ἀ. αὐτοῦ)," thus knitting them into one group[4]. In John, inferior authorities have inserted "his"—naturally, because "his" comes before disciples. But perhaps John did not wish to apply the epithet "his" to "mother,"

---

[1] [2394 a] The other instances are iii. 22, v. 14, vi. 1, vii. 1, xxi. 21. It occurs once in speech, xiii. 7 "But thou shalt know *after these things*."

[2] [2394 b] LXX μετὰ ταῦτα. The more usual Hebrew is (lit.) "*after these words*" μετὰ τὰ ῥήματα ταῦτα, Gen. xv. 1, xxii. 1 etc. Neither μετὰ τοῦτο nor μετὰ ταῦτα is found in Mk or Mt. But Mk-App. xvi. 12 has μετὰ ταῦτα. Lk. has μετὰ ταῦτα, about past action, twice pec. (x. 1, xviii. 4) and once (v. 27) where Mk ii. 13 has πάλιν παρὰ τὴν θάλασσαν, and Mt. ix. 9 ἐκεῖθεν. Lk. has μετὰ ταῦτα twice about the future (xii. 4, xvii. 8).

[3] i. 1, xii. 47, comp. ix. 5, x. 29.

[4] Mk iii. 31, Mt. xii. 46, Lk. viii. 19.

DEMONSTRATIVE [2397]

"brethren" and "disciples" in that impartial way. He may have omitted "his" before "brethren" and inserted it before "disciples" because he has in view—what he tells us later on—that "his brethren did not believe in him[1]."

[2396] This general habit of omitting pronouns makes the following passage all the more remarkable, xii. 16 "*These things* (ταῦτα) his disciples understood not at the first: but when Jesus was glorified, then remembered they that *these things* (ταῦτα) were written (γεγραμμένα) concerning (2339) him, and that they had done *these things* to him." On this Westcott says, "The threefold repetition of the words is to be noticed." He refers to the "threefold repetition" of ταῦτα. Schöttgen[2] gives a multitude of instances in which "this thing," represented by the Hebrew feminine "*this*" (mostly altered as to gender in LXX), is mystically interpreted as referring to the Messiah. The most important is Ps. cxviii. 22—3 "The stone that the builders rejected is become the head of the corner. *This* [*thing*] (αὕτη) is the Lord's doing." This is quoted by our Lord, soon after the Entry into Jerusalem, in Mark and Matthew, who follow the LXX in retaining the literal (but from the Greek point of view quite misleading) feminine[3]. Luke, however, stops short at the word "corner." This, then, is just one of the occasions where we might expect John to intervene (see Index, "John, interventions of").

[2397] There are good reasons for thinking that our Lord's quotation about the "stone" originally terminated with the words "head-stone of the corner," and that an early Christian *congregational ascription of glory, or utterance of hope or thanksgiving*, to God, was

---

[1] [2395 a] vii. 5. Of course it might be urged, on the other side, that by writing ἡ μήτηρ αὐτοῦ καὶ οἱ ἀδελφοὶ καὶ οἱ μαθηταὶ αὐτοῦ, he groups "the brethren" with "the disciples," apart from "the mother." This must be admitted. If therefore a meaning is intended, the meaning is ambiguous (as often in this Gospel) and only to be decided by the sequel, which states that His brethren remained unbelievers.

[2] [2396 a] Schöttg. ii. 45. Gen. ix. 12, 17 "*This* (τοῦτο) is the sign," Ps. xxvii. 3 "In *this* (ταύτῃ) do I trust," Jer. ix. 23—4 "Let him boast in *this* (τούτῳ)" are interpreted of the Messiah.

[3] [2396 b] Mk xii. 11, Mt. xxi. 42 (Lk. om.) παρὰ Κυρίου ἐγένετο αὕτη. Comp. 1 S. iv. 7 "There hath not been *such a thing*," οὐ γέγονεν τοιαύτη, 1 K. xi. 39 "And I will for *this* afflict the seed of David," LXX om., A διὰ ταύτην. Field (on Mt. xxi. 42) says that some modern commentators have committed the error of taking αὕτη as referring to κεφαλή, "This (head of the corner) was from the Lord." I fear we must add Origen (*ad loc.*, Huet i. 468 A) καὶ θαυμαστὴ κεφαλή, and probably Chrysostom. See 2621—2.

variously added (1) by Mark and Matthew, (2) by Luke, (3) by Barnabas[1]. If this was the case, John, taking up Mark's tradition about αὕτη, and converting it into the more intelligible ταῦτα, may have placed the tradition in its right position, *not as an utterance of Christ's, but as an evangelistic statement*, namely, that the Church, in later days, recognised "*these things*," which took place in connexion with Christ's Entry into Jerusalem—meaning the whole, and not excluding the contrast between the fixed rejection by the rulers and the recognition by the multitude (xii. 9—10)—as being divinely ordained.

(iv) Τοιοῦτος

[2398] As to iv. 23 καὶ γὰρ ὁ πατὴρ τοιούτους ζητεῖ τοὺς προσκυνοῦντας αὐτόν, Winer-Moulton (p. 138) parallels it to Mk ix. 37 [ἐν] τῶν τοιούτων παιδίων "one of *such* little children[2]." But John has not prefixed the article as Mark has; and *the article is invariably prefixed in N.T. wherever* τοιοῦτος *is used as a masc. pronoun, referring to some previous description*. It follows that τοιούτους must be taken predicatively, although the construction presents difficulties. Perhaps ζητεῖ is nearly equivalent to "desire" (Dan. vii. 19 Theod. ἐζήτουν, LXX ἤθελον) and the meaning is "*desires [to have]* his worshippers such," as Horace uses "te semper amabilem sperat." for "*hopes [to have]* thee ever amiable." But of course ζητεῖ does not

---

[1] [2397 a] Luke xx. 18 (instead of Mk-Mt.'s continuance of the Psalm quotation) has a prediction that (see Dan. ii. 35—44) "Everyone that falleth on that stone shall be broken in pieces." Barnabas, after the words "He hath made me as a hard rock," continues, vi. 4, λέγει δὲ πάλιν ὁ προφήτης· Λίθον ὃν ἀπεδοκίμασαν οἱ οἰκοδομοῦντες, οὗτος ἐγενήθη εἰς κεφαλὴν γωνίας. καὶ πάλιν λέγει· Αὕτη ἐστὶν ἡ ἡμέρα ἡ μεγάλη καὶ θαυμαστή, ἣν ἐποίησεν ὁ κύριος.
[2397 b] The words in the LXX "This (αὕτη) came (ἐγένετο) from the Lord and it is marvellous *in our eyes*" supplied an extremely appropriate congregational utterance for Greeks, coming after the words "The stone that the builders rejected"—as though the Gentile converts said, "The rulers of Israel, the builders of the Temple, rejected the Stone that was to become the head (κεφαλή), but we accept it, *i.e.* the head, and it is marvellous in our eyes." This would be an error; but, as we have seen, it was one that Origen certainly, and Chrysostom probably, adopted. Both these commentators connect the text with the notion of the cornerstone as uniting the believers in Israel with the Gentiles (Orig. Huet i. 467 E, Chrys. *ad loc.*).

[2] [2398 a] Mk ix. 37, x. 14, Mt. xix. 14, Lk. xviii. 16, Acts xxii. 22, Rom. xvi. 18, 1 Cor. v. 11, vii. 28, xvi. 16 etc. Chrys. *ad loc. el* τοιούτους (Morel. τούτους) πάλαι ἐζήτει seems to have taken τοιούτους non-predicatively, but the usage of all books in N.T. (including 3 Jn 8) is hardly to be disputed.

mean "desire" exactly: and the evangelist may intend to suggest not only what the Father "desires" His worshippers to be, but also the fact that He is "seeking" them out of the world, and "seeking" to help them, as the shepherd "seeks" his flock.

II. PERSONAL

(i) Insertion for emphasis

[2399] In classical Greek the personal inflexion of a verb dispenses mostly with personal pronouns, *e.g.* ὑμεῖς, as subject. But John uses ὑμεῖς about as often as it is used by all the Synoptists together. The main reason is his love of contrast as in viii. 23 " *Ye* (ὑμεῖς) are from beneath; *I* (ἐγώ) am from above: *ye* (ὑμεῖς) are from this world; *I* (ἐγώ) am not from this world[1]." Sometimes, however, emphasis may be intended, and may be in danger of being confused with contrast. Thus, in the first instance where ὑμεῖς occurs, i. 26 (" I (ἐγώ) baptize in water; midst of you standeth [he] whom *ye* (ὑμεῖς) know not") a contrast might be supposed to be intended between "ye" and "I." But there "ye" perhaps means *"even ye*[2], although he is in the midst of you"; and "I" is contrasted, not with "ye" but with "he whom ye know not."

[2400] But a great deal is lost by readers of the English versions of the Fourth Gospel from the general neglect of the translators to distinguish the instances where the English personal pronoun does,

---

[1] [2399 a] There is very little in the Synoptists like this use of ὑμεῖς. The nearest approach to it is the contrast between the "my" of prophecy, meaning God's ("*my* house") and "ye," in Mk xi. 17 (comp. Mt. xxi. 13, Lk. xix. 46) " My house shall be called a house of prayer...but *ye* (ὑμεῖς) have made it a den of robbers": and the Sermon on the Mount contrasts "*I* say unto you" with what was " said to them of old time" (Mt. v. 21—2, 33—4).

[2] [2399 b] "Even ye." Perhaps the emphasis is condemnatory, not "even ye," but " ye of course," " ye, being such as ye are." Comp. v. 44 " How can *ye [being such as ye are]* believe, [ye] that receive glory from one another."

[2399 c] In 1 Jn, there is a clear distinction between "*we write*" and "*I write.*" The Epistle opens with "we" thus (i. 1—10) "That which *we* have heard, that which *we* have seen...And these things *we* (emph. ἡμεῖς) write unto you that our (ἡμῶν, marg. ὑμῶν) joy may be fulfilled.... If we say that *we* have not sinned we make him a liar and his word is not in *us*." After thus writing in the name of the Apostles and Elders generally, describing their testimony, their privileges, and their dangers, the writer passes to his individual testimony (ii. 1) " My little children, these things *I write* unto you," and this is repeated nearly a dozen times, ending with v. 13 " These things *have I written.*" But no pronoun is inserted except for emphasis or antithesis, i. 4 "And these things *we write* (γράφομεν ἡμεῖς) that *our* (v. r. *your*) joy may be fulfilled."

from those where it does not, represent a Greek pronoun. Thus, ii. 18 (A.V.) "What sign shewest thou unto us?" and vi. 30 "What sign shewest thou then?" appear on the same level. But in the latter the pronoun, "thou," is inserted in the Greek; and the context shews that the Jews emphasize the pronoun, possibly meaning *"thou also [like Moses],"* whom they presently mention, or else meaning *"thou on thy side [since thou demandest obedience from us]"*[1]. So in iv. 10 "If thou hadst known...*thou* (σύ) wouldst have asked *him* (αὐτόν)," the second "thou" is emphatic and the meaning is, "*Thou* wouldst have asked *him* [not waiting for *him* to ask *thee*]." There is also a deliberately intended difference between ἡμεῖς οἴδαμεν and οἴδαμεν in the following, ix. 29 "*We* (ἡμεῖς) know that God hath spoken to Moses, but this man—we know not whence he is" where the former means, "We, the guardians of the Law about which you know nothing."

(ii) Ἐγώ

[2401] For ἐγώ with εἰμί, see **2220—8**. For ἐγώ, as denoting emphasis generally, see **2399** and **1713**. The emphatic use of "I" in the testimony of the Baptist—attested sometimes by B alone among the uncial MSS.—has perplexed some, who have not perceived that the Baptist is intended, by the use of this pronoun, to emphasize his own inferiority to Christ, or else the spontaneousness of his testimony, "*I* am not the Christ," "*I* am [but] a voice," "*I* baptize with water," "*I* am not worthy to loose *his* latchet" etc. The following are the instances in Greek: i. 20 ἐγὼ οὐκ εἰμὶ ὁ χρ., i. 23 ἐγὼ φωνή, i. 26—7 ἐγὼ βαπτίζω...οὗ οὐκ εἰμὶ [ἐγώ] ἄξιος[2], i. 30 οὗτός ἐστιν ὑπὲρ οὗ ἐγὼ εἶπον (where Chrys. not only changes ὑπέρ to the more usual περί but also drops ἐγώ), i. 31 (rep. 33) κἀγὼ οὐκ ᾔδειν, *i.e.* "and I *for my part* did not know him, it was God that revealed him to me," i. 31 διὰ τοῦτο ἦλθον ἐγὼ ἐν ὕδατι βαπτίζων, i. 34 κἀγὼ ἑώρακα, *i.e.* "and I, with my own eyes, opened by God, have seen," iii. 28 αὐτοὶ ὑμεῖς

---

[1] [2400 a] In vi. 30 τί οὖν ποιεῖς σὺ σημεῖον; the R.V. "What then doest thou for a sign?" may be intended to emphasize "thou," but there is nothing to make this clear to an English reader. Either italics in the text, or some sign in the margin, might have indicated it. And the absence of any such indication obscures the sense in many passages.

[2] [2401 a] So, too, Mk i. 8 ἐγὼ ἐβάπτισα...αὐτὸς δέ, Mt. iii. 11, Lk. iii. 16 ἐγὼ μέν...αὐτός. But the Synoptists om. ἐγώ in the clause about the shoe-latchet or shoes, οὗ οὐκ εἰμὶ ἱκανός.

μοι μαρτυρεῖτε ὅτι εἶπον [ἐγώ] Οὐκ εἰμὶ ἐγὼ ὁ χριστός, *i.e.* I did not wait for others to dispute my claim to be Messiah, I myself spontaneously denied all claim. Here Alford rejects the first ἐγώ, apparently on the ground that B, alone of the uncials, has it.

(iii) Σύ

[2402] The pronoun "thou" (1726) occurs in John more frequently than in all the Synoptists together. It occurs four times in the short cross-examination of the Baptist by the Jews, four times in the Samaritan Dialogue, and seven times in Christ's Last Prayer— whereas in the whole of Mark's Gospel it does not occur more than ten times. In many cases the Jews use it to Jesus "*Thou* testifiest about thyself," "Art *thou* greater than our father Abraham?" etc. But its frequency extends to the whole of the Gospel and indicates the evangelist's tendency, 1st to lay stress on personality and, 2nd, to express personality in dialogue.

[2403] In xix. 9 "whence art thou (πόθεν εἶ σύ;)?" a difficulty is raised by σύ as well as by πόθεν. As to πόθεν, it is barely conceivable that Pilate might have been so impressed by the charge of the Pharisees (xix. 7 "he made himself a son of God") that he returns to his mysterious prisoner with the question "*From what source, celestial or terrestrial*, art thou?" But, even in that case, there is no need of σύ, which in questions, as in imperatives, sometimes implies contempt (2734). Chrysostom—who apparently had a different reading—says that Pilate, terror-stricken, "begins his examination all over again saying, *Art thou the Christ?* (ἄνωθεν...λέγων Εἰ σὺ εἶ ὁ Χριστός;) But He gives him no answer[1]."

[2404] The Index to Epictetus shews that πόθεν σοι; and πόθεν σύ; might be used, as detached phrases, to mean "How could *you* have the power to do so-and-so?" "How are *you* able to do this or that?"—with a suggestion of incredulity. This suggests another explanation of the words of Pilate. Fresh from the saying of the Pharisees ("He made himself *Son of God*") he comes back into the Praetorium repeating to himself "This man son of God!" and then utters his thought aloud to the prisoner, "*How could you possibly be*

---

[1] [2403 *a*] It is possible that Chrys. has confused the utterance of Pilate with the utterance of the High Priest in Mt. xxvi. 63, see **2734** *d*.

[Son of God]?" πόθεν εἶ σύ[1]; Some might take this as an inquiry about the province from which Jesus came—an inquiry mentioned by Luke alone[2]. John, believing that this was an error, might insert the exact words that caused the error[3]. But see **2733—7**.

III. Relative

(i) "Ος

(*a*) Attraction of the Relative

[2405] In iv. 5 τοῦ χωρίου οὗ ἔδωκεν Ἰ., iv. 14 τοῦ ὕδατος οὗ ἐγὼ δώσω, xvii. 5 τῇ δόξῃ ᾗ (marg. ἥν) εἶχον, xxi. 10 τῶν ὀψαρίων ὧν ἐπιάσατε, the relative pronoun corresponds to the defining relative in English ("that," as in "the water *that* I shall give") and John's adherence to the Greek idiom of the attraction of the relative into the case of the antecedent helps to indicate that the latter without the former is incomplete[4]. Similarly in xv. 20 μνημονεύετε τοῦ λόγου οὗ ἐγὼ εἶπον ὑμῖν, the attracted relative indicates that "the saying" is meaningless until it is defined and completed. The meaning is not "*the word, which* I said," but "*the word that* I said."

[2406] But, if so, why is the relative not attracted—not at least in the best MSS.—in ii. 22 ἐπίστευσαν τῇ γραφῇ καὶ τῷ λόγῳ ὃν εἶπεν ὁ Ἰησοῦς, and in iv. 50 ἐπίστευσεν ὁ ἄνθρωπος τῷ λόγῳ ὃν εἶπεν αὐτῷ ὁ Ἰησοῦς[5]? The answer may be that in these two passages the "saying" is special, and may be called in some sense complete—not "*the word that* Jesus uttered [as a general doctrine]," but (1) "*the* [mysterious] *word* [about destroying the Temple], *which* Jesus then uttered," (2) "*the word* [of healing, 'Thy son liveth'], *which* Jesus

---

[1] [2404 *a*] The insertion of εἶ in such a phrase is, however, improbable. On Epictet. i. 19. 9, for πόθεν σύ, the editor suggests πόθεν σοί. Similarly in Jn, if οι were written over συ, the former might easily be added to the text as ει, resulting in σὺ εἶ. But the subject requires further investigation in connexion with the phrase πόθεν εἰμί, frequent in this Gospel (**2736**).

[2] Lk. xxiii. 6—7.

[3] Against this view, it may fairly be urged that πόθεν σύ, in the Epictetian idiom, suggests an incredulity approaching contempt, whereas Pilate is "afraid"; and, in favour of it, that a character like Pilate's is apt to oscillate between arrogant contempt and servile fear. For the paraphrase of Nonnus see **2734**.

[4] [2405 *a*] The instances given by Bruder (1888) where (in this construction) the antecedent is omitted, are vi. 29 πιστεύητε εἰς ὃν ἀπέστειλεν, vii. 31 πλείονα σημεῖα ποιήσει ὧν οὗτος ἐποίησεν, xvii. 9 περὶ ὧν δέδωκάς μοι.

[5] Here W.H. give ὅν in both passages without marg. altern. although some authorities read ᾧ.

had just uttered." It may be urged that the same reasoning applies to xv. 20, which repeats the word "just uttered" in xiii. 16 "A bondservant is not greater than his lord." True, but it is also *a word that Jesus uttered as a general doctrine* (1784) "A disciple is not above his teacher."

[2407] The same explanation applies to the reading of B in vii. 39 τοῦτο δὲ εἶπεν περὶ τοῦ πνεύματος, ὃ ἔμελλον λαμβάνειν... Here W.H. place ὅ in marg. and οὗ in text. But the former may make better sense if the object is to make a pause after "Spirit." In that case, the meaning is not "the [new] spirit *that* was about to be received," but "the [Holy] Spirit, *which* (i.e. for indeed it) was about to be received." The relative "that" would differentiate the new outpouring of the Spirit from outpourings of the Spirit under the O.T. dispensation, by defining the former as "about to be received by believers." The relative "which" assumes that the readers know "the Spirit" to be "the Holy Spirit," and introduces a new fact about the Spirit, namely, that it was to be received after Christ had been glorified[1].

(β) Ἐν τῷ ὀνόματί coy ᾧ Δέλωκάc μοι (see also 2740—4)

[2408] The relative has been altered by some authorities, because of its difficulty, in xvii. 11—12 "Holy Father, keep them in thy name that thou hast given me (ἐν τῷ ὀνόματί σου ᾧ δέδωκάς μοι) in order that they may be one even as we. When I was with them I kept them *in thy name that thou hast given me* (ἐν τῷ ὀ. σου ᾧ δέδωκάς μοι)." Some in the first clause, and more in the second, have changed ᾧ to οὕς ("*those whom* thou hast given me"), and SS omits both clauses. Chrysostom explains "in thy name" as "through thy help," and reads οὕς in the second clause (if not in the first).

[2409] If the text is correct, it implies a spiritual conception of God's Name and (probably) an indirect attempt to deliver the reader from some popular and philosophic misconceptions, which require a brief notice. All Jews were familiar with the prediction about the Prophet "like unto" Moses (that God's Name was to be "*in him*"), and with the language of Jehovah saying "I will put my name on" persons and places chosen by Him[2]. The Epistle to the Philippians says that God "gave as a free gift (ἐχαρίσατο)" to Jesus "the name that is above every name," in order that "in the name of

---

[1] On the difference between "that" and "which," see **2273** *a*.
[2] Ex. xxiii. 21, Numb. vi. 27, 1 K. viii. 16 etc.

Jesus every knee should bow," whether in heaven or earth or beneath the earth[1]. The Acts of the Apostles[2] relates an attempt of unbelieving Jews to use "the name of Jesus" as a sort of hocus-pocus for the purpose of casting out a devil; and the possibility of such an attempt is recognised in one version of Matthew-Luke's Tradition[3]. The Apocalypse says "To him that overcometh I will *give a white pebble, and on the pebble a new name* written, which none knoweth save he that receiveth it[4]": it describes one sitting on a white horse as "having *a name written that none knoweth save himself,* and clad in a cloak sprinkled with blood, and his name is called the Word of God[5]," and adds, "His servants shall serve him and shall see his face and *his name* [shall be] on their foreheads[6]." These beautiful Apocalyptic traditions may be best and most naturally interpreted in a spiritual sense, but they are open to materialistic perversion.

[2410] Philo apparently implies that "the name of God" represents something inferior to God. The object to aim at is, to be (Deut. xiv. 1) "sons of the Lord God," but, he adds, "If anyone is not yet worthy to be called 'son of God,' let him aim at ordering himself after His firstborn Logos, the Angel, eldest [of angels] as being *Archangel with many names*: for He is addressed as 'Beginning,' and '*Name of God*,' and 'Logos,' and 'the Man according to the Image,' and 'Seeing Israel[7].'" And Justin says "As for name applicable to the Father of all, being unbegotten, there is no such thing... The words 'Father' and 'God' and 'Creator' and 'Lord' and 'Master' are not names, but appellations ($\pi\rho o\sigma\rho\eta\sigma\epsilon\iota s$) derived from beneficent actions and works[8]."

[2411] John's doctrine appears to be that the highest "name" of God is that of Him as Father—only as Father revealed through such

---

[1] Phil. ii. 9. [2] Acts xix. 14.
[3] Mt. vii. 22 "In thy name have we cast out devils," where the parall. Lk. xiii. 25—6 omits the clause.
[4] [2409 a] Rev. ii. 17. $\Psi\hat{\eta}\phi o s$ "pebble," here (as in Acts xxvi. 10 and in Gk generally) probably means a voting tablet either for condemnation or acquittal, so that it may mean "forgiveness of sins." There may be a play on the phrase $\delta\iota\delta\omega\mu\iota\ \psi\hat{\eta}\phi o\nu$ which means "I give my vote." Comp. 1 Jn iii. 20 "If our heart *condemns us not* we have confidence toward God." The context in 1 Jn indicates that this "non-condemnation" proceeds from "loving in deed and in truth": and Rev. ii. 17 perhaps means by "the new name" that new kind of love which the Son brought into the world and which "none knoweth save he that receiveth it."
[5] Rev. xix. 12—13. [6] Rev. xxii. 3—4.
[7] Philo i. 426—7. [8] Just. Mart. 2 *Apol.* 6.

a Son as Jesus Christ. In his Gospel, the word "name," when uttered by Christ, occurs almost always in the phrase (1) "thy *name*," or "the *name* of the (or, my) Father," or else (2) "in my *name*" as being the avenue through which the requests of the disciples are to pass to the Father[1]. Christ's first mention of "the name of my Father" indicates that it is the stamp of the true Deliverer as distinguished from the false deliverer, who "comes in his own name." Hence, "thy name that thou hast given me" means "thy essential being, of Fatherhood, in the form in which thou hast given it to me, the Son." "Thy name," alone, might mean thy name as revealed to Israel under the Law, through Moses; but this "new name" is "the name of Fatherhood as given to the Son in order that He may transmit it to others, making all one in the Family of God[2]."

---

[1] [2411 a] Apart from x. 3 "he calleth his own sheep by name" (and iii. 18 "in the name of the only begotten," which is (**1497, 2066**) not to be taken as an utterance of Christ's) the word "name" is used by our Lord as follows:—v. 43 "I have come in *the name of my Father*...if another come in his own name," x. 25 "the works that I do in *the name of my Father*," xii. 28 "Glorify *thy name*," xvii. 6, 11, 12, 26 "*thy name*"—making seven mentions of the Father's name by the Son.

[2411 b] "*My name*" occurs only in the Last Discourse, addressed to the disciples. Excluding the prediction xv. 21 "all these things will they do unto you because of my name, because they know not...," it is always in the phrase "in my name," concerning the disciples as asking, or the Father as "giving," or "sending" the Spirit, xiv. 13, 14, 26, xv. 16, xvi. 23, 24, 26—seven mentions.

[2] [2411 c] The "name," *i.e.* essence, of the Father (not of the Son) is "*given*" to the Son (not "*revealed*," which would imply unveiling). So in O.T. the Name of God is "put upon" the Temple. The Johannine doctrine bears on superstitious abuses of the name or names of God (see Orig. *Cels.* i. 6 and 24, comp. v. 45), and also on the interpretation of the words in the Lord's Prayer, "Father, be thy *name made holy*." In the Fourth Gospel, Christ only thrice uses the word "holy," namely, here, xvii. 11—12 "*Holy Father, keep them in thy name that thou hast given me*," xiv. 26 "the Paraclete, the *Holy* Spirit," and xx. 22 "Receive the *Holy* Spirit, whosesoever sins ye forgive they are forgiven...." Taken together, the three passages suggest that "holiness" is manifested in connexion with the Holy Spirit, through unity and forgiveness of sins, and that God's "name" is "made holy" when the Spirit attains these objects.

[2411 d] Another aspect of the Johannine doctrine is in the *Didaché* x. 1 "Now after ye are filled (ἐμπλησθῆναι) give thanks thus, 'We give thanks unto thee, *holy Father, for* (ὑπέρ) *thy holy name which* (οὗ) thou didst cause to tabernacle (κατεσκήνωσας) in our hearts,'" where the writer means the relative clause to be essential, "*the* Holy Name of thine *that*" or "*that* Holy Name of thine *which*."

[2411 e] Why does Jn add "*that thou hast given me*" to "thy name"? Probably to lay stress on the *free and full* "*giving*"—"*Not as the world giveth, give* I unto you." This includes the Pauline distinction between attainment

(γ) Ἐντολὴν καινήν...ὅ (1 Jn ii. 8)

[2412] In connexion with the above-mentioned "*new name*" of love, or Father, the following passage also may be mentioned as illustrating the use of the relative, 1 Jn ii. 8 "Again a *new commandment* (ἐντολήν) I write unto you, *which thing* (ὅ) is true in him and in you." Here, the preceding context bids the readers "walk" as Christ "walked," and the following context says that the true light is now shining, and (1 Jn ii. 10) "he that *loveth* his brother abideth in the light." In view of these contexts, the meaning of "*which thing*" appears to be "*which assertion*," namely, the assertion that the "commandment," which he has just called (1 Jn ii. 7) "*not new*," is also, paradoxically, "*new*." To love one's neighbour is a commandment of the Law, "old"; to love as Christ loved us is a commandment of the Son, "new." The only instance in which our Lord uses the word "new" in the Fourth Gospel is "A new commandment give I unto you that ye love one another—even as I loved you that ye also love one another[1]." It is to this saying that the author of the Epistle is referring. The words may be paraphrased: "I have called the commandment 'old,' I now call it 'new': and truly the 'newness' is manifest—manifest in Him, giving His blood for us, manifest in you, made one with Him by His blood[2]."

---

attempted "through works," and "*the free gift*" received through "*faith*." The Hebrew "give" often means "appoint," and "the Law" is said to have been (i. 17) "given through Moses": but the same sentence adds that "the grace" (including all the grace that reached Israel through the Law) came through Jesus Christ.

[1] xiii. 34.

[2] [2412 a] On viii. 40 ζητεῖτέ με ἀποκτεῖναι, ἄνθρωπον ὅς...λελάληκα, where ἄνθρωπον, at first sight, seems needless, see Origen who refers to it in his comment on Ps. lxii. 3 ἕως πότε ἐπιτίθεσθε ἐπ' ἄνθρωπον, saying, Τοῦτο ὅμοιόν ἐστι τῷ Νῦν ζητεῖτέ με ἀποκτεῖναι. Ἄνθρωπον ζητοῦσιν ἀποκτεῖναι· καὶ οἱ ἐπιτιθέμενοι ἀνθρώπῳ ἐπιτίθενται. In the Hebrew of the Psalm, "*man*" appears to be emphatic, Sym. has ἀνδρός, and the Targ. has "*a merciful man*," as though the meaning were: "How long will ye spend your time in setting upon a *man* [*made in God's image*]!" To this emphasis Origen calls attention saying "This [expression of the Psalmist's] is like '*Now ye seek to kill me*' [in the Gospel. In the Gospel] *they 'seek to kill a man*,' and in the Psalm those that 'set upon [him]' set upon '*a man*.'" Perhaps the present text in Origen has dropped ἄνθρωπον, and we ought to read Νῦν ζητεῖτέ με ἀποκτεῖναι, ἄνθρωπον. Ἄνθρωπον....

In Origen's *Comm. Johann.* (on viii. 40) although he does not quote Ps. lxii. 3 ἐπιτίθεσθε, the influence of it may be traced on his statement about τοὺς τῷ λόγῳ τοῦ θεοῦ ἐπιβουλεύοντας that τῷ ἀνθρωπινωτέρῳ αὐτοῦ κ. βλεπομένῳ ἐπιτίθενται.

RELATIVE [2413]

(ii) Ὅστις

[2413] Ὅστις, "whoever," "one that," is mostly used of a class. But it is also used in N.T. of an individual, to mean "the one that," especially at the beginning of a clause that introduces explanatory or illustrative statement[1]. In such cases ὅστις, ἥτις etc. may be rendered "*now he, she* etc.," *e.g.* Gal. iv. 24—6 "One from mount Sinai...*now this* (ἥτις) is Agar... ; but Jerusalem that is above is free, *now this* (ἥτις) is our mother." So in Jn viii. 53 "Art thou greater than our father Abraham (R.V.) *which* (ὅστις) died?" the purpose is to introduce the death of Abraham as illustrative of the necessity that all men should die. We may paraphrase the relative clause as "*One that* [*great as he was*] *died,*" or "*yet he died.*" In viii. 25 "Jesus said unto them (lit.), In the beginning whatever also I speak unto you (τὴν ἀρχὴν ὅτι καὶ λαλῶ ὑμῖν)," some take ὅτι as a conjunction, "because," but it is probably the neuter of ὅστις. This is discussed elsewhere (2154—6).

Subsequently he says οὐκ ἔστιν ὅτε ὁ κατὰ τὸν Ἰησοῦν τροπικῶς νοούμενος ἄνθρωπος οὐκ ἐπεδήμει τῷ βίῳ. These facts bear on the statement made above (1934—5) that ἄνθρωπον is emphatic in viii. 40, which means "a *man, who*"—quite distinct from "a *man that*" meaning "*one that.*"

[2412 b] In vi. 9 ἔστιν παιδάριον ὧδε ὅς ἔχει, some authorities, including ℵ, have ὅ. Some have ἕν before ὧδε. Blass says (p. 317) "better παιδ. ἔχον, Chrys. Nonnus." Some corruption is indicated by the variations of words and order (b e, Syr. (Burk.) Chrys. "there is here a lad," *a* "est puer hic," *f* "est puer unus hic," SS "a certain lad hath on him here"). But ἔχει is probably correct. For Chrys. goes on to say μετὰ γὰρ τὸ εἰπεῖν "Ἔχει πέντε ἄρτους κριθίνους—which suggests that a scribe has given his previous quotation incorrectly. As to the change of gender, comp. 2 S. xiii. 17 ἐκάλεσε τὸ παιδάριον αὐτοῦ τὸν προεστηκότα (unless the particip. is regarded as an appositional noun). Note also that ℵ, which reads ὅ here, substitutes τινα in 1 Mac. xvi. 16 τινας τῶν παιδαρίων, and that D has OC here with a line drawn through the C. The facts indicate that ὅς was the original reading. On xix. 17 Κρανίου Τόπον ὅ, see **2738**.

[1] [2413 a] In the parables, Matthew uses ὅστις to introduce the point of resemblance (of the householder, king, virgins etc.) between the emblem and the reality (*e.g.* "*that* planted a vineyard," "*that* took their lamps" etc.). So in Lk. vii. 37 "a woman *that* was in the city a sinner," the relative clause introduces what is essential to the narrative that follows. Comp. Mk xii. 18 "Sadducees (R.V.) *which* (οἵτινες) say," where the "saying" is not a detached fact but bears on the following discussion. But initial ὅστις means "and accordingly or consequently" in Acts viii. 15 "They sent to them Peter and John, *who accordingly* (οἵτινες) went down and prayed." It has been shewn (**2273** a) that A.V. differs from Shakespeare, and R.V. from both, in the use of relative pronouns; and we must not expect Gk writers always to agree with one another in their use.

(a) ὍCTIC ἄN, or ἐάN

[2414] Ὅστις with ἄν or ἐάν in the Johannine Gospel and Epistles occurs, certainly, only in the neuter, ii. 5 "*Whatsoever* (ἄν) he may say," xiv. 13, xv. 16 "*whatsoever* (ἄν) ye may ask." It is also probable in 1 Jn iii. 20 "[*in*] *whatsoever* (ὅτι ἐάν) our heart may condemn us." Bruder (Moulton) marks under this head xxi. 25 ἔστιν δὲ καὶ ἄλλα πολλὰ ἃ ἐποίησεν ὁ Ἰησοῦς, ἅτινα ἐὰν γράφηται[1]. But ἐάν here is generally regarded as meaning "if," in which case the construction would be quite different from that of ὅστις ἄν (or ἐάν), and the meaning would be "*Of such a kind that* if they should be written[2]." It is certainly strange that ἅτινα and ἐάν should be placed together by any N.T. writer except in the sense of "*whatsoever things*[3]"; and the fact is one of several that render the text extremely doubtful[4]. On ἄν and ἐάν interchanged see 2739.

---

[1] It is not so marked in the original Bruder (1888).

[2] SS "*that* if one by one they were written," *a, b, e, f, ff*, "quae si."

[3] [2414 a] Ἐάν or ἄν, meaning "soever," immediately follows some form of ὅστις in Mk vi. 23 ⌜Ὅτι ἐάν⌝ (marg. ὅτι Ὃ ἐάν), Lk. x. 35, Acts iii. 23, 1 Cor. xvi. 2, Gal. v. 10, Col. iii. 17. I do not know any passage in N.T. where ἐάν, in such a position, means "if," except the one under consideration (if genuine). There is not the same ambiguity about ὅπερ ἐάν, which occurs in *Ox. Pap.* vol. iii. 653 ὅπερ ἐὰν μὴ ποιήσῃς apparently meaning "and unless you do this" (A.D. 162—3). This is closely followed by ὃν ἐὰν σὺ δῷς apparently meaning "whomsoever you appoint," not "whom, if you appoint." For further evidence from the Papyri see 2416 *a*.

[4] [2414 *b*] Origen quotes Jn xxi. 25, as follows (omitting αὐτόν) *Philocal.* 15 φησὶν ὁ Ἰωάννης ὡς ἄρα Οὐδὲ τὸν κόσμον οἶμαι χωρεῖν τὰ γραφόμενα βιβλία, continuing "For the [saying] that 'the world has not room for the books to be written' must be understood not [as being true] on account of the multitude of the writings, as some [say], but on account of the greatness of the acts, since the greatness of the acts cannot possibly be either written or reported by tongue of flesh, nor signified in languages (διαλέκτοις) and sounds of men." He seems to take "the world" as meaning "mankind," and "has not room for" as meaning "has not capability to express." But it is not easy to see how he obtains this meaning: it needs either the omission of τὰ γραφόμενα βιβλία, or else a conjunction οὐδὲ τὸν κόσμον... οὐδὲ τὰ γραφόμενα βιβλία, "neither the world... nor yet books."

[2414 *c*] In a second quotation, after describing Jesus as being (lit.) "a multitude of good [things] (πλῆθος ἀγαθῶν)" Origen says about these "good [things]," (Huet ii. 12) "They have not however *had room found for them* (κεχωρημένων) by writings (ὑπὸ γραμμάτων). And why say I 'by writings,' when John says even (καί) concerning the whole world [that] 'Not even the world itself I think *would have room for* (οὐδὲ αὐτὸν οἶμαι τὸν κόσμον χωρῆσαι) the books to be written'?" Here Origen seems to understand "the world would not have room" for the necessary books as meaning that not only "books," but even the "world," would be insufficient to "find room for" the expression of the acts of the Logos. The context and the quotation would make excellent sense if the two ran thus, in effect, "Why say I '*not by writings*,' when John says '*not even by the world*'?"—omitting "the books to be written."

[**2414** *d*] In a third quotation, the context of which resembles that in the *Philocalia* above, Origen (Huet ii. 201 D *foll.*) says that "writing (γραφή)" in some cases, and "the tongue of man" in others, "have not been capable of expressing, the highest mysteries of God; and he proceeds, "Ἔστι γὰρ καὶ ἄλλα πολλὰ ἃ ἐποίησεν ὁ Ἰ. ἅτινα ἐὰν γράφηται καθ' ἓν οὐδὲ αὐτὸν [τὸν κόσμον is omitted] οἶμαι χωρήσειν τὰ γραφόμενα βιβλία. Both in the *Philocalia* and here, he illustrates his view by St Paul's hearing (2 Cor. xii. 2 foll.) "words not to be uttered."

[**2414** *e*] Again, in a fourth quotation, Origen (Huet ii. 326 D—E) speaks about the numerous words (ῥημάτων) of God "not only those that are written but also those that are (2 Cor. xii. 4) 'not to be uttered, which it is not lawful for a man to speak,' and these about which John says, οὐδ' αὐτὸν οἶμαι τὸν κόσμον χωρῆσαι τὰ γραφόμενα βιβλία": and he alludes to xxi. 25 as shewing that John could have written more Gospels than the world would hold (Huet ii. 88) Ἰωάννου, ὃς εὐαγγέλιον ἓν καταλέλοιπεν, ὁμολογῶν δύνασθαι τοσαῦτα ποιήσειν ἃ οὐδὲ ὁ κόσμος χωρῆσαι ἐδύνατο. He adds ἔγραψε δὲ καὶ τὴν Ἀποκάλυψιν κελευσθεὶς σιωπῆσαι καὶ μὴ γράψαι τὰς τῶν ἑπτὰ βροντῶν φωνάς—apparently as an instance of divinely commanded reticence.

[**2414** *f*] In his Comm. on Lk. iii. 18 "Multa quidem et alia exhortans annunciabat," Origen freely refers to Jn thus, "De Christo refertur quia multa et alia *locutus est quae non sunt scripta in libro isto* quae si scriberentur neque ipsum puto mundum capere potuisse libros qui scribendi erant" (combining xxi. 25 with xx. 30 "not written in this book" and substituting "locutus est" for "fecit" so as to afford a parall. to Lk. iii. 18 "annunciabat"). On Lk. iv. 1 he has "Sicut mundus capere non poterat omnes libros si scripta fuissent quae *fecit et docuit* Jesus." Bearing on the manysidedness of Christ's acts and words is a remark of Origen in his Comm. on Mt. xxvi. 55 indicating that he was disposed to believe that Christ's form was transfigured not only in the Transfiguration but on many other occasions: "Venit autem traditio talis ad nos de eo quoniam non solum duae formae in eo fuerunt, una quidem, secundum quam omnes eum videbant, altera autem, secundum quam transfiguratus est coram discipulis suis in monte, quando et resplenduit facies ejus tanquam sol, sed etiam unicuique apparebat secundum quod fuerat dignus. Et cum fuisset ipse, quasi non ipse omnibus videbatur: secundum quod de manna est scriptum, quando Deus filiis Israel panem misit de coelo omnem delectationem habentem, et ad omnem gustum convenientem: quando desiderio offerentis obsequens, ad quod quis voluerat vertebatur. Et non mihi videtur incredibilis esse traditio haec, sive corporaliter propter ipsum Jesum, ut alio et alio modo videretur hominibus, sive propter ipsam Verbi naturam, quod non similiter cunctis apparet." This belief comes out in the *Acts of John* (§ 2) where Christ standing on the shore of Gennesaret appears to James as a "child" but to John as a man, and afterwards in different shapes.

[**2414** *g*] Again, Pamph. Mart. *Pref.* quotes from Origen "Ejus [Christi] gloriamur esse discipuli, nec tamen audemus dicere quod facie ad faciem ab ipso traditam susceperimus intelligentiam eorum quae in divinis libris referuntur : '*quae quidem certus sum quod ne ipse quidem mundus*' pro virtute ac majestate sensuum '*capere potest*,'" and *ib.* 3 "Sicut scriptum est : '*Ne ipsum quidem*

[2415] On the whole it seems probable that the writer or editors of this Gospel have put down at its close a grammatically irregular utterance (perhaps one of the last utterances) of the aged Disciple, which combined the spiritual meaning of Philo with the hyperbolic expression customary among the teachers of Palestine. It also corresponded to the evangelist's saying in the Prologue that "the law [of God] was given through Moses but the grace and the truth [of God] came through Jesus Christ," and it came well here as a final warning: "Law may be put into writing but Grace and Truth cannot. No, even if a world full of books were written, more books would still need to be written, and yet the Grace of the Father and the Truth of the Father—which were the 'works' of the Son—would remain unexpressed." This statement has been placed in such a context that it might seem to refer to the great number of Christ's "mighty works," or "miracles." But that was probably not the Disciple's intention.

[2416] According to this view, in its original utterance the saying meant, in effect, " *Whatever things* (ἅτινα ἐάν) may be written about the Lord Jesus Christ, in detached narrative, [they will not suffice, nay,] even the whole world will not suffice to hold—[I will not say

---

mundum capere posse arbitror libros qui scriberentur' de gloria et de majestate Filii Dei. Impossibile namque est literis committere ea quae ad Salvatoris gloriam pertinent." Here there is a distinct statement that the truths "cannot be committed to writing." This is quite a different statement from "the world could not hold the books," or "the mind of man could not take in the meaning."

[2414 *h*] Origen's view that χωρεῖν, "make room for," has for its object, not "books" but the attributes of the Logos, agrees both verbally and substantially with Philo (i. 253) τίς ἂν ἐχώρησε θεοῦ λόγων ἰσχὺν τῶν ἁπάσης κρεισσόνων ἀκοῆς... οὐδὲ γὰρ εἰ πλοῦτον ἐπιδείκνυσθαι βουληθείη τὸν ἑαυτοῦ, χωρῆσαι ἂν (ἠπειρωθείσης καὶ θαλάσσης) ἡ συμπᾶσα γῆ, (i. 362) οὐδὲ γὰρ τῶν δωρεῶν ἱκανὸς οὐδεὶς χωρῆσαι τὸ ἄφθονον πλῆθος, ἴσως δὲ οὐδὲ ὁ κόσμος, (ii. 218) ὀρέγω τῷ χάριτος ἀξίῳ πάσας ὅσας ἂν οἷός τε ᾖ δέξασθαι δωρεάς, τὴν δὲ ἐμὴν κατάληψιν οὐχ οἷον ἀνθρώπου φύσις ἀλλ' οὐδ' ὁ σύμπας οὐρανός τε καὶ κόσμος δυνήσεται χωρῆσαι. In the context of the first of these three passages, Philo describes the flow of God's "graces (χάριτας)" ἑτέρας ἀντὶ ἐκείνων καὶ τρίτας ἀντὶ τῶν δευτέρων... in language remarkably like that of John (i. 16 χάριν ἀντὶ χάριτος " grace for grace "); in the context of the second he quotes Proverbs (viii. 22) as attesting the existence of the Wisdom of God (which John calls the Logos) from the beginning. Add Long. *De Subl.* ix. 9 ὁ τῶν Ἰουδαίων θεσμοθέτης...τὴν τοῦ θείου δύναμιν κατὰ τὴν ἀξίαν ἐχώρησε κἀξέφηνεν. Wetstein (*ad loc.*) quotes hyperbolical and literal traditions from the Talmud, that the world and the sky and the sea would not supply paper pens and ink sufficient to write out the knowledge of this or that Rabbi.

the portrait of the Lord, but] the books that would have to be written [in the attempt to represent Him]¹."

SUBJECT²

(i) **Collective or noun group**

[2417] When the subject is a collective noun it may have in agreement with it a singular participle followed by a plural verb as in vii. 49 ὁ ὄχλος οὗτος ὁ μὴ γινώσκων τὸν νόμον ἐπάρατοί εἰσιν, xii. 12 ὁ ὄχλος πολὺς ὁ ἐλθὼν εἰς τὴν ἑορτὴν ἀκούσαντες...ἔλαβον. These two instances favour the plural reading in vi. 22 ὁ ὄχλος ὁ ἑστηκὼς πέραν τῆς θαλάσσης εἶδον (marg. ἰδών)³. In a subsequent clause, referring to "the multitude," the plural would naturally be used as in English, vi. 2 "There followed him a great multitude because *they beheld*" (comp. xi. 42, xii. 9, 18).

[2418] When the verb precedes several nouns that constitute its subject, the verb is mostly in the singular⁴. But in a few cases where perhaps the intention is, from the first, to set a list of names before the reader, the verb is plural, as in xix. 25 "Now *there were standing*...his mother, and his mother's sister, and...," xxi. 2 "*There were* together Simon Peter and Thomas and...." When a second verb subsequently refers to two subjects introduced by a first verb in the singular, the second verb is plural, xii. 22 ἔρχεται Ἀ. καὶ Φ. καὶ λέγουσιν, xx. 3 ἐξῆλθεν οὖν ὁ Π. καὶ ὁ ἄλλος μαθητὴς καὶ ἤρχοντο.

(ii) **Neuter Plural**

[2419] When the subject is a neuter plural, John's usage varies strangely. In most authors, the neuter plural with plural verb can often be explained on the ground that though the author *writes* a

---

¹ [2416 a] Deissmann (pp. 203—5) has given, from Papyri, more than fifty instances of ἐάν with ὅς, ὅσος, ὁπότε, οἷος, ὡς, εἴ τις, ὅστις, ὅπου (from B.C. 27 to A.D. 586). From the same collections of Papyri he gives only eight instances of ἄν with similar words. His conclusion concerning the use of ἐάν for ἄν with these relatival words is, "the first and second centuries A.D. constitute its definite classical period; it seems to become less frequent later." These lists are not put forth as exhaustive; but they decidedly favour the conclusion that in xxi. 25 ἅτινα ἐάν means "whatsoever."

² See also Anacoluthon, Ellipsis, and Number.

³ [2417 a] The changes are interesting in vi. 22—4 "The multitude that was standing (sing.)...[all] *saw* (pl.).... When therefore the m. *saw* (sing. before the vb, εἶδεν ὁ ὄχλος)...they themselves embarked (ἐνέβησαν αὐτοί)...."

⁴ [2418 a] i. 35, ii. 2, 12, iii. 22, iv. 53, xviii. 1, 15. In i. 45 ὃν ἔγραψεν Μ. ἐν τῷ νόμῳ καὶ οἱ προφῆται, the last three words are of the nature of an appendix.

neuter noun, he is *thinking* of a masculine or feminine noun. But xix. 31 ἵνα μὴ μείνῃ ἐπὶ τοῦ σταυροῦ τὰ σώματα...ἵνα κατεαγῶσιν αὐτῶν τὰ σκέλη καὶ ἀρθῶσιν exhibits the two constructions side by side: and it can hardly be argued that σκέλη is more suggestive than σώματα of "a masculine noun." Is it possible that τὰ σκέλη is accusative, a construction very common with κατεαγέναι in such phrases as "to have one's head, skull, collar-bone etc. broken[1]"? This would have the advantage of avoiding the abrupt change of subject in passing from κατεαγῶσιν to ἀρθῶσιν (which, in classical Greek, would require αὐτοί before ἀρθῶσιν: "that their legs should be broken and *the men themselves* (αὐτοί) carried away"). Without αὐτοί, if σκέλη is nominative, the text reads as though the meaning were "that their legs should be broken and carried away." But if σκέλη is accusative, the meaning is "that they should have their legs broken and be taken away." In vi. 13, κλασμάτων...ἃ ἐπερίσσευσαν Aℵ have -σεν, but the tendency to make this correction would be strong in some scribes; W. H. have -σαν without alternative.

[2420] The following variations deserve attention, x. 3—27 τὰ πρόβατα τῆς φωνῆς αὐτοῦ <u>ἀκούει</u>...τὰ πρόβατα αὐτῷ <u>ἀκολουθεῖ</u>, ὅτι <u>οἴδασιν</u>......ἀλλοτρίῳ δὲ οὐ μὴ <u>ἀκολουθήσουσιν</u>......οὐκ <u>ἤκουσαν</u> αὐτῶν τὰ πρόβατα...οὗ οὐκ ἔστιν τὰ πρόβατα ἴδια...ἄλλα πρόβατα ἔχω ἃ οὐκ ἔστιν......καὶ τῆς φωνῆς μου <u>ἀκούσουσιν</u>...τὰ πρόβατα τὰ ἐμὰ τῆς φωνῆς μου <u>ἀκούουσιν</u>. At the beginning of the Parable the sheep are regarded as a flock, collectively, acting in a certain way, "the flock *hearkens* and *follows*." But the thought of motive introduces the thought of individuality and hence the grammatical plural, "*they know...they will not follow.*" Thenceforth individuality and plurality prevail, except in the phrases describing to whom the flock "*belongs*," where personality is merged in collectiveness.

(iii) **Suspended**

[2421] Ὁ πιστεύων, in vii. 38 ("*He that believeth*...rivers...shall flow from his belly") might be defended by some grammarians as implying ὅστις ἂν πιστεύσῃ (where ὅστις might be regarded as having

---

[1] [2419 a] Steph. (κατάγνυμι) qu. Plat. 342 B, 515 E with ὦτα, Pollux iv. 188, with κλεῖν, Demosth. 1268. 3 and many others with κεφαλήν.

[2419 b] The objection to this suggestion is that αὐτῶν should not have been inserted, as "their" is sufficiently expressed by the article. No authority omits αὐτῶν, but *a* renders it "illis." D and SS are missing. Syr. (Walton) has "ut confringerent crura eorum suspensorum atque deponerent eos," and so has the Diatessaron. In Nonnus, πόδες τέμνοιντο favours the usual rendering.

αὐτοῦ for its antecedent). But the construction is Hebraic (1920—2) as well as natural. In one or two passages, a word, or clause, with neuter noun or adjective, might be either subject or object, *e.g.* xv. 2 πᾶν κλῆμα ἐν ἐμοὶ μὴ φέρον καρπὸν αἴρει αὐτό. In the Parable of the Sower, Matthew and Luke have ὁ ἔχων where Mark has ὃς ἔχει[1], but there ὁ ἔχων is the subject of ἀκουέτω.

(*a*) Πᾶν ὃ Δέδωκας (xvii. 2)

[2422] The following requires separate discussion, xvii. 2 (R.V.) "Even as thou gavest him authority over all flesh, *that whatsoever thou hast given him, to them he should give eternal life,*" (A.V.) "*that he should give eternal life to as many as thou hast given him*[2]." R.V., though closer to the Greek than A.V., has substituted "whatsoever" for "all that." Grammatically, the Greek of the italicised words can only be construed as follows: "That he may give all that thou hast given him—[namely] eternal life—to them." But the previous sentence mentions no persons that could be here referred to as "them," so that this makes no sense. D alters "he may give" into "may have" and omits "to them," leaving "that all that thou hast given to him may have eternal life." This makes excellent sense and grammar, but there is no reason for supposing that it was the original text. Later on, we find "Father, [*that*] *which* (ὅ) *thou hast given me*, I will that where I am they also may be with me[3]," which again indicates a desire to give prominence to the clause "*that which thou hast given me*" by assigning to it an irregular position in the forefront of the sentence. In these two passages, "*all that* (πᾶν ὅ) *thou hast given me*" (with or without "all") means the Church collectively, and the subsequent pronoun ("to them," "they also") means the members of the Church individually. In the second of the two passages the pronoun happens to be capable of an appositional construction[4], in the first it is not (1921—2). See also 2740—4.

---

[1] Mk iv. 9, Mt. xiii. 9, Lk. viii. 8: so Mt. vii. 24 πᾶς οὖν ὅστις ἀκούει=Lk. vi. 47 πᾶς ὁ...ἀκούων. Comp. Rev. iii. 21 ὁ νικῶν δώσω αὐτῷ, and Prov. xi. 26, where, with a nom. particip., Aq. alone retains the Heb. idiom, καταράσονται αὐτόν, while Theod. has δημοκατάρατος, Sym. λαοκατάρατος.

[2] xvii. 2 καθὼς ἔδωκας αὐτῷ ἐξουσίαν πάσης σαρκός, ἵνα πᾶν ὃ δέδωκας αὐτῷ δώσει αὐτοῖς ζωὴν αἰώνιον.

[3] xvii. 24. Here D makes no alteration.

[4] [2422 *a*] In xvii. 24, we might theoretically explain the construction as θέλω ἵνα ὃ δέδωκάς μοι—ἐκεῖνοι ὦσιν μετ᾽ ἐμοῦ: but the author must not be supposed to have premeditated any such construction.

(iv) Omitted in partitive clauses

[2423] For the omission of the subject in a partitive clause as in xvi. 17 "[Some] of his disciples therefore said," and for consequent ambiguity, see 2042 and 2213—5.

(v) "They" non-pronominal

[2424] The subject is sometimes omitted by John—not quite after the manner of Mark when he uses the 3rd pers. pl. of a verb to mean "people"—*if "they" can be implied from something in the context*, e.g. ii. 10 "Every man first putteth the good wine [before his guests], and, when [*they*] have drunk freely...¹," iii. 23 "Now John also was baptizing in Ænon...and [*they*, i.e. 'those whom he baptized'] came thither (παρεγίνοντο) and were baptized."

[2425] In xviii. 25 "Now Simon Peter was...warming himself. [They] said therefore...," we must not render "they" by "people" but must go back to xviii. 18 "Now Peter also was standing with *them* and warming himself," treating the intervening words (xviii. 19—24) as a parenthesis². In xix. 29 "there was set there a vessel full of vinegar," the evangelist probably assumes that "vinegar" would be understood to mean "*wine for the soldiers on guard*" (just as, in ii. 10, "wine" implied "wine for the guests"). Consequently he assumes that the following words, "so [they] put a sponge," would be understood to refer to "the soldiers." In xx. 1—2 "Mary Magdalene...seeth the stone taken away from the tomb; she runneth therefore...and sayeth...['They] have taken the Lord out of the tomb,'" "they" cannot mean "people." Mary's mind is full of the thought of Christ and of what His enemies have done to Him. She infers, from what she naturally regards as a hostile act, that the chief priests, not content with killing Him, have removed the body, and "they" means "the chief priests," or "the Lord's enemies."

---

¹ [2424 a] R.V. supplies "men." But "putteth" means "puts on the table," and the subject appears to be "those at the table," not "men [in general]." This is somewhat different from the indefinite "*they*" so frequent in Mark—and common in vernacular English, like the French " on "—where the pronoun does not refer to any noun expressed or implied in the context.

² [2425 a] Similarly, in ix. 24 "[*they*] therefore called," we have to pass over the immediately preceding verse about the man's "parents" and to go back to the statement about "the Jews."

Reviewing the instances, so far, we do not find any in which the missing subject cannot be supplied from the context[1].

[2426] We come now to omissions of the subject in words of our Lord. In one of them, "*they*" appears to refer to "the world" previously mentioned "If *the world* hateth you, reflect that it hath hated me...remember the word that I said unto you, 'The servant is not greater than his Lord.' If [*they*] persecuted me they will persecute you also[2]." But there is nothing for the pronoun to refer to in the earlier instance "If a man abide not in me he is cast forth as the branch [of the vine] and is withered, and THEY gather them and cast them into the fire and they are burned[3]." Here, theoretically, we might supply "people," and if the passage occurred in Mark that would perhaps be the best rendering; but as there has been no previous mention of vine-dressers, and as there has been a previous mention of the Father as "cleansing" the vine, it is probable that THEY—in accordance with frequent Jewish tradition as well as occasional Synoptic usage—means "the powers of heaven" or "the angels."

(vi)   "We" non-pronominal[4]

[2427] "We" non-pronominal—*i.e.* expressed by verbal inflexion and not by pronoun—in 1 Jn i. 1 "that which *we* have heard, that which *we* have seen with our eyes...," appears to mean the writer of the Epistle and his companions, as "we" means in the opening sentences of a Pauline Epistle: but it may mean "we all," "we disciples of Christ," as probably in 1 Jn ii. 28 "And now, little children, abide in him, that, if he shall be manifested *we* [*all*] may have confidence." The most serious ambiguity arising from this use of "we" is in xxi. 24 "*we* know that his witness is true." Are these

---

[1] [2425 *b*] With these contrast Mk i. 32 (Mt. viii. 16 sim.) "But in the evening...[*they*] brought unto him all that were sick" (where Mk i. 29—31 has previously mentioned the healing of Peter's mother-in-law without any suggestion of persons that could be called "they"); the parall. Lk. iv. 40 has "*All that had sick folk*...led them to him."

[2] xv. 16—20, where "the world" is six times mentioned.

[3] xv. 6. On THEY, see **667** *a*, **738** *a—b*. On the alleged omission of an indefinite subject, "any one," and on the question whether ὁ πατὴρ αὐτοῦ is predicate or subject, in viii. 44, see **2378—9**.

[4] [2427 *a*] The difference between the non-pronominal and the pronominal "we" is illustrated by 1 Jn iii. 2, v. 15 (*bis*), 19, 20 οἴδαμεν and iii. 14 ἡμεῖς οἴδαμεν (where "we" is opposed to "the world"). In Jn vi. 42, ix. 24, 29 "*we* (ἡμεῖς) know" implies "*we* know, even if others do not" (**2399—2400**).

the words of the evangelist, and do they mean "*We all* know that the witness of the Son to the Father is true"? Or are they the words of some unknown persons, *e.g.* the elders of the Church of the city where the evangelist was writing, and do they mean, in effect, "*We* [elders of Ephesus, Antioch, or Jerusalem] hereby certify that the witness of this evangelist is true"?

[2428] Before discussing this very important passage, we may mention some instances in which our Lord includes Himself in the non-pronominal "we":—iii. 11 (to Nicodemus) "*We* speak that which *we* know and testify that which *we* have seen and ye receive not our testimony," vi. 5 (to Philip) "Whence are *we* to buy bread that these may eat?" xiv. 31 "Arise, let *us* go (ἄγωμεν) hence." In the first of these, there may be, on the surface, some slight irony—when our Lord ranks Himself with other teachers of spiritual truth, in addressing Nicodemus, who had called Him (iii. 2) "*a* teacher," and whom He had called (iii. 10) "*the* teacher." But there is also an inner meaning, namely that the Son is "not alone" in His testimony, which corresponds to that of "two men[1]," being the testimony of the Father and the Son, so that "we speak" means "the Father and I speak." A similar inner meaning seems to belong to vi. 5 "Whence are *we* to buy bread," where the Johannine "buying"—an entirely new version of the parallel Synoptic "buying[2]"—appears to be typical of the procuring of the Eucharistic "flesh" and "blood," the sacrifice ordained by the Father and offered by the Son. The third instance has been discussed elsewhere, and it has been shewn that "*Arise ye, let us go,*" is a tradition of Mark and Matthew omitted by Luke and liable to be misunderstood as meaning flight, but really meaning appeal to Justice. It ought however to be added that the insertion of "hence" by John ("Arise ye, let us go *hence*") assimilates the words to a famous tradition recorded by Josephus that before Jerusalem was taken by the Romans there was a noise in the Temple as of a rushing host, and the gate opened, and a Voice was heard, "Let us pass hence (ἐντεῦθεν)[3]." Of course these last two passages also have their literal meaning, in which Christ associates Himself with the disciples: but the non-pronominal "we,"

---

[1] viii. 16, 17 and context.

[2] [2428 *a*] Mk vi. 36—7 "that *they* may buy...are *we* to buy," Mt. xiv. 15 "that *they* may buy," Lk. ix. 13 "unless...*we* are to buy." In Mk-Lk. "we" means the disciples. Chrys., however, in Jn, omits the "buying." See **2745**.

[3] See *Paradosis*, **1372—7** and Joseph. *Bell.* vi. 5. 3.

in a saying of Christ, is so fraught with probabilities of latent mysticism that it gives us very little help on the words, not uttered by Christ, now under discussion (xxi. 24) "*We know* that his testimony is true[1]."

---

[1] [**2428 *b***] In ix. 4 "*We* (ἡμᾶς, al. ἐμέ) *must work* (δεῖ ἐργάζεσθαι) the works of him that sent me (με, al. ἡμᾶς)," the insertion of ἡμᾶς differentiates the passage from those quoted above: but it will be discussed here, because, unless it can be shewn to be corrupt, it would seem to shew that, here at all events, Christ does place Himself on a level with His disciples in the emphatic ἡμᾶς. The preceding words are ἵνα φανερωθῇ τὰ ἔργα τοῦ θεοῦ ἐν αὐτῷ, "that the works of God might be manifested in him," *i.e.* in the man born blind. Then follows, in B, ημας δει εργαζεσθε (*i.e.* -αι, to work). Origen twice (Huet i. 125, ii. 25) omits ἡμᾶς δεῖ and quotes the saying as beginning with ἐργάζεσθε "work ye."

[**2428 *c***] D has δι ημας εργαζεσθαι. This might mean "for our sakes. Work ye." But D means δεῖ by δι, "it is necessary for us to work." MSS. often express ει by ι (see Boeckh *Inscr. Gr.* 4588 κε δι = καὶ δεῖ) and errors arise in consequence. Again ἡμᾶς and ὑμᾶς are liable to confusion—as may be seen from Jn viii. 54, 1 Jn i. 4 where W.H. give the two (ὑμῶν and ἡμῶν) as alternatives. Origen, then, might easily have read the words before ἐργάζεσθε as δι' ὑμᾶς "in order that the works of God may be manifested in him, *i.e.* the blind man, *for your sakes*." This would make excellent sense. Comp. xi. 42 (in the Raising of Lazarus) διὰ τὸν ὄχλον...εἶπον, "I said it *for the sake of the multitude*," xii. 30 οὐ δι' ἐμὲ ἡ φωνὴ αὕτη γέγονεν ἀλλὰ δι' ὑμᾶς, "for your *sakes*," and so, xi. 15 χαίρω δι' ὑμᾶς ἵνα πιστεύσητε.

[**2428 *d***] SS has "*and me* it behoves to do...," and so Ephrem (p. 197) "*et me* oportet operari...." The Vat. MS. of the Arabic Diatess. (ed. Hogg) has, as the preceding words, "that *we may see the works* of God *in him*," and the Clementine Homilies (xix. 22 Clark) have "that the *power* of God might be made manifest *through him in healing the sins of ignorance*." SS, Diatess. and the Latin vss all have "me" twice ("it behoves me—him that sent me"), but ℵ*L have "us" twice.

[**2428 *e***] Origen's first quotation is in a comment on Jer. xiii. 16 "Give glory to the Lord your God before (marg.) it grow dark," thus (Huet i. 125) "Perhaps we shall understand this scripture (τὸ γεγραμμένον) by applying (χρησάμενοι) a Gospel saying uttered by the Saviour, which runs thus (οὕτως ἐχούσῃ) 'Work while (ἕως) it is day. There cometh night when no man can work.'" He adds that Christ gives the name of "day" to "this world," contrary to custom. His second is from the early part of his commentary on John (Huet ii. 25) "He says to them that are partakers of His own Light, 'Work *as* (ὡς) it is day. There cometh night when no man can any longer (οὐκέτι οὐδείς) work: when (ὅταν) I am in the world I am the light of the world." It will be observed that in both these quotations Origen omits "the works of him that sent me (or, us)": and the length of the quotation, in the second instance, suggests that he is not quoting from memory but from MS. These and other variations, if they do not demonstrate that the passage is corrupt, suffice to shew that W.H.'s text cannot be relied on as a proof that Jesus here uses ἡμᾶς to mean "My disciples and I."

(a) "We know (οἴΔΑΜΕΝ)" (xxi. 24)

[2429] We return to the discussion of the words "*we know* that his witness is true," in the hope of ascertaining what "we" means. According to the analogy of the Epistle, it might mean (1) the writer, associating himself with others ("*we all* know"), or (2) with some fellow-evangelists or fellow-teachers ("*we* know") as distinct from those who are taught, who might be addressed as "you." Both these meanings occur (2427) in the Epistle. But it might mean (3) "we, the elders of the Church among whom this Gospel has been preached and is now being published, know that the witness of the evangelist is true." This third hypothesis must not be discredited by the mere fact that such an attestation is unique in this Gospel. For how could it well be otherwise? It would come naturally at the end of the book, once for all.

[2430] One argument against this third hypothesis is the fact that it does not come quite at the end of the book. After it there comes one more sentence, which contains the first person singular, xxi. 25 "But there are also many other things that Jesus did, the which (?) *if they are to be written* (ἐὰν γράφηται) *one by one, I think not even the world will hold the books that are [to be] written*[1]." Portions of this sentence are repeatedly (2414 *b—f*) quoted by Origen, and thrice as coming from the evangelist. It could hardly come from any one else, at least in substance[2]. For what mere scribe, or Editor, would venture to append his own expression of personal opinion to such a work as the Fourth Gospel? Moreover, it exhibits a strong sense of the inadequacy of any "books" to represent the multiform action of Jesus—just such a sense as we might suppose likely to be expressed again and again by a very aged

---

[1] [2430 a] Ἔστιν δὲ καὶ ἄλλα πολλὰ ἃ ἐποίησεν ὁ Ἰ., ἅτινα ἐὰν γράφηται καθ' ἕν, οὐδ' αὐτὸν οἶμαι τὸν κόσμον χωρήσειν τὰ γραφόμενα βιβλία. On ἅτινα ἐάν as generally meaning "whatsoever things" but here, possibly if the text is correct, "which things, if," see 2414—6.

[2] [2430 b] Tischendorf says that xxi. 25, in ℵ, is written by a different scribe from the one that wrote the body of the Gospel. But this scribe (according to W.H. *ad loc.*) appears to have been D, the διορθωτής, or corrector, of the MS., who also probably (according to Tischendorf (ℵ p. xxi)) wrote the last leaf of Mk and the first of Lk., as well as what may be described as the title and the salutation in Rev. i. 1—4 "The Revelation...and from the seven Spirits which are before the throne and from Jesus Christ." These facts are consistent with the hypothesis that the change of handwriting may imply some special circumstances but not necessarily interpolation or diminished authority.

disciple of Jesus contrasting his personal recollections of the Lord with "the books that were being written."

[2431] This postscript must be compared with a previous postscript. After the manifestation to Thomas ending with the words, "Blessed are they that have not seen and [yet] have believed," the writer adds, xx. 30—1 "Many other signs therefore did Jesus in the presence of the disciples, which are not written in this book. But these have been written that ye may believe that Jesus is the Christ the Son of God, and that, believing, ye may have life in his name." This apparently deals solely with the Resurrection and the signs wrought by the Lord "in the presence of (2335) the disciples" after the Resurrection, committed to writing in order that, profiting by the rebuke to Thomas, the readers of his narrative ("ye") might be "blessed," "not having seen and yet having believed."

[2432] That would seem to have been a fit termination to the Gospel—a statement of its object, addressed by the impersonal writer to the readers in the second person "that ye may have life in his name." But something seems to have happened to make another termination desirable. The reputed author, or originator—the disciple whom Jesus loved—lived (so says tradition) to a great age prolonged past decrepitude: and it was commonly reported, on the basis of an utterance imputed to Christ Himself, that he was not to die till our Lord's coming. When the old man's end had arrived[1], or drew manifestly near, it would become desirable to contradict this rumour and to shew how it had arisen. For this purpose an account of the utterance and of its occasion and circumstances was committed to writing. And this we find in the last chapter.

[2433] These circumstances would be exceptional, and might well explain an exceptional conclusion. After this Appendix (concerning what may be called the Johannine manifestation of the Resurrection) had been written out, it may have been submitted to the aged Disciple of the Lord, to receive, perhaps, a word or two of writing in his own hand like that at the end of the Epistle to the Galatians "in large letters." If so, it might be difficult to say which

---

[1] [2432 a] The difficult words "This is the disciple that *beareth witness*" and "*he that wrote*" (2166) do not necessarily imply that he was still living to bear witness. On the contrary they might be written (in any Christian Church familiar with the saying (Heb. xi. 4) about Abel) to indicate that the aged Disciple "being dead yet speaketh."

part of the Postscript belonged to the evangelist—who regards himself as writing the Gospel in the Disciple's name—which part (if any) to the Elders of the Church, and which to the Disciple himself[1]. Chrysostom most certainly recognises nothing as coming from Elders. And he quotes οἴδαμεν, once at least, as οἶδα, "*I know*, he says, that the things that he says are true[2]." One might have supposed this to mean that the evangelist was "setting his seal" to the truth of the "testimony" of Christ[3] about which the Gospel speaks so often: but apparently Chrysostom means "I know that the things I said about Him were true." The context is not very clear, and it is possible that Chrysostom may have read οἶδα μέν and ἔστιν δέ, although he quotes the text freely as οἶδα and ἔστι γάρ[4].

[2434] Some variations in the MSS. and Latin versions add to the uncertainty of interpretation[5]. Of course unaccented Greek MSS. would give no guidance as to ΟΙΔΑΜΕΝ whether it was to be taken as two words or one. The main internal evidence for ΜΕΝ, "on the one hand," is found in the following ἔστιν δέ: but this is omitted by SS and by the best Latin versions[6]. Yet ἔστιν δέ is almost certainly

---

[1] [2433 a] The same difficulty of distinction would arise if the Disciple died before this attestation and if the writer of the Gospel or the Elders attached to the MS. a fragment in the Disciple's handwriting recording a favourite saying of his about the inadequacy of books.

[2] [2433 b] Καὶ οἶδα, φησίν, ὅτι ἀληθῆ ἐστιν ἃ λέγει. Above, the text is printed as οἴδαμεν, but this might be an error for οἶδα μέν. Chrys. previously speaks of the evangelist as "testifying to himself (μαρτυρῶν ἑαυτῷ)."

[3] iii. 33 ὁ λαβὼν αὐτοῦ τὴν μαρτυρίαν ἐσφράγισεν ὅτι ὁ θεὸς ἀληθής ἐστιν, comp. viii. 14 ἀληθής ἐστιν ἡ μαρτυρία μου.

[4] [2433 c] The μέν after οἶδα may have been omitted because the rest of the sentence was not given, and the ἔστι γάρ in ἔστι γάρ φησι καὶ ἄλλα πολλά may have been a part of Chrysostom's framework of the quotation, not a part of the quotation itself.

[5] [2434 a] SS has the past ("*bare* witness") and omits ἔστιν δέ, οἶμαι and "itself" (in "the world *itself*"): "This is the disciple that *bare* witness of these things and wrote them and we know that true is his witness. And many other things did Jesus, which if one by one they were [all] written the world would not be sufficient for them." Codex *a* perhaps took the Latin "*his*" for *ihs*, i.e. "Jesus," and it repeats "scimus" and turns "qui" into "quis" thus, "Hic est discipulus qui testificatur de *Jesu* et *quis* scripsit haec *scimus*; et scimus quod verum est testimonium ejus." W.H. give txt ὁ μαρτυρῶν περὶ τούτων καὶ ὁ γράψας ταῦτα, but marg. καί (before μαρτυρῶν) and [ὁ] καί for καὶ ὁ, i.e. ὁ καὶ μαρτυρῶν π. τ. [ὁ] καὶ γράψας ταῦτα.

[6] [2434 b] Οἴδαμεν occurs in 1 Jn iii. 2, v. 15 (*bis*), v. 19, 20, and ἡμεῖς οἴδαμεν

an integral part of the sentence in which it stands. If both οἶδα μέν and ἔστιν δέ belonged to "the disciple whom Jesus loved," the most natural explanation of "*his* testimony" is "*Christ's* testimony"; and the Disciple must here be regarded as declaring his conviction that, whether he is to await the Lord's coming or to die—however much some may have misinterpreted the words "If I will that he tarry"—the Lord's testimony, and especially the testimony after the Resurrection, is absolutely true[1].

[2435] On the whole, the most probable conclusion is that οἴδαμεν is one word and represents the attestation of unnamed persons, and that the words following the attestation in the first person are an addition, supposed to come from the teaching of the aged Disciple, repeating, in effect, what he had said at the conclusion of the first edition of the Gospel. Then he had said that there were many more details, "not written in this book," of that vivid period after the Resurrection during which the Saviour was continually manifesting Himself to the disciples. Now he says that "if these details continue to be written," the world will not "hold" or "contain" all this "writing of books"—and he probably implies also that, "whatever number of these details may be written," the

---

in 1 Jn iii. 14. In all these cases it means "We, the disciples of Christ, know." On the one hand, this might be urged as shewing that οἶδα μέν would be assimilated to the phrase in the Epistle by the error of scribes. But it seems to me a stronger argument, that a writer so fond of οἴδαμεν would not write οἶδα μέν.

[1] [2434 *c*] Strictly after οἶδα μέν we should have something like Eurip. *Hippol.* 1091 ὡς οἶδα μὲν ταῦτ', οἶδα δ' οὐχ ὅπως φράσω: but the clause with δέ strays away as in Jn x. 41 (2169). A much more serious objection is that if the Apostle had meant "Do not lay stress on *me* as bearing witness. It is rather He that beareth witness and I know that *His* witness is true," he would have said ἐκεῖνος, as the Epistle, not αὐτός (2382—4).

[2434 *d*] If οἴδαμεν proceeded from the evangelist as part of the same sentence in which he also says οἶμαι, we should have to suppose the meaning to be "*We* [*the disciples of Christ, all*] *know* that the testimony of the Lord is true, but…," which seems improbable.

[2434 *e*] On Rom. vii. 14 οἴδαμεν γὰρ ὅτι ὁ νόμος πνευματικός ἐστιν, Alford says that Jerome has "*scio*." Gennadius (Cramer) certainly read οἶδα μέν, for he has ἐπίσταμαι ὅτι ὁ νόμος πν. ἐ. Cyril may have done so, for he has ἄμωμόν φησιν εἶναι τὸν νόμον, οἶδε γὰρ ἀμώμους ἀποτελεῖν. This is applied to David, as a parallel to the Apostle, who ἰσχυρίζεται μὲν ὅτι πνευματικὸς ὁ νόμος αἰτιᾶται δὲ τὴν ἀνθρώπου φύσιν. Οἶδε and μέν combine to suggest that he read οἶδα μεν. Origen (Lomm. vii. 31—2) seems to recognise, and to correct, this interpretation, by saying—after quoting the text with "*scimus*"—"Legem vero spiritualem esse *non solus Paulus sciebat*, sed et hi qui ab ipso imbuebantur."

portrait of the Saviour will not be "held" or "contained" in the "books[1]."

TENSE

[2436] Tense-idioms will be conveniently arranged under subdivisions of Mood. Tense-rules are sometimes interfered with by word-rules, *e.g.* the perfects of some verbs are rarely or never used, so that writers may be led to use the aorist for the perfect in those words. Hence the difference between two writers can sometimes be best illustrated by comparing, not their tense-usage in general, but their uses of the tense of one or two words in particular: and the shades of meaning intended by a single writer can often be perceived in the same way.

I. IN THE IMPERATIVE MOOD

(i) **Aorist (first) and Present**

[2437] The first aorist imperative is (1) sometimes more definite, (2) sometimes more authoritative[2], (3) sometimes more solemn[3] than the present imperative, which may denote continuous action. John uses the aorist "abide" in the Lord's mouth, but the present is used

---

[1] [2435 a] It is desirable to make "books" the last word in the English rendering so as to call attention to its emphatic position. Comp. the saying of Papias (Eus. iii. 39. 4) "I did not think I should be so much helped by what I could get from [the] *books* as by the [truths that came] from living and abiding Voice," οὐ γὰρ τὰ ἐκ [τῶν] βιβλίων τοσοῦτόν με ὠφελεῖν ὑπελάμβανον ὅσον τὰ παρὰ ζώσης φωνῆς καὶ μενούσης. Nonnus omits the words καὶ οἴδαμεν ὅτι ἀληθὴς αὐτοῦ ἡ μαρτυρία ἐστίν.

[2] [2437 a] But different writers might take different views of the authoritativeness of the same utterance. Comp. Mk vi. 10, Lk. ix. 4 μένετε, but parall. Mt. x. 11 μείνατε. Here we might say that Mk-Lk. meant "continue to abide." No such explanation avails for Mk vi. 11, Mt. x. 14 ἐκτινάξατε, Lk. ix. 5 ἀποτινάσσετε. But note that Lk. ix. 5 ὅσοι ἂν μὴ δέχωνται...ἀποτινάσσετε, *twice* uses the pres., while Mk vi. 11, Mt. x. 14 ὃς ἂν (Mk + τόπος) μὴ δέξηται... ἐκτινάξατε *twice* use the aorist. Perh. Lk. means "do so *habitually*." Comp. Lk. ix. 23 "take up the cross *daily*" where the parall. Mk viii. 34, Mt. xvi. 24 omit "daily."

[3] [2437 b] "More solemn." *E.g.* Jn xiv. 8 δεῖξον, in Philip's mouth, is "solemn" and reverential (but not authoritative)—like Κύριε, δίδαξον in Lk. xi. 1, ἐμφάνισόν μοι σεαυτόν in the corresponding prayer of Moses (Ex. xxxiii. 13, 18) and ἐλέησον passim. So "thou," in Elizabethan English, is used to the Highest, and to the lowest.

AORIST AND PRESENT IMPERATIVE [2439]

by the writer of the Epistle[1]. The authoritative imperative occurs in the miracle at Cana, ii. 5 (Christ's mother) ποιήσατε, ii. 7—8 (Christ) γεμίσατε,...ἀντλήσατε: at the Cleansing of the Temple, ii. 16 ἄρατε, and ii. 19 λύσατε: in Christ's words to the Samaritan woman, iv. 16 φώνησόν σου τὸν ἄνδρα, and afterwards to the disciples, iv. 35 ἐπάρατε...καὶ θεάσασθε: in the Feeding of the Five Thousand, vi. 10 ποιήσατε: in the Healing of the Blind, ix. 7 ὕπαγε νίψαι: in the Raising of Lazarus, xi. 39, 44 ἄρατε,...λύσατε: in the rejected (937—40) prayer xii. 27 σῶσόν με, and in the accepted prayer (*ib.*) δόξασόν σου τὸ ὄνομα: in the last words to Judas Iscariot, xiii. 27 ποίησον τάχειον: in the Last Discourse, xv. 9 μείνατε ἐν τῇ ἀγάπῃ τῇ ἐμῇ: in the narrative of the Draught of Fish and the subsequent meal, xxi. 10—12 ἐνέγκατε and ἀριστήσατε.

[2438] The instance in the Last Discourse ("Abide in my love") is perhaps the nearest approach to an authoritative command (in John) to obey a moral or spiritual precept. Our Lord never uses (1507 *a*) the authoritative form of the imperative in "believe ye," but frequently the present imperative, which occurs also in vi. 27 ἐργάζεσθε, vii. 24 κρίνετε, and xii. 35 περιπατεῖτε etc.[2] The three Synoptists have "thou shalt love." Two (Mt.-Lk.) have "love ye (ἀγαπᾶτε)." John has neither. Yet his Gospel connects "love" with what Christ calls "my commandment," and his Epistle abounds in "love"—but never "love ye" except in the phrase "love not the world."

[2439] John's avoidance of the aorist imperative of πιστεύω may be illustrated by the charge brought by Celsus against the Christians who, he asserts, authoritatively exclaim "Believe!" (aorist imperative) instead of allowing time for reasonable examination (present imperative) "*Do not spend time in examining* (μὴ ἐξέταζε),

---

[1] [2437 *c*] Jn xv. 4, 9 μείνατε, but 1 Jn ii. 28 μένετε (comp. 2 Tim. iii. 14 μένε). Mk xiv. 34, Mt. xxvi. 38 μείνατε ὧδε is an utterance of the Lord. Lk. xxiv. 29 μεῖνον μεθ' ἡμῶν may represent the (*ib.*) "constraint" put on the unknown Lord by the two disciples ("thou must needs abide with us").

[2] [2438 *a*] In ii. 8 ἀντλήσατε κ. φέρετε, v. 11 ἆρον κ. περιπάτει why have we not ἐνέγκατε (as in xxi. 10) and περιπάτησον? Probably because only the first action is to be done *at once*.

[2438 *b*] The remarks in this section apply only to the first aorist imperative. The second aorist has not this solemn or authoritative meaning. Indeed, in special words, the second aorist may be less authoritative than the present. For example, in iv. 16 φώνησον...κ. ἐλθέ, it is probable that the substitution of ἔρχου for ἐλθέ would have been more solemn (as in i. 46, xi. 34, Rev. vi. 1, 3, 5, 7, xxii. 17 (*bis*), 20) or authoritative (as in Mt. viii. 9, Lk. vii. 8).

but *believe at once* (πίστευσον)¹." The aorist imperative is indeed assigned to Christ once (so W.H. without alternative) by Luke, in the Healing of Jairus's daughter. But the corresponding passage in Mark has the present². Mark again prefers the present imperative in xiii. 21 "If anyone say unto you, 'See, here is the Christ,' (lit.) *Be not disposed to believe* (μὴ πιστεύετε)" where Matthew has (xxiv. 23, 26) "Believe [them] not," μὴ πιστεύσητε. This use of the present imperative (Mk xiii. 21 "*be not disposed to believe*") may perhaps be applied politely to things already done (like the formula "let not my lord say so," applied to what is already said) as in Jn xix. 21 μὴ γράφε, concerning what is already written. It is equivalent to "let not my lord write," and invites Pilate to cancel what he has written³.

[2439 (i)] Both Origen and Chrysostom accept without question the imperative rendering of ἐραυνάω in v. 38—9 τὸν λόγον...οὐκ ἔχετε...ὅτι...οὐ πιστεύετε. ἐραυνᾶτε τὰς γραφάς, ὅτι ὑμεῖς δοκεῖτε ἐν αὐταῖς ζωὴν αἰώνιον ἔχειν· καὶ ἐκεῖναί εἰσιν αἱ μαρτυροῦσαι περὶ ἐμοῦ· καὶ οὐ θέλετε ἐλθεῖν πρός με.... But against this view is the fact that in the few cases where ἐραυνάω is imperative in O.T. and N.T. the aorist is used⁴, and that one of these passages is in John and refers to the searching of Scripture. Chrysostom says that the Jews merely "*read*" the Scripture whereas Christ bade them "*search*" and "*dig*" in them. But the answer is (1) that the Jews *did* "search," (2) that their term "Midrash" implied most diligent "searching," and (3) that the Pharisees themselves exhorted Nicodemus to "search." It is also antecedently more probable that Christ would have advised the Jews to turn their hearts toward the love of God rather than to "*search* the Scriptures." Moreover the indicative agrees better with the indicatives that precede and follow: "*Ye have not* his word in you...because...*ye believe not*. *Ye search* the Scriptures (1722 *g*)

---

¹ [2439 *a*] Orig. *Cels.* i. 9. He might have said μὴ ἐξετάσῃς if he had not wished to emphasize the lingering over the task of examining.

² [2439 *b*] Mk v. 36 μόνον πίστευε, Lk. viii. 50 μόνον πίστευσον καὶ σωθήσεται, "only a special act of faith and she will be healed!" Comp. Epict. *Fragm.* § 3 "If you wish to be good, first *believe once for all* (πίστευσον) that you are bad."

³ The explanation "Do not persist in writing" would apply to Jn xix. 21, but not to Mk xiii. 21.

⁴ [2439 (i) *a*] 2 K. x. 23 ἐραυνήσατε καὶ ἴδετε, Jer. l. 26 ἐραυνήσατε αὐτήν, Jn vii. 52 ἐραύνησον καὶ ἴδε. Comp. Judg. xviii. 2 (A) ἐξεραυνήσατε (of which the pres. imper. does not occur in LXX). Of course these facts prove little except that the pres. imper. was not in common use.

AORIST AND PRESENT IMPERATIVE [2439 (iii)]

[book by book] because ye suppose...and they are they that testify of me, and [yet] *ye desire* not to come to me."

[**2439** (ii)] In xii. 19 οἱ οὖν Φ. εἶπαν πρὸς ἑαυτούς, Θεωρεῖτε ὅτι οὐκ ὠφελεῖτε οὐδέν, A.V. has "Perceive ye...?" R.V. "Behold" imper., but marg. "Ye behold." The indicative is supported by Acts xix. 25—6 ἐπίστασθε—καὶ θεωρεῖτε καὶ ἀκούετε, *i.e.* "ye behold with your own eyes, or see for yourselves," where the Ephesians are asked to "behold" how "this Paul" has perverted almost the whole of Asia—a passage remarkably like the Johannine one, in which a similar charge is brought against Jesus. Θεωρεῖτε is also indicatively used in Acts xxv. 24 and θεωρεῖς in Acts xxi. 20. "Thou seest [for thyself] brother [without words from us] how many myriads there are...." The imperative (twice) in LXX is followed by an accusative or πῶς, and nowhere by a clause with ὅτι[1]. On the whole, the meaning probably is "Ye see for yourselves that ye profit nothing. Behold (ἴδε)! the world hath gone after him." If so, the conclusion slightly confirms the view that ἐραυνᾶτε above (**2439** (i))—which is similarly initial and without ὑμεῖς—is also indicative. Comp. Jas ii. 24 ὁρᾶτε ὅτι ἐξ ἔργων δικαιοῦται ἄνθρωπος where R.V. has "ye see" without alternative[2].

[**2439** (iii)] Λύσατε in ii. 19 "*destroy* this temple and in three days I will raise it up" is explained by Blass (p. 221) as "equivalent to a concessive sentence... = ἐὰν καὶ λύσητε" and illustrated by Soph. *Ant.* 1168 ff. and also (*ib.* p. 321) by "Eph. iv. 26 O.T. ὀργίζεσθε καὶ μὴ ἁμαρτάνετε, which must mean 'angry you may be, but do not sin withal.'" This last passage, however, is from Ps. iv. 4 "Stand in awe (marg. be ye angry) and sin not," and Origen, *ad loc.*, after a long discussion of LXX ὀργίζεσθε, which, he says, may be "indicative (ὁριστικόν)" or "imperative (προστακτικόν)" decides for the former. Of course he may be wrong, but his decision makes it probable that the LXX meant the indicative and that St Paul took it so: "*Ye are*

---

[1] [**2439** (ii) *a*] Comp. iv. 19 θεωρῶ ὅτι προφήτης εἶ σύ, "I see [without more words] that thou art a prophet." The imper. occurs in 2 Macc. vii. 17 θεώρει τὸ μεγαλεῖον αὐτοῦ κράτος. In 4 Macc. xiv. 13 μὴ θαυμαστὸν ἡγεῖσθε...θεωρεῖτε δὲ πῶς..., and in Æschin. p. 13, 19 (quoted by Steph.) θεωρεῖτε τὸ πρᾶγμα μὴ ἐκ τοῦ παρόντος, the contextual μή prepares for, or subsequently suggests, the imperative. In Heb. vii. 4 θεωρεῖτε δὲ πηλίκος οὗτος, the δέ makes it prob. that θ. is imper. ; but it might be a parenthetic indic. following the details about Melchizedek: "But ye see for yourselves how great this man was." Tob. xii. 19 (ℵ) θεωρεῖτε is doubtful. The oratorical imper. is naturally predominant in Demosth. (see Preuss).

[2] On xiv. 1 (R.V.) "Ye believe (marg. Believe)," see **2237** foll.

angry [from time to time, it needs must be so], but[1] do not let your anger become a sin."

[2439 (iv)] What might be called a "concessive" imperative occurs in Eccles. xi. 9 "Rejoice, young man, in thy youth...and *walk in the ways of thine heart and in the sight of thine eyes*, but (Heb. and) know that for all these things God shall bring thee into judgment[2]." This imperative—which might perhaps be better called "minatory," for it implies a threat, "do this if you will, but at your peril," "do this, but take the consequences"—is well instanced in Epict. iv. 9. 18, addressing those who seek other objects than virtue, "If thou seekest...*continue doing as thou art doing* (ποίει ἅ ποιεῖς), not even a god can any longer save thee." This "minatory" imperative is common to all languages, *e.g.* Is. viii. 9 "*Make an uproar* ...and be broken in pieces," Soph. *Ant.* 1168, in effect "*Go on making money* and it will all be a shadow" etc.

[2439 (v)] Whether ii. 19 λύσατε should be called a "concessive" or "minatory," or some other imperative is rather a matter of taste than of grammar. I should prefer to illustrate it by the imperatives in Isaiah vi. 9 "Go and tell this people, Hear ye indeed but *understand not*; and see ye indeed but *perceive not*" uttered in obedience to the command of Jehovah, "*Make the heart of this people fat.*" So after the cleansing of the Temple by Jesus, when the Jews refuse to accept the act, Christ regards them as virtually bent on defiling and destroying the Temple, and says, in effect, "*Destroy it*, then, and I will raise it up." And similarly when Judas, after the washing of feet, and after receiving the "sop," adheres to his treachery and receives Satan into his heart, Christ says, "What thou art doing, *do more quickly.*" With the condemnation of Israel by Jehovah pronounced by Isaiah it is usual to connect the phrase "judicial blindness": and perhaps we might say that John regards the verbs in ii. 19 and xiii. 27 as "judicial imperatives[3]."

---

[1] [2439 (iii) a] The Hebrew *vaw*, "*and*," so often means "but" that the LXX may well have taken it thus here. Indeed Sym. substitutes ἀλλά (as well as ὀργίσθητε to make it clear that *he* takes the verb imperatively).

[2] [2439 (iv) a] Here the LXX has "walk *spotless* in [thy] ways and *not* in the sight of thine eyes and know...." The Targum corrupts the text in the same way so as to make all the imperatives hortative. "*In...thine eyes*" implies self-will.

[3] [2439 (v) a] On ii. 19 Origen (*ad loc.*) says nothing that bears on λύσατε except (Lomm. i. 348) τοῦτον τὸν ναὸν λυθῆναι δεῖ ὑπὸ τῶν ἐπιβουλευόντων τῷ λόγῳ τοῦ θεοῦ. On xiii. 27 ποίησον he says (*ad loc.*) that Christ speaks προκαλούμενος

II. In the Indicative Mood

(i) Aorist

(1) Aorist compared with Perfect

[2440] Commenting on Col. i. 16 "in him all things *were created* (ἐκτίσθη)...all things through him and to him *have been created* (ἔκτισται)" Lightfoot says, "The aorist is used here: the perfect below. Ἐκτίσθη describes the definite historical act of creation; ἔκτισται the continuous and present relations of creation to the Creator: comp. Joh. i. 3 χωρὶς αὐτοῦ ἐγένετο οὐδὲ ἕν with *ib*. ὃ γέγονεν, 1 Cor. ix. 22 ἐγενόμην τοῖς ἀσθενέσιν ἀσθενής with *ib*. τοῖς πᾶσιν γέγονα πάντα, 2 Cor. xii. 17 μή τινα ὧν ἀπέσταλκα with ver. 18 καὶ συναπέστειλα τὸν ἀδελφόν, 1 Joh. iv. 9 τὸν μονογενῆ ἀπέσταλκεν ὁ θεὸς εἰς τὸν κόσμον ἵνα ζήσωμεν δι' αὐτοῦ with ver. 10 ὅτι αὐτὸς ἠγάπησεν ἡμᾶς καὶ ἀπέστειλεν τὸν υἱὸν αὐτοῦ." This comment supplies a clue to several Johannine distinctions between the aorist and the perfect[1]. For example, as regards Christ's "coming into the world," or incarnation, "*I came*" represents the definite act, "*I have come*" the continuous and present relation. But other explanations are sometimes called for by Johannine use, which presents the following paradoxical characteristics[2].

τὸν ἀνταγωνιστὴν (*i.e.* Satan) ἐπὶ τὴν πάλην ἢ τὸν προδότην ἐπὶ τὸ διακονῆσαι τῇ σωτηρίῳ κόσμῳ ἐσομένῃ οἰκονομίᾳ, ἣν οὐκ ἔτι...μέλλειν οὐδὲ βραδύνειν ἀλλ' ὅση δύναμις ταχύνειν ἤθελεν. These last words favour the view taken elsewhere that τάχιον means, not "quickly," but "*more* quickly" (1918, 2554 *b*—*e*).

[2439 (v) *b*] The nearest approach to a judicial imperative in the Synoptists would be, if the text were correct, Mt. xxiii. 32 καὶ ὑμεῖς πληρώσατε: but W.H. marg. gives πληρώσετε with B and *e*, and this reading is now supported by SS. Alford suggests that the v. r. πληρωσετε and επληρωσατε arose from the "imperative not being understood." But it is not more difficult to understand than λύσατε above, for which there is no v. r. Moreover the position of ὑμεῖς before the imperative (without antithesis as in Mt. vii. 12 or μή as in Lk. xii. 29 etc.) is somewhat suspicious.

[2439 (v) *c*] In viii. 38 καὶ ὑμεῖς οὖν ἃ ἠκούσατε παρὰ τοῦ πατρὸς ποιεῖτε, one of several renderings of that difficult passage takes ποιεῖτε as imperative, but reasons have been given (2194 *c*) for taking it as indicative.

[1] [2440 *a*] Comp. xviii. 20 ἐγὼ παρρησίᾳ λελάληκα τῷ κόσμῳ...πάντοτε ἐδίδαξα ἐν συναγωγῇ...ἐν κρυπτῷ ἐλάλησα οὐδέν, where the "*continuous and present relation*" comes first, "*I have spoken* openly"; and this is supported by appeal to the *past*, "*I* ever *taught*," "Not once *spake I* in secret."

[2] [2440 *b*] On iv. 3 ἀπῆλθεν πάλιν εἰς τὴν Γαλιλαίαν, Blass (p. 192) justly says that the aorist "is at least remarkable, since the aorist denotes the journey as completed...." On this, and on the treatment of the passage in the Diatessaron, see 2635 (i).

[2441] On the one hand John uses the aorist where English would use the perfect, *e.g.* x. 32 "many good works *have I shewed* (ἔδειξα) you," xii. 28 "*I have* both *glorified* (ἐδόξασα) it and will glorify it again," xiii. 14 "If *I have washed* (ἔνυψα) your feet," xiii. 18 "I know whom *I have chosen* (R.V. marg. *chose*) (ἐξελεξάμην)," xiii. 34 "As *I have loved* (ἠγάπησα) you," xv. 15 "*I have made known* (ἐγνώρισα) to you," xx. 2 "*They have taken away* (ἦραν)...*they have laid* (ἔθηκαν) him[1]," xxi. 10 "Bring of the fish that *ye have* now *caught* (ἐπιάσατε)." These aorists may be explained in part because Greek does not use the perfect so frequently as in English to denote a recently completed action, but in part by the fact that the Greek perfects of these particular verbs are comparatively seldom used, and John, having no special reason for laying stress on the completion of the action, may prefer the more usual form[2].

[2442] On the other hand John uses the perfect where we might have expected the aorist, or the present, *e.g.* v. 45 "Moses, in whom

---

[1] Yet comp. xi. 34 τεθείκατε.

[2] [2441 *a*] The Greeks seem to have avoided several *active* perfects, *e.g.* of κτίζω, ὁρίζω, ζητέω, γνωρίζω, somewhat as we might avoid the perf. of "awake"—doubting between "have *awaked*" and "have *awoken*" (2747—53). The rarity of a suitable perfect may explain the aorist in vi. 70 (A.V.) "*Have* not *I chosen* you?," but there R.V. has "*Did* not *I choose?*" without alternative, as also in xv. 16—19, where A.V. has "*Ye have* not *chosen* me but *I have chosen* you... *I have chosen* you out of the world." I do not understand why R.V. txt adopts "have chosen" (Westc. "chose") in xiii. 18 alone ("I know whom I have chosen"). "Have," if denoting recent choice, would seem most appropriate to vi. 70.

[2441 *b*] The aorist of ἐκλέγομαι is applied to God or Christ in Mk xiii. 20 διὰ τοὺς ἐκλεκτοὺς οὓς ἐξελέξατο (Mt. xxiv. 22 om. οὓς ἐξ., Lk. diff.), Lk. vi. 13 ἐκλεξάμενος ἀπ' αὐτῶν δώδεκα (Mk-Mt. diff.). Ἐξελέξατο occurs in 1 Cor. i. 27 (*bis*), 28, Jas ii. 5, to describe God as choosing the poor and despised, and Eph. i. 4 has καθὼς ἐξελέξατο ἡμᾶς ἐν αὐτῷ πρὸ καταβολῆς κόσμου. In Acts, it refers to the choosing of apostles or missionaries in i. 2, 24, vi. 5, xv. 7, 22, 25 etc., and only once (xiii. 17) to God's choosing the "fathers" of Israel.

[2441 *c*] It seems clear that Mk xiii. 20 ἐξελέξατο means "chose," emphatically, implying final or irrevocable election or something of the kind. This is also implied in Mk xiii. 22, Mt. xxiv. 24 εἰ δυνατόν (Mt. +καὶ) τοὺς ἐκλεκτούς (which suggests that "the elect" could not possibly be led finally astray) and in Mt. xxii. 14 "many are called but few chosen." But Lk. omits all this, as well as (Mk xiii. 27, Mt. xxiv. 31) the gathering of the "elect."

[2441 *d*] Jn agrees with Lk. in applying ἐκλέξασθαι once to the choice of apostles, but he adds words that destroy the notion of finality, vi. 70 "Have I not [just] *chosen* (2254) *you the twelve*, and one of you is a devil?" On the other hand, later on, he appears to exclude Judas, and to imply a different, spiritual, and final election in xiii. 18 "I know whom *I chose*" following the words (xiii. 11) "Ye are not all clean" (comp. xv. 16, 19).

AORIST INDICATIVE [2443]

ye have hoped (ἠλπίκατε)," xv. 24 "They have seen and *have hated* both me and my Father," xvi. 27 "The father loveth (φιλεῖ) you because *ye have loved* (πεφιλήκατε) me and *have believed* that...," vi. 69 "*We have believed* (πεπιστεύκαμεν)...that thou art the Holy One of God." In modern English, "*I have* believed in him," if the emphasis is laid on "have," may mean "*I have* believed in him, in times past, or up to the present time, but *I do so no longer*." In John the context clearly implies *persistent belief*, and the same applies to the other instances.

[2443] How is this Johannine use to be explained? Probably as a modification of the LXX rendering of the Hebrew perfect in cases where it implies persistence. The Hebrew perfect is frequently used with verbs of "believing," "hoping," "hating," and "loving," to represent a feeling continued from the past into the present. But LXX inadequately renders this almost always by the aorist. Thus St Paul quotes the Psalms "*I have believed* (LXX ἐπίστευσα) therefore I spake," and continues, "We also *believe* therefore also we speak," thus applying the Hebrew perfect (LXX aorist) to himself in the present tense[1]. In that Psalm, A.V. has "*I believed*" and R.V. txt "*I believe*" (marg. "*I believed*"); but elsewhere the two agree in the perfect (Ps. cxix. 66) "*I have believed* in thy commandments." So when the Psalmist repeatedly says to God, "*I have hoped* (ἤλπισα) in thee, or in thy mercy," the meaning (however it may be rendered in English) is "*I steadfastly hope*," or "*my hope is fixed*[2]." The aorist "I hated (ἐμίσησα)" occurs several times in the Psalms, variously translated by R.V. and A.V.; and always in the sense of "*steadfastly hating*." In Proverbs, it is uttered by the Wisdom of God (Prov. viii. 13) "Pride and arrogancy...do I *hate*," and there LXX has the perfect μεμίσηκα, but Symmachus, Theodotion, and "another," have the aorist. The perfect also occurs in Judges xiv. 16 "only *hast thou hated* me (μεμίσηκας) and *hast not loved* me (ἠγάπησας, but A ἠγάπηκας)," where R.V. has "Thou *dost* but *hate* me and *lovest* me not[3]." In all these cases, it is quite clear that the

---

[1] 2 Cor. iv. 13 quoting Ps. cxvi. 10.

[2] [2443 a] Ἤλπισα in the Psalms = Ps. vii. 1, xvi. 1 (R.V. and A.V.) "I do put my trust," xiii. 5 (R.V. and A.V.) "I have trusted," xxxi. 1, 6, 14 (R.V. and A.V.) "I do put my trust," "trust," "trusted" etc.

[3] [2443 b] The Heb. perf., LXX aorist of μισεῖν = Ps. xxvi. 5 A.V. perf., R.V. pres., xlv. 7 A.V. pres., R.V. perf.: in Ps. v. 5, l. 17, cxix. 104, 113, 128, cxxxix. 21, R.V. and A.V. agree in having present. It is interesting to note that in Heb. i. 9,

"hate" described by the Hebrew perfect is a permanent and intense feeling; and the same statement applies to the other verbs. Nothing like this usage can be alleged from Greek literature, and the coincidence of Hebrew usage as to these particular verbs makes it a reasonable conclusion that a Hebrew origin must explain the Johannine use of them.

[2444] In another Hebraic use of the perfect the speaker regards a future action as already accomplished or, as we say, "as good as done." This is particularly common with the verb "give," *e.g.* in Genesis, in promises made by God, "*I have given* you every herb," "Unto thy seed *have I given* (LXX, *I will give*) this land," but also made by Ephron "*I have given* thee the field...*I have given*...*I have given*...," and by Abraham, in return, "*I have given* thee money," where R.V. has thrice "*give*" and once "*will give*," and LXX has δίδωμι and δέδωκα or omissions¹. This Hebraic idiom may have suggested the Johannine phrase "all that *thou hast given* me (or, *hast given* him)" so frequently used (1921, 2454—5) to denote the future Church. It might also explain xvii. 18 "Even as *thou didst send* me into the world, so I also *sent* them into the world." Here the aorist is used in both cases, and "I sent" has been taken by some as

---

quoting Ps. xlv. 7 ἠγάπησας...ἐμίσησας..., R.V.—which usually renders aorists as aorists—follows A.V. in the perfect, "*thou hast loved...and [hast] hated.*"

[2443 c] This Hebraic "Aorist of Persistence" in LXX is quite different from (a) the Greek aorist used to describe what happened before now and will happen again, *i.e.* the aorist of experience or habit. It is also different from (b) the Greek use of (Jelf § 403. 1) ἐπῄνεσα, παρῄνεσα, ᾔνεσα, ἀπέπτυσα, ᾤμωξα, ἐδεξάμην, ἔγνων. Jelf explains these as "referring to a thought supposed to have been long and firmly conceived in the speaker's breast." But in many cases they refer simply to what is "before," *and sometimes only* "*a moment before,*" or "*a moment ago,*" as in Eurip. *Med.* 63—4, where, in answer to the nurse's appeal ("What dost thou mean? Do not begrudge to tell me?") the old servant replies "Nothing. *I changed my mind [just this moment]* about even what I had said before (Οὐδέν, μετέγνων καὶ τὰ πρόσθ᾽ εἰρημένα)." So ἀπέπτυσα may mean "*I spat at [your words as soon as they were uttered]*" etc. In *no instance probably do these aorists contain any notion of anything* "*long and firm.*" Goodwin (*Moods and Tenses* § 60) renders Aristoph. *Eq.* 696 "Ἥσθην ἀπειλαῖς, ἐγέλασα ψολοκομπίαις, "*I am* amused... *I cannot* help laughing," but the English past would there express the sense better "*I was* amused...*I could* not but laugh," as soon as you opened your mouth. So ἥσθην in *Nub.* 174, 1240. And that is the meaning—though perhaps idiomatic English will hardly allow the past tense—in Soph. *Electr.* 668 "*I welcomed* (ἐδεξάμην) your [well-omened] utterance [as soon as uttered]."

¹ [2444 a] Gen. i. 29 δέδωκα, xv. 18 δώσω, xxiii. 11 om., δίδωμι, δέδωκα, xxiii. 13 om.

AORIST INDICATIVE [2446]

referring to the *previous* mission of the Apostles into Palestine. But it is more consonant with the high tone and Hebraic thought of the context to suppose that the Lord, after the manner of Hebrew prophets, mentions the ordained future "sending" into the world at large (not Palestine merely) as already past.

[2445] In xv. 6 (lit.) "If a man be not abiding (μένῃ) in me—[behold] *he was cast* (ἐβλήθη) outside...and was withered," the reader is asked as it were to pause after the statement of the conditional "not abiding." Then he looks back and—the branch "has been cast out." This is not like the Greek instantaneous aorists above mentioned (2443 *c*), *all of which are in the first person*. Probably it springs from Hebrew literature, which regards the sweeping away of things evil as an act of Jehovah so speedy that it is past before there is time to speak of it as future or present : " A thousand years in thy sight *are but as yesterday when it is past, and as a watch in the night. Thou hast carried them away as with a flood*[1]." The most conspicuous instance of this is in Isaiah's prophecy (Is. xl. 6—8 LXX, (lit.)) "All flesh [is as] grass...the grass *was dried up* and the flower *fell away*...but the word of our God *abideth* for ever," which has been reproduced in the Epistle of St James with aorists thus, "Like the flower of the grass he shall pass away. For the sun *rose up* (ἀνέτειλεν) with the scorching wind and *dried up* (ἐξήρανεν) the grass and its flower *fell away* and the fair show of its countenance *perished* (ἀπώλετο)[2]." In the light of these passages, and of the above-mentioned (2443) instances of Hebrew influence on Johannine tense construction, ἐβλήθη appears to be a Hebraic, not a Greek, instantaneous aorist. But see 2754—5.

[2446] According to different contexts, the aorist of the same verb may have very different meanings. For example, in xv. 8, ἐν τούτῳ ἐδοξάσθη ὁ πατήρ μου appears to mean (2393) "Herein [namely, by your abiding in me, the Vine] was my Father glorified,"

---

[1] Ps. xc. 5, Sym. ὡς καταιγὶς ἐξετίναξας αὐτούς.
[2] [2445 *a*] Jas. i. 11, comp. Jas. i. 24, 1 Pet. i. 24. Some excellent Greek scholars call these aorists "gnomic," on which see 2754—5. In view of the Hebrew origin of the quotations, the Hebrew use of the past tense, and the corresponding LXX use of the aorist, Hebrew thought seems to suggest the best explanation of the aorists in Jas. and Pet. "Gnomic" implies an inference of *regularity*: but the context in these Epistles calls attention to *rapidity*. It will be found, however, that an aorist, even in the 3rd pers., when in apodosis, sometimes expresses instantaneousness in non-Hebraic Gk. Hence xv. 6 may be independent of Hebrew influence. But it is certainly not "gnomic."

and the reference is perhaps to the definite fact that when one "branch," Judas, fell away from the Vine, the rest abode in it, or else it is to their whole past "abiding." But in xiii. 31 Νῦν ἐδοξάσθη ὁ υἱὸς τ. ἀνθρώπου κ. ὁ θεὸς ἐδοξάσθη ἐν αὐτῷ, there may be a twofold meaning. The "glorifying" certainly refers to the sacrifice of the Son upon the Cross, and that is future, and the aorist, if referring solely to that, would be the Hebraic aorist of prophetic anticipation above mentioned (2444—5). But it might also refer to the "going out" of Judas, just mentioned, and to the resignation of the Son to the treachery that had (xiii. 21) "troubled" Him "in the spirit," so that He made no further attempt to hinder it. In that case the tense would refer to what has just passed, "Now at last has the Son of man been glorified," because the *spiritual* act had taken place. This latter seems to be the primary meaning.

[2447] In xv. 15 "all things that *I heard* (ἤκουσα) from my Father (R.V.) *I have made known* (ἐγνώρισα) unto you," the R.V. is justified—so far as grammar is concerned—in rendering the two aorists differently, because of the rarity or non-existence (2441 *a*) of the perfect of the latter verb, whereas forms of ἀκήκοα are frequent if we include instances in the Epistle. But the meaning of ἐγνώρισα must depend on the context, which represents Jesus as "*no longer*" calling the disciples "servants" because He has now revealed to them the things that He "heard from the Father." This seems to refer to the recent sign of the Washing of Feet and to the doctrine of "loving" as being the sign of discipleship. If so, the meaning may be, "That which *I heard* from my Father when I came into the world to do His will *I made known to you just now in the Washing of Feet.*"

[2448] In order to distinguish between the aorist and perfect of γινώσκω it is well, in many passages of John, to render the verb "recognise," thus, xvi. 3 "These things they will do because *they did not recognise* (οὐκ ἔγνωσαν) the Father nor me," xvii. 7—8 "Now [at last] (νῦν, **1719** *f*) *have they recognised* (ἔγνωκαν) that all things as many as thou didst give me are from thee, because...and *they recognised* (ἔγνωσαν) truly that I came forth from thee." In the second passage, the perfect describes the present completed result of the previous definite recognition[1]. In xvi. 3, R.V. has "*they have*

---

[1] [**2448** *a*] SS has "And now *I know* that all what thou hast given me is from thyself, because the words that thou didst give to me I have given to them, and

not known": but the aorist should mean "*they did not recognise*" either Father or Son, when the Son announced the Father to them.

[2449] In viii. 29 "And he that sent me is with me: *he did not leave me* (R.V. *hath not left me*) (οὐκ ἀφῆκέν με) alone," the aorist (if not used as a perfect (**2441**) for the rare ἀφεῖκα) would mean that the Father when He *sent* (aorist) the Son into the world did not leave Him alone. R.V. has "*hath not left* me alone," and some have taken these words with the following ones, "because I do always the things that are pleasing to him," as though the Father's presence, throughout the life of the Son on earth, has been the spiritual reward or spiritual consequence of the Son's conduct ("The Father has been with me because I have done right"). But ὅτι means more probably (**2178**) "[I say this] because," introducing the ground of the statement: "The Father when He sent me hither did not deprive me of His presence. [I have a right to say this] because I do such deeds as could not be done without His presence[1]."

---

they have received them from me and they have known truly...," and ℵ has ἔγνων for ἔγνωκαν. Some MSS. support Chrys. in reading ἔγνωσαν for ἔγνωκαν, and one or two have ἐγνώκασιν. Several MSS. omit καὶ ἔγνωσαν. The textual variations of ἔγνωκαν are easily explained as resulting from an original ⲉⲅⲛⲱⲕⲁ and from a failure to perceive the shade of difference indicated by the perfect and the aorist:—"They are *now at last grounded in recognition*...because I have definitely given them the regenerating words of life and they [*at once*] *received* them and [*at once*] *recognised* in truth that I came forth from thee." That is to say, the present steadfastness of the disciples arises not only from the word of Christ but also from a certain affinity between that word and the disciples, which affinity caused them *to receive it at once* with a certain amount of recognition. Comp. i. 12 ὅσοι δὲ ἔλαβον αὐτόν, and note the immediate "reception" of Christ by Andrew and his companion and their brethren and successors.

[1] [**2449 a**] In xii. 40 "He hath blinded (τετύφλωκεν) their eyes and he hardened (ἐπώρωσεν) their heart," πωρόω represents Isaiah's word (vi. 10) " make fat," ἐπαχύνθη, and means not " make stiff " σκληρύνω, but "*make callous.*" Buhl gives no other instance of Heb. "*make fat*" applied to "heart"; and it was very natural that St Paul in writing to the Romans (Rom. xi. 7 οἱ δὲ λοιποὶ ἐπωρώθησαν) and Corinthians (2 Cor. iii. 14 ἐπωρώθη τὰ νοήματα αὐτῶν) should use πωρόω instead of παχύνω in alluding to this famous passage—which describes the "heart" of Israel as "hardened" in the sense of "made callous" although a remnant (Is. vi. 13) was to be faithful. Πωρόω is used by Mk (vi. 52, viii. 17) alone elsewhere in N.T. Its occurrence there, and in Hermas (*Mand.* iv. 2. 1, xii. 4. 4), and always applied to "the heart," suggests that the rare phrase "make the heart callous" found its way into the Roman Church—and thence into the works of Mark and Hermas which have Latin characteristics—through St Paul's Epistle to the Romans. The mention of "blindness" in the context of Isaiah

(2) Aorist of special Verbs[1]

(a) Ἀκούω

[2450] Ἀκούω in the Fourth Gospel may be illustrated by ἀκούω in the Epistle, where ἀκηκόαμεν occurs thrice at the beginning to denote the sum total of the doctrine of Christ possessed by the writers, who "*have heard*" that which was from the beginning; and the same notion of completeness and satisfaction appears in the saying of the Samaritans, "We ourselves *have heard* and know that this is truly the Saviour of the world[2]." Ἠκούσατε occurs five times in the Epistle in connexion with the definite word "heard" by the readers at the beginning of their Christian profession ("*from the beginning*" being thrice inserted to define the aorist). This is the general distinction in the Epistle[3].

(vi. 10) and Jn xii. 40 might lead scribes to confuse πωρόω with πηρόω "make blind" (comp. Job xvii. 7 "mine eye also is *dim*," Β πεπώρωνται, Αℵ[2] πεπήρωνται) and Hesych. explains πεπωρωμένοι as ἐσκληρωμένοι τετυφλωμένοι, but this may mean that he took the verb to mean literally "hardened," and hence "hardened against true impressions," which seemed equivalent to "darkened," or "blind to the truth."

[2449 b] A corrector of Codex B has altered ἐπώρωσεν in xii. 40 to πεπώρωκεν to conform it with the preceding perfect τετύφλωκεν, and this is very natural. There appears no reason for the change of tense, so far as sense is concerned. Perhaps, however, Jn may have been influenced by Pauline and other traditions, which described the act of God in visiting Israel with "callousness of heart" *as a historical fact in the past*. Rom. xi. 7—8 says "That which Israel seeketh after, this it *obtained* (aorist) not (οὐκ ἐπέτυχεν), but the election *obtained* (aorist); but the rest *were made callous* (aorist) (ἐπωρώθησαν), even as it is written, God *gave* (aorist) (ἔδωκεν) them a spirit of torpor, eyes that they should not see...," and LXX also has the aorist in Deut. xxix. 4 "The Lord *gave* not unto you a heart to know and eyes to see and ears to hear...[no, not] unto this day." As Jn xii. 40 deviates from the Heb. and from the LXX, there are special reasons for thinking that the writer may have been influenced by Christian tradition, perhaps oral, which associated the aorist with the "callousness of heart" inflicted on Israel, as by a divine decree, at the time of the Incarnation.

[1] On the aorist of ἀγαπάω, see **1744** (iv) foll.   [2] 1 Jn ii. 1, 3, 5, Jn iv. 42.

[3] [2450 a] There is an apparent inconsistency in 1 Jn ii. 18 καθὼς ἠκούσατε ὅτι ἀντίχριστος ἔρχεται, iv. 3 τοῦτό ἐστιν τὸ τοῦ ἀντιχρίστου ὃ ἀκηκόατε ὅτι ἔρχεται. But the former may be rendered "Even as ye *were taught* at the beginning." The latter may be intended to include a reference to the former: "This is that doctrine of Antichrist as to whom ye *have heard above and on many other occasions* that he must needs come." Καθὼς ἠκούσατε ἀπ' ἀρχῆς occurs also in 2 Jn 6. In Jn xviii. 21 ἐρώτησον τ. ἀκηκοότας means "ask *those who have regularly heard* me." But with οὐ the perfect means (Rom. xv. 21 quoting Is. lii. 15) "have not [up to this time] heard," and comp. Jn v. 37 οὔτε φωνὴν αὐτοῦ πώποτε ἀκηκόατε (**2764**).

AORIST INDICATIVE [2452]

[2451] Ἀκούω in the Fourth Gospel is in the aorist when Christ describes Himself, or is described, as "hearing" from the Father[1]: and this is the case even when "heard" is parallel to "hath seen" as in iii. 32 "That which *he hath seen* (ἑώρακεν) *and [that which he] heard*] (κ. ἤκουσεν) this he testifieth." The explanation here is complicated by the fact that (apart from forms of ὀφθῆναι, ὄψομαι etc.) the perfect of ὁρᾶν is the only part of the verb used by John. He might therefore conceivably use the perfect of ὁρᾶν, concerning spiritual vision, parallel to the aorist of another verb. But the two tenses may be explained as meaning "that which the Son *hath seen* [from the beginning], and *that message which He heard* [*when He came down from the Father to save mankind*]." So, whereas witnesses in Mark say concerning Jesus, "*We heard* him say," witnesses in the Acts say concerning Stephen, "*We have heard* him say." In the former, the meaning is "*we heard on one occasion*," or, "*we heard this definite statement*"; in the latter, "*we have repeatedly heard* him say" words to this effect, as is shewn by the context[2].

[2452] In xi. 41 "Father, I give thanks to thee that thou *didst hear me* (ἤκουσάς μου)," uttered at the grave of Lazarus, the aorist should refer to some definite prayer, and ought not to mean "thou hast always heard me." Origen and Chrysostom both emphasize the fact that no prayer has been mentioned as preceding; and the latter seems to say that there was no real prayer, "*Why*," he asks, "*did He even assume the appearance of praying* (τίνος δὲ ἕνεκεν καὶ εὐχῆς σχῆμα ἀνέλαβεν;)[3]?" But Origen suggests that a prayer, rising in Christ's mind and not yet uttered, was anticipated by the Father, who sent an answer, "It is fulfilled," into the heart of the Son. Some might urge—and with logic on their side—that the prayer must have been uttered some days before, when Jesus first heard "He whom thou lovest is sick" and replied (xi. 4) "This sickness is not unto death but for the glory of God, in order that the Son of God may

---

[1] iii. 32, viii. 26, 40, xv. 15.

[2] [2451 a] Mk xiv. 58 ἡμεῖς ἠκούσαμεν αὐτοῦ λέγοντος, Acts vi. 11—13 ἀκηκόαμεν αὐτοῦ λαλοῦντος ῥήματα βλάσφημα εἰς Μ. κ. τὸν θεόν...οὐ παύεται λαλῶν ῥήματα κατὰ τοῦ τόπου τ. ἁγίου [τούτου] κ. τ. νόμου, ἀκηκόαμεν γὰρ αὐτοῦ λέγοντος....

[3] [2452 a] See the whole context, which shews the influence of controversial considerations: "*Let us therefore ask the heretic*, 'Did He receive the [necessary] impetus (ῥοπήν) from the prayer and [thus] raise up the dead? How then was He wont to do the other works [of His] without prayer?'"—and he quotes Christ's words of authority 'I will, be thou clean' etc.

be glorified through it." But the evangelist may intend to convey to his readers the impression that, although it was revealed to the Son from the first that the sickness would in some way prove to be "not unto death," He nevertheless waited from day to day for further revelation of the Father's will, and that the actual revivification was not effected without an effort on the part of the Son, at the time when He "wept" and "troubled Himself" on His way to the tomb. In any case John—who neither describes Jesus as using the *word* "pray," nor himself speaks of Him as "*praying*"—here teaches the lesson that prayer may be sometimes most efficacious, and perfectly definite, when not expressed in words[1].

(β) Ἀποστέλλω

[2453] Ἀποστέλλω is mostly (15 times) in the aorist, when applied to God as sending Christ, but twice in the perfect, v. 36 τὰ ἔργα ἃ δέδωκέν μοι...μαρτυρεῖ...ὅτι ὁ πατήρ με ἀπέσταλκεν, and xx. 21 καθὼς ἀπέσταλκέ με ὁ πατήρ, κἀγὼ πέμπω ὑμᾶς. In the former, the perfect is perhaps used for parallelism with the preceding perfect δέδωκεν. In the latter, the mission of the Son on earth, being completed or perfected, is appropriately referred to in the complete or perfect tense.

(γ) Δίδωμι

[2454] In the Epistle, δίδωμι is used in the aorist to denote the gifts or commandments given to believers at the commencement of their Christian life; in the perfect, to denote the same gifts when regarded as present possessions. Compare "from the Spirit, which *he gave* us," with "because *he hath given* us of his Spirit[2]." In the Gospel, a corresponding distinction is generally made between the aorist and the perfect with reference to Christ. The aorist usually describes gifts regarded as given by the Father to the Son on His coming into the world to proclaim the Gospel; the perfect

---

[1] [2452 b] Origen (Huet ii. 347) quotes Is. lviii. 9 "While thou art still speaking I will say, lo, I am present," and argues that if Jehovah says this about mere men, He would say about the Lord "*Before* thou speakest, I will say, Lo, I am here." He does not quote Is. lxv. 24 "And it shall come to pass that, *before they cry, I will answer*," where "cry" is κεκράξαι, a word somewhat resembling the remarkable word ἐκραύγασεν in Jn xi. 43. Possibly, "*they*" was an obstacle.

[2] [2454 a] 1 Jn iii. 24 ἔδωκεν, iv. 13 δέδωκεν. Comp. 1 Jn iii. 23 καθὼς ἔδωκεν ἐντολὴν ἡμῖν: and v. 11 ζωὴν αἰώνιον ἔδωκεν ὁ θεὸς ἡμῖν, with iii. 1 ἴδετε ποταπὴν ἀγάπην δέδωκεν ἡμῖν, v. 20 ...ἥκει, καὶ δέδωκεν ἡμῖν διάνοιαν. These are all the instances of aorist and perfect in the Epistle.

describes gifts regarded as having been given to the Son and as now belonging to Him. More particularly, the future Church is frequently mentioned as " all that *thou hast given* me " as though the Son placed Himself in the future and looked back upon the Church as a completed gift. But from a different point of view the collection of faithful believers may be regarded as a gift made to the Son definitely at the Incarnation, and might be called "those whom (or, all that) *thou gavest* me."

[2455] The distinction is illustrated by xvii. 6—9 "I manifested thy name to the men that *thou gavest* me out of the world. Thine they were and *thou gavest* them to me...(9) I ask not in behalf of the world but in behalf of those whom *thou hast given* me." In the opening of the Last Prayer (xvii. 1—2) the Church is called "all that *thou hast given* him," but the aorist is used in the words " As *thou gavest* him authority." Towards the end of the Prayer the aorist is almost, if not entirely, superseded by the perfect, because the mind of Christ is fixed on the completion of God's gifts. But perhaps the aorist is to be read in xvii. 24 " that they may behold the glory that *thou gavest* me (W.H. marg. ἔδωκας, but txt δέδωκας) because thou lovedst me before the foundation of the world." The previous context says (xvii. 22) " The glory that *thou hast given* to me I have given to them, in order that they may be one." Scribes would, therefore, be tempted to conform xvii. 24 to xvii. 22. But xvii. 22 may mean "the glory that *thou hast given me* [*on earth*] so as to shew forth the unity between the Father and the Son," whereas xvii. 24 may mean "the glory that *thou gavest me* [*in the beginning*]," which is explained by "*for thou lovedst me before the foundation of the world*[1]." On πᾶν ὃ δέδωκας, see **2740** foll.

---

[1] [**2455** *a*] B has ἔδωκας here. Δέδωκεν and ἔδωκεν freq. occur as v.r.: see vi. 32, vii. 19, xiii. 15 (Tisch. δέδωκα, but W.H. ἔδωκα without alt.), xvii. 7, 8, 24. In vi. 32 οὐ Μ. ἔδωκεν (marg. δέδωκεν) ὑμῖν τὸν ἄρτον ἐκ τ. οὐρανοῦ the aorist would mean that the bread given on that historic occasion was not the real and true bread; the perfect would mean "M. *has* never *given* you." It follows a quotation (vi. 31) ἄρτον ἐκ τ. οὐρανοῦ ἔδωκεν αὐτοῖς φαγεῖν, from Ps. lxxviii. 24. In vii. 19 οὐ Μ. ἔδωκεν (marg. δέδωκεν) ὑμῖν τὸν νόμον; the aorist would mean "*Did* not M. *give* you the Law from Mount Sinai?" the perfect, in effect, "*Have* you not the Law, *given* you by Moses?" To these and many other passages Lightfoot's explanation (**2440**) applies: the aorist describes a "definite act," the perfect a "continuous and present relation." With οὐ, the aorist means " not, *on a single occasion* "; the perfect "not, *up to this time*."

(δ) Εῖπον

[2456] Εἶπε generally introduces longer and more weighty utterances of Christ than those introduced by the historic present λέγει. In dialogue between Christ and a single person, εἶπε very rarely introduces His words as compared with λέγει. The former is never thus used alone (*i.e.* without ἀπεκρίθη καί) in dialogue, except in a few cases of momentous utterance, six of which are in narratives of miracles[1].

(ε) Ἔρχομαι and ἐξέρχομαι

[2457] Ἔρχομαι and ἐξέρχομαι are used for the most part in the aorist (1637) to describe the Son as coming (or being sent) from the Father, but in the perfect to describe His having arrived in the world. Ἐξελήλυθα never occurs in any context, but ἐλήλυθα occurs three times[2] with εἰς τὸν κόσμον, and once as a sequel to ἐξῆλθον thus, viii. 42 "*I came forth* from God and *am come* (ἥκω); for indeed *I have* not *come* (ἐλήλυθα) from myself, but he *sent* me." In all cases the aorist points to the definite "coming" of the Incarnation. On the curious contrast (viii. 14) between "whence *I came*" and "whence *I come*," see 2482, 2490.

(ζ) Μένω

[2458] Μένω, in a past tense, is used literally of persons remaining in a place in six instances, always in the aorist except x. 40 W.H. txt ἔμενεν, marg. ἔμεινεν. In four of the six instances (i. 39, ii. 12, iv. 40, xi. 6) the aorist is accompanied by a mention of the "days," but not in vii. 9 and x. 40. The explanation of the imperfect in x. 40 may be that the writer means "he *stayed on* there [i.e. *stayed for some time*]" and the context ("many came...and many

---

[1] [2456 a] Jn i. 42 (in the calling of Cephas), iv. 48 (to the nobleman before healing his son), v. 14 (to the impotent man after his being healed), ix. 7, 35, 37 (to the man born blind, "Go, wash," "Dost thou believe," "He that speaketh with thee is he"), xi. 25 (to Martha, "I am the resurrection and the life"), xii. 7 (to Judas, about keeping the ointment for "embalming"), xviii. 11 (to Peter, "Put up thy sword"). Εἶπε, followed by Πάτερ, is also used in xvii. 1 (the Prayer to the Father) and, without Πάτερ, in xix. 30 ("It is finished"). Λέγει on the other hand introduces words of Jesus in dialogue no less than six times in three verses in xxi. 15—17. In Lk. ix. 58—62 εἶπε occurs no less than four times in sayings of Jesus to individuals, and it is his regular word in such cases, comp. Lk. vi. 8, 10, vii. 43—50.

[2] xii. 46, xvi. 28, xviii. 37.

believed on him there") favours this view. In i. 32 "I have beheld the Spirit descending...and it *abode* (καὶ ἔμεινεν) upon him" (where ℵ, *b*, and *e* have "and abiding") the meaning is "it abode once for all."

(3) Aorist for English Pluperfect

[2459] The aorist, *e.g.* ἐποίησε, if preceded (*a*) by ἤκουσαν ὅτι, or (*b*) by ὡς ("when"), is sometimes rendered "he had done" ("*they heard that he had done*," "*when he had done*"). Thus (*a*) iv. 1 "the Lord knew how that the Pharisees *had heard* (ἤκουσαν)," iv. 50 "the man believed the word that Jesus (A.V.) *had spoken* (R.V. *spake*) (εἶπεν)," ix. 35 "Jesus heard that *they had cast* (ἐξέβαλον) him out"; (*b*) ii. 9 "When the ruler of the feast (A.V.) *had tasted* (R.V. *tasted*) (ἐγεύσατο)."

[2460] Quite distinct from these is the use of the aorist to mean "he [previously] *did*"—equivalent to "had previously done"—introducing a mention of something that, in chronological order, should have been mentioned before, *e.g.* v. 13 "But he that had been healed knew not who it was: for Jesus [*previously*] *conveyed himself away* (ἐξένευσεν)," R.V. and A.V. "*had conveyed himself away*." This also appears to be the best rendering of ἦλθον (and perhaps of ἐποίησεν) in iv. 45 "When therefore he came to Galilee the Galilaeans received him, having seen all that *he had done* (ἐποίησεν) in the Feast: for they also themselves *had come* (ἦλθον) to the Feast"—where R.V. and A.V. have "went," but the Latin versions have the pluperfect[1].

[2461] The English pluperfect is perhaps intended in ii. 1—2 "There was a marriage in Cana...and the mother of Jesus was (ἦν) there. *Now there had been invited also Jesus* (ἐκλήθη δὲ καὶ ὁ Ἰ.) and his disciples to the wedding[2]." So, after describing the Entry into

---

[1] [2460 *a*] So, too, has the Syriac (Burk.). The best instance of this—which might be called the aorist of "previousness" or "afterthought"—is Mk vi. 17 (sim. Mt. xiv. 3) ἐκράτησεν "*had laid hold of*," describing Herod's arrest of the Baptist, which had occurred long before. Lk. iii. 19—20 mentions it much earlier.

[2] [2461 *a*] "Vocatus erat" is also read by *a* and *f*. Chrys. expressly reads twice (after ἐν Κανὰ τῆς Γ.) καὶ ἐκλήθη ὁ Ἰ. εἰς τοὺς γάμους. Ἦν δὲ καὶ ἡ μήτηρ τοῦ Ἰ. ἐκεῖ κ. οἱ ἀδελφοὶ αὐτοῦ, or, in Cramer, ἦν δὲ ἡ μ. τοῦ Ἰ. καὶ οἱ ἀδελφοὶ αὐτοῦ ἐκεῖ. Chrys. says that the last sentence was intended to "hint (ἠνίξατο)" that Jesus was not invited as being a "great person" but only as an acquaintance. Nonnus has Χριστὸς...Κλητὸς ἔην σύνδορπος ὁμοκλινέες τε μαθηταὶ Πάντες ἔσαν στοιχηδόν. Ἐς εἰλαπίνην δὲ καὶ αὐτὴ Παρθενικὴ Χριστοῖο θεητόκος ἵκετο μήτηρ. If ἐκλήθη is to be rendered as an aorist, the meaning may be that the mother of Jesus was staying at Cana first and that Jesus was invited thither afterwards.

Jerusalem and the cries of Hosanna, without mention (2756) of the finding of the ass, John adds, apparently as an afterthought, xii. 14 "But Jesus *had found an ass and sat upon it* (εὑρὼν δὲ...ἐκάθισεν)." It is possible then, grammatically, that xix. 39 ἦλθεν δὲ καὶ Νικόδημος might mean "Now there *had come* also Nicodemus." The preceding words are, "He [Joseph] came (ἦλθεν) therefore and took his [Christ's] body," and the question is whether John may mean, not that Nicodemus came *after* Joseph's "coming," but that "he also *had come*" to the tomb, and was waiting for Joseph, having procured the spices in the hope of the success of Joseph's application to Pilate. This, at all events, may be the view of *Acta Pilati* (B) § 11, which represents Nicodemus as saying to Joseph "I am afraid...lest Pilate should be enraged...But if thou wilt go alone, and beg the dead, and take Him, then will I also go with thee, and help thee to do everything necessary for the burial."

[2462] In xviii. 24 Ἀπέστειλεν...αὐτὸν ὁ Ἄννας δεδεμένον πρὸς Καϊάφαν, A.V. has "Now Annas *had sent* him bound," but the correct reading, which gives οὖν between ἀπέστειλεν and αὐτόν, makes this rendering impossible. The οὖν has been omitted by some authorities, and altered by others to δέ, in order to suggest that the previously mentioned examination was identical with the examination described by the Synoptists as occurring before Caiaphas, which is omitted in the Fourth Gospel.

(ii) **Future**, see Present of Prophecy 2484 foll., and οὐ μή 2255

(iii) **Imperfect**

(1) The Imperfect in general

[2463] The imperfect tense, ἐποίουν, may call attention to the beginning of an uncompleted action ("I began to do"), or to its non-completion ("I was [still] doing"), or to its repetition in an incomplete series of actions ("I kept on doing," "I was in the habit of doing"). With a negative, "I did not begin to do" may imply "I shewed no tendency to do," and with special verbs (e.g. "*I shewed no tendency* to help, pity, forgive") the imperfect may imply "I would not." In John, who (in striking contrast with the Synoptists) only once (1674 *a*) uses the verb "begin," the imperfect is frequently used in many shades of meaning not briefly expressible in English.

[2464] The following passage occurs soon after an act of healing on the sabbath. Assuming that no similar act was wrought in the interval, we cannot render ἐποίει "was wont to do these things" and the rendering must be "was beginning to do," thus, v. 16—18 "And for this cause the Jews *began-to-persecute* (ἐδίωκον) Jesus because *he began to do* (ἐποίει)[1] these things on the sabbath. But Jesus answered them, My Father worketh even until now, and I work. For this cause therefore the Jews *began-to-seek* (ἐζήτουν) rather (2733 a) to kill him because he was not only *continuing to break* (or, *thereby breaking*) (ἔλυε) the sabbath, but also *beginning to say*[2] (ἔλεγε) [that] God [was] his own Father......" Here, at all events in the first sentence, the evangelist seems to indicate a "beginning" to persecute, dating from a special act, and perhaps "these things" means "such things as this." In xii. 10—11 "the chief priests took counsel that they might put Lazarus also to death because, for the sake of [seeing] him (1652 b), many of the Jews *were going away and were believing* (ὑπῆγον κ. ἐπίστευον)," the meaning may be either that these things were beginning, or that they were going on under the eyes of the chief priests and would go on till they were stopped. In xiii. 28—9 οὐδεὶς ἔγνω...τινὲς γὰρ ἐδόκουν, the meaning is, "No one [exactly] understood...some *were [at the time] under a vague impression*......[3]."

---

[1] R.V. "did," A.V. "had done."
[2] But see 2468 b. Ἔλεγε may = "he meant," "he *was virtually saying*." On μᾶλλον, not "all the more" but "rather," see 2733 a.
[3] [2464a] So Acts xii. 9 ἐδόκει δὲ ὅραμα βλέπειν. Contrast the definite though erroneous supposition implied in Mk vi. 49 ἔδοξαν ὅτι φάντασμά ἐστιν, Jn xi. 13 ἐκεῖνοι δὲ ἔδοξαν ὅτι περὶ τ. κοιμήσεως τοῦ ὕπνου λέγει.

[2464b] The imperfect of custom is illustrated by Mk xv. 6 κατὰ δὲ ἑορτὴν ἀπέλυεν (Mt. xxvii. 15 εἰώθει...ἀπολύειν), Lk. om., Jn xviii. 39 ἔστιν δὲ συνήθεια ὑμῖν ἵνα ἕνα ἀπολύσω ὑμῖν [ἐν] τῷ πάσχα. The comments of Origen (on Mt. xxvii. 15) and of Cyril (Cramer) make it clear that they know of no such "custom" of pardoning criminals, and that they are at a loss to explain the allusion to it: nor is there any historical evidence of its existence. This may explain Luke's omission. Συνήθεια occurs in N.T. only here and 1 Cor. viii. 7, xi. 16 where it means an "unreasonable habit." Perh. Pilate is supposed by John to mean "a practice that has sprung up through my indulgence towards you." In any case, this is an instance where Lk. omits and Jn intervenes.

[2464c] Κατὰ δὲ ἑορτὴν (A.V. "at [*that*] feast," R.V. txt "at *the* feast" marg. "at *a* feast") is (like καθ' ἡμέραν) ambiguous. The best rendering is "at feast-time," which (according to context) may mean "at [the approaching] feast" or "at [any] feast." SS (in Mt.) has "at *every* Feast" and k (in Mk) has "*singulis* autem diebus festis": D reads τὴν in both. The ambiguity is removed (whether in accordance with fact or not) by Jn's insertion of "the Passover."

[2465] The imperfect of "come," after the aorist of another verb, and before the aorist "came," means "began to come," or "were coming," as follows, iv. 30—40 "They (*i.e.* the Samaritans) *came out* (ἐξῆλθον) from the city and *began to come* (ἤρχοντο) unto him. In the meanwhile......When therefore the Samaritans *came* (ἦλθον) unto him," xi. 29—32 "She (Mary) *arose* (ἠγέρθη) quickly and *began to come* (ἤρχετο) unto him. Now Jesus was not yet...The Jews, then,... followed her...Mary therefore, when she *came* (ἦλθεν) where Jesus was...," xx. 3—4 "Peter therefore *came forth* (ἐξῆλθεν) and the other disciple, and *they began to come* (ἤρχοντο) to the tomb. Now the two were running together; and the other disciple...*came* (ἦλθεν) first." In all these cases the context mentions an interval between the "beginning to come" and the "coming¹." John often uses these imperfects as an introduction to some important action².

[2466] With a negative, the imperfect may mean "was not beginning to do," and this may often mean "had no intention of doing." In ii. 23—4 "many believed (or trusted, ἐπίστευσαν) in his name...but Jesus himself *did not trust* (οὐκ ἐπίστευεν) himself to them," the meaning is "did not *even begin to* trust to them," because He knew their character from the first. It might almost be rendered "would not trust." The same phrase, applied to non-believing Jews in xii. 37 means "*they shewed no tendency to believe*," "did not even make a beginning to believe," and it is followed by xii. 39, "*they were not able to believe*." Nearly the same meaning is in xxi. 12 "no one *shewed a tendency to venture* (οὐδεὶς ἐτόλμα)," or, "*so much as began to venture*." But, in vii. 5 οὐδὲ γὰρ οἱ ἀδελφοὶ αὐτοῦ ἐπίστευον εἰς αὐτόν, the separation of the verb from the negative favours the rendering "not even his brethren *were* [*at that time*] *believing* in him."

---

¹ [2465 *a*] The imperf. is rendered thus, iv. 30 (A.V.) "came," (R.V.) "were coming"; xi. 29 (A.V.) "came," (R.V.) "went"; xx. 3 (A.V.) "came," (R.V.) "went."

² [2465 *b*] In xix. 3 (describing the soldiers mocking Christ), the imperfects, ἤρχοντο, ἔλεγον, and ἐδίδοσαν, mean "*kept coming*," "*kept saying*," "*kept giving*."

[2465 *c*] The imperf. ἐπυνθάνετο might be expected in Jn iv. 52 where, according to Blass (p. 191), "ἐπύθετο is incorrectly used and the correct form ἐπυνθάνετο has weak attestation (in xiii. 24 πυθέσθαι [which should strictly be πυνθάνεσθαι] is only read by AD al...)." In classical Gk, ἐπύθετο would mean "he *ascertained*," and ἐπυνθάνετο would be used (as in Mt. ii. 4, Lk. xv. 26 etc.) to mean "*he tried to ascertain*." In iv. 52 Chrys. has ἐπυνθάνετο and *a, d, f* have "interrogabat," but this attestation is certainly weak. It is noticeable, however, that, in what follows, ℵD *abf* have καί for οὖν (SS om. οὖν) so as to make the

[2466 (i)] When ὅτι ἦν is used after imperfect or aorist statements of perception ("saw that it *was* so"), the natural presumption, in John, is that the meaning is "saw that it *had been*"; for, in order to express "saw that it *was*," John would probably use the present, as in vi. 24 "the multitude *saw that Jesus was not there* (εἶδεν...ὅτι Ἰ. οὐκ ἔστιν ἐκεῖ)" *i.e.* saw [and said to themselves] "Jesus *is* not here" (comp. Mt. xviii. 25 "commanded him to be sold...and all, [said he], that he *hath* (ἔχει)"). With other imperfects, distinguishable from aorists, the imperfect meaning may be retained, *e.g.* xvi. 19 "recognised that they *were and had been desiring* (ἤθελον) to question him," but not with ἦν. In v. 13 οὐκ ᾔδει τίς ἐστιν, D reads ἦν; but the Pharisees have just asked "Who *is it*?" Τίς ἐστιν; and now it is added that the man "did not know [and could not answer this question] *Who is it?*" and then (v. 15) "he said to the Jews (lit.) that '*It is* Jesus.'" In vi. 22 εἶδον (marg. ἰδών) ὅτι πλοιάριον ἄλλο οὐκ ἦν ἐκεῖ, the sense requires "that *there had been* no other boat," and (as there are v. r. εἴδων, ιδον, ειδεν, and *e* has "scirent"), Blass's (p. 192) suggestion that the orig. was εἰδώς is probably right: "the Jews knew there *had been* no other boat there on the previous night." In ix. 8 οἱ θεωροῦντες αὐτὸν τὸ πρότερον ὅτι προσαίτης ἦν, the present ἐστί could not have been used, because the meaning is not "Beheld [and said] He *is* a beggar," but "those who formerly were in the habit of beholding that he *was* a beggar." SS has "those by whom it had been seen that he was begging," and this conveys correctly the pluperfect meaning, that "the begging" belonged to the sphere of the "*had been*[1]."

---

meaning, "He therefore *ascertained* the hour—*and* they said, 'Yesterday about the seventh hour...,'" *i.e.*, in effect, "the father *ascertained* the hour *and* found it was the seventh." But as the text stands, Jn must be admitted to have used ἐπύθετο incorrectly, erring, however, with Plut. *vit. Demetr.* ch. 27 (1076 c) τοῦ Δημητρίου πυθομένου, Τί σοι δοκεῖ; (also *ib.* ch. 28) and with Hesychius, who says, Πυθέσθαι· ἀκοῦσαι, ἐρωτῆσαι, γνώσεσθαι.

[2465 *d*] On the other hand the v.r. xiii. 24 πυθέσθαι may be defended as meaning "*to ascertain*." Similarly, in LXX, πυθέσθαι, "*to ascertain*," in Gen. xxv. 22 and 2 Chr. xxxii. 31, is as justifiable as ἐπυνθάνετο and ἐπυνθανόμεθα, "*tried to ascertain*," in 2 Chr. xxxi. 9 and 1 Esdr. vi. 11; but Esth. iii. 13 πυθομένου is an error for πυνθανομένου which is read by Aℵ². In *Ox. Pap.* 533 (edd.) "sell the grass-seed and *ask* (πύθεσθε)...whether he wants...," I should prefer "*ascertain*." It would be quite correct to say that a man, "*trying to ascertain something* (πυνθανόμενος)" sends messengers "*to ascertain it* (τοῦ πυθέσθαι)."

[1] [2466 (i)*a*] Comp. Mk xi. 32 εἶχον τὸν Ἰωάνην ὄντως ὅτι προφήτης ἦν, Mt. xxi. 26 ὡς προφήτην ἔχουσιν τὸν Ἰ., Lk. xx. 6 πεπεισμένος γάρ ἐστιν Ἰ.

[2467] TENSE

(a) Ἔλεγον

[2467] John very frequently uses ἔλεγον to describe what "was being said" about some one subject, first by some, then by others, of a chattering multitude[1], or what people "began to say," or "said repeatedly" to some one person[2]. But he also uses it sometimes to introduce Christ's sayings, as follows ii. 21 ἐκεῖνος δὲ ἔλεγεν περὶ τοῦ ναοῦ τοῦ σώματος αὐτοῦ, vi. 6 τοῦτο δὲ ἔλεγεν πειράζων αὐτόν, vi. 71 ἔλεγεν δὲ τὸν Ἰούδαν, xii. 33 τοῦτο δὲ ἔλεγεν σημαίνων ποίῳ θανάτῳ ἤμελλεν ἀποθνήσκειν. In all these cases the saying is mysterious and not understood by the hearers, and ἔλεγεν means "*he was saying* [*all the while this or that, though the hearers did not perceive it*]." Once, this is expressed by the pluperfect xi. 13 εἰρήκει δὲ ὁ Ἰ. περὶ τοῦ θανάτου αὐτοῦ. This statement of Christ's meaning follows a statement of the misunderstanding: "Lord, if he is asleep, he will recover. But Jesus *had been saying* [*this*] about his death."

[2468] In each of these instances δέ follows the verb; and δέ, and the context, indicate that the evangelist is adding something to make clear to his readers that which was not clear to the hearers at the time when Jesus was speaking[3]. A somewhat similar meaning may be conveyed by εἶπεν with δέ, as in vii. 39 τοῦτο δὲ εἶπεν (v. r. ἔλεγεν but not marg.) περὶ τοῦ πνεύματος, xxi. 19 τοῦτο δὲ εἶπεν σημαίνων. In both these cases more emphasis is laid upon the weight of the authoritative prediction than on its being misunderstood: and indeed, as to the latter, it is quite possible that Peter is regarded as perceiving that the prediction pointed to a death upon the cross. Λέγω, in Greek literature, must often be rendered "I mean," so that ἔλεγεν may often be rendered "he was [all the while] meaning," as in viii. 27 "They did not understand that *he was* [*all the while*] *meaning* the Father [in speaking] to them[4]."

προφήτην εἶναι. Mk's ἦν, with reference perh. to his recent death, means that "he *had been* a prophet." Acts iii. 10 ἐπεγίνωσκον...ὅτι οὗτος ἦν "began to recognise further that this man *was*..." is rather different. Jn perh. would have here written ἐστίν which (Alf.) is read by some authorities, including Chrys.: but the meaning may be "*had been* but lately sitting as a beggar." The πρότερον in Jn ix. 8 differentiates it from Acts iii. 10.

[1] iv. 33, vii. 11, 12 etc.   [2] iv. 42, v. 10 etc.

[3] [2468 a] Comp. x. 6 ἐκεῖνοι δὲ οὐκ ἔγνωσαν, xi. 13 ἐκεῖνοι δὲ ἔδοξαν, where δέ introduces a statement of misunderstanding.

[4] [2468 b] This sentence may be illustrated by xvi. 17 "what is (emph.) (τί ἐστιν) this that *he says* (λέγει) to us?" which seems to be a blending of (1)

[2469] After ii. 21 "But *he was speaking* (ἔλεγεν) about the temple of his body" there arises some doubt as to the meaning in ii. 22 "When therefore he was risen from the dead, his disciples remembered that *he* (R.V.) *spake* (A.V. *had said*) (ἔλεγεν) this, and they believed the Scripture and the word that Jesus (R.V. and A.V.) had said (εἶπεν)." It is but fair to assume that the writer means two slightly different things by ἔλεγεν and εἶπεν, and that ἔλεγεν in the two consecutive verses has the same meaning. Also "*remembered*" may be used here as in the Entry into Jerusalem, where it is said that the disciples (xii. 16) "remembered that these things were written concerning him [Jesus] and that they had done these things to him"—perhaps (2757) meaning, "*remembered* that Zechariah had written about the King riding on the ass, and *remembered* that certain similar things had happened to Jesus, and *inferred* that 'these things were written concerning him.'" So here, in this prediction about the Temple, "*remembered*" is probably a short way of saying "remembered and recognised"; and ἔλεγεν περί is but a longer form of ἔλεγεν, "he was speaking [about], or speaking [of]," thus: "But *he was [all the while] speaking about* the temple of his body. When therefore he was risen from the dead, his disciples *remembered [and recognised]* that *he was [all the while] speaking [of]* this; and they believed the Scripture and the word that Jesus had said."

[2470] In two instances ἔλεγε appears to be used by John as in Mark to mean "began to say," or "went on to say," or "used to say[1]": vi. 64—5 "...but there are some of you that believe not.—

"What really is this?" τί ἐστιν τοῦτο; (2) "What does he mean?" τί λέγει; (3) "What is he saying to us?" τί λέγει ἡμῖν; in v. 18 ὅτι...πατέρα ἴδιον ἔλεγε τὸν θεόν, the meaning is uncertain (2464) because of the context: but it may mean "because...*he was [virtually] declaring* God [to be] his own father." This differs a little from ἐκάλει. Comp. Mk xii. 37 λέγει αὐτὸν Κύριον "[*virtually*] *declares* him [to be] Lord," where the parall. Mt. xxii. 45, Lk. xx. 44 have καλεῖ, and comp. Mt. vii. 21 οὐ πᾶς ὁ λέγων μοι, Κύριε, Κύριε with parall. Lk. vi. 46 τί δέ με καλεῖτε, Κύριε, Κύριε;

[1] [2470 a] In Mark, ἔλεγεν (which is often (535 (v)) corrected by Matthew and Luke) may sometimes mean "used to say." In the *Aboth* the sayings of a Rabbi are introduced (*a*) sometimes by "*was*," with participle "*saying*," as in i. 2, 3 etc., (*b*) sometimes by "*saying*," without "*was*," as in i. 4, 5, 7 etc., (*c*) very rarely by the past tense, "*said*," in the case of sayings to special persons etc., ii. 7 "he saw a skull...*and he said* to it," ii. 12, 13 "*He said* to them, 'Go and see....'" Dr Taylor renders (*a*) by "*used to say*," (*b*) and (*c*) by "*said*." The

For Jesus knew from the beginning who they were that believed not and who it was that should betray him.—*And he began to say* (καὶ ἔλεγεν), For this cause I have said unto you that no man can come unto me except it be given to him from the Father...," viii. 30—1 "While he was saying these things many believed on him. Jesus therefore *began to say* unto those that had believed him [those that were] Jews." In the former, besides other variations in the text (2636) the Latin *e* has "et dicebat propterea quia nemo," i.e. *"And it was on this account that he said* No man can come unto me[1]." This is equivalent to, "And this was what he meant when he said." But, as the text stands, ἔλεγεν must be rendered as in Mark. These two exceptional instances as compared with the multitude of instances in Mark, make John's ordinary deviation from Mark all the more striking.

(β) Ἤθελον

[2471] Both ηθελεν and ἠθέλησεν occur in John. The latter in i. 43 (R.V. "*was minded to*," A.V. "*would*") means "*it was his pleasure, he resolved*, to go forth to Galilee." Also in v. 35 ἠθελήσατε (A.V. and R.V. "*were willing*") there is perhaps a suggestion of a decision on the part of the rulers of the Jews to accept John the Baptist, "*It was your pleasure* to rejoice for a season[2]." The aorist

---

LXX often renders the Hebrew participle, when used as a tense of the indicative, by the Greek imperfect. These facts indicate that the *habitual sayings* of a Jewish teacher might easily be confused with his *sayings on special occasions*.

[1] To take διὰ τοῦτο as non-initial (as *e* does) would be contrary to Johannine usage (2387—91). For vi. 65 compared with vi. 44, see 2548 *a*.

[2] [2471 *a*] In LXX and N.T., (apart from negative and relative clauses, in which it is very frequent in LXX) ἠθέλησα with an infinitive is rare. In Judg. xx. 5, Tobit iii. 10 (א), it is used of a desire entertained but not accomplished. In N.T. it is similarly used, of a desire frustrated, in Mt. xxiii. 37, Lk. xiii. 34 ποσάκις ἠθέλησα, and in Lk. x. 24 ἠθέλησαν ἰδεῖν (where the parall. Mt. xiii. 17 has ἐπεθύμησαν). Comp. 1 Thess. ii. 18 ἠθελήσαμεν ἐλθεῖν πρὸς ὑμᾶς ἐγὼ μὲν Π. κ. ἅπαξ κ. δίς, κ. ἐνέκοψεν ἡμᾶς ὁ Σατανᾶς, which seems to mean "resolved once, yea twice."

[2471 *b*] In Mt. xviii. 23 (R.V.) "which *would* (ἠθέλησε) make a reckoning," the modern English might be "who *decided* to have an audit," and so Acts xvi. 3 "Paul *decided* that he [Timothy] should go forth with him." So Xen. *Cyrop.* i. 1. 3 "We know that many *made up their minds* (ἐθελήσαντας) to obey," Winer (p. 587) quotes Isocr. *Callim.* 914 οἱ...προκινδυνεύειν ὑμῶν ἠθέλησαν, which should be rendered "*made up their minds* to meet danger for your sake": so in Lucian ii. 408 (*Amor.* 10) ἐθελήσαντας αὐτοὺς ἐπηγόμην, it means "of their own free-will and resolution."

in LXX sometimes means "*it was the pleasure*" of God, or a king, where it conveys the notion of a decree[1]. The meaning of deliberate resolve is also usually conveyed by the aorist when used affirmatively in classical Greek.

[2472] In John, the imperfect ἤθελον occurs (apart from a negative or relative) in vii. 44 τινὲς δὲ ἤθελον...πιάσαι, "now some *would have liked* to have taken him," where it is perhaps (2575) implied that their desire was frustrated because (vii. 30), His "hour was not yet come...." In xvi. 19 ἤθελον (א ἤμελλον) αὐτὸν ἐρωτᾶν the meaning is, "Jesus knew that *they were wishing* to ask him" so that the imperfect has its proper force. In Mark vi. 19, 48 (1735 *b*), Acts x. 10, xiv. 13, xix. 33, ἤθελε refers to a desire given up, or not fulfilled, owing to something intervening. On the strength of these facts, coming to the most important of all the Johannine instances vi. 21 ἤθελον οὖν λαβεῖν, we are justified in saying that the desire must be supposed unfulfilled: "*They began to wish* to take him into the boat." The sequel shews that the wish was not fulfilled, for want of time: "Straightway the boat was at the land[2]."

---

[1] [2471 *c*] Job xxiii. 13 ὁ γὰρ αὐτὸς ἠθέλησε καὶ ἐποίησε, comp. Ps. cxv. 3, cxxxv. 6, Esth. i. 8, 1 K. ix. 1.

[2] [2472 *a*] A.V. "*they willingly received him*" makes quite a different sense. R.V. "*they were willing to receive him*" is ambiguous, for it might mean "they were willing [*as before*]." Chrysostom says, "Why did He *not* go on board the vessel (τίνος δὲ ἕνεκεν οὐκ ἀνέβη εἰς τὸ πλοῖον;)?" So Cramer οὐκ ἐνέβη δὲ εἰς τὸ πλοῖον. On the occurrence of ἤθελεν in the parall. Mk. vi. 48, see **1735 *b***. The 1st pers. in Gal. iv. 20, ἤθελον δὲ παρεῖναι, A.V. "I desire," R.V. "I could wish," Lightf. "I would I had been," is equivalent to our curious expression "*I could have wished*," the literal meaning being "I began to wish but gave it up as the thing was impossible." But the 1st pers. usage is not a safe guide as to the general meaning because it is often used to express modestly a wish that the speaker has *not* given up, as in Hermas *Mand.* v. 7 ἤθελον γνῶναι.

[2472 *b*] Comp. Lk. xxiv. 21 ἡμεῖς δὲ ἠλπίζομεν ὅτι αὐτός ἐστιν ὁ μέλλων λυτροῦσθαι τὸν Ἰσραήλ. R.V. has "But *we hoped* that it was he which should redeem Israel." Apart from the context, "we hoped" might mean "we *hoped* that it was—and it *proved to be so*," and R.V. is not the English of any particular century. A.V. is good seventeenth century English (except for the "which"): "But we trusted that *it had been* he which *should have* redeemed"; and it brings out the non-fulfilment of the "trust," though it does not directly attempt to render the imperfect. The meaning is, "*We were hoping [almost up till to-day* and saying] that 'This is he that is destined to redeem Israel.'" (B has ἠλπίζαμεν, and, in the context γενάμεναι and ἦλθαν (an interesting cluster of forms in -α).) The tense of ἠλπίζομεν, like that of ἤθελον in some of the above-mentioned instances, implies frustration. On ἤθελον implying unfulfilled desire, see **2716—7**.

(iv) **Perfect**

(1) As the result of Johannine style

[2473] It has been pointed out above (2442—3) that, in part, the Johannine perfect corresponds to the LXX aorist representing the Hebrew perfect "I have loved," "I have hated" meaning "I have always loved," "I have always hated," with the implication "I continue to love and hate." We know from Epictetus and Pliny that Roman gentlemen borrowed the Greek κέκρικα to express what the French call *chose jugée*, "*I have decided [once for all]*"[1]. John takes advantage of the Greek distinction—non-existent in Hebrew and Latin—between the aorist and the perfect so as to represent Pilate as saying (xix. 22) ὃ γέγραφα γέγραφα, *i.e.* "What I have written, *I have written [and shall not rewrite]*." This is the usual meaning of the Johannine perfect—permanence. For example, μεμαρτύρηκα (i. 34) might mean "my testimony is completed," as though the Baptist were thinking of himself as released from a completed task. But it probably means "I have witnessed [and abide as a witness]." So in i. 32 "*I have beheld* (A.V. *I saw*) (τεθέαμαι) the Spirit descending," the meaning might be "*I have [just] beheld*"; but—in view of 1 Jn iv. 14 "*we have beheld* (τεθεάμεθα) and testify"—it more probably denotes the *present and permanent result of the vision*, such as Luke (ii. 30) expresses by the Hebraic εἶδον, "mine eyes *have seen [once for all]* (εἶδον) thy salvation[2]."

[2474] The most interesting uses of "the perfect of permanence" are ἤλπικα and πεπίστευκα. As to the former which occurs in v. 45 (R.V.) "Moses, on (εἰς) whom ye have set your hope (ἠλπίκατε) (A.V. in whom ye trust)," there can be no doubt that the perfect in N.T. corresponds to the LXX aorist ἤλπισα above described (2443) and it is fairly frequent in N.T.[3] It may be contrasted with the imperfect

---

[1] [2473 a] Epictetus ii. 15. 5 calls on a friend, who has decided to starve himself to death: "I called on him and began to ask him what had happened [to cause this]. '*I have decided* [κέκρικα],' he replied." Comp. Plin. *Epist.* i. 12. 10 "Dixerat sane medico, admoventi cibum, κέκρικα."

[2473 b] In xx. 23 ἄν τινων κρατῆτε κεκράτηνται, the meaning of κρατέω is doubtful, but the perfect appears to imply instantaneousness, see 2517—20.

[2] Comp. i. 34 ἑώρακα A.V. "I saw," R.V. "I have seen."

[3] [2474 a] 1 Cor. xv. 19 ἐν Χρ. ἠλπικότες ἐσμέν, R.V. "we have hoped in Christ," A.V. "we have hope in Christ"; 2 Cor. i. 10 εἰς ὃν ἠλπίκαμεν, R.V. "on whom we have set our hope," A.V. "in whom we trust"; 1 Tim. iv. 10 ἠλπίκαμεν ἐπὶ θεῷ ζῶντι, R.V. "we have our hope set on the living God," A.V. "we trust in the living God," and sim. in 1 Tim. v. 5, vi. 17.

ἠλπίζομεν describing, in Luke, the disappointed hopes of the disciples a few moments before the manifestation of the risen Saviour (2472 b).

[2475] Πεπιστεύκαμεν occurs in the Epistle 1 Jn iv. 16 "We have a perfect knowledge and *we have a perfect belief*," and in the Gospel vi. 69 "*We have a perfect belief* and we have a perfect knowledge," which have been explained above (1629). In the latter passage Peter speaks, and, in another, Martha, xi. 27 "*I perfectly believe* (πεπίστευκα) that thou art the Christ." Peter's belief fails for a time in the hour of trial, and Martha's faith does not enable her to enter into the Lord's purpose; but these facts do not preclude "I have believed" from meaning, on the lips of the two speakers, *perfect* conviction. And, although the disciples had *not* attained a perfect belief in Christ, they may have "believed perfectly" that He "came forth from God." This might explain an apparent inconsistency where Jesus says (xvi. 31—2), "Ye believe for the moment" and predicts that the disciples will "be scattered," and yet He has previously said (xvi. 27) "ye *have a perfect belief* (πεπιστεύκατε) that I came forth from the Father." Even in the reproof to Thomas in xx. 29, the perfect may retain the meaning of completeness, the reproof being based not on the incompleteness, but on the cause, of the belief[1]. This use of the perfect extends even to the expression of "a perfect hatred" in xv. 24, where—in spite of the saying "No man hath seen God at any time"—Jesus says of the Jews "*They have* both *seen* and *have hated* (καὶ ἑωράκασιν καὶ μεμισήκασιν) me and my Father," meaning that so far as their vision goes, they are *perfect haters* of the Light.

(2) As the result of Johannine thought

[2476] In contrast with πεπίστευκα, ἤλπικα, and μεμίσηκα, the form ἠγάπηκα is not found either in the Gospel or in the Epistle (not at least without a negative to deny the existence of such a "love")[2]. But the perfect of φιλέω occurs once thus, xvi. 27 "For

---

[1] [2475 a] If so, there may be intended a suggestion of incongruity (comp. Rom. viii. 24 "What a man *seeth*, how doth he yet *hope for*?") between "seeing" and "perfect belief": "Because thou hast seen me *thou hast attained [what seemeth to thee] perfect belief*." The only other Johannine instance of πεπίστευκα is in iii. 18 ὅτι μὴ πεπίστευκεν "condemned for not having believed," where the tense may have merely a temporal force ("disbelieved up to this very moment") or may mean "for having no settled belief." Elsewhere it is without the negative. For (viii. 31) πεπιστευκώς, see 2506.

[2] [2476 a] If W.H. txt is correct, the perfect occurs in 1 Jn iv. 10 οὐχ ὅτι ἡμεῖς

the Father himself loveth you because *ye have loved* (πεφιλήκατε) me." It has been maintained elsewhere (**1716** *e, f,* **1728** *m—p,* **2584***c*) that John always uses φιλέω to denote love of a lower kind than that expressed by ἀγαπάω. Using the higher term, St Paul says " Owe no man anything save to love one another[1]"; and perhaps the evangelist thought that "loving," in the higher sense, is the one spiritual action that must never be spoken of as completed. Desiring to describe the disciples as having attained—even before the Resurrection and before the gift of the Holy Spirit—to a complete love of their Master in the lower sense of the word, he uses πεφίληκα.

[2477] If this is the correct explanation of the use of πεφίληκα and the non-use of ἠγάπηκα, it follows that we must be prepared in other instances for similar explanations—that is to say, explanations not based on Greek style like γέγραφα, nor on attempts to render the Hebrew "perfect of permanence," but on Johannine thought. In the first century, when Christian evangelists were comparing or contrasting prophecy with the Gospel, one might say "The prophets *prophesied*," another, "They *have prophesied*." Thus, Matthew and Luke have "All the prophets and the Law *prophesied* until John" and "From that time the kingdom of God is *being preached*[2]." John has "Other men *have laboured* and ye *have entered* into their labours[3]." John often prefers the latter aspect, viewing *the present as a completed result of the past*. Sometimes the perfect may include the notion of instantaneousness—the thought being that one has not time to say "God *is doing*" but must say "God *hath done*." Thus the Epistle to the Hebrews says "In saying 'new covenant,' *he has [by the mere word, at once] made antiquated* the first [covenant][4]." So, when the Lord has washed the feet of the disciples, and when He has for the first time called them "friends," the evangelist may perhaps indicate the sudden introduction of that which is new in the words, " Understand (**2243**) what *I have done* unto you" and "But you *I have called* friends[5]." And when He speaks of the inevitable

---

ἠγαπήκαμεν τὸν θεὸν ἀλλ' ὅτι αὐτὸς ἠγάπησεν ἡμᾶς, "not that *we have loved* God, but that *He loved* us." Here the actual redeeming love of God for man is expressed in the aorist, and the statement in the perfect, "*we have loved* God," is stated only to be denied. But W.H. marg. has ἠγαπήσαμεν.

[1] Rom. xiii. 8 εἰ μὴ τὸ ἀλλήλους ἀγαπᾶν.
[2] Mt. xi. 13 and parall. Lk. xvi. 16.   [3] Jn iv. 38.   [4] Heb. viii. 13.
[5] [2477 a] xiii. 12 γινώσκετε τί πεποίηκα, contrasted with xiii. 14 εἰ ἐγὼ ἔνιψα (but this is partly the result of the general non-use of the perf. of νίπτω), xv. 15 ὑμᾶς δὲ εἴρηκα φίλους.

sequence of divine judgment and reward, He says that the unbeliever "*hath been condemned* already," and that the believer "*hath passed* from death into life[1]." Similarly, placing Himself where He sees future glory and victory as already achieved, He says "*I have been glorified* in them," "*I have conquered* the world[2]." The Johannine perfect is never "used for the aorist" (2747—55).

(3) Second Perfects

[2478] Γέγονα is, no doubt, correctly (so far as tense is concerned) rendered by R.V. in i. 3 "*hath been made*," (A.V. "*was made*"). But there is difficulty in vi. 25 πότε ὧδε γέγονας; (R.V.) "when *camest thou* hither?" The perfect would seem to accord better with "how long" ("How long *hast thou been* here?"). Perhaps it is a condensed expression for "*When* [camest thou, and how] *art thou* [thus suddenly] here?" Some instances in which Matthew applies γέγονε to the fulfilment of prophecy suggest that he uses it as an aorist[3]. But the general Johannine use keeps the sense of the perfect[4]. Nonnus has Πότε δεῦρο παρέπλεες; Chrysostom asks whether πότε may be here used for πῶς, but does not explain γέγονας. The Latin and Syriac versions paraphrase it by "come."

[2479] Κέκραγε in i. 15 Ἰωάνης μαρτυρεῖ περὶ αὐτοῦ κ. κέκραγεν is rendered by R.V. "John *beareth witness* of him and *crieth*," A.V.

---

[1] [2477 b] iii. 18 ἤδη κέκριται, v. 24 μεταβέβηκεν ἐκ τ. θανάτου εἰς τὴν ζωήν, where the judgment and transition are regarded as having actually taken place, not as being vividly predicted by means of a perfect. In xvi. 11, κέκριται applied to the "prince of this world" describes an invisible condemnation that has just been ratified; and xiv. 7 ἑωράκατε describes a vision of the Father that has just been imparted to the disciples.

[2] [2477 c] xvii. 10 δεδόξασμαι ἐν αὐτοῖς, xvi. 33 ἐγὼ νενίκηκα τὸν κόσμον. It would be impossible to say how far these perfects are proleptic, how far regarded as actually expressing completion (in the eyes of God).

[3] [2478 a] Mt. i. 22, xxi. 4, xxvi. 56 R.V. "is come to pass," which seems contrary to English idiom (A.V. "was done"). In 1 K. x. 20 (R.V.) "there *was* not the like made in any kingdom," οὐ γέγονεν is parall. to 2 Chr. ix. 19 οὐκ ἐγενήθη.

[4] [2478 b] Jn i. 15, 30, v. 14, xii. 30, xiv. 22. In 1 Cor. xiii. 11, A.V. "But when *I became* (γέγονα) a man," is rightly corrected by R.V. to "now that *I am become*." Γέγονα (Steph. ii. 623) = "natus sum" in such phrases as "*I am* ten years old," γέγονα ἔτη δέκα, comp. Rom. xvi. 7 "my seniors in Christ (πρὸ ἐμοῦ γέγοναν ἐν Χριστῷ)." Alford and Thayer quote no instance of γέγονα meaning "I am come," or "I came" : ℵD and the Latin and Syriac vss. substitute in Jn vi. 25 some form of the verb "come." The aorist in Jn vi. 21 εὐθέως ἐγένετο τὸ πλοῖον ἐπὶ τῆς γῆς, seems to imply supernatural and instantaneous arrival. Is that the meaning in Jn vi. 25 γέγονας "suddenly come"? See **2758**.

"*bare* witness...and *cried.*" Κέκραγα, "cry aloud," is connected by Origen[1] with the effort of voice needed to make the deaf hear, and is distinguished by him from "cry," βοάω, the word used in the LXX of Isaiah (quoted by the Synoptists) "the voice of one *crying* in the wilderness." John probably associates it with the "*crying aloud*" of Wisdom in the Book of Proverbs "Ye fools, be of an understanding heart." But why does he use the Second Perfect instead of ἔκραξεν? Partly, perhaps, for the purpose of differentiating the cry of the Baptist, whose whole mission was "crying" and "crying aloud," from the "crying aloud" of our Lord Himself, which took place on three special occasions of public teaching or warning, vii. 28, 37, xii. 44, always ἔκραξεν[2]. But partly also the reason may be that he wishes to make the verb of "crying" parallel to the verb of "bearing witness," μαρτυρεῖ—his first use of the historic present (2482) so frequent later on in this Gospel. It is as though the Prologue of the drama had almost concluded, bringing us down from the Word in heaven to the Word on earth ("In the beginning was the Word... and the Word became flesh...full of grace and truth"). Now, before the curtain rises on the terrestrial scene, the dramatist inserts, as it were, a stage direction, "*John is discovered testifying* ('Ι. μαρτυρεῖ) *and crying aloud* (κ. κέκραγεν)."

(v) **Pluperfect**

[2480] The pluperfect is perhaps more frequent in John than in any of the Synoptists, and his use of it (like his use of the perfect) shews a disposition to represent distinctions not capable of being represented in Hebrew (which has no pluperfect). It often expresses

---

[1] [2479 a] Orig. Huet ii. 111 B "But he *cries and cries aloud* (βοᾷ δὲ καὶ κέκραγεν) that those who are far off may hear the speaker, and that those who are dull of hearing (βαρυήκοοι) may understand the greatness of the things that are being spoken." As regards the "*dull,*" lit. "*heavy*" of hearing, comp. Is. vi. 10 (LXX) "For the heart of this people has been made fat and with their ears they *have heard dully* (βαρέως ἤκουσαν)." Those who are "far off" are the Gentiles; those who are "dull of hearing" are the Jews. For the former, "crying" suffices, for the latter, "crying aloud" is resorted to and yet does not suffice. Comp. Prov. viii. 1—5 "Doth not wisdom *cry* (LXX κηρύξεις, but Theod. κεκράξεται)...she *crieth aloud* (ὑμνεῖται)...O ye simple, understand subtilty, and, ye fools, be of an understanding heart." Chrys. has Τί ἐστι τὸ, Κέκραγε; Μετὰ παρρησίας, φησί, μετὰ ἐλευθερίας, χωρὶς ὑποστολῆς ἁπάσης ἀνακηρύττει. But Origen's hypothesis of the "dull of hearing" seems far better. Comp. *Oxyrh. Pap.* 717, a petition of "late 1st cent. B.C.," ἐγὼ οὖν ἐβόων καὶ ἔκραζον...βοῶν καὶ κράζων ὅτι τοῦτό ἐστι....

[2] Comp. xi. 43 ἐκραύγασεν, in the Raising of Lazarus, and see **1752** a—*f*.

a parenthesis, or a statement out of its chronological place, of the nature of an after-thought : iii. 23—4 "Now there-was John also baptizing in Aenon—*for not yet had John been cast* (οὔπω γὰρ ἦν βεβλημένος) *into prison*" (which corrects a misapprehension likely to arise in readers of the Synoptic Gospels[1]) : iv. 8 "for his disciples [*I should have said before*] *had gone away*" : ix. 22 "These things said his parents because they were afraid of the Jews. For [*I should have said that*] some time ago (ἤδη) the Jews *had agreed together*..." : xi. 17—19 "Jesus therefore, having come [thither], found him [Lazarus] already four days in the grave. Now (δέ) Bethany was near Jerusalem...Now (δέ) many of the Jews *had come* to Martha," where the writer goes back from "having come and found" to the circumstances that preceded the "coming" and the "finding" : xi. 30 "Now (δέ) Jesus *had not yet come* into the village" : xi. 57 "Now (δέ) the chief priests and the Pharisees *had given* commandments... that they might take him."

[2481] This tense takes the reader, as it were, behind the scenes —after some mention of deeds or words—to tell him what *really had been the cause* of the result, or what *had been the motive or meaning* of the words. Thus the non-arrest of Jesus is twice explained, vii. 30, viii. 20, "because his hour *had not yet come*." The disciples say about Lazarus "Lord, if he is asleep, he will recover," but the explanation comes, xi. 13 "But Jesus *had said* [*it*] (εἰρήκει, *i.e.* had said "is asleep") concerning his death." In i. 19—24, terminating with the words κ. ἀπεσταλμένοι ἦσαν ἐκ τῶν Φαρισαίων, the reader may naturally ask why these "Pharisees" had not been mentioned in i. 19 along with "priests and Levites." The explanation is, that the deputation is first described from one point of view, as having ecclesiastical status and as baffled in the attempt to extract from the Baptist an answer satisfactory to themselves. Then the Pharisees, who have the status of teachers of the Law, are on the point of stepping in to ask by what right he baptizes, and at this point the evangelist breaks the course of events to tell us that Pharisees "*had been*" (2214) included in the deputation[2].

---

[1] [2480 *a*] Luke (iii. 19—20) narrates the imprisonment of John the Baptist, and then proceeds (iii. 21) "Now it came to pass when all the people were (or, had been) baptized and when Jesus was (or, had been) baptized...." This, if connected with what precedes, might easily give the impression that the imprisonment of the Baptist immediately followed the baptism of Jesus.

[2] [2481 *a*] The pluperf. pass. also occurs in xix. 11 εἰ μὴ ἦν δεδομένον, and xix. 41 ἐν ᾧ οὐδέπω οὐδεὶς ἦν τεθειμένος.

(vi) Present

(1) Historic Present

[2482] The historic present, which is much more frequent in Mark than in the other Synoptists[1], is also a striking characteristic of John. But Mark and John differ in their use of it. For example, before the historic present of ἔρχεσθαι, Mark makes a rule of prefixing καί[2], and uses it rather monotonously. John frequently uses it in asyndeton, often at the beginning of a sentence, and in such a way as to give life and vividness to the narrative, sometimes perhaps also (when applied to the "coming" of our Lord) suggesting that the Messiah is "he that cometh" to deliver (1632—6)[3]. John also, alone of the evangelists, uses βλέπει and—with one Synoptic exception—εὑρίσκει as historic presents[4]. When the risen Saviour came for the first time to the Disciples it is said that He "*came* (ἦλθεν)": but when, after Thomas had refused to believe, He comes to help

---

[1] [2482 a] Comp. *Horae Synopticae*, pp. 114—7, where it is shewn that, of 151 historic presents in Mk, Mt. has only 21, Lk. only 1. In some passages of LXX, the historic present represents the Hebrew "converted future," *e.g.* 1 S. xxxi. 1—3 ἐπολέμουν ... πίπτουσιν ... συνάπτουσιν ... τύπτουσιν ... βαρύνεται ... εὑρίσκουσιν, with parall. 1 Chr. x. 1 foll. ἐπολέμησαν...ἔπεσον...κατεδίωξαν...ἐπάταξαν...ἐβαρύνθη... εὗρον, also 1 S. xxxi. 8 "and it came to pass when (lit. and) they came...then (lit. and) they found," καὶ ἐγενήθη τῇ ἐπαύριον, ἔρχονται οἱ ἀλλ...καὶ εὑρίσκουσιν. Contrast this with parall. 1 Chr. x. 8 καὶ ἐγένετο τῇ ἐχομένῃ καὶ ἦλθον ἀλλ...καὶ εὗρον....

[2] [2482 b] Mk i. 40, ii. 3, 18, iii. 20, 31, v. 15, 22, 38, vi. 1 etc. An exception is v. 35 ἔτι αὐτοῦ λαλοῦντος ἔρχονται, which is the only instance where the parall. Lk. has historic present.

[3] [2482 c] It is applied to Philip and Andrew (twice) in xii. 22 coming to introduce the Greeks, and thrice to Mary Magdalene on the morning of the Resurrection, xx. 1, 2, 18 concluding with ἔρχεται Μ. ἡ Μ. ἀγγέλλουσα τοῖς μ. ὅτι Ἑώρακα τὸν κύριον, where ἑώρακα, of direct speech, is followed by εἶπεν, of reported speech. Somewhat similarly in vi. 24 εἶδεν ὁ ὄχλος ὅτι Ἰησοῦς οὐκ ἔστιν ἐκεῖ, there is a blending of (1) "The multitude perceived and said 'Jesus *is* not *here*,'" and (2) "The multitude perceived that Jesus *was* no longer *there*." The historic present of other verbs is also frequent in (xiii. 4—6) the Washing of Feet and (xx. 1—18) the description of the Resurrection. When John says that the Samaritan woman (iv. 7) "cometh" to draw water—almost immediately after saying that (iv. 4—5) "it was necessary" that Jesus should go through Samaria—and that He "cometh therefore" to a city of Samaria near Jacob's well, he may have in view the coincidence of the two acts of "coming" appointed by a divine "necessity."

[4] [2482 d] Βλέπει i. 29, xx. 1, 5, xxi. 9, 20; εὑρίσκει i. 41, 43, 45, v. 14. The Synoptic exception is Mk xiv. 37, Mt. xxvi. 40 εὑρίσκει αὐτοὺς καθεύδοντας (where parall. Lk. xxii. 45 has εὗρεν).

Thomas and other doubters, it is said that He "*cometh* (ἔρχεται)[1]." The former, like the coming into the world at the incarnation (2457), is described as a matter of past history; the latter as the action of ὁ ἐρχόμενος.

[2483] There is difficulty in xxi. 12—13 "Jesus saith unto them, [Come] hither, break your fast. None of the disciples would be so bold as (ἐτόλμα (2466)) to question him, Who art thou?—knowing [all of them] that it was the Lord. Jesus *cometh* (ἔρχεται 'I.) and taketh the bread and giveth to them, and the fish likewise." If the disciples are commanded to come "hither" by their Master, how is it that He is described as "*coming*" to them? One suggested explanation is that they "hang back[2]." But Peter had previously leaped into the water, uninvited, to hasten towards the Lord. Would he now "hang back"? Even if he had done so, would the beloved disciple "hang back"? Again, the evangelist comments on the mere silence of the disciples ("none of them durst question him"). If there had also been a "hanging back," would not the writer have commented on this also (e.g. "*But when they were afraid and did not draw near*, He Himself came unto them")? It is more in accordance with the tone of this Gospel to suppose that the writer assumed obedience. The Apostles come, as commanded, and recline, as for a meal, around the bread and the fish: then "cometh Jesus," *i.e.* to the disciples assembled round the food[3]. In the Washing of Feet it had been said "He *cometh* therefore to Simon Peter." Now He "*cometh*" to them all, severally. Then He washed their feet for the journey of an evangelist; now He gives them food to prepare them for it. Both are the acts of "*Him that cometh*[4]."

---

[1] xx. 19, 26.

[2] Westc. *ad loc.* "As the disciples hang back, 'Jesus cometh' and gives to them of 'the bread' and 'the fish' which He had Himself provided."

[3] [2483 a] This somewhat resembles Luke's account of Christ's appearing to the disciples and partaking of fish in their presence (Lk. xxiv. 36—42): and it suggests that there may have been various traditions combining a literal and a symbolical meaning (1) about the catching of fish, (2) about a Eucharistic meal (after the Resurrection) in which fish formed a part. In that case, ἔρχεται might be variously interpreted as "cometh to help," "cometh suddenly," or "cometh into the assembly of the disciples."

[4] [2483 b] It is worth noting that, in describing the Eucharist, ἔρχεται is used by Mk xiv. 17 ἔρχεται μετὰ τῶν δώδεκα, where the parall. Mt. xxvi. 20 has ἀνέκειτο, and Lk. xxii. 14 ἀνέπεσεν.

(2) Present of Prophecy and Present of Law

[2484] "Whoever stirs *dies*" contains a prophetic present; but "Whoever is convicted of murder *dies*," and "If a stone is dropped it *falls*," contain ordinary presents, describing what is the law (either conventional or natural). The latter might be called the Present of Law. "The present of law" and "the present of prophecy" are not always easily distinguished, especially in an author prone to contemplate in the present a future—a future when a Law now invisibly at work will be visibly fulfilled. John is such an author, and in his Gospel it is best to take the present (wherever the sense permits) as the present of law, or as the literal present, and not as the present of prophecy. The present in x. 15 "I *lay down* my life for the sheep" is certainly intended to include a reference to the Crucifixion. But it might refer also to the whole of Christ's work as being a "laying down of life," in so far as it realises the ideal of the Good Shepherd, of whom it is said, not that he *will*, if need be, do this, but that he *does* it: x. 11 "The good shepherd *layeth down* his life for the sheep." In iii. 18 "He that believeth in him *is not judged*," the meaning is, "*does not, now or ever*, come under the operation of judgment." That the present is not prophetic is made almost certain by the context, "He that believeth not hath been judged already (ἤδη κέκριται)"—which indicates that "judgment" has been in operation *in time past, up to the present moment*. If a law in present operation is contemplated in the latter clause, it must be contemplated also in the former.

[2485] This notion of a law in present operation occurs also in xii. 25 "he that loveth his life *loseth* (A.V. *shall lose*) (ἀπολλύει) it, and he that hateth his life in this world *shall keep* (φυλάξει) it to life eternal." It seems to mean "*is destroying*," rather than "*loseth*" or "*shall lose*," and the writer desires to suggest the present operation of the corrupting influence of self-love when it takes the form of selfishness. He might have said "*shall lose*" in strict antithesis with "*shall keep*," but he is glad to break the antithesis in order to emphasize the fact that "*he is already losing*[1]."

---

[1] [2485 a] The thought of a law already acting invisibly and soon to be manifested, may perhaps be illustrated by some uses of the phrases (a) "*The hour cometh*," and (b) "*The hour cometh and now is*," especially where the two occur together. The former refers to the time when (iv. 21) Jerusalem and Gerizim will cease to be the special homes of worship; the latter to the earlier and immediate

[2486] (1) The present in x. 32 "For which of those works *are ye stoning* me?" and in xiii. 6 "*Thou* (emph.) *washest* my feet!" is interrogative or exclamatory, and refers to actions of which the beginnings have been described—as it does also in xiii. 27 "What *thou art doing* (ποιεῖς), do more quickly." In xxi. 3 "*I am going* (ὑπάγω) fishing," the phrase "*I am going*" is so suggestive of the future that it may be almost called a form of the future in Greek, as it certainly is in English. This also applies to "*I am coming*," which may be combined with "soon" or other temporal adverbs so as to denote a speedy future. Hence xiv. 3 "If I go...*I come back* (πάλιν ἔρχομαι) (2649 (ii)) and *will receive* you unto myself," "I come" or "am coming" may combine the notion of speed with that of prophetic certainty. The present in xxi. 23 "that disciple *is not to die* (οὐκ ἀποθνήσκει)" and "he said not, '*He is not to die*,'" may perhaps be explained by the Greek usage of that particular word (2530), as in 1 S. xx. 32 "wherefore should he be put to death? (Heb. why shall he die?)," LXX, "Why *dieth* he?" ἵνα τί ἀποθνήσκει;

[2487] (2) In xii. 26 "...let him follow me, and *where I am* (ὅπου εἰμὶ ἐγώ) there shall my minister also be," a suggestion is probably intended that the Son, even while on earth, is in heaven, or with the Father; and the writer wishes to turn the reader's mind to something more than a local heaven. Εἰμὶ ἐγώ is repeated in xiv. 3, xvii. 24, and always precedes the antecedent clause ("that *where I am* ye also may be," "that *where I am* they also may be with me"). It is distinguished by the order of the words from ΕΓΩ ΕΙΜΙ (2226—8). So, too, is the simple εἰμί in xvi. 32 "ye shall leave me alone, and yet *I am* not alone because the Father is with me." Yet even there, "I am" is not prophetic present, but expresses the real, and existing, though invisible fact[1].

---

time when worship is to be (iv. 23) "in spirit and truth." The former is used to predict (v. 28) the resurrection of those "in the tombs"; the latter to predict (v. 25) the proclamation of the Gospel to those who are "dead [in sins]." In xvi. 2, 25, the shorter form is used to predict the persecutions and revelations that await the disciples after Christ's death; in xvi. 32, a version of the longer form, "the hour is coming and hath come," predicts the "scattering" of the disciples on that same night, and, perhaps literally, in that same "hour."

[1] [2487 a] What is the precise difference between vii. 34 ὅπου εἰμὶ ἐγὼ ὑμεῖς οὐ δύνασθε ἐλθεῖν and viii. 21 ὅπου ἐγὼ ὑπάγω ὑμεῖς οὐ δύνασθε ἐλθεῖν? The former is preceded by ἔτι χρόνον μικρὸν μεθ' ὑμῶν εἰμι καὶ ὑπάγω πρὸς τὸν πέμψαντά με, which says, in effect, "*I am* on earth where ye are...I go to the Father where ye cannot be." There is an apparently intentional inconsistency in saying to the

[2488] The following passage is noteworthy because it represents Jesus as varying His own words by converting a future into a present: xvi. 14—15 "He [the Holy Spirit] will glorify me: because *he will take* (λήμψεται) from what is mine and will announce [it] to you. All things as many as the Father hath are mine. For this cause said I that (ὅτι) '*He taketh* (λαμβάνει) from what is mine and will announce [it] to you.'" The change is perhaps best explained, not as though our Lord meant "[Yea, already] he taketh"—for in that case He would have hardly added "I said"—but as a transition of thought from what the Spirit *will* do to what the Spirit *does* in accordance with eternal Law. After a mention, in the future, of what the Spirit *will* do ("*will glorify* me...*will take...will announce*") the Law is stated in the present ("All things that the Father hath *are* mine") which leads to a re-statement of the Lord's words about the action of the Spirit as though He had said "the Spirit *taketh*." But the future is immediately resumed in the phrase "*will announce* [it] to you."

[2489] The present is apparently used as a future in xx. 17 "Touch me not, for I have not yet ascended to the Father: but go unto my brethren and say to them, *I ascend*[1] (ἀναβαίνω) unto my Father and your Father...." In vii. 33—4 Jesus says to the Jews "a little time *I am with you*," and, in the same sentence, "*Where I am ye cannot come.*" Here He says "*I have not yet ascended*" and, in the same sentence, "*I ascend.*" In some authors this present might mean simply "I am on the point of ascending." But this is unusual in John—at least as the sole meaning of the present. More probably the words are intended to suggest the thought of a spiritual ascending, already begun, "*I have not yet ascended...I am ascending.*" The mysterious words "Touch me not for I have not yet ascended" seem to mean that when the Lord had ascended

---

Jews "*Where I am ye cannot come*" immediately after saying "*I am with you*"—the object being to indicate that "*I am*," in the Saviour's mouth, often has a spiritual meaning, especially when it follows such a phrase as "I go to the Father." The two sayings, then, represent the same fact from two points of view, heaven being regarded first as a state in which one *is* and then as a place to which one *goes*—"Where I *am* [i.e. with the Father] ye cannot come. [Do ye not understand this? Then] where I *go*, there ye cannot come." The difficulty of "am" has caused some authorities (**2190** *a*) to take ειμι as εἶμι "I go." So Nonnus, ὀδεύσω.

[1] [**2489** *a*] Origen (Huet ii. 144, 265, 331) freq. (though not always) has πορεύομαι (and so does Chrys. *ad loc.*) for ἀναβαίνω: Nonnus, εἶμι...αὖτις ἱκάνω.

His disciples *would* be able to "touch" Him (perhaps as being the Bread of Life). The Ascension may be regarded in two ways, 1st, as an uplifting from the material earth up to and beyond the material clouds and out of sight, 2nd, as an uplifting of the Messiah in the invisible world, and simultaneously in the hearts of the disciples, to the throne of God. Luke describes the former in the Acts. John may be thinking of the latter here, and, if so, ἀναβαίνω may mean, not "I shall ascend" but "*I am ascending*," i.e. the Father is preparing the moment when the Son shall be exalted to heaven in the sight of angels above and in the hearts of believers below[1].

[2490] In viii. 14 "I know whence *I came* (ἦλθον) and where I go...ye know not whence *I come* (ἔρχομαι) or where I go," a contrast seems to be implied between the particular place from which a traveller may "have come," and the quarter or direction from which a man met in the street may "be coming." Πόθεν ἦλθες would be the more definite, serious, and important question. Πόθεν ἔρχει (almost equivalent to "What have you been recently doing?" "What have you been about?") might be asked out of mere curiosity. The distinction seems intended to express that the Jews have not even an indefinite notion of the origin and mission of the Son[2].

[2491] In xiv. 7 εἰ ἐγνώκειτέ με, καὶ τὸν πατέρα μου ἂν ᾔδειτε· ἀπ' ἄρτι γινώσκετε αὐτὸν καὶ ἑωράκατε (marg. + αὐτόν), the reading is uncertain (2760—6)[3]. If γινώσκετε is correct, it seems to mean "ye are

---

[1] [2489 *b*] Of course the spiritual Ascension may be manifested to believers by a vision of a local Ascension, such as Luke describes in the Acts, and Isaiah in his vision of the Lord in the Temple, "high and lifted up." Origen (Huet ii. 418—9) points out that Christ's *presence with the disciples is dependent on them, as well as on Him*. Where two or three are gathered together in His name, He is "in the midst of them" even after His death. When He says to the disciples (xiii. 33) "Yet a little while am I with you," He does not mean "I shall be dragged away by the guard of the chief priests" but "I shall be parted from you by your want of faith, because ye will be 'scattered' from me." Similarly the moment for His full and final ascension will not have arrived till He can be so "lifted up" as to "draw all men" unto Himself: and until the moment arrives when the disciples will be ready to be "drawn" to Him, the Ascension, for them, is non-existent. For that moment the Lord prepares by calling the disciples "brethren" ("Go unto my brethren and say I am ascending unto my Father and your Father").

[2] [2490 *a*] Chrys. says nothing about this distinction. Origen (Huet ii. 262 c) omits from ποῦ ὑπάγω to ποῦ ὑπάγω (homoeotel., 2549 *a*). On Nonnus see 2759.

[3] [2491 *a*] D and ℵ have εἰ ἐγνώκατε ἐμὲ καὶ τὸν πατέρα μου γνώσεσθαι (*d* scietis) καὶ ἀπάρτι γεινώσκετε (*d* cognoscite) (ℵ γνώσεσθαι) αὐτὸν καὶ ἑωράκατε αὐτόν: Iren.

[2491]

recognising" or "ye begin to recognise." If so, what is the meaning of the addition "and ye have seen"? How can a person begin to "recognise" unless he "has seen" previously? The passage must be compared with that in the Epistle "Every one that sinneth *hath not seen him* [i.e. the Son], *nor even known him*[1]." In both, according to the general Johannine usage, "*hath seen*" must be regarded as indicating not material but spiritual vision, and "seeing" is higher than mere "*recognition*" or "*coming to know*." In ordinary Greek, and indeed in ordinary language of any nation, "knowing" a person would be taken as a later and higher stage than "seeing" him; and Chrysostom (in his comment "those whom we see we may simultaneously see and yet not know") appears to have been misled by ordinary usage into adopting the corrupt "ye shall know (γνώσεσθε)," as though that were the goal to be reached after "having seen (ἑωράκατε)." But John seems to mean, in the Epistle, "hath *not seen nor even recognised*," and, in the Gospel, "Ye are *beginning to recognise,* [*yea*] *and* [*what is more*] *ye have seen*[2]." One may "*recognise*,"

III. 13. 2 "amodo cognovistis eum et vidistis eum," and IV. 7. 3 " Si cognovissetis me et Patrem meum cognovissetis et amodo cognovistis eum et vidistis eum"; *a* " Si me cognovistis et Patrem meum cognovistis: jam ex hoc nostis illum et vidistis illum," *b* and *ff* " Si cognovistis me et Patrem meum cognovistis: et amodo nostis eum et vidistis eum," *f* " Si cognosceretis me utique et Patrem meum cognosceretis et amodo cognoscetis eum et videtis eum"; *e*, alone of the latt. vss., has the present tense of γινώσκω, but in the wrong place as follows, " Si cognovistis me et Patrem meum *cognoscitis* et amodo nostis illum et videtis eum."

[2491*b*] Chrys. is printed by Migne as commenting thus: Πῶς δὲ εἰπών, "Οπου ὑπάγω οἴδατε, καὶ τὴν ὁδὸν οἴδατε, ἐπήγαγεν· Εἰ ἐμὲ ἐγνώκειτε, καὶ τὸν Πατέρα μου ἐγνώκειτε ἄν, καὶ ἀπάρτι γνώσεσθε αὐτόν, καὶ ἑωράκατε αὐτόν; Οὐχὶ ἐναντιολογῶν· ᾔδεσαν μὲν γὰρ αὐτόν, οὐχ οὕτω δὲ ὡς ἐχρῆν. Θεὸν μὲν γὰρ ᾔδεσαν, Πατέρα δὲ οὐδέπω· ὕστερον γὰρ τὸ Πνεῦμα ἐπελθὸν, πᾶσαν ἐν αὐτοῖς κατεσκεύασε τὴν γνῶσιν. Ὁ δὲ λέγει, τοιοῦτόν ἐστιν· Εἰ ᾔδειτε τὴν ἐμὴν οὐσίαν καὶ τὴν ἀξίαν, καὶ τὴν τοῦ Πατρὸς ᾔδειτε. Καὶ ἀπάρτι γνώσεσθε αὐτόν, καὶ ἑωράκατε αὐτόν (τὸ μὲν μέλλοντος, τὸ δὲ παρόντος)· τουτέστιν, δι' ἐμοῦ. Ὄψιν δὲ λέγει τὴν κατὰ διάνοιαν γνῶσιν. Τοὺς μὲν γὰρ ὁρωμένους δυνάμεθα καὶ ὁρᾶν καὶ ἀγνοεῖν· τοὺς δὲ γινωσκομένους οὐ δυνάμεθα γινώσκειν καὶ ἀγνοεῖν. Διὰ τοῦτό φησι· Καὶ ἑωράκατε αὐτόν· ὥσπερ φησίν, "Ὤφθη καὶ ἀγγέλοις (1 Tim. iii. 16). Perhaps ἐγνώκειτε and ᾔδειτε have been confused here in the text or in the comment. But it may be taken as certain that he read γνώσεσθε for γινώσκετε, so that he is able to say, in effect, "the 'knowing' is future, the 'seeing' is present." On Nonnus, see **2760**.

[1] 1 Jn iii. 6 πᾶς ὁ ἁμαρτάνων οὐχ ἑώρακεν αὐτὸν οὐδὲ ἔγνωκεν αὐτόν.

[2] [2491 *c*] Winer-Moulton (p. 342) illustrates this passage by one from Demosthenes *Lacrit*. 597 a (error for 937 a) "Do the terms of the bond bid the defendants to lend our money,—and this, moreover, to *a man with whom we have no acquaintance and whom we have never seen* (ἀνθρώπῳ ὃν ἡμεῖς οὔτε γινώσκομεν οὔθ' ἑωράκαμεν πώποτε)?" But the negative makes a great difference in all phrases

about "knowing." And, if γινώσκω and ὁράω are used by John in a spiritual sense, the usage of Demosthenes may be misleading as a guide to Johannine meaning. In John, when a person is described as "being known," the present, γινώσκω, always implies sympathetic or moral knowledge, insight, understanding, as in i. 48 "Whence *knowest* thou me?"—that is "that I am an Israelite indeed without guile"; ii. 24 "Because of his *knowing* (γινώσκειν) all men" (comp. ii. 25 "he *knew* (ἐγίνωσκεν) what was in man"), x. 14 "I *know* my own and my own *know* me," x. 15 "Even as the Father *knoweth* me," x. 15 "I *know* the Father," x. 27 "I *know* the sheep," xiv. 17 "doth not *know* it—but ye *know* it (*i.e.* the Spirit)." Comp. xvii. 3 "that they may *know* (γινώσκωσιν, Tisch. γινώσκουσιν) thee the only true God," and 1 Jn v. 20 "in order that (ἵνα) *we may know* (γινώσκομεν) the true [one]." In almost all these cases sympathy—and in many of them mutual sympathy—understanding, or insight, is implied.

[2491 *d*] In ii. 24 above, the knowledge or understanding had for its object the weakness or imperfection of human nature: and, still more distinctly the Epistle uses the present, γινώσκω, concerning moral understanding or knowledge of evil, as well as of good, repelling disciples of Christ antipathetically from the evil, and attracting them sympathetically to the good, 1 Jn iv. 2—8 "Herein ye *understand* (γινώσκετε) the Spirit of God...he that *understandeth* God hearkeneth to us... From this we *understand the spirit of truth and the spirit that deceives and leads astray* (τὸ π. τῆς πλάνης). Beloved, let us love one another, because the love [of the brethren] is from God, and everyone that loveth [his brother] is born of God and *understandeth* God."

[2491 *e*] Whence did John derive his use of the present, γινώσκω, to mean personal knowledge and sympathetic insight into character? Probably not from the LXX. The very first use of γινώσκω in LXX (Gen. ii. 17, iii. 5, 22) refers indeed to the "understanding" of good and evil, but this is expressly distinguished from "life," and it brings upon itself the curse of death. Γινώσκω is occasionally applied (2 Chr. vi. 30, Ps. xliv. 21) to God's knowledge of the human heart, in Gen. xxix. 5, and Tobit (*passim*) to "knowing" a person in one's town or village so as to be able to direct a stranger to him. But the style of Genesis and Tobit is not like the style or styles of most of the books of LXX, in which, as a whole, the pres., γινώσκω, signifying knowledge of a person, is very rare. Nor does it appear to be common in the Greek translators of the first century. For example, in Jer. xii. 3 σύ, κύριε, γινώσκεις με, Aq. and Sym. have ἔγνως.

[2491 *f*] More probably John derived his use of the present, γινώσκω, from Greek literature. In Homer and the tragedians it is often used of "distinguishing," or "recognising" persons, and friends, and also of recognising one's own nature and the nature or purpose of others, *e.g.* in Aesch. *Prom.* 309 γίνωσκε σαυτόν, "*recognise* thy weakness," Soph. *Phil.* 1388 "Thou wilt destroy me, *I see through thee* (γινώσκω σε) with these words of thine," comp. Eurip. *Her.* 639, *Hel.* 567, *El.* 768. The Eudemian Ethics of Aristotle (vii. 4) speaks of mothers of children out at nurse as preferring "to *recognise rather than be recognised* (γινώσκειν ἢ γινώσκεσθαι)." In the *Sibylline Oracles* (i. 74 γνωστοὺς δ' οὐκ ἐγίνωσκον) the imperfect means "*recognise* [as having the claims of kindred]." The use of "know" in the sense of "recognising," or "acknowledging," or "appreciating" persons (Gesen. 394 *a*) is fairly common in Hebrew, and is not absent from St Paul (1 Thess. v. 12 εἰδέναι, 1 Cor. xvi. 18 ἐπιγινώσκετε) and from Ignatius (*Smyrn.* 9 καλῶς ἔχει θεὸν κ. ἐπίσκοπον εἰδέναι). But these passages do not contain the pres. γινώσκω. Perhaps John's principal debt is to Plato (**2763** *a—b*).

to some extent, God's being and attributes long before one has "*seen*" Him, in the Johannine sense, as revealed in the Son.

[2492] No one has satisfactorily explained the extraordinary statement attributed to the Pharisees in vii. 52 "Out of Galilee ariseth no prophet (ἐκ τῆς Γ. προφήτης οὐκ ἐγείρεται)." On this, Westcott remarks, "Jonah, Hoshea, Nahum, and perhaps Elijah, Elisha, and Amos were of Galilee." How then could the Pharisees first say to Nicodemus, "Search and see," that is, in effect, "Look at the Scriptures [for you know nothing about them]" and then make such an astounding statement, inviting from Nicodemus an obvious refutation, "Search *ye* the Scriptures—and ye will learn that prophets do 'arise from Galilee'"? The only approach to an explanation is that the present "arises" means "*arises as a rule.*" But this—besides being forced—would expose the Pharisees to the charge of impiety, "Would you lay down 'a rule' for God and assert that He cannot do anything but what you say He does 'as a rule'?" As it stands, the text seems inexplicable. And there is no variation of the text sufficient to afford a solid ground for emendation[1]. Otherwise the conjecture would be obvious that, after the final c in "Galilee," o has dropped out. The result of this would be to convert "*the prophet*" (mentioned just before in vii. 40) to "*prophet.*" Concerning "*the prophet,*" the Pharisees might have traditions identifying His birthplace with that of the Messiah so that they might say "the prophet *ariseth* not from Galilee." In that case the present would be prophetic—"*is not to arise.*"

[2493] In xi. 47 τί ποιοῦμεν, Wetstein simply refers to Acts iv. 16 τί ποιήσωμεν; as though the meaning were "*What ought we to do?*"

---

[1] [2492 *a*] In vii. 52, B and L have ιδε οτι εκ της γ. προφ. ουκ εγειρεται (L εγηγερται). The order is given differently ("a prophet from Galilee") in ℵ ιδε οτι προφ. εκ της γ. ουκ εγειρεται, D ιδε τας γραφας οτι προφ. εκ της γ. ουκ εγειρεται, SS "see that a prophet from Galilee hath not arisen," and in *a* (*b* is missing) and *f*. Origen has (Huet ii. 278 B) the order of B, but οὐκ ἐξέρχεται οὐδὲ ἐγείρεται. There happens to be no other instance in the Gospels of ἴδε ὅτι (Lk. xxiv. 39 ἴδετε ὅτι not being to the point). Ἴδε is used absolutely in i. 46, xi. 34 "come and see." If the Greek ran originally ἐ. κ. ἴδε, Ὁ προφήτης ἐκ τ. Γ. οὐκ ἐγείρεται, "Search and see, The prophet ariseth not out of Galilee," scribes and editors might be inclined to alter ιδε ο προφητης because according to Johannine usage (i. 29, 36, xix. 14, 26, 27) it would mean "Behold, [here is] the prophet." This might explain why D inserts "the scriptures" after "behold." Among other changes, οτι might be substituted for ο. The o before προφήτης is omitted in i. 21 by ℵ and in i. 25 by C. Moreover SS, although it has "*the prophet*" correctly in i. 21—5, has "*a prophet*" incorrectly in vii. 40.

PRESENT INDICATIVE [2494]

But there, as in Lk. iii. 10, 12, 14, Acts ii. 37, the aorist subjunctive is used. Also the subjunctive in Jn vi. 28 (τί ποιῶμεν) (**2512**) indicates that John would have used that mood here if he had meant "*What is to be our course of action?*" If τί ποιοῦμεν; could be used like τί ποιεῖς; "what folly art thou committing?" (Epict. ii. 15. 7, iii. 5. 15, Aristoph. *Nub.* 723, *Vesp.* 1443) it might mean here "How foolishly are we acting in doing nothing!" Such exclamations in the first person are existent in τί φημί; and τί πάσχω; but they are not given in the Thesaurus under ποιῶ.

[**2494**] Philo i. 205 says that τί ἐποίησας is ἴσον τῷ οὐδὲν ἐποίησας or οὐδὲν ἤνυσας, and this meaning,—*i.e.* non-accomplishment—is very suitable here, "What are we accomplishing?" *i.e.* "We are accomplishing nothing." This also brings out more clearly the play upon Christ's "doing" mentioned in the context, saying in effect, "We are *doing nothing* while this man is *doing miracle after miracle*." Moreover it prepares the way for the utterance of Caiaphas, who tells them *what to "do"* ("it is expedient that one man should die"). It is on the same line of thought as xii. 19 "Ye behold that ye *are doing no good* (ὠφελεῖτε οὐδέν). See, the world is going after him!" Up to the time when they exclaim, "what are we *doing*?" they had been "*doing*" nothing: it was (xi. 53) "from that day," that they "took counsel to put him to death." The note of interrogation should follow ποιοῦμεν, and ὅτι, as frequently in John (**2178**), should be taken as an initial "for," thus, "What are we *doing* [apart from talking]? For this man is *doing* signs daily. If we let him continue, he will be our ruin[1]."

---

[1] [**2494***a*] Blass says (p. 210) "The pres. indic. is used very rarely in a deliberative sense in place of the fut. ind. (§ 56, 8): Jo. xi. 47 (Herm. *Sim.* ix. 9. 1) τί ποιοῦμεν; for which there are parallels in colloquial Latin." But he alleges no parallel from Gk and he adds "Plato *Symp.* 214 A πῶς ποιοῦμεν is not quite a similar case; it is not deliberative like τί ποιῶμεν ibid. B, but the present" —*i.e.* the present indicative—"contains a gentle rebuke." This appears to me to apply to τί ποιοῦμεν in John, which also "contains a rebuke" and is distinct from τί ποιῶμεν; For τί ποιοῦμεν; in Epictetus, distinct from τί ποιήσωμεν; see **2766** (i).

III. IN THE INFINITIVE MOOD

(i) **Infinitive compared with ἵνα and Subjunctive**

[2495] The accusative and infinitive as the object of θέλω in affirmations is rare in the Gospels[1]. In xxi. 22—3 (*bis*) ἐὰν αὐτὸν θέλω μένειν, the context is somewhat parallel to that in xvii. 24 θέλω ἵνα ὅπου εἰμὶ ἐγὼ κἀκεῖνοι ὦσιν μετ' ἐμοῦ. The comparison suggests that ἵνα conveys some notion of spiritual effort and purpose (2093—2104), which is not implied in the accusative and infinitive ("if I desire *his abiding*").

(ii) **Aorist and Present**

[2496] The difference between the aorist and the present infinitive, in John, may be illustrated by his use of both after δύναμαι. Where, for example, the infinitive represents what one can *habitually* "do," or "not do," in accordance with the law of one's nature, ποιεῖν is used[2]. And, as John deals principally with this aspect of "doing," he never uses ποιῆσαι, except in xi. 37, "Was not this man [*i.e.* Jesus], who opened the eyes of the blind man, able (lit.) [so] *to do* (ποιῆσαι) that this man also [*i.e.* Lazarus] should not have died (ἵνα καὶ οὗτος μὴ ἀποθάνῃ)?"—where the aorist is used because the reference is not to a course of action, but to a particular act. Hence ἐλθεῖν regularly follows οὐ δύναμαι or οὐδεὶς δύναται, denoting the *definite act* of entering into the Kingdom of God, or of going with Christ on the path of the Cross[3]. Hence, too, a distinction is to be drawn between v. 44 πῶς δύνασθε ὑμεῖς πιστεῦσαι, which may be paraphrased as, "How is it possible for *you* (emph.) so much as to reach the threshold of belief?" and the ordinary course of action contemplated in xii. 39 "For this cause they were not able *to believe* (οὐκ ἠδύναντο

---

[1] [2495 a] With negative, it occurs in Mk vii. 24 οὐδένα ἤθελεν (Tisch. ἠθέλησεν) γνῶναι (contrast Mk ix. 30 οὐκ ἤθελεν ἵνα τις γνοῖ), Lk. xix. 14, 27; without negative in Lk. i. 62 τὸ τί ἂν θέλοι καλεῖσθαι αὐτό. In the Epistles it is more freq., Rom. i. 13, xi. 25, xvi. 19, 1 Cor. vii. 7 etc.

[2] [2496 a] For ποιεῖν with δύναμαι, see v. 19, 30, ix. 16, 33 etc.

[2496 b] There is great difficulty in x. 29 οὐδεὶς δύναται ἁρπάζειν. The Greek MSS. present no variation. But SS, Origen, and perh. Chrys., seem to have read οὐδεὶς ἁρπάζει, and this is prob. right (**2767**).

[3] [2496 c] So, too, ἰδεῖν and εἰσελθεῖν, γεννηθῆναι etc., see iii. 3, 4, 5, vi. 44, 65, vii. 34, 36 etc. Comp. Mk viii. 34, Mt. xvi. 24 ἐλθεῖν with parall. Lk. ix. 23 ἔρχεσθαι (about the path of the Cross) where Lk. indicates continuousness by adding "daily" to "take up the cross."

πιστεύειν)¹." In iii. 27 οὐ δύναται ἄνθρωπος λαμβάνειν, the Baptist is enunciating a general law, that no man can from time to time "receive" except what is given him; but xiv. 17, ὁ κόσμος οὐ δύναται λαβεῖν, perhaps refers to the preceding definite promise "He will give you the Spirit of truth," and means "cannot receive when you receive it." It may however mean "the world cannot even reach the state of reception."

[2497] In xiii. 36—7 (W.H.) οὐ δύνασαί μοι νῦν ἀκολουθῆσαι... διὰ τί οὐ δύναμαί σοι ἀκολουθεῖν ἄρτι; the first clause speaks of the "following" as a new act, the second treats it as the continuance of an old one: "Why can I not *continue following* thee—[both at all times and] at this moment?" Or else the present may mean "*be at this very moment following*" as in xvi. 12 "But (lit.) ye are not able *to [be] bear[ing] them* (βαστάζειν) *at this moment* (ἄρτι)," contrasted with Rev. ii. 2 οὐ δύνῃ βαστάσαι κακούς, "thou art not able *so much as to tolerate* evil [men]," or "*ever to tolerate.*"

[2498] With θέλω and οὐ θέλω the present infinitive means "go on doing," as in vii. 1 "he did not wish *to continue teaching* (περιπατεῖν) (2342 e—f) in Judæa," vii. 17 "If any one be willing *to continue doing* (ποιεῖν) his will" (comp. viii. 44), ix. 27 "Why do ye desire *to be hearing* [it] (ἀκούειν) [*all over*] *again* (πάλιν)?" xxi. 22—3 (*bis*) "If I desire him *to remain permanently* (μένειν)." There is an interesting difference between vi. 21 ἤθελον οὖν λαβεῖν and vii. 44 τινὲς δὲ ἤθελον...πιάσαι, contrasted with xvi. 19 ἤθελον αὐτὸν ἐρωτᾶν. All three refer to particular actions; but perhaps ἐρωτᾶν, "to be asking," means "to ask all about" the mysterious saying, and not merely to put a definite question. Or possibly, as in the Acts, the present may denote an action *almost begun but stopped because Jesus anticipated the question*, "they wished [*and were almost beginning*] to ask²."

---

¹ [2496 d] The latter may mean "form a habit of belief." Comp. Arrian's introductory remarks about the fascination of the uttered words of Epictetus, so that, "whenever he himself was uttering anything, it was inevitable that his hearer should *feel on every occasion* (πάσχειν) what Epictetus desired him *to feel on that special occasion* (ὅπερ ἐκεῖνος αὐτὸν παθεῖν ἠβούλετο)."

² [2498 a] Comp. ἤθελε foll. by Acts xiv. 13 θύειν, xix. 33 ἀπολογεῖσθαι, where the actions are stopped severally, by the Apostles and by the multitude, and see 2472 and 2716—7. Ἠρώτησα suggests "cross-examine" in i. 21 (comp. 19), 25, xviii. 19; but not in ix. 2 ἠρώτησαν αὐτὸν οἱ μαθηταὶ αὐτοῦ λέγοντες, Ῥαββεί, τίς ἥμαρτεν...; Hence it does not seem likely that John would avoid the aorist infin. from a feeling that it suggested disrespect.

IV. In Participles

(i) Aorist

[2499] The aorist participle with the article is comparatively rare in John except in the phrase "he that sent me" or "the Father that sent me[1]." In some instances it occurs in reference to future time, where we might have expected the future participle. But the meaning is "those that [shall] have," as in the Synoptic Tradition, "*But he that shall have endured* (ὁ δὲ ὑπομείνας) to the end, he shall be saved[2]." So in John v. 25—9 "The hour cometh, and now is, when the dead shall hear...and *they that shall have heard* (οἱ ἀκούσαντες, i.e. *really heard*, or *hearkened*, or *obeyed*) shall live...*they that shall have done* (οἱ ποιήσαντες) good......*they that shall have practised* (οἱ πράξαντες) evil...*"*; vii. 39 "Now he spake concerning the Spirit, which they (lit.) were destined to receive that *should [hereafter] have believed* on him (οὗ ἔμελλον λαμβάνειν οἱ πιστεύσαντες (al. πιστεύοντες) εἰς αὐτόν)," xvi. 2 "the hour cometh that every one that *shall have killed you* (πᾶς ὁ ἀποκτείνας ὑμᾶς) shall think......"; xx. 29 "Blessed [are] they that [hereafter (**1554**)] *shall* not *have seen* and *shall [yet] have believed* (μ. οἱ μὴ ἰδόντες καὶ πιστεύσαντες)[3]."

[2500] In xvii. 20, "Neither for these only do I pray, but for them also that (R.V.) *believe* (A.V. *shall believe*) (πιστευόντων) on me through their word[4]," the R.V. might give the impression that "them that believe" denoted the converts already made by the Twelve

---

[1] [2499 a] See Bruder (1888) pp. 588-9. *In the sing., without* πᾶς, *it probably always refers, in John, to a definite person*, as in v. 11, 13, 15, xi. 2, xviii. 14. On iii. 33 probably referring to the Baptist, see **2501—2**.

[2] Mk xiii. 13, Mt. x. 22, xxiv. 13.

[3] [2499 b] In view of the freq. use of μή with participles where οὐ might be logically expected, some may urge that οἱ μὴ ἰ. καὶ π. may refer *to those who, in the course of the last seven days, had believed* in the Resurrection of the Saviour, not having seen it themselves, but having accepted the testimony of the disciples that had seen it. But, if so, would not the Evangelist have stated, however briefly, that certain persons did thus believe? And does it seem likely that he would suppose the Saviour to have thus limited His benediction? Moreover, if that had been the writer's meaning, he could have made it clear by using οὐ as in 1 Pet. ii. 10 and Rom. ix. 25 (from the LXX). In Mt. v. 11 (sim. Lk. vi. 22) (R.V.) "blessed are ye (μακάριοί ἐστε) when [men] shall reproach you (ὅταν ὀνειδίσωσιν ὑμᾶς)," the reference is to future time, although the blessing is indicated (by the insertion of "*are*") as present. Much more might the reference include future time when "*are*" is not inserted (see **1554—5**).

[4] W.H. πιστευόντων. Some authorities read πιστευσόντων.

when previously sent out by Jesus to preach the Gospel. On the other hand, A.V. ("shall believe") has probably followed the inaccurate authorities that have altered the difficult present into an easy future. But οἱ πιστεύοντες may be regarded as a noun, "believers" or "converts"; and, without regarding the present participle as "prophetic," we may say that the prayer "for *the converts through their word*" includes future converts (as well as present) made through the preaching of the apostles and their successors.

[2501] The aorist participle presents difficulty in iii. 32—3, "No one receiveth his testimony. *He that received* (ὁ λαβών) his testimony set his seal [to the statement] (ἐσφράγισεν) that God is true." The words are (Preface, p. ix) part of an evangelistic comment immediately following the Baptist's last words, "He must increase but I must decrease." The "testimony" is that of Christ, and the question arises, What person or persons does ὁ λαβών indicate? It is probably John the Baptist, who was the first to "receive" that "testimony" to the Messianic character of Jesus of Nazareth which was conveyed to the prophet by Christ's inherent grace, truth, and power. This view is confirmed by other passages. If the writer had meant "he that hath at any time received," we should expect, in accordance with Johannine style, either (i. 12) "as many as received (ὅσοι δὲ ἔλαβον)," or (as in vi. 45, πᾶς ὁ ἀκούσας...μαθών and comp. xvi. 2) "every one that hath received," or the plural participle, "those that [shall] have received" (comp. v. 25, 29 οἱ ἀκούσαντες, οἱ τὰ ἀγαθὰ ποιήσαντες)[1].

[2502] The usage of the Gospel, then, suggests a definite person. And the usage of the Epistle tends in the same direction. For there, the aorist participle with ὁ (nom.) in one of the two instances in which it occurs probably refers to Christ, and in the other certainly does so[2]. On the whole, both context and idiomatic usage indicate that the words are a part, so to speak, of the Baptist's epitaph,

---

[1] [2501 a] Besides ὁ καταβάς and ὁ πέμψας, the sing. aor. part. occurs in v. 11 ὁ ποιήσας, v. 13 ὁ δὲ ἰαθείς, v. 15 ὁ ποιήσας, xi. 2 ἡ ἀλείψασα, xi. 37 ὁ ἀνοίξας, xviii. 14 ὁ συμβουλεύσας. All these refer to single persons and definite acts.

[2] [2502 a] Bruder p. 592—3 gives, in the Epistle, about 47 instances of the article with participle; of these about 40 have ὁ (nom.) with pres. particip., but only 2 have ὁ (nom.) with aorist particip., *i.e.* 1 Jn v. 6 ὁ ἐλθών and v. 18 ὁ γεννηθεὶς ἐκ τ. θεοῦ. The latter occurs in the same sentence with πᾶς ὁ γεγεννημένος ἐκ τ. θεοῦ, from which it appears to be deliberately differentiated.

[2503]   TENSE

declaring that he sealed an attestation to the truth of God. This accords with the Johannine account of the Baptist. The Fourth Gospel is the only one that represents the Baptist as declaring that God had said to him, i. 33 "On whomsoever thou shalt see the Spirit descending and abiding on him, he it is that baptizeth in the Holy Spirit." And the next words describe the Prophet as attesting the truth of this message from God: "And I have seen and have borne witness that this is the Elect (815—6) of God¹."

[2503] The aorist and the present participle are used in two different contexts to describe the "descending" of the Son of man, or of the Bread of Life. The first is as follows: "No one hath ascended into heaven but *he that descended* out of heaven², the Son of man." In the next passage, addressed by Christ to the multitude³ after the Feeding of the Five Thousand, ὁ may mean either "the [bread] that," or "the [man] that": "The bread of God is *the [one] that (ὁ) descendeth* from heaven and giveth life to the world⁴." The multitude obviously take "the [one] that" to mean "the *bread* that"; for, without shewing any surprise, they reply "Give us evermore this bread." Then Jesus answers "I am the bread of life," and "*I have descended* (καταβέβηκα) from heaven."

[2504] At this point, "the Jews" are introduced. We are not to suppose that the scene is shifted to Judæa, for we are subsequently told, "these things he said, teaching, in synagogue, in Capernaum⁵." Here, as elsewhere, "the Jews" mean the Pharisees, and more particularly Pharisees of eminence in Capernaum, who had apparently heard of Christ's doctrine to the "multitude." The

---

¹ [2502 b] When Samuel anointed David to be king of Israel on the strength of the word of the Lord 1 Sam. xvi. 12 "Arise, anoint him, for *this is he*," this may be called—and truly, in the spiritual sense—witness from God: but it might also be called a witness from David himself, from the personality of the future king, appealing to the heart of the Prophet and saying "*I am he.*"

[2502 c] Matthew, in a tradition peculiar to his Gospel, indicates the effect that might naturally be expected to be produced upon the Baptist by the personality of Jesus of Nazareth, (606—9) (Mt. iii. 14) "I have need to be baptized by thee"— even before the culminating revelation.

² iii. 13 ὁ ἐκ τοῦ οὐρανοῦ καταβάς. This is either an utterance of Christ to Nicodemus, or an evangelistic comment on Christ's utterance to Nicodemus (which, in that case, terminates with the words "how shall ye believe if I tell you of heavenly things?").

³ Comp. vi. 24—6, which shews that in the following dialogue "the multitude" are the interlocutors, at all events up to vi. 41, where "the Jews" are introduced.

⁴ vi. 33.   ⁵ vi. 59.

narrative—which seems to imply an interval after the address to "the multitude," but does not say how long it was—proceeds thus: "The Jews therefore began to murmur concerning him because he said I am *the bread that descended* (ὁ ἄρτος ὁ καταβάς) from heaven¹." Jesus is not recorded to have said this as yet, but it appears to be their inference from Christ's words "I am the bread" and "I have descended." In replying to them Jesus says, "I am the bread of life. Your fathers ate the manna in the wilderness and died. This is *the bread that descendeth* (ὁ ἄ. ὁ καταβαίνων) from heaven that anyone (τις) may eat of it and not die²." But when He repeats the phrase in the first person, the aorist is used, "I am *the living bread that descended* (ὁ ἄ. ὁ καταβάς) from heaven³." The aorist is also repeated in the last sentence of the discourse, "As the living Father sent me and I live on account of the Father, so he that eateth me he also shall live on account of me. This is the bread that *descended* (ὁ ἄ. ὁ καταβάς) out of heaven...⁴."

[2505] Reviewing all the passages about "the descending bread" we are led to the conclusion that besides the contrast between the bread from heaven and the bread from earth, some distinction is intended between (1) the Bread that is, and has been from the beginning, descending to man from God through the ordinary influences of animate and inanimate Nature⁵, and (2) the definite and supreme gift of that Bread in the Incarnation. The former is expressed by the present, the latter by the aorist.

(ii) **Perfect**

[2506] In viii. 31 "Jesus therefore said to those Jews (R.V.) *which had believed him* (A.V. *which believed on him*), If ye abide in my word...," the words τοὺς πεπιστευκότας αὐτῷ mean (as R.V.) simply "had believed," without conveying any such suggestion of completeness as often attaches itself to the Johannine perfect indicative. For here the context excludes the notion of completeness.

---

¹ vi. 41.   ² vi. 48—50.   ³ vi. 51.
⁴ vi. 57—8, on κἀγώ see **2123—4**.
⁵ [**2505** *a*] Comp. the saying of Deut. viii. 3 quoted in Mt. iv. 4 that man lives "by every word that proceedeth out of the mouth of God," and Heb. i. 1, which indicates that these "words" had been "proceeding" long before the Incarnation. See also below for the illustration of the discrimination between καταβαίνων and καταβάς, applied to "the bread," by the discrimination between ἐρχόμενον and ἦλθεν applied to "the light" (**2508**).

As there is no pluperfect active participle, John, like other authors, employs the perfect participle as an equivalent. The preceding verse says, "*As he spake these things many believed* on him (εἰς αὐτόν)." The perfect participle seems to refer to this *recent* "believing," and to mean "those that *had just entered on belief*[1]." But in any case there is no intention to imply *perfect* belief. On the contrary, the subtle change in passing from "believed *on him*" to "believed *him*," indicates an inferior belief in the latter case (**1522**—3). The context, too, indicates that these believers soon fall away and pass into the bitterest enmity. For such an issue the order of the words is perhaps intended to prepare us: "Jesus therefore said to those that had [just] believed him [being] *Jews*"—a term that in this Gospel almost always means that part of the nation which identified itself with the Pharisees and was systematically hostile to Jesus.

(iii) **Present**

[**2507**] The present participle, with the article, is regularly used by John (as in the LXX "he that curseth (ὁ κακολογῶν) father or mother[2]") in stating a general law so as to include future as well as present, and sometimes referring mainly to the future: xiii. 20 "*He that receiveth* (ὁ λαμβάνων) whomsoever I send (ἄν τινα πέμψω) receiveth me*," vi. 35 "*he that cometh* unto me shall not hunger," vi. 37 "*him that cometh* unto me I will in no wise cast out." In the above quoted instances a class, not an individual, is denoted. But the context shews that an individual, not a class, is denoted in i. 15 (W.H. marg.) "John testifieth concerning him, and crieth aloud, saying, '(lit.) This was he that I said, *He that cometh after me is become before me*'...." Here ὁ ὀπίσω μου ἐρχόμενος, according to Johannine usage, would naturally mean "whosoever cometh after me": but the preceding words, "*This was he that I said*," shew that a special person is intended, and make the meaning clear. W.H.'s text "*This was he that said*" would not make the meaning clear, or

---

[1] [**2506** *a*] The perfect participle often refers to quite recent events in John, *e.g.* ii. 9 "the water *just made* (γεγενημένον) wine...*those that had just drawn* (ἠντληκότες) the water," v. 10, vi. 13 etc.

[**2506** *b*] It has been shewn (**1703** *a*) that John uses the perf. of ὁρᾶν much more freq. than the Synoptists do. But it may be added that he is also far more prone than the Synoptists to the general use of perf. participles.

[2] Ex. xxi. 17 quoted in Mk vii. 10, Mt. xv. 4.

rather would make the meaning different from what is intended. For this and other reasons the marginal reading is preferable[1].

[2508] The present participle without the article is variously interpreted in i. 9 "The true light, which lighteth every human being (πάντα ἄνθρωπον)[2], *coming* (ἐρχόμενον) into the [whole] world." A.V. "every man *that cometh*" is not in accordance with the usage of John, who would probably have written πάντα τὸν ἐρχόμενον if that had been his meaning. R.V. marg. "as he cometh" is liable to the objection that it introduces an inappropriate metaphysical suggestion as to the precise moment when the Light shines on the soul; and it is not supported by the Hebrew phrase "all that come into the world" (which favours A.V. rather than R.V.)[3]. The context, and the tone of the Fourth Gospel, favour the connexion of "*coming*" with "*light*." Like the distinction above (2505) between καταβαίνων and καταβάς, there appears a distinction here between ἐρχόμενον and ἦλθεν, and the passage says, first, that the Light was "*continually coming*" to all mankind (more especially to the prophets and saints) and then that it definitely "*came*" in the Incarnation[4].

---

[1] [2507 a] W.H. marg. ὃν εἶπον, txt ὁ εἰπών. The Syr. and Lat. vss have "*This was he that I said*," or "*about whom I said*." But B has, at end of line, οειπω with a corrector's ℵ above the ο and ο above the ω, C has λεγω ουτος ην ο ειπων with ο ειπων corrected into ον ελεγον : ℵ omits λεγων and has κεκραγεν ουτος ην ο οπισω, a corrector has ins. λεγων...ο ειπων (altered into ον ειπον): D (Latin lost) has κεκραγεν ουτος ην ον ειπον ο οπισω with ΥΜΙΗ (*sic*) above the line after ειπον. The facts point to early confusion between ειπω and ειπο, which might spring from the interchange of ο and ω frequent in MSS. (2691). Origen has (Lomm. i. 154) ὃς μαρτυρῶν κέκραγε, λέγων· 'Ο ὀπίσω..., omitting οὗτος ἦν ὃν εἶπον, (*ib.* 177) ὃν εἶπον, (*ib.* 184) ὃν εἶπον (Huet ὁ εἰπών, but the context, protesting against the view that the Baptist's words are "broken" by the evangelist's, favours εἶπον). Nonnus has εἶπον, Chrys. has it thrice.

[2] [2508 a] See Lightf. on Col. i. 28 where he says that "every man" is "three times repeated for the sake of emphasizing the universality of the Gospel."

[3] [2508 b] *Hor. Heb.* ad loc. quotes four instances of this freq. Heb. phrase, "all that come into the world," but none have "*man*" in the Hebrew.

[4] [2508 c] Comp. i. 9—11 ἐρχόμενον εἰς τὸν κόσμον...εἰς τὰ ἴδια ἦλθεν, "*coming continually* into the world...into his own house he *came* [*once for all*]." Alford says that Origen, Chrysostom and most of the Greek commentators take ἐρχόμενον with ἄνθρωπον. It is true that the Latin translations of Chrys. and Origen have "venientem," but the argument of Chrys. suggests (though it does not prove) that he followed Origen in regarding the metaphor as that of the sun "coming to," and shedding its light on, "the world." Moreover Cramer's version of Chrysostom has πάντας ἦλθε φωτίσαι, and Theodorus says (Cramer) εἰπὼν τὸν ἐρχόμενον εἰς τὸν

[2509] Exact instances of the prophetic present participle in John are very rare. Strictly speaking, if the Holy Spirit must be described as "not yet" being (vii. 39) till Jesus was "glorified," then i. 33 "This is he *that baptizeth* in the Holy Spirit" is prophetic present, and the same must hold good about i. 29 ὁ ἀμνὸς...ὁ αἴρων "the Lamb...*that taketh away* the sin of the world," unless the Lamb of God may be regarded as already beginning to do its work. Both these instances are in words of the Baptist, and perhaps the evangelist deliberately assigns to the last of the prophets the prophetic present. Elsewhere xxi. 20 "Who is it *that delivereth thee up*?" is a repetition of the question xiii. 25 "*Who is it?*" which follows xiii. 21 "One of you *shall deliver me up*," so that it meant "Who is the man *that shall deliver thee up*?" Possibly, then, xxi. 20 is a case of prophetic present. But it must be remembered that xiii. 2 has previously described the intention of "delivering up" as having been put into the heart of Judas, and the Synoptists tell us that the treacherous compact had already been made.

[2510] At an earlier point in the Gospel the future participle is used in connexion with the treachery of Judas, vi. 64 "He knew... and who it was that should deliver him up (ὁ παραδώσων αὐτόν)"— the only instance given by Bruder of a Johannine future participle with the article[1]. Comparing this with xiii. 11 "for he knew him that was delivering him up (τὸν παραδιδόντα αὐτόν)" we can hardly

---

κόσμον περὶ τοῦ δεσπότου Χριστοῦ. Origen *Cels.* vi. 5 quotes Is. lx. 1 "Thy light hath come" to illustrate the "*coming*" of the light "into the world," which he describes as τὸν ἀληθινὸν καὶ νοητόν apparently meaning "the hearts and minds of men." So in his Comm. on Jn (Huet ii. 25) Origen says that, as the material sun is the light of the material world, so the Saviour shines on the reason (τοῖς λογικοῖς καὶ ἡγεμονικοῖς). Comp. Orig. (on Jer. xi. 1—10, *Hom.* ix.) quoting Jn i. 9—11 with the preface ἡ ἐπιδημία [*i.e.* τοῦ Χρ.]...ἐπιλάμψασα ὅλῳ τῷ κόσμῳ. In the Latin Hom. on Ex. xxxv. 5, when Origen quotes Lk. xii. 49 "*I have come* to send fire" with Jn i. 9, "iste ignis (πῦρ) quem venit mittere Jesus illuminat quidem omnem hominem *venientem* (? veniens, ἐρχόμενον)" it is probable that Orig. meant πῦρ ἐρχόμενον to be taken together. See also his Comm. on Judg. ii. 7 (Lomm. xi. 218) "Si enim intelligamus 'lumen verum quod illuminat omnem hominem *venientem* (? error for "*veniens*") in hunc mundum' et praebeamus ei ad illuminandum animas nostras, aut si oriatur nobis sol justitiae, et *mundum animae nostrae* habemus hospitium," where men are apparently said to "have as it were *the world of their soul*" as the abiding-place of the Light." Similarly later on (Lomm. xi. 222) the argument would be improved by substituting "veniens" for "venientem." But Nonnus has ἀνδρῶν Ἐρχομένων ἐπὶ γαῖαν.

[1] Bruder (1888) pp. 588—9.

think it an improbable hypothesis that ὁ παραδιδούς means "engaged in the work of delivering up" and is not a prophetic present.

V. IN THE SUBJUNCTIVE MOOD

(i) Aorist and Present

[2511] That John, more than many Greek authors, utilises the shades of difference between the aorist and the present subjunctive, may be inferred from a single passage x. 38 "in order that ye may *recognise* (γνῶτε) and *go on recognising* (γινώσκητε) that the Father is in me[1]." His usage will be conveniently considered for the most part under the headings of (*a*) Deliberative Subjunctive, (β—ε) ἐάν (or ἄν), (ζ—η) ἵνα, (θ) ὅταν—with which conjunctions the subjunctive most often occurs.

(*a*) In Deliberative Subjunctive

[2512] The deliberative subjunctive in vi. 28 τί ποιῶμεν, "*what must we habitually do*?" (with v.r. ποιησωμεν, -ησομεν, -ουμεν) differs from τί ποιήσωμεν in Luke[2], in that the former indicates a course of action, the latter a special action at a certain crisis. In vi. 5, John agrees with Mark vi. 37 ἀγοράσωμεν "are we to buy [in this emergency]?"—where Matthew and Luke differ from Mark, and John, though agreeing in the deliberative, differs as to the speaker[3]. John's use (though rare) of the deliberative subjunctive bears on xi. 47 τί ποιοῦμεν; shewing that it must not be rendered "what must we do?" since this would have been expressed by him in the usual way, by the subjunctive[4].

---

[1] [2511*a*] Comp. 1 Cor. xiii. 12 "For the moment (ἄρτι) I am [merely] recognising (γινώσκω) in part, but then I shall further recognise (ἐπιγνώσομαι)." Applied to spiritual truth, γινώσκω = "I recognise," ἔγνων = "I recognised at a certain point of time," ἔγνωκα = "I have recognised and possess the recognition," ἐπιγινώσκω = "I have a further recognition," *i.e.* an advanced spiritual knowledge. The Johannine and the Pauline aspects differ. In 1 Cor. xiii. 12 "recognition" is regarded as present and partial when contrasted with the future. In Jn x. 38 it is present and progressive, as contrasted with the past when the believer first recognised (γνῶτε).

[2] [2512*a*] Lk. iii. 10, 12, 14 asked by candidates for baptism.

[3] Mk vi. 37 λέγουσιν αὐτῷ Ἀπελθόντες ἀγοράσωμεν...; Jn vi. 5 ὁ Ἰ...λέγει πρὸς Φίλιππον Πόθεν ἀγοράσωμεν...;

[4] [2512*b*] See 2493—4. In xii. 27, τί εἴπω; if it means "what should I say?" is deliberative subjunctive. If it meant (933 foll., a view now retracted) "Why should I say?" *i.e* "Surely I ought not to say," it would not be what is commonly

[2513] TENSE

(β) With ἐάν (or ἄν), "if"

[2513] In the Synoptists, ἐάν, "if," apart from μή, very rarely occurs—if we except clauses with ἔχω or θέλω—without the aorist subjunctive or some equivalent. There are only two passages of Mark that contain exceptions to this rule[1]. In the two instances

---

called deliberative subjunctive, but a negative interrogative. I cannot, however, find an instance of τί εἴπω; "*why* should I say?" Ps. lxxix. 10 "*Wherefore* should the heathen say?" is in LXX μήποτε εἴπωσιν; (al. εἰς τί λέγει, or ἐρεῖ;). Πῶς εἴπω; "*how* could I say?" might be illustrated by Ps. cxxxvii. 4 πῶς ᾄσωμεν "*how* could we sing?" But τί εἴπω (like τί φῶ; comp. Aristoph. *Nub.* 1378 τί σ' εἴπω;) seems to require the rendering "*what* ought I to say?" It is quite true that (939) "*what* ought I to say?" savours rather of Greek tragedy than of Hebrew literature, and does not at first seem appropriate to the Johannine conception of Christ. But it may be explained by xii. 49 ἐντολὴν δέδωκεν τί εἴπω, "the Father hath given me commandment *what I should say*." The Son, listening for the Father's voice, says, "*what should I say? [*Should I say*] Save me?*"—and then recognises at once that this *should not* be said and utters the prayer that *should* be said.

[2512 c] Irenaeus i. 8. 2 says that the Valentinians, along with "My soul is exceeding sorrowful," and "If it be possible let this cup pass from me," quoted the words καὶ τί εἴπω οὐκ οἶδα, "and what ought I to say? I know not"—as a manifestation of ἀπορία. This at all events proves that in very early times τί was rendered "*what?*" Chrys. paraphrases thus, Ἀλλ' οὐκ ἔχω τί εἴπω, φησίν, ἀπαλλαγὴν αἰτούμενος, διὰ γὰρ τοῦτο ἦλθον εἰς τὴν ὥραν ταύτην, "*I do not know what I should say* petitioning for release." For contextual variations, see **2768—70**.

[1] [2513 a] One of these is Mk xiv. 31 ἐὰν δέῃ, "if it be necessary [*i.e.* the present decree of God]." The other is Mk ix. 43—7 "And if thy hand offend thee...(45) and if thy foot offend thee...(47) and if thine eye offend thee," in which the following variations deserve note:

	ix. 43		ix. 45		ix. 47
B	κ. ἐάν...-ίσῃ	κ.	ἐὰν -ίξῃ	κ.	ἐάν...-ίξῃ
ℵ	,, -ίσῃ		-ίξει	,,	,,
A, C	,, -ίξῃ	,,	-ίξῃ	,,	,,
D	,, -ίξῃ	κἂν	-ίξῃ	κ. ἰ	-ίξει
L	,, -ίσῃ	κ. ἐὰν	-ίσει	κ. ἐὰν	-ίξῃ
a	et si -izaverit	et si	-izat	et si	-izat
b, d	et si -izat	et si	-izat	quod si	-izat
f	et si -izaverit	et si	-izat	quod si	-izat
k	et sic -iziaverit	et si...et	-iziat	et si	-iziaverit

[2513 b] These three sayings about "hand," "foot," and "eye" are given in full by Mk alone. Mt. condenses two of them ("hand or foot") into one. Lk. omits them all. Mk places before them a saying about "a mill-stone" and "whosoever (ὃς ἄν) shall cause to stumble (σκανδαλίσῃ)," Mt. agrees, Lk. varies (ἢ ἵνα σκανδαλίσῃ) but retains "the mill-stone." There, D has, in Mk ix. 42 σκανδαλίξῃ, in Mt. xviii. 6 σκανδαλείσῃ, in Lk. xvii. 2 σκανδαλίσῃ. The hypothesis suggests itself that Mk reflects the influence of oral tradition, and of sayings addressed to converts or to possible converts in different forms on different

AORIST AND PRESENT SUBJUNCTIVE [2514]

where it occurs with the present subjunctive in Matthew, the clause means "If so-and-so be just happening," or, " If so-and-so be going on, [what will be the immediate consequence]¹?" In Luke there are two instances of ἐάν with present subjunctive, and there the force of the present is not so clear².

[2514] In John, ἐάν with the present subjunctive is much more frequent than in the Synoptists, and it is not always easy to perceive the difference of meaning. For example, the aorist is used in viii. 31 "If ye *abide* in my word," viii. 51—2 (*bis*) " If any one *keep* my word," xv. 7 "If ye *abide* in me," xv. 10 "If ye *keep* my commandments." In viii. 31 the apodosis is present, "ye *are* my disciples": does not this seem to shew that "if ye *abide*" means "if ye *are abiding*"? In xv. 7 the apodosis is an imperative "*ask*": and this, too, seems to imply the condition of a *present* "*abiding*," on the strength of which the disciples are encouraged to "ask" at once³. The fact is that, owing to the disuse of some of the old classical Greek conditional forms, a great burden is thrown on this particular form, ἐάν with aorist, just as, in English, a great burden is thrown on such a form as "if he *comes*," which, in spoken English, often does

---

occasions:—at one time, "If thy right hand *should offend thee* (σκανδαλίσῃ)"; at another, "If thy right hand *be [now] offending thee*, cut it off [and come to the Lord Jesus Christ]." I believe it would be found that the misspellings of uncial MSS. are more numerous and striking in Mk than in Mt. and Lk., and that these misspellings—though in part attributable to other causes—may be partially explained by the fact that the author of Mk was comparatively illiterate, and that it was largely based on oral tradition. The same statement would apply, in the Double Tradition, to Mt. as compared with the better spelt version of Lk.

¹ [2513 *c*] Mt. v. 23 "if therefore *thou be in the act of offering* (προσφέρῃς) thy gift and there [on the spot] *shouldst [suddenly] recollect* (κἀκεῖ μνησθῇς)," xv. 14 "But if a blind man *be leading* (ὁδηγῇ) a blind man"—the parall. Lk. vi. 39 has "*Can* a blind man *lead*...?"—"shall they not both fall into the ditch?"

² [2513 *d*] Lk. vi. 33 καὶ [γὰρ] ἐὰν ἀγαθοποιῆτε does not greatly differ (as regards hypothetical force) from Lk. vi. 34 καὶ ἐὰν δανίσητε, and from the aorists in parall. Mt. v. 46—7, ἀγαπήσητε and ἀσπάσησθε. Lk. xix. 31 ἐάν τις ὑμᾶς ἐρωτᾷ is parall. to Mk-Mt. εἴπῃ. Perhaps Lk. vi. 33 ἀγαθοποιῆτε implies continuous action as compared with δανίσητε, and Lk. xix. 31 may mean "If any one venture to ask," or "begin to ask."

³ [2514 *a*] In xv. 7, ὃ ἐὰν θέλητε αἰτήσασθε καὶ γενήσεται, ℵ has αἰτήσεσθε, *a* and *f* have taken αἰτήσασθε as inf. and omit καί—"whatsoever ye desire to ask, [this] shall be done." The imperative is spelt with -αι in A and D. But *d* transl. αιτησασθαι correctly as "petite." Nonnus must have read θέλητε καὶ αἰτήσησθε. He also has Ὑμῖν εἰν ἑνὶ (? corruption of final syll. of ὑμῶν and the following ἐν) πάντα τελείεται.

[2514 (i)]   TENSE

duty for "*if he come*" (which may now be regarded as pedantical), "if he *should come*," "if he *is coming*," and "if he *is about to come*[1]." John accepts, with the Synoptists, the loose aorist with ἐάν, which, though mostly referring to the future, may include the present: but he differs from the Synoptists in that he uses the present with ἐάν, much more frequently than they do, to express something that *may* be at the present time going on, and to introduce the consequence that *must* be (conditionally) going on at the same time, *e.g.* xi. 9 "If any one *be walking* in the day, he is not stumbling."

[2514 (i)] John's free use of ἐάν with present subjunctive allows him to make distinctions not so clearly recognisable in the Synoptists between such phrases as (1) εἰ ταῦτα ποιεῖτε[2], "*if*, *as ye say*, or *if, as I assume, ye are doing* this[3]," (2) ἐὰν ταῦτα ποιῆτε, "*on the supposition that ye are doing* this" or "*put the case that ye are doing* this," (3) ἐὰν ταῦτα ποιήσητε, "*should ye do* this[4]." In xiii. 17 εἰ ταῦτα οἴδατε,

---

[1] [2514 *b*] As for such English phrases as "If he shall come" and "If he shall have come," they are not really English at all, but may perhaps be tolerated occasionally in a treatise like this, which sometimes aims at expressing for readers unacquainted with Greek the different shades of meaning in Greek conditional sentences. "*If* then *we shall shake off* our slavish yoke" *Rich. II.* ii. 1. 291 means "if we *are to*, or *ought to*, shake off"; and even that is quite exceptional.

[2] [2514 (i) *a*] Εἰ conditional with the fut. is non-existent in Jn. In N.T. it is very rare except in Hebraic interrog., *e.g.* Mk viii. 12 εἰ δοθήσεται; and indirect interrog. The fut. occurs (1) after εἰ καί in Mk xiv. 29 (D καὶ ἐάν and subjunct., and par. Mt. xxvi. 33 om. καί) and Lk xi. 8 (D om. εἰ καί):—where the meaning is "I grant that." Elsewhere εἰ and fut. are perh. restricted to phrases about an appointed time of harvest, trial, judgment etc. (1 Cor. ix. 11 μέγα εἰ θερίσομεν, iii. 14 εἴ τινος τὸ ἔργον μενεῖ, iii. 15 εἴ τινος τὸ ἔργον κατακαήσεται). In 2 Tim. ii. 12 εἰ ἀρνησόμεθα, 1 Pet. ii. 20 (*bis*) εἰ ὑπομενεῖτε the futures are prepared for by present verbs, and the fut. means "if [in the hour of trial]."

[2514 (i) *b*] Εἰ with the optative (exc. in the phrase εἰ τύχοι and a few passages in the Acts) does not occur in N.T. except in 1 Pet. iii. 14—17 in connexion with suffering persecution, εἰ καὶ πάσχοιτε...κρεῖττον...εἰ θέλοι τὸ θέλημα τοῦ θεοῦ, πάσχειν.... Emphasis seems to be laid on the hypothesis of a mystery "If ye should *indeed* suffer...if the will of God should [so mysteriously] will."

[3] [2514 (i) *c*] Εἰ, with indic., means "if, as is the fact" in iii. 12, vii. 23, viii. 46, x. 35, 38 etc. It means "if, as you say" in vii. 4, viii. 39, x. 24, xi. 12 etc. Εἴ τις, for ὅστις, occurs more or less freq. in almost every book of N.T., but not in Jn and 1 Jn.

[4] [2514 (i) *d*] In 1 Jn i. 6, 8, 10 ἐὰν εἴπωμεν "*if we should say*" introduces three statements of false doctrine, while i. 7 ἐὰν δὲ...περιπατῶμεν and i. 9 ἐὰν ὁμολογῶμεν introduce the hypothesis of present and continuous Christian life, "*on the supposition that we are walking* or *confessing*"; and this is the general (though not invariable) use in the Epistle.

μακάριοί ἐστε ἐὰν ποιῆτε αὐτά, the meaning is, perhaps, "*If ye know this* [*as ye suppose ye do, though one of you, Judas, knoweth it not*] blessed are ye—*on the supposition that ye are giving effect to your knowledge by action.*" In v. 31 ἐὰν ἐγὼ μαρτυρῶ περὶ ἐμαυτοῦ ἡ μαρτυρία μου οὐκ ἔστιν ἀληθής, "*put the case that I* (emph.) *am bearing witness* about myself; [then] my witness is not true," the meaning seems to be that the Son is not really bearing witness about Himself because, though His lips may utter the words of testimony, the Father is speaking through the Son. This must be compared with viii. 14 "*Even though I* (emph.) *be bearing witness* (κἂν ἐγὼ μαρτυρῶ) about myself, my witness is true[1]."

[2515] Where the protasis contains ἐάν with present subjunctive the apodosis generally contains an indicative present, or imperative[2].

---

[1] [2514 (i) *e*] Comp. Eurip. *Ion* 532 μαρτυρεῖς σαυτῷ. Chrys. *ad loc.* maintains that the meaning is, "If I bear witness about myself, my witness—*according to what you say, you Jews*—is not true." The Jews have said nothing of the kind as yet. But they say it afterwards (viii. 13) and Chrys. maintains that Jesus was here "*anticipating* (προλαβών)" *the charge that the Jews are going to make.* But the context (v. 30 "I am not able to do anything from myself") indicates that Jn has in view the unity of the Son with the Father (as suggested in Is. xi. 3) and that "I" means "I apart from the Father." Subsequently the statement is verbally and superficially contradicted in viii. 14 "Even though I [the Son] be bearing witness about myself, my witness is true"—because the Father is bearing witness through the Son.

[2] [2515 *a*] See v. 31, vii. 37, xi. 9, 10, xii. 26 *a*, xiii. 17, xv. 14. In viii. 16 ἐὰν κρίνω δὲ ἐγώ, the verb is prob. present—the apodosis being "*is.*" Θέλῃ (owing to the rarity of the aorist subjunctive of θέλω) perh. represents the aorist subjunctive in vii. 17 "If any man's *will shall be* (θέλῃ) to do...he *shall know*" (to be contrasted with xxi. 22—3 (*bis*) "If *I will* (θέλω)...what [is] that to thee?"). So in the Epistle, 1 Jn i. 7, 9, ii. 3, 15, iv. 12, v. 14 the verb in the apodosis is present and both protasis and apodosis refer to the present: "If we *be* walking, *be* confessing, *be* keeping his commandments etc...so-and-so follows."

[2515 *b*] The future is exceptionally found in the apodosis in xii. 26 *b* "If any one *be ministering* (διακονῇ) to me, him *will* my Father *honour*," xiii. 35 "Hereby shall men *know* that ye are my disciples, if ye have (ἔχητε) love one to another" (where, however, not much stress can be laid on the pres. ἔχητε, as the aorist subjunctive is rare and does not occur in the Gospel, though found in the Epistle). As to xii. 26 *b* comp. Lk. xii. 37 on the honour that will be paid by the Master to those servants whom "*he shall find* watching": perhaps the meaning is "If any one *be* [*found in the day of visitation*] *ministering* to me." This suggests a similar rendering in xiii. 35 "If ye *be* [*found*] *having* love." But, as to this and xiv. 15 ἐὰν ἀγαπᾶτέ με...τηρήσετε, xiv. 23 ἐάν τις ἀγαπᾷ με...τηρήσει..., it must be noted that the aorist of ἀγαπάω sometimes means (**1744** (iv) foll.) "manifest love by action," and might be unsuitable where the writer desires to say "if ye *be really loving me in your heart* ye will keep my commandments."

[2515 (i)] TENSE

In vi. 62 ἐὰν οὖν θεωρῆτε... Chrysostom reads the aorist ἴδητε while Nonnus paraphrases as ἀθρήσητε—and an aorist in the protasis would of course affect the character of the implied apodosis[1]. The difference between viii. 51—2 ἐάν τις τηρήσῃ (comp. xv. 10 ἐὰν τηρήσητε) and 1 Jn ii. 3 ἐὰν...τηρῶμεν, is that the Gospel declares a future consequence of a future act or state while the Epistle declares the present consequence of a present act or state: "And herein we *recognise* that we [*have recognised and*] know him if we *be keeping* his commandments[2]." In xii. 26, what is the difference intended by the variation of order, ἐὰν ἐμοί τις διακονῇ...ἐάν τις ἐμοὶ διακονῇ? In the former, ἐμοί seems (2553) more emphatic than in the latter: "If a man be servant *of mine* let him follow me on the path of the cross: if a man *be* [*found in the act of*] *serving* me, him will my Father honour." The context shews that διακονῇ in the first clause means "be servant in name and in profession," which may be compared with the tradition in Mark and Matthew "If any one (lit.) *willeth* (εἴ τις θέλει) *to come after me*...let him take up his cross and follow me," where Luke has "If any one *willeth to be* [*daily*] *coming* (ἔρχεσθαι)... let him take up his cross daily (καθ' ἡμέραν) and follow me[3]."

[2515 (i)] Ἐάν with indicative does not occur in John; but it occurs once in the Epistle (1 Jn v. 15) καὶ ἐὰν οἴδαμεν, and it is supported by Blass (p. 214) from 1 Thess. iii. 7 ἐὰν ὑμεῖς στήκετε (-ητε ℵ*DE)—also Job xxii. 3 ἐὰν σὺ ἦσθα—and he says "the only irregularity is that this *present* indicative is occasionally preceded by ἐάν instead of εἰ." The facts alleged hardly justify the phrase "occasionally preceded." For οἴδαμεν is not exactly a present,

---

[1] [2515 c] The Latin versions, including *d*, have "videritis" (D θεωρῆτε). In order to give the usual Johannine force to the pres. subjunct., it would be necessary to suppose that the preceding verbal enunciation of the doctrine of sacrifice by Christ was accompanied by a spiritual act on His part, of the nature of an Ascension (2489) at which the Jews were unconsciously present, "hearing but not understanding, seeing yet not seeing," and that this "seeing yet not seeing" was denoted by θεωρεῖν (2210—2). For Nonnus' version and further details see 2739 *b*.

[2] [2515 d] 1 Jn ii. 3 Καὶ ἐν τούτῳ γινώσκομεν ὅτι ἐγνώκαμεν αὐτόν. See 2491 and 2760—6 on γινώσκω and ἔγνωκα. Here γινώσκομεν appears to mean, not, "we recognise for the first time" or "begin to recognise," but "we spiritually recognise that we have a complete spiritual recognition."

[3] [2515 e] Mk viii. 34, Mt. xvi. 24, Lk. ix. 23. In Jn xii. 26, Chrys. twice reads, in the first clause, ὁ ἐμοὶ διακονῶν, and illustrates it by the Synoptic tradition about "taking up the cross." Cramer has ἐάν τις ἐμοὶ διακονεῖ, but this is in the second clause, "*If any one be* [*found*] *ministering* to me, him will my Father honour."

so that the inference is drawn from a single instance in N.T. Moreover in the LXX, so far as concerns several books at all events, there appear to be no instances of ἐάν with pres. indic. except as various readings[1]. Ἐάν with ἦσθα may be explained by peculiarities connected with ἦσθα, not with ἐάν[2]. So, too, in all probability, may ἐάν with στήκετε[3]. In 1 Jn v. 15 and in the preceding words, there are several variations; אA omit the words in question (prob. through homoeotel.); in 1 Jn ii. 29, ἐὰν εἰδῆτε is corrupted by several

---

[1] [2515 (i) *a*] The Oxf. Conc. gives hardly any instances of ἐάν indic. without †indicating v. r. In Gen., Ex., Lev., Numb., Josh., Job, Psalms and Isaiah, I have not found ἐάν with pres. indic. anywhere except as v.r. and then very rarely, *e.g.* Lev. xxvi. 21 (A) καὶ ἐὰν...πορεύεσθε (comp. xxvi. 23 -ησθε, A -εύσησθε, F -εύεσθε), Is. i. 19 καὶ ἐὰν θέλητε (A θέλετε) foll. by ἐὰν δὲ μὴ θέλητε which A keeps. In N.T., καὶ ἐάν is occasionally foll. by indic. v. r. in such a way as to suggest that a scribe regarded καὶ ἐάν as meaning "even if," "grant that," and thought that it might be foll. by indic. as representing an assumed fact.

[2] [2515 (i) *b*] Phrynichus says, "Ἦς ἐν ἀγορᾷ," σόλοικον. λέγε οὖν "ἦσθα." Ὀρθότερον δὲ χρῶτο (?) ἂν ὁ λέγων, ἐὰν ᾖς ἐν ἀγορᾷ. This apparent "uncertainty about ἦς and ἦσθα" is justly called by Dr Rutherford (p. 240—1) "surprising." But prob. Phrynichus wrote χρω|τω|ι *i.e.* "use the iota subscript" (2772—5). In LXX, ἦς occurs (Oxf. Conc.) 5 times (only 2 without v.r.). Comparing Job xxxviii. 4 ἦς (A ἦσθα) with Job xxii. 3 ἐὰν σὺ ἦσθα (A ᾖς) we may infer that LXX here confused ᾖς and ησθα together—not a difficult matter in view of the general confusion of the forms of the imperfect of εἰμί. Comp. Ex. xxi. 23 ἐὰν δὲ ᾖν (3rd pers.) AF ᾖ, Lev. xxi. 17 στήκετε ᾖ (A ᾖν). In Numb. xxvii. 8 ἄνθρ. ἐὰν ἀποθάνῃ... καὶ υἱὸς μὴ ᾖν (AF ᾖ) αὐτῷ the distance of ᾖν from ἐάν may have caused the ᾖν clause to be taken parenthetically. As regards ᾖν and ᾖ or ᾖ, the insertion or omission of ν may be explained in the usual way (360 *a*). The Editor of certain Berlin Papyri (27 B.C.—250 A.D.) would read ἐὰν ᾖ for ἐὰν ᾖν in some cases where Deissmann (p. 201) would retain the latter; and Deissmann states that "ἐάν with the subjunctive is found three times in the same papyrus" that contains the indicative. See **2771**.

[3] [2515 (i) *c*] As regards 1 Thess. iii. 7 ἐὰν ὑμεῖς στήκετε (-ητε א*DE), comp. Mk xi. 25 W.H. ὅταν στήκετε (but B and Orig. στηκητε, al. στηκειτε, εστηκηται, στητε, εστηκετε, *a, d, f* stabitis, *k* steteritis), and Josh. x. 19 μὴ ἑστήκατε, Aq. Theod. μὴ στήκετε, Symm. μὴ ἀποστῆτε, and note Ex. xiv. 13 στῆτε (A στήκετε), 1 K. viii. 11 στήκειν (A στῆναι). To these add the var. in Jn viii. 44 and Rev. xii. 4, ἕστηκεν (v.r. ἔστηκεν). The facts indicate that forms of στήκω were liable to be confused with forms of ἕστηκα. The perfect subjunctive is rare in Gk. The *Iliad* i. 524 has ὄφρα πεποίθῃς but *Odyss.* x. 335 ὄφρα πεποίθομεν (which Eustath., says Steph. 664 B, derived from πεποίθω, like πεπλήγω and πεφύκω). Isaiah has πεποιθώς with ᾖς and ὦσιν in Is. viii. 13, x. 20, xvii. 8.

[2515 (i) *d*] The conclusion is that particular phrases with οἶδα, εἰμί, and στήκω, do not form a solid basis for inferences about the general usage of ἐάν and ὅταν. Very often *word-usage* might override *grammatical* usage. In London, "We have *drank*" was (at all events between 1865 and 1889) frequently used for

[2516] TENSE

authorities to ἐὰν ἴδητε¹, and if 1 Jn v. 15 originally had ειδομεν, a spelling of ειδωμεν, the former might easily be taken as an error for οιδαμεν. On the whole, however, οἴδαμεν is probably correct. But, if so, it seems used, not to emphasize the indicative, but because the writer avoids the subjunctive εἰδῶ, familiar indeed (2729 a) in the phrase ἵν' εἰδῇς, -ῆτε, but (perhaps on that very account) almost restricted to that phrase—as "hanged," in English, has come to be almost restricted to judicial executions.

(γ) With ἄν and Relative

[2516] Whereas the Gospel has (xiv. 13, xv. 16, xvi. 23) ὅ τι ἄν (or ἄν τι) αἰτήσητε referring to the future, the Epistle has (1 Jn iii. 22) ὃ ἂν αἰτῶμεν (and 1 Jn ii. 5) ὃς δ' ἂν τηρῇ referring to the present². In Jn v. 19 "The Son can do nothing of himself but (R.V.) *what he seeth the Father doing* (ἂν μή τι βλέπῃ τὸν πατέρα ποιοῦντα)," a closer rendering would be "The Son can do nothing of himself—[nothing] unless *he be [at the moment] seeing* the Father doing something," and the reference is to the preceding words, "The Father loveth the Son and is [always] shewing him all things that he himself *is doing*." The exact rendering is of little importance provided that the reader understands that the whole passage (including the statement that "the Son quickeneth whom he will") is not in a prophetic present referring to the future. It regards the incarnate Son as continually "seeing" on earth what the Father is doing in heaven, and as Himself doing the same thing (1607)³.

"we have *drunk*," for seemliness. So (1) the familiar imperative στήκετε might replace the rare ἑστήκητε or στήκητε, (2) εἰδῶμεν, being ambiguous as well as rare, might be replaced by οἴδαμεν, and (3) the two indicative forms ἦσθα and ἦς might be confused with the subjunctive ᾖς.

¹ [2515 (i) *e*] Similar confusions are very frequent in LXX, see Oxf. Conc. εἰδεῖν. Also in Epictet. Index Schweig. has a long note on the confusion between ἵνα εἰδῶμεν and ἵνα ἴδωμεν referring to i. 6. 23, 29. 24, 29. 42 (comp. iii. 9. 14, 21. 6).

² [2516 *a*] 1 Jn iii. 17 ὃς δ' ἂν ἔχῃ τ. βίον τ. κόσμου κ. θεωρῇ...κ. κλείσῃ, may be compared with Mt. v. 23 quoted above (2513 *c*); the man "is staring" stolidly at his distressed brother and then, by a definite act, suddenly shuts up his heart against him. Bruder (1888) prints xv. 7 as the only instance in the Fourth Gospel of ἐάν used for ἄν with relative and subjunct., on which see 2660 *b*. Bruder (Moulton) prints also xxi. 25, perh. by misprint, see 2414—6.

³ [2516 *b*] Another instance of ἄν with pres. subjunct. is ii. 5 ὅ τι ἂν λέγῃ ὑμῖν ποιήσατε, not important, but interesting in view of the freq. use of εἴπω and εἴπωμεν in the Gospel and Epistle, and of the non-occurrence of the subjunctive λέγω, in either, elsewhere. (1) Λέγω is not so formal as εἴπω. (2) Mary probably

(δ) Ἄν τινων κρατῆτε (xx. 23)

[2517] In xx. 23 ἄν τινων (marg. τινος) ἀφῆτε τὰς ἁμαρτίας ἀφέωνται (marg. ἀφίονται) αὐτοῖς, ἄν τινων (marg. τινος) κρατῆτε (D κρατήσητε) κεκράτηνται, the aorist (ἀφῆτε) may imply a definite act "if ye let go," the present (κρατῆτε) a keeping of things as they are, "if ye go on retaining." But the use of κρατέω creates difficulty. It may mean "I hold," "take [hold of]," or, "retain." But does it ever mean "I retain a burden *in its position on someone else*[1]"? There

anticipated *some* immediate action or utterance from her Son; and hence the meaning seems to be "Whatever *he may be shortly saying* to you, obey it [at once]," suggesting that the attendants are to catch up any word that may fall in the next few moments from Jesus. In v. 19 ἄν μή τι, the separation of τι from ἄν seems to differentiate it from ἐάν τις, *i.e.* ὅστις ἄν.

[1] [2517 a] In the Gospels elsewhere, κρατέω (active) (apart from χειρός) is always used with the accusative. When applied to living things, it means "*take hold of*," "*seize*," "*arrest.*" When applied otherwise, it means "*hold fast*," "*keep*," see Mk vii. 3, 4, 8, ix. 10 "*hold fast* tradition" etc. In Lk. the active is never used apart (viii. 54) from χειρός. In the Acts, when the active is applied to persons, it means (iii. 11) "hold fast (in a friendly manner)," (xxiv. 6) "seize" or "arrest." In Rev., it means "hold fast" applied to teaching, but "take" or "lay hold of" applied to (Rev. xx. 2) "the dragon." In Col. ii. 19, 2 Thess. ii. 15, it means "holding fast the head," "traditions," with accus.; but in Heb. iv. 14, vi. 18, "holding fast the confession," "the hope," with genit.; comp. Acts xxvii. 13 δόξαντες τῆς προθέσεως κεκρατηκέναι.

[2517 b] Κρατέω with genit., which (without χειρός) is very rare in N.T., is much more freq. in LXX, where κρατέω sometimes means "conquer" and "control" as well as "hold." In Sir. xxviii. 22 οὐ μὴ κρατήσῃ εὐσεβῶν means "[Death, or the tongue] shall not *rule over* the pious" (comp. Prov. xvii. 2). In Judg. vii. 8 (A) τῶν δὲ τριακοσίων ἀνδρῶν ἐκράτησεν means "*retained* the three hundred men." In classical Gk. the genit. is more freq. than the accus., and κρατεῖν ἑαυτοῦ, ἡδονῶν etc. are frequently used for "*controlling* oneself, pleasures" etc.

[2517 c] Κρατέομαι (passive), in N.T., occurs elsewhere only in Lk. xxiv. 16 "but their eyes *were holden* (ἐκρατοῦντο)," *i.e.* supernaturally bandaged or bound, and Acts ii. 24 οὐκ ἦν δυνατὸν κρατεῖσθαι αὐτὸν ὑπ' αὐτοῦ, which, coming after the expression "*loosed* (λύσας) the pangs of death," indicates that κρατεῖσθαι means "to be held fast," "to remain in bonds," or "to remain shut up in Hades."

[2517 d] SS (Burk.) has, in Jn xx. 23, "and whom ye shall *shut [your door] against—it is shut*," as in Ps. lxix. 15 (quoted by Mr Burkitt *ad loc.*) "Let not the pit *shut* its mouth upon (or, against) me," which suggests that the translator took τίνων as governed by κρατῆτε, and understood the meaning to be "whomsoever ye shut up in prison." Mark and Matthew never use κρατεῖν τινος thus. But they use κρατεῖν τινα as follows:

Mk vi. 17	Mt. xiv. 3	Lk. iii. 20
ἐκράτησεν τὸν Ἰ. κ. ἔδησεν αὐτὸν ἐν φυλακῇ.	κρατήσας τὸν Ἰ. ἔδησεν κ. ἐν φυλακῇ ἀπέθετο.	κατέκλεισεν τὸν Ἰ. ἐν φυλακῇ.

is some reason for believing that John is restating, in a new form, a tradition like those peculiar to Matthew (xvi. 19, xviii. 18) about "binding and loosing." Matthew's traditions have in both clauses an aorist subjunctive in the protasis followed by a perfect participle of permanence in the apodosis, "Whatsoever ye bind (δήσητε)...*shall be once for all bound* (ἔσται δεδεμένον)...whatsoever ye loose (λύσητε) ...*shall be once for all loosed* (ἔσται λελυμένον)[1]."

[2518] If John was writing with allusion to Matthew's tradition, he might naturally wish to differentiate the Christian "loosing" and "binding" from the Jewish "*binding and loosing*" of which, says *Horae Hebraicae* (on Mt. xvi. 19), "one might produce thousands of examples," and in which "*bind*" meant "*pronounce sinful*, or *unclean*" (and hence "forbid," *e.g.* of actions on the sabbath) in allusion to which our Lord said that the Pharisees *bound heavy burdens* on their brethren. Hence, whereas the usual Jewish order (and the order in Matthew) is "bind and loose," John might give prominence to the "loosing" by putting it first, and he describes the "loosing" as a forgiveness of sins.

[2519] The inference is fairly probable that John is writing with some allusion to Matthew's tradition about "binding" and "loosing." Beyond this, it is difficult to advance. The exact meaning is doubtful. The antithesis favours the supposition that (as in R.V.) "sins" must be supplied as the object of κρατῆτε and as the subject of κεκράτηνται. Yet κρατεῖν, in the sense of "hold fast," though most appropriate to "holding fast *hope, tradition, teaching*" etc., seems quite inappropriate to "*sins*." The interpretation suggested by SS of "keeping in prison," cannot be paralleled from N.T., nor from Greek

---

Here Luke substitutes "*shut up*" for the Synoptic "*arrested* and *bound*." And it should be noted that Luke never follows Mark in any of the numerous passages where Mark uses κρατεῖν to mean "take," "arrest." Also, in a metaphorical passage, dealing with remission of sins, where Mark describes the "strong [man]" as being "bound" (Mk iii. 27, Mt. xii. 29 "unless he first *bind* (δήσῃ) the strong [man]") Luke (xi. 22) has "*conquer* (νικήσῃ)."

[2517 e] There are two passages about "binding" and "loosing" (both in the aorist) peculiar to Matthew. One is addressed to Peter, one to the disciples, Mt. xvi. 19 ὃ ἐὰν δήσῃς ἐπὶ τῆς γῆς ἔσται δεδεμένον ἐν τοῖς οὐρανοῖς, κ. ὃ ἐὰν λύσῃς ἐπὶ τῆς γῆς ἔσται λελυμένον ἐν τοῖς οὐρανοῖς, Mt. xviii. 18 sim. with ὅσα ἐὰν δήσητε and ἐν οὐρανῷ. In the latter, the context is connected with forgiveness of sins.

[1] [2517 f] In Jn xx. 23, where there is no ἔσται, the perf. implies also "*at once*." For κρατέω in connexion with "binding" or "casting into prison," comp. Mk vi. 17, Mt. xiv. 3 (**2517** d), Mt. xviii. 28—30, Rev. xx. 2.

literature generally except so far as κρατεῖν with the genitive means "keep in control." Moreover, it interferes with the antithesis.

[2520] But it is worth noting that the author of *Horae Hebraicae* sees in the passage some allusion to the phrase "*delivering over to Satan*," and that this sort of "*delivering over*" in Deuteronomy (xxxii. 30) is rendered by Aquila "*shutting up [in prison]*" συνέκλεισεν. Moreover the Double Tradition has a passage describing how a persistence in injuring one's brethren, followed by a refusal to be reconciled, brings with it a "*delivering over*" and a "*casting into prison*," where the offender is to remain till the last farthing is paid[1]. Chrysostom also, in his brief comment on the Johannine passage, illustrates it by a mention of "a king, who sends rulers with power to *cast into prison* and to let loose from prison[2]." Thus, a number of early Christian and Jewish traditions point to the conclusion, although it cannot be proved, that John may here be referring to "binding" or "imprisoning," and that the tradition meant something to the effect, metaphorically, that whomsoever the disciples from time to time "arrested"—these were "at once and permanently arrested."

(ε) With ἐὰν μή

[2521] Ἐὰν μή with present subjunctive is very rare in N.T. It occurs however thrice in xv. 4—6 "As the branch cannot bear fruit of itself *except it be abiding* in the vine, so neither can ye *except ye be abiding* in me...*Except a man be abiding* in me he is [straightway] cast (ἐβλήθη) (2445) out." The only other instance in the Gospels is Lk. xiii. 3 "*except ye be repenting* (ἐὰν μὴ μετανοῆτε) ye shall all likewise perish," where there is a threat of retribution, as also in the

---

[1] Mt. v. 25—6, Lk. xii. 58—9.
[2] [2520 a] Chrys. *ad loc.* Καθάπερ γάρ τις βασιλεὺς ἄρχοντας ἀποστέλλων ἐξουσίαν εἰς δεσμωτήριον καὶ ἐμβαλεῖν καὶ ἀφιέναι δίδωσιν.... It was the part of a disciple of Christ (Is. lviii. 6) λῦσαι πάντα σύνδεσμον ἀδικίας, but Peter is forced to say to Simon Magus (Acts viii. 23) εἰς σύνδεσμον ἀδικίας ὁρῶ σε ὄντα. The Apostle did not cast Simon Magus into the prison of sin, but was forced to leave him there and to tell him he was there, at the same time warning him to repent. The word seems to have been used by the disciples of Simon Magus (as quoted by Hippol. vi. 19 οὐ γὰρ μὴ κρατεῖσθαι αὐτοὺς ἐπί τινι νομιζομένῳ κακῷ, λελύτρωνται γάρ) to mean that "they were not *under bondage* for any supposed evil [deed]," and it is opposed to being "*ransomed*." In Fayûm Pap. 109 (1st cent.) "whenever you...want to borrow anything from me, (edd.) *I at once give in to you*," εὐθύς σε οὐ κρατῶι, might not the meaning be, "*I do not restrict you*"? Comp. Arrian *Ind.* xvi. 12 of the bit, which κρατέει τὸν ἵππον "*pulls* the horse *up*."

last clause of the Johannine passage. It would make good sense, in both, to supply "found"—with a reference to the Day of Retribution—"*except a man be [found] abiding*," "*except ye be [found] repenting.*" In Luke there follows the usual aorist, xiii. 5 (W.H. txt) "*except ye repent* (ἐὰν μὴ μετανοήσητε) ye shall all likewise perish," but W.H. marg., following B, repeats the present subjunctive[1].

[2522] In Luke xiii. 3 it would have made good sense to render "Except ye *be beginning to repent*," but that would not have suited the Johannine passage well. Nor would it suit what is the only real instance of ἐὰν μή with present in the Epistles, Rom. xi. 23 "And they also, *except they be persisting* (ἐὰν μὴ ἐπιμένωσι) in their unbelief, shall be grafted in[2]." This agrees with the two passages from the Gospels in expressing or implying a warning. The Gospels express a warning of the evil that will follow unless a certain state of things shall be found existing in the Day of Judgment. The Pauline Epistle implies a warning that there will be no change for the better ("grafting in") if a present state of things is persisted in. The only point peculiar to the Johannine passage is that on the repetition of the warning, the writer throws the consequence of the neglect of that warning into the form of an aorist to express instantaneous consequence "he was [then and there] cast out[3]."

[2523] Comparing the Johannine ἐὰν μὴ μένητε with the Johannine ἐὰν μείνητε above discussed, we infer that the former means "If ye be not [found] abiding when the crisis comes there follows instantaneous judgment," while the latter means, simply, "If ye abide,

---

[1] [2521 a] In Lk. xiii. 3—5, *a, e, f* make no distinction between the two subjunctives (having, in both, "nisi poenitentiam egeritis") but *b* has "nisi poenitentiam habeatis...si non credideritis omnes homines peribitis." In Mk xi. 23 ὃς ἂν εἴπῃ...καὶ μὴ διακριθῇ...ἀλλὰ πιστεύῃ, the present, following two parallel aorists, perhaps means "*be [steadfastly] believing*," whereas μὴ διακριθῇ means "not *entertain a momentary doubt.*"

[2] [2522 a] Comp. also passages in which ἐὰν μή is followed by ἔχω : 1 Cor. xiii. 1 ἐὰν λαλῶ...ἀ. δὲ μὴ ἔχω, Jas ii. 14 ἐὰν πίστιν λέγῃ τις ἔχειν ἔργα δὲ μὴ ἔχῃ, Jas ii. 17 ἐὰν μὴ ἔχῃ ἔργα. These three passages are all of the nature of warnings. In 1 Jn iii. 21 ἐὰν ἡ καρδία μὴ καταγινώσκῃ, the verb is repeated from what precedes and μή = *alpha* privative. For Jn v. 19 ἂν μή τι βλέπῃ, see **2516**.

[3] [2522 b] This is certainly more probable than that it is ethical aorist, *i.e.* the aorist that implies a present custom from past actions. The context and the style of the author are against this. It implies instantaneousness, but, as has been shewn (**2445, 2443** *c*), with a different shade of meaning from that of the classical Greek aorist of instantaneousness; nor is it very similar to Jn xiii. 31 νῦν ἐδοξάσθη, where the meaning is helped by νῦν "now at last." See also **2754—5**.

there *will be* blessing," without any reference to impending retribution[1].

(ζ) With ἵνα

[2524] Most Greek writers observe the distinction between the aorist and present subjunctive, as Englishmen observe that between "shall" and "will," unconsciously and without any appearance of deliberately emphasizing the difference. But we have seen above (2511) that John employs the two forms with an unusual deliberateness, even in the same sentence, to distinguish between the beginning of "knowing" and the development of it. A similarly deliberate discrimination is apparent in his references to the beginning and the permanent developments of "*believing* (πιστεύω)," as to which it should be noted that *in every case D alters the present into the aorist*[2].

[2525] Ἵνα with aorist of πιστεύω: i. 7 (The evangelist, concerning the Baptist) "[John]...came for witness...that all might [or, may] believe...," vi. 30 (The multitude, after the Feeding of the Five Thousand) "What, then, doest thou for a sign, that we may see and believe thee?" ix. 36 (The blind man, after being healed) "And who is he, Lord, that I may believe on him?" xi. 15 (Jesus to the disciples, before the raising of Lazarus) "I am glad for your sakes that I was not there, to the intent ye may believe," xi. 42 (Jesus to the Father, before the raising of Lazarus) "Because of the multitude I said it...that they may believe that thou didst send me," xiv. 27—9 (Jesus, to the disciples, when their heart is troubled) "Let not your

---

[1] [2523 a] The hypothesis that ἐὰν μή with pres. subjunct. means "*if one be not found in a certain state when the hour of trial arrives*" is favoured by the frequency of this notion of "finding" in N.T., in connexion with a crisis or day of trial, even when not expressed with these conjunctions. Comp. 2 Cor. v. 3 "*if at least...we shall be found* not naked (εἴ γε...οὐ γυμνοὶ εὑρεθησόμεθα)*,*" ix. 4 ἐὰν... εὕρωσιν ὑμᾶς ἀπαρασκευάστους etc., Rev. ii. 2 εὗρες αὐτοὺς ψευδεῖς, iii. 2 οὐ γὰρ εὕρηκά σου ἔργα πεπληρωμένα. This last passage suggests that Jas ii. 14 ἐὰν πίστιν λέγῃ τις ἔχειν ἔργα δὲ μὴ ἔχῃ may, in the mind of a Jewish writer, suggest the thought of one who, in the midst of his talking about faith, "*is found*,"—when the Judgment arrives—"*having no works to shew*." And perhaps this may be also latent in 1 Jn iii. 21 ἐὰν ἡ καρδία μὴ καταγινώσκῃ, "*if our heart be not found condemning us*" (although there a special preceding context may influence the meaning of the words).

[2] Except in xix. 35 where D is missing.

heart be troubled...I have told you before it come to pass, that, when it is come to pass, ye may believe."

[2526] Ἵνα with present of πιστεύω: vi. 29 (Jesus to the multitude, after the Feeding of the Five Thousand) "This is the work of God, that ye believe on him whom he hath sent," xiii. 19 (Jesus to the disciples, on the night before the Passion) "I tell you before it come to pass, that, when it is come to pass, ye may believe that I AM," xvii. 21 (Jesus to the Father, in the Last Prayer) "That they also may be in us, that the world may believe that thou didst send me," xix. 35 (The evangelist) "And he knoweth that he saith true, that ye also may believe," xx. 31 (The evangelist) "These [things] are written that ye may believe that Jesus is the Christ the Son of God."

[2527] From a comparison of these passages it appears that on the first occasion when our Lord uses the phrase, the present (vi. 29) is employed; it is "the work of God that ye believe on him whom he hath sent." But the multitude, in their reply, speak of an inferior kind of belief, "*believing*" not "*believing on*," and *in the aorist* (vi. 30), "that we may see and believe thee." Again Jesus, when speaking of what takes place for the sake of the disciples or for the sake of the multitude that their faith may be strengthened (xi. 15, 42, xiv. 29) uses the aorist, but when He speaks similarly to His disciples with the addition of the words "that I AM" (xiii. 19), apparently indicating a higher faith, He uses the present, which is also used in the only instance (xvii. 21) where the phrase occurs in Christ's Last Prayer. Moreover the evangelist himself, though he uses the aorist in mentioning belief as the object of the labours of John the Baptist, resorts to the present when he attests (xix. 35) the mysterious blood and water from Christ's side, and when he closes what appears to have been the first draught of his Gospel (2431—2) with the declaration that it is written "that ye may believe that Jesus is the Christ the Son of God."

[2528] The conclusion is that the author prefers the present subjunctive of πιστεύω to denote a continuous faith—that kind of faith for which the Son of God prays and His evangelists labour. The aorist may of course represent a genuine belief, but it is belief in its entrance or first formation, as when the man born blind says, "And who is he, Lord, *that I may [at once] believe* on him?" This conclusion may throw light on the disputed reading in the Epistle, "And this is his commandment *that we should believe* (ἵνα πιστεύσωμεν)

the name of his Son Jesus Christ and love (ἀγαπῶμεν) one another¹."
If the aorist is genuine, as it probably is, it seems intended to denote initial faith, the faith that is connected with baptism and with entrance into the Church², and the meaning is, "that we should [first] believe the name³...and [then habitually] love one another."

[2529] The meaning attached by John to the present subjunctive (not only of πιστεύω but of other verbs such as "know," "love," "remember") and the emphasis that he lays on this grammatical distinction, are illustrated by the fact that it occurs (in connexion with ἵνα) in the Discourse and Prayer on the night before the Passion more often than in all the words of Christ up to that time. That is because the Saviour is represented as so frequently expressing His care for *the permanent future of the Church*—that they "*may be doing*" as He has done, that they "*may be remembering*," "*may be growing in knowledge*," "*may be beholding*" the glory of the Son with the Father, and, above all, "*may be loving one another*⁴."

---

¹ [2528 a] 1 Jn iii. 23. Here ℵAC read πιστεύωμεν. But the authority of B is deservedly great on the use of this particular word. Moreover the naturalness of a tendency to conform the mood of πιστεύω to that of the following ἀγαπῶμεν lessens the weight of the evidence of ℵAC.

² [2528 b] Similarly, in the Epistle, the aorist subjunctive is connected with purification, taking away sins, and being called the children of God (1 Jn i. 9, iii. 1, 5), but the present with the duty of loving, keeping commandments and walking therein (1 Jn iii. 11, iv. 21, v. 3, also 2 Jn 5 and 6 (*bis*)). In 1 Jn ii. 28 ἵνα ἐὰν φανερωθῇ σχῶμεν παρρησίαν κ. μὴ αἰσχυνθῶμεν ἀπ' αὐτοῦ ἐν τῇ παρουσίᾳ αὐτοῦ, there is reference to a definite moment and to a definite action—"coming forward boldly" as distinct from "shrinking back ashamed": 1 Jn iv. 17 ἵνα παρρησίαν ἔχωμεν ἐν τῇ ἡμέρᾳ τῆς κρίσεως implies a state of mind (not a definite action) "*that we may be found possessing boldness*."

³ [2528 c] As πιστεύω τινί is weaker (1480 foll.) than π. εἰς τινά, so "believe the name" would seem to be intended to denote something more rudimentary than "believe *on* the name."

⁴ [2529 a] It may be urged that in xv. 12, 17, the words "that ye may be loving one another" occur as a precept, not as a prayer. But they recur, in effect, as a prayer in xvii. 26 ἵνα ἡ ἀγάπη ἣν ἠγάπησάς με ἐν αὐτοῖς ᾖ κἀγὼ ἐν αὐτοῖς. The greater part of the requests of Jesus for the disciples are expressed with the phrase ἵνα ὦσιν which occurs in xvii. 11, 19, 20, 21, 22, 23, 24, seven times, perhaps meaning that the Church, becoming one with the I AM, may BE, *i.e.* may be essentially and eternally existent. Other requests, for them or for the world, are expressed by xvii. 3 γινώσκωσι, 13 ἔχωσιν, 21 πιστεύῃ, 23 γινώσκῃ, 24 θεωρῶσιν. On the other hand the action requested from the Father is expressed by ἵνα with the aorist subjunct. xvii. 15 τηρήσῃς.

(η) Ἵνα μὴ ἀποθνήςκῃ (vi. 50, in Codex B)

[2530] In vi. 50 (W.H. txt) "This is the bread that is coming down from heaven that a man may eat thereof and *not die* (μὴ ἀποθάνῃ)," W.H. marg. has ἀποθνήσκῃ. Codex B is the only MS. that has this reading. But ἀποθάνῃ is suspiciously easy, ἀποθνήσκῃ labours under no such suspicion. There is nothing on the surface of the context, and nothing in Greek usage generally, that would cause a scribe to correct the aorist to the present. Moreover, B is almost the sole authority for some of the present subjunctives that are undoubtedly a genuine characteristic of John[1]. If B is right, the meaning is "may eat thereof and may *not be [any longer] under sentence of death*." Later on, Christ quotes a Psalm that contains a similar expression, "I said, Ye are gods and all sons of the Highest: but ye are *under sentence of death as [mortal] men* (ὑμεῖς δὲ δὴ ὡς ἄνθρωποι ἀποθνήσκετε)[2]"—where the meaning might be "destined to death," but the notion of a "sentence" is favoured by Deuteronomy xvii. 6 "*He that is under sentence of death* (ὁ ἀποθνήσκων) shall be put to death (ἀποθανεῖται) on the evidence of two or three witnesses." A "sentence" seems also implied by Ben Sira, "From a woman is the beginning of sin, and on account of her *we are all under sentence of death* (ἀποθνήσκομεν)" and perhaps by St Paul, "As in Adam *all are under sentence of death* (ἀποθνήσκουσι) so in Christ shall all be made alive[3]." These facts indicate that W.H. were justified in giving to ἀποθνήσκῃ a place (at least) in their margin: and but little more evidence would be needed to entitle it to a place in the text[4].

---

[1] [2530 a] Great importance must be attached to this fact, and to the untrustworthiness of D, for example, which regularly (2524) corrects the pres. subjunct. of πιστεύω with ἵνα, in Jn, to the aorist.

[2] Comp. x. 34 ἐγὼ εἶπα θεοί ἐστε quoting Ps. lxxxii. 7.

[3] [2530 b] Sir. xxv. 24, 1 Cor. xv. 22. Ἀποθνήσκω, in Gk, would often mean, not what we should express in English by "I am on the point of dying," but "I am on the point of *being put to death*" or "on the point of *being executed*," as in 1 S. xx. 32 "wherefore *should he be put to death* (ἵνα τί ἀποθνήσκει)?" and *Susann*. (Theod.) 43 ἀποθνήσκω μὴ ποιήσασα μηδὲν ὧν οὗτοι ἐπονηρεύσαντο κατ' ἐμοῦ.

[4] [2530 c] It is true that B cannot always be trusted as regards aorist and present subjunctives where the c of the aorist comes next to c or ε, but this is not the case here, and the difference between -θνήσκῃ and -θάνῃ could not be the result of scribal error.

[2530 d] In accordance with the use of ἀποθνήσκει above-mentioned, "*he is under sentence of death*," the phrase might be applied to an apostle on the point of martyrdom (comp. 2 Cor. i. 9 "we have had the answer (marg. sentence)

AORIST AND PRESENT SUBJUNCTIVE [2531]

(θ) With ὅταν

[2531] It is somewhat misleading to say that in N.T. ὅταν with present subjunctive—which is very rare as compared with the aorist—"usually indicates an action of frequent recurrence not limited to any particular time[1]." No doubt, this construction is used sometimes with actions of frequent recurrence, such as "eating," "praying" etc.: but ὅταν with the present does not lay stress on, or imply, frequency. It refers to *coincidence of time* ("*during the time when* this or that is going on," or "*at the moment when* this is beginning"). This is seen clearly in cases where the action is not of frequent recurrence, as in Rev. xviii. 9, "they shall weep and mourn...*when they are watching* (ὅταν βλέπωσιν) the smoke of her burning, standing afar off," 1 Thess. v. 2—3 "The day of the Lord so cometh as a thief in the night. For [*in the moment*] *when they are saying* (ὅταν λέγωσιν) 'Peace and safety,' then sudden destruction cometh upon them," 1 Cor. xv. 24 "Then [cometh] the end [*the hour of consummation*] *when he* [*Christ*] *is delivering up* (ὅταν παραδιδῷ) the kingdom[2]." This applies to one of the three[3] Johannine instances of ὅταν with present subjunctive, vii. 27 (lit.) "The Christ—*when he is in the act of coming* (ὅταν ἔρχηται)—no one is [to be found, in that crisis] understanding (οὐδεὶς γινώσκει) whence he is coming[4]."

(ἀπόκριμα) of death in ourselves," and 1 Cor. iv. 9 "the apostles last, as men appointed to death"). On the other hand οὐκ ἀποθνήσκει might be said of a martyr "*not appointed to death*," *or of one whose sentence was remitted*. Thus the saying about the beloved disciple of whom it was reported among the brethren (Jn xxi. 23) "*he is not to die* (οὐκ ἀποθνήσκει)" (in apparent antithesis to Peter, who was to be crucified) might be connected in some way with various traditions relating how the disciple was actually subjected to punishment that would have been naturally fatal, and how he was miraculously delivered from it.

[1] [2531 a] Winer, p. 387. He adds "or else represents something which in itself is future simply as an event (1 C. xv. 24 where it stands by the side of the aorist conjunctive)." See next note.

[2] [2531 b] 1 Cor. xv. 24 ὅταν παραδιδῷ...ὅταν καταργήσῃ "*when he is delivering up*...*when he has brought to naught*." Ὅταν μέλλῃ is connected with the Day of Consummation in Mk xiii. 4, Lk. xxi. 7, and with the sounding of the seventh trumpet in Rev. x. 7; but not much stress can be laid on these instances of the pres. subjunct. as the aorist ἐμέλλησα is not used in N.T.

[3] [2531 c] "Three," excluding ix. 5 ὅταν ἐν τῷ κόσμῳ ὦ, because ὦ may be regarded as either pres. or aorist subjunctive. In any case the meaning there is not "*Whenever* I am in the world," but "*during the time when.*"

[4] [2531 d] The four instances above quoted all refer to what will take place in a future day of retribution. The last three refer to what is commonly called the

[2532] ῞Οταν ἄγωσιν ὑμᾶς παραδιδόντες in Mk xiii. 11 is parallel to ὅταν δὲ εἰσφέρωσιν ὑμᾶς in Lk. xii. 11 (where the parallel Mt. x. 19 παραδῶσιν has the aorist) and is better interpreted *"In the hour of trial when* men are leading you," than "whenever, as may often happen." Elsewhere ὅταν, in connexion with other verbs, may mean "*in the moment when*" ye are beginning to "pray," "fast" etc., and so in Mt. xv. 2 "They do not wash their hands *just when they are beginning to eat* (ὅταν ἄρτον ἐσθίωσιν)[1]."

Day of the Lord, as to which the prophetic present indicative might naturally be used in the principal verb, and this would favour the sympathetic use of the present subjunctive in subordinate verbs.

[1] [2532 a] See Lk. xiv. 12, 13 "*At the time when you are making* (ὅταν ποιῇς) a dinner or feast" etc., comp. Mt. vi. 2, 5, 6, 16. This is perh. the meaning of Mk xi. 25 (pres. indic.) ὅταν στήκετε προσευχόμενοι "*at the moment when ye stand up in the act of prayer,*" and of Lk. xi. 2 ὅταν προσεύχησθε "*at the moment when ye are praying,* say as follows." This runs into the meaning of "*whenever* ye pray": but "*at the moment when*" is better in some respects, because it suggests a precept to remember to do this or that *at the moment when* one is beginning to do something else. In Mt. x. 23 ὅταν δὲ διώκωσιν, better sense may be made by "*as soon as they begin to persecute*" than "as often as they persecute," or "*whenever* they persecute"—though the latter is of course a possible rendering.

[2532 b] In Mk xiv. 25 (Mt. xxvi. 29) "until that day *when I am drinking* (ὅταν πίνω) it new with you," D reads πίω in Mt. but not in Mk. It seems to be of the nature of a prophetic present after ὅταν, used in connexion with the Day of the Lord, as in 1 Cor. xv. 24 quoted above. The only possible instance of ὅταν with indicative in Lk. is Lk. xiii. 28 marg. ὅταν ὄψεσθε, in connexion with the Day of Judgment.

[2532 c] Lk. xi. 36 εἰ οὖν τὸ σῶμά σου ὅλον φωτινόν, μὴ ἔχον ⌜μέρος τι⌝ σκοτινόν, ἔσται φωτινὸν ὅλον ὡς ὅταν ὁ λύχνος (marg. +ἐν) τῇ ἀστραπῇ φωτίζῃ σε is so difficult that (Burk. vol. ii. p. 295) "the best western MSS. (D *a b e ff i r*) simply substitute Mt. vi. 23[b] for Lk. xi. 35—6," and SS has "Thy body also, therefore, what time there is in it no lamp that shineth, becometh darkened; so what time thy lamp becometh bright, it shineth for thee." The difficulty may be removed by recognising (1) that φωτίζω almost always means "*begin to light up,*" "*bring to light,*" "*dawn on*" (not "shine on" or "steadily enlighten") and that it is especially applied to the light that dawned on Christians in baptism. The present passage warns those who have been (Heb. vi. 4) "once *illuminated* (φωτισθέντας)" against quenching their light. (2) Ἀστραπή does *not* mean "the steady light of a lamp" in any alleged Gk passage, and certainly not in Aesch. fragm. 372 λαμπραῖσιν ἀστραπαῖσι λαμπάδων σθένει where it is applied to the blazing or flashing torches in the Eleusinian mysteries. In Lk. it is applied to a lamp newly brought into a dark room. (3) In Lk. the context speaks of "kindling (ἅψας)," in Mk of a lamp "coming (ἔρχεται)" into a room; and ἀστραπή refers to the first "flash" of the light on those who are in the dark room. (4) ῞Οταν with pres. subjunct. may mean "*just at the moment when.*" Then the sense will be that, if the believer, after receiving the light, keeps it unquenched, he will be "entirely

[2533] Ὅταν θέλητε in Mk xiv. 7 may mean "*whenever* ye will" *i.e.* as often as you like. But it would also make good sense to understand the passage as meaning, in effect, "The poor ye have always with you and ye need not wait long to do them kindnesses, ye are able to do them good *in the very moment in which ye form the wish to do it:* but me ye have not always." In Lk. xi. 21 ὅταν... φυλάσσῃ, the meaning is not, "*Whenever* the strong man guards," but "*During the time when the strong man is guarding his court* his possessions are in peace," and this is contrasted with the aorist ("but when (ἐπὰν δέ) the stronger man comes and conquers (νικήσῃ) him ") which describes a single act[1].

[2534] In the Pauline Epistles, it makes very good sense to suppose that the Apostle meant to say to the Corinthians "[*In the very hour*] *when I am weak* (ὅταν γὰρ ἀσθενῶ) then am I strong," and "we rejoice [*in the very hour*] *when* we are weak[2]." So, too, 1 Cor. iii. 4 ὅταν γὰρ λέγῃ τις does not mean "As often as a man says," but "*In the very moment of saying,*" and the meaning is that a man stamps himself as "carnal" *in the very moment when* he says "I am of Paul" or "I am of Apollos[3]." In Rom. ii. 14, the

---

light, even as *at the moment when* the lamp enlightens him with the flash [of its first coming]." W.H. marg. ἐν, the reading of B, is probably correct, being a literal rendering of the Semitic original, as in Job xxxiii. 30 "to be enlightened *with* the light of the living," A and Theod. τοῦ φωτίσαι αὐτῷ ἐν φωτὶ ζώντων (LXX diff. but ἐν φωτί).

[2532 *d*] Comp. Epict. iii. 17. 1 ὅταν τι τῇ Προνοίᾳ ἐγκαλῇς, ἐπιστράφηθι..., *i.e.*, not, "*Whenever* you accuse," but "*When, at any moment, you are in the act of accusing* Providence, turn and reflect and you will recognise that things have happened according to Reason."

[1] [2533 *a*] In Dan. iii. 5 "at what time," LXX has ὅταν where Theod. has ᾗ ἂν ὥρᾳ, but ἀκούσητε follows, because the meaning is, "*At the instant when ye have heard* the trumpet you must obediently pay worship."

[2533 *b*] In Ex. xxi. 7, Lev. v. 15, where the Heb. has "when," LXX has ἐάν (with aorist subjunct.), but Aq. ὅταν. There is sometimes little difference, in a legal enactment, between (lit.) "When a soul shall have sinned" and "if a soul shall have sinned."

[2] [2534 *a*] 2 Cor. xii. 10, xiii. 9. It is the simultaneousness, not the frequency, that is insisted on—the perfection of "strength," or the "rejoicing," *along with* weakness (2 Cor. xii. 9 "made perfect *in* weakness," *i.e.* in the midst of physical weakness, not by driving it away).

[3] [2534 *b*] Comp. 1 Thess. v. 3 ὅταν λέγωσιν quoted above (2531). So 1 Cor. xiv. 26 "[*Just*] *when ye are assembling* [for sacred worship] (ὅταν συνέρχησθε)— and ought to be thinking of Christ and of Christ's Body, the congregation—each one is perhaps thinking of himself 'I have a Psalm,' 'I have a Doctrine,' 'I have a Revelation.' [Have done with this!] Let all be done to edification." This appears to be the meaning of the passage.

meaning is "*At the moment when* (ὅταν) Gentiles...are doing (ποιῶσιν) by force of nature the works of the Law, these though nominally without Law are really Law to themselves." The foregoing remarks include all the non-Johannine instances of ὅταν with present subjunctive in N.T.; and they indicate that (having quite a different meaning from ὁσάκις ἐάν, "as often as," or "whenever[1]") it emphasizes, not frequency, but *simultaneousness*.

[2535] Of the Johannine instances, vii. 27 ὁ δὲ χριστὸς ὅταν ἔρχηται has been explained above (**2531**) as meaning "[*in the Day of Deliverance*] *when the Christ is in the act of coming*." In xvi. 21 ἡ γυνὴ ὅταν τίκτῃ...ὅταν δὲ γεννήσῃ, the contrast between the two tenses indicates that the meaning is "[in the critical hour] *when she is giving birth* to a child she hath sorrow—but *when she hath given birth* to the child she remembereth no more the sorrow." The only other instance in the Fourth Gospel is viii. 44 ὅταν λαλῇ τὸ ψεῦδος ἐκ τῶν ἰδίων λαλεῖ. This is exactly parallel to the Pauline warning to the Corinthians quoted above (**2534**) "*In the very act of saying* so and so, do ye not prove yourselves to be carnal?" So here, the meaning is "*in the very act of speaking* that which is false he speaketh out of his own (**2728**)," proving himself a liar. There is one instance in the Epistle, 1 Jn v. 2 "Herein do we understand that we are loving the children of God—[*I mean, in the moment*] *when* (ὅταν) *we are loving* God and [*when we*] *are doing* his commandments," where the writer is insisting on the necessary simultaneousness of the fulfilment of the First Commandment and of the Second[2].

---

[1] [**2534***c*] Ὁσάκις ἐάν occurs in 1 Cor. xi. 25, 26, Rev. xi. 6. Ἐάν with pres. subjunct. might almost be translated "whenever" in Mk ix. 45—7 "*whenever* thy foot causes thee to stumble...*whenever* thine eye causes thee to stumble...," Mt. v. 23 "*whenever* thou art offering thy gift," Mt. xv. 14 "*whenever* the blind lead the blind" etc. But in ὅταν time is expressly included, and the emphasis on *time* differentiates ὅταν from ἐάν where both are used with the present.

[2] [**2535***a*] Bruder gives 17 as the total number of instances of ὅταν in Jn. Of these, 13 are followed by the aorist subjunctive, 3 (as above) by the present. One is (ix. 5) ὅταν ἐν τῷ κόσμῳ ὦ. There is only one in the Epistle (as above). The suggestion of a Day of Judgment or hour of crisis, apparently conveyed by ὅταν with pres. subjunct., accords with the similar association of the pres. subjunct., with ἐὰν μή (**2521—3**). In Philo i. 96 Διὸ καὶ Ἀαρὼν ὅταν τελευτᾷ (τουτέστιν ὅταν τελειωθῇ) εἰς Ὢρ, ὅ ἐστι φῶς, ἀνέρχεται, if the bracketed words are not a gloss, the meaning may be "when he is *in the act of attaining the end* through death (*that is, has been perfected*)."

Voice

(i) **Middle**

(a) Αἰτοῦμαι

[2536] Αἰτοῦμαι in N.T. generally means "ask for myself," "ask a favour," and can almost always be thus rendered in the Synoptists[1]. In LXX, the usage varies in different books[2], and also in different MSS.[3] On the whole, the active is used colloquially and for ordinary asking of "food," "money" etc.[4], but the middle in petitions for blessings from God, or for favours from a king, or in elevated style[5]. Variations can generally be explained as in Isaiah, when the prophet says "*Ask as a favour* for thyself (αἴτησαι σεαυτῷ) a sign," and Ahaz replies "I will surely not *ask* (οὐ μὴ αἰτήσω)." The prophet emphasizes "*as a favour for thyself,*" the king emphasizes the negative, "I will *not* ask," i.e. not ask in any way[6]. From meaning "ask a favour," the middle came to mean "ask specially," "ask earnestly," as in Ps. xxvii. 4 "One thing have I *earnestly asked* (ᾐτησάμην) from the Lord," and Prov. xxx. 7 "Two things do I *earnestly ask* (αἰτοῦμαι) from thee." The Epistle of St James implies that Christians

---

[1] [2536 a] Mk vi. 24, 25, x. 38, xv. 8, 43, Mt. xiv. 7, xviii. 19, xx. 22, xxvii. 20, 58, Lk. xxiii. 23, 25, 52. In Mk xi. 24 προσεύχεσθε καὶ αἰτεῖσθε, the parall. Mt. xxi. 22 (which somewhat differs) has αἰτήσητε ἐν τῇ προσευχῇ. Αἰτοῦμαι in Acts is often in a bad sense "asking a favour" that ought not to be granted as also in Mk vi. 25 (the asking for the head of John the Baptist). Αἰτοῦμαι does not occur in the Pauline Epistles, exc. Eph. iii. 13, 20, Col. i. 9 (and αἰτέω only in 1 Cor. i. 22).

[2] [2536 b] Comp. 1 K. iii. 11 ᾐτήσω...οὐκ ᾐτήσω (3 times)...ἀλλ' ᾐτήσω with the parall. 2 Chr. i. 11 οὐκ ᾐτήσω (twice)...καὶ ᾔτησας σεαυτῷ.

[3] [2536 c] In Judg. viii. 26, LXX has active, but A middle. In Dan. (Theod.) vi. 7, 12, 13, txt. has active, but A middle.

[4] [2536 d] Ex. iii. 22, xi. 2, xii. 35, xxii. 14, Judg. i. 14 ἀγρόν (but contrast Josh. xv. 18), v. 25 ὕδωρ, viii. 26 ἐνώτια, 2 K. iv. 3 σκεύη etc. So Ps. lxxviii. 18, cv. 40 of asking food, 2 S. xii. 20, Lam. iv. 4 ἄρτον (but, in the elevated style, Wisd. xix. 11 ᾐτήσαντο ἐδέσματα τρυφῆς).

[5] [2536 e] Αἰτοῦμαι (not αἰτέω) is always used in 1 K. e.g. 1 K. ii. 15, 20 (*bis*), 22 (*bis*), iii. 5, 10, 11 (freq.) etc. and always (4 times) in Joshua.

[6] [2536 f] Is. vii. 11—12. In Mk vi. 22—4, dramatically, Herod Antipas does not dwell upon the fact that he is giving Herodias a gift *for herself*, but simply says—with royal munificence—αἴτησόν με ὃ ἐὰν θέλῃς and ὅτι ἐάν με αἰτήσῃς. But Herodias, with her mind full of the favour she may ask for, says to her mother "*What favour am I to ask* (τί αἰτήσωμαι)?" Mt. xiv. 7 δοῦναι ὃ ἐὰν αἰτήσηται expresses it historically, "to give her *whatever favour she might ask* (ὃ ἐὰν αἰτήσηται)."

fulfilled formally the Lord's command "Ask (αἰτεῖτε) and ye shall receive," but that they did not obtain because they did not "*ask earnestly*" (οὐκ ἔχετε διὰ τὸ μὴ αἰτεῖσθαι ὑμᾶς) or rather they "asked earnestly but wickedly" (κακῶς αἰτεῖσθε)[1]. It was natural that distinctions between the middle and the active should be made by Christians in the first century. For, whereas Mark and Matthew contain a precept about "*asking earnestly*," αἰτοῦμαι, the result being conditional on "believing[2]," Luke omits this precept altogether and merely agrees with Matthew in the unconditional precept "*Ask* (αἰτεῖτε), and it shall be given to you[3]."

[2536 (i)] In the Last Discourse and in the Epistle, John, as will appear below[4], adheres (thrice) to Matthew's and Luke's active,

---

[1] [2536 *g*] Jas iv. 2—3 "Ye have not because *ye ask not earnestly* (διὰ τὸ μὴ αἰτεῖσθαι ὑμᾶς): *ye ask* (αἰτεῖτε) and ye receive not, because *ye ask earnestly in an evil spirit* (διότι κακῶς αἰτεῖσθε) that ye may spend [money] on your pleasures." See Mayor *ad loc.* and his collection of passages from Justin and Hermas containing αἰτέω and αἰτοῦμαι in juxtaposition, *e.g.* Herm. *Vis.* III. x. 7—8 τί σύ... αἰτεῖς ἀποκαλύψεις...; βλέπε μή ποτε πολλὰ αἰτούμενος...Κύριε, τοῦτο μόνον αἰτοῦμαι. Herm. *Mand.* ix. 1—8 insists on the need of "praying earnestly without distraction" (αἰτοῦ...ἀδιστάκτως) and uses the middle about nine times, only twice falling into the active. Mayor suggests αἰτήσῃ in ix. 4 ἐὰν ἀδιστάκτως αἰτήσῃς. But if that is to be altered, must not we also alter ix. 7 τὰ αἰτήματά σου ἃ αἰτεῖς λήψῃ? Is it not natural that in a string of exhortations using the middle αἰτοῦμαι, "*ask earnestly*," the active, αἰτέω—simply "*ask*"—should be sometimes used in clauses describing the spirit in which one is to "*ask*," or promising a reward to petitions "*asked*" in that spirit?

[2] [2536 *h*] Mk xi. 24 πάντα ὅσα προσεύχεσθε καὶ αἰτεῖσθε, πιστεύετε ὅτι ἐλάβετε, καὶ ἔσται ὑμῖν, Mt. xxi. 22 πάντα ὅσα ἂν αἰτήσητε ἐν τῇ προσευχῇ πιστεύοντες λήμψεσθε, after the withering of the fig-tree. Lk. omits both the miracle and this comment.

[3] Mt. vii. 7 (in the Sermon on the Mount), Lk. xi. 9 αἰτεῖτε καὶ δοθήσεται ὑμῖν.

[4] [2536 (i) *a*] Apart from xi. 22 ὅσα ἂν αἰτήσῃ τὸν θεόν addressed by Martha to Jesus, and from the Samaritan dialogue (iv. 9—10 παρ᾽ ἐμοῦ πεῖν αἰτεῖς...σὺ ἂν ᾔτησας αὐτόν) the two voices occur as follows in Jn and 1 Jn:

Active	Middle
xiv. 12—14 ὁ πιστεύων...ποιήσει... κ. ὅτι ἂν αἰτήσητε (marg. αἰτῆτε) ἐν τῷ ὀνόματί μου τοῦτο ποιήσω ἵνα δοξασθῇ ὁ πατὴρ ἐν τῷ υἱῷ. ἐάν τι αἰτήσητέ [με] ἐν τῷ ὀνόματί μου ⌜τοῦτο⌝ (marg. ἐγώ) ποιήσω.	xv. 7 ἐὰν μείνητε ἐν ἐμοὶ κ. τὰ ῥήματά μου ἐν ὑμῖν μείνῃ, ὃ ἐὰν θέλητε αἰτήσασθε κ. γενήσεται ὑμῖν.
xv. 16 κ. ἔθηκα ὑμᾶς ἵνα...κ. ὁ καρπὸς ὑμῶν μένῃ, ἵνα ὅτι ἂν αἰτήσητε (marg. αἰτῆτε) τὸν πατέρα ἐν τῷ ὀνόματί μου δῷ ὑμῖν.	

"*ask*," when he connects "asking" with "receiving" or with "having." But whenever (five times) Christ is represented as using the active, "*in my name*" is added in the context, thus excluding selfish or arbitrary asking. When John for the first time uses the middle, he seems, for the moment, to countenance the most reckless asking of favours—"*ask for yourselves whatsoever ye will* (ὃ ἐὰν θέλητε αἰτήσασθε)": but this is preceded by "if ye abide in me and my words abide in you." And how can the words of the disciples ask recklessly or selfishly "if" Christ's own "words" abide in their hearts and on their lips? This is John's way of saying "If ye steadfastly believe." Only it is not subjective ("believe") but objective: "If ye stand fast in me and I stand fast in you." As regards this "asking of favours" or "asking what ye will," he does not say "*ye shall receive*," but "*it shall be done for you*," resembling Mark's tradition (**2536** *h*) as distinct from Matthew's. In the Epistle, this "asking of favours" is to be "according to the will of God," and the result is, not, "*it shall be done*," but "*He heareth us*."

(β) Ἀποκρίνασθαι

[**2537**] Ἀποκρίνομαι is twice used by John in the first aorist middle (instead of the much more frequent aorist passive) in the passage that describes the first attempt of the Jews to "persecute"

xvi. 23—4 ἄν τι αἰτήσητε τὸν πατέρα δώσει ὑμῖν ἐν τῷ ὀνόματί μου· ἕως ἄρτι οὐκ ᾐτήσατε οὐδὲν ἐν τῷ ὀνόματί μου· αἰτεῖτε καὶ λήμψεσθε.

[**2536** (i) *b*] 1 Jn iii. 21—22 ἐὰν ἡ καρδία μὴ καταγινώσκῃ παρρησίαν ἔχομεν πρὸς τὸν θεόν, κ. ὃ ἂν αἰτῶμεν λαμβάνομεν ἀπ' αὐτοῦ.

1 Jn v. 15 (*b*) [after οἴδαμεν ὅτι] ἔχομεν τὰ αἰτήματα ἃ ᾐτήκαμεν ἀπ' αὐτοῦ.

1 Jn v. 16 ἐάν τις ἴδῃ…αἰτήσει, κ. δώσει αὐτῷ ζωήν.

xvi. 26 ἐν ἐκείνῃ τῇ ἡμέρᾳ ἐν τῷ ὀνόματί μου αἰτήσεσθε, καὶ οὐ λέγω ὑμῖν ὅτι ἐγὼ ἐρωτήσω τὸν πατέρα περὶ ὑμῶν· αὐτὸς γὰρ ὁ πατὴρ φιλεῖ ὑμᾶς ὅτι…

1 Jn v. 14 κ. αὕτη ἐστὶν ἡ παρρησία ἣν ἔχομεν πρὸς αὐτόν, ὅτι ἐάν τι αἰτώμεθα κατὰ τὸ θέλημα αὐτοῦ ἀκούει ἡμῶν.

1 Jn v. 15 (*a*) κ. ἐὰν οἴδαμεν ὅτι ἀκούει ἡμῶν ὃ ἐὰν αἰτώμεθα, οἴδαμεν ὅτι…

[**2536** (i) *c*] In xi. 22 ὅσα ἂν αἰτήσῃ τὸν θεὸν δώσει σοι ὁ θεός, Martha is probably described as applying to Christ, from her own point of view, a word never applied to Him by the evangelist; and the middle "*ask for thyself*," or "*ask earnestly*," or "*ask as a favour*," emphasizes her error. Similarly (**1728** *p*) she uses the word φιλέω to describe Christ's love of Lazarus, whereas John uses ἀγαπάω. Whenever Jn connects "ask" and "give" elsewhere in his own language or in that of Christ, he uses the active, iv. 10, xv. 16, xvi. 23, 1 Jn v. 16, and this accords with the Matthew-Luke Tradition (Mt. vii. 7, Lk. xi. 9).

(v. 16 διὰ τοῦτο ἐδίωκον) Jesus. It was for an act of healing on the Sabbath. Jesus (v. 17) "*made answer* (ἀπεκρίνατο) to them...." It is then said, "On this account therefore did the Jews seek rather to kill him," and again (v. 19) "Jesus therefore *made answer* (ἀπεκρίνατο)." Ἀπεκρίθη occurs in John more than 50 times, but ἀπεκρίνατο only here. It must be rendered according to its frequent use in Greek, "*made answer to the charge*," "*made his defence*." Ὁ διώκων, as a legal term, regularly means "the pursuer," in the Scotch sense, *i.e.* the prosecutor; and the verb often means "prosecute." No doubt, John means "persecute" here; yet he means persecuting with charges of blasphemy implying threats of "prosecution," so that "made his defence" is particularly appropriate to the context, where a charge is being brought against Jesus for the first time in this Gospel. Ἀπεκρίνατο is used only once in the Acts (iii. 12), and there it introduces a speech of Peter "to all the people," not directly of the nature of a defence, but rather an attack upon the Jews for killing Christ. Yet indirectly it is of the nature of a defence or *apologia*. In Mark and Matthew it is used only negatively, describing the refusal of Christ to "make a formal defence" on the day of His trial. Luke has a parallel use of it in somewhat similar circumstances[1]. But Luke also uses the aorist middle once more concerning the public answer given by John the Baptist "to all [men][2]."

---

[1] [2537 *a*] Mk xiv. 61 οὐκ ἀπεκρίνατο οὐδέν (of the silence before the Sanhedrin) (Mt.-Lk. diff.); Mt. xxvii. 12 οὐδὲν ἀπεκρίνατο (of the silence before Pilate) (Mk-Lk. different); Lk. xxiii. 9 (of the silence before Herod). These facts must be contrasted with the frequency of the aorist passive form ἀποκριθείς in all the Synoptists.

[2537 *b*] In LXX, ἀποκρίνασθαι is extremely rare. It occurs in Ex. xix. 19 "Moses spake and God *answered* him by a voice," 1 K. ii. 1 "He [David] *charged* Solomon his son," ἀπεκρίνατο, Aq. etc. ἐνετείλατο, 1 Chr. x. 13 κ. ἀπεκρίνατο αὐτῷ Σ. ὁ προφήτης (not in Heb., "Samuel *made answer* to Saul" when the latter inquired of a soothsayer), Ezek. ix. 11 "*reported the matter*." In Judg. v. 29, of Sisera's mother "making answer" to her own question, LXX has ἀπέστρεψεν λόγους, but A ἀπεκρίνατο ἐν ῥήμασιν. Mic. iii. 11 "the priests *teach* for hire," has the imperf. middle ἀπεκρίνοντο, Aq. Theod. ἐφώτιζον, where LXX perh. took it (as in 1 Chr. x. 13) to mean oracular response. In none of these instances does the middle mean "make answer to a charge"; but in each of them there is some notion of publicity, or oracular response, or solemnity, so that the meaning is different from that of ἀποκριθῆναι.

[2] [2537 *c*] Lk. iii. 10 ἀπεκρίνατο λέγων πᾶσιν. In the account of the trial, Jn does not use ἀπεκρίνατο. But he represents Jesus as freely conversing (ἀπεκρίθη etc.) with Pilate up to the moment when Pilate asked Him "Whence art thou?" Then

[2537 (i)] Under this head it is convenient to consider the middle or intransitive sense of the active form καθίζω in xix. 13 ὁ οὖν Πειλᾶτος…ἤγαγεν ἔξω τὸν Ἰησοῦν, καὶ ἐκάθισεν ἐπὶ βήματος, concerning which it has been suggested in modern times that the verb may be transitive, as in 1 Cor. vi. 4 τούτους καθίζετε, Eph. i. 20 (W.H.) ἐγείρας αὐτὸν ἐκ νεκρῶν καὶ καθίσας ἐν δεξιᾷ αὐτοῦ. Add Hermas *Vis.* iii. 2. 4 ἐγείρει με καὶ καθίζει, "*makes me sit* on the bench to the left," followed by "and she herself, too, sat (ἐκαθέζετο) on the right." But in all these the transitive meaning of the verb is made clear by the context (although in Eph. i. 20 some scribes make it clearer by adding αὐτόν). In xix. 13, αὐτόν might certainly be supplied after ἐκάθισεν[1] if the sense demanded it; but the transitive use of καθίζω would be unique in John[2]; and the phrase καθίσας ἐπὶ τοῦ βήματος, which occurs thrice in the Acts about a judge "*taking his seat* on the tribunal[3]," would here be employed to describe the judge as *causing the accused to sit* on the tribunal! It is needless to dwell on the antecedent improbability that a Roman Governor—even such a one as Pilate—would place an alleged criminal upon the Governor's own seat. No ancient authority is alleged for the interpretation "caused to sit." The *Acta Pilati* (A and B) takes the word intransitively; so do the Latin translators, the Syriac, and Nonnus; and Chry-

---

it is said (xix. 9) "Jesus gave him no *answer* (ἀπόκρισιν)"—a word meaning an answer to a definite question or questions (as in i. 22). It is clear that there were different traditions about Christ's "not making answer" at the trial. By avoiding the traditional phrase οὐκ ἀπεκρίνατο, Jn avoids committing himself to, or against, any one of the three Synoptic accounts.

[2537 *d*] Some MSS. and versions read ἀπεκρίνατο in xii. 23 (W.H.) ὁ δὲ Ἰησοῦς ἀποκρίνεται αὐτοῖς λέγων, preceding the solemn words, "The hour hath come that the Son of man should be glorified." It is the occasion of the arrival of the Greeks and an oracular solemnity is appropriate to the verb of speech. This might be suggested by the unusual present middle, though not so clearly as by the aorist middle. The present is probably the correct reading. Ἀποκρίνεται (pres.) is also used to introduce Christ's indication (xiii. 26) of Judas Iscariot as the traitor, and (xiii. 38) His prediction of Peter's denial.

[1] [2537 (i) *a*] Comp. iv. 47 ἀπῆλθεν πρὸς αὐτὸν καὶ ἠρώτα [v.r. +αὐτόν]…, vi. 15 ἁρπάζειν αὐτὸν ἵνα ποιήσωσιν [v.r. +αὐτόν] βασιλέα, xviii. 12—13 συνέλαβον τὸν Ἰησοῦν καὶ ἔδησαν αὐτὸν καὶ ἤγαγον [v.r. ἀπήγαγον αὐτόν]…. Conversely in xi. 44 λύσατε αὐτὸν κ. ἄφετε αὐτὸν ὑπάγειν, some auth. om. 2nd. αὐτόν.

[2] [2537 (i) *b*] Apart from the spurious viii. 2 καθίσας, Jn has xii. 14 ἐκάθισεν, on which see **2537** (ii). He also has (4) καθῆσθαι and (3) καθέζεσθαι.

[3] Acts xii. 21, xxv. 6, 17. Comp. Epict. iv. 10. 21 "And what is the net result [of being a consul]? Twelve bundles of rods, and three or four times *sitting on a bema* (ἐπὶ βῆμα καθίσαι)!

sostom expressly says that "καθίσαι *makes it clear*" that Pilate professed an intention to "*investigate the matter*" as *a judge*[1].

[2537 (ii)] The suggestion of a transitive meaning in xix. 13 would not have been worth discussing except for its possible bearing on Mk xi. 7 ἐκάθισεν (D καθειζει, *d* sedebat), Mt. xxi. 7 ἐπεκάθισεν (D εκαθητο), Lk. xix. 35 ἐπεβίβασαν. Here Lk. has a transitive meaning, but John not only supports Mt.-Mk in xii. 14 εὑρὼν δὲ ὁ Ἰ. ὀνάριον ἐκάθισεν ἐπ' αὐτό, but also alters the prophecy of Zech. ix. 9 "*riding* on an ass," LXX ἐπιβεβηκώς, to (xii. 15) "seated (καθήμενος)" which accords more exactly with ἐκάθισεν. There was nothing arbitrary in John's action, for the Hebrew word meaning "ride" in Zechariah is also rendered "sit" three or four times in LXX, and indeed the Syriac—in which the Hebrew word exists and is used in the Syriac version of Mk-Mt. here—is rendered by Mr Burkitt "*ride*" in Mk xi. 7, Mt. xxi. 7. There can be little doubt that John, in the Entry into Jerusalem, is writing with allusion to two traditions, possibly arising from variations of ἐκάθισαν (trans.) and ἐκάθισεν (intr.): and, while Lk. adopted the former, "*made to sit*," John supported Mk and Mt. in adopting the latter, "*sat*." Perhaps some tradition followed by Lk. made the same mistake as the LXX made in 2 K. xi. 19 "and he sat," LXX καὶ ἐκάθισαν αὐτόν, A ἐκάθισεν. The spurious Gospel of Peter and Justin Martyr have wild traditions telling how the Jews place Christ on a tribunal or place of judgment[2]. Perhaps

---

[1] [2537 (i) *c*] *Acta P.* (A) 9 τότε ἐκέλευσεν ὁ Π. τὸν βῆλον ἑλκυσθῆναι τοῦ βήματος οὗ ἐκαθέζετο, (B) τότε ἐκάθισεν ὁ Π. εἰς τὸν θρόνον αὐτοῦ ἵνα ποιήσῃ ἀπόφασιν (Evang. Nicod. merely "tunc jussit Pilatus velum solvi"). The Lat. vss have "sedit," SS is missing, but Walton gives all versions (including Syriac) as having "sedit" or "insedit." Nonnus has ἀρτιδόμῳ δ' ἐκάθητο λιθοστρώτῳ παρὰ χώρῳ, Chrys. ἐξέρχεται μὲν ὡς ἐξετάζων τὸ πρᾶγμα (τὸ γὰρ καθίσαι τοῦτο ἐδήλου)· οὐδεμίαν δὲ ποιησάμενος ἐξέτασιν παραδίδωσιν αὐτὸν νομίζων δυσωπήσειν αὐτούς.

[2] [2537 (ii) *a*] Justin Martyr, after quoting from Is. lviii. 2 (LXX) "They ask me now for judgment," adds (*Apol.* 35) "For indeed, as the prophet said, dragging Him along they made Him sit upon a seat of judgment (διασύροντες αὐτὸν ἐκάθισαν ἐπὶ βήματος) and said Judge for us." The Gospel of Peter has (§ 3) "Let us (?) drag (ευρωμεν corrected into σύρωμεν) the Son of God...and they made Him sit on a chair of judgment (ἐκάθισαν αὐτὸν ἐπὶ καθέδραν κρίσεως), saying Judge justly, O king of Israel."

[2537 (ii) *b*] At the same time Jn may also be correcting (**1745**) a misunderstanding arising from Mt. xxvii. 19 καθημένου δὲ ἐπὶ τοῦ βήματος. According to Jn, the βῆμα was not "*the* tribunal" but "*a* tribunal," set up specially in Gabbatha (comp. Joseph. *Bell.* ii. 14. 8) outside the Praetorium. If the sentence was to be pronounced publicly, it could not be done from "*the* tribunal" inside the Praetorium, as the Jews (xviii. 28) would not enter it.

PASSIVE [2540]

some of these were already in the air at the time of the publication of the Fourth Gospel, and the author may have desired, while tacitly refuting them, to use the very phrase that originated them—thus destroying the error by explaining it.

(ii) **Passive**

(a) Ἐκρύβη

[2538] In viii. 59 "They therefore took up stones to cast at him, but Jesus *was hidden* and went out of the temple," xii. 36 "As ye have the light believe in the light that ye may become sons of light. These things spake Jesus and went away and *was hidden* from them," the second aorist passive ἐκρύβη is twice rendered as a middle in R.V. txt and A.V., but as a passive in R.V. marg. In favour of "*hid himself*" may be alleged the usage of LXX. But in LXX ἐκρύβη means "hide oneself in fear," "crouch," "cower," like Adam and Eve in Paradise[1]. Such usage appears inapplicable here.

[2539] In N.T. the 2nd aorist passive of κρύπτω is applied to persons in Heb. xi. 23 "Moses *was hidden* three months," and to things in Mt. v. 14 "a city on a hill cannot *be hid* (κρυβῆναι)," Lk. xix. 42 "but now *are they hid* (ἐκρύβη) from thine eyes," 1 Tim. v. 25 "cannot *be hid* (κρυβῆναι)." Almost all the instances of middle meaning alleged by L. S. may be explained passively, or else they do not affect the usage of the 2nd aorist[2].

[2540] On the side of the middle interpretation, however, we must place Chrysostom, who, though he does not quote ἐκρύβη in the first passage, says "Then He flees back again after the manner of

---

[1] [2538 *a*] Comp. Gen. iii. 8, 10, Judg. ix. 5, 1 S. xiii. 6, xiv. 11, Job xxiv. 4, xxix. 8 etc. Aq. uses it in Gen. xxxi. 27 " why didst thou *flee secretly* (ἐκρύβης τοῦ ἀποδρᾶναι) " LXX om. When κρύπτω is applied to God hiding His face, Aq. has κρύπτω sometimes where LXX has ἀποστρέφω (? for seemliness) *e.g.* Ps. xiii. 1, Is. lxiv. 7. In Is. lvii. 17, "face" is omitted by Heb. but ins. by LXX ἀπέστρεψα τὸ πρόσωπόν μου.

[2] [2539 *a*] Κεκρύφαται Hes. *Op.* 384 of stars, means "they remain hidden," as Steph. " absconditae sunt, Ionice pro κεκρυμμέναι εἰσί." Eurip. *Hel.* 606 οὐρανῷ δὲ κρύπτεται is much more probably passive as is shewn by the context, ἀρθεῖσ' ἄφαντος, οὐρανῷ δὲ κρύπτεται "*lifted out of sight* and *hid* in heaven [by the will of Zeus]": *Cycl.* 615 κρύπτεται ἐς σποδιὰν δρυὸς ἄσπετον ἔρνος, however punctuated, almost certainly means that the stake is "*being hidden*" in the embers. The only remaining instance is an imperfect middle Babr. 5. 4 ἐκρύπτετ' οἴκου γωνίην, rendered by L.S. "*ran to hide himself* in a corner."

man and (?) *hides Himself* (κρύπτεται)[1]," where the parallel "flees" makes it probable that he uses κρύπτεται as a middle. Theodorus expressly explains ἐκρύβη thus, "How ἐκρύβη? Not by coiling himself up in a corner of the Temple in a cupboard...nor yet by twisting round behind a wall or pillar, but making Himself invisible by divine authority (ἐξουσίᾳ θεϊκῇ) to those that were plotting against Him[2]." In the second passage, Chrysostom twice quotes ἐκρύβη and twice explains it as κρύπτεται. Possibly vernacular Greek usage, as well as that of LXX, may have caused Chrysostom to prefer a form less associated with "slinking away[3]": but in any case both these interpreters take ἐκρύβη as middle.

[2541] Some light may be shed on these two passages by another in which Jesus is described as retiring: v. 13 "For Jesus *conveyed himself away* (ἐξένευσεν, אD ἔνευσεν), a multitude being in the place." Here Chrysostom, in quoting, substitutes ἐξέκλινεν, and explains it as ἔκρυψεν ἑαυτόν and ἀναχωρήσας. Now ἐκνεύω is thrice substituted by A for LXX ἐκκλίνω in Judges iv. 18. And (2538 a) the LXX has been shewn to use ἀποστρέφω for κρύπτω concerning the "hiding" of God's "face." Thus it appears that "hiding" and "turning aside" are expressions that might be interchanged in this sense. And, practically, this passage (v. 13) describes a "hiding," or "retiring," as Chrysostom calls it.

[2542] In viii. 59 several MSS. add that Jesus "passed through the midst of them (διελθὼν διὰ μέσου αὐτῶν)" and that He "passed away just as he was (παρῆγεν οὕτως)." The first of these clauses is identical with one in Lk. iv. 30 describing Christ's "passing through" the multitude of Nazareth, when they were attempting to cast Him down a precipice. That escape is generally regarded as miraculous, and the addition of such a clause in Jn viii. 59 indicates that the scribes

---

[1] [2540 a] Εἶτα φεύγει πάλιν ἀνθρωπίνως καὶ κρύπτεται ἱκανὴν διδασκαλίαν αὐτοῖς παραθέμενος.... Chrys. does not quote the text with ἐκρύβη. Cramer prints Τὸ δὲ "ἐκρύβη καὶ ἐξῆλθεν ἐκ τοῦ ἱεροῦ" ἀνθρωπίνως πάλιν ποιεῖ, ἱκανὴν διδασκαλίαν παραθέμενος.... Nonnus has the middle twice, viii. 59 ὑπὸ πτύχα κεύθετο νηοῦ, xii. 36 κεύθετ' Ἰουδαίων χορὸν...ἐάσας.

[2] [2540 b] Cramer *ad loc*. Origen (on Lk. *Hom.* 19, Lomm. v. 156) "...sed quomodo in Joannis evangelio scriptum est quoniam insidiabantur ei Judaei et elapsus est de medio eorum et non apparuit," where the context indicates that he regarded the event as supernatural.

[3] [2540 c] Phrynichus warns people against spelling κρύβεται with a β, and Hesychius gives κρυβόμενος and ὑποπίπτων "cringing," as paraphrases of πτήσσων, "cowering down."

adding it regarded Christ's escape from stoning as miraculous. If so, they must have taken ἐκρύβη as "miraculously concealed himself" or "was miraculously concealed." In any case, this scribal addition indicates a desire to explain the meaning of ἐκρύβη.

[2543] Summing up the evidence, we find the usage of LXX and three Greek commentators favouring the middle "*hid himself*," but the usage of N.T. favouring the passive, "*was hidden.*" The latter ought to count for more than the former[1]. And the passive is also favoured by the context in the last of the three Johannine passages; for it says that the Jews "did not believe" because God had (xii. 40) "*blinded their eyes.*" But some explanation is needed of the motives that induced John to use so ambiguous a phrase. We know from Origen's treatise against Celsus that charges of cowardice were brought by unbelievers against our Lord's character: and if some of these were based on variously expressed traditions that He on certain occasions "*hid himself*," one way of meeting these charges would be to report the tradition in such a way as to shew how it might be misunderstood. Luke had described Christ as "passing through" the Nazarenes, but had not explained how this was effected[2]. John suggests that it was literal and miraculous, but also that it was typical of a spiritual blinding whereby Christ "was hidden" from those who rejected Him[3].

---

[1] [2543 a] Of special importance is Heb. xi. 23, because that Epistle is written by someone familiar with Alexandrian thought, and, to that extent, similar to the author of the Fourth Gospel. The Greek commentators are all late.

[2] [2543 b] Cyril (Cramer, on Lk. iv. 29—30) says of the Nazarenes "Fie on their folly!...*they have eyes and do not see*...and then goes on to say, '*He passed through the midst of them.*'" He does not state that they were literally "blinded," or that Jesus was thus miraculously "hidden" from the Nazarenes. But the juxtaposition of the two traditions shews how the former might originate the latter.

[3] [2543 c] If Chrysostom is right in calling Christ's "conveying himself away" (from the pool of Bethzatha) an act of "hiding," then there are three such acts in John, each followed by an expression of unbelief or hostility on the part of the Jews, or by some evangelistic statement about unbelief (1) "He *conveyed himself away*," (2) "He *was hidden* and went out of the Temple," (3) "He *went away and was hidden from them.*" The last seems intended as a climax, implying the final departure of the Light so that it was "hidden from" the Jews.

BOOK II
ARRANGEMENT, VARIATION, AND REPETITION OF WORDS

CHAPTER I

ARRANGEMENT AND VARIATION

§ 1. *Variation in repetition or quotation*

[2544] It has been shewn in *Johannine Vocabulary* that John uses words with extraordinary discrimination and with subtle shades of meaning. The First Book of *Johannine Grammar* has shewn that the same subtle discrimination pervades his use of grammatical forms and constructions. We have now to consider whether the same characteristics may be traced in his arrangement and variation of words and expressions. Finally we must consider his habit of repetition—a subject that would find no place in a Shakespearian or Euripidean Grammar, but one that will claim a good deal of comment in the following pages. As regards arrangement, John will sometimes be found to combine with parallelism what is commonly called Chiasmus, *i.e.* an order in which the extremes and means of a sentence are alike[1]: and this is so frequent that it will receive a separate section. But the first place must be given to Johannine variation—that is, the habit of repeating the same thing (or representing his various characters as repeating the same thing) in slightly dissimilar words and with slight dissimilarities of order.

---

[1] [2544 *a*] *E.g.* Ps. xxvii. 8 "Seek ye my face: thy face, Lord, will I seek," Ps. cv. 15—16 "Touch not mine anointed and my prophets harm not," "And he called for a famine on the land; every support of bread he brake." In these three sentences, the verbs come at the extremes, and the nouns in the middle. In *parallelism*, the sequence in the first clause would be reproduced in the second, *e.g.* (Ps. cv. 29—33) "He turned their waters into blood, and slew their fish...he smote their vines also and their fig-trees, and brake the trees of their borders." In the first of the three instances of *chiasmus* given above, the two means and the two extremes are identical ("face" "face," "seek" "seek"); in the others, they differ.

[2545] ARRANGEMENT AND VARIATION

[2545] In the list of variations given below, the reader's particular attention is called to the passages, marked †, where an utterance of our Lord is repeated after "I said," "He said" etc. but not with exact accuracy. It is impossible to believe that the evangelist misquoted Jesus or represented Him as misquoting Himself. Our conclusion must therefore be that he wished to compel his readers to perceive that they have not before them Christ's exact words, and that they must think of their spirit rather than of the letter. On at least one occasion Christ is represented as appealing to words that had been previously uttered by Him, but have not been recorded in this Gospel, xi. 40 "Said I not unto thee that, if thou believedst, thou shouldst see the glory of God?" This cannot be identified with any previous utterance of Christ's to Martha[1]. On other occasions (*e.g.* vi. 26—36, and 44—65), the reference is doubtful. Even where Christ is certainly repeating His own words they are never repeated exactly except once (2190 *a*). In that single instance, Jesus says to His disciples xiii. 33 "Even as I said to the Jews, '*Where I go ye cannot come*,' so to you also I say it for the present." He had uttered these exact words (viii. 21) to the Jews. But is it not clear that they are now uttered to the disciples in a meaning made widely different by different circumstances? Probably it is something more than a coincidence that this is the only saying of Jesus quoted by Jesus Himself ("I said"), with exact accuracy[2]. It seems as though the writer wished to bring home to us the truth of Christ's warning, "The spirit it is that giveth life; the flesh profiteth nothing. The words that I have spoken to you are [truly] spirit and are [truly] life[3]."

---

[1] [2545 *a*] Here, Alford describes Jesus as "referring her [*i.e.* Martha] to the plain duty of simple faith insisted on by Him before (*vv.* 25, 26? or in some other teaching?)." Westcott says, "The Lord directs Martha to the deeper meaning of His words....The general description of the victory of faith (*v.* 26) contained necessarily a special promise. The fulfilment of that promise was a revelation of *the glory of God* (*v.* 4) for which Christ had from the first encouraged the sisters to look." The meaning of this is not clear to me. The words in xi. 4 "this sickness is not unto death but for *the glory of God*," were not uttered to Martha and Mary, but at a distance from them. Perhaps, however, Westcott assumes that they were reported to the sisters by their messenger, who had informed Jesus of their brother's sickness.

[2] [2545 *b*] This is all the more extraordinary because the Jews on at least two occasions (vii. 36, viii. 22) quote the words of Jesus at some length and with exact accuracy (2190 *a*).

[3] [2545 *c*] vi. 63. Comp. Orig. Huet ii. 405 D εἴπερ δὲ ἃ ἐλάλει ῥήματα ὁ Ἰησοῦς πνεῦμά ἐστι καὶ οὐ γράμμα, where as elsewhere he indicates that it is

402

The "letter" of words may be described as their "flesh," and the spirit of the words of Christ passes away from us unless we are one with the Person that uttered them, placing ourselves, as far as we can, in His circumstances and receiving from Him His thoughts.

Instances of Variation[1]

[2546] i. 20 Ἐγὼ οὐκ εἰμὶ ὁ χριστός, comp. iii. 28 αὐτοὶ ὑμεῖς μοι μαρτυρεῖτε ὅτι εἶπον [ἐγώ] Οὐκ εἰμὶ ἐγὼ ὁ χριστός, ἀλλ' ὅτι...(2553 a_1).

i. 26—33 Ἐγὼ βαπτίζω ἐν ὕδατι... (31) διὰ τοῦτο ἦλθον ἐγὼ ἐν ὕδατι βαπτίζων... (33) ὁ πέμψας με βαπτίζειν ἐν ὕδατι.

† i. 48—50 ὄντα ὑπὸ τὴν συκῆν εἶδόν σε... (50) εἶπόν σοι ὅτι εἶδόν σε ὑποκάτω τῆς συκῆς (2545).

i. 49 σὺ εἶ ὁ υἱὸς τοῦ θεοῦ, σὺ βασιλεὺς εἶ τοῦ Ἰσραήλ (1966).

ii. 12 καὶ ἐκεῖ ἔμειναν οὐ πολλὰς ἡμέρας, but iv. 40 καὶ ἔμεινεν ἐκεῖ δύο ἡμέρας, and x. 40 καὶ ἔμενεν (marg. ἔμεινεν) ἐκεῖ.

ii. 13 καὶ ἀνέβη εἰς Ἱερ. ὁ Ἰ., but v. 1 καὶ ἀνέβη Ἰ. εἰς Ἱερ., and vii. 14 ἤδη δὲ τῆς ἑ. μεσούσης, ἀνέβη Ἰ. εἰς τὸ ἱερὸν καὶ ἐδίδασκεν.

ii. 14—16 τοὺς πωλοῦντας βόας καὶ πρόβατα καὶ περιστεράς... (16) τοῖς τὰς περιστερὰς πωλοῦσιν.

ii. 18 τί σημεῖον δεικνύεις ἡμῖν, ὅτι ταῦτα ποιεῖς; but vi. 30 τί οὖν ποιεῖς σὺ σημεῖον, ἵνα ἴδωμεν....

iii. 3—5 ἐὰν μή τις γεννηθῇ ἄνωθεν... (5) ἐὰν μή τις γεννηθῇ ἐξ ὕδατος καὶ πνεύματος (2573).

iii. 3—5 οὐ δύναται ἰδεῖν τὴν βασιλείαν τοῦ θεοῦ... (5) οὐ δύναται εἰσελθεῖν εἰς τὴν βασιλείαν τοῦ θεοῦ (2573).

iii. 12 εἰ τὰ ἐπίγεια εἶπον ὑμῖν...ἐὰν εἴπω ὑμῖν τὰ ἐπουράνια.

iii. 31 ὁ ἄνωθεν ἐρχόμενος...ὁ ὢν ἐκ τῆς γῆς...ὁ ἐκ τοῦ οὐρανοῦ ἐρχόμενος....

iv. 10 σὺ ἂν ᾔτησας αὐτὸν καὶ ἔδωκεν ἄν σοι ὕδωρ ζῶν.

iv. 17 ἀπεκρ. ἡ γυνή...Οὐκ ἔχω ἄνδρα. λέγει αὐτῇ ὁ Ἰησοῦς Καλῶς εἶπες ὅτι Ἄνδρα οὐκ ἔχω (2552 and 2553 a_1).

---

through being in the position of the beloved disciple that a believer understands the thoughts of the Son (**1744** (x)). Origen elsewhere connects the Feeding of the Five Thousand with the epithet "fleshly" or "carnal" as referring to the literal interpretation of Scripture (Huet i. 236 D); and he quotes—in connexion with the error of disciples taking "leaven" and "loaves" literally—Gal. iii. 3 "Having begun in the *spirit*," and warns us against "running back to *fleshly things*" (Huet i. 269 D).

[1] Instances marked † are sayings of Christ varied as indicated in **2545**.

iv. 37 ἐν γὰρ τούτῳ ὁ λόγος ἐστὶν ἀληθινός ὅτι..., but ix. 30 ἐν τούτῳ (2553) γὰρ τὸ θαυμαστόν ἐστιν ὅτι....

[2547] v. 26 ὥσπερ γὰρ ὁ πατὴρ ἔχει ζωὴν ἐν ἑαυτῷ, οὕτως καὶ τῷ υἱῷ ἔδωκεν ζωὴν ἔχειν ἐν ἑαυτῷ.

v. 31—2 ἐὰν ἐγὼ μαρτυρῶ περὶ ἐμαυτοῦ ἡ μαρτυρία μου οὐκ ἔστιν ἀληθής·... (32) οἶδα ὅτι ἀληθής ἐστιν ἡ μαρτυρία ἣν μαρτυρεῖ περὶ ἐμοῦ, comp. viii. 13—14 εἶπον οὖν αὐτῷ οἱ Φ. Σὺ περὶ σεαυτοῦ μαρτυρεῖς· ἡ μαρτυρία σου οὐκ ἔστιν ἀληθής· ἀπεκρ. Ἰησ....Κἂν ἐγὼ μαρτυρῶ περὶ ἐμαυτοῦ, ἀληθής ἐστιν ἡ μαρτυρία μου (marg. ἡ μ. μου ἀληθής ἐστιν).

v. 43 ἐγὼ ἐλήλυθα...καὶ οὐ λαμβάνετέ με· ἐὰν ἄλλος ἔλθῃ...ἐκεῖνον λήμψεσθε.

vi. 14 ὁ προφήτης ὁ ἐρχόμενος εἰς τὸν κόσμον, but xi. 27 ὁ χριστὸς ὁ υἱὸς τοῦ θεοῦ ὁ εἰς τὸν κόσμον ἐρχόμενος.

† vi. 26—9 εἴδετε σημεῖα... (29) τοῦτό ἐστιν τὸ ἔργον τοῦ θεοῦ ἵνα πιστεύητε, comp. vi. 36 ἀλλ' εἶπον ὑμῖν ὅτι καὶ ἑωράκατέ [με] καὶ οὐ πιστεύετε (2545, 2161 α).

vi. 31 οἱ πατέρες ἡμῶν τὸ μάννα ἔφαγον ἐν τῇ ἐρήμῳ, καθώς ἐστιν γεγραμμένον..., but vi. 49 οἱ π. ὑμῶν ἔφαγον ἐν τῇ ἐρήμῳ τὸ μάννα καὶ ἀπέθανον, and vi. 58 οὐ καθὼς ἔφαγον οἱ πατέρες καὶ ἀπέθανον (1949—50, 2553 e—f).

[2548] † vi. 33—58 ὁ γὰρ ἄρτος τοῦ θεοῦ ἐστὶν ὁ καταβαίνων ἐκ τοῦ οὐρανοῦ... (41) ὅτι εἶπεν Ἐγώ εἰμι ὁ ἄρτος ὁ καταβὰς ἐκ τοῦ οὐρανοῦ ... (50) οὗτός ἐστιν ὁ ἄρτος ὁ ἐκ τοῦ οὐρανοῦ καταβαίνων... (51) ἐγώ εἰμι ὁ ἄρτος ὁ ζῶν ὁ ἐκ τοῦ οὐρανοῦ καταβάς... (58) οὗτός ἐστιν ὁ ἄρτος ὁ ἐξ οὐρανοῦ καταβάς....

† vi. 38—42 καταβέβηκα ἀπὸ τοῦ οὐρανοῦ... (42) πῶς νῦν λέγει ὅτι Ἐκ τοῦ οὐρανοῦ καταβέβηκα;

vi. 39 ἀλλὰ ἀναστήσω αὐτὸ τῇ ἐσχάτῃ ἡμέρᾳ... (40) καὶ ἀναστήσω αὐτὸν ἐγὼ τῇ ἐσχάτῃ ἡμέρᾳ... (44) κἀγὼ ἀναστήσω αὐτὸν ἐν (2715 b—d) τῇ ἐσχάτῃ ἡμέρᾳ... (54) κἀγὼ ἀναστήσω αὐτὸν τῇ ἐσχάτῃ ἡμέρᾳ.

† vi. 44 οὐδεὶς δύναται ἐλθεῖν ⌜πρός με⌝ (marg. πρὸς ἐμέ) ἐὰν μὴ ὁ πατὴρ ὁ πέμψας με ἑλκύσῃ αὐτόν, comp. vi. 65 εἴρηκα ὑμῖν ὅτι οὐδεὶς δύναται ἐλθεῖν πρός με ἐὰν μὴ ᾖ δεδομένον αὐτῷ ἐκ τοῦ πατρός (2545)[1].

vi. 46 οὐχ ὅτι τὸν πατέρα ἑώρακέν τις εἰ μὴ ὁ ὢν παρὰ [τοῦ] θεοῦ οὗτος ἑώρακεν τὸν πατέρα.

---

[1] [2548 α] Comp. also vi. 45 πᾶς ὁ ἀκούσας παρὰ τοῦ πατρὸς καὶ μαθὼν ἔρχεται πρὸς ἐμέ: vi. 65 seems to combine the positive and the negative statements in vi. 44—5 into a negative, including "draw," "hear," and "learn" in the single term "give." See 2470 and 2636.

vii. 18 ὁ ἀφ' ἑαυτοῦ λαλῶν τὴν δόξαν τὴν ἰδίαν ζητεῖ· ὁ δὲ ζητῶν τὴν δόξαν τοῦ πέμψαντος αὐτὸν οὗτος ἀληθής ἐστιν.

vii. 22 καὶ [ἐν] σαββάτῳ περιτέμνετε ἄνθρωπον. εἰ περιτομὴν λαμβάνει [ὁ] ἄνθρωπος ἐν σαββάτῳ....

vii. 34 ὅπου εἰμὶ ἐγὼ ὑμεῖς οὐ δύνασθε ἐλθεῖν, but viii. 21 ὅπου ἐγὼ ὑπάγω ὑμεῖς οὐ δύνασθε ἐλθεῖν (rep. xiii. 33).

vii. 41 Μὴ γὰρ ἐκ τῆς Γ. ὁ χριστὸς ἔρχεται; οὐχ ἡ γραφὴ εἶπεν ὅτι ἐκ ...ἔρχεται ὁ χριστός;

[2549] viii. 14 οἶδα πόθεν ἦλθον καὶ ποῦ ὑπάγω· ὑμεῖς δὲ οὐκ οἴδατε πόθεν ἔρχομαι ἢ ποῦ ὑπάγω[1]. ὑμεῖς κατὰ τὴν σάρκα κρίνετε.

† viii. 21 καὶ ἐν τῇ ἁμαρτίᾳ ὑμῶν ἀποθανεῖσθε, comp. viii. 24 εἶπον οὖν ὑμῖν ὅτι ἀποθανεῖσθε ἐν ταῖς ἁμαρτίαις ὑμῶν· ἐὰν γὰρ μὴ πιστεύσητε ...ἀποθανεῖσθε ἐν ταῖς ἁμαρτίαις ὑμῶν.

viii. 23 Ὑμεῖς ἐκ τῶν κάτω ἐστέ, ἐγὼ ἐκ τῶν ἄνω εἰμί· ὑμεῖς ἐκ τούτου τοῦ κόσμου ἐστέ, ἐγὼ οὐκ εἰμὶ ἐκ τοῦ κόσμου τούτου (2553 c).

viii. 47 ὁ ὢν ἐκ τοῦ θεοῦ...ὅτι ἐκ τοῦ θεοῦ οὐκ ἐστέ, but x. 26 ὅτι οὐκ ἐστὲ ἐκ τῶν προβάτων τῶν ἐμῶν.

† viii. 51—2 ἐάν τις τὸν ἐμὸν λόγον τηρήσῃ, θάνατον οὐ μὴ θεωρήσῃ εἰς τὸν αἰῶνα.... (52) καὶ σὺ λέγεις Ἐάν τις τὸν λόγον μου τηρήσῃ, οὐ μὴ γεύσηται θανάτου εἰς τὸν αἰῶνα (2576).

ix. 28 Σὺ μαθητὴς εἶ ἐκείνου, ἡμεῖς δὲ τοῦ Μ. ἐσμὲν μαθηταί.

x. 15—17 καὶ τὴν ψυχήν μου τίθημι ὑπὲρ τῶν προβάτων... (17) ὅτι ἐγὼ τίθημι τὴν ψυχήν μου.

---

[1] [2549 a] The txt is doubtful. Origen omits ὑμεῖς δὲ...ὑπάγω. So do (Alf.) Cyr., Aug., and several MSS. Alf. explains the om. by homoeotel.—a hypothesis well illustrated by ℵ where γ, in the first and in the second ΥΜΕΙC, twice ends a line so that the eye might glance from the first γ to the second ΜΕΙC. This however would not explain Chrys. ὑμεῖς δὲ οὐκ οἴδατε, which omits only πόθεν ἐ. ἢ π. ὑ. SS has "ye know *not neither* from whence...*nor* whither...," which would be excellent Gk: *a*, *b*, *e* have "et," *f* has "aut." On the whole, W.H. is probably correct, and the omission and variations have proceeded from two causes, 1st, very early omission through homoeotel., 2nd, a tendency to regard ἢ as corrupt (the Η in D is of an unusual shape and *d* has "et"). If the text is correct, why does Jn use οὐ...ἢ instead of his usual οὐ...οὐδέ (i. 13, 25, vi. 24, xi. 50, xiii. 16, xiv. 17, xvi. 3)? Ἢ is intelligible after negation in iv. 27 "No one however said 'What seekest thou?' or 'Why speakest thou with her?'"—where οὐδέ would have differentiated the two clauses too strongly. Is ἢ used here for the same reason? That Jn *could* have used οὐ...καὶ in a quotation is shewn by Gal. iii. 28 οὐκ ἔνι Ἰουδαῖος οὐδὲ Ἕλλην, οὐκ ἔνι δοῦλος οὐδὲ ἐλεύθερος, οὐκ ἔνι ἄρσεν καὶ θῆλυ (where α. κ. θῆλυ is a phrase from Gen. i. 27). Perhaps ὑμεῖς...ὑπάγω means "ye know not whence I come *or* [*which is the same thing*] whither I go," suggesting that Christ is really speaking of one and the same region—"the bosom of the Father (**2759** *a—f*)." Ἢ, "or," is very much rarer in Jn than in any Synoptist.

[2550] xi. 29—31 ἠγέρθη ταχὺ καὶ ἤρχετο πρὸς αὐτόν...ἰδόντες τὴν Μ. ὅτι ταχέως ἀνέστη καὶ ἐξῆλθεν.

xi. 41 εὐχαριστῶ σοι ὅτι ἤκουσάς μου, ἐγὼ δὲ ᾔδειν ὅτι πάντοτέ μου ἀκούεις.

xii. 26 ἐάν ἐμοί τις διακονῇ...ἐάν τις ἐμοὶ διακονῇ.

† xiii. 10—11 καὶ ὑμεῖς καθαροί ἐστε, ἀλλ' οὐχὶ πάντες... (11) διὰ τοῦτο εἶπεν ὅτι Οὐχὶ πάντες καθαροί ἐστε (2545).

† xiv. 4—18 ὅπου ἐγὼ ὑπάγω οἴδατε τὴν ὁδόν... (18) ἔρχομαι πρὸς ὑμᾶς. Comp. xiv. 28 ἠκούσατε ὅτι ἐγὼ εἶπον ὑμῖν Ὑπάγω καὶ ἔρχομαι πρὸς ὑμᾶς[1].

xiv. 19 ὁ κόσμος με οὐκέτι θεωρεῖ, ὑμεῖς δὲ θεωρεῖτέ με.

xiv. 26—8 ...ὑπομνήσει ὑμᾶς πάντα ἃ εἶπον ὑμῖν ἐγώ.... (28) ἠκούσατε ὅτι ἐγὼ εἶπον ὑμῖν Ὑπάγω....

xv. 4—7 μείνατε ἐν ἐμοί, κἀγὼ ἐν ὑμῖν. καθὼς τὸ κλῆμα...ἐὰν μὴ μένῃ ἐν τῇ ἀμπέλῳ, οὕτως οὐδὲ ὑμεῖς ἐὰν μὴ ἐν ἐμοὶ μένητε... (5) ὁ μένων ἐν ἐμοὶ κἀγὼ ἐν αὐτῷ... (6) ἐὰν μή τις μένῃ ἐν ἐμοί... (7) ἐὰν μείνητε ἐν ἐμοὶ καὶ τὰ ῥήματά μου ἐν ὑμῖν μείνῃ.

xv. 15 οὐκέτι λέγω ὑμᾶς δούλους[2], ὅτι ὁ δοῦλος...ὑμᾶς δὲ εἴρηκα φίλους.

xv. 19 εἰ ἐκ τοῦ κόσμου ἦτε, ὁ κόσμος ἂν τὸ ἴδιον ἐφίλει· ὅτι δὲ ἐκ τοῦ κόσμου οὐκ ἐστέ, ἀλλ' ἐγὼ ἐξελεξάμην ὑμᾶς ἐκ τοῦ κόσμου, διὰ τοῦτο μισεῖ ὑμᾶς ὁ κόσμος.

[2551] xvi. 9—11 περὶ ἁμαρτίας μέν, ὅτι... (10) περὶ δικαιοσύνης δέ, ὅτι..., (11) περὶ δὲ κρίσεως, ὅτι....

† xvi. 14 ἐκ τοῦ ἐμοῦ λήμψεται καὶ ἀναγγελεῖ ὑμῖν, comp. xvi. 15 εἶπον ὅτι ἐκ τοῦ ἐμοῦ λαμβάνει καὶ ἀναγγελεῖ ὑμῖν (2488 and 2583).

† xvi. 16 Μικρὸν καὶ οὐκέτι θεωρεῖτέ με καὶ πάλιν μικρὸν καὶ ὄψεσθέ με, comp. xvi. 19 ὅτι εἶπον Μικρὸν καὶ οὐ θεωρεῖτέ με, καὶ πάλιν μικρὸν καὶ ὄψεσθέ με; (2583 and 2613).

xvii. 2—5 δόξασόν σου τὸν υἱόν, ἵνα ὁ υἱὸς δοξάσῃ σέ,...δώσει αὐτοῖς ζωὴν αἰώνιον· αὕτη δέ ἐστιν ἡ αἰώνιος ζωή...ἐγώ σε ἐδόξασα...καὶ νῦν δόξασόν με σύ.

† xvii. 12 ἐτήρουν αὐτοὺς ἐν τῷ ὀνόματί σου ᾧ δέδωκάς μοι...καὶ

---

[1] [2550 a] Jesus has also previously said xiii. 33 ὅπου ἐγὼ ὑπάγω and xiii. 36 ὅπου ὑπάγω, but never ὑπάγω without ὅπου in the Last Discourse hitherto. Earlier in the Gospel, Jesus says to the Jews vii. 33 ἔτι χρόνον μικρὸν....καὶ ὑπάγω πρὸς τὸν πέμψαντά με and viii. 21 ἐγὼ ὑπάγω καὶ ζητήσετέ με. But xiv. 28 appears to be a free summary of xiv. 4—18.

[2] [2550 b] ? Referring to xiii. 16 οὐκ ἔστιν δοῦλος μείζων τοῦ κυρίου αὐτοῦ οὐδὲ ἀπόστολος μείζων τοῦ πέμψαντος αὐτόν.

ARRANGEMENT AND VARIATION [2552]

οὐδεὶς ἐξ αὐτῶν ἀπώλετο, comp. xviii. 9 ὁ λόγος ὃν εἶπεν ὅτι Οὓς δέδωκάς μοι οὐκ ἀπώλεσα ἐξ αὐτῶν οὐδένα (2740—4).

xvii. 14—16 καὶ ὁ κόσμος ἐμίσησεν αὐτούς, ὅτι οὐκ εἰσὶν ἐκ τοῦ κόσμου καθὼς ἐγὼ οὐκ εἰμὶ ἐκ τοῦ κόσμου.... (16) ἐκ τοῦ κόσμου οὐκ εἰσὶν καθὼς ἐγὼ οὐκ εἰμὶ ἐκ τοῦ κόσμου.

xvii. 18 καθὼς ἐμὲ ἀπέστειλας εἰς τὸν κόσμον κἀγὼ ἀπέστειλα αὐτοὺς εἰς τὸν κόσμον, comp. xvii. 23 καὶ ἠγάπησας αὐτοὺς καθὼς ἐμὲ ἠγάπησας.

xvii. 21—3 ἵνα ὁ κόσμος πιστεύῃ ὅτι σύ με ἀπέστειλας... (23) ἵνα γινώσκῃ ὁ κόσμος ὅτι σύ με ἀπέστειλας, καὶ ἠγάπησας αὐτοὺς καθὼς ἐμὲ ἠγάπησας.

xviii. 29 ἐξῆλθεν οὖν ὁ Π. ἔξω πρὸς αὐτοὺς καί φησιν... (38) καὶ τοῦτο εἰπὼν πάλιν ἐξῆλθεν πρὸς τοὺς Ἰουδ. καὶ λέγει αὐτοῖς...xix. 4 Καὶ ἐξῆλθεν πάλιν ἔξω ὁ Π. (marg. ἐξῆλθεν πάλιν ὁ Π. ἔξω) καὶ λέγει αὐτοῖς....

xviii. 33 εἰσῆλθεν οὖν πάλιν εἰς τὸ πραιτώριον ὁ Π....καὶ εἶπεν αὐτῷ...xix. 9 καὶ εἰσῆλθεν εἰς τὸ πραιτώριον πάλιν καὶ λέγει τῷ Ἰησοῦ....

xviii. 38 λέγει αὐτοῖς Ἐγὼ οὐδεμίαν εὑρίσκω ἐν αὐτῷ αἰτίαν...xix. 4 ἵνα γνῶτε ὅτι οὐδεμίαν αἰτίαν εὑρίσκω ἐν αὐτῷ... (6) ἐγὼ γὰρ οὐχ εὑρίσκω ἐν αὐτῷ αἰτίαν.

xx. 19 οὔσης οὖν ὀψίας...καὶ τῶν θυρῶν κεκλεισμένων...ἦλθεν ὁ Ἰησ. καὶ ἔστη εἰς τὸ μέσον καὶ λέγει αὐτοῖς Εἰρήνη ὑμῖν... (26) ἔρχεται ὁ Ἰησ. τῶν θυρῶν κεκλεισμένων, καὶ ἔστη εἰς τὸ μέσον καὶ εἶπεν Εἰρήνη ὑμῖν.

xxi. 19 Ἀκολούθει μοι... (22) ἐὰν αὐτὸν θέλω μένειν...τί πρὸς σέ; σύ μοι ἀκολούθει[1].

[2552] Several of the foregoing instances indicate a tendency to place the *last* word or clause of a saying *first*, when the saying is repeated:—"*I baptize in water...in water baptizing*" (followed by "*baptize in water*")[2]; "*under the fig tree I saw thee...I saw thee under the fig tree*[3]"; "*I have not a husband*...Well saidst thou '*A husband I have not*[4]'"; "'Our fathers—*the manna they ate in the wilderness*'...'your fathers—*they ate in the wilderness the manna*'" (where the clause "ate in the wilderness" was last and is now first)[5]; "*I have come down from the heaven*...how now saith he, '*From the heaven I have come down*[6]'?"; "not that *the Father some one hath seen*—

---

[1] Only a few of these passages are commented on below, but the textual Index will indicate that many of them are explained elsewhere in comments that include order and emphasis as well as mere grammatical syntax.

[2] i. 26—33.   [3] i. 48, 50.   [4] iv. 17.   [5] vi. 31, 49.

[6] [2552a] vi. 38, 42. But perhaps we ought to take vi. 41—2, the whole saying of the Jews, together, "The Jews...murmured because he said, I am the

except he that is from God, *this [man] hath seen the Father*[1]"; "and on the sabbath ye circumcise a man: if *circumcision is received by* (λαμβάνει) *a man on the sabbath*[2]"; "Can it be that from Galilee *the Christ cometh?*...Did not the Scripture say that from...*cometh the Christ*[3]?" "*in your sin ye shall die...*I said therefore [that] *Ye shall die in your sins*[4]"; "*my life I lay down* for the sheep...because *I lay down my life*[5]"; "I thank thee that *thou heardest me*, but I (emph.) knew that at all times *me thou hearest*[6]"; "he will give him *life eternal*, and this is *the eternal life*[7]"; "*they are not from the world...from the world they are not*[8]"; "*follow me...do thou me follow*[9]."

[2553] It is very natural that what has been last said should sometimes be uppermost in our minds and foremost on our lips when we repeat the substance of a saying. In Greek this alteration of order is far more often possible than in idiomatic English, as the last paragraph shews; but where the Greek order can be followed in English, something is gained in the appreciation of emphasis. Still more is gained by realising that Johannine variations, where they are not deliberately introduced to serve some mystical purpose, spring from the instinct of a dramatist in sympathy with life and living speech. *Wherever a word is placed out of its usual order, or out of the order in which it has previously occurred,* then—unless a change

---

bread that *came down from the heaven*, and they kept saying.... How now saith he *From the heaven I have come down*," so that the Jews repeat the phrase at first in Christ's order "*come down from the heaven*" and then reverse the order, "*from the heaven come down*." Subsequently Christ takes up the words as the Jews have left them, placing "*from the heaven*" first, and emphasizing it as indicating the source of the living bread (vi. 50, 51, 58).

[1] vi. 46.   [2] vii. 22—3.

[3] [2552 b] vii. 41—2. In viii. 51—2, Christ says "*Death shall he surely not behold* for ever," and the Jews repeat it as "*He shall surely not taste death* for ever" (2576).

[4] viii. 21, 24.   [5] x. 15, 17.

[6] [2552 c] xi. 41. In xii. 26 "If me a man (ἐάν ἐμοί τις) be serving, let him follow me...if a man (ἐάν τις) me be serving, my Father will honour him," the position of "me" in "if *me*" makes the pronoun extremely emphatic, and the unusual separation of τις from ἐάν (ἐάν and τις being usually in juxtaposition vi. 51, vii. 17, 37 etc.) suggests "a certain one" (whereas ἐάν τις would be in effect, " whoever") so that the meaning may be paraphrased as "*If an individual* here and there *is singular enough* to wish to serve *me*, let him follow me." In the following clause (ἐάν τις ἐμοί) "me" is still emphatic, but not so emphatic as at first.

[7] xvii. 2.   [8] xvii. 14, 16.   [9] xxi. 19, 22.

is made for clearness¹—*some difference of emphasis may be expected*².

¹ [2553 a_1] If (i. 20) ἐγὼ οὐκ εἰμί had been repeated in iii. 28 after εἶπον, readers might have taken εἶπον ἐγώ together. In iv. 17, καλῶς εἶπες ὅτι οὐκ ἔχω ἄνδρα would have been liable to a momentary misunderstanding; but emphasis, there, seems to me the main cause of the change.

² [2553 a] To take one of the most insignificant instances, relating to "the sellers of doves" in ii. 14—16 τοὺς πωλοῦντας βόας κ. πρόβ. κ. περιστ....τοῖς τὰς περιστερὰς πωλοῦσιν, the author first speaks of those *selling* oxen and sheep and doves," laying a slight emphasis on the "selling" as being a defilement of the temple, and then, owing to our Lord's special mention of the "doves," he lays a slight emphasis on "the doves" by varying the order. In iv. 10 σὺ ἂν ᾔτησας, the unusual position of ἂν calls strong attention to the hypothesis. "Thou, *in that case* [*hadst thou but known*] wouldst have asked him [*instead of waiting for him to ask thee*] and he would have given thee (κ. ἔδωκεν ἄν σοι)." In ii. 18 "What sign shewest-thou?" the order is usual, but vi. 30 "What then doest *thou* (emph.) [*as a*] *sign* (τί οὖν ποιεῖς σὺ σημεῖον)?" the intention is to imply an antithesis between "thou" and "Moses" (previously implied) and also between "sign" and the sign of the "manna" previously mentioned. On the difference between viii. 23 ἐκ τούτου τοῦ κόσμου and ἐκ τοῦ κόσμου τούτου, see **2553** c.

[2553 b] In viii. 47 ἐκ τοῦ θεοῦ οὐκ ἐστέ, both the beginning and the end (but especially the end) are emphatic ("*From God* ye are essentially *not*") as compared with the ordinary and unemphatic order in x. 26 "ye are not from my sheep." In ii. 13 καὶ ἀνέβη εἰς Ἱερ. ὁ Ἰησοῦς the order is to be contrasted with that in v. 1 καὶ ἀνέβη Ἰησοῦς εἰς Ἱερ. and in vii. 14 ἤδη δὲ...ἀνέβη Ἰ. εἰς τὸ ἱερὸν κ. ἐδίδασκεν. In ii. 13, the position of Ἰησοῦς at the end of the sentence, as well as its separation from ἀνέβη, and a previous mention of (ii. 12) "his mother and brethren," seem intended to emphasize "Jesus," as going up to Jerusalem, apart from His family, no longer as a common pilgrim, but by Himself, for the first time, in His character of Saviour (Jesus). This emphasis would be out of place in v. 1, vii. 14.

[2553 c] Ταῦτα τὰ ῥήματα etc., at the beginning of a sentence, in viii. 20, x. 21, means "these words just mentioned" (comp. x. 6, 18, xi. 4, xix. 20). *If it is desired to emphasize "these," "this" etc. in contrast with something else*, it is usual to write τὰ ῥήματα ταῦτα. Consequently, in N.T., "this [*present*] age" is *always* ὁ αἰὼν οὗτος—*except where* Mt. xii. 32 inserts the antithetical clause οὔτε ἐν τούτῳ τῷ αἰῶνι οὔτε ἐν τῷ μέλλοντι (but several authorities correct the unusual phrase). So "*this* [*present*] world" in N.T. is always ὁ κόσμος οὗτος except in Jn viii. 23 ὑμεῖς ἐκ τούτου τοῦ κόσμου ἐστέ, ἐγὼ οὐκ εἰμὶ ἐκ τοῦ κόσμου τούτου. Here again so many authorities have substituted the usual ἐκ τ. κόσμ. τούτ. that Tisch. has adopted it; but the evangelist may use the unemphatic form in the first clause in order to prepare for the emphatic form in the second. In the Samaritan Dialogue, the influence of such phrases as ὁ αἰὼν οὗτος and ὁ κόσμος οὗτος is apparent in iv. 13 πᾶς ὁ πίνων ἐκ τ. ὕδατος τούτου, which means literally the water of this well, but suggests spiritually "*the water of this world*." The woman replies, without any sense of emphasis, δός μοι τοῦτο τὸ ὕδωρ "*give me this water* [*you speak of*]." The emphatic form comes naturally from the Jews at the end of the sentence in vi. 34 πάντοτε δὸς ἡμῖν τ. ἄρτον τοῦτον. Christ uses the unemphatic form in the middle of sentences in vi. 51, 58, but there antithesis is implied in the context so that the emphatic form is not necessary.

[2553 d] What is the difference between the participial clause in vi. 14

ὁ προφήτης ὁ ἐρχόμενος εἰς τὸν κόσμον and in xi. 27 ὁ χρ. ὁ υἱὸς τ. θεοῦ ὁ εἰς τὸν κόσμον ἐρχόμενος? In the former, the multitude emphasize the popular phrase about the Deliverer (**1632** foll.) "He that is to come," and subordinate "the world"; but Martha, having already used the phrases "Christ" and "Son of God," now subordinates the "coming" to the thought of "the world," which the Son is to deliver. In xviii. 38 ἐγὼ οὐδεμίαν εὑρίσκω ἐν αὐτῷ αἰτίαν, xix. 4 οὐδεμίαν αἰτ. εὑρ. ἐν αὐτῷ, xix. 6 ἐγὼ γὰρ οὐχ εὑρ. ἐν αὐτῷ αἰτίαν, Pilate begins and ends by emphasizing his own personal opinion instead of merging it in the official decision of a judge: (1) "*I for my part* find *nothing whatever* in him of guilt [but still instead of acquitting him I ask you whether you would like me to release him as a favour to you]"; (2) "I bring him forth to you outside the palace that ye may recognise that I find *nothing whatever* of guilt in him" followed by an appeal to pity or contempt, "Behold, the man!"; (3) "Take him yourselves and crucify him, for *I for my part* do not find in him guilt." On the third occasion, the phrase "not...guilt" is a little weaker than "no guilt whatever" (οὐδεμίαν αἰτίαν) on the first and second, the emphasis being reserved for the earlier part of the sentence, which is, in effect, "Kill him, *for I, the judge*, pronounce him guiltless."

[**2553** *e*] In discussing (**1949**) vi. 58, οὐ καθὼς ἔφαγον οἱ πατέρες no mention was made of the fact that SS, D, and other authorities, add ὑμῶν, and some add τὸ μάννα. These additions would be naturally suggested (1) by vi. 49, οἱ πατέρες ὑμῶν ἔφαγον...τὸ μάννα, (2) by the fact that οἱ πατέρες in N.T. almost always means the Patriarchs, represented by Abraham, as being receivers of the promises on the basis of which they became fathers of the Chosen People. Fritzsche, on Rom. ix. 5 αἱ ἐπαγγελίαι...οἱ πατέρες, censures Theodoret for supposing that οἱ πατέρες includes those who received promises "through the prophets." Heb. i. 1, however, appears exceptionally to use it thus, when contrasting τοῖς πατράσιν and ἡμῖν. But Jn vi. 58—where there is no such contrast—"*the fathers ate...and died*," if applied to the rebellious fathers of Israel in the wilderness, is unique in its application. It has been suggested above (**1949**) that what Christ taught to Jews in the second person John is summarising for Greeks in the third person. In the former shape, it was: "*Your fathers* ate in the wilderness the manna and died." In the latter it is, "*The fathers* ate and died." By omitting "the manna," and "in the wilderness," John perhaps suggests an application that extends beyond the period of forty years: "From the time of Abraham onwards the fathers of Israel ate [of 'every word that proceedeth out of the mouth of God'] and yet died."

[**2553** *f*] Origen, discussing God's revelations to man before the Incarnation, repeatedly protests against the view that the Apostles were superior in knowledge to "*the Fathers* and the Prophets." In "*the Fathers*" he appears to give the most prominent place to Abraham, then (Huet ii. 96 D) he mentions Moses and Joshua, before passing to Isaiah and Ezekiel. Afterwards he says (*ib.* 98 C) "Consequently, not even the Apostles are to be deemed wiser than *the Fathers, or Moses, and the Prophets.*" He complains that "many" vainly imagine that "the Apostles are wiser than *the Fathers and the Prophets*" and says that "they cancel the gift bestowed on *the Fathers and the Prophets* by God through Christ (through whom all things were made)." These expressions suggest that Origen—whom I have not been able to find quoting Heb. i. 1 "spake *to the Fathers in the Prophets*"—would have preferred to say that "God spake in times past *in the Fathers and the Prophets.*"

§ 2. *Chiasmus*

[2554] Many of the instances in 2546—51 are of the nature of *chiasmus* (2544 a). This is a natural arrangement when the writer wishes to combine parallelism with climax, or with the argument *a fortiori*. For the change of order in the second clause (sometimes taking the reader by surprise) emphasizes both the terms in that clause: "If *the things of earth I said unto you* and ye believe not, how [is it possible that] if *I say unto you the things of heaven*, ye will believe[1]?"; "Ye do not *receive me*...*him ye will receive*[2]"; "Thou art *disciple to him*, but we *to Moses are disciples*[3]." In viii. 13—14, the two halves of an accusation correspond to the two halves of the reply, in chiasmus, thus, (1) "Thou *about thyself testifiest*" to "Even if *I testify about myself*," and (2) "*Thy testimony is not true*" to "*True is my testimony*." In "*Thou lovedst them*, even as *me thou lovedst*," emphasis is laid upon the infinity of the Father's love[4]. So,

---

[1] iii. 12.   [2] v. 43.   [3] ix. 28.

[4] [2554 a] xvii. 23 καὶ ἠγάπησας αὐτοὺς καθὼς ἐμὲ ἠγάπησας. Here the verb is at the extremes. Compare xvii. 18 καθὼς ἐμὲ ἀπέστειλας εἰς τὸν κόσμον, κἀγὼ ἀπέστειλα αὐτοὺς εἰς τὸν κόσμον, where there is neither exact parallelism (καθὼς σὺ ἐμέ...κἀγὼ αὐτούς) nor yet chiasmus.

[2554 b] In xi. 29—31 ἠγέρθη ταχὺ καὶ ἤρχετο πρὸς αὐτόν...ἰδόντες τὴν Μαριὰμ ὅτι ταχέως ἀνέστη καὶ ἐξῆλθεν, the adverb ταχέως—by the repetition of "quickly" in a different form ("[thus] quickly [as I have said"])—seems intended to draw attention to the manner and haste of Mary's "arising." But ταχύ, by its position between ἠγέρθη and ἤρχετο (so that the reader has no time to dwell on the adverb) is subordinated to its verb ἠγέρθη, which is something more than "rising up" and suggests "roused from torpor," "awakened from the lethargy of sorrow." There is no emphasis on ταχύ, for the emphasis is on the "*starting up* ...and *going to him* [i.e. Jesus]." Similarly, in LXX, emphasis is laid, not on the "quickness" but on the "falling away" of Israel in Ex. xxxii. 8, Deut. ix. 12, 16 (A), Judg. ii. 17, with ταχύ *after* various verbs. But the *rapidity* of the falling away of the fickle Galatians is emphasized by ταχέως before the verb in Gal. i. 6 θαυμάζω ὅτι οὕτως ταχέως μετατίθεσθε. The Jews know nothing of the coming of the Teacher, or of the consequent "rousing" of Mary. All they perceive is the *haste* with which she "arose and went out." In N.T., as in LXX, some writers use ταχύ not ταχέως, others ταχέως not ταχύ. It is characteristic of Jn that he uses both with slightly different shades of meaning. For these and other reasons, the conclusion of Blass about ταχέως in xi. 31 (p. 308 "certainly an interpolation") appears to me erroneous.

[2554 c] The Egyptian Papyri have *Oxyr*. 743 (B.C. 2) καλῶς δὲ γέγονεν τὸ ταχὺ αὐτὸν ἐλθεῖν (no great emphasis), 531 (2nd cent.) ἐὰν γὰρ θεοὶ θέλωσι τάχιον πρὸς σὲ ἥξω μετὰ τὸν Μεχεὶρ μῆνα ἐπεὶ ἐν χερσὶν ἔχω ἐπέξιμα ἔργα, i.e. ["I cannot come at once but] I will come *sooner* [*than might be expected under the circumstances*]

[2555]   ARRANGEMENT AND VARIATION

at the conclusion of Christ's last prayer (xvii. 21—3) when He turns for a while from praying for the disciples to pray for the world, the words may be paraphrased, "*in order that the world may grow in belief* (ἵνα ὁ κόσμος πιστεύῃ)...*in order that knowledge may dawn on the world* (ἵνα γινώσκῃ ὁ κόσμος)" so as to indicate that, for the moment, "the world" stands prominent in the thoughts of the Saviour.

[2555] The following are instances of chiasmus in which there is no repetition of a previous saying. Apart from the Prologue, only one or two of them are from strict narrative[1]. The emphasis gained by it for the final word is apparent in such instances as "No one hath ascended into the heaven save he that from the heaven *descended*[2]," and still more in "He that *is* [*essentially*] from the earth

---

after Mecheir is over," Fayum 126 ἀνελθε οὖν ταχέως ὅτι ἐπίγι (*sic*), where the words "for it is pressing" indicate that ταχέως is emphatic.

[2554 d] On Heb. xiii. 23 ἐὰν τάχειον ἔρχηται, Westcott says, "The comparative suggests the occurrence of hindrances which the apostle could not distinctly foresee. Compare *v*. 19"—apparently rendering τάχειον in both verses "more quickly [than might be expected in view of the obstacles]." Τάχιον is read by ℵ as well as other inferior MSS. in 1 Tim. iii. 14 (W.H.) ἐλπίζων ἐλθεῖν [πρὸς σὲ] ἐν τάχει, ἐὰν δὲ βραδύνω. There Chrys. reads ταχέως: but he also paraphrases thus Heb. xiii. 19 as ὥστε με ταχέως ἐλθεῖν πρὸς ὑμᾶς (though he quotes that text with τάχιον) and some scribes might avoid τάχιον owing to the condemnation of it by Lucian (iii. 573) and by Phrynichus. Moreover, if the text was προccεταχειοεαν, an erroneous interpretation of εταχειοε as being εταχειε might explain the dropping of σε and hence of προς σε in some MSS. Ἐν τάχει in N.T. is always connected with divine retribution or angelic command except in Acts xxv. 4. If ἐν τάχει is a corruption of τάχειον, 1 Tim. as well as Heb. might accord with the Papyrus as above quoted (2554 c) in the meaning "sooner than might be expected under the circumstances." Comp. Plut. *Vit. Fab.* § 12 τάχιον μὲν ἢ ἐγὼ προσεδόκων, βράδιον δ' ἢ αὐτὸς ἔσπευδε... which shews how τάχιον might be used of *relative* speed.

[2554 e] Against rendering τάχιον in xiii. 27 "*at once*"—like the imperious θᾶττον in Aristoph.—it may be fairly urged (1) that Steph. gives abundant instances of θᾶττον thus used but none of τάχιον, (2) that ταχύ is repeatedly thus used in N.T. (Mt. v. 25, xxviii. 7, Lk. xv. 22), in LXX (2 S. xvii. 16, Ps. lxix. 17, lxxix. 8, cii. 2, cxliii. 7) and (Deissmann pp. 274—7) in magic adjurations, one of which (3rd century) concludes with the words ἤδη ἤδη ταχὺ ταχύ. If this had been the meaning we should have expected in xiii. 27 ὃ ποιεῖς ποίησον ταχύ.

[1] ii. 15 "And of the money changers he poured out the copper coins and the tables he overturned," vii. 1 "And after these things walked Jesus in Galilee, for he was not willing in Judaea to walk." The latter is not a very exact instance. For vi. 46, vii. 22—3, see 2552.

[2] iii. 13.

from the earth [*essentially*] *is*[1]," i.e. such a one cannot rise above his nature. Only one of the following is certainly a precept, "*Judge not according to appearance, but the judgment that is just judge ye*[2]," but it has been maintained above (**2236—40**) that a precept and not a statement is probably conveyed in "*Believe* (πιστεύετε) *in God, in me also believe*[3]." In xiii. 36—7, emphasis is laid upon the adverbs of time, "Thou art not able *at present* to be my follower, but follower thou shalt be *later on*"—an emphasis repeated in Peter's reply "Why am I not able to be thy follower *at this moment*?" In the opening sentences of the Gospel there is true chiasmus in i. 3 "*All things* through him came into being, and without him came into being *not even one thing*." But the preceding words ὁ λόγος ἦν πρὸς τὸν θεόν, καὶ θεὸς ἦν ὁ λόγος do not contain true chiasmus or, at all events, not such strict chiasmus as appears at first sight. For θεός without the article is distinct from θεός (in πρὸς τὸν θεόν) with it. This passage must be discussed later on (**2594**).

Instances of Chiasmus

[**2556**] i. 1—4 Ἐν ἀρχῇ ἦν ὁ λόγος καὶ ὁ λόγος ἦν πρὸς τὸν θεόν, καὶ θεὸς ἦν ὁ λόγος. Οὗτος ἦν ἐν ἀρχῇ πρὸς τὸν θεόν. πάντα δι' αὐτοῦ ἐγένετο καὶ χωρὶς αὐτοῦ ἐγένετο οὐδὲ ἕν.

ii. 15 καὶ τῶν κολλυβιστῶν ἐξέχεεν τὰ κέρματα καὶ τὰς τραπέζας ἀνέτρεψεν.

iii. 13 οὐδεὶς ἀναβέβηκεν εἰς τὸν οὐρανὸν εἰ μὴ ὁ ἐκ τοῦ οὐρανοῦ καταβάς.

iii. 31 ὁ ὢν ἐκ τῆς γῆς ἐκ τῆς γῆς ἐστίν.

v. 24 ὁ τὸν λόγον μου ἀκούων καὶ πιστεύων τῷ πέμψαντί με...εἰς κρίσιν οὐκ ἔρχεται ἀλλὰ μεταβέβηκεν ἐκ τοῦ θανάτου εἰς τὴν ζωήν.

vii. 1 περιεπάτει [ὁ] Ἰ. ἐν τῇ Γαλιλαίᾳ, οὐ γὰρ ἤθελεν ἐν τῇ Ἰουδαίᾳ περιπατεῖν.

vii. 7 οὐ δύναται ὁ κόσμος μισεῖν ὑμᾶς, ἐμὲ δὲ μισεῖ.

vii. 24 μὴ κρίνετε κατ' ὄψιν ἀλλὰ τὴν δικαίαν κρίσιν κρίνετε.

vii. 28 κἀμὲ οἴδατε καὶ οἴδατε πόθεν εἰμί.

---

[1] [**2555** *a*] iii. 31 ὁ ὢν ἐκ τῆς γῆς ἐκ τῆς γῆς ἐστίν. Here ὁ ὤν—which is frequently used for God, "He that essentially is"—is paradoxically connected with ἐκ τῆς γῆς. Ὁ ἐκ τῆς γῆς would have been quite sufficient to express, unemphatically, "he that is from the earth." At the end of the sentence, ἐστίν receives emphasis from its position and from its relation to the preceding ὤν.

[2] vii. 24.   [3] xiv. 1.

vii. 35 μὴ εἰς τὴν διασπορὰν τῶν Ἑλλήνων μέλλει πορεύεσθαι καὶ διδάσκειν τοὺς Ἕλληνας;

[2557] viii. 18 ἐγώ εἰμι ὁ μαρτυρῶν περὶ ἐμαυτοῦ καὶ μαρτυρεῖ περὶ ἐμοῦ ὁ πέμψας με πατήρ.

ix. 25 Εἰ ἁμαρτωλός ἐστιν οὐκ οἶδα, ἓν οἶδα, ὅτι τυφλὸς ὢν ἄρτι βλέπω.

xii. 31 νῦν κρίσις ἐστὶν τοῦ κόσμου τούτου, νῦν ὁ ἄρχων τοῦ κόσμου τούτου ἐκβληθήσεται ἔξω.

xiii. 20 ὁ λαμβάνων ἄν τινα πέμψω ἐμὲ λαμβάνει, ὁ δὲ ἐμὲ λαμβάνων λαμβάνει τὸν πέμψαντά με.

xiii. 36, 37 οὐ δύνασαί μοι νῦν ἀκολουθῆσαι, ἀκολουθήσεις δὲ ὕστερον ...διὰ τί οὐ δύναμαί σοι ἀκολουθεῖν ἄρτι;

xiv. 1 πιστεύετε εἰς τὸν θεόν, καὶ εἰς ἐμὲ πιστεύετε.

xiv. 7 εἰ ἐγνώκειτέ με, καὶ τὸν πατέρα μου ἂν ᾔδειτε· ἀπ' ἄρτι γινώσκετε αὐτὸν καὶ ἑωράκατε, comp. viii. 19 εἰ ἐμὲ ᾔδειτε, καὶ τὸν πατέρα μου ἂν ᾔδειτε, where there is parallelism.

xvi. 20 κλαύσετε καὶ θρηνήσετε ὑμεῖς, ὁ δὲ κόσμος χαρήσεται.

xvi. 27—8 ...ὅτι ἐγὼ παρὰ τοῦ πατρὸς ἐξῆλθον. ἐξῆλθον ἐκ τοῦ πατρὸς καὶ ἐλήλυθα εἰς τὸν κόσμον· πάλιν ἀφίημι τὸν κόσμον καὶ πορεύομαι πρὸς τὸν πατέρα.

xvii. 11 καὶ οὐκέτι εἰμὶ ἐν τῷ κόσμῳ καὶ αὐτοὶ ἐν τῷ κόσμῳ εἰσίν.

xvii. 16 ἐκ τοῦ κόσμου οὐκ εἰσὶν καθὼς ἐγὼ οὐκ εἰμὶ ἐκ τοῦ κόσμου.

xviii. 36 Ἡ βασιλεία ἡ ἐμὴ οὐκ ἔστιν ἐκ τοῦ κόσμου τούτου· εἰ ἐκ τοῦ κ. τούτου ἦν ἡ β. ἡ ἐμή,......νῦν δὲ ἡ β. ἡ ἐμὴ οὐκ ἔστιν ἐντεῦθεν.

§ 3. *The Possessive Genitive*

[2558] Among Johannine variations of order one of the most frequent is that of the pronominal possessive genitive, which, for the sake of brevity, may be conveniently illustrated by the use of the genitive singular of αὐτός used possessively. "He stretched out *his [own] hand*" would be expressed (1) in Hebrew, briefly, by the inflexional form "*his-hand*," (2) in LXX, lengthily, by τὴν χεῖρα αὐτοῦ, (3) in classical Gk, briefly (as in French) by the article without the pronoun, τὴν χεῖρα—if at least the context made the meaning clear. All the evangelists, John included, freely use (2). But in describing how Peter wounded the High Priest's servant and "cut off *his ear*," all but Luke make αὐτοῦ *precede the article and noun* ("he cut off

ARRANGEMENT AND VARIATION [2558]

of him the ear") expressed by John thus, ἀπέκοψεν αὐτοῦ τὸ ὠτάριον τὸ δεξιόν¹. This αὐτοῦ, *preceding* the article and the noun, must be carefully distinguished from αὐτοῦ *intervening* between the article and the noun, as in τὸ αὐτοῦ ὠτάριον. The *intervening* αὐτοῦ would be *emphatic* and the meaning would be "*his and nobody else's* ear," but the *precedent* αὐτοῦ is *unemphatic* and throws the emphasis on "*ear*," so that it is almost equivalent to "cut off, not his hand, or foot, but his *ear*." Τὸ αὐτοῦ, emphasizing αὐτοῦ, seldom or never occurs in the Gospels², but αὐτοῦ unemphatically preceding the

---

¹ [2558 a] Jn xviii. 10, comp. Mk xiv. 47, Mt. xxvi. 51, Lk. xxii. 50. In Mk xv. 19 ἔτυπτον αὐτοῦ τὴν κεφαλήν, the parall. Mt. xxvii. 30 has ἔτυπτον εἰς τὴν κεφαλὴν αὐτοῦ, and D reads, in Mk, ἔτυπτον αὐτὸν...εἰς τὴν κ., "they smote him on the head," which substantially represents the meaning. Such a genitive in John, Rev., and Epictetus, for the most part *immediately* precedes the article. But this is not always the case in N.T., *e.g.* in Mk vii. 19 οὐκ εἰσπορεύεται αὐτοῦ εἰς τὴν καρδίαν ἀλλ' εἰς τὴν κοιλίαν. But there, too, the unemphatic precedent αὐτοῦ throws the emphasis on what follows. Its precedent position also enables αὐτοῦ to define both καρδίαν and κοιλίαν. See 2559 a and 2783.

² [2558 b] Outside the Gospels, Bruder (1888) indicates Rom. iii. 24 τῇ αὐτοῦ χάριτι, iii. 25 τῷ αὐτοῦ αἵματι, 1 Thess. ii. 19 ἐν τῇ αὐτοῦ παρουσίᾳ. But he omits Tit. iii. 5 κατὰ τὸ αὐτοῦ ἔλεος, Heb. ii. 4 κατὰ τὴν αὐτοῦ θέλησιν and 1 Jn ii. 27 τὸ αὐτοῦ χρῖσμα (2569 a). W.H. mark the txt as doubtful in Jas i. 18 εἰς τὸ εἶναι ἡμᾶς ἀπαρχήν τινα τῶν ⌜αὐτοῦ⌝ (marg. ἑαυτοῦ) κτισμάτων. In all these cases the pronoun is emphatic as when we say "*His* will be done," meaning "God's, not man's." In 2 Pet. iii. 7 W.H. have αὐτῷ (not αὐτοῦ). In such phrases as Rom. i. 20 ἥ τε ἀΐδιος αὐτοῦ δύναμις, i. 21 ἡ ἀσύνετος αὐτῶν καρδία, 1 Pet. ii. 9 τὸ θαυμαστὸν αὐτοῦ φῶς, part of the emphasis of the pronoun is intercepted by the preceding adjective. Comp. Rom. viii. 11.

[2558 c] No satisfactory instances have been alleged where possessive αὐτός comes between the article and the noun without emphasis. Blass § 48. 8 (n. 1) alleges Heb. vii. 18, Herm. *Mand.* vi. 2, and compares Clem. *Hom.* xiv. 7, 10. But in Heb. vii. 18 the context has contrasted the Levitical priesthood and that of Melchizedek; and now the writer says "there is a disannulling of the preparatory command because of the weakness of *that* (διὰ τὸ αὐτῆς ἀσθενές) [*as compared with the strength of this*]." In Herm. *Mand.*, the context has described Hermas as desiring to know the (v. 1—2) ἐνέργειαν of Wrath, and has spoken (vi. 1. 1) of the δύναμιν and ἐνέργειαν belonging to Faith, Fear and Self-control. Now (vi. 2. 1) the Teacher says, "There are two angels with man, one of Righteousness and one of Wickedness," and Hermas replies, πῶς οὖν, κύριε, γνώσομαι τὰς αὐτῶν ἐνεργείας "How shall I recognise the energies of *those* [*as of the rest*] because both the angels dwell with me?" The pronoun is therefore emphasized. Clem. *Hom.* xiv. 7, Schwegler's text, has ὑπὲρ πάντας αὐτοῦ με τοὺς φίλους ἀγαπῶν (not τοὺς αὐτοῦ φίλους) so that it is not to the point. In Clem. *Hom.* xiv. 10 σὺ εἶ Φαῦστος, ὁ ταύτης ἀνὴρ καὶ τῶν αὐτῆς παίδων πατήρ, a husband and father, supposed dead, is being identified in the presence of his wife: "Thou [it seems] art Faustus, the husband of *this woman* and the father of *her* children?" *i.e.* those whom *she*

article occurs occasionally in the Synoptists and very frequently indeed in John. It may be called the unemphatic precedent possessive αὐτοῦ, or "the vernacular possessive" (2776—84)[1]. It occurs in John about eighteen times; but in the Synoptists, taken all together, not much more than half that number.

[2559] The same difference, though not to the same extent, is perceptible in the Johannine and the Synoptic use of μου, σου, and ὑμῶν[2]. Here, too, Luke appears to avoid the precedent unemphatic

---

calls children as mother *you* call children as father. Αὐτῆς appears nearly equivalent to ταύτης, which is perhaps not repeated because the repetition would be monotonous. But the text of this book is so full of errors that τωναυτης may very well be an error, ΤⲰΤΑΥΤΗϹ being read as ΤⲰΝΑΥΤΗϹ.

[1] [2558 d] The "vernacular" possessive—which is freq. in Epictetus and Rev.—appears in i. 27 ἵνα λύσω αὐτοῦ τὸν ἱμάντα τοῦ ὑποδήματος as contrasted with the parall. Mk i. 7, Lk. iii. 16 λῦσαι τὸν ἱμάντα τῶν ὑποδημάτων αὐτοῦ (Mt. diff.). Contrast also xi. 32 ἔπεσεν αὐτοῦ πρὸς τοὺς πόδας with Mk v. 22 πίπτει πρὸς τοὺς πόδας αὐτοῦ (and sim. Mk vii. 25, Lk. viii. 41 Ἰησοῦ, xvii. 16).

[2558 e] Where Mk xi. 15, Mt. xxi. 12 have τὰς τραπέζας τῶν κολλυβιστῶν, Jn ii. 15 has τῶν κολλυβιστῶν ἐξέχεεν τὰ κέρματα καὶ τὰς τραπέζας ἀνέτρεψεν. But the precedent possessive noun stands on a different footing from the precedent possessive pronoun, and is probably emphatic, placed first to define the two following nouns (**2559 a**). The meaning is, "And as for the money-changers he poured out their coins and overturned their tables." Similarly in viii. 17 δύο ἀνθρώπων ἡ μαρτυρία ἀληθής ἐστιν the genitive is manifestly emphatic—"the testimony *of two men*" being required by law to establish truth. So it is in the second clause of x. 4—5 "they know his voice (τ. φ. αὐτοῦ)...they know not *of strangers* the voice (τῶν ἀλλοτρίων τὴν φωνήν)," where ἀλλοτρίων, though precedent, is more emphatic than αὐτοῦ. Ἀλλοτρίων is virtually a noun, and it is emphasized by antithesis. In ix. 27—8 αὐτοῦ and Μωυσέως are perhaps to be regarded as objective genitives "disciples following *him* and *Moses*" and the genitives are emphasized by antithesis. The separation of the genitive from the noun in xx. 23 ἄν τινων ἀφῆτε τὰς ἁμαρτίας makes the intervening ἀφῆτε emphatic, "Of whomsoever ye *forgive* sins," and "forgive" is also emphasized by antithesis with "retain" (mentioned in the context).

[2] [2559 a] I have not found the precedent unemphatic possessive with ἡμῶν in the Gospels unless it occurs in Jn xi. 48 ἀροῦσιν ἡμῶν καὶ τὸν τόπον καὶ τὸ ἔθνος which is almost equivalent to "they will take away from us both Temple and national existence." Phil. iii. 20 ἡμῶν γὰρ τὸ πολίτευμα is differentiated by the initial position of ἡμῶν, and by the intervening γάρ: it means, in effect, "*For us* [whatever it may be for others], our country is in heaven." Rom. xiii. 11 ἐγγύτερον ἡμῶν is prob. (see Steph.) an instance of objective genitive. In 1 Thess. iii. 10 and 13 ἰδεῖν ὑμῶν τὸ πρόσωπον, and στηρίξαι ὑμῶν τὰς καρδίας, the unemphatic ὑμῶν throws the emphasis on what follows, "see you *face to face*," "strengthen [*you not outwardly but inwardly in*] *your hearts*." The unemphatic precedent genitives, ὑμῶν and αὐτῶν occur severally in 1 Thess. v. 23 Αὐτὸς δὲ ὁ θεὸς τῆς εἰρήνης ἁγιάσαι ὑμᾶς ὁλοτελεῖς, καὶ ὁλόκληρον ὑμῶν τὸ πνεῦμα καὶ ἡ ψυχὴ καὶ τὸ σῶμα...

ARRANGEMENT AND VARIATION [2560]

genitive as in his account of the healing of the paralytic compared with that in Mark and Matthew[1]. And in the healing of the centurion's servant, where Matthew, using the unemphatic μου, lays stress upon the condescension of coming all the way to the centurion's "house," instead of healing at a distance ("come to my *house*"), Luke neglects or avoids this distinction[2]. John, since he is continually representing the Saviour as using the words "I" and "my," is bound to use "my" more frequently than the Synoptists: and accordingly he uses μου and ἐμοῦ more frequently than any one of them. But if he wishes to emphasize "my" he mostly uses ὁ ἐμός, and, to increase the emphasis, he repeats the article. Ἐμός is used by John about forty times as against ten times in the rest of the Gospels. Thus he can rise to a climax of pronominal emphasis :—(1) μου τὰ ῥήματα, (2) τὰ ῥήματά μου, (3) τὰ ἐμὰ ῥήματα, (4) τὰ ῥήματα τὰ ἐμά[3]. See 2776—84.

Instances of the Possessive Genitive

[2560] i. 27 ἵνα λύσω αὐτοῦ τὸν ἱμάντα τοῦ ὑποδήματος.

ii. 15 καὶ τῶν κολλυβιστῶν ἐξέχεεν τὰ κέρματα καὶ τὰς τραπέζας ἀνέτρεψεν.

ii. 23 θεωροῦντες αὐτοῦ τὰ σημεῖα ἃ ἐποίει.

τηρηθείη, Acts iv. 5 ἐγένετο δὲ συναχθῆναι αὐτῶν τοὺς ἄρχοντας κ. τοὺς πρεσβ. κ. τοὺς γραμμ.—in both cases before a group of governing nouns, as in Jn xi. 48 before τὸν τόπον κ. τὸ ἔθνος. See **2783**.

[1] [2559 b] Mk ii. 5, Mt. ix. 2 σου αἱ ἁμαρτίαι, Lk. v. 20 σοι αἱ ἁμ. σου : rep. Mk ii. 9, Mt. ix. 5, Lk. v. 23 (D has Mt. ix. 2 σοι αἱ ἁμ., but Lk. v. 20 σου αἱ ἁμ. (correcting Mt. to Lk. and Lk. to Mt. as freq.). D also has Mk ii. 9 σοι αἱ ἁμ., Lk. v. 23 σου αἱ ἁμ.).

[2] [2559 c] Mt. viii. 8 ἵνα μου ὑπὸ τὴν στέγην εἰσέλθῃς, Lk. vii. 6 ἵνα ὑπὸ τὴν στέγην μου εἰσέλθῃς. Mt., by using the unemphatic μου, emphasizes στέγην.

[3] [2559 d] Blass (p. 317) says that ὁ ἐμός "often has so little emphasis that it cannot easily be distinguished from μου : R. x. 1 ἡ εὐδοκία τῆς ἐμῆς καρδίας = τῆς κ. μου G. i. 13, Ph. i. 26." But there is a μέν in Rom. x. 1 ἡ μὲν εὐδοκία τ. ἐ. κ. This, and the context, indicate an antithesis between that which would be well pleasing to the writer's *own* heart and that which may be the will of God for the present. In Gal. i. 12—15, there is a contrast between τὴν ἐμὴν ἀναστροφήν ποτε ἐν τῷ Ἰουδαϊσμῷ i.e. "*my own* [*unconverted*] manner of life" and the previously mentioned change that had come (12) "through the revelation of Jesus Christ"; moreover the sense implies τὴν μὲν ἐμὴν ἀναστροφήν to correspond to (15) ὅτε δὲ εὐδόκησεν. In Phil. i. 25—6 there may be antithesis between ὑμῶν and διὰ τῆς ἐμῆς as freq. in the Pauline Epistles ("*I* shall continue to live that *you* may boast in me," Lightf. compares 2 Cor. i. 14 καύχημα ὑμῶν ἐσμὲν καθάπερ κ. ὑμεῖς ἡμῶν).

iii. 19—21 ἦν γὰρ αὐτῶν πονηρὰ τὰ ἔργα...οὐκ ἔρχεται πρὸς τὸ φῶς, ἵνα μὴ ἐλεγχθῇ τὰ ἔργα αὐτοῦ...ἔρχεται πρὸς τὸ φῶς, ἵνα φανερωθῇ αὐτοῦ τὰ ἔργα ὅτι ἐν θεῷ ἐστιν εἰργασμένα.

iii. 32—3 καὶ τὴν μαρτυρίαν αὐτοῦ οὐδεὶς λαμβάνει. ὁ λαβὼν αὐτοῦ τὴν μαρτυρίαν ἐσφράγισεν....

iv. 16 φώνησόν σου τὸν ἄνδρα, (18) οὐκ ἔστιν σου ἀνήρ.

iv. 34 ἵνα...καὶ τελειώσω αὐτοῦ τὸ ἔργον.

iv. 47 ἵνα...καὶ ἰάσηται αὐτοῦ τὸν υἱόν.

vi. 53, 55 ἐὰν μὴ φάγητε τὴν σάρκα τοῦ ὑ. τοῦ ἀ. καὶ πίητε αὐτοῦ τὸ αἷμα...ὁ τρώγων μου τὴν σάρκα καὶ πίνων μου τὸ αἷμα ἔχει ζωὴν αἰώνιον ...ἡ γὰρ σάρξ μου ἀληθής ἐστι βρῶσις, καὶ τὸ αἷμά μου ἀληθής ἐστι πόσις. ὁ τρώγων μου τὴν σάρκα καὶ πίνων μου τὸ αἷμα ἐν ἐμοὶ μένει.

[2561] vii. 3 ἵνα...θεωρήσουσιν [σοῦ] τὰ ἔργα (marg. τὰ ἔργα σου) ἃ ποιεῖς.

viii. 17 ὅτι δύο ἀνθρώπων ἡ μαρτυρία ἀληθής ἐστιν.

ix. 6 ἐπέθηκεν αὐτοῦ τὸν πηλὸν ἐπὶ τοὺς ὀφθαλμούς.

ix. 10 foll. πῶς [οὖν] ἠνεώχθησάν σου οἱ ὀφθαλμοί; (11) ἐπέχρισέν μου τοὺς ὀ. (rep. 30) (14) ἀνέῳξεν αὐτοῦ τοὺς ὀ., (15) πηλὸν ἐπέθηκέν μου ἐπὶ τοὺς ὀ., (17) ἠνέῳξέν σου τοὺς ὀ. (rep. 26), (21) τίς ἤνοιξεν αὐτοῦ τοὺς ὀ.

ix. 27, 28 μὴ καὶ ὑμεῖς θέλετε αὐτοῦ μαθηταὶ γενέσθαι;...Σὺ μαθητὴς εἶ ἐκείνου, ἡμεῖς δὲ τοῦ Μ. ἐσμὲν μαθηταί.

x. 4, 5 ὅτι οἴδασιν τὴν φωνὴν αὐτοῦ...ὅτι οὐκ οἴδασι τῶν ἀλλοτρίων τὴν φωνήν.

xi. 32 ἔπεσεν αὐτοῦ πρὸς τοὺς πόδας λέγουσα αὐτῷ Κύριε, εἰ ἦς ὧδε οὐκ ἂν μου ἀπέθανεν ὁ ἀδ., contrast ib. 21, Κ., εἰ ἦς ὧδε οὐκ ἂν ἀπ. ὁ ἀδ. μου.

xi. 48 ἀροῦσιν ἡμῶν καὶ τὸν τόπον καὶ τὸ ἔθνος.

xii. 16 ταῦτα οὐκ ἔγνωσαν αὐτοῦ οἱ μαθηταὶ τὸ πρῶτον.

xii. 27 δόξασόν σου τὸ ὄνομα, so xvii. 1 δόξασόν σου τὸν υἱόν.

xii. 40 τετύφλωκεν αὐτῶν τοὺς ὀφθαλμοὺς καὶ ἐπώρωσεν αὐτῶν τὴν καρδίαν, freely quoted from Is. vi. 10 where there is no precedent genitive, but there is a non-precedent genitive τοῖς ὠσὶν αὐτῶν which Jn omits.

xii. 47—8 ἐάν τίς μου ἀκούσῃ τῶν ῥημάτων καὶ μὴ φυλάξῃ...ὁ...μὴ λαμβάνων τὰ ῥήματά μου.

xiii. 1 ὅτι ἦλθεν αὐτοῦ ἡ ὥρα, contrast ii. 4 ἡ ὥρα μου, vii. 30, viii. 20, ἡ ὥρα αὐτοῦ, xvi. 21 ἡ ὥρα αὐτῆς.

xiii. 6 foll. σύ μου νίπτεις τοὺς πόδας; (8) οὐ μὴ νίψῃς μου τοὺς πόδας, (9) μὴ τοὺς πόδας μου μόνον, (12) ὅτε οὖν ἔνιψεν τοὺς πόδας αὐτῶν,

ARRANGEMENT AND VARIATION [2563]

(14) εἰ οὖν ἐγὼ ἔνιψα ὑμῶν τοὺς πόδας, καὶ ὑμεῖς ὀφείλετε ἀλλήλων νίπτειν τοὺς πόδας. See 2564.

xiii. 18 ὁ τρώγων μου τὸν ἄρτον, quoted freely from Ps. xli. 9 ὁ ἐσθίων ἄρτους μου.

[2562] xiv. 1, 27 Μὴ ταρασσέσθω ὑμῶν ἡ καρδία, comp. xvi. 6, 22.

xv. 9, 10 μείνατε ἐν τῇ ἀγάπῃ τῇ ἐμῇ. ἐὰν τὰς ἐντολάς μου τηρήσητε, μενεῖτε ἐν τῇ ἀγάπῃ μου, καθὼς ἐγὼ τοῦ πατρὸς τὰς ἐντολὰς τετήρηκα καὶ μένω αὐτοῦ ἐν τῇ ἀγάπῃ.

xv. 15 οὐκ οἶδεν τί ποιεῖ αὐτοῦ ὁ κύριος.

xvi. 6 ἡ λύπη πεπλήρωκεν ὑμῶν τὴν καρδίαν.

xvi. 22 καὶ χαρήσεται ὑμῶν ἡ καρδία, quoted from Is. lxvi. 14 χαρήσεται ἡ καρδία ὑμῶν[1].

xvii. 6 Ἐφανέρωσά σου τὸ ὄνομα, contrast xvii. 11, 12 ἐν τῷ ὀνόματί σου.

xviii. 10 ἔπαισεν τὸν τοῦ ἀρχιερέως δοῦλον καὶ ἀπέκοψεν αὐτοῦ τὸ ὠτάριον τὸ δεξιόν.

xviii. 37 πᾶς ὁ ὢν ἐκ τῆς ἀληθείας ἀκούει μου τῆς φωνῆς.

xix. 2 στέφανον...ἐπέθηκαν αὐτοῦ τῇ κεφαλῇ.

xix. 29 σπόγγον...προσήνεγκαν αὐτοῦ τῷ στόματι.

xix. 31—4 ἵνα κατεαγῶσιν αὐτῶν τὰ σκέλη... (32) καὶ τοῦ μὲν πρώτου κατέαξαν τὰ σκέλη καὶ τοῦ ἄλλου... (33) οὐ κατέαξαν αὐτοῦ τὰ σκέλη, (34) λόγχῃ αὐτοῦ τὴν πλευρὰν ἔνυξεν.

xix. 35 καὶ ἀληθινὴ αὐτοῦ ἐστιν ἡ μαρτυρία.

xx. 23 ἄν τινων ἀφῆτε τὰς ἁμαρτίας.

xx. 25, 27 ἐὰν μή...βάλω τὸν δάκτυλόν μου...καὶ βάλω μου τὴν χεῖρα εἰς τὴν πλευρὰν αὐτοῦ... (27) Φέρε τὸν δάκτυλόν σου ὧδε καὶ ἴδε τὰς χεῖράς μου καὶ φέρε τὴν χεῖρά σου καὶ βάλε εἰς τὴν πλευράν μου.

xxi. 24 οἴδαμεν ὅτι ἀληθὴς αὐτοῦ ἡ μαρτυρία ἐστίν.

[2563] In some of the instances given above, the pronoun (somewhat like the Latin "ei" in "projecit se *ei* ad pedes") occurs in a phrase mentioning some part of the body where "his," "my" etc. do not exactly mean, or at least do not emphasize, possession. Thus Luke (W.H.) "thou gavest me no water for *my* feet" is expressed in text by μοι, but in margin by preceding μου: and Luke's following words twice use the unemphatic preceding μου to throw emphasis on the homage paid to Jesus by moistening or

---

[1] [2562 a] Note that in three instances, xii. 40, xiii. 18, xvi. 22, when quoting LXX, Jn deviates from it by using a precedent genitive (sim. Rev., see 2781 b).

kissing His "*feet*[1]"—perhaps taking the emphasis off the pronoun and throwing it on the noun "*feet*," because another tradition described an anointing of the "*head*." In John, the "vernacular" possessive occurs repeatedly with "eyes[2]" (in the narrative of the healing of the blind man), also with "heart[3]," "head[4]," "mouth[5]," "legs[6]," "side[7]," "hand[8]." Once it occurs with "right ear"—a noteworthy instance because it occurs in a portion of "the four-fold Gospel," the smiting of the High Priest's servant by Peter: and here, though John agrees with Luke in adding that it was the "*right* ear" (a point omitted by Mark and Matthew) he follows Mark and Matthew against Luke in the use of the "vernacular" possessive[9].

[1] [2563 a] Lk. vii. 44—6 ὕδωρ μοι ἐπὶ πόδας (without the article) but marg. ὕ. μου ἐπὶ τοὺς πόδας: and then, ἔβρεξέν μου τοὺς πόδας...καταφιλοῦσά μου τοὺς πόδας. In his version of the Anointing, Mk xiv. 3 has κατέχεεν αὐτοῦ τῆς κεφαλῆς. Lk.'s use of the precedent possessive here is all the more remarkable in view of his general deviation (2559) from the Synoptic use of it. It is one of many proofs that Lk. contains several documents written in several styles and variously revised.

[2] See ix. 7, 10, 11, 14, 15 etc.   [3] xvi. 6, 22.   [4] xix. 2.
[5] xix. 29.   [6] xix. 31.   [7] xix. 34.   [8] xx. 25.

[9] [2563 b] xviii. 10 ἀπέκοψεν αὐτοῦ τὸ ὠτάριον τὸ δεξιόν. Comp. 1 Cor. viii. 12 τύπτοντες αὐτῶν τὴν συνείδησιν ἀσθενοῦσαν, which is equivalent to "smiting *them* [in the cruellest way, not in the body but] *in the conscience* [and that too when it is] in a state of weakness." So Mk xii. 15 εἰδὼς αὐτῶν τὴν ὑπόκρισιν and parall. Lk. xx. 23 κατανοήσας δὲ αὐτῶν τὴν πανουργίαν mean, in effect, "*detecting them in* their hypocritical craft" (parall. Mt. xxii. 18 γνοὺς δὲ τὴν πονηρίαν αὐτῶν). Mk v. 30 τίς μου ἥψατο τῶν ἱματίων is given in Lk. viii. 46 as ἥψατό μού τις and is repeated in Mk v. 31 without τῶν ἱματίων, the meaning being almost the same as "who *touched me* on, or, *took hold of me* by, the cloak?"

[2563 c] In Acts xvi. 22 περιρήξαντες αὐτῶν τὰ ἱμάτια, one or two inferior authorities read ἑαυτῶν, perhaps because the scribes took the "rending" to be like that of the High Priest in Mk xiv. 63 διαρήξας τοὺς χιτῶνας αὐτοῦ (sim. Mt. xxvi. 65 διέρηξεν τὰ ἱμάτια αὐτοῦ). Rending one's own garments would properly be expressed in classical Gk by the middle περιρήξασθαι τὰ ἱμάτια. "Rending off (περιρήξας) (act.) *the* (τά) garments" (without possess. genit.) regularly describes the action of public or private scourgers in Demosth. 403. 3, Polyb. xv. 3. 4, Plut. *Vit. Poplic.* 6. But Diod. Sic. xvii. 35 and others (see Steph.) use the active for the middle, and perhaps Lk. here used the unemphatic αὐτῶν as an additional indication that the meaning was *not* "their own."

[2563 d] The reader must distinguish between (1) τὰ ῥήματα αὐτοῦ "the *ordinary* possessive," (2) τὰ αὐτοῦ ῥήματα "the *intervening emphatic* possessive," intervening between the article and the noun and emphasizing αὐτοῦ, (3) αὐτοῦ τὰ ῥήματα "the *precedent unemphatic* possessive," *preceding the article and the noun and so unemphatic as to throw emphasis from itself*—unless antithesis exceptionally (2564) compels it to receive emphasis—*on to the contiguous words.* This last, being characteristic of colloquial style, will be often called, for brevity, "vernacular."

[2564] In xiii. 6 σύ μου νίπτεις τοὺς πόδας, the genitive pronoun is emphasized by coming next after another pronoun (2784 c) so that the meaning is, " *Thou! for me!* washest the feet[1]!" This then—owing to special circumstances in the context—is not an instance of the vernacular unemphatic possessive. But it is followed by the true vernacular possessive, xiii. 8 οὐ μὴ νίψῃς μου τοὺς πόδας, "thou shalt *assuredly* never wash my *feet,*" where there is no emphasis on "thou" nor on "my," but on "*assuredly*" and "*feet.*" Then comes the ordinary construction in xiii. 9 μὴ τ. π. μου μόνον, where μὴ...μόνον throws some emphasis on "feet," and xiii. 12 ὅτε οὖν ἔνιψεν τοὺς πόδας αὐτῶν, where there is no emphasis on any particular word. Lastly comes the precept xiii. 14, where ὑμῶν τοὺς πόδας is not an instance of the true vernacular possessive, because "your" is exceptionally emphasized by the previous insertion of an emphatic "I" to which "your" is obviously antithetical. "If therefore *I* (ἐγώ) washed *for you* (ὑμῶν) *the feet*...ye also (καὶ ὑμεῖς) are bound for *one another* to wash the feet (ἀλλήλων νίπτειν τ. πόδας)[2]."

[2565] We are not, of course, to suppose that the evangelist deliberately arranged these variations—which indeed might be to some extent illustrated by an Englishman's unconscious variations of "shall" and "will." But we certainly must suppose that the author of this Gospel had an unusually keen sense of rhythm and dramatic fitness. It may also well be that in the course—perhaps a very long course—of oral teaching, his Gospel assumed a shape in which no phrase or word has been set down except as the result of artistic as well as spiritual evolution. Take, for example, the first utterances of Martha and Mary, when they severally come to meet Jesus before the raising of Lazarus :—

(1) xi. 20—1 ἡ οὖν Μάρθα ὡς ἤκουσεν ὅτι ’Ι. ἔρχεται ὑπήντησεν

---

[1] [2564 a] Comp. xxi. 22 σύ μοι ἀκολούθει (equiv. to "it is for *thee* to follow *me*") where the two pronouns are emphasized by juxtaposition, and μοι is more emphatic than in xxi. 19 ἀκολούθει μοι, "follow me," where there is no antithetical σύ. The meaning is, "That disciple may follow me in his way, which is not the way to the Cross; but you must not follow in his way, but in my way."

[2] [2564 b] So αὐτῶν in xix. 31—4 ἵνα κατεαγῶσιν αὐτῶν τὰ σκέλη is vernacular possessive and unemphatic, "that they might have their legs broken," but τοῦ μὲν πρώτου, though preceding κατέαξαν τὰ σκέλη, is not vernacular because μέν introduces antithesis; and, in οὐ κατέαξαν αὐτοῦ τὰ σκέλη, the effect of antithesis emphasizes αὐτοῦ, so that the meaning is "they brake not *his* legs."

αὐτῷ· Μαριὰμ δὲ ἐν τῷ οἴκῳ ἐκαθέζετο. εἶπεν οὖν ἡ Μάρθα πρὸς Ἰησοῦν, ⌜Κύριε⌝¹, εἰ ἦς ὧδε, οὐκ ἂν ἀπέθανεν ὁ ἀδελφός μου.

(2) xi. 29—32 ἐκείνη δὲ ὡς ἤκουσεν [*i.e.* that Jesus "called" her φωνεῖ σε] ἠγέρθη ταχὺ καὶ ἤρχετο πρὸς αὐτόν...ἡ οὖν Μαριὰμ ὡς ἦλθεν ὅπου ἦν Ἰησοῦς ἰδοῦσα αὐτὸν ἔπεσεν αὐτοῦ πρὸς τοὺς πόδας λέγουσα αὐτῷ, Κύριε, εἰ ἦς ὧδε, οὐκ ἄν <u>μου</u> ἀπέθανεν ὁ ἀδελφός.

[2566] Everything in (1)—the deliberation implied in "going to meet," the weighty word εἶπεν (2456), the ordinary sequence of οὐκ ἂν ἀπέθανεν, and of ὁ ἀδελφός μου—points to deliberate utterance. In (2), Mary's "rising up quickly" (contrasted with the previous "sitting in the house") and her "falling at the feet" of the Saviour when she first catches sight of Him, prepare us for an utterance of passionate emotion. And, as a fact, the ordinary sequence of οὐκ ἄν and verb² is broken by the intervention of μου, and the connexion

---

¹ [2565 a] Κύριε is now known to be omitted by SS. It is also omitted by SS in xiii. 37 where W.H. have ⌜κύριε,⌝ as here. In both cases, scribes have probably added it to assimilate the text to passages in the context inserting κύριε. Peter's omission of "Lord" in xiii. 6 might spring from Peter's haste to expostulate with his Master. Here, Martha is perhaps represented as omitting it because her mind is absorbed in the thought of what might have been ("If only it could have been otherwise!") and an "if" is the first word that escapes from her lips. Mary, though in greater haste than Martha, does not omit "Lord."

² [2566 a] Comp. 1 Cor. ii. 8 "Never the *Lord of glory* would they have crucified (οὐκ ἂν τ. κύριον τῆς δόξης ἐσταύρωσαν)," Heb. iv. 8 "Not about *another* day would he have spoken," οὐκ ἂν περὶ ἄλλης ἐλάλει μετὰ ταῦτα ἡμέρας, *ib.* viii. 7 "not *for a second* [*covenant*] would place be sought," οὐκ ἂν δευτέρας ἐζητεῖτο τόπος.

[2566 b] In view of these instances, and of the reasonableness of emphasizing most pronouns in such a position, it is possible that σοι must be emphasized in Jn xviii. 30 where the evangelist with bitter irony describes the Jews (1885 (ii)) as avoiding external defilement, yet as defiling themselves internally by that which "cometh out of the mouth" in slander, accusing Christ of being an "evil-doer." "If this man had not been an evil-doer we should not have delivered him up *to* [*a just judge like*] *thee*," οὐκ ἂν σοι παρεδώκαμεν αὐτόν. Blass (p. 320) on οὐκ ἂν σοι παρεδώκαμεν, says "better οὐδ' according to the Lewis Syriac." And οὐδέ would certainly be preferable unless an emphasis on σοι could be justified. The variations in the best MSS. as to the position of ἄν in viii. 19 and xiv. 7 proceed in part from scribal doubts as to the relation between the two similar sayings, and in part from a failure to recognise that ἄν, in John, always follows an emphatic word, and that in these two sentences "my Father" is more emphatic than "know." In xviii. 36, ἠγωνίζοντο ἄν (where B marg. has rightly inserted ἄν, casually omitted by B at the end of a line before ἵνα) comes emphatically before a short pause; and this (though not much more striking than xiv. 28 ἐχάρητε ἄν) has caused variations (2739 c). In none of these three passages does there seem good reason for supposing that ἄν was originally omitted. The variations in the Johannine order

between μου and ὁ ἀδελφός is broken by the intervention of the verb. This obliges us to lay stress on ἄν i.e. "*how different it would have been!*" But it is not clear whether the emphasis on ἄν does, or does not, take away the emphasis from the following μου. If σύ had been inserted, we might have felt certain that μου (**2564**) is emphatic. Perhaps the writer draws a contrast between Martha, ending her sentence with "*me*" and Mary, ending hers with "*brother.*" If so, μου is the vernacular possessive. As it is, the conclusion is doubtful[1].

[**2567**] In vi. 51—5, where the Eucharistic doctrine is introduced, the ordinary possessive, ἡ σάρξ μου, occurs, first predicatively ("the bread that I shall give is *my flesh*") and then "except ye eat *the flesh of* (τὴν σ.) *the Son of man.*" After this, when mention is made of drinking the blood and eating the flesh, the unemphatic "his" and "my" are used in order to emphasize "*flesh*" and "*blood*" :—"[yea,] and drink his *blood* (αὐτοῦ τ. αἷμα)…he that eateth my *flesh* (μου τ. σάρκα) and drinketh my *blood* (μου τ. αἷμα)." When a return is made to definition, the ordinary possessive is resumed: "*my* flesh (ἡ σ.

---

of ἄν (*e.g.* viii. 19 τὸν πατέρα μου ἂν ᾔδειτε, viii. 42 ἠγαπᾶτε ἂν ἐμέ, xv. 19 ὁ κόσμος ἂν τὸ ἴδιον ἐφίλει) are mostly explicable by emphasis on special words, but they are irregular enough to perplex scribes (comp. Gal. iii. 21 (W.H.) ἐν νόμῳ ἂν ἦν (marg. ἐκ νόμου ἦν [ἄν])). In xviii. 36 the final ἄν suits well with the imperfect—the meaning being "would be *in that case striving at this very moment*" [comp. Mt. xxvi. 53 "*at this moment*…twelve legions of angels"] "that I might not be delivered to the Jews." Blass (p. 207) says "τοῖς Ἰουδ. is contrary to sense and is omitted by Chrys." But Chrys. *inserts* τοῖς Ἰουδ. *in quoting the passage.* Afterwards, it is true, he omits it. But then he omits not only τοῖς Ἰουδ. but also the rest of Christ's sentence (τοῖς Ἰουδ. νῦν δὲ ἡ βασ. ἡ ἐμὴ οὐκ ἔστιν ἐντεῦθεν). The reason appears to be that he stops short because he sees no ground for special comment on the omitted words. Subsequently he casually repeats the words οὐκ ἐντεῦθεν, shewing that he had the clause before him, though he did not think it worth while to quote it in full or to comment on τοῖς Ἰουδ. Yet in fact there is great force in "*the Jews*," as denoting the real agents, Pilate being a mere puppet. In Lk. xix. 23, Blass (p. 206) takes ἐλθών as = (temporal) protasis, where I should prefer to supply the protasis from the context, "Why didst thou not put my money into the bank…*and* [*then, if thou hadst done this,*] *I on my side* (κἀγώ), when I came home (ἐλθών), should have exacted the sum with interest?"

[1] [**2566** *c*] Some might urge that, if Jn had intended emphasis, he would have used ἐμοῦ, not μου. But ἐμοῦ *is never used in N.T. without* (1) *a preceding preposition* Mt. v. 11, vii. 23, x. 18 etc.; *or without* (2) *antithesis*, Lk. x. 16 ὁ ἀκούων ὑμῶν ἐμοῦ ἀκούει: *or parallelism to a preceding genitive*, Rom. i. 12 ὑμῶν τε καὶ ἐμοῦ, xvi. 2 πολλῶν κ. ἐμοῦ αὐτοῦ, xvi. 13 αὐτοῦ κ. ἐμοῦ. (3) In one exceptional passage the text varies so as to cause suspicion of error Mt. xvi. 23 (BΝ*) σκάνδαλον εἶ ἐμοῦ, v.r. μου ει, ει εμοι, μοι ει, ει μου, where ειμι σοι may have been the original ("I am a stumbling-block [it seems] to thee!").

[2568] ARRANGEMENT AND VARIATION

μου) is true food, and my blood (τὸ ἁ. μου) is true drink." Then, when it has to be insisted that "abiding" in Christ is the result of feeding on the "flesh" and the "blood," the nouns are again emphasized: "He that eateth my *flesh* (μ. τὴν σάρκα) and drinketh my *blood* (μ. τὸ αἷμα) abideth in me[1]."

[2568] Where there is no antithesis we are generally safe in taking the precedent possessive as unemphatic, *e.g.* "I manifested thy *name*," compared with "in *thy* name[2]." But antithesis and chiasmus probably give it emphasis in xv. 10 "ye will abide in my love (μενεῖτε ἐν τ. ἀγ. μου)...even as I...and abide in *his* love (μένω αὐτοῦ ἐν τῇ ἀγ.)[3]." In iii. 19—20, the context is too long to discuss, but the genitives (one of which is separated from its governing noun by a predicative adjective, πονηρά) are perhaps intended to throw the emphasis on what follows in each case[4]. It is however a passage where there is room for difference of opinion.

---

[1] [2567 a] In xx. 25—7, there is perhaps a contrast between the vehement and varied utterance of Thomas and the calm regularity of the Saviour's reproach. Jesus repeats four times the ordinary possessive genitive ("thy finger," "thy hand" etc.). Thomas says "*put my finger* (β. τὸν δ. μου) into the print of the nails, *yea, and put my hand* (κ. β. μου τὴν χεῖρα) into his side." The difference cannot well be expressed in English. But there appears to be intended a climax in the thrusting of the *whole of the* "*hand*" (as compared with "the finger") into the open wound in the side.

[2567 b] In iv. 47 "that he might heal his *son* (ἁ. τὸν υἱόν)" there may be an intention to emphasize "*son*," partly because it illustrated the urgency of the request, partly because some traditions may have differed as to whether (1862 a—c) the sick "boy" was a "*son*" or a "*servant*."

[2] [2568 a] xvii. 6 ἐφανέρωσά σου τ. ὄνομα, comp. xvii. 11, 12 τήρησον (and ἐτήρουν) αὐτοὺς ἐν τῷ ὀνόματί σου.

[3] [2568 b] In iii. 32—3 τὴν μαρτυρίαν αὐτοῦ οὐδεὶς λαμβάνει. ὁ λαβὼν αὐτοῦ τὴν μαρτυρίαν there is no antithesis between αὐτοῦ and another pronoun. The second αὐτοῦ is probably unemphatic, the emphasis being thrown on λαβών, "he that *did* receive" (after the assertion "none receiveth").

[4] [2568 c] iii. 19—20 κ. ἠγάπησαν οἱ ἄνθρωποι μᾶλλον τὸ σκότος ἢ τὸ φῶς, ἦν γὰρ αὐτῶν πονηρὰ τὰ ἔργα. πᾶς γὰρ ὁ φαῦλα πράσσων μισεῖ τὸ φῶς καὶ οὐκ ἔρχεται πρὸς τὸ φῶς, ἵνα μὴ ἐλεγχθῇ τὰ ἔργα αὐτοῦ· ὁ δὲ ποιῶν τὴν ἀλήθειαν ἔρχεται πρὸς τὸ φῶς, ἵνα φανερωθῇ αὐτοῦ τὰ ἔργα ὅτι ἐν θεῷ ἐστιν εἰργασμένα. If this view is correct the meaning is that men as a rule loved darkness "for their *works* were essentially bad (πονηρά)," but that the truth-worker comes to the light "that his *works* may be manifested as being *worked* in God." In both cases the emphasis is taken from "their" and "his," to be thrown on "*works*." But as regards ὁ φαῦλα πράσσων, emphasis is thrown on his personal shrinking from the light lest "*his* works be convicted." In iii. 19 the position of πονηρά before ἔργα makes both words emphatic: "For there was from the first an essential badness in their *works*."

[2569] In ii. 23 "beholding his *signs* (αὐτοῦ τὰ σημεῖα), which he was [continually] doing," and also in vii. 3 "that they may behold thy *works* (if we read σου τὰ ἔργα)," emphasis is laid on "*signs*" and "*works*," and the context implies, perhaps, that the speakers attached more importance to these than to Christ Himself. The same emphasis on the noun is to be laid in the only two instances where precedent αὐτοῦ occurs in the Johannine Epistles: 1 Jn ii. 4—5 "He that sayeth...and keepeth not his commandments (τὰς ἐντ. αὐτοῦ μὴ τηρῶν) is a liar...but whoso keepeth his *word* (ὃς δ' ἂν τηρῇ αὐτοῦ τὸν λόγον)¹, truly in him is the love of God," 3 Jn 9—10 "He that loveth supremacy over them, Diotrephes, doth not fitly receive us: for this cause, if I come, I will call to remembrance [*not his pretensions but*] his *works* (ὑπομνήσω αὐτοῦ τὰ ἔργα)²."

---

¹ [2569 a] On this Westcott says "The position of the pronoun here (αὐτοῦ τὸν λόγον), as contrasted with that which it has in v. 3 (τὰς ἐντολὰς αὐτοῦ), emphasizes the personal idea. The main thought is that the word is His word, the word of God. There is emphasis also on the 'keeping' ὃς δ' ἂν τηρῇ contrasted with ὁ...τὰς ἐντ. μὴ τηρῶν." In view of Jn's frequent use of the "vernacular" αὐτοῦ this interpretation seems untenable. Jn has not here τὸν αὐτοῦ λόγον as in 1 Jn ii. 27 τὸ αὐτοῦ χρίσμα. In αὐτοῦ τὸν λόγον, the emphasis is taken from αὐτοῦ to be thrown on λόγον, which here means "*the* [*spiritual*] *word*" or "the spirit, not the letter," and is stronger than ἐντολάς, "*commandments.*" Comp. xiv. 23—4 τὸν λόγον μου τηρήσει and τοὺς λόγους μου οὐ τηρεῖ. The pl. λόγοι in the Gospel corresponds to the pl. ἐντολαί in the Epistle and both occur in a negative clause while the sing. λόγος is in the positive clause. The position of the pronoun, then, does not "emphasize the personal idea," but throws the emphasis on the spirituality of the "Word" that is to be "kept."

² [2569 b] Somewhat similar is the mention of "those who are puffed up" in 1 Cor. iv. 19, "But I will come quickly unto you...and will acquaint myself not with the speech but with the *power* of them that are puffed up, καὶ γνώσομαι οὐ τὸν λόγον τῶν πεφυσιωμένων ἀλλὰ τὴν δύναμιν."

[2569 c] In ix. 6, the reading is very doubtful. W.H. txt has ταῦτα εἰπὼν ἔπτυσεν χαμαὶ κ. ἐποίησεν πηλὸν ἐκ τοῦ πτύσματος καὶ ⌜ἐπέθηκεν⌝ (marg. ἐπέχρισεν) αὐτοῦ τὸν πηλὸν ἐπὶ τοὺς ὀφθαλμούς. R.V. marg. has "the clay *thereof*," taking αὐτοῦ to refer to πτύσματος, and supplying "his." AC ins. "of the blind man" after "eyes." SS has "and took [it *i.e.* the clay] up [and] smeared [it] upon the eyes of that blind man," D "and smeared upon him (ἐπέχρισεν αὐτῷ) the clay upon his eyes," *d* "et linuit ei lutum super oculos eius," *a* "et linuit oculos ejus," *b* "et superlinuit lutum super oculos illius caeci," *e* "et superunxit oculos caeci," *f* "et superlinivit super oculos caeci," *ff* "et superunxit illud super oculos ejus." (1) Mark's (viii. 23) tradition about healing blindness with saliva, (2) Jewish traditions about such healing, and (3) the possibilities of mystical suggestion in the present passage, combine with (4) the textual variations to make its adequate interpretation at present impossible.

§ 4. *Miscellaneous variations*

[2570] The following miscellaneous variations, taken in their order as they occur in the Gospel, may be of use for reference, and for the purpose of giving the reader a general view of John's style. Many of them have been explained incidentally above: others will be briefly discussed here. A few of them deal with synonyms not discussed in *Johannine Vocabulary*. For example, the use of καταλαμβάνω in the Prologue (i. 5) was discussed in 1735 *e—h*, but the relation between παραλαμβάνω and λαμβάνω in the same context was merely touched on there, and will come first in the instances given below.

In i. 11—12 οἱ ἴδιοι αὐτὸν οὐ παρέλαβον· ὅσοι δὲ ἔλαβον αὐτόν, a distinction is certainly drawn between παρέλαβον and ἔλαβον, and the former is probably used with special reference to οἱ ἴδιοι. The meaning probably is that, when the Son of God came to His own family, none "*received Him fitly as coming from the Father* (παρέλαβον)," but some "*received Him* [*though imperfectly*] (ἔλαβον)[1]."

---

[1] [2570 *a*] Οἱ ἴδιοι αὐτὸν οὐ παρέλαβον and the preceding εἰς τὰ ἴδια ἦλθε are quoted by Clem. Alex. (882—3 εἰς τ. ἴδια, φησίν, ἦλθεν ὁ υἱὸς τ. θεοῦ κ. οἱ ἴδιοι αὐτὸν οὐκ ἐδέξαντο) as referring to "the world (κόσμος)." In that case we might reconcile οὐ παρέλαβον with ὅσοι ἔλαβον by saying that παρέλαβον means a friendly "receiving" (Nonnus, ἐγέραιρον), while ἔλαβον means a less active "receiving" (Nonnus, δέξαντο). Or we might say that John according to his custom (**2628**) states a fact first roughly and inaccurately, and then more exactly.

[2570 *b*] But Chrysostom and Ammonius both take ἴδιοι in a twofold sense, as meaning (1) the world, (2) Israel; and in view of the language of the prophets about the rejection of Jehovah by His own children, and the language of Jesus Himself about "a prophet in his own country," there can hardly be a doubt that both meanings are intended. (1) Applied to the world at large, παρέλαβον may be illustrated by its use in Epictetus to describe our "*receiving from* [*God*]." In one passage he uses παραλαμβάνω (i. 6. 25 τὴν θέαν παρειλήφατε) to describe our reception of the gift of beholding the sights of God's universe. Then he drops the compound preposition (*ib.* 28) "And come now, have you not *received* (εἰλήφατε) faculties?...Have you not *received* manliness? Have you not *received* magnanimity? Have you not *received* patience?" The Logos itself is described as (i. 20. 5) "*received from* [*God*] (παρείληπται) by [human] nature (ὑπὸ τῆς φύσεως)": and concerning the power of the Logos (ἡ λογικὴ δύναμις) it is said that (i. 1. 4) "*it is received from* [*God*]" and, in the same sentence, "*it has come* (ἐλήλυθε)." Elsewhere παραλαμβάνω is used (*Ench.* xxiv. 1, xxv. 1, xxxii. 2) of calling a friend to share one's meal or one's secret plans. (2) From the Jewish point of view, παραλαμβάνω is the regular word for "*receiving* words, or traditions," handed down from a teacher. It is thus used frequently in N.T. The very first words of the Sayings of the Jewish Fathers are "Moses *received* the Law from Sinai,"

[2571] i. 15, 30 ὁ ὀπίσω μου ἐρχόμενος ἔμπροσθέν μου γέγονεν, ὅτι... (30) εἶπον, Ὀπίσω μου ἔρχεται ἀνὴρ ὃς ἔμπροσθέν μου γέγονεν. Hereby the evangelist warns us that when he represents a speaker as apparently repeating a previous utterance, we are not to expect identity of expression. The introduction of ἀνήρ may (2371) allude to the meaning "husband" and may prepare the way for (iii. 29) "bridegroom." But in any case this is one of many passages in which the writer seems to say, "The Baptist and the Lord Jesus said the same things again and again in slightly different ways, and there may be various traditions, all differing and yet all accurate."

[2572] The verb of seeing is thrice varied in i. 32—4 τεθέαμαι τὸ πνεῦμα καταβαῖνον...κἀγὼ οὐκ ᾔδειν αὐτόν· ἀλλ' ὁ πέμψας με...εἶπεν Ἐφ' ὃν ἂν ἴδῃς...κἀγὼ ἑώρακα καὶ μεμαρτύρηκα. This may be paraphrased thus, "*I have beheld* the manifestation of the Spirit...and I for my part did not know him [the Messiah] but he that sent me

---

and the following sentences describe a long succession of teachers as each "*receiving*" from a predecessor.

[2570 *c*] In i. 4—12 the context makes it probable that παρέλαβον refers to the Jews: for it appears to describe three stages of failure, in three negations, with καταλαμβάνω, γινώσκω, and παραλαμβάνω. (1) "The life was the light of men... and the darkness *apprehended it not* (αὐτὸ οὐ κατέλαβεν)." (2) "[The light] was in the world; and the world, through him [or, it], came into being; and the world *recognised him not* (αὐτὸν οὐκ ἔγνω)." (3) "To his own [house] he came, and his own [household] *did not receive him* [as coming] from [the Father of the house] (αὐτὸν οὐ παρέλαβον)."

[2570 *d*] In the Synoptists, παραλαμβάνω is used, with Ἰησοῦν as object, in Mk iv. 36 of the disciples "*taking* Jesus *with them* in the boat," and in Mt. xxvii. 27 of the soldiers of the governor "*taking* Jesus *with them* into the praetorium," where Mk xv. 16 has ἀπήγαγον and Lk. altogether differs. The use of π. to describe "taking prisoners along with one" (or "accepting the surrender of a city" as in 1 Mac. xv. 30 (ℵ) παρελάβετε, LXX κατελάβεσθε) is very rare in Gk, and occurs in canon. LXX perh. only in Lam. iii. 2 παρέλαβέν με κ. ἀπήγαγεν εἰς σκότος. It is therefore worthy of note that Jn, like Mt., has παραλαμβάνω in his account of the Passion. But, in Jn, it is not "the soldiers of the governor" but the "chief priests," who thus "*take with them*" or "*receive*" Jesus; xix. 16—17 "then therefore he [*i.e.* Pilate] delivered him to them [*i.e.* the chief priests] to be crucified. They therefore *received* (παρέλαβον) Jesus." The supposition that the word was applied in diverse traditions to a "reception" of Jesus as a prisoner is confirmed, if the txt is correctly supplied (as it probably is) by *Evang. Petr.* (ed. Robinson) § 1 καὶ τότε κελεύει Ἡρώδης ὁ βασιλεὺς παρ[αλημ]φθῆναι τὸν Κύριον. If Jn deliberately and allusively adapted a version of this ancient tradition, so as to represent the Logos as being, after this fashion, "*received*" *by His own* "*priests*" —*who might be called pre-eminently* "*His own people*"—it is one of the most ironical instances of Johannine irony.

...said, On whomsoever *thou shalt see*...and I [taught by God's word] *have seen [and received the vision]* and have testified" (**1597** foll.). Θεᾶσθαι here means spiritual "seeing" but refers rather to the form ("descent as a dove") of the vision while ἑώρακα refers to the inner meaning of it.

[**2573**] As to iii. 3—5, γεννηθῇ ἄνωθεν compared with γ. ἐξ ὕδατος καὶ πνεύματος, and ἰδεῖν τὴν βασιλείαν τοῦ θεοῦ compared with εἰσελθεῖν εἰς τὴν β. τ. θ., it was noted in **1903** *a* that Chrysostom apparently took ἄνωθεν to mean "*from above.*" It should be added that Origen certainly does this in a passage in which he comments on viii. 23 ὑμεῖς ἐκ τῶν κάτω ἐστέ, ἐγὼ ἐκ τῶν ἄνω εἰμί, iii. 31 ὁ ὢν ἐκ τῆς γῆς...ὁ ἐκ τοῦ οὐρανοῦ ἐρχόμενος, where he says τὰ μὲν γὰρ περίγεια κάτω ἐστί, τὰ δὲ οὐράνια ἄνω, and then, after quoting Matthew's doctrine about the "heart" and the "treasure" being together, he adds: "If a man be treasuring up (θησαυρίζῃ) on earth, [then] as the result of his treasuring up on earth *he becomes 'from below'* (ἐκ τῶν κάτω γίνεται), but if a man is treasuring up (θησαυρίζει) *in the heavens he is born from above* (γεννᾶται ἄνωθεν) *and assumes* (1 Cor. xv. 49) '*the image of the heavenly*[1].'"

---

[1] [**2573** *a*] Huet ii. 280 E—282 C. Comp. Origen's Homily on Gen. i. 6—7, where he refers to the "*living water*" as being that which is "*above the firmament*" and as opposed to the "*water below*," which is the water of death: "Studeat ergo unusquisque nostrum divisor aquae effici ejus quae est supra, et quae est subtus : quo scilicet spiritualis aquae intellectum, et participium capiens ejus quae est supra firmamentum, flumina de ventre suo educat aquae vivae salientis in vitam aeternam, segregatus sine dubio, et separatus ab ea aqua quae subtus est, id est, aqua abyssi, in qua tenebrae esse dicuntur, in qua princeps hujus mundi, et adversarius draco, et angeli ejus habitant, sicut superius indicatum est. Illius ergo aquae supernae participio, quae supra coelos esse dicitur, unusquisque fidelium coelestis efficitur, id est, cum sensum suum habet in arduis et excelsis, nihil de terra, sed totum de coelestibus cogitans, quae sursum sunt quaerens, ubi Christus est in dextra Dei patris."

[**2573** *b*] Toward the end of the first century Christian teachers would find it necessary to emphasize the possibility that a man might be "*born again*" *for evil as well as for good.* This is recognised in some of the Gospels by the Parable of the "seven devils" entering into the man delivered from one devil, and by Christ's description of a proselyte as "*twofold a child of Gehenna*": and Christians might apply this doctrine to Simon Magus and others. Hermas implies this double possibility of proselytism in a passage that contains an attempt to draw a distinction (here made by John) between "*seeing*" and "*entering,*" as regards the "kingdom of God." According to him (*Sim.* ix. 13—15) there are twelve holy Virgins (who are "holy spirits") and twelve unholy, Vexation (Λύπη), Wickedness etc.: "The servant of God that bears these names, though he shall

[2574] iv. 13—14 πᾶς ὁ πίνων...ὃς δ' ἂν πίῃ. Here πᾶς ὁ introduces the multitude of those that go wrong, ὃς δ' ἂν the individual that goes right. Comp. iii. 20 πᾶς γὰρ ὁ φαῦλα πράσσων... with iii. 21 ὁ δὲ ποιῶν τὴν ἀλήθειαν.

vi. 48—51 ἐγώ εἰμι ὁ ἄρτος τῆς ζωῆς...ἐγώ εἰμι ὁ ἄρτος ὁ ζῶν, is not variation but development—a good example of the way in which John leads the reader on from suggestion to statement. "The bread of life" like "the tree of life," is a comparatively simple phrase; but—after the analogy of "the water *of life*" and "*living* (i.e. running) water"—the Teacher passes on to say that the bread is *itself* "*living*," and that it is indeed the "*flesh*" of a living Man. This was a new doctrine for the Jews, though it is only an application to the spiritual world of a physical law—that life feeds on life.

[2575] In vii. 30 ἐζήτουν οὖν αὐτὸν πιάσαι καὶ οὐδεὶς ἐπέβαλεν ἐπ' αὐτὸν τὴν χεῖρα ὅτι οὔπω ἐληλύθει ἡ ὥρα αὐτοῦ, is there any explanation of the sing. χεῖρα here and the pl. χεῖρας in vii. 44 τινὲς δὲ ἤθελον ἐξ αὐτῶν πιάσαι αὐτόν, ἀλλ' οὐδεὶς ἔβαλεν ἐπ' αὐτὸν τὰς χεῖρας? It has been pointed out above (2135 foll.) that ἀλλά as compared with καί represents Greek idiom as compared with Hebrew. So does ἤθελον as compared with ἐζήτουν—which, though meaning in Attic Gk "desire to" (Steph.) before such verbs as πυθέσθαι, ἐκμαθεῖν, εἰδέναι, λαθεῖν, or other verbs expressing what one desires for *oneself*, does not seem to be used as in LXX (Ex. ii. 15, iv. 24, Esth. ii. 21, Ps. xxxvii. 32 etc.) in such phrases as "desire to *kill.*" Possibly, in the same way, χεῖρα may be explained as Hebraic and χεῖρας as Hellenic. At all events, in Esth. vi. 2, where the Heb. has "lay *hand*," the LXX has τὰς χεῖρας (comp. 1 K. xx. 6): and Eustathius (Steph. ἐπιβάλλω 1524 D) speaks of the phrase in the pl., τὸ χεῖρας

---

see the kingdom of God yet shall not *enter* therein," ταῦτα τὰ ὀνόματα ὁ φορῶν τοῦ θεοῦ δοῦλος τὴν βασιλείαν μὲν ὄψεται τοῦ θεοῦ εἰς αὐτὴν δὲ οὐκ εἰσελεύσεται, where the Latin has "spiritus" for ὀνόματα. Irenaeus (i. 13. 6 and i. 21. 1—5) shews that parodies of baptism were common among certain heretics promising a "redemption" or "restitution" that was to be compatible with the grossest immorality. For these reasons it became needful to insist that the "new birth" was not only "*new*" but also "*from above.*"

[2573 c] In addition to the facts adduced in 1903 as to Chrysostom's interpretation of ἄνωθεν it should be added that Cramer has τὸ δὲ ἄνωθεν ἐκ τοῦ οὐρανοῦ οὐ δηλοῖ in a context that indicates either (1) that οὐ δηλοῖ means "does not make clear," or (2) that final -ου in οὐρανοῦ has been repeated as οὐ.

ἐπέβαλε[1]. As to ἐπέβαλεν compared with ἔβαλεν, the latter is perhaps the less aggressive, and John indicates, in vii. 44, that those previously mentioned as longing to capture Jesus dared not now play the part of aggressors even in a minor degree.

[2576] In reply to Christ's words viii. 51 ἐάν τις τὸν ἐμὸν λόγον τηρήσῃ, θάνατον οὐ μὴ θεωρήσῃ εἰς τὸν αἰῶνα, the Jews say, viii. 52 σὺ λέγεις Ἐάν τις τὸν λόγον μου[2] τηρήσῃ, οὐ μὴ γεύσηται θανάτου εἰς τὸν αἰῶνα. "*Taste of death*" is an expression assigned to our Lord by all the Synoptists just before the Transfiguration, and it means *literal* death[3]. But "*behold death*" appears to refer to spiritual death, and perhaps contains an assumption that whatever one "beholds,"—whether it be the true glory of Goodness or the false glory of Satan—one is, as St Paul says, "conformed to it[4]." In what follows, Christ says about Abraham, "He saw it [*i.e.* my day] and rejoiced," *i.e.* he spiritually "saw" the joy of the day of the Messiah and was conformed to that joy so that he himself "rejoiced[5]." Our Lord elsewhere uses the word ἰδεῖν of "seeing the kingdom of God[6]." Here John uses θεωρεῖν—a word that sometimes (1598) means blank, unintelligent, or superstitious vision—perhaps, as being more appropriate to the view of the dark powers of spiritual death[7]. But the Aramaic phrase "*see death*"—as distinct from

---

[1] [2575 a] Aristophanes, however, has sing. in *Nub.* 933 τὴν χεῖρ' ἣν ἐπιβάλλῃς, *Lys.* 440 ταύτῃ τὴν χεῖρ' ἐπιβαλεῖς. Polybius has ἐ. χεῖρας with sing. subj. xviii. 34. 8, and with pl. subj. in iii. 2. 8, iii. 5. 5 : it means "lay sacrilegious hands on" in Lucian (*Tim.* 4, Vol. i. p. 107). Ἐ. χεῖρας occurs in Mk xiv. 46, Mt. xxvi. 50 (where Lk. xxii. 54 (nearly but not quite parall.) has συλλαβόντες), also in Lk. xx. 19 ἐζήτησαν...ἐπιβαλεῖν ἐπ' αὐτὸν τὰς χεῖρας, and Lk. xxi. 12 ἐπιβαλοῦσιν ἐφ' ὑμᾶς τ. χεῖρας αὐτῶν. Ἐπιβάλλω occurs only 4 times in Acts and alw. with τὰς χεῖρας. In 1 Esdr. ix. 20 ἐπέβαλον τὰς χεῖρας (Ezr. x. 19 ἔδωκαν χεῖρα αὐτῶν) means "they gave their hands as a pledge," but Steph. does not quote this or other instances ; and it is difficult to find any reason why Jn should use βαλεῖν χεῖρας here (a very rare constr. if one may judge from Steph. (βάλλω 90 B) who quotes nothing except Zenob. 5. 93 κάτω βαλὼν τὰς χεῖρας εἱστήκει). Possibly he meant "They dared not so much as *move* the hand against him."

[2] [2576 a] Τὸν λόγον μου is not quite so emphatic as τὸν ἐμὸν λόγον, which again is not so emphatic as ὁ λ. ὁ ἐμός would have been. In Jn, ὁ ἐμός occurs thrice, v. 47, vii. 16, viii. 51, whereas ὁ...ὁ ἐμός is much more frequent.

[3] [2576 b] Mk ix. 1, Mt. xvi. 28, Lk. ix. 27, comp. Heb. ii. 9.

[4] [2576 c] See 2 Cor. iii. 18 κατοπτριζόμενοι, Rom. xii. 2 συνσχηματίζεσθε... μεταμορφοῦσθε.   [5] viii. 56.   [6] iii. 3.

[7] [2576 d] This view is favoured by the fact that, when the "seeing" refers to "the kingdom of God" and to "life," Jn has iii. 3 οὐ δύναται ἰδεῖν, iii. 36 οὐκ ὄψεται ζωήν (not θεωρεῖν).

"*taste* death," and without any discrimination between different verbs of seeing—may have referred to Biblical usage, which sometimes attaches to "see" the meaning of "see for oneself," "have personal experience of," "realise[1]." The fact that both Peter and Paul are represented in the Acts as quoting Ps. xvi. 10, to shew that the Messiah was distinguished from David by "*not seeing the pit*," makes it probable that the phrase "*see death*" was variously applied, not without controversy, toward the end of the first century. John here teaches that "*not to behold death*" was a spiritual gift, extending, not only to Enoch, Elijah, and the Lord Jesus Christ, but to all Christ's true disciples. At the same time, he points out that *the Jews confused this with a phrase not used in O.T.*, "*tasting death*," *which they interpreted as referring to physical death.*

[2577] ix. 21—3 πῶς δὲ νῦν βλέπει οὐκ οἴδαμεν, ἢ τίς ἤνοιξεν αὐτοῦ τοὺς ὀφθ. ἡμεῖς οὐκ οἴδαμεν· αὐτὸν ἐρωτήσατε, ἡλικίαν ἔχει...διὰ τοῦτο.. εἶπαν ὅτι Ἡλικίαν ἔχει, αὐτὸν ἐπερωτήσατε (marg. ἐρωτήσατε). The difference between "we know not" and "*we* (ἡμεῖς) know not" is that the latter implies a more emphatic disavowal because the speakers, in the latter case, are more frightened: "But how he now sees we know not. *Or*, who opened his eyes, [if indeed some one opened his eyes]—*we* know nothing about it." In what follows, the fact that the evangelist puts the last words of the parents first in repeating their utterance is in conformity with the rule mentioned above (2552—3). But the change of ἐρωτήσατε to ἐπερωτήσατε is a remarkable concession to dramatic effect or impressionism. "In effect," John seems to say, "what the parents meant was, He is of age, *ask him, [not us, and ask him] as much as you like*[2]."

---

[1] [2576 *c*] See (Buhl 752—3) Is. xliv. 16 "I have *seen the fire*," Eccles. ix. 9 "*See life* with the wife whom thou lovest," Ps. lxxxix. 49 "...and shall not *see death*," Targ. "*see the angel of death*" (comp. Heb. xi. 5 "translated that he should not *see death*"), Ps. xvi. 10 "Neither wilt thou suffer thine holy one to *see corruption* (or, *the pit*)" (quoted in Acts ii. 27 foll. and xiii. 34 foll. as applying not to David but to Christ). In Esth. ix. 26 "that which they had *seen*," LXX has "suffered," πεπόνθασιν. Lk. ii. 26 has μὴ ἰδεῖν θάνατον and Rev. xviii. 7 πένθος οὐ μὴ ἴδω.

[2] [2577 *a*] There is much variety in the O.T. and N.T. use of ἐπερωτᾶν (**456** (ii) *a*). It occurs in Mk (25), Mt. (8), Lk. (17), Jn (2), namely, here and xviii. 7 πάλιν ἐπηρώτησεν, "*repeated his question again.*" The two instances indicate that in both Jn takes ἐπι- to mean "*further*," "*again.*" SS has here "*Lo, he also is of age; from him ye can know.* These things said...Therefore

[2578] In xiii. 33 (rep. from viii. 21) ὅπου ἐγὼ ὑπάγω ὑμεῖς οὐ δύνασθε ἐλθεῖν, which had been uttered to the Jews, the pronouns emphasize the opposition between "*I*" and "*ye*" ("Where *I* go *ye* cannot come")—as also in vii. 34, 36—but when Christ repeats this to Peter, xiii. 36 ὅπου ὑπάγω οὐ δύνασαί μοι νῦν ἀκολουθῆσαι, the pronouns are omitted so as to lay no stress upon personal antithesis but only on present time, "Where I go thou canst not follow me *at present*."

[2579] In xiv. 10—11 οὐ πιστεύεις ὅτι ἐγὼ ἐν τῷ π. καὶ ὁ π. ἐν ἐμοί ἐστιν; the position of ἐστιν at the end of the sentence marks it as emphatic—and all the more emphatic because the meaning would have been clear without it,—"Do ye not believe...that in me the Father *truly is*[1]?" In the repetition, πιστεύετέ μοι ὅτι ἐγὼ ἐν τῷ π. καὶ ὁ π. ἐν ἐμοί, the stress on "is" is dropped by the omission of ἐστιν in order to emphasize "*me*" ("Believe *me*"), and the sentence concludes, "But if [ye can] not [do this], believe *for the mere works' sake*"—thus omitting the whole of the object of "believe" in order to emphasize the cause of belief.

[2580] In xiv. 23—24 ἐάν τις ἀγαπᾷ με τὸν λόγον μου τηρήσει, compared with ὁ μὴ ἀγαπῶν με τοὺς λόγους μου οὐ τηρεῖ, ἐάν τις is more selective than ὁ μή (2552 *c*), and τὸν λόγον represents "the word" taken as a whole, the spirit of Christ's teaching, whereas τοὺς λόγους means the separate doctrines, "does not [even] keep [the letter of] my words." This is the only occasion where Christ in the Fourth Gospel uses the plural λόγοι[2].

[2581] In xv. 9—11 μείνατε ἐν τῇ ἀγάπῃ τῇ ἐμῇ...μενεῖτε ἐν τῇ ἀγάπῃ μου...καθὼς ἐγώ...καὶ μένω αὐτοῦ ἐν τῇ ἀγάπῃ...ἵνα ἡ χαρὰ ἡ ἐμὴ ἐν ὑμῖν ᾖ καὶ ἡ χαρὰ ὑμῶν πληρωθῇ, the phrase ἡ ἐμή emphasizes the "love" and the "joy" so that they are distinguished from the

---

said his parents, *Ask him*." In classical Gk ἐπερωτᾶν sometimes means "*ask in turn*," i.e. "ask after answering," as in Mk xi. 29 (where Mt.-Lk. have ἐρωτᾶν) but Steph. gives no instance where it clearly means "ask further."

[1] [2579 *a*] See Philo i. 267 in 2588 *c*, ὄντως γὰρ ὁ ἀληθινὸς οὗτός ἐστιν, where ἐστιν is similarly emphatic.

[2] [2580 *a*] In the Synoptists, besides other less important passages, λόγοι (Chri.) occurs in Mk xiii. 31, Mt. xxiv. 35, Lk. xxi. 33, "my words shall not pass away"; also in Mt. vii. 24—6 (*bis*) (parall. Lk. vi. 47) "whosoever therefore heareth these words of mine"; also in Mk viii. 38 (parall. Lk. ix. 26) "whosoever shall be ashamed of me and my words" (Mt. om.). Comp. 1 Jn ii. 4—5 where the sing. λόγος in a positive clause with τηρέω is contr. with the pl. ἐντολαί in a negative clause (μὴ τηρῶν) (2569 *a*).

ARRANGEMENT AND VARIATION [2583]

ordinary feelings so called—"the love that is peculiarly mine...the joy that is peculiarly mine"—indicating that a new *kind* of love has been brought into the world by the Son of God.

[2582] In xv. 21 ταῦτα πάντα ποιήσουσιν...ὅτι οὐκ οἴδασιν τὸν πέμψαντά με, and xvi. 3 ταῦτα ποιήσουσιν ὅτι οὐκ ἔγνωσαν τὸν πατέρα οὐδὲ ἐμέ, the exact meaning is hard to give without paraphrase, and is not given by R.V. "know not," "have not known." The first sentence says " They will persecute you, my followers, because they *know not* the nature of him that sent me." Then Jesus shews that this want of knowledge arose, not from intellectual but from moral fault, and lastly He repeats " They will persecute you, I say, because —not having in themselves the spirit of love, the spirit of fatherhood, the spirit of sonship—*they failed to recognise the Father and failed to recognise me,—his Son [when the Father sent the Son to them]*."

[2583] xvi. 14—15 ἐκ τοῦ ἐμοῦ λήμψεται...διὰ τοῦτο εἶπον ὅτι ἐκ τοῦ ἐμοῦ λαμβάνει is a remarkable instance of verbally inaccurate quotation. SS, and the Latin versions except *a*, read λήμψεται for λαμβάνει so as to make the quotation accurate[1]. After saying " He *will take* from what is mine," Jesus explains, that " mine " means "the Father's" because "all things as many as the Father hath *are* mine." Then, having passed into the *present*, while describing the ever present relations between the Father and the Son, He continues in the present tense when repeating what He had previously uttered about the relations between the Holy Spirit and the Son. Another case of variation in repeating occurs in xvi. 16—19 where Jesus says " ye behold me *no longer* (οὐκέτι)," but the disciples repeat it as " ye behold me *not* (οὐ)," and our Lord Himself, accepting their variation, says, " On this matter are ye questioning with one another because I said, A little while and ye behold me *not* (οὐ)!" Perhaps " no longer " was intended to suggest " no longer in the old familiar way, after the flesh." But the disciples, panic-stricken, fasten on the bare negative "not," and their Master adapts His reply to their fears, and accepts their version of His utterance[2].

---

[1] [2583 *a*] ℵ omits the whole of verse 15 (homoeotel.), *e* omits the last part of it (ὅτι ἐκ τ. ἐ. λ. κ. ἀναγγελεῖ) reading " propter hoc dixi vobis pusillum...," *d* has " accipiet " though D has λαμβάνει.

[2] [2583 *b*] In xvi. 16—19 *a*, *d*, *e*, *f* and SS have "non" throughout.

[2583 *c*] On other variations of Christ's sayings see **2545** foll., **2190**. And add ix. 7 ὕπαγε νίψαι εἰς τὴν κολυμβήθραν τοῦ Σ., repeated by the blind man thus, ix. 11 εἶπέν μοι ὅτι "Ὕπαγε εἰς τὸν Σ. καὶ νίψαι.

[2584] In xvii. 12 ὅτε ἤμην μετ' αὐτῶν ἐγὼ ἐτήρουν αὐτοὺς ἐν τῷ ὀνόματι...καὶ ἐφύλαξα, a difference is intended by the difference of verb and tense. Ἐτήρουν, "I was always watching, or keeping my eye on," implies the continually watchful care of the Lord during His incarnate life, on which He is supposed to be, by anticipation, looking back; ἐφύλαξα "I protected" (not "I have protected") implies action regarded simply as past. There is emphasis on "I" as distinct from the Father, "*I* could do it once, now I beseech *thee* to do it." Μετ' αὐτῶν (2349) implies friendly companionship: "As long as I was *side by side with them*," i.e. in the world—a phrase that is supplied by many authorities. On xi. 50 συμφέρει...ἵνα εἷς ἄνθρωπος ἀποθάνῃ, compared with xviii. 14 συμφέρει ἕνα ἄνθρωπον ἀποθανεῖν, see 2104[1].

[2585] xiii. 19 ἀπ' ἄρτι λέγω ὑμῖν πρὸ τοῦ γενέσθαι ἵνα πιστεύητε, ὅταν γένηται, ὅτι ἐγώ εἰμι (marg. ἐγώ εἰμί) is to be compared with

---

[1] [2584 *a*] Another instance of synonymous juxtaposition is in iii. 20, 21, ὁ φαῦλα πράσσων...ὁ ποιῶν τὴν ἀλήθειαν and v. 29 οἱ τὰ ἀγαθὰ ποιήσαντες...οἱ τὰ φαῦλα πράξαντες. In other passages of N.T. a distinction is recognised between these two verbs, and πράσσω—which means "do habitually," "do as a business" —is rather frequently connected with notions of evil: but 2 Cor. v. 10 πρὸς ἃ ἔπραξεν εἴτε ἀγαθὸν εἴτε φαῦλον, and many other passages, indicate that πράσσω may be applied to habitual action good or bad. We shall not find elsewhere in N.T. the thought implied here, that the word "*making*," or "*creating*," ποιέω, is appropriate to good, as distinct from πράσσω which does not imply *creation*.

[2584 *b*] iv. 46—53 presents synonyms that may bear on disputed tradition concerning the boy healed by our Lord at a distance. In Mt. viii. 6 he is called παῖς i.e. "*boy*," which may mean (in the phrase "thy *boy*") "son" or "servant." In Lk. vii. 2, he is called δοῦλος, "*slave*" or "servant." In Jn, the evangelist begins by saying "whose *son* (υἱός) was sick." The father then says, "Come down before my *little child* (παιδίον) dies." Jesus then says, "Thy *son* liveth." Then servants of the father "met him saying, 'Thy *boy* (παῖς) liveth.'" Thus, in Jn, three names are given to the child, all of them compatible with fact, and indicative of the manner in which a mistake might have arisen from mistaking παιδίον, or παῖς, for δοῦλος. See 1862 *a*—*c*.

[2584 *c*] On the synonymous juxtaposition of ἀγαπάω and φιλέω in xxi. 15—17, see 1436 foll., 1716 *d*—*f*, 1728 *m* foll. To the facts there alleged add Origen (on Lam. i. 2 LXX οὐχ ὑπάρχει ὁ παρακαλῶν αὐτὴν ἀπὸ πάντων τῶν ἀγαπώντων αὐτήν· πάντες οἱ φιλοῦντες αὐτὴν ἠθέτησαν ἐν αὐτῇ) οἰόμεθα γὰρ τὸ μὲν ἀγαπᾶν θειότερον εἶναι καί, ἵν' οὕτως εἴπω, πνευματικόν· τὸ δὲ φιλεῖν σωματικὸν καὶ ἀνθρωπικώτερον. No doubt the prophet writes according to the canon of Hebrew parallelism and draws little distinction between the two Hebrew verbs. But the second of the two is more correctly rendered by Aq. and Sym. ἑταῖροι "her *companions*," and Origen is justified by LXX usage in saying that "ἀγαπᾶν is the more divine and, so to speak, the more spiritual, but φιλεῖν is bodily and savours more of men."

xiv. 29 καὶ νῦν εἴρηκα ὑμῖν πρὶν γενέσθαι ἵνα, ὅταν γένηται, πιστεύσητε, and both may be compared with the tradition in Mark and Matthew, "*I have told you beforehand*[1]." The first saying refers to the betrayal by Judas, but this is regarded in the Last Discourse (xiii.—xiv.) as part of a general persecution, which is to befal the Church hereafter, all of which Christ predicts "*before it come to pass.*" The first saying is longer than the second and emphasizes the date ("from this moment") and the object of the prediction, "that ye may grow in the belief (2525—8) that I am [He][2]" (2221 foll.). The second emphasizes the time to come when the coincidence will be observed —between what will have "come to pass," and what was said before it "came to pass"—so as to cause a special belief based on this evidence.

[2586] xix. 8 ὅτε οὖν ἤκουσεν ὁ Π. τοῦτον τὸν λόγον μᾶλλον ἐφοβήθη may be compared with xix. 13 ὁ οὖν Π., ἀκούσας τῶν λόγων τούτων ἤγαγεν ἔξω τὸν Ἰ. In the former, the "hearing" does not produce (1614 *b*) any result beyond emotion; and the clause, being subordinate in thought, is introduced with a subordinate conjunction. In the latter, τούτων is emphasized by position (2553 *c*) and τ. λόγων τούτων by case (1614 *b*)—referring to the words "thou art not Cæsar's friend." This is a charge that Pilate cannot hear unmoved. Now therefore he is goaded to action, and the sentence introduces the action as the consequence, ὁ οὖν Π...ἤγαγεν[3].

---

[1] [2585 *a*] Mk xiii. 23 προείρηκα ὑμῖν πάντα, Mt. xxiv. 25 ἰδοὺ προείρηκα ὑμῖν, following a mention of "false Christs," who would lead astray "if possible, even the elect." All this Lk. omits. A little above, Mk xiii. 6, Mt. xxiv. 5, Lk. xxi. 8, predict the coming of those who will say "I am [He]" or "I am the Christ": and Mk-Mt. (but not Lk.) add "they will lead many astray."

[2] [2585 *b*] The phrase "I am [He]" appears to connect this Johannine tradition directly with Mk xiii. 6 and parall. mentioned above, and hence indirectly with Mk xiii. 23 "I have told you beforehand."

[3] [2586 *a*] On the following minor points there is perh. not evidence enough to establish any conclusion. Εἰς, in Jn, is regularly followed by ἐκ but the Gk mss. omit ἐκ in xix. 34 ἐ. τ. στρατιωτῶν, (*a, e, f* "unus *ex*") and W.H. (following BL) omit it in xii. 4. The great likeness of ειc to εκ in some mss. (*e.g.* D) increases the uncertainty. But in xii. 49 ἐξ ἐμαυτοῦ...ἐλάλησα—as compared with λαλεῖν ἀπὸ ἐμαυτοῦ (or, ἑαυτοῦ) in vii. 17, 18, xiv. 10, xvi. 13—perhaps indicates a more emphatic statement, made at the end of Christ's public teaching, that He did not speak "*out of*" His own treasure but from that which the Father gave Him.

[2586 *b*] According to W.H., Mary Magdalene is called Μαρία in xix. 25, xx. 1, 11, but Μαριάμ in xx. 16, 18. According to Tischendorf, it should be Μαριάμ throughout. If W.H. are correct, the explanation suggests itself that

[2586] ARRANGEMENT AND VARIATION

Μαρία was used in evangelistic narrative up to the point where Jesus called her by her Aramaic name xx. 16 "Mary (Μαριάμ)," and that here, and in the subsequent xx. 18, the Aramaic form was retained.

[2586 c] In xi. 11—12 κεκοίμηται—εἰ κεκοίμηται σωθήσεται, SS has "*is lying down...sleepeth,*" a "*obdormit...dormit,*" b, e, f "*dormit...dormit*" (agreeing with D κοιμᾶται...κοιμᾶται, but d has "*dormivit...dormit*"). Nonnus has εὕδει... κνώσσει. Perhaps the desire to explain the alleged misunderstanding of the disciples caused some translators to represent the disciples as using a different word from Christ's when repeating what He had said. On the other hand an ancient comment (Cramer on xi. 7) boldly asserts "They did not really think it was sleep, but supposed Him to be talking in a dark saying (αἰνίγματι)." The writer declares, not without force, that it would be senseless for the disciples to suppose that their Master would go "fifteen furlongs (sic)" to wake the sleeping man. Cramer (Vol. ii. 316) prints, as from Origen, an explanation suggesting that Thomas supposed the Lord to mean that He was "going down to the place of the [departed] souls (καταβάντος εἰς τὸ τῶν ψυχῶν χωρίον)" to wake Lazarus, and that hence the disciple desired to die with his Master.

[2586 d] In x. 28—9 οὐχ ἁρπάσει τις...οὐδεὶς δύναται ἁρπάζειν, is any difference intended by the variation of οὐ...τις and οὐδείς? The former, in (1) LXX and (2) N.T., means "not a single man." (1) In LXX, οὐκ ἄνθρωπος, or ἄνθρ. οὔ, = "not any one," Heb. "*not a man,*" or "*man not,*" in Josh. i. 5, Ezek. vii. 13 etc. Τις, "any," often = Heb. "man" in the phrase "*if* a man," but never (Oxf. Conc.) in "*not* a man." In 2 S. xix. 22 "shall [any] man die...?," οὐ θανατωθήσεταί τις ἀνήρ, and in Sir. x. 24 οὐκ ἔστιν αὐτῶν τις, the Gk seems to mean "*not a single one.*" Οὐ...τι seems to mean "*not a single thing*" in LXX (where there is no corresponding Heb.) in Job xxxv. 15 οὐκ ἔγνω παράπτωμά τι, Prov. xv. 23 οὐδὲ μὴ εἴπῃ καιριόν τι, Wisd. xi. 24 οὐδὲ γὰρ ἂν μισῶν τι κατεσκεύασας (comp. Judith ii. 13 οὐ παραβήσῃ ἕν τι). (2) In N.T., τις, τι etc., after οὐ or μή, appear to be emphatic in Mk iv. 22 marg., Mt. viii. 28, xi. 27 οὐδεὶς...οὐδὲ...τις, xii. 19, xxii. 46 οὐδεὶς ἐδύνατο...οὐδὲ ἐτόλμησέν τις, Lk. xi. 36 etc. In Mk v. 37 οὐκ ἀφῆκεν οὐδένα the parall. Lk. viii. 51 has οὐκ ἀφῆκεν...τινά (al. οὐδένα). It is very emphatic in 1 Cor. ii. 2, iv. 5, 1 Thess. ii. 9, 2 Thess. iii. 8, 1 Pet. iv. 15 etc. In 2 Pet. iii. 9 μὴ βουλόμενός τινας ἀπολέσθαι ἀλλὰ πάντας...χωρῆσαι shews an exceptional use of the pl. Perhaps the writer means "not desiring that some should perish [while others are saved] but that all should come to repentance."

[2586 e] In Mt. xi. 27, xxii. 46 οὐδὲ...τις is stronger than the *preceding* οὐδείς. Here (x. 28—9) it is stronger than the *following* οὐδείς. The question is at first about "snatching" from the Son, and it is said, emphatically, that "*not any*" can snatch from the Son. Afterwards, when "snatching" from the Father is spoken of, stress is laid, not on "anyone," but on the *notion of "snatching"*:— "*there is no such thing as snatching* from Him,"—where it is better (2767) to read οὐδεὶς ἁρπάζει with Origen; but in any case, the *verb*, not the *pronoun*, is emphatic. If John had wished to emphasize the pronoun he might have used (2257) οὔ... οὐδείς.

CHAPTER II

REPETITION

§ 1. *The nature of Johannine repetition*

[2587] Johannine repetition may be roughly classified as (1) word-repetition, (2) phrase-repetition. In (1), the repetition follows closely in the context, e.g. "*confessed* and denied not and *confessed*." In (2), it is sometimes of the nature of a refrain, as in "A little while and ye shall see me," "Feed my sheep," "All that thou hast given me" etc. Repetition may, or may not, be accompanied with variation of order, such as we find in one of the prayers before sleep in the Jewish Prayer Book: "Behold, He that guardeth Israel will neither slumber nor sleep." This is "*to be said three times*" apparently without variation. But the next sentence is varied thrice, as follows:—"For thy salvation I hope, O Lord. I hope, O Lord, for thy salvation. O Lord, for thy salvation I hope (*to be said three times*)[1]." Few or none of the Johannine variations will be found to present any ambiguity; but they are of importance as illustrating the deliberate and poetic arrangement of large parts of the Fourth Gospel and the weight and mystical meaning attached by the author to certain utterances, and indicated by him in twofold, threefold, and sevenfold repetition.

---

[1] [2587 a] Jewish Prayer Book, transl. by Rev. S. Singer p. 296. In the Confession on a Death-bed (p. 317) "The Lord reigneth; the Lord hath reigned; the Lord shall reign for ever and ever" is to be said three times, and so is "Blessed be His name, whose glorious kingdom is for ever and ever." But "the Lord He is God" is to be said seven times. Presumably, and appropriately, there is to be only one utterance of the final confession of the unity of God: "Hear, O Israel: the Lord our God, the Lord is one." But even here the bald truth might have been expressed by "The Lord our God is one," and the addition of "the Lord" suggests a "threefold effect" like that in the first sentence of the Fourth Gospel.

§ 2. *Jewish canons of repetition*

[2588] Jesus is represented as saying to the Jews "Yea even in your own law it is written that the witness of two men is true." The passage referred to says, "At the mouth of two witnesses or at the mouth of three witnesses shall a matter be established[1]." This would naturally lead to a discussion as to the matters for which, severally, the witnesses should be "two" or "three." Philo says (i. 243) "A holy matter (ἅγιον πρᾶγμα) is approved (δοκιμάζεται) through three witnesses (διὰ τριῶν μαρτύρων)." Commenting on the words of the Psalmist "The Lord spake once, *twice* I have also heard this," he connects terrestrial "hearing" with the imperfect "*duad*[2]." Elsewhere he explains the idiomatic Hebrew reduplications of nouns and verbs as indicating a twofold application to body and to spirit[3]. Scripture, he asserts, never sets down a superfluous word, and never commits "tautology—the worst kind of verbosity[4]."

[2589] In Rabbinical literature we find much allusion to twofold but not much to threefold witness. Philo is fuller on the latter: We must not, he says, delight in casual witness, but must believe that the [Supreme] God is very near us: "For there is no need, says the sacred writer (Deut. xxx. 12), to go away to heaven, nor yet to travel across sea, in search of the Good: for it is near and close to each. And he divides it [*i.e.* the Good] *threefold*—most naturally,

---

[1] [2588 a] Deut. xix. 15, referred to in Jn viii. 17. Westc. says, "The exact form used here is found in St John of the old Scriptures only in this place (compare xx. 31). It is the common form of citation in other books. St John elsewhere uses the resolved form (γεγραμμένον ἐστίν), which is read here by *Cod. Sin.*" Apparently γέγραπται ὅτι is here used to introduce the substance of a quotation not given exactly. It would be absurd to take "*is true*" ("the witness of two men *is true*") as meaning anything more than "*is to be regarded as true.*"

[2] [2588 b] Philo i. 284—5, on Ps. lxii. 11 and lxxv. 8. Ps. lxii. 11 is quoted by *Nedarim* iii. 2 (Schwab viii. 179) to explain the apparent contradictions of the Law; and the Targ. has "God spake *one law*...we *heard it twice* from Moses."

[3] [2588 c] See Philo i. 63 (on Gen. ii. 16 "eating thou mayest eat") and i. 129 (Gen. xxii. 17 "Blessing I will bless") and i. 554 (Ex. xxi. 12 "let him die the death"). On Lev. xviii. 6 (lit. and LXX) "man man shall not approach" Philo says (i. 267) "His saying '*man, man,*' not once but twice, is a sign that the meaning is not the [man] of [mere] body and soul but the [man] of virtue. For this is really the true [man] (μὴ τὸν ἐκ σώματος κ. ψυχῆς ἀλλὰ τὸν ἀρετῇ κεχρημένον δηλοῦσθαι. "Ὄντως γὰρ ὁ ἀληθινὸς οὗτός ἐστιν)."

[4] [2588 d] Philo i. 529 οὐ μακρολογίας τὸ φαυλότατον εἶδος ταυτολογίαν ἐπιτετήδευκε.

'For,' says he, 'it is in thy mouth and in thy heart and in thy hands,' that is, in speech, purpose, and act[1]." Then, after quoting, from Deuteronomy, "Ask thy father, and he shall declare unto thee," he protests that no human "father" can describe the immemorial past, but the "father" must mean "the Right Logos[2]." Afterwards comes the conclusion, "Now a holy matter is approved through three witnesses[3]," where there seems to be an underlying assumption that, since the nature of the highest Good is threefold, the nature of the testimony to the highest truth, and to that which is "holy," must also be threefold[4].

[2590] As regards twofold repetition Philo says that there are "two divine Words (Verba), one, the pillar and support of the world of reason, the other of the world of sense...two Reasons (Rationes) of the twofold Universe, shewing forth foreordained and fixed event, that is to say, the harmonious connexion of all things[5]," and this harmonizes with a mystical view found in Jewish Midrash that "*two words*," when found together in Scripture, denote a twofold fulfilment—"in the kingdom above" and "in the kingdom below[6]."

---

[1] Philo i. 241.
[2] Philo i. 242, quoting Deut. xxxii. 7.
[3] Philo i. 243.
[4] Comp. Philo ii. 19—20 on "the three strangers" seen by Abraham (Gen. xviii. 1 foll.) and (i. 657) on Jacob's pillar as representing a threefold recognition of God.
[5] Philo (*P.A.* 510) (transl.) on Ex. xxv. 11—14.
[6] [2590 a] Thus Schöttg. (ii. 67) quotes *Bammidbar r.* xv. f. 230. 1 as connecting Is. lxii. 10, lvii. 14 "*sternite, sternite, viam*" with Ezek. xi. 19, as implying (1) a "clearing away" of the "stones" by men, and (2) an "eradicating" of the "stony heart" by the Messiah. *Ib.* ii. 71 quotes *Vajikra r.* x. f. 153. 3 "Dixit Deus S. B. ad Iesaiam: 'Omnes prophetae proferunt vaticinia simplicia, tu autem consolationes duplices,'" in support of which are alleged Is. xl. 1 "*Comfort ye, comfort ye*," li. 9 "*Awake, awake*," li. 12 "*I, I,* am he that comforteth you," li. 17 "*Arouse thyself, arouse thyself*," lxi. 10 "*Rejoicing I will rejoice.*"

[2590 b] It is interesting to note how Onkelos (followed by Jer.) deals with the repetition in Ex. xv. 16, which is really nothing but poetic repetition for emphasis: "Until thy people, O Lord, *pass over* [*Arnon*], until thy people whom thou hast redeemed *pass over* [*Jordan*]." All Jewish commentators of the first and second century would agree with Philo that no word of Scripture is "tautological." But they would defend it against the charge of tautology in different ways. Non-mystical writers would try to supply references to two distinct historical events; mystical writers would explain by reference to "the kingdom above" and "the kingdom below."

[2590 c] *Hor. Heb.* (i. 84) quotes (from *Menachoth* ch. x. and *Tosapht.* ibid.) a

St Paul assumes that the Corinthians are familiar with the Deuteronomic saying above quoted—when he says, "This is the *third* time that I am coming to you. At the mouth of *two* witnesses or *three* shall every word be established[1]"—and his Scriptural illustrations of the doctrine about "the second man," who is "of heaven[2]," indicate that Jewish canons of sacred writing would very soon influence writers, and especially mystical writers, of Gospels intended largely for Greeks

§ 3. *Repetition through negation*

[2591] The Fourth Gospel shews traces of another Jewish canon, of which little or no mention seems to have been made by Philo,—namely, that a full statement includes the negative as well as the positive aspect of a fact. Expressions on which it might be based are frequent in O.T., such as "I shall *not* die but live," "The dead praise *not* the Lord…but we will bless the Lord that live," "*Not* unto us, O Lord, but unto thy name," "*Not* their own arm but thy right hand"—all of which are in the Psalms[3]. It does not appear to have been formulated in early Jewish literature; and the principal authority for it is the work *Sohar*, known to be of late origin as a whole but generally acknowledged to contain elements of great

---

quaint tradition combining the "twice" and the "thrice," apparently because the "twice" denoted certainty and the "thrice" certainty about a holy matter (i. 84): "The sheaf of first-fruits was reaped from the Ashes-valley of the brook Kedron. The first day of the feast of the Passover, certain persons, deputed from the Sanhedrim, went forth into that valley…And the reason of the pomp was… because the Baithuseans, or Sadducees, did not think well of doing that action on that day: therefore, that they might cross that crossing opinion, they performed the business with as much show as could be. 'When it was now even, he on whom the office of reaping lay, saith, "The sun is set"; and they answered, "Well."—"The sun is set"; and they answered, "Well."—"With this reaping-hook"; and they answered, "Well."—"With this reaping-hook"; and they answered, "Well."—"In this basket"; and they answered, "Well."—"In this basket"; and they answered, "Well."—If it were the sabbath, he said, "On this sabbath"; and they answered, "Well."—"On this sabbath"; and they answered, "Well."—"I will reap"; and they answered, "Reap."—"I will reap"; and they answered "Reap." This he said *thrice*; and they answered *thrice*, "Well."'"

[1] 2 Cor. xiii. 1.

[2] 1 Cor. xv. 45—7 "*So also it is written*, The first man Adam became a living soul, the last Adam [became] a life-giving spirit.… The second man is of heaven." The amount of quotation in this passage is not clear.

[3] Ps. cxviii. 17, cxv. 17—18, cxv. 1, xliv. 3.

antiquity. Expressed in the words of Grätz[1], who does not err on the side of exaggerating the importance of *Sohar*, the canon is as follows: "All laws of the Torah are to be considered as parts and constituents of a higher world; they resolve themselves into the mysteries of the masculine and feminine principle (positive and negative). Only when both parts meet together does the higher unity arise."

§ 4. *Repetition in the Synoptists*

[2592] The Synoptic Gospels contain but few repetitions. These are mostly in traditions peculiar to one or two writers, and of a very different character from those of the Fourth Gospel. For example, "If thy hand cause thee to stumble," repeated thrice by Mark with the substitution of "foot" and "eye" for "hand"—a tradition condensed by Matthew and omitted by Luke—is manifestly of a concrete and non-mystical character[2]. Non-mystical also, and manifestly rhetorical, are the repetitions of "A greater than Solomon is here" (varied as "A greater than Jonah is here"), "Woe unto you, scribes and Pharisees, hypocrites," "Ye have heard that it hath been said to them of old time," "Thy Father, who seeth in secret, shall reward thee" etc.[3] Emotional repetition of a single word, such as that of Isaiah quoted above (**2590** *a*), is found in Christ's lamentation over the Holy City ("Jerusalem, Jerusalem")[4]: but the Fourth

---

[1] *History of the Jews*, Eng. Transl. iv. 16.

[2] Mk ix. 43—7, Mt. xviii. 8—9.

[3] Mt. xii. 41—2, Lk. xi. 31—2, Mt. xxiii. 14—29, Mt. v. 21, 33, Mt. vi. 4, 6, 18.

[4] [**2592** *a*] Mt. xxiii. 37, Lk. xiii. 34. On the other hand, a mystical meaning is perhaps assumed by the editors or scribes of some early MSS. and versions of N.T. which represent Jesus as saying, "*Young man, young man*," "*Maiden, maiden*," "*Lazarus, Lazarus*." Aphraates says (*Hom.* viii. 6) "By *two words* He raised up each of them"; and "the former is this resurrection, the latter is the future resurrection." Comp. *Beresh. R.* (Wunsche p. 268) on Gen. xxii. 11 "*Abraham, Abraham*," where the reduplication is explained by one Rabbi as indicative of "love and encouragement" but by another thus: "God desired thereby to say to him that it should extend *to him and to his posterity* for merit (es werde ihm und der Nachwelt zum Verdienste (Ruhme) gereichen). There is no generation in which there is not one like Abraham or Jacob (Gen. xlvi. 2 '*Jacob, Jacob*') or Moses (Ex. iii. 4 '*Moses, Moses*') or Samuel (1 S. iii. 10 '*Samuel, Samuel*')." In Ps. xc. 17 (lit.) "and the work of our hands establish thou upon us *and* (R.V. *yea,) the work of our hands establish thou*," the reduplication is omitted by Targ. and by LXX (and the whole is mistransl. by Syr.), but it follows xc. 16 "let thy work appear unto thy servants and thy glory upon *their children*," so that the second clause might well be taken as referring to posterity.

[2593] REPETITION

Gospel contains nothing of this kind. Perhaps the nearest Synoptic approximation to Johannine repetition is in Mark's version of the Rich Ruler, where the words "How hardly shall they that have riches enter into the kingdom of God" are followed by "Children, how hard it is to enter into the kingdom of God[1]"—a repetition that is omitted by the parallel Matthew and Luke. Others might be mentioned, but few or none like those in the Fourth Gospel as will appear later on.

[2593] Repetition by negation in the Synoptists is more frequent comparatively in Mark than in Matthew, and in Matthew than in Luke. Mark alone inserts the negative clauses in "Receiveth *not me* but him that sent me" and "With men it is impossible *but not with God*[2]," and the positive clauses in "Is not able to stand *but hath an end*" and "Hath not forgiveness...*but is liable* to condemnation[3]." Also, where Mark and Matthew write "Have no root...*but believe for a season*," Luke changes the construction so as to avoid οὐκ...ἀλλά[4], and many passages containing this construction are altogether omitted by him or given differently, *e.g.* "The Son of man came *not* to be ministered unto *but* to minister[5]." Where Mark and Matthew say that those who shall be raised from the dead "do *not* marry...*but* are as angels," Luke has "do not marry...for neither can they die any longer, for they are angel-like[6]," and this and other passages indicate that he, or the documents that he followed, sometimes eschewed the construction that abounds in Mark's and Matthew's versions of Christ's words, "*not* this *but* that[7]." But the three Synoptists agree in retaining οὐκ...ἀλλά in the sayings "*Not* they that are whole...*but* they that are sick," "*Not* the righteous *but* sinners," "She is *not* dead *but* sleepeth," "*Not* so with you,

---

[1] Mk x. 23—4.

[2] Mk ix. 37 as comp. with Mt. x. 40, Lk. ix. 48, also Mk x. 27, Mt. xix. 26, Lk. xviii. 27.

[3] Mk iii. 26, Mt. xii. 26, Lk. xi. 18, also Mk iii. 29, Mt. xii. 32, Lk. xii. 10.

[4] Mk iv. 17, Mt. xiii. 21; Lk. viii. 13 οἵ instead of ἀλλά.

[5] Mk x. 45, Mt. xx. 28; Lk. xxii. 27 "But I am in the midst of you as he that serveth."

[6] Mk xii. 25, Mt. xxii. 30, Lk. xx. 35—6.

[7] [2593 a] In Christ's words, besides the passages above quoted or referred to, Mk alone has οὐκ (or μή)...ἀλλά in vi. 9, vii. 19, xi. 23, xiii. 11 a, xiii. 20; Mk-Mt. alone in Mk x. 8 and Mt. xix. 6, Mk x. 40 and Mt. xx. 23, Mk xiii. 11 b, Mt. x. 20. In Mk vii. 15, Mt. xv. 11 and Mk viii. 33, Mt. xvi. 23, Lk. is wanting.

but...," "God is *not* God of the dead *but* of the living," "*Not* my will...*but* thine[1]." The evidence tends to shew that our Lord frequently used this form of speech in His doctrine, and that His usage, in this respect, is better represented by Mark than by Luke.

§ 5. *The Johannine Prologue*

[2594] Before giving a list of Johannine repetitions, twofold, threefold, and sevenfold, it will be convenient to touch on the first six verses of the Gospel from the point of view of the "canon of repetition," including also the "canon of negation" above mentioned (2591), and adding a few remarks on the context. The first sentence, for example, contains three statements about "the Word." Schöttgen tells us that "when one word in the sacred text is twice or thrice repeated, then the Cabbalists multiply that event and make many persons or events out of one[2]." Doubtless it would be an anachronism (as well as a fault of judgment) to impute to John such fancies as these. Yet it is probable that he followed Jewish tradition as well as prophetic inspiration in his three repetitions of "the Word," implying a threefold aspect, first, the Word in itself, and then the Word in two other aspects: "In the beginning was the Word, and the Word was with the Divine Being[3], and Divine Being was the Word." The three relations of the Logos are then summed up thus: "This [*i.e.* the Word conceived as above] was in the

---

[1] [2593 *b*] See the parall. to Mk ii. 17, v. 39, x. 43, xii. 27, xiv. 36. In Mk i. 44 (Mt. sim.) Lk. v. 14 changes μηδενὶ μηδὲν εἴπῃς to παρήγγειλεν...μηδενὶ εἰπεῖν so as to exclude the negative portion of μή...ἀλλά from Oratio Recta.

[2593 *c*] In the Sermon on the Mount, οὐκ...ἀλλά occurs in Mt. v. 17, 39, vi. 13 ("Lead us *not*...*but* deliver us from evil"), vi. 18, vii. 21 : but Lk. omits either the phrase, or the phrase and its context. In Mt. xviii. 22, Lk. omits the phrase.

[2593 *d*] A curious exception to Synoptic usage occurs in Mk iv. 21 μήτι...ἤ... οὐχ ἵνα...; where Mt. v. 15 and Lk. viii. 16, xi. 33 have ἀλλά after a negative. In Mk ii. 22, W. H. bracket the ἀλλά-clause, giving it unbracketed in parall. Mt. Lk.

[2] ii. 361.

[3] [2594 *a*] "With the Divine Being," πρὸς τὸν θεόν. The author might have written πρὸς θεόν here as in i. 6 he has παρὰ θεοῦ, and in xiii. 3 ἀπὸ θεοῦ. But he apparently wishes (as does Philo i. 655) to call attention to the distinction between θεός and ὁ θεός. In the last clause, "the Word" though it comes last (as in Gk) is subject, and we should express it more naturally in English by "the Word was Divine Being." This is stronger than saying "the Word was divine (θεῖος)." It means that the Word must be regarded as "*God*," but never apart from the relationship described as "being with, or towards, *the* [*one*] *God*."

beginning with the Divine Being," a summary that is not tautological; for it teaches us that *the three propositions about the Logos were all true "in the beginning."*

[2595] There follows a sentence in chiasmus, which also contains a negation: "All things through him[1] came into being; and without him came into being not even one [thing]." From the logical point of view the second clause is superfluous; but it is suggestive of the possibility that a thing *might* be "*without him*," i.e. apart from the Word, apart from law, order, and harmony. Grant that "all things came into being" through the Word, does it follow that they may not fall away so as to be "without him"? This phrase prepares the way for the subsequent mention of "darkness" (which is "without the light"). Moreover the sentence, beginning with "all" and ending with "one," suggests (though it does not state) that "without" the Logos or Word, there is no oneness or unity.

[2596] The writer began by three propositions about the Word, telling us first what the Word was "*in*" ("*in* the beginning"). Now he calls our attention to *that which is* "*in*" the Word—first defining it as "life," and then stating two facts about it:—i. 4 "That which *hath come into being*[2] in Him was life, and the life was the light of men; and the light in the darkness shineth and the darkness apprehended it not." But in these three propositions the same subject is not repeated (as it was above, "the Word"). The construction goes forward step by step, the predicate in one clause being repeated as the subject of the next, so as to suggest cause and effect[3]. Moreover, whereas the first verse contained one tense ($\mathring{\eta}\nu$) thrice repeated, this contains three predicative tenses ($\mathring{\eta}\nu$, $\phi a i \nu \epsilon \iota$, and $\kappa a \tau \epsilon \lambda a \beta \epsilon \nu$) suggesting that we have passed from the Eternal "was" into the conditions of change and time. We have also been brought down from "God" to "men." Immediately after the mention of "men" there has come a mention of "darkness" as that in which "the light

---

[1] [2595 a] $\Delta \iota'$ $a\mathring{v}\tau o\hat{v}$, "through him" or "through it." It is most unfortunate that English does not allow us to retain the deliberate ambiguity of the Gk, which gradually prepares the way for the revelation of the Logos or Word, as a Son.

[2] [2596 a] On $\gamma \epsilon \gamma o \nu \epsilon \nu$ see **2478**. It seems to imply that although "all things *came into being*" (aorist) through the Word, yet not "all things" retain the state, so to speak, of "*having come into being*" thus. Only that which retains the state is "life."

[3] [2596 b] Comp. Rom. v. 4—5 "tribulation worketh patience, and patience experience, and experience hope, and hope maketh not ashamed."

[of men] shineth." Last comes a negation, discussed elsewhere (**1735** *e*—*g*), "the darkness apprehended not" the light. This—whether it means "did not overcome" or "did not apprehend" or both—apparently implies something suggestive of failure or conflict.

[2597] After "men" comes mention of "a man," i. 6 "There came into being a man (ἐγένετο ἄνθρωπος) sent from God, his name [was] John." The writer could have said simply, "A man named John was sent by God" or "God sent a man named John." But he apparently wishes to draw a distinction between "*was*" above ("In the beginning *was* the Word") and "came into being" here ("*there came into being* a man"). Perhaps, too, he wishes to suggest a distinction between "the Word *was with God*" and "a man *sent from God.*" Next follows a statement that this man "came to be a witness," which might have been briefly and naturally expressed by saying simply that he "came to be a witness about the light." But this Gospel, in accordance with the canon of twofold repetition, throws the statement into what may be called two "witness-clauses": "This [man] came [*to be*] *for a witness, that he might bear witness* about the light, that all might believe through it (**2302**—**4**)." Then, in accordance with the canon of negation, the fact is restated after a negative: "He was *not* the light, *but* [he came, or, it was ordained (**2063**, **2105** foll.)] in order that he might bear witness concerning the light."

§ 6. *Johannine repetition through negation*

[2598] This is very frequent both in narrative and in words of Christ. In i. 20 "and confessed and *denied not and* (A.V. but) *confessed*," the negative (οὐ) is followed by "*and*" (instead of "*but* (ἀλλά),*" which is almost invariably used). Very frequently the negation means "*not* of man," or "*not* of this or that lower kind," or "*not* evil"; and the affirmation means "*but* of God," or "*but* of a higher kind" or "*but* good," *e.g.* i. 13 "*not*...*nor yet* from the will of man, *but* from God," iii. 16 "should *not* perish *but* should have life eternal," iii. 17 "for God sent *not* his Son...that he should judge the world *but* that the world through him should be saved," v. 24 "Cometh *not* into judgment, *but* hath passed from death into life," v. 30 "I seek *not* mine own will, *but* the will of him that sent me[1]."

---

[1] It is comparatively seldom that οὐκ...ἀλλά introduces evil as in iii. 36 "shall *not* see life *but* the wrath of God abideth on him." But the negation of the good follows the good, without οὐκ...ἀλλά, in xiv. 23—4 "If any one loveth me he will keep my word...*he that loveth me not keepeth not my words.*"

[2599] Instances of repetition with μή are less frequent. The μή clause comes second in iii. 18 "*He that believeth in him is not [to be] judged. He that believeth not* (ὁ μὴ π.) *hath been judged already*"; v. 23 "that all *may honour the Son* even as *they honour the Father. He that honoureth not the Son honoureth not the Father*, who sent him"; xiv. 23—4 "*If any one love me he will keep my word...he that loveth me not keepeth not my words.*" The μή clause comes first in x. 1—2 "*He that entereth not through the door...*is a thief and a robber, *but he that entereth through the door* is shepherd of the sheep," xv. 2 "*Every branch in me that beareth not* (μὴ φέρον) *fruit* he taketh it away, and *every [branch] that beareth fruit* he cleanseth it."

[2600] There is no special ambiguity arising out of these constructions or out of John's general use of the negative. But it is worth noting that οὐ occurs in his Gospel almost as often as in Mark and Luke taken together. And we may often perceive how the negation leads the reader towards an affirmation in a very suggestive and stimulating way, as when our Lord says, "I have *not* come from myself," "I am *not* alone," "I speak *not* from myself," "I seek *not* mine own glory," and "I will *not* leave you orphans[1]," preparing the way for some positive doctrine. The negative, however, is not often thus used in communicating the highest kind of truth. After stating that the Baptist came to bear witness about the light, the evangelist proceeds, " He was *not* the light"; and his description of the "witness" is as follows: "And this is the witness...And he confessed and denied not and confessed, ' I am *not* the Christ'"—the two subsequent answers being also negative ("I am *not*," "*No*")[2]. Then, and not till then, follows the positive testimony. The writer perhaps feels that divine teaching is often a "dark saying" misunderstood for a time, and that the interpreter must explain by negatives, "*not* this *but* that." At all events the last saying of Jesus recorded in this Gospel affords an instance of a "not...but" correcting a misunderstanding : " But Jesus said *not* unto him that he was not to die, *but*...[3]."

§ 7. *Twofold repetition in the Baptist's teaching*

[2601] The teaching of the Baptist, being rudimentary, contains, as might be expected, several instances of twofold repetition. First

---

[1] vii. 28, viii. 16, xii. 49, viii. 50, xiv. 18.
[2] i. 20—21.   [3] xxi. 23.

the evangelist speaks, i. 7—8 "John...came for witness *that he might witness concerning the light*...he was not the light, but [came] *that he might witness concerning the light.*" Then the Baptist (probably, **1927**) speaks, i. 15 (W.H. marg.) "*This was he* (lit.) *that* (ὅν) *I said,*" repeated with variation in i. 30 "*This is he in behalf of whom* (ὑπὲρ οὗ) *I said*[1]." The participial clause "*he that cometh after me*" is also repeated twice[2]. So is the difficult sentence, "*He is become before me because he was first in respect of me*[3]." The mission to "*baptize in water*" is also twice stated as a preparation for something higher[4].

[2602] The words, "*Behold, [here is] the lamb of God*" are twice repeated; first, without mention of any particular hearers, "*Behold, [here is] the lamb of God that taketh away the sin of the world,*" then, in the presence of two of John's disciples, "*Behold, [here is] the lamb of God*[5]." The descent of the Spirit is twice attested, "*I have beheld,*" "*I have seen*"; but it is also predicted by God Himself ("Upon whomsoever *thou shalt see* the Spirit descending"), so that it gives the impression of being twice attested on earth and once from heaven, being one of those "holy things" described by Philo as "approved by three witnesses." Strictly speaking, the

---

[1] [2601 a] See **2369**ᶜ—**71**. The repetitions in the context—i. 14 "We beheld his *glory, glory* as of [the] only begotten," and "full of *grace and truth*" followed by i. 17 "*the grace and the truth*"—probably spring unconsciously from a writer reflecting on the way in which the "glory" of heaven is seen in the "glory" on earth, and in which "the grace and the truth" that were latent in the law of Moses were revealed in the person of the Messiah. See also **2718—22**.

[2] [2601 b] i. 15 ὁ ὀπίσω μου ἐρχόμενος. In i. 26, W.H. have ὀπίσω μου ἐρχόμενος (with Bא¹) without the article; SS has "he that cometh," Origen varies. The testimony of B as to ο following ε is sometimes untrustworthy. In i. 30 ὀπίσω μου ἔρχεται, the vb is indicative.

[3] i. 15, 30, see **1896—1900** and **2665—7**.

[4] [2601 c] i. 26 "*I baptize in water*...," i. 31 "For this cause *came I baptizing in water*...." The mention of "baptizing in the spirit" is assigned, not to the Baptist (as in the Synoptists) but to God, i. 33 "Upon whomsoever thou shalt see the spirit descending...*this is he that is to baptize in the Holy Spirit.*"

[5] [2602 a] This happens on the third day. The account of the first day (i. 19—28) contains the Baptist's *negative* testimony, ending with "one whom *ye know not*..., the latchet of whose shoe *I am not worthy* to loose." The second day (i. 29 "the morrow") contains the first testimony to "the lamb of God," which testimony, however, is not recorded to have produced any effect. The third day (i. 35 "on the morrow again") brings a repetition of the testimony to "the lamb": and this second testimony being uttered in the presence of two witnesses, who immediately become converts, results indirectly in the beginning of the Church of Christ upon earth.

Baptist's testimony may be said to end here. But there is an appeal to it later on in the section describing the close of his mission, where, after negation and antithesis—"I am not the Christ, I am his messenger"; "he, the bridegroom, must increase but I, the bridegroom's friend, must decrease"—there follows a remarkable instance of twofold repetition, "*He that cometh from above is above all. He that is from the earth, from the earth he is, and from the earth he speaketh: he that cometh from the heaven is above all*[1]."

§ 8. *Twofold repetition in Christ's words*

[2603] In Christ's words, the twofold repetitions are for the most part confined to negative or comparatively rudimentary doctrine. The earliest of any importance is expressly said to refer to "earth." It describes the necessity of something more than mere baptism by water, iii. 3 "*Except a man be born from above, he cannot see the kingdom of God,*" iii. 5 "*Except a man be born from water and the Spirit* (2573, 2612) *he cannot enter into the kingdom of God*"—concerning which statements and their context Jesus says, "If I told you *earthly things* and ye believe not, how will ye believe if I tell you heavenly things?" Another twofold protest in behalf of "the spirit" is in iv. 23—4, "the true worshippers *shall worship the Father in spirit and truth*...they that worship him must *worship in spirit and truth.*" The following refers to the resurrection, v. 25—8 "the hour cometh and now is, when *the dead shall hear the voice of the Son of God* and they that shall have heard shall live...the hour cometh when *all that are in the tombs shall hear his voice and shall go forth.*"

[2604] The belief in Christ for His works' sake, being regarded in this Gospel as rudimentary[2], is naturally made the subject of twofold repetition, v. 36 "for the works that the Father hath given me that I may accomplish them, *the very works that I do, bear witness concerning me,*" compared with x. 25 "*the works that I do in the name of my Father, these bear witness concerning me.*" As regards the reduplication in xiv. 13—14 "*Whatsoever ye shall ask in my name this will I do*...*if ye shall ask* [*me*] *anything in my name this will I do,*" it may be intended as a preparation for a further doctrine in xv. 16 "that whatsoever ye may ask the Father in my name he may

---

[1] iii. 28—31.   [2] ii. 23, xiv. 11.

give it to you," and xvi. 23—4 "If ye ask the Father anything he will give it to you in my name. Hitherto ye have asked nothing in my name. Ask and ye shall receive[1]."

[2605] Further instances of twofold negative repetition, in Christ's words, occur as follows: v. 19, 30 "The Son can do, from himself, *nothing*," "I can do, from myself, *nothing*[2]"; v. 30, vi. 38 "I seek *not* mine own will but the will of him that sent me," "*not* that I may do mine own will but the will of him that sent me"; v. 34, 41 "But I receive *not* my witness from man," "I receive *not* glory from man," vii. 6, 8 "My time (καιρός) is *not yet* present," "My time is *not yet* fulfilled." The effect of a twofold repetition is produced both in vii. 34—6 and in viii. 21—2 because Christ first says, and the Jews then repeat, "Where *I* (ἐγώ) am (or, go) *ye* (ὑμεῖς) cannot come." Later on, Christ repeats the second of these sayings to the disciples, xiii. 33 "Ye shall seek me[3], and even as I said to the Jews, 'Where *I* (ἐγώ) go, *ye* (ὑμεῖς) cannot come'—to you also I say it now (ἄρτι)." Then, to Peter, He drops the emphatic pronouns, saying xiii. 36 "Where I go, thou canst not follow me for the present." All this implies that what had been said to the Jews in one sense is repeated to the disciples in another, which is explained to Peter. The following is an utterance of mere condemnation, x. 25—6 "I told you and *ye believe not*......But *ye believe not* because ye are not of my sheep[4]."

---

[1] [2604 a] It might be urged that the twofold use (xii. 23, xvii. 1) of ἐλήλυθεν ἡ ὥρα announcing that the time has come for the sacrifice and for the "glorifying," is to be contrasted with the sevenfold use (2625) of ἔρχεται ἡ ὥρα referring to the time when the sacrifice shall have been consummated in victory. But a closer examination shews that ἔρχεται and ἐλήλυθεν are combined with ὥρα in the description of the bitterest trial of all, which is to leave Christ deserted and "alone," yet "not alone," xvi. 32 ἰδοὺ ἔρχεται ὥρα καὶ ἐλήλυθεν, closely followed by xvii. 1 Πάτερ, ἐλήλυθεν ἡ ὥρα, δόξασόν σου τὸν υἱόν. Hence the more probable view is that ἐλήλυθεν ἡ ὥρα is used thrice as referring to (2589) "a holy matter."

[2] [2605 a] Note the emphasis laid on οὐδέν by its position at the end of the clause or sentence, ποιεῖν ἀφ' ἑαυτοῦ οὐδέν, ποιεῖν ἀπ' ἐμαυτοῦ οὐδέν. The saying is repeated, without δύναμαι, in viii. 28 ἀπ' ἐμαυτοῦ ποιῶ οὐδέν, "from myself I do nothing."

[3] [2605 b] To the Jews Christ had said, viii. 21 "Ye shall seek me and in your sin ye shall die." The disciples were to "seek" Jesus, after His departure, but in a different way (2545).

[4] [2605 c] It may be added that Christ twice says to the soldiers arresting Him (xviii. 4, 7) "*Whom seek ye?*" On this, and on its possible relations with other sayings about "seeking," see 2649 d—e.

[2606] In Christ's words, the pleonastic repetition of a noun or verb may sometimes be sufficiently explained by the desire of emphasis as in x. 32 "Many *deeds* have I shewn unto you [and those] good...For which *deed* of [all] those do ye stone me?" The verb is clearly emphatic in vi. 63 "The words that I have spoken unto you— spirit *they are* and life *they are* (πνεῦμά ἐστιν καὶ ζωή ἐστιν)," x. 10 "that they *may have* life and abundantly *may have* [it]¹." It is interesting—and probably we are intended—to compare Christ's words, x. 18 "*Authority have I* to lay it [*i.e.* my life] down and *authority have I* again to take it," with Pilate's words, xix. 10 "*authority have I* to acquit thee and *authority have I* to crucify"— in view of (1593—4) the two different views of "authority" here contrasted. There is no pleonasm in the following, but the repetition of the noun (instead of using a pronoun) adds weight: iii. 20 "hateth *the light* and cometh not to *the light*," iv. 14 "whosoever shall drink of *the water that I shall give him*...but *the water that I shall give him* shall become...," xii. 47 "for I came not that I might judge *the world* but that I might save *the world*," with which compare iii. 17 "For God sent not the Son into *the world* that he might judge *the world* but that *the world* might be saved through him." In the last two or three instances mystical meaning may be intended.

§ 9. *Twofold repetition in narrative*

[2607] Twofold repetition in narrative may occasionally be intended to emphasize a disputed or doubtful fact, as in the Anointing, where some said that Christ's head was anointed² but John says xii. 3 "She anointed *the feet* of Jesus and wiped with her hair *his feet*." Emphasis is also laid on the piercing of Christ's side by a "soldier" thus, xix. 32 "There came therefore *the soldiers*...but, having come to Jesus...they brake not his legs but one *of the soldiers* with a spear pierced his side." Or it may be used for clearness after a parenthesis as in ii. 9 "But when *the master of the feast* had tasted...*the master*

---

¹ [2606 a] In xii. 49 ἐντολὴν δέδωκεν τί εἴπω καὶ τί λαλήσω, the meaning seems to be, "what I should *say* [*particularly, on each occasion*] and what I should *speak* [*generally, in proclaiming the Gospel*]." Weight is added by the pleonastic repetition of τί, as well as by the two verbs. Comp. Rom. iii. 19 ὅσα ὁ νόμος λέγει τοῖς ἐν τῷ νόμῳ λαλεῖ, "whatsoever the Law *says on any particular occasion* it *invariably proclaims* to those who are in the pale of the Law."

² Mk xiv. 3, Mt. xxvi. 7.

of the feast calleth," or in scorn as in vii. 35 "Will he go to the scattered people of *the Greeks* and teach *the Greeks*?" It is manifestly emphatic in ii. 25 "he needed not that any should testify about *the [nature of] man,* for he knew of himself what was in *the [nature of] man,"* and in the words of Thomas xx. 25 "and [unless] I *put* my finger...and *put* my hand." There is a twofold repetition in i. 20 "He *confessed* and denied not and *confessed,"* and probably a pair of twofold repetitions with slight variations, in xix. 35 "And he that hath seen hath *borne witness* (μεμαρτύρηκεν) and *real-and-true* (ἀληθινή) is his *witness* (μαρτυρία), and he knoweth that he saith *true* (ἀληθῆ)." But on the whole the evangelist's tendency to twofold repetition appears not so much in words as in the insistence on parallelism in events, which is discussed later on (2646—9).

§ 10. *Twofold or threefold repetition*

[2608] In Christ's words, there occurs the twice repeated statement (x. 11, 14) "*I am the good shepherd.*" This describes a condition of conflict intended to prepare the way for victory—the shepherd contending against the wolf—and may be read as a twofold repetition or attestation. But the addition of (x. 11) "*the good shepherd* layeth down his life for the sheep" suggests a threefold repetition of "*the good shepherd,*" as a separate phrase, implying a reference to the sacrifice of Christ, which would be regarded as (2588—9) "a holy matter," to be triply attested. So, too, the triple mention of the vine in xv. 1—5 "*I am the true vine*...if any man abide not in *the vine...I am the vine*"—these being the only instances of "vine" in the Fourth Gospel—suggests a triple attestation. And, if this is so with "*good shepherd*" and "*vine,*" it is probably true about x. 2—9 "But he that entereth through *the door...I am the door of the sheep...I am the door*": and we are to regard the only other mention of "door" (in Christ's words) in this Gospel ("he that entereth not through *the door*...is a thief and a robber") as a negation, serving as a foil to a threefold attestation. With these must be compared the duality of viii. 12 ἐγώ εἰμι τὸ φῶς τ. κόσμου, ix. 5 φῶς εἰμὶ τ. κόσμου supplemented by xii. 46 ἐγὼ φῶς εἰς τ. κόσμον ἐλήλυθα, and that of vi. 35, 48 "I am the bread of life," supplemented by vi. 51 "I am the bread that liveth."

[2609] The same possibility of various interpretation occurs in xii. 45 "*he that beholdeth me beholdeth him that sent me.*" This, if taken with xiii. 20 "*he that receiveth me receiveth him that sent me*," would suggest a twofold statement that the vision, and the reception, of the Messenger on earth, are to prepare the way for a vision, and a reception, of the Sender in heaven; but if the two are combined with xiv. 9 "*He that hath seen me hath seen the Father*"—the three passages suggest a threefold attestation. So, too, the command "Love one another" would be a twofold repetition if taken merely in xiii. 34 "A new command I give you that *ye love one another* even as I loved you that *ye also love one another*"; but it is probably to be taken as repeated a third time in xv. 12 "This is the commandment that is [peculiarly] my own that *ye love one another* even as I loved you" (see also **2612**). On the other hand the statements xiv. 15, 23 "*If ye love me ye will keep my commandments*," "*If a man love me he will keep my word*," are rudimentary and repeated only twice[1].

[**2610**] In the Epistle, duality characterizes the passages that deal with earthly testimony. We may give the name "dual"—or "quadruple" but certainly not "triple"—to the attestation with which the Epistle opens, i. 1 "That which we have heard, that which we have seen (ἑωράκαμεν) with our eyes," followed by (*ib.*) "That which we gazed on (ἐθεασάμεθα) and our hands handled." Similarly ii. 12—13, containing a solemn testimony to all classes in the

---

[1] [**2609** *a*] Ἀνίστημι (trans.) occurs four times in Jn thus, vi. 39 ἀναστήσω αὐτὸ τ. ἐσχάτῃ ἡμέρᾳ—where αὐτό refers to the Church ("all that thou hast given me"), 40 ἀναστήσω αὐτὸν ἐγὼ τ. ἐ. ἡ., 44 κἀγὼ ἀναστήσω αὐτὸν ἐν τ. ἐ. ἡ., 54 κἀγὼ ἀναστήσω αὐτὸν τ. ἐ. ἡ. Here some may say that the language is a varied refrain four times repeated, others that it is first a promise of resurrection to the whole Church, and then a thrice repeated promise to individual believers. The emphasis on "I" in the last three sentences, and the sing. "him," differentiate these three from the first sentence.

[**2609** *b*] In the following three clauses, describing Christ's legacy of "peace" (xiv. 27), the word "*peace*" is twice actually repeated, and a third repetition is suggested. In the first clause it is simply "*peace*," in the second "*my peace*." In the first clause the action is described as "*leaving*"; in the second, as "*giving*"; in the third, as "*giving not as the world giveth*"; and it is no longer δίδωμι "I-give," but ἐγὼ δίδωμι "*I* give." It would be contrary to all rules of literature and good taste—and, we may almost say, of morality—to suppose that the writer deliberately wrote the sentence according to numerical canons. But the passage is one of the most beautiful instances of inspiration working under rule—like the rule of poetic metre for a true poet—rule that gives life and force and harmony to expression: "Peace *I* leave (ἀφίημι) unto you; the peace that is mine *I-give* (δίδωμι) unto you; not as the world giveth *give I* (ἐγὼ δίδωμι) unto you."

Church, repeats twice, to each, "I write," "I have written." It is true that in this Epistle the witness is notably threefold in v. 6—8: "This is he that came by water and blood, Jesus Christ, not in the water alone but in the water and in the blood; and the Spirit it is that witnesseth, because the Spirit is the truth. Because three are they that witness, the Spirit and the water and the blood, and the three make up the one." But even in this passage, the writer seems to indicate by his arrangement of the "three" that "the water" and "the blood" come first as representing the testimony of the life of Jesus *on earth*, and that "the spirit" comes afterwards as witnessing from heaven. The dual form of expression is naturally adopted while the writer is describing the witness of apostles and the manifestation that led to it, and while his mind rests, at the outset, on the dual aspect of the Christian message when the Son was drawing men to the Father and when "the Holy Spirit was not yet": (i. 2 foll.) "And the light (*a*) *was manifested* and (*b*) *we have seen*; and we (*a*) *witness* and (*b*) *declare to you* the life eternal, which (*a*) *was with the Father* and (*b*) *was manifested to us*: (3) what we have (*a*) *heard* and (*b*) *seen*, that we declare also to you, that ye too may have fellowship with us, and indeed our fellowship is with (*a*) the Father and with (*b*) his Son Jesus Christ.... (5) And this is the tidings that we (*a*) *have heard from him* and (*b*) *declare to you*, that (*a*) *God is light* and (*b*) *darkness is not in him at all*."

[2611] Returning to the Gospel we may say in conclusion that the general impression left on us by the form of its ordinary doctrine is that of twofold attestation[1]. In statements made by our Lord

---

[1] [2611 *a*] It is an interesting question whether Jn has any symbolic allusion to twofold attestation in his remarkable use of ἀμὴν ἀμήν (instead of the Synoptic single ἀμήν) and ἀπεκρίθη κ. εἶπεν (instead of the Synoptic ἀποκριθεὶς εἶπεν) as introductions to utterances of Christ. In both of these, his deviation from Synoptic usage must have seemed very strange to readers of the earlier Gospels. It may be illustrated by the surprise that would have been felt by readers of Boswell's biography coming upon a new life of Dr Johnson in which "*Sir, Sir*" was regularly substituted for "*Sir*."

[2611 *b*] Ἀμὴν ἀμήν occurs twenty-five times (ἀμήν never) and is used in predictions (i. 51, xiii. 21, xiii. 38, xxi. 18) of good and of evil including the prediction of betrayal. It introduces (viii. 58, x. 7) "I am [he]" and "I am the door," and on the other hand (vi. 26) "Ye seek me...because ye have eaten of the loaves," and (viii. 34) "Everyone that doeth sin is a slave," and it is thrice used (iii. 3, 5, 11) in the Dialogue with Nicodemus. The facts suggest no special doctrine for which the phrase is reserved.

[2611 *c*] Ἀπεκρίθη (Ἰησοῦς) κ. εἶπεν, in its last three instances, is used where

about Himself, the duality of "I am the good shepherd," "I am the light of the world," "I am the door," "I am the bread of life," "I am the vine," is supplemented in such a way as to suggest a trinity; but for the most part the doctrine is distinctly dual, especially in the teaching of the Baptist. That there should be passages in which the distinction is not clearly drawn is fit and natural in a work that expresses spiritual truth with dramatic yet natural vividness. A book made up of manifest twofold, threefold, and sevenfold repetitions, broken by regular and systematic variations, would be intolerably artificial. But the work we have before us betrays nothing that could fairly be called artificiality—at least in a Jew, trained to the study of the Bible in the literary school of Philo (though raised up above the narrower formalities of that school by the Spirit of Christ), and committing to paper some among many traditions of the Christian Church, with his paraphrases and explanations of them, according to the manner and pattern of the Hebrew Scriptures and Jewish Targums. One reason for duality of form may have been that he was profoundly impressed by the Lord's statement that His doctrines, without the Spirit, were "dark sayings." Hence perhaps, in a point of detail, the contrast between the Gospel and the Epistle as to the "blood and water" from the Cross. The Gospel says, "He that hath seen *hath borne witness* and true is his *witness*[1]." The Epistle speaks of "water" and "blood" and "spirit." The latter suggests trinity; the former duality—because "the Holy Spirit was not yet."

---

there is some misunderstanding in the context, as where the Voice from heaven is taken by some to be "thunder," and Christ (xii. 30) explains that it came for the sake of the multitude. It also introduces the saying to Peter (xiii. 7) "What I do, thou knowest not now," and the answer to "Judas not Iscariot" (xiv. 23) who cannot understand how a manifestation can be made to the disciples and not to the world. At the outset of the Gospel it is used twice (i. 48, 50) in the Dialogue with Nathanael, once before the words (misunderstood) (ii. 19) "Destroy this temple," and thrice (iii. 3, 5, 10) in the Dialogue with Nicodemus, who is supposed not to understand even elementary truths. Subsequently it is used (iv. 10, 13) in the Dialogue with the Samaritan woman, who takes the Doctrine of Water literally, and (from vi. 26 to viii. 14) several times in discussions with literalising or hostile controversialists. The facts suggest that the phrase introduces elementary doctrine or explanation of misunderstanding.

[1] xix. 35 followed by καὶ ἐκεῖνος οἶδεν ὅτι ἀληθῆ λέγει, on which see **2383—4** and **2731**.

§ 11. *Threefold repetition*

[2612] It is obvious that a threefold repetition of the same saying, with little or no variation, and in the same context, would be monotonous and unimpressive, except in special circumstances where a refrain is intended, as in the threefold question to Peter, "Lovest thou me?" followed by the threefold precept "Feed my sheep": and, even there, the three utterances are not quite identical. Hence, if the writer introduces this form of doctrine in Christ's words, it is diversified in various ways. For example, the commandment "love one another" might be regarded as repeated twice as a commandment and once more as a sign (xiii. 34—5) "A new commandment give I you that *ye love one another*; even as I loved you that *ye* (emph.) *also love one another*: herein shall all know that ye are my disciples if *ye have love among one another*": but it is also repeated once again (2609) as a commandment. It has been pointed out (2608) that this variation so affects such sayings as "I am the good shepherd" that we may regard them as either twofold or threefold repetitions; and the same statement applies to the doctrine about new birth, which, though called an "earthly" doctrine from one point of view (iii. 12), may be regarded as "heavenly" since it concerns the Holy Spirit (iii. 3—7) "Verily, verily, I say unto thee, except a man *be born from above*...Except a man *be born from water and the spirit*... Marvel not that I said unto thee, Ye must *be born from above*[1]." In the prediction of the suffering of the Good Shepherd, the monotony of a repetition of "I lay down my life for the sheep" is avoided by dropping "for the sheep" in the second clause, and "my life for the sheep" in the third, and by substituting for them phrases suggesting the resurrection and the spontaneousness of the sacrifice (x. 15—18) "*I lay down my life* for the sheep...For this cause doth my Father love me because *I lay down my life that I may receive it again*...No man hath taken it from me, but *I lay it down of myself*." The result is a threefold repetition of nothing but "I lay down": yet the meaning is clear and the threefold effect is retained.

[2613] A triple effect is imparted to a long saying of Christ in the following passage by the questioning of the disciples and the

---

[1] [2612*a*] That "baptism" in 'water implied something more than mere washing in water, might be called an earthly doctrine. But what that "something more" was, and whence it came, might be called a heavenly doctrine.

explanation of their Master: xvi. 16—19 "*A little, and ye no longer behold me*, and *again a little, and ye shall see me*...What is this that he saith to us, *A little, and ye behold me not, and again a little, and ye shall see me?*...Jesus...said to them, Question ye with one another concerning this that I said unto you, *A little, and ye behold me not, and again a little, and ye shall see me?*" In the following, which states the absolute knowledge (οἶδα) of the Father possessed by the Son, a third clause is introduced negatively: viii. 55 "Ye have no understanding of (ἐγνώκατε) him. But *I know* (οἶδα) him. And, if I say *I know* (οἶδα) him not, I shall be a liar like unto you. But *I know* (οἶδα) him[1]." As in the Dialogue with Nicodemus a triple repetition of the verb "*to be born*" was accompanied with a double repetition of other circumstances, so there is a triple repetition of "*he that feedeth*," with variations, in the following: vi. 54—7 "*He that feedeth* on my flesh and drinketh my blood hath life eternal...*he that feedeth* on my flesh and drinketh my blood abideth in me...*he that feedeth* on me, he (emph.) shall live on account of me."

[2614] Concerning the Wind or Breath or Spirit Christ says (iii. 8) that man (1) hears its voice, but knows not (2) whence it comes, and (3) whither it goes. This may refer to (1) the work, (2) the origin, and (3) the object of the Holy Spirit, and may suggest a threefold aspect of it. Certainly the Spirit's "convicting" influence is triply described later on as referring to (xvi. 8) "*sin*," "*righteousness*," and "*judgment*." It is also thrice mentioned (xiv. 17, xv. 26, xvi. 13) as "*the spirit of truth*[2]." And in the following passage—along with an implied threefold statement that what the Spirit will "declare" comes from Him who is speaking, indicated by the thrice repeated "*me*" or "*mine*"—the words "*He shall declare unto you*" occur as a triple refrain (xvi. 13—16) "For he shall not speak from himself, but what he heareth that shall he speak and things to come (1) *he shall declare unto you*. He shall glorify me, for he shall take from *mine* and (2) *he shall declare unto you*. All things that the Father hath are *mine*. For this cause said I that he taketh from *mine* and (3) *he shall declare unto you*." The thought of the Spirit is

---

[1] [2613 a] See **1621**—9 for the difference between οἶδα and γινώσκω. In only one other passage (vii. 29) does Jesus use the words οἶδα αὐτόν of God, so that the total number of positive repetitions is three.

[2] [2614 a] The Paraclete is mentioned positively thrice (xiv. 16, 26, xv. 26) and negatively once (xvi. 7) "For if I go not away the Paraclete will surely not come unto you."

connected with the thought of unity—unity both in the being of God and in the Church; and the prayer for this, which is uttered, first for the Church as a whole, and then for the Apostles in particular, is thrown (in both cases) into a threefold form (xvii. 21) "That all may be one:—even as (1) thou, Father, art in me, and (2) I in thee, that (3) they, also, may be in us," (xvii. 23) "that they may be one as we are one:—(1) I in them, and (2) thou in me, that (3) they may be perfected into one[1]." Negative doctrine would naturally be seldom expressed with threefold repetition; but when it points to the divine unity an exception may be expected, as in viii. 16 "*I am not alone*," viii. 29 "He [*i.e.* the Father] *hath not left me alone*," xvi. 32 "And *I am not alone* because the Father is with me."

[2615] As regards the use by the evangelist (in his own person) of threefold repetition, it is most prominent in the Prologue, which begins with a triple mention of "the Word" in the same sentence, commented on above (**2594**). The last words of the Prologue (i. 18) are not quite certain, but they are probably—as has been maintained above (**1964**)—"God no one hath seen at any time. Only begotten, God (R.V. Son), HE THAT IS in the bosom of the Father, he hath declared him." If so, instead of one name (R.V. txt) "*the only begotten Son*," we may suppose the writer to mean two names, making a total of three: (1) "*Only begotten*," (2) "*God*," (3) "*He that is in the bosom of the Father.*" These will correspond to the three clauses in the first verse: (1) "*In the beginning*," (2) "*with God*," (3) "*God.*" This is far more symmetrical than the view that the Prologue begins with three clauses describing the Word, and ends with two.

[2616] The act of "lifting up the eyes" is thrice attributed to Jesus. Once also He uses the phrase as a precept, iv. 35 "*Lift up your eyes* (ἐπάρατε τ. ὀ.) and behold the lands how that they are

---

[1] [2614*b*] To these might have been added Christ's triple repetition of the doctrine that "*the Son of man* (or, *I*) *must be lifted up*" in iii. 14, viii. 28, xii. 32, the last being "if *I be lifted up* from the earth I will draw all men unto me."

[2614*c*] There remain threefold repetitions of words partly by Christ partly by the evangelist. Of these, εὐχαριστέω (vi. 11, 23, xi. 41) is probably accidental. But Jn's statement that Christ (xi. 33) "*troubled* (ἐτάραξεν) *himself*," and (xiii. 21) "*was troubled in spirit*," may be intended to be read along with (xii. 27) "*Now is my soul troubled*," as a threefold repetition (**920**). There is also His doctrine of "the way," introduced with the words (xiv. 4) "Ye know *the way*," to which Thomas answers, "How can we know *the way*?" whereon Jesus replies "I am *the way, and the truth, and the life*," which has decidedly the effect of a threefold repetition.

white for harvest." This is obviously a spiritual act. Philo (on Gen. xviii. 2) treats it as such when he describes how Abraham, seated at the door of his tent, "lifted up his eyes" and beheld the three divine Persons to whom he ministered and gave bread (1608). It is a commonplace in Jewish tradition that whatever Abraham does in service to God, God will do, in return, to Abraham's seed. Most appropriately, therefore, before the Feeding of the Five Thousand, John says that the Logos (vi. 3—5) "sat" with His disciples on the mountain[1] and *"lifted up [his] eyes* (ἐπάρας οὖν τ. ὀ.) and beheld that a great multitude was coming unto him," *i.e.* He sees the spiritual harvest, the seed of Abraham after the spirit, the future Church. Then, as Abraham gave bread to the three Persons, so He gives bread to Abraham's children.

[2617] On the second occasion it is said (xi. 41) "*He lifted [his] eyes upward* (ἦρεν τ. ὀ. ἄνω) and said, 'Father, I thank thee that thou didst hearken to me...,'" before the raising of Lazarus; and, on the third (xvii. 1) "These things spake Jesus, and, *having lifted up his eyes to the heaven* (ἐπάρας τ. ὀφθαλμοὺς αὐτοῦ εἰς τ. οὐρανόν), he said, 'Father, the hour hath come...'" In Isaiah (li. 6) "*Lift up your eyes to the heavens* and look upon the earth beneath" introduces a contrast between the eternal righteousness of God and the perishableness of men, and Ibn Ezra says (though dissenting) "Philosophers derive from this verse the doctrine of the immortality of the soul of man." Having regard to the Scriptural use of the phrase, to the comments of Philo, and to the metaphorical use of it as a precept by Christ, we are justified in concluding that John attaches a spiritual meaning to the thrice repeated act of our Lord, and that the last is regarded as the climax of the three. No outward action, it is true, accompanies the third utterance; but it prepares the way for the sacrifice on the cross[2].

---

[1] [2616 *a*] As regards the "mountain," Philo appears twice to use forms of the word ὀρικός of thoughts, "high," "uplifted." But his use of the word is based on a mistransl. of Numb. xx. 19 "by the highway," παρὰ τὸ ὄρος, which he explains by (i. 297) ὑψηλαῖς καὶ μετεώροις δυνάμεσι...καὶ ὀρικῶς ἕκαστα σκοπεῖν, playing on ὀρικῶς and ὁρικῶς, of which the latter means "proceeding by definition." So in i. 299 ἀδύνατον γὰρ τὸν μὴ ταῖς ὑψηλαῖς καὶ ὀρικαῖς χρώμενον ὁδοῖς ἀπογνῶναι μὲν τὰ θνητὰ μετακλῖναι δὲ καὶ μεταναστεῦσαι πρὸς τὰ ἄφθαρτα. Steph. recognises ὀρεικός as applied to a mountainous district in Polybius, but not ὀρικός as above.

[2] [2617 *a*] It may be noted that θεᾶσθαι is twice applied to Jesus, once (i. 38) when He sees the two disciples "following," once (vi. 5) when He sees "that a great multitude is coming to him." The two disciples are the firstfruits of the

[2618] The word κράζω, "cry aloud," applied to our Lord by Matthew alone (or possibly by Matthew and Mark)[1] is applied to Him thrice by John on three solemn occasions. It has been pointed out (1752 *a—f*) that there may have been various traditions as to the Messiah's *not "crying aloud,"* based on Isaiah xlii. 2, which may have induced evangelists to refrain from assigning this act to Him at any time, or at all events till the "victory" consummated in the crucifixion. The first Johannine mention of it applied to Christ is in vii. 28, "Jesus then *cried aloud* in the temple teaching and saying, Ye know both me and ye know whence I am; and I am not come of myself, but he is true that sent me, whom ye (emph.) know not." This clearly "witnesses" to the Father. The second is in vii. 37, "In the last day, the great one, of the Feast, stood Jesus, and *cried aloud* saying, If any man thirst, let him come to me and drink. He that believeth in me—as said the Scripture—rivers from his belly shall flow forth, [yea,] of living water." This "witness"—the evangelist himself tells us in the next verse—"he spake concerning the Spirit." The third and last (xii. 44—50) introduces the final public utterance of Jesus on finding Himself rejected by His countrymen, and it is a series of statements concerning Himself:— that He represents the Father; that He has come as the Light of the World; that His word will judge those who reject Him; and that His utterances are the words of the Father. Of these three utterances we may say, roughly, that they severally witness to the Father, the Holy Spirit, and the Son. Thus the peculiar nature of the subject-matter supplies, in itself, some kind of probability that the author deliberately chose this special and unusual word (κράζω) to emphasize the public threefold witness of Jesus to a "holy matter."

[2619] Corresponding to the threefold "crying aloud" of Christ in His preaching of the Gospel we might naturally expect to find a threefold manifestation of Himself after the Resurrection: and this is stated as a fact (xxi. 14) "This is now *the third time* that Jesus

---

Church; the Five Thousand are a type, though an elementary one, of the Church as a whole. There is, therefore, an inward similarity between the two scenes, however much they outwardly differ. Βλέπω is only applied once to Christ, and then describes the Son (v. 19) "*noting*" the acts of the Father in heaven. Philo, too (1607), uses the same word to describe the Eldest Son "*noting*" the acts of the Father "as patterns for His own action."

[1] [2618 *a*] Mt. xxvii. 50. Some authorities add it in Mk xv. 39, including ACD *ff*, *k* and SS. These passages describe Christ's death.

was manifested to the disciples (having been raised from the dead)." Having previously mentioned one manifestation to Mary and two to the disciples, John might have said, "This is now the *fourth* time." But presumably he lays stress on *"to the disciples"* here, meaning that it was *"the third" to them collectively*, excluding manifestations to single persons. The first Epistle to the Corinthians enumerates three manifestations to collective witnesses thus, (xv. 6—8) "He appeared to Cephas, then to (1) *the Twelve*; then he appeared to (2) *five hundred brethren at once*;...then he appeared to James; then to (3) *the apostles all* [*together*] (τοῖς ἀποστόλοις πᾶσιν). But last of all he appeared as unto one born out of due time, yea, even to me." If both writers were to be supposed to have known all the manifestations, and to be here enumerating all the manifestations they knew, it would follow that the manifestation here mentioned by John in which Christ sends forth Peter and his companions to "feed the sheep" is identical with the one described by Paul as being "to the apostles all [together]." But John mentions only seven disciples as being present.

[2620] More probably there were a vast number of manifestations during the period described by Luke in the Acts (i. 3) as one of "forty" days: and John uses the phrase "this is now *the third* time" in order to describe that particular one (out of a very large number) which he intends to place third and last, as being the crowning manifestation (apart from the one to Mary Magdalene)[1]. In confining himself to *"three"* manifestations, he would be following Hebrew precedent, as to phrases about Jehovah making His face to shine on Israel. This refrain is thrice repeated in one of the Psalms[2], and the phrase occurs in the Blessing of Israel, which contains the name of Jehovah in threefold repetition[3]. In view of these circum-

---

[1] [2620 *a*] Cramer has the following (on Jn xxi. 14) Διὰ τί εἶπε, "τοῦτο ἤδη τρίτον ἐφανερώθη ὁ Ἰησοῦς τοῖς μαθηταῖς αὐτοῦ ἐγερθεὶς ἐκ νεκρῶν;" δεῖξαι θέλων ἐκ τούτου ὅτι οὐ συνεχῶς ἐπεχωρίαζεν αὐτοῖς οὐδὲ ὁμοίως· καὶ ἐνταῦθα μὲν οὐ λέγει ὅτι ἔφαγε μετ' αὐτῶν· ὁ δὲ Λουκᾶς ἀλλαχοῦ αὐτὸ φησιν, ὅτι συναλιζόμενος αὐτοῖς ἦν· τὸ δὲ πῶς, οὐχ ἡμέτερον εἰπεῖν. Chrysostom (Migne) has, more briefly, Ὅτι δὲ οὐδὲ συνεχῶς ἐπεχωρίαζεν οὐδὲ ὁμοίως, λέγει ὅτι Τρίτον τοῦτο ἐφάνη αὐτοῖς ὅτε ἠγέρθη ἐκ νεκρῶν. See **2715**.

[2] Ps. lxxx. 3, 7, 19.

[3] [2620 *b*] Numb. vi. 24—6 "*Jehovah* bless thee and keep thee! *Jehovah* make his face to shine upon thee and be gracious unto thee. *Jehovah* lift up his countenance upon thee and give thee peace." Here the dual clauses in the three

stances it is probably not accidental that the evangelist, besides inserting "*third*," mentions the verb φανερόω thrice, in connexion with Christ's resurrection, xxi. 1—14 "Jesus *manifested* himself again to the disciples on the sea of Tiberias. Now he *manifested* himself thus......This is the third time that Jesus *manifested* himself to the disciples." How simple, in the first verse, to have written merely, "Jesus *manifested* himself again thus...Tiberias," using the verb once! How can we possibly acquit the writer of that "tautology" which Philo so gravely rebukes—unless he wrote with a sense of the spiritual meaning and weight conveyed by this threefold repetition?

[2621] The following passage contains a curious instance of the threefold repetition of a mere pronoun, which, in an ordinary writer, would naturally be set down to mere slovenliness of style:—xii. 16 "*These things* (ταῦτα) his disciples recognised not at the first. But, when Jesus was glorified, then they remembered that *these things* had been written concerning him, and [that] they did *these things* to him." What are "*these things*"? The previous narrative describes Jesus entering into Jerusalem riding on an ass: and it might be supposed by one familiar with the Synoptists—who say that the disciples found the ass and (according to Luke) placed Jesus upon it—that John refers to this action of the disciples. But John says expressly, "*Jesus, having found an ass, sat on it.*" Consequently "*these things*" must refer to the fact that the multitude welcomed Jesus as king in the words of the Psalms (cxviii. 25—6) crying "Hosanna, blessed is he that cometh in the name of the Lord." Now in the LXX of this Psalm "these things," or its equivalent, occurs in a very peculiar form. The whole of the Psalm may be regarded as Messianic, and part of it is quoted by all the Synoptists as being uttered by Jesus soon after the Entry, "The stone that the builders rejected...." Then follow words, omitted by Luke, but quoted by Mark and Matthew as follows; "*This* (αὕτη) is from the Lord[1]"—meaning "*this thing*" or "*these things*," where the evangelists (following the LXX) curiously reproduce a Hebrew feminine use of the demonstrative pronoun.

[2622] Westcott, at this point, reminds his readers that (1) the cry of Hosanna is from Ps. cxviii. 25, and adds, on "*these things*,"

---

sentences suggest a blessing in heaven fulfilled upon earth: and the threefold repetition suggests that the words contain "a holy matter" (2588—9).

[1] Mk xii. 11, Mt. xxi. 42.

the remark, "(2) The triple repetition of the words is to be noticed." But he does not connect the two statements. Schöttgen, however, calls attention to the fact that the Hebrew feminine pronoun occurring here is interpreted by the Cabbalists in a symbolical sense as referring to the Messiah, and he quotes a very large number of passages in which the pronoun is similarly symbolized[1]. But in Greek the feminine is so unintelligible that even Origen misunderstands it and refers it to the preceding κεφαλή[2], and perhaps the difficulty of it was the reason, or one of the reasons, that induced Luke to omit it, and to substitute something about a "stone" of a very different kind. The facts, taken as a whole, point to the conclusion that there was early difficulty as to the meaning of the words "*This* (αὕτη) was from the Lord"—quoted from the Psalm that was connected on the one hand (through the cry of the multitude) with the "Hosanna" in the Entry into Jerusalem, and, on the other (through our Lord's quotation about "the *stone* that the builders rejected"), with Christ's doctrine about the rejection of the Messiah or about the Stone of Israel. Luke at all events omits both the cry "Hosanna" (1816 *b*) and the difficult "this" or "these things." John (besides following Mark and Matthew in retaining "Hosanna") paraphrases and amplifies an explanation of "these things" that contains a latent symbolism. See 2757.

[2623] Another parallel instance of threefold repetition, as to a fulfilment of prophecy, only touched on by Mark and Matthew and given quite differently by Luke, refers to the "sponge" full of vinegar given to Christ at the crucifixion. John introduces this as part of the total "accomplishment" (2115) of the will of the Father by the Son "in order that the Scripture might be perfected" and as prefaced by a special utterance of our Lord, "I thirst." Then he says xix. 29—30 "A vessel lay [near] full of *vinegar*. A sponge therefore full of *the vinegar*...they brought near to his mouth. When therefore he received *the vinegar* Jesus said, It is finished...[3]."

---

[1] [2622 *a*] Schöttg. ii. 45, "de Cabbala Exegetica," places Ps. cxviii. 23 first in the list of these interpretations. *Ib.* p. 140 places Dan. ii. 35 (on "the stone") first, and then (after Ezek. i. 28) Ps. cxviii. 23. It will be remembered that Lk. xx. 18, instead of the quotation about αὕτη, has "everyone that falleth on this stone," which W.H. also bracket in Mt. xxi. 44.

[2] [2622 *b*] Origen (on Mt. xxi. 42) Huet i. 468 A. Field (*ad loc.*) refers only to modern commentators, not to Origen, but calls the explanation "objectionable."

[3] [2623 *a*] Comp. Mk xv. 36, Mt. xxvii. 48, Lk. (of the soldiers of Herod

§ 12. *Sevenfold repetition*

[2624] The number "seven" occurs in Revelation more often than in all the rest of N.T. taken together. In the Fourth Gospel, which was probably written by some one connected with the author of Revelation, "seven" never occurs at all (though fairly frequent in the Synoptists). But the Gospel is *permeated structurally with the idea of* "*seven*," as might be expected from one accepting the tradition about (Rev. iii. 1) "*the seven spirits of God.*" John records only seven "signs," a small number as compared with the greater number of the "mighty works" recorded by the Synoptists. Again in xii. 1 "Jesus, six days before the passover, came to Bethany," Westcott says, "St John appears to mark the period as the new Hexaemeron, a solemn period of 'six days,' the time of the new Creation. His Gospel begins and closes with a sacred week." But an ordinary reader might easily overlook the "sacred week" here, and still more easily that at the outset. For there it is (we may almost say) carefully disguised from those who are not on the alert for mysteries by the phrases (i. 29) "on the morrow," (i. 35) "on the morrow," (i. 43) "on the morrow"; (ii. 1) "on the third day": and the reader has to go through an addition of $1 + 1 + 1 + 3$, before he realises that "those who see" are intended to "see" here a solemn period of six days of spiritual creation. Again, a searching analysis of the work is needed before one realises that the witness to Christ is, as Westcott shews again, of a sevenfold character[1].

[2625] As soon as this symbolism is recognised, we are led to enquire whether it may not be also latent elsewhere. Thus, the words I AM, though in their full sense occurring only once (viii. 58) are repeated elsewhere in Christ's words five times (directly or indirectly) before the arrest of Jesus (iv. 26, vi. 20, viii. 24, viii. 28, xiii. 19), so as to make up six; and then at the arrest we have a single threefold testimony as follows:—xviii. 5—8 "He saith unto

---

Antipas) xxiii. 36. Jn, alone of the Gospels, mentions "Scripture" in connexion with this incident. Very early writers connect "gall" with the "vinegar" in such a way as to shew that they regarded the action as predicted in Ps. lxix. 21. Jn does not mention "gall," and leaves it open to suppose that he may have included in "Scripture" the words Ps. xlii. 2 "My soul is athirst."

[1] [2624 a] According to Westcott (xlv—vii) it is (1) the witness of the Father; (2) the witness of Christ Himself; (3) the witness of works; (4) the witness of Scripture; (5) the witness of the Forerunner; (6) the witness of disciples; (7) the witness of the Spirit.

them '*I am* [he]'...(6) When therefore he said unto them '*I am* [he]'...(8) Jesus answered, I said unto you '*I am* [he].'" The supposition of a sevenfold intention is somewhat confirmed by the fact that "I am" certainly occurs seven times in the sevenfold representation of His relationship to mankind: (1) vi. 35 etc. "*I am* the Bread of Life"; (2) viii. 12 etc. "*I am* the Light of the World"; (3) x. 7 etc. "*I am* the door"; (4) x. 11 etc. "*I am* the Good Shepherd"; (5) xi. 25 "*I am* the Resurrection and the Life"; (6) xiv. 6 "*I am* the Way, the Truth, and the Life"; (7) xv. 1 etc. "*I am* the True Vine." Again, in the last words of Jesus, when He is reviewing the whole of His teaching, He uses seven times (xiv. 25, xv. 11, xvi. 1, 4, 6, 25, 33) the expression "*These things have I spoken to you* (ταῦτα λελάληκα ὑμῖν)" (which occurs nowhere else in the Gospel[1]), and also, in connexion with promises (xiv. 13, 14, 26, xv. 16, xvi. 23, 24, 26), the phrase "*in my name.*" There is also fair evidence for a sevenfold repetition of ἕν in the expression of the divine unity in the words of Jesus, first (x. 30) "I and the Father are one"; and then in prayer that men may be one in that unity (xvii. 11, 21 (twice)[2], 22 (twice), 23). Again, whereas the noun "*love*" is not mentioned at all by Mark and only once by Matthew and Luke, John uses it seven times, and always in the words of Jesus[3]. The promise "*thou shalt*, or, *ye shall, see*" occurs also seven times, almost always in reference to "glory" or resurrection[4], and so does the prediction "*the hour is coming*[5]."

[2626] In concluding the instances of repetition, we may add that the "Law" is mentioned six times (vii. 19 (twice), 23, viii. 17, x. 34, xv. 25) in the words of Jesus, an imperfect number as appropriate to the imperfect law as is the number "six" applied to the water-pots which were (ii. 6) for "the purification of the Jews." We

---

[1] [2625 *a*] On the mystical meaning that may attach to "these things," see 2621—2.

[2] [2625 *b*] The evidence of C for the omission of ἕν is here discredited by the fact that it omits it previously (against all the MSS.) missing the meaning.

[3] [2625 *c*] But the first of these (v. 42 "the love of God") is negative. The others are xiii. 35, xv. 13 ἀγάπην, xv. 9 ἐν τῇ ἀ. τῇ ἐμῇ, xv. 10 ἐν τῇ ἀ. μου, xv. 10 αὐτοῦ ἐν τῇ ἀ., xvii. 26 ἡ ἀ. ἣν ἠγάπησάς με.

[4] [2625 *d*] i. 39, 50—51, xi. 40, xvi. 16, 17, 19. In xvi. 17 the words are Christ's but repeated by the disciples.

[5] [2625 *e*] Ἔρχεται ὥρα is in iv. 21, v. 28, xvi. 2, 25 also (with καὶ νῦν ἐστίν) in iv. 23, v. 25; also (with καὶ ἐλήλυθεν) in xvi. 32.

might have expected perhaps that the Paraclete would have been mentioned "three" or "seven" times. But the mentions are four. Of these, the fourth is negative, xvi. 7 "If I go not away, *the Paraclete will not come unto you*," and possibly this may be intended to be excluded from the total. Westcott (p. xiv) reckons as five the quotations from Scripture in Christ's words; but if we add viii. 17 "It is written in your law, *The witness of two men is true*," the number is six. If we also add xix. 28 "In order that the Scripture might be perfected he saith '*I thirst*,'" the number is seven[1].

[2627] What was said as to threefold must be repeated as to sevenfold repetition. Several instances of the latter are certain, but some are doubtful, *e.g.* the repetition of "love" which perhaps, instead of being taken as one group of seven, might be grouped as two pairs of three positive statements with one negation. The same word may be differently regarded by the author in different circumstances. Φανερόω applied to the Son in the Gospel is repeated thrice. But when applied to the Father and to the Son in the Epistle it is repeated seven times. Making every allowance for doubtful cases and different aspects, we find enough to assure us that the author of this Gospel was largely influenced by a habit of sevenfold grouping that affected his whole narrative as well as particular words and phrases in it.

---

[1] [2626 *a*] In xix. 28, W.H. print "I thirst" as a quotation from Ps. lxix. 21 εἰς τὴν δίψαν μου ἐπότισάν με ὄξος. But Jn may contemplate also Ps. xlii. 2 ἐδίψησεν ἡ ψυχή μου. The five quotations mentioned by Westcott are vi. 45 (Is. liv. 13), vii. 38 ("Even as the Scripture said, '*River of water*...,'" on which Westcott remarks "there is no exact parallel. The reference is probably general"), x. 34 (Ps. lxxxii. 6), xiii. 18 (Ps. xli. 9), xv. 25 (Ps. xxxv. 19 and Ps. lxix. 4). Westcott is justified in excluding i. 51 ("the angels of God ascending...") on the ground that "Scripture," "law," "written," etc. do not occur in the context. But I do not understand why he includes vii. 38 and excludes viii. 17.

CHAPTER III

CONNEXION OF SENTENCES

§ 1. *Self-corrections*

[2628] One occasional Johannine characteristic, which might be alleged as being incompatible with the view that the author paid much attention to words or aimed at strict accuracy, is that he occasionally sets down what he himself, by subsequently repeating it accurately, admits to be inaccurate, *e.g.* iii. 32—3 "*No one receiveth* his testimony. *He that* [*hath*] *received* his testimony [hath] set his seal [to this] that God is true," viii. 15—16 "Ye judge according to the flesh, I *judge no one.* Yea, and *if I judge,* my judgment is real and true." Somewhat different is iv. 1—2 "When therefore the Lord recognised that the Pharisees [had] heard [the saying] that 'Jesus is making more disciples and *baptizing* [*more*] *than John*[1]'—and yet Jesus himself did not baptize, but his disciples [did]." This last statement may be defended as strictly accurate. The writer tells us, not what Jesus *did*, but what the Pharisees *heard* that He was doing—a very different thing. But this illustrates the evangelist's way of putting before his readers the popular view, or roughly accurate view, and then correcting it. And this may explain iii. 33. In comparison with the world-wide acceptance that might have been expected, it might be said that "*no one*" accepted the testimony of the Logos. So, as to viii. 16, Christ came not to judge but to save the world: yet indirectly He would necessarily judge those that rejected Him, in so far as any moral ideal "judges" those that behold it and reject it.

---

[1] [2628 a] W.H. have βαπτίζει [ἢ] 'Ιωάνης, but the omission of H may be expl. by the similarity of IHI coming together.

[2629] In this last passage there may have been a desire to subordinate the literal view of Christ as the future Judge, seated on the clouds of heaven, in order to give more prominence to (1581—5, 1714, 1859) the righteousness and present power of divine judgment. And this indicates that John's other so-called "inaccuracies" are really deliberate. The Pauline Epistles in various phrases describe "*all*" mankind as "concluded in *unbelief*," and John, in effect, may desire to say the same thing when he speaks of "*no one*" receiving the testimony of the Logos[1]. Possibly, too, the evangelist was moved by the fact that Christ Himself frequently expressed a truth briefly and broadly at first and then "narrowed it down" afterwards. This manner of speaking is at all events manifest when He says "I *go not* up to this feast," and yet "*went*" (only not after the manner of "going up" expected by His brethren)[2], and "Ye will leave me *alone* and yet I am *not alone*[3]," and "*My* teaching is *not mine*[4]," and when He first says, concerning the Paraclete, "He will take of *mine*," and then explains that He has said "*mine*" because "All that the Father hath is *mine*[5]."

[2630] As compared with the first and the third of Christ's utterances about "requesting[6]" the Father (xiv. 16 κἀγὼ ἐρωτήσω τὸν πατέρα καὶ ἄλλον παράκλητον δώσει ὑμῖν and xvii. 9 ἐγὼ περὶ αὐτῶν ἐρωτῶ) there is some difficulty in a second one (xvi. 26 ἐν ἐκείνῃ τῇ ἡμέρᾳ ἐν τῷ ὀνόματί μου αἰτήσεσθε, καὶ οὐ λέγω ὑμῖν ὅτι ἐγὼ ἐρωτήσω[7] τὸν πατέρα περὶ ὑμῶν· αὐτὸς γὰρ ὁ πατὴρ φιλεῖ ὑμᾶς). The first says "*I will request the Father* and he will give you another Paraclete," the third, addressed to the Father, says "*I request concerning them*," i.e. the disciples, the second, "*I say not to you that I will request the Father concerning you*, for the Father of himself loveth you." But if

---

[1] [2629 a] On i. 11 οὐ παρέλαβον...ὅσοι δὲ ἔλαβον see 2570.

[2] vii. 8—10.   [3] xvi. 32.   [4] vii. 16.

[5] xvi. 14—15. Perhaps to these we might add "the hour cometh and hath come," on which see 1639 a, b, 2485 a, 2604 a. On v. 31 "If I am bearing witness about myself my witness is not true," contrasted with viii. 14 "Even though I be bearing witness about myself my witness is true," see 2514 (i).

[6] [2630 a] "Request," though in some respects not a very good rendering of ἐρωτάω, is used here to distinguish it from αἰτέω "ask" and αἰτοῦμαι "ask for a gift" (or "ask earnestly"). On the rendering "question," see 2630 c.

[7] [2630 b] Chrys. reads οὐκ ἐρωτήσω and so does Cramer. SS has "I say not unto you that I will beseech my Father—*but* my Father himself hath loved you," *a* has "et ego rogabo propter vos."

the context be examined, it will appear that our Lord is distinguishing between two stages of spiritual development for the disciples. He first says that, if the disciples love Him, they will keep His commandments even though they may have momentarily deserted Him, and He will "request" the Father to give them another Paraclete. Then He leads them to a higher stage, xvi. 23—6 "In that day ye shall *request* nothing from me…. These things have I spoken to you in proverbs"—which we might perhaps call metaphors, or parables—"the hour cometh when I shall no longer speak to you in proverbs but shall announce to you plainly about the Father. In that day ye shall ask-for-gifts (αἰτήσεσθε) in my name, and *I say not [now] to you that I will request the Father* about you; for the Father of himself loveth you…." Here He speaks of what He will *not* do after the Resurrection and after the outpouring of the Holy Spirit. And this is quite compatible with the fact that just before His arrest —while the disciples are still in the stage of "dark sayings" and without the Spirit—He pours forth one last "request" for them[1].

---

[1] [2630 c] Ἐρωτήσω τὸν πατέρα can hardly mean "I will question the Father," for—apart from other objections—ἐρωτάω, meaning "question," in Jn, is always followed by a direct or indirect interrogative, i. 19, 21, 25, v. 12, ix. 2, 15, 19, xvi. 5, xviii. 21, or has something in the context that implies questioning (ix. 19, 21, xvi. 19, 30, xviii. 19, 21) (xvi. 23 is doubtful and perhaps includes both "ask a question" and "ask a boon").

[2630 d] Ἐρωτάω, in Alexandrian Greek of the 1st and later centuries, very freq. means "I ask whether you are pleased to do so and so," and is used in invitations to dinner and polite requests generally (*Oxyr. Pap.* i. no. 110 and 111 etc.). Hence ἐρωτηθείς (*Oxyr. Pap.* ii. no. 269) (perh. literally "*being asked what your pleasure is*") means "*please*" (A.D. 57). Comp. *ib.* i. no. 113 ἐρωτηθεὶς εὖ ποιήσεις ἀγοράσεις "I beg you to be good enough to…buy," ἐρωτηθεὶς ἀγόρασον, "I beg you to buy" (2nd century), iv. no. 744 ἐρωτῶ σε κ. παρακαλῶ σε (B.C. 1) etc.

[2630 e] From classical Gk no instances of ἐρωτάω, "ask a boon," are given by Steph., but the germ of it may perh. be traced in Eurip. *Phœnissæ* 15, where the childless Laius ἐλθὼν ἐρωτᾷ Φοῖβον ἐξαιτεῖ θ' ἅμα i.e. he not only asks Apollo whether it is the divine will that he should have children, but also asks for the boon. There is a close connexion between "Is it thy will?" and "Let it be thy will." Jn uses αἰτέω concerning the disciples "asking" (not concerning Christ, except in the words of the Samaritan Woman iv. 9 (act.) and Martha xi. 22 (mid.)) but ἐρωτάω concerning the Son when He describes Himself as "requesting" that the Father's good will may be fulfilled for the Church (xiv. 16, xvi. 26, xvii. 9 (*bis*), 15, 20).

[2630 f] The distinction apparently drawn in xvi. 26 between αἰτήσεσθε and ἐρωτήσω invites comparison with 1 Jn v. 16 ἐάν τις ἴδῃ τὸν ἀδελφὸν αὐτοῦ ἁμαρτάνοντα ἁμαρτίαν μὴ πρὸς θάνατον, αἰτήσει, καὶ δώσει αὐτῷ ζωήν, τοῖς ἁμαρτάνουσιν μὴ πρὸς

θάνατον. ἔστιν ἁμαρτία πρὸς θάνατον. οὐ περὶ ἐκείνης λέγω ἵνα ἐρωτήσῃ. This is preceded by the statement "If we *ask a gift* (αἰτώμεθα) *according to his will* he heareth us. And if we know that he heareth us [as to] whatsoever we *ask as a gift* (αἰτώμεθα), we know that we have our (lit.) askings [the things] that we have asked from him (ἔχομεν τὰ αἰτήματα ἃ ᾐτήκαμεν ἀπ' αὐτοῦ)." It would be pedantry to express in a translation intended for general readers the precise differences between αἰτέω, αἰτοῦμαι, and ἐρωτάω: but it would be an insult to the writer to suppose that he did not discriminate between them. The impression left on the reader is that ἐρωτάω means asking with a question as to what God's will may be, "*if it be thy will*," "*if it be possible*."

[2630 *g*] If that is the distinction in Jn, the meaning of 1 Jn v. 16 (*b*) may be, "There is a sin [that tends] toward death. *I am not* [*now*] *speaking about that, in order that he should ask* [*if it be possible, that it may be forgiven, or stopped before it be too late*]." In other words, the writer distinguishes between two classes of sins. About one class of sins he says, in effect, λέγω ἵνα αἰτήσῃς. About the other—which would require ἐρώτησις not αἴτησις—he does not say λέγω ἵνα μὴ ἐρωτήσῃς. He simply says οὐ λέγω ἵνα ἐρωτήσῃς, "I am not at this moment enjoining such an ἐρώτησις, I am not now talking about that."

[2630 *h*] Comp. Hermas *Vis*. iii. 10. 1—6 ἠρώτων ἵνα μοι ἀποκαλύψῃ...ἕτερον δεῖ σε ἐπερωτῆσαι ἵνα σοι ἀποκαλυφθῇ...πᾶσα ἐρώτησις ταπεινοφροσύνης χρῄζει...τί σὺ ὑπὸ χεῖρα αἰτεῖς ἀποκαλύψεις ἐν δεήσει; βλέπε μήποτε πολλὰ αἰτούμενος βλάψῃς σου τὴν σάρκα, where ἐρωτᾶν ἵνα expresses "request" for a revelation, and this "request" is afterwards called an "*asking*" or an "*urgent asking*." If we had before us the whole Christian literature of 50—150 A.D. we should probably find many such distinctions between verbs of praying. For example, δέομαι is never used by Mk, Jn, Heb., Pet., Jas, and Rev. Παρακαλέω, to mean "beseeching the Lord" (as in 2 Cor. xii. 8), is very rare in N.T. (apart from "beseeching" Christ to heal etc. in the Gospels. Jn consistently represents the Son, when praying to the Father, as ἐρωτῶν, not προσευχόμενος, nor δεόμενος, nor αἰτῶν, nor αἰτούμενος, nor παρακαλῶν. It is true that the Epistle says (1 Jn ii. 1) "If any man sin, we have a *Paraclete*"—("one called in to aid," "advocate," **1720** *k*)—"with the Father, Jesus Christ the righteous"; but this does not mean that the Paraclete "*beseeches*" (παρακαλεῖ) the Father. The Johannine doctrine is that the Son, when on earth, offered "requests" to the Father, but that, in heaven, "request" became unmeaning in the unity between the Father and the Son.

[2630 *i*] Westcott (on 1 Jn v. 16) says, "It is interesting to notice that ἐρωτᾶν is used in this sense of Christian prayer for Christians in a very early inscription in the Roman Catacombs: ΖΗϹΗϹ ΕΝ ΚѠ ΚΑΙ ΕΡѠΤΑ ΥΠΕΡ ΗΜѠΝ (Northcote and Brownlow, Roma Sotteranea, ii. 159)." It is much to be regretted that Westcott neither adds the evidence shewing that this inscription is "very early," nor gives any indication as to the rarity or frequency of ἐρωτάω in this sense in other "very early" inscriptions. I have not been able to find in Boeckh more than the following, which may be the one he has in view, "9673 Romae lapis nuper repertus in coemeterio Callisti. Edidit Rénier apud Perretum Les catacombes de Rome VI. p. 28 et 178, qui habet a Bonnettyo Annales de philosophie chrétienne IV. série, tom. IX. p. 111, quem librum inspicere mihi non licuit. Versus duos extremos citat etiam Wiseman Fabiola p. 147." The inscription is κατ[αθεσις] τη προ ιγ καλ[ανδων] ιουν[ιων] Αυγενδε ζησαις εν κω και ερωτα υπερ ημων. Boeckh makes no further remarks. Κατάθεσις, here abbreviated as κατ, is not given by Steph., L. S., or Sophocles, in the sense of "interment"—which it seems to have

§ 2. *Parentheses*

[2631] When a clause with "therefore (οὖν)" follows a parenthesis, the "therefore" ought to look back beyond the parenthesis to some preceding statement, *e.g.* iv. 7—9 "Jesus saith to her, 'Give me to drink' (for his disciples had gone away into the city to buy food). The Samaritan woman *therefore* saith unto him...." Here οὖν means "in consequence of Christ's request." But, if we remove the marks of parenthesis, it might seem that the woman uttered this *because the disciples had gone away*, and it is perhaps partly because of this ambiguity, and partly because of a feeling that the chronological order should be kept, that SS rearranges the whole text as follows:—

iv. 6—9 (Gk)	iv. 6—9 (SS)
"Now (δέ) there was there Jacob's spring. Jesus *therefore*... sat...over the spring. It was about the sixth hour. There cometh a woman from Samaria to draw water. Jesus saith to her, Give me to drink.—*For his disciples had gone away into the city to buy food*.... The woman of Samaria *therefore* saith to him, How dost thou—*being a Jew*—ask drink from me...?"	"Now there was there Jacob's spring of water, *and* Jesus came [and] sat over the spring...... *And his disciples had entered that town that they might buy themselves food*; and when Jesus sat down it was about the sixth hour, and a certain woman had come from Samaria to draw water. Jesus saith to her, Give me water to drink. That Samaritan woman saith to him Lo, *thou art a Jew*; how askest thou me for water to drink...?"

Here the Syriac once omits "therefore" and once renders it by "and." It also connects with the context the detached or parenthetical "it was about the sixth hour" by means of a "when." But the most important change is that SS places the parenthesis about the departure of the disciples earlier, in its chronological order.

---

here, and in 9598, 9610, 9649, 9651, 9660, 9663, 9675, 9831 (comp. 9661 κατετέθη). It occurs also in *Oxyr. Pap.* 475. 31 "burial." There are some hundreds of Christian sepulchral inscriptions given by Boeckh in the adjacent pages, and I have been unable to find any other that has ἐρῶτα. It should be added that κατάθεσις generally occurs at or near the end of an epitaph (except where the epitaph states nothing but the fact of κατάθεσις and the date) and not, as here, at the beginning. If genuine, ἐρῶτα would seem to be quite exceptional like μέμνησο [τοῦ σοῦ πατέρος] *ib.* 9865.

[2632] The arrangement of SS is chronological, but it is not Johannine. John does not accumulate his descriptions of scenery and circumstance at the beginning of a scene as in a stage direction, but prefers to give them in parentheses, each in its turn as it is wanted. Thus, after the words of Christ's mother, "Do whatsoever he may say unto you," John inserts "*Now there were there stone waterpots...holding two measures or three*"—but not till the insertion is made absolutely necessary as a preparation for Christ's following words, "Fill *the waterpots* with water[1]." Again, it is not till after Christ's exclamation "I thirst," that we read "*A vessel lay near full of vinegar.* A sponge, therefore, full of *the vinegar*...they brought near to his mouth. When therefore he received *the vinegar*, Jesus said, *It is finished*[2]." In these passages, "*the* waterpots" and "*the* vinegar" would be unintelligible without what we may call the immediately preceding and parenthetical stage direction[3].

---

[1] ii. 5—7.   [2] xix. 28—30.

[3] [2632 a] SS is wanting for these two passages. But, so far as the faithful representation of Johannine connexion of sentences depends—as it does very largely—upon the faithful representation of the Johannine οὖν, we must pronounce SS worthless, as may be seen from its renderings of οὖν in ii. 18 om., ii. 20 om., ii. 22 "but," iii. 25 "now," iv. 1 "now," iv. 5 "and," iv. 6 "and," iv. 9 (see **2631**), iv. 28 "and," iv. 33 om. Compare also the Gk and Syr. of xxi. 7:

Gk	SS
"Simon Peter therefore, having heard [that] 'It is the Lord,' girt himself with (lit.) the coat—*for he was naked*—and cast himself into the sea. But the other disciples came in the little boat,—*for they were not far from the land, but about two hundred cubits off*—dragging the net *of the fish*."	"Now Simon, when he heard it was our Lord, took his coat [and] put [it] on his loins ∧ and fell into the lake and was swimming and coming, *because they were not far from the dry land*. And the rest of the disciples were coming in the boat drawing that net ∧."

Here SS omits "for he was naked" and the curious addition "of the fish." It also places the parenthesis "for...land" earlier in the narrative, just as it did in the Samaritan Dialogue (**2631**).

[2632 b] In vi. 10 "Jesus said Make the men sit down.—*Now* (δέ) *there was much grass in the place*—The men therefore (οὖν) sat down," Syr. (Burk.) has "Go make the folk sit down [to meat] companies by companies. Now the green grass was plentiful in that same spot, and the folk sat down [to meat]," but SS "He saith to them: Make the folk sit down [to meat]. Now the green grass was plentiful in that same place. He saith to them: Go, make the folk sit down [to meat] *on the herbage*." Mk vi. 39 has ἐπέταξεν αὐτοῖς ἀνακλιθῆναι (marg. ἀνακλῖναι) πάντας, συμπόσια συμπόσια, ἐπὶ τῷ χλωρῷ χόρτῳ, which seems to have influenced the Syriac.

[2632 c] There are two parenthetic clauses, followed by "*then therefore*," in

[2633] A parenthesis is frequently followed by a resumptive οὖν, which, in some cases, may mean "consequently" but in others little more than "well, then" (or "to return, then") : ii. 16—18 " Make not my Father's house a house of merchandise.—*His disciples remembered that it is written, ' The zeal of thine house shall eat me up.'*—The Jews *therefore* answered and said..."; iii. 23—5 "And they used to come to [John] and to be baptized.—*For John had not yet been cast into prison.*—There arose *therefore* a questioning...about purifying"; iv. 8—9 "Jesus saith to her, Give me to drink.—*For his disciples had gone away...to buy food.*—The woman *therefore* saith to him...." So probably we should regard as parenthetical all that comes between iv. 26 "Jesus saith to her *I am* [the Messiah]" and iv. 28 "The woman *therefore* left her waterpot...[1]." In the following, however, the italicised words are probably not parenthetical, vi. 3—5 "Now (δέ) Jesus went up to the mountain and there he sat with his disciples. *Now there was* (ἦν δέ) *near at hand the passover, the feast of the Jews.* Jesus *therefore* having raised his eyes and having beheld that a great multitude was coming to him..." The mention of the passover may have a mystical meaning connected with what follows. Jesus is described as "raising his eyes" to the contempla-

---

xi. 12—14, "The disciples therefore said to him, 'Lord, if he is asleep he will be saved [from death].'—*But* (δέ) *Jesus had spoken about his death. But* (δέ) *they supposed that about the falling asleep of slumber he was speaking.*—Then therefore (τότε οὖν) Jesus said to them plainly, 'Lazarus is dead.'" SS renders δέ first by "*now*" and then by "*and*"; and, for "then therefore," it has "again," thus: "They say to him : 'Our Lord, if he sleepeth, he will live.' *Now Jesus on* [*the ground*] *that Lazar was dead had said* [*it*] *to them, and they were supposing that of sleep he said it.* Again *Jesus said to them plainly*, 'Lazar is dead.'"

[2632 d] In xix. 23 "The soldiers therefore...took his upper garments (and made four parts, for each soldier a part)—*and the tunic.* Now the tunic was without seam...," John passes rapidly over the "garments," for which there was no need to draw lots, to the "tunic," for which there was the need; and he twice mentions the "tunic," partly perhaps because the Synoptists had wholly omitted this detail. SS and D are wanting here. But this twofold mention of the tunic is avoided by most of the Latin and other versions by dropping "and the tunic." Thus they also avoid the parenthesis: *e* has "simili modo et tunicam. Erat autem ei tunica...," thus avoiding the parenthesis in a different way.

[1] [2633 a] The intervening words describe the arrival of the disciples: "And they were marvelling that he was speaking with a woman. No one however said, What seekest thou? or why speakest thou with her?" This does not seem to contain a reason for the woman's departure. But the astounding utterance "I am [the Messiah]" may be intended to explain her sudden departure and her leaving her waterpot behind her—either in amazement or in reverence for the "prophet."

tion of the New Passover, of which a type was to be presented in the Feeding of the Five Thousand. In xi. 4—6 "'This sickness is not unto death....'—*Now* (δέ) *Jesus loved...Lazarus.*—When *therefore* he heard that he was sick, he abode at that time two days in the place where he was...," οὖν may mean "well, then," or it may mean that, because He knew that the sickness was "not unto death," Jesus "consequently" abode where He was[1].

[2634] In some instances a δέ clause is followed by an οὖν clause that might express the consequence of the former, as in xviii. 1—3 "...Jesus went forth...where was a garden...*But* (δέ) Judas also... knew the place...Judas *therefore*...cometh." In this case it is reasonable to take the δέ clause as not parenthetic. But in what follows, xviii. 5—6 "He saith to them 'I am [he].'—*Now* (δέ) there stood Judas...with them.... When *therefore* he said to them, 'I am [he]' they went away backward and fell on the ground," the δέ clause seems parenthetic, and the "falling" is described as the effect of the majestic and mysterious utterance "I am [he]." In the following, the οὖν clause may be regarded possibly as the sequel of the immediately preceding sentence but more probably as looking back past a parenthesis, xi. 12—14 "His disciples therefore said, Lord, if he is fallen asleep he will recover.—*But* (δέ) Jesus had said [the words] concerning his death. *But* (δέ) they thought that he was saying [them] about falling really asleep.—Then *therefore* Jesus said to them plainly, 'Lazarus is dead[2].'"

---

[1] [2633 *b*] In the following, δέ (or οὐδέ) introduces a parenthetical clause, which is followed by an οὖν clause: vi. 10 Ποιήσατε...ἀναπεσεῖν (ἦν δὲ χόρτος πολὺς ἐν τῷ τόπῳ). ἀνέπεσαν οὖν, vii. 3—6 εἶπον οὖν πρὸς αὐτὸν οἱ ἀδ. αὐτοῦ...φανέρωσον σεαυτὸν τῷ κόσμῳ (οὐδὲ γὰρ οἱ ἀδ. αὐτοῦ ἐπίστευον εἰς αὐτόν). λέγει οὖν αὐτοῖς ὁ 'Ι., vii. 38—40 ὁ πιστεύων...ὕδατος ζῶντος (τοῦτο δὲ εἶπεν...ἐδοξάσθη). ἐκ τοῦ ὄχλου οὖν...ἔλεγον, xi. 1—3 ἦν δέ τις ἀσθενῶν...Μαρ. κ. Μάρθ. τῆς ἀδελφῆς αὐτῆς (ἦν δὲ Μαρ. ἡ ἀλείψασα...) ἀπέστειλαν οὖν αἱ ἀδελφαί, xi. 29—31 ἐκείνη δὲ...ἤρχετο πρὸς αὐτόν (οὔπω δὲ ἐληλύθει ὁ 'Ι....) οἱ οὖν 'Ιουδαῖοι...ἠκολούθησαν..., xi. 50—3 συμφέρει ὑμῖν ἵνα εἷς ἄνθρωπος ἀποθάνῃ... (τοῦτο δὲ ἀφ' ἑαυτοῦ οὐκ εἶπεν...) 'Απ' ἐκείνης οὖν τῆς ἡμέρας ἐβουλεύσαντο..., xii. 5—7 Διὰ τί...οὐκ...ἐδόθη πτωχοῖς; (εἶπεν δὲ τοῦτο...). εἶπεν οὖν ὁ 'Ιησοῦς, xii. 32—4 πάντας ἑλκύσω πρὸς ἐμαυτόν (τοῦτο δὲ ἔλεγεν σημαίνων...). ἀπεκρίθη οὖν αὐτῷ.... In xviii. 10—11, Christ's reply is to an action Σ. οὖν Π....ἀπέκοψεν αὐτοῦ τὸ ὠτάριον τὸ δεξιόν (ἦν δὲ ὄνομα τῷ δούλῳ Μάλχος). εἶπεν οὖν ὁ 'Ι. In all these cases οὖν follows a parenth. with δέ or οὐδέ.

[2] [2634 *a*] There is something extremely impressive in the reticence of the clause that defines the personality of Barabbas (in contrast with the details of Lk. xxiii. 19, 25). Coming at the end of a section, the clause is rather an appendix than a parenthesis, xviii. 40—xix. 1 "They therefore cried aloud again, saying 'Not

[2635] After xi. 57 "He will surely not come to the feast.—Now (δέ) the chief priests...had given commandment...so that they might take him," a new section begins, xii. 1 " *Therefore* Jesus...came to Bethany." The δέ clause cannot here be called parenthetical: but it takes the reader behind the scenes to the previous plotting of the chief priests, after having exhibited on the stage the gossipping multitude. As to the οὖν clause it is perhaps not merely resumptive but describes Jesus as knowing the danger and *"consequently" advancing to meet it*. This view is supported by the sentence following the arrival of Judas with the soldiers, xviii. 4 "Jesus, *therefore, knowing all things that were coming on him*, went forth, and saith to them, 'Whom seek ye?'" In many cases opinion may be divided as to whether a δέ clause is, or is not, parenthetical: but it is certain that οὖν (far more frequently than δέ) *introduces* the more weighty words and deeds of Christ[1], and that an οὖν clause is often *preceded* by a parenthetical, explanatory, or subordinate statement.

[2635 (i)] A parenthesis on a very large scale—a great parenthetic work of Christ in the conversion of Samaria—may possibly be indicated by the extraordinary construction in iv. 1—3 ὡς οὖν ἔγνω ὁ κύριος...ἀφῆκεν τὴν Ἰουδαίαν καὶ ἀπῆλθεν πάλιν εἰς τὴν Γαλιλαίαν, on which Blass (p. 192) truly says that it "is at least remarkable, since the aorist denotes the journey as completed, whereas in verses 4 ff. we have an account of what happened on the way, and the arrival in Galilee is not reached till verse 45." The Diatessaron places iv. 3 *a*

---

this [man] but Barabbas.—*Now I should explain that* (δέ) *B. was a robber*.—Then therefore [without more delay] (τότε οὖν) Pilate took Jesus and scourged [him]."

[1] [2635 *a*] The difference is particularly noticeable in the last nine chapters where δέ is not applied thus except in xiii. 1, xix. 9, xxi. 1, 4, 19. Contrast the frequency of οὖν, xiii. 6, 12, 26, 27, 31, xviii. 4, 7, 11, xix. 5, 26, 30, xx. 19, 21, xxi. 5, 15. Of the five instances of δέ, one (xix. 9) introduces a negation, and one (xxi. 19 τοῦτο δὲ εἶπε σημαίνων) is a subordinate or parenthetic statement of the meaning of what Christ has previously said, and this characterizes some of the earlier instances of δέ, *e.g.* ii. 21 ἐκεῖνος δὲ ἔλεγε..., vi. 6 τοῦτο δὲ ἔλεγε πειράζων, vi. 71 ἔλεγε δὲ τὸν Ἰούδαν, vii. 39 τοῦτο δὲ εἶπε, xi. 13 εἰρήκει δὲ ὁ Ἰησοῦς.

[2635 *b*] Δέ, when introducing a word or deed of Jesus, often follows an adv. phrase or participle, i. 38 στραφεὶς δέ, iv. 43 μετὰ δὲ τὰς δύο ἡμέρας, vi. 12 ὡς δὲ ἐνεπλήσθησαν, vi. 61 εἰδὼς δὲ ὁ Ἰ., vii. 9 ταῦτα δὲ εἰπών, vii. 10 ὡς δὲ ἀνέβησαν, vii. 14 ἤδη δέ, etc. Such as the following are comparatively rare, ii. 24 αὐτὸς δὲ Ἰ. οὐκ ἐπίστευεν αὐτόν, v. 17 ὁ δὲ ἀπεκρίνατο, vi. 3 ἀνῆλθε δὲ εἰς τὸ ὄρος, vi. 20 ὁ δὲ λέγει αὐτοῖς, Ἐγώ εἰμι, viii. 59 Ἰ. δὲ ἐκρύβη etc.: xi. 41, xii. 23, 44 are exceptional and introduce acts or words of importance, but the rule remains as above.

early (sect. 6) immediately before the Baptist's imprisonment: "And [so] he left Judaea (Lk. iii. 19—20) And Herod...shut up John in prison. (Mt. iv. 12) And when Jesus heard that John was delivered up he went away (ἀνεχώρησεν, lit. retired) to Galilee." Long afterwards (sect. 21), omitting iv. 3 *b*, it has (after Mk vii. 31—7) iv. 4 "*And while he was passing through* the land of Samaria he came to one of the cities of the Samaritans," omitting the very important phrase in iv. 4 "*it was necessary*" (before "that he should pass through Samaria")[1]. Origen *ad loc.* has a long discussion on iv. 35 "four months," shewing that various inferences were drawn, from this expression, as to the date of the Samaritan dialogue. Πάλιν in iv. 3 is omitted by A, and is only added in the margin by B. Its omission suggests motives based on chronology. Πάλιν makes it almost necessary to suppose that Christ, having come up from Galilee to Jerusalem for the first Passover recorded in this Gospel, was now "going away to Galilee *again*," i.e. *back, without any very long interval, and certainly without any intervening visit to Galilee*. It was "*a return journey*." By omitting "*again*," the Diatessaron leaves itself free to regard the Samaritan Dialogue *as a much later event than the delivering up of John the Baptist*.

[2635 (ii)] Chrysostom, quoting the passage at some length, has Ὡς οὖν ἔγνω ὁ Ἰησοῦς...ἀνεχώρησεν ἀπὸ τῆς Ἰουδαίας καὶ ἦλθεν εἰς τὴν Γαλιλαίαν, and he repeats ἀναχωρέω twice later on "Why, pray, did He *retire* (ἀνεχώρει)?"—using the same word as that in Mt. iv. 12 quoted above. The context shews why he favoured this reading. He points out that the Gospel was in the first instance offered to the Jews, and that it was Jewish rejection that caused Jesus to preach the Gospel to the Samaritans, as it caused the Apostles to preach to the Gentiles. The visit to Samaria, he says, "was a *parergon* of His journey[2]." This seems to give us a clue to the Johannine expression and arrangement. John might have written continuously that Jesus, finding that His success was being magnified at the cost of the Baptist, (iv. 3) "left Judaea and went away back to Galilee, (iv. 44)

---

[1] [2635 (i) *a*] Nonnus has Καί μιν ἔτι χρέος εἷλε δι' εὐύδρου Σ.: ἔδει might be confused with the following δε, or read as ἔδε, *i.e.* ἐν δέ (with foll. inf.).

[2] [2635 (ii) *a*] Δεικνὺς ὁδοῦ πάρεργον αὐτὸν τοῦτο ποιούμενον, printed in Cramer ὥσπερ ἔργον αὐτὸν ποιούμενον τὴν τῆς Σαμαρείτιδος ὁδόν. In what precedes, Chrys. has ἀναχωρήσας γοῦν πάλιν τῶν αὐτῶν εἴχετο ὧν καὶ πρότερον. Οὐ γὰρ ἁπλῶς ἐπὶ τὴν Γαλιλαίαν ἀπήρχετο. This combines ἀναχωρέω and ἀπέρχομαι.

for Jesus himself testified that a prophet in his own country hath no honour." But he desires to insert a *parergon*, or at least what some might call by that name—the conversion of Samaria. This *parergon* he expresses by a long parenthesis. According to his custom he gives the reader an impression at first erroneous and then corrected. "He left Judaea and *went away back to Galilee*." Then follows the correction "*But it was necessary* that he should pass through Samaria": and every sympathetic reader of the Fourth Gospel would at once understand that "necessary" implied "the will of the Father" and that this "necessity" would issue in some divine consequence. If this view is correct, John's use of the aorist ἀπῆλθεν is remarkable but not erroneous.

§ 3. *Instances of doubtful connexion*

[2636] In i. 43—5 "...and he findeth Philip. And Jesus saith to him, Follow me. *Now* (δέ) Philip was from Bethsaida, sprung from[1] the city of Andrew and Peter. Philip findeth Nathanael...," δέ probably introduces a reference to the previous discipleship of Andrew and Peter, as if to say, *Now I ought to explain that* Philip was connected locally with Andrew and Peter, and they may have mentioned him to the Lord, who accordingly came to "find" him[2]. The Latin and Syriac versions vary as to the italicised words in vi. 64—5 "'But there are some of you that believe not.'—For Jesus knew from the beginning...who was to betray him.—And *he proceeded to say* (καὶ ἔλεγεν) *For this cause have I told you* that no one can come unto me except...," SS has "*He saith to them Therefore I have said to you*[3]," a "et dicebat: propterea dixi vobis, Nemo...," e "et dicebat propterea quia," Chrysostom omits "you that (ὑμῖν ὅτι)." Perhaps some rendered καὶ ἔλεγεν διὰ τοῦτο, "and it was for this cause that he said [previously]": but, if that had been the meaning, the text would probably have been διὰ τοῦτο εἶπεν or διὰ τοῦτο εἰρήκει. "For this cause" appears to mean "Because of the fundamental difference

---

[1] [2636 a] On ἀπό and ἐκ here, see **2289—93**. SS has "Now Philip, his kin was from Bethsaida, from the city of Andrew and of Simon."

[2] On vii. 22 οὐχ ὅτι τοῦ M. ἐστὶν ἀλλ' ἐκ τῶν πατέρων, see **2218—19**, and on iv. 9 οὐ γὰρ συγχρῶνται Ἰ. Σαμαρείταις, see **2066**.

[3] [2636 b] vi. 65 καὶ ἔλεγεν Διὰ τοῦτο εἴρηκα ὑμῖν ὅτι οὐδεὶς δύναται.... Comp. ix. 23 διὰ τοῦτο οἱ γονεῖς αὐτοῦ εἶπαν..., and especially xiii. 11—12 ᾔδει γὰρ τὸν παραδιδόντα αὐτόν· διὰ τοῦτο εἶπεν ὅτι Οὐχὶ πάντες καθαροί ἐστε.

between the unbelieving or selfish theory of things, and the believing or unselfish theory"; and this is implied in "there are some of you that believe not"; *i.e.* ye believe not in a Father but believe in your own worldly interests and in nothing else[1].

[2637] In xviii. 10 "Simon Peter *therefore* having a sword drew it...," οὖν cannot be resumptive of anything said about Peter, as he is not mentioned in the preceding context. Nor does οὖν introduce a consequence of the preceding words, which are "'...If therefore ye seek me let these depart'—that there might be fulfilled the word that he spake 'Whom thou hast given me of them I have lost none.'" Perhaps we may assume that the words "let *these* depart" implied that Christ Himself would *not* "depart" but surrendered Himself, and that Peter "*therefore*" intervened to prevent the surrender[2].

[2638] In xx. 10—11 "The disciples *therefore* went away to their own homes. But Mary was standing at the tomb. As *therefore* she was weeping, she glanced into the tomb," SS has "*now*" for the first "therefore" and "*and*" for the second, and makes one sentence of the whole. But W.H. regard the words "But Mary" as beginning a new section. Probably the first οὖν means "as the result of all that preceded," namely, the entering into the sepulchre. Οὖν is here nearly equivalent to μὲν οὖν, and as μέν ends a book of Thucydides

---

[1] [2636 c] In iii. 15 ἵνα πᾶς ὁ πιστεύων ἐν αὐτῷ ἔχῃ ζωὴν αἰώνιον, R.V. txt has "that whosoever *believeth may in him* have eternal life," but marg. "*believeth in him.*" (1) The former is supported by the following facts. Πιστεύω ἐν occurs nowhere in N.T. exc. Mk i. 15 "believe in the gospel" (**1480** *a*). (2) The variations here, εἰς αὐτόν, ἐπ' αὐτόν, ἐπ' αὐτῷ, indicate that ἐν was in the original text and caused difficulty to scribes assuming its connexion with πιστεύω. (3) It is in Jn's manner to have an adverbial phrase with ἐν before its verb when the phrase is emphatic or metaphorical as i. 1 ἐν ἀρχῇ ἦν etc. and comp. especially v. 39 ἐν αὐταῖς ζωὴν αἰ. ἔχειν, and 1 Jn passim. (4) It is also characteristic of Jn to introduce a new doctrine, first in broad and general terms, and then to "narrow down" (**2290**). So here the first two mentions of "believing" use the verb absolutely, iii. 12—15 "ye *believe* not...everyone that *believeth*." Then comes iii. 16 "everyone that *believeth in* (εἰς) *him*," where "him" refers to the previously mentioned "Son of man."

[2] [2637 *a*] It is surprising that the Latin versions here retain "therefore"; but SS has "*now*," and D τότε. It should be added that, in the context, almost every sentence of narrative is introduced with οὖν as though indicating that the delivering up of Christ took place in the regular sequence of divinely decreed cause and effect: and the evangelist may regard Peter's impulsive action as a part of the whole foreordained series.

and δέ begins the next[1], so here οὖν ends the account of what the two disciples saw, and δέ introduces the weeping of Mary as a preparation for what she, in her turn, was destined to see. The effect of the particles is something of this kind: "So the upshot of it all was that the two disciples went back to their several homes. One indeed believed. But neither he nor Peter had any message of glad tidings to convey to the Eleven. So *they* went away, and *that was all as far as they were concerned*. *But* Mary on the other hand abode by the tomb in tears. While *therefore* she wept she received a vision of angels and then a manifestation of the Saviour Himself. And so she returned, not to her home but to the disciples, the first to proclaim the Gospel of the Resurrection."

[2639] There is a parenthesis with asyndeton (according to W.H.) in the following, ii. 16—18 "'Take these things hence......make not my Father's house a house of merchandise.'—His disciples remembered[2] that it is written, 'The jealousy for thy house shall eat me up.'—The Jews *therefore* answered and said to him....." The variations of the authorities that insert conjunctions to destroy the asyndeton indicate that W.H. are right. But the question arises, *When* did the disciples remember this? At once, or after Christ's resurrection? In favour of the former it may be urged that several authorities insert "*at the time*," or something to that effect, and that, if John had meant "after the resurrection" he would have inserted the words as he does in ii. 22 "*When therefore he was raised from the dead* his disciples remembered....." But on the other side it may be replied that (1) John may have assumed that the clause "when he was raised from the dead," which he is purposing to introduce immediately, will modify "remembered" in both cases; (2) the hypothesis that the disciples spontaneously called to mind a prediction (virtually) of their Master's death at the very outset of His career perhaps never entered the mind of the evangelist and is certainly very improbable; (3) John habitually represents the disciples as misunderstanding much, and as foreseeing nothing, that relates to Christ's sacrifice; (4) the meaning "remembered [in after times]"

---

[1] Thuc. iii. 116 ταῦτα μὲν κατὰ τὸν χειμῶνα τοῦτον ἐγένετο... iv. 1 τοῦ δ' ἐπιγιγνομένου θέρους....

[2] [2639 a] SS as elsewhere (2631—2) avoids or softens the parenthetic abruptness by inserting "When he did these things" before "his disciples." D is wanting. Chrys. and *a* ins. τότε, A and *b* ins. δέ, *e* has "et continuo," *f* "et" (*b* also strangely has "discipulus ejus").

accords best with the two other passages that describe the disciples as applying Scripture to our Lord, so as to make a threefold mention of this "remembering[1]."

[2640] The discussion of the Johannine οὖν in narrative cannot be quite satisfactory because it is not at present capable of illustration from contemporary or earlier writers. In LXX, from the beginning of Numbers to the end of Chronicles, the Oxford concordance does not give thirty instances of οὖν, and, of these, none are in narrative[2]. In the Gospels, narrative οὖν is almost[3]—and in Revelation[4] it is quite—non-existent. In classical and non-classical Greek the Thesaurus gives no examples that can be fairly said to establish precedents or parallels for the Johannine usage. But some quotations from a Byzantine writer in the Thesaurus shew a tendency to use narrative οὖν abundantly in the sense "I say," "to resume": and these, although much later than the Johannine period, preclude a critic from deciding that John's usage is a mere idiosyncrasy of the writer[5]. Whatever may be the causes of the usage, there can be no

---

[1] [2639 b] Perhaps we might add, as a fifth reason, that if John had meant to modify ἐμνήσθησαν by τότε he could have inserted τότε (as Chrysostom does) or something of the same kind, e.g. "in that very hour."

[2] [2640 a] Οὖν is frequent in Genesis, but not in narrative. From Genesis to the end of Chronicles, narrative οὖν is non-existent except in a few instances in Exodus, as follows. In Ex. iv. 4 it occurs, like Johannine δέ, in parenthesis, "'stretch forth thy hand and grasp the tail.'—Having *therefore* (Heb. *and*) stretched out his hand he grasped the tail and it became a rod in his hand—'in order that they may believe.'" (LXX ἔκτεινας οὖν, F καὶ ἔκτεινας.) In Ex. viii. 10, 19, εἶπεν οὖν, and εἶπαν οὖν (Heb. "and") occur in rapid dialogue, and *ib.* 17 "And the Lord said...stretch... And they did so and Aaron stretched," LXX omits "and they did so and" and substitutes οὖν i.e. "*accordingly*." It occurs also in Ex. xiv. 6 ἔζευξεν οὖν, xxxii. 26 συνῆλθον οὖν, and is a remarkable feature in this book.

[3] [2640 b] Οὖν narr. is in Mt. i. 17 πᾶσαι οὖν αἱ γ., xviii. 26, 29 (parab.) and xxvii. 17 συνηγμένων οὖν, Lk. iii. 7, xiii. 18 ἔλεγεν οὖν, xix. 12 εἶπεν οὖν. (In Lk. xx. 29 the Sadducees say ἑπτὰ οὖν ἀ. ἦσαν, where Mk xii. 20 has no conjunction and Mt. xxii. 25 has δέ.) In Acts, narrative μὲν οὖν is freq. but this is quite distinct from narrative οὖν which is very rare (perh. only is in x. 23, xvi. 11, xxii. 29, xxv. 1, 17 (? speech), 23). On οὖν in Christ's words in the Synoptists see **2191 a**.

[4] [2640 c] The absence of οὖν narr. in Revelation is important because, like the Acts, it is largely made up of narrative, so that we might have expected narrative οὖν in abundance if it had been written by the hand that wrote the Fourth Gospel.

[5] [2640 d] In the following, οὖν is repeated resumptively after clauses such as ἐξ ἐκείνου τοῦ χρόνου, Steph. v. 2391 "Mire Jo. Malalas p. 29, 19: Οἱ οὖν Σύροι Ἀντιοχεῖς ἐξ ἐκείνου τοῦ χρόνου ἀφ' οὗ οἱ Ἀργεῖοι ἐλθόντες ἐξήτησαν τὴν Ἰὼ ποιοῦσιν οὖν τὴν μνήμην· neque enim delendum videtur alterutrum. Simplex sic est p. 59,

doubt that the differences in the Greek Gospel between John's frequently repeated "and" and "but" and "therefore"—so often covered up by the Syriac and Latin translators—do help in a very remarkable manner to suggest relative importance and unimportance in the events of the Gospel; and the use of "therefore" often helps the reader to receive the impression that what Christ said or did was not an accident but a consequence, an effect proceeding from a cause, and that cause from a cause still higher, reaching to the First Cause of all.

16: Τὰ δὲ μεταγενέστερα βασίλεια Αἰγυπτίων, λέγω δὲ ἀπὸ τοῦ Ναραχὼ καὶ κάτω, συνεγράψατο οὖν ταῦτα Θεόφιλος· 101, 13: Καὶ οὐ παρεχώρησεν, ἀλλ' εὐθέως ἀπὸ τοῦ κόπου...συμβαλὼν οὖν μάχεται· 195, 4: Καὶ εἰσελθόντα πρὸς αὐτὴν ἅμα τοῖς... πρεσβευταῖς γνωρίσασα οὖν αὐτόν· 238, 4: Ἀκηκουῖα δὲ τοῦ...Χριστοῦ τὰ ἰάματα, ὃς ...θεραπεύει, πρὸς αὐτὸν οὖν κἀγὼ...ἔδραμον· et similiter 362, 12; 380, 1. Ceterum imprimis part. οὖν frequentari ab scholiastis notavit Dobr. ad Aristoph. Pl. 973, p. 120, qui exx. illic citatis facile plurima ex schol. Aristoph. et aliis adjicere potuisset."

[2640 e] The foll. are not in narr., but they are useful as illustrating the various uses of οὖν: Fayûm Pap. 133 (4th century) καθ' αὐτὴν οὖν τὴν ὄψιν, μὴ πισθεὶς οὖν τοῖς καρπώναις, τὴν τρύγην ποίησε, "*so I say* at sight of this—not listening, *I say*, to the fruit-buyers—make the vintage." Note also the strange use of οὖν at the beginning of the following letter, ib. 114 (A.D. 100) "L.B.G. to his son S. greeting. *To repeat what I said* (οὖν)—*on receipt of my letter you will oblige me by sending Pindarus...to me at the city* (εὖ οὖν πυήσας κομισάμενος μου τὴν ἐπιστολὴν πέμσις μυ Πίνδαρον εἰς τὴν πόλιν)." This may perhaps be explained as a repetition of the phrase in a letter from L.B.G. to S. a few days before (ib. 113). "Be sure to send Pindarus...*you will oblige me therefore immediately by sending him immediately* (sic) (εὖ οὖν πυήσας ἐξαυτῆς πέμσις αὐτὸν ἐξαυτῆς)." The later of these two letters (no. 114) indicates that G. was vexed with his son for delaying—on the pretext that he was busy threshing—to send some fish: "Send the fish on the 24th or 25th for Gemella's birthday feast. *Finally* (ο(ὖ)ν) don't talk nonsense about your threshing." Two previous letters from Gemellus (111 and 112) after a long list of minute instructions, end thus μὴ οὖν ἄλλως πυήσῃς, "*So*, (or, *finally*) don't neglect these instructions," and the same formula occurs in 115, 118, and 119, besides being conjecturally supplied in 116. Note the curious spelling of ποιεῖν as πυεῖν.

APPENDIX I

TWOFOLD MEANINGS AND EVENTS

§ 1. *Our Lord's Sayings*

[2641] It belongs to a Commentary, not to a Grammar, to illustrate in detail the double and mystical meanings that underlie large portions of the Fourth Gospel. But they may be briefly touched on here, as the recognition of them sometimes influences the grammatical interpretation or the textual reading, as, for example, will appear (**2648**) in relation to i. 28 W.H. "Bethany," R.V. txt. "Bethany" but marg. "Bethabarah" or "Betharabah."

[2642] To begin with our Lord's sayings, John himself tells us that the words "Destroy this temple...[1]" were misunderstood by all till after Christ's resurrection, and that the disciples understood "our friend Lazarus has fallen asleep[2]" to refer to literal sleep. Before the Feeding of the Five Thousand, Jesus says to Philip, "Whence shall we buy bread that these may eat[3]?" and though John does not say that this had a double meaning, he adds "But this he said, tempting him"—implying that the words did not mean what anyone, taking them literally, would have supposed them to mean. As regards the prophecy "A little while and ye behold me no more and again a little while and ye shall see me[4]," he says that the disciples were perplexed about it, and implies that they misunderstood it even after Christ's further comment. The utterance to the Lord's mother, "My hour is not yet come[5]," and the prediction to Peter "Thou

---

[1] ii. 19.   [2] xi. 11.   [3] vi. 5.   [4] xvi. 16.
[5] [2642 a] ii. 4. In **2230** it was said that this verse could present no doubt about its meaning to "contemporary" Greeks. This limitation contemplated Nonnus' interpretation of Christ's words to Mary τί ἐμοὶ καὶ σοί; which he

shalt follow me hereafter[1]," are not commented on, but the impression left on the reader is that neither of these utterances is supposed by the evangelist to have been understood at the time. The second of these, in a slightly varied form ("Follow me"), occurs again in a mysterious connexion later on, after the prediction "When thou shalt grow old, thou shalt stretch out thy hands, and another shall gird thee and carry thee whither thou wouldest not[2]," to which is added "This he said signifying by what manner of death he should glorify God." But it seems doubtful whether the prediction was understood at the time. Almost the last words of Christ uttered to the multitude are "And I, if I be lifted up from the earth, will draw all men unto me[3]," and John adds expressly "This he said signifying by what manner of death he was destined to die"—namely, "lifted up" on the cross. No doubt, the evangelist included (here and elsewhere) the notion of "exaltation," or "ascension."

---

paraphrases as τί μοι, γύναι, ἠέ σοι αὐτῇ; Nonnus wrote in the fifth century, and he descibes Mary at Cana thus:—

Ἐς εἰλαπίνην δὲ καὶ αὐτὴ
παρθενικὴ Χριστοῖο θεητόκος ἵκετο μήτηρ,
ἀχράντῳ παλάμῃ γαμίης ψαύουσα τραπέζης,
παιδοτόκος φυγόδεμνος, ἀεὶ μεθέπουσα κορείην.

It is probable that his translation of τί ἐμοὶ κ. σοί was influenced by poetic and theological feeling.

[1] xiii. 36.   [2] xxi. 18—19.

[3] [2642 b] xii. 32—4. "*Lift up*" implies (1) Gen. xl. 13 "exalting," (2) *ib.* 19 "executing." Is it not possible that there may be some connexion between the prediction that Christ would be "*lifted up*" and the prediction that He would "give" His "*flesh*" for the world? Comp. Gen. xl. 17—19 where the baker dreams that "the birds" eat bread from the baskets on his head and Joseph explains it, "Pharaoh shall *lift up* thy head from off thee and shall *hang thee on a tree* and the birds shall eat thy *flesh* from off thee." Thus, such a saying as "*the crucified feeds many*" would seem likely to be known to Jews from Jewish sources apart from the Greek sayings quoted above (**2211** c), to which add Artemid. iv. 49 "To fancy oneself crucified signifies glory and wealth: glory, because the crucified is *lifted higher* [*than others*], wealth because *he feeds many birds* (πολλοὺς τρέφειν οἰωνούς)." The same writer applies the phrase "*he feeds many*" to one condemned to fight with wild beasts in the arena, (ii. 54) "To fight with wild beasts is [a] good [sign] for a poor man, for *he will be able to feed many* (πολλοὺς γὰρ ἕξει τρέφειν). For indeed the man condemned to fight thus feeds the wild beasts from his own flesh (κ. γὰρ ὁ θηριομαχῶν ἀπὸ τῶν ἰδίων σαρκῶν τὰ θηρία τρέφει)." Τρέφω is used for feeding slaves in *Pap. Oxyr.* iii. 489, ll. 9, 17, and in the phrase "*board* and clothing" for apprentices, *ib.* iv. 725, ll. 15, 45. "Pasco" is applied to the feeding of slaves by their masters and of crows by the slaves on the cross (Hor. *Ep.* i. 16. 48 "non pasces in cruce corvos," and see Juv. iii. 141, annot. Mayor).

But the multitude apparently recognise neither of these meanings. They reply "How sayest thou that the Son of man must be lifted up? Who is this Son of man?" The Gospel leaves us under the impression that all Christ's sayings were of the nature of "proverbs" till the Holy Spirit came. The very last saying of all is recorded to have given rise to a false impression about the disciple whom Jesus loved—namely, that "he would not die[1]."

§ 2. *The Sayings of the Disciples and of the Evangelist*

[2643] Here there is perhaps only one saying of which it can be distinctly said that the speaker meant one thing and unconsciously predicted another, namely, the utterance of Peter, "Lord, *I will lay down my life* for thy sake[2]." Luke's version is, "I am *ready* to go with thee to prison and to death[3]." The latter was not true. The former proved true, though not in the way anticipated by the speaker. There is no double meaning in "Now speakest thou clearly[4]"— uttered by the disciples to their Master at the very moment when they had been warned that the time was yet to come when He would cease to speak in "proverbs"—but there is an irony. As regards the saying of Philip "We have found Jesus the son of Joseph, [Jesus] of Nazareth[5]"—if we were certain that John accepted the tradition of the birth at Bethlehem there would be, here too, a touch of gentle irony in representing Philip as thus deluded and as nevertheless believing. But John's meaning may be that Philip's view of facts on earth was not incompatible with belief that Jesus was the incarnate Son of God from heaven. Another saying of Philip is that "Two hundred pennyworth of bread" would not suffice to give even "a little" to the Five Thousand[6]. This, in view of the prevalence of inner mystical interpretations in this Gospel, may have a double meaning: but in any case it will be found that double meaning in the sayings of the disciples is not so frequent as in those of non-believers (2645).

[2644] There is little of double meaning or irony in the comments of the evangelist made in his own person. He prefers for the most part to exhibit the Jews or Pilate as the mouthpieces of Providence uttering condemnations on themselves or testifying to the Messiah;

---

[1] xxi. 23. [2] xiii. 37. [3] Lk. xxii. 33.
[4] xvi. 29. [5] i. 45. [6] vi. 7.

or else to relate events in such a way as to suggest that while man after the flesh struts on the stage in front and says "I have authority," the hand of the real "authority," behind the curtain, directs all the puppet's movements. But under the head of evangelistic irony we may perhaps put down the statement that although many of the Jews in Jerusalem, beholding Christ's signs, "*trusted* in his name," Christ "did not *trust* himself to them[1]." Later on, when he sums up the cause of Christ's being rejected by the rulers, there is no irony but merely grave condemnation in the words, "They loved the glory of men rather than the glory of God[2]."

[2644 (i)] As regards the double meaning in xix. 30 κλίνας τὴν κεφαλήν it has been maintained elsewhere that the natural meaning is "rested the head," and that John intends, as the primary meaning (1456), "laying His head to rest on the bosom of the Father." Since that passage was written I have found the following in Origen's Latin commentary on Matthew (xxvii. 50 ἀφῆκεν τὸ πνεῦμα) "If we have understood the meaning of '*bending the head*' (inclinare caput) …let us be urgent so to keep our own lives that in our departure we too may be able…to deliver up our spirit even as Jesus, who *bent the head and took His departure in the act of resting it as it were on the lap of the Father who could cherish it and strengthen it in His bosom* (sicut Jesus, qui inclinavit caput et quasi supra Patris gremium illud repausans exiit, qui poterat illud in sinu suo favere et confortare)." And he proceeds to repeat "*inclinasse caput super gremium Patris*," and "*inclinare caput super gremium Dei.*"

§ 3. *The Sayings of Others*

[2645] Caiaphas is expressly asserted to have said, "It is expedient for you that one man should die for the people," under the influence of the spirit of prophecy[3], because Jesus "was destined to die for the nation, and not for the nation only but also that he might gather together into one the children of God that were scattered abroad." Similarly unconscious utterance of divine truth by unworthy and sinful agents is implied, though not stated, about other sayings indicating the sovereignty of Jesus and the destruction of the Jews. Thus Pilate writes the title "*King of the Jews.*" The chief priests—who are uniquely called on this occasion "chief priests

---

[1] ii. 23—4.   [2] xii. 43.   [3] xi. 50—1.

*of the Jews*¹"—say, "Write not '*King of the Jews.*'" But Pilate replies, "What I have written, I have written." Elsewhere the Pharisees predict, in effect, the conversion of the world to Christ, "Behold, the world hath gone after him²." And, to one writing thirty years after the fall of Jerusalem, the following, in spite of the conditional clause, would read like an unconscious prophecy, " If we let him alone thus, all will believe in him, and *the Romans will come and take away both our place and our nation*³." In the days of the descendants of Gideon, the trees of the field chose the bramble to be their king, and fire was to come out from the bramble upon them⁴; so, in the Fourth Gospel, the Jews cried, " We have no king but Caesar⁵," and fire came out from Caesar to destroy their city. Other ironies may probably be found in Pilate's exhibition of "the [ideal] man" with the saying, "Behold the man⁶!" and in the sayings of the multitude, "Surely he will not come up to the feast," "Who is this Son of man?" "Will he go to the dispersion of the Greeks and teach the Greeks⁷?" As to Pilate, the whole of the Dialogue between him and Christ inside the Praetorium, and between Pilate and the Jews outside it, reads like an ironical drama on the subject of "False Authority, or the Ruler that is a Slave." But on this subject enough has been said elsewhere (**1562—94**) to illustrate the Johannine irony latent in Pilate's words, "I have authority to release thee and I have authority to crucify thee⁸."

§ 4. *Events*

[**2646**] On two occasions Christ "was hidden" from the Jews. In both, a literal meaning is intended, but a spiritual meaning also is almost certainly included. In both cases apparently the "hiding" takes place in the Temple⁹, and in the context of both there are mentions of "light" and "blindness" which imply that the Shechinah is being described as withdrawn first for a time, then finally. The

---

¹ [**2645** *a*] xix. 21. "Chief priests" occurs in Jn nine times elsewhere, but never with this addition.
² xii. 19.   ³ xi. 48.   ⁴ Judg. ix. 14—15.
⁵ xix. 15.   ⁶ xix. 5.
⁷ xi. 50, xii. 34, vii. 35.   ⁸ xix. 10.
⁹ viii. 59, xii. 36. The Temple is not actually mentioned in xii. 36, but it follows the entrance into Jerusalem which is connected by the Synoptists with the entrance into the Temple.

[2647] TWOFOLD MEANINGS AND EVENTS

Jews, it is said, came up to the passover—the passover of the crucifixion—"*to purify themselves*[1]": at the same time they discuss the question of Christ's venturing to come up to the Feast, and decide that He will "surely not come." They speak as spectators, neither for, nor against, Christ. But this mention of "*purifying*" prepares the way for the hypocrisy of their rulers, who, soon afterwards, "*defile* themselves" (as Matthew's Gospel implies[2]) by letting slander "go forth out of their mouth" ("if this man were not an evil-doer we should not have delivered him up unto thee[3]") and yet "entered not into the palace that *they might not be defiled*[4]."

[2647] Of a different kind are certain arrangements and connexions of events that indicate a recognition of the mysterious ways in which the circle of things comes round, and history repeats itself, yet with the strangest vicissitudes[5]. Thus it is implied (2624) that the public life of Christ opens with a six days' work preparing the way for the Feast at Cana when the wine was changed to water, and that it closes with a six days' work preparing the way for the Passover, the sacrifice of the Paschal Lamb, whence issued the water and the blood. The typical meaning of the Feast at Cana is indicated by the words "my hour *is not yet come*" in the former narrative, compared with the words "the hour *is come*," which precede the latter[6]. Again, in summing up Christ's work before the seventh and greatest "sign" (the raising of Lazarus) it is said, "He went away again beyond Jordan *into the place where John was at the first baptizing*...and they said, 'John indeed did no sign, but all things whatsoever John spake of this man were true[7].'"

[2648] This last passage represents Jesus—after being rejected by the Jews, who try to stone Him—as retreating, so to speak, before achieving His crowning victory: and He goes back "into the place where John was at the first baptizing," *i.e.* where the Gospel began. This place the Fourth Gospel—alone of the Gospels—has previously described by name, "*Bethany beyond Jordan*[8]"; and now, after mentioning this retirement, it proceeds to describe a summons to

---

[1] xi. 55. [2] Mt. xv. 11, 18.
[3] xviii. 30. [4] xviii. 28.
[5] Philo i. 298 χορεύει γὰρ ἐν κύκλῳ λόγος ὁ θεῖος, ὃν οἱ πολλοὶ τῶν ἀνθρώπων ὀνομάζουσι τύχην.
[6] ii. 4, xvii. 1. [7] x. 40—42, see 2649 (i).
[8] i. 28.

another "Bethany" ("a certain man was sick, Lazarus of *Bethany*"). To this Bethany, which might be called "*Bethany on this side Jordan*," Jesus now journeys and raises Lazarus from the dead. The third and last mention of this "Bethany this side Jordan" is the following: "Jesus therefore, six days before the Passover, came to Bethany[1]." At the first Bethany He was baptized for the work of His life on earth: at the second Bethany He is described as being anointed for His death and sacrifice.

[2649] Among minor interesting repetitions is the twofold use of ἐμβλέψας, where John the Baptist is said to have "looked intently on Jesus" before pronouncing Him to be the Lamb of God, and, a few verses afterwards, Jesus "looked intently" on "Simon son of John" before saying, "Thou shalt be Cephas," *i.e.* Peter or Stone[2]. Perhaps the evangelist regarded both the Baptist and the Messiah as perceiving by divine intuition what was in those whom they severally "looked on." Another interesting repetition (with variation) occurs in the first words of Jesus as Preacher of the Gospel and in His first words after He has risen from the dead. To Andrew and Andrew's nameless companion the Lord says, "*What seek ye*[3]?" After the life of the incarnate Son is closed on earth, and when the disciples have gained through sorrow and tears new insight into what that life has been, the voice of the risen Saviour utters, as its first words, to Mary, "Why weepest thou? *Whom seekest thou*[4]?" There are passages in O.T. and Philo that indicate how this question might be traditionally regarded as one of mystical meaning[5].

---

[1] xii. 1.
[2] [2649 *a*] i. 36, 42. Comp. Judg. vi. 14 "and the Lord *looked on* him (Gideon)," LXX ἐπέστρεψεν, "turned," al. exempl. ἐπέβλεψεν, "looked on"—whereby Gideon is endowed with strength ("Go, in this thy strength"). So in Lk. xxii. 61 "the Lord *turned and looked* on Peter (στραφεὶς ὁ κύριος ἐνέβλεψεν τῷ Πέτρῳ)." Lk. and Jn are the only two evangelists that describe Jesus as "looking intently on Peter." Mk x. 27, Mt. xix. 26, use ἐμβλ. of Christ "looking intently" on the discouraged disciples; in the same context, however, Mk x. 21 uses it of Christ looking on the rich young man, who "went away sorrowing" (**1744** i—xi).
[3] i. 38.   [4] xx. 15.
[5] [2649 *b*] Almost the first use of ζητέω in LXX (the only earlier one being Gen. xix. 11 "seeking the door") is the question of the unnamed man (Gen. xxxvii. 15 "a certain man") to the wandering Joseph "*What seekest thou?*" Philo (i. 196) regards Joseph as the type of the wandering soul to whom the ideal Man (ὁ πρὸς ἀλήθειαν ἄνθρωπος)—who dwells in our hearts—speaks as a Convicter (ἔλεγχος) asking us what we regard as the object of our life. By this "man"—whom the Targum calls the Man of God or Gabriel—Philo means the

[2649 (i)] TWOFOLD MEANINGS AND EVENTS

[2649 (i)] Concerning the retirement beyond Jordan, x. 40 καὶ ἀπῆλθεν πάλιν[1] πέραν τοῦ Ἰορδάνου, Alford refers to i. 28, but Westcott says "the reference is probably to some recent and unrecorded visit. The events of i. 28 are too remote." Both seem to assume that πάλιν means "again." But πάλιν means (1) "*back*" *locally*, as well as (2) "again" *temporally*[2], and John frequently has (1) with verbs of

---

Logos. So here the incarnate Logos puts to the two companions the question, "*What seek ye?*" The probability of a mystical meaning is increased by the occurrence, in the context (i. 38), of the phrase "Come and ye shall see" (**1598**).

[2649 *c*] In Genesis, the answer of Joseph to the "man" is "I seek my brothers," and the "man" guides him so that he may find them. So, concerning the two companions, it is said that "Andrew first *findeth his own brother*," and it is implied that Andrew's companion does the same.

[2649 *d*] It is worth noting (1) that Elenchos, the Convicter, is supposed by Philo to put this question to *every wandering soul, who may answer it wrongly or rightly*, and (2) that the question (xviii. 4, 7) "*Whom seek ye?*" is put—in a very different sense and in very different circumstances—to Judas and his companions when arresting Jesus. These men are quite ready with an answer. They are the "darkness," in one sense apprehending the light, but in another sense "not apprehending it." They want "Jesus of Nazareth." The answer to this is I AM, which causes them to "fall to the ground." Then, when they persist in their hostility, they are allowed to "apprehend" the Logos by binding Him and leading Him away as a prisoner.

[2649 *e*] Origen (Huet ii. 83 C—D) points out that the question addressed to Christ "*Where abidest thou?*" implies that they "*long to behold the habitation of the Son of God*" and that their "*seeking*" implies that they will "*find*." To the two companions Christ does not say at once where He "abides," but only, "Come, and ye *shall see*." Elsewhere Christ says (**2263** *e—f*), "The slave abideth not in the house for ever, *the Son abideth* [*in the house*] *for ever*," meaning in *the home, or bosom of the Father*. In Luke, Jesus (in the days of His youth) says (Lk. ii. 49) "Wist ye not that I must needs be in my *Father's* [*abiding-place*]?" If it be admitted that "Come and ye shall see!" means, in its inner sense, "Come unto me and ye shall experience the peace of those at home with God," then there is a parallelism between this promise and the fuller revelation to Mary Magdalene about that home : xx. 17 "Go unto my brethren and say to them, *I ascend unto my Father and your Father and my God and your God*."

---

[1] [2649 (i) *a*] SS and *e* omit πάλιν. So does Chrys., in quoting; but he paraphrases it as ἀναχωρεῖ and discusses it as being a retreat. Nonnus, ἐχάζετο, om. πάλιν. Perhaps SS and *e* were influenced by the notion that πάλιν must mean "a second time" and must imply a reference to a recent visit.

[2] [2649 (i) *b*] See Steph. (87 B) quoting Aristarchus as to Homer's use, Τὸ πάλιν οὐκ ἔστιν ἐκ δευτέρου ὡς ἡμεῖς, ἀλλ' ἀντὶ τοῦ ἔμπαλιν ἐρεῖ, ἐναντίως, and giving copious instances of both uses, and of πάλιν ἐλθεῖν = "redire." He also quotes a schol. on *Il*. ii. 276 τὸ δὲ πάλιν, εἰς τοὐπίσω· τὸ δὲ αὖτις χρονικόν, ἐξ ὑστέρου. Comp. 1 Jn ii. 8 πάλιν ἐντολὴν καινὴν γράφω, i.e. "*on the other hand*."

TWOFOLD MEANINGS AND EVENTS [2649 (ii)]

motion. Luke scarcely ever uses πάλιν[1]. Matthew uses it rarely in comparison with Mark, John more frequently than either[2]. Matthew and Luke frequently deviate from Mark's phrases with πάλιν[3]. One reason may have been that, when used with verbs of motion, πάλιν is ambiguous, since it may mean (1) "coming *back* to one's home, or to a place recently left," (2) "coming *a second time* to a strange city." Another reason may have been that the Greek word sometimes represented a Semitic original that might have various meanings[4]. At all events in xviii. 33 εἰσῆλθεν οὖν πάλιν does not mean "entered *a second time*" (for no previous entry has been mentioned): but, "went *back*," into the palace, comp. xx. 10 "went *back* (ἀπῆλθον πάλιν) to their homes": and in the present passage John seems to shew that he means "back" by adding "to the place where John was at the first baptizing," as if to say that the Saviour, before working His greatest sign, *went back* to the place where He had begun the Gospel. These passages make it probable that others should be similarly translated, *e.g.* iv. 3 "*went away back* (ἀπῆλθεν πάλιν) to Galilee," iv. 46 "*he came back therefore* (ἦλθεν οὖν πάλιν) to Cana of Galilee" (*i.e.* on the eve of working a new "sign" He came back to the place where He had worked His old and first "sign"), vi. 15 "he *retreated* (lit.) *back* (ἀνεχώρησεν πάλιν) to the mountain." He had not "retreated" before; He had "sat" there; now He retires "*back*" to the mountain.

[2649 (ii)] Πάλιν coming at the beginning of a sentence, *without any mention of motion in the preceding sentence*, naturally means "again" in the sense of "a second time." But πάλιν with a verb of motion may mean either "*a second time*" (as in "he came to London

---

[1] [2649 (i)c] Only thrice, Lk. xiii. 20, xxiii. 20, and vi. 43 οὐδὲ πάλιν δένδρον σαπρόν, "nor, *on the other hand*, does a bad tree..."—not a freq. use of πάλιν. If this was derived from a Græco-Hebraic document, we should suspect that the original was πᾶν, "not *any* tree." See the parall. Mt. vii. 17—19.

[2] [2649 (i)d] Mk about 27 times, Mt. about 16, Jn about 40.

[3] [2649 (i)e] Mk ii. 1, Mt. ix. 1, Lk. v. 17; Mk ii. 13, Mt. ix. 9, Lk. v. 27; Mk iii. 1, Mt. xii. 9, Lk. vi. 6; Mk iii. 20, Mt. xii. 22, Lk. xi. 14. All these Lk.-parallels are greatly modified by D, which inserts πάλιν in Lk. v. 27, vi. 6.

[4] [2649 (i)f] In the canonical books of LXX, πάλιν may be roughly regarded as an experimental way of rendering the Heb. "*I* [*re*]*turn and do*," i.e. "*I do again*,"—a rendering rare in later books. It occurs Gen. (10), Ex. (4), Lev. (1), Num. (1), Deut. (1), Josh. (1), Judg. (4), never in S. or K. and only once in Chron. That it is characteristic of a free Gk. transl. is shewn by the fact that it occurs (5) in 1 Esdr., (0) in Ezra, and (10) in Job. The freq. use of πάλιν is one of many characteristics common to Genesis and Mark.

again") or "*back*" (as in "turn *again*, Whittington"). In John, the general rule is that πάλιν after a verb of motion means "back," but πάλιν before a verb of motion may mean either "back" or "again" and the meaning depends on the preceding context. In xiv. 3, where Christ has previously said, "If I go [away]," πάλιν ἔρχομαι, coming in the middle of a sentence, is best rendered "I come back." So, too, in xvi. 28 ἐξῆλθον ἐκ τ. πατρὸς κ. ἐλήλυθα εἰς τ. κόσμον· πάλιν ἀφίημι τ. κόσμον..., though πάλιν comes at the beginning of a clause, the meaning is not "*a second time* I leave the world," but "*reversely*, or *returning back*, I leave the world," referring to what precedes. In xi. 7—8 ἄγωμεν εἰς τὴν Ἰ. πάλιν...πάλιν ὑπάγεις ἐκεῖ; the meaning of the first πάλιν seems to be "*back-again*"; and in the reply, the second πάλιν may have a temporal meaning, the local adverb being ἐκεῖ emphatic: "*A second time* dost thou go *there* (1527)?" In the description of Pilate's going to and fro between Jesus in the palace and the Jews outside, it has been shewn above that πάλιν at least once means "back," but once it may mean "a second time," xviii. 33 foll. εἰσῆλθεν οὖν πάλιν (*back*)...(38) πάλιν ἐξῆλθεν (*a second time* went out)...(xix. 4) (ἐξῆλθεν πάλιν ἔξω) went out *again* outside [or, went out *back* to the Jews *outside*]...(9) εἰσῆλθεν εἰς τὸ π. πάλιν (went into the palace *back again*, or *again*)."

[2649 (iii)] In xiii. 12 (W.H.) ὅτε οὖν ἔνιψεν...καὶ ἔλαβεν τ. ἱμάτια αὐτοῦ καὶ ⌜ἀνέπεσεν, πάλιν⌝ εἶπεν αὐτοῖς, the punctuation of W.H. txt would connect πάλιν with εἶπεν, "said to them *a second time*." But W.H. marg. ἀνέπεσεν πάλιν "lay down in his place *again*" is far more in accordance with Johannine usage and is probably supported by Origen (*ad loc.* τὸ σχῆμα τοῦ δειπνοῦντος ἀναλαβών, "*resuming* the appearance of one at a meal"), by Chrysostom (ἀνέλαβε τὰ ἱμάτια αὐτοῦ καὶ κατεκλίθη), and by Nonnus (παλίνορσος ἑοὺς ἔνδυνε χιτῶνας Καὶ παλάμης ἀγκῶνα παλινδίνητον ἐρείσας...εἶπεν...). This punctuation is also supported by *a* and *b* (*e* and *f* leave the connexion doubtful).

APPENDIX II

READINGS OF CODEX VATICANUS NOT ADOPTED BY WESTCOTT AND HORT

[2650] Where W.H. deviate from B, the following list reproduces B's text[1]. Adjacent to each reading of B is placed W.H.'s text in round brackets together with W.H.'s signs (⌐ ¬ and [ ]) of doubtful readings. Where readings agreeing with B are placed by W.H. at the foot of their page, the fact is indicated by "marg. as B." The context is given in some cases rather fully, because it often supplies manifest evidence as to the reasons for W.H.'s deviation. For example, the reader will soon discover that the scribe's error of repeating c twice, or of inserting o after c, or after ε, occurs so often as to make him in some cases an unsafe guide as to the article. The list was compiled from Tischendorf's edition of B (Leipsic, 1867).

[2651] Since the compilation, I have compared Tischendorf's edition, in a few instances, with Danesi's photograph of B. The results indicate some apparent errors in the text (or omissions in the notes) of the former, given below. It must be premised that the original writing of B has been coarsely inked over by a subsequent scribe, who has sometimes altered the text. For example, in i. 18, the photograph shews εω at the end of a line as part of εωρακεν, but the ω shews signs of having been originally o, and Tischendorf prints εορακεν and calls attention to the ω as a correction. This he also does elsewhere, not only in ix. 37 where ω is written above o, but in cases where (occasionally) the correction, if it exists, is not visible to

---

[1] [2650 a] The list does not give all the peculiarities of B's spelling rejected by W.H., *e.g.* the frequent use of ει for long ι—much more rarely (2654 b) for short ι—nor insertions or omissions of -ν *ephelkustikon*. But it gives B's abbreviations, ιc̄ (for Ἰησοῦς), θc̄ (for θεός), κc̄ (for κύριος), χc̄ (for Χριστός).

[2652] READINGS OF CODEX VATICANUS

a non-expert. This being the case, readers of Tischendorf and of the photograph naturally assume that the former will either reproduce in his pages the exact text of the latter with all its errors or else, in his notes, will call attention to the reading shewn by the photographic text as a correction of the original text. We are all the more entitled to expect this because Tischendorf, as a rule, agrees exactly with the photograph even where the text contains a palpable error, as in Jn v. 7 προc for πρo and Mk vi. 48 περιπαντωΝ for περιπατωΝ.

[2652] In these circumstances I have thought it worth while to call attention to the following discrepancies between the photograph and Tischendorf, as to which Tischendorf is silent. I have included cases where the photograph shews a correction above the line, *e.g.* Βαcιλεγει with c above, printed by Tischendorf βασιλευσ ει without note. Probably Tischendorf has commented on these and other differences elsewhere, but it is important to the possessor of the edition of Tischendorf above described that he should be aware of its deficiencies. The omission of c before ε, as in Βαcιλεγcει, is a common error of B, illustrating the tendency of the scribe to drop, or repeat, such letters as o, c, θ, and ε, as in Mk vi. 22 where Tischendorf rightly gives B's error in his text ειελθογcηc, adding, in a note, that the corrector has changed it to ειcελθογcηc. This bears upon the evidence of B in readings where the question turns on the insertion or omission of the article, o, in juxtaposition with similar letters. There may be other deviations in Tischendorf. These are merely what came under my notice in examining a few passages in the Fourth Gospel.

[2653]   TISCHENDORF   PHOTOGRAPH
   i. 45 ο προφηται   οιπροφηται
   i. 49 συ βασιλευσ ει cγΒαcιλεγει (with c above)
  iii. 27 λαμβανειν   λαμΒαινειν
   v. 15 ανθρωποσ   ανθρωποο
   v. 35 αγαλλιασθηναι   αγαλλιαθηναι
  vi. 15[1] ερχεσθαι   ερχεcθε
 viii. 39 εποιειτε   εποιειτε (2078—9)

---

[1] [2653 a] Tisch. corrects this error in a note, Introd. p. xli. "Alfordus testatur ερχεσθε pro ερχεσθαι, id quod nos fugit."

NOT ADOPTED BY WESTCOTT AND HORT [2654]

Tischendorf	Photograph
ix. 2 η οι γονεισ	ΗΟΙΟΙΓΟΝΕΙC
	ΑΙ
ix. 7 ερμηνευεται	ΕΡΜΗΝΕΥΕΤΕ
x. 6¹ τινα η	ΤΙΝΔΗΝ
xii. 27—8 πατερ...πατερ	ΠΔΤΕΡ...ΠΔΤΗΡ
xii. 43 υπερ	ΗΠΕΡ
	Ν
xviii. 17 ουν τω	ΟΥΤΩ
	Ε
xix. 31 επει παρασκευη	ΕΠΙΠΔΡΔCΚΕΥΗ
xx. 20 τον ιν̄	ΤΟΝ ΚΝ̄

§ 3. List of Readings

[2654]² Chap. i. 4 το φως και (f. τὸ φῶς τῶν ἀνθρώπων καί), 9 αληθεινον³ (f. ἀληθινόν), 12 ελαβαν (f. ἔλαβον), 13 ανθρωπων (f. αἱμάτων), ουδε εκ θεληματος σαρκος αλλ⁴ (f. οὐδὲ ἐκ θ. σ. οὐδὲ ἐκ θελήματος ἀνδρὸς ἀλλ᾽), εγενηθησαν (f. ἐγεννήθησαν), 14 χαριτος αληθειας (f. χ. καὶ ἀ.), 18 εορακεν (Tisch.) (f. ἑώρακεν), 21 συ ουν τι Ηλειας ει (f. Τί ⌜οὖν; [σὺ] Ἡλείας⌝ εἶ;, marg. Τί οὖν σύ; Ἡλείας εἶ;), 23 εφει (Tisch.) (f. ἔφη), 27 ουκ ειμι εγω αξιος (f. ὁ. ἐ. [ἐγὼ] ἄξιος), 35 ειστηκει (f. ἱστήκει), 41 ευρεσκει (f. εὑρίσκει), 48 προ του σαι (f. π. τ. σε).

Chap. ii. 1 τη τριτη ημερα (f. τῇ ⌜ἡμέρᾳ τῇ τρίτῃ⌝, marg. as B), 6 τρις (f. τρεῖς), 17 εστιν γεγραμμενον (f. γεγρ. ἐστίν), 19 και τρισιν

---

¹ [2653 b] Tisch. has no footnote, but says in Introd. p. xli. "τινα η ut M²; male M¹ τινα ην." The photograph has clearly ΤΙΝΔΗΝ.

² [2654 a] Om. = "omits"; f. = "for," e.g. "ελαβαν (f. ἔλαβον)" means that B has ελαβαν for W.H. ἔλαβον. This Appendix does not, as a rule, include the corrections of B mentioned by Tisch. as made by subsequent scribes. In some cases where Tisch. has been found to differ from the photograph and may be presumed to have differed because he thought he detected the original lettering under the coarse "inking over" of a secondary scribe, "Tisch." is inserted to indicate the fact.

³ [2654 b] Ἀληθινός is spelt without ε always later on (iv. 23, 37, vi. 32 etc.). Conversely, Νικόδημος occurs in iii. 1, but Νεικόδημος in iii. 4, 9, vii. 50, xix. 39.

⁴ [2654 c] Alford explains this omission by "homoeotel." But if the eye of the copyist had passed from the end of the first θεληματος to the end of the second, overlooking the intervening words, he would have written ουδε εκ θεληματος ανδρος αλλ. Homoeoteleuton, therefore, does not explain the omission. And the change (in the same sentence) of αιματων to ανθρωπων indicates that other than mere transcriptional causes have been at work.

[2655] READINGS OF CODEX VATICANUS

ημεραις (f. καὶ [ἐν] τρ. ἡμ.), 23 εν τω πασχα τη εορτη¹ (f. ἐν τ. πάσχα ἐν τῇ ἑ.).

Chap. iii. 4 λεγει προς αυτον Νεικ. (f. λ. πρ. ἀ. [ὁ] Ν.), 5 απεκριθη ο ἰ̅ς̅ (f. ἀ. [ὁ] Ἰησ.), 8 αλλα ουκ (f. ἀλλ᾽ οὐκ), 23 ην δε και ο Ιω. (f. ἦν δὲ καὶ [ὁ] Ἰω.), 27 ουδε εν αν (f. οὐδὲν ἐάν), 28 ειπον εγω ουκ ειμι εγω ο χ̅ς̅ (f. εἶπον [ἐγώ] Οὐκ ἐ. ἐ. ὁ χρ.), 34 ου γαρ εκ μετρου διδωσιν² (f. οὐ γ. ἐκ μ. δ. τὸ πνεῦμα).

[2655] Chap. iv. 1 ἰ̅ς̅ πλειονας μαθητας...και βαπτιζει Ιωανης (f. ⌜Ἰησ. πλ. μαθ....βαπτίζει [ἢ] Ἰωάνης⌝), 3 απηλθεν εις την Γ.³ (f. ἀπῆλθεν πάλιν εἰς τ. Γ.), 5 ο εδωκεν Ιακωβ τω Ιωσηφ (f. ὃ ἔδ. Ἰ. [τῷ] Ἰ.), 6 ουτω επι (f. οὕτως ἐπί), 9 ου γαρ συνχρωνται Ιουδαιοις⁴ Σαμαρειταις (f. [οὐ γὰρ σ. Ἰουδαῖοι Σ.]), 15 μηδε διερχομαι (f. μ. διέρχωμαι), 17 ειπεν αυτω (f. ἐ. [αὐτῷ]), 40 συνηλθον (Tisch.)⁵ ουν προς αυτον οι Σ. ηρωτων (f. ὡς οὖν ἦλθον πρὸς αὐτὸν οἱ Σ. ἠ.), 42 ελεγον (f. ἔλεγον [ὅτι]), την λαλιαν σου (f. τὴν ⌜σὴν λαλιάν⌝, marg. as B), 46 ηλθεν ουν παλιν εν Κανα της Γ. (f. ἦλθ. οὖν π. εἰς τὴν Κ. τῆς Γ.), 51 λεγονταις⁶ (f. -τες), 52 την ωραν εκεινην (f. τ. ὥραν παρ᾽ αὐτῶν), ειπον (f. εἶπαν), ωραν εβδομην αφηκεν αυτην⁷ ο πυρετος (f. ὥραν ἑ. ἀ. αὐτὸν ὁ π.), 54 τουτο δε παλιν (f. τοῦτο [δὲ] π.).

Chap. v. 2 Βηθσαιδα (f. ⌜Βηθζαθά⌝, marg. as B), 5 τριακοντα οκτω (f. τρ. [καὶ] ὀκτώ), 7 προς⁸ εμου (f. πρὸ ἐμοῦ), 14 αυτον⁹ ἰ̅ς̅ (f. ἀ. [ὁ] Ἰησ.), 15 ανηγγειλεν (f. ⌜εἶπεν⌝, marg. as B), 19 απεκρινατο ουν και

---

¹ [2654 d] Comp. vi. 4 (B) τὸ πασχα η εορτη των Ιουδαιων which might mean "the passover, [that is to say, not the Paschal offering but] the feast so called." If that is the meaning of the scribe in ii. 23, τη εορτη is appositional, not temporal, dative. But see 2715 c.

² In iii. 34, after διδωσιν, a space is left sufficient for more than one letter, and the margin adds το π̅ν̅α̅. The next words are ο πατηρ.

³ B marg. ins. παλιν (see 2635 (i)).

⁴ B has repeated the first c of cαμαρειταιc as the last c of ιουδαιοιc (see 2652).

⁵ The phot. shews ογνηλθον (with small superlinear ωc before ογν and cγν after it), which might easily be confused with cγνηλθον. See Tisch. Introd. p. xl.

⁶ Comp. i. 48 σαι for σε (where, however, σαι comes just above another σαι and might have been copied from the latter) and vi. 24.

⁷ Did the scribe take αυτην as agreeing with ωραν "the seventh hour precisely"?

⁸ προc arises from the corrupt addition of c between the two similar letters o and ε. In iv. 6 c was omitted through the juxtaposition of ε.

⁹ Αὐτόν coming at the end of a line is written αγτο̅, and o may have been omitted after it owing to the identity of the two letters.

NOT ADOPTED BY WESTCOTT AND HORT [2656]

ελεγεν (f. ἀπεκρ. οὖν [ὁ Ἰησοῦς] κ. ἔλεγεν), 35 αγαλλιασθηναι[1] (Tisch.) (f. ἀγαλλιαθῆναι), 44 του μονου ου[2] (f. τ. μόνου [θεοῦ] οὐ), 45 εστιν ο κατηγορων υμων προς τον πατερα[3] Μωυσης (f. ἔστιν ὁ κ. ὑμῶν Μ.), 47 πιστευετε[4] (f. ⌜πιστεύσετε⌝, marg. as B).

[2656] Chap. vi. 12 περισσευοντα (f. περισσεύσαντα), 15 ερχεσθε (2653 a) (f. ἔρχεσθαι), 17 ουπω προς αυτους εληλυθει ο ΙΣ (f. οὔπω ἐλ. ⌜π. ἀ. ὁ. Ἰησ.⌝, marg. οὔπω ἐλ. Ἰησ. π. αὐτούς), 19 ω[5] σταδιους (f. ὡς στ.), 22 περα[6] της (f. πέραν τῆς), 23 εκ της[7] Τιβεριαδος (f. ἐκ Τ.), 24 ζητουνταις[8] (f. ζητοῦντες), 25 και μη[9] ευροντες αυτον περαν της θαλασσης (f. καὶ εὑρόντες ἀ. π. τ. θ.), 30 ινα ειδωμεν (f. ἵνα ἴδωμεν), 36 εωρακατε με (f. ἑ. [με]), 43 μετα[10] αλληλων (f. μετ' ἀλλήλων), 44 προς[11] εμε (f. ⌜πρός με⌝, marg. as B), 46 εορακε (Tisch.) (2651) (f. ἑώρακεν), παρα θυ[12] (f. π. [τοῦ] θεοῦ), εορακεν (Tisch.) (f. ἑώρακεν), 50 φαγη και μη αποθνησκη[13] (f. φ. κ. μ. ⌜ἀποθάνῃ⌝, marg. as B), 51 ζησεται εις (f. ζήσει εἰς), 52 την σαρκα αυτου φαγειν (f. τ. σ. [αὐτοῦ] φ.), 53 αυτοις ΙΣ[14] (f. ἀ. [ὁ] Ἰησ.), φαγηται (f. φάγητε), 60 ειπον (f. εἶπαν), 64 αλλ εστιν (f. ἀλλὰ εἰσίν).

---

[1] [2655 a] The phot. clearly shews ΑΓΑΛΛΙΑΘΗΝΑΙ. Codex L has ἀγαλλιασθῆναι, which may have arisen from a supposed analogy in ἀγαλλιάσθωσαν (freq. in LXX). But ἀγαλλιασθῆναι belongs of right to ἀγαλλιάζω, which means (Steph.) "I reproach or revile." Clem. Alex. 815 quotes Ps. cxviii. 24 (LXX ἀγαλλιασώμεθα) ἀγαλλιαθῶμεν.

[2] Θεοῦ being written ΘΥ might be inserted by some MSS. and omitted by others, between -ΟΥ and ΟΥ. (See also 1895 and 2664.)

[3] [2655 b] Perh. rep. by B from what precedes (μὴ δοκεῖτε ὅτι ἐγὼ κατηγορήσω ὑμῶν π. τὸν πατέρα). SS omits π. τ. π. in both clauses.

[4] The variation might arise from C inserted or omitted before ε.

[5] C is dropped before C.

[6] [2656 a] ΠΕΡΑΤ in a MS. that used abbreviations might be easily copied as ΠΕΡΑΤ in a MS. that did not use them. Conversely (2651) in Mk vi. 48 B has ΠΕΡΙΠΑΝΤΩΝ for ΠΕΡΙΠΑΤΩΝ.

[7] This is the first mention of Tiberias. On the article with names, see 1967 foll.

[8] See above, i. 48, iv. 51.

[9] [2656 b] Perhaps the scribe meant "and because they had *not* found him on the east side of the sea, they now ask him how he had come from the east to the west." In xv. 7, μή is ins. where it is very difficult to make sense of it (see 2660 b).

[10] Comp. iii. 8 ἀλλὰ οὐκ.

[11] B has C and ε together.

[12] An error might arise from the similarity of ΤΟΥ and ΘΥ.

[13] On this, see 2530.

[14] [2656 c] B has ΑΥΤΟΙΣΙΣ, where O might easily have been dropped, or inserted.

[2657] READINGS OF CODEX VATICANUS

Chap. vii. 1 περιεπατει ι̅ς̅ (f. π. ⌈ὁ⌉ Ἰησ.), 3 σου τα εργα α ποιεις (f. ⌈σοῦ⌉ τὰ ἔργα⌉ ἃ ποιεῖς, marg. τὰ ἔργα σου ἃ ποιεῖς), 4 ζητει αυτο¹ εν παρησια ειναι (f. ζητεῖ⌈αὐτὸς⌉ (marg. αὐτό) ἐν παρρησίᾳ εἶναι), 6 παρεστιν² ετοιμος (f. ἐστιν ἕτοιμος), 12 αλλοι δε (f. ἄλλοι [δέ]), 22 ουκ οτι (f. οὐχ ὅτι), και σαββατω (f. κ. [ἐν]³ σαββάτῳ), 23 ει περιτομην λαμβανει ο⁴ ανθρωπος (f. εἰ π. λ. [ὁ] ἄνθρωπος), χολαται⁵ (f. χολᾶτε), 28 διδασκων ο ι̅ς̅ (f. δ. [ὁ] Ἰησ.), 37 εστηκει⁶ (f. ἱστήκει), προς εμε (f. πρός με), 38 ει⁷ εμε (f. εἰς ἐμέ), 39 του πνευματος ο (f. τ. π. ⌈οὗ⌉, marg. ὅ), ουπω γαρ ην πνευμα αγιον δεδομενον (f. ὁ. γ. ἦν πνεῦμα), 40 ελεγον οτι (f. ἔ. [ὅτι]), 42 ουκ η (f. οὐχ ἡ), 43 σχιμα (f. σχίσμα), 47 απεκρ. ουν οι Φ. (f. ἀπεκρ. οὖν [αὐτοῖς] οἱ Φ.).

[2657] Chap. viii. 12 ελαλησεν ι̅ς̅ (f. ἐ. [ὁ] Ἰ.), 14 η μαρτυρια μου αληθης εστιν (f. ⌈ἀλ. ἐ. ἡ μ. μου⌉, marg. as B), 15 καταта⁸ την σαρκα (f. κατὰ τ. σ.), 16 εγω και ο πεμψας με πατηρ (f. ἐ. κ. ὁ π. με [πατήρ]), 25 ειπεν αυτοις ι̅ς̅⁹ (f. ἐ. ἀ. [ὁ] Ἰ.), 28 ειπεν ουν ο ι̅ς̅ οτι οταν¹⁰ (f. ἐ. οὖν ὁ Ἰ., Ὅταν), ο πατηρ μου (f. ὁ πατήρ), 34 αυτοις ι̅ς̅¹¹ (f. ἀ. [ὁ] Ἰ.), δουλος εστιν της αμαρτιας¹² (f. δ. ἐστιν [τῆς ἁμαρτίας]), 39 αυτοις ι̅ς̅¹³ (f. αὐτοῖς [ὁ] Ἰ.), εποιειτε (Tisch.) (2653) (f. ⌈ποιεῖτε⌉, marg. as B), 41 ειπον (f. εἶπαν), 42 αυτοις ι̅ς̅¹⁴ (f. ἀ. [ὁ] Ἰ.), ει ο θ̅ς̅ ο¹⁵ πατηρ υμων ην (f. εἰ ὁ θεὸς π. ὑ. ἦν), 52 ειπον (f. εἶπαν), θανατον ου μη θεωρηση εις τον αιωνα¹⁶

---

¹ [2656 d] D and Syr (Burk.) also read αὐτό (but SS αὐτός), Alford says that E has αὐτόν. It is a case where ΑΥΤΟC if genuine would precede ε.

² Perh. repeated from (vii. 6) οὔπω πάρεστιν.

³ Ἐν, temporal, is omitted by B in ii. 19, 23 and xviii. 39 (**2715** c).

⁴ See **1961**.

⁵ See above i. 48, iv. 51, vi. 24, 53.

⁶ Comp. above, i. 35, and see **2661** c.

⁷ c dropped from εις before ε in εμε.

⁸ [**2657** a] Meaningless rep. of syll., comp. below, (xi. 11) ταυταυτα and the instances quoted by W.H. ii. 234, Mk ix. 25 εγω εγω επιτασσω (f. ἐγὼ ἐπιτάσσω), Acts xviii. 17 τουτωντων τω (for τούτων τῷ).

⁹ This is written ΑΥΤΟΙC at the end of a line and Ι̅C̅ at the beginning of the next. See **2656** c.

¹⁰ Ὅτι "recitativum" is inserted here, as in vii. 40. But here the archetype may have written οτ twice (**2657** a), ΟΤΟΤΑΝ, corrected by B to ΟΤΙΟΤΑΝ.

¹¹ ΑΥΤΟΙCΙ̅C̅ as usual.

¹² As above (v. 45), B repeated πρὸς τὸν πατέρα from a preceding clause, so here it perh. repeats τῆς ἁμαρτίας from the preceding πᾶς ὁ ποιῶν τὴν ἁμαρτίαν.

¹³ The facts are as in viii. 25 above.

¹⁴ ΑΥΤΟΙCΙ̅C̅.   ¹⁵ θ̅C̅Ο.

¹⁶ [**2657** b] In viii. 51 Jesus had said θάνατον οὐ μὴ θεωρήσῃ ἐ. τ. ἀ., and the Jews in viii. 52 repeat what He had said. According to W.H. they repeat

NOT ADOPTED BY WESTCOTT AND HORT [2658]

(f. οὐ μὴ γεύσηται θάνατον εἰς τὸν αἰῶνα), 56 ινα ειδη (f. ἵνα ἴδῃ), 57 ειπον (f. εἶπαν), εορακες (Tisch.) (f. ⌜ἑώρακας⌝, marg. ἑώρακέν σε)[1], 59 ι̅ς̅ εκρυβη[2] (f. Ἰ. δὲ ἐκρύβη). Chap. ix. 2 η οι οι γονεις (2653) (f. ἦ οἱ γονεῖς), 4 ημας δει εργαζεσθε[3] (f. ἡ δ. ἐργάζεσθαι), 7 ερμηνευετε[4] (f. ἑρμηνεύεται), απηλθεν βλεπων (f. ἀπῆλθεν οὖν καὶ ἐνίψατο καὶ ἦλθεν βλέπων[5]), 9 αλλ ομοιος (f. ἀλλὰ ὅμοιος), 10 πως ηνεωχθησαν (f. πῶς [οὖν] ἠ.), 16 αλλοι δε (f. ἄλλοι [δέ]), 22 ειπον (f. εἶπαν), 26 ειπον (f. εἶπαν), 27 τι ουν παλιν θελετε ακουειν (f. τι πάλιν θ. ἀ., marg. as B), 28 ειπον (f. εἶπαν), Μωσεως[6] (f. Μωυσέως), 31 αλλα εαν (f. ἀλλ' ἐάν), 36 και τις εστιν, εφη, κυριε (spelt κ̅ε̅)[7] (f. ⌜ἀπεκρίθη ἐκεῖνος [καὶ εἶπεν] Καὶ τίς ἐστιν⌝, κύριε, marg. as B), 37 (2651) εορακας (f. ἑώρακας), 40 ειπον (f. εἶπαν), 41 αυτοις ι̅ς̅[8] (f. ἀ. [ὁ] Ἰ.).

[2658] Chap. x. 1 αμην αμην υμιν λεγω (f. ἀ. ἀ. λ. ὑμῖν), 6 (Tisch.) τινα η[9] α ελαλει αυτοις (f. τίνα ἦν ἃ ἐ. ἀ.), 7 ειπεν ουν παλιν ι̅ς̅ αμην αμην υμιν λεγω (f. εἶπεν οὖν π. [ὁ] Ἰ., ἀ. ἀ. λέγω ὑμῖν), 18 ταυτην[10]

---

it inexactly, but, according to B, exactly. SS has viii. 51—2 "...death he shall not taste for ever... dost thou say, 'He that keepeth my word shall not taste death?'". Apparently these two high authorities both err by conforming inconsistent passages, but B conforms the second to the first, SS the first to the second. On misquotations in this Gospel, see **2544** foll.

[1] Comp. xvii. 7 (B) εδωκες: SS has "Fifty years old thou art not and A. hath seen thee?" ℵ has ἑώρακέν σε.

[2] This is written as parts of two lines, thus: ι̅ϲ̅ ΚΡΥΒΗ.

[3] In vii. 23 χολαται was for χολᾶτε, and here -ε is generally taken as a late inaccuracy for -αι, but see **2428** b foll.

[4] Tisch. prints ερμηνευεται, but the photogr. clearly has -τε with superlinear ΔΙ. See **2653** and note on ix. 4 above.

[5] [2657 c] SS has "'Go, wash thy face with a baptism of Shiloah'; and when he washed his face his eyes were opened." In the words of Christ, a and b omit "wash," e om. "wash" after "go," but has "...Siloam quod interpretatur missus et lava oculos tuos." Apparently B's omission is caused by homoeoteleuton. It is not corrected in the margin.

[6] But correctly spelt Μωυσει afterwards in the same verse.

[7] [2657 d] Nonnus has ἀνὴρ δ' ἠρεύγετο φωνήν, Κοίρανε, τίς πέλεν οὗτος, indicating that he had before him κε (for καί τίς ἐστιν; and that he read κε as κ̅ε̅ i.e. κύριε: ℵ actually has ειπεν κ̅ε̅ τις εστι with ϗ added above the line. Possibly the misunderstanding of καί, as requiring an additional verb, caused the addition of εἶπεν ("answered and [said]").

[8] ΑΥΤΟΙϹΙϹ.

[9] [2658 a] Inserted above, because, if true, the reading might be of great importance. But the photograph has clearly ΗΝ (**2653**).

[10] [2658 b] B om. την next to την, comp. below xiii. 7 με for μετα before τα, xiv. 10 λεγω om. after εγω.

εντολην (f. ταύτην τὴν ἐ.), 23 περιεπατει ιϲ (f. π. [ὁ] 'Ι.), 24 εκυκλευσαν (f. ⌜ἐκύκλωσαν⌝, marg. as B), ειπε¹ ημιν (f. εἰπὸν ἡμ.), 25 απεκριθη αυτοις ιϲ² (f. ἀπ. αὐτ. [ὁ] 'Ι.), Ειπον υμιν και ουκ επιστευσατε (f. ἐ. ὑ. κ. οὐ πιστεύετε), 34 απεκριθη αυτοις ιϲ (f. ἀπ. αὐτ. [ὁ] 'Ι.), 39 εζητουν παλιν αυτον πιασαι (f. ἐζ. [οὖν] ⌜αὐτ. πάλιν⌝ πιάσαι, marg. ἐζ. [οὖν] [πάλιν] αὐτ. πιάσαι).

Chap. xi. 11 ...εν αυτω ταυταυτα ειπεν (f. ἐν αὐτῷ. ταῦτα εἶπεν), 12 ειπον ουν (f. εἶπαν οὖν), 15 αλλ αγωμεν (f. ἀλλὰ ἀγ.), 20 Μαρια δε (f. ⌜Μαριὰμ⌝ δέ, marg. as B), 21 Ει ης ωδε (f. ⌜Κύριε, εἰ⌝ ἦς ὧδε, marg. as B), 24 αναστησεται εν τη αναστησει³ εν τη (f. ἀ. ἐ. τ. ἀναστάσει ἐ. τ.), 27 εγω πιστευω⁴ οτι (f. ἐ. πεπίστευκα ὅτι), 37 ειπον (f. εἶπαν), 38 ενβρειμωμενος (f. ἐμβριμώμενος), 39 τεταρτεος⁵ (f. τεταρταῖος), 44 λεγει ιϲ αυτοις (f. λέγει [ὁ] 'Ι. αὐτ.), 46 ειπον (f. εἶπαν), 52 αλλα ινα (f. ἀλλ' ἵνα), 54 παρησια (f. παρρησίᾳ).

[2659] Chap. xii. 3 ηλειψεν τους ποδας ιυ (f. ἤ. τ. π. [τοῦ] 'Ι.), η δε οικια επλησθη εκ της οσμης (f. ἡ. δ. ὁ. ἐπληρώθη ἐκ τ. ὀ.), 4 λεγει δε Ιουδας (f. λέγει [δὲ] 'Ι.), 9 ηλθον (f. ἦλθαν), 10 εβουλευσαντο δε και οι αρχ. ινα και (f. ἐ. δὲ οἱ ἀρχ. ἵνα καὶ), 12 ακουσαντες οτι ερχεται ο ιϲ (f. ἀ. ὅτι ἔρχεται 'Ιησ.), 13 (Tisch.) εκραυγασαν⁶ Ωσαννα (f. ἐκραύγαζον Ὠσ.), 18 δια τουτο υπηντησεν αυτω και ο οχλος (f. διὰ τοῦτο καὶ ὑπήντησεν αὐτῷ ὁ ὄχλος), 21 προσηλθον (f. προσῆλθαν), 28 πατερ⁷,

---

¹ [2658 c] Comp. xiii. 24 εἰπέ. On aor. imp. in -ον see 2437—9. Comp. Mt. iv. 3 εἰπόν (Tisch. εἰπέ), Lk. iv. 3 εἰπέ: but Mt. viii. 8, Lk. vii. 7 (a humble request) εἰπέ. Mk xiii. 4 εἰπὸν ἡμῖν πότε ταῦτα ἔσται is par. to Mt. xxiv. 3 εἰπὸν (Tisch. εἰπέ) ἡμῖν. Lk. xxii. 67 εἰ σὺ εἶ ὁ χρ. εἰπὸν ἡμῖν is exactly parall. to the present passage, and prob. the original had ειπο̄ (for εἰπόν) copied by B as ειπε.

² From this point the reader will not be reminded that B's omission of ο between αὐτοῖς and 'Ιησοῦς may be connected with the abbrev. spelling of the latter, giving ΑΥΤΟΙϹ ΙϹ, as here and ix. 41, x. 34 etc. In x. 7, 23 the omission of ὁ before 'Ιησοῦς cannot be thus explained.

³ Mechanical repetition of αναστη- for αναστα-.

⁴ [2658 d] The phot. has ΠΙϹΤΕΥΚΑ (with πε above), but there are traces of ω under ΚΑ. Tisch. prints πιστευω and adds note "pro πιστευω ipse *substituit πεπιστευκα."

⁵ [2658 e] On the interchange of ε and αι see i. 48, iv. 51, vi. 24, 53, vii. 23, ix. 4, xiv. 13, xv. 16.

⁶ [2659 a] The photograph has ΕΚΡΑΥΓΑΖΟΝ, with slight indications of erasure under Ζ, and Tisch. says "ex εκραυγασαν B³ fecit εκραυγαζον."

⁷ [2659 b] The phot. clearly has ΠΑΤΗΡ here with the accent on Η though it has ΠΑΤΕΡ in the previous verse with the accent on Α. On the possible difference between the two when used as vocatives, see 2052—3. There is no trace of correction or erasure in the photograph; and Tisch.'s silence indicates that he has printed ΠΑΤΗΡ as πατερ by error.

NOT ADOPTED BY WESTCOTT AND HORT [2659]

δοξασον μου[1] το ονομα (f. π. δ. σου τὸ ὄ.), 29 ο οχλος ο εστως (f. ὁ [οὖν] ὄ. ὁ ἑ.), 43 μαλλον υπερ την δοξαν (f. μ. ⌜ἤπερ⌝ τ. δ., marg. as B) 46 ινα ο πιστευων (f. ἵνα πᾶς ὁ π.).

Chap. xiii. 7 γνωση δε με[2] ταυτα (f. γ. δ. μετὰ ταῦτα), 9 λεγει αυτω Πετρος Σιμων[3] (f. λ. ἀ. Σ. Π.), 10 ουκ εχει χρειαν ει μη τους ποδας νιψασθαι (f. οὐκ ἔ. χ. [εἰ μὴ τ. π.][4] νίψασθαι), 14 B repeats twice ει ουν εγω ενιψα υμων τους ποδας ο κ̅ς̅ και ο διδασκαλος, 18 επηρεν[5] εμε την

---

[1] [2659 c] The photograph has, at the end of the line (which terminates with abbreviated letters), ʉ for м (as freq.), o (small) above ʉ, and, below the ʉ, the tail of a γ, making the usual abbreviation of μου, thus: ΔΟΖΑϹΟΝʉ̣. If the original was ΔΟΖΑϹΟ̄ΟΥ with the last letters written small, the mistake might easily be made by mechanical copyists, first writing ΔΟΖΑϹΟΝΟΥ and then reading this as ΔΟΖΑϹΟ̄ΜΟΥ.

[2] τα dropped next to τα and supplied by corrector above the line, comp. above, x. 18 την om. next to την.

[3] [2659 d] A noticeable variation of the usual order. The corrector has not rectified the error. In xiii. 21 there is also an unusual order in ἀμὴν ἀμὴν ὑμῖν λ.

[4] [2659 e] ℵ omits (as R.V. marg.) the words bracketed by W.H. "save the feet." But the omission may be thus explained. The context is:—

ΟΥΚΕΧΙΧΡΕΙΑΝΝΙ
ΨΑϹΘΑΙ.

Now ει "if" in this MS. (ℵ) is sometimes written ι (Mt. vi. 30, 2 Cor. ii. 2 corr. p.m., Lk. xii. 28). Suppose it to have been written so here in the archetype of ℵ thus:—

ΟΥΚΕΧΙΧΡΕΙΑΝΙ
ΜΗΤΟΥϹΠΟΔΑϹΝΙ
ΨΑϹΘΑΙ.

The ordinary error of homoeoteleuton would explain how the scribe mistook the final ΝΙ in the second line for the final ΝΙ in the first, and omitted the second line. Then it would be natural to divide the words as ΧΡΕΙΑ ΝΙΨΑϹΘΑΙ taking the former as χρεῖᾱ, *i.e.* χρείαν. The spelling of ΕΙΜΗ as ΙΜΗ would facilitate the corruptions Η and ΗΜΗ which some MSS. present. If "save the feet" is inserted, there is perhaps an allusion to the Levitical "washing (νίπτω)" of the hands and feet of the priests (Ex. xxx. 19, 20, 21) following the "bathing" (Ex. xxix. 4) by which they had been consecrated. And, in the context, the expression "*ye are clean, but not all*," suggests a parallelism between Jn and Ezr. vi. 20 "*all of them were clean as one* [*man*]." Jn is describing a preparation for the New Passover, and Ezra a preparation for the old one. It must be admitted, however, that Origen not only twice omits εἰ μὴ τοὺς πόδας but argues on the omission (*ad loc.*, Lomm. ii. 406—7). He inserts the clause in his (Latin transl.) comm. on Lev. (Lomm. ix. 181) but nothing in the context is based on the insertions, comp. **2079** *c*.

[5] [2659 f] The omission of επ following, at a little distance, a previous επ, seems to be a fault of the same kind as the omission of τα next to τα (xiii. 7)

πτερναν (f. ἐπῆρεν ἐπ' ἐμὲ τ. π.), 21 αμην αμην υμιν λεγω οτι (f. ἀ. ἀ. λέγω ὑμῖν ὅτι), 23 ον ηγαπα ι̅ς̅ (f. ὃν ἡ. [ὁ] Ἰ.), 26 αποκρινεται ουν ι̅ς̅... βαψας ουν ψωμιον (f. ἀποκρ. οὖν [ὁ] Ἰ....β. οὖν [τὸ] ψ.), 28 τουτο ουδεις εγνω (f. τοῦτο [δὲ] οὐδ. ἔ.), 37 λεγει αυτω ο Πετρος (f. λ. ἀ. [ὁ] Π.).

[2660] Chap. xiv. 6 λεγει αυτω ο[1] ι̅ς̅ (f. λέγει αὐτῷ Ἰησ.), 9 λεγει αυτω ο ι̅ς̅ (f. λέγει αὐτῷ [ὁ] Ἰησ.), 10 ου πιστευσεις[2] οτι (f. οὐ πιστεύεις ὅτι), τα ρηματα α εγω[3] υμιν απ εμαυτου ου λαλω (f. τ. ῥ. ἃ ἐγὼ λέγω ὑμῖν ἀπ. ἐ. οὐ λ.), 11 δια τα εργα αυτου πιστευετε μοι (f. δ. τ. ἔ. ⌈αὐτὰ⌉ π., marg. as B), 13 οτι αν αιτηται[4] εν τω ονοματι μου (f. ὅτι ἂν ⌈αἰτήσητε⌉ (marg. αἰτῆτε) ἐν τῷ ὀ. μου), 14 εαν τι αιτησητε με εν τω ο. μου (f. ἐάν τι ἀ. [με] ἐν τ. ὀ. μ.), 16 ινα μεθ υμων εις τον αιωνα η (f. ἵνα ⌈ῇ μεθ' ὑμ. εἰς τ. ἀ⌉., marg. as B).

Chap. xv. 5 χωρις εμου ου δυνασθε ποιειν ουδε εν[5] εαν... (f. χ. μ. οὐ δ. π. οὐδέν. ἐάν...), 7 Εαν μη[6] μεινητε εν εμοι... ο αν θελητε αιτησασθε (f. ἐὰν μείνητε ἐν ἐμοί...ὃ ἐὰν θελ. αἰτ.), 9 ε (f. ἐν)[7], 13 μειζονα ταυτης αγαπην ουδε εις[8] εχει (f. μ. τ. ἀ. οὐδεὶς ἔχει), 16 εξελεξασθαι[9] αλλ (f. ἐξελέξασθε ἀλλ'), οτι αν αιτητε τον πατερα (f. ὅτι ἂν ⌈αἰτήσητε⌉ τὸν π., marg. as B).

---

and to be one of a group of errors (xiii. 7—21) shewing the scribe in an unusually careless mood. But carelessness would not explain the insertion of ει μη τους πόδας in xiii. 10, as to which B is probably correct.

[1] [2660 a] Here, and in xiv. 9, xviii. 37, B ins. ο (where W.H. om. or bracket it) before ι̅c̅. In xx. 21 B has ο ι̅c̅ where W.H. have [ὁ Ἰησ.].

[2] Perhaps c was inserted as redupl. of ε (2650).

[3] λεϝω om. after εϝω (2658 b).

[4] -αι for -ε, see 2658 e.

[5] Οὐδὲ ἕν at the end of the sentence would resemble οὐδὲ ἕν adopted by W.H. in i. 3, where ℵD have οὐδέν. Comp. οὐδὲ εἷς in xv. 13 (B).

[6] [2660 b] Comp. vi. 25 where μή is ins. Here, if the archetype spelt ει as ι, confusion might be caused by εανμινητε with μι repeated by clerical error εανμιμινητε. In the same verse (xv. 7) B, alone of the uncials, reads αν for εαν. If εαν is right, this (and perh. xxi. 25) would be an instance, exceptional in John though frequent in the Synoptists, of ἐάν, for ἄν, with relative. But the reading is doubtful, for ℵ reads ὅσα ἐάν, A δ ἐὰν θέλετε, e "quod vultis." Ὅσα ἄν is read by ℵC as ὅσα ἐάν in xi. 22, and ὅσα itself is elsewhere confused with ἅ or ὅ. Perhaps here the original was οcαν or οcααν, corrected by B to οαν, by ℵ to οcαεαν, and by others to οεαν. The tendency to read ὅσα ἐάν would be increased by its frequency in Mt. (vii. 12, xviii. 18 (bis), xxiii. 3 etc.). [In 1 Jn iii. 22, W.H. print ὃ ἂν αἰτῶμεν (with B) without alternative.]

[7] This is not a mistake of ε̄ for ε at the end of a line: ε is in the middle of the line and ν added by a corrector above the line.

[8] Comp. ουδε εν in xv. 5 (B).

[9] On the interchange of -αι and -ε, see 2658 e.

NOT ADOPTED BY WESTCOTT AND HORT [2661]

Chap. xvi. 2 πας ο αποκτεινας[1] δοξη (f. π. ὁ ἀ. [ὑμᾶς] δόξῃ), 13 οσα ακουσει[2] λαλησει (f. ὅσα ⌜ἀκούει⌝ λαλήσει, marg. as B), 18 ουκ οιδαμεν (f. οὐκ οἴδαμεν [τί λαλεῖ])[3], 25 παρησια (f. παρρησίᾳ).

[2661] Chap. xvii. 7—8 παντα οσα εδωκες[4] μοι...τα ρηματα α εδωκες μοι (f. π. ὅσα ⌜ἔδωκάς⌝ (marg. δέδωκάς) μοι...τὰ ῥ. ἃ ⌜ἔδωκάς⌝ (marg. δέδωκάς) μοι), 11 Πατηρ[5] αγιε (f. πάτερ ἄγιε), ινα ωσιν εν καθως και ημεις (f. ἵνα ὦσιν ἐν καθὼς ἡμεῖς), 12 οτε ημεν[6] μετ αυτων (f. ὅτε ἤμην μετ' ἀ.), 15 ουκ ερωτω ινα αρης αυτους εκ του[7] πονηρου (f. οὐκ ἐρ. ἵνα ἄρ. αὐτ. ἐκ τοῦ κόσμου ἀλλ' ἵνα τηρήσῃς αὐτοὺς ἐκ τ. π.), 17 αγιασον αυτους εν αληθεια (f. ἀγ. αὐτ. ἐν τῇ ἀλ.), ο λογος ο σος η αληθεια[8] εστιν

---

[1] ΥΜΑC could be supplied from what precedes; but it has prob. been omitted by B owing to the similarity of ΝΑC, which begins a line, to the last three letters of ΥΜΑC.

[2] [2660 c] 'Ακούσει is confirmed by SS, a, and f "audierit" (d has "audierit" =D ἀκούσει). The act. fut. (instead of mid.) is non-classical and has been corrupted by scribes in 2 S. xiv. 16, Is. vi. 9, Mt. xii. 19; but it is read by B in Jn v. 25, 28, x. 16 (where W.H. adopt it, in spite of variations) and is prob. correct here.

[2660 d] Winer-Moulton (p. 99) recognises ἀκούσω in Mt. xii. 19, xiii. 14, Rom. x. 14 (Rec.), Jn xvi. 13, but adds, "'Ακούσομαι, however, is the more common future in the N.T. especially in Luke, see Acts iii. 22 (vii. 37), xvii. 32, xxv. 22, xxviii. 28 (Jn v. 28)." But Acts iii. 22 is a quotation from Deut. xviii. 15, and Acts vii. 37 is an interpolation from Acts iii. 22. Acts xvii. 32 and xxv. 22 contain the words of Athenian philosophers and a Roman Governor—whom Luke could hardly represent as using the active future. It is antecedently probable that Luke would generally prefer the middle future, when writing in his own person or in that of St Paul (Acts xxviii. 28); but Acts xxviii. 26 reproduces ἀκούσετε from Is. vi. 9. Mt. xii. 19 has ἀκούσει τις, where Is. xlii. 2 (LXX) has ἀκουσθήσεται, indicating a preference for the active fut., even against LXX. If we follow B as to the text of Jn it will not be true to say that "ἀκούσομαι is the more common future in the N.T." The truth seems to be that Matthew and John prefer the active whereas Luke prefers the middle.

[3] [2660 e] In xvi. 18, some auth. om. ἔλεγον οὖν, some om. ὃ λέγει, SS has, after "unto my Father," simply "What is then this 'A little' that he saith?"

[4] Comp. ἑόρακες in viii. 57.

[5] [2661 a] Contrast xvii. 5 (B) συ πατερ, D συ πατηρ with xvii. 11 (B) πατηρ αγιε, (D) πατερ αγιε, and see 2052—3, also 2659 b.

[6] In xi. 15, B has ἤμην correctly.

[7] Error of homoeoteleuton, caused by repetition of ἐκ τοῦ.

[8] [2661 b] B's (probable) errors both come at the end of lines—where the letters might have been originally small and obscure in the archetype. Ἐν ἀληθείᾳ, "in truth," might mean little more than "truly." Ἡ ἀλ. as a predicate, "thy name is *the truth*," would be contrary to the usage of Ps. cxix. 142 ὁ λόγος σου ἀλήθεια, ib. 151 πᾶσαι αἱ ὁδοί σου ἀλήθεια. B's txt would contain a kind of play on "truth": "Sanctify them not in mere name and not with mere external purifications but *in truth*. Thy word is *the truth* [*of which I speak*]."

(f. ὁ λ. ὁ σὸς ἀλ. ἐστιν), 18 B repeats twice καγω απεστειλα αυτους εις τον κοσμον, 19 και υπερ αυτων εγω αγιαζω εμαυτον (f. καὶ ὑ. ἀ. ⌈ἐγὼ⌉ ἁγ. εμ.), 24 την δοξαν την εμην ην εδωκας μοι (f. τὴν δ. τὴν ἐ. ἣν ⌈δέδωκας⌉ μοι, marg. as B).

Chap. xviii. 2 συνηχθη ι̅ς̅ μετα των μαθητων αυτου εκει[1] (f. σ. Ἰ. ⌈ἐκεῖ μετὰ τῶν μ. αὐτοῦ⌉, marg. as B), 3 εκ των αρχ. και των Φ. (f. ἐκ τῶν ἀρχ. καὶ [ἐκ] τῶν Φ.), 5 εγω ειμι ι̅ς̅[2] ιστηκει δε (f. ἐγώ εἰμι (marg. + Ἰησοῦς) ἱστήκει δέ...), 7 ειπον (f. εἶπαν), 15 γνωστος ην (f. ⌈ἦν γνωστός⌉, marg. as B), 17 ου τω[3] (f. οὖν τῷ), 20 παρησια (f. παρρησίᾳ), 36 ηγωνιζοντο ινα[4] (f. ἠγ. ἂν ἵνα), 37 απεκριθη ο[5] ι̅ς̅ (f. ἀπ. [ὁ] Ἰ.), 39 απολυσω υμιν τω[6] πασχα (f. ἀπ. ὑμ. [ἐν] τῷ π.).

[2662] Chap. xix. 5 εξηλθεν ουν ι̅ς̅ (f. ἐξ. οὖν [ὁ] Ἰ.), ιδου[7] ανθρωπος (f. ἰδοὺ ὁ ἄνθρ.), 12 λεγοντες αν τουτον (f. λ. Ἐὰν τοῦτον), 17 ο λεγετε[8]

---

[1] On the position of ἐκεῖ see 1527.

[2] [2661 c] Hitherto B has had ΕΙϹΤΗΚΕΙ (i. 35, vii. 37) not ΙϹΤΗΚΕΙ (as also in xx. 11), but here (xviii. 5) and in xviii. 16, 18, xix. 25 the text has had ΙϹΤΗΚΕΙ and a corrector has prefixed ε. In consequence of the initial ΙϹ here, the original scribe, by an error of repetition, has probably added ΙϹ, and it has been taken to mean Ι̅Ϲ̅ i.e. Ἰησοῦς. B's habit of repeating syllables makes its testimony for Ἰησοῦς (against almost every authority, but *a* has "*Jesus* autem") of very little value. Moreover there is some antecedent probability that ἐγώ ειμι might be intended to convey a double meaning (2220—8) which would be destroyed by inserting Ἰησοῦς.

[3] [2661 d] B has, at the beginning of a line, ΟΥΤω with part of a very small Ν above the line. Tisch. is silent. If the Ν was added by the original scribe, it might be explained by his copying from a MS. that had ΟΫ. See 2656 a.

[4] [2661 e] The ι (faintly written) of ΙΝΑ comes at the end of a line and the ΝΑ at the beginning of the next: ΑΝ may have dropped before ΙΝΑ. Above the faint ι at the end of the line there is written a small ΑΝ, and the ι is rewritten before the beginning of the next line, in the margin. Alford places ἄν earlier after ὑπηρέται (οἱ ὑπηρέται ἂν οἱ ἐμοὶ ἠγωνίζοντο ἵνα). In B, ΥΠΗΡΕΤΑΙ comes at the end of the line with some indistinctness in the ΑΙ, suggesting that it might be easily reduplicated as ΑΝ.

[5] [2661 f] Contrast ἀπεκρίθη Ἰ. in xviii. 8, 34, 36 and ἀπ. αὐτῷ Ἰ. in xviii. 20, 23, xix. 11. There is a blank space here (enough for a letter or a little more) after απεκριθη. Perh. an obscure ΟΫ was in B's archetype.

[6] For the omission of ἐν before the dative of time, see above, ii. 19, 23, vii. 22, and 2715 c.

[7] [2662 a] The omission of ο between γ and Α cannot easily be explained—unless indeed the scribe felt that the article implied contempt (1960). Read in the light of prophecy, the phrase "Behold a man" might suggest Zech. vi. 12 ἰδοὺ ἀνήρ, referring to the future Builder of the Temple.

[8] -ε for -αι, see 2658 e.

NOT ADOPTED BY WESTCOTT AND HORT [2663]

εβραιστι Γολγοθ· οπου (f. ὃ λέγεται Ἑβρ. ⌜Γολγοθά⌝ (marg. Γολγόθ) ὅπου), 23 τεσσαρα (f. τέσσερα), αρραφος (f. ἄραφος), 24 ειπον (f. εἶπαν), 28 ῑ̄ς ειδως (f. ⌜εἰδὼς ὁ Ἰ.⌝, marg. as B), 30 οτε ουν ελαβεν το οξος ῑ̄ς (f. ὅτε ὀ. ἔ. τὸ ὄξος [ὁ] Ἰ.), 31 η ημερα εκεινη του σαββατου (f. ἡ ἡμ. ⌜ἐκείνου⌝ τοῦ σ., marg. as B), 38 ὧν μαθητὴς ῑ̄υ (f. ὧν μ. [τοῦ] Ἰ.).

Chap. xx. 11 Μαρια δε ειστηκει (f. Μ. δὲ ἱστήκει), 13 τι κλαιεις και λεγει αυτοις (f. τί κλαίεις; λέγει αὐτοῖς), 17 μη απτου μου (f. ⌜μή μου ἅπτου⌝, marg. as B), 20 ιδοντες τον ῑ̄υ (Tisch.)[1] (f. ἰδόντες τὸν κύριον), 21 ειπεν ουν αυτοις ο ῑ̄ς[2] παλιν (f. εἶπεν οὖν αὐτοῖς [ὁ Ἰησοῦς] πάλιν), 23 αν τινος αφητε τας αμαρτιας αφειονται αυτοις αν τινος κρατητε κεκρατηνται (f. ἄν ⌜τινων⌝ (marg. τινος) ἀφ. τὰς ἀμ. ⌜ἀφέωνται⌝ (marg. ἀφίονται) αὐτοῖς· ἄν ⌜τινων⌝ (marg. τινος) κρατῆτε κεκράτηνται), 25 εορακαμεν (f. ἑωράκαμεν), 29 λεγει αυτω ῑ̄ς (f. λ. ἀ. [ὁ] Ἰ.).

Chap. xxi. 3 εξηλθον (f. ἐξῆλθαν), 10 and 12 λεγει αυτοις ῑ̄ς (f. λ. ἀ. [ὁ] Ἰ.), 12 ουδεις εντολμα (Tisch.)[3] (f. οὐδεὶς ἐτόλμα), 17 και ειπεν κυριε (spelt κ̄ε̄) παντα συ οιδας (f. καὶ εἶπεν αὐτῷ κύριε πάντα σὺ ὀ.), 24 ουτος εστιν ο μαθ. ο και μαρτυρων (f. οὗτος ἐ. ὁ μ. ὁ (marg. ins. καὶ) μαρτυρῶν).

§ 4. *Pause-spaces in B*

[2663] Pauses in B are often represented by spaces of varying size. W.H. frequently disagree from these, *e.g.* they make no pause before i. 15 Ἰ. μαρτυρεῖ, i. 18 θεὸν οὐδεὶς ἑώρακεν, ii. 19 ἀπεκρίθη Ἰ., ii. 20 εἶπαν οὖν οἱ Ἰουδ., iv. 28 ἀφῆκεν οὖν τὴν ὑδρίαν, iv. 45 ὅτε οὖν ἦλθεν εἰς τὴν Γαλ., v. 5 ἦν δέ τις ἄνθρωπος, v. 17 ὁ δὲ ἀπεκρίνατο αὐτοῖς, vi. 3 ἀνῆλθεν δὲ εἰς τὸ ὄρος, vi. 7 ἀπεκρίθη αὐτῷ Φιλ., vi. 15 Ἰ. οὖν γνούς, vi. 47 ἀμὴν ἀμὴν λέγω ὑμῖν, vi. 51 ἐγώ εἰμι ὁ ἄρτος ὁ ζῶν, vii. 6 λέγει οὖν αὐτοῖς ὁ Ἰ., vii. 33 εἶπεν οὖν ὁ Ἰ., vii. 43 σχίσμα οὖν ἐγένετο, viii. 13 εἶπον οὖν αὐτῷ οἱ Φαρ., viii. 17 καὶ ἐν τῷ νόμῳ δὲ τῷ ὑμετέρῳ, viii. 18 ἐγώ εἰμι ὁ μαρτυρῶν, viii. 51 ἀμὴν ἀμὴν λέγω ὑμῖν. In all these (except ii. 20, vi. 47, vii. 43, viii. 17, 18, 51, where space is left for only one letter) space is left for one and a half or more

---

[1] [2662 b] The phot. clearly shews κ̄ν̄, *i.e.* κύριον. If Tisch. regarded the bent part of the κ as a later addition, he would (no doubt) have stated his view in a footnote. He seems to have overlooked the matter, or else it is a misprint (like ο προφηται in i. 45 (**2653**)).

[2] In B, οῑς is almost certainly an erroneous reduplication of οις in αυτοις.

[3] [2662 c] The photograph shews ετολ at the end of a line and μα at the beginning of the next. The μ is curtailed at the beginning: but there is no sign of ν before τ.

letters. The scribe seems to have used pause-spaces for two purposes, (1) to call special attention to some of Christ's weightier sayings, (2) to indicate that the evangelist is passing to a new aspect of an old subject—often after some parenthesis or digression. In particular the scribe is fond of making pauses before an οὖν clause, and he does this (where W.H. have none) not only in the cases indicated above (iv. 28, 45 etc.) but also before viii. 24 εἶπον οὖν ὑμῖν, ix. 24 ἐφώνησαν οὖν, xii. 19 οἱ οὖν Φαρ., xii. 28 ἦλθεν οὖν φωνή, xiii. 6 ἔρχεται οὖν, xix. 5 ἐξῆλθεν οὖν, xix. 6 ὅτε οὖν εἶδον, xx. 6 ἔρχεται οὖν. Perhaps the scribe regarded οὖν in some of these cases as similar in meaning to μὲν οὖν, "Well, then," "And now, to proceed" etc., so that it came well at the beginning of a new section.

NOTES

ON PRECEDING PARAGRAPHS

SUMMARY

[2664] On μόνος (1895)
[2665—7]   ,, πρῶτός μου (1896—1901)
[2668]   ,, the emphasis of adverbs (1902)
[2669]   ,, βασιλεύς and ὁ βασιλεύς (1966)
[2670]   ,, the article with Ἱεροσόλυμα (1970)
[2671—4]   ,, the article with ΚεΔρων (1970)
[2675—7]   ,, ἄλλος and ἕτερος (1972)
[2678]   ,, the accusative of time (2013)
[2679—82]   ,, the article used vocatively (2051)
[2683]   ,, ix. 30 ἐν τούτῳ γάρ (2068)
[2684]   ,, ὁ δέ, ἡ δέ (2071)
[2685]   ,, ἤπερ (2092)
[2686—7]   ,, ἵνα (2093)
[2688—9]   ,, viii. 56 ἠγαλλιάσατο ἵνα (2097)
[2690]   ,, ἵνα with indicative (2114)
[2691]   ,, St Paul's autograph (2114)
[2692]   ,, iv. 45 καὶ αὐτοὶ γάρ (2167)
[2693]   ,, ὅπως ἄν (2173)
[2694]   ,, ὅτι=ὥστε (2186)
[2695]   ,, ὅτι μή (2187)
[2696]   ,, ὡς (2201)
[2697]   ,, iii. 16 οὕτως...ὥστε (2203)
[2698]   ,, ἄν with indicative (2213)
[2699—700]   ,, Lk. xxiv. 39 ἐγώ εἰμι αὐτός (2224)
[2701—3]   ,, xxi. 5 παιδία μή τι προσφάγιον ἔχετε (2235)
[2704]   ,, x. 12 ὁ...οὐκ ἂν ποιμήν (2253—4)
[2705]   ,, ζῶ διὰ σέ (2297)
[2706—13]   ,, various meanings of εἰς (2305—8)
[2714]   ,, iii. 34 ἐκ μέτρου (2324)

SUMMARY

[2715]	On	διά with genitive applied to time (2331)
[2716—7]	,,	vi. 21 ἤθελον οὖν λαβεῖν (2346)
[2718—22]	,,	i. 30 ὑπὲρ αὐτοῦ (2369)
[2723]	,,	ix. 21 αὐτὸς περὶ ἑαυτοῦ (2374)
[2724—6]	,,	vi. 15 αὐτὸς μόνος (2375)
[2727]	,,	ζητεῖ αὐτὸς (marg. αὐτό)...εἶναι (2375 a)
[2728]	,,	viii. 44 ἐκ τῶν ἰδίων λαλεῖ (2378)
[2729]	,,	ἐκεῖνος (2381—5)
[2730]	,,	v. 32 ἄλλος...ὁ μαρτυρῶν (2384)
[2731]	,,	xix. 35 καὶ ἐκεῖνος οἶδεν (2384)
[2732]	,,	vii. 11 ποῦ ἐστὶν ἐκεῖνος (2385)
[2733—7]	,,	xix. 9 πόθεν εἶ σύ (2403)
[2738]	,,	xix. 17 Κρανίου Τόπον ὅ...(2412)
[2739]	,,	ἄν and ἐάν interchanged (2414)
[2740—4]	,,	xvii. 2 πᾶν ὃ δέδωκας (2422)
[2745—6]	,,	vi. 5 πόθεν ἀγοράσωμεν (2428)
[2747—53]	,,	the non-use of some active perfects (2441 a)
[2754—5]	,,	the "gnomic" aorist (2445 a)
[2756]	,,	xii. 14 εὑρὼν ὀνάριον (2461)
[2757]	,,	xii. 16 καὶ ταῦτα ἐποίησαν (2469)
[2758]	,,	vi. 25 πότε ὧδε γέγονας (2478)
[2759]	,,	viii. 14 καὶ ποῦ ὑπάγω...ἢ ποῦ ὑπάγω (2490)
[2760—6]	,,	xiv. 7 ἀπ' ἄρτι γινώσκετε αὐτόν (2491)
[2766 (i)]	,,	xi. 47 τί ποιοῦμεν (2493)
[2767]	,,	x. 29 οὐδεὶς δύναται ἁρπάζειν (2496 b)
[2768—70]	,,	xii. 28 πάτερ δόξασόν σου τὸ ὄνομα (2512 c)
[2771]	,,	ἐάν with indicative (2515 (i))
[2772—5]	,,	iota subscript (2515 (i) b)
[2776—84]	,,	the possessive genitive (2558—69)
[2785—90]	,,	the "epistolary" aorist (2691 d)
[2791—7]	,,	ἄλλος in Epictetus and John (2730)
[2798—9]	,,	"authority" in Epictetus (2740—4)

NOTES

ON PRECEDING PARAGRAPHS

On μόνοс (1895)

[2664] On v. 44 τὴν δόξαν τὴν παρὰ τοῦ μόνου [θεοῦ], Origen's Greek comment (correctly given by Huet's (i. 392) text and Lommatzsch's footnote) omits θεοῦ, though the Latin translator inserts it. Origen *De Orat.* 19 (Lomm. vol. xvii. 162) quotes the text fully πῶς δύνασθε...... παρὰ τοῦ μόνου θεοῦ οὐ ζητεῖτε, *with* θεοῦ, but proceeds to comment on it *without* θεοῦ, as τὴν κυρίαν δόξαν καὶ ἀληθῆ τὴν ἀπὸ [reading ἀπό for παρά, as also in the quotation above mentioned] τοῦ μόνου τὸν τῆς δόξης ἄξιον......δοξάζοντος, which rather suggests that θεοῦ may have been added in the quotation by the scribe. Codex D, though it has θγ at the end of a line, has a little interval between it and the preceding word. Euseb. P. E. 653 *b* has, καὶ ὁ σωτήριος δὲ λόγος φησί· Δόξαν τὴν παρὰ ἀνθρώπων ζητεῖτε καὶ τὴν δόξαν τὴν παρὰ μόνου τοῦ ἑνὸς οὐ ζητεῖτε[1]. See also 2724—6 on αὐτὸς μόνος.

---

[1] [2664 a] As regards xvii. 3 τὸν μόνον ἀληθινὸν θεόν (comp. Rom. xvi. 27 μόνῳ σοφῷ θεῷ, Jude 25 μόνῳ θεῷ σωτῆρι, Rev. xv. 4 μόνος ὅσιος) it seems in accordance with the Gk usage in Herod. i. 25 μοῦνος δὴ...ἐξεῦρεν, Judith xi. 8 μόνος ἀγαθός (sc. εἶ), and it is paraphr. by Nonnus, Ὄφρα σε γινώσκωσι θεὸν μόνον ἐλπίδα κόσμου, *i.e.* ὅτι μόνος εἶ "that thou alone art the hope of the world." The Heb. "only," applied to God, is a declinable phrase, adverbial in meaning, but adjectival in form, meaning "by himself, herself, themselves" etc. When applied to God, it is rendered by adj., μόνος, in LXX. Μόνον in 2 Chr. xviii. 30 ἀλλ' ἢ τὸν βασ. Ἰσρ. μόνον, Esth. i. 16 οὐ τὸν βασ. μόνον, may theoretically be adv., but it may be adjectival, "the king *alone*," as when applied to God. *There is no instance where this Heb. word can be safely said to be rendered in LXX adverbially*, exc. Gen. xlvii. 26 χωρὶς τῆς γῆς τῶν ἱερέων μόνον : and even here A has μόνων corresponding to the Heb. "of the priests *by themselves*." In LXX, μόνος, when applied to God in prayer, mostly comes at the end of its clause 2 K. xix. 15 σὺ εἶ ὁ θεὸς μόνος, *ib.* 19 σὺ κύριος ὁ θεὸς μόνος, comp. Ps. lxxxvi. 10, Is. xxxvii. 20 etc.,

On πρῶτός μου (1896—1901)

[2665] On i. 15 πρῶτός μου (1900) comp. Philo ii. 366—7 ὅπερ γὰρ πόλεως βασιλεύς, τοῦτο καὶ κώμης ὁ πρῶτος, καὶ οἰκίας ὁ δεσπότης, καὶ νοσούντων ἰατρός, καὶ στρατοπέδου μὲν στρατηγός, ναύαρχος δ' ἐπιβατικοῦ..., also *Inscr. Gr.* 5754 Λ(ούκιος)......ἱππεὺς Ῥωμαίων, πρῶτος[1] Μελιταίων καὶ πάτρων..., and Acts xxviii. 7 (referring, like the inscription, to Malta) τῷ πρώτῳ τῆς νήσου. These facts shew that, in the first century, "the headman," or "patron," of a village or district might be officially known as the "First." And the extract from Philo indicates that, as a soldier or sailor might say "my general" or "my captain," so a provincial villager might say "my *First*" meaning "my Patron," or "Patronus." All these terms might be used metaphorically. The context in Philo deals with true and false sovereignty (like the Johannine Parable of the Shepherd) and likens the village chief, or "First," not only to a King but also to a Physician. This

---

but note Dan. iii. 45 Theod. σὺ εἶ κύριος θεὸς μόνος καὶ ἔνδοξος, LXX σὺ εἶ μόνος κύριος ὁ θεὸς καὶ ἔνδοξος. It probably combined the notions of (1) unity, (2) unapproachableness or uniqueness. Nonnus, in v. 44, has Μούνου παγγενέταο θεοῦ.

[2664 *b*] xi. 52 οὐχ ὑπὲρ τοῦ ἔθνους μόνον is paraphr. by Nonnus οὐ περὶ μούνου ἔθνεος, adjectively. This late position of adverbial μόνον (though Steph. gives only Lycurg. p. 151, 7 as an instance) is freq. in Epictetus, comp. i. 6. 17, i. 9. 4, i. 19. 17 etc., and even i. 28. 13 ἀπολώλει ἡ Ἰλιὰς οὐ μόνον ἀλλὰ καὶ ἡ Ὀδύσσεια (? οὐ μόνον δέ). It occurs also in Mk vi. 8 εἰ μὴ ῥάβδον μόνον (not μόνην), Mt. v. 47 τοὺς ἀδελφοὺς ὑμῶν μόνον, xxi. 19 εἰ μὴ φύλλα μόνον (where Mk om. μόνον). Lk. nowhere uses the adv. μόνον exc. in viii. 50 μόνον πίστευσον : but a bracketed passage in Lk. xxiv. 12 has τὰ ὀθόνια μόνα, where (**1804**) the parall. Jn xx. 3—11 speaks of "linen cloths," with "apart" in the context. Schweig. Index to Epict. says about μόνον "Saepe adverbium hoc ponitur ubi adjectivum expectasses: verbi causa, ποιοῦντες ταῦτα, non μόνα i. 9. 5 n.: ἐφ' ἡμῶν μόνον dant MSS. i. 6. 12 ubi vulgo μόνων."

[1] [2665 *a*] The omission of the article meets the very natural objection that we should expect the article before πρῶτος meaning "the first man," or "*the* chief." Comp. *Ox. Pap.* 299. 4 (late 1st cent.) Διονυσίῳ προσ(τ)άτῃ Νεμερῶν, and edd. n. "cf. 239. 11, 290. 21. The προστάτης κώμης was probably the village 'sheikh' and chief of the πρεσβύτεροι or council of elders." Comp. *Tebtun. Pap.* 120, 122, 129 (B.C. 97 or 64). In the 6th cent., we find *Ox. Pap.* 155. 11 "to my master, John, the all-magnificent *comes* and my *patron* (προστάτῃ) from Theophilus, citizen." In all these instances the article is omitted before προστάτης.

[2665 *b*] In Mk xii. 28 πρώτη πάντων, the text varies greatly, and the genitive is generally taken as partitive. In Aristoph. *Av.* 468, ἐμοῦ πρῶτον means "[kings over] me in the first place." The way for πρῶτος κώμης would be prepared by such expressions as Aristoph. *Eq.* 6 πρῶτος Παφλαγόνων (with a play on the phrase), *ib.* 130 ὃς πρῶτος ἕξει τῆς πόλεως τὰ πράγματα, *ib.* 325 πρῶτος ὤν. Polyb. has the pl. i. 31. 5 ἐξέπεμψαν αὐτῶν τοὺς πρώτους ἄνδρας.

[2666] NOTES ON PRECEDING PARAGRAPHS

increases the probability that the Fourth Gospel might use the phrase to represent in vernacular Greek the Baptist's recognition of Jesus as his Rabbi, or Superior, or Head.

[2666] The words πρῶτος or πρώτιστος were Hebraized. Levy quotes a saying that an earthly ruler, differing from God, puts his name first and then his title: "N. N. the Augustulus, N. N. the *Protata*" which Levy renders "der Prior." Also, in connexion with Mordecai and Haman, a proclamation uses the phrase "*Proté* of the Jews," "*der Vornehmste* der Juden[1]." Origen, *Josh. Hom.* i. 5 (Lomm. xi. 16) quotes xv. 18 "odit vos hic mundus quia me *priorem vestrum* odio habuit," which may mean "your *prior, primate*, or *chief*," and, at all events, does not mean "*before* it hated you." Nonnus paraphrases πρῶτός μου ἦν in i. 15 as μεν ἦν πρώτιστος, but omits it in i. 30. In xv. 18, Nonnus has Ὑμείων ὅτι μᾶλλον ἐπεσβολίῃσιν ἐλέγχων Πρῶτον ἐμὲ στυγέεσκε, which seems to combine (1) "Hated me *above you*, or, *more than you*," (2) "Hated me *first*."

[2667] In favour of the rendering πρῶτός τινος "before anyone" there has been urged the occurrence of σοῦ πρῶτός εἰμι in an ancient papyrus[2]. But the phrase is not used independently there. It occurs in a "magical" papyrus containing the name *Iao* and describing a contest between two Æons. *Iao* is mentioned by Irenaeus and Origen[3] in connexion with very early heresies, and it is described by the former as a magic word the pronouncing of which plays a prominent part in the Valentinian system; but, more particularly, "the little *Iao*" is connected in the Pistis Sophia with the birth of John the Baptist which was (according to the Pistis Sophia) brought about by Christ[4]. In the contest described by the Papyrus, the Gospel comparison between the Baptist and Christ is transmuted into a conflict between a lesser and a greater Æon, with

---

[1] Levy iv. 112 a. The latter word is also used (*ib.*) to mean "of superior quality." Krauss refers to many other passages.

[2] See the *Classical Review* xv. 437, a paper by Dr J. H. Moulton who adds (in the *Expositor* x. 133) "The phrase σοῦ πρῶτός εἰμι (second or third century) shews that in this word [viz. πρῶτος] it was the superlative which ousted the comparative and not vice-versa as elsewhere."

[3] Iren. i. 4. 1, Orig. *Cels.* vi. 31.

[4] Pist. Soph. ch. 12 "I implanted in her [the mother of John the Baptist] the power that I received from the little *Iao*," comp. *ib.* ch. 371 "the great *Iao*." The Papyrus (*Leyden Pap.* ed. Leemans, Lugduni, 1885, Pap. W. pag. 12 a) mentions "a great god" appearing after the pronunciation of *Iao*.

a curious confusion of the Synoptic ἰσχυρότερός μου and the Johannine πρῶτός μου, only with σου for μου[1]:—"Having seen that he was *mightier than himself* he withstood him saying, *I am [born] (?) before thee* (σοῦ πρῶτός εἰμι)[2]." Another reminiscence (apparent in the Papyrus) of John the Baptist seems to point to the Johannine distinction between Christ as the Word and the Baptist as "a Voice." The Papyrus describes the begetting of these two Æons by God through various sounds, and then God decides the superiority of the rivals not according to the date of birth but according to the sound from which they were born: "Thou art from sound (ἠχοῦς): but he is from utterance (φθόγγου)[3]. So utterance is better than sound." The writer may take σοῦ πρῶτος to mean "*I was born before thee*," or "*I am thy elder brother [and therefore thy better]*[4]." But whatever his meaning might be, he could but help us as an interpreter, and not a very intelligent one, writing about a century and a half after the evangelists. Similarly, but much more intelligently, Theobald or Pope might help us to interpret Shakespeare; but they would not be independent witnesses testifying to Elizabethan usage. The indices of the Egyptian Papyri (1898—1904) indicate no instance of πρῶτος with genitive.

On the emphasis of adverbs (1902)

[2668] The initial adverbial phrase in iv. 31 ἐν τῷ μεταξὺ ἠρώτων αὐτὸν οἱ μαθηταί is emphatic, not only because of its position but also because of its extreme rarity. Μεταξύ is almost non-existent in LXX. In the Gospels elsewhere it occurs only as a preposition (4). Here Syr. (Burk.) and SS have "*now*" or "*and*," *b* "*postmodum autem*," *d*, *e*, "*inter haec*," *f* "*inter haec autem*." Hesychius explains μεταξύ as ἐξαίφνης (conj. ἑξῆς), μετ' ὀλίγον, ἀνὰ μέσον, and μ. means "afterwards" in Acts xiii. 42 εἰς τὸ μ. σάββατον, Clem. Rom. 44 (*bis*),

---

[1] Mk i. 7, Mt. iii. 11, Lk. iii. 16, Jn i. 15.
[2] Another version (pag. 5 *a*) says ἤρισεν αὐτῷ ὁ πρότερος λέγων, ἐγὼ τούτου ἰσχυρότερός εἰμι.
[3] Then follow the words ἔστε (*i.e.* ἔσται) δὲ ἐξ ἀμφοτέρων ἡ δύναμις, σου ὕστερον φωνουμένου. The other version (p. 5 *a*) says ὁ θεὸς ἔφη τῷ ἰσχυρῷ, σὺ μὲν ἀπὸ ποππυσμοῦ τυγχάνεις, οὗτος δὲ ἐξ ἠχοῦς· ἔσεσθε ἀμφότεροι ἐπὶ πάσης ἀνάγκης (having previously said ἐγεννήθη θεὸς ἐκ τοῦ ἤθους (for ἠχοῦς) ὃς πάντων ἐστὶν κύριος).
[4] Comp. *As You Like It* i. 1 "I know you are my eldest brother...the courtesy of nations allows you *my better* in that you are *the firstborn*."

Barn. 13 etc.¹ But Jn appears to use the phrase in its classical sense "*in the intervening* [*time*]," namely, between the departure of the Samaritan woman (iv. 28 ἀπῆλθεν) and the anticipated arrival of the Samaritan men, who "were coming" (iv. 30 ἐξῆλθον ἐκ τῆς πόλεως καὶ ἤρχοντο). The appropriateness of the phrase will not be understood till we perceive that *the context deals with the thought of* "*intervening time.*" Jesus has just sown the seed of the Gospel in Samaria. The Samaritans, who are speedily to bring forth the harvest—confessing (iv. 42) "This is of a truth the Saviour of the world"—are on their way to the Saviour. "*During the interval*" Jesus utters His doctrine about the *interval* between the sowing and the harvest:—"*Say ye not, 'it is four months'?* Nay, the harvest is ready."

On βαcιλεγc **and** ὁ βαcιλεγc (1966)

[2669] On the difference between i. 49 "*King* of Israel" and xii. 13 "*the King* of Israel" see 2233—4, where it is shewn that all the Gospels agree that Pilate asked Christ whether He was "*the king* of the Jews," but the fourth Gospel alone implies that Christ refused this title, while accepting that of "*king.*" The LXX has βασιλεὺς Ἰσραήλ predicatively in 1 K. xxii. 32 φαίνεται β. Ἰ. οὗτος, *ib.* 33 οὐκ ἔστιν β. Ἰ. οὗτος (and 2 Chr. xviii. 31—2), but the absence of the article is not distinctive there, for the context contains 1 K. xxii. 31 καὶ βασιλεὺς Συρίας ἐνετείλατο. Jn does not shrink from using *the article with a predicate concerning Christ: but in all such cases the article implies uniqueness in the universe* (not like Mk vi. 3 οὐχ οὗτός ἐστιν ὁ τέκτων;), as "the light of men," "the light of the world," "the good shepherd," "the way," "the truth" etc. In x. 2 "He that entereth through the door is *shepherd* (ποιμήν ἐστιν) of the sheep," R.V. has txt "*the shepherd,*" marg. "*a shepherd.*" But "the good shepherd" comes later, and the intention here seems to be to prepare the way for it by something intermediate between "a

---

¹ [2668 *a*] Xen. *Conviv.* i. 14 ἐν τῷ μεταξὺ παυσάμενος...συγκαλυψάμενος κατέκειτο looks, at first sight, like another instance of "afterwards": but I think the writer has in his mind i. 16 ἀνεκαλύψατο, so that ἐν τ. μ. means "for the time." The passage at all events shews how the meaning "afterwards" might naturally arise. Origen explains twice (*ad loc.*) ἐν τ. μ., as meaning that the disciples did not like to ask their Master to eat in the presence of the woman or before the Samaritans—not a very satisfactory explanation, but one that at all events recognises that the insertion of so unusual a phrase needs to be explained. Nonnus has Ἔνθα χρόνου μεσσηγύ, πρὶν ἄστεος ἔκτοθι βαίνειν Στεινομένων νεφεληδὸν ἐπήτριμα κύματα λαῶν.

NOTES ON PRECEDING PARAGRAPHS [2671]

shepherd" (which might suggest "one of many shepherds") and *"the [ideal] good shepherd"* presently to be mentioned.

On the article with Ἱεροcόλγμα (1970)

[2670] John is the only writer in N.T. that uses the article with the declinable name Ἱεροσόλυμα, ii. 23, v. 2 (where it may be intended to "carry the reader back" to Jerusalem mentioned in v. 1, and may be explained as "anaphoric"[1]), x. 22 ἐγένετο τότε τὰ ἐνκαίνια ἐν τοῖς Ἱ. (v.r. ἐγένετο δὲ τὰ ἐ., and ἐν Ἱ.), xi. 18 ἦν δὲ Βηθανία ἐγγὺς τῶν Ἱ. In the last of these passages the article perhaps emphasizes the *local* meaning:—"near *the city walls*," "near *the* [*city of*] Jerusalem." Similarly, in the first two books of Maccabees, "Jerusalem," though used without the article more than 20 times, is used with it in 2 Macc. xi. 8 πρὸς τοῖς Ἱ. "hard by *the* [*walls of*] *Jerusalem*," and xii. 9 "so that the flashes of the light were visible *up to the* [*walls of*] *Jerusalem* (εἰς τὰ Ἱ.), two hundred and forty furlongs." In John, the context is local in v. 2 ("near the sheep pool") and in x. 22 (which mentions "Solomon's porch"). In ii. 23 the name cannot very well be "anaphoric" to ii. 13 which seems rather too far off for that hypothesis. Perhaps the meaning is "When he was [with the multitude of the pilgrims assembled] *inside the* [*walls of*] *Jerusalem* at the Passover, many believed on him[2]."

On the article with Κεδρων (1970)

[2671] The article (τῶν) in xviii. 1 (R.V. txt) "He went forth... over the brook *Kidron*" (marg. "ravine of *the* (τῶν) *cedars*")—on

---

[1] [2670 a] Ἀναφορικόν is used (Steph.) by the Greek Grammarians to denote the "*relative*" pronoun, but it is applied by Blass p. 153 to the definite article in v. 2; and "anaphoric" is a very convenient term to denote ὁ when meaning "*the above-mentioned*."

[2] [2670 b] Along with Jn's peculiar use of τὰ Ἱεροσόλυμα may be mentioned his use of τὴν γῆν in iii. 22 (comp. iv. 3 (D and latt.)) εἰς τὴν Ἰουδαίαν γῆν, where it would be unreasonable to suppose that he meant the same thing as the ordinary τὴν Ἰουδαίαν (vii. 3, xi. 7). The context indicates that Jesus came *from Jerusalem* so that He could not be said to come "*into Judæa*": but He comes from the Judæan *capital* "into the Judæan *land*," *i.e.* into the country round about Jerusalem, comp. Mk i. 5 ἡ Ἰουδαία χώρα (**334**) distinguished from "the men of Jerusalem." Mt. ii. 6 γῇ Ἰούδα seems to be an error for Mic. v. 2 "Ephrathah," and the meaning of it is doubtful. In 2 S. xv. 23 καὶ πᾶσα ἡ γῆ ἔκλαιεν...καὶ πᾶς ὁ λαὸς παρεπορεύοντο, the Heb. "land" is rendered by the Targ. (Walton) "habitatores terrae," but the Targum word mostly means "sojourners" (Levy *Ch.* i. 173 a). It might suggest "country folk," peasants, called in Hebrew "people of the land."

[2672] NOTES ON PRECEDING PARAGRAPHS

which Blass (p. 315) says that the text is "in ℵBCD etc. stupidly corrupted¹"—may certainly be explained, and possibly justified, by the following considerations. The exact meaning of the Hebrew name "*Kidron*" is unknown; but it is generally connected with *Kedar* "*dark*"—an epithet that might easily be given, from natural causes, to a ravine or to the torrent in it. According to *Hor. Heb.* i. 85 (and *ib*. on Jn xviii. 1) the ravine had come to be used as an open sewer, and, in the Talmud, *Kedar* signifies "*dung*." These two facts might suggest for the name an unsavoury origin against which some might be glad to protest by deriving it from the Greek κέδρος, which was adopted as a late Hebrew word². Accordingly a Talmudic tradition describes two "cedars" of portentous size on the neighbouring mount of Olives. This hill ran down to the Kidron, and cedars on the slope might be supposed to give the name to the ravine³.

[2672] In the MSS. of the LXX the accent of the word varies, and (being of little authority) will be omitted in the following quotations (as also all distinctions between κ and K); but it is important to note that the LXX always spells the name with ε. The first place where it occurs describes the passage of David across Kidron, and the MSS. vary as follows, 2 S. xv. 23 (lit. Heb.) "and all the people passing and the king passing in the torrent Kidron and all the people passing on the face of the way of the wilderness," B καὶ πᾶς ὁ λαὸς παρεπορεύοντο ἐν τῷ χειμάρρῳ τῶν κεδρων καὶ ὁ βασιλεὺς διέβη τὸν χειμάρρουν κεδρων...⁴, A κ. π. ὁ λ. παρεπορεύοντο καὶ ὁ βασιλεὺς παρερχόμενος ἐν τῷ χειμάρρῳ τῶν κεδρων..., Luc. κ. π. ὁ λ. διεπορεύετο καὶ ὁ β. διεπορεύετο ἐν τῷ χειμάρρῳ κεδρων...⁵. There

---

¹ W.H. follow BC των κεδρων, ℵD have του κεδρου with *a* and *b*.

² [2671 *a*] Levy *Ch*. ii. 347 *a* has κέδρος, and Levy iv. 249 *a* has κέδρινον.

³ [2671 *b*] J. *Taanith*. iv. 6 (Schwab vol. vi. p. 191). Under one of these cedars were "four shops" selling things needed for purification, and under the other were sold "pigeons sufficing for the sacrifices of all Israel." Cedars of such immense size could almost certainly not have grown on Mount Olivet. If they had grown there, they would almost certainly have found some other mention in Jewish tradition.

⁴ [2672 *a*] Swete prints the first κεδρων as a paroxyton plural noun, τῶν κέδρων, the second as an oxyton sing. name, Κεδρών, *i.e.* (1) "the ravine *of the cedars*," (2) "the ravine *Kedron*, or *Cedar-grove*." He prints τῶν κέδρων "*of the cedars*," in 1 K. xv. 13. Comp. Euseb. *Onomast*. p. 273 χειμ. ἡ φάραγξ Κεδρών, but p. 303 Χειμ. Κέδρων.

⁵ [2672 *b*] Luc., at the end, has (2674 *a*) κατὰ τὴν ὁδὸν τῆς ἐλαίας τῆς ἐν τῇ ἐρήμῳ.

514

is no v. r. in 1 K. xv. 13 ἐν τῷ χειμ. τῶν κεδρων (but Luc. om. τῶν). Elsewhere τῶν is omitted before κεδρων (1 K. ii. 37, 2 K. xxiii. 6 etc.) as it is also before "Arnon," "Kishon" etc. when they are preceded by the word "torrent" or "ravine" (χειμάρρους)[1]. It looks as though some tradition connecting "Kidron" with "cedars" has left its influence on one or two passages where that ravine is mentioned, and especially the one in which David is described as passing over it *in sorrow*[2], so that it is described by some as "the ravine *of the cedars.*"

[2673] In Josephus, κεδρων (which occurs nine times) is never clearly an indeclinable noun and is sometimes clearly declinable[3]. This proves nothing as to the sense he attached to the name, for it is in accordance with his custom of making "Arnon" and "Sihon," etc. as well as "Simon," declinable. But it is significant that he often attaches to κεδρων the word "*called.*" Now it is the custom of this historian to speak of "the mountain *called* of Olives," "the tomb *called* the Potter's," "the camp *called* of the Assyrians," *in such a way as to suggest that the Greek word connected with "called" is to be translated, as explaining the origin of the place-name. This leads to the conclusion that according to analogy he intends his readers to translate κεδρων by "cedars" and not to transliterate it as "Kedron."* It may mean κέδρων "of cedars" or κεδρών "cedar-grove": but in either case, *it must be translated*[4]. It may be noted also that

---

[1] [2672 c] The article is ins. between "the torrent" and "Bosor" ("the torrent the Bosor") by LXX in 1 S. xxx. 10, 21 (τ. χ. τ. Βοσόρ, or Βεανά) and by Luc. in 1 S. xxx. 9; but that is because the Heb. has "*the* Bosor" quite exceptionally. The Heb. has not "*the* Kidron."

[2] [2672 d] Jerome (*Onomast.* p. 53) has "Cedron, *tristis maeror* siue dolor."

[3] [2673 a] In the following, ἐλαιων as well as κεδρων will be left unaccented: *Ant.* viii. 1. 5. διαβαίνειν τὸν χειμάρρουν κεδρωνα (v.r. κεδρωνος, and so Hudson), ix. 7. 3 εἰς τὴν φάραγγα τὴν κεδρωνος, *Bell.* v. 2. 3 κατὰ τὸ ἐλαιων καλούμενον ὄρος... φάραγγι βαθείᾳ διειργόμενον ἢ κεδρων ὠνόμασται, v. 4. 2 κατὰ τὸ τοῦ Γναφέως προσαγορευόμενον μνῆμα...εἰς τὴν κεδρωνα καλουμένην φάραγγα, v. 6. 1 ἄχρι τοῦ κεδρωνος...καὶ τὴν κεδρωνα καλουμένην φάραγγα, v. 7. 3 κατὰ τὴν Ἀσσυρίων παρεμβολὴν καλουμένην ἐπισχὼν πᾶν τὸ μεταξὺ μέχρι τοῦ κεδρωνος, v. 12. 2 ἀπὸ τῆς Ἀσσυρίων παρεμβολῆς...ἔνθεν διὰ τοῦ κεδρωνος ἐπὶ τὸ ἐλαιων ὄρος, vi. 3. 2 τῆς κεδρωνος καλουμένης φάραγγος.

[4] [2673 b] Contrast *Ant.* iv. 5. 1 ἐπὶ τὸν ποταμὸν (Niese) Ἀρνῶν' ὃς ἐκ τῶν... (v.r. ἀρνῶνος, ἀρνῶνα, ἀρνῶν, ἀρνών) iv. 5. 2 τριῶν ποταμῶν...τοῦ μὲν Ἀρνῶνος... (without καλουμένου etc.) where the name has nothing to do with "lambs" and is *not* to be translated. Scribes might well be perplexed by the various ways

Josephus—when describing the flight of David from Jerusalem—though he does not mention κεδρων, uses ελαιων as a declinable noun (*Ant.* vii. 9, 2) διὰ τοῦ Ἐλαιῶνος ὄρους "through the mountain [called the] *place of olives*[1]." Blass (pp. 32, 64, 85) would emend Ἐλαιῶνος both here and in Acts i. 12. But there is good reason to think that Ἐλαιών, the Latin Olivetum, or Olive-grove, might be a form that recommended itself both to Josephus and to Luke, when writing in an elevated style, in preference to the more popular name "mount *of olives*."

[2674] If John had written τὸν χειμ. κεδρων, meaning "the brook *Kidron*," without explaining it as he explains "Siloam," "Gabbatha," "Golgotha" etc., (1) he would have gone contrary to his usage by introducing a place-name with the definite article without explaining it; (2) he would have adopted a Hebraic construction contrary to his usage; (3) he would have gone the way to mislead Greek readers (who would naturally suppose it to mean "cedars"). But by writing τῶν κεδρων without explanation (1) he writes intelligibly for Greeks, (2) he adopts the exact language of the LXX describing the exile of David from Jerusalem, (3) he falls in with a seemly tradition (possibly Jewish as well as Greek) that the name meant "the torrent, or

---

of representing the names of places with the meanings of their names *e.g.* Gen. xxvi. 33 ἐκάλεσεν τὸ ὄνομα αὐτοῦ Ὅρκος, Josh. v. 3 ἐπὶ τοῦ καλουμένου τόπου Βουνὸς τῶν ἀκροβυστιῶν. See **2680** *c*.

[1] [**2673** *c*] In *Ant.*, the only other mention is xx. 8. 6 πρὸς ὄρος τὸ προσαγορευόμενον ἐλαιων ἔρχεσθαι where Niese om. ἔρχεσθαι but adds that two MSS. insert it. Hudson inserts it without comment, and it is needed to complete the sense. Hence we may read ἐλαιών' ἔρχεσθαι as Niese reads in iv. 5. 1 Ἀρνῶν ὅς (**2673** *b*). But Joseph. *Bell.* ii. 13. 5 and v. 2. 3 has τὸ ἐλαιων καλούμενον ὄρος, v. 3. 5 ἐπὶ τοῦ ἐλαιων ὄρους (v.r. καλουμένου ὄρους), v. 12. 2, vi. 2. 8 τὸ ἐλαιων ὄρος—agreeing with the use of the LXX and of Mk-Mt., who all say "mount *of Olives*." It may be taken as certain that Josephus never regards ἐλαιων as an indeclinable noun, for he dislikes and avoids such nouns as far as possible—as may be seen from his use of Σιναῖον ὄρος (never Σινά), Γαλάδης or Γαλαδηνή (never Γαλαάδ exc. as a personal name), and from his avoidance (or mention as declinable nouns) of the names "Canaan," "Hor," "Horeb," and "Seir." Note also the way in which he introduces Gerizim (*Ant.* iv. 8. 44) δυοῖν ὁροῖν, Γριζαίου (with v.r.) μὲν τοῦ..., only by degrees falling into the use of the indeclinable form. These facts illustrate the divergence between Acts i. 12 ἀπὸ ὄρους τ. καλουμένου ἐλαιωνος (a declinable noun) and Lk. xix. 29, xxi. 37 πρὸς (or εἰς) τὸ ὄρος τὸ καλούμενον ἐλαιων, where a declinable noun is out of the question, as it would have to be accus. ἐλαιωνα. The former is Luke's own use, the latter is that of Synoptic Tradition.

ravine, of the cedars." This reading is also supported by the best MSS.[1]

On ἄλλος **and** ἕτερος (1972)

[2675] On v. 32 ἄλλος ἐστὶν ὁ μαρτυρῶν (1972) Blass (p. 180) most appropriately quotes Aesch. *Suppl.* 230 f. κἀκεῖ δικάζει...Ζεὺς ἄλλος. See Lightf. (Gal. i. 6—7) "ἄλλος adds, while ἕτερος distinguishes," and "ἕτερον implies a difference of kind, which is not involved in ἄλλο," "ἄλλος is another as 'one besides,' ἕτερος another as 'one of two'"; and from this notion of "two," often implying *contrast*, ἕτερος sometimes comes to mean "different." If ἄλλος means "another of the same kind" here, it has a bearing on the relation between the Speaker and God, who is the "*other*." But there is some difficulty in proving that John observes the distinction, as he uses ἕτερος only once, xix. 37 "*another* (ἑτέρα) scripture saith." He has previously quoted one scripture from the Law (Ex. xii. 46 "not a bone shall be broken") and he may mean that "*a second and independent* scripture" from Prophecy predicted the "piercing." Heb. v. 6 καθὼς κ. ἐν ἑτέρῳ λέγει is not a certain parallel (R.V. "as he saith also in another [place]") for Westc. *ad loc.* alleges no instance of τόπῳ omitted, and Clem. Rom. viii. ἐν ἑτέρῳ τόπῳ ("in *another* [or, *second*] passage") suggests that τόπῳ would have been inserted had that been the meaning; moreover Chrys. *ad loc.* (τίς ἐστι κατὰ τὴν τάξιν Μελχ.; οὐδεὶς ἕτερος...οὐδένα ἂν ἔχοι τις ἕτερον δεῖξαι) rather suggests that he took ἕτερος to mean "*other* [*than Christ*]." The use of ἕτερος and ἄλλος is different in different authors; *e.g.* in Dan., LXX freq. has ἄλλος and ἕτερος whereas Theod. has ἕτερος freq., ἄλλος never. In Is. lxv. 15 "*another* name," *i.e.* different, LXX has καινόν, Aq. and Sym. ἕτερον. In N.T., the Petrine and Johannine Epistles never use ἕτερος, and Jude only uses it once (verse 7) in the phrase "*strange* flesh," according to the LXX use of the word in "*strange* gods" etc.

[2676] The Pauline Epistles observe the distinction pointed out

---

[1] [2674a] In the description of David's flight (2 S. xv. 23 foll.), the Bible mentions both "Kidron" and "Olivet." Josephus mentions only Olivet. Luc. in 2 S. xv. 23 adds (2672 b) "of the olive," beside mentioning "the ascent of the Olives" in *ib.* 30. In the Gospels, where Mk-Mt. mention "Mount of Olives" and "Gethsemane," Lk. has "Mount of Olives" alone, Jn κεδρων alone, but SS in Jn has "the torrent of Cedron, a *hill* where..." and so Diatess. It is almost certain that at a very early time a parallel must have been perceived between the going forth of David and that of Christ; and the parallel may have influenced the latest of the Gospels most.

[2677] NOTES ON PRECEDING PARAGRAPHS

by Lightf. on Gal. i. 6 εἰς ἕτερον εὐαγγέλιον, ὃ οὐκ ἔστιν ἄλλο, "to a *different* Gospel, which is not *another* [of the same kind]...." So Rom. ii. 1 "thou judgest *thy neighbour* (τὸν ἕτερον)," ii. 21 "thou that teachest *some one else* (ἕτερον without τόν)," vii. 3 "if she become [wedded] to a *new husband* (ἀνδρὶ ἑ.)," 4 "that you should become [wedded] to a *new* [husband] (εἰς τὸ γενέσθαι ὑμᾶς ἑτέρῳ)," vii. 23 "But I note a *new-and-strange* (ἕτερον) law in my members," viii. 38—9 "nor [evil] angels, nor principalities, nor powers,...nor any *other* [*however new and strange*] created thing (κτίσις ἑτέρα)." There is perhaps a play on ἕτερος in xiii. 8—9 "he that loveth *his neighbour* (τὸν ἕτερον) hath fulfilled Torah; for the [command], Thou shalt not commit adultery...and every *other* [*however separate and distinct*] (ἑτέρα) commandment is summed up in this," where perhaps there is also an allusion to the fact that the second half of the Decalogue (which deals with man's duty to man) was recognised as (Philo ii. 189, 201 etc.) ἡ ἑτέρα πεντάς, "the *second and distinct* Pentad." And perhaps Chrysostom is right here in saying that the Apostle means that the love of man includes the love of God. It would be possible similarly to go through the other Pauline Epistles (excluding the pastoral ones) and to shew that ἕτερος always has a shade of difference from ἄλλος, *e.g.* in 2 Cor. xi. 4 ἄλλον Ἰησοῦν...πνεῦμα ἕτερον...εὐαγγέλιον ἕτερον "*another* Jesus...a *different* [Holy] Spirit...a *different* Gospel." Even in 1 Cor. xii. 8—10 where ἑτέρῳ twice intervenes between ἄλλῳ, the writer means "one ...another...*some one else*...another...*someone else*," and he omits δέ after ἑτέρῳ to gain emphasis by abruptness.

[2677] These details support Lightfoot's view of Gal. i. 6 against that of Blass, who sees (p. 318) "no distinction." They also shew that each author must be judged by himself. Perhaps in Lk. and Acts the use varies according to the documents compiled by the author. In Lk. xvi. 18 γαμῶν ἑτέραν means (as in Rom. viii. 3) "marrying a *new* wife," but the parall. Mk x. 11, Mt. xix. 9 have ἄλλην. John, being a peculiarly discriminative writer, probably means (xix. 37) "a *different and independent* prophecy" or a "*second* prophecy" (not "another of the same kind"). In Jn v. 43 ἐὰν ἄλλος ἔλθῃ, we might have expected ἕτερος as in Mt. xi. 3, Lk. vii. 19 "Are we to expect a *different* [deliverer]?" but Jn means "If *another* come [*professing to be of the same kind as myself*]," like the Pauline (2 Cor. xi. 4) ἄλλον Ἰησοῦν. On Lk. vii. 19 ἕτερον προσδοκῶμεν perh. softened to Lk. vii. 20 ἄλλον προσδοκῶμεν see **1856**.

On the accusative of time (2013)

[2678] In Mk xiii. 35 ὀψὲ ἢ μεσονύκτιον (v. r. -ίου) ἢ ἀλεκτοροφωνίας, it is usual (Swete *ad loc.* and Blass p. 311) to take μ. as accus. But it would be difficult to explain the abrupt change from accus. to genit. More probably μ. is adverbial. See Wetst. *ad loc.* who first quotes Phrynichus as saying that μεσονύκτιον is "poetic," and then Theocr. xiii. 69, xxiv. 11, in both of which passages the word is adverbial (μεσονύκτιον, in the latter, being illustrated by Kiessling from Anacr. iii. 1 μεσονυκτίοις ποθ' ὥραις). This adverbial use distinguishes Mk from Lk., who (like Lucian and Plutarch) uses μ. as a noun, Lk. xi. 5, Acts xvi. 25, xx. 7[1].

On the article used vocatively (2051)

[2679] As regards xx. 28 Ὁ κύριός μου (in the confession of Thomas) it must be noted that the vocative with ὁ in idiomatic Greek differs in tone and usage from the vocative with the Hebrew article. The latter is frequently solemn and addressed to God; the former is often vernacular and imperious as being addressed to a slave, or to a policeman, or to a nameless person in a crowd, or to some one whose name the speaker humorously affects to have forgotten[2].

---

[1] [2678 a] For a curious phrase, prob. indicating point of time, see Berl. Pap. i. no. 69 (A.D. 120) δραχμάς...ἃς καὶ ἀποδώσω σοι τῷ ἔγγιστα δοθησομένῳ ὀψωνίῳ. This is rendered in *Class. Rev.* (1901) vol. xv. p. 438 "with your next wages," as meaning accompaniment; but the document is an I. O. U. given by Valerius Longus ἱππεύς to Julius Agrippianus ἱππεύς, of the same Τύρμη, as follows : ὁμολογῶ ἔχιν παρά σου χρῆσιν ἔντοκον ἀργυρίου σεβαστοῦ νομίζματος δραχμὰς ἑκατὸν τεσσεράκοντα, ἃς καὶ ἀποδώσω σοι τῷ ἔγγιστα δοθησομένῳ ὀψωνίῳ. We cannot suppose that one soldier would say to another in the same squadron "I will pay you so-and-so *with your next wages.*" Perhaps—as in English we say "*at* the next prize-distribution," "*at* the next feast" (where "*at*" means "at the time of" or "when it comes round")—so these military men were in the habit of saying among themselves "*at next pay*" meaning "*at next pay [day].*"

[2] [2679 a] Aristoph. *Ach.* 54 "the police [there], off with him]," οἱ τοξόται, *Ran.* 40 ὁ παῖς, and 521, ὁ παῖς, ἀκολούθει lit. "the boy [in attendance]," Xen. *Anab.* i. 5. 16 (in a hasty and unceremonious speech dispensing with the usual ἄνδρες) Κλέαρχε καὶ Πρόξενε καὶ οἱ ἄλλοι οἱ παρόντες Ἕλληνες, οὐκ ἴστε ὅ,τι ποιεῖτε. Perh. too we should follow Steph. in reading ὁ (not with Stalb. ὦ) in Plato *Symp.* 172 "*Mr Phalerian* (ὁ Φ.), said he, you there (οὗτος), Apollodorus!" Athen. xiii. 580 D Μειράκιον, ὁ καλός, φησί, addressed to a young butcher with a play on the word καλός (sometimes written up in the streets as a sign of affection). Blass p. 86 quotes Aristoph. *Acharn.* 242 πρόϊθ' εἰς τὸ πρόσθεν ὀλίγον ἡ κανηφόρος which sounds better than the regular and formal (Dind.) προίτω 's τὸ πρόσθεν... : but something would depend on the degree of respect attached to the young lady. This idiom is of a piece with the appellative οὗτος, the French "chose," and English slang equivalents.

When Mark uses this vocative in the Hebrew sense, he is careful to prefix the Aramaic original[1]. When he uses it imperiously, he does not insert the Aramaic[2]. In expressing the solemn vocative of "Father," divergences would naturally arise in Greek. The Aramaic is *Abba*, the article, or vocative case, being in the suffix. This might be expressed by (1) πάτερ, (2) ὁ πατήρ, or (3) πατήρ (setting aside Hebraic ὦ as meaning in LXX something different from the Greek ὦ). The first of these (supplemented by ἡμῶν in Mt.) has been adopted in the Lord's Prayer, the second (supplemented by 'Αββά) in Mk; John, as we have seen (2052—3), uses both (1) and (3) and appears to distinguish between them.

[2680] These facts should keep the reader's mind open to the possibility of exceptional Johannine usage as to the vocative of κύριος. The vocative κύριε occurs repeatedly in the Egyptian papyri, and it is also used in Talmudic Hebrew and Aramaic, meaning "my lord" or "sir," besides being applied (2049 foll.) to God in the LXX and elsewhere. It might, therefore, imply no special reverence; and Mark puts ῥαββί, but never κύριε, into the mouths of the disciples addressing Jesus[3]. In the healing of the leper, where Matthew and Luke have κύριε, Mark omits it[4]. The Matthew-Luke tradition represents Christ as condemning those who say to Him Κύριε, Κύριε, without doing His commandments[5]. Origen, in a comment on Jn xiii. 13 ὑμεῖς φωνεῖτέ με Ὁ διδάσκαλος καὶ Ὁ κύριος, remarks on the uselessness of

---

[1] [2679 b] Mk v. 41 Ταλειθά κούμ ὅ ἐστιν μεθερμηνευόμενον Τὸ κοράσιον, σοὶ λέγω, ἔγειρε, Mt. ix. 25 om., Lk. viii. 54 ἡ παῖς ἔγειρε, and Mk xiv. 36 'Αββά, ὁ πατήρ, Mt. xxvi. 39 πάτερ μου, Lk. xxii. 42 πάτερ.

[2] [2679 c] Mk ix. 25 τὸ ἄλαλον καὶ κωφὸν πνεῦμα (Mt.-Lk. om.), Delitzsch does not ins. the Heb. article. Lk. has the vocative article in xii. 32 μὴ φοβοῦ τὸ μικρὸν ποίμνιον, and a quasi-vocative article in vi. 25 οὐαὶ ὑμῖν, οἱ ἐμπεπλησμένοι, but xi. 39 νῦν ὑμεῖς οἱ Φ....καθαρίζετε seems rather appositional than vocative. Μακάριοι οἱ πτωχοί is followed in Mt. v. 3 by αὐτῶν but in Lk. vi. 20 by ὑμετέρα, as though vocative; and a corresponding difference continues in the contexts.

[3] [2680 a] Κύριε, in Mk, is uttered only by the Syrophœnician woman (Mk vii. 28). The disciples, including Judas, use ῥαββί thrice, Mk ix. 5, xi. 21, xiv. 45.

[4] Mk i. 40, Mt. viii. 2, Lk. v. 12.

[5] [2680 b] Mt. vii. 21 οὐ πᾶς ὁ λέγων μοι Κύριε, Κύριε, Lk. vi. 46 τί δέ με καλεῖτε Κύριε, Κύριε; On the latter of these Alf. makes no remark, but Steph. gives nothing like the constr.; D has λεγεται, *i.e.* λέγετε, and so have Clem. Alex and Iren. (dicitis); SS and Diatess. have "Not all that *say unto me, 'My Lord, my Lord.'*" Mt. vii. 22—3 describes the rejection of some, who cry Κύριε, Κύριε. The parall. Lk. xiii. 25 describes the rejection of some, who cry Κύριε.

some utterances of Κύριε, Κύριε, and he adduces 1 Cor. xii. 3 εἰπεῖν Κύριος Ἰησοῦς, and speaks of τὸ καλῶς εἰπεῖν τῷ Σωτῆρι τὸ Ὁ διδάσκαλος. He leaves on us the impression that he does not regard ὁ διδάσκαλος as a Hebraic vocative, but as a title used in the nominative: "Ye address me [using] the [title] Teacher and the [title] Lord[1]," and that this seems to him more weighty than the ordinary vocative κύριε, which might mean merely "Sir." He is, of course, writing not about the difference of cases but about the difference of spirit: yet he seems to assume that the Johannine ὁ κύριος, though not predicatively used, implies a confession of lordship.

[2681] In the Apocalypse, κύριε, ὁ θεός is thrice used[2] vocatively. In Rev. iv. 11 ἄξιος εἶ, ὁ κύριος καὶ ὁ θεὸς ἡμῶν—where A.V. follows an inferior text with simply κύριε—the rendering (in view of the non-existence of ὁ κύριος as a vocative anywhere and the threefold κύριε ὁ θεός in this very book) seems to be "Thou, [being] our Lord and our God, art worthy"; but it differs very little from a vocative.

[2682] Returning to the confession of Thomas, most readers will feel that the ordinary vocative κύριέ μου would have been comparatively common-place, and that it would also have almost required to be followed by some appeal for help, or some ascription of praise. Thomas's silence is far more effective. We have also to consider that the Saviour has previously approved of the appellation ὁ διδάσκαλος καὶ ὁ κύριος: and there is an appropriateness in His leading them on from that to the still higher ὁ κύριος καὶ ὁ θεός. It has been noted above (2680 b) that, where Matthew has ὁ λέγων μοι, Κύριε, Luke has the rare or unique με καλεῖτε, Κύριε, apparently meaning καλεῖτε λέγοντες. Similarly, John might use εἶπεν αὐτῷ in the sense of ἐκάλεσε or εἶπε φωνῶν. These facts favour the view of R.V. (against the one suggested in 2051) that καί means "and" (not "also") and that the meaning is "Thomas said to him [the words] 'My lord—and my God[3].'"

---

[1] [2680 c] Lobeck p. 517 quotes Dio Cass. lvii. 14. 860, Pausan. viii. 41. 479 and ix. 25. 76, Aesch. De fals. l. p. 275, Plutarch, De Garrulitate ch. xxii. to shew that the nominative may follow the phrases ἐπωνυμίαν λαβεῖν etc. (=καλεῖσθαι). More remarkable are (ib.) Phot. Bibl. lxxx. p. 192 ᾧ κλῆσιν ἔθεντο Φαλεντινιανός, Dio Cass. xliii. 13. 349 βιβλίον γράψας ὃ Ἀντικάτων ἐκάλεσε. In xiii. 13 Nonnus has accus. κοίρανον and διδάσκαλον.

[2] Rev. xi. 17, xv. 3, xvi. 7.

[3] [2682 a] Origen (on xiii. 13) has εἰπεῖν τῷ Σωτῆρι τὸ Ὁ διδάσκαλος. Having regard to the frequent interchange of o and ω in the first century, it is quite

[2683] NOTES ON PRECEDING PARAGRAPHS

On ix. 30 ἐν τούτῳ γάρ (2068)

[2683] In ix. 30 ἐν τούτῳ γὰρ τὸ θαυμαστόν... *a, b,* and SS omit γάρ. D, *e* and Walton's Syriac have οὖν. A and others have ἐν γὰρ τούτῳ. Also *e* must have read τοῦτο for ἐν τούτῳ (and Scrivener's *Adversaria* mentions τοῦτο as a Gk reading). Τό before θαυμαστόν is omitted by AD and others. Diatess. has "From this is the wonder." Blass (p. 275) remarks that the words are "equivalent to an interrogative οὐ γὰρ ἐν τούτῳ." This suggests that οὐ interrogative may have been dropped by most MSS. but may have been read by D and *e* as οὖν supplanting γάρ. But οὐ γάρ interrogative, though good classical Greek, does not occur in John, who frequently uses it in statement (iii. 17, 34, iv. 9, xii. 47 etc.). Nonnus has Τοῦτο γάρ ἐστι τὸ θαῦμα πολὺ πλέον ὅττι περ ὑμῖν Ὁὗτος ἔην ἄγνωστος, shewing that he read γάρ[1]. Did he also read τοῦτο with *e*, and, if so, ἐν as ἕν meaning "unique," "preeminent"? Comp. Epict. i. 17. 13 ἆρ᾽ οὖν τοῦτό ἐστι τὸ μέγα καὶ τὸ θαυμαστόν...; "Is this, then, the great [object], *the wonderful [ideal]*...?"

On ὁ δέ, ἡ δέ (2071)

[2684] In John, ὁ δέ, ἡ δέ etc. is far rarer than in any other Gospel and almost always occurs in the phrase "*and,* or *but,* he said."

---

possible that in xx. 28 the original was ΕΙΠΕΝΑΥΤΟΤΟΟΚΥΡΙΟC and that the second ΤΟ has been omitted. Τό, when thus or similarly used, and also when prefixed to interrogations, is very liable to corruption, as in Mk ix. 23, Mt. xix. 18, Lk. i. 62, xix. 48, Gal. iv. 25, 1 Thess. iv. 1 etc.

[2682 *b*] Nonnus has Θωμᾶς δ᾽ ὑστερόμητις ἀμοιβάδα ῥήξατο φωνήν, Κοίρανος ἡμέτερος καὶ ἐμὸς θεός, where the change of pron. ("*our...my*") is rather startling. But perhaps he felt that "*my Lord*" was liable to be confused with "*my lord,*" which means little more than "Sir." "*My God*" could not be thus misunderstood: and the sing. "*my*" was preferable here as it expressed Thomas's personal conviction that his "lord" was also "God." I do not however think that Nonnus means "our Lord [is] *also* my God" as suggested in **2051**.

[1] [2683 *a*] Comp. *Fayûm Pap.* 123 (Edd.) "Having been molested I was unable to come down...let us get from him the rest of the oil if you agree. [*I say,* '*molested,*'] *for* Teuphilus the Jew has come (ἐλήλυθεν γὰρ Τ. Ἰουδαῖος) saying 'I have been pressed in as a cultivator, and I want to go to Sabinus.' [*This is strange*] *for* he did not ask me to be released at the time that he was impressed (οὔτε γὰρ εἴρηχε ἡμ(ῖ)ν ἀγόμενος ἵνα ἀπολυθῇ), but has suddenly told me to-day (ἀλλὰ αἰφνιδὶ [[.]]ως εἴρηχεν ἡμῖν σήμερον. [*You need take no steps at present*] *for* I will find out whether he is speaking the truth (γνώσομαι γὰρ εἰ ἀληθῶς λέγι)."

[2683 *b*] The translation given above is that of the editors, except that they have omitted a rendering of γάρ in each case, and I have inserted it together with a conjectural addition of the ellipsis implied. Note also (1) εἴρηχεν (*sic*) used for εἶπεν once at least, if not twice, (2) the use of οὔτε...ἀλλά.

In iv. 32, v. 17, vi. 20, R.V. has "*But* he [Jesus] said," in vii. 41 "*But* some said," in xx. 25 "*But* he [Thomas] said"—because in all these cases there is adversativeness. Besides iv. 32, v. 17, vi. 20, it is used once more (xxi. 6 R.V. "and he said") of Jesus, in His reply to the saying of the disciples that they have taken no fish. Perhaps it would be best to render it "*but*," so as to suggest adversativeness: "They said, We have taken nothing [and were on the point of desisting from fishing], *but* he said, 'Cast the net…and ye shall find fish.'" Then all the four passages where John uses ὁ δέ concerning Jesus will represent Him as correcting or comforting the disciples or opposing the Jews.

On ἤπερ (2092)

[2685] Ἤπερ occurs emphatically with μᾶλλον in Xen. *Conv.* i. 15 οὔτε γὰρ ἔγωγε σπουδάσαι ἂν δυναίμην μᾶλλον ἤπερ ἀθάνατος γενέσθαι, "I could no more be serious than become immortal," implying "I could not possibly become immortal." Comp. Orig. *Comm. Joann.* Lomm. i. 262 εὐδοκοῦντος τοῦ θεοῦ μᾶλλον ἡμᾶς ἀναδέξασθαι… αἰκίας…ἤπερ ἀπαλλαγῆναι τῶν τοσούτων νομιζομένων κακῶν, and *ib.* ii. 252 συναρπάζειν μᾶλλον καὶ σοφίζεσθαι δύναται…ἤπερ πείθειν (v.r. εἴπερ πείθει). For Eustathius on *Iliad* i. 117 see Steph. ἤπερ.

On ἵνα (2093)

[2686] John's predilection for ἵνα does not appear to be sufficiently recognised in Blass's remarks (p. 223) (*a*) "John, Matthew, and Mark employ it very freely. Luke much more rarely especially in the Acts," (p. 321) (*b*) "Probably even in the Gospels its insertion is often the work of scholiasts": (*c*) "in Jo. v. 36 read τελειῶσαι with Tert.," (*d*) "in xi. 31 κλαῦσαι (without ἐκεῖ) with Syr. Lew. and Chrys.," (*e*) "[in] xi. 55 [read] ἁγνίσαι with Chrys.," (*f*) "[in] xii. 20 [read] προσκυνῆσαι with Syr. Lew. and Chrys."

[2687] To begin with (*a*). Since John employs ἵνα about (1726) as often as Mk, Mt. and Lk. all together[1], it is reasonable to expect, in him, many uses of it that would seem suspicious in the other evangelists but (*b*) are not to be suspected, in his Gospel, of being "the work of scholiasts." (*c*) As regards Tertullian's rendering of v. 36 ἵνα τελειώσω (*Prax.* 31) "consummare," it should be noted

---

[1] [2687 *a*] Jn abt 150, Mk 65, Mt. 40, Lk. 50. These figures are hardly compatible with the inference suggested above that Luke uses ἵνα "much more rarely" than the other evangelists, including Matthew. It would be less misleading to say that *Lk. uses ἵνα more freq. than Mt. in his Gospel*, but *less freely in the Acts* (12 times).

that whereas the Latin versions agree with the Greek order, Tertullian disagrees; and it is quite possible that he wrote "dedit ut consummarĕ," and that the dropping of "ut" after "-it" has led to the reading "consummare[1]." Chrysostom twice quotes the verse with ἵνα[2], Nonnus paraphrases it as ὄφρα τελέσσω. The ancient Latin translations have "ut." John himself repeats this very phrase with ἵνα. Why should all these witnesses weigh less than a possibly corrupt text in Tertullian? (d) In xi. 31, it is true that SS renders εἰς τὸ μνημεῖον ἵνα κλαύσῃ ἐκεῖ. ἡ οὖν M. "to the grave...*to* weep: and she Mary"; but this, besides being slight evidence, may be the result of textual corruption[3]. In any case Chrys. does not *quote* this passage without ἵνα, but merely refers to it in a paraphrase, "all began to follow her as though she were going away to weep (ὡς κλαῦσαι ἀπερχομένῃ)." Nonnus has ὄφρα. (e) In xi. 55 ἀνέβησαν... ἵνα ἁγνίσωσιν ἑαυτούς it is true that Mrs Lewis renders SS freely by "to," but SS has "[*in order*] *that*" and Mr Burkitt has "*that*." Chrysostom condenses and paraphrases three verses thus (xi. 55—7) πολλοὶ δὲ ἐκ τῆς χώρας ἀνέβησαν ἁγνίσαι ἑαυτούς. καὶ ἔδωκαν παραγγελίας οἱ ἀρχιερεῖς καὶ οἱ Φ. ἵνα πιάσωσιν αὐτόν. Nonnus has ὄφρα. (f) In xii. 20 ἦσαν δὲ Ἕλληνές τινες ἐκ τῶν ἀναβαινόντων ἵνα προσκυνήσωσιν ἐν τῇ ἑορτῇ, SS has "to," and Chrysostom has ἦσαν δέ τινες τῶν Ἑλλήνων ἀναβάντες προσκυνῆσαι εἰς τὴν ἑορτήν. This is the nearest approach to evidence of an original infinitive. But it is quite unconvincing. It simply shews that Chrysostom would himself prefer the inf. to ἵνα after verbs of motion and that he sometimes lapses into it when he quotes freely or paraphrases. As regards SS, or any

---

[1] [2687 b] Both here and in xvii. 4 δέδωκάς μοι ἵνα ποιήσω, D reads the aorist (ἔδωκεν or ἔδωκας). Translators with this reading would naturally use the imperf. subjunct. "consummarem," and indeed in xvii. 4 the Latin versions have "ut facerem." To go further into the question would require an examination of Tertullian's general rendering of ἵνα clauses and of the instances in which he allows himself to use the infin. after "dedit." Even in the absence of such evidence, it is safe to say that error is more likely to be in Tertullian's present text than in the general consent of all the Greek texts and commentators.

[2] [2687 c] Chrys. also thrice quotes the passage with ἔδωκεν for δέδωκεν,—which favours the view that Tertullian may have written "dedit" as an aorist. Cramer prints a quotation of the words as ἵνα ποιῶ (for ἵνα τελειώσω).

[3] [2687 d] It is pretty certain that SS has read εκειη as though it were εκειη i.e. "she." This explains its omission of "there." Reading the context thus incorrectly, the translator may have dropped ινα after ιον and taken κλαυcη as κλαυcαι to make sense.

translation, its evidence, on this point, may be very slight. Comp. i. 27 ἄξιος ἵνα λύσω (2104 a) where there is no suspicion of any various reading. The Latin versions mostly have "dignus *solvere*," Vulg. "*ut solvam*," mm "*ut solvere*" (sic); but it would be absurd to deny that John wrote ἵνα, although the parallel Synoptists have ἱκανός with infinitive.

On viii. 56 ἨΓΑΛΛΙΆCΑΤΟ ἽΝΑ (2097)

[2688] On viii. 56 ἠγαλλιάσατο ἵνα ἴδῃ, Blass (p. 225) says "the meaning can only be 'to long with ecstasy' ' to rejoice that he should see'": and he compares Herm. *Vis.* iii. 8. 1 (misprinted iii. 8. 7) περιχαρὴς ἐγενόμην τοῦ ἰδεῖν, and iii. 10. 6 περὶ τούτων περίλυπος ἤμην λίαν τοῦ γνῶναι, also (p. 321) Libanius (A.D. 350) *Apol. Socr.* § 68 τέρποιτο ἰδεῖν 'in the prospect of seeing.' But, according to this view, Herm. *Vis.* iii. 10. 6 ought to mean "I was very sorrowful *that I should know*," or "*in the prospect of knowing*," which is the opposite of what is meant. In both passages of Hermas, περιχαρής and περίλυπος appear to be used like πολλὴν χαρὰν (or λύπην) ἔχων followed by a genitive governed by the implied noun. Comp. (if the text is correct) Joseph. *Ant.* xix. 2. 3 περιχαρὴς κ. ἐλπίδος κ. φρονήματος. In any case, these instances afford little guidance as to the way in which John would use ἀγαλλιᾶσθαι ἵνα. Nonnus has ἰδεῖν ἠγάλλετο[1], which Steph. (162 c) quotes, in about seven columns of instances, as the sole instance of an inf. with this verb. Steph. also gives (*ib.*) one instance of the accus., but in that and in every other case the verb refers to past or present causes of joy and never means "look forward with joy to the future." In John, some reference to the future is needed, because of the following words, "and he saw." We can hardly suppose that John meant "Rejoiced *because he saw, and he saw*."

[2689] The probable explanation is that ἠγαλλιάσατο—which

---

[1] [2688 a] 'Αγάλλομαι mostly means "I am proud of," but Irenaeus i. 2. 1 says " And according to them [the Valentinians] Nous alone took pleasure (ἐτέρπετο) [in] contemplating the Father, and *exulted* (ἠγάλλετο) [in] considering His immeasurable greatness." Nonnus could not use ἠγαλλιάσατο in a hexameter: and the aorist ἠγήλατο appears (Steph.) to have been rare: *b* has "laetabatur," *e* "exultatus est" (as also in v. 35). The Latin renderings of Origen vary as follows (Lomm. vi. 38, viii. 216 "desideravit *ut videret*," vi. 279 "exsultavit *ut videret*," ix. 145 "concupivit *videre*," xiv. 425 "quia desideraverit *videre*"). They afford a useful warning against the danger of inferring a Johannine infin. from an infin. in a Latin translation.

[2689] NOTES ON PRECEDING PARAGRAPHS

may be here conveniently rendered "exulted" to distinguish it from ἐχάρη "rejoiced"—expresses the Jewish tradition that Abraham was filled with a divine "strength[1]" and "joy in believing[2]," *in order that*, in accordance with the divine decree, he might receive the reward of the vision of the Day of the Lord[3]. Origen expressly

---

[1] [2689 a] Comp. Rom. iv. 20 "he (*i.e.* Abraham) was *strengthened* (ἐνεδυναμώθη) *in*, or *by, faith* (τῇ πίστει)," Heb. xi. 11 "By *faith* also Sarah herself received strength (δύναμιν)."

[2] [2689 b] Comp. Rom. xv. 13 "Now may the God of hope fill you with all *joy* and peace *in believing*."

[3] [2689 c] Comp. 1 Pet. i. 6—9 "In whom ye exult (ἀγαλλιᾶσθε), though now for a little while ye have been put to grief...that the proof of your faith...might be found unto praise and glory...at the revelation of Jesus Christ : whom, not having seen, ye love ; [looking] to whom, though now ye see not, yet believing, ye *exult* (ἀγαλλιᾶτε ? -ᾶσθε) with joy unspeakable..., *receiving the end of your faith the salvation of your souls*." The context here implies that the "exultant" faith itself—as well as the "proof" of their faith—is ordained to lead the believers to the "*end*," *namely* "*salvation*."

[2689 d] The *thought* runs through the whole of the Bible that "exultant joy" in God is a gift from God, or a virtue to be practised : but the *word* (which Steph. does not quote from any source but LXX or Christian writings) does not occur (in any form) in the LXX till 2 S. i. 20 R.V. "lest the daughters of the uncircumcised *triumph*" (LXX ἀγαλλιάσωνται, but Aq. and the rest, γαυριάσωσι). When ἀγαλλιάομαι occurs as rendering Hebrew, it is restricted (with six exceptions) to the Psalms (about 50) and Isaiah (10). In 3 Macc. ii. 17, as in 2 S. i. 20, it is used in a bad sense, being perh. used like ἀγάλλομαι "plume myself," "boast." It represents 7 (not 8, as Oxf. Conc.) Hebrew words including "sing," "boast," etc., but Aq. appears to have restricted it to "exultation" in a good sense. In N.T. the verb (with the exc. of Mt. v. 12 ἀγαλλιᾶσθε, parall. Lk. vi. 23 σκιρτήσατε) is restricted to Lk., Jn, Acts, 1 Pet. and Rev. Consequently, although the Pauline Epistles emphatically inculcate the virtue or duty of "*rejoicing*," we might easily miss the connexion between this and the "*exultation*" of Abraham : but the Apostle certainly regards "joy" or "rejoicing" as a gift—like "faith" and "hope"—to be used *with a view to* the ultimate seeing of the truth "face to face." Paul, like John, would maintain that we are to "*exult*," *that we may* "*see*" *Christ's* "*day*."

[2689 e] The non-use of ἀγαλλιάομαι in the Pentateuch perhaps prevented Philo from using the word largely (if at all) ; but he (i. 602—3) dwells on the "*laughter*" of Abraham (Gen. xvii. 17) "Then Abraham fell upon his face and laughed—" reminding us that "Isaac" means "laughter," that the soul, so to speak, "rejoices before joy," and that "hope anticipates the coming good and indicates it to the soul that is to be its permanent possessor." Philo's *Quaest. in Gen.* (on Gen. xvii. 17) says that the "falling on the face" implied "an act of adoration and an excess of divine ecstasy" and also an act of confession, and adds "jure autem risit *exsultans* de promissione magna spe adimpletus." Compare Rom. iv. 18—21 ἐπ' ἐλπίδι ἐπίστευσεν εἰς τὸ γενέσθαι αὐτὸν πατέρα πολλῶν ἐθνῶν...δοὺς δόξαν τῷ θεῷ καὶ πληροφορηθείς.

says that Abraham was *not* one of those who "desired to see" the Day of the Lord—and he adds that Abraham "rejoiced" in offering up his son Isaac—a sacrifice universally recognised as a type of the crucifixion[1]. Irenaeus also couples the ἀγαλλίασις of Abraham with that of Mary the Lord's mother[2]: and probably it is implied that in

---

[1] [2689 f] See Origen Lomm. i. 178 quoting Jn viii. 36 and saying οἱ τετελειωμένοι καὶ διαφέροντες (sc. προφῆται) οὐκ ἐπεθύμησαν ἰδεῖν ἃ εἶδον οἱ ἀπόστολοι (referring to Mt. xiii. 17) τεθεωρήκασι γὰρ αὐτά (taking ἐπεθύμησαν to mean "desired in vain"). His words in Lomm. ii. 300 ἀφ' οὗ ἰδὼν τὴν Ἰησοῦ ἡμέραν ἠγαλλιάσατο καὶ ἐχάρη, give at first the impression that he took ἵνα ἴδῃ to mean ὅτι εἶδεν: but a comparison of all his quotations indicates that the ἵνα ἴδῃ is so overshadowed in his mind by εἶδεν that he scarcely touches on the former. In his commentary on Rom. iv. 24 (Lomm. vi. 279) he mentions the "exultation" of Abraham after saying that the patriarch "offered up his only son *rejoicing* (gaudens)," and on Gen. xxi. 8 (Lomm. viii. 215) he treats the "*joy*" of Abraham as equivalent to "*Isaac*," so that "*Isaac* crescebat"="*gaudium* crescebat Abrahamo." Before his first quotation of the passage, Origen (Lomm. i. 152—3) maintains at great length that, as Christian apostles and martyrs were "adorned" or "prepared" (κοσμούμενοι, ἐκοσμήθησαν τῷ μάρτυρες εἶναι) so patriarchs and prophets "have received as a gift [given] by God the [task of] preannouncing Christ, having perceived Him [in the mind] (τὸ προκαταγγεῖλαι Χριστὸν, νοήσαντες αὐτὸν, δῶρον ὑπὸ θεοῦ εἰλήφασι), teaching......As now 'he that hath not known the Son hath not the Father (1 Jn ii. 23),' so also we must perceive that it was of old. Wherefore (διόπερ) Abraham 'exulted [with exultation given from God] in order that he might see the day of Christ'...." A gloss quoted in the notes to Hesychius on ἀγαλλίαμα quotes ἀγάλλω as meaning κοσμῶ, and possibly Origen may have in his mind some allusion to this meaning of the kindred word. In fine, we cannot be certain that Origen took ἵνα as meaning "in order that," but it is certain that he regarded the ἀγαλλίασις as something more than a subjective "longing."

[2] [2689 g] Irenaeus iv. 5. 3—4 has "...'*exultavit* ut videret..., et gavisus est.' Quid enim? 'Credidit Abraham Deo...(Rom. iv. 3, Gen. xv. 6),'" and "'Propheta ergo cum esset A. et videret in Spiritu diem adventus Domini et passionis dispositionem...*exultavit vehementer*. Non incognitus igitur erat Dominus Abrahae cuius diem *concupivit* videre." Either this is inconsistently translated or Irenaeus halted between two meanings, "exultare," and "concupiscere." The translator also renders ἐχάρη first "gavisus est" and then "exultavit vehementer"—or else Irenaeus interchanged ἐχάρη and ἠγαλλιάσατο. The context speaks of Abraham as "following the Logos...*in order that* (ἵνα) he might find his abiding city (πολιτευθῇ) with the Logos" and as "willingly (προθύμως)" giving up his son as a sacrifice to God, "*in order that* (ἵνα) God also might be pleased to give *His* son as a sacrifice for us." There is a suggestion (though no more) that Irenaeus took ἵνα ἴδῃ to mean "*in order that* [Abraham] might see [the Incarnation and the Sacrifice of Christ typified in the sacrifice of Isaac]."

[2689 h] Elsewhere Irenaeus paraphrases thus, iv. 7. 1 "Abraham...*concupivit eam diem videre*, uti et ipse complecteretur Christum: et per Spiritum prophetiae eam videns *exultavit*," where the last word seems to confuse ἠγαλλιάσατο and ἐχάρη. He passes at once to Simeon's utterance ("viderunt oculi mei salutare

[2689]   NOTES ON PRECEDING PARAGRAPHS

both cases this exultant and ecstatic belief was a gift from God *with a view to* (ἵνα) the fulfilment of divine purpose. The Epistle to the Romans (iv. 18) says the same thing in different words, when it declares that Abraham "believed *to the intent that* [*in accordance with God's will*] *he might become* (εἰς τὸ γενέσθαι αὐτόν) the father of many nations[1]." John elsewhere uses the very exceptional passive form (ἀγαλλιαθῆναι) concerning the Pharisees, who were willing (?) "to be gladdened," for a season, in the light of John the Baptist[2].

---

tuum") and that of Mary, "Magnificat...et exultavit," and concludes "Bene igitur Dominus noster...dicens, Abraham pater vester exultavit ut videret diem meum et vidit, et gavisus est" (quoted similarly in ii. 22. 6).

[2689 *i*] This mention of the Magnificat (Lk. i. 47) ἠγαλλίασεν τὸ πνεῦμά μου raises the question whether ἠγαλλίασεν (or -σε), read by all MSS. there, means something different from ἠγαλλιάσατο. The active is not found in LXX anywhere, nor in N.T. elsewhere exc. in 1 Pet. i. 8 (where B has preserved it), and Rev. xix. 7 χαίρωμεν καὶ ἀγαλλιῶμεν (where several authorities have ἀγαλλιώμεθα). 1 Pet. and Rev. may have used the active in a special sense as will be seen below (2689 *l*). But that Lk. should use it thus is improbable, as he has the middle thrice (in Lk. and Acts together) and applies it once to Christ Himself. A Greek tradition printed as Origen's in connexion with his Latin comment on Lk. i. 47, says τὸ δὲ πνεῦμα αὐτῆς ἠγαλλιάσατο...εἶτα ἠγαλλιάσατο τὸ πνεῦμα αὐτῆς, and Cramer prints a comment, διὸ καὶ ἠγαλλιάσατο τὸ πνεῦμά μου. This may be the true reading. If ηγαλλιασα came at the end of a line and τοτο πνευμα at the beginning of the next, it would be very natural that the first το should be dropped, and α changed to ε for sense.

[1] [2689 *j*] Εἰς τό in the Pauline Epistles almost always expresses, not result alone, but *aim—the aim of God*, underlying and controlling the motions of men. This is especially the case in the Epistle to the Romans (i. 11, iii. 26, iv. 11 εἰς τὸ εἶναι...εἰς τὸ λογισθῆναι, iv. 16, vii. 4 etc.). Of course where εἰς τό is connected with a special phrase like ἐπιθυμίαν ἔχων (Phil. i. 23) it may mean "pointing towards" without this notion of divine control. But the whole atmosphere of the Epistle to the Romans is full of the thought of God's preordinance; and iv. 18 εἰς τὸ γενέσθαι, both from a literary and from a grammatical point of view, must be regarded as implying that thought.

[2] [2689 *k*] On v. 35 ἠθελήσατε ἀγαλλιαθῆναι πρὸς ὥραν ἐν τῷ φωτὶ αὐτοῦ, Chrysostom says "they merely *admired* (ἐθαύμασαν) for a season," Cramer has ἀπεδέξαντο πρὸς ὥραν, SS "ye wished to *make your boast* for the hour in his light," Nonnus ἐφαιδρύνασθε...ἀγαλλόμενοι. Clem. Alex. (815) substitutes ἀγαλλιαθῶμεν for ἀγαλλιασώμεθα in quoting Ps. cxviii. 24. In many Christian writers (*e.g.* Chrys. on Gal. vi. 17 ἀγάλλεται τραύματα περιφέρων, but Vulg. ἀγαλλιάζεται) there is much confusion between ἀγάλλομαι "*boast* [of what is my own]," and ἀγαλλιάομαι "*rejoice*, or, *sing praises* [to the glory of God]." Field (on Ps. xxxiii. 1) has πανταχοῦ τὸ, ἀγαλλιᾶσθε, ὁ μὲν Ἀκύλας, αἰνεῖτε, ὁ δὲ Σύμμαχος, εὐφημεῖτε, ἡρμήνευσεν: and it is true that Aq. substitutes "praise" for the LXX ἀγαλλ. when the word means "jubilare," *e.g.* Ps. v. 11, xx. 5, xxxiii. 1. This shews that, in the second century at all events, students of the Bible gave thought

528

Here he uses the middle, probably with some general allusion (as Chrysostom says)[1] to the "day" of the Lord's sacrifice, and, if so, with a special allusion to the Psalmist's words, "This is *the day that the Lord hath made*, Let us *exult* and be glad in it[2]." But the principal allusion seems to be to the "laughing" of Abraham before the birth of "Laughter" *i.e.* Isaac, when he lay prostrate, adoring the goodness of God, abased (as Philo says) in the flesh, but lifted up in the spirit, rapt into the seventh heaven, *in order that he might*

---

to this particular word, and prepares us to believe that some, without going with Aquila so far as to change the *word*, might change its *form*, representing the mere passive feeling of joy by ἀγαλλιαθῆναι or other passive forms, but the active outburst of ecstatic joy—expressing itself in responsive praise and magnifying of God for His mercies—by active or middle forms.

[2689 *l*] This may explain 1 Pet. i. 6—9, which should perhaps be punctuated thus, ἐν ᾧ ἀγαλλιᾶσθε—ὀλίγον ἄρτι, εἰ δέον, λυπηθέντες...ἵνα τὸ ⌜δοκίμιον⌝...ἐν ἀποκαλύψει Ἰησοῦ Χριστοῦ—ὃν οὐκ ἰδόντες ἀγαπᾶτε, εἰς ὃν ἄρτι μὴ ὁρῶντες πιστεύοντες δὲ ἀγαλλιᾶτε (so B and Orig.) χαρᾷ ἀνεκλαλήτῳ καὶ δεδοξασμένῃ, κομιζόμενοι τὸ τέλος τῆς πίστεως, σωτηρίαν ψυχῶν. Here sense requires (1) a marked difference between ἐν ᾧ ἀγαλλιᾶσθε and εἰς ὃν πιστεύοντες ἀγαλλιᾶτε, (2) a climax in the latter. "Some Latin fathers and inferior Vulg. MSS.," says Hort, take the former (ἀγαλλιᾶσθε) as fut. "exultabitis." But a better meaning may be expressed in the foll. paraphrase, "In whom ye *are made to rejoice*—in spite of your momentary sufferings, which shall result to your good in the day of the final revealing of Jesus Christ—whom, I say, not having seen, ye love, *to whom* even now, though not seeing, yet believing, *your hearts go out in ecstasy with a joy ineffable and divinely glorified*." The Apostle speaks of the "rejoicing" of the Christian first from a passive, then from an active, point of view. The active joy is called "glorified" because it is purified from all thought of self, as the rejoicer merges himself in God—like Abraham (Rom. iv. 20) "giving glory to God."

[1] [2689 *m*] Chrys. "He seems to me to speak here of the day of the Cross, which day he typically predicted (προδιετύπωσε) in the sacrifice of the ram and of Isaac," Cramer diff. and adds "He praises Abraham as having been filled with joy because of the cross (ὡς εὐφρανθέντα διὰ τὸν σταυρόν) wishing to shew that he does not unwillingly come to the suffering (δεῖξαι θέλων ὅτι οὐκ ἄκων ἐπὶ τὸ πάθος ἔρχεται)"—which last words might apply to Abraham or to the Saviour.

[2] [2689 *n*] Clem. Alex. (815) quotes "This is the day etc." with a general reference to τὴν δι' υἱοῦ ἐνέργειαν in the *creation* of the world, not in its *redemption*. But Origen (Ps. cxviii. 24) *ad loc*. "For what could possibly equal this day in which the reconciliation of God came to men...and paradise was opened and we received again our ancient country and the curse was blotted out and sin destroyed ...wherefore let us too *exult* (ἀγαλλιασώμεθα) and be glad in it."

[2689 *o*] Clem. Alex. 973 gives a Valentinian quotation of viii. 56 stopping at τὴν ἡμέραν τὴν ἐμήν, and continuing thus, τὴν ἐν σαρκὶ παρουσίαν. ὅθεν ἀναστὰς ὁ κύριος εὐηγγελίσατο τοὺς δικαίους τοὺς ἐν τῇ ἀναπαύσει καὶ μετέστησεν αὐτούς... apparently referring it to Abraham in Hades waiting to be liberated by the Saviour.

see—and help all mankind to see—the vision of the Father sacrificing Himself in the sacrifice of the Son[1].

On ἵνα with indicative (2114)

[2690] The instances of ἵνα with fut. in John are so few that no safe inference is possible as to any difference of meaning. In vii. 3 ἵνα...θεωρήσουσιν (v.r. -ήσωσιν) there may be an intention to blend purpose with assured result. In xvii. 2 ἵνα...δώσει (v. r. δωση, δωσω etc.) compared with Lk. xx. 10 ἵνα δώσουσιν and 1 Cor. ix. 18 ἵνα θήσω, it is possible that the use of the future may have been facilitated by the tendency to substitute for forms of the 2nd aorist active (see Blass, p. 43) forms of the 1st aorist active in -σα, which resembled forms of the future. It would be an anachronism to suppose in N.T. the late Gk aorists ἔδωσα[2] and ἔθησα: but, long before these forms came into use, there might be a tendency to avoid the 2nd aorists of verbs in -μι, because of their perplexing irregularity and erroneous use as in *Ox. Pap.* cclxix. col. ii. 8—12 (A.D. 57) ἐάν σοι δῦ (for δῷ) τὸ ἀργύριον δῦς (for δὸς) αὐτῷ ἀποχήν, καὶ ἐὰν εὕ[ρ]ῃς ἀσφαλὴν (*sic*) δῦς (for δὸς) αὐτῷ τὸ ἀργύριον ἐνένκαι μοι, and *Fayûm* cix. 4 τοὺς τρεῖς στατῆρες (*sic*) οὕς εἴρηκέ σοι Σέλευκος δῶναί (for δοῦναί) μοι ἤδη δὸς Κλέωνι. It is probable that ἵνα with *particular futures that had an aorist subjunctive sound would come into use long before* ἵνα *became customary with the future in general*. But the future after ἵνα would also displace, at a comparatively early date, *irregular and rare forms of the subjunctive*.

On St Paul's autograph (2114)

[2691] As regards the interchange of ο and ω in a passage written or partly written by St Paul's own hand, compare the Fayûm Papyri 110 foll., which gives several letters from one

---

[1] [2689 *p*] Lk. x. 21 ἠγαλλιάσατο, applied to Christ, and parall. to Mt. xi. 25 ἀποκριθείς, precedes an utterance of "confession" (ἐξομολογοῦμαί σοι) to the Father. The relation between Lk. and Mt. is too difficult a question to be discussed here. But it may be noted that elsewhere in N.T. (exc. Jn v. 35) both the verb and the noun almost always describe ecstatic joy in man tending to the glorifying of God.

[2] [2690 *a*] In Mk vi. 37 Swete reads δώσωμεν (with אBD 33 etc., v.r. δωσομεν and δωμεν), but W.H. has δώσομεν. Possibly, the original was δωσωμεν, with ω for ο, intended as a fut., and the scribes of אB and D retained ω because of the preceding ἀγοράσωμεν, taking both words as delib. subjunct., whereas the meaning was "*Are we to* buy...*and shall* we give?" Hesychius explains προέμενος as προδώσας, and Lobeck's Phrynichus (p. 719—20) gives many instances of corruptions arising from a preference of debased first aorist forms.

Gemellus¹. The first of these is dated A.D. 94. In this the spelling

---

¹ [2691 a] How much was written by the Apostle himself cannot be decided apart from the meaning of the aorist in Gal. vi. 11 ἴδετε ⌜πηλίκοις⌝ (marg. ἡλίκοις) ὑμῖν γράμμασιν ἔγραψα τῇ ἐμῇ χειρί, R.V. "See with how large letters I *have written* unto you with mine own hand," marg. "*write*." Lightf. renders this "'*I write*,' the epistolary aorist conveniently translated by a present"; and he quotes *Mart. Polyc.* § 1 ἐγράψαμεν ὑμῖν, ἀδελφοί..., at the very beginning of the epistle, to shew that the "epistolary aorist" may refer to words that follow. But that epistle, having been written in compliance with a request from the brethren addressed (*ib.* § 20), might naturally begin thus, "*We have written*, brethren [as you desired]"—especially if (as is very likely) the facts of the martyrdom were written first and the introduction added afterwards. Lightfoot quotes no other instance outside N.T.

[2691 b] As regards N.T., in Philem. 18—19 "If he...oweth thee aught, *put that to mine account*; *I Paul have written* (R.V. write) *it* (ἔγραψα) with mine own hand, I will repay it," the aorist probably refers to "put...account" (repeated, in effect, in "I will repay it"); and *ib.* 21 ἔγραψά σοι refers to all that precedes. In Rom. xv. 15, ἔγραψα refers (Fritzsche) to previous portions of the letter. In 1 Cor. v. 9—11 ἔγραψα ὑμῖν ἐν τῇ ἐπιστολῇ...νῦν δὲ ἔγραψα ὑμῖν, both aorists —however τῇ ἐπ. may be explained—appear to refer to something previously written; and this is certainly true of 1 Cor. ix. 15 (οὐκ ἔγραψα δὲ ταῦτα, which refers to *ib.* 3—14), 2 Cor. ii. 3, 4, 9, vii. 12. The past meaning of the aorist is made all the more probable since that St Paul frequently uses γράφω or γράφομεν (1 Cor. xiv. 37, 2 Cor. i. 13, xiii. 10, Gal. i. 20, 2 Thess. iii. 17, 1 Tim. iii. 14) when he really means the present "I am writing." In 1 Pet. v. 12, ἔγραψα comes at the close of the epistle and means (as R.V.) "*I have written*." In 1 Jn ii. 13, 14 (*bis*), 21, 26, v. 13, ἔγραψα is to be distinguished from *ib.* i. 4 γράφομεν and ii. 1, 7, 8, 12, 13 (*bis*), γράφω, and Westcott—who rightly regards ἔγραψα as a true aorist—supposes, between the two tenses in ii. 13, "a pause in thought if not a break in the composition of the letter." Even without that hypothesis, the aorist causes no difficulty, "I *write* (pres.) unto you, children, because...[Another reason why] I *wrote* (aor.) unto you, children, [was] because...." In any case, ἔγραψα in these Johannine passages means (R.V. txt) "have written" or (R.V. marg.) "wrote." Ἐπέστειλα (R.V. "I have written") occurs at the close of the Epistle to the Hebrews (xiii. 22).

[2691 c] Lightf. refers to the "epistolary" use of ἔπεμψα. This aorist, in Acts xxiii. 30, occurs at the end of a letter in which Claudius Lysias says, in effect, to Felix, "Along with this letter *I have sent* you a prisoner." It occurs also in 2 Cor. viii. 18, 22, ix. 3, Eph. vi. 22, Col. iv. 8 about sending "brethren" or friends, *who, in all cases, bring the Apostle's letter with them*. Similarly, in an English letter, many would prefer to say "I *have enclosed*, or, *enclose*, a cheque" (though strict logic would require "I *shall enclose*") meaning "*you will find that I have enclosed*." If we were to say "I *shall enclose*, or, *shall send*, a cheque," it might often lead the reader to suppose that a cheque would be sent later on. The same objection would apply to πέμψω in a Greek letter. We cannot argue from this obviously convenient use of ἔπεμψα that letter-writers would adopt an obviously inconvenient use of ἔγραψα—inconvenient, because it would merely

[2691] NOTES ON PRECEDING PARAGRAPHS

is excellent. In the second we have ὡδοῦ for ὁδοῦ, [κ]όμῃ for κώμῃ and λέγον for λέγων, in five consecutive lines, and similar substitutions occur in later letters. The reason for the difference is that *the first letter was written for Gemellus by a scribe, but the second and following ones by Gemellus himself*: and *he himself regularly confused o and ω*. In the LXX, comp. Gen. iv. 5 "his countenance fell," LXX συνέπεσεν τῷ προσώπῳ, Aq. ἔπεσε τὸ πρόσωπον αὐτοῦ, Josh. xv. 8 LXX ἐπὶ νότου, A νώτου, Sir. xliii. 26 LXX εὐωδία for אC εὐοδία etc. In Gal. vi. 8—12, beside the interchanges of o and ω mentioned in **2114**, B clearly shews ηλικοις for πηλίκοις, a very minute π being perhaps inserted above the line, and περιτεμεσθαι occurs at the beginning of the line for περιτέμνεσθαι. The photo-

represent the same thing as the epistolary γράφω, which is very frequent, whereas the epistolary πέμπω nowhere occurs in N.T.

[**2691** *d*] Chrys. on Gal. vi. 11 takes ἔγραψα to refer to "the whole letter.' He and a "vir...eruditus" mentioned by Jerome—but Wetst. and Migne give Jerome's evidence very differently (**2785** foll.)—regarded the "large letters" as the uncouth handwriting of one unaccustomed to write Greek. Theodorus, on the other hand, thinks that the Apostle, "being on the point of sharply attacking (μέλλων καθάπτεσθαι) his adversaries, used larger letters [than usual] emphasizing [the fact] that he himself neither blushes nor denies what was being said (ἐμφαίνων ὅτι οὔτε αὐτὸς ἐρυθριᾷ οὔτε ἀρνεῖται τὰ λεγόμενα)." The "vir...eruditus"—about whom Jerome adds (Migne) "miror quomodo rem ridiculam locutus sit"—was not improbably Chrysostom himself, though Migne dissents from this conclusion. In any case, Jerome's own explanation is quite unsatisfactory, as he translates πηλίκοις as though it were ποίοις. As to the view of Theodorus, favoured by Lightfoot, that "large letters" might correspond to our underlining, no evidence for it is alleged by Lightfoot, nor has any been (so far as I know) adduced from the numerous papyri discovered since. Lightfoot wrote. Lucian's two mentions of "great letters" refer only to placards and public inscriptions (i. 750 *Herm.* 11, ii. 903 *De Gymnas.* 22).

[**2691** *e*] *A man writing, contrary to his custom, in "large letters," could not reproduce the peculiarities of his handwriting in a natural manner.* But St Paul says "See with what *large letters I have written with my own hand*" in such a way as to suggest that they could recognise his handwriting, as in 2 Thess. iii. 17 "the salutation of me Paul *with mine own hand, which is the token in every epistle, thus I write*." It is probable that this "token" was written in large letters, and that St Paul, on the very rare occasions when he wrote Greek at all, always wrote thus. But the special peculiarity about the autographic writing to the Galatians was that it extended to a passage of some length. Some of this almost certainly preceded the word ἴδετε. Perhaps (as Chrysostom maintained) it extended to the whole of the epistle. If so, we need not, of course, adopt the view that the writer "gloried in his imperfect knowledge" (**2788**); he may be referring to the laborious "large letters" as a proof that he loved the Galatians. When forced to rebuke them more bitterly than he had rebuked any other church, he would not rebuke them through the hand of an amanuensis.

graph also shews something wrong in the accentuation of χειρί and perhaps in the following o, of ΧΕΙΡΙΟ. It may be urged that Gemellus, though a man of means, was not highly educated, whereas St Paul, as a youth, perhaps studied at Tarsus. But Augustus is said by Suetonius to have been a bad speller (2790). And if a Roman Emperor, why not a Jew—who probably had little practice in Greek writing during his training under Gamaliel in Jerusalem, and who certainly wrote Greek, for the most part, through an amanuensis?

On iv. 45 καὶ αὐτοὶ γάρ (2167)

[2692] In iv. 45 καὶ αὐτοὶ γὰρ ἦλθον, why is special emphasis apparently laid on αὐτοί? Καὶ γὰρ αὐτοί, "for they also," would have emphasized the pronoun; but καὶ αὐτοὶ γάρ seems to give a special emphasis. Does it mean "*even* the despised Galilaeans"? Chrys., in his comments, suggests this view, calling attention to the contempt with which they were regarded by the Jews. But he omits αὐτοί (though Migne's Latin translation supplies it). Origen (*ad loc.*), besides quoting with αὐτοί, appears to attempt to explain it thus, Πλὴν ἔξεστι Γαλιλαῖον ὄντα ἑορτάζειν ἐν Ἱεροσολύμοις γινόμενον, ὅπου ὁ ναὸς τοῦ Θεοῦ, καὶ θεωρεῖν πάντα ὅσα ἐποίει ἐκεῖ ὁ Ἰησοῦς... Ἀρχὴ γὰρ ἡ ἐν Ἱεροσολύμοις ἑορτὴ τοῖς Γαλιλαίοις ἐστὶ τοῦ καὶ δέξασθαι τὸν υἱὸν τοῦ Θεοῦ ἐλθόντα πρὸς αὐτούς. This seems to mean, "Though the Galilaeans were at a distance from Jerusalem and somewhat despised, it was quite lawful for *them* [*as distinct from the Samaritans mentioned in the preceding chapter*] to keep the Feast in Jerusalem and [*hence possible for them*] to behold Christ's works there... [And this is essential to the narrative] for the Feast in Jerusalem was, in effect, the beginning of the Gospel for them." He proceeds to argue that the Galilaeans would not have received Jesus if they had not gone up to the Feast in Jerusalem. Nonnus inserts αὐτοί, calling the Galilaeans ἑσμὸς θεοστόργων and adding Καὶ γὰρ ἐς ἱερὸν ἦμαρ ἐπεστιχόωντο καὶ αὐτοί. Steph. 521 B—D gives freq. instances of καὶ γάρ but none where the phrase is broken by an intervening noun or pronoun.

On ὅπως ἄν (2173)

[2693] Ὅπως ἄν, in the Psalms, is the regular equivalent of the Heb. "*in order that*," "*for the sake of*," when used with verb, Ps. ix. 14, xxx. 12, xlviii. 13, li. 4, lx. 5, cviii. 6 etc. The same Heb. is rendered by Aq. (fragm. ed. Taylor) in 2 K. xxiii. 24 ὅπως where LXX has ἵνα (before (ἀνα)στήσῃ). In Proverbs, the same Heb. (occurring thrice) is rendered once εἰ γάρ, twice ἵνα, and in Job

[2694] NOTES ON PRECEDING PARAGRAPHS

(occurring twice) once καὶ τότε, and once ἢ ἵνα. In Egypt. Pap. Indices ὅπως with subjunct. is mostly confined to petitions but occurs twice (*Oxyr.* 532. 13, *Fayûm* 121. 10) in private letters.

On ὅτι = ὥστε (2186)

[2694] Ὅτι is equivalent to ὥστε, "so that" in xiv. 22 Κύριε, τί γέγονεν ὅτι ἡμῖν μέλλεις ἐμφανίζειν σεαυτὸν καὶ οὐχὶ τῷ κόσμῳ; The Diatessaron, it is true, renders this "*What is the purpose of thy intention to* shew thyself...." But this indicates the reading τί ἐστιν ὅτι, the reading of D, SS (Chrys. has 1st τί ὅτι, and 2nd τί ἔστιν ὅτι;). Nonnus has Κοίρανε, πῶς τεὸν εἶδος ὁμοφρονέων ἀναφαίνεις Μούνοις σοῖς ἑτάροισι καὶ οὐ θηήτορι κόσμῳ; Theoretically, τί γέγονεν ὅτι might be rendered, "*Why hath it come to pass that...?*" But ὅτι, "*so that,*" is very common in O.T. in such phrases as "What is man *that*...?" (Heb. ii. 6, qu. Ps. viii. 4), "*What* have I done *that*...?" and this is probably the meaning here: "Lord, *what* [*new thing*] *hath come to pass so that* thou dost purpose...?" It is one of the very few certain instances of ὅτι "*so that,*" in N.T.[2] The Thesaurus quotes no instances of ὅτι meaning ὥστε except from Scholiasts on Theocritus[3]. This Johannine instance of ὅτι in interrogation is quite distinct from the Byzantine and post-Christian use of it after τοσοῦτος etc. (2697).

On ὅτι μή (2187)

[2695] On iii. 18 ὁ μὴ πιστεύων ἤδη κέκριται ὅτι μὴ πεπίστευκεν εἰς τὸ ὄνομα τοῦ μονογενοῦς υἱοῦ τοῦ θεοῦ[4], Blass says (p. 255) that it

---

[1] [2694a] See Gen. xx. 9, 10, Judg. xiv. 3, 1 S. xx. 1, 1 K. xviii. 9 etc. In Gen. xx. 10 "What sawest thou *that* thou hast done?" LXX has τί ἐνιδὼν (Sym. ἰδών) ἐποίησας; but Aq. τί εἶδες (Theod. ἑώρακας) ὅτι ἐποίησας; In Gen. xl. 15 "I have done nothing *that* they should have placed me in the dungeon," LXX has ἀλλά. In all these cases the Heb. conj. is כִּי, which may mean "*but*," "*for indeed*," "*since*," as well as "*that*."

[2] [2694b] In Mk iv. 41, Mt. viii. 27, Lk. viii. 25, ὅτι may have been used by the writers to mean "such that," or "for indeed." In Lk. iv. 36 ὅτι (which has caused v.r. in parall. Mk i. 27) prob. means "because" or "for indeed."

[3] [2694c] On Theocr. ix. 25 μέγας...τοσοῦτον ὅτι...διέκοψα, on *ib*. x. 14 ἐς τοσοῦτον ὅτι. Classical Greek might have used ὥστε μέλλει here. But ὥστε with indic. is almost non-existent in LXX, and (except as meaning initial "wherefore") occurs in N.T. perh. only in Gal. ii. 13 and Jn iii. 16. This tradition about "Judas not Iscariot" or "Judas Thomas" is perh. derived from some special source. The indices of the Egyptian Papyri give no instance of ὅτι "so that."

[4] [2695a] Syr. Curet. (Burk.) "But he that believeth not is guilty, in that he believed not in the name of the only Son of God," SS "and he that believeth not in him is judged on [the ground] that he believed not in the name of the approved Son (*sic*)."

is the only exception to the rule of using οὐ—"unless indeed the late form ὅτι μή should be taken as an indication of the spuriousness of the subordinate clause which is omitted by Chrys. and is very tautological." But ὅτι μή is found in Joseph. *Ap.* i. 23 διήμαρτον ὅτι μὴ ταῖς ἱεραῖς ἡμῶν βίβλοις ἐνέτυχον, and Epict. iv. 4. 8 ὅταν γὰρ ἐσθίῃς, ἄχθῃ ὅτι μὴ ἀναγινώσκεις (besides later writers such as Justin Martyr and Lucian), so that the construction, relatively to John, can hardly be called "*late.*" Chrys., it is true, omits the words, but the context indicates that he merely omits them because they seemed to him unnecessary for the purpose of his comment. Nonnus paraphrases them fully. Origen appears to have read them, if we restore a missing μή in a passage distinguishing between "believing in him" and "believing in his name[1]." Origen's argument is condensed, but it seems to be this: "Christ says 'He that *believeth in me* is not judged,' but not 'He that *believeth in my name* is not judged.' He does not go on to say 'He that *believeth not in me* hath been judged already' [He says simply 'he that *believeth not*,' meaning '*believeth not in any way*']: for perhaps 'he that believeth *in His name,*' does at all events (μέν) believe; wherefore he does not deserve to 'have been judged already,' though inferior to him that '*believeth in Him.*'" From this it appears probable that Origen assumed in this context the existence of a negative clause about "not believing *in the name*," though he does not quote it. He actually quotes it in his commentary (Latin) on the Epistle to the Romans[2]. In his commentary on the Psalms he stops short, as Chrys. does, at the word κέκριται, but it is for brevity; and there he

---

[1] [2695 b] Orig. (on Jn ii. 23—5, Lomm. i. 371). Φησὶ γὰρ ὁ κύριος, "'Ὁ πιστεύων εἰς ἐμὲ οὐ κρίνεται," οὐχὶ δέ "'Ὁ πιστεύων εἰς τὸ ὄνομά μου οὐ κρίνεται." Οὐκέτι δέ φησιν "'Ὁ [μὴ] πιστεύων εἰς ἐμὲ ἤδη κέκριται·" τάχα γὰρ "ὁ πιστεύων εἰς τὸ ὄνομα αὐτοῦ" πιστεύει μέν, διόπερ οὐκ ἔστιν ἄξιος "ἤδη κεκρίσθαι," ἐλάττων δέ ἐστι τοῦ πιστεύοντος εἰς αὐτόν. For ὅτι μή in Epictetus, see also iv. 4. 11 κλαίῃ... ὅτι μὴ ἔξω γυμνάζεται and iv. 5. 8—9 (thrice) ἐλοιδόρησέ σε ὁ δεῖνα. Πολλὴ χάρις αὐτῷ ὅτι μὴ ἔπληξεν....

[2] [2695 c] Lomm. vi. 99 "Omnis qui credit in me non judicabitur. Qui autem non credit, jam judicatus est quia non credit in nomine unigeniti Filii Dei." Both in Gk and Latin, Origen has "He that believeth in *me*" (for "believeth in *him*"). So has Irenaeus v. 27. 2. The reason is, that all three quotations are preceded by "*The Lord said,*" or words to that effect, and "*The Lord said,* 'He that believeth in *him*'" would be liable to misunderstanding as meaning "He that believeth in *God.*" But the quotations afford an instructive illustration of the manner in which a saying about "the Son of God" or "the Son of man" might be altered to a saying in the first person.

adds "But I understand the words 'he that believeth not' to stand for 'he that disbelieveth¹.'." This may partly explain John's exceptional use of μή. It may be taken as a sort of *alpha* privative. "The *disbeliever* (ὁ μὴ-πιστεύων)" is condemned because "he has *disbelieved* (μὴ-πεπίστευκεν)." But the precedent μὴ πιστεύων occurs also in 1 Jn (2187) where ὅτι οὐ follows; so that it does not suffice as a complete explanation.

On ὡc (2201)

[2696] Ὡς, "donec," is mentioned in Steph. (p. 2108 A) only as an unsatisfactory rendering in *Odyss*. iii. 301 where ὡς "when," or ὥς "thus," is to be preferred. It certainly seems to mean "while" (less probably "as") in Ignat. *Smyrn*. 9 ὡς [ἔτι] καιρὸν ἔχομεν, 2 Clem. Rom. 8 ὡς οὖν ἐσμὲν ἐπὶ γῆς, 9 ὡς ἔχομεν καιρόν. But two of these three passages appear to be quotations of Gal. vi. 10 ὡς καιρὸν ἔχωμεν (prob. a misspelling (2114, 2691) of ἔχομεν) R.V. "*as we have opportunity*"; and, even if the quoters regarded ὡς as equivalent to ἕως, it by no means follows that they were right. In the Indices of the Egyptian Papyri ἕως is fairly frequent, but not ὡς except once in ὡς ἄν. In Lk. xii. 58 ὡς γὰρ ὑπάγεις (R.V.) "*as thou art going*" there is apparently no notion of "as long as" till Luke adds ἐν τῇ ὁδῷ (Mt. v. 25 ἕως ὅτου εἶ...ἐν τῇ ὁδῷ)—*i.e.* "[being still] in the way." In modern Greek (Blass p. 332), ὡς is said to be used for ἕως in such a phrase as ὡς ἔτι ζῶ, but in non-modern Greek, there appears to be no evidence at present for such a usage of ὡς with indicative except that given above. In Gal. vi. 10, there seems to be a reference to the preceding words: "Let us not faint, *for in its own* [i.e. *the harvest's*] *appointed time* (καιρῷ γὰρ ἰδίῳ) we [workmen] shall reap the harvest if we faint not. Well then *as we* [workmen] *have an appointed time* (ἄρα οὖν ὡς καιρὸν ἔχομεν, not -ωμεν) let us work...." In view of the exceptional misspellings in the context of Gal. vi. 10 the conclusion is uncertain, but probably ὡς is not used for ἕως, and the passage means either "*as* we have an appointed time²," or "*according as* we have opportunity."

---

¹ [2695 d] On Ps. lxxii. 4 (Lomm. xiii. 2) Ἀκούω δὲ τοῦ "ὁ μὴ πιστεύων" ἀντὶ τοῦ "ὁ ἀπιστῶν." Clem. Alex. 641 actually uses ἀπιστεῖν in quoting iii. 18, ὁ ἀπιστήσας, κατὰ τὴν σωτήριον φωνήν, ἤδη κέκριται.

² [2696 a] Ὡς ἄν is prob. (Steph.) for ἕως ἄν "as long as" in Soph. *Ajax* 1117 ὡς ἂν ᾖς οἷός περ εἶ in view of Plato *Phaedr*. 243 E ἕωσπερ ἂν ᾖς ὃς εἶ, and comp. Soph. *Phil*. 1330, *Œd. Col.* 1361 and possibly (Steph.) Hippocr. 418. 5 μηδ' ὡς ἄν

On οὕτως...ὥστε (2203)

[2697] Concerning iii. 16 οὕτως γὰρ ἠγάπησεν...ὥστε τὸν υἱὸν τὸν μονογενῆ ἔδωκεν Blass (p. 224) says "the correct reading in place of ὥστε is ὅτι, which is doubly attested by Chrys. (in many passages) and Nonnus § 78, 6." But Chrysostom, while *quoting the whole text* with ὅτι, comments thus, οὕτως ὑμᾶς ἠγάπησεν ὡς ὑπὲρ τῶν δούλων δοῦναι τὸν υἱόν. Subsequently, he says ἅπερ ἐπήγαγε λέγων ὅτι τὸν υἱὸν αὐτοῦ τὸν μονογενῆ ἔδωκεν. Here ὅτι should prob. be printed as "recitativum"; but its use suggests how easily ὅτι τὸν υἱόν might creep into the text in the place of ὥστε τὸν υἱόν when the words were quoted. Moreover this use of ὅτι after οὕτως, τοσοῦτος etc. does not appear to exist till quite late. We must carefully distinguish between (1) the LXX use of ὅτι "so that" (2694) after questions and negations, and (2) the Byzantine or post-Christian use of ὅτι, "so that," after τοσοῦτος etc.[1] To impute to John the idiom οὕτως... ὅτι may have been natural for Chrysostom or for a scribe of Chrysostom's text, but for John himself (so far as evidence is alleged) it would apparently have been an anachronism. Οὕτως...ἵνα "so greatly...that" he might have written, along with Epictetus[2]:

---

v.r. μὴ δὲ ως. But these are all with pres. subjunct., and must be carefully distinguished from ὡς ἄν with aorist subjunct. "whenever," or "when," which occurs in Herodotus, Cebes (Steph.), Josh. ii. 14, iii. 8, 13 etc. *Tebt. Papyr.* xxvi. l. 2 (B.C. 114) ὡς ἂν ἀναγνῶτε, and in 1 Cor. xi. 34, Phil. ii. 23. Rom. xv. 24 ὡς ἂν πορεύωμαι is either quite exceptional "*when* I am taking my proposed journey," or "*provided that* I journey." In vernacular English, "as long as" sometimes means "*provided that*."

[2696 b] 'Ως in Mk ix. 21 (B ἕως, al. ἐξ οὗ and so Lat. and Syr.) πόσος χρόνος ἐστὶν ὡς τοῦτο γέγονεν means "since." SS has "behold since," which is like Judg. xvi. 13 "hitherto," B "*behold*" ἰδού (confusing the Heb.), A ὡς νῦν, al. (Field) ἕως νῦν. Ezr. ix. 7 ὡς ἡ ἡμέρα αὕτη is corrupted in 1 Esdr. viii. 74 to μέχρι τῆς σήμερον ἡμέρας suggesting that ὡς has been read as ἕως. Conversely Ezr. vi. 20 "as one" is rendered ἕως εἷς, al. (Field) ὡς εἷς. These facts (and others in Steph., and see Herm. *Vis.* iii. 8 ὡς, v.r. ὅς and ἕως) indicate frequent scribal confusion of ὡς and ἕως, but they do not shew that early Christian writers used the former for the latter.

[2696 c] In xii. 35—6 περιπατεῖτε ὡς τὸ φῶς ἔχετε... ὡς τὸ φῶς ἔχετε πιστεύετε, the repetition, and the reversed order of the words accord (2554) with Johannine usage. Blass's suggestion (p. 332) to read (with ℵ) 1st ἕως and 2nd ὡς would not accord with it so well.

[1] [2697 a] For the latter, Jannaris (p. 416) quotes only Theod., Apophth., J Moschos, Leont. Neap., J Canan.

[2] [2697 b] Comp. Epictet. ii. 2. 16 οὕτω μωρὸς ἦν ἵνα μὴ ἴδῃ... ; ii. 22. 9 σαίνοντα...ἀλλήλοις ἵν' εἴπῃς (*so as to make you say*) Οὐδὲν φιλικώτερον, iii. 1. 12 τί

[2698] NOTES ON PRECEDING PARAGRAPHS

but not οὕτως ὅτι. As to Nonnus, Passow reads οὕτω...ἵνα, with ὅτι as a rejected reading.

On ἄν with indicative (2213)

[2698] On ἄν with indic. in hypothetical sentences Blass says (205) "the insertion of ἄν is not obligatory," and he refers to viii. 39, xv. 24, xix. 11 and Gal. iv. 15. But in viii. 39 it is maintained (2079) that B has preserved the right reading, and that ἄν is not omitted. In xv. 24 οὐκ εἴχοσαν, xix. 11 οὐκ εἶχες—and, we may add, xv. 22 οὐκ εἴχοσαν—the phrase is always of one kind and negative, and does not afford a basis for a general statement that ἄν is not obligatory. In Gal. iv. 15 μαρτυρῶ γὰρ ὑμῖν ὅτι, εἰ δυνατόν, τοὺς ὀφθαλμοὺς ὑμῶν ἐξορύξαντες ἐδώκατέ μοι, the Apostle describes hyperbolically the past affection of the Galatians by a reference to stories like that told by Lucian (ii. 548, *Tox.* 40) of friends cutting out their eyes for friendship's sake. Perhaps ἄν is omitted (though the writer may have been combining in his mind (1) "*If it had been possible,* you *would have* cut out your eyes," (2) "*If I may say so,* you *did* cut out your eyes "), but in any case the sentence is exceptional.

εἶδεν ἐν ἐμοὶ ὁ Ἐ. ἵνα...περιΐδῃ; "what did E. see in me *so as to make him neglect me?*"; iii. 12. 10 οὕτω προβήσῃ ἵνα...εἴπῃς "you will make *such progress as to be able to say*" etc. But in i. 19. 13, ii. 3. 3, and iii. 22. 63, placed by Schenkl under τοιοῦτος ἵνα with query, ἵνα (see context) is probably not dependent on τοιοῦτος but means "in order that." In the Pauline Epistles, ἵνα may possibly mean "so that" in 1 Thess. v. 4 "ye are not in the darkness *that* (ἵνα)," but it is more in accordance with Pauline thought and usage to take it as meaning "it is not ordained for you *that.*" And in 1 Cor. ix. 24 οὕτως τρέχετε ἵνα almost certainly means "Thus, as I have described, must ye run *in order that* ye may attain." The notion of an overruling Providence, or of an ordained conflict, is also probably present in Gal. v. 17 ταῦτα γὰρ ἀλλήλοις ἀντίκειται ἵνα μὴ ἃ ἐὰν θέλητε ταῦτα ποιῆτε, where Chrys.'s paraphrase is ἵνα μὴ συγχωρῇς τῇ ψυχῇ πορεύεσθαι ἐν ταῖς ἐπιθυμίαις αὐτῆς ταῖς πονηραῖς, shewing that he took ἵνα to mean "in order that." But Cramer prints a comment of "another," who says τὸ γὰρ ἵνα οὐκ ἐπὶ αἰτίας εἶπεν ἀλλ' ὡς ἀκόλουθον κατὰ τὸ οἰκεῖον ἰδίωμα.

[2697c] In the Egypt. Pap. ὥστε τινι occurs about money received by, or given to, someone "*as for someone else,*" in *Oxy.* vol. iii. 529, 582, *Fayûm* xvii. 2, and ὥστε with the infin., in wills and contracts, meaning "on condition of doing" (as in classical Gk.). Other notable uses are *Oxy.* vol. iv. 743 (B.C. 2) ὥστ' ἂν τοῦτό σε θέλω γεινώσκειν, "wherefore I should like you to understand," *Tebtun.* lviii. 35 (B.C. 111) ὥστ' ἂν σὺν τοῖς θεοῖς καταστοχήσαμεν αὐτοῦ "*wherefore* (D.V.) we shall probably secure him" [This is quite distinct from ὥστ' ἂν in the phrase "so that the damage might be estimated at" (*Tebt.* xxxviii. 25, xxxix. 33 etc.)], *Fayûm* xxiv. 15 (A.D. 158) ἐπιστολῆς...ὥστε αὐτοὺς ἀνέρχεσθαι, "a notice... ordering them to return."

Winer quotes ix. 33 οὐκ ἠδύνατο, but this is negative. In Rom. vii. 7 τὴν ἁμαρτίαν οὐκ ἔγνων εἰ μὴ διὰ νόμου, τήν τε γὰρ ἐπιθυμίαν οὐκ ᾔδειν εἰ μὴ ὁ νόμος ἔλεγεν, the meaning of the first clause is "I *did* not recognise sin *except* through Law..." and then the second clause says, in effect, "I *did* not know covetousness—*except that* the Law [stepped in and] said, Thou shalt not covet." Similarly Acts xxvi. 32 ἀπολελύσθαι ἐδύνατο ὁ ἄνθρωπος οὗτος εἰ μὴ ἐπεκέκλητο Καίσαρα, is equivalent to "*It was possible* [up to the moment of his appeal] for this man to have been released at once—*only* he had appealed to Caesar"; but the last clause is changed into a protasis by using "*if not*" instead of "*only*," "*if* he had *not* appealed (ἐπεκέκλητο)." The facts indicate that in N.T. hypothetical ἄν is not omitted except in special circumstances[1].

On Lk. xxiv. 39 ἐρώ εἰμι ἀγτός (2224)

[2699] In our discussion of ἐγώ εἰμι, it was said that the text of Lk. xxiv. 39 was "doubtful." W.H. print ἐγώ εἰμι αὐτός without alternative, following אBL *b, f*. But (1) SS has here the same Syriac as in Mk vi. 50, Mt. xiv. 27, Jn vi. 20, where there is ἐγώ εἰμι without αὐτός. (2) The Palestinian Lectionary also has the same Hebrew in Lk. xxiv. 39 as in Mt. xiv. 27. (3) Epiphanius twice (i. 1002 A and ii. 95 D) quotes ὅτι ἐγώ εἰμι without αὐτός (once with αὐτός (i. 1003 B) but with καὶ τοὺς τύπους τῶν ἥλων inserted). (4) The treatise on the Resurrection attributed to Justin § 9 (594 D) has εἶπεν αὐτοῖς Οὔπω ἔχετε πίστιν; φησίν, Ἴδετε ὅτι ἐγώ εἰμι, and continues κατανοήσαντες ὅτι αὐτός ἐστι καὶ ἐν τῷ σώματι, implying that the αὐτός belonged to the inference of the disciples, not to the words of Christ. (5) One of Epiphanius' quotations without αὐτός (i. 1002 A)

---

[1] [2698 *a*] Ἄν hypothetical is omitted in *Ox. Pap.* 526, 2nd cent., a private letter ("badly written and obscurely worded") εἰ καὶ μὴ ἀνέβενε ἐγὼ τὸν λόγον μου οὐ παρέβενον, "Even if he were not going I should not have broken my word" (perh. "I was not going to break my word"), *ib*. 530, 2nd cent.,—a very well written letter—εἰ πλεῖον δέ μοι παρέκει[το] πάλιν σοι ἀπεστάλκειν (Edd.) "If I had had more I would have forwarded a further sum," where "a further sum" represents πάλιν. This seems rather harsh, and, if πάλαι occurred in the Indices of the Papyri, I should venture to suggest πάλαι ἄν "If I had had more money at home *I should have sent* [*this*] *long ago*." In 2 Cor. xii. 19 πάλαι has been corrupted into πάλιν so that A.V. has "again," and πάλαι ἄν might be still more easily corrupted thus. The omission of ἄν in negative sentences may sometimes be explained by the hypothesis that the speaker has in his mind (1) "It was not so at first, *but* something happened to bring it about," which passed into (2) "It was not so *and would not be so now, but that* something happened to bring it about."

has ἐγώ εἰμι καὶ οὐκ ἠλλοίωμαι[1] and so has (Resch *ad loc.*) John Damasc. Fid. Orthod. p. 303. This looks like a negative paraphrase of αὐτός taken as ὁ αὐτός. (6) The Latin *a* has "quoniam ego sum: *ipsi* tractate," having apparently read ἐγώ εἰμι· αὐτοὶ ψηλαφήσατε. (7) The Latin and Greek authorities are divided as to the position of αὐτός, many having it before ἐγώ εἰμι but some between ἐγώ and εἰμι. (8) Αὐτοί ἐσμεν is frequent in Greek literature (Steph. p. 2558 c) but means "we are *by ourselves*." Of αὐτός εἰμι Steph. gives no instance. If it existed, it would naturally mean "I am *alone*, or, *by myself*[2]." (9) Ignatius, quoting a passage closely resembling Lk. xxiv. 39, asserts that the Lord said (*Smyrn.* §3) "see that (or, because) *I am not a bodiless demon* (δαιμόνιον)," and makes no mention of the words ἐγώ εἰμι αὐτός in any order.

[2700] The most probable conclusion from all these facts is that Lk. xxiv. 39 ἐγώ εἰμι αὐτός is an attempt—not perhaps Luke's attempt but incorporated by Luke in his Gospel—to render the Hebrew (2224) "*I* [*am*] *He*," more fully than it is rendered by the "*I am*" of Mk-Mt. (2220). But ἐγώ εἰμι αὐτός—being neither exactly Greek nor exactly Hebrew idiom—caused great perplexity. Some altered the order, to αὐτὸς ἐγώ εἰμι meaning "I myself am [present]." This would be Greek, if εἰμί could stand for πάρειμι, but is (probably) not what Lk. meant. Others took it as ἐγώ εἰμι ὁ αὐτός, "I am *the same*." This, being negatively paraphrased (as in Epiphanius and John of Damascus), became "I am not *made another*." "Another" is used in Isaiah (xlii. 8) as a parallel to "idols"; and it is used, in New Hebrew, (Levy i. 57 a) of things evil and impure about which one would fain not speak. The Ignatian legend might be explained by some as a mere inference

---

[1] [2699 a] This is somewhat similar to Mal. iii. 6 "I the Lord change not," ἐγὼ Κύριος ὁ θεὸς ὑμῶν καὶ οὐκ ἠλλοίωμαι.

[2] [2699 b] Αὐτός occurs thus with the particip. of εἰμί in *Iliad* viii. 99 αὐτός περ ἐών, προμάχοισιν ἐμίχθη, where the schol. says Καίπερ μόνος ὤν. Of course, one is free to theorize or conjecture that αὐτός, in ἐγώ εἰμι αὐτός, may mean the same as in Αὐτὸς ἔφα, or the same as in some other special Greek idiom. But, until the discovery of at least one instance of ἐγώ εἰμι αὐτός *actually thus used*, the most reasonable explanation is that it is not idiomatic Greek at all, but an attempt to render literally in Greek some non-Greek tradition that does not bear a literal rendering. The nearest approach to Lk.'s phrase that I have found is Epict. iv. 1. 152 "Diogenes was free...not that he was free-born (for he was not) *but that he was himself* (ἀλλ' ὅτι αὐτὸς ἦν)," *i.e.* his true self, or unsubjugated by external influences.

or paraphrase based on the words "I am myself." But, in view of these traditions about "*another*" in Jewish and Christian writers, it is not improbable that something more than mere inference originated the traditions about a "bodiless demon."

On xxi. 5 παιδία, μή τι προσφάγιον ἔχετε; (2235)

[2701] In xxi. 5 παιδία, μή τι προσφάγιον ἔχετε; questions suggest themselves as to (1) παιδία, (2) μή τι, (3) προσφάγιον. (1) If Christ is to be regarded as presenting the appearance of a man much older than the disciples, παιδία may be taken as "children." Otherwise such an address from an apparent stranger causes difficulty. Chrys., as printed by Migne, omits παιδία, but a version in Cramer inserts it. Both versions say that Christ asked whether the disciples had any fish "as though He were intending to buy from them[1]." Nonnus paraphrases παιδία as παῖδες ἁλὸς δρηστῆρες, and perhaps agrees with Chrysostom as to the object of the question[2]. In the *Acts of John* (§ 2) Christ is said to have appeared to James as a little child, but to John, simultaneously, as a man with a long beard and head partly bald. This was "on the shore." The writer of the *Acts* appears to have interpreted John here as meaning that Jesus appeared as one of venerable aspect addressing the disciples as "children."

[2702] (2) As regards the interrogative, is it neutral, or does it expect a negative answer? Μή τι, with a following noun with which τι agrees, does not occur anywhere in N.T. as far as I have found. Μήτι occurs in all the Gospels, and thrice in John, as an interrogative, always expecting a negative[3]. In LXX, μήτι is repeatedly used by

---

[1] [2701 a] Chrys. (Migne) Λέγει οὖν αὐτοῖς (Cramer + Παιδία) Μή τι προσφάγιον ἔχετε; τέως ἀνθρωπινώτερον διαλέγεται [Cramer om. τ. ἀ. δ.], ὡς μέλλων τι ὠνεῖσθαι [Cramer -ήσασθαι] παρ' αὐτῶν. ὡς δὲ ἀνένευσαν μηδὲν ἔχειν....

[2] [2701 b] Ἰχθυβόλους δ' ἐρέεινεν ἐθήμονας ἰχθυβολῆας, Πλωτὰ τελεσσιγόνοιο κομίζετε δεῖπνα θαλάσσης, Παῖδες ἁλὸς δρηστῆρες; where κομίζετε seems to mean "Are ye catching?" He proceeds, ἀμειβόμενοι δὲ μαθηταὶ Οὐδὲν ἔχειν ἀνένευον—which resembles Chrys.'s comment.

[3] [2702 a] Μήτι is in iv. 29 μήτι οὗτός ἐστιν ὁ Χριστός; viii. 22 μήτι ἀποκτενεῖ ἑαυτόν; xviii. 35 μήτι ἐγὼ Ἰουδαῖός εἰμι; In xxi. 5 W.H. give μή τι without option. But Greek MSS. having ΜΗΤΙ—or, if a scribe has added accents, ΜΉΤΙ—afford no guidance as to the separation or union of ΜΗ and ΤΙ : ℵ has ΜΗ to which a corrector has added ΤΙ, L has ΜΙΤΙ, SS "*have ye not*," and so *gat*. "pulmentarium *non* habetis," *b, f* "*numquid* pulmentarium habetis," *e* "*numquid* habetis pulmentarium," *d* "*numquid aliquid* manducare habetis"—but the photograph of D and *d* shews no difference between ΜΗΤΙ or *numquid* here (xxi. 5) and in Mk iv. 21, where everyone takes it as μήτι—*a* has "habetis *aliquid* pulmentum *vos*." The

[2702] NOTES ON PRECEDING PARAGRAPHS

Aquila to represent "Num?" and, so far as Oxf. Conc. shews (under μή τις, μή τι), τι never agrees with a following noun¹. In N.T. μήτι variations indicate an early difficult tradition, most probably μήτι (not μή τι). In the following paragraphs, for convenience, μήτι will be printed as one word.

[2702 *b*] Westcott says (*ad loc.*) "The form of the question in the original (μήτι) suggests a negative answer. See iv. 29," *i.e.* μήτι οὗτός ἐστιν ὁ χριστός;— where A.V. has "*Is not* this the Christ?" R.V. "*Can* this *be* the Christ?" and Westcott says, "The form of the sentence grammatically suggests a negative answer (iv. 33) but hope bursts through it." Μή interrogative may perhaps always be rendered by "can it be that?" and μήτι by "can it be in any way possible that?" In Plato and Xenophon and other classical writers, μή interrogative is sometimes used courteously or ironically to suggest that the possibility may be realised—"*can it be that* we are mistaken?" but μή is never used by them for ἆρ’ οὐ. In the Pauline Epistles, μή is used in passionate rejections of blasphemy as Rom. iii. 5 μὴ ἄδικος ὁ θεός; ix. 14 μὴ ἀδικία παρὰ τῷ θεῷ; ix. 20 μὴ ἐρεῖ τὸ πλάσμα; 1 Cor. i. 13 μὴ Παῦλος ἐσταυρώθη; (comp. Rom. iii. 3, xi. 11, 1 Cor. x. 22 etc.) and always expects a strong negative reply. There is the same indignant fervour in Rom. x. 18—19 μὴ οὐκ ἤκουσαν...μὴ Ἰσρ. οὐκ ἔγνω, "*will any one venture to say that they did not hear...and that Israel did not know?*" 1 Cor. ix. 4—5 (*bis*) μὴ οὐκ ἔχομεν ἐξουσίαν, "*will any one deny* that we have authority?" xi. 22 μὴ γὰρ οἰκίας οὐκ ἔχετε εἰς τὸ ἐσθίειν καὶ πίνειν; Here, after saying that some of the Corinthians drink too much at the Lord's Supper, he adds "[*Shame on you!*] *For can it be that ye have not houses for ordinary eating and drinking?*" Μήτι interrogative occurs thrice in the Epistles and always introducing a shameful or absurd hypothesis, 2 Cor. i. 17 "Did I shew fickleness (μήτι ἄρα τῇ ἐλαφρίᾳ ἐχρησάμην)?" *ib.* xii. 18 "Did Titus take advantage of you (μήτι ἐπλεονέκτησεν ὑμᾶς T.)?" Jas. iii. 11 μήτι ἡ πηγὴ ἐκ τῆς αὐτῆς ὀπῆς βρύει τὸ γλυκὺ κ. τὸ πικρόν;

[2702 *b*₁] But it is in Epictetus that μή and μήτι are most prominent: and there, so far as I can judge from verifying about thirty of Schenkl's very numerous instances, μή always expects a negative answer as in i. 11. 18 "Is there incompatibility between natural affection and reason?" and μήτι is still stronger, often propounding an absurd proposition for a negative reply *e.g.* ii. 19. 15 "Is it a vice to be shipwrecked (μήτι κακία ἐστὶ τὸ ναυαγῆσαι)?" In one instance (i. 16. 10 μήτι (or μή τι) ἀχρηστότερον τριχῶν;) τι or μήτι has a predicative adj. agreeing with it. Schweigh. Index says of μή that it is sometimes (nonnunquam) *interpreted interrogatively where it might be rendered negatively*; and this at least is certain that any pupil in Epictetus's lecture-room hearing the philosopher begin a sentence with μήτι would anticipate some question that required a negative answer. And the style of Epictetus is so similar to that of John that the Epictetian usage strongly increases the probability that the Johannine μήτι προσφάγιον ἔχετε must have been written with a similar meaning. In later Greek writers, *e.g.* Clem. Alex., μήτι "is it possible that?" is found occasionally meaning "perhaps." But Clement as compared with Epictetus, for the purpose of illustrating John, is like Dryden compared with Bacon, for the purpose of illustrating Shakespeare.

¹ [2702 *c*] Μήτι interrog. and requiring a negative answer (*generally to an indignant question*) is very often used by Aquila (where LXX differs) in Exod. ii. 14 (LXX μή), Is. vii. 13, lxvi. 9 etc. In Is. vii. 13 μήτι (LXX μή) ὀλίγον; Job x. 3 μήτι (LXX ἤ) ἀγαθόν; there is no connexion between τι and ὀλίγον or ἀγαθόν.

often introduces an impossibility (*e.g.* "Do men gather grapes from thorns?") and implies a very strong negative[1]. But there is a difficulty here if the words mean, "*Is it possible* that ye have caught fish?" The difficulty would not be much diminished by reading μή, separated from τι, since μή, too, expects a negative answer[2]. Chrysostom and Nonnus presumably interpreted μήτι as "perhaps," taking the language to be that of a peasant dealing with fishermen, "*Might you be having* some fish for sale?" But this is a late usage not justified by LXX, N.T., Epictetus, or Aquila. The Johannine meaning appears to be widely different. The Lord does not ask for information. He *knew that the disciples had caught no fish and that it was not possible for them to have caught fish;* because they had been toiling without Him in the "night" of spiritual darkness and had not cast the net on the "right side" of the ship. This is mystically described by representing the Master of the fishermen as standing on the shore, witnessing the unavailing efforts of His servants and calling to them, in effect, "Children, ye have toiled long, *but can ye say that ye have caught anything? Ye cannot say it.*" This is the only way in which the words of the Gospel could be understood by a Christian at the beginning of the first century familiar with the language of the Gospels, or by a convert or enquirer familiar with the doctrine of Epictetus.

[2703] (3) As regards προσφάγιον, why is not the word ὀψάριον attributed to Jesus here as it is later on (xxi. 10 ἀπὸ τῶν ὀψαρίων, and comp. xxi. 9)? Προσφάγιον appears to have been later, and more vernacular, than ὀψάριον[3]. In classical Greek, it might naturally be

---

[1] [2702 *d*] Mk iv. 21 μήτι ἔρχεται ὁ λύχνος...; xiv. 19 (Mt. xxvi. 22, 25) μήτι ἐγώ; Mt. vii. 16 μήτι συλλέγουσιν etc.; Lk. vi. 39 μήτι δύναται τυφλός...; Jn iv. 29 μήτι οὗτός ἐστιν ὁ Χρ.; viii. 22 μήτι ἀποκτενεῖ ἑαυτόν; xviii. 35 μήτι ἐγὼ Ἰουδαῖός εἰμι;

[2] [2702 *e*] Comp. iii. 4 μὴ δύναται; iv. 12 μὴ σὺ μείζων εἶ; iv. 33 μή τις ἤνεγκεν; vi. 67 μὴ κ. ὑμεῖς θέλετε ὑπάγειν; vii. 31 μὴ πλείονα...ποιήσει; vii. 41 μὴ γὰρ ἐκ τῆς Γ. ὁ Χρ. ἔρχεται; vii. 47 μὴ καὶ ὑμεῖς πεπλάνησθε; etc. This last illustrates xviii. 17, 25 μὴ καὶ σὺ ἐκ τ. μαθητῶν εἶ; and shews how "Is it possible that?" may be used sometimes to mean "*It is surely not possible that*" but sometimes, in special contexts, ironically, to mean "*It is perhaps after all possible that.*" Μή in vii. 47 means the former; in xviii. 17, 25 the latter.

[3] [2703 *a*] See Steph. 2024 B "Eust. p. 867, [54] ἐπὶ τοῦ ἁπλῶς προσοψήματος, ταυτὸν δ' εἰπεῖν κοινῶς προσφαγίου, τὸ Ὀψάριον λέγεται. [Schol. Hom. *Il.* 1, 489] Itidem Suidas, Ὄψον πᾶν τὸ προσόψημα ἢ προσφάγιον. Similiter et Hesych.: Ὄψον, προσφάγιον. [Et Etym. M. p. 646, 14]. Hoc alioqui vocab. neuter

[2703] NOTES ON PRECEDING PARAGRAPHS

taken as a form of πρόσφαγμα "a preliminary victim." The context clearly implies that the "fish," of which the disciples partake, is a sacramental food, and a "breakfast" to strengthen the disciples for the work of evangelists. Origen (Lomm. i. 259—62), commenting on "the Lamb of God that taketh away the sins of the world," and on the sacrifice of the lamb in the morning as "*the beginning of the sacrifices*," goes on to speak of the lamb in the language of Revelation, as "*standing, as having been slain as a victim* (ἑστηκὸς ὡς ἐσφαγμένον)." Christ, "standing on the shore" of Tiberias at the moment of sunrise, might be a type of the sacrifice that is "sent up at the moment of the enlightening of the soul (ἅμα τῷ φωτίζεσθαι τὴν ψυχὴν ἀναπεμπόμενος)." Regarded in this light, προσφάγιον might have an inner meaning intelligible to none but the initiated—including an allusion to the ΙΧΘΥΣ[1], or ONE FISH, which in this very narrative appears as a eucharistic type of Christ:—"Ye have not yet received THE FISH. Ye have not yet partaken of that sacrificial victim which was slain before the foundation of the world (Rev. xiii. 8), without which the eyes of your souls cannot be enlightened nor can ye see how to cast the net of the Church 'on the right side' of the ship[2]."

---

in serie alphabetica in numerum eorum quae exponuntur retulit: unde conjicere licet plebeium fuisse, aut vetustioribus Graecis incognitum." Hence Lk. xxiv. 41 might very well prefer βρώσιμον, and the next note will shew that a Christian writer substitutes βρώσιμον for προσφάγιον in paraphrasing Jn.

[1] On "the earliest extant reference to the emblem of the ΙΧΘΥΣ," see Lightf. *Ignat.* vol. i. p. 181.

[2] [2703 *b*] The comment of Origen is lost. That of Chrys., and others printed by Cramer, seem to mix together the literal and the metaphorical, and perhaps the accounts of Lk. and Jn and the story of the Walking on the Waters. Chrys. says that Christ "was not continuously present with the disciples, and the Spirit had not yet been given to them," and they were "not yet commissioned (ἐγκεχειρισμένοι)." In the previous context he says Christ "appeared (ἐφάνη)" to the disciples and "*flew away* (ἀπέπτη)," then appeared once again "and again *flew away*; then, after this, [appeared] on (ἐπί, *i.e.* by) (**2340**—**6**) the sea and again with the accompaniment of their exceeding fear (μετὰ πολλοῦ τοῦ φόβου)." By this "fear" he appears to mean their fear of the Jews: for he says that Christ had taken away most of their alarm so that they could now "peep forth (προκύπτειν) from the house and go about everywhere." But still he adds, "Having therefore nothing to do they came to fish and even this they did in the night because they were in great alarm (περιδεεῖς)." He adds, "This Luke, too, says, but this is not the same [as Luke's account] but different (τοῦτο καὶ ὁ Λουκᾶς φησιν, ἀλλ' οὐκ ἔστι τοῦτο ἐκεῖνο, ἀλλ' ἕτερον)"—where he seems to refer to Luke's account of Peter fishing all through the night and then saying to Jesus in alarm "Depart from me,

NOTES ON PRECEDING PARAGRAPHS [2704]

Oh x. 12 ὁ...οὐκ ὢν ποιμήν (2253—4)

[2704] In x. 12 ὁ μισθωτὸς καὶ οὐκ ὢν ποιμήν, A has δέ after, ℵD have it before, μισθωτός : *a* has "qui mercenarius est et non est pastor," *e* "mercinarius (sic) autem" (om. "et qui non est pastor"), Syr. Curet. (Burk.) "but the hireling, *the false one*," SS om. "the false one" and substitutes nothing. Nonnus has ὁ δὲ μίσθιος οὐ πέλε ποιμήν. The use of οὐκ, instead of μή, may be due to one of two causes. (1) "Hireling and not Shepherd" may go together as though the Greek were ὁ μισθωτὸς-καὶ-οὐ-ποιμὴν ὤν. (2) Οὐ may be regarded as part of the name of the "hireling," who is the antithesis of the Shepherd, just as the Heb. of "not" is part of the names (Hos. ii. 23 "Lo-ruhamah," "Lo-ammi") "Not-beloved (*or*, pitied)" and "Not-my people"—which are rendered in LXX τὴν Οὐκ ἠγαπημένην and τῷ Οὐ λαῷ μου (comp. Rom. ix. 25, 1 Pet. ii. 10). Some sense of this may have induced the Curetonian translator to paraphrase the clause as "*the false one*," perhaps meaning "*the No-shepherd*." Ὤν might have been omitted by John without destroying the sense; but

---

O Lord" (not to Luke's account of the alarm of the disciples when Christ appears to them after the Resurrection).

[2703 *c*] Another comment (Cramer) says, "Those that were before the disciples (οἱ πρὸ τῶν μαθητῶν, ? πρό = " at the head of," more prob. read προτοίτων = πρῶτοι τῶν, "chief of the disciples") being in the dizziness and darkness of error that was sent from evil spirits (ἐν σκοτοδινίᾳ ὄντες τῆς δαιμονιώδους πλάνης) persuaded (ἔπεισαν) no one, or very few—which is as good as 'nothing'" (comp. xxi. 3 "caught (ἐπίασαν) *nothing*") "...nay even the multitude of the Gentiles was not caught in the net [of the Gospel]...But when the Sun of Righteousness came, He that hungereth for the salvation of men, He found nothing *to eat*" (the writer uses βρώσιμον as in Lk. xxiv. 41, not προσφάγιον as in Jn xxi. 5) "and told them that the evangelic word must be cast forth, that is to say the 'right (δεξιά)' teaching" (comp. xxi. 6 "on the *right* (δεξιά) side of the ship") "compared to which the Law and the prophets being cast forth are conceived as the left side." Nonnus spells πιάζειν "take (fish)" with an ε, which would increase the likeness between επεισαν and επιεσαν suggesting an early play upon the two words preserved in this tradition.

[2703 *d*] Compare the three following traditions of Chrysostom: (1) (On vi. 21) Ἀλλ' οὐδὲ τοῖς μαθηταῖς ὤφθη ἐπὶ πολὺ τοῦτο ποιῶν, ἀλλὰ ἅμα τε ὤφθη καὶ ἀπέστη ἀπ' αὐτῶν, (2) (On xxi. 1) Ὁρᾷς ὅτι οὐ συνεχῶς αὐτοῖς ἐπιχωριάζει, οὐδ' ὥσπερ ἔμπροσθεν; Ἐφάνη γοῦν τῇ ἑσπέρᾳ καὶ <u>ἀπέπτη</u>· εἶτα μετὰ ὀκτὼ ἡμέρας πάλιν ἄπαξ, καὶ πάλιν <u>ἀπέπτη</u>· εἶτα μετὰ ταῦτα ἐπὶ τῆς θαλάσσης, καὶ πάλιν μετὰ πολλοῦ τοῦ φόβου...ταλαιπωρουμένοις ἐφίστατο ὁ Ἰησοῦς (Cramer, ἐπιστὰς δὲ αὐτοῖς ταλαιπωρουμένοις), (3) (On Acts i. 3) (Cramer) ἐφίστατο γὰρ καὶ <u>ἀφίστατο</u> πάλιν. The comparison suggests that there has been a confusion between ἀπέπτη and ἀπέστη.

perhaps it emphasizes the non-reality, "*is not really* Shepherd." According to this view, John would have written ὁ μὴ ποιμὴν ὤν as he has written (x. 1) ὁ μὴ εἰσερχόμενος, if he had meant "he that is not a shepherd." But he means something different; in effect, he is declaring that the hireling is "*no* shepherd."

On ζῶ διά cέ (2297)

[2705] A very important illustration of ζῶ διὰ σέ occurs in a passage where Epictetus describes the philosopher as using similar language in the moment of death, iii. 24. 95 foll. "For this cause the man that is really good—bearing in mind both who he is and whence he has come, and by whom he has been brought into being—is wholly absorbed in this one thought, *how he can fill his appointed place in orderly and willing obedience to God*: Dost thou will me to exist yet [longer]? [Then I will do so], as a free man and noble, as thou hast willed: for thou hast made me unshackled in my own sphere. But, on the other hand [*perhaps*] thou hast no further need of me ('Ἀλλ' οὐκέτι μου χρείαν ἔχεις;)? I praise and bless thee (Καλῶς σοι γένοιτο) [then]! Even up to this day I *kept on abiding [on earth] simply for thy sake, and for no other* (καὶ μέχρι νῦν διὰ σὲ ἔμενον, δι' ἄλλον οὐδένα)." Here the context indicates that διὰ σέ means "for thy service," "in orderly and willing obedience (εὐτάκτως καὶ εὐπειθῶς)" to God. Other instances are iv. 1. 163 ἔξελθε διὰ τὰ παιδία, "escape *for the sake of the children*," i.e. *to do them service*, iv. 8. 17 ὅσα καλῶς ἐποίουν...οὐ διὰ τοὺς θεατὰς ἐποίουν, ἀλλὰ δι' ἐμαυτόν, "not *for the sake of the spectators* but *for my own sake*," where he proceeds to exemplify the statement by using a dative of advantage, ἤσθιον ἐμαυτῷ καλῶς, "I used to eat decently *for my own sake*." Comp. i. 17. 18 οὐδὲ γὰρ Χρυσίππου χρείαν ἔχομεν δι' αὐτόν ...οὐδὲ γὰρ τοῦ θύτου δι' αὐτόν, where he subsequently (i. 17. 29) explains that he goes to the θύτης or "sacrificer," οὐκ αὐτὸν θαυμάσας "*not out of reverence for him*" but out of reverence for his teaching. No doubt Epictetus frequently uses διά τινα to mean "*thanks to so-and-so*," but that is not the meaning in any of these passages. Where the verb employed with διά τινα is passive or neutral, διά may mean "*thanks to*." But often, where it implies action and active service, it means "*for the sake of*."

On various meanings of εἰc (2305—8)

[2706] The peculiarity, and the importance, of i. 18 ὁ ὢν εἰς τὸν κόλπον are in danger of being obscured by vague affirmations that "εἰς is used for ἐν in Byzantine and modern Greek," and that the same use is to be found in N.T. generally and in John elsewhere, e.g. ix. 7 ὕπαγε νίψαι εἰς τὴν κολυμβήθραν τοῦ Σ. (ὃ ἑρμηνεύεται Ἀπεσταλμένος). This last, however, may be illustrated (2305 a) from the use of λούω, βάπτω, and βαπτίζω in other authors[1]: and it affords no ground for thinking that John would use εἰς for ἐν with εἰμί.

[2707] Again, as to xix. 13 ἤγαγεν ἔξω τὸν Ἰησοῦν καὶ ἐκάθισεν ἐπὶ βήματος εἰς τόπον, the εἰς is shewn by the context not to be connected with ἐκάθισεν in the sense of "on" (which is represented by ἐπί) but to mean "[going out] to," being influenced by ἤγαγεν ἔξω, and the preposition helps to illustrate two points on which John lays stress (1745 a) namely, that Pilate had to go out to the Jews as the Jews would not come into his palace, and that the sentence was pronounced outside the palace in a place where a special tribunal was erected. That John would not have used καθίζω εἰς we may perhaps infer from vi. 3 ἀνῆλθεν δὲ εἰς τὸ ὄρος Ἰ. καὶ ἐκεῖ ἐκάθητο, as compared with Mk xiii. 3 καθημένου αὐτοῦ εἰς τὸ Ὄρος (Mt. xxiv. 3 ἐπὶ τοῦ Ὄρους). Καθίζω εἰς is classical Greek, but John does not use it[2].

[2708] Among other N.T. meanings of εἰς not found in John, is "near" or "at" before place-names, e.g. "the things that happened [away] at Capernaum," "Philip was found [away] at Azotus," "to be at Jerusalem by the feast," "that Paul was in custody [away] at Caesarea[3]." This can hardly be paralleled from classical authors. The meaning "with a view to," "in regard to," "in relation to" —very common in Thucydides, when used with verbs of action generally and of "expending" in particular, and also to denote friendly or unfriendly relations[4]—is frequent in the Pauline Epistles,

---

[1] [2706 a] See Steph. on βάπτω and βαπτίζω with εἰς and even (109 A) πρός, and comp. Mk i. 9 ἐβαπτίσθη εἰς τὸν Ἰ. (where Mt. and Lk. differ). Blass (p. 123) says, on ix. 7, "νίψαι however appears not to be genuine." But the omissions of it, and the variations of its position in several authorities, may perhaps be explained by (1) its unusual position, (2) a desire to conform the text to ix. 11 εἰπέν μοι ὅτι Ὕπαγε εἰς τὸν Σιλωάμ καὶ νίψαι. If νίψαι had been interpolated into ix. 7 from ix. 11, would it not have been interpolated in the same order, i.e. at the end of the sentence? In any case the nature of the verb, and of the context, which implies motion, make εἰς in ix. 7 easily explicable, as also in Mt. ii. 23, iv. 13, Lk. xxi. 37.

[2] [2707 a] Chrys. (on Jn vii. 1) says ὅτε γὰρ εἰς τὸ ὄρος ἐκάθητο, φησίν, ἦν ἡ ἑορτὴ τοῦ πάσχα. Quoting John loosely, he falls into language like that of Mark describing Christ as seated on the Mount of Olives.

[3] Lk. iv. 23, Acts viii. 40, xx. 16, xxv. 4.

[4] [2708 a] Comp. ἁμαρτάνω εἰς in Æsch. Prom. 945, Mt. xviii. 21, Lk. xvii. 4. Jn, in the Gospel, uses ἁμαρτάνω always (thrice) absolutely; in 1 Jn,

[2709] NOTES ON PRECEDING PARAGRAPHS

and may perhaps explain the curious idiom in Mark—altered by many scribes and by the parallel Matthew—about breaking loaves "*to* the five thousand[1]." But it is not found in John.

[2709] Another important use of εἰς, dating from the best classical writers, is with verbs of speaking or proclaiming. Sometimes it distinguishes speaking publicly to an assembly from speaking privately to a council. It is never used, in this sense, of addressing a single person. It is appropriate to the far-reaching and public nature of the message of the Gospel, and John lays stress on the publicity of Christ's teaching; but he never uses this idiom[2].

---

where it occurs (10) more freq. than in any book of N.T., it is always absolute or with cognate accusative.

[1] [2708 b] Mk viii. 19—20 ὅτε τοὺς πέντε ἄρτους ἔκλασα εἰς τοὺς πεντακισχιλίους..., ὅτε τοὺς ἑπτὰ εἰς τοὺς τετρ., parall. to Mt. xvi. 9—10 τοὺς πέντε ἄρτους τῶν πεντακισχιλίων (D τοῖς πεντ.)...τοὺς ἑπτὰ ἄρτους τῶν τετρ. (D τοῖς τετρ.). The text in Mk is greatly confused. As regards "the four thousand," the Syriac has the preposition "to" or "for." Delitzsch has it in both clauses. This preposition might be interpreted as "*belonging to*," or "*of*." Comp. Ezr. x. 13 "and the work is not *for* (ל) one day," εἰς ἡμέραν μίαν where 1 Esdr. ix. 11 has taken the meaning to be "*belonging to* one day," i.e. "*of* one day," ἡμέρας μιᾶς.

[2708 c] But ἔκλασα εἰς, besides perhaps expressing the Semitic Original exactly, harmonizes with the classical Greek use of εἰς with verbs of spending. From this came the use of εἰς in accounts of expenditure (Deissmann p. 118) "*to* lamps, so much" or "*to* a sick horse, so much" etc. So here, there is a suggestion of items, "*to* five thousand men, five loaves," "*to* four thousand men, seven loaves." "To," in this sense, would not often be used with persons except when regarded as labourers; but Deissmann, who calls this, when used of persons, "dativus commodi," quotes (*ib.*) τὸν εἰς Τάγην οἶκον ᾠκοδομημένον "the house built *with a view to* [the occupation of] Tages." If Tages was a labourer or bailiff the house might be built "with a view to" Tages but *for the advantage* of his employer. Having regard to this usage, it is best to render Mt. xx. 1 μισθοῦσθαι εἰς τὸν ἀμπελῶνα "hire *with a view to* the vineyard," not "hire [*and bring*] *into* the vineyard." In Mt. v. 22 ἔνοχος εἰς τὴν γέενναν—coming as a climax after ἔνοχος· τῇ κρίσει and τῷ συνεδρίῳ—probably combines two meanings, 1st, a penalty *extending to* Gehenna, 2nd, the penalty of being cast *into* Gehenna. For the first, comp. Numb. xxxii. 15 "*as much as*, or *even* (ל) all this people," εἰς ὅλην τὴν συναγωγὴν ταύτην.

[2] [2709 a] Comp. Mk i. 21 (W.H. marg.) καὶ εὐθὺς τ. σαββ. ἐδίδασκεν εἰς τὴν συναγωγήν, (txt) τ. σαββ. ⌈εἰσελθὼν εἰς τὴν συν. ἐδίδασκεν⌉, Mt. om., Lk. iv. 31 καὶ ἦν διδάσκων αὐτοὺς ἐν τοῖς σαββ.: Mk i. 39 καὶ ἦλθεν (SS, latt., ACD ἦν) κηρύσσων εἰς τὰς συναγωγάς, Mt. iv. 23 περιῆγεν...διδάσκων ἐν ταῖς σ. αὐτῶν κ. κηρύσσων, Lk. iv. 44 καὶ ἦν κηρύσσων εἰς τὰς σ. Here Mk is doubtful. Lk. iv. 44 appears to use εἰς with a notion of extension or far-reaching publicity, sending forth the message of the Gospel into the synagogues, as in Lk. vii. 1 ἐπλήρωσεν...εἰς τὰς ἀκοὰς τοῦ λαοῦ (perhaps with a suggestion of εἰς τὸ μέσον). As a proof that Luke considers the phrase good Greek, note Acts xvii. 20 εἰς τὰς ἀκοὰς ἡμῶν, uttered by

NOTES ON PRECEDING PARAGRAPHS [2711]

[2710] As regards John's use of στῆναι εἰς τὸ μέσον (2307) compared with Luke's στῆναι ἐν μέσῳ, we may adduce Mk iii. 3 ἔγειρε εἰς τὸ μέσον, D ἔγειρε καὶ στηθει (sic) ἐν μέσῳ, d "in medium," Lk. vi. 8 ἔγειρε καὶ στῆθι εἰς τὸ μέσον, D ἐν τῷ μέσῳ, d "in medio," which shew how easily the two constructions might be interchanged according as the notion of coming *into* an assembly was prominent or latent. Comp. Xen. *Cyropaed.* iv. 1. 1 στὰς εἰς τὸ μέσον[1]. Reasons have been given (2307) for thinking that John might deliberately prefer εἰς because of its spiritual suggestiveness.

[2711] More direct in its bearing on the Johannine ὁ ὢν εἰς are phrases in Mark where εἰς οἶκον or εἰς τὴν οἰκίαν is used in connexion with Christ[2]. But the text of these is doubtful. Nor do the Papyri,

---

philosophers (see ἀκοαί, "ears," in Lucian (iii. 585) *Philop.* § 1). Acts ii. 22 ἀποδεδειγμένον ἀπὸ τοῦ θεοῦ εἰς ὑμᾶς perh. means "approved from God in the sight of [all of] you," or "approved [as being sent] from God to [all of] you." Comp. Herm. *Vis.* ii. 4. 3 πέμψει οὖν Κλήμης εἰς τὰς ἔξω πόλεις...Γραπτὴ δὲ νουθετήσει τὰς χήρας...σὺ δὲ ἀναγνώσῃ εἰς ταύτην τὴν πόλιν μετὰ τῶν πρεσβυτέρων... τῆς ἐκκλησίας, where the meaning seems to be "read [*publicly*] to [the people of] this city with the elders." Comp. Mk xiii. 10 καὶ εἰς πάντα τὰ ἔθνη πρῶτον δεῖ κηρυχθῆναι (Mt. xxiv. 14 κηρυχθήσεται...τοῖς ἔθνεσιν) and 1 Pet. i. 25 τὸ ῥῆμα τὸ εὐαγγελισθὲν εἰς ὑμᾶς (Hort) "which was preached [reaching even] to you," Lk. xxiv. 47 καὶ κηρυχθῆναι...μετανοίαν ⌜εἰς⌝ ἄφεσιν ἁμαρτιῶν εἰς [reaching even to] πάντα τὰ ἔθνη, and Rom. viii. 18 τὴν μέλλουσαν δόξαν ἀποκαλυφθῆναι εἰς ἡμᾶς.

[2709 *b*] That λέγειν εἰς in this *public* sense is good Greek, appears clearly from Thucydides, especially when he describes the fear of Alcibiades lest the Spartan ambassadors should convert the Athenians to peace "if they should say the same things [*publicly*] *to the Demos*" that they had said, less publicly "*in the Boulé*," v. 45 ἢν ἐς τὸν δῆμον ταῦτα λέγωσιν (following λέγοντες ἐν τῇ βουλῇ, and preceding ἐς τὸν δῆμον παρελθόντες) and comp. i. 72 ἔφασαν βούλεσθαι καὶ αὐτοὶ ἐς τὸ πλῆθος αὐτῶν εἰπεῖν, iv. 58 ἐς τὸ κοινὸν τ. δὴ λόγους εἶπεν. In this sense, λέγειν εἰς *could not be used about addressing a single person.* [In Herod i. 86 οὐδέν τι μᾶλλον ἐς ἑωυτὸν λέγων ἢ ἐς ἅπαν τὸ ἀνθρώπινον the meaning is, "*with reference to.*"] Εἰς ὦτα may be used of one person or many; but probably Mt. x. 27 εἰς τὸ οὖς *i.e.* "secretly," is deliberately altered into πρὸς τὸ οὖς by Luke (xii. 3) who uses εἰς ὦτα for publicity in Acts xi. 22 ἠκούσθη δὲ ὁ λόγος εἰς τὰ ὦτα τῆς ἐκκλησίας (as well as in the sense of penetration in Lk. i. 44 ὡς ἐγένετο...εἰς τὰ ὦτά μου). Luke's liking for εἰς in connexion with the spread of the Gospel may be illustrated by the Pauline doctrine, Rom. x. 18 μὴ οὐκ ἤκουσαν; μενοῦνγε, (Ps. xix. 4) Εἰς πᾶσαν τὴν γῆν ἐξῆλθεν ὁ φθόγγος αὐτῶν.

[1] [2710 *a*] In 1 Pet. v. 12 εἰς ἣν στῆτε—regard being had to *ib.* i. 8 εἰς ὃν and *ib.* iii. 20 εἰς ἣν and to their several contexts—we should probably take εἰς ἣν as combining two meanings (1) "*looking to which*" or "*with a view to which*," and (2) "*in which.*"

[2] [2711 *a*] Comp. Mk ii. 1 (om. by parall. Mt.-Lk.) εἰσελθὼν πάλιν εἰς Καφ.... ἠκούσθη ὅτι ⌜ἐν οἴκῳ ἐστίν⌝, where marg. has εἰς οἶκόν ἐστιν, SS is wanting, Latt.

[2712] NOTES ON PRECEDING PARAGRAPHS

so far as is at present alleged, give a safe instance of εἰς τόπον εἶναι. Blass (p. 122 n.) quotes Berlin Pap. (3rd cent.) Vol. ii. 385 εἰς Ἀλεξανδρείαν ἐστί. But the context somewhat favours the view that the person spoken of is not actually at Alexandria but is coming there. Moreover the text has εσσι. And the editors regard this as a misspelling for εἶσι "will be going." If this is the meaning it may be illustrated by *Ox. Pap.* (2nd cent.) 529 ἐγὼ δὲ εἰς Κόπτον μετὰ τοῦ ἡγεμόνος εἰμι, "*I am going* to Coptus." I am informed that in *Tebtun. Pap.*, Part II. (416) not yet published (1905), a rather illiterate letter contains ἐγενάμην ἐν Ἀλεξανδρείᾳ followed by ἐγενάμην εἰς Ἀλ. But γίγνεσθαι εἰς is quite different from εἶναι εἰς, of which (at present) no certain instance is adduced from papyri.

[2712] These passages in Mark about the house or home of Christ, being omitted by Matthew and Luke, may be expected (2396) to be referred or alluded to by John. But the other details above mentioned appear in no way to help us to explain, indeed they make it more difficult to explain—except upon mystical and spiritual grounds—why John, who generally avoids εἰς for ἐν, writes ὢν εἰς τὸν κόλπον about the Son of God at the beginning of his Gospel and ἐν τῷ κόλπῳ about the beloved disciple toward the end of it. That he had some peculiar meaning in εἰς is made all the more probable because, so far as is alleged, εἰς κόλπον without a verb

---

"in domo," but *e* "domi." Again, after the words "let not man put asunder," common to Mk and Mt., Mk alone has x. 10 καὶ εἰς τὴν οἰκίαν πάλιν οἱ μαθηταὶ... ἐπηρώτων (Lk. om. the whole) SS "when he entered the house again," *a* "domi," *b* "in domum," *f*, *k* "in domo." The mention of πάλιν in Mk ii. 1, x. 10 suggests that in both cases the meaning is (as SS in the latter) "when he entered the house again."

[2711 *b*] Mk xiii. 16 has ὁ εἰς τὸν ἀγρόν where parall. Mt. xxiv. 18, Lk. xvii. 31 have ὁ ἐν τῷ (Lk. om. τῷ) ἀγρῷ. In this last passage, the antithesis between the previously mentioned "on the housetop" and "into the field" resembles that in 1 S. ix. 26 "*on the housetop*...went out...*abroad*," LXX ἕως ἔξω but Ἄλλος (Field) has εἰς ἀγρόν. In 1 S. a verb of motion is expressed. Mark perh. intends to imply one, "the [man that is] on the housetop" being contrasted with "the [*man that has gone out*] to the field [to labour]." The fact that both Mt. and Lk. substitute ἐν for εἰς indicates that Mk's idiom was of the nature of a mannerism. Neither εἰς οἶκον nor εἰς ἀγρόν could very well have a Semitic origin, as the Semitic preposition used in "at home" and "abroad" is almost always "*in*," not "*to*." Lk. xi. 7 εἰς τὴν κοίτην εἰσίν (D and latt. ἐν τῇ κοίτῃ) has not been illustrated by other examples, and it appears alien from Hebrew and Latin. The meaning may be "[recently come] *to* bed."

550

of motion occurs nowhere in the Bible, nor in Greek literature, whereas ἐν κόλπῳ is very common, and is familiar to all in the phrase "in Abraham's bosom[1]." It is therefore natural to infer that εἰς has a spiritual meaning—somewhat as in the Pauline Epistles where men are said to be baptized, or confirmed, or fulfilled, or made to grow, "*into* Christ," and where it is said concerning God, Rom. xi. 36 εἰς αὐτὸν τὰ πάντα, and 1 Cor. viii. 6 ἡμεῖς εἰς αὐτόν (**1475**)[2].

[**2713**] One explanation may be that, as the beloved disciple is said to be (xiii. 23) "lying *in* the bosom" of the Lord when he asks Him to reveal a secret, so the Son is described as being "*into* the bosom of the Father*"* because He is regarded as the revealing Mediator passing from man to God and from God to man. But, beside this, it is not improbable that John is alluding to ancient traditions about Christ's "home." It has been maintained elsewhere (**1451—8, 1839 foll., 2644** (i)) that John's description of Christ as "laying his head to rest" on the Cross contains an allusion to the Matthew-Luke saying "The son of man hath not where to lay his head to rest." If that is so, we may still more reasonably expect some Johannine allusion to Mark's repeated traditions about a "house" or "home" into which Christ enters—traditions almost always omitted by Matthew and Luke[3]. The discussion of these must be reserved for a future treatise. On the single occasion on which John associates the mention of a house with Christ's teaching or action Origen calls the "house" (**2329**) "omnem hujus mundi domum ac totius ecclesiae domum." An attempt will be made in a future treatise to shew that John desires to meet various unprofitable and conflicting traditions about Christ's "house" by saying, at the outset of his Gospel, that He was to be regarded as being in no earthly house, but as being in heaven—even while on earth—leading men "to the bosom of God."

On iii. 34 ἐκ μέτρογ (**2324**)

[**2714**] On iii. 34 οὐ γὰρ ἐκ μέτρου δίδωσιν, Chrys. agrees with Apollinarius in taking ἐκ μέτρου as μέτρῳ, "We all have received the

---

[1] *Hor. Heb.* on Lk. xvi. 22—3, and comp. 2 S. xii. 3 (Heb., Gk, and Targ.).

[2] [**2712** *a*] The Pauline Epistles exemplify all the uses of εἰς above mentioned except "at" with places, which would naturally be rare in hortatory language. Εἰς is also very rare, in any sense, in Revelation.

[3] [**2713** *a*] Mk ii. 1, iii. 20, vii. 17, 24, ix. 28, 33 (but see Mt. xvii. 25), x. 10. See also Mt. ix. 28 (which is in the style of Mk).

energy of the Spirit *by measure* (μέτρῳ)...but He has it *without measure* (ἀμέτρητον)." Wetstein gives a great number of instances from Greek, Latin, and Hebrew (including *Vajikra R.* 15 "Spiritus S. non habitavit super Prophetas nisi mensura quadam") of "*by* measure" or "*according to* measure"; but none have "*from* measure." Nonnus, however, takes the words to imply a spontaneous stream, as distinct from "measures" of water, οὐρανόθεν γὰρ Οὗτος ὃν ἐς χθόνα πέμψε θεὸς χραισμήτορα κόσμου Πατρῴης σοφίης αὐτόσσυτον ὄμβρον ἰάλλει· Οὐ γὰρ μέτρα λόγοιο φέρει Λόγος, ἀλλά οἱ αἰεὶ Μούνῳ πνεῦμα δίδωσιν ἀειλιβέος ῥόον ὀμφῆς: and this suggests the most satisfactory solution. John has in view the living water of the Spirit (Ps. xxxvi. 8—9 "Thou shalt make them drink *of the river of thy pleasures*, for with thee is *the fountain of life*") as compared with draughts from the "*measured vessel*" (comp. ii. 6 μετρητάς) of the Law. Μέτρῳ might have meant linear (not liquid) measure as μέτρον means in Rev. xxi. 17. But ἐκ μέτρου could not mean this and might therefore seem preferable[1].

On Διά with genitive applied to time (2331)

[2715] Διά, with genitive, applied to time, means "passing through." If the time means the *whole* of a life, age, year, month, or day, διά often means "*throughout*" (ὅλος being often inserted); but, if there is no such notion of wholeness, it means "*passing through one period to a period that follows*," i.e. "after an interval of." *This is always the meaning where a number is mentioned.* Διὰ νυκτός, however (Steph.) is sometimes loosely used to mean "*by* night." Plutarch *Quaest. Rom.* 279 F οὐκ...μετὰ φωτὸς...ἀλλὰ διὰ σκότους may throw light on Acts v. 19 (comp. xvi. 9, xvii. 10, xxiii. 31) where an angel opens the door for Peter "*by* night," suggesting perhaps that the deliverance took place, in part, "*by means of*," or "*with the aid of*," night. Steph. gives *no instance in which διά is used with a number of years, days, etc. to mean anything but "after the interval of."* Most frequently "*after the interval of* the third, fourth

---

[1] [2714 a] A generic term for Heb. liquid measure occurs (Buhl 487 b) in Lev. xix. 35 ξύγος, Ezek. iv. 11, 16, μέτρον, 1 Chr. xxiii. 29 LXX om. (or includes that and another word under μέτρον) but al. (prob. Aquila) ἀποσιρωτόν (Field) " ut praepositio quidem primam vocis Hebraeae literam repraesentet," and he compares Ps. cxxxviii. 20 ἀπ-έννοια. This suggests that, in connexion with this particular word for "measure," the "praepositio" ἐκ might arise from "prima vocis Hebraeae litera," and the same statement applies to another Heb. word meaning "*measure*" in Sir. xxxi. 27 (*Jewish Q.* 1889, p. 6)."

NOTES ON PRECEDING PARAGRAPHS [2715]

year etc." means "*every* third or fourth year." But Herod. i. 62 διὰ ἑνδεκάτου ἔτεος, describing the long interval during which Pisistratus waited to effect his return to Athens, appears to mean "after an interval extending to the eleventh year" (not, as L.S., "in the course of the eleventh year")[1]. The facts confirm the view taken in 2331 that διά in Acts i. 3 means "after an interval of." Ἐν, rather than διά, would be used to express "in the course of[2]."

---

[1] [2715 a] In an extremely obscure passage, Lucian *Hist. Conscr.* 21 (ii. 30) ridicules a fabulous account of a death by self-starvation undergone by Severianus, who attacked Osroes and was taken prisoner and killed by him. Lucian says that "the man's suffering" was, in fact, a matter of three days only; whereas men starved to death mostly last as many as seven days—"unless one were to resort to the supposition that Osroes εἱστήκει περιμένων ἔστ' ἂν Σ. λιμῷ ἀπόληται καὶ διὰ τοῦτο οὐκ ἐπήγαγε (v.r. ἐπῆγε) διὰ τῆς ἑβδόμης." The meaning is disputed. But it affords very slight ground for supposing that διὰ τεσσαράκοντα ἡμερῶν can mean "through forty days." Like the extract from Herodotus it describes an interval of prolonged waiting, and the final words seem to ridicule the notion that Osroes stood waiting "*till the expiration of the seventh day.*" It certainly does not mean "*during* the seventh day."

[2] [2715 b] As regards ἐν, "in the course of," or "during," in vi. 39—54 (see **2548**) the MSS. vary greatly, between τῇ, and ἐν τῇ, before ἐσχάτῃ ἡμέρᾳ. W.H. gives, in order, two instances without ἐν, a third with ἐν (vi. 44), and a fourth without ἐν. As ∈N follows (or would follow), in some of these cases, ΑΥΤΟ or ΑΥΤΟΝ, it might be easily dropped or inserted, after the similar letters O or ON. But ἐν τῇ ἐσχάτῃ ἡμέρᾳ occurs, without v.r., in xi. 24 ἐν τῇ ἀναστάσει, ἐν τ. ἐ. ἡ., xii. 48 ἐκεῖνος κρινεῖ αὐτὸν ἐν τ. ἐ. ἡ. Both there, and in vii. 37 ἐν δὲ τῇ ἐ. ἡ...τῆς ἑορτῆς, the preposition seems to mean "in the course of"; and "the last day" is regarded, not as a date or a point of time, but as a period *in the course of which* great events take place. If this view is correct, ἐν τῇ ἐ. ἡ. in vi. 44 may be regarded as a climax, the weightiest of the three utterances in vi. 39—44, and vi. 54 as being a separate utterance.

[2715 c] As regards σαββάτῳ with or without ἐν, the preposition may be regarded as emphasizing the sacred period of rest *during* which work may not be done. But it is very doubtful whether John ever omits ἐν with this word. B and some latt. versions omit it once, so that W.H. bracket it, in vii. 22—3 καὶ [ἐν] σαββάτῳ περιτέμνετε...εἰ περιτομὴν...λαμβάνει ἐν σαββ....ὑγιῆ ἐποίησα ἐν σαββ. But the latt. vss. omit it also in v. 16 ταῦτα ἐποίει ἐν σαββάτῳ. And B, before other words, (against W.H.) omits ἐν temporal in ii. 19, 23, xviii. 39. In ii. 19, 23, ἐν, if inserted by B, would come at the end of a line and would be liable to omission as being written in small letters. In xviii. 39, ∈N might be dropped after ΥΜΙΝ, especially if the latter was written ΥΜ∈ΙΝ in B's archetype. In ii. 19, vii. 22 ∈N follows ΚΑΙ, and the latter, if written Κ∈ in B's archetype, might easily cause the omission of a following ē meaning ∈N. *A priori* one might maintain that, in vii. 22—3, σαββάτῳ was used at first unemphatically to be followed by a more emphatic ἐν σαββάτῳ: but the evidence negatives this supposition.

[2715 d] Ἐν, or κατά, is always used by Mk, Mt., and Jn with ἑορτή to express

[2716] NOTES ON PRECEDING PARAGRAPHS

On vi. 21 ἤθελον οῦν λαβεῖν (2346)

[2716] Nonnus paraphrases this Καί μιν ἑλεῖν μηνέαινον (sic) ἐς ὁλκάδα· καὶ μένος ἄλμης *Ην τότε, καὶ πέλεν ὅρμος, ἐπεὶ θεοδινέϊ παλμῷ Οἷα νόος πτερόεις, ἀνέμων δίχα, νόσφιν ἐρετμῶν, Τηλεπόροις λιμένεσσιν ὁμίλεεν αὐτομάτη νηῦς[1], where μενέαινον implies earnest desire that was not fulfilled because the vessel was brought to shore by a heavensent blast before the disciples could receive Jesus on board. Chrys. takes the same view, twice repeating that Christ "*did not go on board*," and attempting to give a reason for it[2]. Both take ἤθελον as denoting unfulfilled desire.

[2717] In the LXX, forms of ἤθελον are very rare as compared with those of ἠθέλησα. The 3rd pers., ἤθελον, ἤθελε, without οὐ, hardly occurs outside apocryph. exc. in Judg. xiii. 23 εἰ ἤθελεν ὁ Κύριος where Theod. (and sim. A) has ἐβούλετο (and see other instances from LXX in 1735 *b*). Many Indices do not distinguish between θέλω and ἐθέλω, so that statements must be cautiously based on them. In Egypt. Pap. Indices, ἐθέλω is very rare; but ἠθέλησα is sometimes used about authoritative resolutions of those in power, and οὐκ ἠθέλησεν means "he refused"; ἤθελεν occurs (according to the Indices) only once, and then apparently of unfulfilled desire[3].

"during" or "in the course of." Lk. alone has the dat. without prep. in Lk. ii. 41 ἐπορεύοντο...τῇ ἑορτῇ, "at the feast." Strictly, Lk. should have said "*for the feast*," or "*to the feast*" (as Jn vii. 8, 10, xi. 56, xii. 12 εἰς τὴν ἑορτήν) and hence D ins. ἐν, *d* "in die festo," *b* "in diem sollemni (*sic*)," *e* "ad dies solomni (*sic*)," *f* "in die solemni," *a* "die sollemni."

[1] [2716 *a*] For μενεαίνω signifying vain desire see *Il*. xv. 617 ἀλλ' οὐδ' ὣς δύνατο ῥῆξαι μάλα περ μενεαίνων and comp. *Il*. xv. 104. *Ην τότε is perh. an imitation of Virgil's "sed *fuit*," "*was a thing of the past*:" ΗΤΟΤΕ might easily spring, as a corruption, from ΗϹΤΟΤΕ *i.e.* ἧστό τε, but (Steph.) ἧμαι does not appear to be used of "settling down." Θεοδινέϊ παλμῷ may be illustrated from Chrys. (*ad loc.*) οὐ γὰρ μόνον ἀσφαλῆ ἀλλὰ καὶ ἐξ οὐρίων αὐτοῖς παρέσχε τὸν πλοῦν.

[2] [2716 *b*] Τίνος δὲ ἕνεκεν οὐκ ἀνέβη εἰς τὸ πλοῖον;...οὐκ ἐνέβη δὲ εἰς τὸ πλοῖον, ἵνα τὸ θαῦμα μεῖζον ἐργάσηται. Chrys. supposes that Christ first walked on the sea, and then, "*as soon as He had appeared to the disciples, in the same moment, removed to the land*, (ἅμα τε ὤφθη καὶ ἀπέστη ἀπ' αὐτῶν)." He quotes vi. 21 ἤθελον λαβεῖν αὐτόν· καὶ εὐθέως τὸ πλοῖον ἐγγὺς τῆς γῆς ἐγένετο. Perhaps ℵ means this in substituting ἐπὶ τὴν γῆν εἰς ἣν ὑπήντησεν "the land to which Jesus *came to meet them*." Origen (on *Prov*. xxx. 19) has εὐθέως γὰρ ἐγένετο τὸ πλοῖον ἐπὶ τὴν γῆν εἰς ἣν ὑπῆγον, θείᾳ δυνάμει.

[3] [2717 *a*] See *Oxy. Pap*. ii. no. 237, col. vii. 10, 18, 19 etc. Here, and in several other passages of this long petition, the word seems to mean "willed," "decreed," "decided" (once τεθελήκασι). In *Fayûm Pap*. 131. 7 οὐκ ἠθέλησεν means "refused." In *Oxy*. iii. no. 472. 14 "*did not wish* (οὐκ ἤθελεν) her to survive him" the context indicates that the desire was frustrated.

According to the Indices of Lucian and Aristotle, ἤθελον does not occur in those authors, although ἐθέλω and θέλω are frequent in them[1]. The fact that ἤθελον occurs twice at no great interval in Test. xii. Patr. and that it is used by Hermas to express a modest wish[2], indicates that it may have been freely used by some writers; but its rarity in the writers above-mentioned and its non-existence in Mt.-Lk., confirm the view taken elsewhere (1735 b) that in the Walking on the Waters John's use of ἤθελον is connected with Mark's use of ἤθελεν[3].

On i. 30 ὑπὲρ ἀγτοΥ (2369)

[2718] On this passage Blass (p. 135) says that the use of ὑπέρ

---

[1] [2717 b] Lucian's Index has *Dial. Marin.* xiii. 2 (i. 321) οὐκ ἔθελες, "you did not wish," but nowhere ἤθελες or ἠθέλησας. Schenkl's Index to Epictetus gives ἤθελον (without ἄν) 1st pers. sing. "*I could have wished*," "*I should have liked*" (in vernacular English, "I only wish") in i. 10. 6 "I *only wish* I could stand by him and remind him" (comp. iv. 1. 143 "I *only wish* I could stand over one of these people" and Gal. iv. 20 ἤθελον δὲ παρεῖναι, i. 29. 35 "I should have liked to go on still as a pupil," and sim. i. 29. 38, ii. 8. 16 etc., almost always of impracticable (and often of unreasonable) desires. So in 2nd pers. i. 1. 18 (and comp. iii. 23. 13) Τί οὖν; ἤθελες πάντας τραχηλοκοπηθῆναι; "*would you have liked* to see all the world beheaded?" and 3rd pers. ii. 9. 22 οἷον εἴ τις δέκα λίτρας ἆραι μὴ δυνάμενος, τὸν τοῦ Αἴαντος λίθον βαστάζειν ἤθελεν "as though a man unequal to carrying ten pounds *would like* to lift the stone of Ajax!" In ii. 17. 33 ἤθελον δ' ἀσφαλῶς ἔχειν the desire is scoffed at by Epictetus (σὺ θεὸς εἶ, ὦ ἄνθρωπε) as absurdly ambitious. It occurs with a neg. in iv. 11. 24, "God forbid! I would not wish such a thing, even if it were to make me a wise man (οὐδ' εἰ σοφὸς ἔμελλον εἶναι ἤθελον)." Schenkl gives only one instance of ἤθελες ἄν (iii. 17. 4) "could you possibly have wished," referring to a disgraceful action.

[2717 c] Schenkl's very copious Index gives no instance of ἤθελε in Epictetus. Swete's note on Mk vi. 48 is "Vg. *volebat* praeterire eos...With the feigned purpose comp. Lc. xxiv. 28 and see Mc. v. 36, vii. 27." But ἤθελεν (so far as I know) never means "he feigned," and the passages referred to in Mk and Lk. do not contain ἤθελεν.

[2] [2717 d] Test. xii. Patr. *Rub.* § 1 εἰ μὴ Ἰακώβ...προσηύξατο περὶ ἐμοῦ...ὅτι (?) ἤθελε Κύριος ἀνελεῖν με, *ib. Sym.* § 2 κ. ἐλθὼν Ῥουβὴμ ἐλυπήθη· ἤθελε γὰρ αὐτὸν διασῶσαι.... In Herm. *Mand.* v. 1. 7, ἤθελον γνῶναι, "volebam cognoscere," is like our "*I wanted* to know—in case you can spare me five minutes—whether you think...," which does not imply that the "want" is given up.

[3] [2717 e] Mt. xiv. 25 ἦλθεν πρὸς αὐτούς has neither ἤθελον nor ἤθελεν. Possibly there may have been some Gk confusion between ΗΛΘΕΝ and ΗΘΕΛΟΝ or ΗΘΕΛΕΝ. In Jn vi. 21, the Cureton. Syr. (Burk.) has "*And they were willing that they should receive* him," but SS "*and when they took* him"; ℵ has ἦλθον for ἤθελον, an interchange like that in 2 S. xxiii. 9, where B* reads ἤθελε for ἦλθε.

[2719] NOTES ON PRECEDING PARAGRAPHS

for περί as in λέγειν ὑπέρ "to speak about," (1) "is common in Attic and Hellenistic Greek," (2) "as also in the LXX," (3) that it "is found more rarely [in N.T.] and is almost confined to Paul," and he instances "Jo. i. 30 ὑπὲρ οὗ (περὶ οὗ ℵᶜA al.) εἶπον, 2 Cor. viii. 23 εἴτε ὑπὲρ Τίτου ('as concerning'), xii. 8 ὑπὲρ τούτου παρεκάλεσα ('on this account,' 'on behalf of this')...2 Thess. ii. 1, καυχᾶσθαι ὑπέρ often in Paul, also φυσιοῦσθαι ὑπέρ, φρονεῖν ὑπέρ (in Phil. i. 7 'to think upon' in iv. 10 'to care for')." (4) On Jn i. 30 he adds (p. 313) "better ὅν without prep. Nonn. Chrys."

[2719] (1) A distinction should be drawn *between* ὑπέρ τινος *masc. and* ὑπέρ τινος *neuter*. The former almost always means "*in behalf of*," or at all events suggests some *interest* in the person mentioned. Comp. *Il*. vi. 524 ὑπὲρ σέθεν αἴσχε' ἀκούω πρὸς Τρώων implying that Hector blushes for his brother Paris, whom he would gladly defend, when he hears the Trojans revile him, Soph. *Œd. Tyr.* 1444 οὕτως ἄρ' ἀνδρὸς ἀθλίου πεύσεσθ' ὑπέρ (*i.e.* taking any interest in the fallen king), Lucian *De Salt.* 9 (ii. 273) of Achilles "receiving good news about (πυνθανόμενος ὑπέρ)" his son. In Plat. *Legg.* 776 E, the meaning may well be that Homer, "making proclamation *in behalf of Zeus* (ὑπὲρ τοῦ Διὸς ἀγορεύων)," has "openly declared" or "given sentence" that Zeus takes away half a man's being when he takes his freedom: that is, he speaks for the god, though not in the first person, as though he were in the counsels of Zeus[1].

---

[1] [2719 a] Plato 776 E may be punctuated thus, ὁ δὲ σοφώτατος ἡμῖν τῶν ποιητῶν καὶ ἀπεφήνατο ὑπὲρ τοῦ Διός, ἀγορεύων, "*has actually given sentence in the name of Zeus*, making public proclamation thereof." Comp. *ib*. 580 B ἴθι δή μοι, ἔφην ἐγώ, νῦν ἤδη ὥσπερ ὁ διὰ πάντων κριτὴς ἀποφαίνεται, καὶ σὺ οὕτω, "as the judge *gives his sentence* [as to which chorus is first, which second] so do you," followed by μισθωσώμεθα οὖν κήρυκα "*let us hire a herald*" to proclaim the sentence. Homer, then, seems to be the "herald" giving sentence in behalf of Zeus. Conversely, comp. Epict. ii. 23. 7 τί γάρ ἐστι τὸ ἀποφαινόμενον ὑπὲρ ἑκάστης τούτων τῶν δυνάμεων...with *ib*. μήτι τῆς ὁρατικῆς ποτ' ἤκουσας λεγούσης τι περὶ ἑαυτῆς; "What is it that *declares in behalf of* each of these faculties?...Did you ever hear the faculty of sight uttering a word *about* itself?" *i.e.* there is a higher power that speaks *in behalf of*, or *as the interpreter of*, its servants, for they cannot speak *about* themselves. Apart from Xen. *Cyrop*. (discussed in **2370 a**), Steph. gives no other instances except from an affidavit in Demosth. 554, 11 ἡ εἰσαγγελία ἐδόθη...ὑπὲρ Ἀριστάρχου, and Aeschin. 22, 12 (ch. 154 Teubn. p. 157) ὑπὲρ αὐτῶν ψηφιεῖσθαι ὧν ἡ δίωξις ᾖ. As to the former, since a contest is said to be "*in behalf of* (ὑπέρ) life or death," ὑπέρ τινος (masc.) came to be used in an action of a public character (εἰσαγγελία), perh. meaning at first "*in behalf of*," and then "*for or against*," comp. Arrian *Alex*. i. 25. 8 τί χρὴ ὑπὲρ Ἀλεξάνδρου

γνῶναι. In Aeschin., the preceding words (τί ὑμεῖς ὀμωμόκατε;) and the context, indicate that αὐτῶν is neut., as in the accepted Latin transl. "Vos quid jurastis? *De iis rebus* pronuntiaturos quæ in accusatione præscriptæ sunt." Steph.'s numerous instances from Polyb. are all neuter. Lucian's Index gives abundant instances of ὑπέρ with gen. of person, but all mean "*pro*," exc. perhaps *Phal. prior* 10 (ii. 197) ἄλλα μὲν ὑπὲρ ἐμοῦ ἀκηκοώς, ἐπεὶ δ' ἐπειράθη ἀπῆλθεν ἐπαινῶν με where the Latin gives "*de me*," and the meaning may be "in controversy for and against me." [If the meaning had been "other [good things] in my favour," we should have expected ἄλλα τε...καί.]

[**2719** *b*] In Arrian's *Exped. Alex.* ὑπέρ is freq. used with genit. of person and verbs of writing, inquiring etc. In his preface, distinguishing between γράφω περί and γράφω ὑπέρ, he says, ὅσα μὲν (?) ταῦτὰ ἄμφω περὶ Ἀλεξάνδρου...ξυνέγραψαν ταῦτα ἐγὼ ὡς πάντῃ ἀληθῆ ἀναγράφω...Ἄλλοι μὲν δὴ ἄλλα ὑπὲρ Ἀλεξάνδρου ἀνέγραψαν, οὐδ' ἔστιν ὑπὲρ ὅτου πλείονες ἢ ἀξυμφωνότεροι ἐς ἀλλήλους. The ἄμφω are Ptolemaeus and Aristobulus, and he proceeds to explain that these two wrote without being influenced by love of gain or other pressure. These two write in a detached and disinterested way "*about*" Alexander; the others "*in behalf of*," or "*in praise of*" him (or perhaps "in a controversial spirit about him"). He proceeds (*ib.*) to say that he has neglected mere idle oral tradition or talk "in favour of" Alexander (πάντῃ ἄπιστα ὡς λεγόμενα μόνον ὑπὲρ Ἀ.). It is perh. significant that vi. 2. 6 ὑπὲρ Ἀλεξάνδρου ξυνέγραψε is followed by ἐψεύσατο. Of course ὑπέρ with genit. of person may mean "*about*" a man, or men, when regarded impersonally, as an enemy, a nation etc., as in Arr. *Alex.* i. 5. 3 ὑ. τῶν Αὐταριατῶν, ii. 6. 2 ὑ. Δαρείου, v. 5. 1 ὑ. Ἰνδῶν. The Index to Arrian contains several instances where ὑπέρ τινος masc. means "in behalf of," as in N.T.

[**2719** *c*] Ὑπέρ, in ἀποφαίνεσθαι ὑπέρ, has been shewn (**2719** *a*) to mean "*in behalf of*," or "*in the name of*." Contrast Epict. iii. 18. 4 περὶ Σωκράτους δ' οὐκ ἀπεφήναντο οἱ δικασταί;—i.e. "gave sentence *about* Socrates." Epictetus appears never to use ὑπέρ for περί. The former, when used with the genitive, he mostly connects with verbs that imply anxious effort to gain some prize, retain some possession, or defend some person. His view is (ii. 16. 41, and comp. iv. 10. 22) that it is right to "strive even to desperation *for the sake of* (ὑπέρ) tranquillity, freedom, noblemindedness," for these things are parts of oneself; but it is only fools that would be anxious *for the sake of* a mere possession. Hence the parenthesis with ὑπέρ in the following, amidst a group of περί clauses, ii. 13. 11 ἀλλὰ περὶ τοῦ σωματίου ἀγωνιῶμεν—ὑπὲρ τοῦ κτησειδίου (comp. iii. 18. 3 ἐπὶ τὸ σωμάτιον—ἐπὶ τὸ κτησείδιον)—περὶ τοῦ τί δόξει τῷ Καίσαρι, περὶ τῶν ἔσω δ' οὐδενός. This might be paraphrased: "But we are anxious *about* the paltry body— [anxious] *for the sake of* that most trumpery possession!—*about* what Cæsar will think—but never a jot *about* the things within us." The ὑπέρ clause anticipates and meets the objection: "Why of course a man is anxious for the sake of his body!" and the meaning is, we are anxious *for the sake of* external unrealities, but we are not anxious, not even in the lowest sense, "*about*" internal realities. In i. 19. 26 ὑπὲρ ἱερωσύνης ἐλάλει μοι, ὑπέρ appears from the context to mean "*about the advisableness of attempting to obtain*" such an office (for it does not seem likely that ὑπέρ could mean "to secure my interest for his application"). The closest approximation of ὑπέρ to περί that I have been able to find is in iv. 1. 105 where εὐχαριστεῖν (elsewhere twice used with ἐπί) is used with ὑπέρ: but even here ὑπέρ probably represents a feeling less detached and more emotional than would be represented by περί. Similarly, in English, when we say "sorry or thankful *for*"

[2720] NOTES ON PRECEDING PARAGRAPHS

[2720] (2) In LXX, ὑπέρ with gen. is very rare except in the titles of Psalms and in the phrases ὁ ὑπέρ and ὑπὲρ οὗ. In the Pentateuch, it occurs only in Deut. xxiv. 16 (*bis*) "the fathers shall not be put to death *for* the children" and xxviii. 23 ὁ οὐρανὸς ὁ ὑπὲρ κεφαλῆς σου. Different authors and MSS. use ὑπέρ and περί differently. As to genit. of person, note Judg. vi. 31 "Will ye plead *for* Baal?" ὑπέρ, A περί, 1 S. ii. 25 "who shall entreat *for* him?" ὑπέρ, A περί, but 1 S. i. 27 "*for* this child I prayed" ὑπέρ (no v.r.), 2 S. vii. 25 and parall. 1 Chr. xvii. 23 (David to God) "thou hast spoken *concerning* thy servant and *concerning* his house," S. LXX περί (once), Luc. ὑπέρ (*bis*), Chr. LXX πρός and ἐπί¹. There are probably *very few instances of ὑπέρ with genit. of person in canonical LXX meaning "about*," except in the various reading (Luc.) of David's prayer quoted above².

[2721] (3) In N.T., ὑπέρ with genit. is relatively very much more frequent than in LXX. It occurs nearly twenty times in the

---

(but "angry or delighted *at*") there is a notion of having received something "[*in return*] *for*" which we make an emotional response of sorrow or thankfulness.

[2719 *d*] Ὑπέρ with genit. of pers. occurs in Epict. *Fragm.* (3 Schenkl, 136 Schweig.) ὑπὲρ ἡμῶν βεβούλευται to mean "in behalf of" and also with γράφω i. 9. 27, where γράφω ὑπέρ τινος means "write *in behalf of*" or "a letter of introduction for," rep. i. 9. 33 ὑπὲρ τούτου τί ἄλλο ἢ ἀνάγκη γράφειν ἐπιστολὰς ὡς ὑπὲρ νεκροῦ; Here there seems to be a play on writing a letter of introduction for the sake of helping a helpless creature and writing a letter of request for the sake of recovering a dead body to give it burial. It may be doubted whether the genit. is masc. or neut. in ii. 16. 42 ἄρχειν με θέλεις, ἰδιωτεύειν, μένειν, φεύγειν, πένεσθαι, πλουτεῖν; ἐγώ σοι ὑπὲρ ἁπάντων τούτων πρὸς τοὺς ἀνθρώπους ἀπολογήσομαι· δείξω τὴν ἑκάστου φύσιν οἵα ἐστίν, but τούτων, if not masculine, is at least personal in effect. The Philosopher says to God, "Make me play what part thou wilt, Ruler, Citizen, etc. I will justify thy ways to men, *representing these characters* [*in accordance with thy will*]." The discrimination between περί and ὑπέρ in Epictetus strongly confirms the conclusion that John likewise discriminated between them.

¹ [2720 *a*] As to genit. of thing, comp. 1 Esdr. vii. 8 ὑπὲρ ἁμαρτίας with Ezr. vi. 17 περὶ ἁμαρτίας and Dan. ii. 18 "mercies *concerning* this secret" (where there is a notion of intercession) LXX περί, Theod. ὑπέρ, with *ib.* vii. 16 "*concerning* all this" LXX ὑπέρ, Theod. περί. Comp. also Ezr. x. 19 (about sacrifice) περὶ πλημμελήσεως with parall. 1 Esdr. ix. 20 ὑπὲρ τῆς ἀγνοίας. In 2 S. vii. 19 "spoken of thy servant's house," vii. 28 "promised unto thy servant," the LXX has ὑπέρ, perh. (1) taking "house" as a thing, and (2) confusing "unto" with "in behalf of," but the parall. LXX in 1 Chr. xvii. 17, 26 has ἐπί in both cases.

² [2720 *b*] In 1 and 2 Macc., ὑπέρ with genit. occurs about 28 times, and when used with genit. of person, it alw. means "in behalf of" exc. in 2 Macc. ix. 8 "*above* [the level of] men."

Gospels (as compared with twice in the Pentateuch and Joshua) always with *genit. of person*, and—*unless it can be proved that* i. 30 *is an exception*—*always meaning* "*in behalf of*[1]." This also is its meaning in the Acts where the genitive is always personal, or quasi-personal, referring four times (out of seven) to sufferings "in behalf of the Name [of the Lord]." In the Pauline Epistles it occurs about ninety times, and in almost every instance it means "*in behalf of*" *some person, or some name, or cause, for which the Apostle contends as though contending for a person, or some object for which he is striving, or praying, or interceding*: and in the very few instances in which this meaning is not expressed, it is probably always implied[2].

[2722] (4) As regards the alleged omission of ὑπέρ by Chrys. and Nonnus in i. 30 οὗτός ἐστιν ὑπὲρ οὗ, Migne prints two quotations of it by Chrys. thus (1) Οὗτος ἦν περὶ οὗ εἶπον· Ὁ ὀπίσω μου ἐρχόμενος ἔμπροσθέν μου γέγονεν, (2) Οὗτος ἦν ὃν εἶπον· Ὀπίσω μου ἔρχεται ἀνὴρ ὃς ἔμπροσθέν μου γέγονεν, and a subsequent quotation of i. 15 thus (3) ὀπίσω μου ἔρχεται ὃς ἔμπροσθέν μου γέγονεν although he has previously quoted i. 15 (*ad loc.*) thus (4) οὗτος ἦν ὃν εἶπον, ὁ ὀπίσω μου ἐρχόμενος ἔμπροσθέν μου γέγονεν. It will be observed, 1st, that Chrys. does not omit a prep. in his first quotation of i. 30 (though he

---

[1] [2721 *a*] Mt. has it only in v. 44 (Lk. vi. 28) προσεύχεσθε ὑπὲρ (Lk. περί) τῶν διωκόντων. Where Mk xiv. 24 has ὑπὲρ πολλῶν, Mt. xxvi. 28 has περί, and bracketed Lk. xxii. 19, 20 has ὑπὲρ ὑμῶν.

[2] [2721 *b*] The single doubtful case of pers. genit. is Rom. ix. 27 Ἡσαίας δὲ κράζει ὑπὲρ τοῦ Ἰσραήλ, where Fritzsche may be right in alleging Arrian *Exp. Al.* vi. 2. 6 ὑπὲρ Ἀλεξάνδρου, "about Alexander" (**2719** *b*), so that Israel is not a *person*, but a historical subject. But note the obvious contrast in Rom. xi. 2 Ἠλείᾳ...ὡς ἐντυγχάνει...κατὰ τοῦ Ἰσραήλ. In Rom. xi. 2, Elijah intercedes *against Israel* and is rebuked by the answer that *there is* "*a remnant.*" In Rom. ix. 27, Isaiah "cries *in behalf of Israel*" and announces that *there will be a* "*remnant.*" 2 Cor. viii. 23 εἴτε ὑπὲρ Τίτου means "*whether* [*I have to stand up in defence*] concerning Titus and his relations with you and myself"—I maintain that he has done you no wrong. In 2 Thess. ii. 1, ὑπὲρ τῆς παρουσίας means—as Lightf. expresses it, "roughly and broadly paraphrased"—"to advocate the true view of the coming." Phil. i. 7 καθώς ἐστιν δίκαιον ἐμοὶ τοῦτο φρονεῖν ὑπὲρ πάντων ὑμῶν, means that the Apostle is bound to feel confident, hopeful, and thankful "*in behalf of*" his Philippian converts.

[2721 *c*] Ὑπέρ, when used with a verb and such phrases as vi. 51 "the life of the world," xi. 4 "the glory of God," Acts ix. 16 "my name," Rom. xv. 8 "the truth of God," 2 Cor. i. 6 "your comforting," 2 Thess. i. 4 "your endurance"—whether the verb be "contend" or "speak as an ambassador" or "boast" or whatever else—manifestly implies a *personal interest* "*in behalf of*" *some person or some personified thing*.

has περί for ὑπέρ), 2nd, that he alters ἐστίν to ἦν in both his quotations of i. 30 (conforming them to i. 15), 3rd, that he omits the important word ἀνήρ in his first quotation of i. 30. These variations detract from the value of his testimony and indicate that he mixed i. 30 and i. 15. The same statement applies to Nonnus so far as concerns ἦν in i. 30 Οὗτος ἔην ὃν ἔειπον, ὀπίστερος ἔρχεται ἀνήρ. Even Origen uses περί in his commentary on Samuel (1 S. xxviii. 18 foll.) οὗτός ἐστι περὶ οὗ ἐγὼ εἶπον, Ὁ ὀπίσω μου ἐρχ., also omitting ἀνήρ[1]. It has been shewn above (2371) that ἀνήρ, if it means "husband" or "bridegroom[2]," goes far to explain ὑπέρ. This view is confirmed by the fact that, when Origen says that the Baptist called Christ not only ἀμνός but also ἀνήρ, he quotes the text correctly with ὑπέρ, and he does it again later on[3]. The evidence from Chrys. therefore indicates nothing except that he did not understand the three points that differentiate i. 30 from i. 15, namely, ἐστίν for ἦν, ὑπὲρ οὗ for ὅν, and the important insertion of ἀνήρ. A review of all the evidence makes it almost certain that John did not use ὑπέρ for περί.

On ix. 21 αὐτὸς περὶ ἑαυτοῦ (2374—80)

[2723] ix. 21 αὐτὸς περὶ ἑαυτοῦ λαλήσει, if translated according to classical Greek usage, would closely connect αὐτὸς περὶ ἑαυτοῦ making αὐτός little more than a preparation for emphasizing ἑαυτοῦ "he will speak—*he about his own self*," i.e. about himself and nothing else.

---

[1] [2722 a] Lomm. xi. 328 Οὗτος οὖν ὁ σκιρτήσας πρὸ γενέσεως, Ἰωάννης ὁ εἰπών· "οὗτός ἐστι, περὶ οὗ ἐγὼ εἶπον· ὁ ὀπίσω μου ἐρχόμενος ἔμπροσθέν μου γέγονε." καὶ "ὁ πέμψας εἰπέ μοι· ἐφ' ὃν ἂν ἴδῃς τὸ πνεῦμα καταβαῖνον, καὶ μένον, οὗτός ἐστιν ὁ υἱὸς τοῦ θεοῦ." οὗτος, φασίν, οὐκέτι ᾔδει Ἰησοῦν Χριστὸν ἐν κοιλίᾳ. Ἤιδει γὰρ αὐτόν. Ἀλλὰ δι' ὑπερβολὴν δόξης ὅμοιόν τι τῷ Πέτρῳ πεποίηκεν. Origen is quoting freely but Lomm.'s text is also corrupt. We should prob. ins. the words bracketed as follows, οὗτος, φασίν, οὐκέτι ᾔδει Ἰησοῦν Χριστὸν [ὃν] ἐν κοιλίᾳ [ᾔδει]· ᾔδει γὰρ αὐτόν, ἀλλὰ δι' ὑ..., "They assert that he no longer knew Jesus Christ [whom] in the womb [he had known]. Absurd (2068a) ! For he knew Him,...but...."

[2] [2722 b] Origen (2722 c) ranks the Baptist's testimony as to ἀνήρ along with his testimony as to ἀμνός, suggesting that he laid stress on the former; but his comment *ad loc.* is lost. Cramer *ad loc.* prints (as one of several explanations of ἀνήρ given by Ammonius) ἢ ὅτι πάσης τῆς λογικῆς φύσεως, ὅ ἐστι τῆς Ἐκκλησίας, νυμφίος ἐστίν.

[3] [2722 c] Lomm. i. 47 οἷον ὁ Ἰωάννης αὐτὸν ἀμνὸν θεοῦ ἀναγορεύει λέγων, Ἴδε... καὶ ἄνδρα διὰ τούτων, Οὗτός ἐστιν ὑπὲρ οὗ ἐγὼ εἶπον ὅτι Ὀπίσω μου..., rep. *ib.* p. 156. In both passages, Origen, or the scribe, has perhaps rep. οπι (of ὀπίσω) as ὅτι. Nonnus (on Jn i. 13) seems to take αἵματα as referring to (2269) the mother and ἀνήρ to the father, Οὓς φύσις οὐκ ὤδινε λεχωιὰς, οὐ βίος ἔγνω Ἀνδρομέου βλάστημα θελήματος, οὐδὲ καὶ αὐτὴ Σαρκὸς ἐρωτοτόκοιο γαμήλιος ἤροσεν εὐνή.

Thus ὁ δὲ Κάτων αὐτὸς ἑαυτὸν ἀνεῖλεν would not mean "Cato *himself* [virtuous though he was] committed suicide" but "Cato killed himself *with his own hand,*" as in Xen. *Anab.* ii. 4. 10 οἱ δὲ Ἕλληνες ὑφορῶντες τούτους αὐτοὶ ἐφ᾽ ἑαυτῶν ἐχώρουν "but the Greeks...marched *entirely by themselves,*" not "the Greeks *themselves* by themselves." So 2 Cor. i. 9 ἀλλὰ αὐτοὶ ἐν ἑαυτοῖς τὸ ἀπόκριμα τ. θ. ἐσχήκαμεν means "we have had in our *own* selves the sentence of death" (R.V. "we ourselves"—less suitably if it means "we ourselves [as distinct from others].") But where the context makes αὐτός emphatic so that one pauses on it, it may be separated from the ἑαυτοῦ-phrase, as possibly in 2 Cor. x. 12 ἀλλὰ αὐτοί—ἐν ἑαυτοῖς ἑαυτοὺς μετροῦντες...οὐ συνιᾶσιν. ἡμεῖς δὲ οὐκ.... There W.H. make no stop after αὐτοί, but αὐτοί seems to refer emphatically to "certain persons" mentioned above and contrasted with "we" thus: "but *they*—measuring themselves by themselves...have no understanding, but *we*...." So probably in Rom. viii. 23 οὐ μόνον δέ, ἀλλὰ καὶ αὐτοί—τὴν ἀπαρχὴν τοῦ πνεύματος ἔχοντες [ἡμεῖς]—καὶ αὐτοὶ ἐν ἑαυτοῖς στενάζομεν, "we ourselves, we ourselves, I say, having in ourselves..." (not "in our own selves"). In Jn ix. 21 the context exhibits the timorous parents shifting responsibility from themselves to their son, laying an increasing stress on the antithesis between "*we*" and "*him*": "We (unemph.) know that this is our son...but how he now seeth we (unemph.) know not, or (2759 *a—f*) who [as it is said] opened his eyes *we* (emph.) (ἡμεῖς) know not. Ask *him* (αὐτόν)—he is of age—*he* (αὐτός) shall speak concerning himself"—where "he" means "*he himself,*" apart from us and uninfluenced by us.

On vi. 15 ἀΥτὸc μόνοc (2375)

[2724] Origen, commenting on Christ's retirement to Ephraim (xi. 54) and mentioning other retirements, quotes vi. 15 γνοὺς ὅτι... ἀνεχώρησεν εἰς τὸ ὄρος and adds ἀλλ᾽ οὐ μετὰ τῶν μαθητῶν ἀλλὰ μόνος (not αὐτὸς μόνος)[1]. The Latin *b* also omits "ipse." Chrys. has γνοὺς ὅτι...ἀνεχώρησεν εἰς τὸ ὄρος, and proceeds to comment, without adding αὐτὸς μόνος. Both Origen and Chrys. omit the preceding πάλιν (in

---

[1] [2724 *a*] Origen elsewhere (on Mt. xv. 29 ἀναβὰς εἰς τὸ ὄρος ἐκάθητο ἐκεῖ) says that the mountain represents the Ecclesia, and he argues that the disciples (Lomm. iii. 122) went up with their Master. This is before the Feeding of the Four Thousand. The going up to the mountain at first *with* the disciples affords a contrast with the going up to the mountain afterwards *without* the disciples (αὐτὸς μόνος).

[2725] NOTES ON PRECEDING PARAGRAPHS

ἀνεχώρησεν πάλιν εἰς τὸ ὄρος). Nonnus does not express αὐτός or πάλιν in his paraphrase, Οὔρεος ὑλήεντος ἐρημάδα δύσατο πέτρην. Δύσατο, implying "*hiding*," resembles ἐκρύβη in Epiphanius (117 D *Haer*. xxix. 2) γνοὺς ἀνεχώρησε καὶ ἐκρύβη ἐν Ἐφραὶμ πόλει τῆς ἐρήμου (after the words ἦλθον γὰρ (φησὶ τὸ εὐαγγέλιον) χρῖσαι αὐτὸν εἰς βασιλέα) which also omits the words αὐτὸς μόνος. SS supports W.H. as to αὐτὸς μόνος, but the Curetonian Syr. has "he left them and *fled* again to the hill alone," φεύγει is also the reading of א*, and Chrys., in his comment, uses this word, ὁ δὲ Χριστὸς φεύγει. Τί δήποτε; Strangely enough, a little afterwards, Chrys., who has omitted the words πάλιν and μόνος in describing Christ's retirement, inserts them in the Walking on the Waters[1]. D and *d* add κἀκεῖ προσηύχετο after αὐτὸς μόνος, א has μόνος αὐτός.

[2725] In xii. 24 αὐτὸς μόνος μένει there is no various reading. Latin versions of Origen twice paraphrase it as "doth not bring forth fruit." Chrys. first quotes the greater part of xii. 24, including αὐτὸς μ. μένει, then explains ἦλθεν ἡ ὥρα, then ὁ κόκκος...ἀποθάνῃ, but makes no attempt to explain αὐτὸς μ. μένει. But Origen elsewhere (in his comment on Jeremiah xi. 19 in which he finds a reference to the "wood" of the cross) quotes xii. 24 ἐὰν μὴ κόκκος (for ὁ κ.) ...αὐτὸς μόνος μένει and adds that, but for the crucifixion, ἔμεινεν ἂν μόνος ὁ κόκκος. There is nothing in his comment to shew clearly at first whether he took αὐτός to mean "*it*" (as A.V.) or "*by itself*" (as R.V.), but when he repeats the words, he transposes them into a form that may be rendered thus, "Consider therefore His saying [and ask] whether He has not intended (βεβούληται) this [*i.e.* a reference to the cross] saying, 'The grain of wheat, *except it*, [or, *it itself*] *fall into the earth and die* (ὁ κ. τ. σίτου, ἐὰν μὴ πεσὼν εἰς τὴν γῆν ἀποθάνῃ αὐτός), abideth alone (μόνος μένει)'"—if we punctuate after αὐτός. Nonnus brings out the predicative meaning of αὐτός, "by itself and fruitless," with great force[2].

[2726] Αὐτὸς μόνος must be distinguished from μόνος αὐτός (which א reads in Jn vi. 15). The latter, according to the analogy of δεύτερος, τρίτος etc. followed by αὐτός, would mean "alone by himself." It occurs two or three times in Lucian to mean "unique[3]."

---

[1] [2724 *b*] Τίνος οὖν ἕνεκεν ἀφίησιν αὐτοὺς καὶ ἀναχωρεῖ; μᾶλλον δέ, τίνος ἕνεκεν φαίνεται πάλιν μόνος ἐπὶ τῆς θαλάσσης βαδίζων;

[2] [2725 *a*] Τότε μοῦνος ἐτώσιος αὐτόθι μίμνει Ἄσπορος, ἀχρήιστος, ἀνήροτος, ἄμμορος ἄρπης.

[3] [2726 *a*] Lucian *Demon*. 29 (ii. 386) μόνος αὐτός ἐστι καὶ πρῶτος τῶν διαλεκτι-

But αὐτὸς μόνος might have various meanings according to its context *e.g.* "*he himself* [did it, and that too] alone and unaided," or "[He is] by himself [quite] alone," or "[existing] by himself [and] alone[1]." In vi. 15, αὐτὸς μόνος, coming at the end of the sentence is peculiarly emphatic (more so than in xii. 24) and the general confusion of the text, together with the difficulty of the phrase, suffice to explain the omission (by some) of αὐτός, or of μόνος, or of both. But the peculiar language springs from peculiar circumstances. In Gethsemane, Christ's disciples were to "leave" Him "alone" (xvi. 32). After the Feeding of the Five Thousand (as Origen suggests[2]) they perhaps went, from one point of view, still further from their Lord, if they abetted the multitude against Him, and desired to see Him "made a king" by force. If ever the Son could be called "alone"—though He could not really *be* "*alone*" because the Father "was with" Him—it was on this occasion; and this perhaps is the meaning of the final αὐτὸς μόνος, "—by Himself, even the disciples being against Him, taking His way *alone*." In reality, as Origen says, it was not Christ that was left "alone." It was the disciples. And this sinister word "alone" ending the narrative of the Five Thousand, prepares the way for the Walking on the Waters, which describes the disciples as leaving their Master and failing in faith.

On vii. 4 ζητεῖ ἀΥτός (marg. ἀΥτό)...εῖΝΑΙ (2375 *a*)

[2727] In vii. 4 οὐδεὶς γάρ τι ἐν κρυπτῷ ποιεῖ καὶ ζητεῖ ⌜αὐτὸς⌝

κῶν, "that he is *unique* and first" (see **1895** *c*), *Gymnas.* 40 (ii. 921) μὴ ἐρήμην, ὦ γενναῖε, μηδὲ τῶν ἀνδρῶν ἀπόντων, μόνος αὐτός (*alone by yourself*) λέγων οἷον κρατεῖν. The meaning is ironical in both these cases. *Harmon.* 3 (i. 855) μόνος αὐτὸς ἀμείνων ἂν ἦσθα, seems to mean "*You alone by yourself* would have been better than all these together."

[1] [2726 *b*] L. S. quotes αὐτῷ μόνῳ and καθ' αὑτοὺς μόνοι from Plato, but not αὐτὸς μόνος, nor does Mitchell's Index. Aristoph. *Ran.* 78 Ἰοφῶντ' ἀπολαβὼν αὐτὸν μόνον means "taking aside Iophon *by himself alone*," emphasizing the secrecy. Long. *De Sublim.* 35 τοῦ γηγενοῦς ἐκείνου καὶ αὐτοῦ μόνου...πυρός, referring to the flames of Etna, might mean "*unique*" fire, but Dr Roberts (p. 238) indicates a parall. in Pind. *Pyth.* i. 21—4 πυρὸς ἁγνότατα...παγαί and renders αὐτοῦ μόνου "pure and unmixed" (comp. Steph. 2508 A quoting Demetr. *De Eloc.* 144 τὸ δὲ αὐτίτης πεποιημένον ἐκ τοῦ αὐτός). On αὐτός meaning "alone," see **2699**.

[2] [2726 *c*] Lomm. ii. 368 (on xi. 50). Origen speaks of the disciples as βουληθεῖσιν ἂν μετὰ τῶν θελόντων ποιῆσαι αὐτὸν βασιλέα, ἵν' ἤδη γένηται καὶ κοσμικῶς αὐτῶν βασιλεύς, *i.e.* their king after the manner of this world, which might be paraphrased as "according to the manner of 'the prince of this world.'" The crisis resembled that in the Temptation (Mt. iv. 9, Lk. iv. 6).

(marg. αὐτό) ἐν παρρησίᾳ εἶναι, there is probably a contrast between the "*works*" mentioned in vii. 3 ("that thy disciples also may behold *thy works* which thou art doing") and the *worker* ("himself")—as in x. 38 ("Even if ye believe not *me* believe the *works*," and comp. xiv. 11). Missing this contrast, some scribes have dropped αὐτός as superfluous or have supposed ΑΥΤΟCΕΝ to be an error for ΑΥΤΟΕΝ[1]. Chrys. quotes οὐδεὶς γὰρ ἐν κρυπτῷ τι...αὐτός, but afterwards refers freely thus, Τὸ μὲν οὖν εἰπεῖν, Οὐδείς τι ἐν κρυπτῷ ποιεῖ, δειλίαν ἐγκαλούντων ἐστίν...τὸ δὲ ἐπαγαγεῖν ὅτι Ζητεῖ ἐν παρρησίᾳ εἶναι, φιλοδοξίας. Under the circumstances this can hardly be taken as proof that he did not read αὐτός. For ζητεῖ αὐτός quoted apart from its context would be liable to misunderstanding. It should be added, however, that SS has "wisheth *himself* that *it* (or, *he*) should be in the open," which suggests that it may have read αὐτὸς αὐτό. Nonnus certainly did not read αὐτό, but he may have omitted the pronoun altogether: Οὐ γάρ τις...ὑποκόλπιον ἔργον ὑφαίνει...ἀμφαδίην δ' ἐθέλει θρασὺς ἔμμεναι—where he combines the two meanings of παρρησία, (1) publicity (ἀμφαδίην), (2) boldness (θρασύς). The textual evidence against αὐτό, when combined with the fact that παρρησία is regularly applied to *persons*, not to reports, makes it certain that αὐτό is corrupt, and probable that αὐτός is correct.

On viii. 44 ἐκ τῶν ἰδίων λαλεῖ (2378)

[2728] R.V. "speaketh of his own" leaves it an open question whether ἐκ is (1) partitive (**2214**) "[some] of," or (2) significative of origin (as in Mt. xii. 34 (sim. Lk. vi. 45) ἐκ τοῦ περισσεύματος τῆς καρδίας τὸ στόμα λαλεῖ). Probably it is the latter ("from"). But "speaketh from [a source] belonging to him" seems (but see **2728** *d*) to make very poor sense as compared with Mt.-Lk. where the meaning is "speaks, because he cannot help it—the stream of words bursting forth from the fountain in the heart." Chrys. says "Man uses falsehood not as *belonging to him* (ἰδίῳ) but as *alien* (ἀλλοτρίῳ), but he [that is, Satan, uses it] as *belonging to him*." By "belonging to him" he means "*one of his family*" as appears from his preceding

---

[1] [2727 *a*]. There are many variations in ℵ, D and latt. and syr. vss., as to the order of the words and transl.: ℵ and *b* have ποιῶν for ποιεῖ καί, *e* has "in auctoritate" for ἐν παρρησίᾳ and omits γάρ, *ff* has "Nemo quid facit in occulto. Quid facit quaerit ipse": *b* and *e* omit "ipse". Ἐν κρυπτῷ τι, the reading of D and most latt., seems to lay less stress on τι than is laid in οὐδεὶς γάρ τι ἐν κρ. The latter may have been supposed by the scribe of B to mean "doeth a *certain thing in secret*" in contrast with "wisheth *it to be* [*known*] *in public*."

statement that Satan was the *origin and parent* of falsehood (ἔτεκε τὸ ψεῦδος πρῶτος) in the words to Eve ("Your eyes shall be opened"). Origen *ad loc.* refers to the "spirit" that "stood before the Lord" in order to cause the death of Ahab, saying "I will go forth and *be a spirit of falsehood in the mouth of all his prophets.*" The lying "spirit," on that occasion "spake from his own (ἐκ τῶν ἰδίων ἐλάλησε)" *i.e.* from the false prophets whom he had made "his own" by placing the spirit of falsehood in them. This view explains the Johannine connexion between "speaking from his own" and "ye are from the devil as your father," which otherwise is obscure[1].

---

[1] [2728 *a*] Comp. Mt. x. 20, "it is not ye that speak but the spirit of your Father that *speaketh in you*," where it would have made good sense to substitute "*speaketh from you*," as the "speaking" goes forth from the disciples to the world. Nonnus gives no help as to the meaning of "his own," Φθέγγεται ἐξ ἰδίων ὅτι λοίγιον ἦθος ἀέξων Ψεύστης αὐτὸς ἔφυ Ψευδήμονος ἐκ γενετῆρος, where Nonnus appears to take a view thrown out by Origen at the outset of his comment on the passage (Lomm. ii. 241) ἀμφίβολος ἡ λέξις ἐστί· δηλοῦται γὰρ ἀπ' αὐτῆς ἓν μέν, ὡς ἄρα ἔχει ὁ διάβολος πατέρα.

[2728 *b*] In viii. 44 R.V. and A.V. may intend "speaketh *of* his own" to mean "speaketh *from*." Comp. vii. 17, 18, xiv. 10, xvi. 13, λαλεῖν ἀπό, xii. 49 λαλεῖν ἐκ, where A.V. has "speak *of*" (but R.V. has "speak *from*"). In xviii. 34 (as in viii. 44) ἀπὸ σεαυτοῦ...λέγεις is rendered by R.V. as well as A.V. "*of* thyself." Shakespeare uses "of" for "from" in "of one's self, himself etc.," and (in very rare cases) with a verb of speech as prob. in *All's Well* i. 3. 7 "when *of ourselves* we publish them" *i.e.* our own praises. "Sayest thou this *of thyself*?" is therefore justifiable: but there is probably nothing in English literature to justify such a phrase as "speaketh *of his own*" in any sense but "speaketh *about his own*."

[2728 *c*] Origen (Lomm. ii. 267) calls attention to the contrast between the spirit of falsehood—which speaks ἐκ τῶν ἰδίων—and the Holy Spirit, Τὸ μὲν οὖν ἅγιον πνεῦμα...οὐκ ἐκ τῶν ἰδίων λαλεῖ ἀλλ' ἀπὸ τοῦ λόγου τῆς ἀληθείας (comp. xvi. 13 οὐ γὰρ λαλήσει ἀφ' ἑαυτοῦ).

[2728 *d*] The above comment, on viii. 44 ἐκ τῶν ἰδίων, should have included some notice of Epictetus's use of τὸ ἴδιον. By ἴδια he means "essential property." Etymologically, a man's "*property*," being that which is "peculiar" to him, ought to include—if the question is of the difference between man and non-human creatures—such possessions as his reason, temperance, charity, etc. But in Gk, as in English, τὰ ἴδια had come to mean mostly a man's house, estate, etc. Against this popular use Epictetus protests, as when he bids us (iv. 5. 15—16) "mourn over one whose fate it has been, not to die, but, while still living, to *lose his essential property* (ἀπολέσαι τὰ ἴδια), not his patrimony or paltry plot of ground...(for none of these things is *proper* (ἴδιον) to the man)...but the qualities of man (τὰ ἀνθρωπικά), those characteristics with the stamp of which upon his mind he has come [into the world] (τοὺς χαρακτῆρας οὓς ἔχων ἐν τῇ διανοίᾳ ἐλήλυθεν)." Elsewhere he says of a man's "rooted convictions (δόγματα)" or "motives"— a very different thing from our "dogma"—iv. 4. 44 "these are a man's *essential property*, the things that make his actions also either vile or honourable (ταῦτα γάρ

On ἐκεῖνος (2381—5)

[2729] The insertion of a superfluous ἐκεῖνος for the sake of emphasis was explained above (1920) as mainly due to Hebrew influence. But it is in part traceable to a universal desire, among those who speak naturally, to put the subject they are going to talk about at the head of the sentence, as often in old-fashioned English songs ("our captain he did say"). Comp. the use of αὐτῷ in *Ox. Pap.* 299 (late 1st cent.) Λάμπωνι μυοθηρευτῇ ἔδωκα αὐτῷ διὰ σοῦ ἀραβῶνα (δραχμὰς) η ἵνα μυοθηρεύσει ἔντοκα. καλῶς ποιήσεις πέμψεις μοι αὐτάς. καὶ Διονυσίῳ προσ[τ]άτῃ Νεμερῶν κέκρηκα (δραχμὰς) η καὶ ταύτας οὐκ ἔπεμψε, ἵνα εἰδῇς, ἔρρωσ(ο), which edd. transl. "Regarding Lampon the mouse-catcher I paid him for you as earnest money 8 drachmae in order that he may catch the mice while they are with young. Please send me the money. I have also lent Dionysius, the chief man of Nemerae, 8 drachmae, and he has not repaid them, to which I call your attention. Good-bye[1]."

On v. 32 ἄλλος...ὁ μαρτυρῶν (2384)

[2730] In v. 32 ἄλλος ἐστὶν ὁ μαρτυρῶν, Nonnus has Ἄλλος ἀνὴρ πέλε μάρτυς taking ἄλλος to mean the Baptist, as Chrysostom does (2384): and ℵ*D *a*, *e*, and SS, read οἴδατε for οἶδα in what follows ("*Ye know* that his witness is true"), indicating that they, too, took

---

ἔστι τὰ ἴδια ἑκάστου, τὰ καὶ τὰς πράξεις αἰσχρὰς ἢ καλὰς ποιοῦντα)." Comp. ii. 4. 1 ἀνατρέπει τὸ ἴδιον (*i.e.* faithfulness) τοῦ ἀνθρώπου, ii. 12. 14 τὸ...μάλιστα ἴδιον Σωκράτους, ii. 26. *tit.* τὸ ἴδιον τοῦ ἁμαρτήματος. These facts indicate that, in the Epictetian sense, ἐκ τῶν ἰδίων might mean nearly the same thing as "from the abundance of the heart," and that this is one of the two meanings intended.

[1] [2729 *a*] Note here, for future reference (1) διὰ σοῦ used by an illiterate writer for διὰ σέ "on thy account," "for thy sake" (**2294, 2705**), (2) ἵνα with the future (**2114**), (3) καλῶς ποιήσεις πέμψεις either misspelt for κ. π. πέμψας, or more prob. taken by this writer as meaning "you will kindly send," (4) ἵνα εἰδῇς (familiar to us in N.T.) used for "[I write this] that you may know [it]." Ἵν' εἰδῇς, used absolutely in Euripides, means "that you may know [the facts]," and is sometimes used towards enemies, "that you may know [what I think]," as in *Hec.* 1243, where Agamemnon tells Polymestor what he thinks of him. Comp. *And.* 589 "that you may know [what will be the result of your insolence]," *Ion* 35 "that you may know [the truth]," *Orest.* 534 "that you may know [my mind, I say] 'Do not go against the Gods.'" So Ulysses to Philoctetes in Soph. *Phil.* 989 "It is Zeus, it is Zeus—that you may know [the truth]—who bade me do this." In the Papyrus, it seems to mean "[I write] that you may know [the fact that I have not been paid]." The prevalence of εἰδῇς in this particular phrase might result in the correct use of forms in the 2nd pers., εἰδῇς, -ῆτε (comp. Mk ii. 10, Mt. ix. 6, Lk. v. 24, Eph. vi. 21, 1 Tim. iii. 15, 1 Jn ii. 29, v. 13), after other forms, *e.g.* εἰδῶ, -ῶμεν, had fallen into disuse (see **2690**).

the meaning to be "Ye, Jews, know that *the Baptist's* witness is true." But (1) whereas there is no difficulty in supposing that Jesus appeals to the testimony of God (as a physician might appeal to Nature) there is some weakness in supposing that Jesus, as it were, calls into court a human witness to Himself and then adds "*I know that this man speaks the truth.*" [This objection is removed by א*D etc., but at the cost of altering the text.] (2) As John was probably by this time in prison, or dead, and as he is described by the context in the past tense ("He *was* the lamp") it is not likely that he would be described here in the present (ἐστίν). (3) The whole passage appears to mean: "There is another witness now witnessing about me—I do not speak of John, who witnessed in the past—a present witness and a greater witness than John, I mean the works given me by my Father." (4) This explanation suits ἄλλος (2675—7) "*another of the same kind as myself*" (*a d* and *ff* "alter," not "alius" as the rest) by which the evangelist suggests Christ's unique unity with the Father. (5) Origen (2794—5) probably agrees with Cyprian, who (*Epist.* lxvi. 2, ed. Hartel, vol. ii. p. 727) quotes v. 31—2 as shewing that "The Lord Himself...was unwilling to be believed on His own testimony, but preferred to be approved by the judgment and testimony of *God the Father.*" On ἄλλος in Epictetus see 2791 foll.

On xix. 35 καὶ ἐκεῖνοc οἶΔεν (2384)

[2731] On xix. 35 καὶ ἐκεῖνος οἶδεν, paraphrased by Nonnus as ἴδμεν, comp. Barn. ix. 8—9 δηλοῖ οὖν τὸν μὲν Ἰησοῦν ἐν τοῖς δυσὶν γράμμασιν καὶ ἐν τῷ ἑνὶ τὸν σταυρόν. οἶδεν ὁ τὴν ἔμφυτον δωρεὰν τῆς διδαχῆς αὐτοῦ θέμενος ἐν ἡμῖν. The writer has been enlarging on the mystery of "the three letters" that point to Jesus and His crucifixion, and he concludes, "*He knoweth* [*the truth of this mystery*]— even He who set in us the implanted gift of the Teaching." The parallel in the two appeals ("*He knoweth*") is made the more remarkable by a parallel corruption of the texts. As Nonnus tried to make sense by reading οἴδαμεν, so the Latin translator of Barnabas ("scitote quia") read οιδατε (or ? ιστε) οτι, and א has οτι for ο and διαθηκης for διδαχης. Corresponding to John's use of ἐκεῖνος to mean the Lord or Master, is the ancient Greek use of αὐτός in αὐτὸς ἔφα, "He [the Master] said it," meaning Pythagoras, frequently referred to in Greek literature, and used of God in Heb. xiii. 6 "Be ye free from the love of money...for HE (R.V. himself) hath said...," where Wetst. refers to Josh. i. 5 and adds "κατ' ἐξοχήν, *i.e.* Deus."

[2732] NOTES ON PRECEDING PARAGRAPHS

On vii. 11 ποΫ́ ἐcτὶν ἐκεῖνοc (2385)

[2732] In vii. 11 Ποῦ ἐστὶν ἐκεῖνος, whereas Chrys. asks why the Jews will not call Christ by His name and decides that it is because of their detestation of Him, Nonnus apparently takes the pronoun as ="ille" in a good sense, Καί μιν Ἰουδαῖοι φιλίῃ μάστευον ἀνάγκῃ Πῆ μοι ἔβη; ποῖ κεῖνος; The double meaning is illustrated by Mt. xxvii. 19 τῷ δικαίῳ ἐκείνῳ, ib. 63 ἐκεῖνος ὁ πλάνος. The context in vii. 11 allows of Nonnus' interpretation; but that of Chrys. is favoured by ix. 12 ποῦ ἐστὶν ἐκεῖνος; xix. 21 ἐκεῖνος εἶπεν, where it is almost certainly contemptuous as well as hostile. On Acts v. 28, Blass (p. 171) says "D has τοῦ ἀνθρ. ἐκείνου· for τ. ἀ. τούτου of the other MSS. (the latter is due to ἐπὶ τῷ ὀνόματι τούτῳ in the same verse)." Against this are the following facts: (1) the Latin of D in Acts v. 28 has "huius"; (2) the Gk, though it shews signs of an original εκεινογ, has τογτογ written over it, not above the line but in the line; (3) in the line above, there happens to be Γειν which may have led the scribe to write εκεινογ by a mere lapse.

On xix. 9 πόθεν εἶ cγ́; (2403)

[2733] Alford and Westcott take πόθεν εἶ σύ; to mean, in effect, "Whence art thou? [*Art thou from heaven?*]" This suits the charge brought by the Jews in xix. 7, "He made himself *the Son of God.*" It also suits xix. 8 μᾶλλον[1] ἐφοβήθη, since "fear" would be natural in a Governor if he suspected that he had scourged a god or angel from heaven, as Pentheus had dealt with Dionysus. The words may be intended *by John* to include this meaning, just as (2645) "Behold, the Man!" may be intended *by John* to include the meaning with which Christians utter the latter. That *Pilate*, however, intended them thus is improbable for the following reasons.

[2734] We have seen (2403) that Chrysostom describes Pilate as "*beginning the examination over again.*" Similarly says Nonnus, but

---

[1] [2733 a] No mention has been previously made of Pilate's "fearing." Hence it would seem we must render "he was *rather* terrified [*than incensed against the prisoner as the Jews had hoped*]." Similarly, in v. 18, μᾶλλον ἐζήτουν αὐτὸν οἱ Ἰ. ἀποκτεῖναι does not mean "they sought *more [earnestly than before]* to kill him." For the previous context has made no mention of "killing," but only, v. 16 "*began to persecute* Jesus." Some MSS., it is true, after "persecute," add "and sought to slay him": but this is only because the scribes have misinterpreted μᾶλλον later on, which means "they *rather* sought to kill him [*than merely to persecute him as before*]." SS and Nonnus omit μᾶλλον in v. 18 and Nonnus (SS is wanting) in xix. 8.

more in detail, " He began to question Jesus the second time *in the customary language*, '*Who art thou* (τελέθεις)? *Whence art thou* (εἶ σύ)¹?'" The phrase "customary language" appears to mean that a magistrate would begin the examination, whether of a witness or of an accused person², by asking his name and domicile—as Minos asks that of Scipio Africanus, when the latter demands a hearing—"*Who and whence are you?*" Outside the Greek Testament, πόθεν εἶ does not seem to be used without τίς³, and σύ is not usually inserted. According to this view, Pilate—terrified rather than goaded into severity by the charge of the Jews "He made himself the Son of God"—may be seeking to gain time, and to find a way of releasing Jesus without irritating the Jews, by asking Jesus about His birth and domicile in the usual form, which he ought to have used at first⁴. This is a rational supposition. But in that case, it may be urged that Pilate would have said τίς καὶ πόθεν, according to Greek usage (and as Nonnus has it), and that he would not have inserted the superfluous σύ, which, in non-hebraic Greek, savours rather of familiarity, or contempt, or hatred, than of reverence, when used in questions or commands⁵.

¹ [2734 a] Ἰησοῦν δ' ἐρέεινε τὸ δεύτερον ἠθάδι μύθῳ, Τίς τελέθεις; πόθεν εἶ σύ;

² [2734 b] Lucian, *Dial. Mort.* xii. 7 MIN. Τίς γὰρ εἶ, ὦ βέλτιστε; ἢ πόθεν ὢν ἐρεῖς; ΣΚΗ. Ἰταλιώτης, Σκηπίων, στρατηγός.

³ [2734 c] Steph. quotes many instances such as Hom. *Il.* xxi. 150 τίς πόθεν εἰς ἀνδρῶν; Soph. *Phil.* 56 τίς τε καὶ πόθεν πάρει; also from Plato and later authors, but none of πόθεν εἶ without τίς. Rev. vii. 13 τίνες εἰσὶν καὶ πόθεν ἦλθον refers to those previously described as vii. 9 ἐκ παντὸς ἔθνους καὶ φυλῶν καὶ λαῶν καὶ γλωσσῶν, now brought into the City or Congregation of God.

⁴ [2734 d] Chrys. has Εἶτα Πιλᾶτος μὲν φοβεῖται...αὐτοὶ δὲ...οὐ πεφρίκασιν, ἀλλ' ἀναιροῦσιν αὐτὸν ὑπὲρ ὧν ἐχρῆν προσκυνεῖν, *i.e.* Pilate on the one hand "fears" instead of being incensed against Jesus; the Jews, on the other hand, desire to kill Him for the very reasons for which they should have done Him homage. There is perh. a latent reference to μᾶλλον ἐφοβήθη, *i.e.* to Pilate's feeling "fear," *rather than* desiring to kill Jesus as the Jews hoped. Chrys. continues, Διὰ τοῦτο οὐκέτι αὐτὸν ἐρωτᾷ, Τί ἐποίησας; ἀλλ' ἄνωθεν πάλιν, ὑπὸ τοῦ φόβου κατασειδόμενος, ποιεῖται τὴν ἐξέτασιν, λέγων, Εἰ σὺ εἶ ὁ Χριστός; ἀλλ' οὐκ ἀπεκρίνατο. The Latin of Chrys. renders ἄνωθεν "a sublimioribus," but ἀ. π. must mean here "all over again." Jn, however, does not contain the words εἰ σὺ εἶ ὁ Χριστός nor anything like them. Nor do the Synoptists attribute them to Pilate. Either Chrys. (or a scribe) has attributed to Pilate the words of the Highpriest (Mt. xxvi. 63 εἰ σὺ εἶ ὁ Χριστός) or the text is corrupt.

⁵ [2734 e] A superfluous σύ is freq. in Aristophanes after κάκιστε etc., and comp. Soph. *Phil.* 927 ὦ πῦρ σύ, Eurip. *And.* 261 ὦ βάρβαρον σὺ θρέμμα. When not required for sense *e.g.* after an imperative, it is either antithetical to another

[2735] NOTES ON PRECEDING PARAGRAPHS

[2735] In O.T., "Whence [art] thou (or [are] ye)?" is at least once distinguished from "Whence comest thou?" and means "What is thy birth and origin?" The Hebrew regularly omits the verb and inserts the pronoun, contrary to the Greek idiom. On two occasions the LXX inserts both verb and pronoun, thus mixing the two idioms. The question is from a superior to an inferior except when Jacob modifies it by adding "brethren[1]."

[2736] These facts shew that if Pilate recommenced his examination as Nonnus and Chrysostom suggest—a view that is favoured by Mark (xv. 4) who alone says "but Pilate began to question him *again* (πάλιν)"—he might begin with a question about the name and domicile of the accused, and that this, in Biblical Greek, might be expressed by πόθεν εἶ σύ; This might commend itself to John because of its inner and mystical meaning. Throughout his Gospel, πόθεν εἰμί and πόθεν ἔρχομαι refer to the Father from whom the Son was born and from whom He came[2].

---

pronoun, or emphatic as in vernacular English ("come here, *you* rascal"), or familiar. It does not appear to be used in reverential requests, *e.g.* with Ζεῦ, by the tragedians (**2776** *b*).

[1] [2735 *a*] Comp. Gen. xxix. 4 Ἀδελφοί, πόθεν ἐστὲ ὑμεῖς; οἱ δὲ εἶπαν, Ἐκ Χαρράν ἐσμεν, where the meaning may be "What is your country?" and the Heb. (as always) omits the verb, 1 S. xxx. 13 τίνος σὺ εἶ καὶ πόθεν εἶ (to a slave); 2 S. i. 13 πόθεν εἶ σύ; This last—since it follows i. 3 "Whence *comest* thou?"—would seem to mean, "*What is thy country and extraction?*" The man answers "I am the son of a stranger, an Amalekite." In Josh. ix. 8, "Who [are] ye and whence come ye?" LXX, through Heb. corruption, has πόθεν ἐστέ (Aq. τίς ὑμεῖς) καὶ πόθεν παραγεγόνατε; Philo i. 470 quotes Gen. xxix. 4 without ὑμεῖς.

[2] [2736 *a*] In the Synoptists, Christ is represented by Mt. as using πόθεν in connexion with John's baptism, xxi. 25 πόθεν ἦν; ἐξ οὐρανοῦ ἢ ἐξ ἀνθρώπων (where Mk-Lk. om. πόθεν, and Orig. Lomm. iii. 55 reads πότερον and elsewhere (Huet) omits ἐξ οὐρανοῦ ἤ, prob. by homoeotel.). In Mk, the people of Nazareth use it about Christ's powers, Mk vi. 2 πόθεν τούτῳ ταῦτα; The parall. Mt. xiii. 54, 56 uses it twice thus. Both Mk and Mt. mention in the context a discussion about Christ's parentage. Mk's two other uses of πόθεν are viii. 4 πόθεν......ἐπ' ἐρημίας; (Mt. xv. 33 πόθεν...ἐν ἐρημίᾳ), and Mk xii. 37 πόθεν αὐτοῦ ἐστιν υἱός; (Mt.-Lk. πῶς). In both, πόθεν might imply *impossibility*.

[2736 *b*] According to the usage of Epictetus, πόθεν τούτῳ; would imply a denial, "*This man could not possibly possess these powers.*" Comp. iii. 13. 12 πόθεν γὰρ αὐτῷ ταύτην [*i.e.* τὴν εἰρήνην] κηρύξαι; "for *what power has he to* preach peace?" iii. 21. 10 πόθεν σοι μεταδιδόναι τούτων ὧν οὐκ ἔχεις; "*what power have you* to impart to others things you don't yourself possess?" Sometimes πόθεν is without a verb, as in Epict. iii. 24. 70 "Who then has authority over me? Philip, or Alexander, or Perdiccas or the Great King? *Whence do they get* it (πόθεν αὐτοῖς)?" In i. 19. 9 a tyrant says "I will shew you that I am your lord," and

[2737] The evidence from Luke and from the *Acta Pilati*[1] indicates that John is not inventing a saying for Pilate but is utilising, in a form quite different from Luke's, a tradition that the Roman governor asked some question about Christ's origin.

---

the philosopher replies πόθεν σύ; and in iii. 1. 36 (see Schweig. Index) some MSS. read the nom. πόθεν γὰρ ἐκεῖνος, but the best MSS. have ἐκείνῳ.

[2736 c] In Jn, πόθεν is freq. used by Christ to express His coming from the Father, as in viii. 14 <u>οἶδα πόθεν ἦλθον καὶ ποῦ ὑπάγω, ὑμεῖς δὲ οὐκ οἴδατε πόθεν ἔρχομαι ἢ ποῦ ὑπάγω,</u> vii. 28 <u>κἀμὲ οἴδατε καὶ οἴδατε πόθεν εἰμί.</u> The Jews are represented as using the phrase about Jesus in a local sense, vii. 27 τοῦτον οἴδαμεν πόθεν ἐστίν (*i.e.* His native place). They proceed, ὁ δὲ Χριστὸς ὅταν ἔρχηται οὐδεὶς γινώσκει πόθεν ἐστίν (a phrase quite distinct from the one implying rejection or disowning in Lk. xiii. 25—7 (*bis*) οὐκ οἶδα ὑμᾶς πόθεν ἐστέ). How could they make this last statement in view of the Jewish belief that the Messiah was to be born in Bethlehem? *Hor. Heb.* (on vii. 27) refers to Jer. *Berach.* fol. 5. 1 and to other traditions asserting that the Messiah, after being born, was snatched away or hidden. *Sanhedr.* 97 a speaks of "Messiah, treasure-trove, and a scorpion" as three things that come when one does not think of them (comp. Lk. xvii. 20 "without observation"), and the Jew in Justin's Dialogue (*Tryph.* 8) mentions a belief that Messiah "if he is really born, is unknown and does not yet know his own self, or possess any power, till Elias shall anoint him." Traditions as to the material and local "whence" the Messiah was to come—on the clouds of heaven, or riding on an ass down from Mount Olivet, or, as Tacitus says, "from the East," or from Nazareth, or from Bethlehem—might so overshadow the spiritual "whence," that John might naturally desire to emphasize the latter.

[1] [2737 a] Luke, alone of the Synoptists, explains how such a question might have arisen. He represents the Jews as using, concerning the origin of the Christian heresy, the phrase (Lk. xxiii. 5) "*beginning from Galilee.*" On this, Pilate questions them and ascertains that Jesus came from the jurisdiction of *Herod* [*tetrarch of Galilee*]. A rival tradition (in which the three versions of the *Acta Pilati* (ix. 4) agree) says that the Jews mentioned, not *Galilee*, but "*Bethlehem*," as the implied birthplace, and mentioned Herod [*the King*] as having sought for the infant Jesus. Pilate questions them as to whether this was the Jesus whom "*Herod sought.*"

[2737 b] Mk, in his description of Christ's silence, has xv. 4 ὁ δὲ Π. πάλιν ἐπηρώτα αὐτὸν [λέγων] Οὐκ ἀποκρίνῃ οὐδέν; ἴδε <u>πόσα σου κατηγοροῦσιν</u> (without mention of previous silence). Mt., after mentioning Christ's silence, has xxvii. 13 τότε λέγει αὐτῷ ὁ Π., Οὐκ ἀκούεις <u>πόσα σου καταμαρτυροῦσιν</u>; but here B has οσα, D τοσα; the *Acta Pilati*—though reading τι ουτοι or τι οτι or "quid est quod isti" here (ii. 2)—have, later on (ix. 5) "*thine own nation, or race, hath convicted thee.*" This would agree with John, "*thine own nation...delivered thee up to me, what hast thou done?*" which Jn places at the beginning of the trial. Πόθεν, which often means "for what cause?" "from what motive?"—might very well come at the end of Pilate's words thus: "Dost thou not hear? Thine own people accuse thee? *Whence* [*is this*]?" If this were reported in the third person, καὶ ἐπηρώτα αὐτὸν πόθεν, or πόθεν ἦν, it might give rise to the tradition presented in different forms by Lk., Jn, and *Acta Pilati*.

But it is far from sufficient to shew that Pilate uttered the Johannine question. To understand its inner meaning we must go back to the last words of Pilate's previous dialogue with Jesus (xviii. 38) "*What is truth?*" and to the sequel—"Having said this he went out again." This does not imply (as Bacon assumes) that Pilate was "jesting"; but it does imply that "he did not stay for an answer." Though we may be unable to believe that Pilate uttered the words— at least in this abstract sense—it is easy to see the deep mystical meaning capable of being attached to them as representing the restless and unsatisfied scepticism of the upper classes of the Empire. The Roman world asks the Truth to reveal itself, and then, "goes out" from its presence without waiting for the revelation. Hence, afterwards, when it asks the Truth a second question, "*Whence art thou?*" the Truth is silent. The question and the silence are dramatically appropriate. But this very appropriateness—suggesting that the Son of God was judicially hidden from the eyes of the unjust judge—makes it likely that a symbolistic evangelist would accept on slight evidence a non-historic tradition, or interpretation of tradition, that lent itself to symbolism. This likelihood combines with the divergence and confusion of all the Gospel traditions at this point, and with the uncertainty as to the witnesses of the dialogue between Christ and Pilate, so as to make it impossible to feel sure that Pilate uttered the question in any sense at all—least of all in the sense "What is thy parentage, human or divine[1]?"

On xix. 17 Κρανίου Τόπον ὅ (2412)

[2738] In xix. 17 εἰς τὸν λεγόμενον Κρανίου Τόπον, ὃ λέγεται Ἑβραϊστὶ ⌜Γολγοθά⌝ (marg. Γολγόθ), some MSS. alter ὅ to ὅς, others omit ὃ λέγεται, and Blass (p. 77) would read Κρ. Τ., Ἑβρ. δὲ Γ. But the question is complicated by the fact that the same repetition

---

[1] [2737 c] The dialogue between Christ and Pilate is comparatively little quoted by early Christian writers and is given in a confused form, in parts almost amounting to a parody, by *Acta Pilati*. For example, Mk xv. 12 (Mt. xxvii. 22) τί οὖν ποιήσω; addressed by Pilate to the *Jews*, appears, in all three versions of the *Acta* (iv. 3), as addressed by him to *Jesus*, A τί ποιήσω σοι; (B) τί θέλεις ποιήσω σοι; Lat. "Quid faciam *tibi*?" Cyprian *Adv. Jud.* § 6 quotes xix. 15 thus "Ignoramus qui sit hic, non enim est rex noster: habemus alium regem Caesarem"—no doubt quoting from memory and perhaps blending ix. 29, but still giving us an insight into great possibilities of early confusion of the text. We have seen above (**2734** d) that perhaps even so late a writer as Chrysostom blends an utterance of Pilate with an utterance of the High Priest.

of λεγ. is found in Mt. xxvii. 33 εἰς τόπον λεγόμενον Γολγοθά, ὅ (al. ὅς) ἐστιν Κρανίου Τόπος λεγόμενος (D om. λεγόμενος) where Mk xv. 22 has ἐπὶ τὸν Γολγοθὰν τόπον (D τόπον Γολγοθά), ὅ ἐστιν ⌈μεθερμηνευόμενος⌉ (marg. and D -όμενον) Κρανίου Τόπος, but Lk. xxiii. 33 (omitting Γολγοθά) has simply ἐπὶ τὸν τόπον τὸν καλούμενον Κρανίον. Confusion seems to have arisen from the fact that the place was really called "Skull," but was known to many Christians as The Place of the Skull. The very extraordinary text in Mk (W.H. txt) seems to mean "to the place [called] Golgotha which [word] is Place of Skull rendered into [Hebrew]," making μεθερμηνευόμενος agree with τόπος! For the most part an Aramaic word would be put first, then ὅ ἐστιν, and then the Gk equivalent. But in xix. 17 the Greek comes first, and ὅ may refer either (1) to Κρανίου as a Gk neuter noun, or (2) to Κρανίου Τόπον regarded as a place-name and therefore as neuter. Having regard to the fact that this is a case where Lk. is omitting and Jn intervening to support Mk-Mt., we must be prepared for a mixture of traditions, and the safest plan seems to be to adopt W.H.'s txt, though we must leave in doubt the precise antecedent of ὅ. The repetition of λέγεται may indicate that the place was "(popularly) called (in Greek)" by one name and "(correctly) called in Hebrew" by another.

On ἄν and ἐάν interchanged (2414)

[2739] Since ὅς ἄν might be expressed by ἐάν τις, some writers might like, in the former phrase, to spell ἄν as ἐάν—thus emphasizing its conditional meaning and distinguishing it from ἄν in apodosis. On the other hand, writers that freely use ἄν (as in classical Greek) for "if" in protasis, would not recognise the use of this distinction. John, alone of writers of N.T., uses ἄν for "if"—almost, however, if not entirely, restricted to the phrase ἄν τις. As he also freely uses ἐάν τις, it may be presumed that he uses ἄν τις to express the condition with less emphasis, so as to approximate to ὅστις ἄν. Ἐάν after a relative occurs frequently in Mark and Matthew, but only in one passage of W.H.'s text of Luke (xvii. 33 ὅς ἐὰν ζητήσῃ... ὅς δ' ἂν ἀπολέσει). In John it occurs in xv. 7 ὅ ἐὰν θέλητε (ℵ ὅσα) and in xxi. 25. As to the latter, see 2414 on the question whether ἐάν means "if" or "soever[1]."

---

[1] [2739 a] In v. 19 "nothing, except," οὐδὲν, ἂν μή, W.H. read ἂν without altern. on the authority of ℵB, but in both MSS. ΟΥΔΕΝ comes at the end of the line, which, in their archetype, may very well have originally terminated with

[2740] NOTES ON PRECEDING PARAGRAPHS

On xvii. 2 πᾶν ὅ δέδωκας (2422)

[2740] In xvii. 2 δόξασόν σου τὸν υἱόν, ἵνα ὁ υἱὸς δοξάσῃ σέ, καθὼς

ογΔεε so that the second ε was dropped and ΑΝ at the beginning of the next line was supposed to mean "if." In xii. 32 W.H. read κἀγὼ ἂν ὑψωθῶ, without altern., on the authority of B alone, but there again ΑΝ comes at the end of the line. In the other instances, ἄν is followed by τις, xiii. 20, xvi. 23, xx. 23 (*bis*). In Acts ix. 2 ὅπως, ἐάν τινας, א reads ἄν at the end of a line. Chrys. quotes viii. 14 κἂν ἐγώ correctly, and then καὶ ἐὰν ἐγώ immediately afterwards. He also quotes vi. 62 as ἂν οὖν ἴδητε (W.H. ἐὰν οὖν θεωρῆτε).

[2739 *b*] As regards vi. 62 discussed in 2210—2, 2515, and just mentioned as misquoted by Chrys. (in Migne) as ἂν οὖν ἴδητε—it should be added that Cramer prints a version containing the context of Chrys. (τὸ τὰ ἀπόρρητα φέρειν εἰς μέσον) but having ἐάν with indic. pres., ἐὰν οὖν θεωρεῖτε. SS has "but [what] if *ye shall see*," and the Latin versions have "videritis." The indices give no reference to this passage in the works of Clement of Alexandria, or Origen. Nonnus has εἰ δέ κεν ἀθρήσητε...τί ῥέξετε τοῦτο μαθόντες; not only paraphrasing the protasis with an aorist subjunctive but also consistently supplying an apodosis in the future. These facts increase the uncertainty of interpretation. But it still remains probable that the difficult θεωρῆτε is the correct reading, corrupted by translators and commentators into something that gives a more intelligible and materialistic meaning than the evangelist himself intended. According to Johannine usage, ἐὰν θεωρῆτε should mean either "*if ye be at this moment* beholding," or "*if ye be found in the day of visitation* beholding."

[2739 *c*] An omission may be here supplied as to the Johannine use of ἄν with indic. in apodosis touched on in 2566 *b*. Outside Jn, Bruder (1888) gives *no instance of* ἄν *before a pause in N.T.*, the nearest approach being Mt. xxiv. 43 ἐγρηγόρησεν ἄν καὶ οὐκ ἂν εἴασεν...where Bruder inserts a comma after the first ἄν, but W.H. rightly omit it, and the parall. Lk. xii. 39 has in W.H. txt ἐγρηγόρησεν ἄν καὶ οὐκ ἀφῆκεν, but marg. simply οὐκ ἂν ἀφῆκεν. Jelf § 431, in a page on "the position of ἄν," gives no instance of ἄν at the end of a clause. But (*ib.* § 432) in a page on "the repetition of ἄν" he gives a large number of instances where it is repeated in order to emphasize the condition. In a few of these (not distinguished by Jelf from the rest) ἄν comes before a pause, Aesch. *Ag.* 340 οὐ τἂν...ἀνθαλοῖεν ἄν, Eur. *Hipp.* 961 τῆσδ' ἂν γένοιτ' ἄν, *Hec.* 359 ἴσως ἄν...τύχοιμ' ἄν. Jelf adds Plato 31 A ὑμεῖς δ' ἴσως τάχ' ἄν...κρούσαντες ἄν με...ῥᾳδίως ἂν ἀποκτείναιτε, εἶτα τὸν λοιπὸν βίον καθεύδοντες διατελοῖτ' ἄν. But there (εἶτα being equiv. to "and then") διατελοῖτ' ἄν seems to be parall. to ἂν ἀποκτείναιτε so that ἄν is not reduplicated. This passage, then, resembles xiv. 28 ἐχάρητε ἄν and xviii. 36 ἠγωνίζοντο ἄν quoted in 2566 *b* as placing a non-reduplicated ἄν at the end of a clause. No doubt there are other instances in Greek, but Jelf does not mention any and they are probably rare.

[2739 *d*] As regards the position of ἄν in viii. 19, xiv. 7 τὸν πατέρα μου ἂν ᾔδειτε (where Bruder, 1888, has ἄν final), it follows the rule (Jelf § 431. 2) that ἄν is generally joined to the predicate, as in ἔλεγον ἄν, or to "*that member of the sentence on which most emphasis is laid.*" What is peculiar to these two Johannine passages is that the "*member*" is not here a single word (as in οὐκ ἄν, πάλαι ἄν, τάχ' ἄν, ταῦτ' ἄν) but a phrase, τὸν πατέρα μου.

ἔδωκας αὐτῷ ἐξουσίαν πάσης σαρκός, ἵνα πᾶν ὃ δέδωκας αὐτῷ δώσει αὐτοῖς ζωὴν αἰώνιον, there are striking variations in the MSS., in Chrysostom, Nonnus, and Epiphanius, who repeatedly reads δός for δώσει¹. Origen's comment is lost; but elsewhere he blends xvii. 11 with xvii. 21 πάτερ ἅγιε, δὸς ἵνα... in a manner resembling the tradition of Epiphanius². Ὅ, πᾶν ὅ, and ὄνομα ὅ, with the aorist or perfect of "give," occur frequently in John, and seldom without important variations. Sometimes the neuter is changed to the masculine; or the clause about "giving," or the word "name," is omitted, so as to substitute "*he that* gave" for "*that which* he gave," "*those whom*

¹ [2740 a] W.H. have καθὼς ἔδωκας αὐτῷ ἐξουσίαν πάσης σαρκός, ἵνα πᾶν ὃ δέδωκας αὐτῷ δώσει αὐτοῖς ζωὴν αἰώνιον. Some MSS. read δωση, δωσω and δως. D has εχη for δώσει αὐτοῖς, and some conflation of these two readings (δως being spelt (2114) as δος) might give rise to a tradition δος εν [ε]αυτοις εχειν which Epiphanius (Resch) five times repeats (e.g. Epiph. 753 A *Haer*. lxix. 28 etc., φησὶ γοῦν ὁ κύριος· δὸς αὐτοῖς ζωὴν ἔχειν ἐν ἑαυτοῖς· αὕτη δέ ἐστιν ἡ αἰώνιος ζωή...).

[2740 b] Chrys. appears to quote xvii. 2 in two forms, of which the first is ἵνα πᾶν ὃ δέδωκας αὐτῷ μὴ ἀπόληται. But perhaps μὴ ἀπόληται is not a quotation but a preparatory paraphrase; "'*Even as thou gavest him authority over all flesh, that all that thou hast given him*'—may not perish, for to benefit is always 'glory' to God." Later on, having explained that "authority over all flesh" does not imply authority over those that refuse to believe, he resumes the text correctly thus, ἵνα πᾶν ὃ δέδωκας αὐτῷ δῷ αὐτοῖς ζωὴν αἰώνιον. But he proceeds to apologize for it, as it were, by saying that Jesus speaks here about Himself ἀνθρωπινώτερον, whereas the evangelist takes higher language. His meaning seems to be that Jesus says, in effect, "the Father hath given me eternal life," whereas John says "He *was* life," and "He *was* light." This implies the rendering "that all that He [the Father] hath given to Him [to the Son] He [the Son] may give to them—[*namely*] *eternal life*."

[2740 c] Nonnus has...ὡς πόρες αὐτῷ Σαρκὸς ὅλης βροτέης πρυμνήσιον ἡνιοχεύειν Βούλομαι εἰν ἑνὶ πάντας, ὅσοις πάρος ὤπασας αὐτός, Ζωὴν θεσπεσίην αἰώνιον ἀμφιπολεύειν Ὄφρα σε γινώσκωσι θεὸν μόνον... "I desire that in unity (εἰν ἑνί) all on whom thou thyself by preordinance (πάρος) hast bestowed it may follow after eternal life, in order that they may know...." Comp. xvii. 11 τήρησον αὐτοὺς ἐν τῷ ὀνόματί σου ᾧ [where he read οὕς] δέδωκάς μοι, which he paraphrases as φύλαξον ὁμόφρονας. The two passages suggest that Nonnus vaguely felt that these phrases about "giving" were connected with the unity of the Church and might be rendered by "at one" and "likeminded." Also, in xvii. 2 he seems to have read ᾧ δέδωκας αὐτό for ὃ δέδωκας αὐτῷ.

² [2740 d] Lomm. xiii. 304 πάτερ ἅγιε, δὸς ἵνα καθὼς ἐγὼ καὶ σὺ ἕν ἐσμεν (and sim. Lomm. xxv. 54) and xiv. 118, with "I ask" for "give," "Pater sancte, *rogo ut sicut ego*...." These quotations blend xvii. 11 with xvii. 21. They may have arisen from regarding ἵνα as meaning "Oh, that!" "Would that!" In xvii. 2, ἵνα following the imperat. δόξασον may have been taken as meaning ["Do this, I pray thee] in order that," or "[I desire that thou wouldest do this] in order that," and hence Nonnus may have rendered it Βούλομαι.

thou hast given" for "*that which* thou hast given" etc. Sometimes the word "give," sometimes the whole clause about "giving," is omitted. The Latin translations of Origen repeatedly exhibit these deviations; and even in Christ's utterance to the Samaritan woman "If thou knewest *the gift of God, and* who it is that saith unto thee, 'Give me to drink,'" the translation of Origen omits the italicised words[1].

[2741] Most unfortunately, Origen's Greek comment is missing on almost every one of the passages where this difficult phrase occurs. But textual evidence and antecedent probability support W.H. in retaining ὅ against ὅς and οὕς, and indicate that the phrase "*that which thou hast given me*," even when it denotes the Church, points back to the unity between the Father and the Son and to the unity between God and man. Origen, in his commentary on Romans (xvi. 20 "The grace of our Lord Jesus Christ"), says, "the grace of God and the grace of our Lord Jesus Christ is to be taken as one and the same, '*For as the Father maketh alive whom he will, the Son also* (et) *maketh alive whom he will*'; and '*As the Father hath life in himself, to the Son also* (et) *he hath given to have life in himself*': so also the grace that the Father gives the Son too gives": he adds, "Gratia ergo est, quicquid habet is, qui non fuit, et est, accipiens ab eo, qui semper fuit, et est, et erit in aeternum[2]."

[2742] These words of Origen's explain not only why the word "give" occurs more frequently in John than in the Synoptists but also why it is applied by him so frequently to the Father and to the Son. What "*grace*" is in the Pauline Epistles, "*giving*" is in the

---

[1] [2740 e] Comp. xvii. 24 πατήρ, ὃ δέδωκάς μοι, θέλω ἵνα ὅπου εἰμὶ ἐγὼ κἀκεῖνοι ὦσιν μετ' ἐμοῦ, a very difficult passage but susceptible of a mystical rendering (2741). The words ὃ δέδωκάς μοι are omitted in the Latin transl. of Origen in Lomm. vi. 393, vii. 92, x. 265, 370, xi. 155, xii. 231, (?) xv. 82 : xvii. 12 ἐτήρουν αὐτοὺς ἐν τῷ ὀνόματί σου ᾧ δέδωκάς μοι καὶ ἐφύλαξα καὶ οὐδεὶς ἐξ αὐτῶν ἀπώλετο εἰ μή..., is rendered (Lomm. vi. 104) "Omnes, inquit, quos dedisti mihi servavi et nullus ex eis periit...": iv. 10 εἰ ᾔδεις τὴν δωρεὰν τοῦ θεοῦ καὶ τίς ἐστιν is (vi. 199) "Si scires quis est...."

[2] [2741 a] Origen here blends Jn v. 21 and v. 26 (Lomm. vii. 448). According to this view, if χάρις is received only by a human being ("qui non fuit et est"), as distinct from a divine one, we might expect some evangelists to prefer not to use such expressions as Lk. ii. 40, 52 about Christ, although Origen accepts and explains them as applying to Christ's human nature. Jn and Lk., alone of the evangelists, use χάρις. And both apply it to Christ. But they apply it very differently (1775).

Fourth Gospel. The Father is represented above as "giving" to the Son "*to have life in himself*" and also the power of "making alive." That which the Son "*makes alive*" is the Church. The Father, therefore, virtually "*gives*" the Church to the Son. Elsewhere, it is implied that the Father has "given" His "*name*" to the Son (xvii. 12 "thy name that thou hast given me"), that is, the essential being of the true Son of God. This implies unity with the Father ("I and the Father are one" etc.) and the possession of the love of the Father (xv. 10 "ye will abide in my love...I abide in his love," xvii. 26 "that the love wherewith thou lovedst me may be in them and I in them"). There is also a gift of peace, a peace above the peace of the world ("My peace I give unto you—not as the world giveth"). When, therefore, the Son prays to the Father for the disciples "Keep them *in thy name that thou hast given me*," He means "keep them in thy love and peace, at one with me, as I am with thee[1]."

---

[1] [2742 a] The "*giving*" of the Father to the Son is connected with the following nouns or phrases:—iii. 34 "the Spirit," iii. 35 "all things," v. 22 "all judgment," v. 26 "to have life in himself," v. 27 "authority to do judgment," v. 36 "the works that the Father hath given me," vi. 37 "all that the Father is giving (or, giveth) to me," vi. 39 "all that he hath given to me," x. 29 (W.H. txt) "my Father, that which he hath given to me," xii. 49 "He (αὐτός) himself hath given me commandment what I should say," xiii. 3 "the Father gave all things into his hands," xiv. 31 "even as the Father gave me commandment" (following the words "that the world may know that I love the Father"). Here Tisch. and Alf. read ἐνετείλατό μοι with ADא. Nonnus, too—who in xii. 49 has ζείδωρον ἔχω παρὰ πατρὸς ἐφετμήν—has here κυβερνητῆρι πατὴρ ἐπετέλλετο μύθῳ. It is certainly strange that no MSS. should alter "give commandment" in xii. 49 and that so many should alter it here. But ἐνετείλατο so distinctly means the commandment of a law-giver or master (*e.g.* Mk xiii. 34) that it is difficult to believe that John could have used it here.

[2742 b] There remain the instances in the Last Prayer:—xvii. 2 "thou gavest him authority over all flesh," *ib.* "that all that thou hast given to him he should give to them eternal life," *ib.* 4 "having perfected the work that thou hast given to me that I might do it," *ib.* 6 "the men that thou gavest me out of the world ...thine they were and thou gavest them to me," *ib.* 7 "all things as many as thou gavest (marg. hast given) me are from thee," *ib.* 8 "the words that thou gavest (marg. hast given) me," *ib.* 9 "I ask...about them that thou hast given me," *ib.* 11 "keep them in my name that thou hast given me," *ib.* 12 "I was keeping them in thy name that thou hast given me," *ib.* 22 "the glory that thou hast given me," *ib.* 24 "Father, that which (ὅ) thou hast given me, I will that where I am they also may be with me," *ib.* 24 "that they may be beholding the glory that is mine [the glory] that thou hast given (marg. gavest) to me," xviii. 9 "those whom thou hast given me I have not lost [a single] one (οὐδένα) of them" (referring to xvii. 12), *ib.* 11 "the cup that the Father hath given me." There is nothing

[2743] Nonnus paraphrases the words "the Father hath life in himself" as "provideth the *all-motherly life of the world* (παμμήτορα κόσμου ζωήν)," an epithet applied to the Earth by Æschylus (*Prom.* 90) and Philo. As the Psalmist says (Ps. cxlv. 16) "Thou openest thy hand and satisfiest the desire of every living thing," so Philo (i. 32) says that the poets were right to call the earth "All-mother," and that "Nature has bestowed on her, as being the most ancient and fruitful of mothers, the streams of rivers and fountains, *like breasts*,"—a saying that would appeal to worshippers of the "many-breasted" image of "Diana of the Ephesians." Another epithet of the earth was Pandora, the All-giver, applied by Philo to the earth in the passage just quoted, and by Cleanthes (in the masculine) to Zeus. In the Sermon on the Mount, our Lord refers to the Father as the Giver of the sunshine and the rain. Elsewhere He speaks of the Father as giving (Mt. vii. 11) "good gifts" to them that ask Him. For "good gifts" the parallel in Luke (xi. 13) substitutes "the Holy Spirit." John (iv. 10) speaks of "the gift of God," meaning "the living Water," which must be interpreted as the Holy Spirit. The Spirit, as being God's "gift," and "the gifts of the Spirit," are mentioned throughout the Epistles. When John describes the Father as "giving" the bread of heavenly life and the water of the Holy Spirit to men, and also as giving life in Himself, and in His Name, to the Son, he appears to be attempting to raise his readers above formal notions about "grace (χάρις)" and "reward (μισθός)," into a high spiritual sphere where God is regarded not only as the All-giver, but also as the Self-giver, so that "that which he hath given" to the Son means not only this or that divine attribute, but the Pleroma or Fulness, of all the divine attributes,—the Father giving His own Fulness to the Son, and, through the Son, dispensing gifts from His Fulness to men. This language would be intelligible to Greeks as well as Jews and would avoid the notion of "*favouritism*" suggested by the word "grace" or "favour" in Greek[1].

---

like this in the Synoptists exc. Mt. xxviii. 18 "all authority is given to me in heaven and upon the earth."

[1] [2743 a] Epictetus, like John, prefers to speak of God as "giving" rather than to speak of His grace or χάρις. He twice (i. 16. 15 Schweig. n. "beneficia," ii. 23. 2) uses the pl. (as Philo does, **2285** *b*, *c*) to mean God's "gifts" to man; but he much more frequently uses the sing. and then it almost always means "gratitude" (mostly from man to God), *e.g.* iii. 5. 10 νῦν με θέλεις ἀπελθεῖν ἐκ τῆς πανηγύρεως; ...χάριν σοι ἔχω πᾶσαν ὅτι ἠξίωσάς με συμπανηγυρίσαι σοι. On the doctrine that

[2744] If this was John's meaning, we can understand why he may have in some cases strained the Greek language to suggest, without too sharply defining, all that the Son of God implied when He spoke of the Father as "*giving.*" For example, x. 29 ὁ πατήρ μου ⌜ὃ δέδωκέν μοι πάντων μεῖζόν ἐστιν⌝, if it refers to the Church as being the new-created Cosmos, may mean that the Church includes (and is therefore "greater than") all things, or superior to all enemies. But it may also refer to the redeeming Love of the Father—to the (Eph. iii. 18—19) "breadth and length and height and depth" of the love of God in Christ "which passeth knowledge," by which the Church is "filled unto all the fulness of God." At the same time it suggests the Father as a Fountain of Giving—"*The Father, that which hath given to me*"—a Being that desires to be known as "the Being that gives[1]." We can also understand how some found difficulty in the thought as well as in the Greek. The reception of gifts, they may have said, is "grace"; and then they may have added, with Origen (**2741**), "Grace, or the reception of gifts, belongs to *man, who once was not, and now is* (qui non fuit, et est)—receiving from Him that ever was and is and shall be to all eternity." The inference followed that Christ was *not* to be regarded as a recipient of "gifts[2]." This, as well as the crabbed Greek, may have caused the corruption of the

---

"a man has nothing that he has not received from God" no Christian teacher can be more fervid (iv. 1. *103*) "And after all this, canst thou—having received everything from Another, yea, even thine own self's self (καὶ αὐτὸν σεαυτόν)—canst thou, I say, chafe against and chide *Him that gave* (τὸν δόντα) if He take aught away from thee? Who art thou [to dare this]? And for what hast thou come [into this world]? Did not *He* (ἐκεῖνος) bring thee on the stage (εἰσήγαγεν)? Did not *He* shew thee the light? Did He not *give* thee fellow-workers? Senses? Reason? And in what character did He bring thee on the stage (ὡς τίνα δὲ εἰσήγαγεν;)? Was it not as a mortal?...Art thou not willing, then, after beholding the procession for as long a time as *hath been given* to thee...to depart with homage and thankfulness for the things thou hast heard and seen?"

[1] [**2744***a*] For example, in xvii. 24 "Father, *that which thou hast given me*, I desire that where I am they also may be with me," it seems probable that the italicised words mean something more than "as for that portion of the human race which thou hast given me." They suggest a spiritual conception that puts the reader on his guard against supposing that "*with me*" means "*in the same place with me*," instead of meaning in the unity of the Giver and the Receiver, the Father and the Son.

[2] [**2744***b*] Comp. Eph. iv. 8 "Having ascended on high...*he gave* gifts to men." This is from Ps. lxviii. 18 "Thou hast *received* gifts among men," LXX ἔλαβες δόματα ἐν ἀνθρώπῳ. The Targum however paraphrases with St Paul (Walton) "Docuisti verba Legis, *dedisti* dona filiis hominum."

[2745] NOTES ON PRECEDING PARAGRAPHS

Johannine doctrine expressed in πᾶν ὃ δέδωκε, which teaches that it is the glory of the Son to receive everything from God and to give everything to man[1].

On vi. 5 πόθεν ἀγοράϲωμεν (v.r. -ομεν). (2428)

[2745] Chrysostom, after explaining why Christ selected Philip as the disciple to be questioned, drops *"buy"* and inserts *"so many"* in the question thus, " And see what He saith (καὶ ὅρα τί φησιν ἐκεῖνος), *Whence [can there come] to us so many loaves that these may eat* (πόθεν ἡμῖν ἄρτοι τοσοῦτοι ἵνα φάγωσιν οὗτοι;)?" Later on he describes *the disciples* as having been, at first, so unbelieving as to say, "*Whence shall we buy loaves* (πόθεν ἀγοράσομεν ἄρτους;)?"—words that occur nowhere in N.T. except in vi. 5 (v.r.), which assigns them to *Christ*[2].

---

[1] [2744 c] In support of the masc. reading οὕς in xvii. 12 ἐτήρουν αὐτοὺς ἐν τῷ ὀνόματί σου <u>οὕς</u> (for W.H. <u>ᾧ</u>) δέδωκάς μοι...καὶ οὐδεὶς ἐξ αὐτῶν ἀπώλετο...it may be urged that Jn himself refers to the words thus xviii. 9 "the word that he said, '*Those whom* (οὕς) thou hast given me I have lost (ἀπώλεσα) not one of them.'" To this however it may be replied that, if the quotation had been intended to be exact, ἀπώλετο would have been repeated. It is not exact. It refers to the general tenor of Christ's prayer for His disciples (xvii. 1—26) in which ὧν δέδωκας, ὃ δέδωκας, ᾧ δέδωκας, and ἃ δέδωκας occur in connexion with His thought of them. In particular, John may be referring to xvii. 9—12 ἐρωτῶ...περὶ ὧν δέδωκάς μοι...ὅτε ἤμην μετ' αὐτῶν ἐγὼ ἐτήρουν αὐτούς...καὶ οὐδεὶς ἐξ αὐτῶν ἀπώλετο. Nonnus paraphrases xviii. 9 as Τούτων οὐδὲν ὄλωλα (v.r. -λε) τά μοι πόρες, and xvii. 12 as Αὐτὸς ὅλους ἐφύλασσον ἀπήμονας· οὐδέ τις αὐτῶν [Οὓς πόρες υἱέϊ σοῦ βροτέης σωτῆρι γενέθλης] Ὤλετο. He appears, as elsewhere, to have taken "in thy name, which thou hast given me" to mean vaguely "in peace and unity" (which he expressed by "whole and entire, unharmed"). An interpolator has added something about "giving"—"which thou didst give to thy Son the Saviour of the race of mortals."

[2] [2745 a] Chrys. says, in the context, (1) "The other evangelists say that the disciples came to [Jesus] and questioned and besought so that He should *not* send them away fasting (ἐρωτᾶν καὶ παρακαλεῖν ὥστε μὴ ἀπολῦσαι αὐτοὺς νήστεις): but this one [John] introduces [the fact] that Philip was asked by Christ (οὗτος δὲ εἰσάγει τὸν Φ. ἐρωτηθῆναι παρὰ τοῦ Χριστοῦ)." (2) Then, after assigning to Christ the question, " *Whence [are there]* to us so many loaves that these may eat?" he proceeds, "So also in the Old Testament He said to Moses. For He did not work the sign till He had asked him, *What ever* (τί ποτε) *is in thy hand?*" Here we should have expected a reference to the question of Moses (Numb. xi. 13) " *Whence [is there] to me* flesh to give to all this people?" But he quotes Ex. iv. 2 " *What is this* (τί τοῦτό ἐστιν) in thine hand?"—which does not seem to apply to anything in the Feeding of the Five Thousand (unless it refers to the tradition peculiar to Mk vi. 38 "*How many loaves have ye?*" comp. 1 S. xxi. 3 "Now therefore what is *under thine hand? Give me five loaves*....") (3) Chrys. continues, "And having been asked he answereth (καὶ ἐρωτηθεὶς ἀποκρίνεται) saying, *Loaves of [the value of] two hundred denarii suffice not that each should take a little*. But this he said tempting him, for he himself knew what he was intending to do."

Nonnus has "*buy*" (in a different word—πριάμεσθα, not ἀγοράσωμεν) but introduces "*so many*" in connexion, not with the loaves, but with the people, "whence are we [to be] buying an abundance of loaves *for so many men* (τοσσατίοισιν)?"

[2746] Origen nowhere quotes vi. 5. Nor does he refer to Christ's question about "buying"—though he refers more than once to "buying food," on the part of the disciples, as signifying the attempt (and failure) to obtain spiritual truth[1]. He certainly regarded the bread in the Feeding of the Five Thousand as having a Eucharistic meaning, and as signifying the flesh or body of Christ. But, if he accepted, as Christ's, the question, "*Whence are we to buy loaves?*" he would probably interpret it as mystically meaning (in accordance with a frequent meaning (2736 *a, b*) of "Whence?") that *the Bread could not be bought*. It was bread stamped with the sign of the Cross, or imbued with its savour, *given* by the Lamb of God "without price[2]."

On the non-use of some active perfects (2441 *a*)

[2747] The best illustration of the non-use of active perfects, as compared with the use of passives, is to be found in κτίζω "create,"

There can be no doubt that "he said" here means "*He* said," that is, Christ. But the extract, with the words so strangely transposed, shews how easily "said, tempting him," might form part of a tradition that Philip or some other disciple "tempted" Christ, by questioning Him as Moses questioned God. In "so that He should *not* send them away fasting," μή seems to be a corrupt insertion: "The disciples, *in effect*, said to Christ, 'Send them away fasting.'" Or else Chrys. has attributed to the disciples the expression of Christ's own feeling, "I am unwilling to send them away fasting." This commentary—which is the earliest we possess on the Johannine miracle—must be described as chaotic.

[1] [2746 *a*] Origen on Mt. xiv. 15 represents Christ as saying to the disciples, in effect, "These people *have need of me*, not of food from the villages." A little before this, he speaks of "the bread" and "the cup" of the Lord, and illustrates Christ's healing of the sick before the miracle, by reference to 1 Cor. xi. 30 "For this cause [i.e. *desecration of the Eucharist*] *many of you are weak and sickly*." When the disciples abandon Jesus near Sychar, Origen says (on iv. 8) that they had gone into the city "to buy food or [in other words]—having found agreeable food among the heterodox—doctrines of a sort that suited them (λόγους τινὰς ἁρμόζοντας)."

[2] [2746 *b*] Comp. Clem. Alex. 75—6 on Is. lv. 1 "without price," where the bastard or son of perdition is said to "buy for money" what the true child of God receives "without price," created by God for the child's "*eucharistic banquets* (ταῖς εὐχαρίστοις τρυφαῖς)." A connexion between the Bread and the Cross was traced from the LXX of Jer. xi. 19 "let us cast wood into his bread," ἐμβάλωμεν ξύλον εἰς τὸν ἄρτον αὐτοῦ, by Origen (*ad loc.*) as well as by Justin Martyr (*Tryph.* 72). Origen illustrates it by the wood cast by Moses into the bitter water.

applied to the Creator throughout the whole of the Greek Testament and *frequently used in the perfect passive*, ἔκτισται¹, but *never in the active*, ἔκτικα. Prof. Jannaris (*Gk Gr.* p. 189) gives ἔκτικα, without reference. L.S. give "κέκτικα Diod." Diod. Sic. Index gives no such instance. But Steph. gives "Perf. κεκτικέναι τὴν Ῥώμην ap. Diodor. (ex Georg. Syncell.) vol. 2, p. 636, 67." This may be corrupt, but it is instructive. The rule is that when a verb begins with κτ the perfect should begin with εκτ: but it is broken with κτάομαι. Whoever wrote κεκτικέναι may have thought himself entitled to break it with κτίζω. All other Greek writers (so far as Steph. alleges) appear to have left the active perfect of κτίζω alone. And yet there are abundant cases in LXX where the passive perfect is used and where the active perfect would have been, though not necessary, at all events suitable, as in Ps. lxxxix. 12 "*Thou hast created* the north and the south*,*" where the LXX has ἔκτισας.

[2748] Take also ζητέω and ὁρίζω. Veitch quotes Dinarchus for ἐζήτηκα—non-occurrent in Aristoph., Demosth., Aristot., O.T., N.T. and Steph., though the latter mentions ζητεῖται and ἐζήτηται as frequent in scholiasts. Its use by Dinarchus accords with the unfavourable judgment pronounced on him by Dionysius. The active perfect of ὁρίζω occurs once in Demosth. (doubtful), once in Aristot., never in N.T.; the passive perfect is frequent².

[2749] In support of the statement that "the perfect sometimes stands for the aorist even in *A* [i.e. Classical Antiquity]" Jann. p. 439 quotes (*a*) "Thuc. i. 21 οὔτε ὡς ποιηταὶ ὑμνήκασι...οὔτε ὡς λογογράφοι ξυνέθεσαν," (*b*) "Demosth. 7, 29 τὴν χώραν ἣν οἱ Ἕλληνες καὶ βασιλεὺς ὁ Περσῶν ἐψηφίσαντο καὶ ὡμολογήκασιν ὑμετέραν εἶναι," and, for post-classical Greek, (*c*) "Polyb. iii. 1. 2 ἐν τῇ τρίτῃ βύβλῳ" (Schweig. βίβλῳ) "δεδηλώκαμεν· ὁμοίως δὲ καὶ τὰς αἰτίας ἐν αὐτῇ ἐκείνῃ διεσαφήσαμεν." But, in (*a*), the perf. expresses the permanent works of the ancient poets regarded as a present possession for their posterity, while the aorist refers to comparatively recent compilations, with perhaps a special allusion (Classen) to Herodotus. In

---

¹ [2747 *a*] Comp. *Col.* i. 16 ἐν αὐτῷ ἐκτίσθη τὰ πάντα...τὰ πάντα...εἰς αὐτὸν ἔκτισται. The distinction here drawn between "*were* created" and "*have been* created" might (it would seem) be just as logically made between "thou *didst create*" and "thou *hast created.*" But it is not made anywhere in the Gk Test. by the use of the act. perf. of κτίζω.

² [2748 *a*] As an instance of variation, note the abnormal perf. in Eurip. *Iph. Aul.* 595 ἐβλαστήκασι, but the normal pluperf. in Thuc. iii. 26 ἐβεβλαστήκει.

(b),—beside the fact that the perf. of ψηφίζομαι in active sense (Steph.) appears to be extremely rare or non-existent—the aorist of ψ. naturally expresses *past* decrees, and the perf. ὡμολογήκασιν the resultant, permanent, and *present* agreement. In (c), there is no reason for saying that Polybius uses δεδηλώκαμεν for ἐδηλώσαμεν[1]. It would be less misleading to say that, as the perf. act. of διασαφέω was very rare (in Steph. it is non-existent) and the aorist very frequent, he used *the aorist,* διεσαφήσαμεν, *for the perfect,* διασεσαφήκαμεν. But we may give both tenses their several value thus: "I *have indicated* above...and similarly I *clearly shewed.*" In English, we should often prefer to use the past thus, after the complete present; and Polybius, too, may have preferred it.

[2750] Again, Jann. p. 439 alleges from Mt. xiii. 46, and Hermas, "and so on in all post-Christian compositions," a number of perfects, including πέπρακε, "he sold," to illustrate "the full development of this usage" of the perfect for the aorist "during the latter part of *G* [the Graeco-Roman period]." But πιπράσκω *never had an active aorist from the beginning of Greek literature*—so that the use of its perfect as aorist cannot prove "development."

[2751] Jann. p. 439 also refers, for further illustrations of this "development," to "Hebr. 11, 17. Cp. John 4, 6. 6, 3. 6, 9." In iv. 6, κεκοπιακώς means "being completely tired out." In vi. 3, ἐκάθητο is not a perfect and has no manifest bearing on the point; the other reference is perhaps a misprint. In Heb. xi. 17 πίστει προσενήνοχεν Ἀβραὰμ τὸν Ἰσαὰκ πειραζόμενος, καὶ τὸν μονογενῆ προσέφερεν, the contrast between the perfect and the imperfect is most instructive. The perf. means that Abraham, through God's guidance, *has offered up* the typical sacrifice just as Moses (Heb. xi. 28) "*has instituted* (πεποίηκεν)" the typical Passover, and it is one of many perfects (see Westc. on Heb. vii. 6 δεδεκάτωκεν) shewing that the writer regarded Biblical events as *present* possessions for those who accept the Bible as God's word. See 2758.

[2752] Jann. p. 439 alleges only one instance of the "perf. for aorist" from LXX, "Ex. xxxii. 1 καὶ ἰδὼν ὁ λαὸς ὅτι κεχρόνικε Μωϋσῆς καταβῆναι ἐκ τοῦ ὄρους, ἀνέστη" (Swete συνέστη) "ὁ λαὸς ἐπὶ Ἀαρών."

---

[1] [2749 a] In English we should more often say "I *have shewn* above that this is the case" than "I shewed." Demosthenes (Preuss) uses δεδήλωκα five times, never ἐδήλωσα. The Index to Polybius gives ii. 22. 11 δεδηλώκαμεν but no instance of ἐδηλώσαμεν.

[2753] NOTES ON PRECEDING PARAGRAPHS

This might have been illustrated by Tob. x. 4 where Tobit's mother says to her husband, ἀπώλετο τὸ παιδίον διότι κεχρόνικεν "He must be dead because *he has been [so] long [away]*," i.e. "he is putting off his coming" (comp. *ib.* ix. 4 "my father counteth the days"). Here the perf. is clearly *not* used for an aorist but rather for a *present*. A close examination of Ex. xxxii. 1 shews that the perf. is there, too, used rather as a present than an aorist, somewhat like Jn vi. 24 ὅτε οὖν εἶδεν ὁ ὄχλος ὅτι Ἰησοῦς οὐκ ἔστιν ἐκεῖ (**2466** (i)). Ex. xxxii. 1 means, in effect, "When the people saw [what was happening and said] Moses *is disappointing us*, or, *not keeping to his time*[1]."

[2753] These details have been discussed in order to shew the futility of the attempt to judge Johannine by Byzantine Greek (in which the perfect is unquestionably sometimes used for the aorist). In criticizing the Fourth Gospel, credit must be given by the critic to the evangelist for a careful use of tense forms above, not below, the average of Greek authors. John may occasionally use an aorist where Englishmen would use a perfect or a pluperfect: but such uses will be found to be in accord with the rules of contemporary Greek, written or vernacular. And the notion that he "uses" one Greek tense "for" another Greek tense must be shunned as an *ignis fatuus*[2].

---

[1] [2752 *a*] So Buhl 97 *a* "beschämt machen." Gesen. Oxf. 101 *b* "delay in shame." Jer. Targ. adds "when they saw that the time he had appointed to them had passed."

[2] [2753 *a*] These facts illustrate such passages as xii. 19 ἴδε, ὁ κόσμος ὀπίσω αὐτοῦ ἀπῆλθεν (R.V.) "Lo, the world is gone after him," where the rendering "*is gone*" may seem to demand ἀπελήλυθεν, so that, if R.V. is right, some might say "here we have a case where Jn uses one Gk tense for another." Certainly, it can hardly be maintained that the Pharisees mean "the whole of Jerusalem *went after him [a few hours ago when he rode into the City]*": but the following facts shew that Jn could not have said ἀπελήλυθεν because, besides being extremely rare, it had acquired a special meaning, which would have been unsuitable here.

[2753 *b*] Ἀπελήλυθα *does not occur once, in any form of the indicative perfect, in the whole of Aristophanes and Demosthenes*. The Oxf. Conc., amid more than three columns of different forms of ἀπέρχομαι, gives (as far as I have found) *no form* of ἀπελήλυθα *except in* 2 S. iii. 22—4 "He [*i.e.* David] had sent him [*i.e.* Abner] away and he had gone away (ἀπελήλυθει) in peace..., they told Joab saying, 'Abner...came to the king, and he hath sent him away (ἀπέσταλκεν) and he *went away* (ἀπῆλθεν) in peace.' Then Joab came to the king and said, 'What hast thou done...Why is it that thou hast sent him away (ἐξαπέσταλκας, *sent him right away*) and *he is quite gone* (ἀπελήλυθεν ἐν εἰρήνῃ)?'" Here (besides repeating "in peace," which does not bear upon the point in question) the LXX clearly uses

On the "gnomic" aorist (2445 a)

[2754] Jelf § 402. 1 says that the aorist "is used to express an action which took place repeatedly in past time," and goes on to say that "the imperfect also has an iterative force." I should prefer to say that the so-called "gnomic" aorist tells the hearer simply and indefinitely that "so-and-so *happened*," leaving him to take the hint and to *infer* that it will happen again. *This "gnomic," "empiric," or "suggestive" aorist is quite different from the aorist of instantaneousness.*

[2755] Special contexts, however, may make it doubtful whether an aorist is "*gnomic*" or "*instantaneous.*" Thus Jann. p. 436 places under empiric or gnomic aorists, and Jelf § 403. 2 under aorists that "express future events which must certainly happen," Demosth. 20, 9 which describes how, when a tyrant has attained power through

---

the perf. ἀπελήλυθεν emphatically to represent the emphatic Hebrew (lit.) "*going hath gone,*" i.e. "*is quite gone,*" or "*gone for good,*" "*gone past recall.*" [For the same reason the LXX puts into Joab's mouth ἐξαπέσταλκας "*sent him right away*" as compared with the preceding ἀπέσταλκεν "sent him away"—a distinction not in the Hebrew.]

[2753 c] As to N.T., though various forms of ἀπέρχομαι occupy more than two columns of Bruder, *no form of ἀπελήλυθα occurs except in* Jas i. 24 κατενόησεν γὰρ ἑαυτὸν καὶ ἀπελήλυθεν rendered by Mayor "just a glance and *he is off,*" where the perf. expresses the completeness of the action as well as the suddenness of it—"he *is gone for good.*" Compare the Demosthenic use of ἐξέρχομαι; it occurs frequently in the aorist indic. but only once (Preuss) in the perf. indic. (xxiii. 204) concerning the good old habit of punishing the guilty, which ἐξελήλυθεν ἐκ τῆς πόλεως, "*has quite vanished* out of the City."

[2753 d] In xii. 19 ἀπῆλθεν, SS has "goeth," Nonnus ὀδεύει, ff "sequitur,"—indicating that the translators felt (as it was right to feel) that the aorist had more than the usual aorist meaning. Ἀπελήλυθεν being out of the question, Jn has used ἀπῆλθεν as the best Gk writers often use the aorist to include a meaning that would be expressed in English by "*have.*" Similarly our English aorist ("I saw") includes meanings that would be expressed in French by a perfect ("I *saw him* yesterday," "je *l'ai vu* hier "). But we should not admit that such a use of "I saw" was "using one tense for another." It is our regular tense in such circumstances.

[2753 e] In xii. 19 ἴδε, ὁ κόσμος, SS, DL, latt., Nonnus, and other authorities, add ὅλος. Chrys. does not. But he *calls attention to the fact that κόσμος is here used in the sense of ὄχλος.* Possibly this may explain the remarkable prevalence of the interpolated ὅλος. Ὄχλος may have been first placed in the margin, or above the line, as an explanation of κόσμος. Then it may have been introduced into the text so as to give ὁ κόσμος ὄχλος—in which ὄχλος was afterwards corrected to ὅλος. Comp. Oxf. Conc. on 2 Macc. vi. 3 (R) ὄχλοις (A, as in Swete, ὅλοις). This view is confirmed by the reading of ff, "ecce *unus populus* sequitur post illum," "*the multitude as one man.*"

[2756] NOTES ON PRECEDING PARAGRAPHS

villainy, ἡ πρώτη πρόφασις καὶ μικρὸν πταῖσμα ἄπαντα ἀνεχαίτισε καὶ διέλυσεν. This should be compared with 24, 21 which says that, while a state is waging a distant war, ἀφανῆ τὰ κακὰ τοῖς πολλοῖς ἐστιν, ἐπειδὰν δὲ ὅμορος πόλεμος συμπλακῇ πάντα ἐποίησεν ἔκδηλα. Probably the aorist in both passages is not "gnomic." It does not however seem to indicate certainty so much as instantaneousness; and this is confirmed by many other instances of the aorist in apodosis. The essence of the "gnomic" aorist is that it expresses *nothing but indefinite past action*. When the protasis *defines the circumstances of the action, e.g.* by a clause with ὅταν, the aorist in the apodosis cannot be "gnomic"—if "gnomic" (2754) implies an indefinite "happened." Consequently after a ὅταν clause, an aorist, if it occurs where a present might have been expected, may be used to denote instantaneousness[1]. It is therefore possible that the instantaneous aorist in xv. 6 ἐβλήθη, being preceded by the protasis ἐὰν μή τις, may not be Hebraic, though it is in accordance with Hebraic Greek. But, in any case, the purely gnomic aorist of the type of *Il.* ix. 320 κάτθαν' ὁμῶς ὅ τ' ἀεργὸς ἀνὴρ ὅ τε πολλὰ ἐοργώς is certainly alien from the style of O.T. and N.T. and probably non-occurrent in the latter.

On xii. 14 εὑρών...ὀνάριον **(2461)**

[2756] The Diatessaron omits the whole of the clause about Christ's finding the ass. SS omits *"finding"* ("Now Jesus was riding on [an ass]"). Origen (Lomm. i. 316 foll.) points out that the Johannine and the Synoptic accounts are, according to the letter, inconsistent: but both he and Chrys. mention the "finding" by Christ; and Chrys. tries to reconcile it with the Synoptic account[2].

---

[1] [2755 a] Comp. the following passages where a protasis with ὅταν, εἰ etc., defines the circumstances: (a) Eurip. *Med.* 130 μείζους δ' ἄτας ὅταν ὀργισθῇ δαίμων οἴκοις ἀπέδωκεν, (b) *ib.* 245 ἀνὴρ δ' ὅταν τοῖς ἔνδον ἄχθηται ξυνών, ἔξω μολὼν ἔπαυσε καρδίαν ἄσης, (c) *Il.* xvii. 99 ὁππότ' ἀνὴρ ἐθέλῃ...τάχα οἱ μέγα πῆμα κυλίσθη, (d) *Il.* ix. 413 εἰ μέν κ' αὖθι μένων...ἀμφιμάχωμαι, ὤλετο μέν μοι νόστος, (e) Plato 462 D ὅταν...δάκτυλός του πληγῇ...πᾶσα ἡ κοινωνία...ᾔσθετό τε.... Jelf calls (a) and (b) aorists of iteration, but the rest aorists of certainty. I should be disposed to say that the aorist, in all of them, denotes *instantaneous consequence implying certainty*. Add Epict. iv. 10. 27 ὅταν θέλῃς, ἐξῆλθες "at the instant you desire, *you are out [of prison]*." Ὅταν or ἤν is expressed by the participle in Soph. *Ant.* 709 ὅστις γὰρ...φρονεῖν μόνος δοκεῖ,...οὗτοι διαπτυχθέντες ὤφθησαν κενοί.

[2] [2756 a] Chrys., πῶς δὲ οἱ ἄλλοι φασὶν ὅτι μαθητὰς ἔπεμψε καὶ εἶπεν, Λύσατε τὴν ὄνον καὶ τὸν πῶλον (Cramer, τὸν πῶλον καὶ τὸν ὄνον), οὗτος δὲ οὐδὲν τοιοῦτόν φησιν, ἀλλ' ὅτι Ὀνάριον εὑρὼν ἐπεκάθισεν (Cramer, ἐκάθισεν); Ὅτι ἀμφότερα γενέσθαι εἰκὸς ἦν, καί, μετὰ τὸ λυθῆναι τὴν ὄνον, ἀγόντων τῶν μαθητῶν εὑρόντα αὐτὸν

Nonnus omits εὑρών, but has ἰθύνων[1]. The very great difficulty implied in εὑρών and its frank acceptance by Origen—whose spiritual interpretation of the text raises him above all danger of harmonistically corrupting it—make it certain that εὑρών is genuine. Some may have omitted or corrupted εὑρών for the sake of reconciling the Johannine with the Synoptic account.

On xii. 16 ἐμνήcθηcαν ὅτι ταῦτα...καὶ ταῦτα ἐποίηcαν (2469)

[2757] In xii. 16, R.V. renders κ. ἐποίησαν "and *that* they had done," making ἐποίησαν depend on the ὅτι in the preceding words, ὅτι ταῦτα ἦν ἐπ' αὐτῷ γεγραμμένα, and accordingly supplying "*that*" in English. But a second "*that*" is not inserted in the Greek, nor in SS, nor in the Latin versions. Nonnus also (ed. Passow) has Καὶ οἱ ταῦτα τέλεσσαν at the beginning of a new sentence, pointing to a reading of ἐποίησαν as independent of ὅτι[2]. If John had wished to say "remembered *that*...and *that*," there seems no obvious reason why he should not have repeated ὅτι after καί, as he does elsewhere when he wishes to say "*because (of)...and because*," and once "*that... and that*[3]." Here, however, he may have wished to combine the fact that "these things had been written," and the fact that the

---

ἐπικαθίσαι. Chrys. omits the difficult Synoptic words "*Ye shall find* an ass," but, even when they are omitted, how he can say that Christ "*found*" what the disciples brought to Him I cannot understand. No doubt, εὑρίσκω, besides meaning "find" in the sense of "discover," means also "find" in the sense of "earn," "procure": but can Chrys. possibly be suggesting that the disciples first "*found*" the ass in the former sense, and Christ afterwards "*found*" it in the latter? Also, it is not clear whether αὐτὸν ἐπικαθίσαι means "He Himself (emph.) sat on [it]," or, "He (unemph.) sat on [it]." Previously Migne's text has τὸ δὲ [ἐπὶ] ὄνον (Cramer, τὸ δὲ ὄνον) καθίσαι which Chrys. explains as a prediction that Christ "was destined to subject (ὑποχείριον ἔχειν) the unclean race of the Gentiles (τῶν ἐθνῶν)." Cramer's text takes ὄνον as accus. gov. by καθίσαι.

[1] [2756 b] Ἰθύνων ἀχάλινον ὄνον ταλαεργὸν ὁδίτην, Ἑξόμενος νώτοισιν ἀπειρήτοιο φορῆος. Possibly ἰθύνων is to be explained from poetic desire of symbolism, and to be illustrated by Origen (Lomm. i. 331) who describes Christ as ἡνιοχῶν τοὺς ἐκ περιτομῆς καὶ ἐθνῶν πιστεύοντας having previously mentioned the "ass" as the type of the Jews, and the "colt" as the type of the Gentiles.

[2] [2757 a] Nonnus has, τότε πάντες ἀνεμνήσαντο μαθηταὶ "Ὅττι σοφῇ τάδε πάντα πέλει κεχαραγμένα βίβλῳ. Καὶ οἱ πάντα τέλεσσαν.... Burkitt has "they remembered that these things had been written of him, and these things did they (*not*, they did) to him." Walton, without inserting "that," removes ambiguity by the Latin subjunctive "quod ea *essent* scripta de eo et haec *fecissent* ei." In xiii. 3 (see below) "knowing *that*...and *that*," Syr. (Burkitt) has "was knowing *that*... and *was knowing that*."

[3] [2757 b] ii. 25 "*because of* (διὰ τὸ)...and *because* (ὅτι)," xiii. 3 "*that* (ὅτι)...and *that* (ὅτι)," 1 Jn ii. 21 "*because* (ὅτι)...and *because* (ὅτι)."

[2758] NOTES ON PRECEDING PARAGRAPHS

pilgrims or disciples "had done these things" in fulfilment of the prophecy, as *one fact of coincidence "remembered" by the disciples*. He also wishes (2396—7) to convey a suggestion of divine fulfilment of prophecy by the triple repetition of "these things" in one sentence. But it is not surprising that the words have been variously interpreted and perhaps corrupted[1].

On vi. 25 πότε ὧδε γέγονας **(2478)**

[2758] It is of course possible that Nonnus and Chrysostom may have found no difficulty in regarding γέγονας as aorist because, by their time, the 2nd perf. had come to be thus used. Is γέγονεν thus used in Origen (Lomm. i. 278) πυνθανομένοις ἡμῖν περὶ τοῦ

---

[1] [2757 c] Origen says (*Comm. Matth.*, Lomm. iv. 46) ὁ δὲ Ἰωάννης ἀντὶ τοῦ "ἐπιβεβηκὼς ἐπὶ ὑποζύγιον καὶ πῶλον νέον" πεποίηκε "καθήμενος ἔρχεται ἐπὶ πῶλον ὄνου." ὅστις ἐμφαίνων ὅτι γνώσεως δεῖται τὸ κατὰ τὸν τόπον, ἐπιφέρει, τό "Ταῦτα δὲ οὐκ ἔγνωσαν οἱ μαθηταὶ αὐτοῦ τὸ πρότερον." This not only gives ἔγνωσαν correctly (which D reads as ενοησαν) but shews that Origen perceived its force. The meaning is not "knew" but "*recognised*" or "*understood*"; and Origen accordingly says that the subject required *gnosis*, i.e. spiritual understanding or recognition. Origen stops short at πρῶτον (which he read, or remembered, as πρότερον): but we cannot infer that he was unacquainted with the following words ἀλλ' ὅτε...ἐποίησαν αὐτῷ. He is not here commenting on Jn but on Mt., and he quotes enough for his purpose.

[2757 d] Chrys. on the other hand seems either to miss the meaning of ἔγνωσαν if he is paraphrasing, or else to misquote, if he is quoting, in the following (*ad loc.*) Τοῦτο δὲ οὐκ ᾔδεσαν, φησίν, οἱ μαθηταὶ αὐτοῦ ὅτι ἦν ἐπ' αὐτῷ γεγραμμένον...ὅρα δὲ φιλοσοφίαν εὐαγγελιστοῦ, πῶς οὐκ ἐπαισχύνεται τὴν προτέραν αὐτῶν ἀγνοίαν ἐκπομπεύειν. "Ὅτι μὲν οὖν γέγραπται ᾔδεσαν· ὅτι δὲ ἐπ' αὐτῷ γέγραπται, οὐκ ᾔδεσαν. He makes no mention of "remembering" and omits the whole of the clause about "doing." Thus the whole is condensed into a statement that the disciples "*knew*" Zechariah's prophecy but "did not *know*" that it applied to Christ—perfectly intelligible, but not what the evangelist meant.

[2757 e] These two criticisms—of Origen and Chrysostom—should be borne in mind as giving a clue to their different methods. Origen is a scholar; Chrysostom —at least as represented by his Johannine commentary in its extant form—is rather a preacher. Origen gives full value to each word, Chrysostom criticizes on the unscholarly basis of a belief—too common in our own days—that the evangelist "uses one word for another." Origen is often fanciful and minutely diffuse in allegorization—as in this instance where he gives copious details about the typical meaning of the ass and the foal—but he rarely tampers with, and does not very often even paraphrase, his text. Chrysostom is much less imaginative but also much less faithful to his author. As for the mysterious purpose of Providence latent under τὸ τῆς ὄνου, all he says is καὶ τοῦτο μέγα ἦν, "*this, too, was great*"— he means by, "*too*," that it was "great" like the mystery in "Destroy this temple"—but he does not make up for this brevity by any compensating explanation of the verbal difficulties of the clause about "remembering," which he does not quote.

Πότε (Huet has gap in text, but πότε in marg. with Cod. Bodl.) γέγονε πρῶτον ἐν τῇ Καφαρναοὺμ ὁ Χριστός...? Unless other instances of Origen's aoristic use of γέγονεν are produced, this might best be rendered, "*When is it on record that Christ was first* at Capernaum?" In the context, Origen appeals to the exact words (λέξις) of the evangelists. Comp. Orig. on Ps. xxi. 4 where LXX has ᾐτήσατο... ἔδωκας, and Origen says (Lomm. xii. 80) ᾐτήσατο...καὶ εἴληφεν, "he [Hezekiah] asked...and *is recorded to have received*." According to this view, γέγονεν, like the perfects in the Epistle to the Hebrews (**2751**), represents, in Origen, a past event as a present record[1]. And if it does so in Origen, perhaps it may do so in the formula frequently used by Matthew to introduce prophecy (**2478** *a*) "*It is on record that this came to pass* in order that it might be fulfilled..."

On viii. 14 καὶ ποῦ ὑπάγω...ἢ ποῦ ὑπάγω (**2490**)

[**2759**] On viii. 14 οἶδα...καὶ ποῦ ὑπάγω· ὑμεῖς δὲ οὐκ οἴδατε πόθεν ἔρχομαι ἢ ποῦ ὑπάγω. ὑμεῖς... Blass remarks (p. 324) "Chrys. and Nonnus omit ἢ...ὑπ." This is true of Chrys. who quotes thus, κἂν ἐγὼ μαρτυρῶ περὶ ἐμαυτοῦ, ἡ μαρτυρία μου ἀληθής ἐστιν. ὅτι οἶδα πόθεν ἔρχομαι καὶ ποῦ ὑπάγω· ὑμεῖς δὲ οὐκ οἴδατε πόθεν ἔρχομαι,—and there stops. But can we feel sure that he does not stop because he has quoted enough to be the basis of his comment? After two short sentences, he quotes again καὶ ἐὰν ἐγὼ μαρτυρῶ περὶ ἐμαυτοῦ ἀληθής ἐστιν μαρτ. μου, ὅτι οἶδα πόθεν ἔρχομαι—and there stops. If we had this quotation alone, we might say that he omitted in his text the clause καὶ ποῦ ὑπάγω. But he has quoted it above. Again, after one more sentence, he quotes, Ὑμεῖς δὲ οὐκ οἴδατε—and there stops; but the reason obviously is that he does not want to repeat what he has said. Ammonius (Cramer) says, Ὑμεῖς δὲ διὰ τοῦτο μὲν οὐκ οἴδατε, ἐπειδὴ οὐδὲν θέλετε τοῦ φαινομένου νοεῖν. οὐκ εἶπε δέ, Θεός εἰμι, ἀλλά, Πόθεν ἔρχομαι καὶ ποῦ ὑπάγω· ἐθελοκάκουν (*sic*) γὰρ καὶ προσεποιοῦντο

---

[1] [**2758** *a*] See **2751** and contrast the perf. of *recorded action* with the imperf. of *habitual action*, and with the aorist of *special action*, in Epict. ii. 12. 15 εἰ θέλετε γνῶναι πόσην ἐν τούτῳ δύναμιν εἶχεν (sc. Σωκράτης) (*habitually possessed*) ἀνάγνωτε τὸ Ξενοφῶντος Συμπόσιον καὶ ὄψεσθε πόσας μάχας διαλέλυκε "how many quarrels *he is recorded to have peacefully settled*," iv. 5. 3 "See in the pages of Xenophon (παρὰ Ξενοφῶντι)...how many quarrels *he is recorded to have settled* (λέλυκε), how again [*in the several dialogues in which their names are mentioned*] *he tolerated* (ἠνέσχετο) Thrasymachus, Polus, and Callicles, how *he habitually tolerated* his wife (πῶς τῆς γυναικὸς ἠνείχετο)." So Origen (Lomm. ii. 366) after saying γέγραπται (xi. 54) γάρ...ἀπῆλθεν, proceeds, καὶ οὐ μόνος γε ἐκεῖ ἀπελήλυθεν, *i.e.* is recorded to have departed.

[2759]   NOTES ON PRECEDING PARAGRAPHS

μὴ εἰδέναι. This shews how commentators, even though they had the full W.H. text before them, might stop short at οὐκ οἴδατε (and perhaps at πόθεν ἔρχομαι) because those words sufficed to indicate the argument as to Christ's divine origin. The omission of ὑμεῖς δέ …ὑπάγω by Origen, Cyril, and Augustine (Alf.) (through homoeotel.) indicates a lacuna in very early MSS. Nonnus has Μοῦνος ἐγὼ νοέω πόθεν ἤλυθον ἢ πόθι βαίνω. Ὑμεῖς δ' οὐκ ἐδάητε πόθεν γενόμην πόθεν ἔστην. John uses ἔστη with εἰς but not with ἐκ or ἀπό, and *it is improbable that Nonnus would paraphrase* πόθεν ἔρχομαι *by two clauses*—the second so meaningless and farfetched as πόθεν ἔστην. *More probably Nonnus paraphrased* ἢ ποῦ ὑπάγω *as* ΠΟΘΙΔΕCΤΗΝ, where ΙΔ might easily be corrupted into ΙΝ. Then ΠΟΘΙΝ would be amended into ΠΟΘΕΝ. Πόθεν γενόμην πόθι δ' ἔστην would correspond to πόθεν ἔρχομαι ἢ ποῦ ὑπάγω in John, and would also harmonize with the preceding πόθεν ἤλυθον ἢ πόθι βαίνω in Nonnus himself (see 2549 a)[1].

---

[1] [2759 a] Ammonius, apparently commenting on the object of οὐκ οἴδατε in viii. 14, οὐκ οἴδατε πόθεν ἔρχομαι ἢ ποῦ…, has καί for ἤ, thus repeating the previous clause πόθεν ἔρχ. καὶ ποῦ ὑπάγω. This is not so strange as Nonnus's substitution of ἤ for καί in the previous clause. Ἤ is comparatively intelligible after a negative (οὐκ οἴδατε), but not after a positive (οἶδα). It was briefly suggested in **2549** a that ἤ in viii. 14 prob. means "*or* [*which is the same thing*]." In view of a frequent confusion between ἤ and καί elsewhere, and of arguments—based on these two conjunctions—about the Lord's Supper, the following additional facts about οὐ… καί and οὐ…ἤ are here submitted.

[2759 b] In Genesis and Exodus, when A.V. "nor" is represented by Heb. "and," it corresponds to οὐδέ or μηδέ in Gen. xxi. 23, xlv. 6, Ex. xii. 9, xxiii. 26, but to καί in Gen. xlix. 10, Ex. xiii. 22 (R.V. "and"), xx. 10, xxiii. 32, xxxiv. 10. In Dan. xi. 24, LXX has οὐδέ but Theod. καί, and so Heb. Οὐ…οὐδέ is clear but not literal. Οὐ…καί is literal but not clear, *e.g.* "thou shalt *not* sow with wheat *and* barley" would be a literal transl. of Heb., in which it would mean "with wheat *or* barley,"—*neither* being allowed. But in English and Greek it might mean "thou shalt not sow with wheat *and* barley [*together*]"—*one* being allowed. In 2 K. xxiii. 10 "that no man might make his son (Heb.) *and* (R.V. and A.V. *or*) his daughter pass through the fire," Sym. has ἤ for "*and*." As his style somewhat resembles that of Luke, the instance will prepare us to find οὐ…ἤ in the Acts.

[2759 c] From classical Gk (from which Blass p. 266 and the Thesaurus quote no instance) Winer-Moulton (p. 550) alleges only Thuc. i. 122, which I should punctuate thus, οὐκ ἴσμεν ὅπως τάδε τριῶν…ἀπήλλακται—ἀξυνεσίας ἢ μαλακίας ἢ ἀμελείας. Here the negation "we do not see the way to an acquittal" is equivalent to the affirmation "there must be a verdict of guilty." This necessitates an appositional clause :—"that is to say, guilty, not of all three, but of the first, *or* the second, *or* the third of the three." Both in rhythm and in grammatical construction, the passage is inappropriate as an illustration of N.T. usage.

[2759 d] Winer-Moulton (but not Blass) refers to Acts xxiv. 12 καὶ οὔτε ἐν τῷ ἱερῷ εὗρόν με πρός τινα διαλεγόμενον—ἢ ἐπίστασιν ποιοῦντα ὄχλου—οὔτε ἐν ταῖς συναγωγαῖς. But if this is punctuated as above, it appears that ἢ introduces a parenthetical clause and that οὔτε prepares the way for οὔτε not for ἢ. And this gives the clue to other instances, *e.g.* Acts i. 7 οὐχ ὑμῶν ἐστὶν γνῶναι χρόνους ἢ καιρούς "It is *not* for you to know the times—*or* [*rather I should say*] appointed seasons," preparing the way for the words, "which the Father placed under his own authority," Acts xvii. 29 "we ought *not* to suppose that the divine [being] is like gold—*or* [*may be*] silver *or* stone—the sculpturing of art and of human device." So, too, Rom. iv. 13 "For *not* through Torah [was] the promise to Abraham—*or* [*as it might also be said*] to his seed," ix. 11 "*not* yet having been born *nor even* having done anything—good *or* bad (μηδὲ πραξάντων τι—ἀγαθὸν ἢ φαῦλον)."

[2759 e] A more interesting instance is Acts xi. 8 μηδαμῶς, κύριε, ὅτι κοινὸν ἢ ἀκάθαρτον οὐδέποτε εἰσῆλθεν εἰς τὸ στόμα μου, in a Petrine speech, corresponding to Acts x. 14 μηδαμῶς, κύριε, ὅτι οὐδέποτε ἔφαγον πᾶν κοινὸν καὶ ἀκάθαρτον. In Acts x. 14, several authorities have altered καί to ἤ to make the text correspond to Peter's report of his own words; but it has been pointed out (**1913**) that Luke in writing the Petrine speech has allowed himself more freedom than in the Petrine narrative of the facts. The narrative retains the old Hebraic idiom οὐδέποτε...πᾶν: and the καὶ ἀκάθαρτον (which, coming at the end of the sentence, cannot be parenthetic) is also to be explained as Hebraic. But when writing a speech for Peter—a speech that, without shorthand writers, or a miracle, or both, cannot possibly be regarded as giving the Apostle's exact words—Luke allows himself to drop some Hebraisms; and, like Symmachus above (**2759** *b*), he substitutes ἤ for the Hebraic καί.

[2759 *f*] We pass to 1 Cor. xi. 27 ὃς ἂν ἐσθίῃ τὸν ἄρτον ἢ πίνῃ τὸ ποτήριον τοῦ κυρίου ἀναξίως, ἔνοχος ἔσται τοῦ σώματος καὶ τοῦ αἵματος τοῦ κυρίου. This may be illustrated by Lev. xx. 9 ὃς ἂν κακῶς εἴπῃ τὸν πατέρα αὐτοῦ ἢ τὴν μητέρα αὐτοῦ θανάτῳ θανατούσθω· πατέρα αὐτοῦ ἢ μητέρα αὐτοῦ κακῶς εἶπεν, ἔνοχος ἔσται. Here the Heb. has "*and*" twice, but the obvious inconvenience of allowing a man to suppose that he may ill-treat "his father *or* his mother," because the Law merely forbade him to ill-treat "his father *and* his mother" has led the LXX here and in Ex. xxi. 15, 17, Deut. xxvii. 16, Prov. xx. 20 (and comp. Mk vii. 10, Mt. xv. 4) to render the Heb. "*and*" by the Gk "*or*." In 1 Cor. xi. 22—9, the whole passage assumes the "eating *and* drinking" (*ib.* 22 ἐσθίειν καὶ πίνειν, 26 ὁσάκις γὰρ ἐὰν ἐσθίητε...καὶ...πίνητε, 28 ἐσθιέτω καὶ...πινέτω, 29 ὁ γὰρ ἐσθίων καὶ πίνων) of the Lord's Supper, and teaches the preparation for it. But when the Apostle comes to warn the Corinthians about the danger of eating *and* drinking irreverentially, he naturally substitutes "*or*" for "*and*" in order to shew that *either* act was liable to penalty. There is no question of οὐ—ἤ here, nor is the ἀ in ἀναξίως regarded as a negative. The construction would have been the same if the adverb had been ὑπερηφανῶς.

[2759 *g*] In explaining viii. 14, we must have regard to the fact that (1) it would have made good sense to repeat οὐ...καί instead of introducing οὐ...ἤ. (2) Also (**2549** *a*) ἤ is rare in Jn as compared with the Synoptists. (3) It has been just shewn that οὐ...καί and οὐ...ἤ are interchanged by various writers and scribes in a manner that suggests a thoughtful distinction between the two. (4) Ἡ is used by Jn (**2549** *a*) where οὐδέ would differentiate too strongly. These facts confirm the view taken in **2549** *a* that "*or*" means "*or* [*which is the same thing*]."

[2760]   NOTES ON PRECEDING PARAGRAPHS

On xiv. 7 ἀπ' ἄρτι γινώσκετε αὐτόν (2491)

[2760] The context (W.H.) εἰ ἐγνώκειτέ με, καὶ τὸν πατέρα μου ἂν ᾔδειτε· ἀπ' ἄρτι γινώσκετε αὐτὸν καὶ ἑωράκατε (al. + αὐτόν) is rendered by SS "If me ye have not known, *my Father also will ye know?* And from now ye know him and have seen him." Nonnus has Εἰ δὲ θεορρήτῳ με σοφῷ γινώσκετε μύθῳ, Ἐξ ἐμέθεν γνώσεσθε καὶ ὑψιμέδοντα τοκῆα· Ἄρτι δέ μιν <u>φράσσασθε</u> καὶ ὑψιμέδοντα μαθόντες. The last line shews that he took γινώσκετε to be imperative, "If ye recognise me...ye shall from me recognise the Father also. [*Nay*] *but at once understand Him learning the* Father *also* [*as well as myself*]." This makes good sense, meaning in effect, "Do I say ' *Ye would have known* '? Nay, begin to know Him at once [through me], and [then] ye [will] have seen [Him]." The sequence "Do this, and straightway that will have followed" is like Lk. xi. 41 "*Give* for alms...and behold all things *are clean.*" It should be added that Irenæus iii. 13. 2—quoted above (**2491** *a*)—places these words out of their order as part of Christ's reply to Philip.

[2761] Epiphanius (i. 919) wedges between two quotations of "He that hath seen me hath seen the Father" a statement about Christ as ὁ λέγων ὅτι ὁ γινώσκων ἐμὲ γινώσκει τὸν πατέρα. The most probable explanation of this is that he is borrowing unintelligently (as he often does) from Hippolytus (*adv. Noet.* 7), who, after quoting "He that hath seen...the Father," adds, "That is to say, *If thou hast seen me thou mayest know the Father through me.*" Epiphanius seems to have mistaken a version of this (conforming "*seen*" to "*know*") for an actual saying of Christ. Hippolytus—after saying that the Father is known through *the "image" like Him*—continues "*But if thou didst not know the image, which is the Son, how wouldest* (θέλεις) *thou see the Father?*" It will not escape the reader that this is like SS "*If me ye have not known, my Father also will ye know?*" Corruption of the text may have done something to produce these variations, but paraphrase probably contributed more.

[2762] Is Nonnus right in taking xiv. 7 γινώσκετε imperatively? The answer depends partly on the general Greek use, and the particular Johannine use, of γινώσκετε, partly on the place assigned by John to "knowing" in his theory of revelation and redemption. Nonnus renders it by the subjunctive ἐσαθρήσητε in xiv. 17, where the subjunctive is difficult to explain as an imperative but perhaps

NOTES ON PRECEDING PARAGRAPHS   [2763]

more difficult as an indicative[1]. In xiii. 12 where W.H. punctuate γινώσκετε τί πεποίηκα ὑμῖν; Nonnus has εἶπεν ἑοῖς ἑτάροις γινώσκετε τοῦτο καὶ αὐτοί punctuated by Passow interrogatively but probably imperative, "Understand this *ye, too,* [my disciples]," implying a precept to understand it even as, or in the sense in which, their Master understands it[2]. In xv. 18 γινώσκετε ὅτι ἐμέ...μεμίσηκεν, Nonnus has Τοῦτο χαμαιγενέων γινώσκετε μάρτυρες ἔργων. This is ambiguous, but μάρτυρες suits best with an imperative rendering, "I call on you to bear witness and to recognise that they persecuted me": and it is so taken by the Latin versions and SS. Nonnus, then, in two out of four instances certainly renders γινώσκετε by an imperative or subjunctive; in two, where he retains γινώσκετε, he probably intends the imperative.

[2763] Γινώσκετε occurs only twice in Aristophanes, once interrogative, once doubtful[3]. In Demosthenes it occurs four times indicatively (but in such a context as to present no ambiguity) and always in connexion *with the "recognition" of character, good or bad*; once imperatively, at the end of a speech, bidding the jurors recognise or decide that which is just[4]. In Epictetus, there is

---

[1] [2762 a] xiv. 17 ὑμεῖς γινώσκετε αὐτό, ὅτι παρ' ὑμῖν μένει καὶ ἐν ὑμῖν ἐστίν (marg. ἔσται): Nonnus, (1) Ἐσαθρήσητε δὲ μοῦνοι Ὑμεῖς ἔνθεον εἶδος ἀθηήτοιο προσώπου Ὅττι μεθ' ὑμείων μενέει καὶ ὁμόστολον ἔσται Ὑμῖν, πάντας ἔχον νοερὸν δόμον.... Nonnus must have read μενεῖ (not μένει) (1960 a). This is parall. to xiv. 19 ὑμεῖς δὲ θεωρεῖτέ με, ὅτι ἐγὼ ζῶ καὶ ὑμεῖς ζήσετε, which Nonnus paraphrases thus, (2) Ἀλλ' ἐμὲ μοῦνοι Λεύσσετε καὶ μετὰ γαῖαν ἀεὶ ζώων ὅτι μίμνω, Καὶ δι' ἐμὲ ξύμπαντες ἀεὶ ζώοιτε καὶ ὑμεῖς. Λεύσσετε, a poetic word, seems alw. imperative, *e.g.* Soph. *Oed. R.* 1524, *Ant.* 940, Eurip. *Or.* 977, *Med.* 161, and prob. (see p. 678 note 1) *Iliad* i. 120 (comp. *Odyss.* xxiii. 124 ταῦτά γε λεύσσε). Nonnus seems to mean (1) "But *ye* [*I pray*] *do ye*—alone and apart from the world—*fix your eyes* on the divine form of the invisible Person [and perceive] that it will abide with you as in a home," (2) "But *do ye* [*I pray*]—alone and apart from the world—*behold* me even after [my life on] earth how that ever living I abide," taking ὅτι, after the verbs of "seeing," as "that" (not "because") as in iv. 35 "behold the fields...*that*."

[2762 b] In xiv. 17, Chrys., as printed by Migne and Cramer, has μένει, but a great part of the comment is consistent with the hypothesis that he wrote μενεῖ. Chrys. also twice repeats μόνοι, as Nonnus does, εἶπεν ὅτι Πρὸς ὑμᾶς μόνους ἔρχεται, and again, "Lest they should say, How then saidst thou to the Jews, *From henceforth ye shall not see me?*—He destroys the [apparent] contradiction by saying *To you alone* (λύει τὴν ἀντίθεσιν εἰπών, Πρὸς ὑμᾶς μόνους)."

[2] [2762 c] Chrys. and Origen give no guidance on this point. Nor do the Latin vss. SS has the interrogative.

[3] *Thesm.* 606 interrog., *Fragm.* 203 (meaning doubtful).

[4] Demosth. (Preuss) Indic. xviii. 10, 276, xxiv. 59, xxxix. 2. Imper. xxxiii. 38 ὑμεῖς οὖν, κατὰ τοὺς νόμους, γινώσκετε τὰ δίκαια.

[2763] NOTES ON PRECEDING PARAGRAPHS

abundant use of the aorist, and of γνῶθι σαυτόν, but Schenkl's Index under "γινώσκω c. accus." gives no instance of any form of the present. On the other hand, Plato, while emphasizing, as the great precept of life, γνῶθι σεαυτόν, insists repeatedly on τὸ ἑαυτὸν γινώσκειν as being the fulfilment of this precept, and connects the phrases with a distinction between material and spiritual knowledge of oneself[1]. The Fourth Gospel teaches that "eternal life" consists (xvii. 3) in the "knowledge (γινώσκωσιν)" of the true God and of Jesus Christ. It is hardly possible that the evangelist was ignorant that he thus came into collision with the doctrine taught by the successors of Plato and popularised by his own contemporary, Epictetus, and it is almost certain that the collision was deliberate. It may be asked why the evangelist, if he wished to record a precept of Christ about "knowing," did not use the unambiguous aorist, but it has been pointed out (1626)

---

[1] [2763 a] Comp. Plato *Phileb.* 48 C—D γνῶθι σαυτόν...τοὐναντίον μὴν ἐκείνῳ δῆλον ὅτι τὸ μηδαμῇ γινώσκειν αὑτόν, 1 *Alc.* 131 A ὅστις ἄρα τῶν τοῦ σώματός τι γινώσκει τὰ αὑτοῦ ἀλλὰ οὐχ αὑτὸν ἔγνωκεν...οὐδεὶς ἄρα τῶν ἰατρῶν ἑαυτὸν γινώσκει, καθ' ὅσον ἰατρός, where the first words mean "whosoever *recognises*, or *knows intelligently*, something of his bodily system, has *obtained the knowledge* of his possessions, not of himself." In 1 *Alc.* 133 B—D it is said that the soul, if it is to know itself, "must look to (βλεπτέον εἰς) the soul, and especially to that province (τόπον) of the soul wherein exists the soul's [constituent] virtue," that nothing belonging to the soul "is more divine than this the centre of knowledge and wisdom (θειότερον ἢ τοῦτο περὶ ὃ τὸ εἰδέναι τε καὶ φρονεῖν ἐστίν)," and "the intelligent knowledge of oneself we agree in calling healthymindedness (τὸ δὲ γινώσκειν αὑτὸν ὁμολογοῦμεν σωφροσύνην εἶναι)." In *Charm.* 164 D, 165 B, it is said that σωφρόνει, not χαῖρε, is the best greeting, and that σωφρονεῖν means γνῶθι σαυτόν: then follows σχεδὸν γάρ τι ἔγωγε αὐτὸ τοῦτό φημι εἶναι σωφροσύνην, τὸ γινώσκειν ἑαυτόν. This *gnosis* is subsequently connected with οἶδα thus, *ib.* 167 A ὁ ἄρα σώφρων μόνος αὐτός τε ἑαυτὸν γνώσεται καὶ οἷός τε ἔσται ἐξετάσαι τί τε τυγχάνει εἰδὼς καὶ τί μή, καὶ τοὺς ἄλλους...ἐπισκοπεῖν τί τις οἶδε καὶ οἴεται, εἴπερ οἶδε, καὶ τί αὖ τις οἴεται μὲν εἰδέναι, οἶδε δ' οὔ...καὶ ἔστι δὴ τοῦτο...τὸ ἑαυτὸν αὐτὸν γινώσκειν, τὸ εἰδέναι ἅ τε οἶδε καὶ ἃ μὴ οἶδεν.

[2763 b] Γινώσκω, in connexion with "knowing" other persons than oneself, and as distinct from "seeing" these persons, is discussed at great length by Plato, beginning with ἐπιγινώσκω thus, *Theaet.* 193, Σωκράτης ἐπιγινώσκει Θεόδωρον καὶ Θεαίτητον, ὁρᾷ δὲ μηδέτερον, μηδὲ ἄλλη αἴσθησις αὐτῷ πάρεστι περὶ αὐτῶν. After this first hypothesis, a second, and its consequence, are stated thus, Δεύτερον τοίνυν, ὅτι τὸν μὲν γινώσκων ὑμῶν, τὸν δὲ μὴ γινώσκων, αἰσθανόμενος δὲ μηδέτερον, οὐκ ἄν ποτε αὖ οἰηθείην ὃν οἶδα εἶναι ὃν μὴ οἶδα. In a third hypothesis this collocation of οἶδα and γινώσκω is repeated; and the two verbs are manifestly intended to be distinguished. Applied to facts of science, γινώσκω means "recognise" or "know intelligently" in *Ion* 537 E, "I *recognise* that these fingers are five: you *recognise* the same facts...we both *recognise* them by arithmetic."

that John expressly distinguishes the aorist from the present as though the latter represented a higher stage than the former; and he may also have been influenced by the use of the aorist in Jeremiah (xxxi. 34) quoted in the Epistle to the Hebrews (viii. 11) "They shall no more teach...saying *Know* (γνῶθι) the Lord." The Fourth Gospel is full of subtle distinctions between γινώσκω and οἶδα that could not have originated from Aramaic utterance, if exactly translated[1], but may well have originated from Greek paraphrase. *A priori* it is quite reasonable to suppose that John represented Christ as holding up to His disciples "the Father" and not "yourselves" as the object of the highest knowledge, and that the precept to "*know*" was expressed so as to exclude the Delphic "*know once for all,*" γνῶθι, and to imply "*knowing by degrees*" or "*growing in recognition and sympathy,*" γινώσκετε. In the absence of help from Origen and Clement of Alexandria the conclusion must be left uncertain, but it is not improbable that Nonnus is right in his imperative rendering of this ambiguous form.

[2764] Of course, the fact that John's *expression* of the doctrine of "knowing" God is in part Greek and Platonic, is not inconsistent with the fact that the *thought* is Jewish, or Hebrew, and Biblical. In John, "knowing" and "seeing" go together, and therefore the "knowing" may be illustrated by v. 38 οὔτε εἶδος αὐτοῦ ἑωράκατε, an amazing phrase—"ye have neither seen *his form* (εἶδος)"—considering that "*his*" means the Father's! Chrysostom's explanation is, in effect, "*Ye have not seen his form, because there was no form to see*"! God, he urges, is "above all outward fashion." Nor will he accept the notion of a spiritual form: "He means, not that God has a form *but not a visible* one (οὐ θεατὸν δέ), but that *none of these things concerns God* (ἀλλ' ὅτι οὐδὲν τούτων περὶ θεόν)." At the same time he dismisses the statements that Moses heard the voice of God and that Isaiah saw Him, and represents Christ as "*goading the Jews into philosophic dogma* (εἰς φιλόσοφον αὐτοὺς ἐνάγει δόγμα)."

[2765] But the fact appears to be that "form" here alludes to the ancient Jewish tradition about Penuel, the *Face of God*, twice called by the LXX *the Form* (εἶδος) *of God*, a phrase unique in the whole of

---

[1] [2763 c] There do not exist in Heb. two words corresponding to οἶδα and γινώσκω. In Jerem. xxxi. 34 γνῶθι τὸν κύριον...πάντες εἰδήσουσίν με, the Heb. of "*know*" is the same word in both cases. It is not therefore exactly translated by LXX.

the Bible[1]. It was there that Jacob said "*I have seen God face to face*"; and from this fact Philo, though erroneously, explains the name of "Israel," there given to Jacob, as *Seeing God*. Those who took this view would discern in the words addressed to Nathanael, i. 47 "Behold an *Israelite* indeed," the meaning, "Behold *one that sees God*," and would find an appropriateness between this and the following words, (i. 50) "*Thou shalt see* greater things than these…" followed by an allusion to the ladder of heaven and the angels ascending and descending over the head of Jacob.

[2766] Again it was said of Moses that (Ex. xxxiii. 11) "the Lord *spake unto Moses face to face."* Combining this with Jacob's "*seeing the Lord face to face*," we can understand how our Lord, in a spiritual sense, not casting away the traditions of His nation, but interpreting them, while condemning the Scribes and Pharisees for degenerating from the true Israel, might say something that might be paraphrased for Greeks thus "Ye are not genuine sons of Israel, who '*saw the form of God*'; ye are not genuine disciples of Moses, who '*heard the voice of God*'; ye have neither *heard his voice* at any time nor *seen his form*[2]."

On xi. 47 τί ποιοῦμεν; (2493)

[2766 (i)] As regards the distinction between τί ποιοῦμεν; and τί ποιήσωμεν; it may be illustrated from Epictetus, who—besides frequently using τί ποιήσω; parall. to deliberat. subjunct. (i. 27. 7, iv. 10. 1 etc.) so that it is proved to be subjunctive, and (i. 22. 17) τί οὖν ποιήσωμεν;—has the indicative in a passage where he is maintaining that "man is born for faithfulness (πρὸς πίστιν γέγονεν)." An intruder (ὁ δέ)[3], notorious for adultery, ironically replies (ii. 4. 2) ἀλλ' ἄν..., ἀφέντες τοῦτο τὸ πιστὸν πρὸς ὃ πεφύκαμεν, ἐπιβουλεύωμεν τῇ γυναικὶ τοῦ γείτονος, τί ποιοῦμεν; Presumably the man means "*What*

---

[1] [2765 a] Gen. xxxii. 30—1. Aquila (once at all events) has πρόσωπον ἰσχυροῦ the literal rendering. Clem. Alex. 132 has εἶδος θεοῦ. Both he and Origen (on Gen. xxxii. 30) explain the "angel" or "face of God" as being the Logos, and represent the "wrestling *with* (συμπαλαίω)" as "wrestling *on the side of*," meaning that *He assisted Jacob in wrestling against Satan*—Clem. at least certainly, Origen probably. In LXX, "the form *of the glory of God*" etc. may be found elsewhere, but not "*the form of God*."

[2] [2766 a] See **1716** h for another allusive phrase (in connexion with theophanies) in the use of ἐμφανίζω occurring in xiv. 21—22, and in one passage of the Pentateuch Ex. xxxiii. 13—18 where Moses says to God ἐμφάνισόν μοι σεαυτόν.

[3] Ὁ δέ, in Epict. (Schenkl) means some one replying to a *speech* or *letter*. But here it may mean Epictetus replying to the *intrusion*. If so, he himself utters ἀλλ' ἄν...τί ποιοῦμεν; See context.

are we doing, in effect [except disproving this fine theory about natural faithfulness, since our conduct shews that men are naturally unfaithful]?" The sequel is, "Why, *what else* [*are we doing*] (τί γὰρ ἄλλο) except destroying and slaying?" "Whom?" "The [ideal] man of faith [within us]." In ii. 3. 5 ἐπὶ δὲ τοῦ βίου τί ποιῶ; νῦν μὲν λέγω ἀγαθόν, νῦν δὲ κακόν, the meaning is "What am I in the habit of doing?" But the context suggests "*What* [*good*] *am I doing*?"—as in i. 25. 29 "revile a stone—and *what* [*good*] *will you do* [*by it*] (καὶ τί ποιήσεις)¹?"

On x. 29 ογΔεὶc Δγ́ΝΑΤΑΙ ἁρπᾶzειν (2496 *b*)

[2767] In x. 28—9 οὐχ ἁρπάσει τις...οὐδεὶς δύναται ἁρπάζειν the difference intended between ἁρπάσει and δύναται ἁρπάζειν (if the latter is correct) must depend to some extent upon the whole context (2740—4), and especially on the object of ἁρπάζειν, which is implied in W.H.'s text, but inserted by Chrys. and Latin versions².

---

¹ [2766 (i) *a*] Another Epictetian use of τίς, illustrative of a v.r. in Jn, is τί δοκεῖτε; τί δοκεῖς; introducing an absurd hypothesis, *e.g.* i. 26. 5 ἐπεὶ τί δοκεῖς; ὅτι θέλων περιπίπτω κακῷ;...μὴ γένοιτο, iv. 8. 26 τί δοκεῖτε;...μὴ γένοιτο, ii. 2. 15 ἐπεὶ τί δοκεῖς; ὅτι...θέλων Σωκράτης...ἂν ἔλεγεν...; This may explain the reading of D (2184) τί δοκεῖτε ὅτι...in Jn xi. 56 τί δοκεῖ ὑμῖν; ὅτι οὐ μὴ ἔλθῃ... A scribe may have thought that the context introduced an absurd hypothesis and that τί δοκεῖτε ὅτι was the correct phrase for this. D, however, by retaining οὐ μή, gives the meaning "What think ye? [Anything so absurd as] that he will not come to the feast?"—which is probably the opposite of what is intended. Τί δοκεῖ ὑμῖν, if the text is correct, seems to mean "what is your serious opinion?" and so Nonnus, Ὑμῖν φραζομένοισι τί φαίνεται; The original may have been τί δοκεῖτε; οὐ μὴ ἔλθῃ... If δοκειτε, spelt δοκειται, came to be regarded as two words, it might lead to δοκει οτι and to the insertion of υμιν before or after δοκει (as Origen variously places it).

[2766 (i) *b*] The questions put by the Jews to the Baptist i. 19—21 σὺ τίς εἶ;... [σὺ] Ἠλείας εἶ; may be illustrated by Epict. iii. 1. 22—3 σὺ οὖν τίς εἶ...λέγε αὐτῷ, ἄν σοι δόξῃ, Σὺ δὲ τίς εἶ..., μὴ δὴ λέγε τῷ ἐξαιρέτῳ, Σὺ οὖν τίς εἶ, where the Athenians are supposed to put this question rudely to Socrates—whom they dislike for attempting to reform them—and to be rebuked for it. So, too, there is rude abruptness in iii. 22. 91 σὺ εἶ ὁ Διογένης, ὁ μὴ οἰόμενος εἶναι θεούς; and it elicits a rebuke. It illustrates the abruptness of Pilate's first question to Christ, xviii. 33 σὺ εἶ ὁ βασιλεὺς τῶν Ἰουδαίων;

² [2767 *a*] Chrys. quotes οὐδεὶς δύναται ἁρπάζειν αὐτὰ ἐκ τῆς χ. τ. πατρός μου, having previously read ὁ πατήρ ὅς (for ὅ) ἔδωκέ μοι. He means by αὐτά the sheep of the flock (called αὐτά in the preceding verse). But *a, e, f* having read ὅ ("pater quod dedit mihi") supply the neut. sing. αὐτό ("nemo potest rapere illud"). Previously, Chrys. has οὐδεὶς δύναται ταῦτα ἁρπάσαι (for οὐχ ἁρπάσει τις αὐτά) ἐκ τῆς χειρός μου, paraphrasing "no one will snatch" as "no one can possibly

Chrys. confuses together the clauses about "snatching" from the Son and "snatching" from the Father; and Nonnus blends them into one ("Nor could anyone snatch my flock that knows [me] from *our* hand[1]"). Origen in two passages omits δύναται and has οὐδεὶς ἁρπάζει ἐκ τῆς χειρὸς τοῦ πατρός, or ἐκ τῶν χειρῶν αὐτοῦ, and in one of these, while repeating οὐδεὶς ἁρπάζει, he explains it as meaning οὐδεὶς δύναται ἡμᾶς λαβεῖν[2]. SS also omits δύναται ("There is no one that doth snatch away from the hand of the Father"). In the LXX, the present infinitive, after δύναται, occurs rarely as compared with the aorist, and, when it does occur, mostly implies continuance[3]. But continuance is out of the question in x. 29. In some cases, LXX adds δύναται to express the Hebrew interrogative, *e.g.* "Shall I bear?" (i.e. "*Shall I be able* to bear?") "Did he deliver?" (i.e. "*Was he able* to deliver[4]?"). So, where Matthew has (vii. 4) "How *wilt thou say* (πῶς ἐρεῖς) to thy brother?" Luke has (vi. 42) "How *canst thou say* (πῶς δύνασαι λέγειν)?" Probably x. 29 (W.H.) is corrupt, and we should read ἁρπάζει for δύναται ἁρπάζειν.

On xii. 28 πάτερ, Δόξασόν σου τὸ ὄνομα (2512 c)

[2768] After δόξασον, B has an abbreviated μου (ṃ̊) at the end of a line, and ΤΟΟΝΟΜΑ at the beginning of the next: L has ϲΟΥ at

---

snatch"; but a little later on, he writes as if the phrase οὐδεὶς ἁρπάζει were applied to the Father (τί οὖν; εἰ διὰ τὴν δύναμιν τοῦ πατρὸς "οὐδεὶς ἁρπάζει"...) and also applied to the Son (εἰπὼν ὅτι Οὐδεὶς ἁρπάζει αὐτὰ—no longer ταῦτα—ἐκ τῆς χειρός μου), and then argues as though he had read ἁρπάζειν in connexion with the Father: εἰ γὰρ μὴ τοῦτο, ἀκόλουθον ἦν εἰπεῖν ὅτι "Ὁ πατὴρ ὃς ἔδωκέ μοι μείζων πάντων ἐστὶ καὶ οὐδεὶς δύναται ἁρπάζειν αὐτὰ ἐκ τῆς χειρός μου." Ἀλλ' οὐκ εἶπεν οὕτως ἀλλ' "ἐκ τῆς χειρὸς τοῦ πατρός μου."

[1] [2767 b] Οὐδέ τις ἁρπάξειεν ἐμὴν πινυτόφρονα ποίμνην Χειρὸς ἀφ' ἡμετέρης. Nonnus probably means "no one could [possibly] snatch" to be emphatic.

[2] [2767 c] Lomm. ii. 144 and xv. 318 (comm. Jerem.). This is important as indicating that, in Origen's view, if δύναται had been inserted, the aorist infin., not the pres., should have followed.

[3] [2767 d] When pres., it mostly denotes continuance or habit, as in Gen. xiii. 6 οὐκ ἐδύναντο κατοικεῖν, xxxvi. 7 οὐκ ἐδύνατο ἡ γῆ...φέρειν αὐτούς, xxxvii. 4 οὐκ ἐδύναντο λαλεῖν, xliii. 32 οὐ γὰρ ἐδύναντο...συνεσθίειν, xlv. 1 οὐκ ἠδύνατο... ἀνέχεσθαι, xlviii. 10 οὐκ ἠδύνατο βλέπειν (where ἔτι might very well have been inserted as it is in Ex. ii. 3 οὐκ ἠδύναντο αὐτὸ ἔτι κρύπτειν), xviii. 18 οὐ δυνήσῃ ποιεῖν, "you will not be able to continue doing" etc.

[4] [2767 e] Deut. i. 12 πῶς δυνήσομαι μόνος φέρειν; Heb. (lit.) "*How shall I bear?*" Comp. 2 K. xviii. 24 ἀποστρέψετε with the parall. Is. xxxvi. 9 δύνασθε ἀποστρέψαι, and 2 K. xviii. 34 ἐξείλαντο with the parall. Is. xxxvi. 19 ἐδύναντο ῥύσασθαι, where there is no "able" in the Heb. of either passage.

the end of a line and ΤΟΝΥ͞Ν *i.e.* τὸν υἱόν at the beginning of the next: ℵ has coy at the end of a line, and ΤΟΟΝΟΜΑ at the beginning of the next. D has ΟΝΟΜΑ at the end of a line, and adds εν τη δοξη η ειχον παρα σοι προ του τον κοσμον γενεσθαι (see xvii. 5). Nonnus follows L, having Υἷα τεὸν κύδαινε, and this is the reading of a MS. in the Ferrar group (πάτερ ἅγιε δόξασόν σου τὸν υἱόν). Resch *ad loc.* quotes Augustine, "*clarifica me* ea claritate...mundus fieret" and Jerome "*glorifica me* gloria...mundus esset," as being uttered immediately before the Voice from heaven; and Aphraates, "*Jesus said*—I have glorified it and will glorify it."

[2769] SS, which agrees with W.H. up to "glorify thy name," proceeds "*And in the same hour was heard*" (instead of "there came therefore"), D has καὶ ἐγένετο for ἦλθεν οὖν and Nonnus has πέλε. The facts indicate that there was early confusion as to the words that followed δόξασον. The causes may have been, in part, a desire to paraphrase for Greeks the meaning of "Name," and to shew that "glorify thy Name" meant in effect "glorify thy Son"; in part, from an early confusion caused by Greek corruption of the letters ΤΟΝΥ͞Ν and ΤΟΟΝΟΜΑ. If, in some early MSS., ΤΟΟΝΟΜΑ was written ΤΟΥΝΟΜΑ —by crasis, as in Mt. xxvii. 57—ΤΟΥΝ, at the end of a line, might easily be read as ΤΟΥ͞Ν, "the Son."

[2770] Origen, commenting on Christ's recognition of the ordinance of all things by the Father in accordance with the set "hour," says, "Dicit in aliquo loco ad matrem suam *Nondum venit hora mea.* Item, *Nunc anima mea...propter hoc veni in hanc horam.* Item, *Pater, venit hora, clarifica Filium tuum ut et Filius tuus clarificet te*[1]." If the second "item" were omitted, this would place the words "Glorify thy Son" immediately after that utterance of Christ which preceded the Voice from heaven, in such a way as to lead readers to take the two separate sayings as a single continuous one. This indicates another way in which to explain the extraordinary misquotation of Augustine and Jerome. They may have been influenced by *some collection of Christ's sayings about the "hour."* Some confusion arising from the repetition of ὥρα may perhaps account for the phrase in SS, "*and in the same hour.*"

On ἐάν with indicative (2515 (i))

[2771] Deissmann (p. 201) calls attention to the fact that Berl.

---

[1] On Mt. xxvi. 1 (Lomm. iv. 388).

[2772] NOTES ON PRECEDING PARAGRAPHS

Pap. 48. 13 (which he dates 2nd—3rd cent. A.D.) has ἐάν with the indic. and also thrice with the subjunct. The sentence with the indic. runs thus, ἐὰν δέ σοι δόξῃ καὶ περὶ τῶν ἐριδίων, ἐὰν δὲ μὴ ἐνῆν ἐρ[ί]δια, [χ]άριν ποίσας π[έ]μψεις μοι…i.e. "If you would be pleased [to do this] also in the matter of the fleeces [I should be obliged], but, *if it should turn out that the fleeces were not practicable*, kindly send…." The first subjunctive is ἐὰν οὖν δοκῇ σοι, the third is ἐὰν ἀναβῇς τῇ ἑορτῇ (2715 d). Deissmann gives another instance of ἐάν with ἦν from Berl. Pap. 300. 5 (148 A.D.) ἀπαιτήσαντα τοὺς μισθωτὰς, κἂν δέον ἦν μισθώσαντα ἢ αὐτουργήσαντα. Here, as above, the meaning is "*and, if it should turn out to have been* needful." The MS. is illiterate. But there seems a fair probability that the writer really meant, not κἂν ᾖ "*even if it be*," but κἂν ἦν, which he intended to be taken as above.

On iota subscript (2515 (i) b)

[2772] Phrynichus says ἧς ἐν ἀγορᾷ σόλοικον. λέγε οὖν ἦσθα. He then adds—according to the printed text—" but the [person] saying ἐὰν ᾖς ἐν ἀγορᾷ would use [ᾖς] *more correctly*," ὀρθότερον δὲ χρῶτο ἂν ὁ λέγων, ἐὰν ᾖς ἐν ἀγορᾷ. But how can what is *absolutely correct*, ἐὰν ᾖς, be described as "*more correct*"—and, more amazing still, "more correct" than what is described as σόλοικον? Dr Rutherford (p. 240) calls attention to this language as indicating "uncertainty," which he justly calls "surprising." Coming from Phrynichus, not a lenient critic, it is incredible. But Lobeck adds a note that suggests a corruption in Phrynichus's text, "Ex Ed. Pr. et Phavor. restitui ἄν, quod Nunnesius praetermisit. Vulgo ὀρθώτερον."

[2773] Omitting ἄν, we obtain χρωτοο. Now Phrynichus, in his *Ecloga*, when he tells his readers what to say, uses λέγε, ἐρεῖς, most frequently, and χρὴ λέγειν rarely, but never χρῶτο with or without ἄν. On the other hand he has (Lobeck p. 37) τῷ ἄπειμι χρῶ, and (p. 175) τὸ ῥάπισμα οὐκ ἐν χρήσει· χρῶ οὖν τῷ κρείττονι. *A priori*, then, χρῶ τῷ is more likely here than χρῶτο. And, if we accept χρῶ, we reject ἄν, with "Nunnesius."

[2774] To this it may be objected that the text has χρωτο not χρωτω. But the text (according to Lobeck "vulgo") also has ὀρθώτερον for ὀρθότερον, indicating that the scribe, like the farmer Gemellus (2691), confounded o and ω, an extremely frequent error. And Jann. *Gk Gr.* par. 20ᶜ alleges "τō for τῶι H. Röhl 503 twice," and also quotes "Strabo 14, 41 πολλοὶ χωρὶς τοῦ ι γράφουσι τὰς δοτικὰς καὶ (add ὑποτακτικάς) ἐκβάλλουσι δὲ τὸ ἔθος φυσικὴν αἰτίαν οὐκ ἔχον," i.e. "Many write the datives and [add subjunctives] without the *iota*" [i.e. the iota commonly called subscript] "and reject the custom, having [indeed] no reason in nature."

[2775] These facts suggest that the real question in Phrynichus's mind is not of a *grammatical* nature—whether ἐὰν ᾖς is "more correct" *grammatically* than the "soloecism" ᾗς. It is a question of *orthography—whether* ΗΣ, *when subjunctive, should be written with, or without, the iota subscript*. Strabo, as alleged above, seems to have disliked the use of the iota subscript, and indeed the papyri indicate that it was greatly abused[1]. But the use of the *iota* in ᾖς subjunctive was certainly convenient, and Phrynichus seems to have come to the conclusion that it was also "more correct[2]." According to this view, the text of Phrynichus must be read, ὀρθότερον δὲ χρῶ τῷ ι λέγων, Ἐὰν ᾖς ἐν ἀγορᾷ, "But when you mean, 'If you be in the market-place,' *use the iota*, [*thus writing*] *more correctly* [*than those who do not use it*]."

On the Possessive Genitive (2558—69)

[2776] The vernacular possessive genitive[3]—called hereafter, for brevity, the vernacular possessive, or vernacular genitive—is not only unemphatic, but, so to speak, *under-emphasized, in order to emphasize the context*. It occurs in Plato's *Phaedo* (117 B) where, in answer to the question of Socrates "what must one do [after taking the hem-

---

[1] [2775 a] Comp., as one of many specimens, *Fayûm Pap.* (1st cent.) 137 θεῶι με(γά)λο μεγάλωι. χρημάτισον μοι, ἢ μείνωι...ἢ μέλ(λ)ω ἐντυνχάνιν ; τουτωι ἐμοὶ χρημάτισον (answer me this). This also illustrates ωι for ο (in τουτωι).

[2] [2775 b] It has been suggested to me that ὀρθότερον—instead of implying that two views of ης are more or less right—may be a "litotes," or under-statement, like Kemble's reproof to George IV., "It would *better* become your Royal Highness's mouth to say 'oblige' (instead of *obleege*)," meaning that "obleege" was *not "becoming"* at all. But ὀρθότερον λέγειν is used by Plato 165 B, 362 A, Aristot. *Phys. Ausc.* iv. 13. 8, of "*the more correct*" *of two* assertions, and Phrynichus himself says (Lobeck p. 235) Διόσκουροι, ὀρθότερον Διόσκοροι. It is true that he adds γελάσεις οὖν τοὺς σὺν τῷ υ λέγοντας. But he must have known that both were right, since Plato and Thucydides (Lobeck) use the form at which he says his readers may laugh as not being the usual Attic one.

[3] [2776 a] i.e. for example, (1) αὐτοῦ coming *before the article and the noun*, αὐτοῦ ἡ κεφαλή, as distinct from (2) the possessive genitive in the order usual in the Synoptists and in the LXX ἡ κεφαλὴ αὐτοῦ, and from (3) the very rare emphatic genitive ἡ αὐτοῦ κεφαλή, see **2558**. It may be in some slight degree illustrated by "me" and "to me" in English, where "me" may be either emphatic or unemphatic ("Give *me* the book," or "Give me the *book*"), but "to me" is necessarily emphatic ("Give the book *to me*").

[2777] NOTES ON PRECEDING PARAGRAPHS

lock]?" the jailer replies "you must just drink it off and walk about, till you feel a *weight* in your *legs* (ἕως ἄν σου βάρος ἐν τοῖς σκέλεσι γένηται)": also *Symp.* 215 E where it is parallel to the unemphatic *dativus commodi* μοι, "When I am in the act of listening to Socrates my heart leaps up with more than corybantic bounds (πολύ μοι μᾶλλον ἢ τῶν κορυβαντιώντων ἥ τε καρδία πηδᾷ)...but listening to Pericles...I used to feel nothing like this, and [though my outer man was moved] my *soul* was not [thus] instantaneously whirled away (οὐδὲ τεθορύβητό μου ἡ ψυχή)...." It might fairly be called a *genitivus commodi* or *incommodi*. So, the innkeeper in Aristophanes uses σου and μου as *genitivus incommodi* in *Ran.* 572—3 "How dearly I should love to *smash* your *grinders with a stone* (ὡς ἡδέως ἄν σου λίθῳ τοὺς γομφίους κόπτοιμ' ἄν) for *gobbling up* my *property* (οἷς μου κατέφαγες τὰ φορτία)," *ib.* 1198—1200 οὐ κατ' ἔπος γέ σου κνίσω τὸ ῥῆμ' ἕκαστον, ἀλλά...ἀπὸ ληκυθίου σου τοὺς προλόγους διαφθερῶ[1].

[2777] The same use of an unemphatic pronoun, in order to throw the emphasis on other words in the context, is noticeable in the position of σε in adjurations, Soph. *Phil.* 468 πρός νύν σε πατρός ...ἱκνοῦμαι, *Oed. C.* 1333 πρός νύν σε κρηνῶν...αἰτῶ. The speaker merely touches the personality and passes from it to dwell on some circumstance of the person. It is particularly convenient where more than one noun is connected with the pronoun, as in the sarcastic Athenian utterance to the poor trustful Melians (Thuc. v. 105) "But as for your fanciful way of looking to Lacedaemonians, which makes you trust that their fear of disgrace will force them to help you—while congratulating your innocence we do not envy [your] insanity (μακαρίσαντες ὑμῶν τὸ ἀπειρόκακον οὐ ζηλοῦμεν τὸ ἄφρον)."

[2778] The vernacular possessive is a frequent characteristic of Epictetus. The following shews that μου and σου for example are used, not to mean "belonging to me, or to you," but to emphasize the context, while merely indicating the personality:—i. 4. 13 Σὺ οὖν ἐνταῦθά μοι δεῖξόν σου τὴν προκοπήν. καθάπερ, εἰ ἀθλητῇ διελεγόμην, Δεῖξόν μοι τοὺς ὤμους· εἶτα ἔλεγεν ἐκεῖνος, Ἴδε μου τοὺς ἁλτῆρας. The preceding context is about "progress," προκοπή. The student has

---

[1] [2776 *b*] In Aristoph. *Ran.* 1201 ἀπὸ ληκυθίου; σύ; τοὺς ἐμούς; would perhaps be an exaggeration of the true punctuation, but it would be truer than Dindorf's ἀ. ληκυθίου σὺ τ. ἐ.; The σύ is initial, emphatic, and insulting, as in *ib.* 1205 ἰδού, σὺ δείξεις;

NOTES ON PRECEDING PARAGRAPHS [2779]

boasted of his *progress*—"in Chrysippus." So many treatises! He can now read Chrysippus by himself! Epictetus replies, I don't want progress "in Chrysippus" but progress *in right thought and right action*. "Do you, then, in these points shew me your *progress*." In what follows (δεῖξόν μοι τοὺς ὤμους) he could not say δεῖξόν μοί σου τ. ὤ. because that would have emphasized the two pronouns by juxtaposition (2564, 2783). So he omits σου. But here the unemphatic μοι helps to throw emphasis on τοὺς ὤμους. Similarly in the pseudo-athlete's answer the emphasis is thrown forward from the unemphatic "my" to the following noun, "Look at my *dumb-bells*." The poor creature has no *acts* on view—only *preparations for acting*. Similarly in i. 18. 16 ἀπώλεσά μου τὸ ἱμάτιον is parallel to ἀλγῶ τὴν κεφαλήν where no pronoun is inserted[1].

[2779] The ordinary possessive genitive *after the noun*, in Epictetus, is more emphatic, or, at all events, not unemphatic. It may be illustrated by i. 1. 23 "'I will bind you.' 'Man! what do you mean? Me? *My leg* you will bind (τὸ σκέλος μου δήσεις),"—that is, "*the leg that belongs to me*, a *possession of mine*, not my very self." In the next sentence, he does not say τὴν προαίρεσίν μου, for that would be an admission that the "will," like the "leg," was a mere possession; so he continues, τὴν προαίρεσιν δὲ οὐδ᾽ ὁ Ζεὺς νικῆσαι δύναται, "But *the* will not even Zeus can conquer[2]." "The leg my possession" resembles "the corpse my possession"—which cannot be expressed in English—in i. 19. 9 "'I will shew you I am [your] master.' 'You? Impossible!—But you are master of *my corpse* (τοῦ νεκροῦ δέ μου κύριος εἶ). Take it!'" A querulous egoist complains i. 6. 30 αἱ μύξαι μου ῥέουσι, "*my nose* is running," and Epictetus, imagining himself an egoist, says (ii. 18. 17) "I stroke *my [own] head* (καταψῶ τὴν κορυφήν μου) and say, 'Well done, Epictetus!'" Again, the exceptional creature says to its censor iii. 1. 23 "Don't require me to be like the rest. Or, if you must blame, blame *my [inherent] nature* (τῇ φύσει μου)[3]."

---

[1] Comp. i. 4. 24 and 29, i. 11. 4, and many more instances in Schenkl's Index under Ἐγώ.

[2] [2779 a] The "will," or προαίρεσις, is the man himself, iii. 1. 40 "You are not flesh, or hair, but *will* (προαίρεσις)," iv. 5. 11 "Are you a mere utensil? No, you are *will* (οὔ, ἀλλὰ προαίρεσις)."

[3] For instances of the possessive μου after its noun, see Schenkl's Index, in which there are fewer of these than of the vernacular genitive.

[2780] NOTES ON PRECEDING PARAGRAPHS

[2780] The vernacular and unemphatic αὐτοῦ and αὐτῶν is also frequent in Epictetus, and, in some of these instances, emphasis appears to be laid on what precedes as well as on what follows, *e.g.* i. 19. 4 "What! Do I not attend to my donkey? Do I not *wash* his *feet* (οὐ νίπτω αὐτοῦ τοὺς πόδας)?" ii. 8. 26 "Does the statue of Zeus in Olympia draw up [his] eyebrow? On the contrary his *look is fixed* (ἀλλὰ πέπηγεν αὐτοῦ τὸ βλέμμα)"—where the parallelism shews the pronoun to be unemphatic, iii. 20. 14 "what will you make of sickness? I will *reveal* its *nature* (δείξω αὐτῆς τὴν φύσιν)," iii. 22. 75 "See how low (ποῦ) we are bringing down our Cynic! *after what a fashion* we are despoiling him of his *kingdom* (πῶς αὐτοῦ τὴν βασιλείαν ἀφαιρούμεθα)¹!"

¹ [2780 *a*] Comp. ii. 18. 22 διαπαίζοντα αὐτοῦ τὴν ὥραν, ii. 21. 15 and many other instances in Schenkl: iii. 5. 12 Ἀλλ' ἡ μήτηρ μου τὴν κεφαλὴν νοσοῦντος οὐ κρατήσει. Ἄπιθι τοίνυν πρὸς τὴν μητέρα is placed by Schenkl as an instance of precedent μου, but the Latin has "mea mater." Probably Schenkl is right, and, as τὴν μητέρα means "[your] mother," so ἡ μήτηρ means "[my] mother"—"Mother will not hold my head when it aches."

[2780 *b*] For ἡμῶν as a vernacular genitive see Epict. ii. 12. 11—12 "We are absolutely unable to move him by these means, and consequently, as is natural, perceiving this inability of ours (ταύτης ἡμῶν τῆς ἀδυναμίας) we give the matter up," where ἡμῶν is so unemphatic that Mrs Carter's transl. omits it in English. The difference between the moderately emphatic ἡμῶν in οἱ πολῖται ἡμῶν and the vernacular and unemphatic ἡμῶν in ἡμῶν οἱ πολῖται is neatly illustrated in ii. 20. 22—4 where a philosopher is first requested to prove that religion is a good thing "in order that *the citizens of our state* (οἱ πολῖται ἡμῶν) may honour the divine Being": then, after being thanked for the proof, he offers to prove the contrary, and having done so, is thanked ironically, thus, "Well done, Mr Philosopher! You have done a service to *our citizens* (ἡμῶν τοὺς πολίτας)"—almost equivalent to "you have done the citizens a service for us, or, at our request." Another instance of the unemphatic ἡμῶν when citizens speak of "our city"—in a context that has previously implied "our"—contains also the unemphatic μου and the emphatic τὰ ἐμά. The philosopher is describing the castle of his mind, iv. 5. 24—5 "These reptiles [ἀνδράποδα ταῦτα, *i.e.* the mocking world] do not know in the least either who I am or where I find the Good and the Evil (οὐδὲ ποῦ μου τὸ ἀγαθὸν καὶ τὸ κακόν): for they have no way of getting at *what is really mine* (ὅτι οὐ πρόσοδος αὐτοῖς πρὸς τὰ ἐμά). Just so, those who dwell in a strong city mock at their besiegers: ['Yesterday,' they say, 'things might have been different,] but, as it is (νῦν δ'), what trouble these fellows are taking—and all for nothing! Our wall is secured (ἀσφαλές ἐστιν ἡμῶν τὸ τεῖχος), we have food for any length of time, and every preparation made.'"

[2780 *c*] Ὑμῶν is a vernacular genitive following an emphatic ὑμεῖς in iii. 16. 13 "The physicians send away their chronic patients for change of air (ἄλλον ἀέρα). And they do right. You, too, [must do the same]. Make a thorough change of habits, fix your fundamental conceptions (πήξατε ὑμῶν τὰς ὑπολήψεις)."

[2781] This vernacular genitive may be frequent in some authors and rare in others. In the LXX, for example, in such language as "I know their sorrows, their imagination, thy rebellion and thy stiff neck, thy pride and the naughtiness of thine heart, your thoughts, their works and their thoughts, your manifold transgressions," the possessives are all represented (Ex. iii. 7, Deut. xxxi. 21, 27, 1 S. xvii. 28, Job xxi. 27 (Symm.), Is. lxvi. 18, Amos v. 12) by the ordinary genitive. But in Rev. ii. 9 "I know thy tribulation and poverty," ii. 19 "I know thy works and love and…," and iii. 1, 8, 15 "I know thy works," the vernacular genitive is used. It follows that in N.T. books in which LXX style is prominent—*e.g.* in the Acts and some portions of Luke that are in the literary style, or else moulded on the LXX—the vernacular genitive must not be expected[1].

[2780 d] But ὑμῶν is emphasized by antithesis in the following contrast drawn by Epictetus between men of the world and his pupils ("you") in their present undeveloped state. He asks them, first, whether *they* have the power of Socrates, to twist people round to his own view, iii. 16. 6—7 "How could *you* possibly have it (πόθεν ὑμῖν)? Nay, it cannot be but the men of the world will twist *you* round. Why then are *they your* superiors (ἐκεῖνοι ὑμῶν ἰσχυρότεροι, **2564**, **2783**)? Because *they* talk their rotten [stuff] from convictions [of the heart]. But *you* [preach] your healthy [doctrine] from the lips, for which cause it is nerveless and dead; and it is sickening to listen to *your* sermons (ὑμῶν τοὺς προτρεπτικούς). Thus *you* are vanquished by the men of the world." There is an intervening verb between ἡμῶν and its noun in the following, and ἡμῶν is emphasized by an antithesis carried on from the context which describes how, when we were children and fell down, "the nurse would not scold *us* but would beat the *stone*," iii. 19. 5 "Again [in boyhood] if we don't find a meal ready, the moment we come from the bath, the private tutor never dreams of checking *our* greediness (οὐδέποθ' ἡμῶν καταστέλλει τὴν ἐπιθυμίαν ὁ παιδαγωγός) but gives the *cook* a flogging."

[1] [2781 a] The non-use of the vernacular genitive may sometimes result in a want of clearness as to emphasis. For example, Luke uses the ordinary possessive sometimes where it is certainly unemphatic Acts i. 9 βλεπόντων αὐτῶν ἐπήρθη κ. νεφέλη ὑπέλαβεν αὐτὸν ἀπὸ τῶν ὀφθαλμῶν αὐτῶν, i. 18 ἐξεχύθη πάντα τὰ σπλάγχνα αὐτοῦ, but sometimes where it might well be emphatic as in i. 19 ὥστε κληθῆναι… τῇ διαλέκτῳ αὐτῶν, i. 20 (LXX) τὴν ἐπισκοπὴν αὐτοῦ λαβέτω ἕτερος. [Of course μου in Acts i. 8 ἔσεσθέ μου μάρτυρες is quite distinct from the vernacular genitive. There is no article, and μου μάρτυρες is predicative.]

[2781 b] Contrast Rev. x. 9 πικρανεῖ σου τὴν κοιλίαν ἀλλ' ἐν τῷ στόματί σου ἔσται γλυκύ, *ib.* xiv. 18 πέμψον σου τὸ δρέπανον τὸ ὀξύ, xviii. 4—5 ἐξέλθατε…ἵνα μὴ συνκοινωνήσητε ταῖς ἁμαρτίαις αὐτῆς…ὅτι ἐκολλήθησαν αὐτῆς αἱ ἁμαρτίαι ἄχρι τοῦ οὐρανοῦ—all of which allude to LXX, but the reader will find no vernacular genitives in the LXX passages indicated by W.H. (comp. **2562** a).

[2781 c] In the Gospel, Lk. has the vernacular genitive in vii. 48 ἀφέωνταί σου αἱ ἁμαρτίαι, xv. 30 οὗτος ὁ καταφαγών σου τὸν βίον, xvi. 6 δέξαι σου τὰ

[2782] NOTES ON PRECEDING PARAGRAPHS

[2782] In the Synoptists, the vernacular genitive manifestly throws emphasis on the context in Mk ix. 24 βοήθει μου τῇ ἀπιστίᾳ, and probably in Mt. xvi. 18 ἐπὶ ταύτῃ τῇ πέτρᾳ οἰκοδομήσω μου τὴν ἐκκλησίαν. In Mt. ii. 2 εἴδομεν γὰρ αὐτοῦ τὸν ἀστέρα, the Magi assume that "the [great blazing] star" pointed to the expected King, so that they ask, in effect, "Where is the King? For we have seen *the star* that is his sign." These, and three instances in Luke (2781 c), are peculiar to single evangelists. See also 2558 a.

[2783] In the Pauline epistles the vernacular μου is frequent when the Apostle assumes that his disciples will be kind to him but wishes them to be kind in a certain way and so subordinates the personal pronoun to the noun of circumstance, Phil. ii. 2 "*complete* my *joy* (π. μου τὴν χαράν)," *ib.* iv. 14 "*sharing in* my *affliction* (σ. μου τῇ θλίψει)," Col. iv. 18 "*remember* my *bonds* (μ. μου τῶν δεσμῶν)." When he uses ὑμῶν thus, there is sometimes an additional reason, namely, that (besides throwing emphasis on the context) it is the common precedent genitive of a number of nouns Col. ii. 5 βλέπων ὑμῶν τὴν τάξιν καὶ τὸ... Of course, however, where there is antithesis—and especially where two pronouns are in juxtaposition (2564)—the precedent pronoun may be emphatic 1 Cor. ix. 11 μέγα εἰ ἡμεῖς ὑμῶν τὰ σαρκικὰ θερίσομεν[1];

γράμματα rep. xvi. 7. All these are peculiar to Luke, and in what may be called his vernacular style. Lk. xix. 35 ἐπιρίψαντες αὐτῶν τὰ ἱμάτια is parall. to Mk xi. 7 ἐπιβάλλουσιν αὐτῷ τὰ ἱμάτια αὐτῶν (v.r. ἑαυτῶν and αὐτοῦ), Mt. xxi. 7 ἐπέθηκαν ἐπ' αὐτῶν τὰ ἱμάτια (v.r. + αὐτῶν). This must be discussed in a future treatise.

[2781 d] The vernacular possessive introducing a group of nouns is followed by the ordinary possessive in Rev. ii. 19 οἶδά σου τὰ ἔργα καὶ τὴν ἀ. καὶ τὴν π. καὶ τὴν δ. καὶ τὴν ὑπομονήν σου καὶ τὰ ἔργα σου τὰ ἔσχατα πλείονα τῶν πρώτων, where (1) the writer could not well have said καὶ σου, and (2) the twofold repetition (κ. τ. ὑ. σου κ. τ. ἔ. σου) shews that emphasis is intended—"the patience *that you shew* and the deeds *that you do*." The vernacular is also followed by the ordinary possessive in Rev. x. 9 καὶ πικρανεῖ σου τὴν κοιλίαν ἀλλ' ἐν τῷ στόματί σου ἔσται γλυκὺ ὡς μέλι, where the unemphatic σου throws the emphasis on πικρανεῖ and τὴν κοιλίαν, but the writer could not have said ἀλλ' ἐν σου τῷ στόματι, and besides he wished to throw the emphasis on γλυκὺ ὡς μέλι. The two passages shew that the unemphatic σου is not likely to be used after an unemphatic word.

[1] [2783 a] 2 Pet. iii. 1—2 Ταύτην ἤδη...δευτέραν ὑμῖν γράφω ἐπιστολήν, ἐν αἷς διεγείρω ὑμῶν ἐν ὑπομνήσει τὴν εἰλικρινῆ διάνοιαν, μνησθῆναι τῶν προειρημένων ῥημάτων ὑπὸ τῶν ἁγίων προφητῶν καὶ τῆς τῶν ἀποστόλων ὑμῶν ἐντολῆς τοῦ κυρίου καὶ σωτῆρος is such amazing Greek that it is hard to say what precisely the writer meant. But perhaps the first ὑμῶν is under-emphasized in order to emphasize the following words. As for the second ὑμῶν, R.V. renders it "*your* Apostles"—an astonishing

[2784] Space does not admit of a fuller discussion of the Pauline distinction between the vernacular and the ordinary possessive genitive. It is sufficient to have shewn that the former is characteristic of Aristophanes, Paul, Epictetus, and, generally, of what may be described as "spoken Greek." Often, it cannot be expressed in English. But it adds greatly to the force of the Fourth Gospel, and John's abundant use of it as well as of the ordinary genitive should protect us from the danger of imagining that he uses the two promiscuously. It is an instance of what Winer-Moulton calls "an effort to throw an unemphatic word into the shade[1]" and what Blass calls "the tendency which from early times exists in Greek as in cognate languages, to bring unemphasized (enclitic) pronouns and the like as near as possible to the beginning of the sentence (though not to put them actually at the beginning)[2]."

---

phrase. To take it as meaning "*your* Lord and Saviour" would perhaps not be much more astonishing.

[1] [2784 a] Winer-Moulton p. 689. But in view of its use by the jailer in the *Phaedo* and the inn-keepers in the *Frogs*, and in the perfectly spontaneous little dialogues of Epictetus, and in the uncouth inartistic effusions of the author (or authors) of Revelation, and in some of the most impassioned parts of the impassioned epistles of St Paul—combined with its extraordinary prevalence in the Fourth Gospel, a work that breathes of a most divine inspiration—"effort" does not seem to be the happiest of expressions for this very natural construction. Nor is the unemphatic word exactly "*thrown* into the shade." It *is* in the shade, but "the shade" is its natural place. For, being really not so much a genitive of possession as a *genitivus commodi*, it takes the place of the *dativus commodi*.

[2] [2784 b] Blass p. 288 quotes Rom. i. 11 ἵνα τι μεταδῶ χάρισμα ὑμῖν πνευματικόν, Acts xxvi. 24 τὰ πολλά σε γράμματα εἰς μανίαν περιτρέπει, Heb. iv. 11 ἵνα μὴ ἐν τῷ αὐτῷ τις ὑποδείγματι πέσῃ, 1 Cor. v. 1 ὥστε γυναῖκά τινα τοῦ πατρὸς ἔχειν. On this last, he says that the object is "also to emphasize both γυν. and πατρός." I should extend this remark to his other instances, in all of which the context seems to me to be emphasized by the unemphatic pronoun; and this applies to Jn ix. 6 ἐπέχρισεν αὐτοῦ τὸν πηλὸν ἐπὶ τοὺς ὀφθαλμούς, if (2569 c) the text is sound.

[2784 c] Blass includes xiii. 6 σύ μου νίπτεις τοὺς πόδας, in which however, owing to the juxtaposition of pronouns (2564, 2783), μου (as well as σύ) appears to me to be emphasized. So too is ὑμῶν by the context in Mt. xxiii. 8 (*bis*) "But be not *ye* (ὑμεῖς) called Rabbi, for one is *your* teacher (εἷς γάρ ἐστιν ὑμῶν ὁ διδάσκαλος)...."

[2784 d] Blass adds "Lk. xviii. 18 καὶ ἐπηρώτησέν τις αὐτὸν ἄρχων λέγων. But here again there is no obligation to use this order of words: thus we have 2 Cor. xi. 16 κἂν ὡς ἄφρονα δέξασθέ με, where no doubt the object was to give δέξασθε the prior position." I should rather be disposed to explain it by the preceding words, μή τίς με δόξῃ ἄφρονα εἶναι, εἰ δὲ μήγε κἂν ὡς ἄφρονα δέξασθέ με, ἵνα κἀγώ...the personality being first under-emphasized and then, to some extent, emphasized,

[2785] NOTES ON PRECEDING PARAGRAPHS

On the "epistolary aorist" (2691 d)

[2785] Jerome comments on Gal. vi. 11 thus (Migne): "*Videte qualibus litteris scripsi vobis;* non quod grandes litterae fuerint (hoc quippe in Graeco sonat πηλίκοις), sed quod suae manus essent eis nota vestigia." This (1) renders πηλίκοις by "qualibus" "*of what sort*," (2) appears to deny that the "letters" were "*great*," or at any rate that the "greatness" was the point to which attention was called, (3) asserts that they were written by the Apostle's "*own hand*." Later on, (4) he illustrates (or quotes[1] an illustration of) "mea manu" from Jerem. xxxvii. 2 "sermo Dei qui factus est *in manu* Jeremiae" (where "manu" does not mean lit. "hand") and says (or quotes a saying) that St Paul writes "grandes litteras" to-day to everybody—giving both to "*hand*" and to "*great*" a spiritual significance—"magnae sunt litterae quia in litteris magnus est sensus."

[2786] Between these two distinct interpretations Migne's edition of Jerome inserts the following, "In hoc loco vir apprime nostris temporibus eruditus[2], *miror quomodo rem ridiculam locutus sit*[3]. Paulus, inquit, Hebraeus erat et Graecas litteras nesciebat. Et quia necessitas expetebat, ut manu sua epistolam subscriberet[4], contra consuetudinem curvos tramites litterarum, vix magnis apicibus exprimebat: etiam in hoc suae ad Galatas indicia caritatis ostendens, quod propter illos id quoque quod non poterat, facere conaretur. Grandibus ergo Paulus litteris scripsit epistolam, quia sensus erat grandis in illis...." If the text is correct, Jerome appears to be sneering at, and parodying, the view held by Chrysostom, who connects St Paul's writing with ἠναγκάσθη, ἀναγκαίως, ἠναγκάσθην (Jer. "necessitas") and who represents St Paul as saying "I do not know how to write *very well* (ἄριστα)"—which Jerome parodies by saying that he "attempted to do what he *was not able to do.*" In Jerome's last quoted sentence ("grandibus *ergo* Paulus...sensus erat

---

"receive *me* [as being your Father in Christ] that I, too, may...." Comp. *ib.* xi. 1 ὄφελον ἀνείχεσθέ μου μικρόν τι ἀφροσύνης· ἀλλὰ καὶ ἀνέχεσθέ μου, where there is first under-emphasis and then emphasis.

[1] Most probably it is a quotation, and not Jerome's own view (see **2786**), but the passage is very obscure.

[2] [**2786** a] Migne has the following note "Quanquam hoc ferme Chrysostomus sentiat, quod Hieron. impugnat, illum tamen hic denotari non puto." Migne gives no reasons for this opinion.

[3] Wetst. omits the italicised words.

[4] Wetst. has "scriberet."

grandis") the "ergo" introduces obscurity. It may mean "consequently, as this 'vir eruditus' says," or "consequently, I suppose, this 'vir eruditus' would infer." It can hardly mean "consequently, as I infer from my own statement of the facts."

[2787] Jerome repeatedly says that the Apostle began to write with his own hand from Gal. vi. 11. But his evidence is discredited (1) by the fact that he mistranslates one of the two words (πηλίκοις) on which the argument turns. (2) He may have been misled as to ἔγραψα by the Latin epistolary usage of the past tense. (3) There is a tone of bitterness about his remarks indicating that the question had become controversial, and not auguring well for a dispassionate conclusion based on evidence.

[2788] Lightfoot (*ad loc.*) asks "Does he (*i.e.* St Paul), as *Chrysostom* and others have supposed, point to the rude ill-formed[1] characters...as though he gloried in his imperfect knowledge of Greek?" I can find nothing in Migne's or Cramer's version indicating that Chrysostom—whose name I have italicised above—supposed the apostle to have "gloried" in anything of the kind. Cramer prints something of the kind as from Theodorus, but even his words (2691*d*) οὔτε αὐτὸς ἐρυθριᾷ do not refer to any such "imperfect knowledge." Chrysostom says, οὐδὲν ἄλλο αἰνίττεται, ἀλλ᾽ ὅτι αὐτὸς ἔγραψε τὴν ἐπιστολὴν ἅπασαν· ὃ πολλῆς γνησιότητος (see Steph. and comp. preceding γνησίων "relations") σημεῖον ἦν *i.e.* "a sign of *great natural affection*," and he adds that Paul wrote with his own hand, partly to refute those who asserted that he did not really condemn the Judaizing doctrine but partly "*owing to love* (δι᾽ ἀγάπην)." He concludes, τὸ (al. τῷ) δὲ "πηλίκοις" ἐμοὶ δοκεῖ οὐ τὸ μέγεθος, ἀλλὰ τὴν ἀμορφίαν τῶν γραμμάτων ἐμφαίνων λέγειν (al. λέγει) μονονουχὶ λέγων, ὅτι οὐδὲ ἄριστα γράφειν εἰδώς, ὅμως ἠναγκάσθην δι᾽ ἐμαυτοῦ γράψαι ὥστε συκοφαντῶν ἐμφράξαι τὸ στόμα. These words do not deny that the "letters" were "large"; they merely suggest that the Apostle *emphasized, not their largeness but their uncouthness*, saying in effect "I cannot write [in Greek characters] very well, but yet I was constrained to write with my own hand so as to stop the

---

[1] [2788*a*] Lightf. says, "πηλίκοις denotes size only, not irregularity." But it does not need much imagination to see that a large O, or Θ, or C, written by a Jew, unaccustomed to the round characters of Greek writing, was likely to be "irregular" in proportion to its "largeness"—very much like a child's "large hand" in English, which he is taught to write "large" because the "largeness" brings out the "irregularity" that has to be corrected.

[2789] NOTES ON PRECEDING PARAGRAPHS

mouth of slanderers." The whole of the context implies that there is no "glorying," but an affectionate allusion to his inability to write Greek in anything but a laborious, uncouth "large hand."

[2789] In Jerome, the interpretation that explains πηλίκοις by "grandis sensus"—supposing it to be, not Jerome's, but one ridiculed by him—may be explained as part of the view adopted by Chrysostom and perhaps borrowed by Chrysostom from Origen, whose commentary on this Epistle was freely used by Jerome. Origen may have said that St Paul's "large letters" were *not only literally large but also a sign of the largeness of his affection* and spiritual sympathy with the Galatians. Chrysostom expresses the same thing, only without this symbolism. Jerome literalises and laughs at it. If Origen had taken Jerome's view of the epistolary aorist, it seems probable that, on a point of this controversial character, the Latin Father would have appealed to one Greek Father against the rest. At the outset of his Galatian commentary, Jerome expressly says that he has read that of Origen[1]. In one passage he extracts nearly two columns from it continuously[2]. In another he quotes a passage of some length without acknowledgment[3]. In a third, he assails the opinions of Origen[4]. Not improbably Jerome is here again dissenting from Origen as well as Chrysostom—under cover of a "vir apprime nostris temporibus eruditus," who, whether he is Chrysostom or not, appears to have expressed Chrysostom's view with considerable verbal similarity. It may be added that when Jerome wrote this commentary (388 A.D.) he had only recently commenced his long residence in Palestine (which began in 386 A.D.)[5].

---

[1] [2789 a] Jerome pp. 369—70 (Migne pp. 332—3) " Quid igitur, ergo (? ego) stultus aut temerarius qui id pollicear quod illo (? ille) non potuit? Minime. Quin potius in eo, ut mihi videor, cautior atque timidior quod, imbecillitatem virium mearum sentiens, *Origenis Commentarios sum secutus*. Scripsit enim ille vir in Epistolam Pauli ad Galatas quinque proprie volumina, et...tractatus quoque varios ...legi haec omnia."

[2] Migne pp. 434—6.

[3] See Migne's note, p. 391 n., " Haec ex Origine (*sic*) pene ad verbum descripsit," and Migne appends more than a dozen lines from Origen.

[4] See Migne's note, p. 349 n., " Haec, ut et inferior totus contextus, Origenem ejusque asseclas verissime petunt: hanc enim ille (sc. Origenes) blasphemiam incurrit...."

[5] *Dict. Christ. Biogr.* " Hieronymus," vol. iii. p. 48.

[2790] Wetst. on Gal. vi. 11 quotes "*Plotinus* de Porphyrio, ἔγραφε δὲ οὐδὲ εἰς κάλλος ἀποτυπούμενος τὰ γράμματα, οὔτε εὐσήμως τὰς συλλαβὰς διαιρῶν, οὔτε τῆς ὀρθογραφίας φροντίζων, ἀλλὰ μόνου τοῦ νοῦ ἐχόμενος," and Suetonius says of Augustus (§ 88) "*Orthographiam*, id est formulam rationemque scribendi a grammaticis institutam non adeo custodit ac *videtur eorum potius sequi opinionem qui perinde scribendum ac loquamur existiment*...."

On ἄλλος in Epictetus and John (2730)

[2791] The use of ἄλλος in v. 32 ἄλλος ἐστὶν ὁ μαρτυρῶν to mean the Father may be illustrated by its use in Epictetus to denote God, whom he regards as the Friend and Father of all good men, providing for His children all that they need, so that the philosopher may say (iii. 13. 13—14) "Now no evil can possibly befall me...all is peace, all is calm,...*Another*, who makes [my wants] His care, supplies food, *Another* [not myself, gives me] raiment, *Another* gave [me] perceptions, *Another* gave [me] [mental] anticipations: and when at any moment I find Him stopping this continual supply of the necessaries [of life] [then, I know] He is sounding the retreat, He has opened (ἤνοιξε) the door and He is saying, 'Come'"; iii. 1. 42—3 "But mark what Socrates says...'Equip thy will, eradicate base convictions.' 'What about the body, then?' '[Deal with it] according to its nature. These things *Another* has made His care; leave them in His hands.'"

[2792] This Being, whom Epictetus (iii. 3. 1—10) reverentially calls "*Another*," Ἄλλος, is not Different, Ἕτερος, from men—any more than Caesar is "different" from his subjects. He is the Good (τὸ ἀγαθόν) and He has stamped His image on "goodness" as His "current coin (νόμισμα)" and has given this current coin to man so that he can keep it if he pleases. Not even Zeus can take it from him. Man can keep it as Zeus keeps it[1]. As the banker or the greengrocer cannot refuse the legal "good coin," namely, Caesar's coinage, so, in the spiritual world, the bad and the good cannot refuse that coinage which represents, for them, "the good[2]." If a bad man

---

[1] [2792 a] Epict. iii. 3. 5—10 οὕτω γὰρ πέφυκα· τοῦτό μοι τὸ νόμισμα δέδωκεν ὁ Θεός...ἐκ ταύτης γὰρ τῆς οὐσίας τίς δύναται ἐκβαλεῖν; οὐδ' ὁ Ζεύς. οὐδὲ γὰρ ἠθέλησεν. ἀλλ' ἐπ' ἐμοὶ αὐτὸ ἐποίησε, καὶ ἔδωκεν οἷον εἶχεν αὐτός—ἀκώλυτον, ἀνανάγκαστον, ἀπαραπόδιστον.

[2] [2792 b] Epict. iii. 3. 3 ὡς γὰρ τὸ τοῦ Καίσαρος νόμισμα οὐκ ἔξεστιν ἀποδοκιμάσαι τῷ τραπεζίτῃ οὐδὲ τῷ λαχανοπώλῃ, ἀλλ' ἂν δείξῃς—θέλει οὐ θέλει—προέσθαι αὐτὸν δεῖ τὸ ἀντ' αὐτοῦ πωλούμενον, οὕτως ἔχει καὶ ἐπὶ τῆς ψυχῆς.

chooses a bad coinage—he is constrained by the Law to take that. A thievish proconsul comes into your province; you capture him with money: an adulterer, with women. They must perforce take the bribe. To a sportsman you offer a fine horse or hound: "Cursing and groaning [at his fate] he will sell you for it what you will. *For Another constrains him in his heart* (ἔσωθεν), *He that hath appointed this current coin* (ὁ τὸ νόμισμα τοῦτο τεταχώς)[1]." Elsewhere (i. 25. 13), when the philosopher is asked by a controversialist to "suppose himself" to be "in evils (ἐν κακοῖς)," he replies that he cannot suppose this—meaning that he, a son of God (2799 *e*), never deserted by God, cannot be in real "evils"—and he phrases it thus, "*Another* prevents me." And, in case any of his pupils should be brought before kings and rulers to testify for the truth, he prepares them thus: "When thou art going into [the judgment hall of] some one in power remember that *there is also Another noting from above all that goes on*, and that thou must please Him rather than the man in power[2]."

[2793] We pass to the Johannine use of ἄλλος. In xiv. 16 "If ye love me ye will keep my commandments: and I will request the Father and *he will give you another Paraclete* (ἄλλον παράκλητον δώσει ὑμῖν)," SS has "*another*, the Paraclete." A Paraclete (1720) meant a "friend in court," an "*alter ego*," an unpaid advocate. "We know not how to pray as we ought," says the Epistle to the Romans (viii. 26), "but the Spirit itself maketh intercession for us"; and Mark

---

[1] [2792 *c*] Epict. iii. 3. 13 "Ἄλλος γὰρ αὐτὸν ἀναγκάζει ἔσωθεν ὁ τὸ νόμισμα τοῦτο τεταχώς. Schweig. "Is *alius*, quem dicit (cf. iii. 1. 43 n.) Deus est; qui talem naturam constituit hominis ut qua in re is suum Bonum ponit, ei rei possit non caetera omnia postponere... Est autem hominis culpa, si ibi Bonum suum ponit ubi Deus illud non posuit."

[2] [2792 *d*] Epict. i. 30. 1. Comp. Acts iv. 19 "But Peter and John answered and said unto them," *i.e.* to the Jewish rulers sitting in judgment, "*Whether it be right in the sight of God to hearken unto you rather than unto God, judge ye.*" Steph. (who indeed does not quote any of these instances) does not appear to contain any use of ἄλλος in this Epictetian sense. It can hardly be Hebraic. "Other" and "another," in O.T., when connected with God or man, are generally used in a bad sense, *e.g.* "they followed after *other* Gods," "my glory I will not give to *another*," "there is no *other* God" etc. The notion of "*another*" world, "*another*" judgment, might naturally be developed in Gk literature out of such passages as Aesch. *Supp.* 228—31 οὐδὲ μὴ 'ν Ἅιδου θανὼν Φύγῃ μάταιον αἰτίας πράξας τάδε. Κἀκεῖ δικάζει τἀμπλακήμαθ᾽, ὡς λόγος, Ζεὺς ἄλλος ἐν καμοῦσιν ὑστάτας δίκας. But I have found no such use of ἄλλος.

has, "It is not ye that are the speakers but the Holy Spirit[1]." Hence a Christian, speaking in the reverential language of Epictetus, might say, "I do not know how to pray, *Another* teaches me," or "I do not know how to speak before princes and rulers, *Another* speaks for me and in me." *Paraclete*, or *Parclete*, was recognised as an Aramaic word and may have been used sometimes as a proper name, sometimes as a common noun. This is the first place where it is mentioned in N.T. and the meaning, according to SS, may be paraphrased thus: "If ye do your part, ye will not be left unaided. The Father will send you *Another*, a Spirit like yours but beyond yours, [as] *Paraclete* [to you]." This removes a difficulty that attends the ordinary translation "He will give you *another Paraclete* besides myself" or "in the place of myself." For the latter assumes that Christ has called Himself a Paraclete in the previous context. This is not the case. Without any such previous mention it is difficult to attach any great force to "another" in the sense "another than myself": but it is both appropriate and forcible if it means "*other than yourselves*"—promising the disciples that they will not be left to their own unaided efforts[2].

[2794] Origen quotes xiv. 16 thus (Lomm. x. 127, about the "well" in Numb. xxi. 16) "Et rursus tertium puto videri puteum posse, cognitionem Spiritus Sancti. Alius enim et ipse est a Patre, et Filio, sicut et de ipso nihilominus in Evangelio dicitur *Mittet vobis Pater alium paracletum spiritum veritatis*," where "mittet" represents δώσει and "Pater" is supplied from the context. Before this, Origen says, "Alius enim a Patre Filius, et non idem Filius qui

---

[1] [2793 a] Mk xiii. 11, parall. Mt. x. 20 "but the Spirit of your Father that speaketh in you," parall. Lk. xii. 12 "For the Holy Spirit shall teach you..." (see *Synopticon* p. 127 A).

[2] [2793 b] The passage is quoted inaccurately (Resch) by Ephrem, Epiph. (thrice) and Eusebius. To his instances add Origen (Lomm. x. 127) "*mittet vobis alium paracletum.*" Chrys. and Nonnus both lay stress on ἄλλον, as meaning "another like myself," Chrys. ὡς ἐμέ, Nonn. Χριστῷ σύγγονον ἄλλον ὁμοίϊον. Chrys. also lays stress on it as indicating "the difference of hypostasis," and he uses it against "those infected with the Sabellian disease."

[2793 c] The Greeks seem to have regarded Hercules as the type of "the friend in need," and, besides calling a friend ἄλλος ἐγώ, they had the proverb ἄλλος Ἡρακλῆς, ἄλλος οὗτος (? αὐτός). Comp. Aristot. *Eth. Magn.* ii. 15 (Weise) ἄλλος οὗτος Ἡ. ἄλλος φίλος (?) ἐγώ, *Eth. Eudem.* vii. (viii.) 12 (Weise) ὁ γὰρ φίλος βούλεται εἶναι, ὥσπερ ἡ παροιμία φησίν, ἄλλος Ἡ., ἄλλος οὗτος. Is there some allusion to the story that Hercules helps those who help themselves?

et Pater, sicut ipse in Evangeliis dicit: *Alius est qui et testimonium de me dicit, Pater.*" For this, Lommatzsch's footnote refers the reader to viii. 18 "I am he that beareth witness about myself and *the Father that sent me beareth witness.*" But more probably the reference is to v. 32 "*Another is he that beareth witness concerning me,*" and "Pater," as in xiv. 16, is supplied for sense. It was shewn above (2730) that ἄλλος in v. 32 was taken by Chrysostom and Nonnus as referring to John the Baptist, but by Cyprian as referring to the Father. Origen, it would seem, takes the latter view.

[2795] In accordance with the difference of context, "another" means "another than *myself*" in v. 32, and "Another than *yourselves*" in xiv. 16—in both cases, however, referring to a supernatural power. In iv. 37 ἄλλος ἐστὶν ὁ σπείρων καὶ ἄλλος ὁ θερίζων, the meaning of ἄλλος is defined (1) by the following ἄλλος, (2) by the statement that it is a "proverb." Hence ἄλλος is here correctly rendered "one," and refers primarily to man and to the facts of social life, "*one soweth, another reapeth.*" But Christ goes on to say that this worldly proverb is "really and genuinely true" in another interpretation, and that a spiritual one, namely referring to the spiritual harvest (1727 *i*). Hence it is not fanciful to see a latent allusion to the invisible "Sower," the Holy Spirit: "He that soweth is *Another* [one without whom all human sowing by prophets and apostles would be vain]."

[2796] What is the meaning of "another" in the prediction of Peter's martyrdom xxi. 18 "*Another* (ἄλλος) shall gird thee"? Several authorities and MSS. read the plural ἄλλοι. And indeed, if the "girding" and the following words allude—as everyone admits—to Peter's crucifixion, how can the plural be dispensed with? Even if one man could perform the binding, how could one man perform the lifting up on the cross or the carrying to the cross[1]? The sense seems to demand, "Others shall bind thee round the loins and carry thee where thou wouldst not be [*i.e.* to the cross][2]." But what if the evangelist here again uses "*Another*" to mean "One stronger than thyself," namely, Christ, or the Spirit of Christ, which constrains

---

[1] [2796 *a*] Οἴσει has been altered by ℵ to ποιήσουσιν, and by D to ἀπάγουσιν (comp. Mk xv. 22 φέρουσιν αὐτὸν ἐπὶ τὸν Γολγοθὰν τόπον, where Mt.-Lk. differ).

[2] [2796 *b*] Nonnus, Ὀψὲ δὲ γηράσκων τανύσεις σέο χεῖρας ἀνάγκῃ Καί σε περισφίγξουσιν ἀφειδέες ἄνερες ἄλλοι, Εἴς τινα χῶρον ἄγοντες ὃν οὐ σέο θυμὸς ἀνώγει.

the Apostle to go on the Path of the Cross¹, and which "girds" him for the conflict—as the Psalmist (xviii. 32) says, "It is God that *girdeth me with strength*"?

[2797] Chrysostom takes pains to explain the final words in "shall carry thee *where thou wouldest not*," as implying "weakness after the flesh." In the *Martyrium Petri et Pauli* and the *Acta Petri et Pauli*, Peter is described as retiring from Rome, and Christ as commanding him to return, in order to be crucified, saying "Follow me" and "Fear not, because I am with thee²." Thus, in effect, Christ "girds" him with strength and "carries" him "whither he would not." Perhaps, however, in the Johannine tradition, there is no reference to a temporary weakness of the Apostle just before his martyrdom, but the meaning of the whole is an antithesis—rather implied than clearly expressed—between "doing one's own will" in youth, and "doing the will of *Another*" in old age: "When thou wast young thou wast strong [as thou didst suppose] in thine own strength and didst walk according to thine own will; but when thou shalt be old thou shalt stretch out thy hands [on the cross]³, and *Another* shall gird thee [for thy martyrdom] and shall carry thee [to the cross, obedient now to His will] where according to thine own [present] will thou wouldest not (οὐ θέλεις) be carried⁴."

On "authority" in Epictetus (2740—4)

[2798] Epictetus looks forward to the hour of death when he will stretch his hands up to God and say "Because thou (emph.) didst beget me I give thee thanks for the things thou gavest...take them back again and dispose them in what place thou wilt: for *they were all thine; thou* (emph.) *hast given them to me*." The things

---

¹ Comp. 2 Cor. v. 14 "the love of Christ constraineth us" and other passages in which Christ is said to "apprehend" *i.e.* take captive, or lead in triumph, His disciples (Phil. iii. 12, 2 Cor. ii. 14).

² [2797 a] *Acta Petri et Pauli* § 82, sim. *Mart. P. et P.* § 61.

³ [2797 b] SS, "thou wilt *lift up* thine hands," suggests prayer rather than crucifixion. The "spreading out of the hands" on the cross was regarded in ancient times as typifying prayer or intercession.

⁴ [2797 c] Instead of οποyογθελεις, D has οποyсγθελεις (with a small οy above θελεις) which would mean "*Another* shall carry thee whither [in thy present love for thy Lord]—*thou desirest to go*." This is an intelligible and a beautiful meaning. But it is almost certainly a corruption arising from (1) a casual confusion of οy and сy, (2) a desire to remove the difficulty explained by Chrysostom.

[2798] NOTES ON PRECEDING PARAGRAPHS

given are described in the context as "perceptions" and "preconceptions," "helps received from thee that I might understand thy ordinance [of the universe] and might follow it[1]." Over this internal and spiritual realm the philosopher has "authority," unshackled, unhindered[2]. No one can take it from him—this "authority" to be virtuous, temperate, courageous, untroubled. No doubt, occasionally, Epictetus suggests that this absolute fearlessness and rectitude of conscience gives the philosopher some "*authority*" over *others*. This comes out clearly in a passage where he proclaims the superiority of Diogenes, the natural king—the wielder of the sceptre[3]

---

[1] [2798 a] Epict. iv. 10. 14—16 ἃς ἔλαβον ἀφορμὰς παρὰ σοῦ πρὸς τὸ αἰσθέσθαι σου τῆς διοικήσεως καὶ ἀκολουθῆσαι αὐτῇ, τούτων οὐκ ἡμέλησα...Ὅτι με σὺ ἐγέννησας χάριν ἔχω ὧν ἔδωκας· ἐφ' ὅσον ἐχρησάμην τοῖς σοῖς ἀρκεῖ μοι. πάλιν αὐτὰ ἀπόλαβε καὶ κατάταξον εἰς ἣν ἂν θέλῃς χώραν. σὰ γὰρ ἦν πάντα, σύ μοι αὐτὰ δέδωκας. These last words remind us of Jn xvii. 6 "*Thine they were and thou gavest them to me.*" But, in John, "*thine*" is masc. and means "the disciples." In Epictetus, "*thine*" is neut. and means the will and the power to be virtuous. No doubt, in John also, "*all that thou hast given me*" is frequently neuter. But, even when neuter, it includes the thought of the Church as partaking in the spiritual unity of the Father and the Son (2740—4).

[2] [2798 b] Epict. *Ench.* i. 1—2 ἐφ' ἡμῖν μὲν ὑπόληψις, ὁρμή, ὄρεξις, ἔκκλισις... καὶ τὰ μὲν ἐφ' ἡμῖν ἐστι φύσει ἐλεύθερα, ἀκώλυτα, ἀπαραπόδιστα. The self-controlled movements of the mind are (*ib.*) "*our own works* (ἡμέτερα ἔργα)" and are "in our power (ἐφ' ἡμῖν)," and the philosopher says, iv. 10. 30, ἀρκεῖ μοι ὧν ἔχω ἐξουσίαν, "sufficient to me are those things over which I have *authority*," iii. 3. 9—10 "can anyone defraud me of my trustworthiness or of my love for my brethren? This is an estate from which none can eject me—not even Zeus! Not that He would desire it for a moment. Nay, He has placed this at my own disposal, and gave it to me even as He Himself possessed it—*unhindered, unconstrained, unshackled.*"

[3] [2798 c] See iii. 22. 57 "the sceptre of Diogenes," *ib.* 63 "the sceptre and the kingdom" of the Cynic. The whole chapter deals with the essential nature of royalty, which belongs to the Cynic because men recognise in him both their unselfish Benefactor and their natural Master. How is it possible, asks the pupil, that a naked, homeless, squalid creature—without a slave to attend him, or a country to call his own—can live a life of equable happiness? To which Epictetus replies, iii. 22. 46—50 "Behold, God hath sent unto you the man that shall demonstrate in act this possibility. Behold, [all of] you, that I am without country, home, possessions, slaves, making my bed on the ground—no wife, no children, no paltry palace, only the earth and the sky and one poor cloak! And what do I want? Am I not painless! Am I not fearless? Am I not free? When saw ye me missing anything that I longed for? Or falling into any evil that I shunned? What fault found I ever, either with God or man? When did I accuse anyone? Saw ever anyone my face clouded with gloom? How do I confront the great men before whom you stand frightened and abashed? Do

of man's conscience—to Nero, Sardanapalus, Agamemnon, and Alexander: "These kings and tyrants were wont to receive[1] from their armed guards the [privilege of] rebuking this man or that and the [brute] power of even inflicting punishment on offenders—and this though they themselves were bad: but on the Cynic this authority is bestowed not by arms and guards but by the conscience" —*i.e.* the consciousness[2] of being a disinterested toiler for mankind, of being a friend of Zeus, and of knowing men (whom he counts as his brethren or children), as a general knows his soldiers, so that he may reprove them freely[3]. Still, this "authority" is shackled and hindered. The only absolute "authority" given to man is over his own heart.

[2799] On the other hand there is the false "authority" of the despot, which so imposes on the pseudo-philosopher that he cries

I not treat them as [cringing] slaves (ἀνδραπόδοις)? *Who that sees me does not think that he beholds his own [true] King and Master?*"—This, says Epictetus, is the Cynic's message, this is his true character.

[1] [2798 *d*] iii. 22. 94 Lit. "*were wont to supply* to these kings." Mrs Carter's transl. has the pres. "give." But Epictetus is looking back at the long line of *kings of the old dispensation* (comp. Jn x. 8 "*all that came before me are thieves and robbers*") including (iii. 22. 30) Agamemnon, "though he was better than Sardanapalus and Nero." Not that Epictetus denies Agamemnon the title of "shepherd." "Shepherd in truth," he says (iii. 22. 35), "for you weep like the shepherds, when a wolf has snatched away one of their sheep!" The "shepherd" as fighting for the sheep against the wolf is not considered by Epictetus. He dislikes the metaphor: "And these [Greeks]," he says, "are sheep indeed, who are ruled over by you." As for the true Cynic, he is to abstain—at all events (iii. 22. 67) during the present state of society—from the distractions of wife and children so that he may devote himself wholly to his subjects, who include the whole human race, and may play his part as the king (*Iliad* ii. 25) "to whom the nations are entrusted and [the burden of] so many cares," going about the world and doing good as Ruler and as Healer (iii. 22. 72).

[2] [2798 *e*] "The consciousness," txt iii. 22. 95 ὅταν ἴδῃ ὅτι ὑπερηγρύπνηκεν ὑπὲρ ἀνθρώπων. But the sense is improved by reading εἰΔΗ. It has been shewn (2659 *e*) that ℵ sometimes uses ι for ει. Moreover B—which frequently uses ει for long ι—sometimes uses ει for short ι as (2654 *b*) in Jn i. 9 αληθεινον, Jas iii. 7 ανθρωπεινη, *ib.* iv. 14 ατμεις. And, in Epictetus itself, Schweig. Index testifies that ἐὰν εἰδῶ, *sciam*, "interdum perperam cum ἐὰν ἴδω permutatur." See also 2515 (i) *e*. By reading ὅταν εἰδῇ here ("*Knowing* as he does," or "*conscious* as he is") we shall keep the connexion between εἰδῇ and the preceding συνειδός. It is the *Cynic's own "conscience"*—as well as the conscience of those whom he controls—that gives him a kingly power over his subjects.

[3] [2798 *f*] iii. 22. 96 "speak freely," διατί μὴ θαρρήσῃ παρρησιάζεσθαι πρὸς τοὺς ἀδελφοὺς τοὺς ἑαυτοῦ, πρὸς τὰ τέκνα, ἁπλῶς πρὸς τοὺς συγγενεῖς; On the prominence of παρρησία in Jn see **1917** (i)—(vi).

out "But he has *authority* to kill me[1]!" To this Epictetus replies elsewhere that the despot *has* "authority" over our body and other possessions but not over our will. To the objection "So you philosophers teach people to despise kings!" he replies, "God forbid! Which of us teaches [anyone] to lay claim, in rivalry with them, to the things over which they have *authority*? Take my body —[we say]—take goods, take reputation, take my friends and relations...'Yes,' [says the despot], 'but I desire also to rule your [inmost] convictions.' And who gave you this *authority*[2]?" It follows that the despot's "authority" is a mere vapour[3], and that the pupils of Epictetus might ask to be allowed to release themselves from it by self-slaughter: "Here [on earth, are] robbers and thieves and courts of justice and so-called despots, who fancy they have some sort of *authority* over us—simply because of [their hold on] our paltry body and its possessions. Suffer us [O Epictetus] to shew them that they have *authority* over nothing[4]." According to

---

[1] [2799 a] Epict. ii. 13. 22—3. The immediate reply to this is that such a man must not pretend to be a philosopher: "As long as you give people this grip on you through your body your course must be *always to follow the stronger* (ἀκολούθει παντὶ τῷ ἰσχυροτέρῳ)" *i.e.* not the good and wise, but the strong, the tyrant. The bitter phrase, "follow the stronger," helps us to understand why Jn would prefer i. 15 πρῶτός μου to the Synoptic ἰσχυρότερός μου (**2667**).

[2] [2799 b] Epict. i. 29. 9—11. Did God, then, give the tyrant this "authority"—transient and unreal though it is—over the bodies of men? Epictetus *implies* that He did, in a passage (iii. 22. 5 foll.) where God is represented as allotting their several parts to the sun, to the heifer (which has to run away from the lion), to the bull (which has to fight), to Agamemnon and to Achilles: but he never says that God assigned a part to Thersites. The burden of this difficulty is thrown (iv. 1. 100—1) on the ὁρμάς—the "*tides*," or "*motions*," of God's universe, which we must carefully consider: "Our will is unshackled," but "the body of clay—*how was He able* to make that unshackled? Therefore He *made subject to the [ever moving] circle of the universe* (ὑπέταξεν οὖν τῇ τῶν ὅλων περιόδῳ) possessions, utensils, house, children, wife. Why, then, should I fight against God?"

[3] [2799 c] Epictetus imagines his well-trained pupil, after an interview with the "great man," the possessor of false "authority," exclaiming i. 30. 6—7 "Why all these preparations to meet nothing at all? Was *this* his *authority*? *This*, his antechambers, his gentlemen of the chamber, his yeomen of the guard!...These things were nothing, and I was preparing for things great."

[4] [2799 d] Epict. i. 9. 15. Epictetus will not consent, he bids his pupils await God's sign. In iv. 10. 29, τὰ ἀλλότρια ὄψεται αὐτὰ ὃς ἂν φέρῃ, ὡς ἂν δίδωται παρὰ τοῦ ἔχοντος ἐξουσίαν...ἀρκεῖ μοι ὧν ἔχω ἐξουσίαν...τὰ δ' ἄλλα ὡς ἂν θέλῃ ὁ ἐκείνων κύριος, some have taken ὁ ἐκείνων κύριος as God. But κύριος *is almost always used*

Epictetus, then, as also according to the Fourth Gospel, all men that receive the Logos of God receive authority over the will within them, which enables them to conform their will to His and to become His children; and this—the authority to lead a virtuous life—is the only real authority[1]. The authority to pronounce judgment is not real authority unless the judge knows the truth[2]. That power which has "authority" to bestow the greatest "profit" is "divine ($\theta\epsilon\hat{\iota}o\nu$)[3]."

---

by Epict. in a bad sense. His advice everywhere is, in effect, "Call no man *lord.*" Here ὁ ἐκείνων κύριος means "the lord or master of those transient objects." Comp. ii. 2. 25—6 "But if you gape after external objects, you must needs wobble *at the dictate of the lord* (ἄνω καὶ κάτω κυλίεσθαι πρὸς τὸ βούλημα τοῦ κυρίου). *And who is 'lord'* (τίς δ' ἐστὶ κύριος)? *He that has [from time to time] authority over the things that you covet or avoid.*"

[1] [2799 e] Jn i. 12 "But as many as received him [the Logos or Light] to them gave he *authority* to become children of God." Epictetus frequently describes the Cynic as (i. 9. 6) "Son of God" (comp. i. 3. 2 "knowing that thou art *son of Zeus*"), i. 19. 8—9 "When the tyrant says to anyone 'I will fetter your leg,' the man that consistently honours (τετιμηκώς) his leg says 'Don't, for pity's sake!' But the man [that honours] his own will says, 'If it appears advisable to you, fetter it.' 'Won't you bend?' [says the tyrant]. 'I will not bend.' 'I will shew you that I am lord (κύριός εἰμι).' 'You! Impossible! (πόθεν σύ;) I have been freed by Zeus. Do you really suppose that He would purpose to allow *His own Son* (τὸν ἴδιον υἱόν) to be made a slave? But of my corpse you are lord. Take it.'"

[2] [2799 f] Epict. i. 29. 50 "'But,' say you, '*the authorities* (ὁ ἔχων τὴν ἐξουσίαν) have given sentence [saying] *I judge you [guilty] of impiety and profanity.*' What [harm] is there [in that] for you?" i. 29. 52 "This man, whoever he be, that has *authority* to sentence you—does he know what piety or impiety is?" Such "judgments" therefore are futile, i. 25. 2 "What can henceforth cause us trouble or fear? Can it be any of the objects of our life? No one has any *authority* over these. As for the things over which the others have *authority*, we do not care a jot for them," ii. 13. 14 "Consequently, Zeno, for his part, felt no anxiety when he was going before Antigonus. For what the former admired, the latter had no *authority* over...but Antigonus was anxious at the prospect of meeting Zeno," iii. 24. 48 "And further remember that [in going to a great man] you have in effect gone to a shoemaker or greengrocer, to one that has *no authority over anything that is great or serious*—though he may sell [his goods] at a great price." These extracts have a bearing on Pilate's judgment. Pilate sat as judge to decide the truth: but he confessed that he did not know what it was ("what is truth?"). He also "was afraid," as Antigonus before Zeno.

[3] [2799 g] "Profit," ὠφέλεια (Epict. seldom uses σωτηρία except in a fashionable asseveration). Comp. Epict. iv. 1. 61 ἐννοοῦμεν γὰρ ὅτι τὸ ἔχον ἐξουσίαν τῆς μεγίστης ὠφελείας θεῖόν ἐστι. But, says the context, we think the things of greatest "profit" are wealth, office, etc. Then it follows that (*ib.* 59—60) "those who have *authority* over these things are our *lords*," and "thus then we have many *lords* (κυρίους)" because we have many worldly desires. It is assumed that

[2799] NOTES ON PRECEDING PARAGRAPHS

These and many other passages indicate that educated Greeks at the beginning of the first century must have been familiar with the contrast between true authority and false so vividly exhibited in the Fourth Gospel (**1594**).

---

the only true Lord is He that can bestow on us the only true "profit," namely, virtue. In his doctrine about lordship, Epictetus had to deal with the difficulty that "lord" was regularly used in conversation to mean little more than "Sir." He does not forbid the use of the word thus, provided that it be used merely as a form. But iv. 1. 57 "If you hear anyone say heartily and feelingly (ἔσωθεν καὶ ἐκ πάθους) '*Lord*,' then—though twelve fasces go before him—call him '*Slave*.'"

[2799 (i)] **Addendum on** ὅτε. Jn's use of ὅτε differs little from the Synoptic, exc. in the frequency of the phrase "there cometh an hour...*when* (ὅτε)...," iv. 21, 23, v. 25 (but v. 28 ἐν ᾗ), xvi. 25. In ix. 4 "there cometh *night, when*," W.H. make no pause; but a comma is required after νύξ, to distinguish it from "*a night when*." In v. 25 ἔρχεται ὥρα, καὶ νῦν ἐστίν, ὅτε, a pause is also necessary, to avoid the familiar juxtaposition ἔστιν ὅτε, and also for the sense, "there cometh an hour [appointed by God], and even now it is [here], *when*...." Here "when" is almost equivalent to ἐν ᾗ "in which hour," or "in that hour" (as in v. 28). In xvi. 2, 32, "the hour cometh" is not followed by ὅτε but by ἵνα—probably because here the phrase exceptionally introduces, not an "hour" of blessing or resurrection but an "hour" of persecution or trial, and it is desired to emphasize the fact that this trial is part of God's purpose, ordained "*in order that*" the trial may come to pass.

[2799 (ii)] **Addendum on** ϹΎΝ. Jn agrees with Demosthenes and Epictetus in hardly ever using σύν (while abundantly using μετά with gen.). Σύν is also non-occurrent in Rev. These facts stamp σύν as belonging to literary as distinct from spoken Greek. Accordingly σύν occurs in 1 Esdr. ii. 7, viii. 14 where μετά occurs in the parall. Ezr. i. 4, vii. 16; and the instances of σύν in Luke (including Gospel and Acts) as compared with all the rest of N.T. are as three to two. Σύν with neut. pl. "*along with* these things," may have various meanings (Lk. xxiv. 21 "*along with*" [i.e. *in addition to*] but Nehem. v. 18, Epict. *Ench.* xxxii. 3, xxxiii. 13 "*along with* [*and in spite of*]"). Σύν with persons regarded statistically may mean "reckoned up with," contrasted with μετά which implies helpful companionship, as in Epict. i. 24. 19 "*I reckon myself with* the multitude (συγκατατάττω ἐμαυτὸν σὺν τοῖς πολλοῖς) *and walk companionably with* many individuals (καὶ μετὰ πολλῶν περιπατῶ)." In σὺν θεῷ, σὺν τῷ δικαίῳ, οἱ σὺν αὐτῷ, etc. the dat. mostly represents God, a Cause, a Leader *on whose side* (not "*by whose side*," παρά) one is fighting or working and with whom one identifies oneself (as with Christ in the Pauline Epistles). Σύν occurs thrice in Jn, xii. 2, xxi. 3 (which need no comment), xviii. 1—2 ταῦτα εἰπὼν Ἰησοῦς ἐξῆλθεν σὺν τοῖς μαθηταῖς αὐτοῦ...εἰσῆλθεν αὐτὸς κ. οἱ μαθηταὶ αὐτοῦ...συνήχθη 'Ι. ἐκεῖ μετὰ τῶν μαθητῶν αὐτοῦ. Both here and elsewhere Christ is described by Jn as in helpful companionship with (μετά) the disciples, but not elsewhere as σὺν τ. μαθηταῖς. Nonnus omits the σύν clause, and so does Chrysostom (exc. in the title of his homily). But Origen quotes it. Doubtless it is genuine and bears upon Lk. xxii. 39 "*according to the* (τό) *custom...there followed him* [*also*] *the disciples.*" Did space allow, it might be shewn that Lk. and Jn appear to take different views of "*the custom*"—Jn interpreting it as referring to Christ's customary reception of the disciples in a certain place. But the discussion of this point must be deferred to a treatise on "Johannine Interventions."

[2799 (iii)] **Addendum on** λόΓοc (**sing. and defined**) **in Christ's words**

(1) IN THE SYNOPTISTS. The first Synoptic mention is in the Parable of the Sower Mk iv. 14 ὁ σπείρων τὸν λόγον σπείρει, parall. Mt. xiii. 19 παντὸς ἀκούοντος τὸν λόγον τῆς βασιλείας, Lk. viii. 11 ὁ σπόρος ἐστὶν ὁ λόγος τοῦ θεοῦ (foll. by Lk. viii. 21 μήτηρ μου καὶ ἀδελφοί μου οὗτοί εἰσιν οἱ τὸν λόγον τοῦ θεοῦ ἀκούοντες καὶ ποιοῦντες, which is parall. to Mk iii. 35 ὃς ἂν ποιήσῃ τὸ θέλημα τοῦ θεοῦ, Mt. xii. 50 ὅστις γὰρ ἂν ποιήσῃ τὸ θέλημα τ. πατρός μου τ. ἐν οὐρανοῖς). The only other mention in Lk. is xi. 28 (pec. to Luke) μενοῦν μακάριοι οἱ ἀκούοντες τὸν λόγον τ. θεοῦ καὶ φυλάσσοντες. Apart from the Sower and its explanation (and Mk vii. 29 "for this *saying* go thy way") Christ's only use of ὁ λόγος, in Mk, is in the charge brought against the Pharisees that they make void "*the word of God*"—which enjoins the honouring of parents—for the sake of their tradition (Mk vii. 13, Mt. xv. 6 txt "the word of God," but marg. "law of God"). The impression given by these passages is that "*the word*" in Mk iv. 14 means the word of God as set forth in the fundamental principles of the Law of Moses, interpreted and expanded in the Sermon on the Mount—the law enjoining the love of God and of "neighbour"—dealing primarily with motives, and claiming to override the sabbath in respect of works of healing, but not as yet illustrated by Christ's Sacrifice on the Cross.

(2) IN JOHN. (*a*) "*My word*," "*his word*," "*thy word*." The first Johannine mention of ὁ λόγος (apart from iv. 37 "the saying [about the harvest]") is in v. 24 ὁ τὸν λόγον μου ἀκούων καὶ πιστεύων τῷ πέμψαντί με ἔχει ζωὴν αἰώνιον. This is part of Christ's reply to the Jews, who first persecute and then desire to kill Him for healing on the sabbath, and for saying "My Father worketh hitherto and I [too] work." Chrysostom (twice, but varying with pl. and sing.) quotes this as "*my words*," and so does Nonnus. But "*the word*" seems to mean the word of the Son, which is also that of the Father—*the word, or law, of love and kindness exemplified in the healing on the sabbath*—which is a principle, or seed, of spiritual life, so that it abides in men, if they make room for it in their hearts by "belief," as above stated, v. 24 "He that heareth *my word* and believeth him that sent me hath eternal life," v. 38 "Ye have not *his word* abiding in you," viii. 37 "*My word* hath no place in you," viii. 51—2 (*bis*) "if any one keep *my word*"; or else men may be described as abiding in it, viii. 31 "If ye abide in *my word.*" Concerning this "*word*" of the Father, the Son says, viii. 55 "I know him [*i.e.* the Father] and I keep *his word.*" In the Last Prayer He thrice calls it "*thy word*" thus, xvii. 6 "They have kept *thy word*," xvii. 14 "I have given unto them *thy word*," xvii. 17 "*thy word* is truth"—which implies that the vital recognition of the true relation between God and man, and between man and man, has been implanted by the Son of God in the hearts of men His brethren. After saying (xiv. 23) "If any one love me he will keep *my word*," Christ is represented as implying the identity between the "word" of the Son and that of the Father in

xiv. 24 "and *the word* that ye hear (or, are hearing) is *not mine* but [*the word*] *of the Father* who sent me."

(*b*) "*The word of God*," in Jn, occurs only in x. 35 " If he called them 'gods' unto whom *the word of God came* (πρὸς οὓς ὁ λόγος τ. θεοῦ ἐγένετο)," referring to Ps. lxxxii. 6 " I said ye are gods, and all of you sons of the Most High, nevertheless ye shall die like men." The Psalm is about "judges" to whom "the word of the Lord came"—as it is freq. said to "come" to prophets (*Through Letter* etc. 850 ἐγένετο πρός)—to enable them to judge justly, as the Spirit of God was imparted to the Seventy through Moses (Numb. xi. 25) for the same purpose. The judges mentioned by the Psalmist judge unjustly. Nevertheless it is implied that they had in themselves the potentiality to become "gods" and the "sons of God" because He offered them His Word, *i.e.* the seed of spiritual life, though they rejected it. See Origen (on *Rom.* iii. 4, Lomm. vi. 155—6).

(*c*) "*The word that is in their own law*, [*there*] *written*" occurs in xv. 25 referring to Ps. xxxv. 19 "They hated me without a cause." On viii. 43 "my speech...*my word*," see **2251**, and on xv. 20 "*the word* that I said unto you" see **2405—6**.

(*d*) "*The word that I spake* (ὁ λ. ὃν ἐλάλησα)—that (ἐκεῖνος) shall judge him" (xii. 48), describes "the word" as rejected, so that it can no longer be an internal source of life, a friendly ally, but is forced to become an external judge. This must be contrasted with xv. 3 "Already are ye clean because of *the word that I have spoken* (λελάληκα) *to you*: abide in me, and I too in you"—where "*the word*" is the new Law of Love inculcated in the Washing of Feet. This "word" has been taken by the disciples into their souls. Judas indeed rejected it; but concerning the rest it is afterwards said, xvii. 6 "they have kept *thy word*." The cleansing influence of the Logos may be illustrated from Epictetus, who says, iv. 11. 4 "But since it is impossible that man's (αὐτῶν) being should be completely clean (καθαράν)...*the word*, received from [God], so far as is possible, attempts to make it cleanly (ὁ λόγος, παραληφθείς, εἰς τὸ ἐνδεχόμενον, ταύτην καθάριον ἀποτελεῖν πειρᾶται)." But Epictetus regards ὁ λόγος as little more than "reason." John uses ὁ λόγος in the words of Christ to represent not only the *word* announcing the sonship of man to God, but also the *thought* of sonship, so taken into man's heart that the personal Son enters along with the thought, as into a home, and makes His abode there—or else so rejected that it becomes a Judge.

(*e*) "*Their word*"—Christ's last mention of λόγος—occurs in xvii. 20 "I pray...for them that believe on me through *their word*," contemplating a time when "*the word*" of the Son, transmitted to the disciples and assimilated by them so that it becomes "*their word*," will be **a** power diffusing belief in the Son throughout the world.

INDICES

INDICES

TO "JOHANNINE VOCABULARY"

		PAGE
I.	New Testament Passages	625
II.	Subject-Matter (English)	641
III.	Words (Greek)	646

TO "JOHANNINE GRAMMAR"

I.	New Testament Passages	652
II.	Subject-Matter (English)	666
III.	Words (Greek)	677

INDICES TO "JOHANNINE VOCABULARY"

I. NEW TESTAMENT PASSAGES

[*The references are to paragraphs, indicated by black numbers, which, in this Index, run from* **1438** *to* **1885**. *To save space, the thousand figure is not printed.*]

MATTHEW			MATTHEW			MATTHEW		
		PAR.			PAR.			PAR.
1	20	749 c	4	16	710 c, 863 a	6	28	859
	21	865		18	725 b		29	864
	23	728 l_2	5	3–11	859 e	7	1	714 d, 859 a
	24	865		4	674		3–5	851 d
2	2	641 b		6	750 b, 854 b		7–8	852 b
	3	644, 727 b		8	857 c		13	764, 810 a
	4	863		11	554		16	864
	6	682 j, 862		12	851 b		22	478 a
	7	749 c		14	748		22–3	484, 764 a
	8	644, 675 b, 751		14–16	715 g		25	862
	9	725 d		15	858		27	862-3
	11	644, 754		16	728 h		27–9	573-4
	13	749 c		18	860		28	865 b
	16	686		19	708 i		29	562
	18	674		22	682 a	8	2	644
	19	749 c		23–4	851 d		4	695 b, 833 e, 885 a
	23	860		25	565, 714 e, 719 h, 852 c		5–6	862 b, c
3	2	690 a		37	753		8	862 a, b, c
	3	726		44	856, 885 f		9	574 a, 718 c, 855
	6	678 a, 861 a		47	753		10	477 b, 673 d
	8	852	6	9	851 a_1		11	851 a, 856
	9	851 a		14–15	711 a		13	477 a, 862 b, c
	10	858		17	728 a		14	834 a–b
	11	686 f, 833 d		19–20	858		17	679 d, 724 a, 853
	16	866 (iv)		23	864 a, 866		19	839 foll.
4	1–11	854 a		24	854 d		20	452-8, 609 b, 839 foll., 858 a
	6	863		25	865			
	9	565, 643		26	856			
	10	643		27	856, 862			
	15	714 b						

This Index extends from **1438** *to* **1885** (*printed* **438—885**).

INDICES TO "JOHANNINE VOCABULARY"

MATTHEW		MATTHEW		MATTHEW	
	PAR.		PAR.		PAR.
8 22	720 f	11 6	859 e	13 58	673 d
24	680 a	7	604 a, 689 e, 856	14 5	708 c
26	477 b			14	763 b
34	755	8	755	20	692 c
9 2	834 a–b	10	681 a	21	693 c
6	562, 575, 594 c	11	683 b	22	735 a
8	575	13	860	23	718 i, 813 a
9	604 a	16	861	24	813 a, 833 b, 864
11	718 a	17	857		
16	815 d	19	775 a, 854, 864, 866 b	25	718 i
17	751 b, 853 a			26	727 b
18	644, 765 a, 852 c	20	708 c	27	713 h, 811 e
		22	859 b	33	644, 727 j
22	477 b, 864 b	23	851, 866 a	15 2	728 a
23	852 c	24	859 b	3	714 h, 824–31
27–30	742	25	678 a, 852, 860, 864–5	14	861
28	477 a			17	817 a
29	477 b	26	852	22	713 b
30	713 e, 811 b, 885 a	27	810 c, 852	24	723 j
		28	810 c	25	644
36	708 c	29	865 a	28	477 b, 533
38	853	12 13	728 e	16 9	721 h, 728 l
10 1	580 a	14	695 c	18	709 a
2	709 a	15	810	23	864 b
3	714 c	16	752 b	24	792 b, 842
5	863	18	674	27	712 i
6	723 j	19	752 b foll.	28	530 a, 710 c
8	751 a	20	689 e, 751	17 8	855
10	852	21	855	11	634 b
11	707 a, 751	30	863	14	862 d
13	853 a	34	864	18	862 d
15–16	859	41	859 b	20	477 b
18	695 b, 725 c	42	859 b, 864	26	712 e, 751 b
20	720 k	45	856 a, 858	18 2	793
21	679	48–9	749 a	3	676 a, 865 a
22	713 f	50	728 g	4	865 a
24	723 h–i	13 10	720 a, b, 802 a	6	686 b
24–8	775 a, 784–92	11–13	721 c	8	734 b
25	723 h–i	13	612–3, 724 f	9	682 a
26	716 i, 738 a, 852, 859 d	15	683 e	11	692 e
		16	560, 859 e	15	851 d, 852 a, 855
27	863 a, 866	19	854 a		
28	565–6	21	811 f	16	696 e, 707 c, 725 e
32	861 a	22	676		
34	854 e	24	692 i	20	793
35	860	28–48	864	21	779 a, 781, 852 a
36	787 a, 792 a	31	692 i		
37	450, 792 a, 866 b	35	721 c	26	644
		39	854 a	31	720 f
38	792 b	46	753	19 1	865 b
40	671 b, 721 f	53	865 b	4	708 a
40–1	825–31	54	696 d, 720 h, 864	8	708 d
42	728 b			16	852 c
11 1	865 b	55	714 c, 777	17	714 h
3	632, 856 a	57	720 h	28	859 a

This Index extends from **1438** to **1885** (*printed* **438—885**).

NEW TESTAMENT PASSAGES

MATTHEW		MATTHEW		MATTHEW	
	PAR.		PAR.		PAR.
20 4	691 e	23 34	678, 854 c	26 25	696 e
11	449 a, 718 a, 853	35	860	28	690 a
19	678	37	674, 682 f, 859	30	794
20	644	39	633	31	862
21	712 i, 753	24 6	719 a, 728 l	33	438 a
22–3	678 c	7	680 a, 687 a, 718 d	34	718 i
25	570–1	8	708 d	36	634
26	717 d-e-f	9	713 f	38	707 a
27	717 f, 723 h	12	716 c, 851 c	39	716 b, 728 g
28	579	14	695 b	40	634
30	737 a, 813	21	708 d	44	695 e
32	725 b-c	23	477 a	45	634
34	477 b	26	477 a	48	716 g, 866 b
21 1	775 e	27	866	50	862
2–7	861 b	30	712 i	51	738 b, 866 c
5	456 a, 634, 754 a, 757	31	682 f	54	722 d
8	720 f	38	680 b, 710 h, 755 a	55	857
9	633, 816 b	42–4	634 a	56	722 d
12	812 b	43	858	59	695 c
15	816 b	45	862 e, 866	61	675 c
16	860	46	859 e	64	713 i
19	712 d	47	865	67	737 e
21	467	49	752	71	860
23–7	562	50	856	73	716 b, 727 j
24	857 b	51	860	27 1	754
25	477 a	25 1	720 f, 755	6, 9	755
27	841	4	720 f	11	725 c-e
32	477 a	7	720 f	15	711 e, 735 b
42	722 c, 811 e	9	852	19	745, 750
43	687 a, 718 d	19	634 b	27	814 c, 815 c
22 7	861	21	862 e	28	805–6
8	853	23	862 e	29	689 e, 734 a, 805–6, 814 b
11	604 a, 853	24	754		
12	853	24–6	856	30	689 e
15	695 c, 723 b	35	750 b	33	807, 810
16	727 d, m	36	810 b	40	675 c
24	721 e	37	750 b	44	817 c
27	866	38–44	810 b	45	710 b
29	722 d	40	749 a	48	689 e, 813 c
32	851 a	41	854 a	49	756
36	860	42	750 b	50	752 d
44	680, 856	44	750 b	51	707 e
23 3	714 h	26 1	865 b	52	693 a, 858
6–7	866 b	2	678	53	716 h
11	717 d-e	4	723 b, 811	54	727 j
12	865 a, 866 a	5	711 e	59	716 a, 857 c, 866 (i)–(iv)
23	477 b, 697, 716 c, 851 c, 859 b	8	810 a		
		9	742 a, 814 a	62	717 h
		10	728 j	66	754
26	857 c	12	734 e, 751 c	28 1–2	680 a, 832 b
27	861	18	834 e	5	681 d
28	753	24	653, 713 a, 816 a	6	858
31	859			7	802 a
				8	675 b

This Index extends from **1438** *to* **1885** (*printed* **438—885**).

INDICES TO "JOHANNINE VOCABULARY"

MATTHEW		MARK		MARK	
	PAR.		PAR.		PAR.
28 9	644	4 11–12	612–13, 721c	7 4	689c
10	749	15	854a	5	677b
13	858	17	811f	6	688a
15	713m	19	676, 833c	9	714h, 824–31
17	644	21	715g	13	824a
18	562, 590	22	686c, 716i,	22	811
19	485c		738a, 859d	23	677b
20	793	26–8	515	26	713b
		30	686a	29	477b
	MARK	33	721c	33	693d, 737b
1 1	708f	34	720a–d, 721c	35	852b
2	681a	39	832c	8 6–7	692i
4	690a, 734c	40	477b, 728l	17	728l, 737c
5	678a, 861a	41	681c	18	721h
7	686f, 833d	5 6	644	21	728l
10	852b, 866 (iv)	12	723d	23	693d, 737b
15	467, 480a	14	675b	32	712f, 744 (xi)a
16	725b	19	653, 675b	34	792b, 842
19	716b	22	765a, 852c	35	720f
20	736b	29	736c	38	697, 711a, 712i
22	562	33	727m	9 1	530a, 710c
22–7	572–4	34	477b, 653,	12	634b
24	835		728e, 854e	17	862d
30	834a	36	477a, 507a,	18	735e
39	884c		533	23	533
43	713e, 811b–c	41	728l_2	24	862d
44	653, 695b,	6 1	634a, 720h	34	570d, 683b
	833e, 885a	2	696d, 864	35	717d–g
45	738	3	686, 714c, 777	36	721g, 793
2 1	884c	4	720f, h	37	721f, 826–31
4	834a, 884a	6	673d	40	885f
4–12	673, 736a, 834a	7	562, 580a	41	691b, 728b
10	525a, 562,	10	707a	42	686b
	575, 594c	11	695b	43, 45	734b
11	653	19	735b	10 1	634a
12	575	20	832	6	708d
14	604a	21	738	15	865a
15	834b	26	832a	17	852c
16	718a	30	675b	21	716d, 744 (i)–
21	815d, 853a	31	716b, 810c		(xi)
28	525a	34	763b	34	686
3 3	793	37	710e, 734d	37	712i
6	695c	41	692i	38–9	678c
7	810, 834c	42	692c	42	570–1, 594a
8	834c	45	735a	42–3	683a
15	562, 580a	47	718i, 813a	43	810
16	709a	48	634a, 718i,	43–4	717d–g
18	714c, 726		735b–c,	44	723h
20	634a		833b	45	579
29	712d	50	713h, 727b,	46	737a
31	725a, 737		811e	49	725b–c
33–4	749a	52	737c	51	737d
35	728g	55	673, 736a	52	477b
4 10	720a–b, 802a	7 2	677b	11 1	775e
11	530a	3	713m, 728a	2	653, 728l

This Index extends from **1438** *to* **1885** (*printed* **438—885**).

NEW TESTAMENT PASSAGES

MARK			MARK			MARK		
		PAR.			PAR.			PAR.
11	2–7	861 b	14	6	728 j	16	11	604 a, 856
	7	720 f		8	734 e, 751 c		12	597 b, 686 c,
	9	816 b		11	686			687 e, 716 i,
	10	633 a, 816 b		13	653, 728 b,			738 a, 856 a
	12	717 h			834 e		14	597 b, 686 c,
	14	712 d		17	634 a			708 c, 716 i,
	15	812 b		21	653, 713 a,			738 a, 856
	17	675			816 a		16–17	477 a, 487
	18	739–40		26	794			
	22	467		29	438 a			LUKE
	25	697, 711 a,		30	718 i			
		725 a, 737		34	707 a	1	2	708 f, 719 h
	28	594		35	716 b		3	707 e
	28–33	562		36	697, 711 a,		6	734 c
	29	857 b			728 g		9	770
	31	477 a		37	634 a		12	727 b
	32	688 a		41	634 a, 695 e		13	708 b
12	2	723 h		44	716 g, 866 b		17	501 a
	4	723 h, 832		47	738 b		30	775 c
	10	722 c		49	722 d foll.		31	865
	11	811 e		51–2	810 b		33	712 d
	13	723 b		54	711 f, 715 g,		47	774 a, 851 b
	14	727 d, m			735 d		51	766
	17	687		58	675 c, 679 b		52	865 a
	22	866		62	713 i		53	768
	24	722 d		63	696 e		55	712 d
	26	684, 837 a,		65	737 e		57	708 b
		851 a		67	735 d		59	709 c
	30–33	716 d		70	716 b, 727 j		69–77	774 b
	32	727 m	15	1	815 b		75	854 b
	36	680, 856		6	711 e		79	710 c
	37	739–40		12	707 g	2	3	720 f
	40	834 d		16	814 c, 815 c		8	862
	44	715 f		17	734 a, 805–6,		11	774 a
13	2	679 b			814 b		21	709 c
	7	719 a, 728 l		19	644, 689 e		22	833 e
	8	680 a, 687 a,		20	686		25	734 c
		708 d, 718 d		22	728 l₂, 807, 810		34	764
	9	695 b, 725 c		29	675 c		36	734 c
	11	720 k		31	686		39	720 f
	12	679		32	817 c		40	775 c
	13	713 f		33	710 b, 864 a		41–2	711 e
	19	708 d		34	728 l₂,		43	774 c
	20	592, 709 b		36	689 e, 813 c		44	767
	21	477 a		38	707 e		46	857
	26	712 i		39	727 j		52	775 c
	27	682 f		46	691, 716 a,	3	2	764 b, 857
	32	697, 711 a			857 c, 866		3	690 a
	34	723 h, 728 h			(i)—(iv)		6	592
14	1	723 b, 811	16	1	832 b		8	851 a, 852
	2	688 a, 711 e		2	815 a		9	858
	3	736 d, 834 b		6	858		12	690 f
	4	810 a		7	802 a		13	772 b
	5	710 e, 738. 811		9	815 a		14	690 f, 852
		a–c, 814 a		10	802 a		15	885 b

This Index extends from **1438** *to* **1885** (*printed* 438—885).

629

INDICES TO "JOHANNINE VOCABULARY"

		LUKE			LUKE			LUKE
		PAR.			PAR.			PAR.
3	16	686 f, 833 d, 899	6	28	885 f	9	1	580 a
	18	674		32–4	775 c		4	707 a
	19	855		35	856		5	695 b
	21	866 (iv)		37	714 d, 859 a		8	749 c
	22	767		38	769		12	858 a
4	1	772 a		39	861		14	693 c
	2–13	854 a		40	723 h, 775 a, 784–92		16	692 i
	6–7	565					17	692 c
	7–8	643		41–2	851 d		23	792 b, 842
	11	863		43	707 g		26	712 i
	16	778		44–5	864		27	530 a, 696 a, 710 c, 727 j
	17–19	690 b	7	1–10	862 b			
	19	768		2	862 b		29	767, 769
	20	719 h		3	713 m		32	802 a, 865
	21	722 c		5	687 a, 718 e		35	833 a
	22	775 c, 777–8, 857 a, 859		7	862 a, b		38	771, 862 d
				7–8	718 c, 855		42	862 d
	23	778		9	477 b, 673 d, 864 b		47	793 a
	24	720 f, h					48	717 e, 721 f, 826–31
	25	727 m		12	771, 775 e			
	29	606 a		13	779 a		50	885 f
	32	562		19	632, 779 a, 856 a		55	864 b
	32–6	572–4					56	692 e
	34	835		23	859 e		57	839 foll.
	38	834 a		24	604 a, 689 e, 856		58	452–8, 609 b, 839 foll., 858 a
5	1	725 b, 769						
	2	736 e		25	769		60	720 f
	2–6	763		27	681 a	10	1	779 a
	3	716 b		28	683 b		2	853
	4	763 a, 775 e		32	857, 861		3	859
	6, 8	834 c, 835 b		34	775 a, 866 b		6	853 a
	14	695 b, 833 e, 885 a		35	854, 864		7	707 a, 852, 860
				37	834 b			
	19	884 a		38	768 a		8	692 j
	24	562, 575, 594 c		44	728 b, 768 a, 864 b	12, 14		859 b
	25	834 a					15	851, 866 a
	26	575		47	560 a		16	671 b, 825–31, 832 a
	27	604 a	8	9	720 a, b, 802 a			
	29	834 b		10	612–3, 721 c		17	478 a
	30	449 a, 718 a, 853		12	854 a	17–20		589
				13	811 f		19	567, 580 a
	36–7	853 a		14	676, 715 f		21	678 a, 851 b, 860, 864–5
	37	751 b		17	716 i, 738 a, 859 d			
6	8	793				21–2		852
	11	695 c		19	884 a		22	810 c
	13	833 a		21	728 g, 749 a		23	560, 859 e, 864 b
	14	709 a		24	832 c			
	15	726		25	477 b		26	860
	16	714 c		28	644		32	770
	17	725 b		29	833 b		38	771 a
	20–2	859 e		41	765 a, 852 c		39	717 b, 771 b, 779 a
	21	750 b, 854 b		42	771			
	22	554		48	477 b		40	717 a, e, 771 a
	25	768		50	477 a, 507 a, 533		41	771 a, 779 a
	27	856						

This Index extends from **1438** *to* **1885** (*printed* **438–885**).

NEW TESTAMENT PASSAGES

	LUKE			LUKE			LUKE
	PAR.			PAR.			PAR.
10 42	709 b, 771 b, 833 a		12 58	565–6, 569 d, 714 e, 775 e, 852 c		17 8	712 g
						9	775 c
11 2	851 a_1					10	723 h, 861
6	692 j		59	566		24	866
9	852 b		13 1	862		27	710 h
10	852 b		4	773		32	721 h
21	720 f		14	728 j		34	718 i
22	771 c		15	779 a, 861 b		18 6	779 a
23	863		19	720 f		11	725 d, 866
26	856 a, 858		20	707 g		13	720 f, 725 d, 760
28	859 e		24	764			
31	864		27	764 a		14	865 a, 866 a
31–2	859 b		28	851 a		18	852 c
35	864 a, 866		29	856		35	737 a
36	775		32	774 c		37	860
39	779 a		34	674, 682 f, 720 f, 859		40	725 b, c
41	857 c					42	477 b
42	477 b, 697, 716 c, 851 c, 859 b		35	633		19 7	718 a
			14 1	765 a		8	779 a
			7	833 a		9	774 b
			11	865 a, 866 a		10	692 d
49	854 c		21	861		11	531, 693 e
51	860		25	864 b		13	720 f
12 2	738 a, 852, 859 d		26	450, 713 f, 720 f, 792 a		17	862 e
						20	760
3	784, 863 a, 866		27	720 f, 792 b		21–2	856
			29	686		23	772 b
4	565, 723 i, 775 a, b, 784–92		33	720 f		29	775 e
			15 2	718 a		30–5	861 b
			12	715 f		36	720 f
5	565		20	720 f		38	633 a, 816 b
8	861 a		30	715 f		42	719 b, 859 c
11	567 a, 569 a		16 4	720 f		48	739
20	718 i		5	720 f		20 2–8	562
21	884 c		6	767		3	857 b
23	865		7	767		5	477 a
24	856		8	715 g, 720 f, 782–3, 866		11	672, 832
25	856, 862					12	672
27	859, 864		11	727 f, 764		17	722 c
33	858		12	851		20	567 a, 569 a, 723 b
35	712 g, 858		13	854 d			
37	712 g		16–17	860		21	727 d, m
39	858		20–5	770		29	721 g
42	779 a, 862 e, 866		22–3	769		32	866
			24	728 b, 765		37	771, 775 e, 851 a
43	859 e		25	674, 715 f, 719 b		43	680, 856
44	696 a, 727 j, 865					46	866 b
			17 2	686 b		47	834 d
45	752		3	851 d		21 3	696 a, 727 j
46	856, 860		3–4	852 a		4	715 f
48	692 j		4	781		9	719 a
51	854 e		5	781, 779 a		10	687 a, 718 d
53	860		6	467, 477 b, 779 a		11	680 a
55	862					12	725 c
57	691 e, 714 e, f		7	862			

This Index extends from **1438** *to* **1885** (*printed* **438—885**).

631

INDICES TO "JOHANNINE VOCABULARY"

	LUKE			LUKE			JOHN
	PAR.			PAR.			PAR.
21 13	695 b, 763 b		23 48	760		1 11	624 a, 637 a,
15	720 k		49	767			720 d, 735 f
16	679		51	544, 713 m		12	481, 483–7,
17	713 f		53	716 a, 719 a,			576, 676 a,
20	770			728 l, 857 c,			721 f
27	712 i			866 (i)–(iv)		13	484, 708 k,
36	725 d		56	832 b			728 g
22 1	711 e		24 1	765, 832 b		14	604, 712 j,
2	723 b		3	779 a, 801 b			744 (x) a,
3	692 b, 765		4	832			771, 772 a,
5	774		5	858 a			885 e, 885
6	678 a		9	802 a			(ii) c
10	728 b, 834 e		12	600 b, 673 e,		14–17	727 n, 775 c
15	833 c			716 a, 726 b,		15	635, 885 g
17	721 f			772, 798–		16	727 n
19–20	885 f			804, 866		18	604 b, 605, 769,
22	653, 713 a,			(iii) a			771, 884 c
	816 a		13	798 foll.–804,		19	688, 770
23	772 b			864		20	679–80
25	570–1, 594 d		17	725 d		21	885 d
26	717 e, f, 810		20	765 a		22	723 e, 885 d
30	859 a		23	802		23	696 c, 728 f,
31	779 a		24	802 a			885 (ii) a
32	695 h		25	477 a		25	680, 885 d
33	438 a, 843		26	722 e foll.		26	725 a, g, 737,
37	770		27	722 e foll., l			796
42	728 g		29	858 a		26–7	635
45	713 d, 771, 858		32	722 e foll., l,		27	635, 686 f,
47	716 g, 866 b			775 e			833 d, 852
50	738 b		34	560		28	708 g
51	738 b, 866 c		35	769		29	607, 635, 717 h,
53	567		36	725 b, 793–7,			885 (ii) a
55	711 f			804 a, 884 c,		30	635, 885 g
56	711 f, 715 g			854 e		31	684 c, 716 j
59	727 m		36–43	794–7		32	604, 707 a
60	693 e		38	727 b		33	707 a, 723 e
61	779 a, 864 b		39	713 j, 861		34	606, 676 c
63	737 e		40	804 a		35	717 h
66	692		41	796 a		36	885 (ii) a
70	713 i		43	768 b		37	720 m
23 2	687 a, 718 e		44	724 f, 722 e		38	604, 694 c,
7	567 a		45	722 e, l			720 m,
11	676 d, 806 a		52	644			728 d, l_2,
13	765 a						864 b
15	772 b			JOHN		39	598, 609 a, 610,
20	707 g						885 d
22	695 e		1 1	708 f		41	717 c, 720 e, i,
23	769		1–5	443			m, 728 l_2
28	864 b		5	735 e–h, 885		42	439, 675, 709 a,
29	708 b			(ii) c			714 a, 728 l_2
33	807, 810		6	734 c, 885 e		43	717 h, 720 m
35	676 c, 765 a		7	464, 481–2		45	720 m, 778
41	772 b		8	708 k, 748 a		46	598 a, 609
44	710 b		9	635, 727 g, 775		47	702 a, 713,
46	692 j		9–11	483			727 l, 811

This Index extends from **1438** *to* **1885** (*printed* **438—885**).

632

NEW TESTAMENT PASSAGES

JOHN

	PAR.		
1	47–50	610	
	48	885 i	
	49	684 c	
	50	464, 481, 488, 598, 885 i	
	51	524, 598, 672, 852 b, 866 (iv), 884 d	
2	1	686 d, 695 d, 853	
	2	675, 686 d, 853	
	4	719 a, 728 l	
	5	717 d	
	6	833 e, 885 (ii) b, c	
	7	707 d, 728 b, 885 (ii) c	
	8	719 d, 885 (ii) a	
	9	717 d, 885 (ii) a	
	10	752, 885 (ii) a	
	11	464, 489–90, 712 j	
	14	885 (ii) b	
	15	686, 751 b, 812 b, 885 (ii) a–c	
	16	885 (ii) a	
	17	721 i, 860, 885 (ii) b	
	18	885 d	
	19	679 b, 708 i, 722 k	
	20	675 c, 885 d	
	21	507	
	22	491, 721 i, 722 a, l, 860	
	23	483–4, 493 a, 598	
	23–4	464, 481	
	24–5	626	
3	1	734 c, 765 a, 852 c	
	2	544, 718 j	
	3	676 a, 685 a, 707 e	
	4	885 (ii) a	
	5	685 a, 728 b	
	7	673 a, 707 e	
	8	614 b, 655, 728 c, d, 862	
	10	684 c	
	12	464, 494, 520 a, 885 (ii) a	
	14	494, 524, 728 f, 866 a	

JOHN

	PAR.	
3	16	693 b, 716 e, 744 (vi) foll., 771
	16–18	498
	16–21	497 a
	17	581–5, 677 d, 692 f
	18	486, 502, 582–5, 677 d, 771
	19	582–5, 710 a, 716 e, 728 h, 744 (vi) a, 859 b
	20	728 h, 772 b, 885 (ii) c
	21	728 h, 772 b
	22	481, 493, 885 (ii) a
	23	707 f, 721 n
	24	438 b, 688
	25	713 l, 833 e, 885 (ii) b
	28	681 a
	29	860
	30	684, 885 (ii) a
	31	635, 707 e
	32	606
	33	727 d foll., 754
	35	716 e
	36	501, 885 (ii) a
4	1	780
	1–3	493
	2	481, 853 a
	5	687 c, 726
	6	885 (ii) b
	6–14	736 c
	8	865
	9	713 l, 863, 885 (ii) c
	10	682 g, 885 (ii) a
	10–15	728 b
	11	765, 885 d
	12	683 c, 885 (ii) b
	14	712 d, 885 (ii) a
	16	652 a
	18	719 d
	19	598
	20	647
	20–4	640, 647–51
	21	464, 503–7
	22	647–8, 713 m, 774 b
	23	719 c, 885 (ii) b
	23–4	640–51, 727 p

JOHN

	PAR.	
4	24	647
	25	635, 717 c
	27	673 a
	28	885 (ii) c
	31	860
	34	456, 774 c
	35	604, 608, 674 b, 885 (ii) c
	36	691 b, 727 a
	36–7	693
	36–8	856
	37	727 i
	39–42	503–7
	42	727 k, 774 a
	43	777–8
	44	720 h, 755, 777–8
	45	606 a, 689 c, 721 f
	46	885 (ii) a
	47	683 e
	48	464, 508–9, 524 a, 533
	49	676 b, 885 (ii) a
	50	508–9
	51	862 a
	52	863, 885 (ii) a, b
	53	464, 509, 684 a
5	2	708 h, 713 g, 885 (ii) a–c
	2–7	720 n
	3	685 c, 834 a, c
	4	728 e
	5	683 d
	6	610, 834 a
	6–15	728 e
	8–11	673, 736 a
	10	683 d–e, 685
	13	683 e, 885 (ii) a
	14	852 a
	16	854 c
	18	673 b, 708 i
	19	607
	20	596, 673 b, c, 716 e, 728 p
	21	716
	21–3	581–5
	24	614 b, 710 d, 860
	24–47	510–11
	25	719 c
	25–8	614 c, 710 d
	26–7	576–8, 581
	27	581–5
	28	673 a

This Index extends from 1438 to 1885 (printed 438—885).

INDICES TO "JOHANNINE VOCABULARY"

JOHN

	PAR.	
5	29	585 a, 772 b, 859 b, 885 (ii) c
	30	581–5, 691 e, 728 g
	34	692 g
	35	685 d, 748 a, 851 b, 858, 885 (ii) c
	36	774 c
	37	605, 614 b, 767
	38	520 a, 707 a
	39	492, 722 g, 885 (ii) a
	43	720 i
	44	885 e
	45	855
	46	492
	47	492, 767
6	1	726 e, 811 d
	2	598, 605 a, 606 a
	3	885 (ii) a
	5	604, 608
	6	695 a
	7	710 e, 734 d, 852
	9	708, 885 (ii) b
	10	765
	11	735 b
	12	768
	13	708, 885 (ii) a
	14	635, 727 k
	15	810
	16	718 i, 813 a
	17	710 b, 718 i, j
	18	683 a, 832 c, 862
	19	598, 833 b, 864
	20	681 d, 713 h, k, 811 e
	21	652 a, 721 f, 735 b, c
	22	885 (ii) c
	23	726 e, 736 e, 780
	24	736 e
	26	692 c
	26–36	512–16
	27	707 a, 754
	29	512–13, 547
	30	513
	31	717, 728 f
	32	727 h
	33	512 a

JOHN

	PAR.	
6	35	517, 684
	36	512 b, 532, 605
	37	752 f
	38	728 g
	39	721 e
	40	517, 598, 721 e
	41	718 b
	42	624, 719 d, 777, 857 a
	43	718 b
	44	517, 710 g, 721 e
	45	885 e, 885 (ii) a
	46	605, 885 e
	47	518 a
	49	717, 728 f
	50	710 f
	51	712 d
	51–63	712 b
	52	885 (ii) b
	54	518 a, 721 e
	54–8	710 h
	55	727 e, 885 (ii) b
	56	707 a
	57	884 b
	58	712 d
	59	694 b, 777
	60	754
	61	694 a, 718 b
	62	885 d
	63	519, 716
	64	520 a
	64–70	464
	67	652 a, 695 i, 835 b
	68	519
	69	519, 629, 835
	70	695 i, 709 b, 854 a
	71	695 i, 724 c
7	2	885 (ii) c
	3	652 a, 860
	5	520
	6	688, 719 a, 728 l, 862
	6–8	695 f
	7	728 h
	8	719 a
	10	738
	12	682
	13	681 c
	14	885 (ii) b
	15	673 a, 767
	18	720 i, 727 d foll., 764 a

JOHN

	PAR.	
7	21	673 a
	22	709 c
	23	708 i, 709 c, 728 e, 885 (ii) c
	24	691 e, 714 f, 859 a, 885 (ii) b
	26	727 k, 765 a, 885 b
	27	624–5, 635
	27–8	728 c
	28	624, 727 h, 752 f
	30	728 l
	31	464, 521
	33	655, 716 b
	35	702, 713 b, 728 d
	37	683 a, 725 f, g
	37–8	521, 722 k
	38	728 b, 885 (ii) c
	39	521 a, 637 b
	40	614 c, 727 k
	42	635, 679 a, 692 h, 696 b, 722 k, 853
	43	815 d, 884 a
	44	735 b
	48	520, 765 a
	49	885 (ii) a
	51	765 a
	52	885 (ii) a
8	3–4	735 h
	4	694 c
	5	726 a
	9	884
	11	852 a
	12	748 a
	14	624, 637 a, 655, 728 c–d
	15	581–5, 714 f, 859 a
	16	661, 714 f, 727 h
	17	696 e, 707 c, 715 b
	18	522
	19	624, 626
	20	728 l
	24	522, 713 k, 885 d
	25	708 e
	26	727 d foll.

This Index extends from **1438** *to* **1885** (*printed* **438—885**).

NEW TESTAMENT PASSAGES

JOHN			JOHN			JOHN		
		PAR.			PAR.			PAR.
8	28	713 k, 866 a	9	21	719 d, 856	11	3	716 e, 728 o–p
	29	885 (ii) a		22	726, 774, 861 a		4	529, 710 d, 712 j
	30	464		23	672 c, 856			
	30–1	523		24–5	693		5	728 p, 744 (vi) foll.
	31	707 a, 727 l		28	885 (ii) b			
	32	727 q–r		29	625, 728 c		8	527 a, 652 a, 719 g, 726 a
	32–6	712 e		30	728 c, 811 e			
	33	692 h, 854 d		31	693, 885 (ii) b		9	607, 863
	33–6	751 b		32	672 a, 728 k		10	718 h, 863
	33–58	851 a		35–8°	524–5		11	652 c, 693 a, 858
	34–5	723 i		38	464, 647			
	35	684 a, 712 d		39	581–5, 594, 637 a		12	693 a, 858
	36	885 d					13	710 d, 865, 885 (ii) b
	37	692 h, 817 a		39–41	607			
	38	885 d		41	707 a, 719 b		14	528
	39	676 a, 728 h	10	1–5	721 a		15	528, 545
	40	719 b		1–10	858		16	710, 885 (ii) c
	41	728 h		3	601, 614 a, c, 852 b		18	864
	42	637 a, 856					19	885 (ii) b
	43	614		4	601		20	636, 771 b
	44	708 e, 711 d, 725 a, 727 p, 737, 833 c, 854 a, 885 (ii) a, c		5	682 c		21–2	529, 719 e
				6	594, 721 a		23	534
				9	692 g		23–6	529–34
				10	637 a, 753		25	534
				11	715 d		26	507 b, 529 a, 710 f, 712 d
				12	682 c, 736 b, 863		27	464, 636
	45–6	522		13	736 b		28	535, 862
	47	614 b, d		14	626, 885 j		30	696 b
	49	832		15	626, 715 d		31	684 a, 885 (ii) b
	50	582		16	614 a, c, 723 j, 862		33	466, 610, 713 e, 727 b, 811 b, c
	51–2	710 d, 712 d, 714 h						
	53	683 c, 885 c		17–18	587–9, 715 d		34	609
	55	624, 686 a, 714 h, 861, 885 (ii) c		18	576–8		35	885 (ii) a
				19	815 d		36	716 e, 728 p
				20	885 (ii)		38	636, 713 e, 769, 811 b, c
	56	478, 610, 851 b		21	679 c			
	59	726 a, 859 c		22	885 (ii) a		39	885 (ii) b, c
9	1	610, 687, 813, 885 (ii) a		23	864, 885 (ii) c		40	529–34, 598, 712 j
				24	770			
	2–3	852 a		28	712 d		41	608
	4	718 h, 735 a		29	683 c		42	528, 885 (ii) b
	5	748 a		31–3	726 a		43	683 a, 752 a, f
	6	693 d, 737 b, 885 (ii) b, c		33	674		44	652 a, 760, 885 (ii) b
				34	715 b, 722 k			
	6–15	709		35	708 i, 722 k		45	604
	7	652 a, 720 n, 728 l_2		36	674, 835 a		47	692
				37–8	526		48	536, 702, 718 f, 721 k
	7–11	773		38	626			
	7–25	607		40	527			
	8	737 a, 885 (ii) b		42	527		49	768
	9	686 a, 861	11	1	696 b, 734 c, 770, 771 a, b		50	688 a, 718 f, 770
	11	652 a, 885 (ii) a						
	16	693, 815 d		2	734 c, 768 a, 780		50–2	885 h
	18	526					51	768

This Index extends from **1438** *to* **1885** (*printed* **438—885**).

635

INDICES TO "JOHANNINE VOCABULARY"

JOHN		JOHN		JOHN	
	PAR.		PAR.		PAR.
11 51–2	718 *f*	12 35	657, 716 *b*, 735 *e*, 748 *a*, 775 *d*	13 18	884 *d*, 885 (ii) *b*
52	676 *a*, 682 *f*			19	545–6
53	536			20	671 *b*, 721 *f*, 723 *e*, 826–31
54	710, 728 *f*				
55	885 (ii) *a*	36	539–40, 715 *g*, 748 *a*, 775 *d*, 782–3, 859 *c*, 866		
57	695 *c*, 771			21	727 *b*, 811 *c*
12 1	717 *h*, 770			22	607, 832
2	717 *a, e*, 771 *a*			23	596 *a*, 744 (vi) foll., 769
3	684 *a*, 717 *b*, 736 *d*, 753, 768 *a*, 771 *b*, 885 (ii) *b*	37	540		
		38	766, 852	24	885 (ii) *b*
		38–40	673 *b*	25	744 (x), 760
		39	540	26	724 *c*, 765
4	810 *a*	39–40	612–13	26–30	724 *e*
5	710 *e*, 738, 814 *a*	40	683 *e*, 737 *c*, 813, 885 (ii) *c*	27	692 *b*, 885 (ii) *c*,
				29	885 (ii) *a*
6	858, 885 (ii) *a*			30	544 *a*, 710 *b*, 718 *j*
7	734 *e*	41	610, 712 *j*		
8	688 *b*	42	464, 726, 765 *a*, 861 *a*, 884 *a*	33	658, 676 *a*, 716 *b*, 843, 885 (ii) *c*
9	652 *b*, 739–40, 884 *a*				
		42–3	540–1		
11	537–8, 652 *b*, 884 *a*	43	744 (vi) *a*	34	843
		44	752 *f*	36	658, 719 *c*, 728 *d*, 866
12	636, 739–40	44–5	598		
13	633 *a*, 635–6, 674, 684 *c*, 752 *a*, 755, 816 *b*, 885 (ii) *a, c*	44–6	543–4	37	692 *a*, 715 *d*, 843, 885 *h*
		44–8	825–31, 832 *a*		
		47	614 *c*, 637 *a*, 692 *g*	38	679, 692 *a*, 715 *d*, 843, 885 *h*
		47–8	582–5		
14	861 *b*, 885 (ii) *b*	50	885 *d*	14 1	546, 727 *b*
15	456 *a*, 636, 674 *b*, 677, 678 *d*, 754 *a*, 756, 861 *b*	13 1	680 *c*, 720 *d*, 744 (vi) foll., 860	1–12	464
				2	682 *h*, 684 *a*
		1–3	657–8	2–3	661, 688 *c*
		2	724 *c*, 854 *a*	3	637
16	721 *i*, 860	3	637 *a*	4	658, 696 *c*
20	647, 713 *b*	4	712 *g*, 885 (ii) *b*	5	728 *d*
20–1	538, 702	5	674 *a*, 712 *g*, 768 *a*, 885 (ii) *b*	6	696 *c*, 727 *q*
21	677 *a*			7	605, 626
23	639 *b*			8	852
24	681, 692 *h*			9	605, 626 *b*
25	450, 713 *f*, 716 *e*, 728 *p*, 866 *b*	6	636	10	546, 707 *a*
		7	626	11	546
		8	860	12	546, 662
		10	728 *a*	15	714 *h*
26	717 *d*	10–11	545 *a*, 857 *c*	16	708 *a*, 712 *d*, 720 *j*
27	639 *b*, 692 *g*, 719 *f*, 727 *b*	14	861, 885 *d*		
		15	885 (ii) *c*	17	627, 727 *p*
		16	672, 683 *c*, 723 *i*, 775 *a*, 784 foll.	17–19	598
29	672			18	637
30	692 *a*			19	716 *b*
31	719 *f*, 859 *b*				
32	517, 710 *g*, 866 *a*	17	784 foll., 859 *e*	21	597 *b*, 716 *h*, 885 *j*
		18	680 *b*, 709 *b*, 710 *h*, 722 *k*, 755 *a*,		
33	710 *d*, 724 *b*			22	714 *c*, 716 *h*
34	538–9, 704, 866 *a*			23	637 *b*
				26	720 *j*, 723 *e*

This Index extends from **1438** *to* **1885** (*printed* **438—885**).

636

NEW TESTAMENT PASSAGES

JOHN			JOHN			JOHN		
		PAR.			PAR.			PAR.
14	28	637, 658, 662, 683 c	16	21	721 h, 811 f, 865	18	13	764 b, 768, 885 (ii) b
	29	546		22	598, 719 c, 885 d		14	688 a, 885 h
	31	627		25	675 b, 694 d, 712 f		15	767, 885 (ii) c
15	1	684, 727 h		25–9	721 b		16	767
	2	674		26	708 a		18	711 f, 735 d, 885 (ii) c
	2–6	885 (ii) b		27	548, 596 a, 637 a, 716 f, 728 p		20	672 b, 694 b, 712 f
	3	857 c						
	4–5	674, 707 a						
	6	674, 682 a, 858, 864		28	637 a, 662–3		22	737 e
				29	662–3		24	764 b
	9–10	707 a		30	464, 548, 637 a		25	679, 735 d
	12	843		31	464, 548		26	680, 709 d, 734 b, 738 b, 866 c
	13	715 d		32	639 a, b, 674 b, 863			
	14	596, 775 a, b, 784–92		33	549, 771 c, 811 e, f		27	679
	15	596, 717 g, 723 i, 775 a, b, 784–92	17	1	639 b		28	745 a, 814 c, 815 b, 885 (ii) b
				1–2	590–2, 608			
				2	576–8		29	885 (ii) b
	16	659–60, 676 c		3	627		31	685, 715 b
	19	716 f, 728 p		4	774 c, 884 e		32	710 d, 724 b
	20	683 c, 721 h, 723 i, 775 a, b, 784–92, 854 c		5	712 j, 719 f		35	713 l, 718 f
				7	719 f		36	685 a, 713 m, 719 b, h, 764
				8	464, 550, 637 a, 727 l			
	21	625, 626 c, 692 a		9	708 a		37	614 c, 727 r
				12	591, 722 k, 810 a		38	727 r
	22	719 b, 834 d					40	752 a
	24	605, 719 b		13	719 f	19	2	676 d, 734 a, 805–6, 814 b, 885 (ii) b
	25	715 c, 751 a		15	708 a			
	26	720 j, 723 e, 727 p		17	727 q		3	737 e
				18	723 g		4	707 g
	27	708 e		19	692 a, 885 h		5	674 b, 734 a, 755, 805 a, 885 (ii) b
16	1	545, 694 a		20	708 a			
	2	679, 726, 885 (ii) b		20–1	464, 550			
				22	712 j		6	721 g, 752 a
	3	626 c		23	627, 774 c, 884 c		7	861
	4	708 e, 721 h					8	614 b
	5	658, 728 d		24	712 j, 858		9	728 c, 814 c
	5–7	662		25	629 a, 691 e		10	577, 593
	6	713 d, 771	18	1	885 (ii) b, c		11	570 c, 577, 707 e, 884 f
	7	720 j, 723 e		3	815 c, 885 (ii) b, c			
	8	582–5					12	752 a, 764, 788 a
	8–10	854 b		5	860			
	9	464, 547		6	885 (ii) c		12–16	593–4
	10	658		7	672 c, 860		13	614 b, 713 g, 745, 750, 885 (ii) b
	11	582–5		8	652 a, 885 d			
	13	727 p, 861		10	680, 709 d, 710 g, 734 b, 738 b, 885 (ii) b			
	16	597					15	752 a
	16–19	598 c, 716 b					17	713 g, 792 b, 807, 810
	19	735 b						
	20	857		11	508, 678 c, 885 (ii) b		18	796
	20–22	713 d, 771						
	21	676 b, 708 b,		12	738, 815 c		19	860, 885 (ii) c

This Index extends from **1438** *to* **1885** (*printed* **438—885**).

637

INDICES TO "JOHANNINE VOCABULARY"

JOHN		JOHN		JOHN	
	PAR.		PAR.		PAR.
19 20	689 a, 713 c, g, 721 l, 885 (ii) c	20 14	725 f	21 9	607, 711 g, 763, 769
		15	728 d, 885 (ii) b	10	719 g, 723 b
		16	694 c, 713 g, 737 d	11	683 a, 710 g, 712 a
23	707 e, 885 (ii) a, c	17	695 g, 719 a, 728 l, 749	12	602, 751, 780, 810 c
24	679, 722 k, 769–70	18	599 a, 601, 694 d, 885 (ii) a	12–13	636
25	885 (ii) b			14	597 b, 686 c, 695 e, 716 j, 738 a
26	596 a, 610, 744 (vi) foll.	19	636, 681 c, 725 f, 796–7, 804 a, 813 a, 854 e, 858, 884 c		
26–30	752 f			15	714 a, 728 p, 885 (ii) a
27	721 f			15–17	437–41, 714 a, 728 p
28	722 k, 750 b, 774 c				
28–30	865 b	20	780		
29	813 c, 864, 885 (ii) c	21	723 e–g, 854 e	16	862, 885 (ii) b
		22	721 f, 885 (ii) a	17	624 b, 695 e, 728 p, 885 (ii) b
30	451–8, 462 a–c, 839 foll., 858 a	23	682 d, 691 a, 721 j		
		24	695 i, 710	18	693 g, 712 g, 735 b, 843, 885 (ii) a
31	683 a, 885 (ii) c	25	465, 552–8, 885 (ii) b, c		
31–3	751				
32	678 b, 817 c, 885 (ii) e	26	636, 725 f, 796–7, 854 e, 858, 884 c	19	710 d, 712 h, 724 b, 843
33	775 d, 885 (ii) c	27	681 b, 862 e	20	596 a, 607, 638, 695 h, 744 (vi) foll., 760
34	756	29	465, 554–60, 599, 601, 749 b, 859 e		
35	465, 551, 606, 727 h				
36	722 k, 861	30	768 b	20 foll.	638–9
37	687 e, 722 k, 856 a, 885 (ii) a	31	465, 553, 561	22	735 a
		21 1	597 b, 686 c, 716 j, 726 e, 738 a, 811 d	23	708 j, 735 a
38	541, 681 c			25	885 (ii) b
39	544, 718 j, 754, 885 (ii) a, b	2	710, 727 a		ACTS
		3	544 a, 652 a, 718 j, 719 g, 723 b	1 4	794 a
40	600, 716 a, 734 e, 751 c, 832 b, 866 (i)–(iv)			14	749 d
				15	708 j
				16–20	722 h
		3–8	736 e	25	720 i
20 1	607, 710 b, 718 j, 815 a	4	725 b, f, 754, 884 c	2 1	727 a
				14	725 e
2	596 a, 728 d, p	4–9	763	17	592
3–11	798–804	5	676 b, 796 a, 885 (ii) b	38	485 c
4	727 a, 885 (ii) c			5 15	736 a
5	600–1, 607, 716 a, 726 b	6	691 d, 693 f, 710 g, 712 a, 763 a, 834 c	20	725 e
				6 3	772 a
7	760, 866 (ii)–(iv)			7 43	645 a
8	465, 552–60, 722 a foll.	7	596 a, 602, 712 g, 744 (vi) foll., 780, 810 b	55	772 a
				55–6	725 h
8–10	673 e			8 16	485 c
9	491, 722 a–l			19	594 a
11	466, 560, 600, 726 b, 775 d	7–8	560	27	645 a
		8	712 a, 734 d, 736 e, 862, 885 (ii) c	32–5	772 h
12	672, 858			9 33	736 a
13	728 d			42	476 a

This Index extends from **1438** *to* **1885** (*printed* 438—885).

NEW TESTAMENT PASSAGES

ACTS			ROMANS			GALATIANS		
		PAR.			PAR.			PAR.
10	10	735 *b*	8	17	844	1	6	673 *d*
	25	645 *a*		35, 37	744 (iv)	2	4	884 *a*
	43	476 *a*	9	11	478		9	720 *c*
	48	485 *c*		17	722 *h*		16	474, 722 *i*
11	17	476 *a*		21	583 *a*		20	517, 744 (iv),
	24	772 *a*		32	478			(x)
	28	724 *b*		33	474	3	6	474
12	4	723 *c*	10	9–11	541		8, 10,	
	21	745 *a*		11	474, 722 *h*		22	722 *i*
13	41	507 *b*		14	474		27	475 *a*
14	2	708 *j*		21	501 *a*	4	10	648 *b*
	13	735 *b*	11	2	722 *h*		19	598 *b*
	17	853 *a*		6	478		20	735 *b*
	23	476 *a*, 692 *j*		32	722 *i*		30	722 *h*
16	19	710 *g*	12	21	771 *c*	5	1	725 *a*
	31	476 *a*, 507 *a*	13	1	569 *b, c*		12	709 *d*, 734 *b*
	34	692 *j*	14	3–22	714 *g*		13	717 *f*
17	3	692 *j*		4	725 *a*		EPHESIANS	
	22	725 *e*	15	24	604 *b*	2	4–5	744 (iv) *a*
	27	617, 804 *b*	16	5	722 *j*	3	10	569 *a*
18	12, 16,						19	629
	17	745 *a*		1 CORINTHIANS		5	2	744 (iv)
19	4	476 *a*					8	715 *g*, 782
	5	485 *c*	1	13, 15	485 *c*		25	744 (iv)
	32	504 *b*		22	479	6	12	569 *a*
	33	735 *b*	2	11	727 *o*		PHILIPPIANS	
20	28	720 *i*	4	5	714 *g*	1	14	744 (iv) *b*
21	30	710 *g*		11	842		19	763 *b*
22	19	476 *a*	5	3	714 *g*		29	474
	23	752 *a*	6	12	594 *a*	2	15	748 *a*, 749 *c*
23	13, 21	504 *b*		19	740	3	12	735 *j*
	35	814 *c*	7	31	570 *c*	4	13	744 (iv) *a*
24	11	645 *a*	8	10	834 *b*		COLOSSIANS	
25	6, 10,		9	1–5	594 *a*	1	4	475
	17	745 *a*		18	570 *c*		13	568, 569 *d*, 570 *e*
	27	724 *b*	10	2	475 *a*		16	569 *a*
26	19	501 *a*		27	692 *j*	2	5	475
27	12	504 *b*	11	18	507 *b*		9	772 *a*
	21	725 *e*	12	13	475 *a*		10, 15	569 *a*
28	23	504 *b*	13	2	478		16	648 *b*
				7	474 *a*, 507 *b*	4	12	725 *d*
	ROMANS		14	25	645			
1	30	501 *a*	15	3–4	722 *e*		1 THESSALONIANS	
2	1–27	714 *g*		5	560, 802	1	9	727 *f*
	8	501 *a*		5–8	597 *b*, 716 *j*	2	7	662
	17	648		6	504 *b*	4	8	828 *a*, 832 *a*
3	4	771 *c*		24	569 *a*		14	474 *a*
	20–8	478	16	13	725 *a*	5	5	715 *g*, 782–3
4	2–6	478		22	630–1, 728 *q*			
	3	474, 722 *h*					2 THESSALONIANS	
	5, 24	474		2 CORINTHIANS		2	11, 12	474 *a*
6	3	475 *a*					16	744 (iv) *a*
	6	517	3	17	727 *q*			
7	19	772 *b*	11	32	723 *c*			

This Index extends from **1438** *to* **1885** (*printed* **438—885**).

639

INDICES TO "JOHANNINE VOCABULARY"

1 TIMOTHY		
		PAR.
1	12	744 (iv) a
	16	474 c
	18	692 j
4	13	638, 735 a
5	18	722 h
6	3	677 a

2 TIMOTHY		
1	12	474 c
2	2	692 j
	12	844
3	2	501 a

TITUS		
1	16	501 a
3	1	569 a
	3	501 a
	8	474 c
	15	728 q

PHILEMON		
	5	475

HEBREWS		
1	6	645
2	9	712 h
	12	794
	15	811 c
4	3	476 b, 853 a
5	8	845
6	4	485 a
7	2	728 l_2
	23	504 b
8	2	727 h
9	24	727 h
10	7, 9	637 a, 856
	32	485 a
11	1	478 c
	6	476 b
	18–19	722 e
	21	645
	34	858 a
12	2	475 b

JAMES		
1	25	600 b, 726 b, 800
2	8	722 h
	17	478
	19	476
	23	476, 596 a, 722 h, 790 b

JAMES		
		PAR.
4	4	716 f
	5	722 h

1 PETER		
1	8	475
	12	600 b, 726 b, 800 b
	21	475
	24	592
2	4	677 a
	6	722 h
4	19	692 j
5	3	594 a

"2 PETER"		
1	13	832 c
	20	722 i
3	1	832 c

1 JOHN		
1	1	604, 804 b
	1–5	616–20
	9	764 a, 848, 861 a
2	1	720 j
	3, 5	628
	7	687 d
	8	727 g
	9–10	539
	11	656
	12	553 a
	18, 29	628
3	1	609
	8, 12	728 h
	17	603 a
	18	728 h, 744 (v)
	19	628
	23	487 b, 553 a
	24	628
4	2	628
	3	722 k
	6	628, 727 p
	7	628
	9	498, 723 g
	10	723 g
	12	604
	14	604, 723 g, 774 a
	16	629
	17	585 a, 859 b
	18	651, 681 c
5	6	637 a, 727 p
	10	491 b

1 JOHN		
		PAR.
5	10–13	487 a
	13	553 a
	16	609
	17	764 a
	20	627, 856

3 JOHN		
	14	609

JUDE		
	6	800 b

REVELATION		
1	1	724 b
	4	639
	5	696 e
	13	794
2	1	794
	13	696 e
	17	711 h
	26	564, 594 b
3	7–14	727 f
	9	744 (iv)
	14	696 e
	19	728 q
	20	725 h
5	6	794
6	8	563, 594 b
	10	727 f
7	17	794
9	3, 10, 19	563
	20	646
11	3	696 e
	6	563, 594 b
12	10	563
13	2–12	564 a
	7	594 b
	8, 12	646
14	9, 11	646
	18	564, 594 b
16	9	564 b, 594 b
17	6	696 c
	12, 13	564
18	1	564
19	20	723 c
20	4	646
	6	564
22	14	564 c, 594 b
	15	728 q
	17, 20	631

This Index extends from **1438** *to* **1885** (*printed* **438—885**).

INDICES TO "JOHANNINE VOCABULARY"

II. SUBJECT-MATTER (ENGLISH)

[*For Synoptic and Johannine words not in this Index, see the English alphabetical lists in* **1672—96** *and* **1707—28**]

Aaron, "the holy one of God" **835** *a*
Abide **707**; "abiding in" **659-60**; "abiding," higher than "believing" **547**
Above, from, **707**
Abraham, God's "friend" **596** *a*, **789** *a*, **790**; his faith **472-8**
Adders, deaf **614** *d*
Allusiveness, in Jn **438-9, 446**; specimens of **450-8, 762-3, 797, 804, 831**
Alone, "the linen cloths alone" **804**
Ambiguities, verbal **444-5, 529**, and see Index to "Johannine Grammar"
Annas **764**
Aphesis, the sabbatical "release" **690**
Apostles or Missionaries in the first century **594** *a*
"Appeared to" or "was seen by" (ὤφθη) **597** *b*
Apprehend (καταλαμβάνω) **735** *e*
Authority **562-94**; "receiving authority," explained by Origen **484**

Baptism, baptizing **485, 487, 493**
Baptist, see "John"
Begin (vb.), only once in Jn **674** *a*
Beginning (n.) **708** *d*

Beholding (θεωρέω) **597** foll., **723**; sometimes unintelligent **598**
Belief or faith, not used by Jn as noun **467**; Mk's doctrine of **467**; meaning of, influenced by Christianity **473**; "thy faith hath saved thee," unique agreement as to, in the Triple Tradition **477**; insignificance of "faith" in the teaching of Epictetus **479**; a lower and a higher **505**; inferior to "knowledge" **559**
"Believe" or "trust," a key-word in the Fourth Gospel **463—561**
Benefactor, a name assumed by several Eastern kings **571**
Blood and water, the fountain of **606**
Bowing the head **451** foll.
Bread **699**; "the true bread" **513**
Break (bread) **675**
Brother (metaph.), not used in Jn till after the Resurrection **701**; "the brethren" **708**; "my brethren" **748-9**
Burial of the Lord, the, verbal differences as to **866** (i)—(iv)

Child **676**; "authority to become children of God" **579**; "receiving little

This Index extends from **1438** *to* **1885** (*printed* **438—885**).

children" 698; "children of light" 782

Coming, vbs denoting 630–9; the coming of the Lord 630 foll.; "come and see," a Talmudic formula 609; "He that cometh," a technical Jewish term 633; "thy king cometh" 634; s. also 624 a

Compassion 677

Cross, the, taking up, bearing etc. 792 b, 842; in connexion with "following" Christ 843

Cry aloud 752 a foll.

Darkness 710; degrees of 544
Dative w. πιστεύω 470–90
Deaf, the, not mentioned in Jn 614
Debts, remission of, in the sabbatical year 462, 690; Mt. has "debts" for "sins" in the Lord's Prayer 462
Destruction, parall. to "Judas Iscariot" 810 a; "the son of destruction" to be "destroyed" 591
Devils, authority to cast out 580 a
Diminutives, Jn's use of 736 e, 738
"Disciple that Jesus loved, the" 744 (x); at Christ's tomb 600
Double Tradition, defined 447 foll.

Edition, a second, hypothesis of in Lk. 871 a
Elenchos, the convicting Logos or Spirit 609 a
Enemies, "a man's enemies shall be they of his own household" 792 a
Enlightened, "those who were once enlightened" = "baptized" 485 a
"Eternal," applied by Jn to nothing but "life" 705
Euergetes and *Kakergetes* 571
"Eyes, lifting up the," symbolical 608

Faith, see "Belief"
Family of Heaven, the 698
Father, divine 711
Fear (*i.e.* worship) the Lord 643 a, 651

Fellowship 619, 700
Fire of coals 711
Five Thousand, Feeding of the 512
Flesh, metaph. 699; "all flesh" 592
Following Christ 840–3
Forgive, forgiveness 682; authority to forgive 575
Free (adj.) 712; "I am free and a friend of God" 788 a
Freedom 727 q; Epictetus on "freedom" and "slavery" 717 g
Friend, "my friends" 775 a, 784; distinction between "friends" and "servants" 789–91; "a friend of Caesar" 788 a; "I am free and a friend of God" 788 a

Galilaeans, the, described differently by Lk. and Jn 606 a
Galilee, the sea of 811 d
Glory, glorifying 712; in Jn, of a spiritual nature 489–90
God, "knowing God," "not knowing God" 622
Going, vbs denoting 652–64; "go and bear fruit" 659–60
Golgotha 807
"Government, the," Jewish traditions on 570
Greater, of persons 683
Greek, classical, fails to represent Semitic traditions about trust in God 470; low-class 732, 736, 737
"Grow in the understanding of God" 627

"Hating one's own life" 450, 713 f, 761, 792 a
Head, "bow the head," meaning of 451 foll., 839
Hearing, the Johannine and the Synoptic view of 612
Heaven, the opening of 530 b, 866 (iv)
Hebrew, "believing" or "trusting," meaning of, in Hebrew 469–71

This Index extends from **1438** *to* **1885** (*printed* **438—885**).

SUBJECT-MATTER (ENGLISH)

Hell, "destroying in hell," parallel to "casting into hell" **566**
Hillel, abrogated the Remission of Debts **462, 690**
"Holy One of God, the," **835**
Hosanna **807**
Household, "they of his own household," Heb. "men of his house," Syr. "sons of his house,"="friends" **787**

I AM [HE] **522**
"Israelite, an" **727** *l*

"Jews, the," the term how used in Jn **647, 713**
John, St, the Baptist **482**
John, St, the Evangelist, see "Johannine Grammar" Contents, *passim*, and, in Index, "Allusiveness," "Ambiguity," "Emphasis," "Metaphor," "Mysticism," "Narrowing down," "Quotation"
"Joseph, son of" **776–8**
Jubilee, the,=the Sabbatical Year **690** *b*
Judas Iscariot, parall. to "destruction" **810** *a*
Judging, judgment **714**; not in Triple Tradition **714** *d*; "judgment," not used by Mk **585**; "day of j." not mentioned in Jn **585** *a*; "authority to do judgment" **581–5**
"Judgment seat, *a*" or "*the*" **745**

Kingdom, antithesis between k. and "authority" **568**; "the k. of God, of heaven" **685** *a*
Knowing, vbs denoting **621–9**

"Law, your" **715**
Life, "hating one's own life" **450, 713** *f*, **792** *a*; "authority to lay down one's life" **594**
Light, children (or sons) of **782**; the Light of the world **748**

Logos, the, described by Philo as "standing" **725** *g*
Look, "stoop (?) and look in" **798**
Loosing the shoe **833** *d*
"Lord, the," meaning "Jesus" **779** foll.
Love, different words for **436, 596, 716, 728** *m—p*; the n. not used by Mk **697**
Luke, a compiler of traditions in various styles **758**; hypothesis of a second edition in his gospel **871** *a*; his view of "authority" **565–71**; avoids ὑπάγω **653**; Jn differs from **606** *a*, **778**; where Lk. omits, Jn intervenes **792**

Manifest (vb) **716**
Maran atha **630–1**
Mark, his doctrine of belief or faith **467**
Marvel (see "Wonder") rebuked by Jesus **673** *a*
Mary Magdalene at Christ's tomb **601**
Meant (ἔλεγε) **491** *a*
"Meek," an epithet om. by Jn in quoting Zechariah **456**
Metaphors, Johannine **699, 867**
Midst, "standing in the midst," used of Jesus **793–7**
Might, mighty **686**; "mighty work" **686** *e*
"Minister" and "slave," apparently used by Mk as parallel terms **717** *g*
"Multitude, the great" **739–40**

Name, the, believing in **483**
"Narrowing down" **481**
Nathanael, his profession of belief **488**; the calling of **671** *b*
"Nazareth where he was brought up" **778**
Nicodemus, the dialogue with **493–6**; "a ruler of the Jews" **765** *a*
Night (metaph.) **718**
"Nos qui cum eo fuimus" **802** *a*
"Now," different meanings of **719**

"Own, his" **720**

This Index extends from **1438** *to* **1885** (*printed* **438—885**).

INDICES TO "JOHANNINE VOCABULARY"

Parable, see "Proverb"
Paraclete, the **720**
Paul, St, his view of "belief" **475, 478**
Perfect belief, knowledge etc. **629**
Peter, St, at Christ's tomb **600**
Phantasm, phantom, or spirit **813** *a*
Praetorium, not in Lk. but in Acts **814** *c*
Praying ($\pi\rho o\sigma \epsilon \acute{u}\chi o\mu a\iota$) not mentioned by Jesus in Jn **649**
Prepositions in the Four Gospels **881–5**
"Privately," not used by Jn of Christ's teaching **672** *b*
"Proverb" and "parable" **721**

"Qui cum eo fuimus" **802** *a*
Quotation, Johannine, of Zechariah, inaccurate **456, 757**; from Scripture, how introduced **722** *h*

Rebelling **502**
Receiving (persons) **689, 721**; "receiving little ones" **829**
Recognising **629** *a*
"Reigning with Christ" **844**
Rejection, Mk, Lk., and Jn on **823** foll.
Remission of sins **690**
Resurrection, Christ's, revealed differently to different persons **600**
"Retaining sins" **721**
Revelation, "God revealed Himself by degrees" **600** *a*
Righteous, only once in Jn **668**; applied to God **691** *e*
"Rising again," an ambiguous term **529**

Sabbatical Year, the **690** *b* foll.
Salim **721**
Samaritan Woman, the, dialogue with **647–51**
Scripture, "believing the s." **491–2**; "another s." **722**; "the s.," "this s." **722**; "the scriptures" **722**
"Sea of Galilee, the" **811**

Seeing, vbs denoting **597—611, 723**; Philo on Gen. i. 31, "God saw ($\epsilon \tilde{\iota}\delta \epsilon \nu$) his works" **611** *a*
Sending, vbs denoting **723**; "He that sent me" **723**
Serpent in the Wilderness, the **495, 517**
Servant **723**; bondservant **785**; distinction between "servants" and "friends" of God **704, 789–91**
"Signs," i.e. miracles **521**
Simon, father of Judas Iscariot **724** *c*; Simon, in Heb. confusable w. "those with us" **802** *a*
Sing, Christ singing **794**
Single Tradition, defined **447**
Sins, remission of **690**; Mt. substitutes "debts" for "sins" in the Lord's Prayer **462**
"Slave" and "Minister," used by Mk as parallel terms **717** *g*
Sleep, "He giveth unto his beloved in sleep" **515**
"Son of man" **525** *a*, **539** *a*, **704**; the Eldest Son "looking at the Father's acts" **607**; Sons of Light **782**
"Spirit, a," = phantasm, or phantom **813** *a*; a spirit or messenger, in Epictetus **727** *o*
Spirit, the, "the Spirit of truth" **720** *l*, **727** *p*; Spirit or wind, $\pi\nu\epsilon\tilde{\nu}\mu a$ **655**
Standing, applied to Jesus **725, 793–7**; to God, Wisdom etc. **725** *g*
Stretching out the hands **693**
Stumbling **545–6**
Synonyms, see note on next page

Talmud, the, on authority **569** *c*, **570** *a*
Testimony, see "Witness"
"The Lord (Jesus)," in narrative **779**
Tradition, see Double, Single, and Triple Tradition
Transliteration **728** l_2
Triple Tradition, defined **447**; does not agree in a single saying of Christ using the verb "believe" **477**

This Index extends from **1438** *to* **1885** (*printed* **438—885**).

SUBJECT-MATTER (ENGLISH)

Trouble **727**; "freedom from trouble" in Epictetus **706**, **727** *c*
True, truly, truth **727**; "knowing truth" **703**
Trusting or believing **469–78**
Truth, see "True"
"Twelve, the," how mentioned by Jn **671** *b*

Understanding (God or man) **624–9**; implies sympathy **626**

"Verily" and "Verily verily" **696** *a*
Vine, metaphor of the **660**

Water **699**
Wind or Spirit, πνεῦμα **655**
With, "those with us," confusable in Heb. w. "Simon" **802** *a*
Witness **696**; believing witnesses **522**; witness = testimony **703**
Wonder, in a bad sense **671** *a*, **673** *a—e*; "I saw and wondered," a phrase used by Greek tourists **673** *e*
Worshipping **640–51**; different from "prostration" **643**; "we worship that which we know" **647**

This Index extends from **1438** *to* **1885** (*printed* **438—885**).

Addendum on "Synonyms"

By "synonyms" are meant (**1595**) "words so far alike that at first the reader may take the thought to be the same, though it is always really different." A more exact term—if it were English—would be "*homoionyms*." Strictly speaking, some might say that *there are no "synonyms" in John*, i.e. no words that convey precisely the same shade of meaning.

INDICES TO "JOHANNINE VOCABULARY"

III. WORDS (GREEK)

[*The main object of this Index is to guide the reader to some paragraph in "Johannine Vocabulary" where a characteristic Johannine word is mentioned or discussed. It does not contain e.g. ἄρτος, σάρξ, or ὕδωρ, because these words are not characteristically Johannine. But "bread," "flesh," and "water," in the English Index, will guide the reader to passages illustrating the Johannine characteristic use of these common words.*

For conjunctions, prepositions, pronouns etc., the reader is referred to Index III. of "Johannine Grammar."]

Ἀβραάμ 851
ἀγαθός 682
ἀγαλλιάω 851
ἀγανακτέω 684
ἀγαπάω and φιλέω 436, 596, 716, 728 m—q, 744 (i)—(xi)
ἀγάπη 716, 851
ἀγαπητός 674
ἀγγελία 620
ἀγγέλλω 885 (ii)
ἄγγελος 672
ἁγιάζω 835 a, 851
ἅγιος, ὁ ἅ. τοῦ θεοῦ 835
ἁγνίζω 885 (ii)
ἀγωνίζομαι 764
ἀδελφός, οἱ ἀδελφοί 708, ἀδελφός σου 851
ᾅδης 851
ἀδικία 764
ἀθετέω 823—32
αἰγιαλός 750
Αἰνών 707
αἴρω, ἀ. ὀφθαλμούς 608, ἀ. σταυρόν 792 b
αἰών 672 a, εἰς τὸν ἀ., εἰς τοὺς ἀ. 712 d, 728 k
αἰώνιος 710, 715
ἀκάθαρτος 695
ἀκάνθινος 734, 805 a

ἀκούω, w. accus. and w. gen. 614 a—c
ἀκυρόω 824 a
ἀλήθεια 727
ἀληθής 727, 810, ἀ. and ἀληθινός 727 h—i
ἀληθινός 727, 764, ἀ. and ἀληθής 727 h—i
ἀληθῶς 727
ἁλιεύω (Jn xxi. 3) om. in 885 (ii)
ἀλλά 708, ἀλλ' εἰς and ἄλλος 756
ἄλλομαι 885 (ii)
ἄλλος, and ἀλλ' εἰς 756
ἀλλότριος 851
ἀλόη 885 (ii)
ἁμαρτάνω 852
ἁμαρτία, ἄφεσις ἁμαρτιῶν 690
ἁμαρτωλός 693
ἀμήν 696
ἀμνός 885 (ii)
ἀμπελών 696
ἀναγγέλλω 616, 620
ἀναγινώσκω 689
ἀνάκειμαι 689 d
ἀνακλίνω 689
ἀναπίπτω 689 d
ἀνάστασις 529 c

ἀνατρέπω 885 (ii)
ἀναχωρέω 810
ἄνεμος 696
ἀνέρχομαι 885 (ii)
ἀνθρακιά 711
ἀνθρωποκτόνος 885 (ii)
ἀνίημι 752 b
ἀνίστημι tr. 721, intr. 672
Ἄννας 764
ἀνοίγω 852, 866 (iv)
ἀντιλέγω 764
ἀντλέω 710
ἄνω, -θεν 707
ἄξιος 852
ἀπαγγέλλω 616, 675
ἀπαρνέομαι 679
ἀπειθέω 501, 885 (ii)
ἀπέχω 679
ἀπιστέω, -ία, -ος 681
ἀποβαίνω 763—4
ἀποδίδωμι 687
ἀποθνῄσκω 710
ἀποκαλύπτω 738 a, 852
ἀποκόπτω 709 d, 734
ἀπόκρισις 765
ἀπολύω 679
ἀπορέω 832
ἀποστέλλω 723 d
ἀπόστολος 672

This Index extends from **1438** to **1885** (printed **438—885**).

WORDS (GREEK)

ἀποσυνάγωγος 726
ἅπτομαι 695
ἀπώλεια 810
ἄρα 695
ἄραφος 885 (ii)
ἀργύριον 686
ἀρεστός 885 (ii)
ἀριθμός 765
ἀριστάω 765
ἀρκέω 852
ἀρνίον 885 (ii)
ἁρπάζω 750
ἄρτι 719, 750
ἀρχή 708, 810
ἀρχιτρίκλινος 885 (ii)
ἄρχομαι 674
ἄρχων 765, 852
ἄρωμα 832
ἀσθένεια 679 d, 724, 853
ἀσθενέω 724
ἀσθενής 724, 750
ἀτιμάζω 832
ἀταραξία 727 c
αὐξάνω 684
αὐτόματος 515 a
ἄφεσις 682, ἄ. ἁμαρτιῶν 690
ἀφίημι 682; ἀ. φωνήν, 752 e
ἀφοράω εἰς 475

Βαθύς 765
βαΐον 885 (ii)
βάλλω, βεβλημένη 834 a
βαπτίζω 485 c
βάπτισμα 673
βαπτιστής 673
βάπτω 765
βασιλεία 685
βασιλικός 885 (ii)
βαστάζω σταυρόν 792 b
Βηθανία...πέραν τοῦ Ἰορδάνου 708
Βηθαθά, v.r. Βηθσαιδά etc. 708
Βηθλεέμ 853
βῆμα 745, 750
βιβρώσκω 885 (ii)
βίος 694
βλασφημέω, -ία 674
βλέπω 600, 607, 723
βοάω 752 e
βουλεύομαι 766
βοῦς 766
βραχίων 766
βραχύ 766
βρέφος 676
βροντή 734

βρῶσις 746, 750

Γαββαθά 712
γαζοφυλάκιον 832
γαμέω, -ος etc. 686, 853
γάρ 712
γε 853
γέεννα 683
γείτων 766
γεμίζω 832
γενεά 682
γενετή 885 (ii)
γεννάω 708
γέρων 885 (ii)
γεωργός 684
γηράσκω 885 (ii)
γίνομαι 734, γ. and ἦν 734 c
γινώσκω 621–9, 715, 738 a
γλωσσόκομον 885 (ii)
γνωρίζω 766
γνωστός 767
γογγύζω 689 b, 718, 853
γογγυσμός 718
Γολγοθά 810
γράμμα 767
γραμματεύς 692
γραφή, sing. and pl. 692, 722
γράφω, τὸ γεγραμμένον τοῦτο 722 c
γρηγορέω 696
γυμνός 810
γυνή (wife) 696

Δαιμονίζομαι 679
δαιμόνιον 679
δακρύω 885 (ii)
Δανείδ 679
δεξιός 691
δέομαι 853
δεῦτε 810
δέχομαι 689, 721 f, 825–31
δέω 866 (iii)
διά 692 a, διά τινα 652 b, 884 ab
διάβολος 665 a, 854
διαγογγύζω 689 b
διάγω 794 a
διαδίδωμι 767
διαζώννυμι 712
διακονέω 717
διάκονος 717, 810
διακόσιοι 734
διαλογίζομαι, -ισμός 689
διαμερίζω 679
διασπορά 713 b, om. in 885 (ii) a

διατρίβω 885 (ii)
διδακτός 885 (ii)
διδάσκαλε (voc.) 694
Δίδυμος 710
διεγείρω 832
δίκαιος 691, 727 f
δικαιοσύνη 854
δικαιόω 854
διψάω 750
διώκω 854
δόλος 811
δόξα 712
δοξάζω 712
δουλεύω 854
δοῦλος 717 f, 723, 790 foll.
δύναμις 669, 686
δυνατός 686
δώδεκα, οἱ δ. 695
δωρεά 885 (ii)
δωρεάν 746, 751
δῶρον 682

Ἑαυτοῦ, -ῶν 720 f
Ἑβραϊστί 713
ἐγγίζω 687
ἐγγύς 718
ἐγώ and εἰμί 713
ἔθνος 687, 718
ἔθος 767
εἶδον 610–11, ἰδεῖν 609, ἰδών 599
εἶδος 767
εἰμί 707, 713, ἦν and ἐγένετο 734 c
εἰρήνη 854
εἰς for ἐν 884, w. βαπτίζεσθαι 475 a, w. πιστεύω 470 foll.
εἷς? ἀλλ᾽ εἷς read as ἄλλος, 756
εἰσάγω 767
εἰσέρχομαι, parall. to προσέρχ. 801 a, b
ἑκατοντάρχης 676
ἐκβάλλω (δαιμόνια) 679
ἐκδύω and ἐνδύω 806
ἐκεῖ 527 a
ἐκκεντέω 885 (ii)
ἐκλέγομαι 709, 833
ἐκλεκτός 676
ἐκμάσσω 762, 768
ἐκνεύω 885 (ii)
ἐκτείνω χεῖρα(ς) 693
ἐκχέω 751 b
ἐλαιῶν (al. -ών) 687
ἐλαττόω 885 (ii)
ἐλάττων 885 (ii)
ἐλαύνω 833

This Index extends from 1438 *to* 1885 (*printed* 438—885).

647

INDICES TO "JOHANNINE VOCABULARY"

ἐλέγχω 855
ἐλεέω 677
ἐλεημοσύνη 855
ἔλεος 677, 727 n., 855
ἐλεύθερος 712, 751
ἐλευθερόω 712
ἕλιγμα 885 (ii)
ἑλκύω 710
Ἕλληνες, -ιστί 713
ἐλπίζω 855
ἐμαυτοῦ, -όν 718, 855
ἐμβριμάομαι 713, 811
ἐμός 718
ἐμπαίζω 686
ἐμπίμπλημι 768
ἐμπόριον 885 (ii)
ἔμπροσθεν 681 a
ἐμπτύω 693
ἐμφανίζω 597 b, 716, 751
ἐμφυσάω 885 (ii)
ἐν 881-2, w. πιστεύω 470, 480
ἐνδύω 689, ἐ. and ἐκδύω 806
ἐνειλέω 866 (i) foll.
ἕνεκα 692, 884
ἐνθάδε 768
ἐνιαυτός 768
ἐνκαίνια 885 (ii)
ἐνταφιάζω 734 e, 751
ἐνταφιασμός 732, 734
ἐντεῦθεν 768
ἐντυλίσσω 855, 866 (i) foll.
ἐνώπιον 768
ἐξάγω 833
ἐξέρχομαι 637 a
ἔξεστιν 594 a, 685
ἐξετάζω 751
ἐξηγέομαι 769
ἐξομολογέομαι 678
ἐξουσία 562-94
ἐξουσιάζω 570 b
ἐξυπνίζω (Jn xi. 11) om. in 885 (ii)
ἑορτή 711
ἐπαίρω 855
ἐπαιτέω 737 a
ἐπάρατος 885 (ii)
ἐπαύριον 811
ἔπειτα 769
ἐπενδύτης (Jn xxi. 7) om. in 885 (ii)
ἐπερωτάω 672
ἐπί 884, πιστεύω ἐ. 470–77
ἐπίγειος 885 (ii)
ἐπιγινώσκω 685

ἐπιθυμία 833
ἐπίκειμαι 769
ἐπιλέγομαι 885 (ii)
ἐπιστρέφω 695
ἐπισυνάγω 682
ἐπιτίθημι, v.r. περιέθηκαν 805
ἐπιχρίω 885 (ii)
ἐπουράνιος 885 (ii)
ἑπτά, ἑπτάκις 692
ἐραυνάω 885 (ii)
ἐργάζομαι 513, 728
ἔργον 728
ἔρημος 679, 728
ἑρμηνεύω 713, 728 l_2
ἔρχομαι 630–9, ἔρχομαι and ἦλθον 624, ὁ ἐρχόμενος 633, ἐλήλυθα 637 a, ἐλήλυθεν ὥρα, ἔρχεται ὥρα 639 a—b
ἐρωτάω 708
ἐσθίω 680
ἔσχατος 685, ἐ. ἡμέρα 715
ἕτερος 687, 856
ἑτοιμάζω, ἕτοιμος 688
εὐαγγελίζομαι, εὐαγγέλιον 670, 682
εὐδοκέω, -ία 696
εὐθέως 693
εὐθύνω 885 (ii)
εὐθύς (adv.) 693
εὐλογέω, εὐλογητός 674
εὐνοέω 714 e
Ἐφραίμ 710
ἐχθές 885 (ii)
ἐχθρός 680, 792 a, 856
ἔχω 796 a
ἕως conj. 735, prep. 884

Ζῆλος 885 (ii)
ζήτησις 885 (ii)
ζωή 715
ζώννυμι 712
ζωοποιέω 716

Ἡ 647 c
ἡγεμών 682
ἤθελον etc. s. θέλω
ἥκω 637 a, 856
Ἠλείας 680
ἡλικία 856
ἧλος 885 (ii)
ἤπερ 647 c

Θάλασσα 811
θάνατος 710
θανατόω 679
θαρσέω 811

θαυμάζω 671 a, 673 a—e
θαυμαστός 811
θεάομαι 604, 723, 856
θέλημα 728
θέλω, ἤθελον, -ησα, -α 735 b, c
θεός, ὁ 497 a
θεοσεβής 885 (ii)
θεραπεύω 683
θερίζω 856
θερμαίνομαι 735
θεωρέω 598 foll., 723
θήκη 885 (ii)
θλῖψις 811
θρέμμα 885 (ii)
θρηνέω 857
θυγάτηρ 678
θυρωρός 735

Ἰάκωβος 684 d
ἰάομαι 683
ἴδε 674, 812
ἰδεῖν 609–11, s. εἶδον
ἴδιος 720, κατ' ἰδίαν 672, οἱ ἴδιοι and τὰ ἴδια 720 d; (τις) τῶν ἰδίων 630
ἰδού 674
ἱερεύς 688
Ἱεροσολυμεῖται 735
ἱκανός 683
ἱμάς 833
ἱματισμός 769
ἵνα 726
Ἰουδαῖος 713
Ἰούδας, οὐχ ὁ Ἰσκαριώτης 714
Ἰσραήλ 684
Ἰσραηλείτης 713
ἵστημι 725, σταθῆναι and στῆναι 725 b—e, ἑστώς of God 725 g, ἔστη εἰς μέσον or ἐν μέσῳ, of Jesus 793 foll.
ἰσχυρός, ἰσχύς, ἰσχύω 686, 693
Ἰωάνης (Peter's father) 714
Ἰωσήφ (Mary's husband) 857

Κἀγώ 857
καθαίρω 885 (ii)
καθαρίζω 676
καθαρισμός 833
καθαρός 857
καθέζομαι 857
καθεύδω 693
Καιάφας 857

This Index extends from 1438 to 1885 (printed 438—885).

648

WORDS (GREEK)

καιρός 695
καίω 858
κακῶς ἔχων 679
κάλαμος 689
καλέω 675
Κανᾶ 709
κατά 884, κατ' ἰδίαν 688
καταβολή 858
κατάγνυμι 751
κατάκειμαι 834
κατακλίνω 689
κατακρίνω 677
κατακυριεύω 570
καταλαμβάνω 735
καταλύω 679
κατανοέω 800 a
κατεξουσιάζω 570
κατηγορία 885 (ii)
κατοικέω 858
Κέδρων (τῶν) 885 (ii)
κεῖμαι 858
κειρία 885 (ii)
κεντυρίων 676
κερδαίνω 682
κέρμα 686, 885 (ii)
κερματιστής 885 (ii)
κεφαλή, s. κλίνω
κῆπος 769
κηπουρός 885 (ii)
κηρύσσω 688
Κηφᾶς 709
κλάδος 674
κλάω 675
κλείω 858
κλέπτης 858
κλῆμα 674, 885 (ii)
κληρονομέω, -ία, -ος 684
κλίνω 858, κλίνω κεφαλήν 451-8, 462, 839
Κλωπᾶς 885 (ii)
κοιμάομαι 693, 858
κοίμησις 885 (ii)
κοινός 677 b
κοινόω 677
κοινωνία 700 a
κόκκος 692 h
κολάζω 723 c
κόλασις 723 c
κολλυβιστής 812
κόλπος 769
κολυμβήθρα 720
κομψότερον ἔχειν 885 (ii)
κοπιάω 859
κόσμος 728
κράβαττος 673, 736
κράζω 752 a—f
κρατέω 691, κ. ἁμαρτίας 721
κραυγάζω 752 a—f

κρίθινος 708
κρίνω 677 d, 714, 859
κρίσις 859
κρύπτω 859
κτήματα 694
κυκλόω 770
κύπτω, forms of 799 c
κυριεύω 570
κύριος (ὁ), of Jesus 770
κωφός 679

Λαγχάνω 770
Λάζαρος 770
λάθρᾳ 752
λαλέω 724
λαλιά 752
λαμβάνω 689 c, 721, 735 f, λ. σταυρόν 792 b
λαμπάς 746, 752
λαός 688, parall. to ὄχλος 739
λατρεία 885 (ii)
λέγω hist. pres. 804 a, ἔλεγε 491 a
λέντιον 885 (ii)
λέπρα, -ός 685
Λευείτης 770
λιθάζω 726
λίθινος 885 (ii)
λιθοβολέω 859
λιθόστρωτος 885 (ii)
λίτρα 885 (ii)
λογίζομαι 770
λόγος, s. Joh. Gr. Index
λόγχη 752
λοιδορέω 885 (ii)
λούω 728
λύκος 859
λυπέομαι 727 c, 812
λύπη 771
λύχνος, -ία 685
λύω 679 b

Μαίνομαι 885 (ii)
μακάριος 859 e
Μάλχος 885 (ii)
μανθάνω 812
μάννα 717
Μάρθα 717, 771
Μαριά(μ) (the mother of Jesus) 686
Μαριά(μ) (sister of Lazarus) 771
μαρτυρέω 703, 726, 859
μαρτυρία 695 b, 726, 834
μαρτύριον 695, 726
μάρτυς 696, 726
μάστιξ (disease) 692

μάχομαι 885 (ii)
μέγας 683
μεθερμηνεύω 728 l_2, 812
μεθύω 752
μείζων, of persons 683
μένω 707
μερίζω 679
μέριμνα 676
μέρος 860
μέσος, s. ἵστημι, 793 foll.
μεσόω 885 (ii)
Μεσσίας 717
μεστός 753
μεταβαίνω 860
μετανοέω, -οια 691
μεταξύ 860
μετρητής (Jn ii. 6) om. in 885 (ii)·
μηδείς 885
μήποτε 885
μηνύω 771
μιαίνω 885 (ii)
μικρόν (adv.) 716, 812
μικρός 686
μιμνήσκομαι 721 i, 860
μισέω 713
μισθός 691
μισθωτός 736
μνημονεύω 721
μονή 707
μονογενής 771
μόνος, τὰ ὀθόνια μόνα 804

Ναζωραῖος 860
Ναθαναήλ 718
νάρδος 736
νεύω 885 (ii)
νεφέλη 676
νήπιος 676, 860
νηστεύω, νηστεία, νῆστις 681
νικάω 771
Νικόδημος 718
νιπτήρ 885 (ii)
νίπτω 728, 813
νοέω 813
νομή (Jn x. 9) om. in 885 (ii)
νόμος 715, 860
νόσος 679, 724 a
νύμφη 860
νῦν 719
νύξ 718
νύσσω 753

Ξύλον 885 (i)

Ὁδηγέω 861

This Index extends from 1438 to 1885 (printed 438—885).

649

INDICES TO "JOHANNINE VOCABULARY"

ὁδοιπορία 885 (ii)
ὁδός 696
ὄζω 885 (ii)
ὀθόνιον 716, 772, 804
οἶδα 621—9, 715
οἰκία 684
οἰκοδεσπότης 684
οἰκοδομέω 675
οἶκος 684
οἶμαι 885 (ii)
ὀκτώ 772
ὀμνύω 694
ὅμοιος 861
ὁμοιόω 686
ὁμολογέω 678 a, 861
ὁμοῦ 727
ὀνάριον 885 (ii)
ὄνομα 553 a, πιστεύω εἰς τὸ ὄ. 483
ὄνος 861
ὄντως 834
ὅπλον 885 (ii)
ὅπως 695
ὅρασις 601
ὁράω 601, 605-6, 723, ὤφθη 597 b
ὀργίζομαι 861
ὅρκος 687
ὀρφανός (Jn xiv. 18) om. in 885 (ii)
ὀσμή 885 (ii)
ὀστέον 861
ὅστις 885
ὅτε 775 e
ὅτι 726, πιστεύω ὅ 476
οὐαί 696
οὐ μόνον 753
οὖν 883, 885
οὔπω 719
οὖς 680, 866 c
οὐχί 861
ὀφείλω 861
ὀφθαλμοὺς αἴρω 608
ὄχλος and λαός 739, ὁ ὄ. πολύς 739-40
ὀψάριον 712
ὀψία 813
ὄψις 885 (ii)

Παιδάριον 736 e, 885 (ii)
παιδίον 676
παῖς 862
παλαιός 687
παρά 885
παραβαίνω 824 a
παραβολή 669, 687, 721 a
παράγω 687, 813
παράδοσις 695

παρακαλέω 674
παράκλητος 720
παρακύπτω 600, 726, 772, 798—804
παραλαμβάνω 689 c, 735 f, 781 a
παραμυθέομαι 885 (ii)
παρατίθημι 692
παραχρῆμα 693, 862
πάρειμι 862
παρέρχομαι 631, 687, 735 c
παροιμία 669, 721
παρρησία 744 (xi) a, (ἐν) π. 712, 719
πάσχω 694
πατήρ 711
πεινάω 684
πειράζω, -ασμός 695
πέμπω 723, ὁ πέμψας (με) 723 e
πενθερός 885 (ii)
πεντήκοντα 834
πέραν τοῦ Ἰορδάνου 714, 813
περί 885, οἱ π. Πέτρον 802 a
περιάπτω 711 f
περιβάλλω 676, 806 a
περιδέω 885 (ii)
περιίστημι 885 (ii)
περιπατέω 656
περισσός 753
περιτέμνω 772
περιτίθημι 809, 813, περιέθηκαν v.r. for ἐπέθηκαν 805
περιτομή 709
πέτρα 691
πηγή 736
πηλός 709
πῆχυς 862
πιάζω 723
πιπράσκω 808, 814
πιστεύω pp. xi—xii, 463—561, 681, perf. 472, 519, 629
πιστικός 736
πίστις 478 c, 681, π. θεοῦ 467
πιστός 681, 736 d, 862
πλείων 504 b
πλέκω 809, 814
πλευρά 753
πλῆθος 834
πλήρης 772
πλήρωμα 814
πλησίον 687
πλοιάριον 736

πλούσιος 691
πλοῦτος 691
πνεῦμα 655, 720 k, ἐνεβριμήσατο τῷ π. 811 b
πνέω 862
πόθεν 728
ποιέω 513, 772
ποιμαίνω 862
ποίμνη 862
πολλάκις 814
πολύς, ὁ ὄχλος π. 739-40
πολύτιμος 753
πορεύομαι 652-64
πορνεία 814
πορφύρεος 885 (ii)
πόσις 885 (ii)
πόσος 683
πότερον (Jn vii. 17) om. in 885 (ii)
ποτήριον 678
ποῦ 728
πραιτώριον 809, 814
πράσσω 772
πρεσβύτεροι 680
πρό, π. μικροῦ 799 b, π. προσώπου 681 a, π. τοῦ (inf.) 863
προάγω 682
προβατική 885 (ii)
προβάτιον 885 (ii)
πρόβατον 723
προέρχομαι 682
προπορεύομαι 682
προσαιτέω 885 (ii)
προσαίτης 737
προσέρχομαι 649, 677, 801 a—b
προσευχή 688
προσεύχομαι 649, 688
προσκόπτω 863
προσκυνέω 640-51
προσκυνητής 885 (ii)
προσφάγιον 796 a, 885 (ii)
πρόσωπον, πρὸ π. 681 a
πρότερον, (τό) adv. 708
προτρέχω 773
πρόφασις 834
πρωί 815
πρωία 754
πρῶτος 682
πτέρνα 885 (ii)
πτύσμα 885 (ii)
πτύω 693 d, 737
πτωχός 688
πυνθάνομαι 863
πῦρ 682
πῶλος 677
πωρόω 737

This Index extends from 1438 to 1885 (printed 438—885).

WORDS (GREEK)

Ῥαββεί 694 c, 815
Ῥαββουνεί 694 c, 737
ῥάπισμα 737
ῥέω 885 (ii)
Ῥωμαῖοι, -αϊστί 721

Σαδδουκαῖος 692
Σαλείμ 721
Σαμαρείτης 863
Σαμαρεῖτις 885 (ii)
Σαμαρία 773
Σατανᾶς 692
σεισμός 680
σημαίνω 724
σημεῖον 669
Σιλωάμ 773
Σίμων (father of Judas Iscariot) 724
Σιών 754
σκανδαλίζω, -ον 545, 694
σκέλος 885 (ii)
σκηνοπηγία 885 (ii)
σκηνόω 885 (ii)
σκληρός 754
σκορπίζω 863
σκοτία, -ος 710, 863, 864
σμύρνα 746, 754
Σολομών 864
σουδάριον 773
σοφία, -ός 696, 864
σπεῖρα 809, 815
σπείρω 693
σπέρμα 692
σπλαγχνίζομαι 677
σπόγγος 815
σπόρος 692
στάδιος 864
σταυρός, -όω 678, 792 b
στέφανος 815
στῆθος 773
στήκω 725, 737
στοά 885 (ii)
στόμα 864
στρέφω 864
σύ 726
συγγενής 773
συλλέγω 864
συμφέρω 754
συνάγω 682 f
συναγωγή 694
συναλίζομαι 794 a
συνανάκειμαι 689
συνεισέρχομαι 885 (ii)
σύνεσις, συνετός 695, 865
συνέχω 834 a
συνήθεια (Jn xviii. 39) om. in 885 (ii); see 2464 b
συνίημι 695
συνμαθητής 885 (ii)

συνσταυρόω 678, 817 c
συντίθεμαι 774
σύρω 885 (ii)
Συχάρ 726
σφραγίζω 754
σχίζω 866 (iv)
σχίσμα 815
σχοινίον 885 (ii)
σώζω 692
σῶμα 674
σωτήρ 774
σωτηρία 774

Ταπεινός, -όω 865
ταράσσω 727
τάχειον 885 (ii)
ταχέως 774
τε 865
τεκνίον 676 a, 885 (ii)
τέκνον 676
τελειόω 774
τελέω 865
τέλος 680
τελώνης 689
τέρας 816
τεταρταῖος 885 (ii)
τετράμηνος 885 (ii)
τηρέω 714, 816
Τιβεριάς 726
τίθημι 659 a, τ. ψυχήν 715
τίκτω 865
τιμή 746, 755
τίτλος 885 (ii)
τότε 695
τριακόσιοι 738
τρίτον, ἐκ τρίτου 695, (τὸ) τρίτον 834
τρίτος 695
τροφή 865
τρώγω 680 b, 710, 755
τύπος 885 (ii)
τυφλόω 885 (ii)

Ὑγιής 728, 816
ὑδρία 885 (ii)
ὕδωρ 728, 834
ὑμεῖς 728
ὑμέτερος 774
ὑπάγω 652-64, 713, 816
ὑπάντησις 755
ὕπαρξις θεοῦ 476 b
ὑπάρχοντα, τά 694, 865
ὑπέρ 692 a, 885
ὑπηρέτης 719
ὕπνος 865
ὑπό 885
ὑπόδειγμα 885 (ii)
ὑποκρίνομαι, -κρισις, -κριτής 684
ὑπομιμνήσκω 775

ὕσσωπος 885 (ii)
ὕστερον 866
ὑφαντός 885 (ii)
ὕψιστος 683
ὑψόω 711 c, 866

Φαγεῖν 680 b
φαίνω, ἐφάνη 749 c, 885 (ii)
φανερός 686
φανερόω 597 b, 716, 738
φανερῶς 738
φανός 885 (ii)
φαῦλος 885 (ii)
φεύγω 682
φιλέω and ἀγαπάω 436, 595-6, 716 d—f, 728 m—q
φιλία 716 f
Φίλιππος 720
φίλος 775, 866
φοβέομαι 643 a, 681
φόβος 681
φοῖνιξ 885 (ii)
φορέω 755
φραγέλλιον 885 (ii)
φρέαρ 775
φρόνιμος 866
φυλακή 688, 696
φωνέω 752 e
φῶς 715, 866, φ. κόσμου 748
φωτίζω 485, 775

Χαμαί 885 (ii)
χάρις 775
χείμαρρος 885 (ii)
χειμών 816
χιλίαρχος 738
χολάω 885 (ii)
χορτάζω 692
χωλός 685
χωρέω 816
χωρίον 816

Ψεῦδος 885 (ii)
ψεύστης 885 (ii)
ψηλαφάω 617, 804
ψῆφος 711 h
ψύχος 885 (ii)
ψωμίον 724

Ὠ 687
ὧδε 683
ὡς (when) 775
ὡσαννά 816
ὡσεί 693
ὥσπερ 866
ὥστε 693
ὡτάριον 736 e, 738, 866 c
ὠτίον 866

This Index extends from 1438 *to* 1885 (*printed* 438—885).

INDICES TO "JOHANNINE GRAMMAR"

I. NEW TESTAMENT PASSAGES

[*The references are to paragraphs, indicated by black numbers, which, in this Index, run from* **1886** *to* **2799**. *The thousand figure is not printed. An asterisk distinguishes numbers up to* [2]000.]

MATTHEW			MATTHEW			MATTHEW		
		PAR.			PAR.			PAR.
2	2	782	9	2	559 b	14	7	536 f
	6	670 b		9	394 b		15	428 a, 746 a
	23	292		21	270 a		21	009–10
3	11	899*, 981*, 998*, 401 a		28	239		23	962*
			10	11	437 a		25–6	341–6
4	8	962*		14	437 a		26	220
	13	292		19	532		27	914 a*, 220-2, 699
	18	342 f		22	322, 499			
	23	709 a		23	532 a	15	2	532
5	3	679 c		27	709 b		6	799 (iii)
	11	499 b	11	3	940*		11	959*, 646
	12	689 d		8	216 b		14	513 c, 534 c
	14	539		13	477		18	646
	15	948*, 275 b		18	253 a		29	724 a
	22	708 c		25	689 p	16	9–10	708 b
	23	513 c, 534 c		25–7	165		18	782
	25–6	520		27	586 d, e		19	517–19
6	4	377 a	12	14	173		23	566 c
	26	144		25	261 b		24	437 a, 496 c, 515
7	4	767		29	517 d		28	576
	7	536		32	553 c	17	1	962*
	11	743		46	395		17	364 a
	16	702 d		50	799 (iii)	18	8–9	592
	21	263, 680 b	13	2	342 f		18	517–9
	22	335 a, 409		13–14	093 b	19	3	379
	24–6	580 a		14	144		9	677
	27	915*		19	799 (iii)		26	649 a
8	6	584 b		21	039	20	1	708 c
	8	559		56	364 a		12	272 a
	27	162 a	14	3	460 a, 517 d		18	265 b

This Index extends from **1886** to **2799**. Before numbers with * supply **1**, e.g. [1]999*; before others, **2**, e.g. [2]000.

NEW TESTAMENT PASSAGES

MATTHEW		MATTHEW		MARK	
	PAR.		PAR.		PAR.
20 28	593	27 13	737 *b*	4 26	917 *a* *
21 1	310 *a*	15	464 *b–c*	36	272, 570 *d*
7	537 (ii), 781 *c*	19	294 *a*, 537 (ii) *b*,	41	162 *a*, 694 *b*
11	292		732	5 11	962 *
12	558 *e*	27	570 *d*	22	558 *d*
22	536	30	558 *a*	27	270 *a*
23	971 *, 342 *e*	33	738	28	270 *a*
25	906 *, 953 *	48	623	30	270 *a*, 563 *b*
42	356, 396 *b*, 621	55	318	35	482 *b*
22 12	253 *a*	57	291, 769	36	237 *a*, 439 *b*
18	563 *b*	62	087–8	37	586 *d*
46	586 *d, e*	63	732	41	679 *b*
23 8	784 *c*	28 1	310	6 3	363 *a*, 364 *a*
25	329 *a*	6	171 *e*	10–11	437 *a*
30–2	950 *a* *	7	186 *a*	17	460 *a*, 517 *d*
32	439 (v) *b*	10	307 *b*	22–4	536 *f*
24 3	707	18	742 *b*	32	020
5	220 *a*, 585 *a–b*			36–7	428 *a*
8	197 *a*		MARK	37	512, 690 *a*
13	322, 499	1 5	670 *b*	38	745 *a*
14	709 *a*	7	899 *, 043,	45	089 *a*
18	711 *b*		558 *d*	46	962–3 *
23	439	8	981 *, 998 *,	48–9	341–6, 472
25	186 *a*, 585 *a–b*		401 *a*	49	220
26	439	9	292, 706 *a*	50	914 *a**, 220–1,
30	317 *f*	16	342 *f*		699
35	255, 580 *a*	21	709 *a*	52	449 *a*
26 5	918 *	27	694 *b*	7 13	799 (iii)
7	607	32	425 *b*	15	959 *
14	928 *a* *	39	709 *a*	18	261 *b*
18	364 *a*	2 1	711 *a*	8 17	449 *a*
20	483 *b*	4	294 *a*	19–20	708 *b*
21	945 *	5	559 *b*	32	917 (iii)–(vi)*
22	702 *d*	7	155 *a*	34	437 *a*, 496 *c*, 515
23	945 *	13	394 *b*	38	580 *a*
25	702 *d*	19	235 *a*	9 1	576
28	721 *a*	27	959 *	2	962 *
29	532 *b*	3 3	710	11	155 *a*
30	307 *c*	6	173	19	363 *a*, 364 *a*
39	679 *b*	9	294 *a*	21	696 *b*
40	482 *d*	13	962 *	24	782
47	928 *a* *	25	261 *b*	25	679 *c*
50	575 *a*	26	593	28	155 *a*
51	558 *a*	27	517 *d*	37	398, 593
56	111, 478 *a*	29	593	43–7	513 *a*, 592
61	331	31	395	45	534 *c*
63	734 *d*	35	799 (iii)	47	534 *c*
64	915 (vi) *a**,	4 1	342 *f*	10 2	379 *a*
	220 *a*, 245 *a*	12	093 *b*	10	711 *a*
65	270 *b*, 563 *c*	14	799 (iii)	11	677
72	960 *b* *	17	039, 593	21	649 *a*
74	914 *, 960 *b* *	21	948 *, 275 *b*,	23–4	592
27 2	969 *		372 *a*, 593 *d*,	26	366 *c*
12	537 *a*		702 *d*	27	593, 649 *a*

This Index extends from **1886** *to* **2799**. *Before numbers with* * *supply* **1**,
e.g. [1]999*; *before others*, **2**, *e.g.* [2]000.

653

INDICES TO "JOHANNINE GRAMMAR"

MARK		MARK		LUKE	
	PAR.		PAR.		PAR.
10 33	265 b	14 63	270 b, 563 c	6 39	513 c, 702 d
45	167, 593	71	960 b*	42	767
11 1	310 a	72	914*	43	649 (i) c
7	537 (ii), 781 c	15 1	969*	46	680 b
8	047	4	736, 737 b	47	580 a
15	558 e	6	464 b–c	49	915*
23	521 a	14	068 a	7 1	709 a
24	536	16	570 d	2	584 b
25	532 a	19	558 a	6	559
27	342 e	22	738	19	940*
28	971*	23	380 b	33	253 a
30	906*, 953*	36	623	44	563 a
32	466 (i) a	40	318	47	178 a
12 11	356, 396 b, 621	42	048, 087–8	48	781 c
12	366 c	43	291	8 1	374 a
15	563 b	16 2	310	10	093 b
25	593	6	171 e	11	799 (iii)
28	665 b			13	039
37	468 b		LUKE	16	948*, 275 b, 372 a
41	333 a	1 3	904*	19	294 a, 395
13 3	707	37	356 a	21	799 (iii)
6	585 a–b	45	356 a	25	162 a
8	197 a	2 30	473	32	962*
10	709 a	41	715 d	46	563 b
11	532	3 16	899*, 981*, 998*, 043, 401 a, 558 d	50	237 a, 439 b
13	322, 499			51	586 d
16	711 b			54	679 b
20	078 a, 441 b–c	18	335 a, 414 f	9 4	437 a
21	439	19–21	460 a, 480 a	5	437 a
23	585 a–b	20	517 d	13	428 a
31	255, 580 a–b	4 1	072	17	329 (i) a
35	678	14–15	374 a	23	437 a, 496 c, 515
14 2	918*	16	292	26	580 a
3	563 a, 607	30	542–3	27	576
7	533	31	709 a	28	962*
10	928 a*	36	694 b	37	331 e
17	483 b	40	425 b	41	364 a
18	945*	44	709 a	10 21	689 p
19	702 d	5 1	342 f, 354	21–2	165
20	945*	2	354	11 2	532 a
24	721 a	3	342 f	7	711 b
25	532 b	14	593 b	9	536
26	307 c	19	294 a	13	743
31	513 a–b	20	559 b	21	533
36	679 b	27	394 b	22	517 d
37	482 d	6 6	983 a*	36	532 c
43	911*, 928 a*	8	710	39	329 a
46	575 a	11	173	41	760
47	558 a	12	962*	42	033 a
49	111, 363 a, 364 a	20	679 c	12 3	709 b
58	331, 451	23	689 d	11	532
61	537 a	25	679 c	24	144
62	220 a, 245 a	33	513 d	32	679 c

This Index extends from **1886** *to* **2799**. *Before numbers with* * *supply* 1, *e.g.* [1]999*; *before others*, 2, *e.g.* [2]000.

NEW TESTAMENT PASSAGES

LUKE		LUKE		JOHN	
	PAR.		PAR.		PAR.
12 58–9	520	23 5	737 *a*	1 15–34	601–2
13 3	521–2	9	537 *a*	16	146 *a*, 414 *h*
5	521	33	738	16–18	pref. p. vii
26	335 *a*	34	318 *b*	17	301, 411 *e*
28	532 *b*	36	623	18	938*, 964*,
14 12, 13	532 *a*	38	339, 347		275 *a*, 308–
33	261 *b*	48	317 *i*, 318		9, 382, 615,
15 30	318 *c*	49	318 *a*		706 foll.
16 6	781 *c*	51	291	19	481
16	477	53	257 *b*	19–21	766 (i) *b*
18	677	53–4	087–8	20	189, 401, 598
17 20	736 *c*	24 1	310	20–1	600
31	711 *b*	12	664 *b*	21	940*, 965*,
33	739	21	472 *b*		248 *c*, 498 *a*
18 5	322	36	307	22	113
31	265 *b*	36–42	483 *a*	23	401
19 2	374 *a*	39	220–1, 269 *d*,	24	214, 481
28–9	310 *a*		699–700	26	998*, 399
31	513 *d*	41	703 *a*, *c*	26–7	401
35	537 (ii), 781 *c*	43	335	26–33	552
42	539	47	709 *a*	27	094 *a*, 104 *a*,
20 1	342 *e*				558 *d*, 687
2	971*		JOHN	28	968 *c**, 172,
4	906*, 953*				648
10	690	1 1	937*, 994 *a**,	29	938*, 509, 624
18	397 *a*, 622 *a*		308, 363–8,	30	896*–900*,
23	563 *b*		395		927*, 330,
21 1	333 *a*	1–2	386		360, 369–
8	220 *a*	1–8	594–7		71, 401,
12	197 *a*	3	301, 440, 478		478 *b*, 571,
18–19	322	3–4	996*		666, 718
33	255, 580 *a*	5	141		foll.
22 3	928 *a**	6	937*, 277, 358	31	064, 387
14	483 *b*	7	302–4, 525–8	31–3	401
19	721 *a*	7–8	063	32	952–5*, 458,
20	721 *a*	8	105–7, 112, 382		473
27	593	9	277, 508	32–4	572
33	643	9–11	508 *c*	33	947*, 981*,
39	307 *c*, 799 (ii)	10	301		336, 382,
42	679 *b*	11–12	570		509
45	482 *d*	12	268–9, 448 *a*,	34	386 *a*, 401, 473
47	928 *a**		799 *e*	35	624
48	072	13	268–9, 371 *a*,	36	649
50	983 *a**, 985 *a**,		654, 722 *c*	38	279 *a*, 649
	558 *a*	14	946*	41	901 *b**, 985*
53	111, 364 *a*	14–17	284–7	42	456 *a*, 649
54	575 *a*	14–18	180	43	471, 624
58	960 *b**	15	896*–900*,	43–5	970*, 636
60	914*, 960 *b**		925–7*,	44	289
61	649 *a*		330, 371,	45	931–2*, 418 *a*,
67	220 *a*		478 *b*, 479,		643
69	915 (vi) *a**		507, 571,	45–6	289
70	220 *a*, 245 *a*		665–6, 722,	46	932*, 245,
23 1	969*		799 *a*		248 *c*

This Index extends from 1886 *to* 2799. *Before numbers with* * *supply* 1, *e.g.* [1]999*; *before others*, 2, *e.g.* [2]000.

655

INDICES TO "JOHANNINE GRAMMAR"

JOHN		JOHN		JOHN	
	PAR.		PAR.		PAR.
1 47–51	765	3 10	966*, 248	4 7	482 c
48	995 a*, 278, 372, 491 c, 552	11	428	8	310, 480, 746 a
		12	256, 554	9	pref. pp. viii–ix, 066, 273
		13	931–2*, 141. 211, 265 a, 275, 503		
49	966*, 669			9–10	536 (i) a
50	189, 236, 241, 248 c, 372, 552	15	636 c	10	980 a*, 400, 553 a, 743
		15–21	pref. pp. vii–viii, 066	11	258
51	958*, 265 a, 275, 336, 626 a	16	917 a*, 986*, 203, 262, 697	12	374 a
				13	553 c
2 1	985*, 624			13–14	574
1–2	461	17	301, 606	14	039, 255, 314–16, 405
3	031	18	986*, 181, 187, 253, 475 a, 477 b, 484, 695	16	437–8
4	229–30, 642, 647			17	552
5	414, 437, 516 b			18	894*, 915 (ii)*
5–7	632			19	439 (ii) a
6	070, 281–3	19	092, 181	20	245
7–8	437–8	19–20	568 c	21–3	019, 061, 485 a
9	939*, 016–8, 069 a, 281–3, 459, 506 a, 607	20	574, 584 a, 606	23	167, 398
		21	185 a, 574, 584 a	23–4	603
		22	670 b	24	994 a*
10	424	22–3	277 a	25	939*, 382
11	386 (i)	23	424	25–6	205, 221 b
12	374, 394, 395	23–4	480	26	940*
13	553 b	23–5	633	26–8	633
14–16	553 a	25	349–50	27	231 b foll., 338
15	929*, 558 e	27	496	28	310
16	437	28	189 c, 330, 401	29	702 b, d
16–18	633, 639	28–31	602	30	465
18	179, 183 a, 400	29	939*, 571	31	668
19	439 (iii)–(v)	30–6	pref. p. viii	34	994*, 095, 298
19–20	331	31	904*, 555 a	35	185, 230 (ii)–(iii), 246 a, 437, 616, 762 a
20	021–4, 146, 248 c	32	451		
		32–3	501, 568 b, 628	36	287 b, 313
21	382, 467–9	33	270 c	36–7	392
22	406, 469	34	324, 654, 714	37	980 a*, 795
23	069 a, 569, 654, 670	35	334 c	38	477
		36	576 d, 598	39	041, 273
23–4	466, 644	4 1	198, 459	40	465, 655
24	995 a*, 254	1–2	628	42	929 a*, 989*, 450
24–5	959*, 374, 491 c, d	1–3	635 (i)		
		2	374 a	43	994 b*
25	094 a, 104 a, 607	3	440 b, 649 (i), 670 b	43–4	067
				45	167, 273, 460, 692
3 1	071 a, 290 a	4	272 a, 635 (i)		
2	933*	4–5	482 c	46	071 a, 198, 649 (i)
3	576 d	5	970*, 198, 310, 368 a, 405		
3–5	573, 603			46–53	584 b
3–7	903–8*, 612	6	916*, 198, 272, 751	47	567 b
5	316 a			48	232, 366 b, 456 a
8	614	6–9	631		

This Index extends from **1886** *to* **2799**. *Before numbers with* * *supply* **1**, *e.g.* [1]999*; *before others,* **2**, *e.g.* [2]000.

656

NEW TESTAMENT PASSAGES

JOHN		JOHN		JOHN	
	PAR.		PAR.		PAR.
4 50	406, 459	5 38–9	439 (i), (ii)	6 30	400, 525–8, 553 a
52	465 c	39	383 a	31	552
52–3	013, 025–6, 206	39–40	141	32	455 a
53	374 a	41	605	33	974*, 503
5 1	951 a*, 394	42	032–40	34	553 c
2	216, 670	43	145, 554, 677	34–6	056
3	930*	44	895*, 923*, 145, 399 b, 496, 664	35	255, 507, 625
4	334 d, 348			36	161, 189
5	071 a			37	507
6	248 c, 279 a	45	973*, 235 a, 442–3, 474	38	952 a*, 552 a, 605
6–7	206 a				
7	093 b	46	339	39	921–2*, 213, 262
9	914*	47	989*, 256		
11	380 b, 438 a	6 1	045	39–54	609 a, 715 b
11–12	206	1–15	963*	40	093, 096
13	031, 460, 466 (i), 541	2	417	41	504
		3	707, 751	41–2	552 a
14	456 a, 478 b	3–5	616, 633	42	932*, 970*, 427 a, 552 a
15	466 (i)	4	931*, 654 d		
15–18	389	5	279 a, 366 b, 428, 512, 642, 745–6		
16	537, 715 c			43	349
16–18	464			44	715 b
17	915 (vi)*, 226 b, 537	6	374, 467–8	44–5	548 a
		7	643	45–6	218–19, 357–9
18	468 b, 733 a	9	056, 412 b	46	386, 552
19	148, 382, 516, 537, 605, 617 a, 739 a	10	009–11, 070, 437, 632 b	48–50	504–5
		11	198	48–51	574, 608
20	114, 375	13	985*, 267, 329 (i), 419	49	950 a*, 552, 553 e
21	148, 741 a				
21–3	066 b	14	940*, 553 d	49–51	956–7*
23	128	15	198, 375, 649 (i), 724 foll.	50	530
24	477 b, 799 (iii)			51	074, 076, 504–5
25	485 a, 499, 603, 799 (i)				
		16	336	51–5	567
26	039, 148, 741 a	17	031	53	039
26–7	066 b	18	929 a*	54	715 b
28	485 a, 603	19	909*	54–7	613
29	499, 584 a	19–21	340–6	56	124 a
30	514 (i) e, 605	20	205, 220–2, 699	56–7	297–300
31	514 (i)	21	909*, 914*, 472, 478 b, 498, 716–7	57	957*, 124, 151
31–2	972*				
32	384, 675, 730, 791–5			57–8	504–5
		22	417, 466 (i)	58	949–50*, 952–7*, 122 b, 553 e
34	605	22–4	417 a		
35	275 b, 471, 655, 689 k	24	466 (i), 482 c, 752	60	041
				61	248 c, 279 a
36	230 a, 384, 453, 604, 686–7	25	478, 758	62	172 a, 192, 210–12, 265 a, 515, 739 b
		27	931*, 312–13, 438		
37	450 a	28	493, 512		
37–8	038–40, 259	29	968 b*, 096, 382, 405 a, 526–8	63	975–7*, 257 b, 545 c, 606
38	178, 382, 764–6, 799 (iii)				

This Index extends from **1886** *to* **2799**. *Before numbers with* * *supply* **1**, *e.g.* [1]999*; *before others*, **2**, *e.g.* [2]000.

A. VI. 657 42

INDICES TO "JOHANNINE GRAMMAR"

JOHN

PAR.

6	6₃₋₄	056 *b*
	6₄	251 *a*, 254, 510
	6₄₋₅	470, 636
	6₅	548 *a*
	6₇	235
	68–9	226 *c*
	69	442–3, 475
	70	441 *a–d*
	71	928*, 931*, 945*, 467–8
7	1	498
		931*, 951*
	2	114, 147, 569, 690, 727
	4	917 (i), (vi)*, 202, 375 *a*, 727
	5	395 *a*, 466
	6–8	989*, 605
	8–10	264–5, 629
	9	458
	10	202, 375
	11	385, 732
	13	917 (i), (vi)*
	14	264–5
	15	253
	16	989*, 629
	16–17	250
	17	498, 515 *a*, 586 *a*
	18	386
	19	248 *b*, 455 *a*
	21–2	388
	22	949–50*, 218–19
	22–3	961*, 552, 715 *c*
	23	244, 248 *c*
	24	438
	26	917 (vi)*, 057, 139 *a*
	27	531, 535, 736 *c*
	27–8	142
	28	200 *a*, 479, 600, 618, 736 *c*
	29	151, 613 *a*
	30	138, 472, 481, 575
	31	074–5, 405 *a*
	32	991 *a* *
	33–4	489
	33–5	082

JOHN

PAR.

7	34	487 *a*
	34–6	171 *d*, 190 *a*, 578, 605
	35	046, 179, 248 *b*, 607, 645
	37	168, 479, 618
	37–8	039, 129
	38	921–2*, 315–16, 421, 626 *a*
	39	407, 468, 499
	40	213
	41–2	068, 289, 552
	42	932 *a* *
	44	138, 472, 498, 575
	45	991 *a* *, 385
	48	057
	49	924*, 253, 266, 417
	51	960*
	52	185 *a*, 439 (i) *a*, 492
8	6, 9	348
	11	915 (vi) *a* *
	12	608, 625
	13–14	554
	14	457, 490, 514 (i), 549, 736 *c*, 739 *a*, 759
	15–16	628
	16	074–6, 159, 207, 515 *a*, 600, 614
	16–17	428
	17	988*, 558 *e*, 588 foll., 626
	18	794
	19	148, 566 *b*, 739 *d*
	20	138, 333–4, 481
	21	487 *a*, 545, 552, 578
	21–2	190 *a*, 605
	22	185 *a*, 702 *d*
	23	399, 553 *c*
	24	189, 192, 221 *b*, 552
	24–5	223–8
	25	154–6, 413
	26	062, 451
	27	468
	28	221 *b*, 605 *a*

JOHN

PAR.

8	29	449, 614
	30–1	470
	31	366 *b*, 506, 514
	35	263 *e–g*
	36	192
	37–8	193–4
	38	027, 355, 357–9, 439 (v) *c*
	39	078–9, 213 *a*, 698
	40	934–5*, 412 *a*, 451
	41	932*, 194 *c*
	42	326, 382, 457
	43	251
	44	932*, 194 *b–c*, 326, 378–9, 498, 535, 728
	45	177 *a*
	47	389, 553 *b*
	50	973 *a* *, 600
	50–1	978*
	51	989*
	51–2	514–15, 552 *b*, 576, 657 *b*
	52	017
	53	923*, 413
	54	927 *a* *, 979*
	55	160, 613
	56	935*, 097, 688–9
	57	146, 248 *c*
	58	221 *b*, 625
	59	072, 538–43, 646
9	2	098
	3	063, 106–7, 112
	4	089, 428 *b–e*
	5	531 *c*, 608
	6	569 *c*, 784 *b*
	7	305, 437, 456 *a*, 583 *c*, 706
	8	466 (i)
	9	189, 205, 221 *b*, 265 (i)
	11	305, 381, 583 *c*, 706 *a*
	12	732
	13	931*, 018, 351 *b*

This Index extends from **1886** *to* **2799**. *Before numbers with* * *supply* **1**, *e.g.* [1]999*; *before others*, **2**, *e.g.* [2]000.

NEW TESTAMENT PASSAGES

	JOHN			JOHN			JOHN	
		PAR.			PAR.			PAR.
9	14	071 a	10	26-7	987*	11	32	465, 565-6, 558 d-e
	16	386 b		27	491 c		33	198, 614 c
	17	018, 183, 274		28-9	139, 586 d-e, 767		34	441
	18	931*, 018		29	053 b, 496 b, 744		37	496
	19	248 c					38	198
	21	723		32	441, 486, 606		39	437
	21-3	577		34	190 c		40	189, 545
	22	480		35	143, 799 (iii)		41	052, 452, 552 c, 617
	24	425 a, 427 a		35-6	921*, 244, 248 c		42	058, 294, 525-8
	25	274, 351, 381		36	190 b		44	437
	27	498		37	256		45	941-4*
	27-8	558 e		38	893*, 511		45-6	380
	28	554		40	968 c*, 172, 458, 649 (i)		47	991 a*, 493-4, 512, 766 (i)
	29	400, 427 a, 737 c		40-2	647		48	559 a, 645
	29-30	068, 142 a		41	075 a, 169		50	104, 645
	30	218 c, 393, 683	11	1	071 a, 290		50-1	645
	33	079 b, 698		2	276		52	664 b
	34-5	248 c		4-6	633		54	917 (vi)*, 199, 352 a, 724
	35	242, 456 a, 459		6	198, 458		55	646, 686-7
	36	113, 157, 381, 525-8		7	394		55-7	687
	37	980 a*, 163, 456 a		7-8	649 (ii)		56	184, 349, 766 (i) a
	40	215, 351		8	146, 248 c		57	991 a*, 173, 480, 635
	41	190 b		9	514			
10	1	265 b-c		11	394, 642	12	1	172, 199, 288, 624, 635, 648
	2	669		11-12	586 c			
	2-9	608		12-14	632 c, 634			
	3-12	267		13	382, 464 a, 467-8, 481		3	168, 329, 607
	3-27	420		14	917 (i), (ii)*		4	928*, 945*, 586 a
	4	330 a		14-15	099-102			
	4-5	558 e		15	525 foll.		5	945*
	5	255		16	928*		7	103, 352 b, 456 a
	6	251, 382		17	198			
	8	361-2, 798 d		17-19	480		9	941 a*
	10	606		18	670		9-12	992*
	11	484, 608, 625		18-19	941-4*		10	147
	12	704		19	990-1*, 360		10-11	464
	12-13	179		20-1	565-6		11	041, 294 a
	14	608		22	915 (i)-(v)*, 536 (i) a, c, 660 b		12	278, 417
	14-15	125-6, 491 c					13	966*, 047, 669
	15	484, 552		25	456 a, 625		14	461, 537 (ii), 756
	15-18	612		26	242, 248 c, 262, 545 a			
	16	151		27	940*, 475, 553 d		15	537 (ii)
	17	391, 552					16	339, 360, 396-7, 469, 621-2, 757
	18	606		29	902 b*, 465, 565-6			
	22	670						
	23	969 a*		29-31	902 b*, 554 b		18	152-3, 386 b
	24	917 (vi)*		30	480		19	439 (ii), 494, 645, 753 a-e
	25	186 a, 604		31	902 b*, 941-4*, 686-7			
	25-6	605						

This Index extends from **1886** *to* **2799**. *Before numbers with* * *supply* **1**, *e.g.* [1]999*; *before others*, **2**, *e.g.* [2]000.

INDICES TO "JOHANNINE GRAMMAR"

	JOHN			JOHN			JOHN	
		PAR.			PAR.			PAR.
12	20	046 b, 686–7	13	10	263, 265 (i), 659	14	7	915 (vi)*, 243 a, 477 b, 491, 566 b, 739 d, 760 foll.
	21	289		11	190 a, 263, 265 (i), 510			
	22	418, 482 c						
	23	537 d, 604 a		12	243, 248 c, 270, 477, 564, 649 (iii), 762		8	437 b
	24	948*, 375, 725					9	248 c, 609
	25	313 b, 485					10–11	579
	26	487, 515, 552 c		13	051 d, 195, 680		11	080, 238, 727
	27	057, 231 b, 325, 389 a, 437, 512 b–c, 614 c		14	931*, 195, 441, 477, 564		12	151
				15	127 a		12–14	536 (i)
				16	550 b		13	414, 516
	27–8	052, 053 c, 659		17	514 (i)		13–14	604, 625
	28	958*, 162, 441, 768 foll.		18	105–12, 263, 441		15	987*, 515 b, 609
	30	110 b, 478 b, 611 c		19	915 (vi)*, 995 a*, 221 b, 526–8, 585		16	931–2*, 630, 793–5
	32	642, 739 a					16–17	352–3
	33	467–8		20	507, 609, 739 a		17	243 a, 491 c, 496, 762
	34	642, 645		21	945*, 614 c			
	35	923*, 201, 342 h, 438		23	277, 308		18	600
				24	249, 252, 465 c–d		19	149, 177, 230 (i), 241 a, 762 a
	35–6	201, 696 c		25	917*			
	36	238, 342 h, 538, 646		26	537 d			
	37	031, 466		27	918*, 437, 439 (v), 486, 554 e		21	980*, 987*, 373
	37–40	390					22	928 b*, 265 (i), 478 b, 694, 766 a
	39	466, 496						
	40	093 b, 114, 449 a–b		28–9	464			
				29	926 b*			
	43	092, 369		30–2	914*		23	515 b, 609
	44	072, 479		31	446, 522 b		23–4	569 a, 580
	44–50	618		33	082, 127 a, 190, 489 b, 545, 578, 605		24	799 (iii)
	45	609					25	625
	46	933*, 262, 457, 608					26	931–2*, 411 c
				33–7	915 (vi)*		27	957 a*, 993*, 122 b, 609 b
	46–7	159		34	894 b*, 094, 116, 127 a, 130, 412, 441, 609			
	47	395, 606					27–9	525–8
	48	978*, 799 (iii)					28	550 a, 739 c
	48–9	179					29	186 a, 585
	49	293 b, 375, 586 a, 606 a, 742 a		34–5	036 b, 612		29–30	915 (v)*
				35	332, 393, 515 b		30–1	106–8
				36	082, 578, 605, 642		31	428, 742 a
	49–50	195				15	1–5	608, 625
13	1	319–23		36–7	497, 555		2	920–2*, 421
	1–4	279		37	565 a, 643		2–5	921*
	3	327, 334 c		37–8	248 c		3	353, 799 (iii)
	4	270		38	537 d		4	208, 437 c
	6	200, 236 a, 248 c, 483, 486, 564, 784 c	14	1	889*, 236–40, 555		4–6	521
				1–3	080–6, 186		5	386
				3	159, 486–7, 649 (ii)		6	919*, 266, 426, 445, 755
	7	394 a		4–6	614 c		7	514, 516 a, 536 (i), 660 b, 739
	8	564		6	301 a, 625			
	8–9	208–9, 564						

This Index extends from **1886** *to* **2799**. *Before numbers with* * *supply* **1**, *e.g.* [1]999*; *before others*, **2**, *e.g.* [2]000.

NEW TESTAMENT PASSAGES

	JOHN			JOHN			JOHN	
		PAR.			PAR.			PAR.
15	8	114, 393, 446	16	20	058	17	11–12	408–11, 568
	9	127, 437		21	948 a*, 535		12	584, 742, 744 c
	9–11	988*, 581		21–2	149, 196–7		14	552
	9–12	987*		22	915 (vi) c*,		15	325
	10	131, 514, 568			077, 169		16	552
	12	096, 131, 529 a,		23	516, 630 c,		17	661
		609			739 a		18	127, 132, 444,
	13	095		23–4	536 (i), 604			554 a
	15	901*, 441, 447,		24	915 (vi) b*		19	369, 376 a
		451, 477,		25	917 (i), (ii),		19–24	529 a
		550			(vi)*, 485 a		20	074–5, 304,
	16	120–1, 313, 414,		26	536 (i), 630			500, 799 (iii)
		441 a, d,		27	931 a*, 246,		20–4	118–9
		516, 536 (i),			326–8,		21	208 b, 308,
		604			442–3,			376 a,
	16–20	426			475–6			526–8, 554,
	17	529 a		28	326–8, 457,			614, 740
	18	896*, 901*, 243,			649 (ii)		21–2	127 b, 132 a
		666, 762		29	917 (i), (ii), (vi)*,		21–5	052–3
	19	387, 441 a, d			643		22	455
	20	405–6		30	104 a, 246, 327,		23	306, 554, 614
	20–1	059			332		24	151, 422, 455,
	21	582		30–1	248 c			487, 495,
	22	213 a, 698		31–2	475			740 e, 744 a
	24	161, 213 a, 442		32	246, 485 a, 487,		25	164–5
		–3, 475, 698			604 a, 614,		26	014, 164 b,
	24–5	105–12			629, 799 (i)			529 a
	25	799 (iii)		33	058, 477	18	1	374 a, 671–4
	26	931–2*	17	1	958*, 456 a,		1–2	799 (ii)
	27	074			604 a, 617,		1–3	634
16	1–7	060			647		3	994 b*
	2	093 b, 485 a,		1–2	455		4	200, 605 c, 635,
		499, 799 (i)		1–11	052			649 d
	2–11	999*		2	921*, 936*, 114,		5	189, 205, 221 b
	3	448, 582			117, 266,		5–6	634
	4	254 a			422, 552,		5–8	625
	5	139 a			690, 740–4		6	205, 221 b
	7	104		2–24	742 b		7	605 c, 649 d
	8	367, 614		3	936*, 095, 114,		8	189, 191, 205,
	8–11	182			168, 491 c,			221 b
	9–10	074–5			664 a		9	190, 742 b,
	9–11	077, 169		4	340, 687 b			744 c
	11	477 b		4–5	915 (v)*		10	985*, 558 a,
	12	497		5	995 a*, 027,			563, 637
	13–16	614			355, 405,		11	232, 377, 456 a,
	14–15	488, 583, 629			768 foll.			742 b
	15	189		6	455, 568, 798 a		14	104
	16	190 d, 642		7–8	448, 455 a		16	931–2*, 986*,
	16–19	583, 613		8	246, 328, 376 a			368
	17	190 d, 213,		9	405 a, 455, 630		16–17	985 b*
		423, 468 b		9–12	744 c		17	381
	19	248 c, 349,		10	332, 477		18	351 a
		466 (i), 472,		11	376 a, 529 a,		20	917 (vi)*,
		498			661, 740			251 b, 440 a

This Index extends from **1886** *to* **2799**. *Before numbers with* * *supply* **1**,
e.g. [1]999*; *before others*, **2**, *e.g.* [2]000.

INDICES TO "JOHANNINE GRAMMAR"

JOHN		JOHN		JOHN	
	PAR.		PAR.		PAR.
18 21	381, 450 a	19 28	115, 394, 626 a	20 28	679 foll.
22	245, 248 c	28–30	279 a, 632	29	236, 241, 248 c, 475, 499
24	462	29	425		
25	425	29–30	623	30	335, 414 f
27	914*	30	456 a, 644 (i)	30–1	431–5
28	048, 646	31	048, 087–8, 115, 267, 419	31	526 foll.
29	969*			21 1	917 a*, 340–6, 620
30	277, 566 b, 646	31–4	564 b		
31	969 b*	32	607	2	418
33	234, 248 c, 649 (i), 766 (i) b	33	336	3	486
		34	914*, 586 a	4	137, 307 a, 336, 341 a
		35	151 a, 383–4, 526–8, 607, 611, 731	5	235 b–d, 701–3
33 foll.	649 (ii)			6	684, 703 c
34	090–1, 245 a, 248 c, 250 b	37	317–18, 675–7	7	632 a
35	702 d	38	291, 394	8	020, 288
36	988*, 566 b	39	461	9	703
37	185 b, 233–4, 245 a, 248 c 457	41	257 b	10	213, 405, 441, 703
		20 1	310–11		
		1–2	425, 482 c	10–12	437
38	553 d, 737	1–18	482 c	11	281, 283 c
39	094 a, 248 c, 464 b–c	2	367, 441	12	924*, 273, 466
		3	418	12–13	483
39–40	209	3–4	465	13	335 a
40	969 a*, 070	3–11	664 b	14	619–20
19 3	465 b	4	918*	15–17	248 c, 456 a, 584 c
4	553 d	6–7	377		
5	960*, 200, 645	7	305	18	211 c, 796–7
6	553 d	10–11	638	19	468, 552, 564 a
7	403, 733	11	073, 368	19–21	209
8	586, 733 a	12	171–2, 216 b, 368	20	509
9	403–4, 537 c, 733 foll.			21	209, 386 c
		13	050, 185 d	22	229–30, 552, 564 a
10	231 a, 606, 645	14	137		
11	904*, 213 a, 698	15	377, 649	22–3	089, 495, 498, 515 a
		16	586 b		
12	969 a*	17	265 a, 307 b, 489	23	074–5, 185 b, 486, 530 d, 600, 642
13	537 (i)–(ii), 586, 707				
		18	925–6*, 190 c, 482 c, 586 b	24	166, 386, 427–35
14	048, 088				
15	245, 248 c, 645, 737 c	19	031, 200, 307–9, 482	25	335 a, 414–16, 430–5, 660 b, 739
16–17	570 d	20	384 a		
17	738	21	127, 132, 453		
17–18	171	22	411 c		ACTS
19	347	23	473 b, 517–20, 558 e, 739 a	1 3	331 c, 620, 715
21	966 a*, 439, 645, 732			7	759 d
		24	928*, 073	8, 9	781 a
22	473	25	255 a, 607	12	673
23	904 a*, 071, 270, 632 d	25–7	567 a	18–20	781 a
		26	307–9, 331 d, 482	2 22	709 a
24	270, 335 a	27	384 a	3 12	537
25	928*, 217, 355, 418, 586 b	27–8	049–51	13	385 a

This Index extends from **1886** *to* **2799**. *Before numbers with* * *supply* **1**, *e.g.* [1]999*; *before others*, **2**, *e.g.* [2]000.

662

NEW TESTAMENT PASSAGES

ACTS

		PAR.
3	17	915 (i)*
4	5	559 a
5	28	732
6	11–13	451
7	19	949 a*
9	2	739 a
10	14	913 a*, 759 e
	16	913*
	36–8	292 a
	41	335 a
11	8	913 a*, 759 e
	10	913*
	22	709 b
14	1	917 a*, 203 b
16	22	270 b, 563 c
17	1	171 c
	20	709 a
	29	759 d
19	14	409
	25–6	439 (ii)
20	22–32	915 (i) c*
21	20	439 (ii)
23	30	691 c
24	12	759 d
25	7	335 a
	24	439 (ii)
26	5	904*
	24	784 b
	27	242
	32	698
28	7	665

ROMANS

1	11	784 b
	20, 21	558 b
2	14	534
3	19	606 a
	24, 25	558 b
	27	265 (i) a
4	13	759 d
	18	689
7	7	698
8	18	709 a
	23	723
	29	897 b*, 901*
9	11	759 d
	27	158, 721 b
10	1	559 d
	11	262 a
	18	702 b
11	7–8	449 a–b
	23	522
	36	294
13	11	559 a
15	15	691 b
16	20	741
	27	664 a

1 CORINTHIANS

1	7–8	322
2	8	566 a
	11	959*
3	4	534
4	9	530 d
	19	569 b
	21	332 a
5	1	784 b
	9–11	691 b
6	14	162 c
8	12	563 b
9	4	702 b
	11	783
	15	691 b
	18	690
	22	440
11	22	702 b
	27	759 f
	30	746 a
12	3	680
	8–10	676
13	1	522 a
	11	478 b
	12	915 (vi) c*, 511 a
	13	313 a
14	26	534 b
15	6–8	619
	19	474 a
	20	901*
	22	530 b
	24	531
	47	906*, 953 a*
16	10	364 b

2 CORINTHIANS

1	9	530 d, 723
	10	474 a
	14	559 d
	23–4	219 b
3	12	917 (ii) a, (v)*
	14	449 a
4	13	443
5	3	523 a
	8	364
	10	584 a

2 CORINTHIANS

		PAR.
7	9	915 (ii) a*
8	9	243 a
	23	721 b
9	4	523 a
10	12	723
11	1	784 d
	4	676
	16	784 d
12	4	414 e
	10	534 a
	17–18	440
13	9	534 a

GALATIANS

1	6–7	675–7
	12–15	559 d
	18	364 b
2	5	364 b
	13	694 c
3	7	243 a
4	9	904*
	15	698
	20	472 a, 717 b
	24–6	413
	25–6	906*, 907 c*
5	17	697 b
6	9–12	114
	10	696
	11	691 a–e, 78, 90

EPHESIANS

2	4	014
	13	909*
4	8	744 b
	26	439 (iii)
6	3	114

PHILIPPIANS

1	7	721 b
	25–6	559 d
2	1–2	036 b
	2	783
	9	409
	22	243 a
3	20	559 a
4	12	162 b
	14	783

This Index extends from **1886** *to* **2799**. *Before numbers with* * *supply* **1**, *e.g.* [1]999*; *before others*, **2**, *e.g.* [2]000.

INDICES TO "JOHANNINE GRAMMAR"

COLOSSIANS

	PAR.
1 15	897 b*
16	294, 440, 747 a
18	897 b*
24	915 (ii) a*
2 5	783
15	917 (i) *
4 18	783

1 THESSALONIANS

1 7–8	991*
2 16	322
19	558 b
3 7	515 (i)
10	559 a
13	559 a
4 9	379 a
5 1	379 a
2–3	531
3	534 b
4	697 b
23	322, 559 a

2 THESSALONIANS

2 1	721 b
5–6	915 (ii) *
10	033 a
3 5	033 b
17	691 e

1 TIMOTHY

3 14	554 d
4 10	474 a
13	089
5 25	539

2 TIMOTHY

2 12	322 b

TITUS

3 5	558 b

PHILEMON

18–19	691 b
19	219 a

HEBREWS

1 1	949*, 553 e
14	265 (i)

HEBREWS

	PAR.
2 4	558 b
6	694
9	576 b
10	294
12	307 b
4 8	566 a
11	784 b
5 6	675
6 5	016 a
7 4	439 (ii) a
6	751
18	558 c
25	322 c
8 7	566 a
11	763
12	255
13	477
10 17	255
37	230 (i)
11 17	751
23	539, 543 a
28	751
12 23	901*
13 6	203 b, 731
19	918*, 554 d
23	918*, 243 a, 554 d

JAMES

1 11	445
17–18	904 a*, 907 a*
18	558 b
24	753 c
2 14	522 a, 523 a
17	522 a
19	242 a
24	439 (ii)
3 15	904 a*
17	904 a*
4 2–3	536 g
4	034 a
5 11	322 b

1 PETER

1 1	046
3	907 a*
6–9	689 c, l
20–1	304 a
23	907 a*, 313 a
25	709 a
2 9	558 b
4 8	036 b

1 PETER

	PAR.
5 10	377 a
12	691 b, 710 a

"2 PETER"

3 1–2	783 a
9	586 d

1 JOHN

1 1	427, 450
1 foll.	399 c, 610
3	074, 450
4	399 c, 691 b
5	181, 450
2 1	159, 399 c, 630 h
2	075, 159
3	392, 515
4–5	569, 580 a
5	033–40, 516
6	132 b, 382
7	254 a, 412
7–8	894 b*
8	412
12	610
12–14	691 b
15	034 a
16	262 b
18	915 (iii) *, 450 a
19	106, 110, 263 c–d
21	262 b, 691 b
23	262 b
24	254 a
24–7	922*
26	691 b
27	104 a, 201, 558 b, 569 a
27–8	915 (iii)*
28	427, 437 c, 528 b
29	243 a, 515 (i)
3 1	391, 454 a
2	915 (iv)*, 427 a, 434 b
3	132 b, 382
5	382
6	262 b, 491
7	132 b, 382
9	262 b
10	262 b
12	957*

This Index extends from **1886** *to* **2799**. *Before numbers with* * *supply* **1**, *e.g.* [1]999*; *before others*, **2**, *e.g.* [2]000.

664

NEW TESTAMENT PASSAGES

1 JOHN		1 JOHN		REVELATION	
	PAR.		PAR.		PAR.
3 14	178 a, 427 a, 434 b	5 13	399 c, 691 b	1 5	897 b*, 901*
15	039, 262 b	14	181, 536 (i)	7	317 e
16	035 foll., 382	15	121 a, 159, 427 a,	17	900*
17	035 foll., 516 a		434 b,	2 2	497
20	409 a, 414		515 (i),	7	920*
21	522 a, 523 a		536 (i)	9	781
21-2	536 (i) b	16	121 a, 536 (i),	17	409
22	335, 516, 660 b		630 f, i	19	781 d
23	454 a, 528	18	262 b, 502 a	3 1	624
23 foll.	035 foll.	19	427 a, 434 b	3	013
24	454 a	20	936*, 114,	10	175 a
4 2	243 a		427 a,	12	920*
2-8	491 d		434 b,	16-17	175
3	915 (iv)*, 262 b, 450 a		454 a, 491 c	21	920*, 421
				4 11	681
9	297, 304			6 8	332 a
9-10	218, 440	2 JOHN		10 9	781 b, d
10	476 a			12 7	350 b
13	454 a	5	915 (iv)*	14 18	781 b
14	473	6	450 a	15 4	664 a
16	036 b, 475	9	262 b	18 4-5	781 b
16-19	036			7	175 a
17	382, 528 b	3 JOHN		9	531
5 2	037, 535			19 7	689 i
3	037	9-10	569	11	362 a
6-8	610	10	258	12	409
8	306, 383			13	409
10	187	JUDE		21 6	377 a
11	454 a	25	664 a	22 3-4	409

This Index extends from **1886** *to* **2799**. *Before numbers with* * *supply* **1**, *e.g.* [1]999*; *before others,* 2, *e.g.* [2]000.

665

INDICES TO "JOHANNINE GRAMMAR"

II. SUBJECT-MATTER (ENGLISH)

Abba **679**
Abide, abiding **915** (iii)*, **352**, **437**, **458**, **514**, **521**; Origen on **649** e; imperat. **437**; "a. in the house" **263** e–f; "a. (?) unto eternal life" **312** foll.; "a. alone" **375**
Aboth, the, quotations in, how introduced **470** a
Above, "from a.," in Jewish literature **906***; "born from a." **903*** foll.
Abraham, his love of man, Philo on **935***; his "laughing," Philo on **097**, **689** e; Origen on **689**
Abruptness of style **932***, **996*** foll., **136**–40, **766** (i) b
Accent (Greek) **960** a*, **190** a, **429**–**35**, **671**–4, **762** a–b
Accusative, absolute or suspensive **012**; adverbial **009**–11; cognate **014**, **036** a; (?) of respect **267**, **419**; of time **013**, **678**; accus. and infin. **375** a, **495**; for accus. w. special verbs, see the several verbs in Index III
Active (voice) and middle **563** c, **689** i
Adjectives, predicatively used **894***; special **895***–**901***, **664**–7, s. Index III, also Article **982***–9*, Ellipsis **216**, Emphasis **982*** foll., **993***
Adverbs, how emphasized **902***, **554** b, **668**; their position **636** c; intensive, rare in Jn **902***; special **903**–18*, s. Index III
Adversative particles, s. Conjunction and Connexion
Advocate, s. "Paraclete"
Afterthought, in Jn **461**; how introduced **633**–4; expr. by pluperf. **480**; s. Self-correction and Impressionism
"All that thou hast given me (or, him)," = "the future Church" **921***, **262**, **422**, **444**, **454**, comp. **740**–4
Allusiveness, in Jn **901** b*, **966** a*, **992***, **009** foll., **211** b, **265** b, **269**, **275** b, **372** a, **517**–20, **537** (ii), **584** b, **689**, **764**–5; s. also "John, intervention of," and Mysticism
"Alone," applied to God **895***, **664**, comp. **168**; "by himself alone" **375**, **724**–6; adv. **664** b
Ambiguity, causes of **886***, **893***
(i) in the meaning and reference of words: "first," "before," or "chief" **901***, **665**–7; "from above" **903*** foll.; "and now" **915** (i)* foll.; "thus" **916***; "boldly" or "plainly" **917** (i)* foll.; "(more) quickly" **918***; "the Jews" **941***; "the fathers" **949**–50*; "the heaven" **952**–8*; "the man" **959**–61*; "the prophet" **965***; "taste" or "taste that" **016**; "that" or "because" **083**, **181**–6, **219**; "they went out [as our soldiers, *or*, as deserters]" **110** a–b, **263** c; "and" or "and yet" **141** foll.; "and" or "also" **149** foll.; "[in] the beginning" or "at all" **154**; "and if" or "even if" **159**; "and," "both," or "also" **166**; "that" used for inverted commas **189** foll.; "lifted up" for "crucified" **211** c; "why?" or "what?" **231** b; "from the beginning" **254**; "blood" pl.

This Index extends from **1886** *to* **2799**. *Before numbers with* * *supply* 1, *e.g.* [1]999*; *before others*, 2, *e.g.* [2]000.

SUBJECT-MATTER (ENGLISH)

268; "we all" 287; "out of" and "from" describing extraction and domicile 289 foll.; "because of" or "for the sake of" 294 foll.; "through him" or "through it" 302 foll., comp. 378–9; "to" or "into" 310; "looking to" (in hope or fear) 317; "to the end" or "to the utmost" 319 foll.; "keep out of" or "take out of" 325; "in front of" or "superior to" 330; "on the sea" or "near the sea" 342; "along with" or "against" 349; "questioning" or "quarrel" 350; "in" or "among" 353 *a*; "before me" 361 foll.; "he knoweth" or "He (*i.e.* the Lord) knoweth" 383–4, 731; "that," "because" or "whatever" 413; "if" or "soever" 414; "at feast time" = "at that feast" or "at any feast" 464 *c*; "apprehend" *i.e.* "understand" or "take captive" 596; "again" *i.e.* "a second time" or "back" 635 (i), 649 (i)–(ii); "another" or "Another (*i.e.* God)" 793 foll. (comp. 384, 730)

(ii) in forms or inflexions : indic. or imperat. 889*, 915 (iii) *b**, 079, 193, 194 *c*, 236 foll., 240 *a*, 439 (ii), 491, 760; particip. = "because" or "though" 924 *a**, 273; particip. pres. w. ἦν 277; "he that received" or "he, who received" 501–2; present, ordinary or prophetic 484 foll.; "hid himself" or "was hidden" 538–43; dat. of time 021; genit. subjective or objective 032 foll., voc. or nom. 049 foll.; 1st pers. pl. inflexion, "we," meaning of 427 foll.

(iii) in connexion or arrangement: 921*; apposition 928*, 933*, 937* foll.; asyndeton 996* foll.; connexion of "for" (conj.) 067 foll.; "but" adversative or consecutive 071 foll.; "because" 099 foll.; "accomplished in order that" or "saith in order that" 115; "in order that...in order that" 116 foll.; "even as" suspensive or explanatory 122–32; "because" suspensive or explanatory 175 foll.; "because" or "I say this because" 178 foll.; "I should have told you that" or "I should have told it to you, because" 186; "not ...all" *i.e.* "not any" or "not every" 260 foll.; connexion of participle 277; "leaping to life" or "leaping, to life" 314 (comp. 312–13); "filled [full] of fragments" or "baskets of fragments" 329 (i); "for this cause [above mentioned, or, now to be mentioned]" 387 foll.; "everyone that cometh" or "the light...coming 508; "and they did" or "and [that] they did" 757; words of Christ and words of the evangelist (or others) not clearly distinguished 917 *a**, 936*, 957*, 066, s. Speech

(iv) in omission of words (s. also Asyndeton): "the [one] that is descending 974*, 503; "that [? spirit] which giveth life" 975* foll.; "but [? it was ordained] in order that" 105 foll.; "[I say this] because" 180 foll.; "This man what [shall he do? less prob. shall become of him?]" 209; "If therefore...[what then will ye do?]" 192 and 210 foll.; "[some] from" *i.e.* "some of" or "[sent] from" 214–15; "[daughter] of" or "[wife] of" 217; "[I do] not [say] that" or "[I say this] not because" 219; "I AM [HE] 220 foll.; omission of interrogative particle 236 foll., and see especially 240 *a*; comp. 142 *a*; "his own [family, or possessions]" 378, 728

(v) miscellaneous 372 *b*, 570 *b*

Anacoluthon 919–27*, 957*; w. subj. suspended 920–2*, 421, (?) 422

Anaphoric article, the 670 *a*

Anew, s. "New"

Anointing of David, the 502 *b*

"Another," meaning God, in Epictetus 791–2; connected with the Paraclete in Jn 793

"Answered and said," a Johannine phrase 271; "made public answer" 537

Antithesis 209, 263 *f*, 553 *a*, 568; s. Emphasis

Aorist: imperat. aor. and pres. 437–9; indic. aor. and imperf. 465 *c*, 584; aor. and perf. 440–9, 753; aor. for Eng. pluperf. 459–62; infin. aor. and pres. 496–8, 767; particip. aor. 276, 499–505; subjunct. aor. and pres. 511–35; aor. of experience or habit 443 *c*, 522 *b*, instantaneousness 443 *c*, 522 *b*, 755, persistence 443 *c*; anticipatory 635 (ii), epistolary 691 *a* foll., 785–90; "gnomic" and "instantaneous" distinguished 754–5; aor. of special verbs, see Index III

This Index extends from **1886** *to* **2799**. *Before numbers with* * *supply* **1**, *e.g.* [1]999*; *before others*, **2**, *e.g.* [2]000.

Apocalypse, the, s. Revelation
Apodosis, ellipsis of **192**; see also Index III ἄν, ἐάν, εἰ, ἵνα, καθώς, καί, ὅταν, ὅτι
Aposiopesis, s. Ellipsis
Apposition, w. proper names **928***; in subdivisions **929–30***; explaining or defining **931–6***; w. particip. **937–45***; noun repeated in **946***; pronoun in appos. w. preceding subject **947***, **386**
Aramaic, s. Hebrew
Arimathaea, Joseph of **291**
Arrangement and Variation **544** foll.
Artemidorus (*Oneirocritica*) quotations from **907** *d**, **211** *b*, *c*, **216** *b*, **642** *b*
Article, the, w. nouns in general **948*** (s. also **194** *b*); w. "fathers" **949–50***; "feast" **951***; "heaven" **952–8***; "king" **966***, **669**; "man" **959–61***; "mountain" **962–3***; "only begotten" **964***; "prophet" **965*** (comp. **492**); "teacher" **966***; "the woman [of the house]" *i.e.* "wife" **948***; w. names of persons **967–70***; w. names of places **670** foll.; in "the [? daughter] of" **217**; w. "God," Philo on **594** *a*; "the love" (like "the Name," "the Will") **035**; w. adjectives **982–9***; w. infin. **995***; w. particip. **275–6**, **507**; w. particip. and "is" or "are" **971–81***; quasi-vocative **049** (comp. **679** foll.); omitted or misplaced **990–4***; reduplicated **982*** foll.; in Codex B **652**; "Teuphilus [the] Jew" **683** *a*
Ascending **211** *a* foll., **489**; "a. to heaven" **211–12**, **275**
Asking **516**, **536** foll.; "a." and "requesting" **630**
Asyndeton **996*** foll.; instances of, classified **000–8**; used by Jn w. historic pres. **482**; introducing parenthesis **639**
Attraction of relative **405–7**
Authority **250**; "I have a." **644**; Epictetus on **798–9**

B *i.e.* Codex Vaticanus, readings of, rejected by W.H. **650–62**; pause-spaces in **663**; important readings of, in special passages **053** *c*, **079**, **166**, **401**, **407**, **428** *b*, **455** *a*, **507** *a*, **521**, **530**, **768**; its authority great on πιστεύω **528** *a*; its weak points **895***, **925** *a**, **961***, **968** *a**, **530** *c*, **650–2**; interchanges -αι and -ε **658** *e*
Baptist, John the, **898*** foll., **927***, **303**, **330**, **350**, **371**, **479**, **480** *a*, **501–2**; his "testimony" **401**; twofold repetition in his teaching **601** (comp. **927***)
Before (ambig.) **330**, **361**
Began to do, to say etc., expr. by imperf. **463**, **470**
"Beginning, from the" **251** *a*, **254**
Beholding **318**, **473**, **516** *a*; in a bad sense **212**
Belief **475**
Believe, believing etc., **302–4**, **438–9**, **466**, **475**, **496**, **499**, **506**, **695**; aor. and pres. **438–9**, **524** foll.; imperf., ambig. **466**; perf. meaning "have fixed belief" **442**, **474–5**; "believe ye," ambig. **238** foll.; "believe" and "know" in juxtaposition **226** *c* (see also *Joh. Voc.* **1463—1561**)
Bethany, connected w. Lazarus **290**; twofold mention of **641**; beyond Jordan **648**
Bethlehem **289**
Binding and loosing **517** *e* foll., **517–9**
Blending two constructions **923***, **189** *c*, **468** *b*, **482** *c*
Blinding (metaph.) **449** *a*
Blood, of Christ **269** *b* foll.; of the circumcised **269** *e*; of the passover **269** *e*
Boldness of speech, Christ's, why emphasized **917** (i)* foll.
Bread, the, that descended from heaven **503** foll.; "buying b." **745–6**
Brethren, Christ's **395**; "He is not ashamed to call them b." **307** *b*
Bridegroom, the **371**
Buying (metaph.) **745–6**; "buying food," Origen on **746**

Cana, the "sign" at **281–3**; meaning of the name **386** (i)
Case, s. Accusative, Dative, Genitive etc., also Contents p. xv
Causation, notion of, prominent in Jn **174**; expr. by conjunct. **174** foll.; by particip. **271–3**; by prepos. **295**
Cedars on Mt of Olives **671**
Chiasmus **544**, **554–7**, **568**
Choosing, God's **441** *b* foll.
Chronological order, not always followed by Jn **632**
Chrysostom, compared with Origen **757** *e*; ?alluded to by Jerome **786**; quoted or referred to **897***, **903***, **916***, **934***, **942***, **020**, **062** *b*, **066**, **083**, **091–2**, **102** *a*, **115**, **122** *b*, **124–5**, **154–6**, **163**, **169**, **181**, **184** *a*, **195**, **199**, **207**, **209**, **211**, **212** *b*, **214** *a*, **215**, **218** *a*, **231** *b*,

This Index extends from **1886** *to* **2799**. *Before numbers with* * *supply* **1**, *e.g.* [1]**999***; *before others*, **2**, *e.g.* [2]**000**.

SUBJECT-MATTER (ENGLISH)

232, 240 a, 263 g, 264 a, 268, 281 a, 290, 300 a, 308 a, 322 c, 323 a, 329 (i), 331 c, 338, 342 h, 350 d, 351, 355, 357, 362, 372 c, 384–5, 386 (i), 396 b, 397 b, 398 a, 401, 403, 408, 412 b, 433, 439 (i), 452, 461 a, 465 c, 466 (i) a, 472 a, 478, 479 a, 489 a, 491 b, 508 c, 512 c, 514 (i) e, 515 e, 520, 537 (i) c, 540–1, 543 c, 549 a, 554 d, 566 b, 570 b, 573, 620 a, 630 b, 635 (ii), 649 (i)a; 649 (iii); 675–6, 686–7, 689 k, m, 691 d, 692, 694–5, 697, 701 a, 703 b, d, 707 a, 714, 716, 718, 722, 724–5, 727–8, 730, 732, 734, 736, 739 a foll., 740 b, 745, 753 e, 756, 757 d–e, 758–9, 762 b, 764, 767, 786, 788, 793 b, 794, 797, 799 (ii), 799 (iii)

Clean, man made clean by the Logos 799 (iii)
Codex Bezae, s. D
Codex Vaticanus, s. B
Come, applied to Christ 440, 482, 490; aor. 457; imperf. 465; pres. 482–6; "he that is to come" 940*; "he that cometh after me" 507; "coming into the world" 508; "came" and "have come" 440; "the hour cometh" and "hath come" 485 a, 604 a
Comparative degree 896*—901*, 918*, 092, 772, 775 b; comp. 733 a
Concessive particles 158–60
Conditional sentences 078–86, 158–9, 513–5, 517–23
Conjunctions: for most, s. Contents pp. xv–xvii; for others, s. Index III; for omission of conjunctions, s. Asyndeton
Connexion of sentences or clauses 996*, 278–9, 628 foll.; adversative or consecutive 069–76; with "and" or "and yet" 136–45; with "that" or "because" 174–86; doubtful instances 278, 414, 636–40, s. also Conjunctions and Pronouns
Consecutive particles 191—200, 203, 694, 697
Constructio ad Sensum, s. Anacoluthon
Convicting Spirit, the 649 b, d
Corrective manner, a Johannine characteristic 939*, 380, 628–30
Correspondence between the visible and the invisible 122 foll., 148
Crasis 150, 151, 383, 769
Cross, taking up the 515
Crucified, "the crucified feeds many" 211 c, 642 b
Crucifixion 211 b–c

Crying and crying aloud 479, 618

D, i.e. Codex Bezae, corrects irregularity 926*, 990*, 014, 258, 422; alters pres. to aor. subjunct. 524, 530 a; some readings of 942*, 053 c, 422, 428 b, c, 637 a, 664, 797 c
Dative, of instrument 020; of time (completion) 021–4; of point of time 025–6; of advantage, 776, 784 a; w. special prepositions 027, 338, 355, 357–9; w. special verbs 019, 506
Daughter (or wife?) ellipsis of the word 217
Day, "three days," "third day" etc. 331; day of judgment, the 521–2, 535 a
Dead, the, (?) prayer for the intercession of 630 i
Death, "tasting of d." and "beholding d." 576
Decalogue, the, second half of 676
Deliberative subjunctive 512, 766 (i)
"Delivering over to Satan" 520
Demonstrative, s. Pronouns
Descending from heaven 275; of the Son of man 503
Digression, causes anacoluthon 923–4*
Diminutives 235 d (s. *Joh. Voc.*)
Disciple, the beloved, Origen on 545 c
Dispersion of the Greeks, the 046
Distributive use of ἀνά 281 foll.
Domicile and birthplace, how denoted 289–93
Double Tradition, the, parallels between, and Jn 026, 165; "laying the head to rest" 644 (i)
Dove, "as a d." 955*
Dreams, Artemidorus on 211 c, 642 b
Drinking and eating at the Lord's Supper 759 f
Dying 530, 576

Eating in the presence of Christ or the disciples 335; "eating and drinking" at the Lord's Supper 759 f
Ellipsis, of two kinds 204; contextual 205–9; idiomatic 213 foll.; of apodosis 210–12; of "some" 213–5; (?) of "gate" 216; of "daughter" or "wife" 217; of copula 229–30; w. "I am" 220 foll.; between "but" and "in order that" 063–4, 105–12; s. also 386 c, 698
Emphasis, caused by insertion of word not needed for sense, e.g. of pron. 375, 399; of "is" 972*; of redupl. article with adj. 982* foll., 993*;

This Index extends from 1886 *to* 2799. *Before numbers with* * *supply* 1, *e.g.* [1]999*; *before others*, 2, *e.g.* [2]000.

caused by unusual position **515, 553**, *e.g.* of pron. **552** *c*, **553** *a*, *c*, **692**; of "this" **553** *c*; of adverbs **554** *b*, **668** (comp. **902***); of "is" **353**, **553** *b*, **555** *a*, **579**; caused by chiasmus, **555**; by antithesis **564** *b*, **566** *c* (which may be expressed or implied **399**); on two pronouns in juxtaposition **564, 783, 784** *c*; on contingency **566**; diverted from possessive genit. to noun **558, 569, 776–84**; confusable w. contrast **399**; s. also **902*, 979** *a**, **983*, 993*, 267, 555, 566** *a*, *b*, **605** *a*
Entering the Kingdom of God **496**
Ephesians, Diana of the **743**
Epictetus, quoted or referred to **907** *c**, **917** (v)*, **960** *c**, **049, 228** *a*, **229–30, 297** *c–e*, **305** *a*, **334** *d*, **404, 439** *b*, **439** (iv), **473** *a*, **493, 532** *d*, **570** *b*, **664** *b*, **683, 695, 697** *b*, **702** *b*, **705, 717** *b–d*, **719** *a*, *c–d*, **728** *d*, **736** *b*, **743** *a*, **755** *a*, **758** *a*, **763, 766** (i), **778–80, 791–2, 798–9, 799** (ii), **799** (iii)
Epistle, of St John, the first: general "duality" of its style **610**; its use of "now" **915** (iii–iv)*; of "we" **399** *c*; of "He" absolutely to mean Christ **382**; of "the true [One]" **936***; of "the love of God" to mean "God's love for men" **032** foll.; its emphasis on "confidence" **917** (ii)*; its universal negations **262** *b*; on "asking" and "requesting" **121** *a*, **630** *f–g*; peculiarities of construction or meaning in **159, 392, 515–6, 528**
Eucharist, symbols of **746**
Exclamatory Tone, s. Interrogation

Face of God, the **765**
Father, ambig. **193, 359**; "*the* fathers" and "*your* fathers" **949–50*, 553** *e–f*
Feast, "the [principal] feast [of the Jews]" **951***; "at feast-time" ambig. **464** *c*
Feminine, in Heb. and LXX, a cause of error **621–2**; s. also "sheep-gate" **216**
First, different meanings of **899*** foll., **665–7**
Fish, a symbol **703**
Following **497**
Form of God, the **765** *a*
Fruit (metaph.) **120**
Future regarded as past **444**; included in pres. partic. **507**; fut. partic. a corrupt reading **500**; fut. in apodosis **515** *b*; fut. and subjunct. w. οὐ μή **255**; w. ἵνα **114, 690**; s. also **484, 660** *c–d*, **762** *a* and **960** *a**

Galilee, "from out G." **289**; "out of G....no prophet" **492**; "sea of G." **045**
Gender, **216, 378, 621–2, 738**
Genitive, absolute **028–31**; objective **558** *e*; objective or subjective **032–40**; partitive **041–2**; before nouns **043**; in special passages **044–8**; possessive **558–69**; unemphatic or "vernacular" possessive **563** *d*, **776** foll.; emphatic possessive **558** *b*, **563** *d*; ordinary possessive **558, 563** *d*, **779, 781** *a–b*; for gen. w. special verbs, s. the several verbs in Index III
Gennesar **045** *a*
Gennesaret supplanted by "Tiberias" **045**
Giving **454–5**; Hebraic use of "I have given" **444**; "g. by measure" **714**; "g. commandment" **742** *a*; "giving," in Jn, parall. to "grace" in the Pauline epistles **742–3**; "all that thou hast given" **740–4, 798** *a*
Glorify, "glorifying God" **117**; "the Father was glorified" **393, 446**
Glory **211** *a–b*; connected with spiritual unity **946*, 455**
Gnomic aorist **754–5**
God, "the face of" **765**; "the form of" **765** *a*; "the word of" **799** (iii)
Gods, "I said ye are g." **799** (iii)
"Going up to the feast" **265**; to Jerusalem **265** *b*, s. "Ascending"
Golgotha **738**
"Grace and truth" **286, 415**; "grace" corresponds to the Johannine "giving" **742–3**
Greek, non-classical, disuses the optative **252**; uses μή with particip. **253** *a*; literary as distinct from vernacular **799** (ii); later Greek introduces other developments not found in Jn **694, 697, 702, 718–22**; the futility of judging Jn's Gk as Byzantine **747–53**
Greeks, "the Dispersion of the G." **046**

Hardened, confusable with "blinded" **449** *a*
Harvest, waiting for **230** (iii)
Hate, "hating one's father" **228** *a*; "I hated," meaning "I steadfastly hated" **443**; "I have hated" **475**
He = HE **382** foll.
Head, "laying the head to rest," Origen on **644** (i), **713**

This Index extends from **1886** *to* **2799**. *Before numbers with* * *supply* **1**, *e.g.* [1]**999***; *before others*, **2**, *e.g.* [2]**000**.

SUBJECT-MATTER (ENGLISH)

Healing at a distance 026
Hearing 450 foll., 586
Heaven, "the h. opened" 958*; "from h." and "from the h." 952* foll.
Hebrew or Aramaic, influence of, in N.T. 915(v)*, 920*, 938*, 019, 041, 133–4, 137, 145, 260 foll., 277, 332, 347, 443–5 (see especially 445 a), 482 a; Hebraized Gk 216, 666, 671, 793
Hellenistic, s. Greek
Herod the Great and Herod Antipas 737 a
Hide, "Jesus hid himself" 538 foll., 724
Hireling, the years of a 230 (ii)
Historic present 482
Holy 411 c, d
Homoeoteleuton 490 a, 549 a, 654 c, 657 c, 659 e, 736 a, 759
Hoping 474, 476
Horse, allegorized by Origen 362 a
Hour, the, "cometh," "cometh and now is," "hath come" etc. 485 a, 604 a; the hour of trial 523 a (see also 770 and 799 (i))
House, allegorized by Origen 329; mention of, peculiar to Mk 711–13

I emphatic 401; in the Baptist's testimony 401; Epictetus on "the I" 228 a
I AM and "I am" 205, 220 foll., 487 a
Illuminating 532 c
Imperative, aor. and pres. 437–9; imp. pres. confusable w. indic. 439 (ii), with interrog. 238–44 (especially 240 a, 243 a); first aor. imp. authoritative 437; differently used by different writers 437 a; (?) "concessive" 439 (iii–v), might be called "judicial" 439 (v); implied by prohib. conjunct. 208–9; expressed or implied before "but if not" 080; s. also 233
Imperfect 463–6; imperf. and aor. 584; of special verbs 467–70; with neg. = "would not" 466; "it was" or "it had been" 466 (i)
Impersonal, s. Subject
Impressionism, results in anacoluthon 925* foll.
"In you" may mean "among you" 353 a
Inaccuracies, so called, deliberate 629
Indefinite "they" 424 a
Indicative: tenses of 440–94, and see Contents p. xxii; interrog. or non-interrog. 238–44; confusable w. imperat. 193, 194 c, 439 (ii–iii), 760; for subjunct. 114, 515 (i), 771
Indirect interrogative 249–51
Infinitive, aor. and pres. 496–8, 767; compared w. ἵνα and subjunct. 495; accus. and infin. 375 a, 495; infin. w. article 995*
Instantaneous aorist 755
Instrument, expr. in Hebrew by "in" 332; instrumental dative 020
Intercession of dead for living, (?) prayer for 630 i
Interrogation expr. by particles 231–5; without particles 236–48; sometimes exclamatory 142, 146, 486; confusable w. imperat. and affirmation 238–44 (esp. 240 a); indirect 249–51
Iota subscript 515 (i) b, 772–5
Irony, in Jn 960*, 046, 570 d, 643–5
Isaac, *i.e.* "laughter" 689
Ishmael, (?) alluded to 263 e
Israel = "seeing God" 765

Jacob, described as seeing God 765
Jerome, (?) alludes to Chrysostom 786; mentions Origen 789 a
Jew, "a Jew" 350; "the Jews" (?) = citizens of Jerusalem 942*; "many of the Jews," ambig. 941* foll.
Jewish canons of repetition 588, and of negation 591; Jewish Prayer-Book, repetition in 587 a; s. Hebrew
John the Baptist, s. "Baptist"
John the Evangelist, style of (see Allusiveness, Ambiguity, Anacoluthon, Asyndeton, Emphasis, Epistle, Impressionism, Irony, Metaphor, Mysticism, Narrowing Down, Parenthesis, Quotation, Repetition, Self-correction, Symbolism, Variation) shews traces of more than one writer 891–2*; intervention of, where Lk. omits or deviates from Mk 917* (iii) foll., 918*, 945*, 963*, 039, 045, 047, 048, 088, 173, 293, 346 a, 396, 464 b, 480 a
Joseph (husband of Mary), Jesus called "son of J." 289, 643
Joseph (son of Jacob) seeking his brethren 649 b–c
Josephus, his rendering of Heb. names 673
Judges, addressed in the words "I said ye are gods" 799 (iii)
Judging, judgment, 334 b, 695, 799; how regarded by Christians 182 a

Kidron 671–4

This Index extends from **1886** *to* **2799**. *Before numbers with* * *supply* **1**, *e.g.* [1]999*; *before others*, **2**, *e.g.* [2]000.

INDICES TO "JOHANNINE GRAMMAR"

King, "a k." and "the k." 245 *a*, 669; the natural k. 798
Knowing 491 foll., 511, 515, 760 foll.; "knowing" in juxtaposition w. "believing" 226 *c*; "I know" 448 *a*; "they have not known" 448; "know ye" ambig. 243, 762 foll.; "know thyself" 126, 763

Latin versions 895 *a**, 901 *a**, 926 *a**, 118 *d*, 154 *d*, 168 *a*, 190 *a*, 210 *a*, 289 *a, b, c*, 290 *a*, 331 *b*, 343 *a*, 350 *c*, 491 *a*, 569 *c*, 687, 702 *a*, 711 *a*, 715 *d*, 727 *a*, 767 *a*; infin. and subjunct. in 687, s. also 688 *a*
Latinisms 213 *a*, 258, 288
Law, the 286; "Present of Law" 484
Life, hating, loving, losing one's life 485
Lifted up = crucified 211 *b, c*; double meaning of 642 *b*
Lifting up the eyes 616-7
Logos, the 269 *b*, 308, 410; action or agency of 296 *a*, 301; titles of 938*, 964*, comp. 410
Looking to 317
Loosing sins 517; binding and loosing 517 foll.
Lord, used by Epict. in a bad sense 799 *d*; meanings of "my lord" 050
Losing one's soul 228 *b*
Love, "love of God," two meanings of 032 foll.; "the Love," like "the Name," "the Will" 035
Loving 476, 529 *a*; loving one another 529
Luke, literary style of 781, 799 (ii); various styles in his Gospel and the Acts 913*, 563 *a*, 677, 686, 759 *e*; peculiarities of 737 *a*; optative in 252; differs in construction from Jn 972*, 995*, 191 *a*, 307, 593, 799 (ii); deviates from Mk, or omits what is in Mk, where Jn intervenes 917 (iii)* foll., 918*, 945*, 039, 045, 047, 088, 173, 276, 293, 346 *a*, 396, 464 *b*, 480 *a*

Man, emph. 412 *a*; "the man" 959-60*; "the new man" 959*; perh. = "husband" or "bridegroom" 371, 722; the ideal, in Philo 649 *b*; in Epictetus 960 *c**
Manifestations of Christ 331 *c* foll., 414 *f*, 619 foll., 699, 701-3, 715
Mark, style of 065, 380 *b*, 513 *b*, 649 (i) *f*, 686; his use of hist. pres. 482; of article 967*; of the word "house" 711; Mk regarded as a Petrine Gospel 913*; similarities in Mk and Jn 917 (vi)*, 112, 238, 240, 380 *b*, and s. "John, intervention of"
Mary "those that had come to M." 380
Master, the natural m. of men 798 *c*
Matthew, John agrees with 026, 537 (ii) *b*; Mt's use of "this is come to pass" 478 *a*, 758; s. also *Joh. Voc.* 1745-57
Mean, "he meant to say" 467 foll.
Messiah, Talmudic Traditions about 736 *c*
Metaphor 948*, 955-8*, 120, 197 *b*, 211 *a* foll., 230 (ii-iii), 281-3, 300, 329, 346 *a, c*, 355, 449 *a*, 520, 642 *b*
Middle voice 536 foll., 660 *d*, 688, 689 *i-l*
Mis-spelling, s. Spelling
Mood 889*, 252; see also Imperative, Indicative etc., Tense, and Contents p. xxi foll.
Moses, Chrysostom on 745 *a*
Motion, implied without verbs of motion 305
Mountain, the, meaning of 962*
Mysticism, 890*, 985*, 134, 168, 265, 281-3, 329, 384, 426, 483 *a*, 543, 587-627, 611 *a*, 641-9, 702-3, 712-3, 731, 736-7, s. also Metaphor

Name, God's 409-10; "my n." 411 *b*; "a new n." 409, 412; "thy n." and "thy Son" 769; "thy n. that thou hast given me" 744 *c*
Names: Proper names in apposition 928*; article with 967* foll.; indeclinable, with article 968*; declinable and indeclinable 672 foll.
"Narrowing down" 290 (esp. 290 *b*); 908*, 303, 310, 629, 636 *c*
Nazareth 289; "Jesus from N." 292
Negation, repetition through 591, 598
Negative particles 253-65, 704; double negative 257; negative w. imperf. 466
Net, of the Gospel, the 703 *c*
Neuter plural 267, 419-20
New 907*; the word in Aramaic and Greek 906*; "the n. birth" 906* foll.; "the n. man" 959; "a n. commandment" 412; "a n. name" 409, 412
Nicodemus in *Acta Pilati* 461
Nominative 049-51, s. Subject
Nonnus, quoted or referred to 156 *a*, 235 *c*, 338 *a*, 350, 384 *a*, 386 *c*, 386 (i) *n*, 419 *b*, 435 *a*, 461 *a*, 478, 487 *a*, 489 *a*, 508 *c*, 514 *a*, 515, 537 (i) *c*, 540 *a*, 586 *c*, 635 (i) *a*, 642 *a*, 649 (iii), 657 *d*, 664 *a, b*, 666, 668 *a*, 682 *b*, 683, 687-8, 689 *k*, 692, 694, 701 *b*, 702, 703 *c*, 704, 714,

This Index extends from 1886 *to* 2799. *Before numbers with* * *supply* 1, *e.g.* [1]999*; *before others,* 2, *e.g.* [2]000.

SUBJECT-MATTER (ENGLISH)

716, 722, 724–5, 727, 728 *a*, 730–2, 733 *a*, 734, 736, 739 *b*, 740 *c*, 742 *a*, 743, 744 *c*, 745, 753 *d*, *e*, 756, 757, 758, 759, 760, 762, 766 (i) *a*, 767, 768–9, 793 *b*, 796 *b*, 799 (ii), 799 (iii)
Nouns, indeclinable 968*, 970*, 673 *c*; neut. pl. 267, 419–20; repeated in apposition 946*; genitive before 043, 558 foll., 776 foll.; with article 948* foll.
Number, sing. and plur. 266–70
Numbering the people, under the Law 010
Numbers, mystically allegorized 281–3; "perfect" 283 *c*

One, meaning unity 118 *b*
One, meaning "anyone" 379
Only, "the o. man of Italy" 895*
Only begotten, with and without article 964*
Openly, confidently, or plainly 917 (i–vi)*, 727, comp. 798 *f*
Optative 252, 514 (i) *b*
Oratio Obliqua 189
Order, chronological, broken 460; of words 544–86, 776 foll., s. Emphasis and Variation
Origen, compared with Chrysostom 757 *e*; mentioned by Jerome 789 *a*; quoted or referred to 895*, 897*, 903 *a*, 934*, 942–4*, 965*, 022 *a*, 079 *c*, 110 *b*, 118 *b*, *c*, 184 *a*, 209, 218 *a*, 222 *a*, 263 *d*, 269 *a*, 275 *a*, 283 *c*, 285–6, 304 *b*, 307 *d*, 316 *b*, 324 *c*, 329, 329 (i), 335 *a*, 338, 346 *a*, 357, 362 *a*, 386 (i), 396 *b*, 397 *b*, 412 *a*, 414 *b–h*, 428 *b* foll., 430, 434 *e*, 439 *a*, 439 (i), (iii), (v) *a*, 452, 464 *b*, 479, 489 *a*, *b*, 490 *a*, 492 *a*, 507 *a*, 508 *c*, 540 *b*, 543, 545 *c*, 549 *a*, 553 *f*, 573, 584 *c*, 586 *c*, 622, 635 (i), 644 (i), 649 *e*, 649 (iii), 659 *e*, 664, 666–7, 668 *a*, 680, 682 *a*, 685, 688 *a*, 689, 692, 695, 703, 713, 716 *b*, 722, 724, 725, 726, 728, 730, 736 *a*, 740–2, 744, 746, 756, 757 *c*, *e*, 758, 759, 765 *a*, 766 (i) *a*, 767, 770, 793 *b*, 799 (ii), 799 (iii)
Orthography 114, 691; Augustus, negligent of 790

Papyri, quoted or referred to 049, 114, 173 *a*, 235 *d*, 252, 282 *a*, 332 *a*, 334 *d*, 386 *a*, 414 *a*, 416 *a*, 465 *d*, 479 *a*, 520 *a*, 554 *c*, 630 *d*, *i*, 640 *e*, 642 *b*, 665 *a*,

667, 678 *a*, 683 *a*, *b*, 690, 691, 693, 696, 697 *c*, 698 *a*, 708 *c*, 711, 717, 729, 771, 775 *a*
Paraclete, the 932*, 352–3, 793
Parallelism, as distinct from Chiasmus 544 *a*
Parenthesis 070 foll., 164, 168, 180, 631 foll.; w. Asyndeton 639; avoided by SS 631; comp. 018
Participle 271–9; in apposition 937* foll.; w. negative 253–4, comp. 704; aor. 499—505; fut. a false reading 500; fut. comprehended in present 500; perf. 506, 517; pres. 351, 507–10; probably expressing cause 924 *a*, 273; see also Article and Genitive Absolute
Partitive Genitive 041 foll.
Passive voice, avoided by Jn 373; passive and middle 538–43
Patriarchs, the 949–50*
Paul, St, the Apostle, his handwriting 114, 691, 785–90; his view of God's preordinance 689 *j*
"Pause-spaces" in Codex B 663
Penuel, meaning of 765
Perfect tense, as result of Johannine style 473–5; as result of Johannine thought 476–7; compared with aorist 440 foll.; meaning "it is on record that" 758; denoting instantaneousness and permanence 517–20; in Heb. 443; second perf. 478–9; some act. perfects in Gk seldom used 441, 747–53; perf. partic. 506; s. also 683 *a*, *b*
Personal, s. Pronoun
Pharisees 214–5; chief priests and P. regarded as one council 991 *a**
Philo, on the "laughing" of Abraham 097; quoted or referred to 890*, 895*, 905*, 907 *c**, 917 (v)*, 935*, 964*, 097, 223, 275 *b*, 281, 283 *b*, *c*, 285, 295–6, 307 *d*, 346 *a*, 386 (i), 410, 414 *h*, 494, 535 *a*, 579 *a*, 588–90, 594 *a*, 602, 616, 617 *a*, 647 (n.), 649, 665, 676, 689 *e*, 743, 765
Philosophers and kings 799
Phrynichus on ἧς 772 foll.
Pilate's judgment 799 *f*
Plato, on "knowing" 763 *a–b*; his use of the "vernacular genitive" 776
Pleonasm for emphasis 606
Pluperfect 480–1; aor. for Eng. p. 459–62; no p. in Heb. 480; no p. partic. in Gk 506
Plural 417; pl. vb w. sing. noun 278;

This Index extends from 1886 *to* 2799. *Before numbers with* * *supply* 1, *e.g.* [1]999*; *before others*, 2, *e.g.* [2]000.

pl. referring to sing. 266; neut. pl. 267, 419-20
Position of words, 544-86; see also Emphasis and Variation
Possessive adjectives 987-9*
Possessive genitive 558-69, 776-84
Prayer 452; the Lord's Prayer, reference to, in Jn 053
Praying 536; the Son not described as "praying" to the Father 630 h
Predicate, when before subject 994*; p. in one clause subject of next 596; "such" used as p. 398
Preordinance, divine 093, 102-5, 109-10
"Preparation of the Passover," meaning of 048
Prepositions 280 foll., and see Contents pp. xix–xx
Present, imperat. 437-9; indic. 482-94; historic 482-3; of prophecy and of law 484-94; infin. 496-8; aor. and pres. infin. in LXX 767; particip. 507-10; pres. part. w. "was" 277; subjunct. 511-35
Privately, Christ does not teach privately 202, 348, 251 b
Pronouns, demonstrative 374-98; personal 399—404; relative 405-16; ins. for emphasis 399 foll.; in appos. to preceding subject 947*; ambiguous 378-9; emphasized by juxtaposition 784 c; see also possessive genit. 558-69 and 776-84
Proper names, s. Names
Prophecy, "present of p." 484, 509
Prophet, "a, or the, p." 492 a; "the p." 940*; "art thou the p.?" 940*, 965*
Prophetic present 484, 509
Proselytes 907-8*
Punctuation 996*, 186, 225 a, 248 a, 278, 314, 372 b, 414, 508, 799 (i), s. Connexion of Sentences
Purpose, how expressed in Jn 093, 097, 173, 524-9, 686-90, 693, comp. 995*

"Question" (vb) meaning interrogate 498, 577
"Questioning" (n.) meaning discussion or dispute 349-50
Quotations and repetitions 190 a–c, 275 a; variation in 544; of Christ's words by Himself 545; conformed to txt. rec. 269 a, 357 b; introduced in Aboth 470 a; s. also 079 c, 412 b, 745 a

Rab, root of "Rabbi," two meanings of 899*

Rachel, regarded by Justin, Iren., and Orig. as type of the Church 944*
Reception of Christ 448 a
Recognition 491, s. "knowing"
Regeneration 903* foll., 268 foll.; "from above" 573
Relative (Pronoun) 405-16; attraction of 405; s. also 738
"Remembering" after the Resurrection 469
Repetition, or Refrain 587 foll.; variation in 544 foll.; in Jewish Prayer Book 587 a; Jewish Canons of 588; through negation 591, 598; in Synoptists 592; of Vocatives 592 a; twofold, in the Baptist's teaching 601-2; in Christ's words 603 foll.; in narrative 607; twofold or threefold 608-11; threefold 396, 612-23; sevenfold 624-7
Resumptive clauses 633
Resurrection, manifestations after the 335, 699-700, 703 b, d; the period of 331 c, comp. 715
Retaining sins 517-20
Revelation of St John, the 890*, 892*, 964*, 011, 176, 270 c, 288, 329, 349, 624, 640, 781, 799 (ii)
"Right side of the ship, the" 703 c

Samuel, the call of 307 d
Saul, Abba 227
Saying, vbs of 456, 469, comp. 251 b; "began to say" 467, 470
Scripture 339; difficulty of identifying 129; Orig. on lit. interpretation of 545 c; Christ's quotations from 626; "searching the scriptures" 439 (i)
Sea, "on, or near, the s." 340-5; Jesus standing "by the s." 354
"Searching the scriptures" 439 (i)
Seeing = experiencing 576 e; s. and beholding 572; s. and knowing 491, 764-6; s. the kingdom of God 573
Self-correction 628 foll., 635 (ii)
Sending 277, 440, 453
Sentences, connexion of 628 foll.
Septuagint, variety of styles in 349 a, 536, 649 (i) f, 689 d, comp. 911*
Serving 515
"Seven," the number, in Revelation 624; sevenfold repetition 624 foll., comp. 411 a–b, 529 d
"Sheep-gate, the," an error 216
Singular number 418; referred to as pl. 266

This Index extends from 1886 to 2799. Before numbers with * supply 1, e.g. [1]999*; before others, 2, e.g. [2]000.

SUBJECT-MATTER (ENGLISH)

"Six," the number 283 *b*; six days, mystically implied 647
Slave, the, does not "abide in the house" 263 *e*
Son of God 410, 798–9
Sower, Parable of the, "word" how used in 799 (iii)
"Speaketh of his own" 728
Speaking, vbs of, see "Saying"
Speech, direct or reported 926*, 189; speech confusable w. narrative or comment (see Preface, pp. vii–ix) 936*, 949*, 956–7*, 066, 128, 203, comp. 925*; speech assigned wrongly by Chrys. 734 *d*, 745 (see esp. 745 *a*), by Cyprian 737 *c*, by Aphraates 768, comp. 061; change of "him" to "me" in 695 *c*
Spelling, St Paul's 691; Augustus's 790; misspellings freq. in Mk 513 *b*
Spirit 315 foll., 407; different meanings of 976 *a**; not given "from a measure" 714; "the Holy S." 488; "the S. of truth" 352
SS (see p. xxv) 926 *a**, 942 *a**, 944 *a**, 977*, 990*, 079, 083, 186 *b*, 235 *a*, 329 (i) *b*, 448 *a*, 517 *d*, 632 *a*, *b*, *c*, 739 *b*, 756, 760, 769; its avoidance of parenthesis 631, 632 *a*, 639 *a*
Stand, "Jesus stood" 307 *a* foll., 703, 710
Stone (metaph.) 397; "a white s." 409; "the s. that the builders rejected" 622
Style, Johannine 891–3*, 112, 132, 134, 455; its abruptness 135; contrasts 140 *a*; rarely resembles that of Lk. 335 *a*; s. "Ambiguity," "Epistle," "Hebrew," "Speech"
Subject 417 foll.; collective or noun-group 417–8; neut. plur. 419–20; suspended 421–2; omitted in partitive clauses 041–2, 213–5; "they" non-pronominal 424–6; "we" non-pronominal 427–35; "[any]one" 379
Subjunctive aor. and pres. 893*, 511–35; deliberative 512, 766 (i); in final clauses 093 foll., 524–30, 687–9; in conditional clauses 513–5, 517–23; in temporal clauses 531–5; after the indef. relative 516; in strong negation 255
Suspensive sentences 122 foll., 175 foll.
Symbolism, s. Metaphor and Mysticism
Synonyms (on the meaning, see p. 645 n.) 630 *h*; juxtaposition of 570, 576–7, 584 *a–c*, s. *Joh. Voc.* p. 151

Tabernacles, the feast of 265 *a*
Talmud, the 196
Tautology, Philo on 588 *d*
Teacher, "thou art the t. of Israel" 966*
Temple, the, rebuilding of 021 foll.
Tense 893*, 436, 753, s. Contents, p. xxi—xxiii, also Aorist, Future etc.
They, non-pronominal 424; THEY 426
Third day, the 982*
This, "this is he" etc. 957 *b**; "this [thing] is the Lord's doing" 396
Thomas, his confession of faith 049–51
Three Witnesses 588–9
Threefold repetition 612–23, comp. 411 *c*; thr. rep. of "remembering" 639; twofold or threefold rep. 608–11
Tiberias, the sea of 045
Time, completion of 021 foll.; duration of 013 *b*, comp. 678; interval of 331 *c*, 715; point of 013, 025, 331; simultaneousness of 531
Transliteration 216, 666, 671 *a*, 793
Transposition 915 (ii), (iii); s. Emphasis and Variation
Treasury, the 333
Two, "t. witnesses" 588; "t. or three firkins" 281–3
Twofold attestation 589; twofold meanings and events 641–9, comp. 172; twofold repetition: in the Baptist's teaching 601–2; in Christ's teaching 603–6; in narrative 607; twofold or threefold rep. 608–11

Understanding, or knowledge, moral 491 *d*

Variation in repetition or quotation 544 foll.; in sympathy w. meaning 565; miscellaneous 570 foll.
"Vernacular genitive, the" 558 foll., 776–84
Vernacular and literary Gk 781, 799 (ii)
Vocative 052–3; expr. by article 679 foll.
Voice, middle 536–7; passive 538–43; s. also 563 *c*, 689 *c* foll.

Walking 342; = "teaching" *ib*.
Water, connected with "life" 314; "rivers of w." 316 *b*
"We," meaning of 287; non-pronominal 427
"Which" and "who" in A.V. and R.V. 273 *a*
Wife (?) ellipsis of the word 217

This Index extends from 1886 *to* 2799. *Before numbers with* * *supply* 1, *e.g.* [1]999*; *before others*, 2, *e.g.* [2]000.

INDICES TO "JOHANNINE GRAMMAR"

"Will of God, the," parall. to "the word of God" **799** (iii)
"With "="in the sight of" or "in the house of" **355**; ambig. **363**, **799** (ii); "questioning w." **349**
Witnesses, "two" and "three" **588**; "three" **306**
Witnessing **383–4**
Wonder, in bad sense **338**
Word, "the word," "the word of God," "my word" etc. **799** (iii)

Worshipping **019**
"Would"="was minded to" **471**; "would not," how expr. **463**; "would have liked" **472**, **498**

Year, the agricultural, how divided by the Jews **230** (iii); "forty and six years" an error **021–4**

This Index extends from **1886** *to* **2799**. *Before numbers with * supply* **1**, *e.g.* [1]999*; *before others*, **2**, *e.g.* [2]000.

INDICES TO "JOHANNINE GRAMMAR"

III. WORDS (GREEK)

[*This Index deals mainly with conjunctions, prepositions and pronouns. Nouns and verbs in it are regarded mainly in their grammatical and syntactical aspects and not so much with reference to their separate meanings—for which the reader is referred to Index III of "Johannine Vocabulary." If a word, e.g. ἀγαπάω, is occasionally mentioned in a non-grammatical aspect, it is because of a desire to supply some defect in "Johannine Vocabulary," e.g. the testimony of Origen to the difference between ἀγαπάω and φιλέω (2584 c).*]

'Α- privative expr. by οὐ 143, 248, 256
'Αββά 679
ἀγαλλιάομαι: w. ἵνα 097, 688–9; -αθῆναι v. r. -ασθῆναι 655 a; active form of 689 i
ἀγαπάω: aor. 323, 515 b; aor. and perf. 443; perf. 476–7; ἡ ἀγάπη ἣν ἠγάπησάς με 014; Origen on ἀ. and φιλέω 584 c
ἀγάπη 581; rarely w. objective genitive 033 foll.; ἡ ἀ., in Jn, "the love of God revealed to men" 035
ἀγοράζω: ἀγοράσωμεν in Mk and Jn 428 a, 512, 745–6
ἀγρός: εἰς ἀγρόν 711 b
ἄγω: ἄγωμεν 428
ἀδελφός: τοῖς ἀ. μου 307 b
-αι interchanged w. -ε 428 b, 514 a, 658 e
αἷμα and αἵματα 268
αἰτέομαι, s. αἰτέω
αἰτέω: pres. and aor. subjunct. 516; ἀ. and αἰτέομαι 536; ἀ., αἰτέομαι, and ἐρωτάω 630 f foll.; προσεύχεσθε καὶ αἰτεῖσθε 536 a; αἰτήσασθε imper. or infin. 514 a

αἰτία, ἡ 295 b
αἰών: εἰς τὸν ἀ. 312; οὐ (or μή)...εἰς τὸν ἀ. 263 e–g
ἀκοαί= "ears" 709 a
ἀκούω: aor. and perf. 450–2; fut. act. 660 c–d; w. accus. and w. gen. 586
ἀληθεινος in Codex B 654
ἀλλά: =contrariety, "not this but that, or, something more" 055–7; = difference, "nevertheless" 058–9; in special passages 060–2; ἀλλ' ἵνα 063–4, 105–12, 387, in the Synoptists 111; ἀλλ' οὐχὶ πάντες 265 (i); οὐκ... ἀλλά 593; οὐ followed by καί instead of ἀλλά 598; οὔτε...ἀλλά in Papyri 683 a, b
ἀλλήλων: μετὰ ἀ. 349
ἅλλομαι 314–6
ἄλλος: ἄλλος ἐστιν 972*, 675 foll., 730; ἄλλος and δι' ἄλλον in Epict. 791 foll., 297 e; ἄλλα πολλά 335 a; ἄλλος and ἕτερος 675–7
ἀμὴν ἀμήν 611 a, b
ἄν: its omission 079, 213 a, 698; its position 566, before a pause[1] 739 c;

---

[1] To the instances of ἄν at the end of a sentence add Lucian *Hermotim*. § 24 (i. 762) ἴσως γὰρ ἂν αὐτὰ ἤδη ἀμφὶ τὰ προάστεια καὶ πρὸς ταῖς πύλαις ἦν ἄν.

This Index extends from 1886 *to* 2799. *Before numbers with* * *supply* 1, *e.g.* [1]999*; *before others*, 2, *e.g.* [2]000.

INDICES TO "JOHANNINE GRAMMAR"

ὅστις ἄν, ὃ ἄν (or ἐάν) etc. 516 ; ὥστε ἄν...θέλω 697 c ; ἄν and ἐάν interchanged 739 ; ἄν "if," only in Jn 739 ; s. also ἐάν
ἀνά 281–3
ἀναβαίνω 264 a, 265 ; with ἑορτή 264–5, 771 ; quoted as πορεύομαι 489 a
ἀνήρ: applied to Christ 371, 722 b, c ; distinct from ἄνθρωπος 009, 571 ; θέλημα ἀνδρός 269 ; ἰδού ἀνήρ in Zech. 662 a
ἄνθρωπος 386 b ; emphatic 412 a ; how used in Jn 934* ; ὁ ἄ. 959–61* ; ὁ ἄ. in Epict. 960 c* ; ἄ. contrasted w. λόγος 277, distinct from ἀνήρ 009, 571 ; οὐκ ἄ. or ἄ. οὐ in LXX 586 d
ἀνίστημι in repetition 609 a
ἀντί 284–7
ἀντλέω 281 foll.
ἄνωθεν 903–8*, 403, 573, 734 d
ἀπάρτι, s. ἄρτι
ἀπέρχομαι : w. ἐν 334 d ; ἀπελήλυθεν and ἀπῆλθεν 753 a foll.
ἀπό : transposed 288 ; ambig. 215 b, 291 ; ἀπό and ἐκ meaning "[some] of" 213–5, denoting domicile and birthplace 289–93, interchanged in LXX 293 a, w. λαλέω 293 b, 586 a ; ἀπό, ἐκ, and παρά, w. ἐξέρχομαι 326–8
ἀποθνήσκω : οὐκ ἀποθνήσκει 486 ; ὁ ἀποθνήσκων "he that is under sentence of death " 530 ; ἵνα μή ἀποθνήσκῃ v.r. for ἀποθάνῃ 530
ἀποκρίνομαι: ἀποκριθείς 271 ; ἀπεκρίνατο and ἀπεκρίθη 537 ; ἀπεκρίθη ('Ιησ.) καὶ εἶπεν 611 a–c ; ἀπεκρίθη w. Ἰησ. (not w. ὁ Ἰησ.) 968*
ἀπολύω : κατὰ δὲ ἑορτὴν ἀπέλυεν 464 b
ἀποστέλλω : aor. and perf. 440, 453 ; ἀπεσταλμένος παρὰ θεοῦ contrasted w. ἦν πρὸς τὸν θεόν 277 ; ἀ. and ἐξαποστέλλω 753 b

ἀποτινάσσω : ἀποτινάσσετε and ἐκτινάξατε 437 a
ἀριθμός : τὸν ἀ., adv. accus. 009
ἄρτι and νῦν 915 (i)–(vi)*, 246
ἄρτος : ὁ ἄ. ὁ καταβαίνων and ὁ ἄ. ὁ καταβάς 504 ; ὁ ἄ. οὗτος and οὗτος ὁ ἄ. 553 c
ἀρχή : τὴν ἀρχὴν ὅτι καὶ λαλῶ ὑμῖν 154–6 ; ἀ. τῶν σημείων 386 (i) ; ἐξ ἀ. and ἀπ' ἀ. 254 a
ἀσθενέω : ἀσθενούντων, ambig. 930*
ἀστραπή 532 c
αὕτη s. οὗτος
αὐτός 374–80, meaning "God" 731, change from to ἐκεῖνος 302 ; αὐτοῦ etc. possessive, emphatic and non-emphatic 558, om. or rep. 395 ; αὐτοῦ ambig. 378–9 ; αὐτόν ins. and om. 537 (i) a ; αὐτὸς ὁ 931 a* ; αὐτὸς μόνος and μόνος αὐτός 724–6 ; αὐτὸς περὶ ἑαυτοῦ 723 ; ἐγώ εἰμι αὐτός 220, 221 a, 224, 699—700 ; δι' αὐτοῦ ambig. 302, 595 a ; αὐτοί ἐσμεν "we are by ourselves" 699 ; καὶ αὐτοὶ γάρ emph. 692 ; αὐτός v. r. αὐτό 727 ; αὐτοῖς [ὁ] Ἰησοῦς, why a doubtful reading 656 c

Βαΐα : τὰ β. τῶν φοινίκων 047
βαπτίζω : w. εἰς 706 a
βασιλεία : εἰσελθεῖν εἰς, or ἰδεῖν, τὴν β. τοῦ θεοῦ 573
βασιλεύς : with and without article 966*, 669 ; σὺ λέγεις ὅτι β. εἰμι 245 a ; s. also 798–9
βασιλικός : ἐκ τῶν βασιλικῶν 215 b
βαστάζω : aor. and pres. infin. 497
Βηθανία : ἀπὸ Β. 290
Βηθλεέμ : ἀπὸ Β. 289
βῆμα 537 (ii) b
βλέπω : hist. pres. 482 ; βλέπετε, initial, imperat. 237[1]

---

[1] In 2237 it was said that "βλέπετε would naturally be imperative." In N.T., βλέπετε—except with relative or negative—is almost always (abt 20) initial and, when initial, alw. imperative (1 Cor. i. 26 being no exception). In Poet. Scen. βλέπετε is only in Eurip. Cyc. 211 (imperat.). Initial ὁρᾶτε in Poet. Scen., though possibly interrog., prob. always means "See!"—Aesch. Prom. 119 "See [me outraged because of my love for mankind]!," Ag. 1217 "See [these spectres]!," Soph. El. 1228–30 "See [Orestes restored to life]!" to which the Chorus replies "We do see," Oed. Col. 871—2 "See [these insults]!" to which Oedipus replies, "They do see," Ant. 806 "See [me led away to death]!," Eurip. Fragm. Alcm. 11 "See [the tyrant in exile]!" In Aristoph., too, ὁρᾶτε initial, or after a pause, is almost alw. imperative, or may be so taken. In N.T., ὁρᾶτε is alw. imperat. exc. perh. in Jas ii. 24 ὁρᾶτε ὅτι (after βλέπεις ὅτι) R.V. "ye see that"; and, even there—in view of Epictet. iii. 13. 9 ὁρᾶτε γὰρ ὅτι, "videte enim" and the frequency

This Index extends from **1886** *to* **2799**. *Before numbers with* * *supply* **1**, *e.g.* [1]999* ; *before others*, **2**, *e.g.* [2]000.

Γαζοφυλάκιον: ἐν τῷ γ. and κατέναντι τοῦ γ. 333-4
γάρ: Synoptic and Johannine use 065-6; sometimes an indication of evangelistic origin 066 *b*; in special passages 067-8, 683; καὶ γάρ 167, comp. 692; οὐ γάρ, not interrogative in Jn 683; various ellipses before 683 *a*
γεμίζω: w. ἐκ 329 (i)
γέμω: w. ἐκ 329 *a*
γεννάομαι 904-8*, 573
γεύομαι: w. accus. 016-18; γ. θανάτου 576
γῆ: εἰς τὴν Ἰουδαίαν γῆν 670 *b*; γῆ Ἰούδα 670 *b*
γίνομαι: ἐγένετο contrasted w. ἦν 277, 596-7; γέγονα 396 *b*, 478 *b*; γέγονεν ἵνα 478 *a*; γέγονα and ἐγενόμην 440; γέγονας 758; γενάμεναι 472 *b*
γινώσκω: aor. and perf. indic. 448, 511 *a*; aor. and pres. subjunct. 511; ἔγνων 328, 511 *a*, 582; ἔγνων = "I knew [at once]" 443 *c*; γινώσκετε ambig. 243, 491, 760; γινώσκετε combined w. ἑωράκατε 491; γ. and οἶδα 491, 757 *d*, 763; γνῶθι σαυτόν and τὸ ἑαυτὸν γινώσκειν 763
γνωρίζω: aor. 447
Γολγοθά 738
γράμμα: πηλίκοις γράμμασιν 691 *d*-*e*, 785-90
γράφω: ἐπ' αὐτῷ γεγραμμένα 339; δ γέγραφα γέγραφα 473; ἔγραψα in letters 691 *a* foll., 785-90
γυνή: w. article 948 *a**; ? ellipsis of γ. or θυγάτηρ 217

Δέ: consecutive or adversative 069-73; third word, or later, in its clause 074-6; denoting antithesis 209; introducing parenthesis 633 *b*; in doubtful connexion 636; a δέ-clause before an οὖν-clause 634; w. ἔλεγεν 468; w. pluperf. 480; καί...δέ 076; μέν...δέ 077; μέν ends Thucyd. iii. 116 foll. by δέ *ib.* iv. 1 638; s. also 635 (i) *a*
δεῖ: ἔδει 272 *a*, 635 (i) *a*; δει written δι, confusable with δι' (prep.) 428 *c*
δεκάς 283 *c*

διά: w. accus. of pers. 294—300, 705; w. gen. of pers. 301-4; w. gen. of time 331 *c* foll., 715; δι' ὅν...καὶ δι' οὗ 294; οὐ διὰ τοῦ θεοῦ ἀλλὰ παρ' αὐτοῦ 296 *a*; διὰ τί; 231 *c*; διὰ τοῦτο 387 foll.; (?) δι' ὑμᾶς 428 *c*; διὰ σοῦ for διὰ σέ 729 *a*
διασπορά: ἡ δ. τῶν Ἑλλήνων 046
διδάσκαλος: w. article 966*, 195, ? vocatively used 680
δίδωμι: aor. and perf. 454-5; imperf. 465 *b*; pres. and perf. in LXX 444; ὃ δέδωκάς μοι 422; πᾶν ὃ δέδωκας 740-4; ἔδωκεν, v. r. for δέδωκεν 687 *c*; late forms of, *e.g.* ἔδωσα 690; δός, v.r. in ch. xvii. 740
διώκω: ὁ διώκων "the prosecutor" 537
δοκέω: aor. and imperf. 464 *a*; μὴ δοκεῖτε 235 *a*; τί δοκεῖ ὑμῖν and τί δοκεῖτε 766 (i) *a*
δοξάζω: aor. 441; various meanings of ἐδοξάσθη 446
δοῦλος 263 *g*, 584 *b*
δραχμαί om., *e.g.* ἀραβῶνα (δ.) ἡ "eight [drachmae] as earnest money" 729
δύναμαι: w. aor. and pres. infin. 496, 767; δύναται ἁρπάζειν and ἁρπάσει 767; δ. ins. by LXX = Heb. interrog. 767
δύο 281-3

E, θ, ο and c interchanged in B 650-2
-ε interchanged w. -αι 428 *b*, 658 *e*
ἐάν or ἄν: w. aor. and pres. subjunct. 511, 513-5; w. indic. in 1 Jn 515 (i), comp. 771; ἐὰν μή 521-3, w. pres. subjunct. in connexion w. the hour of trial 523 *a*; ἐάν τις 580; ἐάν and τις separated 552 *c*; καὶ ἐάν 158-9; ἄν τινων κρατῆτε 517-20; ἐὰν οὖν θεωρῆτε 210-12; ὅστις ἐάν ambig. 414-6; ὅστις ἄν, ὃ ἄν (or ἐάν) etc. 516, 660 *b*; ἄν and ἐάν interchanged 739; ἐάν for ἄν in Papyri 416 *a*
ἑαυτοῦ: ἐν ἑαυτῷ, -οῖς, how used in Jn 039; πρὸς ἑαυτούς 366 *c*; αὐτὸς περὶ ἑαυτοῦ 723
ἐγγύς 909*
ἐγείρω: προφήτης οὐκ ἐγείρεται 492

---

of ὅρα ὅτι in Epictet., as well as i. 3. 9 ὁρᾶτε οὖν καὶ προσέχετε—the meaning may be "*see* [*and note*] that." These facts bear on 2762 *a*, which rendered *Il.* i. 120 λεύσσετε imperatively, though rendered in Monro's *Hom. Gramm.* p. 190 "*ye see.*" The scholiast says, "ὁρᾶτε, βλέπετε," perh. intending not only to explain the poetic λεύσσετε by a prose word, but also to shew that it was imperative, like initial ὁρᾶτε and βλέπετε.

This Index extends from 1886 *to* 2799. *Before numbers with* * *supply* 1, *e.g.* [1]999*; *before others*, 2, *e.g.* [2]000.

INDICES TO "JOHANNINE GRAMMAR"

ἐγώ 401; ἐγώ εἰμι 220 foll.; ἐγώ εἰμι αὐτός 221 a, 224, 699 foll.; ὅπου ὑπάγω and ὅπου ἐγὼ ὑπάγω 578; λέγω om. after ἐγώ 658 b, 660; ἐμοῦ, not in N.T. without (1) prepos. (2) antith. or parall. (3) v.r. 566 c; μου emph. and non-emph. 559, 776 foll.; μου, v.r. for μοι 563; μου and σου confused 768; με ταῦτα for μετὰ ταῦτα 659; s. also ἡμεῖς

ἐθέλω, s. θέλω

εἰ: written ι 659 e, comp. 428 c, 515 (i) e, 650 a, 654 b, 798 e; corresponding to ἄν, in words of the Lord 078–9; εἰ w. fut. 514 (i) a, w. optat. 514 (i) b; εἰ οὐ 256; εἰ δὲ μή 080–6, in LXX foll. imperat. 080

εἶδον: ἰδεῖν "to experience" 576 e; ἰδεῖν τὴν βασιλείαν and εἰσελθεῖν εἰς τὴν β. 573; τεθέαμαι...ἐφ' ὃν ἂν ἴδῃς...ἑώρακα 572; ἴδη and ειδη confused 515 (i) e, 798 e¹

εἶδος θεοῦ 765 a

εἰμί: ἐγώ εἰμι 220 foll.; ἐγώ εἰμι αὐτός 224, 699—700; ὅπου εἰμί (v.r. εἶμι) ἐγώ and ὅπου ἐγὼ ὑπάγω 190 a, 487 a; πόθεν εἶ σύ 733–7; ellipsis of ἐστί 229–30 (i); ἐστί w. particip. 971–81*; εἰσὶν οἵ 971 c *; ἦν, contrasted w. ἐγένετο 277, 596–7; ἦν w. pres. particip. 277; ὅτι ἐστίν and ὅτι ἦν after εἶδον 466 (i); ὁ ὤν in various phrases 938 *, 964 *, 275, 308, 358, 711 foll.; ὁ...οὐκ ὤν 704; ὤν referring to the past 274; ἵνα ὦσιν, seven times repeated in the Last Prayer 529 a; forms of εἰμί emphasized 972 *, 979 a–d *, 553 b, 555 a, 579; repeated for emphasis 606², ἐὰν σὺ ἦσθα 515 (i); ἦς and ἦσθα 515 (i) b; Phrynichus on the spelling of ης 772–5; ἔσσι 711

εἶμι: not used in N.T. 171 d, v.r. for εἰμί 190 a, 487 a; εἰς Κόπτον εἶμι 711; (?) εἶσι spelt εσσι 711

εἶπον 456; ὃν εἶπον v.r. ὁ εἰπών 925 a *, 507 a; εἶπε, differently used by Lk. and Jn 456 a; εἶπεν and ἔλεγεν 469; εἰρήκει 481; τί εἴπω; τί σ' εἴπω; 512 b; εἶπόν and εἰπέ 658 c; εἶπον ἂν ὑμῖν ὅτι 083–6, 186; εἶπον with and without ὅτι 189 foll.; εἴρηχεν, in Pap., = εἶπεν 683 a, b

εἰρήνη: ἐ. τὴν ἐμὴν 609 b

εἰς: without verb of motion 305–9, 706 foll.; "to" or "into" 310–11; εἰς ζωὴν αἰώνιον 312–6; ὄψονται εἰς 317–8; εἰς τέλος 319–23; περιπατέω εἰς 342 h; πιστεύω εἰς 506 (and s. πιστεύω); ὁ ὢν εἰς τὸν κόλπον 308–9, 706, 711 foll.; εἰς and ἐπί 310, 316 b; ἔστη εἰς v.r. ἐπί 307 a; εἰς τό in St Paul's Epistles 689 j; λέγω εἰς implying publicity 709

εἷς: used with dative 118 b; εἷς καθ' εἷς 348; εἷς [ἐκ] 586 a; εν "one" in juxtaposition with εν "in" 118 b; ουδε εν or ουδεν 660

εἰσέρχομαι: εἰσελθοῦσαι 311; ἐ. εἰς, or ἰδεῖν, τὴν βασιλείαν τοῦ θεοῦ 573

εἶτα, see below³

εἰώθα: εἰώθει parall. to imperf. 464 b

ἐκ: "from" or " (some) of" 042, 213–5; "native of" (but ἀπό "resident in") 289–93; ἐκ and ἀπό in LXX 293 a; ἐκ and ἀπό w. λαλέω 293 b, 586 a; ἐκ w. ἐξέρχομαι 326–8, w. πληρόω 329, w. γεμίζω 329 (i), w. σώζω and τηρέω 325; ἐξ ἡμῶν 110 a–b, 263 c foll.; ἐκ μέτρου 324, 714

ἐκεῖ ἡ conf. w. ἐκείνη 687 d

ἐκεῖνος 381–5, 729; emph., change to from αὐτός 302; contemptuous 732; meaning "HE" 132 b, 382, 731; ἐκεῖνη conf. w. ἐκεῖ ἡ 687 d; κἀκεῖνος 150–1

ἐκκεντέω 317 h

ἐκλέγομαι: aor. 441, and see esp. 441 b foll.

ἐκλεκτός: v.r. for υἱός 386 a

ἐκμάσσω: ἡ ἐκμάξασα 276

ἔκμετρος 324 d

---

¹ For ἴδε, see *Joh. Voc.*, where it should have been added that ἴδε, foll. by nom. without verb, is pec. to Mk and Jn.

² Comp. Epict. i. 14. 13—14 μέμνησθε μηδέποτε λέγειν ὅτι μόνοι ἐστέ· οὐ γὰρ ἐστέ. ἀλλ' ὁ Θεὸς ἔνδον ἐστί, καὶ ὁ ὑμέτερος Δαίμων ἐστί.

³ εἶτα occurs Mk (2), Mt. (o), Lk. (1), Jn (3), comp. Mk iv. 28 εἶτεν (*bis*). In canon. LXX, εἶτα occurs only in Job (12, with v.r.), Prov. (2). It is one of several points in common between the style of Job and Mk. In N.T. (outside Gospels) it is only in 1 Cor. xv. 5 (txt), 7 (txt), 24, 1 Tim. ii. 13, iii. 10, Heb. xii. 9, Jas i. 15.

This Index extends from 1886 *to* 2799. *Before numbers with* * *supply* 1, *e.g.* [1]999 *; *before others*, 2, *e.g.* [2]000.

WORDS (GREEK)

ἐκνεύω : ἐξένευσεν, v.r. ἔνευσεν 541
ἐκτινάσσω: ἀποτινάσσετε and ἐκτινάξατε 437 a
ελαιων : how accented 673
Ἕλληνες : ἡ διασπορά τῶν Ἑ. 046
ἐλπίζω: imperf. 472 b, 474; ἠλπίζαμεν 472 b; perf. 442, 474
ἐμβλέπω : twofold use of ἐμβλέψας 649
ἐμός : ὁ ἐμός...and ὁ...ὁ ἐμός 987–9*; ὁ ἐμός, ἡ ἐμή etc. emphatic 559, 581
ἔμπροσθεν 896*, 330
ἐν : temporal 025–6, 331, om. by B 661, ins. and om. before ἡμέρᾳ, ἑορτῇ, and σαββάτῳ 715 b–d; instrumental and quasi-instrumental 332; = "into" 334 c, d; ἐν τούτῳ 332, 392; ἐν τῷ γαζοφυλακίῳ 333–4
ἕνεκα 300
ἐντέλλομαι 742 a
ἐντολὴ καινή...ὁ 412
ἐνώπιον 335
ἐξ 281–3
ἐξεραυνάω 439 (i) a
ἐξέρχομαι 263 c foll., w. ἀπό, ἐκ, and παρά 326–8; aor. 457; ἐξῆλθον ambig. 110 a–b
ἐξουσία 798–9
ἑορτή : w. article 951*; ἀναβαίνω εἰς ἑ. 264–5; κατὰ δὲ ἑορτὴν 464 c; ἐν ins. and om. before 715 d, comp. 771
ἐπαίρω τοὺς ὀφθαλμούς 616–7
ἐπεί and ἐπειδή 087–8
ἐπερωτάω and ἐρωτάω 577
ἐπί : w. accus. 336, 342 d, i; w. dat. 337–9; w. gen. 340–7; ἐπί and εἰς 307 a, 310, 316 b; ἐπὶ τούτῳ 338; ἐπὶ τὴν θάλασσαν and ἐπὶ τῆς θαλάσσης 340–6; ἔστη ἐπί 336; ἐπ' αὐτῷ γεγραμμένα 339; ἐπιγραφὴ ἐπ' αὐτῷ 339; ἐπὶ τοῦ σταυροῦ 347
ἐπιβάλλω χεῖρας 575 a
ἐπιβλέπω : ἐπιβλέψονται πρός με 317 c
ἐπιγινώσκω 511 a
ἐπιγραφὴ ἐπ' αὐτῷ 339
ἐπιεικῶς 233 a
ἐπικαθίζω : ἐπεκάθισεν v.r. ἐκάθισεν 756 a
ἐπιτίθεμαι : how used by Origen 412 a
ἐραυνάω : of "searching" the Scriptures 439 (i); ἐραυνᾶτε ambig. ib.
ἐργάζομαι 226 b; ἐργάζεσθαι v.r. -θε 428 b
ἔρχομαι : aor. and perf. 326, 457; aor. and pres. 490; hist. pres. 482; ἤρχοντο 465; ἦλθαν 472 b; ἦλθεν and ἤθελον 342 d, 346, 717 e; ἐρχόμενος and ὁ ἐρχόμενος 940*, 277, 553 d; ὁ ὀπίσω μου ἐρχόμενος 507; ἐρχόμενον (neut. or masc.) εἰς τὸν κόσμον ambig. 277,

508; ἕως ἔρχομαι 089; ἔρχεται...καὶ ἐλήλυθεν 604 a, 625 e; ἔρχεται...καὶ νῦν ἐστίν 799 (i); s. also εἰς 310–11
ἐρωτάω 498, 630; ἐ., αἰτέομαι, and αἰτέω 630 f–h; ἐ. and ἐπερωτάω 577; ἐ. in Alexandrian Gk 630 d; (?) ερωτα υπερ ημων in Christian tombstone 630 i
ἑταῖροι in Aquila = φιλοῦντες in LXX 584 c
ἕτερος : ἕτερος and ἄλλος 675–7; πολλά... καὶ ἕτερα 335 a
ἔτι : ἔ. μικρόν 230 (i); ἔ. τετράμηνός ἐστιν 230 (ii) foll.
ἔτος : ἔτεσιν, dat. pl. of duration, when used 021
εὐθέως, εὐθύ, and εὐθύς 910–15*
εὑρίσκω : hist. pres. 482; εὑρών om. in xii. 14 756
εὐχαριστέω 614 c
ἐφάλλομαι 315
ἔχω : ἔχεις τι; 235 b foll.
ἕως (conj.) 089; (?) ὡς for ἕως 201, 696; ἕως ἔρχομαι 089

Ζάω : w. διά and accus. of pers. 297, 705; w. πρός and accus. of pers. 366; σοὶ ζῶ, ἤτοι διὰ σέ 297 c
ζητέω 375 a, 398; w. infin. 575, 727; first use of in LXX 649 b; forms of 748
ζήτησις 349, 350 a
ζωή : εἰς ζωὴν αἰώνιον 312–6

Ἡ 090–1; after negative (οὐ...καὶ and οὐ...ἤ) 549 a, 759; omitted 628 a
ἡ τοῦ Ἀ. ? the [wife, or, daughter] of A. 217
ἡμεῖς : perh. applied to Christ 428 b; how used in 1 Jn 399 c; ἡ. πάντες 287; ἡμῶν and ὑμῶν in v.r. 428 c
ἡμέρα : τρίτῃ ἡμέρᾳ, διὰ τριῶν ἡμερῶν, ἐν τρισὶν ἡμέραις etc. 331; καθ' ἡμέραν, inserted by Lk. 515; ἐν ins. and om. before 715 b–d
ἤπερ 092, 685
Ἡρώδης 737 a

Θ, Ε, Ο and C interchanged in B 650–2
θάλασσα : ἐπὶ τὴν θ., ἐπὶ τῆς θ., and παρὰ τὴν θ. 340–6, 354, and see specially 341 and 344
θάνατος : w. γεύομαι, θεωρέω, and ἰδεῖν 576
θᾶσσον 918 a*
θεάομαι : twice applied to Christ 617 a; τεθεάμεθα 473; τεθέαμαι...ἐφ' ὃν ἂν ἴδῃς...ἑώρακα 572

This Index extends from **1886** *to* **2799.** *Before numbers with* * *supply* **1**, *e.g.* [1]999*; *before others*, **2**, *e.g.* [2]000.

θέλημα ἀνδρός and θ. σαρκός 269; θ. τ. θεοῦ parall. to λόγος τ. θεοῦ 799 (iii)
θέλω: ἤθελεν of unfulfilled desire 716–7; (?) ηθελεν, ηθελον and ηλθεν 342 d, 346, 716–7; ἤθελεν and ἠθέλησεν 471–2, 716–7; w. accus. and infin. 495; ἔθελες 717 b
θεός: the distinction between θεός and ὁ θεός 594 a; παρὰ θεῷ 027, 355; ὁ ὢν παρὰ [τοῦ] θεοῦ 358; εἶδος θεοῦ 765 a
θεωρέω 210–12, 318, 576, 739 b; θεωρεῖτε ambig. 439 (ii)
θυγάτηρ: (?) ellipsis of θ. in the phrase ἡ τοῦ 'A. 217

I: sometimes written ει, and ει written ι 659 e, comp. 428 c, 515 (i) e, 650 a, 654 b, 798 e
ἰδεῖν, ἰδών etc., s. εἶδον
ἰδίαν: κατ' ἰδίαν 348
ἴδιος: τὸν ἀδελφὸν τὸν ἴδιον 985–6*; ἐκ τῶν ἰδίων 378, 728; οἱ ἴδιοι 570 a–b
ἰδού 246
Ἱεροσόλυμα w. article 670
Ἰησοῦς: with and without article 968*; in B written IC, liable to confusion 661 c; Ἰησοῦν (ΙΝ) and Κύριον (ΚΝ) confused 662 b; αὐτοῖς [ὁ] Ἰησοῦς, why a doubtful reading 656 c
ἱμάτιον: sing. and pl. 270; in ellipsis 216 b
ἵνα: freq. in Jn 686; expresses or implies purpose 093–6; special passages 097—103; ἵνα and subjunct. compared w. infin. 104, 495; ἵνα w. indic. 114, 690; w. aor. and pres. subjunct. 511, 524–30; omission of principal vb before ἵνα 105–12; dependent on vb implied in question 113; its connexion 115; ἵνα...ἵνα 116–21; ἀλλ' ἵνα 063–4, 105–12; ἠγαλλιάσατο ἵνα ἴδῃ 097, 100, 688–9; ἵνα τί; not used in Jn 231 c; οὕτως... ἵνα 697; ἵνα εἰδῇς "to tell you the plain truth" 729 a; ἔρχεται ὥρα...ἵνα 799 (i)
Ἰουδαῖος: οἱ Ἰουδαῖοι 941* foll.; πολλοὶ ἐκ τῶν 'I. 941–2*; εἰς τὴν Ἰουδαίαν γῆν 670 b
ἵστημι: ἔστη εἰς (v.r. ἐπί) 307 a; στῆναι εἰς τὸ μέσον 710; ἑστῶτα, of God 307 d
ἰσχυρότερός μου in Synoptists 667, 799 a
ΙΧΘΥΣ 703
Ἰωάνης with and without article 968 c*
Ἰωσήφ with and without article 970*

Κἀγώ: in crasis 150; after καθώς 123–7
καθαρός in Jn, and καθάριος in Epictet. connected with ὁ λόγος 799 (iii)
κάθημαι: forms of 751; καθημένου εἰς 707
καθίζω: trans. and intrans. use 537 (i)–(ii); ἐκάθισεν εἰς 707; ἐκάθισεν v.r. ἐπεκάθισεν 756 a; τὸ ὄνον (sic) καθίσαι 756 a
καθώς: suspensive 122, followed by κἀγώ or καί in apodosis 123–7; supplementary 128–32; ἵνα...καθὼς... ἵνα 117–8
καί: in narrative (Hebraic) 133–4; connecting affirmation and negation 135; meaning "and yet," "but," 136–45, 265 (i) b, 439 (iii); parall. to μέντοι 137; exclamatory 146; meaning "[indeed] and" 157; meaning "also" 147, 152–6; in apodosis 123–7, 148; in crasis 150; omitted between two adjectives 168; καὶ ὑμεῖς 149; κἀγώ 123–7; κἀκεῖνος 151, 383; κἄν 160; καὶ γάρ 167 (comp. 692); καὶ ἐάν 158–9; καὶ νῦν, varies in meaning 915 (iii); καὶ...δέ 076; καί...καί 161–6; οὐ...καί instead of οὐ...ἀλλά 598; τὴν ἀρχὴν ὅτι καὶ λαλῶ ὑμῖν 154–6; written ΚΕ and confused with ΚΕ i.e. κύριε 657 d; οὐ...καί and οὐ...ἤ 549 e, 759; καί and ἤ interchanged 759 a foll.
καινός: ἐντολὴν καινήν 894 b*; ἐντολὴν καινήν...δ 412
καιόμενος 275 b
κἀκεῖνος 151, 383
καλέω and λέγω 468 b; καλέω foll. by accus. and voc. 680 b
καλῶς ποιήσεις 729 a
κἄν 160
κατά 348; εἰς καθ' εἷς 348; κατ' ἰδίαν 348; κατὰ δὲ ἑορτήν 464 c
κατάγνυμι: ἵνα κατεαγῶσιν αὐτῶν τὰ σκέλη 267, 419
κατάθεσις: inscr. on Christian tombstone 630 i
καταλαμβάνω 596
κατευθύνω 033 b
Κεδρων: how accented 671–4
κλάδος 047
κλάσματα 329 (i)
κλίνω κεφαλήν 644 (i), 713
κοιμάομαι: double meaning of 586 c
κόκκος: w. article 948*
κόλπος: ὁ ὢν εἰς τὸν κ. τοῦ πατρός 308, 706 foll.

This Index extends from **1886** *to* **2799**. *Before numbers with* * *supply* **1**, *e.g.* [1]999*; *before others*, 2, *e.g.* [2]000.

κομίζομαι 230 (i) a
κόπτω : κόψονται 317 c foll., v.r. ὄψονται 317 d
Κόρινθος : πλοῦς εἰς Κ.¹ 263
κόφινος 329 (i)
κόσμος 508 c ; ὁ κ. οὗτος and οὗτος ὁ κ. 553 c ; in connexion with χωρεῖν 414 b ; ἐρχόμενον εἰς τὸν κ. 508
κράβαττος 206 b
κράζω : thrice applied to Christ 618 ; κέκραγε 479
Κρανίου Τόπον ὃ λέγεται...Γολγοθά 738
κρατέω : how used in the Gospels 517 a foll. ; ἄν τινων κρατῆτε 517–20
κρίμα or κρίσις 799 f
κρίνω : κέκρικα, how used 473 ; κέκριται 695 ; κρίνει, unaccented, fut. or pres. 960 a *
κρύπτω : the meaning of ἐκρύβη as applied to Jesus 538–43, 724
κτίζω : ἐκτίσθη and ἔκτισται 440 ; forms of 747
κύριος : ὁ κύριός μου 049, 679 foll. ; παρὰ κυρίου 356 ; κύριε 680 foll., ins. or om. 565 a ; written κε and confusable w. καί (κε) 657 d ; κύριον (κν) confused w. Ἰησοῦν (ιν) 662 b ; used by Epict. in a bad sense 799 d
κώμη 746 a

Λαλέω and λαλιά 251 ; λαλέω w. ἐκ and ἀπό 293 b, 586 a ; ἐκ τῶν ἰδίων λαλεῖ 728 ; ταῦτα λελάληκα ὑμῖν, seven times repeated 625
λαμβάνω : ἔλαβον and παρέλαβον 570 ; λήμψεται and λαμβάνει 488, 583
λαοί (pl.) "peoples," used of the Jews 317 h
λέγω : imperf. 467–70 ; ἔλεγεν and εἶπεν 469 ; λέγω and καλέω 468 b ; σὺ λέγεις and ὑμεῖς λέγετε 234 b, 245 ; ὅταν λέγωσιν 531 ; λέγω om. after ἐγώ 658 b, 660
λίθος 396–7
λόγος : distinct from λαλιά 251 ; ὁ λόγος ἦν foll. by ἐγένετο ἄνθρωπος 277 ; ὁ λόγος in Christ's words (1) in the Synoptists and (2) in Jn 799 (iii) (1) and (2) ; ὁ λόγος μου, τ. θεοῦ, ὁ σός etc. in Jn 799 (iii) 2 ; λόγοι (pl.), in Christ's words, only once in Jn 580

λούω : w. εἰς 305 a
λύχνος : w. article 948 b * ; ὁ λ. ὁ καιόμενος 275 b

Μαθητής 545 c
μακάριος : μακάριοί ἐστε ὅταν 499 b
μᾶλλον 733 a, w. ἤ and w. ἤπερ 092
Μάρθα : τὰς περὶ Μάρθαν, v.r. for Μάρθαν 990*, 360
Μαρία and Μαριάμ 586 b
μαρτυρέω : perf. 473 ; μαρτυρεῖς σαυτῷ 514 (i) e ; ἄλλος...ὁ μαρτυρῶν 730
μαρτυρία 383
μάχαιρα : ἐν μαχαίρῃ 332 a
μέν 169–70 ; μὲν...δέ 077, in Mt.-Lk., where not in Mk-Jn 998 * ; μέν ends Thucyd. iii. 116 foll. by δέ ib. iv. 1 638 ; μὲν οὖν 335 a
μέντοι 170, parall. w. καί 137
μένω 263 e–f, 312, 313 a ; aor. and imperf. 458 ; ἔμεινα 458 ; μένετε ambig. 915 (iii) * b ; μένετε and μείνατε 437 a–e ; μένει and μενεῖ 762 a ; ἐὰν μὴ μένητε and ἐὰν μείνητε 523 ; μ. μετά 352
μετά : w. accus. 349 ; w. gen. 349–53 ; μ. τοῦτο and μ. ταῦτα 349 a, 394 ; μ. Ἰουδαίου 349–50 ; οἱ μ. αὐτοῦ ὄντες 351 ; μένω μ. 352 ; μετά τινος compared w. παρά τινι 352–3, and σύν τινι 799 (ii)
μεσονύκτιον 678
μέσος : στῆναι εἰς τὸ μέσον and στῆναι ἐν μέσῳ 710
μετανοέω : pres. and aor. subjunct. 521–2
μεταξύ 668
μετρητής 281–3
μέτρον, μέτρῳ, ἐν μέτρῳ, ἐκ μέτρου 324, 714
μή (interrog.) 235 ; μή τι or μήτι 701–2
μή (neg.) : encroaches on οὐ 253–4 ; implies imperat. 208–9 ; w. particip. 499 b ; w. πᾶς 260 foll. ; ὅτι μή 187, 695 ; οὐ μή 255
μικρόν : ἔτι μικρόν 230 (i) foll.
μισέω : aor. and perf. 443, 475
μισθός 287 b
μονογενής 938*, 964*, 308
μόνον (adv.) 664 b
μόνος : applied to God 895*, 664, comp. 168 ; μόνους inserted paraphrastically

---

¹ Lucian *Hermotim*. § 27 foll. (i. 767) takes Corinth as the ideal city to which all the seekers of truth are journeying.

This Index extends from 1886 *to* 2799. *Before numbers with* * *supply* 1, *e.g.* [1]999*; *before others*, 2, *e.g.* [2]000.

INDICES TO "JOHANNINE GRAMMAR"

762 b; αὐτὸς μόνος and μόνος αὐτός 375, 724–6

N dropped or inserted, εκεῖη confused w. εκειη 687 d
Ναζαρέτ: τὸν ἀπὸ Ν. 289
νῦν and ἄρτι 915 (i)–(vi)*, 246; καὶ νῦν varies in meaning 915 (iii)*; καὶ τὰ νῦν 915 (i) c*

Ο, ε, θ, and c interchanged in Β 650–2
ο and ω interchanged in MSS. 928 a*, 114, 691
ὁ and ὄν, v.r. 925* foll.
ὁ, ἡ, τό: see Index II "Article"
ὁ δέ 684
οἶδα: οἶδα and γινώσκω 491, 757 d, 763; οἴδαμεν "we know" (?) οἶδα μέν 429–35; καὶ ἐκεῖνος οἶδεν 384 b, 731; ἐὰν οἴδαμεν 515 (i); ἵνα εἰδῇς "to tell you the plain truth" 729 a; ειδη and ιδη confused 515 (i) e, 798 e
οἰκία, οἶκος: Mark's use of εἰς οἶκον or εἰς τὴν οἰκίαν 711 a
ὅλος and ὄχλος 753 e
ὄνομα: ἐν τῷ ὀ. σου ᾧ δέδωκάς μοι 408 (comp. 740–4); τογν[ομα], confusable w. τογν "the Son" 768–9
ὅπου 171–2; ὅπου εἰμί (v.r. εἶμι), ὅπου ὑπάγω, and ὅπου ἐγὼ ὑπάγω 190 a, 487 a, 578
ὅπως 173; ὅπως ἄν 693
ὁράω: perf. 475, ἑόρακεν and ἑώρακεν 651; τεθέαμαι...ἴδης...ἑώρακα 572; ἑωράκατε and γινώσκετε 491; ὄψονται εἰς 317; ὄψονται v.r. for κόψονται 317 d; ὁρᾶτε, after pause, mostly imperat. or interrog., see n. on p. 678.
ὀρθογραφία 790
ὀρθότερον: meaning of 775 b
ὁρίζω: forms of 748
ὅρος: w. article 962–3*
ὅς (demonstr.): ὅς δέ 380 b
ὅς (rel.): in attraction 405–7; ἐν τῷ ὀνόματί σου ᾧ δέδωκάς μοι 408–11; ἐντολὴν καινήν...ὅ 412; Κρανίου Τόπον ὃ λέγεται... 738; δι' ὅ, δι' οὗ, ὑφ' οὗ etc. 294–5; ὃς ἄν and ὃς ἐάν 739; v.r. οὕς, ὅ, ᾧ 740 foll., 744 c
ὅσος: ὅσα ἐάν 660 b
ὅστις 413; ὅ,τι ἄν (or ἐάν) 414, 516;

ἅτινα ἐὰν γράφηται 414–6; ὅστις ἄν 739
ὅταν: parall. to ᾗ ἂν ὥρᾳ 533 a; w. aor. and pres. subjunct. 511, 531–5; ὅταν λέγωσιν "in the moment when they are saying" 531, in Epict. "when, at any moment" 532 d¹
ὅτε 799 (i)
ὅτι: (1) suspensive and (2) explanatory 174–7; suspensive, a characteristic of Jn and Rev. 176, 236; in LXX 390 a; (?) "that" or "because" 181–6, 219; introducing (1) cause of action or (2) ground of statement 178–80; recitativum 189–90; not used interrogatively in Jn 231 c; ὅτι after vbs. of seeing 762 a; ὅτι v. r. τί ὅτι etc. in LXX 231 d foll.; ὅτι μή 187, 695; οὐχ ὅτι 188, 218–9; εἶδον ὅτι ἦν 466 (i); τὴν ἀρχὴν ὅτι καὶ λαλῶ ὑμῖν 154–6; ὅτι = ὥστε 694; οὕτως... ὅτι 697; τί ὅτι and τί ἔστιν ὅτι, for τί γέγονεν ὅτι 694; ὅτι...καὶ ὅτι 757 b
οὐ(κ) (interrog.) 231; οὐκοῦν 233–4; οὐ μή 232; οὐχί 231 (and see οὐχί below)
οὐ(κ) (neg.): encroached on by μή 253; v. r. for οὔπω 264–5; οὐ and οὐκέτι 583; οὐ μή w. fut. and subjunct. 255; εἰ οὐ 256; οὐ...μόνον 147 b; οὐ...οὐδείς 257; οὐ...οὐκέτι 257 a; οὐ combined w. πᾶς 260–3; οὐ followed by καί instead of ἀλλά 598; οὐ(κ)...ἀλλά 593; Xenophon uses οὐκ, ἀλλά, but Epictetus οὐ, ἀλλά 265 (i) c; οὐχί 265 (i); οὐ = ἀ- privative 143, 248, 253 a, 256; οὐ γάρ, not interrog. in Jn 683; ὁ...οὐκ ὤν 704; οὐ...καί and οὐ...ἤ 549 a, 759; οὐ...τις and οὐδείς 586 d, e; ου confused w. συ 797 c
οὐδέ: v. r. for οὔτε 258; introducing parenthesis 633 b; ουδε εν or ουδεν 660
οὐδείς: καὶ οὐδείς 139; οὐ...οὐδείς 257; οὐ...τις and οὐδείς 586 d, e; οὐδέν, emphasised by position 605 a; ουδεν or ουδε εν 660
οὐκέτι: repeated as οὐ 583; οὐ...οὐκέτι 257 a
οὐκοῦν 233–4
οὐ μή 232, 255
οὐ μόνον 147 b
οὖν: in Christ's words 191–7; in narrative of Christ's acts 198—200; after parenthesis 631 foll.; in LXX 640;

---

¹ Add Epict. i. 24. 20 ὅταν σοι φαίνηται...ἀπαλλάσσου.

This Index extends from **1886** *to* **2799**. *Before numbers with* * *supply* 1, *e.g.* [1]999*; *before others*, 2, *e.g.* [2]000.

WORDS (GREEK)

in Papyri 640 e; "pause spaces" before οὖν in B 663; v. r. τότε 637 a
οὔπω: v.r. οὐ 264-5
οὐρανός: with and without article 952-8*
οὔτε...καί 258-9; οὔτε...ἀλλά (in Pap.) 683 a, b
οὗτος 386-97; how emphasized 553 c; οὗτός ἐστιν etc., used in testimony 957 b*; αὕτη "this [thing]" 396, 621-2; διὰ τοῦτο 387-91; ἐν τούτῳ 332, 392-3; ἐπὶ τοῦτο and ἐπὶ τούτῳ 338; μετὰ τοῦτο and μετὰ ταῦτα 349 a, 394; ταῦτα thrice repeated 396, 621, ταύτην ἐποίησεν ἀρχὴν τῶν σημείων 386 (i)
οὕτως "unpremeditatedly" 916-7*; οὕτως...ὥστε 917 a*, 203, 697; οὕτως ...ἵνα or ὅτι or ὡς 697
οὐχ ὅτι 188, 218
οὐχί: interrog. 231 a; ἀλλ' οὐχὶ πάντες 265 (i)
ὄχλος 417; ὁ ὄχλος πολύς 153 a; ὄχλος and ὅλος 753 e
ὀψάριον 235 d, 703
ὄψομαι s. ὁράω

Παιδάριον...ὅς 412 b
παιδίον 701-3
παῖς, παιδίον, and δοῦλος 584 b
πάλαι ἄν (?) confused w. πάλιν 698 a
πάλιν: double meaning of 635 (i), 649 (i)-(iii), 711 a; ? confused w. πάλαι ἄν 698 a
παντέλειος: an epithet of the number "ten" 283 c
παρά: w. accus. 354; w. dat. 352-3, 355, 363; w. gen. 356; w. gen. and dat. interchanged 357-9; παρὰ τὴν θάλασσαν 341, 344, 354; παρὰ θεῷ 027; παρὰ τῷ θεῷ 355; παρὰ τῷ πατρί and παρὰ τοῦ πατρός 357; ὁ ὢν παρὰ [τοῦ] θεοῦ 358; οὐ διὰ τοῦ θεοῦ ἀλλὰ παρ' αὐτοῦ 296 a; παρά, ἀπό, and ἐκ w. ἐξέρχομαι 326-8
παραδίδωμι: παραδοῖ 252; ὁ παραδιδούς 510
παράκλητος 630 h, 791-7
παραλαμβάνω: in Epict. 570 b; παρέλαβον and ἔλαβον 570
παρασκευή: π. τοῦ πάσχα 048; ἐπεὶ ἦν π. 087 a
πάρειμι 225 a
παρέρχομαι 342 d
παρρησία 917 (i)-(vi)*, 727; connected w. Epict. 917 (v)*, 798 f
πᾶς: combined w. οὐ or μή 260-3; πᾶν

ὃ δέδωκεν (δέδωκας) etc. 921-2*, 422, 740-4; περιπάντων, for περιπατῶν 651; οὐ...πᾶν Hebraic 759 e
πάσχα: παρασκευὴ τοῦ π. 048; τὸ πάσχα ἡ ἑορτή 654 d
πατήρ: used vocatively, πάτερ, πατήρ, and ὁ πατήρ, 052-3, 661 a, 679, v. r. in B 659 b; παρὰ τῷ πατρί, παρὰ τοῦ πατρός, and παρὰ τοῦ θεοῦ 355-9; οἱ πατέρες 949-50*, 553 e; οἱ π. and οἱ π. ὑμῶν 957*
πατριάρχαι 949 a*
παχύνω 449 a
πέμπω: ἔπεμψα, in letters 691 c
περα for περαν 656 a
περί 360, 370; τὰς π. Μάρθαν 990*; π. and ὑπέρ 718, 719 b
περιπατέω 342 a foll., diff. from βαδίζω 342 b, = "teach" 342 e; περιπατῶν corrupted to περιπάντων 651
περιρρήγνυμι: active and middle, w. ἱμάτια 270 b, 563 c
πηγή 316 b
πηλίκοις: πηλίκοις γράμμασιν ἔγραψα 691 a-e, 785-90
πιάζω: ἐπίασαν οὐδέν and οὐδένα ἔπεισαν 703 c
Πιλᾶτος: with and without article 969*
πιπράσκω, forms of 750
πιστεύω: w. dat., εἰς, ἐν, see Joh. Voc. Index III and esp. 1470; πίστευε and πίστευσον 439 b; πιστεύετε ambig. 237-40; perf. 442, 474; τοὺς πεπιστευκότας αὐτῷ 506; οὐκ ἐπίστευον 466; οἱ πιστεύοντες, meaning of 500; aor. and pres. subjunct. 525 foll.; πιστεύσωμεν v. r. -εύωμεν 528; pres. subjunct. altered by D into aor. subjunct. 530 a; π. διά τινος 304 a
πίστις s. Joh. Voc. Index III
πιστός 304 a
πλήν: v. r. for πρὸ προσώπου 361 a
πληρόω: w. ἐκ 329
πλησίον "near" 368 a
πλοῖον: ἐδράσωμεν τὸ π. 346 c
πνεῦμα: τὸ π. ἐστι τὸ ζωοποιοῦν 975-7*
πόθεν: π. εἶ σύ; 403, 733-7; ποθεν, a corruption of ποθι 759
ποιέω: π. and ἐργάζομαι 226 b; π. and πράσσω 584 a; ἐποίουν 463-4; ποιεῖτε ambig. 194 c, 359; τί ποιοῦμεν; τί ποιῶμεν; and τί ποιήσωμεν; 493, 512, 766 (i); καλῶς ποιήσεις 729 a; ἤκουσαν ὅτι ἐποίησεν 459
πολύς: πολλοί sometimes ambig. 941*; πολλοὶ τῶν, not in Jn 041; πολλοί... ἐκ τῶν Ἰουδαίων 941* foll.; ὕδατα

This Index extends from 1886 to 2799. Before numbers with * supply 1, e.g. [1]999*; before others, 2, e.g. [2]000.

685

πολλά 270 c; ἄλλα πολλά, πολλὰ... καὶ ἕτερα and πολλὰ...καὶ ἄλλα 335 a
πονηρός: σώζω, τηρέω etc. ἐκ τοῦ πονηροῦ (ambig.) 325
πορεύομαι and ὑπάγω 082[1]; π. substituted for ἀναβαίνω 489 a
πόσος: ποσα v. r. οσα and τοσα 737 b
ποτέ 351 b
πότερον 250
πράσσω and ποιέω 584 a
πρό: πρὸ ἐμοῦ 361-2; πρὸ προσώπου 330, v. r. πλήν 361 a; πρὸ ἐξ ἡμερῶν τοῦ πάσχα 288; πρό corr. to πρός 651, 655
πρόβατα (pl.): collective and non-collective 420
προβατική 216
πρός: w. accus., w. vb of rest 363-6, w. vbs of speaking 366 b-c, repeated after vb of motion 367; w. dat. 368; εἶναι πρός τινα 363a; ἦν πρὸς τὸν θεόν, contrasted w. ἀπεσταλμένος παρὰ θεοῦ 277; τί πρὸς σέ; 229; πρός a corruption of πρό 651, 655
προσάββατον 048
προσεύχομαι 630 h; προσεύχεσθε καὶ αἰτεῖσθε 536a
προσκυνέω: w. accus. and w. dat. 019
προσφάγιον 235 d, 701-3
πρόσωπον: πρὸ π. 330, v. r. πλήν 361 a
προφήτης: with and without article 940*, 965*; προφήτης for ὁ προφήτης (?) 492a; διὰ τοῦ π. 301
πρωι for πρωτον 901 b*
πρῶτον, s. πρῶτος
πρῶτος followed by genitive 896* foll., 665-7; πρῶτον ὑμῶν ambig. 901*; πρῶτος or πρώτιστος Hebraized 666
πρωτότοκος 897*
πύλη 216 a
πυνθάνομαι: aor. and imperf. 465 c-d
πωρόω: v. r. πηρόω 449 a; aor. and perf. 449 a-b

Ῥαββεί 680
ῥάβδος: ἐν ῥάβδῳ ἐλθεῖν 332 a

C, ε, θ and ο interchanged in B 650-2
σάββατον: σαββάτῳ and ἐν σαββάτῳ 715c
σάρξ: θέλημα σαρκός 269; τὰς σάρκας ἀπολλύουσιν οἱ σταυρωθέντες 211 c

σημεῖον 386 b; ἀρχὴ τῶν σημείων 386 (i)
σκανδαλίζω: variations of ὃς ἂν σκανδαλίσῃ 513 b
σκέλος: ἵνα κατεαγῶσιν αὐτῶν τὰ σκέλη 419
σταυρόω: ὑψηλὸς ὁ σταυρωθεὶς καὶ πολλοὺς τρέφει...τὰς σάρκας ἀπολλύουσιν οἱ σταυρωθέντες 211 c
στήκω: στήκετε w. ἐάν and ὅταν 515 (i)
στιβάδας: v.r. στοιβάδας 047
σύ 400 a, 402-4; σὺ λέγεις 234 b; πόθεν εἶ σύ 733-7; σύ with vocat. and imperat. 734 e; σου and μου confused 768; σου unemph. 776 foll.; συ confused w. ου 797 c
συμφέρον: how used by Epict. 228 a
σύν 799 (ii)
συνειδός 798 e
συνζητέω 349
συνήθεια 464 b
σώζω: w. ἐκ 325

Ταράσσω: applied to Christ 614 c
τάχειον "more quickly": not the same as ταχέως 918*, 439 (v) a, 554 c-e
ταχέως, ταχύ, ἐν τάχει 554 b-d
τε: how used in Jn 929*
τέλειος: applied to numbers 283 c
τέλος "eminence" 320 a; εἰς τ. 319-23
τετράμηνος: ἔτι τ. ἐστιν 230 (ii) foll.
τηρέω: w. ἐκ 325; pres. and aor. subjunct. 515; ἐτήρουν...καὶ ἐφύλαξα 584
τί, s. τίς
Τιβεριάς 045
τίθημι: late aor. of 690
τις: omitted 379 b; τινί supplied w. ἔξεστιν 379 a; ellipsis of τινές 213 foll.; ἐάν τις 580; ἐάν separated from τις 552 c; οὐ...τις and οὐδείς 586 d, e
τίς; τί; (direct interrogative) τί; διὰ τί; ἵνα τί; 231 b-e; τί; τί ὅτι; and ὅτι, in v.r. 231 d; τί ὅτι; τί ἔστιν ὅτι; and τί γέγονεν ὅτι; 694; τί λαλεῖς; ambig. 231 b; τί εἴπω; prob.= "what should I say?" 512 b, c; τί ποιοῦμεν; τί ποιῶμεν; τί ποιήσωμεν; distinction between 493, 512, 766 (i); τί ἐμοὶ καὶ σοί; 229-30; οὗτος δὲ τί; 209, 386 c; τί πρὸς σέ; 229; τίνα ἦν ἃ ἐλάλει 251; τίς ἐστιν ὁ παραδώσων 251 a; τί δοκεῖς; in Epict. 766 (i) a

---

[1] Add Epict. iii. 24. 44—7 θέλεις με...πορεύεσθαι;...διὰ τί μὴ ἀπέλθῃς;...τί οὖν ἔτι πορεύομαι; ἵνα ἀπέλθῃς.

This Index extends from 1886 to 2799. Before numbers with * supply 1, e.g. [1]999*; before others, 2, e.g. [2]000.

WORDS (GREEK)

τοιοῦτος 398 ; τοιαύτη "such a thing" 396 b
τόπος : ? ellipsis of τόπῳ 675
τοσοῦτοι v.r. 745
τότε : v.r. for οὖν 637 a
τρεῖς 281-3, s. "Three" and "Threefold"
τρέφω : ὁ σταυρωθεὶς πολλοὺς τρέφει 211 c, 642 b

Ὑδρία 281 a
ὕδωρ : ὕδατα πολλά 270 c ; ἐπὶ τὰ ὑ. 342 d
υἱός : ? interchanged w. παῖς 584 b ; v.r. ἐκλεκτός 386 a ; ΤΟΥΝ i.e. τὸν υἱόν, confusable w. ΤΟΥΝ in τοὔνομα 768-9
ὑμεῖς : Jn's use 399 ; καὶ ὑμεῖς 149 ; (?) δι' ὑμᾶς 428 c ; ὑμῶν, unemph. 559 a ; ὑμεῖς in LXX before ambig. forms in -ετε 243 a ; ὑμ- and ἡμ- confused 428 c
ὑμέτερος : rare and emphatic 988*
ὑπάγω 486 ; distinct from πορεύομαι 082 ; ὅπου ὑ. (and ὅπου ἐγὼ ὑ.) and ὅπου εἰμι (v.r. εἶμι) 487 a, 578 ; ὑπῆγον 464
ὑπέρ 369-71 ; ὑπὲρ οὗ 927 b*, 360 ; ὑπέρ τινος masc. and neut. 718-22 ; ὑπέρ and περί 719 a-c
ὑπεραγαπάω 323 b
ὑπό : w. accus. 372 ; w. gen. 373 ; ὑ. and ὑποκάτω 372
ὑποκάτω 372
ὑπομένω 322 b ; ὁ ὑπομείνας 499
ὑψηλός : applied to ὁ σταυρωθεὶς 211 c
ὑψόω : applied to Christ 614 b

Φανερόω : thrice applied to Christ's Resurrection 619
φέρω : "bear fruit" 120 b

φημί rare in Jn, freq. in Acts[1]
φιλέω 328, 584 c ; perf. 442, 476-7 ; Origen's distinction between φ. and ἀγαπάω 584 c
φοῖνιξ : τὰ βαΐα τῶν φοινίκων 047
φυλάσσω : ἐτήρουν...καὶ ἐφύλαξα 584
φυλή : αἱ φυλαὶ τῆς γῆς 317 e-f
φωτίζω 532 c

Χάρις : Philo on 285 b ; Epictetus on 743 a
χείρ : in var. phrases w. εἰς and ἐν 334 c ; χεῖρα or χεῖρας w. βάλλω and ἐπιβάλλω 575
χόρτος 632 b
χρονίζω : forms of 752
χώρα : ἡ Ἰουδαία χ. 670 b
χωρέω 414 b foll.

Ψῆφος : δίδωμι ψῆφον 409 a

Ω and ο interchanged 114, 691
ὠδῖνες 197
ὥρα : combined with ἔρχεται and ἐλήλυθεν 604 a, 625 e ; τὴν ὤ. ταύτην "about this time" 013 ; (ἐν) ἐκείνῃ τῇ ὤ. 025 ; ὤ. ἑβδόμην 013, 206 ; ᾗ ἂν ὤ. parall. to ὅταν 533 a ; ὤ. ἵνα and ὤ. ὅτε 799 (i), s. also 770
ὡς : (?) for ἕως 089, 201, 696 ; "as it were" 202 ; ὡς δέ "so when" 069 ; ὡς ἂν 696 a ; οὕτως...ὡς, for οὕτως ὥστε 697
ὥσπερ 066 b
ὥστε 203, 694 c ; οὕτως ὤ. 917 a*, 697 ; in Egypt. Pap. 697 c
ὠφέλεια : how used by Epict. 798-9

---

[1] It should have been stated in 2456 a that Jn—who uses φημί only in i. 23, ix. 38, xviii. 29—never applies it (as the Synoptists do) to Christ. Mt. and Lk. agree (agst Mk) in applying it to Christ in His answer to Pilate, "Thou sayest it." It is a mark of classical style. In Pentateuch, of seven instances, five are in the prophecy of Balaam, Numb. xxiv. 3—15. In N.T., it occurs mostly in Acts, 24 times. In the Synoptists, Mt. uses it most freq. (17), Mk (6), Lk. (7). It is never used by three Synoptists in common. Lk. mostly uses it in traditions peculiar to himself.

This Index extends from 1886 *to* 2799. *Before numbers with* * *supply* 1, *e.g.* [1]999*; *before others*, 2, *e.g.* [2]000.

www.ingramcontent.com/pod-product-compliance
Lightning Source LLC
Chambersburg PA
CBHW052107010526
44111CB00036B/1545